International Trade Law

International Trade Law

A Comprehensive Textbook

Volume Four:
Preferences, Labor, Environment, and Intellectual Property

FIFTH EDITION

Raj Bhala

BRENNEISEN DISTINGUISHED PROFESSOR
THE UNIVERSITY OF KANSAS, SCHOOL OF LAW
LAWRENCE, KANSAS

SENIOR ADVISOR
DENTONS U.S. LLP
KANSAS CITY, MISSOURI

"ON POINT" COLUMNIST
BLOOMBERGQUINT
MUMBAI, INDIA

CAROLINA ACADEMIC PRESS
Durham, North Carolina

ISBN   978-1-5310-1438-4
eISBN 978-1-5310-1439-1
LCCN 2019937680

Carolina Academic Press
700 Kent Street
Durham, North Carolina 27701
Telephone (919) 489-7486
Fax (919) 493-5668
www.cap-press.com

Printed in the United States of America

For Shera and Her Generation,
That They Are Not Scourged by Poverty, Extremism, or a Clash of Civilizations,
But Rather Blessed by Peace through Sustainable Trade and Development.

And for the Glory of God.

Summary of Contents

Part and Chapter titles are for all four Volumes of *International Trade Law, Fifth Edition*. Please see individual Volumes for detailed Table of Contents.

VOLUME ONE
INTERDISCIPLINARY FOUNDATIONS AND
FUNDAMENTAL OBLIGATIONS

Acknowledgments
Note on Pedagogy
Note on Sources
Preface to 5th Edition
Introduction: 10 Propositions

Part One: Moral Foundations of Free Trade
    Chapter 1   Philosophical and Religious Theories
    Chapter 2   Four Types of Justice
    Chapter 3   Theory and Practice of Ethics

Part Two: Transactional Foundations of Free Trade
    Chapter 4   Documentary Sale
    Chapter 5   Trade Finance

Part Three: Economic Foundations of Free Trade
    Chapter 6   Classical and Neo-Classical Free Trade Theory
    Chapter 7   Modern Free Trade Theory
    Chapter 8   Questioning Capitalist Free Trade Theory
    Chapter 9   Communist Trade Theory
    Chapter 10   Trade Patterns
    Chapter 11   Trade and Factors of Production
    Chapter 12   Economics of Protection

Part Four: Historical Foundations of Free Trade
    Chapter 13   American Trade History
    Chapter 14   Presidential Powers and Trade
    Chapter 15   GATT Rounds through 1970s
    Chapter 16   Uruguay Round (1986–1994) and Birth of WTO (1995)
    Chapter 17   Doha Round (November 2001–March 2018)

Part Five: Institutional Foundations of Free Trade

Chapter 18 Structure of WTO and GATT-WTO Law

Chapter 19 GATT-WTO Accession Process

Chapter 20 WTO Accession Case Studies

Part Six: Adjudicatory Foundations of Free Trade

Chapter 21 Pre-Uruguay Round GATT Civil Procedure (1948–1994)

Chapter 22 Post-Uruguay Round WTO Civil Procedure (1995–)

Chapter 23 Participation and Capacity Problems

Chapter 24 Resource and Interpretation Problems

Chapter 25 Enforcement Problems

Part Seven: Product Relationships for Legal Foundations of Free Trade

Chapter 26 Like Products

Chapter 27 Directly Competitive Or Substitutable Products

Part Eight: Legal Foundations of Free Trade: Five Pillars of GATT-WTO Law

Chapter 28 First Pillar: GATT Article I and MFN Treatment

Chapter 29 Second Pillar: GATT Article II and Tariff Bindings

Chapter 30 Second Pillar (Continued): Tariff Changes

Chapter 31 Third Pillar: GATT Article III:1-2 and National Treatment for Fiscal Measures

Chapter 32 Third Pillar (Continued): GATT Article III:4 and National Treatment for Non-Fiscal Measures

Chapter 33 Fourth Pillar: GATT Article XI and QRS

Chapter 34 Fourth Pillar (Continued): GATT Article XIII and Administering QRS

Chapter 35 Fourth Pillar (Continued): TBTs as NTBs

Chapter 36 Fifth Pillar: GATT Article X and Transparency

Part Nine: Exceptions: Cracks in Pillars of GATT-WTO Law

Chapter 37 Non-Application, Waivers, Preferences, And Remedies

Chapter 38 GATT Articles XII and XVIII and Bop Crises

Chapter 39 GATT Article XX General Exceptions

Chapter 40 GATT Article XX(a) Morality Exception: Islamic Jurisdictions, Alcohol, and Pornography

Chapter 41 GATT Article XX(a) Morality Exception (Continued): Animal Rights and Money Laundering

Chapter 42 GATT Article XX(a) Morality Exception (Continued): Censorship

Part Ten: Trade and Agriculture

Chapter 43 Ag Market Access

Chapter 44 Ag Export Subsidies

Chapter 45 Domestic Ag Support

Chapter 46 Green Box Controversies

Chapter 47 SPS Measures

Part Eleven: Trade and Services
Chapter 48 Services Classifications and Supply Modes (GATS Parts I, V–VI)
Chapter 49 General Obligations And Exceptions (GATS Part II)
Chapter 50 Specific Commitments And Exceptions (GATS Parts III–IV)

VOLUME TWO
CUSTOMS LAW AND NATIONAL SECURITY

Part One: Country of Origin
Chapter 1 Marking
Chapter 2 Non-Preferential Rules of Origin
Chapter 3 Classic Marking Disputes

Part Two: Entry of Merchandise
Chapter 4 Types of Entry
Chapter 5 Foreign Trade Zones

Part Three: Customs Classification
Chapter 6 Tariff Schedules
Chapter 7 Conceptual Classification Categories
Chapter 8 Classification Conundrums
Chapter 9 More Classification Conundrums

Part Four: Customs Valuation
Chapter 10 Valuation Methodologies
Chapter 11 Valuation Conundrums

Part Five: Special Customs Law Opportunities
Chapter 12 Drawback
Chapter 13 Pre-Shipment Inspection
Chapter 14 Trade Facilitation

Part Six: Border Security
Chapter 15 Post-9/11 Customs Law Paradigm Shift
Chapter 16 Post-9/11 Border Security Initiatives

Part Seven: Defining "National Security"
Chapter 17 Multilateral and American Legal Frameworks
Chapter 18 Section 232

Part Eight: Trade Sanctions
Chapter 19 Morality of Trade Sanctions
Chapter 20 Iran Trade Sanctions: 1979 Hostage Crisis–2012
Chapter 21 Iran Trade Sanctions (Continued): Increasing the Pressure and
            Getting a Deal, 2012–2018
Chapter 22 Iran Trade Sanctions (Continued): 2018 Iran Nuclear Deal
            Withdrawal and Aftermath

Part Nine: Export Controls
    Chapter 23 Nuclear Items
    Chapter 24 Military Goods
    Chapter 25 Dual Use Items

VOLUME THREE
REMEDIES

Part One: Remedies against "Unfair" Trade: Antidumping Law
    Chapter 1 Political Economy of Dumping and Ad Duties
    Chapter 2 Procedures: Original Investigations through Final Determinations
    Chapter 3 Procedures (Continued): After Final Determinations
    Chapter 4 Data Issues in Ad Cases
    Chapter 5 Dumping Margin Calculation
    Chapter 6 Dumping Margin Calculation Issues: Viability, Below-Cost Sales, and Merchandise Comparisons
    Chapter 7 Dumping Margin Calculation Issues (Continued): Proxies for Normal Value
    Chapter 8 Dumping Margin Adjustments: Adjustments to Normal Value
    Chapter 9 Dumping Margin Adjustments (Continued): Adjustments to Export Price or Constructed Export Price
    Chapter 10 Injury

Part Two: Remedies against "Unfair" Trade (Continued): Countervailing Duty Law
    Chapter 11 Political Economy of Subsidies and CVDs
    Chapter 12 Definition of "Subsidy," First Element: "Financial Contribution"
    Chapter 13 Definition of "Subsidy," Second Element: "Benefit" Conferred
    Chapter 14 Definition of "Subsidy," Third Element: Specificity Test
    Chapter 15 Traffic Light System: Red Light (Prohibited) Subsidies
    Chapter 16 Traffic Light System (Continued): Yellow Light (Actionable) Subsidies
    Chapter 17 CVDs against Pre-Privatization Subsidies

Part Three: Remedies against "Unfair" Trade (Continued): Causation in Antidumping and Countervailing Duty Cases
    Chapter 18 Theories of Causation
    Chapter 19 Proving Causation: GATT-WTO Jurisprudence
    Chapter 20 Proving Causation (Continued): American Jurisprudence

Part Four: Disciplines on Fishing Subsidies
    Chapter 21 Issues and Consequences
    Chapter 22 Post-2013 Bali Ministerial Conference Efforts

Part Five: Remedies against "Fair" Trade: Safeguards
Chapter 23 Rationales for Safeguards
Chapter 24 Legal Criteria for General Safeguards
Chapter 25 America's Safeguard: Section 201 Escape Clause

Part Six: Remedies against Non-Market Economies
Chapter 26 Ad Cases against Nmes
Chapter 27 Cvd Cases against Nmes
Chapter 28 Market Disruption

Part Seven: Unilateral Remedies
Chapter 29 Rationales for Unilateral Retaliation
Chapter 30 Section 301
Chapter 31 Section 301 and Sino-American Trade War

Part Eight: Currency Manipulation
Chapter 32 GATT Article XV and IMF Article IV
Chapter 33 Alternative Strategies

VOLUME FOUR
PREFERENCES, LABOR, AND THE ENVIRONMENT

Part One: Rationales for FTAs
Chapter 1 Economic Aspects of FTAs
Chapter 2 Political Aspects of FTAs
Chapter 3 National Security Aspects of FTAs

Part Two: Common Legal Features of FTAs
Chapter 4 GATT-WTO Disciplines on FTAs
Chapter 5 Special Disciplines for India and Pakistan
Chapter 6 Preferential Roos
Chapter 7 Preferential Roos (Continued): NAFTA Case Study
Chapter 8 Preferential Roos (Continued): Additional Issues

Part Three: Legal Commitments in FTAs
Chapter 9 Typical FTA Market Access Obligations
Chapter 10 Liberalizing Services Trade through FTAs
Chapter 11 Liberalizing and Protecting FDI through FTAs
Chapter 12 Additional Commitments in "Deep" FTAs

Part Four: Preferences for Poor Countries: Development Economics
Chapter 13 Measuring Growth, Development, and Poverty
Chapter 14 Economic Growth Models: Stages Of Growth and Sources of
           Growth
Chapter 15 Economic Growth Models (Continued): Industrialization and
           Labor Surplus

Chapter 16 Trade Policy, Growth, and Poverty: Export Orientation
Chapter 17 Trade Policy, Growth, and Poverty (Continued) Import
           Substitution
Chapter 18 Modern Indian Trade History

Part Five: Preferences for Poor Countries (Continued): Trade Laws
Chapter 19 Special and Differential Treatment
Chapter 20 Generalized System of Preferences
Chapter 21 Special Help for Africa?

Part Six: Trade And Labor
Chapter 22 International Labor Law and Trade Restrictions
Chapter 23 Substantive Labor Obligations in FTAs
Chapter 24 Resolving Labor Disputes under FTAs
Chapter 25 Theory of TAA
Chapter 26 Practice of TAA

Part Seven: Trade and the Environment
Chapter 27 GATT Article XX(b) and XX(g) Jurisprudence
Chapter 28 Environmental Provisions in FTAs
Chapter 29 Trade and Climate Change

Part Eight: Trade and Intellectual Property
Chapter 30 IP Overview
Chapter 31 Substantive Trips Agreement Obligations
Chapter 32 Compulsory Licensing, Evergreening, and Patented
           Pharmaceuticals
Chapter 33 IP Enforcement

Contents

About the Author   xxi
Table of Abbreviations   xxiii

Chapter 1 · Economic Aspects of FTAs   3
    I. Terminological Distinctions and Examples   3
    II. Global Statistics and Trends   9
    III. Overview of U.S. FTAs   9
    IV. Job Creation or Destruction?   11
    V. Trade Creation or Diversion?   29
    VI. Stepping Stones or Fortresses?   42
    VII. Diversity in Ambition of FTAs: Breadth, Depth, and Timing   46
    VIII. Case Study: *CAFTA-DR*   49

Chapter 2 · Political and Security Aspects of FTAs   53
    I. Competitive Liberalization and Its Defects   53
    II. Choosing FTA Partners   59
    III. Political Criteria   60
    IV. Case Study: Taiwan, *TIFA*, But No FTA   61
    V. Case Study: Panama and Three FTA Issues   67
    VI. Political Economy Criteria   72

Chapter 3 · Security Aspects of FTAs   75
    I. Choosing FTA Partners Based on National Security Criteria   75
    II. Case Study: Egypt, QIZs, and Israeli Content   77
    III. Case Study: Korea and *KORUS*   81
    IV. Case Study: *KORUS* and Kaesong   93
    V. Case Study: Pakistan, ROZs, and Islamist Extremism   97
    VI. Case Study: Turkey   100
    VII. Competitive Imperialism   101

Chapter 4 · GATT-WTO Disciplines on FTAs   125
    I. Poor Countries, *ITO Charter* Article 15, and GATT Article
        XXIV Origins   125
    II. Purpose of RTAs, Article XXIV:4, and Article XXIV:10 Waiver   130
    III. First Discipline: "Substantially All" Test in Article XXIV:8   133
    IV. Second Discipline: "Higher or More Restrictive" Test in
        Article XXIV:5   136

V. Compensatory Adjustments, Article XXIV:6, and Case Studies of
    EU and Gabon   143
VI. Third Discipline: Notification under Article XXIV:7   145
VII. Are RTA Disciplines Parlous?   148

Chapter 5 · Special Disciplines for India and Pakistan   151
I. Historical Context of Article XXIV:11: August 1947 British
    Partition of India   151
II. Applying Article XXIV:11 to Indo-Pakistani Trade   155
III. Open Questions about Indian Subcontinent and Article XXIV:11   161

Chapter 6 · Preferential ROOs   165
I. Indispensability   165
II. Three Generic Categories   166
III. Four Problems   174
IV. Israeli Origin, Occupied Territories, and February 2010 ECJ
    Brita Case   181
V. Middle East Politics and QIZs   185

Chapter 7 · Preferential ROOs (Continued): *NAFTA* Case Study   189
I. Overview of Eight Types of Preferential ROOs in *NAFTA* and
    Other FTAs   189
II. Type 1: Goods Wholly Obtained Rule   191
III. Type 2: Originating Materials Rule   192
IV. Type 3: Substantial Transformation Rule   192
V. Type 4: Value Added Test   196
VI. Type 5: Hybrid Rule   198
VII. *NAFTA* Renegotiations on 62.5% Auto RVC   200
VIII. *NAFTA* 2.0 Hybrid Auto ROO: 75% RVC and Minimum Wage   203
IX. From Hybrid Auto ROO to Overall Trilateral Deal   209
X. Type 6: Assembled Goods Rule   231
XI. Type 7: Specified Process Rule   231
XII. Type 8: *De Minimis* Test   236

Chapter 8 · Preferential ROOs (Continued): Additional Issues   237
I. Tariff Shift and 2006 *Cummins* Case   237
II. *NAFTA* Certificate of Origin and 2006 *Corrpro* Case   242
III. Trans-Shipment and *Singapore FTA*   248

Chapter 9 · Typical FTA Market Access Obligations   251
I. Check List   251
II. "Ambitious" Elimination of Trade Barriers?   254
III. Case Studies on Ambition: *Singapore* and *Chile FTAs*   257
IV. Case Study on Negotiating Objectives: *Australia FTA*   258
V. Sensitive Products and Sectors   261
VI. Case Studies on Sensitive Products: Agricultural Products and T&A   262

VII. Case Study on Enhanced Market Access for Agricultural Goods
and T&A: *NAFTA* 2.0   268
VIII. Sensitivities and Bilateral and Special Safeguards   278
IX. Case Study on Safeguards: 1998 *NAFTA Corn Brooms* Case   285
X. Case Study on Enhanced Market Access for Industrial Goods:
NAFTA 2.0   289
XI. Managed Trade in Goods?   292

Chapter 10 · Liberalizing Trade in Services through FTAs   297
I. Financial Services and Capital Controls   297
II. Freer Trade or Safer Roads? *NAFTA* Cross Border Trucking Case   299
III. Case Study on Non-Discrimination and Data Localization: *NAFTA* 2.0   312
IV. Managed Trade in Services?   315

Chapter 11 · Liberalizing and Protecting FDI through FTAs   317
I. Overview of FTA Investment Chapters   317
II. FDI Market Access Rules   323
III. FDI Non-Discrimination Rules   327
IV. Rules on Compensation for Expropriation   329
V. Overview of Institutions and Dispute Resolution Mechanisms   333
VI. Critique of ISDS Mechanisms   339
VII. *NAFTA* 2.0 ISDS Cut Back   348
VIII. FDI and Competition Policy, and SOEs   350

Chapter 12 · Additional Commitments in "Deep" FTAs   353
I. "Deep," "Second Generation," or "21st Century" FTAs   353
II. *NAFTA* Chapter 20 Case Study   353
III. Economic Significance of Government Procurement   358
IV. Managed Trade in Government Procurement   359
V. Malaysian Social Engineering through Government Procurement   359
VI. Exporting American IP Standards and Pushing *TRIPs*
Plus Commitments   360
VII. El Said Argument on *TRIPs* Plus Commitments   368
VIII. Case Study on *TRIPs* Plus Commitments: *NAFTA* 2.0   371
IX. Securitization and Relationship between *TRIPs* Plus and
Other FTA Obligations   378
X. Cultural Industries Exceptions and 1997 *Canada Magazines* Case   378
XI. International Digital Trade   391
XII. Case Study on Digital Trade: *NAFTA* 2.0   394

Chapter 13 · Measuring Growth, Development, and Poverty   399
I. What Is "Growth"?   399
II. What Is "Development"?   405
III. Absolute Poverty   415
IV. Top-Bottom Ratio   418
V. Gini Coefficient   419

Chapter 14 · Economic Growth Models: Stages of Growth and
        Sources of Growth   427
        I. 1960 Rostow Stages of Growth Theory   427
        II. Essential Growth Model Concepts   431
        III. Harrod-Domar One-Sector Growth Model   438
        IV. Sources of Growth Accounting   440

Chapter 15 · Economic Growth Models: Industrialization and
        Labor Surplus   447
        I. Transformation from Agriculture to Industry   447
        II. Concept of Labor Surplus and Its Shift   451
        III. Background to Labor Surplus Models   456
        IV. 1964 Fei-Ranis Labor Surplus Model   473
        V. Critique of Labor Surplus Models   479
        VI. Neo-Classical Two-Sector Model   482
        VII. Patterns of Development and 1975 Chenery-Syrquin Study 486

Chapter 16 · Trade, Growth, and Poverty: Export Orientation   489
        I. Industrialization and Unbalanced Growth   489
        II. Growth, Poverty, and Kuznets Inverted U Theory   495
        III. Piketty Critique of Kuznets Curve   497
        IV. Terms of Trade   497
        V. Export Orientation versus Import Substitution   498
        VI. Market-Based Theory for Export Orientation   499
        VII. Risk of Immiserizing Growth   501
        VIII. Evidence for Export Orientation   502
        IX. Evidence Questioning Export Orientation   509

Chapter 17 · Trade, Growth, and Poverty (Continued):
        Import Substitution   515
        I. Marxist Intellectual Heritage of Import Substitution   515
        II. Frank and Dependency Theory   521
        III. Prebisch-Singer Thesis   523
        IV. Policy Implications of Prebisch-Singer Thesis   527
        V. Evidence for Import Substitution   529
        VI. 1981 Lord Bauer Rebuttal   534

Chapter 18 · Modern Indian Trade Policy   539
        I. 15 August 1947 Partition   539
        II. Socialism, Nationalism, and Anti-Colonialism   541
        III. Three Hallmarks of Post-Partition Socialist Style Planning 544
        IV. 1970s: Inefficiencies   546
        V. 1991 First Generation Reforms   549
        VI. 1990s and Early 2000s: Reforms Sputter   555
        VII. Path Ahead   563
        VIII. New Era with Prime Minister Modi?   570

Chapter 19 · Special and Differential Treatment 575
   I. Prebisch, Baran, and Intellectual Background for Non-Reciprocal
      Trade Preferences and GATT Part IV 575
   II. 1958 *Haberler Report* 577
   III. Substantive Content of Article XXXVI:8 579
   IV. Collaboration, GATT Article XXXIII, and 1980 *Sugar Refunds* Case 583
   V. Summary Tables of S&D Treatment in GATT-WTO Texts 584
   VI. Reciprocity and European Preferences for Former Colonies 635
   VII. December 2013 Bali *Monitoring Mechanism Decision* 636

Chapter 20 · Generalized System of Preferences 639
   I. Background to *GSP* 639
   II. Designation as BDC 644
   III. Case Study of Bangladeshi Worker Rights 652
   IV. Eligible Articles and Extensive Ineligibility List 654
   V. Sleeping Bags, Import Sensitivity, and Politics 658
   VI. *GSP* Preferential ROOs 659
   VII. Discretionary Graduation and CNLs 668
   VIII. Non-Discriminatory Discrimination or Divide and Rule?
      1979 Tokyo Round *Enabling Clause* Paragraph 2(a) Defense and
      2004 *EU GSP* Case 674
   IX. NTMs and RTAs: 1979 Tokyo Round *Enabling Clause* Paragraphs
      2(b)–(c) Defenses and 2019 *Brazil Tax* Case 688

Chapter 21 · Special Help for Africa 707
   I. Background on *AGOA* 707
   II. Devilishly Protectionist Details 711
   III. Trade Distortion? 724
   IV. Economic Dependency? 726
   V. Social Justice? 728

Chapter 22 · International Labor Law and Trade Restrictions 733
   I. ILO Overview 733
   II. Defining "Internationally Recognized Worker Rights" Based on
      ILO *Conventions* 740
   III. EU *Social Charter* 744
   IV. Push versus Pull Debate on Labor Rights in Poor Countries 749
   V. GATT Article XX(e) Prison Labor Exception 751
   VI. U.S. Section 307 Ban on Merchandise from Convict, Forced, or
      Indentured Labor 752
   VII. Section 307 Cases 754
   VIII. End of 85-Year-Old Consumptive Demand Exception 758

Chapter 23 · Substantive Labor Rules in FTAs 761
   I. Controversy 761
   II. November 2013 ILO Study on Significance 761

III. Four Models   763
IV. Special Importance of Model 4   767
V. Case Study of Collective Bargaining and ILO Implementation:
    NAFTA 2.0   768
VI. Provisions for Women and LGBTQ+ Persons   770

Chapter 24 · Resolving Labor Disputes under FTAs   773
I. Procedures under 1994 *NAFTA Labor Side Agreement*   773
II. Procedures under 2012 *Colombia TPA*   791
III. Cases under 1994 *NAFTA Labor Side Agreement*   802
IV. 2001 *Jordan FTA* and Jordanian Labor Conditions   803
V. 2006 *Bahrain FTA* and Arab Spring   805
VI. 2006 *CAFTA-DR* Chapter 16 and Enforcing and Guatemalan and
    Dominican Labor Law   806
VII. 2009 *Oman FTA* and Omani Labor Law Reform   811

Chapter 25 · Theory of TAA   815
I. Compensating "Losers" from Free Trade   815
II. Statutory Evolution   817
III. Five Non-Fiscal Policy Questions   838
IV. Generosity, Catholic Social Justice Theory, and Funding   839

Chapter 26 · Practice of TAA   843
I. Federal and State Involvement   843
II. Primary and Secondary Worker, and Farmer, Eligibility Criteria   845
III. Service Sector and Public Agency Worker Eligibility Criteria   850
IV. Four Types of Worker Benefits   852
V. Firm Eligibility   861
VI. Rebuilding Communities   862
VII. Proving Causation and 2013 *Western Digital* and 2014 *Boeing* Cases   864
VIII. Efficacy   866

Chapter 27 · GATT Article XX(b) and XX(g) Jurisprudence   871
I. Extraterritorial Measures, Primary Boycotts, and 1992 *Tuna-
    Dolphin I* Case   871
II. Extraterritorial Measures, Secondary Boycotts, and 1994 *Tuna-
    Dolphin II* Case   878
III. Eco-Labeling and 2012 *Tuna Dolphin* Case   879
IV. Two-Step Test, Differential Regulations, and 1996 *Reformulated
    Gas* Case   883
V. The Introductory Provisions of Article XX of the General Agreement:
    Applying the *Chapeau* of the General Exceptions   889
VI. Two-Step Test, Species Protection, and 1998 *Turtle-Shrimp* Case   891
VII. Passing Two-Step Test and 2001 *Asbestos* Case   905
VIII. Failing Two-Step Test and 2014 *China Rare Earths* Case   909
IX. Products versus Processes   911

Chapter 28 · Environmental Provisions in FTAs 913
   I. Six Metrics to Compare FTA Environmental Provisions 913
   II. Case Study: 1994 *NAFTA Environmental Side Agreement* 914
   III. Case Study: Contrasting Environmental Dispute Settlement under
      2005 *Singapore FTA*, 2005 *CAFTA-DR*, and 2009 *Peru TPA* 923
   IV. Case Study: 2012 *KORUS Environmental Chapter* 928
   V. May 2007 Bipartisan Trade Deal and Expansion of *NAFTA* 932
   VI. Case Study on Wildlife and Timber Trafficking, and IUU Fishing:
      NAFTA 2.0 933

Chapter 29 · Trade and Climate Change 937
   I. Synopsis of Scientific Evidence Concerning Climate Change 937
   II. Environmental Kuznets Curve 946
   III. Three Relationships between Trade and Climate Change 947
   IV. International Efforts to Mitigate Climate Change 950
   V. BTAs and GATT-WTO Rules 955
   VI. Failed Doha Round Environmental Negotiations 959
   VII. Toward a Plurilateral *Environmental Goods Agreement* 967

Chapter 30 · Overview of IP 977
   I. IP Types 977
   II. Leading International IP Treaties 980
   III. Importance of IP in Manufactured Products 984
   IV. Interests of Rich and Poor Countries 987
   V. 1994 Smith Argument on *TRIPs Agreement* Implementation 989
   VI. 1990 Raghavan Recolonization Argument 993
   VII. 1994 Ringo African Dilemma Argument 996
   VIII. Extended Transition Periods and December 2005 Hong Kong
      Ministerial Conference 1000

Chapter 31 · Substantive *TRIPs Agreement* Obligations 1003
   I. Purposes and Cornerstones 1003
   II. Summary Table to Navigate *TRIPs Agreement* 1004
   III. Special Points about Copyright Protection 1007
   IV. Mail Boxes and 1998 *India Patent Protection* Case 1008
   V. Substantive Holdings of 1998 *India Patent Protection* Case 1011
   VI. Jurisprudential Hypocrisy as to What "Law" Is? 1020

Chapter 32 · Compulsory Licensing, Evergreening, and
Patented Pharmaceuticals 1023
   I. Dreaded Diseases and Generic Medicines 1023
   II. Doha Round December 2005 Hong Kong Ministerial
      Conference and First Waiver from Article 31(f) 1024
   III. 2007 *Rwanda* Case Invoking Article 31(f) Waiver 1026
   IV. Doha Round December 2005 Hong Kong Ministerial
      Conference and Two Additional Waivers 1027

V. 2007 Thai and Brazilian, and 2012 Indian, Compulsory
License Cases 1028
VI. Evergreening and 2013 Indian Supreme Court *Novartis* Case 1030

Chapter 33 · IP Enforcement 1033
I. Infringement, Exclusion and Seizure, and Section 337 Elements 1033
II. Section 337 Operation 1036
III. Exclusion Orders 1037
IV. Presidential Discretion, Patent Hold Up Behavior, and
2011–2013 Apple-Samsung Cell Phone Patent War 1041
V. GATT Consistency of Section 337 and 1989 *Section 337* Case 1044
VI. Gray Market, Section 337, 1999 *Gamut* Case, and 2005 *SKF* Case 1045
VII. Refusing Protection and 2002 *Havana Club* Case 1054
VIII. Special 301 Black Listing 1065
IX. 2014 Case of India on Special 301 Priority List 1070

Index 1079

About the Author

Raj is the inaugural Leo. S. Brenneisen Distinguished Professor (2017–present) at the University of Kansas School of Law, before which he held the inaugural Rice Distinguished Professorship (2003–2017). Both are university-level chairs, the highest accolade for scholarship and research in Kansas. He served as KU's Associate Dean for International and Comparative Law (2011–2017).

Raj is Senior Advisor to Dentons U.S. LLP, the world's largest law firm, focusing on international and comparative legal matters. He practiced law at the Federal Reserve Bank of New York, where he twice won the President's Award for Excellence, thanks to his service as a delegate to the United Nations Conference on International Trade Law, and to the world class New York Fed lawyers who mentored him.

A Harvard Law School (J.D.) graduate, *cum laude*, Raj completed Master's degrees at the London School of Economics, in Economics, and Oxford (Trinity College), in Management-Industrial Relations, as a Marshall Scholar. His undergraduate degree (in Economics), *summa cum laude*, is from Duke, where he was an Angier B. Duke Scholar and inducted into *Phi Beta Kappa*. He graduated from the University School-Milwaukee. At each institution, he was blessed with great teachers.

Raj is author of one of the world's leading textbooks, *International Trade Law: A Comprehensive Textbook*, the 1st edition of which was published in 1996, and which has been used at over 100 law schools around the world. He wrote the first treatise on GATT in nearly 50 years, *Modern GATT Law*, and the first major book on the *Trans Pacific Partnership*, *TPP Objectively*. His book *Trade, Development, and Social Justice* applies Catholic social teaching to GATT special and differential treatment rules.

Raj is the first non-Muslim American scholar to write a textbook on Islamic Law, *Understanding Islamic Law (Sharī'a)*, which is used for courses in law schools and for U.S. Special Operations Forces. His new book projects are *Business Law of Modern India* and *Principles of Law, Literature, and Rhetoric*. "On Point" is his column, which Bloomberg Quint (India) publishes (www.bloombergquint.com).

He has been privileged to live, work, and/or explore about 50 countries across six continents, including India and Pakistan, Israel and most of the Gulf Arab countries, and China and (the separate customs territory of) Taiwan. His abiding professional goal is to educate for peace, that is, to enhance human capital and legal capacity for economic development, political stability, and international understanding.

He is an avid distance runner and has completed three of the "World's Major Marathons" (Boston twice, Chicago, and New York), and is a (rather poor) student of Shakespeare and Hindi. His Wikipedia entry is https://en.wikipedia.org/wiki/Raj_Bhala.

Table of Abbreviations

AANZFTA	ASEAN-Australia-New Zealand Free Trade Agreement
AB	WTO Appellate Body
ABA	American Bar Association
ABI	Automated Broker Interface
ACDB	WTO Accession Commitments Data Base
ACFTU	All China Federation of Trade Unions
ACP	African, Caribbean, and Pacific
ACS	Automated Commercial System
ACTRAV	Bureau for Workers' Activities (ILO)
ACWL	Advisory Center on WTO Law
AD	Antidumping
AD Agreement	WTO Antidumping Agreement (Agreement on Implementation of Article VI of the General Agreement on Tariffs and Trade 1994)
ADB	Asian Development Bank
ADP	Automatic data processing
ADVANCE Democracy Act	2007 Advance Democratic Values, Address Non-democratic Countries and Enhance Democracy Act
AECA	Arms Export Control Act of 1976
AEO	Authorized Economic Operator
AFA	Adverse Facts Available
AfDB	African Development Bank
AFIP	*Administración Federal de Ingresos Públicos* (Argentina, Federal Public Revenue Administration)
AFL-CIO	American Federation of Labor-Congress of Industrial Organizations
AFTA	ASEAN Free Trade Area
Ag	Agriculture
AGOA	2000 African Growth and Opportunity Act

AGOA II	(included in 2002 Trade Act)
AGOA III	2004 African Growth and Opportunity Acceleration Act
Agriculture Agreement	WTO Agreement on Agriculture
AI (1st meaning)	Artificial Intelligence
AI (2nd meaning)	Avian Influenza
AID	U.S. Agency for International Development
AIG	American Insurance Group
AIIS	American Institute for International Steel
AIPAC	American Israel Public Affairs Committee
AIOC	Anglo Iranian Oil Company
ALBA	Bolivarian Alliance for the Peoples of our America
ALJ	Administrative Law Judge
ALOP	Appropriate Level Of Protection
ALT	Alternate (alternate proposed text)
AMA	American Medical Association
AmCham	American Chamber of Commerce
AMPS	Acrylamido tertiary butyl sulfonic acid
AMS (1st meaning)	Aggregate Measure of Support
AMS (2nd meaning)	Agriculture Marketing Services (USDA)
ANAD	National Association of Democratic Lawyers (Mexico)
ANZCERTA	Australia-New Zealand Closer Economic Relations Trade Agreement (CER)
AoA	WTO Agreement on Agriculture
AOG	All Other Goods
AOR	All Others Rate
APEC	Asia Pacific Economic Cooperation (forum)
APOC	Anglo Persian Oil Company
AR	Administrative Review
ARI	Additional (United States) Rules of Interpretation
ARP Act of 2000	2000 Agricultural Risk Protection Act
ARRA	2009 American Recovery and Reinvestment Act
ARS	Advance Ruling System
ASA	American Sugar Alliance

ASCM	WTO Agreement on Subsidies and Countervailing Measures (SCM Agreement)
ASEAN	Association of South East Asian Nations
ASP	American Selling Price
ATAP	1996 Agreement Concerning Certain Aspects of Trade in Agricultural Products (1985 U.S.-Israel FTA)
ATC	WTO Agreement on Textiles and Clothing
ATPA	1991 Andean Trade Preferences Act
ATPDEA	2002 Andean Trade Promotion and Drug Eradication Act
ATT	2014 U.N. Arms Trade Treaty
AU$	Australian Dollar
AUD	Australian Dollar
AUV	Average Unit Value
AV	Audio-Visual
AVE	*Ad Valorem* Equivalent
B&H	Brokerage and handling (costs)
B&O	Washington State Business and Occupation Tax Rate Reduction
BA	Bankers Acceptance
BBS	Bangladesh Bureau of Statistics
B.C.	British Columbia
BCI	Business Confidential Information
BCR	Blue Corner Rebate (Thailand)
BDC	Beneficiary Developing Country
BDS	Boycott, Divestment, and Sanctions
Berne Convention	1886 (1971) Berne Convention for the Protection of Literary and Artistic Works
BFA	Banana Framework Agreement
BIA	Best Information Available (Pre-Uruguay Round U.S. term for Facts Available)
BILA (ILAB)	Bureau of International Labor Affairs (U.S. DOL OTLA)
BIS (1st meaning)	Bank for International Settlements
BIS (2nd meaning)	Bureau of Industry and Security (U.S. DOC)
bis (3rd meaning)	second version (of a text), again, repeat
B.I.S.D.	Basic Instruments and Selected Documents

BIT	Bilateral Investment Treaty
BJP	Bharatiya Janata Party (India)
BNA	Bureau of National Affairs (International Trade Reporter and International Trade Daily)
BOJ	Bank of Japan
BOK	Bank of Korea
Bolero	Bills of Lading for Europe
BOP	Balance Of Payments
BOT	Balance Of Trade
BP	British Petroleum
bpd	barrels per day
Brexit	Withdrawal of the U.K. from EU
BRICS	Brazil, Russia, India, China, and South Africa
BSE (1st meaning)	Bombay Stock Exchange
BSE (2nd meaning)	Bovine Spongiform Encephalopathy (Mad Cow Disease)
BSSAC	Beneficiary Sub-Saharan African Country
BTA (1st meaning)	Bilateral Trade Agreement
BTA (2nd meaning)	2002 Bio-Terrorism Act (Public Health Security and Bioterrorism Preparedness and Response Act of 2000)
BTA (3rd meaning)	Border Tax Adjustment
BTD	May 2007 Bipartisan Trade Deal
C&F	cost and freight
CAA	1979 Clean Air Act
CA$	Canadian Dollar
CAD	Canadian Dollar
CAPES	*Centre d'Analyse des Politiques, Economiques et Sociales* (Burkina Faso)
CAFTA-DR	*Central American Free Trade Agreement—Dominican Republic*
CAN	Community of Andean Nations
CANACAR	*Camara Nacional del Autotransporte de Carga*
CAP (1st meaning)	Common Agricultural Policy (EU)
CAP (2nd meaning)	Carolina Academic Press
CASA	*Construcciones Aeronáuticas SA* (Spain)
CB	citizens band (radio)

CBD	U.N. Convention on Biological Diversity
CBE	Commander of the Most Excellent Order of the British Empire
CBERA	1983 Caribbean Basin Economic Recovery Act
CBI (1st meaning)	Caribbean Basin Initiative
CBI (2nd meaning)	Central Bank of Iran
CBO	Congressional Budget Office
CBOT	Chicago Board Of Trade
CBP	U.S. Customs and Border Protection ("U.S. Customs Service" until 1 March 2003)
CBSA	Canadian Border Services Agency
CC	Cooperative Country (Argentina)
CCB	U.S. Conference of Catholic Bishops
CCC (1st meaning)	U.S. Commodity Credit Corporation (USDA)
CCC (2nd meaning)	Customs Cooperation Council (renamed WCO in 1994)
CCC (3rd meaning)	Commerce Country Chart
CCFRS	Certain cold flat-rolled steel
CCI	Countervailing Currency Intervention
CCL	Commerce Control List
CCP	Chinese Communist Party (or CPC, Communist Party of China)
CCPA	U.S. Court of Customs and Patent Appeals (abolished 1982; transfer to Federal Circuit)
CCS	Carbon Capture and Storage
CDC (1st meaning)	U.S. Centers for Disease Control
CDC (2nd meaning)	Canadian Dairy Commission
CDC (3rd meaning)	Chilean Distortions Commission
CDM	Clean Development Mechanism
CDSOA	2000 Continued Dumping and Subsidy Offset Act (Byrd Amendment)
CEC	Commission for Environmental Cooperation (*NAFTA*)
CEMAC	*Communauté Économique et Monétaire de l'Afrique Centrale*
CEP	Constructed Export Price
CEPR	Center for Economic and Policy Research
CER	Australia-New Zealand Closer Economic Relations Trade Agreement (ANZCERTA)

CET	Common External Tariff
CETA	Comprehensive Economic and Trade Agreement
CFC	Controlled Foreign Corporation
CFIUS	Committee on Foreign Investment in the United States
C.F.R. (1st meaning)	Code of Federal Regulations
CFR (2nd meaning)	Council on Foreign Relations
CGE	Computable General Equilibrium
CH	Order of the Companions of Honor
CHIPS	Clearing House Interbank Payment System
CIA	U.S. Central Intelligence Agency
CIC	Citizenship and Immigration Service for Canada
CIF (c.i.f)	Cost, Insurance, and Freight
CIP	Chhattisgarh Industrial Program (India)
CISADA	2010 Comprehensive Iran Sanctions, Accountability, and Divestment Act
CISG	Convention on Contracts for the International Sale of Goods (U.N.)
CIT	U.S. Court of International Trade (New York, N.Y.)
CITA	U.S. Committee for Implementation of Textile Agreements
CITES	1973 Convention on International Trade in Endangered Species of Wild Fauna and Flora
CITT	Canadian International Trade Tribunal
CJ	Commodity Jurisdiction
CKD	Complete knock down
CME	Chicago Mercantile Exchange
CMI	*Comité Maritime International* (IMO)
CMM	Conservation Management Measures
CMO	Common Market Organization (EU)
CNCE	*Commission Nacional de Comercio Exterior* (Argentina)
CNL	Competitive Need Limitation
CNY	Chinese Yuan
COBRA	Consolidated Omnibus Budget and Reconciliation Act (multiple years)
COCOM	Coordinating Committee on Multilateral Export Controls
COGS	Cost of Goods Sold

COMESA	Common Market for Eastern and Southern Africa
CONNUM	Control Number
COP	Cost of Production
COS	Circumstances of Sale (dumping margin calculation adjustment)
COSCO	Chinese Ocean Shipping Company
CPA	Certified Public Accountant
CPC	U.N. Central Product Classification list
CPSC	U.S. Consumer Product Safety Commission
CPTPP	Comprehensive and Progressive Agreement for Trans Pacific Partnership (entered into force 30 December 2018, informally called TPP 11)
CQE	Certificate of Quota Eligibility
Crop Year 2001 Act	Crop Year 2001 Agricultural Economic Assistance Act
CRS	Congressional Research Service
CRTC	Canadian Radio-Television and Telecommunications Commission
CSCL	China Shipping Container Lines
CSI	Container Security Initiative
CSP (1st meaning)	Conferences of States Parties
CSP (2nd meaning)	Certificate of Supplementary Protection (CETA)
CSPV	Crystalline Silicon Photovoltaic cells, modules, laminates, and panels (solar panels)
CTC	Change in Tariff Classification
CTD	WTO Committee on Trade and Development
CTESS	WTO Committee on Trade and Environment in Special Session
CTH	Change in Tariff Heading
CTHA	WTO Chemical Tariff Harmonization Agreement
CTPA	United States—Colombia Trade Promotion Agreement
C-TPAT	Customs—Trade Partnership Against Terrorism
CTSH	Change in Tariff Sub-Heading
CU	Customs Union
Customs Valuation Agreement	WTO Agreement on Customs Valuation (Agreement on Implementation of Article VII of the General Agreement on Tariffs and Trade 1994)

CUFTA (CUSFTA)	Canada — United States FTA
CV	Constructed Value
CVA	Canadian Value Added
CVD (1st meaning)	Countervailing Duty
CVD (2nd meaning)	Chronic Venous Disorder
CVI	Chronic Venous Insufficiency
CVID	Complete, Verifiable, Irreversible Disarmament
CWP	Circular Welded carbon quality steel Pipe
CY	Calendar Year
DAHD	Department of Animal Husbandry, Dairying, and Fisheries (India)
DARPA	U.S. Defense Advance Research Project Agency
DCR	Domestic Content Requirement
DCS	Destination Control Statement
DDA	Doha Development Agenda
DDTC	U.S. Directorate of Defense Trade Controls (Department of State)
DeitY	Department of Electronics and Information Technology (MCIT, India)
DFQF	Duty Free, Quota Free
DGFT	Director General of Foreign Trade (part of Ministry of Commerce, India)
DHS	U.S. Department of Homeland Security
DJAI	*Declaración Jurada Anticipada de Importación* (Argentina, Advance Sworn Import Declaration)
DIEM	*Derechos de Importación Específicos Mínimos* (Argentina, Minimum Specific Import Duties)
DIFMER	Difference in Merchandise (dumping margin calculation adjustment)
DIY	Do It Yourself
DM (1st meaning)	Dumping Margin
DM (2nd meaning)	*Deutsche Marks*
DMA	Domestic Marketing Assessment
DMZ	De-Militarized Zone
DOC	U.S. Department of Commerce
DOD	U.S. Department of Defense

DOE	U.S. Department of Energy
DOJ	U.S. Department of Justice
DOL	U.S. Department of Labor
DOT	U.S. Department of Transportation
DP (DPW)	Dubai Ports Dubai Ports World
DPA	Deferred Prosecution Agreement
DPCIA	1990 Dolphin Protection Consumer Information Act
DPRK	Democratic People's Republic of Korea (North Korea)
DRAM	Dynamic Random-Access Memory
DRAMS	Dynamic Random-Access Memory Semiconductor
DSB	WTO Dispute Settlement Body
DSM	Dispute Settlement Mechanism
DSU	WTO Dispute Settlement Understanding (Understanding on Rules and Procedures Governing the Settlement of Disputes)
DVD	Digital Video Recording
EA	Environmental Assessment
EAA	1979 Export Administration Act
EAC (1st meaning)	East African Community
EAC (2nd meaning)	East Asian Community
EAC (3rd meaning)	Environmental Affairs Council (CAFTA-DR, KORUS)
EADS	European Aeronautic Defense and Space Company NV
EAR	Export Administration Regulations
EBA	Everything But Arms
EBOR	Electronic On Board Recorder
EC (1st meaning)	European Commission
EC (2nd meaning)	European Communities
ECA (1st meaning)	Economic Cooperation Agreement
ECA (2nd meaning)	Agreement between the Government of the United States of America and the Government of the Republic of Korea on Environmental Cooperation (KORUS)
ECA (3rd meaning)	Export Controls Act of 2018 (part of 2018 NDAA)
ECAT	Emergency Committee for Foreign Trade
ECB	European Central Bank

ECC (1st meaning)	Environmental Cooperation Commission (CAFTA-DR)
ECC (2nd meaning)	Extraordinary Challenge Committee (NAFTA)
ECCAS	Economic Community of Central African States
ECCN	Export Control Classification Number
ECE	Evaluation Committee of Experts (NAFTA)
ECFA	Economic Cooperation Framework Agreement
ECHR	European Court of Human Rights
ECJ	European Court of Justice
ECLAC	Economic Commission for Latin America and the Caribbean
E-Commerce	Electronic Commerce
ECU	European Currency Unit
ED	Economic Development Administration (of DOC)
EDBI	Export Development Bank of Iran
EDC	Export Development Corporation (Canada)
EDI	Electronic Data Interchange
EEC	European Economic Community
EEZ	Exclusive Economic Zone
EFSA	European Food Safety Authority
EFTA	European Free Trade Association
EGA	WTO Environmental Goods Agreement
EIB	European Investment Bank
EIF	Enhanced Integrated Framework (formerly "IF," or "Integrated Framework")
EIG	*équipement d'intérêt general* (France)
ELLIE	Electronic Licensing Entry System
ELS	Extra Long Staple (cotton)
EN	Explanatory Note
ENFORCE Act (TFTEA, TEA)	2015 Trade Facilitation and Trade Enforcement Act
EOBR	Electronic On Board Recorder
EP	Export Price
EPA (1st meaning)	Economic Partnership Agreement
EPA (2nd meaning)	U.S. Environmental Protection Agency
EPI	Economic Policy Institute
EPZ	Export Processing Zone

ERP	Effective Rate of Protection
E-SIGN	2000 Electronic Signatures in Global and National Commerce Act
ESCS	European Steel and Coal Community
ESL	English as a Second Language
ESP	Exporter's Sales Price (Pre-Uruguay Round U.S. term for Constructed Export Price)
ERP	Effective Rate of Protection
ET (EST)	Eastern Time (Eastern Standard Time)
ETA	Employment and Training Administration (of DOL)
ETI Act	2000 Extraterritorial Income Exclusion Act (U.S.)
ETP	Eastern Tropical Pacific (Ocean)
ETS	Emission Trading Scheme
EU	European Union
EV	Electric Vehicle
Ex-Im Bank	U.S. Export-Import Bank
FACT Act of 1990 (1990 Farm Bill)	1990 Food, Agriculture, Conservation and Trade Act
FAIR Act of 1996 (1996 Farm Bill)	1996 Federal Agricultural Improvement and Reform Act
FAO	Food and Agricultural Organization
FAS	Foreign Agricultural Service (of USDA)
FAST	Free And Secure Trade
FATA	Federally Administered Tribal Areas (Pakistan)
FATF	Financial Action Task Force
FBI	U.S. Federal Bureau of Investigation
FCIC	U.S. Federal Crop Insurance Corporation (USDA)
FCPA	1977 Foreign Corrupt Practices Act
FDI	Foreign Direct Investment
Federal Circuit	U.S. Court of Appeals for the Federal Circuit (Washington, D.C.)
Fed. Reg.	Federal Register
FERC	U.S. Federal Energy Regulatory Commission
FF	*French Francs*
FFTJ	Fittings, flanges, and tool joints

FICCI	Federation of Indian Chambers of Commerce and Industry
FIFA	*Fédération Internationale de Football Association*
FINCEN	U.S. Financial Crimes Enforcement Network (Department of the Treasury)
FIRRMA	Foreign Investment Risk Review Modernization Act of 2018 (part of 2018 NDAA)
FIT	Feed-in tariff
FMCSA	Federal Motor Carrier Safety Administration
FMSA	2011 Food Safety Modernization Act
FMV (1st meaning)	Foreign Market Value (Pre-Uruguay Round U.S. term for Normal Value)
FMV (2nd meaning)	Fair Market Value
FMVSS	Federal Motor Vehicle Safety Standards
FOA	Facts Otherwise Available
FOB (f.o.b.)	Free On Board
FOP	Factors of Production
FOREX	Foreign Exchange
FPA	Foreign Partnership Agreement
FPC	U.S. Federal Power Commission (predecessor of DOE)
FRAND	Fair, Reasonable, and Non-Discriminatory (terms)
FRCP	U.S. Federal Rules of Civil Procedure
FRCrimP	U.S. Federal Rules of Criminal Procedure
FRE	U.S. Federal Rules of Evidence
FRS	Fellowship of the Royal Society
FRSA	Fellowship of the Royal Society for the Encouragement of Arts, Manufactures, and Commerce
FSA (1st meaning)	U.S. Farm Services Agency
FSA (2nd meaning)	Food Safety Agency (EU)
FSC	Foreign Sales Corporation
FSRI Act of 2002 (2002 Farm Bill)	2002 Farm Security and Rural Investment Act
FTA	Free Trade Agreement
FTAA	Free Trade Area of the Americas
FTAAP	Free Trade Agreement of the Asia Pacific Region
FTC	Free Trade Commission (NAFTA)

FTZ (1st meaning)	Foreign Trade Zone
FTZ (2nd meaning)	Free Trade Zone
FY	Fiscal Year
FX	Foreign Exchange
G7	Group of Seven Industrialized Nations
G8	Group of Eight Industrialized Nations
G20	Group of Twenty Developed Nations
G33 (or G-33)	Group of 33 Developing Countries
G&A	General and Administrative expenses
GAAP	Generally Accepted Accounting Principles
GAIN	USDA FAS Global Agricultural Information Network
GAO	U.S. Government Accountability Office
GATB	General Agreement on Trade in Bananas (15 December 2009)
GATS	General Agreement on Trade in Services
GATT	General Agreement on Tariffs and Trade (GATT 1947 and/or GATT 1994)
GATT 1947	General Agreement on Tariffs and Trade 1947 and all pertinent legal instruments (Protocols, Certifications, Accession Protocols, and Decisions) entered into under it before entry into force of the WTO Agreement (1 January 1995)
GATT 1994	GATT 1947 plus all pertinent legal instruments (1994 Uruguay Round Understandings and Marrakesh Protocol) effective with the WTO Agreement (1 January 1995)
GCC	Gulf Cooperation Council
GDP	Gross Domestic Product
GE	General Electric
GI	Geographical Indication
GILTI	Global Intangible Low-Taxed Income
GL	General License
GM	Genetically Modified, Genetic Modification
GMO	Genetically Modified Organism
GNH	Gross National Happiness
GNI	Gross National Income
GNP	Gross National Product
GOI	Government of India

GPA	Government Procurement Agreement (WTO Agreement on Government Procurement)
GPO	Government Pharmaceutical Organization (Thailand)
GPS	Global Positioning System
GPT	General Preferential Tariff
GRI	General Rules of Interpretation (of the HS)
GSM	General Sales Manager
GSP	Generalized System of Preferences (U.S.)
GSP+	Generalized System of Preferences Plus (EU)
GTA	Global Trade Atlas
GW	gigawatt
H5N1	Avian Flu (virus)
HCTC	Health Care Tax Credit
HDC	Holder in Due Course
HDI	U.N. Human Development Index
Helms-Burton Act	1996 Cuban Liberty and Democracy Solidarity (*Libertad*) Act
HFCS	High Fructose Corn Syrup
HHS	U.S. Department of Health and Human Services
HIPC	Highly Indebted Poor Country
HKMA	Hong Kong Monetary Authority
HM	Her (His) Majesty
HMG	Her (His) Majesty's Government
HNW	High Net Worth
HOEP	Hourly Ontario Energy Price
Homeland Security Act	2002 Homeland Security Act
HPAE	High Performing Asian Economy
HPAI	High Pathogenic Avian Influenza
HPC	High Performance Computer
HPNAI	High Pathogenic Notifiable Avian Influenza
HQ	Headquarters
HS	Harmonized System
HSBC	Hong Kong Shanghai Banking Corporation
HSBI	Highly Sensitive Business Information

HTS	Harmonized Tariff Schedule
HTSUS	Harmonized Tariff Schedule of the U.S.
HVAC	Heating, Ventilation, and Air Conditioning
IA (1st meaning)	Import Administration (U.S. DOC)
IA (2nd meaning)	Information Available
IA (3rd meaning)	Internal Advice
IADB	Inter-American Development Bank
IAEA	International Atomic Energy Agency
IBRD	International Bank for Reconstruction and Development (The World Bank)
IBT (1st meaning)	International Brotherhood of Teamsters
IBT (2nd meaning)	International Business Transactions
IC (1st meaning)	Indifference Curve
ICs	Indigenous Communities (Inuit and other indigenous communities)
ICAC	International Cotton Advisory Committee
ICC	International Chamber of Commerce
ICE	U.S. Immigration and Customs Enforcement
ICFTU	International Confederation of Free Trade Unions
ICJ	International Court of Justice
ICOR	Incremental Capital Output Ratio
ICS	Investment Court System
ICSID	International Center for the Settlement of Investment Disputes
ICTSD	International Center for Trade and Sustainable Development
IDB	Integrated Database
IDF	Israeli Defense Forces
IEC	Importer-Exporter Code (India)
IEEPA	1977 International Emergency Economic Powers Act
IFPRI	International Food Policy Research Institute
IFSA	2006 Iran Freedom Support Act
IFTA	1985 United States-Israel Free Trade Implementation Act
IGBA	1970 Illegal Gambling Business Act
IGG	*itinéraire à grand gabarit* (France)
IIPA	International Intellectual Property Alliance

ILAB (BILA)	Bureau of International Labor Affairs (U.S. DOL OTLA)
ILC	International Law Commission
ILO	International Labor Organization
ILRF	International Labor Rights Forum
ILSA	1996 Iran and Libya Sanctions Act (called ISA after IFSA)
IMC	Industrial Metal and Commodities
IMF	International Monetary Fund
IMF Articles	Articles of Agreement of the International Monetary Fund
IMO	International Maritime Organization (CMI)
IMTDC	iron mechanical transfer drive component
Incoterms	International Commercial Terms (ICC)
INR (1st meaning)	Initial Negotiating Right
INR (2nd meaning)	Indian *Rupee*
INS	U.S. Immigration and Naturalization Service (reorganized partly into ICE in March 2003)
IO	International Organization
IP	Intellectual Property
IPCC	Intergovernmental Panel on Climate Change
IPIC Treaty (Washington Treaty)	1989 Intellectual Property in Respect of Integrated Circuits
IPOA	International Plan Of Action
IPOA-IUU	International Plan Of Action to Prevent, Deter, and Eliminate Illegal, Unreported, and Unregulated Fishing (FAO)
IPPC	1952 International Plant Protection Convention
IPR (1st meaning)	Intellectual Property Right
IPR (2nd meaning)	International Priority Right
IRC	U.S. Internal Revenue Code
IRG (IRGC)	Iranian Revolutionary Guard Corps (Islamic Revolutionary Guard Corps)
IRISL	Islamic Republic of Iran Shipping Lines
IRQ	Individual Reference Quantity
IRS	U.S. Internal Revenue Service
ISA	Iran Sanctions Act of 1996, as amended, *i.e.*, Iran Sanctions Act of 2012 (formerly ILSA)
ISDS	Investor-State Dispute Settlement

ISIL	Islamic State in the Levant (ISIS)
ISIS	Islamic State in Shams (ISIL)
ISO	International Organization for Standardization
ISTC	International Sugar Trade Coalition
IT	Information Technology
ITA (1st meaning)	WTO Information Technology Agreement (1996)
ITA (2nd meaning)	U.S. International Trade Administration (DOC)
ITA II	Information Technology Agreement (2015)
ITAR	International Traffic in Arms Regulations
ITC	U.S. International Trade Commission
ITDS	International Trade Data System (electronic single window for import-export data)
ITO	International Trade Organization
ITO Charter (Havana Charter)	Charter for an International Trade Organization
ITRD	International Trade Reporter Decisions
ITSR	Iranian Transactions and Sanctions Regulations (31 C.F.R. Part 560)
ITT	ITT Corporation
ITT NV	ITT Night Vision
ITU	International Telecommunications Union
IUU	illegal, unreported and unregulated
JADE Act	2008 Tom Lantos Block Burmese JADE (Junta's Anti-Democratic Efforts) Act
J&K	Jammu and Kashmir (Indian-Administered Kashmir)
JFTC	Japan Fair Trade Commission
JIA	Japanese Investigative Authority
JNPT	Jawaharlal Nehru Port Terminals (Mumbai, India)
JPC	Joint Planning Committee (India)
JV	Joint Venture
KCBT	Kansas City Board of Trade
KDB	Korea Development Bank
KEXIM	Export-Import Bank of Korea
KFC	Kentucky Fried Chicken
KfW	*Kreditanstalt für Wiederaufbau* (Germany, Credit Agency for Reconstruction)

kg	kilogram
KMA	Kubota Manufacturing of America
KMT	*Kuomintang*
KORUS	Korea — United States Free Trade Agreement
KPPI	*Komite Pengamanan Perdagangan Indonesia* (competent international trade authority)
KSA	Kingdom of Saudi Arabia
KU	University of Kansas
kWh	Kilowatt hour
L/C	Letter of Credit
LAN	Local Area Network
LAP	Labor Action Plan (Colombia TPA)
LCA	Large Civil Aircraft
LCD	Liquid Crystal Display
LDBDC	Least Developed Beneficiary Developing Country
LDC (1st meaning)	Least Developed Country
LDC (2nd meaning)	Less Developed Country (includes developing and least developed countries)
LDC (3rd meaning)	Local distribution company
LGBTQ+	Lesbian, Gay, Bisexual, Transgender, Queer (or Questioning), and others
LLDC	Landlocked Developing Country
LNG	Liquefied Natural Gas
LNPP	Large Newspaper Printing Press
LOC	Line of Control (Kashmir)
LPAI	Low Pathogenic Avian Influenza
LPMO	Livestock Products Marketing Organization (Korea)
LOT	Level of Trade (dumping margin calculation adjustment)
LPNAI	Low Pathogenic Notifiable Avian Influenza
LPMO	Livestock Product Marketing Organization (Korea)
LRW	Large Residential Washer
LTFV	Less Than Fair Value
LWR	Light-Walled Rectangular pipe and tube
LWS	Laminated Woven Sacks
MAD	Mutually Assured Destruction

MAFF	Ministry of Agriculture, Forestry, and Fisheries (Korea)
MAI	Multilateral Agreement on Investment
MAP	Monitoring and Action Plan
Marrakesh Protocol	Marrakesh Protocol to GATT 1994
MAS	Monetary Authority of Singapore
MBB	*Messerschmitt-Bölkow-Blohm GmbH* (Germany)
MCIT	Ministry of Communications and Information Technology (India)
MCL	Munitions Control List
MCTL	Military Critical Technologies List
MDG	Millennium Development Goal
MDL	Military Demarcation Line (DMZ)
MEA	Multilateral Environmental Agreement
MEFTA	Middle East Free Trade Agreement
MENA	Middle East North Africa
METI	Ministry of Economy, Trade, and Industry (Japan, formerly MITI)
MFA	Multi-Fiber Arrangement (1974-2004)
MFN	Most Favored Nation
MHI	Mitsubishi Heavy Industries, Ltd.
MHT	*Matra Hautes Technologies* (France)
MIIT	Ministry of Industry and Information Technology (China)
MITI	Ministry of International Trade and Industry (Japan)
MMA	Minimum Market Access (quota)
MMBtu	Million British Thermal Unit
MMPA	1972 Marine Mammal Protection Act
MNC	Multinational Corporation
MNE	Multinational Enterprise
MOCI	Ministry of Commerce and Industry (India, Saudi Arabia)
MOCIE	Ministry of Commerce, Industry, and Energy (Korea)
MOFAT	Ministry of Foreign Affairs and Trade (Korea)
MOFCOM	Ministry of Commerce (China)
MOI (MOI Test)	Market Oriented Industry
MOTIE	Ministry of Trade, Industry, and Energy (Korea)
MOU	Memorandum of Understanding

MP	Member of Parliament
MPC	Marginal Propensity to Consume
MPF	Merchandise Processing Fee
MPS	Marginal Propensity to Save
MRA	Mutual Recognition Agreement
MRE	Meals Ready to Eat
MRL	Maximum Residue Level
MRM	Marine Resource Management
MRS	Marginal Rate of Substitution
MRT	Marginal Rate of Transformation
MSF	*Médecins Sans Frontières*
MSME	Micro, Small, and Medium Sized Enterprise
MSP	Ministry of Social Protection (Colombia)
MST	Minimum Standard of Treatment
mt	metric ton
MTA (1st meaning)	Multilateral Trade Agreement
MTA (2nd meaning)	Metropolitan Transit Authority (New York City)
MTB	Miscellaneous Trade Bill (multiple years)
MTN	Multilateral Trade Negotiation
MTO	Multilateral Trade Organization
MTOP	Millions of Theoretical Operations per Second
MVTO	Motor Vehicles Tariff Order (Canada)
MY	Marketing Year
NAD Bank	North American Development Bank (NAFTA)
NAAEC	North American Agreement on Environmental Cooperation (NAFTA Environmental Side Agreement)
NAALC	North American Agreement on Labor Cooperation (NAFTA Labor Side Agreement)
NAFTA	North American Free Trade Agreement (NAFTA 1.0 and/ or NAFTA 2.0)
NAFTA 1.0	North American Free Trade Agreement (original FTA that entered into force 1 January 1994)
NAFTA 2.0	North American Free Trade Agreement (revised FTA based on August 2017-September 2018 renegotiations, formally entitled USMCA, signed 30 November 2018)
NAI	Notifiable Avian Influenza

NAM (1st meaning)	U.S. National Association of Manufacturers
NAM (2nd meaning)	Non-Aligned Movement
NAMA	Non-Agricultural Market Access
NAO	National Administrative Office (NAFTA)
NATO	North Atlantic Treaty Organization
NASA	U.S. National Aeronautics and Space Administration
NBP	National Bank of Pakistan
NCC (1st meaning)	National Chicken Council
NCC (2nd meaning)	Non-Cooperative Country (Argentina)
NCM	Non-Conforming Measure
N.C.M.	*Nomenclatura Común MERCOSUR* (*MERCOSUR* Common Nomenclature)
NCTO	National Council of Textile Organizations
NDA	National Democratic Alliance (India)
NDAA	U.S. National Defense Authorization Act (annual policy bill for DOD and national security since 1962)
NDRC	National Development and Reform Commission (China)
NEI	National Export Initiative
NEP	New Economic Policy (Malaysia)
NFIDC	Net Food Importing Developing Country
NFTC	National Foreign Trade Council
NG	Natural Gas
NGR	Negotiating Group on Rules (WTO Doha Round)
NHI	National Health Insurance (Korea)
NHT	National Hand Tools Corporation
NIC	Newly Industrialized Country
NICO	Naftiran Intertrade Company
NIEO	New International Economic Order
NIOC	National Iranian Oil Company
NITC	National Iranian Tanker Company
NJPA	National Juice Products Association
NLC	National Labor Committee (U.S.)
NLCF	National Livestock Cooperatives Federation
NLD	National League for Democracy (Burma)
NMDC	National Minerals Development Corporation (India)

NME	Non-Market Economy
NMFS	U.S. National Marine Fisheries Service (DOC)
NNSA	U.S. National Nuclear Security Administration (DOE)
NOAA	U.S. National Oceanic and Atmospheric Administration (DOC)
NO_x	Nitrogen oxides
NPA	Non-Prosecution Agreement
NPC	National People's Congress (China)
NPF	Non-Privileged Foreign status
NPL	Non-Performing Loan
NPT	1968 Nuclear Non-Proliferation Treaty
NRA	National Rifle Association
NRC	U.S. Nuclear Regulatory Commission
NRI	Non-Resident Indian
NRL	Nuclear Referral List
NSA	U.S. National Security Agency
NSC	National Securities Commission (Argentina)
NSG	Nuclear Suppliers Group
NSIBR	National Security Industrial Base Regulations
NSM	Jawaharlal Nehru National Solar Mission (India)
NSPD	National Security Presidential Directive
NSS	WTO SPS National Notification System
NTA	National Textile Association (U.S.)
NTB	Non-Tariff Barrier
NTC	National Trade Council (United States)
NTE (1st meaning)	National Trade Estimate Report on Foreign Trade Barriers (USTR)
NTE (NTE sector) (2nd meaning)	Non-Traditional Export (sector)
NTM	Non-Tariff Measure
NTR	Normal Trade Relations
NV	Normal Value
NVOCC	Non-Vessel Operating Common Carrier
NWFP	North West Frontier Province (Pakistan) (Khyber Pakhtunkhwa)

N.Y. Fed (FRBNY)	Federal Reserve Bank of New York
NYU	New York University
NZ$	New Zealand Dollar
NZD	New Zealand Dollar
OAS	Organization of American States
OBE	Officer of the Most Excellent Order of the British Empire
OBRA	Omnibus Budget and Reconciliation Act (multiple years)
OCD	Ordinary Customs Duties
OCR	Out of Cycle Review
OCTG	Oil Country Tubular Goods
ODA	Official Development Assistance
ODC	Other Duties and Charges
OECD	Organization for Economic Cooperation and Development
OED	Oxford English Dictionary
OEE	U.S. Office of Export Enforcement (BIS)
OEM	Original Equipment Manufacturer
OFAC	U.S. Office of Foreign Assets Control (Department of the Treasury)
OIC	Organization of Islamic Conference
OIE	World Organization for Animal Health (*Office International des Epizooties*)
OMA	Orderly Marketing Arrangement
OMO	Open Market Operation
OOIDA	Owner-Operator Independent Drivers Association
OPA	Ontario Power Authority (Canada)
OPEC	Organization of Petroleum Exporting Countries
OPIC	U.S. Overseas Private Investment Association (U.S. International Development Finance Corporation)
OPZ	Outward Processing Zone (KORUS)
OTC	Over the Counter
OTCA	1988 Omnibus Trade and Competitiveness Act
OTCG	Oil Country Tubular Good
OTDS	Overall Trade distorting Domestic Support
OTEXA	Office of Textiles and Apparel (U.S. DOC)
OTLA	Office of Trade and Labor Affairs (in DOL)

OTR	Off-The-Road
PAP	People's Action Party (Singapore)
PAPS	Pre-Arrival Processing System
Paris Agreement	December 2015 Paris Climate Accord, or Paris Climate Agreement, under UNFCCC
Paris Convention	1883 Paris Convention for the Protection of Industrial Property
PASA	Pre-Authorization Safety Audit
PBC (PBOC)	People's Bank of China
PBS	Price Band System
PBUH	Peace Be Upon Him
PC	Personal Computer
PCA	Post-Clearance Audit
PCAST	President's Council of Advisors on Science and Technology (United States)
PCB	Printed Circuit Board
PCG (PCG fibers)	Polyvinyl alcohol (PVA), cellulose, and glass fibers
PDV	Present Discounted Value
PEO	Permanent Exclusion Order
PF	Privileged Foreign status
PFC	Priority Foreign Country
PhRMA	Pharmaceutical Manufacturers of America
PLO	Palestine Liberation Organization
PM	Prime Minister
PNTR	Permanent Normal Trade Relations
PNW	Pine wood nematode
POI	Period of Investigation
POR	Period of Review
POW-MIA	Prisoner of War — Missing in Action
PP	Purchase Price (Pre-Uruguay Round U.S. term for Export Price)
PPA	Power Purchase Agreement
PPF	Production Possibilities Frontier
PPM (1st meaning)	Parts Per Million
PPM (2nd meaning)	Process and Production Method

PPP	Purchasing Power Parity
PPS	Probability-Proportional to Size
PRC	People's Republic of China
PROEX	*Programa de Financiamento às Exportações* (Brazil)
PRO-IP Act	2008 Prioritizing Resources and Organization for Intellectual Property Act
PRS	Price Range System
PSA	Port of Singapore Authority
PSH	Public Stock Holding
PSI	Pre-Shipment Inspection
PSI Agreement	WTO Agreement on Pre-Shipment Inspection
PSRO	Product Specific Rule of Origin
PTA (1st meaning)	Preferential Trade Agreement, or Preferential Trading Arrangement
PTA (2nd meaning)	Payable through account
PTO	U.S. Patent and Trademark Office
PV	Photovoltaic
PVA (PVA fibers)	Polyvinyl alcohol fibers
PVC	Polyvinyl chloride
QE	Quantitative Easing
QIZ	Qualified Industrial Zone
QR	Quantitative Restriction
R&D	Research and Development
R&TD	Research and Technological Development measures
RAM	Recently Acceded Member (of WTO)
RBI	Reserve Bank of India
RCC	United States—Canada Regulatory Cooperation Council
RCEP	Regional Comprehensive Economic Partnership
RCMC	Registration-cum-Membership Certificate (India)
rDNA	recombinant deoxyribonucleic acid
REER	Real Effective Exchange Rate
RFMO	Regional Fisheries Management Organization
RMA (1st meaning)	Risk Management Association (U.S.)
RMA (2nd meaning)	Risk Management Authorization
RMB	*Ren min bi* ("people's money," the Chinese currency)

RMG	Ready Made Garment
RMI (DRM)	Rights Management Information (Digital Rights Management)
ROA	Return on Assets
Rome Convention	1964 Rome Convention for the Protection of Performer, Producers of Phonograms and Broadcasting Organizations
ROO	Rule Of Origin
ROW	Rest Of World
ROZ	Reconstruction Opportunity Zone
RPG	Rocket-propelled grenade
RPL	Relative Price Line
RPT	Reasonable Period of Time
Rs.	*Rupee*
RTA	Regional Trade Agreement
RTAA	Re-employment Trade Adjustment Assistance
RVC	Regional Value Content
S&D	Special and Differential
SAA	Statement of Administrative Action
SAARC	South Asia Association for Regional Cooperation
SACU	Southern African Customs Union
SADC	Southern African Development Community
SAFE Port Act	2006 Security and Accountability for Every Port Act
SAFTA	South Asia Free Trade Agreement
SAGIA	Saudi Arabian General Investment Authority
SAMA	Saudi Arabian Monetary Authority
SAPTA	South Asia Preferential Trading Arrangement
SAR	Special Administrative Region
SARS	Sudden Acute Respiratory Syndrome
SCGP	Supplier Credit Guarantee Program
SCM	Subsidies and Countervailing Measures
SCM Agreement	WTO Agreement on Subsidies and Countervailing Measures (ASCM)
SCP	Sugar Containing Product
SDF	Steel Development Fund (India)
SDG	United Nations Sustainable Development Goal

SDN	Specially Designated National
SE	*Secretaría de Economía* (Secretariat of Economy, Mexico, formerly *SECOFI*)
SEBI	Securities and Exchange Bureau of India
SEC	U.S. Securities and Exchange Commission
SECOFI	Secretary of Commerce and Industrial Development (*Secretario de Comercio y Fomento Industrial*), *i.e.*, Ministry of Commerce and Industrial Development (Mexico, renamed SE in December 2000)
SEI	Strategic Emerging Industry (SEI Catalogue—China)
SEIU	Service Employees International Union
SENTRI	Secure Electronic Network for Travelers Rapid Inspection
SEP	Standard Essential Patent
SEZ	Special Economic Zone
SFO	Serious Fraud Office
SG&A	Selling, General, and Administrative expenses
SG$	Singapore Dollar
SGD	Singapore Dollar
SCI	*Secretaría de Comercio Interior* (Argentina, Secretary of Domestic Trade)
SIE	State Invested Enterprise
SIFI	Systemically Important Financial Institution
SIFMA	Securities Industry and Financial Markets Association
SIL	Special Import License (India)
SIM	*Sistema Informático MARIA* (Argentina, AFIP electronic portal information system)
SIMA	Special Import Measures Act (Canada)
SKD	Semi-knock down
SMART	Secondary Materials and Recycled Textiles Association
SME (1st meaning)	Small and Medium Sized Enterprise
SME (2nd meaning)	Square Meter Equivalent
SMS	Supply Management System (Canada)
SNAP	Supplemental Nutritional Assistance Program
SNAP-R	Simplified Network Application Process—Redesign
S.O.	Statutory Order (India)

SOCB	State Owned Commercial Bank (China)
SOE	State Owned Enterprise
SOF	Special Operations Forces
SOGI	Sexual Orientation and Gender Identity
SPD	Solar Power Developer
SPI (1st meaning)	Seven Pillars Institute for Global Finance and Ethics
SPI (2nd meaning)	Special Program Indicator
SPS (1st meaning)	Sanitary and Phytosanitary
SPS (2nd meaning)	Single Payment Scheme
SPS Agreement	WTO Agreement on Sanitary and Phytosanitary Measures
SPV	Special Purpose Vehicle
SRAM	Static Random Access Memory (chip)
SRO	Special Remission Order (Canada)
SSA	Sub-Saharan Africa
SSAC	Sub-Saharan African Country
SSF Guidelines	Voluntary Guidelines for Securing Sustainable Small-Scale Fisheries in the Context of Food Security and Poverty Eradication (FAO)
SSG	Special Safeguard
SSM	Special Safeguard Mechanism
SSN	Resolutions of the National Insurance Supervisory Authority (Argentina)
STDF	WTO Standards and Trade Development Facility
STE	State Trading Enterprise
STO	Special Trade Obligation
SUV	Sport utility vehicle
SVE	Small, Vulnerable Economy
SWAT	Strategic Worker Assistance and Training Initiative
SWIFT	Society for Worldwide Interbank Financial Telecommunications
T&A	Textiles and Apparel
TAA (1st meaning)	Trade Adjustment Assistance
TAA (2nd meaning)	Trade Agreements Act of 1974, as amended
TAAEA	2011 Trade Adjustment Assistance Extension Act
TAA Reform Act	2002 Trade Adjustment Assistance Reform Act

TABC (TBC)	Trans-Atlantic Business Council (also abbreviated TBC)
TABD	Trans-Atlantic Business Dialogue
TAC	Total Allowable Catch
TB	tuberculosis
TBT	Technical Barriers to Trade
TBT Agreement	WTO Agreement on Technical Barriers to Trade
TCOM	Total Cost of Manufacturing
TCP (1st meaning)	Third Country Price
TCP (2nd meaning)	*El Tratado de Comercio entre los Pueblos*, ("Trade Treaty for the Peoples")
TCS	Tata Consulting Services
TDA	2000 Trade and Development Act
TDEA	1983 Trade and Development Enhancement Act
TDI	Trade Defense Instrument
TDIC	Tourism Development and Investment Company (Abu Dhabi, UAE)
TEA (1st meaning)	Trade Expansion Act of 1962, as amended
TEA (2nd meaning)	Trade Enforcement Act of 2015, as amended (same as TFTEA)
TED	Turtle Excluder Device
TEO	Temporary Exclusion Order
ter	third version (of a text)
TEU	Twenty Foot Equivalent Unit
TFA	WTO Agreement on Trade Facilitation (Trade Facilitation Agreement)
TFAF	Trade Facilitation Agreement Facility
TFP	Total Factor Productivity
TFR	Total Fertility Rate
TGAAA	2009 Trade and Globalization Adjustment Assistance Act
TIEA	Tax Information Exchange Agreement
TIFA	Trade and Investment Framework Agreement
TIPI	Trade and Investment Partnership Initiative
TIPT	Trade and Investment Partnership Initiative
TISA (TiSA, TSA)	WTO Trade in Services Agreement
TN	NAFTA business visa

TNC	WTO Trade Negotiations Committee
TOT	Terms of Trade
TPA (1st meaning)	Trade Promotion Agreement
TPA (2nd meaning)	Trade Promotion Authority (Fast Track)
TPBI	Thai Plastic Bags Industries
TPC	Technology Partnerships Canada
TPEA	2015 Trade Preferences Extension Act
TPF	United States — India Trade Policy Forum
TPL	Tariff Preference Level
TPM (1st meaning)	Trigger Price Mechanism
TPM (2nd meaning)	Technological Protection Measure
TPP	Trans Pacific Partnership
TPP 11	CPTPP (entered into force 30 December 2018)
TRA	Trade Readjustment Allowance
TRB	Tapered roller bearing
TRIMs	Trade Related Investment Measures
TRIMs Agreement	WTO Agreement on Trade Related Investment Measures
TRIPs	Trade Related Aspects of Intellectual Property Rights
TRIPs Agreement	WTO Agreement on Trade Related Aspects of Intellectual Property Rights
TRO	Temporary Restraining Order
TRQ	Tariff Rate Quota
TSA	U.S. Transportation Security Administration
TSUS	Tariff Schedule of the United States (predecessor to HTSUS)
T-TIP	Trans-Atlantic Trade and Investment Partnership
TV	Television
TVE	Town and Village Enterprise
TVPA	2000 Trafficking Victims Protection Act
TWEA	1917 Trading With the Enemy Act
TWN	Third World Network
UAW	United Auto Workers
UBC	University of British Columbia
U.C.C.	Uniform Commercial Code
UCLA	University of California at Los Angeles

UCP (1st meaning)	Uniform Customs and Practices
UCP (2nd meaning)	Unified Cargo Processing
UE	United Electrical, Radio and Machine Workers of America
UES	United Engineering Steel (U.K.)
UETA	1999 Uniform Electronic Transactions Act
UF	Ultra-filtered (milk)
UF_6	Uranium Hexafluoride
UI	Unemployment Insurance
UIEGA	2006 Unlawful Internet Gambling Enforcement Act
U.K.	United Kingdom
U.K.CGC	U.K. Carbon & Graphite Company
UMR	Usual Marketing Requirement (FAO)
UMTS	Universal Mobile Telecommunications System
UN	United Nations
UNCAC	United Nations Convention Against Corruption
UNCITRAL	United Nations Commission on International Trade Law
UNCLOS	United Nations Conference on the Law of the Sea Treaty
UNCTAD	United Nations Commission on Trade and Development
UNEP	United Nations Environmental Program
UNFCCC	United Nations Framework Convention on Climate Change
UNICA	Brazilian Sugarcane Industry Association
UNITA	National Union for the Total Independence of Angola
UNODA	United Nations Office of Disarmament Affairs
UPA	United Progressive Alliance (India)
UPOV	International Union for the Protection of New Varieties of Plants, referring to 1961 International Convention for the Protection of New Varieties of Plants (revised 1972, 1978, 1991)
UPS	United Parcel Service
UPU	Universal Postal Union
URAA	1994 Uruguay Round Agreements Act
U.S.	United States
USAPEEC	USA Poultry and Egg Export Council
U.S.C.	United States Code
USCCAN	United States Code Congressional and Administrative News

USMCA	United States-Mexico-Canada Agreement (revised FTA based on August 2017-September 2018 renegotiations, informally called NAFTA 2.0, signed 30 November 2018)
USML	United States Munitions List
USP	United States Price (Pre-Uruguay Round U.S. term encompassing both Purchase Price and Exporter's Sales Price)
U.S.S.R.	Union of Soviet Socialist Republics
USTR	U.S. Trade Representative
USW (1st meaning)	United Steel, Paper and Forestry, Rubber, Manufacturing, Energy, Allied Industrial and Service Workers International Union
USW (2nd meaning)	United Steel Workers of America
VAT	Value Added Tax
VC	Venture Capital
VCR	Video Cassette Recorder
VEO	Violent Extremist Organization
VER	Voluntary Export Restraint
VEU	Validated End User
Vienna Convention	1969 Vienna Convention on the Law of Treaties
VOC	Volatile organic compound
VRA	Voluntary Restraint Agreement
VW	Volkswagen AG
W120	WTO services classification list (based on CPC)
WA	1995 Wassenaar Arrangement
WAML	Wassenaar Arrangement Munitions List
WCO	World Customs Organization (formerly CCC until 1994)
WHO	World Health Organization
WIPO	World Intellectual Property Organization
WMD	Weapon of Mass Destruction
WMO	World Meteorological Association
WTO	World Trade Organization
WTO Agreement	Agreement Establishing the World Trade Organization (including all 4 Annexes)
WWF	World Wildlife Fund
XITIC	Xiamen International Trade and Industrial Company

ZAC	*zone d'aménagemement concertée* (France)
ZTE	Zhongxing Telecommunications Corp.
1916 Act	Antidumping Act of 1916, as amended (repealed)
1930 Act	Tariff Act of 1930, as amended
1934 Act	Reciprocal Trade Agreements Act of 1934
1934 FTZ Act	Foreign Trade Zones Act of 1934, as amended
1974 Act	Trade Act of 1974, as amended
1978 Act	Customs Procedural Reform and Implementation Act
1979 Act	Trade Agreements Act of 1979
1984 Act	International Trade and Investment Act of 1984 (Trade and Tariff Act of 1984)
1988 Act	United States—Canada Free Trade Implementation Act
1990 Act	Customs and Trade Act of 1990
1993 NAFTA Implementation Act	North American Free Trade Implementation Act of 1993
2002 Act	Trade Act of 2002
2003 Act	Burmese Freedom and Democracy Act of 2003
2007 Act	Implementing Recommendations of the 9/11 Commission Act of 2007
2010 Act	Omnibus Trade Act of 2010
3D	Three dimensional
3PLs	Third Party Logistics Providers
3Ts (3T Issues)	Taiwan, Tiananmen, and Tibet
4Ts (4T Issues)	Taiwan, Tiananmen, Tibet, and The Party (CCP)

Part One

Rationales for FTAs

Chapter 1

Economic Aspects of FTAs[1]

I. Terminological Distinctions and Examples

- "RTA" and "PTA"

Roughly 30% of total U.S. imports are accounted for by a free or preferential trading arrangement (with *NAFTA* and *KORUS* being statistically pre-eminent). But, to appreciate that fact begs an important technical matter of terminology. There is a distinction among the terms RTA, FTA, and CU. The term RTA is an umbrella covering both FTAs and CUs. Sometimes, the term PTA, is used as a synonym for RTA. The term RTA is misleading. It suggests all countries that are in a particular FTA or CU are located in the same geographic region. America and Bahrain are not in the same region, yet have an FTA. That also is because RTA intimates all countries in a region are members of an RTA. Belize and Panama are not members of the *CAFTA-DR*.

The term PTA avoids this misconception. However, "PTA" can be confused with preferential arrangements for developing and least developed countries, such as the GSP and *AGOA*. Thus, there is no perfect term or acronym to cover FTAs and CUs.

Among RTAs, the balance of attention of many international trade lawyers and scholars, and the business media, focuses on FTAs. Accordingly, this and subsequent Chapters frequently employ the rubric of "FTAs." However, many of the legal and policy principles are applicable to CUs, and where appropriate, attention is dedicated to them.

- "FTA"

GATT Article XXIV:8 embeds the distinction between an FTA and CU. This provision not only provides the exemption from the MFN obligation of GATT Article I:1 necessary to create an RTA, but also defines the two creatures. An FTA is an arrangement between two or more countries removing all, or substantially all, barriers to trade between or among them. The arrangement may be bilateral, *i.e.*, between two countries, such as the FTAs the U.S. has with Israel and Bahrain. Or, an FTA may be plurilateral, *i.e.*, among a group of countries, such as the *NAFTA*,

---

1. Documents References:
   (1) *Havana (ITO) Charter* Articles 43–45
   (2) GATT Article XXIV
   (3) Relevant Provisions in FTAs

which covers Canada, Mexico, and the U.S., *COMESA*, (an FTA with aspirations to be a CU), which covers 20 African nations, and *CAFTA-DR*, which covers Costa Rica, El Salvador, Guatemala, Honduras, Nicaragua, plus the Dominican Republic and U.S.

Each Party to an FTA retains its sovereignty as to setting trade barriers vis-à-vis products originating from third countries (*i.e.*, non-FTA members). For example, assume neither the U.S. nor Bahrain has an FTA with Brazil. The U.S. might impose a 2.5% tariff on passenger automobiles from Brazil, whereas Bahrain retains a 5% duty on the same vehicles. Under the *U.S.-Bahrain FTA*, however, the FTA parties have agreed to the same duty on vehicles traded between them — zero.

- "TCP"

Inspired partly by socialist-oriented Latin American leaders during the first decade of the new millennium, such as Bolivian President Evo Morales (1959–, President, 2006–) and Venezuelan President Hugo Chávez (1954–2013, President, 2002–2013), "PTA" took on another meaning: "Peoples Trade Agreement." The Spanish acronym is "TCP," for *El Tratado de Comercio entre los Pueblos, i.e.,* "Trade Treaty for the Peoples." A PTA in this sense is an economic alternative and political challenge to an FTA. In April 2006, Bolivia and Venezuela joined Cuba in a 10-point PTA. The first point says the trilateral accord

> is a response to the failed neo-liberal model, based as it is on deregulation, privatization and indiscriminate opening of markets.[2]

Accordingly, the PTA aims to promote

> a model of trade integration between people that limits and regulates the rights of foreign investors and multinationals so that they serve the purpose of national productive development.[3]

What motivated Bolivia, Venezuela, and Cuba to sign a PTA?

One answer is they resurrected — consciously or not — Socialist-style trade policies popular in Latin America in the 1950s and 1960s. Leading economists like Paul Baran (1909–1964), Raul Prebisch (1901–1986), and Sir Hans Singer (1910–2006) advocated these policies. Another answer is a genuine sense a conventional market capitalist FTA will not work for them. President Morales vowed in March 2006 Bolivia "never" would negotiate an FTA with the U.S., and in August 2006 Bolivian Vice President Álvaro García Linera (1962–) explained:

> Bolivia wants trade relations with the entire world. I traveled to the United States to try to advance a trade pact. But, we can't just have free trade under the old rules, because it is too aggressive for our economy.

---

2. *Quoted in* Lucien O. Chauvin, *Venezuela, Bolivia, and Cuba Sign Alternative "Trade Treaty for the Peoples,"* 23 International Trade Reporter (BNA) 692 (4 May 2006). [Hereinafter, *Venezuela, Bolivia.*]

3. *Quoted in Venezuela, Bolivia.*

For example, how is a small farmer in Bolivia going to compete with farmers from countries that use the latest tractors and other technologies? It's like trying to make the 2nd century compete with the 21st century. The same goes for our urban small businesses. How are we going to compete with giant factories under such conditions?[4]

Interestingly, a third answer is soybean economics provoked the Bolivia-Venezuela-Cuba PTA. When Colombia signed an FTA with the U.S. on 27 February 2006, it agreed to purchase a 600,000-ton quota of American soybeans. Until that point, Bolivia had shipped 500,000 tons of soybeans to Colombia, worth $166 million (in 2005). The *Colombia TPA* thus diverts soybean trade away from Bolivia and toward America. Bolivian President Morales responded immediately with the PTA proposal. Andean region politics reinforced his call.

The *Community of Andean Nations (CAN)* — founded in 1969, and comprised of Bolivia, Colombia, Ecuador, Peru and Venezuela — had been disintegrating. Not only Colombia, but also Peru (in April 2006), signed FTAs with the U.S. Further, in December 2005, *MERCOSUR* admitted Bolivia and Venezuela to full membership (though actual admission was deferred for political reasons, so Venezuela did not join until July 2012, and effective 1 December 2016 was suspended temporarily, and on 5 August 2017 indefinitely, while Bolivia remains an associate member). In April 2006, Venezuelan President Hugo Chavez (1954–2013, President, 1999–2013) announced his country was withdrawing from *CAN*, and called the Peruvian President, Alejandro Toledo (1946–, President, 2001–2006), a traitor to South America for signing an FTA with America.

- "CU"

A CU is one step deeper than an FTA in terms of economic integration. The members of a CU — which may be bilateral or plurilateral — agree to delete all, or substantially all, barriers to internal trade between or among them. In that sense of internally free movement of goods, and an attendant set of rules to determine origin within the grouping, a CU is like an FTA. However, the CU Parties also agree to a CET, which means they establish the same trade barriers on the same categories of products in the HS — a unified set of customs laws and procedures. In brief, a CU is a single market both as among the members and vis-à-vis the rest of the world.

Of course, it is not easy for countries to agree on a unified tariff schedule, and harmonize their NTBs. They must not only coordinate their foreign economic policy, but also integrate this homogenous outlook with their domestic commercial, financial, and investment needs and interests. No one country can impose its trade policies on the others in the grouping. That is as true for customs duties as it is for NTBs (such as technical standards), investment rules, and IP protection. Not surprisingly, therefore, there are fewer examples of CUs in the world than there are

---

4. *Quoted in* James Langman, *Bolivia Looks for New Kind of Trade Pace With U.S., While Seeking ATPDEA Extension*, 23 International Trade Reporter (BNA) 1198–2000 (10 August 2006).

FTAs, and often countries seeking an RTA start with an FTA, and then articulate a desire to move to a CU in the future.

For example, *MERCOSUR*, initially established in 1991, has Brazil, Argentina, Paraguay, and Uruguay as founding members, plus Venezuela. Brazil, Argentina, and Venezuela are, respectively, the first, second, and third largest South American economies, accounting for roughly 60% of the GDP of the continent (as of July 2012, though by March 2018, Colombia had easily overtaken Venezuela). But, *MERCOSUR* countries share a legacy of import substitution protectionist policies, and they compete against one another in some products. Autos and footwear are examples. So, they do not have a unified CET that applies horizontally to all tariff lines. Rather, the *MERCOSUR* CET is set at 11 different levels, from zero to 20% depending on the product, and was phased in from its initial agreement in 1995 through 2014. The average *MERCOSUR* CET is 14%–15%. On most imported products, the CET is below 20–22%. In December 2011, they agreed to a waiver list of 100 products per country, whereby they could raise duties up to 35%. Such items include automobiles, which is unsurprising as Argentina and Brazil both produce them, and for which 35% is their maximum WTO bound rate. In July 2012, fearing competition from Chinese and other aggressively priced exports, *MERCOSUR* doubled the size of the waiver list to 200 items.

Arguably, *MERCOSUR* is a "bad customs union." That was the characterization of Uruguay President Jose Mujica in March 2013. He cited the many exceptions to the CET, along with unilateral Argentine import and foreign exchange restrictions following the 2008 global economic crisis. He also pointed to political quarrels, such as the suspension of the membership of Paraguay when the other members deemed the impeachment trial of its President undemocratic. Perhaps most damning was the self-imposed isolation of *MERCOSUR* from the U.S. and Europe. In 2005, *MERCOSUR* rejected an American proposal to create a hemispheric FTA, and its FTA negotiations with the EU, launched in 1995, dragged on to no end. Understandably, the U.S. turned to the Asia-Pacific region *TPP*, and to the EU for an FTA, leaving *MERCOSUR* adrift.

The most obvious and successful (at least until the Eurozone crisis that started in late 2009) example of a CU is the EU. However, it actually is a step beyond a CU, insofar as most of the Union members (with the notable exceptions of the U.K. and Denmark) have accepted a common currency—the *euro*. In other words, the EU boasts not only a single market that is the hallmark of a CU, but also monetary union. Such union necessitates prior agreement on convergence criteria, for example, permissible government budget deficits. In addition to the EU, other examples of CUs include *MERCOSUR* and *SACU*.

Price differentials between the U.S. and Canada intimate the difference between a CU and FTA. Despite the 1988 FTA between these Parties, superseded by *NAFTA* in 1994, prices of like products commonly purchased by consumers on either side of the border are unequal. It would be wrong to expect retail or wholesale price convergence: because the U.S. and Canada are not in a CU, they do not share a CET.

In 2012, Canadian retail prices on regularly-bought items were 27% higher than those in the U.S. (though in 2002 they were 22% less, and remained low through the mid-2000s).[5] While neither the U.S. nor Canada imposes tariffs on goods originating from the other (or Mexico), each levies duties on merchandise from non-*NAFTA* Parties (save for those countries with which they have a different FTA). Canada's tariffs on a variety of goods, such as cheese, eggs, milk, poultry, and yogurt, are higher than those of America. Its relatively higher duty rates are part of Canada's long-standing supply management system for dairy and other products, and translate into higher retail prices. Contributing further to price differentials are higher costs of doing business in Canada (because of stricter regulation and higher fuel, income, and property taxes), lower density in the Canadian market, and less competition among wholesalers.

- Arab Islamic CU: GCC

While the Near East boasts an ancient history of trading, among Arab countries for most of the 20th and early 21st centuries, trade languished. Conflict, imprudent economic policies, outright corruption, the scourge of Islamist extremism, plus the lingering effects of colonialism, are among the culprits. But, Arab countries have made efforts to foster regional trade. An illustration of a CU in the Arab Islamic world was formed in 1981 in Riyadh, Saudi Arabia. Six Arab countries in the Gulf (that is, the Persian or Arabian Gulf) region—Bahrain, Saudi Arabia, Kuwait, Oman, Qatar, Saudi Arabia, and the UAE—agreed to form the "Cooperation Council for the Arab States of the Gulf," of "GCC." As a Persian country, Iran is not a member. The other proximate Arab nations, Iraq and Yemen, also did not join, though Yemen (as of 2015) seeks membership, though it (unlike the GCC Parties, and unlike Iraq) has no Gulf coastline.

The purpose of the GCC is to promote stability and economic cooperation in the region. Thus, in 1991, during the first Gulf War, the GCC formed a regional military force with Egypt and Syria, which was used to liberate Kuwait and is available for peacekeeping purposes. The GCC also has a fund for Arab development. Most notably, in January 2003, the GCC eliminated tariff and many NTBs on trade among member states, and established a CU.

Specifically, at a December 2001 GCC Heads of State Summit, GCC leaders agreed to an across-the-board CET of 5% on imports originating from non-GCC countries, with implementation in January 2003. Considerable challenges face the GCC, such as agreement on a list of products as to which a tariff higher than the 5% CET will apply. Some GCC countries have tariffs of 15–20% or more on certain products—Bahrain, for instance, has a 20% duty on 12-millimeter steel bars. Some of them impose a duty of 100% or more on goods the consumption of which

---

5. *See* Nicholas Li, *Sticker Shock: The Causes of the Canada-U.S. Price Differential*, C.D. Howe Institute, University of Toronto (6 May 2014), www.cdhowe.org/pdf/Commentary_409.pdf; Peter Menyasz, *Study Blames Tariffs for Price Gap, Not Anticompetitive Behavior in Canada*, 31 International Trade Reporter (BNA) 918 (15 May 2014).

Islamic Law (*Sharīʿa*) forbids, namely, alcohol, pork, and pork products. On alcohol (as discussed in a separate Chapter), Bahrain puts a 125% duty, and Oman and Qatar a 100% duty, but Saudi Arabia bans importation of all these goods under GATT Article XX(a). Most GCC countries impose a 100% tariff on tobacco products. Additional challenges the GCC faces in achieving a CU include agreement on harmonizing technical standards, and distributing revenues.

Like the EU, the GCC aspires to create a common currency, and thus achieve monetary union. The GCC articulated this goal in 2001, along with convergence criteria to achieve it, namely:

(1) Each GCC country would maintain an inflation rate of 2% or less.

(2) Each GCC would limit its annual fiscal deficit to no more than 3% of GDP.

Following the EU model, the GCC believed that along with dismantling trade barriers, a single currency would boost intra-regional trade.

The original target date for GCC monetary union was 1 January 2010, with the new currency to float freely by 2015. To meet this deadline, Kuwait agreed in January 2003 to end its 27-year-long link to a basket of currencies. (Kuwait was the only GCC country to peg its currency to a unit other than the U.S. dollar. The other GCC countries linked their currencies to the dollar.) Yet, the GCC did not meet its interim 2005 deadline for meeting convergence criteria, especially inflation rates, which vary considerably in the Gulf Region. Given the real-world experience of the EU in forming a monetary union, the ECB (among other entities) provided technical assistance on convergence criteria, including the formation of a common currency, the name of such currency, and the location of a central bank. In September 2006, the GCC agreed to put its Central Bank in Abu Dhabi. As for the currency name, it might be "*karam*"—the Arabic word for "generosity."

Nevertheless, in March 2009 the GCC had no choice but to postpone its planned monetary union. Several GCC countries had implemented unilateral measures to support growth and help their own banking systems, particularly in the global economic recession that struck following the September 2008 collapse of Lehman Brothers on Wall Street. Oman declared it would not join the currency union. The GCC had yet to agree on a common regulatory or monetary policy framework to cover critical issues like reserve management. None of the six GCC governments had endorsed formally a single currency agreement. Implementing even the first convergence criterion was not possible, because the GCC had not harmonized statistical and data collection and evaluation, and thus had no common measure for inflation. In an effort to maintain some momentum toward monetary union, the GCC planned to launch a Monetary Council, as a precursor to a Central Bank, sometime in 2009.

That effort failed when, in May 2009, the UAE pulled out of the agreement to form a common currency. It did so because the GCC, possibly under heavy Saudi pressure, opted to move the site for the GCC Central Bank to Riyadh.

Interestingly, in June 2010, Jordan, Lebanon, and Syria joined with Turkey to agree on establishing an FTA and free travel zone. Frustrated at continued rebuffs by the EU to join that CU, Turkey turned to the Arab world. Since the era of the Ottoman Empire (11th century–1923), Turkey had been a bridge between East and West. Turkey thus signed FTAs with Egypt, Jordan, Morocco, Palestine, Syria, and Tunisia.

II. Global Statistics and Trends

No one possibly can know every detail of each RTA.[6] There are too many of them. There were over 300 RTAs in force as of October 2011, an increase from 70 in 1990. The average WTO Member was Party to 13 RTAs. The number of FTAs and CUs well exceeded the number of countries on earth, and that number continues to rise.

By May 2018, the WTO reported 459 RTAs (including FTAs, CUs, economic integration agreements, and partial scope agreements) in force, with some Members party to over 20 deals. There was a period in which only one Member — Mongolia (which acceded to the WTO effective 29 January 1997) — was not in any FTA or CU. But, with the *Japan-Mongolia Free Trade Agreement and Economic Integration Agreement*, which was signed on 10 February 2015 and entered into force on 7 June 2016, that period ended (*i.e.*, by June 2016, every WTO Member was Party to at least one RTA). About two-thirds of all RTAs are between or among developing countries, and referred to as "South-South" RTAs (because so many poor countries are in the Southern Hemisphere).

III. Overview of U.S. FTAs

Tor scholars, students, and practitioners engaged in trade matters involving the U.S., it is important to memorize the countries with which America has an FTA, and thereby be able to spot when an FTA issue actually or potentially arises. The U.S. is a party to the following FTAs:

(1) *Israel FTA*, effective 30 August 1985.

(2) *CUFTA*, effective 1 January 1989 (but legally most provisions suspended by *NAFTA*).

(3) *NAFTA*, effective 1 January 1994.

(4) *Jordan FTA*, effective 17 December 2001.

---

6. *See* RAJ BHALA, DICTIONARY OF INTERNATIONAL TRADE LAW (3rd ed. 2015) (containing Annexed Tables with legal and political facts about the FTAs in which the U.S. is involved, and summarizing substantive market access provisions concerning goods, services, and government procurement in those FTAs).

(5) *Singapore FTA*, effective 1 January 2004.

(6) *Chile FTA*, effective 1 January 2004.

(7) *Australia FTA*, effective 1 January 2005.

(8) *Morocco FTA*, effective 1 January 2006.

(9) *CAFTA-DR*, effective 1 March 2006 with El Salvador, and 1 April 2006 with Guatemala, Honduras, and Nicaragua, implemented the Dominican Republic on 1 March 2007, and narrowly approved in an October 2007 referendum in Costa Rica, where it took effect on 1 January 2009.

(10) *Bahrain FTA*, effective 1 August 2006.

(11) *Oman FTA*, effective 1 January 2009.

(12) *Peru FTA*, effective 1 February 2009.

(13) *Colombia FTA*, signed 22 November 2006, and enacted in October 2011 following agreement by Colombia in April 2011 on *Action Plan Related to Labor Rights* to strengthen worker protections and deal with violence against trade unionists, and effective 15 May 2012.

(14) *Panama FTA*, signed in December 2006, but with the labor provisions left open pending guidance from Congress, and enacted in October 2011 following agreement by Panama in spring 2011 to address concerns about labor rights and in April 2011 to enhance tax transparency, and effective 31 October 2012.

(15) *KORUS*, signed in March 2007, revised under an April 2008 *Beef Import Protocol* and January–February 2011 *Supplemental Agreement* covering auto trade, enacted in October 2011, and effective 15 March 2012.

Further, every international trade lawyer should be aware of a number of intriguing features evident from these FTAs, which provoke many questions. Consider:

(1) The time between commencing negotiations and entry into force. What factors affect the gap?

(2) The votes in Congress on each FTA, including the overall vote and "no" vote by political party, and political control in Congress at the time of the vote. Is there anything left of the famed post–Second World War bipartisan consensus in favor of free trade?

Obviously, there are an enormous number of FTAs—planned, in negotiations, and implemented—not involving the U.S.

For instance, Australia, Japan, Mexico, New Zealand, and Singapore have FTA "dockets," as it were, differing in activity, history, and purpose. So, too, does the EU. Indeed, it has entered into, and continues to pursue, "association agreements." These free trade deals are more than an economic link. They are designed as the first step toward accession into the EU, at least for some of the former Soviet bloc countries. It is dubious as to whether the EU ever would admit all of the countries in the Mediterranean region with which it has such agreements.

IV. Job Creation or Destruction?

• Theoretical Points

RTAs are far more than economic creatures. They also are political bodies, which is apparent from watching their treatment on Capitol Hill. Sometimes, economic issues dominate the debate. Beef, dairy and sugar lobbies had serious reservations about the *Australia FTA*. But, often other factors enter into the legislative process. *NAFTA* almost was derailed by a 10–10 authorizing vote in the Senate Finance Committee, the *Jordan FTA* was held up for a year over ideology, and labor rights and social issues loomed large in the rows over the *CAFTA-DR* and *Colombia FTA*. Moreover, RTAs may be about the cultural identity of a region. By integrating governments and communities of the members, they may give them a collective voice in the global economy. For instance, Malaysian Prime Minister Mahathir Muhammad (1925, PM, 1981–2003, 2018–) adamantly opposes American membership in the FTA of *ASEAN*. Were the far larger U.S. a member of the *ASEAN FTA* (*AFTA*), it would drown out the distinct voice of the smaller South East Asian countries, and meddle in their internal and regional affairs.

Thus, it is unfair to judge the success of RTAs solely on neoclassical economic grounds. Yet, so they are: whether they "are good" or "make sense" depends on their economic performance. The analysis is both theoretical and empirical in nature. To begin, as a general economic benefit RTA advocates say in virtually all countries with which the U.S. has entered into an FTA, there has been an increase in *per capita* GNP, and sometimes acceleration in the rate of growth of *per capita* GNP. The elimination of trade barriers—that is, deeper cuts in tariffs and NTBs than occur in a multilateral trade round under GATT-WTO auspices—by a fewer number of countries at least correlates with the *per capita* income changes. Whether this elimination is a statistically significant causal factor, much less the most important one, in boosting income, is another question. Even if it is, changes in income distribution and poverty levels are a key, hotly contested matter.

The effects of RTAs on income levels, growth, and distribution are connected with a bottom-line question that virtually all workers, whether blue or white collar, whether in agriculture, manufacturing, or services, ask—or ought to ask—when their government contemplates an RTA: what will this mean for my job? In the most general sense, the answer is that an RTA presents both risks and opportunities. Hence, the appetite of any individual for an RTA may depend on her risk profile.

Knowing this question resonates in the minds of many workers, much of the empirical economic research focuses on whether more jobs are created than are lost in each of the member countries of an RTA. Free trade theory is misinterpreted if it is believed there are no "losers" from trade liberalization. The reduction of tariff and NTBs is supposed to reward industries that have a comparative advantage, and punish those that do not. In turn, productive resources (labor, land, human capital, physical capital, and technology) are supposed to be reallocated from the "losing" to the "winning" sectors.

Moreover, recall the Stolper-Samuelson Theorem predicts trade liberalization will lead to a reduction in the returns to labor in the labor-scarce country. That is, wages will fall in that country, and rise in the labor-surplus country. The reason is that the labor-scarce country will specialize in the export of goods that use intensively in their production other factors (such as land and capital) in which that country has a surplus. In contrast, the labor surplus country will export labor-intensive goods, thereby capitalizing on its comparative advantage derived from its labor surplus position. Thus, the demand for labor will fall in the labor-scarce country, causing a drop in wages, while it will rise in the labor-surplus country, causing a rise in wages.

Politicians have their own version of the Stolper-Samuelson Theorem. During the 1992 Presidential campaign, candidate Ross Perot warned of a "giant sucking sound." He meant *NAFTA* would cause a net loss of American jobs to Mexico, and forecast it would be around 5.9 million. In 1995, and again in 1998, perennial presidential candidate Patrick Buchanan warned the real income of American workers would continue to erode as *NAFTA* forced them to compete with Mexican laborers earning one tenth of their wages. The Administrations of Presidents George H.W. Bush (1924–, President, 1989–1993) and Bill Clinton (1946–, President, 1993–2001) countered with rosy forecasts about hundreds of thousands of new jobs resulting from freer trade with Mexico and Canada, which in turn would stimulate American economic growth. Both sides lacked common sense. On the one hand, as the *Wall Street Journal* pointed out in 1997, Americans had been losing jobs long before *NAFTA* was invented. On the other hand, how could it possibly be that freer regional trade alone—and not macroeconomic, technological, or demographic forces—would produce so many new jobs?

Similar extreme claims were made in 2011 amidst debates over America's FTAs with Colombia, Korea, and Panama. Representing Corporate America, the American Chamber of Commerce claimed *KORUS* would generate 280,000 jobs (but failure by Congress to pass it could cost 380,000 jobs due to export sales lost to the EU and other foreign countries that had duty-free access to Korea). The liberal Economic Policy Institute, funded partly by labor unions, said *KORUS* would cost 159,000 manufacturing jobs.[7] The Administration of Barack H. Obama (1961–, President, 2009–2017) claimed *KORUS* would yield a net job increase of 70,000. The Administration urged the Colombia and Panama FTAs would lead to job gains in

7. *See* Richard McGregor, *Congress Set to Back Free Trade Deals*, Financial Times, 4 October 2011, at 4.

export sectors benefitting from reduced trade barriers in those countries, but not to job losses, because 90% of the products from those two countries already entered the U.S. duty free under a preferential trade program.[8]

• **Late 20th Century Empirical Research**

The effects of an FTA on jobs and wages are not the only repercussions of importance. Does an FTA boost overall economic growth? Advocates of *NAFTA* assert the Mexican economy outperforms economies in the rest of Latin America. They proudly proclaim that annual trilateral trade in merchandise among the *NAFTA* Parties crossed the 1 trillion dollar mark in 2011. Critics charge other non-*NAFTA* causes are at play, and the period of investigation can make all the difference in reaching a result like "the Mexican economy grew by 3% while other Latin economies grew by 2.5%." Has an FTA affected migration patterns? Advocates of *NAFTA*, like former Mexican President Salinas, said the U.S. would get both more tomatoes and tomato workers. Opponents said migration is driven more by demographic trends than an FTA. Has an FTA had negative externalities? Advocates and opponents of *NAFTA* argue about implications of the accord on the environment, labor, and narcotics trafficking.

Nevertheless, in the minds of most average citizens in most countries, the job and wage effects of an FTA loom the largest. For all the opportunity it creates, trade liberalization also causes anxiety. The American public is deeply skeptical about job and wage effects of FTAs. In a 1998 NBC/*Wall Street Journal* poll, 58% of Americans surveyed said foreign trade had been bad for America because cheap imports have led to wage declines and job losses. The skepticism persists to the present day. No doubt such polls, read by politicians, help explain close votes on Capitol Hill on many trade deals, such as *CAFTA-DR*. In many countries, the public shares the skepticism of Americans about trade liberalization. Is this sentiment, and hard-fought political battles, warranted?

That is, what do the empirical analyses about job creation versus destruction—most of which use *NAFTA* as their case in point—say? Some economists counsel that studying the "job count" effects of an FTA is a fool's errand. That advice has not put a halt to the research. So numerous are the studies that even a brief synthesis of the majority of them is impossible. Moreover, *NAFTA* is different from all other American FTAs because of the trade shares involved, *i.e.*, it is so much larger than other deals. However, a peek at just a few, conducted in the wake of *NAFTA*, suggests the difficulty in providing an unambiguous answer.

In 1996, the North American Integration and Development Center at the University of California at Los Angeles published the results of a comprehensive study funded by the U.S. government. It found *NAFTA* created about 49,000 jobs through exports to Mexico. Imports from Mexico had cost more than 38,000 jobs. The net

---

8. *See* Len Bracken, *Unions, Lawmakers Dispute Jobs Claims from FTAs; Hoyer Foresees TAA Passage*, 28 International Trade Reporter (BNA) 1611 (6 October 2011).

effect was 11,000 new jobs, an insignificant amount among roughly 125 million American jobs. In other words, the UCLA study said that both sides were wrong. Significantly, the study stressed that the 1995 Mexican *peso* crisis, during which the value of the Mexican *peso* fell dramatically relative to the U.S. dollar, had more to do with boosting Mexican exports to the U.S. than did *NAFTA*. Interestingly, in 1997 the Toronto-based C.D. Howe Institute reached a similar conclusion with respect to Canada: neither *NAFTA* nor its predecessor, *CUFTA*, had produced a dramatic effect on Canadian jobs, hence free trade between Canada and the U.S. could not be blamed for Canada's disappointing labor market performance.

In 1997, the Institute for Policy Studies, an independent center, teamed with the Great Cities Institute of the College of Urban Planning and Public Affairs at the University of Illinois at Chicago. They issued a report rebutting Clinton Administration claims that export growth resulting from *NAFTA* and the Uruguay Round agreements would translate into new jobs. The study pointed out the global economy was dominated by MNCs, which have no incentive to create jobs in the U.S. vis-à-vis any other location. That is, there was no guarantee that MNCs would use additional profits earned through increases in exports of their product to finance new jobs in the U.S. To the contrary, MNCs might use these profits to finance activities that actually lower employment (and wages) in the U.S., *e.g.*, mergers, outsourcing, and downsizing. However, the Illinois study did not provide much in the way of empirical assessments. It also seemed somewhat undercut by a 1998 survey released by the Center for Strategic and International Studies, a Washington, D.C., think tank. That survey found the vast majority of North American businesses polled either employed more, or kept the same number of, workers since *NAFTA* entered into force on 1 January 1994. Of 361 American, Canadian, and Mexican businesses, only 11% reported fewer employees since *NAFTA* took effect, and only one such company blamed *NAFTA* for job losses.

A 1997 study by the Economic Policy Institute did stake out a position on the actual effect of *NAFTA* on American employment. The EPI is a non-profit research group funded by labor unions and corporations. A *NAFTA* critic, it teamed up with some other critics (the Institute for Policy Studies, International Labor Rights Fund, Public Citizen's Global Trade Watch, Sierra Club, and U.S. Business and Industrial Council Educational Foundation) to produce a report entitled *The Failed Experiment—NAFTA at Three Years* (June 1997). This study said America's trade deficit with Mexico and Canada rose dramatically since the entry into force of *NAFTA* on 1 January 1994. In consequence, America lost 420,000 jobs—251,000 Americans lost their jobs because of the worsened trade balance with Mexico, and 169,000 Americans were thrown out of work because of the deterioration in the bilateral trade balance with Canada. The study was careful to point out *NAFTA* hardly was the only, or even major, cause of the bilateral trade deficits. The Mexican *peso* crisis and depreciation of the Canadian relative to the U.S. dollar were key factors, too. Thus, the stunning 420,000 figure could not be pinned entirely on *NAFTA*. In November 1999, the EPI updated its analysis. In the new study, *NAFTA's*

Pain Deepens, the EPI reported job losses of more than 440,000 as a result of *NAFTA* and attendant trade deficit. California was the biggest job loser — 44,132. Displaced workers who did manage to find new jobs took an average 16% pay cut.

In 1997, the Clinton Administration weighed in on the empirical effects of *NAFTA*. Not surprisingly, its report — *Study on the Operation and Effects of the North American Free Trade Agreement* (July 1997) — contended 2.3 million American jobs depended on exports to Mexico and Canada. Of these, roughly 90,000 to 160,000 were newly created jobs thanks to *NAFTA*. Also in 1997, the ITC said the effects of *NAFTA* on domestic employment could not be discerned, because of the high employment rate in the U.S. since *NAFTA* entered into force. These studies, while hardly supporting *NAFTA's* critics, suggested the Bush and Clinton Administrations oversold the positive effects of *NAFTA* on jobs. Paper agreements cannot create socioeconomic miracles.

- **Early 21st Century Empirical Research**

The studies continued into the new millennium, of course. In 2000, the North American Integration and Development Center at UCLA reported *NAFTA* created in the range of 130,000 to 208,980 new jobs. In July 2001, the EPI issued another study claiming *NAFTA* had cost America jobs. This study, which assumed trade deficits remain the same, put the job loss figure at 733,060. In 2003, a study associated with the *NAFTA* Trade Adjustment Assistance program examined data from 1994–2002. It recorded 413,123 job dislocations. That suggests a rate of dislocation of about 50,000 per year. However, this study errs in both over- and under-counting. An estimate covering 1994–2017 said 930,000 jobs were certified under TAA as lost to *NAFTA*.[9] That updated estimate thus suggested both a rate of about 40,000 a year, and a deceleration from the early years of the FTA.

In May 2011, the EPI updated its research yet again. In the last year before *NAFTA* entered into force, 1993, the U.S. ran a trade surplus with Mexico of $1.6 billion, but now ran a deficit of $97.2 billion. The EPI said since 1994, the U.S. trade deficit with Mexico caused the loss (*i.e.*, destruction) or displacement (*i.e.*, shifting to Mexico or Canada) of 682,900 jobs. The U.S. lost an average of 40,000 jobs annually. These effects were felt in all 50 states, plus the District of Colombia and Puerto Rico, but the hardest hit (in order, measured by the share of jobs displaced) were Michigan, Indiana, Kentucky, Ohio, and Tennessee. Of all jobs displaced, 60.8% (or 415,000) were in the manufacturing sector, particularly computers and electronic parts (22% of the total, or 150,300), and motor vehicles (15.8%, or 108,000).

Also in May 2011, the American Chamber of Commerce tried to rebut the EPI empirical results. Between 1993–2007, said the Chamber, the American economy

---

9. *See* Letter from Rep. Pramila Jayapal (Democrat-Washington) and 21 other freshman Democratic Members of the House of Representatives to USTR Ambassador Robert E. Lighthizer, 17 November 2017, www.citizenstrade.org/ctc/wp-content/uploads/2017/11/JayapalNAFTALetter1117.pdf.

generated a net increase of 28 million jobs. Trade with Mexico and Canada trebled to $1 trillion, and these two *NAFTA* Parties bought over one-third of America's exports. Further, American manufacturing exports to Mexico and Canada garner annual average revenue of $25,000 per American industrial worker, thus contributing significantly to that worker's annual average wage of $37,000. However, did the Chamber confuse correlation with causation: was the net job gain due to *NAFTA*?

Moreover, did the Chamber consider linkage effects? Setting aside exact amounts, it is safe to say *NAFTA* has created service sector jobs, but cost unionized manufacturing jobs, in the U.S. This shift may well have (1) led to greater distributional inequities (in effect, white-collar service workers get wealthier, blue collar production workers poorer), (2) undermined collective bargaining efforts (because of the loss of unionized jobs), but also (3) boosted productivity in both service and manufacturing sectors. These links are precisely what the AFL-CIO think have happened because of *NAFTA* during its first two decades of operation.[10] It calculates a loss of at least 700,000 American jobs to, plus a yawning trade deficit with, Mexico thanks to 20 years of *NAFTA*.[11]

To add to the skepticism were four significant studies, two each on *NAFTA* and *KORUS*. The first one came in February 2014 from the Center for Economic and Policy Research.[12] The CEPR study argued Mexico failed to emerge as a First World nation during its 20-year experience with *NAFTA*, and in fact its economic performance during those two decades had lagged. It was 18th out of 20 Latin countries in respect of average annual *per capita* GDP growth. Its unemployment rate was 3.1% in the 4 years prior to *NAFTA* (1990–1994), fell to 2.2% in 2000, but in 2014 was at 5%. Worst of all was the Mexican poverty rate in 2012 was 52.3%—about the same the year *NAFTA* took effect.

In March 2014, the AFL-CIO produced another critical study: *NAFTA at 20*.[13] This study reported *NAFTA* caused "stagnant wages, increased inequality, and weakened social protections," and "failed to ensure the kind of social distribution necessary to achieve sustainable economic growth." Were the CEPR and AFL-CIO correct, or did they confuse correlation and causation?

---

10. *See* Brian Flood, *Environmental, Labor Reps Criticize NAFTA In Anticipation of Deal's 20th Anniversary*, 30 International Trade Reporter (BNA) 1650 (24 October 2013) (reporting the comments of Cathy Feingold, Director of International Affairs, AFL-CIO).

11. *See* James Politi, *Contentious Pact Continues to Generate a Sparky Debate*, Financial Times Special Report—The Future of NAFTA, 3 December 2013, at 2.

12. *See* Rossella Brevetti, *Minority Leader Pelosi Delivers Strong Criticism of Pending TPA Proposal*, 31 International Trade Reporter (BNA) 373 (20 February 2014).

13. *See* AFL-CIO, *NAFTA at 20* (March 2014), www.aflcio.org/content/download/121921 /3393031/March2014_NAFTA20_nb.pdf; Michael Rose, *AFL-CIO Report Denounces NAFTA, Argues for New Approach to Trade Pacts*, 31 International Trade Reporter (BNA) 621 (3 April 2014).

Also in March 2014, the EPI and Public Citizen's Global Trade Watch each examined the effects of *KORUS*, which entered into force on 15 March 2012.[14] During these two years, Korea became Americas' 6th largest trading partner—a fact the USTR touted. But, at what price? EPI recalled *KORUS* supporters said the deal would create 70,000 new jobs in the U.S. from exports. In fact, *KORUS* cost America 60,000 jobs, because of its ever-increasing bilateral trade deficit with Korea. Global Trade Watch pointed out that in 21 of the 22 months since *KORUS* had been in effect, exports of goods from the U.S. to Korea fell below the average monthly level of the last year before *KORUS* was law.

• **Pre- Versus Post-*NAFTA* Mexican Experience**

A line of critique catalyzed by Dani Rodrik and his 1997 book *Has Globalization Gone Too Far?* highlights instances in which FTAs have not resulted in the anticipated benefits of supra-normal growth or poverty alleviation. Mexico, following the 1 January 1994 entry into force of *NAFTA*, is an example.[15] Mexico's average GDP growth rate from 1994–2016 was about 2.5%, about the same as that of the U.S. and Canada. But, that was less than half the GDP growth rate in the developing world. Egypt, Turkey, and even sanctions-ridden Iran outperformed Mexico. Worse yet, because Mexico's population grew by faster than 2.5%, its *per capita* income fell. Much of Mexico's GDP gains were captured by upper classes. So, almost 25 years of *NAFTA* experience did not produce a convergence of the three Parties in terms of *per capita* GDP, nor did it reduce income inequality in Mexico. Indeed, as of November 2017, Mexico had the most unequal income in the OECD. Though growth rates expectedly decelerate as a country moves into the middle-income category, in the 25 years before *NAFTA*, Mexican *per capita* GDP grew nearly twice as fast as after *NAFTA*.

But, was *NAFTA* to blame? Almost certainly not. Mexico suffered from crime, especially narco-terrorism. Its drug war, lasting over 10 years, took an estimated 1% off of GDP annually. Corruption took its toll, too, with state governments misappropriating $1.4 billion in federal funds in 2015.

Mexico also suffered from poor macroeconomic policy. For example, after the 1994–1995 *Tequila* Crisis in which the *peso* was devalued, Mexico's central bank adhered to tight monetary policy to fight inflation, but had no legal authority to orient that policy toward growth. Mexican fiscal policy is tight, too—another legacy of that Crisis. Among the OECD, Mexico runs a notably balanced budget, which

---

14. *See* Robert E. Scott, *U.S.-Korea Trade Deal Resulting in Growing Trade Deficits and Nearly 60,000 Lost Jobs*, 14 March 2014, *posted at* www.epi.org/blog/korea-trade-deal-resulted-growing-trade/; Public Citizen, Global Trade Watch, *Korea FTA Outcomes on the Pact's Second Anniversary—U.S. Exports to Korea Are Down, Imports from Korea Are Up, Auto and Meat Sectors Hit Particularly Hard*, March 2014, www.citizen.org/documents/Korea-FTA-outcomes.pdf.

15. *See* Eric Martin & Nacha Cattan, *NAFTA's Ugly Reality: U.S.-Mexico Wage Gap Is Actually Widening*, 34 International Trade Reporter (BNA) 1594 (30 November 2017).

means it earns high investment credit ratings, but does not spend on infrastructure and human capital development. And, aside from the auto sector, Mexican industries got little in the way of infant industry protection to prepare them for integration into *NAFTA* and the global economy.

• **Bottom Line?**

Is there an empirical "bottom line"? Probably not, other than to say common sense matters. For example, using trade balance statistics to measure free trade benefits, such as the availability of a greater diversity of lower-priced goods and services, may be nonsensical. Likewise, common sense is needed in respect of job creation claims. During the first several years after *NAFTA* entered into force (on 1 January 1994), empirical estimates of its impact on aggregate employment range from gains of 160,000 jobs to losses of 420,000 jobs.

Almost certainly, neither extreme is accurate. Truth lies somewhere in between. A 1997 study by the ITC, *The Impact of the North American Free Trade Agreement on the U.S. Economy and Industries: A Three-Year Review*, confirmed this point.[16] It found no discernible impact of the agreement on aggregate American employment. A number of studies have shed light on the impact of *NAFTA* on specific sectors. For example, American corn exports have put Mexican corn farmers under serious pressure, and Oxfam reported Mexico lost 1.3 million farm jobs in the first decade of *NAFTA*. But, the overall impression from sectoral analyses is "it depends," namely, on the sector, researcher and methodology, and period of investigation.

That truth lies in the middle was confirmed by a February 2013 CRS study. It examined the effects of the first 20 years of *NAFTA*, 1993 through 2012, and concluded:

> *NAFTA* did not cause the huge job losses feared by the critics or the large economic gains predicted by supporters. The net overall effect of *NAFTA* on the U.S. economy appears to have been relatively modest, primarily because trade with Canada and Mexico account for a small percentage of U.S. GDP.[17]

More surprisingly, the CRS study suggested *NAFTA* might not even have been necessary to generate trade among its three Parties. During the first two decades of *NAFTA*, trade between America and Mexico grew 506%, and between America and Canada 192%.[18] But, during that period, U.S. trade with non-*NAFTA* countries increased by 279%. The inference from these statistics is that without *NAFTA*, American exports to and imports from Canada and Mexico would have grown

---

16. *See* United States International Trade Commission Publication 3045 (June 1997).

17. M. Angeles Villarreal & Ian F. Fergusson, Congressional Research Service, *NAFTA at 20: Overview and Trade Effects* (21 February 2013), www.fas.org/sgp/crs/row/R42965.pdf [hereinafter, February 2013 CRS *NAFTA at 20 Study*]; Shawn Donnan, *World Faces Up to the Era of Regional Agreements*, Financial Times Special Report—The Future of NAFTA, 3 December 2013, at 1.

18. February 2013 CRS *NAFTA at 20 Study*, at 10.

impressively. Put differently, *NAFTA* helped, but too much political fuss was made about it.

That truth is in the middle also was confirmed in the January–February 2014 *Foreign Affairs* issue. In *NAFTA at Twenty*, it gave three different "takes" on the accord:[19]

First: The American View — Carla Hills

". . . By uniting the economies of Canada, Mexico, and the United States, *NAFTA* created what is today a $19 trillion regional market with some 470 million consumers. . . . *NAFTA* was the first comprehensive free-trade agreement to join developed and developing nations, and it achieved broader and deeper market openings than any trade agreement had before.

NAFTA did that by eliminating tariffs on all industrial goods, guaranteeing unrestricted agricultural trade between the United States and Mexico, opening up a broad range of service sectors, and instituting national treatment for cross-border service providers. It also set high standards of protection for patents, trademarks, copyrights, and trade secrets. To preserve the rights of investors, it prohibited barriers such as local-content and import-substitution rules, which require producers to ensure that specified inputs are produced domestically.

. . .

[T]hanks to *NAFTA*, North Americans not only sell more things to one another; they also make more things together. About half of U.S. trade with Canada and Mexico takes place between related companies, and the resulting specialization has boosted productivity in all three economies. For every dollar of goods that Canada and Mexico export to the United States, there are 25 cents' worth of U.S. inputs in the Canadian goods and 40 cents' worth in the Mexican goods. By way of comparison, there are four cents' worth of U.S. inputs in Chinese goods going to the American market and two cents' worth for Japanese goods.

. . .

. . . Last year [2012], roughly 14% of U.S. exports went to Mexico — more than went to Brazil, Russia, India, and China combined. Indeed, Mexico buys more U.S. goods than the rest of Latin America combined, and more than France, Germany, the Netherlands, and the United Kingdom combined.

---

19. *See NAFTA at Twenty: Three Takes on the Historic Free-Trade Agreement*, 93 FOREIGN AFFAIRS issue 1 (January–February 2014) (containing Carla A. Hills, *NAFTA's Economic Upsides — The View from the United States*, Michael Wilson, *NAFTA's Unfinished Business — The View from Canada*, and Jorge G. Castañeda, *NAFTA's Mixed Record — The View from Mexico*), www.foreignaffairs .com/issues/2014/93/1.

Although economists still debate whether *NAFTA* has caused a net gain or a net loss in U.S. jobs, they agree that the market openings it created have generated more export-related jobs in the United States, which pay an average of 15 to 20% more than those focused purely on domestic production.

. . . Mexico represents a major market opportunity for U.S. entrepreneurs large and small. But small U.S. enterprises, lacking the global reach of major corporations, benefit in particular from Mexico's proximity and openness. Mexicans purchase about 11% of the exports of small and medium-size U.S. companies, which account for more than half of all job creation in the United States. Even Mexican exports worldwide benefit the U.S. economy, because of their high percentage of U.S. content. And making the picture even brighter, for every dollar that Mexico earns from its exports, it spends 50 cents on U.S. goods.

. . .

Another of *NAFTA's* positive effects has been the increased sharing of talent. . . . Canadians constitute about three percent of the United States' total foreign-born population, and Mexicans constitute about 30 percent. Americans make up about 4% percent of Canada's foreign-born population and roughly 70% of Mexico's. The Canadians and Mexicans who live in the United States are younger than the overall U.S. population. And . . . immigrants in the United States are almost twice as likely to start a new business as native-born Americans."

Second: The Canadian View—Michael Wilson

". . . [T]hose of us who championed *NAFTA* hoped the agreement would be something more: a means to deepen integration among the three economies. Unfortunately, when measured against this more ambitious benchmark, *NAFTA* has fallen well short of expectations.

. . .

. . . [T]he reality is that two decades after *NAFTA* came into force, efforts to advance the cause of North American economic integration have stalled. One reason for the lack of progress lies in the deep-seated skepticism of free trade prevalent among average Americans, which U.S. policymakers have never been able to overcome. Canadians . . . are more supportive of open trade with the United States, which they credit with boosting the Canadian economy. . . .

The 9/11 attacks also played a role in setting back economic integration. Both Canada and the United States understandably tightened their border security in response, but the new restrictions profoundly reduced the relative ease of movement between the two countries. . . .

. . .

Moreover, efforts at further economic integration would require a change in the orientation of the Office of the U.S. Trade Representative. Whether hemmed in by the realities of U.S. politics or simply reflecting a mercantilist mindset, that office has long shown little interest in taking a joint approach to trade policy with Canada and Mexico. . . .

. . .

. . . Canada exports more oil to the United States than does any other country: at least 2.3 million barrels a day, or 99% of Canadian crude oil exports. That oil makes a vital contribution to U.S. energy security and will do so for the foreseeable future, even after taking into account the rapid growth in U.S. domestic production caused by the shale oil boom."

Third: The Mexican View — Jorge G. Castañeda

". . . It would be overly simplistic to credit *NAFTA* for Mexico's many transformations, just as it would be to blame *NAFTA* for Mexico's many failings.

The truth lies somewhere in between. Viewed exclusively as a trade deal, *NAFTA* has been an undeniable success story for Mexico, ushering in a dramatic surge in exports. But if the purpose of the agreement was to spur economic growth, create jobs, boost productivity, lift wages, and discourage emigration, then the results have been less clear-cut.

. . .

Without a doubt, *NAFTA* has drastically expanded Mexican trade. Although exports began increasing several years before the treaty was finalized, when . . . [Mexico joined GATT] . . . in 1985, *NAFTA* accelerated the trend. . . . Manufactured goods, such as cars, cell phones, and refrigerators, compose a large share of these exports, and some of Mexico's largest firms are major players abroad. . . . [T]he corollary of that export boom — an explosion of imports — has driven down the price of consumer goods, from shoes to televisions to beef. Thanks to this "Walmart effect," millions of Mexicans can now buy products that were once reserved for a middle class that was less than a third of the population, and those products are now of far superior quality. If Mexico has become a middle-class society, . . . it is largely due to this transformation, especially considering that Mexicans' aggregate incomes have not risen much, in real terms, since *NAFTA* entered into force.

NAFTA also locked in the macroeconomic policies that have encouraged . . . these gains for the Mexican consumer and the country. . . . [O]ver the long run, the authorities have kept in place sound public finances, low inflation, liberal trade policies, and a currency that has been unpegged and, since 1994, never overvalued.

. . . Although no clause in *NAFTA* explicitly mandated orthodox economic management, the agreement ended up straitjacketing a government accustomed to overspending, overpromising, and underachieving. It prevented Mexico from returning to the old days of protectionism and large-scale nationalizations and caused the prices of tradable goods on both sides of the border to converge. . . . *NAFTA* made Mexico's traditional gargantuan deficits no longer viable, since they were now generators of currency crises, as in late 1994.

. . .

. . . *NAFTA* helped open Mexicans' minds. . . . [B]y increasing all types of cross-border exchanges, the treaty accelerated the shift toward an attitude that has stressed Mexico's victimization less and been less introspective and history-obsessed. . . .

Despite the real benefits *NAFTA* has wrought for Mexico, the economic growth so many of the treaty's advocates imagined would ensue has remained elusive. . . . . . . [Between 1994 and 2013], Mexico experienced two years of major economic contraction (1995 and 2009), two years of zero growth (2001 and 2013), and four years of high performance (1997, 2000, 2006, and 2010). But the country has averaged only 2.6% annual GDP growth.

Meanwhile, Mexico's *per capita* income has just barely doubled over the past 20 years, rising, in current-dollar terms, from $4,500 in 1994 to $9,700 in 2012 — growing at an average yearly rate of just 1.2%. Over the same period, Brazil, Chile, Colombia, Peru, and Uruguay experienced far greater growth in *per capita* GDP. And as a percentage of the United States' *per capita* income, Mexico's has barely budged, drifting from 17 percent in 1994 to 19% today. Real GDP per hours of work has increased by a meager 1.7%, meaning that productivity has remained flat, although there has been some improvement in the automobile sector (which was already doing well in the early 1990s), in the aeronautic sector (which did not yet exist), and in a number of so-called *maquiladoras*, factories in free-trade zones, in the north. Accordingly, real incomes in the manufacturing sector and the rest of the formal economy have remained stagnant, even if the fall in the price of some goods has softened the blow for workers.

One important reason for these disappointing results is Mexico's failure to develop at home enough of what economists call "backward linkages:" connections to upstream industries that produce the materials for assembly further down the supply chain. In 1994, 73% of Mexico's exports were composed of imported inputs; by 2013, the number had actually risen, to 75%. As a result, employment in the manufacturing sector has stayed unchanged, and so have salaries. Not even the tourism industry, Mexico's largest employer, has performed that well. The number of Americans visiting Mexico today is twice what it was two decades ago, but Mexico's market share of U.S. tourism has stayed flat, and the sector is growing at the same rate as before. Similarly, the *maquiladoras* created only about 700,000 jobs over the past 20 years, or, on average, 35,000 per year. During this period, roughly one million Mexicans entered the job market every year, and the country's population rose from approximately 90 million to 116 million, which explains why the average wage differential between U.S. and Mexican workers has not shrunk.

... [T]he number of Mexican-born people living in the United States, legally and otherwise, jumped from 6.2 million in 1994 to almost 12 million in 2013. (And that second number takes into account the temporary slowdown in Mexican immigration to the United States between 2008 and 2012 and the nearly one million deportations of Mexicans from there between 2009 and 2013.) Thus, *NAFTA* has also failed to achieve its goal of discouraging emigration: as Mexican President Carlos Salinas said when the treaty was up for debate, 'we want to export goods, not people.'

The absence of backward linkages in Mexico's export sector stems from foreigners' unwillingness to invest in Mexico, a problem that dates back to the 1980s. That decade, the country's economy collapsed . . . . The only alternative was to dramatically boost foreign direct investment, chiefly from the United States. And the only avenue for that was *NAFTA* . . . . Through *NAFTA*, Mexico sought to increase its foreign direct investment as a percentage of GDP to as much as 5%, far above what it had ever been before.

That didn't happen. . . . If one takes the average of foreign direct investment for 2012 (a very bad year) and 2013 (a very good year), one finds that Mexico now receives only around $22 billion annually in foreign direct investment—slightly less than 2% of GDP, well below the figures for Brazil, Chile, Colombia, Costa Rica, and Peru.

Foreign investors have proved particularly unwilling to channel capital into export-industry supply chains. . . . [T]he overall level of capital formation . . . has averaged about 20% of GDP since the mid-1990s. At that rate, Mexico can attain only the mediocre growth it has known for 20 years. In other words, despite impressive trade numbers, *NAFTA* has delivered on practically none of its economic promises.

. . .

A relevant question . . . is how the Mexican economy would have performed without *NAFTA*. It is difficult to see why it would have fared much worse. . . . [G]rowth was greater in other Latin American countries that did not have free-trade agreements with the United States for all of the 1990s and much of the next decade, including Brazil, Chile, Colombia, Peru, and Uruguay. Moreover, Mexico grew faster in *per capita* terms from 1940 to 1980, and the population was rising then at a faster rate than it is now. . . . [T]here is little reason to believe that in the absence of *NAFTA*, Mexico's productivity, attractiveness for foreign investment, employment levels, and wages over the past 20 years would have been systematically lower, unless the government had attempted a return to the [unsustainable, anti-free market] policies of the 1970s and early 1980s—an improbable scenario."

The authors make these "takes" particularly notable: Carla Hills (1934–) was the USTR responsible for negotiating *NAFTA*, Michael Wilson (1937–) was the Canadian Minister of International Trade involved in those talks, and Jorge Castañeda (1953–) served as the Mexican Foreign Minister.

In all instances, note the importance of the investigation period. Opponents of *NAFTA* sometimes speak as if job loss is permanent unemployment. In many, if not most, instances, that is not true. Job loss typically is temporary dislocation. Further, depending on the period, a certain set of exchange rates will prevail. It is difficult for an exporter to compete with over-valued exchange rates. That is true even if that exporter otherwise has a global comparative advantage. Change the period of research, and the exchange rate may change, too, yielding different results.

Fortunately, the *Financial Times* of London has kept its wit amidst confusion sewn by economists across the centuries. In 1997, it queried:

Which of the following have been caused by the *North American Free Trade Agreement*?

1. The loss of 500,000 U.S. jobs.
2. A 2 m[illion] rise in Mexican unemployment.
3. The *peso* crisis.
4. More hepatitis and chronic diarrhoea in Mexico.
5. Two armed uprisings south of the Rio Grande.
6. Malfunctioning toilets at the office of the U.S. Trade Representative.

Answer: None or all of the above, depending on whom you ask.[20]

Obviously, trade policy on RTAs might be simpler to formulate if statistics and econometrics all pointed in one direction, job creation or job destruction. They do not, and perhaps never will. Each study is unique in the exact issue it addresses, assumptions it makes, data sets it uses, and methodologies it applies. No study is entirely free from seepage of researcher bias, or bias of the entity that funds the study, into the analysis.

Most importantly, the effect of *NAFTA*—or, for that matter, any RTA, or trade liberalization in general—on jobs should not be overestimated. A range of macroeconomic factors (*e.g.*, monetary policy, exchange rate movements), technological developments (*e.g.*, labor-saving devices), and demographic conditions (*e.g.*, aging

---

20. Nancy Dunne, Stephen Fidler & Patti Waldmeir, *Old Wounds to Reopen: An Imminent Report on NAFTA Could Affect Future U.S. Trade Policy*, FINANCIAL TIMES, 30 June 1997, at 21.

and immigration) affect trends, not only in employment, but also in wages, output, and trade balances. The effect of robots cannot be over-estimated. Between 1980 and 2015, the U.S. lost 6.4 million manufacturing jobs—over one-third of its industrial employment base.[21] One way to appreciate that RTAs were not the only (and probably not the most significant) cause is to consider this contrast highlighted by a Brookings Institution research:

> In 1980, it took *25 jobs* to generate $1 million in manufacturing output in the U.S. Today [November 2016], it takes *just 6.5 jobs* to generate that amount—and that's after five more stable years [2011–2015] of little change.
>
>   . . .
>
> By all means, the nation should demand fair trade and aggressively employ the anti-dumping provisions in existing trade pacts to rebalance the playing field. By all means, the nation should address the disrupted careers, depressed wages, and sense of marginalization of the nation's dislocated production workers. And by all means the nation should bolster its critical manufacturing sector. *But to hang frustrated workers' hopes of relief on large-scale hiring in an increasingly automated, hyper-efficient manufacturing sector appears to be severely misdirected. It would be far better to focus on preparing workers for the rise of the robots than to promise them jobs that will be done by machines.*[22]

Thus, beware of pundits that point only to trade as a cause of change. Beware, too, of the difference between (1) aggregate employment effects and (2) localization of job losses in certain sectors (*e.g.*, T&A) in an RTA country may have lost its comparative advantage. In sum, quantitative analyses inform the debate about RTAs. But, they ought not to drive it, be relied upon as dispositive, or considered enduring. They depend on the biases of the analyst and vary with the period from which the analyst extracts data.

- **Micro-Level Effects**

Repercussions of an FTA or CU should be evaluated not just from a macroeconomic perspective, but also from a microeconomic one. Depending on the specific agricultural, industrial, or service sector, the causal implications of an RTA differ. Again, consider *NAFTA*:

(1) In Canada:

Not known for oenological strength, Canadian vintners have improved thanks to competition wrought by free trade. As the *Financial Times* reported:

---

21. *See* Mark Muro & Sifan Liu, *Why Trump's Factory Job Promises Won't Pan Out—In One Chart*, Brookings, 21 November 2016, www.brookings.edu/blog/the-avenue/2016/11/21/why-trumps-factory-job-promises-wont-pan-out-in-one-chart/. [Hereinafter, Muro & Liu.]

22. Muro & Liu (emphasis added).

You can taste the difference that freer trade with the U.S. has made to Canada. Before the *Canada-U.S. Free Trade Agreement*, the precursor to *NAFTA*, Canadian wine was notorious. That agreement, which took effect at the start of 1989, removed tariff protection and exposed Canadian producers to competition from U.S. wine.

Helped by government subsidies to replace old vines with higher-quality varieties, the Canadian industry began to produce much better wines. The FT's [renowned wine critic] Jancis Robinson [OBE] reported this year [2013] that the wines from British Columbia and Ontario had "improved considerably." She was "seriously impressed" by some.

That may be one reason why freer trade in North America commands strong support from the Canadian public.[23]

Note the Canadian government intervened in wine trade in one respect: it assisted its vintners to meet American competition.

Among wine producing countries with which America has an FTA is Israel. Has the 1985 *Israel FTA* led to better Israeli wine? Arguably, no, because Israeli producers are not subject to the same degree of foreign competition under the *FTA* as are their Canadian counterparts under *NAFTA*.

The original *Israel FTA* deal did not cover all agricultural products. So, in 1996, they added to the FTA an *Agreement Concerning Certain Aspects of Trade in Agricultural Products (ATAP)*. *ATAP* provided for duty-free or other preferential treatment of certain agricultural products, was extended in 2003, and then followed by a new agreement in 2004 that was extended in December 2009 through 31 December 2010. Yet, American vintners still face significant barriers to the Israeli wine market, as the USTR explained:

> Under the current *ATAP*, Israel granted U.S. wine exports an annual TRQ of 200,000 liters of duty-free imports of wine. In addition, U.S. exports in excess of the quota limit are charged a tariff lower than Israel's MFN rate. However, the current method of quota allocation for wine creates a significant challenge for importers of U.S. wine. Quotas are issued arbitrarily, sometimes through a lottery system to groups that do not make use of the licenses they are allocated. Further compounding the problem, the reallocation of quotas at the end of a period often occurs too late to make it commercially viable for another importer to utilize the remaining quota. Wine importers note that the Israeli government does not require Israeli wine producers to follow the detailed labeling requirements of the official standard for wine, while these rules are strictly enforced on imported wines. Sales of U.S. wines to Israel are about $700,000 per year. Industry

---

23. Ed Crooks, *Canada's Strongest Ties Are with its Close Neighbor*, Financial Times, 3 December 2013, at 3.

estimates that the elimination of trade barriers could result in increased exports worth up to $10 million per year.[24]

These barriers arise because *ATAP* did not liberalize agricultural trade as dramatically as did *NAFTA*. It allowed the Israeli government to grant American agricultural products access to the Israeli market under one of three schemes: (1) unlimited duty free access, (2) TRQs (with annual increases in the in-quota quantity of each TRQ through 2008), or (3) preferential tariffs set at least 10% below the Israeli MFN rate for the product in question.[25] Wine fell into the second category.

The contrasting treatment of wine under the trade agreements with Canada and Israel show the hazards of general characterizations of the effects of free trade, even on a particular sector. The "devil" truly is "in the details." A lawyer-like analysis of how a particular FTA treats a sector, and what sort of government interventions and protections it permits, must be considered.

(2) In Mexico:[26]

The Mexican manufacturing sector benefited enormously: by 2013, industrial products accounted for 80% of Mexican exports. Mexico was the largest producer in the world of flat screen TVs, and a top producer of aircraft and medical equipment, and cars. Its high tech sector benefited, too, with aerospace, computers, electronics, machinery, and high tech items accounting for over 17% of Mexican GDP, ahead of China and behind only Germany and Korea.

The Mexican industrial boom was predictable under the Heckscher-Ohlin and Stolper-Samuelson Theorems. The Theorems predicted that with free trade, Mexico would specialize in making and exporting goods that use intensively in their production the factor with which Mexico is relatively well endowed, and that factor would benefit from free trade. Mexico is relatively well endowed with unskilled and semi-skilled labor, which are used intensively in the production of many industrial products.

(3) In the U.S.:

In 1950, the first pipeline to carry oil from Canada to America was constructed, and with its oil boom in the 1970s, Mexico became a key supplier of crude to the U.S. Thanks to the discovery of shale reserves in the U.S., and the development of hydraulic fracturing and horizontal drilling, oil and NG flow in the opposite direction. America exports petroleum products and NG to its *NAFTA* partners, particularly Mexico, with its energy needs for its large population and emerging economy. *NAFTA* Chapter 6 is dedicated to energy, and facilitates trade in energy by

---

24. UNITED STATES TRADE REPRESENTATIVE, NATIONAL TRADE ESTIMATE REPORT ON FOREIGN TRADE BARRIERS 191–192 (March 2010), www.ustr.gov/sites/default/files/uploads/reports/2010/NTE/2010_NTE_Israel_final.pdf. [Hereinafter, 2010 NTE.]

25. *See* 2010 NTE, at 191.

26. *See Exporting Mexico Joins Global League*, FINANCIAL TIMES SPECIAL REPORT—THE FUTURE OF NAFTA, 3 December 2013, at 4.

forbidding or otherwise disciplining import or export restrictions via incorporating GATT provisions:

Article 603: Import and Export Restrictions

1. Subject to the further rights and obligations of this Agreement, the Parties *incorporate* the provisions of the *General Agreement on Tariffs and Trade* (GATT), with respect to prohibitions or restrictions on trade in energy and basic petrochemical goods. The Parties agree that this language does not incorporate their respective protocols of provisional application to the GATT.

2. The Parties understand that the provisions of the GATT incorporated in paragraph 1 *prohibit*, in any circumstances in which any other form of quantitative restriction is prohibited, *minimum or maximum export-price requirements* and, except as permitted in enforcement of countervailing and antidumping orders and undertakings, minimum or maximum import-price requirements.

    . . .

5. Each Party may administer a system of import and export licensing for energy or basic petrochemical goods *provided that* such system is operated in a manner consistent with the provisions of this Agreement, including paragraph 1 and Article 1502 (Monopolies and State Enterprises).

Article 604: Export Taxes

No Party may adopt or maintain any *duty, tax or other charge on the export of any energy or basic petrochemical good* to the territory of another Party, unless such duty, tax or charge is adopted or maintained on:

(a) exports of any such good to the territory of all other Parties; and

(b) any such good when destined for domestic consumption.

Article 605: Other Export Measures

Subject to Annex 605, a Party may adopt or maintain a restriction otherwise justified under Articles XI:2(a) or XX(g), (i) or (j) of the GATT with respect to the export of an energy or basic petrochemical good to the territory of another Party, *only if*:

(a) the restriction *does not reduce the proportion of the total export shipments* of the specific energy or basic petrochemical good made available to that other Party relative to the total supply of that good of the Party maintaining the restriction as compared to the proportion prevailing in the most recent 36 month period for which data are available prior to the imposition of the measure, or in such other representative period on which the Parties may agree;

(b) the Party *does not impose a higher price for exports* of an energy or basic petrochemical good to that other Party than the price charged for such good when consumed domestically, by means of any measure such as licenses, fees, taxation and minimum price requirements. The foregoing provision does not apply to a higher price that may result from a measure taken pursuant to subparagraph (a) that only restricts the volume of exports; and

(c) the restriction *does not require the disruption of normal channels of supply* to that other Party or normal proportions among specific energy or basic petrochemical goods supplied to that other Party, such as, for example, between crude oil and refined products and among different categories of crude oil and of refined products.[27]

"Thanks to *NAFTA*," obtaining a license to export to a *NAFTA* Party "is easy."[28] Thus, conceived as helpful to secure American imports by diversifying away from potentially unstable Arab sources, *NAFTA* helps America enhance its exports.

V. Trade Creation or Diversion?

- **Viner's 1950 Study**

Asking whether entry into an RTA results in net job gain or loss to a country assumes the view of an individual RTA member country. A second critical question is asked from a "bird's eye" view of the entire RTA: does the RTA stimulate more trade than it diverts, that is, does the "trade creation" effect overwhelm, or is overwhelmed by, the "trade diversion" effect? In 1997, the WTO opined Mexico's trade was too biased in favor of *NAFTA*. Complex ROOs, for instance, had diverted trade toward America and Canada, and away from more efficient suppliers. In 1992, just before *NAFTA* entered into force, the share of Mexico's merchandise trade with America was 75%. In 1996, shortly after the agreement took effect on 1 January 1994, the share had risen to 80%. By 2015, American and Mexican manufacturing production was highly integrated, with considerable back-and-forth trade: the U.S. was the origin of 40% of the inputs in goods made in Mexico and then exported to America. Concomitantly, Mexican inflation rates tracked those of its *NAFTA* partners, and its exchange rate against the greenback and loonie (*i.e.*, U.S. and Canadian dollars, respectively) was relatively stable.

---

27. Emphasis added.

28. Ed Crooks, *Revolution in Shale Transforms Market*, Financial Times Special Report— The Future of NAFTA, 3 December 2013, at 2.

The WTO advised Mexican industry would be better off if concessions granted to the U.S. and Canada were extended to all of Mexico's trading partners. The WTO's advice—sensible as it may be—also reflects its role as the flagship institution to advance multilateral trade liberalization. The WTO's concern about trade creation versus diversion is hardly new. The problem was identified, in conceptual terms, as far back as 1950 by the famous economist Jacob Viner (1892–1970), in a book entitled *The Customs Union Issue*. To be sure, by definition an RTA means preferential treatment is given to suppliers in member countries, so increased trade activity among the preferred suppliers is bound to occur. But, asked Viner, will it occur to an adverse degree? Following the approach of Viner and his successors, the application of neo-classical economic tools provides a model of the trade creation versus diversion issue. By "trade creation," Viner meant a shift in demand for imports from an inefficient to an efficient source. By "trade diversion," he meant a shift of imports from an efficient to an inefficient source.

Consumers enjoy a greater range of goods at lower prices when their country joins an RTA. After all, as the member countries of the RTA reduce trade barriers among themselves, the price of intra-regional imports falls, which then stimulates demand for these imports. Thus, trade creation ought to result from demand stimulation caused by the drop in trade barriers. Certainly, there are hidden assumptions here: consumers are motivated solely (or primarily) by price in deciding what to buy, and the goods produced within and outside the RTA are substitutes. Whether these assumptions are valid depends on 2 key empirical measures: the elasticity of demand, and the elasticity of substitution, respectively. Nonetheless, the basic insight is that trade creation through an RTA entails a shift from home country production to imports from a partner country as a result of a decline in the price of the good in question.

As for trade diversion, this effect is expected because of the elimination of barriers among only the RTA Party countries. Non-Parties do not benefit from the intra-regional tariff cuts. Consumers in the Party countries are likely to shift to the now lower-priced intra-regional imports, and away from the relatively higher priced substitute products they formerly bought from non-Party countries. In other words, what was imported from non-Parties before will be imported from Parties. The shift of imports from outside the RTA to a partner country is, of course, trade diversion from the outside countries. Again, this effect assumes price is the only (or, at least a main) determinant of consumer preference, and that the goods produced within and outside the RTA are alike.

Not all economists worry about trade diversion. Former U.S. Treasury Secretary and Harvard President Lawrence Summers finds it "surprising that this issue is taken so seriously—in most other situations, economists laugh off second best considerations and focus on direct impacts." Part of what motivates this comment is a belief trade diversion is a minor nuisance. But, Professors Jagdish Bhagwati, Arvind Panagariya, and others reject Summers argument. They challenge the premise that economists do not pay attention to second-best solutions. In practice, economists study these solutions. And, the first-best solution, non-discriminatory trade liberalization—*i.e.*, movement toward a multilateral free-trade regime—is by definition ruled out (at least for the short term) when a group of countries bands together to form an RTA. RTAs are an inherently second-best solution to the problem of trade liberalization. Because they are a widely used alternative, their potential effects (including trade diversion) demand attention.

Related to the long-standing controversy about trade creation and diversion is the problem of bilateral trade deficits. Does entry into an RTA mean a member will experience a trade deficit with another or other members? The question is especially poignant if the member enjoys a surplus with another member before the RTA takes effect, as America did vis-à-vis Mexico before *NAFTA* entered into force on 1 January 1994. *NAFTA* critics cite the post-*NAFTA* bilateral deficits as evidence the accord is not working to the advantage of the U.S. Similar concerns surround the *Israel FTA* and *Jordan FTA*: have these deals helped Israel and Jordan, respectively, more than America? If the yardstick is percentage increases in export growth, then critics of these *FTAs* can point to data showing (for example) Israeli exports to the U.S. grew by 10% (but American exports to Israel grew by a smaller amount), and Jordanian exports to the U.S. tripled (but not so with flows in the other direction). Of course, this criticism depends on the period from which data are extracted.

One resolution to the problem of bilateral trade deficits among RTA partners is to question the question. Do bilateral trade deficits really matter? If so, then why do they matter? Assuming bilateral trade deficits are important (and not all economists would agree on that point), and assuming there are no advantages from an RTA to offset a deficit (a dubious assumption), then a second response is "it depends." Many factors affect a trade balance, other than trade barriers. Exchange rates, savings rates, consumption trends, product innovation (partly because of technological change) are among the variables. These variables fluctuate over time, again underscoring the importance of the period of investigation.

• Neo-Classical Economic Analysis

Both the trade creation and trade diversion effects can be represented graphically, as below. Suppose four-door, non-sport utility passenger automobiles with V-6 engines are made in Argentina. They are not made in great supply, because the industry is an infant one. Still, suppose it is an industry Argentina hopes to develop. Graph 1-1 depicts the market for these cars in Argentina, and Table 1-1 summarizes the effects of two alternative regimes: a tariff on all imports, and an FTA (or CU) favoring imports from a member country but discriminating against third country merchandise.

The line DD represents demand for this product in Argentina. SS represents domestic supply of these cars in Argentina. Assume Argentina trades cars with two other countries, Brazil and Japan. Both countries manufacture cars that, while not identical with, are substitutable for the Argentine product. Brazil is especially eager to develop its car industry further, because like Argentina, it sees this industry as

Graph 1-1. Argentine Car Market

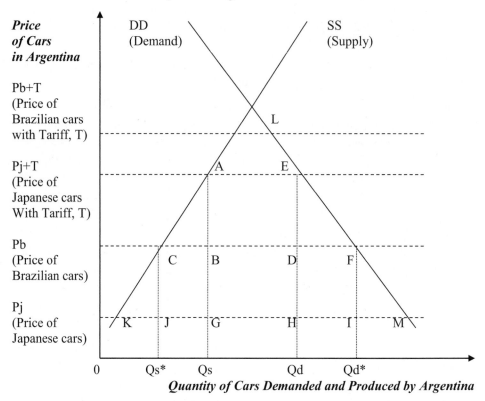

Quantity of Cars Demanded and Produced by Argentina

central to its economic future. This belief is common among developing countries, as China, India, Indonesia, Malaysia, and Vietnam evince. However, history manifests its patent falsity. Countries like Finland, Norway, Singapore, and Switzerland all developed without a domestic car industry. The belief also is economically misguided, because there is tremendous over-capacity in the world car market.

Suppose Argentina has in place a tariff on all imported automobiles, including the cars from Japan and Brazil. The value of the tariff is T, and it is plainly designed to protect domestic car producers. The price of the Japanese cars rises to Pj+T, and the value of the Brazilian model increases to Pb+T. Again, the price of the Japanese cars remains relatively lower, so Argentina will import more Japanese than Brazilian cars. Indeed, it may be safe to say that the tariff compels Argentina to import from Japan, not Brazil, *i.e.*, the tariff will have priced the Brazilian model out of the market.

How many cars will Argentina import? The answer depends on the number of cars produced in Argentina. The price of the cars made by their Japanese competitors, inclusive of the tariff, is Pj + T. At that price, Argentine car companies have an incentive to produce the quantity Qs. Likewise, at that price, Argentine consumers will demand the quantity Qd cars. Plainly, Argentine demand outstrips Argentine supply by the amount Qd − Qs. Therefore, Japanese cars are needed to plug the

Table 1-1. Summary of Effects of FTA (or CU)

Variable	With Tariff, T, Imposed by Argentina on Brazilian and Japanese Cars	With FTA (or CU) involving Argentina and Brazil, but not Japan (No Tariff on Brazilian Cars. Tariff remains on Japanese Cars. If customs union, Tariff is a Common External Tariff.)
Argentine Demand	Qd Relevant price is Pj+T, reflecting consumer preference for cheaper Japanese cars over Brazilian cars.	Qd* Relevant price is Pb, reflecting consumer preference for duty-free Brazilian cars over Japanese cars, to which the Tariff, T, applies. Argentine consumers demand more cars at lower price Pb than at Pj+T.
Argentine Supply	Qs Based on price Pj+T for Argentine cars.	Qs* Based on price Pb for Argentine cars. Argentine producers make fewer cars at lower price Pb than at Pj+T. Gap filled by trade creation (imports from Brazil).
Imports	Qd – Qs All imports from Japan.	Qd* – Qs* All imports from Brazil.
Tariff Revenue	AEHG To Argentine government, equal to Tariff, T, multiplied by import quantity.	None (foregone). Possibly *de minimis* amount collected on small number of Japanese imports.
Trade Creation	None	Increase in imports, which is the difference between from Qs* – Qs and Qd* – Qd.
Trade Diversion	None (assuming Tariff is applied on MFN basis)	
Change in Consumer Surplus	Not applicable If compare against free trade, where relevant price is Pj, then loss of EMPjPj+T	Increases by EFPbPj+T
Change in Producer Surplus	Not applicable If compare against free trade, where relevant price is Pj, then gain of AKPjPj+T.	Decreases by ACPbPj+T
Difference between Changes in Consumer and Producer Surplus	Not applicable If compare against free trade, where relevant price is Pj, then AEMK.	EFCA

(continued)

Table 1-1. Summary of Effects of FTA (or CU) (*continued*)

Net Welfare Effect	Not applicable If compare against free trade, where relevant price is Pj, then AGK and EHM, which is AEMK minus the tariff revenue, AEHG.	ABC and DEF Tariff revenue AEHG is foregone. ABC reflects lower prices. DEF reflects expanded consumption opportunities.
Dead Weight Loss	Not applicable. If compare against free trade, where relevant price is Pj, then AGK is dead weight loss because of inefficient Argentine production encouraged by the Tariff, T, and EHM is dead weight loss because of diminished consumption opportunities.	BDHG Graphically, BDHG is the difference between EFCA (which reflects the Consumer and Producer Surplus changes) and AEHG (foregone tariff revenue). Conceptually, BDHG suggests Argentina would be better off under free trade, *i.e.*, by eliminating the Tariff, T, on all car imports. Then, the Price would be Pj, and the quantity imported Qd* − Qs*

gap. Argentina will import Qd − Qs cars from Japan at a price of Pj+T. The Argentine government will collect a tariff revenue of AEHG, which reflects the quantity imported (Qd − Qs) multiplied by the amount of the tariff (the increase from Pj to Pj+T, *i.e.*, T).

In any event, the price of the Brazilian cars is Pb. The Japanese model is price Pj. They are free trade prices. Obviously, Japan is a more efficient producer than Brazil, because Pj is less than Pb. Thus, *ceteris paribus* (*i.e.*, all other things being equal), Argentina will import more Japanese than Brazilian cars. Observe the intersection of the demand and supply curves corresponds to a price level above the prices of Brazilian and Japanese cars. After all, Argentine cars (reflected by SS) are relatively uncompetitive.

Now suppose opposition from Argentine car producers (and, probably, other groups) is overcome. Argentina joins an FTA with Brazil, but not Japan. Eventually, Argentina and Brazil hope to become a CU, but they agree to start with the creation of an internal free market before implementing a CET. The central obligation each country must perform to give birth to an FTA is to eliminate tariffs on goods traded between them. Thus, Argentina must drop its tariff, T, on cars from Brazil. The tariff remains in effect for cars from non-member countries, *i.e.*, countries outside the FTA like Japan.

The trade diversion effect is evident from the fact that the price of cars from Brazil falls to Pb, but the price of cars from Japan remains at Pj+T. Pb is less than Pj+T, hence Argentine consumers are likely to switch, *ceteris paribus*, from the higher-priced Japanese car to the now cheaper Brazilian model. That is, the gap between Argentine supply and demand, Qs − Qd, used to be filled by Japanese cars. Now, the Brazilians take over. The change is, of course, a diversion of trade from a non-member of the free trade area (Japan) to a member of that area (Brazil).

The trade creation effect also is apparent from the Graph. The price of imported cars has fallen from Pj+T to Pb. The fall in the import price should generate additional imports, and indeed it does. At Pb, Argentine companies produce Qs* cars, but Argentine consumers demand Qd* cars. The domestic demand-supply gap has yawned from Qd – Qs to Qd* – Qs*. The difference between Qs* and Qs, and between Qd* and Qd, is trade creation. The trade created from Qs to Qs* results from the fact that Argentine companies produce fewer cars at the lower price, Pb. The trade created from Qd to Qd* follows from the increased demand among Argentine consumers for cars at that lower price. Thus, Brazilian car companies not only fill the Qd* – Qs* void, but the quantity they export to Argentina exceeds the quantity Japanese companies previously had exported.

Trade diversion and creation are not the only effects the Graph shows. Most obviously, Argentina loses the tariff revenue, AEHG, which it previously collected. After all, no longer is Argentina importing Qd – Qs cars from Japan at a price of Pj+T inclusive of the tariff T. Now, it imports Qd* – Qs* cars from Brazil at a price of Pb. To be sure, Japanese cars remain available at a price of Pj+T, but it is assumed they are not imported in significant quantities because of their much higher price relative to the Brazilian models. Accordingly, any tariff revenues from Japanese imports are *de minimis*.

There is another subtle, but important, lesson from the graph. At the lower import price, Pb, Argentine consumers gain. Their gain is represented by the triangles ABC and DEF. The gain of triangle ABC arises because Argentine consumers no longer have to pay higher prices to Argentine car companies. Instead of buying Qs cars from them at a price Pj+T (assuming the Argentine car companies charged the same price as the Japanese producers plus the tariff), Argentine consumers reduce purchases of Argentine cars to Qs*, and pay Pb instead of Pj+T. The gain of triangle DEF can be thought of as a consequence of the fact Argentine consumers can buy more imported cars at a cheaper price. Their demand has grown from Qd to Qd*, and they pay Pb instead of Pj+T.

Another way to see that the triangles ABC and DEF represent a gain to Argentine consumers is to consider the changes in consumer and producer surplus. The demand curve DD represents the quantity of cars Argentine consumers are willing and able to buy at a given range of prices. It slopes downward because as the price of cars falls, consumers want more cars, *ceteris paribus*. Points on the demand curve, but above the actual price, are points at which consumers buy cars for a price that is less than the amount that they are willing and able to pay — *i.e.*, the consumers operating on these points of DD "get a good deal." For example, consider point L. A consumer operating at this point is willing and able to pay a price for cars higher than Pj+T, namely, Pb+T. But, she need not pay this exorbitant amount because the going price is Pj+T. She is happy, and more generally, the points beneath DD and above the actual price constitute the zone of consumer surplus, because consumers save money when they buy. "Consumer surplus" is the difference between the price that consumers are willing to pay for a product, and the price they actually pay.

As for the supply curve SS, it represents the quantity of cars Argentine producers are willing and able to manufacture at a given range of prices. It slopes upward because as the price of cars rises, producers are willing to make more cars (again, *ceteris paribus*). A point on SS above the going price for cars is a "good deal" for producers. Producers operating at such a point manufacture cars that fetch a price that is higher than the price they require in order to coax them to manufacture. For example, consider point K. Argentine producers are willing and able to manufacture cars and sell them for a low price, Pj. But, they need not do so, because the actual price is Pj+T. They benefit from the difference between what they would have sold for, and what they actually received. Put differently, points above SS comprise the zone of producer surplus, because producers make extra money. "Producer surplus" is the difference between the price at which producers would like to supply a product, and the price at which they actually supply it.

To see how the triangles ABC and DEF represent a gain to consumers from the creation of the free trade area, compare consumer and producer surplus before and after the creation. First, what areas represented consumer and producer surplus when Argentine consumers faced a price of Pj+T, and Argentine producers charged this price? For consumer surplus, the answer is the large area marked off by point E, across to the left to Pj+T, and upwards to the demand curve DD. For producer surplus, the answer is the large area demarcated by point A, across to the left to Pj+T, and downwards to the supply curve SS.

As explained above, when Argentina joins the free trade area and removes the tariff, T, on Brazilian cars, the price of these imports falls to Pb. When that occurs, consumer surplus expands, and producer surplus contracts. Consumer surplus becomes the area from point F, across to Pb, and up to the demand curve DD. The increase in consumer surplus is EFPbPj+T. Producer surplus falls to the area from point C, across to Pb, and down to the supply curve SS. The decrease is ACPbPj+T. The difference between the increase in consumer surplus (EFPbPj+T) and the decrease in producer surplus (ACPbPj+T) is the trapezoid EFCA.

Of this trapezoid, it was established earlier AEHG is tariff revenue the Argentine government no longer collects after entry into the free trade area. The difference between the trapezoid EFCA and the forgone tariff revenue AEHG are the triangles ABC and DEF, and the rectangle BDHG. So, the difference between the increase in consumer surplus, on the one hand, and the decline in producer surplus plus the lost tariff revenue, on the other hand, includes the net gain to consumers, the triangles ABC and DEF.

What about the rectangle BDHG? It represents still another subtle but interesting lesson from the graph. We can say that it is part of the "dead weight loss" that arises as a result of the free trade area. The trade diversion effect that occurs when Argentina and Brazil enter into the accord is not necessarily healthy, certainly not in the short-run anyway. Brazil is an inefficient producer relative to Japan, yet the free trade area diverts trade in Brazil's favor. From the standpoint of economic welfare, Argentina would have been better off had it eliminated the tariff, T, for all car imports regardless of their origin. Then, the price of cars sold in Argentina would be Pj, that is, the price of the most efficient producer, Japan. Because Argentina imports from a higher-cost producer, Brazil, Argentine consumers pay Pb instead of Pj. The difference between these prices, Pb − Pj, multiplied by the quantity imported, Qd* − Qs*, is the extra cost of importing from the higher-cost producer. It is represented by the rectangle CFIJ, which includes BDHG.

The general point, then, is that a free trade area always is less satisfactory, from a neoclassical economic perspective, than a complete free trade regime. The reason is that only in a free trade regime are imports assuredly coming from the cheapest-cost producer. In a free trade area, imports may be sourced from an inefficient producer, resulting in foregone opportunities or savings, collectively known as a dead weight loss. As Professors Bhagwati and Panagariya conclude: "our analysis enables us to examine and reject the much-cited claim that it is wrong to worry about trade diversion and that PTAs are generally as good as non-preferential trade liberalization."[29] Put succinctly, not all forms of trade liberalization are equal.

A final subtle lesson from the Graph is aesthetic. Neo-Classical economic graphs are like some of Mondrian's paintings. Both have plenty of nice, neat lines that make up squares, rectangles, triangles, trapezoids, etc. As a general rule, in the economic graphs, welfare effects on consumers and producers are triangular in shape. Tariff revenue effects are rectangles. As for Mondrian paintings . . . well, perhaps that is why they are art.

So, what is the "bottom line" of the Neo-Classical economic analysis of the free trade area between Argentina and Brazil? If the question invites comparison with pure free trade, then the answer was just revealed. If, however, the question asks for an evaluation of the free trade area on its own merits, then the answer is uncertain. True, as a general matter, the consensus of economic studies on RTAs show the gains from trade creation outweigh losses from trade diversion. But, a complete evaluation requires an inquiry into whether, excluding the loss of government tariff revenue, the net welfare effect of an RTA is negative. The answer, graphically, is the consumer gain of ABC + DEF minus the cost of buying from an inefficient producer, CFIJ. It is not possible to say whether the gain outweighs the loss without knowing more about these empirical facts: the shape of the demand curve, shape of the supply curve, and height of the tariff. That is, figures for the elasticities of demand and supply, and size of the tariff, T, are needed.

---

29. Jagdish Bhagwati & Arvind Panagariya, *Preferential Trading Areas and Multilateralism — Strangers, Friends, or Foes?*, *in* THE ECONOMICS OF PREFERENTIAL TRADE AGREEMENTS 1–55, at 3 (Jagdish Bhagwati & Arvind Panagariya eds. 1996).

Moreover, the search for a "bottom line" conclusion based on one sector is rather artificial. Argentina and Brazil are diverse economies, and any RTA can be trade-creating in one sector, and trade-diverting in another sector. To determine the implications of an RTA in an aggregate sense, a more comprehensive and nuanced analysis is needed. Multi-sectoral, CGE and "gravity" models provide this sort of analysis. (Interestingly, CGE models give lower predictions on the increases in trade caused by an FTA than do gravity models.) An even broader answer would include the effect on sectors and countries around the world, *i.e.*, a world welfare analysis.

• **Tariff Redistribution Effect**

The aforementioned "bottom line" based on simple Neo-Classical analysis is not the full story. Suppose in the Argentina-Brazil FTA, there is more trade creation than trade diversion, so the consumer gain outweighs the cost of buying from an inefficient producer. Can it be said unequivocally Argentina is better off? No. The Neo-Classical analysis neglects income distribution effects that arise from the re-distribution of tariff revenue. Because of this effect—a re-distribution of tariff revenue from Argentina to Brazil—it is quite possible Argentina experiences a net welfare loss, even if trade creation overwhelms trade diversion (indeed, even if there is no trade diversion at all).

When Argentina eliminates its tariff, T, on Brazilian cars, the terms of trade between Argentina and Brazil in the car sector change in favor of Brazil. That is, Brazil exports more cars to Argentina, and thus Brazilian car producers earn more profits. At the same time, the Argentine government loses tariff revenue, which in absence of corruption presumably was put to use for the benefit of the Argentine people through appropriate fiscal expenditures. Income is thus distributed from Argentina to Brazil: less is collected by the Argentine government and spent on the Argentine polity, and more is earned by Brazilian car manufacturers.

How large is this income re-distribution? The answer depends on the size of the initial tariff, T, the initial volume of car exports from Brazil to Argentina, and the extent to which Argentina opens its market to Brazilian cars. The greater the initial tariff, the greater the volume of Brazilian car exports before the creation of the RTA, and the larger Argentina's market opening, the greater the potential loss to Argentina. A greater initial tariff and import volume means that Argentina had been collecting a large amount of tariff revenue before it joined the RTA. (Recall tariff revenue is calculated as the amount of the tariff multiplied by the quantity of imports.) A large market opening means Argentina risks being flooded with Brazilian cars. The corollary to the ostensible "bottom line" is that a country can lose from liberalizing trade under a preferential trade arrangement, even if that arrangement creates more trade than it diverts.

• **Dynamic Considerations and Margins of Preference**

Aside from the controversial assumptions on which it rests, one of the central difficulties of the neoclassical analysis of trade creation and diversion, even as supplemented by an examination of income re-distribution, is that it is static. For example, over time, Brazilian car companies can reap economies of scale that, in turn, may allow them to increase their efficiency. The elimination of the tariff as between Argentina and Brazil will mean that Brazilian producers no longer are hamstrung by the dis-economies inherent in a single modest market, but rather can take advantage of the combined Argentine-Brazilian market.

However, whether Brazilian car companies actually become more efficient, or whether they produce in the cozy free trade arrangement without cutting costs and boosting output, remains to be seen. If barriers to FDI are low, then Japanese car companies may respond to the free trade area by building factories in Brazil. The presence, or even the threat, of these factories may motivate Brazilian auto executives and workers. It may even result in joint ventures between Brazilian and Japanese producers, which in turn results in technology transfer from the Japanese to the Brazilian partners. However, at the outset it is not at all clear that Brazil should be in the car business, and any dynamic gains will by definition not materialize for some time.

In addition, the neoclassical economic analysis does not explicitly account for margins of preference. This term refers to the difference between an MFN tariff and the preferential (*e.g.*, duty-free) rate associated applicable to a particular category of merchandise. The higher the MFN tariff, the greater the margin of preference. In turn, the greater the margin, the greater the trade (and investment) diversion effects of an RTA. Finally, the greater the diversion, the greater the potential damage to less developed countries not included in an RTA or other PTA (*e.g.*, countries receiving special and differential treatment pursuant to the Tokyo Round *Enabling Clause*, and countries like Bangladesh that are not *AGOA* beneficiaries). Thus, if MFN tariff rates decrease through multilateral trade rounds, or if new RTAs enter into force that embody broader, deeper tariff cuts than extant accords, then margins of preference diminish.

- *MERCOSUR* and Alleged Trade Diversion

The graphical example used above concerning the car trade in Latin America is not entirely hypothetical. In 1996–1997, one of the most publicized real-world examples of the trade diversion question materialized. The conventional wisdom about *MERCOSUR* was it had created billions of dollars' worth of trade among its members, and simultaneously paved the way for the members to compete in the global economy. An unpublished study, leaked to the press, by the principal economist in the World Bank's international trade division, Alexander J. Yeats, challenged the conventional wisdom. It argued *MERCOSUR* was repeating the policy folly of autarky and import substitution, which crippled Latin economies in the 1950s and 1960s, at a regional level.

The title of the Yeats study bore all the marks of controversy, differing significantly from the normally soporific rubrics of World Bank research. Yeats called it *Does MERCOSUR's Trade Performance Justify Concerns About the Global Welfare Reducing Effects of Regional Trading Arrangements? YES!* The study concluded that inefficient industries were prospering behind high trade walls built by *MERCO-SUR*. The sectors in which intra-*MERCOSUR* trade had grown most rapidly were capital-intensive goods like cars, buses, agricultural machinery, and refrigerators. But, *MERCOSUR* members produced these goods inefficiently: the goods were too expensive, and of too poor a quality, to sell to anyone but *MERCOSUR* customers.

The auto sector was a prime example. In 1988, trade in motor vehicles among Argentina, Brazil, Paraguay, and Uruguay was just $207 million. (In December 2005, Bolivia and Venezuela joined these 4 countries as full *MERCOSUR* members.) By 1994, intra-*MERCOSUR* trade in autos exploded to $2.1 billion. In part, the explosion resulted from the separate—and very significant—barriers that *MERCOSUR* members maintained individually to third-country auto imports, despite their commitment to formation of a customs union. Brazil imposed tariffs as high as 70% on imported vehicles, and Argentina and Uruguay had quotas on foreign vehicle imports.

To be fair to Brazil and Argentina, as a result of *MERCOSUR* obligations, tariffs on autos had fallen from as high as 100% to 20%. Predictably, auto imports into *MERCOSUR* surged, and Brazilian car producers cried they would collapse without protection. They got it, in the form of 70% tariffs (though by 1998 the duty had fallen to 49% for autos produced by companies without Brazilian subsidiaries). Argentina, however, kept a lid on its tariffs, at around 30%. Likewise, Uruguay's rate was 23%, and Paraguay's rates ranged from 10% to 15%. To complicate matters further, trade was managed: as between Argentina and Brazil, each country agreed to export no more than U.S. $1.95 worth of auto and auto parts for each $1 it imported from the other country.

Starting on 1 January 2000, *MERCOSUR* implemented a unified auto import policy consisting of a CET of 35%. This rate applies to passenger cars, trucks, and busses. (Lower rates, between 14–18%, apply to auto parts.) The CET was reached only after considerable squabbling between Brazil, which seeks to develop a car industry, and its *MERCOSUR* partners, which—save for Argentina—did not want to raise their auto tariffs to the 35% level. Effective 1 July 2008, Brazil and Argentina agreed to liberalize trade in autos between them, and establish joint production of 6 million vehicles annually—5 million units in Brazil, and 1 million units in Argentina—by 1 July 2013. Yet, the liberalization was not full, as a managed trade element remained. Under the deal, Argentina obtained the right to sell to Brazil $2.50 worth of autos and auto parts for every dollar it imported from Brazilian carmakers, whereas Brazil agreed to remain with the limit of exporting no more than $1.95 of cars and car parts for every dollar it imported from Argentine producers. In August 2010, Brazil and Argentina proposed to extend the arrangement to the other *MERCOSUR* states.

Three adverse effects resulted from the protection of inefficient industries behind *MERCOSUR's* trade walls. First, and most obviously, *MERCOSUR* consumers were harmed. They paid more, but got less in terms of quality, for capital-intensive goods. In microeconomic terms, there was a large loss of consumer surplus. Insofar as many of the goods were intermediate ones used in the production process for other products, producers of the other products were injured.

Second, factors of production were misallocated away from more competitive industries. When *MERCOSUR's* CET ultimately fell, the industries most likely to succeed in the global economy would not have received necessary labor, land, physical capital, human capital, and technology to ensure world-class performance. Conversely, there would have been over-investment in the industries least likely to succeed.

Third, non-*MERCOSUR* countries that produced capital-intensive goods were damaged. The cheaper, higher quality items produced by third-country suppliers were not admitted into *MERCOSUR* in the volumes, and at the prices, that free trade logic would dictate. This effect, plus mis-allocation of *MERCOSUR's* productive resources, amounted to trade diversion. The discrimination against these third-country products in favor of intra-*MERCOSUR* trade distorted the normal, free-market pattern of international trade flows. *MERCOSUR* members were concentrating on selling products, which were not internationally competitive, to one another. This concentration on the wrong products, and on each other's markets, plainly was caused by the higher tariffs and NTBs *MERCOSUR* maintained on third-country products than on products from its members.

Concomitant with trade diversion was investment diversion. Japanese and American auto producers scrambled to build plants in *MERCOSUR* countries to get inside the fortress. Absent the need to leap-frog *MERCOSUR's* CET, this flow of FDI might have been channeled elsewhere. Major multinational car companies — Ford, Fiat, General Motors, Renault, Peugeot, and Volkswagen — all built production facilities in Argentina and Brazil to make cars for domestic markets and export.

The WTO added a fourth adverse effect *MERCOSUR* had on the economies of its member countries, particularly Uruguay, that might just as easily have been included in the Yeats study. In a 1998 *Trade Policy Review Mechanism (TPRM)* report, the WTO warned that Uruguay relied too heavily on trade with its *MERCO-SUR* partners. For instance, between 1992–1998, more than half of all of Uruguay's merchandise exports went to a *MERCOSUR* country, with Brazil alone accounting for almost 40% of the shipments. Deliveries to the rest of the world had declined. By not diversifying its export customers and import sources, Uruguay was vulnerable to vicissitudes in Argentina, Brazil, and Paraguay. A safer strategy was to hedge against regional downturns by having significant export and import ties with third countries. Insofar as *MERCOSUR*-induced trade diversion inhibited diversification, it was not in Uruguay's long-term economic interest.

The Yeats study was a political headache for the World Bank, and the Bank proceeded to create a public relations disaster for itself. Officially, it supported *MER-COSUR*, and its policy is to avoid public criticism of World Bank members. Brazil accused Yeats in thinly veiled terms of using his position to draw public attention to his views. The Bank felt compelled to distance itself from the study, saying it was iconoclastic and did not represent official policy. It refused to release the study (though in 1997 it apparently reversed course and published it as Policy Research Working Paper 1729), and forbade Mr. Yeats from speaking to the press. Critics of the study said Yeats was wrong to have drawn the inference of trade diversion from data on exports. They pointed out imports from other *MERCOSUR* countries had grown faster than imports from third countries, but the gap was not significant, and certainly far less great than that between the growth of intra-*MERCOSUR* exports versus third-country exports. Still, the Bank appeared to be stifling honest intellectual discourse that was in the best interests of developing countries. One *Wall Street Journal* editor asked sarcastically: "So we have an economist in the international trade division at the World Bank who is not supposed to have professional opinions about world trade. What is he supposed to do?"

The Yeats study should compel consideration of yet one more adverse repercussion: the effects of regionalization on the multilateral trading system. Does *MERCOSUR's* experience challenge the integrity of the multilateral trading system? How might that integrity be preserved? It is difficult to argue the criteria of GATT Article XXIV are sufficiently strict to ensure formation of an FTA or CU does not undermine multilateral trade liberalization. Yet, WTO Members have done nothing to impose new strictures on the formation of RTAs. Low intra-regional barriers, coupled with high external ones and protectionist preferential ROOs, characterize trade in various sectors of some RTAs. The current lax criteria help explain why there are now over 100 regional trade groupings, and virtually every WTO Member belongs to at least one of them.

VI. Stepping Stones or Fortresses?

• Stepping Stones Argument and Related Advantages

A key issue in the controversy over the position and role of RTAs in the world trading system is their effects on that system. Do they lead to broader, deeper integration among a larger number of countries? Or, do they become endpoints? If negotiating an RTA is a precursor to, or catalyst for, multilateral trade talks, then so much the better. If they exhaust legal capacity that could be allocated to advancing multilateralism, and leave countries satisfied with their own regional blocs, then so much the worse.

Advocates of FTAs and CUs have some historical evidence in their favor. Consider European integration. To be sure, its purpose was to put a stop to European wars, not catalyze multilateral trade efforts. Three important steps in the integration process had a salubrious effect on them. First, the creation of the EC by the 1957 *Treaty of Rome* led to the 1962 *Trade Expansion Act* (*TEA*) in the U.S., and the 1964–1967 Kennedy Round. Second, EC expansion in 1973 to include the U.K.

contributed to momentum for the 1976–1979 Tokyo Round. Third, deepening amalgamation (including monetary union) through the 1992 *Treaty of Maastricht*, though finalized near the end of the Uruguay Round, reinforced multilateral trade liberalization efforts.

Another example is from "Down Under." In January 1983, the original *CER* between Australia and New Zealand entered into force. At that time, the *CER* did not include services. In 1988, they added a *CER Services Protocol* to cover all services sectors. That development helped position these countries for MTNs on *GATS*.

As still another example, Chapters in *NAFTA* are one intellectual origin of some WTO agreements. One story about the genesis of *NAFTA* is the U.S. was frustrated by its inability in 1982 to persuade other countries to commence a new round of MTNs. So, America shed its reluctance to make use of GATT Article XXIV, and sought trade liberalization on a regional level. Having done this, it pursued multilateral trade talks, beginning in 1986, and on a more-or-less parallel track. Consequently, some Uruguay Round texts read similarly to Chapters of *NAFTA*. Many provisions in the *TRIPs Agreement* look like Chapter 17 in *NAFTA*, on Intellectual Property. There also is a reasonably close correspondence between provisions in the *GATS* and *NAFTA* Chapters (12 and 14) on Services and Financial Services (respectively). The resemblances suggest the *NAFTA* Parties took their FTA agreement as a basis, if not model or precedent, for a multilateral bargain. That should not be a surprise. Having negotiated an FTA, they hardly would want to see it undermined by a WTO deal.

RTA advocates also point out negotiating an FTA or customs union is a process that yields learning-by-doing. Negotiators become educated and experienced. They can leverage their enhanced legal capacity to negotiate RTA expansions or WTO deals—contexts in which the issues may be more complex than before. Mexican and Korean trade negotiators are examples. Some Mexican negotiators helped Central American officials prepare for *CAFTA-DR* talks with the U.S. by providing training courses on their experience with the U.S. and *NAFTA*. Korean negotiators worked on trade deals with New Zealand and Singapore, before "big league" talks with America and Japan. The capacity building effect is especially important for developing countries and LDCs. As the number of countries, with a team of savvy, sophisticated negotiators, expands, in theory reaching a multilateral bargain ought to be a more efficient process with better outcomes than otherwise would have occurred.

• **Fortress Argument and Related Drawbacks**

RTAs do not necessarily lead to grander trade liberalization. The claim of competitive liberalization—that pursuing freer trade on any one level (bilateral, regional, or multilateral) stimulates and reinforces that pursuit on the other two levels—has not been put to a serious test. That is because a large number of RTAs (perhaps most in the world), especially FTAs, entered into force since Uruguay Round negotiations concluded on 15 December 1993.

What if members of an FTA or CU become self-satisfied with their arrangement, and retreat into it? Then, they effectively undermine the multilateral trading system. Consider the fact that while *CUFTA* preceded *NAFTA*, *NAFTA* has not led to an *FTAA* — i.e., *NAFTA* has yet to lead to hemispheric integration. Similarly, the many RTAs the U.S. negotiated and signed between 2000 and 2004, namely, with Australia, Bahrain, *CAFTA-DR*, Chile, Jordan, Morocco, and Singapore, did not contribute to a successful outcome in the Doha Round. To the contrary, they were a hedge against the failure of that Round. Another way to put the question is as follows: Are negotiations for an RTA and multilateral trade liberalization dependent on or independent of one another? That is, what relationship, if any, exists between the time paths of these sets of negotiations?

If they are dependent, then each negotiation could be a spur for the other. There could be a domino effect, whereby non-parties seek to join the RTA for fear of a loss of competitiveness. This effect could stimulate multilateral talks, as more and more non-parties seek to maintain or enhance their competitive positions. However, if RTA and multilateral talks are not related, then formation of an RTA could be the end of the line for many years. Economists like Professor Jagdish Bhagwati fear exactly this independence. RTAs, they say, are more often than not stumbling blocks to broader trade liberalization. Once created, they become economic fortresses. In some instances, member countries may feel their RTA market is large enough internally, and covers a sizeable enough percentage of export markets. They have little short- or medium-term incentive to expand the RTA or pursue a multilateral trade round. Likewise, industries in the member countries may be successful in lobbying their governments to eschew further, progressive trade liberalization that might expose them to third country competition.

With RTAs pursued independently of, and undermining, multilateral trade liberalization, the result is a proliferation in legal complexity. That is most evident in the area of preferential rules of origin. Each RTA will have its own such ROOs. The result is a global trading system that, to use Professor Bhagwati's metaphor, looks like a spaghetti bowl. Trade barriers (including, possibly, SPS and TBT measures), and thus market access, vary depending on the country of origin of the imported article — a *prima facie* incongruity with the MFN concept. In turn, the tariff and NTBs to market access rely on monstrously complex preferential ROOs, which is good work for customs lawyers, but distasteful to exporters and importers.

Spaghetti, of course, is not what businesses — especially multinational corporations — order. They engage in global production, attempting to source inputs based on comparative costs to realize economic efficiencies. At the top of their menu is clear soup. They consider whether the margin of preference accorded by an RTA vis-à-vis the otherwise-applicable MFN rate for their merchandise is a benefit that offsets the cost of compliance with the rules of origin of the RTA. The lower the margin of preference, and the more onerous the rules, the more likely they will elect to pay the MFN rate.

As a historical point, the inconsistency of RTAs with America's MFN policy since the Inter-War Period is worth highlighting. The U.S. followed a conditional MFN strategy from the birth of the republic through the 1920s. The result was discrimination against certain countries. In 1924, the Economic Advisor to the U.S. Secretary of State wrote a memo to the Secretary advocating an end to conditional MFN treatment. The memo argued conditionality creates antagonism, promotes discord, and discourages commerce. By the time of the GATT negotiations, in 1946–1947, America was firmly committed to an unconditional MFN policy. Similarly, the U.S. understood discrimination in favor of RTA partners meant discrimination against the rest of the world. By being selective in economic friends, America risked making economic—and political—enemies. (Of course, in the post–Second World War era, the EU took the opposite approach. The very creation of this customs union led to the greatest discrimination against non-European countries in history. Hence, Union membership is a highly contentious affair.) However, the aggressive FTA policy the U.S. has pursued since roughly the late 1990s, which has created a patchwork of bilateral and regional FTAs, undermines the unconditional MFN pillar of GATT.

Still another concern about FTAs and CUs, redolent of the rubric of "trade diversion," is "attention diversion." Do RTA negotiations create a disincentive to pursue multilateral reform because of the resources they consume? Does the large size of the EU as a CU make reform of the CAP more difficult, and increasingly so with EU expansion, than would be true in pursuing agricultural reform with just one European country? Even for a relatively well-lawyered body like the USTR, negotiating an RTA takes time and energy. There is learning-by-doing, and thus efforts to use a template from prior agreements. But, there are *sui generis* features to every RTA.

Moreover, completion of an FTA or CU is only the beginning. Monitoring compliance with any RTA obligation is necessary, which consumes precious government resources. During the Clinton Administration, the U.S. brought an average of 10 cases per year to the WTO as a complainant. As of May 2003, during the Bush Administration, that average had dropped to about two cases per year. Might a reason for the decrease be a pre-occupation with FTA deals? Overall, to what extent is this resource allocation justified if other FTA members are not commercially significant? Perhaps the answer hinges on whether the FTA serves an important non-commercial purpose. For example, Israel accounted for roughly 1% of total American trade. Jordan accounted for about 2/10 of 1% of total American trade. By contrast, trade with America's *NAFTA* partners, Canada and Mexico, accounted for 30 times (or more) than with Israel or Jordan. Yet, the USTR devoted more than 1% of its resources to administering the FTAs with Israel and Jordan. The same point can be made with the *Singapore FTA* and *Chile FTA*. While Singapore and Chile are diversified economies in terms of their imports and exports (though Singapore does not export agricultural products), Singapore and Chile account for only about 2% of total American trade.

"Negative precedents" are another potential drawback of RTAs. Suppose an RTA contains weak disciplines (*e.g.*, it permits certain kinds of discriminatory treatment) and a poor dispute settlement mechanism (*e.g.*, it is slow and lacks strong enforcement tools). Suppose, too, partial sectoral coverage and product exclusions diminish its commercial significance. This kind of RTA, comprised of "WTO minus" duties (*i.e.*, below levels set by extant WTO accords), is not a benchmark for multilateral trade liberalization. Rather, it is a negative precedent for future WTO rounds. From a global systemic perspective, an RTA with "WTO plus" rights and obligations would be preferable.

A serious worry is whether an FTA or CU evolves from a trade fortress into a military fortress. If so, then it may create peace and security within the bloc, but not spread "peace through trade" outside the bloc. In the 1930s, President Franklin Delano Roosevelt's visionary Secretary of State, Cordell Hull (1871–1955), sensed a great danger from trade blocs. A division of the world into blocs threatened international prosperity and security. Global prosperity hardly was likely if countries retreated behind regional fortresses. They might facilitate militarism on a regional basis. Their trade fortresses might go to war with one another when they felt their markets were threatened. Hull read the history of the 19th and early 20th century in this fearsome light. He believed passionately a free, open global trading system was the best guarantor for livelihood and peace. His belief translated into Anglo-American plans for the post–Second World War trading system.

Whether RTAs are stepping stones or fortresses depends partly on negotiating dynamics. By definition, any RTA discussions involve fewer countries than the number of WTO Members. Negotiations almost surely are easier with a relatively smaller number. Though that is no guarantee of success, *prima facie* the time and energy of bargaining among, say, five like-minded countries are reduced, and the logistics easier, than talks among 160 countries. During the Doha Round, neither the U.S. nor the EU relished the prospect of repeated confrontations with developing and least developed countries, and business communities in both America and the EU often seemed content with the RTA deals their governments concluded. Small wonder why—during this Round—the two trade hegemons aggressively pursued RTAs with a select number of countries. However, that pursuit exacerbated rich–poor tensions in the Round. Negotiations with some countries sowed resentment among countries not invited to the table. Thus piqued, excluded countries—many of which were developing and least developed—were both less committed to a successful multilateral outcome, and less inclined to compromise with America and the EU in multilateral talks.

VII. Diversity in Ambition of FTAs: Breadth, Depth, and Timing

Conventional wisdom holds "globalization" is the word defining the present era of international trade history. Paradoxically, interest and activity in regionalism has rarely if ever been higher than today. From a multilateralist perspective, RTAs are supposed to be an exception to the rule of MFN treatment. Yet, are they the rule, and MFN treatment the exception? Are FTAs and CUs proliferating to a degree that puts the WTO at risk of being a sideshow and talk shop? It is tempting to infer an affirmative answer simply from the large and increasing number of RTAs. That answer troubles advocates of multilateralism. However, 5 points ought to qualify this answer.

First, many FTAs (and CUs) are under negotiation. Many of them never will come to fruition. Second, a large number of FTAs are between or among former Soviet republics. The extent to which these accords are operative varies. Third, at the WTO, there may be some double counting of FTAs. Once an FTA is notified to the WTO, it is counted once under Article XXIV of GATT. It also may be counted a second time under Article V of the *GATS*. Fourth, more than half of the FTAs involve LDCs, and about one-fourth of FTAs involving these countries are between or among them and the EU. So, proliferating regionalism—if indeed the adjective is accurate—has development implications. Fifth, and perhaps most importantly, not all FTAs are alike.

Rather, FTAs vary considerably according to their economic ambition. Three key variables gauge this ambition: breadth, depth, and timing. "Breadth" refers to how comprehensive an FTA is, *i.e.*, its scope—wide or narrow. Does it cover all sectors and products in the economies of the member countries? Or, does it exempt a large number of sectors? Does it leave out a few sensitive sectors or products that account for a large volume or value of trade? The extreme free-trade possibility is complete coverage of all goods and services. In practice, however, coverage is always less than 100%, at least in the immediate and short term.

For example, the 1 January 1983 *CER* between Australia and New Zealand, and 1994 *NAFTA*, are comprehensive FTAs. The May 2003 *U.S.-Singapore* and June 2003 *U.S.-Chile FTAs* boast even more features than *NAFTA*. (Likewise, the EU is a thorough CU.) America insists on comprehensive FTAs, *i.e.*, deals covering goods, services, and IP. America points out its approach respects GATT Article XXIV, which requires an FTA or CU cover substantially all trade.

Even with comprehensive accords, there is room for broader integration. Regarding *NAFTA*, in energy and energy services, especially oil and gas, restrictions on cross-border investment exist, and in security, risk management issues remain. But, that room is small in comparison with many FTAs involving less developed countries. These deals tend to contain exceptions so extensive it is almost laughable to call them "free trade" agreements. The FTAs between the EU and Mexico, Chile and Mexico, and Colombia and Mexico are all less ambitious than *NAFTA*. The *EU-Mexico FTA* leaves out agriculture. The FTA of the *ASEAN*, *AFTA*, omits services, leaves out major agricultural products, and allows some members—those with national car projects like Indonesia and Malaysia—to maintain trade barriers on autos and auto parts. Consider whether any EU type FTA or association agreement satisfied the GATT Article XXIV obligation? Would *NAFTA* and the EU itself be among the few instances of compliance?

"Depth" refers to the extent of reduction of tariffs and NTBs—deep or shallow? For each merchandise category, the extreme free-trade possibility is complete elimination of all barriers. Does the FTA slash all tariffs to zero, eradicate all quantitative restrictions, and move aggressively against abuse of SPS and TBT measures? Or, is the FTA shallow in these respects? That is, does it allow for non-zero tariffs on some merchandise, and the re-imposition of tariffs (sometimes called "tariff snap backs") under certain circumstances? Does it leave plenty of room to deploy TBT and SPS measures for protectionist purposes?

"Timing" concerns the speed with which an FTA liberalizes trade—fast or slow? The extreme free-trade possibility is immediate elimination of all tariff and non-tariff barriers on all goods and services. In practice, that speed never is reached. Rather, FTAs create staging categories, and slot products into the categories. Barriers fall at different rates, depending on the category of the merchandise in question. Timing also refers to the realization of benefits from an FTA. Static gains, profiled in neo-classical economic analysis of RTAs, emphasize increased imports and exports. But, dynamic gains, too, may be achieved. For example, if an FTA creates a better business climate and stimulates foreign and domestic investment, then capital formation and productivity may increase.

As intimated, the three variables—breadth, depth, and timing—are manifest in detailed provisions, which fall into three categories:

(1) *Concession Exclusions*

Goods or sectors agreed upon as "sensitive" are excluded from trade liberalizing concessions. The exclusion may be permanent or for a sustained, definite period, or it may be subject to negotiation after a certain date.

(2) *Tariff Phase Outs*

Goods or sectors not rising to the level of "sensitive," but still of concern, are excluded from immediate duty-free treatment. Tariff reduction schedules are set, with longer durations for goods of greater concern. Likewise, for such goods, tariff cuts may be skewed toward the end of the phase out period, *i.e.*, over half of those cuts come in the second half of the phase out period.

(3) *Tariff Contingencies*

Goods or sectors—whether or not sensitive or of concern—may be subject to a contingent tariff program. One such program is a TRQ, on which the U.S. insists in its FTAs. Another example is a special safeguard. Using this remedial device, MFN duties may be re-imposed on a product category if imports in that category from an FTA partner are below a threshold price or above a threshold volume.

Where in an FTA are these kinds of provisions found? The truth is they are not always "in" the text of the FTA. For political reasons, governments sometimes place them in not-so-transparent side letters to an FTA.

The three variables determine the significance of economic benefits an FTA generates. Succinctly put, an FTA is less economically meaningful if it is (1) narrow in coverage, (2) shallow in barrier reductions, and (3) slow in phasing out barriers. In turn, an FTA that is not economically meaningful, in terms of bringing about economic benefits both in the short and long term, is not sustainable. In other words, it will fail to generate economic gains. That is true even if political and national security factors commend the FTA. To the extent political and national security aims depend on economic gains, they will not be realized.

Further, an FTA that lacks economic ambition indicates irresolute political behavior. Such an FTA suggests difficult domestic political decisions in member countries are not being made. The governments are not pursuing full economic reform, but rather exempting certain preferred constituencies. An FTA lacking in ambition also may become obsolete shortly after signature. It may not be an enduring model accord that can be used for "boilerplate text." Rather, with new economic developments, there are demands for new and different deals, stylized to fit idiosyncrasies of a business climate that, too, will change.

VIII. Case Study: *CAFTA-DR*

• Origins

It would be a grave error to believe the same criteria motivate all countries in every proposed or actual FTA or CU to negotiate and enter into a deal. Any one country may have multiple justifications for seeking an RTA. Or, in the same RTA, one dominant motive may impel one country, whereas another reason may drive its partner. In brief, a concatenation of economic and non-economic criteria may explain the genesis of, and be the sustenance for, an FTA or CU. To illustrate this point, consider *CAFTA–DR*.

The Presidents of five Central American countries—Costa Rica, El Salvador, Guatemala, Honduras, and Nicaragua—proposed the idea of an FTA when President Bill Clinton visited the region in 1997. Those Presidents called for enhanced benefits under the *CBI*, a PTA sponsored by the U.S., or *NAFTA* parity, as a short-term measure, and an FTA as a long-term strategy. President Clinton explained to them that FTA negotiations were not possible at that juncture, given his lack of delegated trade negotiation authority from Congress. In 2002, during a visit to the OAS, President George W. Bush announced he would pursue an FTA—and, by then, had the authority to do so.

• Development Economics

Arguably, an FTA with the U.S. was the most significant pro-development idea to emerge from Central America in decades. Central America has a history of failure to achieve economic integration, dating as far back as independence from Mexico in the 1920s. The region has established every possible institution and accompanying bureaucracy to link the national economies closely, but none has generated substantive results. Border disputes stretching back decades occasionally turn into bloody clashes.

In all material respects, Costa Rica, El Salvador, Guatemala, Honduras, and Nicaragua are tiny relative to the U.S. These Central American countries (as of May 2005) have 12% of the population of the U.S., 4.5% of the territory of the U.S., and 0.5% of the GDP of the U.S. Their combined GDP is $59 billion, below that of Chile. From their perspective, the U.S. market is critical. Remittances from their expatriate workers (legal and illegal) in the U.S. are a key source of income, and for some countries the largest source. These countries ship 50% of their exports to the U.S., and 45% of their imports come from the U.S. The converse is not true. For the U.S., which is the fifth largest Spanish-speaking nation in the world, the countries are commercially insignificant. They represent 1% of total U.S. trade (exports and imports).

By suggesting an FTA, the Central American leaders signaled their interest in broad, deep integration with the U.S. and each other, as opposed to five bilateral hub-and-spoke links with the U.S. as the hub, and their commitment to economic and legal reform. To be sure, an FTA cannot solve all problems. Sound macroeconomic management, infrastructure development, pro-competitive policies, salubrious education and social policies, and legal capacity building are indispensable if trade liberalization is to help generate income and reduce poverty. What use is duty-free access to the giant American market if there is not enough reliable electricity to power factories to make goods for export, if workers are insufficiently trained to perform even semi-skilled manufacturing tasks, road networks from factories to ports are better suited for mules than container-carrying trucks, and the ports themselves are bedeviled with antiquated cranes and corrupt officials? Note the link between this question and government procurement. A Chapter in *CAFTA-DR* on government procurement that encourages transparency in bidding and brings top-notch providers of infrastructure goods and services to the region would contribute to economic growth. Examine *CAFTA-DR* to see if it contains one.

- **Negotiating Objectives**

From the outset, Panama was not involved in the *CAFTA-DR* negotiations. It is relatively richer than the Costa Rica, El Salvador, Guatemala, Honduras, and Nicaragua. Ranked by the U.N. HDI among 173 countries (as of May 2003), the U.S. is six, Costa Rica is 43, and El Salvador, Guatemala, Honduras, and Nicaragua all are below 100. Indeed, save for Panama and Costa Rica, poverty rates are higher in Central America than the rest of Latin America.

Moreover, being service-oriented, the economy of Panama is structurally quite different from the rest of Central America. Services (such as banking and finance, and transportation) account for a far greater percentage, and agriculture and T&A far lesser percentages, of employment and GDP in Panama than in the other Central American economies. The Canal Zone, and importance it plays in world trade and the Panamanian economy, also accounts for the unique situation of the country.

Finally, psychologically and culturally, Panama sometimes considers itself part of Central America, and sometimes part of South America. Panama is not part of the Central American Common Market, an RTA created in the 1960s which remains inchoate, and which lacks a CET on some products. But, the Dominican Republic is not part of this Common Market either, and it is a *CAFTA-DR* member. Query whether *CAFTA-DR* envisages the possibility of Panama docking onto the accord, and whether it is possible for *CAFTA-DR* itself to dock onto *NAFTA*.

Thus, for Costa Rica, El Salvador, Guatemala, Honduras, and Nicaragua, economic criteria dictated the choice of each other and the U.S. as FTA partners. The specific negotiating objectives of the Central American countries included:

(1) Secure guaranteed, DFQF access to the largest market in the world (the U.S.), particularly for products of keen export interest, such as T&A.

(2) Create a hedge against unilateral preference grants by the U.S., such as the CBI.

(3) Enhance overall economic development.

However, the mismatch in material positions meant economics had little power to explain the U.S. interest in *CAFTA-DR*. Neither did generosity toward five poor countries play a role. To the contrary, geopolitical and security objectives motivated the American side.

America's history pre-*CAFTA-DR* with Central America resonates between the extremes of benign neglect and over-engagement. In the 1990s, more illegal immigration into the U.S. originated from Central than South America, despite the fact the former region has a considerably smaller population base than the latter region. Central America also devolved into a base for drugs, narco-terrorism, and money laundering. From the U.S. vantage, as long as Central America remains poor, it is unstable and insecure, and the U.S. vulnerable. That is because poverty creates conditions hostile to peace. It swells the ranks of persons willing or susceptible to engage in bad acts. Surely something is amiss when (as was true as of May 2003) Norway and Mongolia each pay the same amount of tariff duty to the U.S. — about $23 million — but Norway has $5.2 billion of exports to the U.S., and Mongolia just $132 million. U.S. tariffs on goods that matter to Third World countries — such as cotton, footwear, peanuts, and T&A — are high, in the range of 40% to 60%. Thus, an FTA with Central America made sense for U.S. political and security objectives. It could strengthen Central America by helping each country achieve its economic objectives. Specifically, by improving terms of entry for Central American products to the U.S. market, employment in export-sectors of Central America could increase, leading to rising living, labor, and environmental standards.

• **Legal Results**

Consider the legal obligations created by *CAFTA-DR*. To fulfill its criteria, did the U.S. have to make major concessions? To what extent is it an optimal negotiating strategy to try extracting maximum economic concessions from Central American countries? Might undue American pressure put both sides in a mercantilist position? Evidently, the criteria motivating the Central American countries and U.S., while different, proved complimentary. The economic development interests of the five tiny countries meshed with political and security goals of their giant partner. In July 2006, the accord passed the House of Representatives, albeit by the slimmest margin of any trade deal in American history—217 to 215 (with two politicians not voting)—and cleared the Senate by a 55–45 margin. *CAFTA-DR* took effect on 1 March 2006.

Chapter 2

Political and Security Aspects of FTAs[1]

I. Competitive Liberalization and Its Defects

Does the strategy of competitive liberalization work in practice? Allegedly, former Singaporean Prime Minister Lee Kuan Yew (1923–2015, PM, 1959–2000) developed the strategy in 1993, in the context of the APEC forum. In the context of a domestic economy, it means implementing economic reforms to enhance international competitiveness. To help achieve this goal, trade liberalization is necessary at three levels — multilateral, regional, and bilateral. In turn, developing FTAs and customs unions, on a regional or bilateral basis, can lead to liberalization multilaterally through the WTO.

Prime Minister Lee argued that if the U.S. were serious about competitive liberalization of its domestic economy, then it would invite any Asian country to join *NAFTA* that also was committed to deregulation. There would be tension with some Asian countries, in which changing economic structures and policies is a slow process (*e.g.,* Japan). But, within five years any recalcitrant Asian country would acquiesce, liberalize expeditiously, because it could not afford to stay out of an FTA with the U.S.

In brief, competitive liberalization means moving as aggressively as possible toward the goal of global free trade by pursuing trade liberalization on three levels — multilateral, regional, and bilateral — simultaneously. In theory, at least, this pursuit is mutually reinforcing. For example, an FTA can encourage movement in WTO negotiations, and *vice versa*, as Susan Schwab explains:

> My experience as U.S. Trade Representative [for President George W. Bush (1946–, President, 2001–2009] is that they [bilateral, regional, and multilateral trade deals] are in fact mutually reinforcing. The negotiated bilateral and regional deals are gold-standard agreements. They are very deep in that virtually everything opens up. It's not a way of negotiating around sensitivities but a way of coming to grips with sensitivities. Here in these

---

1. Documents References:
   (1) *Havana (ITO) Charter* Articles 43–45
   (2) GATT Article XXIV
   (3) Relevant Provisions in FTAs

bilateral negotiations, you develop a precedent that could at some point be translated in a multilateral setting. In some cases, you really need a multilateral approach to get at issues like piracy and counterfeiting. I have found in Geneva our very best allies for a strong Doha Round have been current and former [free trade] partners.[2]

Thus, none other than a leading advocate of competitive liberalization, Fred Bergsten, the Director of the Institute for International Economics in Washington, D.C., urged creation of an *FTAAP* in August 2006, right after the Doha Round negotiations collapsed in July.[3]

His argument is two-pronged. First, an *FTAAP* would revive the Doha Round, the way the first APEC summit shocked Uruguay Round negotiators into completion of that Round, after they missed an initial 1990 deadline. They missed it because of EU obstinacy against reform of the CAP. When EU negotiators learned the November 1993 APEC summit yielded a commitment to free trade (which APEC leaders reiterated at their 1994 summit), they agreed to CAP reforms—knowing the alternative to a failed Uruguay Round was a vast FTA in the Asia Pacific region. Bergsten urged that even the prospect of an *FTAAP* is leverage to complete a multilateral trade round. After all, the 21 APEC members account for over one-half of world GNP and nearly one-half of world trade. Better to have a successful multilateral round than be left out of an *FTAAP*. The gains from an *FTAAP* would be for members, and non-members would suffer trade diversion.

However, the *Financial Times* casts serious doubt on the Bergsten argument:

> [T]he argument is tenuous, being based on a version of history subscribed to in Washington but nowhere much else.
>
> It holds that the Uruguay Round came to closure in 1993 because APEC leaders scared a recalcitrant Europe into resuming negotiation by making a vague, U.S.-inspired call for closer intra-regional links. But if Europe was swayed at all it was because it feared the U.S. was preparing to unplug itself from multilateralism—not because it seriously believed a grouping as formless, disparate and strife-ridden as APEC could agree on much. The conventional explanation of the Uruguay Round's endgame remains the most plausible: Europe's internal agricultural reforms allowed it to offer just enough on farm trade to escape blame for scuppering the talks, while the U.S. settled for a far weaker deal than it had been holding out for.[4]

The best alternative to multilateralism, then, is not bilateralism or regionalism, but unilateralism, that is, unilateral dismantling of trade barriers, exactly as

---

2. Renuka Rayasam, *Free-Trade Evangelist*, U.S. NEWS & WORLD REPORT, 21 August 2006, at 22 (Q&A: Susan Schwab).

3. Fred Bergsten, *Plan B for World Trade: Go Regional*, FINANCIAL TIMES, 16 August 2006, at 9.

4. Guy de Jonquières, *Do-it-Yourself is Free Trade's Best "Plan B,"* FINANCIAL TIMES, 24 August 2006, at 9.

David Ricardo's Law of Comparative Advantage suggests, and as Australia, Chile, China, Hong Kong, Singapore, and to a lesser degree, India, all have done in recent decades, with ensuing net welfare gains. Moreover, neither the quote from Ambassador Schwab nor the *FTAAP* idea mentions underlying domestic catalysts—or retardants—for competitive liberalization. In truth, competition is driven—or held back—by domestic-level economic reforms, *i.e.*, deregulation. Might it, then, be more accurate to call the strategy "complimentary liberalization," or (as it euphemistically is sometimes dubbed) "parallel liberalization"?

Labels aside, it is necessary to examine domestic-level reform strategies and visions, neither of which is homogeneous or static across countries. For many countries, including some APEC members, the important part of the rubric "Doha Development Agenda" was the middle word. Would competitive liberalization advance development, and in particular, would address growing income disparities?

Consider Asian free trade bastions like Singapore:

> The social contract under which Singaporeans gave up certain civil liberties in return for prosperity is under threat.
>
> . . .
>
> Shortly after the [May 2006 general] election [in which the ruling People's Action Party (PAP) experienced an 8 percentage point drop in support], the government revealed that the income gap was bigger than at any time since independence in 1965. The bottom 30 percent of households have seen incomes fall since 2000.
>
> Singapore's Gini coefficient, a measure of income inequality, places the city state at 105th in the world, between Papua New Guinea and Argentina.
>
> "A two-speed, dual economy appears to be emerging in Singapore," said Citigroup.
>
> "Globalization, for a small open economy, may be having a disproportionately large impact."[5]

China faces the same problem on a much larger scale.[6] A time series analysis of relevant statistics, including Gini coefficients, indicates in 1986, income distribution in China resembled Germany and Sweden. By 2006, the rich-poor gap had widened to a degree making China more unequal than Russia or the U.S., and approaching Brazil and Mexico. Why? China's development model, which favored investment on the coast, a large number of labor surplus workers shifting from non-productive work in the rural sector into manufacturing and service jobs, and corruption were among the culprits. Aggressive trade liberalization may well have been at least a handmaiden.

---

5. John Burton, *Singapore's Social Contract Shows Signs of Strain*, Financial Times, 19–20 August 2006, at 3.

6. Richard McGregor, *China Seeks to Reduce Gap Between Rich and Poor*, 8–9 July 2006, at 2.

Whatever label is used for "competitive liberalization," the policy presumes shared interests within and among countries in freer bilateral, regional, and multi-lateral trade. In turn, it presumes interests are impelled by shared, or at least complementary, visions of desirable domestic policies and the role of each country in the trading system.

Competitive liberalization also suffers from conceptual and practical problems. Consider the following questions.

- **First: Integration of Reforms?**

How does trade liberalization feed back to domestic-level reforms? This question is particularly acute in special or sensitive sectors like agriculture and T&A.

- **Second: Bicycle Theory?**

How do multilateral, regional, and bilateral trade liberalization efforts relate to each other? Is the "Bicycle Theory" of trade negotiations correct, whereby these efforts must continue (as a cyclist must keep pedaling to move forward) or they will come to a halt (as a cyclist would stop, even fall off)? Competitive liberalization presumes there are three bicycles, and trade talks at the multilateral, regional, or bilateral level spur such talks on another level, or the other two levels. But, is the right metaphor for trade negotiations not a bicycle, but a hedge. The *Financial Times*' Guy de Jonquières puts the concern this way:

> Washington has claimed . . . that its use of muscular bilateral trade diplomacy will re-energize the multilateral trading system by unleashing a wave of "competitive liberalization." The Doha [Round] debacle has exposed that theory for what it is. In practice, bilateralism has fed off itself, intensifying the rush into preferential deals while draining energy from the Doha talks, polarizing the U.S. Congress and further diminishing its appetite for trade initiatives of all descriptions.[7]

Moreover, a reverse causal directional arrow may exist: stalled or failed talks at one level (*e.g.*, the Doha Round) may bring out calls for talks at another level (*e.g.*, bilateral FTAs).[8] There is plenty of evidence in favor of a reverse directional arrow.

Israel, for example, began pursuing FTA negotiations with *MERCOSUR* in December 2005, the month of the unsuccessful WTO Hong Kong Ministerial Conference, and talks continue apace.[9] India boasted FTAs with Singapore, Sri Lanka, and Thailand. In light of the July 2006 collapse of Doha Round negotiations, India

---

7. Guy de Jonquières, *Do-it-Yourself is Free Trade's Best "Plan B,"* FINANCIAL TIMES, 24 August 2006, at 9.

8. *See, e.g.*, Christopher Swann & Edward Alden, *Focus on Bilateral Trade Deals, Bush is Urged*, FINANCIAL TIMES, 4 April 2006, at 7 (discussing advice to President George W. Bush from Rep. Bill Thomas, Chairman, House Ways & Means Committee, to focus efforts on FTAs, because the U.S. and EU have irreconcilable differences in the Doha Round).

9. David Haskel, *MERCOSUR, Israel to Exchange Duty-Free List of Products for Inclusion in Free Trade Pact*, 23 International Trade Reporter (BNA) 542 (6 April 2006).

announced it would pursue FTAs vigorously, including with the EU and Japan. Even Chile, well disposed to unilateral trade barrier reduction, has not sat on the sidelines. It had FTAs with China and South Korea, a "Partial Scope Agreement" with India, and (as of June 2006) was discussing a comprehensive "Economic Association Agreement" with Japan.

• **Third: Collective Action Problem?**

WTO Members did not commit themselves to ensuring regional integration complement their Doha Round negotiations. They could have entered into an "RTA Peace Clause," whereby they placed a standstill on all new FTAs and CUs until they completed the Round. Instead, they raced each other to seal RTA deals.

Does this behavior suggest it would be easier for WTO Members to reach consensus in an MTN round if they do not have the option to join an FTA? That is, does this option give them an exit strategy? If so, then is there a collective action problem: no one Member is willing to forego the RTA option unless all other Members do, but each Member passes the responsibility to others to take the lead in exerting discipline?

• **Fourth: Erosion of Global Economic Order?**

Is competitive liberalization a fair concept, particularly when it discriminates through an RTA, within the context of non-discriminatory treatment under GATT-WTO rules, and results in elaborate preferential ROOs in each FTA or CU? Arguably, competitive liberalization means competitive discrimination, trade diversion, and erosion of the global economic order. That is the argument of the ADB, which in *The Routes for Asia's Trade* (2006) warned FTAs undermine global trade liberalization and exacerbate divisions within Asia, leaving the poorest countries worst off.[10]

To take a technical example, suppose under *NAFTA's* Yarn Forward ROO, the U.S. accords duty-free treatment to cotton shirts imported from Mexico, but only if they are made from yarn spun into cotton fabric in Mexico. The U.S. imposes a tariff on the same kind of shirts if the yarn is spun into fabric in Pakistan. Logically, Mexican garment manufacturers will source the input (yarn) from within *NAFTA*. Economically, the U.S. has exported its tariff to Mexico, *i.e.*, the effect of the origin rule is as if Mexico imposed a tariff on the Pakistani input. That effect undermines any previously-agreed multilateral tariff reduction on the input.

The foundation of the global economic order is the multilateral trading system, characterized by non-discriminatory treatment and the progressive lowering and binding of barriers. A preference granted to one country is discrimination visited on all other countries. Because discrimination is incongruous with the multilateral

---

10. *See* Asian Development Bank, The Routes for Asia's Trade (2006), www.adb.org; Jonathan Hopfner, *ADB Suggests Asian Nations Face Risks with Pursuit of Bilateral Free Trade Deals*, 23 International Trade Reporter (BNA) 611–12 (20 April 2006).

trading system, it erodes the global economic order. Nonetheless, WTO Members, and GATT contracting parties before them, have entered into FTAs and CUs— under the cover of GATT Article XXIV and *GATS* Article V.

Consider Mongolia. This country had been (as of August 2006) the only WTO Member not to have joined an RTA. As Damedin Tsogtbaatar of the Mongolian Development Strategy Institute explained, Mongolia put more into the WTO than it had obtained from it, because it "chose, ironically, a rather Buddhist path of self-perfection and good WTO-consistent behavior, without regard to whether other countries were doing the same."[11] Yet, query whether this "Buddhist path" is what other WTO Members ought to follow, and thus whether competitive liberalization is a road for apostates. Indeed, if every WTO Member (as of August 2006—149 of them) had struck a bilateral FTA with every other Member, then there would have been 11,026 bilateral deals.

- **Fifth: International Rule of Law?**

How does competitive liberalization contribute to the international rule of law? On the one hand, adjudicatory mechanisms and outcomes under an RTA may prove useful as guidance, even path-breaking in legal theory or rationale, for WTO Panels and the Appellate Body. They also may provide for forum selection, and contribute to healthy competition among adjudicators in different bodies by encouraging them to better quality proceedings and outcomes. In brief, there may be a "race to the top."

On the other hand, RTA dispute settlement schemes may lead to forum shopping. They also may present an un-level playing field. Would, for example, it be preferable to resolve alleged trade violations of China through *ASEAN* or through the WTO *DSU*?

- **Sixth: Alignment of Benefits?**

Does competitive liberalization fail to align properly economic and non-economic benefits from trade liberalization? Consider rents from tariffs in comparison with rents from IP. Tariff rents come from government collection of tariff revenue. IP rents are associated with the ability of a patent, trade or service mark, or copyright owner to exclude all others from manufacturing, distributing, or licensing the good or service embodying the IP, and thus to hold a monopoly position on that good or service.

Suppose competitive liberalization were extended to the extreme through RTAs, whereby the U.S. had an FTA with every country in the world. Rents from tariffs would disappear. That is because with all trade accorded duty-free treatment, neither the U.S. nor its FTA partners gain tariff revenue. Would IP rents disappear?

The answer is "no." Holders of patents, trade and service marks, and copyrights— from Adidas to Sony Pictures, from Amazon.com to Roche—would press the

---

11. *Quoted in Least Favored Nation*, The Economist, 5 August 2006, at 68.

U.S. and its FTA partners for textual provisions to ensure strict IP protection and enforcement. Thus, exporters and importers of goods would enjoy the disappearance of tariff rents. IP holders would enjoy the maintenance of IP rents. This alignment could create tension.

The first group (exporters and importers) would focus on the economic dimensions of the FTAs. The second group (IP rights holders) would be sensitive to IP infringement, and urge rigorous prosecution and penalties. The first group would prefer diplomatic peace to preserve its economic benefits. The diplomatic interests of the second group might call for confrontation to enforce their IP rights, possibly with some disruption in the economic *status quo*. In brief, competitive liberalization might not necessarily bring into alignment all economic and non-economic features of RTAs.

- **Seventh: Administration?**

Finally, competitive liberalization suffers from an administrative problem. It is a strategy only rich countries can pursue effectively. It requires a considerable number of talented international trade lawyers to pursue three-track negotiations, and the lawyers on each track must coordinate with the lawyers on all other tracks. That is a challenge even for the USTR, and *a fortiori* it is a close-to-insurmountable task for trade ministries in the Philippines, Suriname, or Togo.

Clearly, then, from a systemic perspective, competitive liberalization is at best an imperfect justification for an active FTA policy.

That said, the fundamental point to observe is that competitive liberalization itself is not a purely economic strategy. As suggested, encouraging trade negotiations on three tracks simultaneously is a self-interested hedge against the political risk of failure on one or two of the tracks. In American terms, it avoids the U.S. "putting all its trade eggs in the multilateral basket." More bluntly, it ensures U.S. efforts to obtain market access in other countries are not subject to a veto by any one country, such as France or India, or by any one domestic constituency, such as steel or T&A interests. If blockage occurs on one level, then progress might be made on another level.

II. Choosing FTA Partners

What priorities ought to govern the decision to enter into negotiations for an FTA or CU? That is, what are the criteria by which to decide potential RTA partners? For much of GATT history, with the notable exception of economic integration in Europe beginning in 1950, FTAs and CUs were a sideshow in the international trade arena. But, as of May 2003, there were 155 FTAs notified to the WTO, and an additional 83 that had been concluded but not notified. At that time, the U.S. was a partner in three of the 155 (and two of the 83), and the EU (or *EFTA*), a partner in 59 of the 155 (and 6 of the 83).

These figures continue to grow. Overall, there are 459 FTAs and CUs in the world (as of May 2018, and dozens more planned or under negotiation). This number is almost thrice the number of WTO Members, and more than double the number of countries in the world. If the global trading system is characterized by regionalism and bilateralism, then which actual and potential RTAs ought to be highest on the negotiating agenda for a country? As the number of RTAs suggests, these questions are relevant to most countries. Mexico, for example, has a network of FTAs, including *CPTPP*, with nearly five dozen countries across the world. Indeed, Mexico had a post-*NAFTA* FTA binge. Mexico had just one FTA, with Chile, in 1994.

No less than two dozen countries have asked the U.S. for an FTA. How should the U.S. pick among them? Should the criteria be exclusively, or primarily, economic? What would the specific criteria be? How would they apply in particular contexts? For example, how might an FTA between the U.S. and Thailand benefit each country economically? Thailand is a major production base for Japanese and other foreign auto and auto parts producers. What would be the effect of an FTA on the auto industry in each country, and third countries? Conversely, what factors are or should be relevant from the perspective of other countries in contemplating, negotiating, and implementing an FTA with the world's superpower?

Economic research, starting with Jacob Viner's classic study, *The Customs Union Issue* (1950), has evaluated the complex effects of RTAs on trade activity. For the consensus of mainstream economists, the general theoretical conclusions are:

(1) It is better to liberalize trade unilaterally, even without reciprocal concessions from trading partners. This conclusion follows from the standard Smith-Ricardo arguments for free trade.

(2) It is better to negotiate trade liberalization through a multilateral forum, rather than regional or bilateral fora. This conclusion follows from the analysis of trade creation versus trade diversion.

Obviously, these conclusions do not dispose of efforts to enter sub-multilateral trade deals. There may be practical economic blessings and curses—what might be called "political economy" factors—from an RTA. In turn, once political calculations enter into RTA decision-making, then so also do national security considerations.

III. Political Criteria

Evidently, the plethora and dispersion of actual and potential RTAs means they are more than just economic creatures. Political factors may impel countries to a deal. An obvious example is direction from a legislature or domestic constituencies. Article I, Section 8, Clause 3 of the U.S. Constitution gives Congress the power to regulate trade with foreign nations. Congress may delegate that power to the Executive Branch, and thereby authorize the President to conduct trade negotiations at the multilateral, regional, or bilateral level. Such delegations typically entail Congressional guidance as to countries with which the President should seek an FTA.

That is the case for *CBI*, an ongoing initiative created under the 1983 *CBERA* (which was expanded in 1990 and amended in 2000). The *CBI* calls for negotiations with Central and Southern American nations. Similarly, through the 2000 *AGOA* (as subsequently amended), Congress pushed for FTAs in Sub-Saharan Africa. In both instances, FTAs with the U.S. create the potential to support regional integration. Immigrant communities in the U.S.—Central Americans and Africans, respectively—helped to support *CBI* and *AGOA*.

Notably, America's first FTA with a sovereign nation came in April 1985 when it signed an accord with Israel. (The *Canada-U.S. Auto Pact* of 1965 obviously precedes this accord, but it covers only trade in auto and auto parts.) The *U.S.- Israel FTA* came a decade after the EU signed a free trade accord with Israel, in 1975. It also helped unblock a debate in Congress over trade delegation authority to the President for what would be the Uruguay Round. In October 2000, the U.S. signed an FTA with Jordan. Both countries were members of the GATT-WTO system when their FTAs occurred: Israel acceded to GATT on 6 April 1962, and Jordan joined the WTO on 11 April 2000. These FTAs are unambiguous examples of trade policy being used as a tool of foreign policy. That is, America's foreign policy interests in Israel and Jordan outweigh any domestic economic sensitivity to particular imports from these countries.

At the same time, the *Israel* and *Jordan FTAs* exemplify the way in which a politically-driven bargain can broaden ties among the member countries. Before these deals, political and military affairs dominated the relationships between the U.S. and Israel, and the U.S. and Jordan. After the FTAs took effect, indeed as they were negotiated, tomato growers and sweater producers became interested in the relationships. In other words, an FTA can expand the range of constituencies actively engaged in a foreign linkage. That expansion can yield not only net economic benefits among the members, but also reinforce mutual political and military ties.

IV. Case Study: Taiwan, *TIFA*, But No FTA

- **China, Taiwan, and Official American Recognition**

Since 1 January 1949 when the CCP, led by Mao Zedong, took control of the Mainland, the Mainland has asserted sovereignty over the island of Formosa, or Taiwan. The victorious CCP drove from power the Nationalists led by General Chiang Kai-Shek, who fled to Taiwan. Conversely, Taiwan never relinquished its claim to sovereignty over the Mainland. To this day, officially, each side claims it is the rightful "one" China. The debacle of the Mainland turning "Red" not only exacerbated Cold War tensions and led to fears of country after country falling into the

Communist orbit like dominoes—the "Domino Theory"—but also caused fearsome events in the U.S. "Who lost China?" was a debate that turned ugly during the McCarthy Era, as many Americans were accused—rightly or not—of being Communists or Communist sympathizers. Not until the post-9/11 Era, and the disclosure in June 2013 by former intelligence officer turned whistleblower, Edward Snowden, that the NSA systematically spied on Americans and foreigners alike, did a national security problem abroad so challenge civil liberties at home.

In any event, until the 1970s, America stuck with Taiwan. Like South Korea, Taiwan was the loyalist of allies, backing America in every war—including Vietnam—and boasting a robust market-oriented economy. Politically, both countries moved, albeit hesitatingly, towards multi-party democracies.[12] Culturally, their people shared America's pastime—baseball. But, demographics alone made that policy unsustainable: there were one billion "Red" Chinese, but only about 20 million Taiwanese (1.2 billion and 23 million, respectively, as of June 2013). Moreover, America realized the Communist threat was not monolithic. After all, the Sino-Soviet split dated back to the late 1950s.

So, in February 1972, the most ardent of Cold Warriors, President Richard Nixon (1913–1994, President, 1969–1974), authorized his controversial Secretary of State, Henry Kissinger (1923–), to visit the Mainland. Soon thereafter, President Nixon himself met Chairman Mao Zedong (1893–1976, in office, 1949–1976). The days of sticking with Taiwan as the official one China were numbered. In 1979, President Jimmy Carter (1924–, President, 1977–1981) normalized relations with the PRC, and de-recognized the Republic of China (Taiwan).

• **What Is in a Name?**

To this day, CCP officials fume at applying the rubric "country" or "nation" to Taiwan. They adhere to the "one country, two systems" characterization of their former Chairman, Deng Xiaoping (1904–1997, in office, 1978–1989), who spearheaded economic reforms on the Mainland in 1978–1979. Thus, from the perspective of the CCP, there can be only one China participating in an IO, such as the U.N. Taiwan was booted out of the U.N. in 1971, replaced by the Mainland. Likewise, no country can have official relations with both. So, the U.S. maintains its "official" Embassy in Beijing, and has an "unofficial" embassy in Taipei through the American Chamber of Commerce (AmCham).

The WTO is a key exception. Both the Mainland and Taiwan are Members. But, Taiwan acceded as the "Separate Customs Territory of Taiwan, Penghu, Kinmen and Matsu." A "Customs Territory" that is "Separate" from what? The Mainland.

---

12. For an argument FTAs are not necessarily a force for political stability, namely, their effectiveness as such is more perception than reality, at least in the context of FTAs entered into by China, where China's political stability seems more to be a cause of its free trade policies than a consequence of those policies, see Gonzalo Villalta Puig & Vinci Chan, *Free Trade as a Force of Political Stability? The Case of Mainland China and Hong Kong*, 49 THE INTERNATIONAL LAWYER number 3, 299–323 (winter 2016).

Notwithstanding political disputes over names and recognition, Taiwan has been throughout the post–Second World War era a robust trading nation, and one of the four Far East Tigers, or Dragons, along with Hong Kong, Korea, and Singapore. Its importance to the U.S. has been significant.[13] In 1989, it was the 6th largest trading partner of the U.S., and the ninth largest market for American exports. In 2012, it was America's 11th largest trading partner, and 16th largest market. The decline in that period, however, excludes data on Taiwan's position in the supply chain for goods: such goods incorporate Taiwanese parts, are assembled outside of Taiwan, and thereafter exported from their third country assembly points to the U.S.

- **Strategic Ambiguity**

Since 1979, the U.S. has pursued a policy toward the two entities characterized as "strategic ambiguity." On the one hand, the 1979 *Taiwan Relations Act* (22 U.S.C. §§ 3301 *et seq.*) reaffirms America's commitment to a "One China Policy," a product of the famous February 1972 *Shanghai Communiqué* worked out between Chinese Premier Zhou Enlai (1898–1976) and American Secretary of State Henry Kissinger (1923–). On the other hand, the same *Act* commits the U.S. to providing military and economic assistance to Taiwan.

Strategic ambiguity has not inhibited commercial relations between the U.S. and Taiwan, and in 1994 the two sides signed a *TIFA*. Taiwan (as of March 2013) is the 11th largest trading partner of the U.S., and 15th largest market for American exports. Indeed, American trade with Taiwan far exceeds trade with any other East Asian nation, save for the PRC and Korea. Conversely, America is Taiwan's third largest trading partner, and the largest source of FDI in Taiwan.

- **Trade Disputes**

Strategic ambiguity also has not kept the two countries from trade spats. In 1998, the U.S. suspended *TIFA* talks, displeased at three aspects of Taiwan's trade policy: reluctance to open its rice market; slow progress on opening service markets; and poor enforcement of IP rights. Subsequently, a fourth area of dispute arose that held up *TIFA* talks: Taiwanese SPS measures.[14] Concerned about Mad Cow disease, Taiwan banned American beef in 2003 and 2005. It replaced the ban with limited restrictions in 2006. Between 2007 and 2012, the two countries sparred over whether Taiwan was correct in one such restriction: a ban on imports of American beef from cattle 20 months of age or less because of Mad Cow disease risk. America insisted its beef was free from the disease. Taiwan thought otherwise.

From January 2011 until July 2012, they quarreled over inclusion in American beef of ractopamine, a veterinary drug that is a feed additive used to boost protein deposits in carcasses and thereby create lean muscle mass in cattle, pigs, and

---

13. *See* Brian Flood, *Taiwan Pursing Multiple Trade Pacts, Congressional Research Service Says,* 31 International Trade Reporter (BNA) 230 (30 January 2014).

14. *See* Shirley A. Kan & Wayne M. Morrison, U.S.-Taiwan Relationship: Overview of Policy Issues, Congressional Research Service 7-5700, R41952 34–36 (27 October 2014), www.crs.org.

turkeys. Taiwan admitted the shipments had trace amounts well below the maximum residue levels (MRLs) for human health safety set by the *Codex Alimentarius* Commission (though *Codex* had not adopted formal, science-based MRLs). But, Taiwan ordered retailers to remove American beef from store shelves, in keeping with its zero-tolerance policy for this additive. China, the EU, Russia, and Thailand had the same policy.

America countered ractopamine is legally acceptable in America (having been approved by the FDA in 1999 for use in cattle and swine) and 25 other countries (including Australia, Brazil, Canada, Indonesia, Korea, Mexico, and Philippines). The U.S. accused the Taiwanese government of sowing public misperception the additive is risky with a live TV press conference ordering the removal. Was protectionism afoot?

The U.S. said as much: in 2007 Taiwan conducted a risk assessment on ractopamine, and notified the WTO it would set a MRL for it, until domestic pig farmers demonstrated against the proposal. In March 2012, Taiwan announced — amidst strong protests from its civil society community — that it would open its beef market conditionally to certain types of meat containing ractopamine residues, thus abandoning its zero-tolerance policy. The allowed products had to bear a special label, and were subject to strict enforcement of a MRL. Finally, in July–August 2012, the Taiwanese legislature amended its *Act Governing Food Sanitation (Food Safety Act)*, granting authority to regulators to set MRLs for permitted beta-agonists, which is the class of drugs to which ractopamine belongs, in domestic and imported meat. Taiwan's Department of Health used the authority by adopting the ractopamine MRL standard of *Codex*, namely 10 parts per billion. In March 2013, *TIFA* talks resumed for the first time since their suspension in 2007. However, 4 years on, in March 2014, American pork exporters remained frustrated: Taiwan refused them market access unless they certified their products were free of ractopamine.

- **Logic of *Taiwan FTA***

Yet, the damage to Taiwanese-American trade relations, in terms of lost time and opportunities, had been done. For several years, the two countries failed to fulfill the *TIFA* obligation that they hold senior level consultations at least annually. How strong is the commercial logic for a *U.S.-Taiwan FTA*? For the U.S., the largest export benefit from an FTA with Taiwan would be in the auto and auto parts sector. But, American auto and auto producers suspect an FTA would make little difference in practice, because Taiwan eventually would eliminate its ban on imports from China of these products. An FTA would be all but irrelevant if America forges a *TPP* that includes Taiwan.

Suppose auto and auto parts could be exported directly from China to Taiwan. American producers in China would benefit — without an FTA with Taiwan. For Taiwan, the U.S. is the most important trading partner (measured in terms of two-way trade, *i.e.*, exports plus imports), though exports from Taiwan to China are increasingly important. The biggest export gain for Taiwan from an FTA with the U.S. would be concentrated in the T&A sector, in which it holds a clear comparative advantage over the U.S. Neither country would see agriculture as a major issue in an FTA with the other, largely because Taiwan is not a major agricultural exporter, and thus not a threat to American farmers.

In a study of the potential benefits from such an accord, the ITC suggested overall economic gains would be modest. As AmCham in Taipei pointed out in a May 2006 *Taiwan White Paper*, many benefits could be had without an FTA, but rather through removing restrictions on transactions across the Taiwan Strait. Such restrictions inhibit imports into Taiwan from the Mainland of certain products, investment in the Mainland, travel from the Mainland to Taiwan by employees of multinational (including Taiwanese) companies, transfer from Taiwan to the Mainland of commercial technology, and direct air and shipping links between Taiwan and the Mainland. In turn, cross-Strait integration is retarded, and Taiwan segregates itself from Greater China and the global economy.

By inference, therefore, geopolitical calculus over economics might be the more compelling logic for a *Taiwan FTA*. An agreement between the two sides would have significant political benefits. It would formalize the close relationship between the U.S. and Taiwan, and suggest the former regards, or at least treats in a *de facto* way, the latter as an independent nation. It also would challenge the efforts of China to isolate Taiwan, both diplomatically and in international trade.

An FTA between the U.S. and Taiwan might well mortify the CCP, whereas American leadership might embolden allies. For years, Taiwan tried to conclude bilateral trade accords with Australia, Japan, and Singapore, but they have been standoffish, fearful of annoying China. A *Taiwan FTA* would be less about trade between the parties and more about a stark political statement to the giant country across the Formosa Straits. That statement would reinforce the re-balancing of American military forces to the Pacific region by 2020, to a 60–40 rather than 50–50 split with the Atlantic area, announced by the Administration of President Barack H. Obama in June 2012. It also would underscore the questioning by his successor, Donald J. Trump, of America's "One China Policy," in place since the 1972 *Shanghai Communiqué*.[15] Taiwan was quick to take note, and in January 2017 indicated it would drop trade barriers to American products to secure a free trade deal.

Should, then, the criteria for choosing RTA partners include, even be dominated by, political factors? An FTA or CU can broaden and deepen links among member countries. Such integration can, in turn, be furthered through monetary and political union—as the EU shows. No longer is the remark of American Secretary of State Henry Kissinger—to the effect, when you want to speak to "Europe," whom

---

15. This states: "The United States acknowledges that Chinese on either side of the Taiwan Strait maintain there is but one China and that Taiwan is a part of China. The United States does not challenge that position."

do you call?—accurate. Europe, generally, speaks with one voice on an array of political issues.

• **Taiwanese FTA Policy**

Taiwan did not sit forlornly hoping for an FTA with the U.S. It forged an active FTA policy, including negotiated bilateral deals with Guatemala, Nicaragua, and Panama, and in May 2007, after one year of bargaining, it signed its first "multilateral FTA" with El Salvador and Honduras.[16] Under the *Taiwan-El Salvador-Honduras FTA*, which took effect on 1 January 2008, 57.1% of Taiwanese exports to El Salvador (3,590 products), and 61.9% of its exports to Honduras (3,881 products) got duty free treatment. Among the delighted constituencies were Taiwanese producer-exporters of certain agricultural items, electronics, golf clubs, hand tools, home appliances, rubber products, screws and nuts, and tires. Conversely, Taiwan accorded duty free status to 64.4% of El Salvadorian imports (5,688 products), and 69.4% of Honduran imports (6,135 products).

Most notably, as Taiwan and America quarreled over ractopamine, Taiwan signed a Taiwan-China Cross-Straits *ECFA*, which entered into force in September 2010, strengthening its ties with the PRC. The *ECFA* amounts to a "Greater China FTA," linking Taiwan more closely with the Mainland, Hong Kong, and Macau. Overall, between May 2008 and August 2012, Taiwan and the Mainland signed 18 economic accords. Their August 2012 investment protection and customs cooperation pact (1) establishes an arbitral mechanism for private companies to resolve business disputes outside of court (using a Taiwanese or Chinese arbiter as agreed by the disputing parties), (2) sets up mediation for commercial disputes between a private company and host-country government, and (3) obligates the countries to collaborate on tariff classification, origin of goods verification, smuggling, and new customs rules notifications.

Moreover, eager to become a "free trade island," Taiwan set up free economic zones. In 2003, the Taiwanese government established Kaohsiung (the largest international harbor on the island) as a free trade zone with efficient distribution flows and logistic management capabilities. Such zones are designed to keep pace with *KORUS* and other FTAs in the region to which Taiwan is not a party, and also to bolster the attractiveness of Taiwan as an FTA partner, for example, with Japan, New Zealand, and Singapore, with which Taiwan sought economic cooperation arrangements.

Possibly, Taiwan could benefit economically from the *FTA* in conjunction with closer trade relations between the U.S. and Central America under the *CAFTA-DR*. How might Taiwanese producer-exporters use the *FTA* and *CAFTA-DR* to facilitate access for their products into the American market? Observe the *FTA* is clever for Taiwan for diplomatic reasons, too. It is an opportunity for a modicum of influence in a world in which a dwindling number of countries grant it official recognition.

---

16. Yu-Tzu Chiu, *Taiwan Signs Free Trade Pact with El Salvador and Honduras*, 24 International Trade Reporter (BNA) 700 (17 May 2007).

- July 2013 *New Zealand-Taiwan Economic Cooperation Agreement*

The U.S. might rightly be criticized for behavior that is both politically pusillanimous and economically inefficient in not forging an FTA with Taiwan. Those epithets cannot be hurled at New Zealand. In July 2013, New Zealand signed an FTA with Taiwan. That came just five years after New Zealand entered into an FTA with China, and after a year of negotiations with Taiwan. Also, in 2013, Taiwan inked an *Agreement between Singapore and Taiwan on Economic Partnership*.

New Zealand has a "No Surprises" Policy with the Mainland in respect of relations with Taiwan, and officially recognizes Beijing. So, the deal is not officially called an "FTA," but rather an "*Economic Cooperation Agreement*" (*ECA*). The counterparty is not dubbed "Taiwan," but rather given the WTO Member label—"Separate Customs Territory of Taiwan, Penghu, Kinmen and Matsu." Moreover, the signing ceremony was at Victoria University in Wellington, not in an official government building, and no government ministers attended.

The *New Zealand-Taiwan ECA* made good sense for both sides. For Taiwan, it was the first free trade deal inked with a member of the OECD. For New Zealand, Taiwan is its eighth largest export market (as of June 2013), and 12th largest trading partner (as of June 2012), in the world.

New Zealand has a keen export interest in agricultural products. Before the *ECA*, New Zealand exports of primary goods faced Taiwanese tariffs of 20%–25%, with duties on deer velvet and fresh milk of up to 500%. With the *ECA*, tariffs on 44% of exports from New Zealand to Taiwan were eliminated immediately. The items included apples, cherries, rock lobsters, wine, and nearly all dairy products. Two years later (2015), tariffs on beef were eliminated, and three years later (2016), tariffs on kiwi fruit were cut to zero. So, four years after the *ECA* (2017), 98.7% of exports from New Zealand to Taiwan were duty-free, and in eight years (2021) the percentage rose to 99.5%.

Two other features of the *ECA* were notable, both involving services. Before the deal, there was a limit of 7 flights per week between New Zealand and Taiwan. The ECA removed this cap. Also, the deal expanded access for TV and film co-productions. With movies like *The Whale Rider* (2002), *Lord of the Rings* (2001–2003), and *The Hobbit* (2012), the Kiwi film industry is world class. Taiwan is exempt from the restrictions China imposes on foreign films entering the Mainland. So, under the *ECA*, New Zealand productions could enter the vast Chinese market via the "back door" of Taiwan.

V. Case Study: Panama and Three FTA Issues

- SPS Side Letter on Food Safety

Few FTA stories are entirely happy. Political factors can be a significant impediment to, and even vitiate (at least temporarily), a proposed FTA. Negotiations between the U.S. and Panama, conducted between April 2004 and December 2006 are an example. The countries, sharing a common destiny dating back over a century to the construction of the Canal Zone, seemed poised for an easy FTA negotiation.

Panama—unlike the *CAFTA* countries—has a small agricultural sector, and thus poses little challenge to entrenched U.S. lobbying interests in sectors like sugar. Further, even without an FTA, 96% of Panamanian exports enjoyed duty-free access to the American market (many through preferences, particularly the *CBI*). Yet, 3 issues almost proved politically insurmountable in the FTA talks—SPS, labor rights, and lobbying.

First, the U.S. insisted Panama sign a Side Letter on SPS measures that obligated Panama to recognize all American testing procedures and measures for food and beverage products. Bitter historical experience, albeit from when Panama was under military dictatorship, in which American exports were blocked for political reasons veiled by SPS concerns, impelled the U.S. to take this position. The U.S. asserted other countries with which it had or was seeking an FTA, such as Colombia and Oman, had agreed to an SPS Side Letter. Panama countered with a demand to see those Letters. The U.S. refused, forcing Panama to attempt to get them directly from the other countries. In February 2006, Panama further countered with a request to visit the U.S. to review the USDA food safety and inspection system. The logic was that if the U.S. demands Panama accept American SPS standards, then Panama would like to see what the system is and how well it works. Surprisingly, the initial American response was negative, but the U.S. ultimately relented. Interestingly, Panama urged the U.S. to put a negotiated text on the recognition of SPS measures not in a Side Letter, but in the FTA document itself. The U.S. refused.

From the political angle of Panama, the Side Letter was the SPS equivalent of dollar-ization, *i.e.*, dropping its own currency, adopting the U.S. dollar, and thus being entirely subject to monetary policy set by the Federal Reserve. The government of Panama would have to accept for Panamanian citizens whatever food and beverage risk assessment testing the U.S. government set for American citizens. To be sure, the U.S. levels might well be higher than all or almost all Panamanian levels. Yet, politically, Panamanian leaders would have to defend the delegation, if not abdication, of the sovereign right to set SPS standards—a right guaranteed by the WTO *SPS Agreement*—to the giant country to the north. Indeed, in early 2006, the Panamanian Agriculture Minister, Laurentino Cortizo, resigned, saying an FTA would increase the risk of his country importing animal diseases.

Also, from a Panamanian political vantage point, the U.S. failed to differentiate among Central American nations. Pursuant to *CAFTA-DR* negotiations, the U.S. was largely successful in obtaining recognition from the likes of El Salvador to accept the equivalency of U.S. meat and poultry inspection and other SPS standards. The U.S. refused to implement *CAFTA-DR* with respect to El Salvador on the target date of 1 January 2006, because that country had not recognized the

American standards as equivalent. Only with recognition did implementation follow, on 1 March 2006.

But Panama is not El Salvador, which is poorer, more agrarian, and weaker. Thus, Panama is less susceptible than El Salvador to American pressure in the form of "do this or we don't implement." Of course, the American side had its own political concerns: in the TPA legislation by which Congress delegated power to the President to conduct FTA talks, Congress required the U.S. export its equivalency standards. Might it be inferred as a general proposition that the deal, if any, trade negotiators bring home depends in large part on negotiating parameters set by their political masters?

• **Labor Laws in Canal Zone**

Second, the U.S. told Panama it would have to change its labor law, which meant a possible change to its constitution, to grant workers in the Panama Canal Zone the right to strike. Panama responded Canal Zone jobs are among the most highly sought after in the country. That is because of their relatively higher pay, benefits, and working conditions. Workers there have little interest in that right, but even if they did, Panama could not afford granting this right, and it would not be in America's interests to do so.

Panama is a unique Latin American country. Like the U.S., for Panama, services (especially banking, the Colon Free Zone, tourism, and transshipment of cargo) account for the predominant source of national income—roughly 77% of GDP (as of June 2007). The Canal alone contributes about 6% to Panama's GDP. Trade through the Canal represents 5% of world trade, and the U.S. is the largest user of the Canal (with about 70% of total cargo, and 54% of vessels originating in or destined for the U.S.) By 2014, Panama plans to add a $5.25 billion third lane (specifically, two large flights of three locks), and widen and deepen the 50-mile Canal. Its goal is to increase capacity and allow the largest and most modern container vessels to sail directly from Asia to the U.S. Eastern Seaboard. (When the Canal opened in 1914, the 12 locks could handle the biggest ships of the day.) In part, China's rise as a producer and exporter of manufactured goods necessitates expansion, as the Canal operates at 90% capacity. Expansion means the Canal could accommodate ships up to 366 meters long and 49 meters wide, and which can carry 12,000 TEUs of containers—i.e., ships larger than currently exist, and twice the size of the biggest vessels now able to use the Canal.

Any strike or serious labor disruption not only could hamper expansion plans, but also cripple operations in the Canal Zone, with adverse knock-on effects for the country and world trade. For example, if a vessel is too large for the Canal, or if the Canal is closed, the alternative Asia-to-East Coast route is through the Suez Canal—which is further, longer, and entails political risks associated with transport in the Middle East—or from Asia to the West Coast, and then across America by rail. Quite rightly, Panama asked, did the U.S.—indeed the world trading community—seriously believe a right to strike in the unique Canal Zone context, would be a responsible economic, political, and national security gesture? From a historical perspective, the U.S. position was ironic: an American-engineered revolution in Colombia led to Panamanian independence in 1903, and Panama obtained full control of the Canal from the U.S. on 31 December 1999.

· Lobbying

Third, the U.S called upon Panama to persuade the American Congress to accept a *U.S.-Panama FTA*. This demand came at a time when a former Congressman from Ohio — Ambassador Robert Portman — held the position of USTR. Skilled in Capitol Hill Politics, the USTR appreciated the significant opposition to FTAs, especially from Democratic Party members. However, from Panama's vantage point, the USTR was calling on its government to do the work of the USTR. If Panama agreed, then it would be in the position of negotiating not with one executive branch agency (the USTR), but with dozens of different interest groups embodied in 435 House members and 100 Senators. The Panamanian response was firm and called for reciprocity. If the Panamanian Ambassador to the U.S. had to lobby Democrats on the Hill for an FTA, then the American Ambassador to Panama would have to lobby Panamanian lawmakers.

Evidently, with that response, the FTA talks ended in the Spring 2006. For Panama, prospective economics benefits from a deal were less than the political costs associated with American demands. Roughly three-quarters of Panamanian exports go to the U.S., even without an FTA. The average MFN tariff imposed by these exports is quite low, especially if T&A products are excluded. Thus, for most of its exports, the margin of preference Panama would gain from an FTA is modest. As for T&A, with competition from China, India, and Vietnam, Panama appreciates its future is not in this sector. It encourages adjustment of factor resources to other sectors, especially services, which account for 70%–80% of its GDP.

Similarly, for the U.S., political costs outweighed prospective economic gains. An FTA with Panama would provide American manufacturers with another platform from which to export, based on relatively cheap labor. But, politically, no American administration can articulate openly FDI overseas as a reason for establishing an FTA. That would translate as factory closures (or non-openings) in the U.S., and thus job loss (or non-creation) for Americans. Accordingly, only significant concessions from Panama that could be touted publicly would persuade a skeptical Congress to pass an FTA.

Surprisingly, a few days before Christmas 2006, the USTR announced it had struck a deal with Panama. Panama accepted U.S. SPS standards on meat and poultry, and apparently had agreed to do some lobbying on Capitol Hill, too. Over 50% of U.S. farm exports (including beef, certain processed goods, poultry, soybeans, wine and distilled spirits) receive duty-free treatment upon entry into force of the FTA, as do Panamanian T&A articles — if they use U.S. or Panamanian yarn or fabric. U.S. financial providers also obtain enhanced market access, U.S. government contractors benefit from greater transparency, and U.S. investors are guaranteed national treatment—all important with respect to the Panama Canal expansion, for example. Notably, in February 2007, while the FTA was before Congress, Panamanian President Martín Torrijos (1962, President, 2004–2009) traveled to Washington, D.C., and personally called on the leadership of the House Ways and Means Committee—the third time he had met with the Committee Chairman (Charles Rangel, Democrat-New York). Clearly, Panama had conceded it would have to share the burden of proof that Congress should pass the FTA.

When is a deal truly complete? When negotiators inked the Panama FTA in December 2006, they left open its Chapter on labor standards. Pending guidance from Congress, labor issues had to be resolved. Supposedly they were when the countries reached a deal to incorporate the May 2007 understanding between the Administration of President George W. Bush (1946–, President, 2001–2009) and Congress on enhanced labor and environmental provisions. So, the U.S. and Panama signed the FTA in June 2007. Yet, Congress remained unsatisfied. In March 2009, Congress raised new issues, including a demand that Panama address American concerns it is a tax haven depriving the U.S. of corporate tax revenues, and it has not met its 2002 pledge to share information about tax matters.

- **Changes Panama Accepted**

Not until Spring 2011 was the deal complete, and Congress did not approve it until October 2011. Under pressure emanating from the U.S. Congress and Administration of President Barack H. Obama (1961–, President, 2009–2017), Panama agreed to the following changes in its labor, tax, and securities rules:

(1) Labor Law Amendments:

(a) Panama issued executive decrees against the misuse of sub-contract and temporary contract labor, strengthening collective bargaining and the right to strike, and preventing employers from interfering with union activities.

(b) The Ministry of Labor issued a resolution to increase the number of inspections in the maritime sector.

(c) Panama agreed to eliminate restrictions on labor rights in free trade and export processing zones to give the right to strike and collective bargaining rights to all workers in those zones (including the special economic zone of Barú), and eliminate an exemption from these rights for temporary workers hired for up to three years.

(2) Tax Law Changes:

In April 2011, Panama's legislature approved a U.S.-Panama *Tax Information Exchange Agreement* (*TIEA*), which the two countries had signed in November 2010. (*See* Law 33, Official Gazette of Panama, 20 June 2010.)

The *TIEA* makes it more difficult for Panama to be a tax haven. It allows each country to seek evidence from the other on civil and criminal tax matters in accordance with international conventions on information exchange (including the 1985 *Hague Convention on the Law Applicable to Trusts and Their Recognition*, which entered into force in 1992, and which Panama joined in connection with the *TIEA*), beginning on or after 30 November 2007, even if the evidence sought is not of interest to the domestic authority from which it is sought.

(3) Securities Laws Changes:

Panama changed its law on anonymous accounts, called "Bearer Shares," obligating law firms that incorporate a business to engage in due diligence to verify the true owners of the business and provide this information to the Panamanian government, *i.e.*, to "Know Your Client." (See Law 2, Official Gazette of Panama, 1 February 2011.)

The Panamanian case study is one of several FTAs, including the accords with Korea and Colombia, which illustrates a key fact about U.S. trade policy: no longer is an FTA just about trade, as was true with Israel and Canada, nor even just about trade, labor, and the environment, as was the case with *NAFTA*. The U.S. uses FTAs to pursue a range of additional goals, including gathering evidence against suspected tax evaders. Depending on its prospective FTA partner, America tailors FTAs to its liking to solve specific trade-related or even non-trade problems that it identifies as part of its national interest. In this sense, are FTAs more attractive than multilateral trade deals under WTO auspices?

VI. Political Economy Criteria

- **Sensitive Sectors and Legislative Support**

In theory and practice, it is not always easy to separate political from economic factors that are pertinent to FTAs. Trade policy initiatives, including FTA and CU proposals, may arise from an admixture of the two. An obvious example concerns sensitive sectors and the link to selling a deal to national legislatures.

The U.S. consciously examines the pattern of exports of a prospective RTA partner before considering whether to commence discussions with that country. The "hard" case is a pattern revealing the other country has a keen interest in access to the American market for products the U.S. regards as sensitive. Assuredly, any FTA with that country will be difficult to sell to domestic producers of the like product regarded as sensitive by the U.S. Those producers will exert influence against the FTA on Capitol Hill. To overcome their opposition, the U.S. will need to show enormous gains on other fronts, meaning that the other country will have had to make correlating concessions. Such concessions, however, may create political headaches for that country.

Conversely, the "easy" case, of course, is a country with an export interest in few if any sensitive products. Opposition may arise from civil society, that is, from NGOs, including activists for labor and environmental rights, and for religious freedom. But, few if any domestic economic constituencies will mobilize against the deal. The U.S. may not need to press relentlessly for full and immediate market access in every goods and services sector (although a template-like approach to FTA negotiations that is both ill-considered and insolent may lead the USTR to do so). Assuming NGO opposition is addressed through appropriate provisions in the FTA, or in acceptable, transparent Side Letters, then legislators on Capitol Hill may have little trouble supporting the deal.

- **Locking in Reform in a Coalition of Well Performing**

Another clear manifestation of the political economy of RTAs concerns liberalization. Sustaining momentum for, and solidifying, economic and political reforms are potential gains from an RTA. A country politically serious about real economic liberalization is likely to be a country serious about an RTA. The link between an RTA and reform may be especially apparent when negotiations pair a relatively larger and smaller country, or a developed and developing country. The RTA can be both a catalyst and *raison d'être* for reform in a smaller or developing country, and thus a persuasive tool against recalcitrant traditionalism.

Thus, in evaluating countries, the U.S. considers whether top political leadership of a prospective FTA partner is fully committed to reform, and both willing and able to deliver on legal commitments. Three indicators of this commitment are:

First: WTO Performance

Has a would-be FTA partner been slack in implementing multilateral trade commitments? If so, then why would the U.S. expect it to behave differently in an FTA? However, is it appropriate for the U.S. to demand that the country commit to cooperating with the U.S. in the WTO? Calling upon the country, as an equal WTO partner, to take a problem-solving approach to multilateral trade controversies is one thing. Conditioning an FTA on that country supporting American positions in the WTO is quite another thing.

Second: Negotiation Team

How capable and skillful is the trade negotiating team of a country that is a would-be FTA partner with the U.S.? Sending a team lacking in legal capacity is a poor harbinger of life after an FTA. It suggests the team may make commitments it neither understands fully nor appreciates how to implement rigorously.

Third: TIFAs

Has a would-be FTA partner entered into a *TIFA* with the U.S.? These modest documents are frameworks on which the U.S. prefers to build (and sometimes insists on building) an FTA. Morocco, Bahrain, Egypt, Indonesia, the Philippines, and Thailand are among the many countries that have signed *TIFAs*.

In sum, in selecting countries for an FTA, the U.S. seeks a "coalition of the well performing," with the U.S. setting criteria for performance and judging its quality.

Consider whether *NAFTA* helps lock in reforms in Mexico. No longer does Mexico experience pendulum-like swings between economic liberalization and nationalization and state planning. Mexico has used *NAFTA* successfully to complement domestic economic liberalization, and thereby attract FDI from developed countries. Observe, then, a corollary point: competition for FDI is an incentive for a poor country to eschew isolationism and push for an FTA.

Such competition is nearly pointless if a poor country retains high trade barriers, discriminatory standards, and import substitution policies. Conversely, an FTA is a statement about commitment to economic reform and the rule of law. Two other examples of how an RTA can help catalyze and sustain political momentum for economic reforms are the U.S. FTAs with Israel (signed in April 1985) and Jordan (signed in October 2000).

Chapter 3

Security Aspects of FTAs[1]

I. Choosing FTA Partners Based on National Security Criteria

- *MEFTA*, Morocco, Australia

To what extent do and should national security criteria affect choice of RTA partners? The American strategy, articulated in May 2003 by President George W. Bush (1946–, President, 2001–2009), to achieve a *Middle East Free Trade Agreement (MEFTA)* by 2013, answers: "a lot." Underlying *MEFTA* is a belief in a causal nexus: from free trade to economic growth; then to poverty alleviation; then to social and political stability; then to political reform; and then to combatting terrorism. *MEFTA* could bring prosperity and democracy to a region in which extremists hideously twist the good and true name of Islam to define a monstrous future. Toward *MEFTA*, the U.S. built a network of FTAs with Bahrain, Jordan, Morocco, and Oman, but progress in this modern-day incarnation of the "peace through trade" vision of Cordell Hull (1871–1955), Secretary of State to President Franklin Roosevelt (1882–1945, President, 1933–1945) slowed under President Barack H. Obama (1961–, President, 2009–2017).

Consider the *U.S.-Morocco FTA*. Morocco is a middle-income developing country, with roughly the same *per capita* GNP as Egypt (U.S. $1,300). Morocco is not a large market for U.S. products. But, American exporters certainly prefer duty-free access to that market than the average MFN tariff Morocco imposes of 34%. In fact, such treatment puts the Americans on a level playing field with their European competitors. Because of an association agreement between the EU and Morocco, all tariffs on industrial trade between the EU and Morocco are scheduled to fall to zero by 2012.

Still, from the American side, national security was a (if not the) prime criterion, in the FTA. Morocco has a long history of friendship with the U.S., which the FTA cements. For decades, Moroccan foreign policy has urged restraint by Israelis and Palestinians. Morocco also has a demonstrable record of fighting terrorism. For the U.S., the FTA logic was to help accelerate economic development, and thereby

---

1. Documents References:
   (1) *Havana (ITO) Charter* Articles 43–45
   (2) GATT Article XXIV
   (3) Relevant Provisions in FTAs

alleviate economic conditions that may breed extremist behavior. Ultimately, whether the logic is fanciful depends on domestic economic and political reform, infrastructure development, and the enhancement of legal capacity, in Morocco itself. Without such change, the full benefits of an FTA are not attainable.

Interestingly, from the perspective of Morocco, an FTA with the U.S. satisfied more than national security criteria. Morocco saw an FTA with the U.S. as an opportunity to gain leverage with the EU. The largest trading partners for Morocco (as of May 2003) are France (to which Morocco ships 34% of its exports, and from which Morocco obtains 24% of its imports), Spain (13% and 10%, respectively, of exports and imports), and the U.S. (3% and 6%, respectively). Consequently, the prospect of an FTA with the U.S. created for Morocco the risk of trade diversion from the EU to the U.S., and a loss of tariff revenue collected on American products. Morocco viewed this scenario as an opportunity, however. It could bargain more aggressively with the EU, at least subtly playing it and the U.S. off against each other.

- **Australia**

National security also is the logic of the post-9/11 U.S. deal with Australia. The "Lucky Country" is a key American ally in the War on Terror, and in countering if not containing Chinese expansionism. That is, it is naïve to see the *U.S.-Australia FTA* as something other than a device for America to cement a strategic military relationship. Indeed, sometimes it is bluntly observed that Australia has embraced the role scripted for it by the U.S. — Deputy Sheriff in the Asia-Pacific region.

In contrast, New Zealand was not included in these *FTA* talks. New Zealand's stance on the Iraq War, and its desire to remain nuclear free, explain why. New Zealand did not support the U.S. position in 2003 in the U.N. Security Council as to the use of force in Iraq. Moreover, New Zealand prohibits U.S. Navy ships that are nuclear powered or nuclear armed from docking in its ports. Similarly, the *U.S.-Singapore FTA* was signed at the White House on 6 May 2003. While the *Chile FTA* was ready for signature, the U.S. deferred signature for a month, until 6 June 2003. Chile did not support the U.S. position in the Security Council on war in Iraq. The diplomatic affront had little practical effect, however, as both FTAs entered into force on 1 January 2004. Is it wise to define FTA policy by opposition to a specific war or nuclear weapons generally?

- **No Bright Line**

One obvious inference from the FTA case studies (in this and separate Chapters) is there is no bright line between an economic, political, and national security assessment of an FTA. That is especially true for the U.S. Accounting for roughly 25% of world GNP (and higher on PPP terms), the U.S. has economic — and concomitant political — interests in every region of the world. It must pursue balance among different regions in establishing and strengthening its FTA networks. Put bluntly, the global superpower must not be a regional FTA player, and must fashion its FTA policy in conjunction with its national security interests. Arguably, every

FTA or CU the U.S. even contemplates has a national security dimension. In the post-9/11 world, the U.S. is explicit that it expects from any prospective FTA partner cooperation—or better—on foreign policy and security matters.

Consider the *U.S.-Peru TPA*, signed in April 2006. One argument for the deal was it would support Peru in the Andean region, which is plagued by economic and political instability, including narco-terrorism, which threaten U.S. security. The causal nexus is the *PTPA* would be part of a strengthened, transparent legal framework for trade and FDI, and such economic activity would generate employment opportunities in Peru, enlarging the number of people with a stake in the *status quo*. The U.S. made the same argument in favor of the *Colombia TPA*, concluded in February 2006 and enacted in October 2011.

II. Case Study: Egypt, QIZs, and Israeli Content

· **Upheaval**

Egypt has a roughly U.S. $500 billion economy (on the eve of the Arab Spring, December 2010, in PPP terms) and market of 90 million people. The EU and U.S. are its largest trading partners, and it gets (as of December 2011) $1.3 billion per year in U.S. military aid. Is Egypt a viable potential FTA partner for the U.S.? Could a *U.S.-Egypt FTA* address an admixture of national security, political, and economic interests?

Politically, Egypt has long been a (if not the) leader in the Arab world, and a uniquely influential country in the Middle East. Egypt hosted the Arab League when that body was founded in 1945. It was the first country to sign a peace treaty with Israel, the 1979 *Camp David Accords* brokered by President Jimmy Carter. Egypt exports political ideas, including in 1958 socialism and pan-Arabism through the ultimately unsuccessful United Arab Republic. It also exports its culture around the Middle East, including the Egyptian dialect of Arabic, through cinema, music, and television. Egypt also exports its human capital. Roughly two million Egyptians work in the Middle East outside of their home country, many as teachers, including law professors at Arab law faculties.

In the breathtaking Arab Spring of 2011, Egypt overthrew 4 decades of oligarchic, military-dominated leadership. In late 2011 and early and mid-2012, it held elections. Liberal, secular parties competed with the Freedom and Justice Party of the Muslim Brotherhood, and the *Al Nour Salafi* Islamist Party, for power in the Egyptian parliament and ultimately, the Presidency. They did so in a climate of sputtering FDI, tourism, and trade. Surely it would be in American national security interests to encourage moderate, reform-minded electoral results by improving the economic prospects of middle-class and poor Egyptians. Such improvement would make their extremist alternatives less attractive. Might an FTA provide the necessary fillip for economic growth? Whatever the answer, in July 2013, the military replaced the Brotherhood-led government.

Economically, Egypt is not Chile, but one inference from the Arab Spring is that it seems to want, and need, to be. The *per capita* GNP of Egypt (at just U.S. $6,200 in PPP terms as of December 2010) is markedly lower than that of Chile. Unlike Chile, Egypt has not completed economic liberalization, and hardly is a model reform country. Some U.S. trade policy officials argue a country ought to reform economically first, and then enter into FTA talks. But, that stance potentially pre-empts an FTA, because if a country has implemented meaningful reforms, then it might not need an FTA. In other words, an FTA can accelerate a reform process that is inchoate in a country like Egypt.

Egypt took some important stabilization measures in the 1990s. It reduced its fiscal (budget) deficit from 20% to 1% of national income. It unified its FX rates into a single rate, devalued its currency (the Egyptian pound), anchored the exchange rate, and finally floated the currency. The Egyptian Central Bank tamed inflation (to a rate of about 5% in the 1990s), and shifted its monetary policy to target inflation.

To be sure, there are political and economic factors mitigating against rash conclusion of an *Egypt FTA*. The U.S. criticized the way in which Egypt handled its fall 2005 presidential elections, including suppression of opposition candidates (some of which were fielded by the Muslim Brotherhood), its conviction (on charges of forgery) of Ayman Nour, the runner up in these elections, and its postponement of municipal elections (which had been slated for April 2006). Structural reform in the Egyptian economy is lagging. Privatization of SOEs is needed, and exchange rate deviation from PPP needs to be addressed. Trade laws require further liberalization. Egypt has virtually eliminated all of its import bans, implemented the WTO *Agreement on Customs Valuation*, and joined both the *Basic Telecommunications Agreement* and the *ITA*. But, many of its WTO commitments are weak. Query, then, would an FTA encourage broader and deeper reform of the political economy, or should it be a pre-condition to a deal?

• **QIZs Instead of FTA**

In lieu of an FTA, the U.S. agreed to a substantively thin "strategic partnership agreement" with Egypt in June 2009, and touts QIZs as a way for Egypt to boost its trade with America. In 1996, Congress authorized the QIZ program through an amendment to the 1985 *United States-Israel Free Trade Implementation Act*.[2] In November 1996, President Bill Clinton (1946, President, 1993–2000) issued Proclamation Number 6955 to grant preferential trade treatment for merchandise from the West Bank, Gaza Strip, or QIZs. The policy goal was to reward Egypt for signing a peace treaty with Israel (which it did in 1979), and to promote peace and development through trade between Israel and its neighbors. In 1999, Jordan became the first neighbor to take advantage of the QIZ opportunity. Any product "originating" in a QIZ receives DFQF in the U.S. market. In December 2004, Egypt agreed to set

---

2. *See* 19 U.S.C. Section 2112 note.

up the QIZs, signing the "Qualified Industrial Zones Protocol" with the U.S. and Israel. The Protocol has no end date.

Over 700 Egyptian companies (as of April 2010) benefit from the duty-free access to the American market. The QIZs (as of March 2013) are set out in six Egyptian geographical areas:

(1) Greater Cairo—encompassing Giza, Shubra Al Kheima, Nasr City, 10th Ramadan City, 15th May City, Badr City, 6th October City, Obour City, Kalyoub City, and the industrial area in Gesr El Suez.

(2) Alexandria—including Amereya, New Amereya, Borg El Arab, and Dekheila.

(3) Suez Canal Region—covering covers Port Said, Ismailya, and Suez.

(4) Central Delta Region—namely, the governorates of Gharbiya, Dakahlya, Monofiya, and Dammietta.

(5) Al Minya.

(6) Beni Suief.

There are calls from both commercial and political quarters to expand the number of QIZs, including (via a petition from Egypt and Israel to the USTR in October 2007) to establish one in impoverished Upper Egypt. From time to time, the USTR adjusts the precise definitions of a particular QIZ, thus affecting eligibility of products for duty-free treatment. For example, in March 2013, the USTR liberalized eligibility for the above-listed QIZs to cover merchandise from all current or future production facilities in them.

Under the QIZ rules, "origination" is defined via a value-added test. At least 35% of the value of the article, in terms of labor and material (*i.e.*, components), must be added through processing (growth, production, or manufacturing) in the QIZ. The product must be exported directly from the QIZ to the U.S. without passing through any other country.

- "Israeli" Content Issue

There is a key "catch" with political and national security dimensions: the agreement mandates of the 35%, a certain percentage must come from Israel. Egyptians must use some Israeli content to get duty-free American treatment. Originally under the *QIZ Protocol* (Article II:D(1)(a)), of the 35%, 11.7% had to originate in Israel, and the remaining 23.3% in Egypt. The figures were renegotiated, to 10.5% Israeli value added and 24.5% Egyptian value added.

Is content be "Israeli" if it is from the Occupied Territories, *i.e.*, the lands Israel captured in the June 1967 Arab-Israeli War, West Bank, East Jerusalem, Golan Heights, or Gaza? About 500,000 Israeli settlers, plus 2.5 million Palestinians, live in the West Bank and East Jerusalem. In a 2004 Advisory Opinion, the ICJ held the settlements illegal, and all governments consider them so. Israel points to the

Old Testament and historical events to support its claim to the West Bank and East Jerusalem.

On the one hand, the *Protocol* (in Article II:D(2)) states that:

Only Israeli companies operating in areas under Israel's customs' control shall be recognized for the purposes of applying the Israeli contribution.[3]

Does Israel exercise "customs control" over the Occupied Territories? On the other hand, President Clinton's 1996 Proclamation (in Paragraphs 2–3) says the U.S. considers products from the West Bank and Gaza as "Israeli":

2. Section 9(c) of the [*United States-Israel Free Trade Area Implementation*] *Act* [*of 1985*, as amended] authorizes the President to proclaim that articles of Israel may be treated as though they were articles directly shipped from Israel for the purposes of the *U.S.-Israel Free Trade Agreement* (the *"Agreement"*) *even if shipped to the United States from the West Bank, the Gaza Strip, or a qualifying industrial zone*, if the articles otherwise meet the requirements of the Agreement.

3. Section 9(d) of the *Act* authorizes the President to proclaim that the cost or value of materials produced in the West Bank, the Gaza Strip, or a qualifying industrial zone may be included in the cost or value of materials produced in Israel under section 1(c)(i) of Annex 3 of the *Agreement*, and the direct costs of processing operations performed *in the West Bank, the Gaza Strip, or a qualifying industrial zone* may be included in the direct costs of processing operations performed in Israel under section 1(c)(ii) of Annex 3 of the *Agreement*.[4]

The EU takes a stricter line against Israel than the U.S.: products originating in an Israeli settlement on the West Bank, and those in East Jerusalem and the Golan Heights, are ineligible for benefits under an EU-Israel PTA, the *EU-Israel Association Agreement*. In 2005, the EU and Israel agreed on a technical arrangement under which customs authorities of EU countries to identify distinctly exports from settlements to the EU. In 2009, Her Majesty's Government advised U.K. supermarkets to label products from settlements as such to distinguish them from Palestinian-grown or made goods.

Similarly, in May 2012, South Africa announced Israeli goods produced in the Occupied Territories must not bear a "Made in Israel" label, but rather one showing they are from the Territories. Then, South African consumers could decide whether they wanted to buy such goods. Israel denounced the decision as "tainted

---

3. Protocol Between the Government of the Arab Republic of Egypt and Between the Government of the State of Israel on Qualifying Industrial Zones, www.qizegypt.gov.eg/About_Textprotocol.aspx.

4. Presidential Proclamation 6955 of 13 November 1996, ¶¶ 2–3, 61 Fed. Reg. 58761 (18 November 1996) (emphasis added).

with what seems to be racist motivation."[5] Throughout the South African apartheid era, Israel was one of the few countries keeping strong ties with the white minority government.

Does the Israeli content requirement promote peace and commerce between Egypt and Israel? Foreign direct investors come from East Asia and Turkey, eager to jump the high-tariff walls the U.S. levies on T&A merchandise. Egypt is a BDC under the U.S. GSP program, but most T&A articles are not eligible for GSP treatment. Not surprisingly, 80% of the QIZ companies (as of March 2010) produce T&A articles. Popular textile exports are bed sheets and towels. Popular apparel exports are RMGs like jackets, pants, pullovers, shirts, shorts, t-shirts, tops, and twin sets. Enterprises in the QIZ tend to import fabrics, chemicals, zippers, threads, packaging material, and other accessories for RMGs from Israel to produce finished T&A merchandise. Top American importers from QIZ exporters are Gap, Gloria, Levi Strauss, J.C. Penny, Levi Strauss, Van Heusen, and VF Jeanswear. So, who are the real beneficiaries of the QIZs? Do QIZs help Palestinians and bolster the Middle East peace process?

III. Case Study: Korea and *KORUS*

- **History and Significance of Korea**

Another manifestation of economic and political criteria for forging an FTA that are intermingled with national security considerations is a major bargain between the U.S. and Korea, called "*KORUS.*" Formal negotiations commenced in June 2006. The two sides signed the deal in Seoul, on 1 April 2007, within 25 minutes of expiry of the deadline under U.S. *TPA* for notifying Congress of an agreement. The negotiators deftly took advantage of a weekend, plus the difference between Korean and Eastern Standard Time. (It was 11:35 p.m. EST on 31 March when they inked the deal.)

After years of economic controversy and political wrangling, Congress finally approved *KORUS* in October 2011, and it entered into force on 15 March 2012. For its part, Korea made 22 changes to its laws to implement *KORUS*. These changes bespeak the breadth of scope of the FTA, and how intrusive an FTA can be in terms of compelling changes to domestic legal regimes of one or more of the Parties. They affected (*inter alia*) the following Korean rules: *Copyright Act*; *Design Protection Act*; *Patent Act*; *Pharmaceutical Affairs Act*; *Trademark Act*; *Utility Model Act*; *Individual Consumption Tax Act*; *Local Tax Act*; *Enforcement Regulation on Clean Air Act*; *Enforcement Regulation on Electrical Appliances Safety Control Act*; *Notice on the Recognition Criteria for Equivalence for Motor Vehicle Standards*; *Regulation on Health Care Insurance Benefit*.

---

5. *See* Wendell Roelf, *S. Africa Wants Change in Import Labels, Angers Israel*, REUTERS, 21 May 2012, www.bilaterals.org (quoting Yigal Palmor, Israeli Foreign Ministry Spokesman).

For Korea, *KORUS* meant Korea extended coverage through its network of FTAs to 44 countries, 27 of which were the EU states. Thus, adding the U.S. to the EU was a significant gain for Korean producer-exporters and consumers of imported products.

Indubitably, *KORUS* is the most important FTA implemented by the U.S. since *NAFTA*. In the world (as of 2011), Korea is the 13th largest economy, 11th largest market, seventh largest goods exporter and importer, 10th largest services exporter, and sixth largest services importer. Korea is America's seventh largest trading partner (with $72 billion in two-way trade goods, and $14 billion in two-way services trade, in 2005), and sixth largest market for U.S. farm goods. Conversely, importing 17% of Korea's global exports, America is Korea's third largest market. Overall, imports and exports account for roughly two-thirds of Korea's GDP.

Thus, *KORUS* is the most commercially significant FTA the U.S. has, save for *NAFTA*. In announcing negotiations, however, President George W. Bush made clear more than economics were at stake: "[The two countries] have a strong alliance and are bound together by common values and a deep desire to expand freedom, peace, and prosperity throughout Asia and the world."[6] Once North Korea successfully tested a nuclear device, in October 2006, it was obvious an FTA ought to be viewed in geopolitical terms. *KORUS* is a device to merge trade and security issues, and a tool to strengthen the economic and military alliance between the countries that began over a half century ago when President Harry S. Truman (1884–1972, President, 1945–1953) intervened in the Korean War.

- **Agricultural Goods**

Manifestly, a central challenge facing the U.S. in negotiating FTAs with North East Asian countries — Korea and Japan, in particular — are agricultural barriers imposed by them. With 3.5 million farmers who make themselves heard through bodies like the Korean Advanced Farmers Federation, Korea had a three-pronged strategy in FTA talks:

    (1) exclusion of sensitive agricultural commodities;

    (2) long-term tariff reduction schedules for some farm products; and

    (3) contingent tariff programs, such as TRQs and special safeguards for other products.

Not surprisingly, the Korean pre-*KORUS* trade-weighted average duty rate on agricultural products was 64.1% (the simple average is 52%), with tariffs as high as 500% (as of 2005). (America's average farm tariff is 12% (as of 2005).)

Yet, on both agricultural and industrial products, *KORUS* yielded most economic gains for the U.S., most of which came through improved terms of trade

---

6. *Quoted in* Christopher S. Rugaber, *U.S., Korea Launch FTA Talks, Will Seek To Reach Agreement by End of This Year*, 23 International Trade Reporter (BNA) 207–09 (9 February 2006).

(*i.e.*, cheaper import prices and higher export prices). To be sure, DFQF immediately upon EIF treatment did not occur on 100% of merchandise trade. Over 100 products, including garlic, onions, and pepper, benefit from long-term protection in Korea, that is, extended tariff phase out periods, and rice is entirely excluded. Still, gains came from enhanced market access through lowering tariffs and NTBs. Fruit of the vine, as it were—that is, wine, along with beer and whiskey—are examples.

KORUS obligated Korea to phase out its 30% tariff on beer over seven years, and eliminate immediately its 20% and 15% duties on whiskeys and wines, respectively. Moreover, in February 2012, Korea amended its *Liquor Tax Law* to abolish a ban in place since 1983 against direct sales to domestic consumers by alcoholic beverage importers. Purportedly justified as a way to prevent tax avoidance in the supply chain of imports, the ban meant importers had to sell through retailers, wholesalers, retailers, restaurants, or hotels. In August 2012, Korea again amended that *Law* to eliminate a stiff capital requirement of 50 million *won* (U.S. $44,000) for a license to import alcoholic beverages. To be sure, while dubbed a "free" trade deal, *KORUS*— like any other FTA—does not level completely the competitive playing field for every good and service. Korea still imposes liquor taxes and surcharges that inflate the import price of alcoholic beverages, with beer costing 168% of its CIF price (as of August 2012). Such post-border measures are not always transparent, and thus not always easy to discipline via an FTA.

- **Industrial Goods, Including Autos**

On industrial goods, the Korean pre-*KORUS* trade-weighted average duty rate is 4.5%, but on autos it is 8% (in contrast with the U.S. rate of 2.5%)—on top of an engine displacement tax the U.S. contended discriminates against foreign-produced cars because the amount tax depends on engine size, and foreign cars have larger-sized engines than Korean cars. Among OECD countries (of which Korea is one), imported cars account for 40% of the market, but in Korea the figure is 2.7% (as of 2005). In bilateral Korean-American auto trade (as of March 2012, just before *KORUS* was implemented), Korea exported over 400,000 cars to the U.S., but imported just 10,000 cars from America.

Notably, under the originally-negotiated provisions of *KORUS*, in the auto sector Korea agreed to:

(1) Drop immediately the 8% tariff on 2 of the 3 major auto import categories covering U.S. priority passenger vehicles and trucks.

(2) Eliminate the engine displacement-based taxes (*e.g.*, Korea's Annual Vehicle Tax, Special Consumption Tax, and Subway/Regional Development Bond).

(3) Establish an Automotive Working Group to review auto-related regulations, promote good regulatory practices in Korea, ensure Korea shares the same information on technical standards with U.S. automakers as it does with Korean companies, and serve as an early warning system against possible future market access barriers.

(4) Create an enhanced dispute settlement mechanism for controversies over auto-related measures, requiring a decision by a panel within 6 months of commencing a case, and allowing the winning country to snap back the tariff at issue to the pre-*KORUS* MFN level.

For its part, the U.S. agreed to phase out its 2.5% car tariff, and 25% truck tariff, on Korean vehicles across 10 years (starting with small-engine capacity cars, in which Korea has a keen export interest).

- **Government Procurement**

Some of the gains to the U.S. from *KORUS* are in the area of government procurement. The U.S. waived the obligation of Korea to adhere to the plurilateral WTO *GPA*, because Chapter 17 and Annex 17-A, which cover government procurement, provide for greater market access than does the *GPA*. In particular, *KORUS* prohibits a procuring entity from imposing as a condition for award of a contract that a bidder for the contract have been awarded a contract previously, or have work experience in the territory of that entity. In contrast, the *GPA* mandates only reciprocal opportunities in Korea, hence Korea could impose such a condition.

- **NTBs**

Gains to the U.S. from *KORUS* come from removing NTBs, especially opaque, unpredictable, and discriminatory regulations, and anti-competitive practices of the giant industrial conglomerates, or *chaebols*. Such barriers plague agricultural products:

(1) Quotas raise rice imports from 4% to just 8% of domestic consumption between 2005–2015.

(2) Korean SPS measures shut out U.S. beef, starting in December 2003, over concerns about mad cow disease (with a partial reopening in September 2006 for boneless beef from cattle less than 30 months old, followed in April 2007 by import clearance from Korea's National Veterinary Research and Quarantine Service of a 6.4 metric ton shipment of beef from Creekstone Farms of Kansas, and by a May 2007 declaration by the OIE that the U.S. had "controlled risk" status on beef, *i.e.*, it had sufficient safety precautions to prevent exports of tainted beef). Korea had been the third largest market for U.S. beef exports, but during the closure Australian beef imports into Korea soared.

(3) A Korean Ministry of Health and Welfare rule (effective 1 January 2007) mandates all restaurants with a floor space of 300 square meters or more display on menu boards and signs the country of origin of beef they serve, with criminal penalties of up to a $31,200 fine and three-year prison term for violation.

NTBs also impede market access for autos (*e.g.*, Korea-specific emission standards), as well as banks, insurance companies, pharmaceutical firms, software businesses, and telecommunications providers. Overall, with coverage of farm and auto trade, the net welfare gains from *KORUS* proved important (though, predictably, accompanied by trade diversion). Conversely, had *KORUS* excluded the agricultural sector alone, then over half of all forecast gains would have disappeared.

However, significantly, *KORUS* does not cover rice. Korea insisted upon its exclusion. Korea maintained an import quota of (as of May 2015) 408,700 metric tons, which was global (eliminating in January 2015 country-specific quotas for Australia, China, Thailand, and the U.S.) Its out-of-quota MFN tariff on rice was a whopping 513%. Moreover, Korea made no formal commitment on SPS measures in respect of U.S. beef.

• **Services**

As did agricultural products and autos, services posed a hurdle in the *KORUS* negotiations. Korea was willing to concede only gradual liberalization in sectors in which the U.S. holds a comparative advantage. In the end, Korea conceded to a Negative List approach to liberalizing services trade (whereby access is provided in all sectors unless specifically exempted). Accordingly, it granted enhanced market access for AV and broadcasting services, e-commerce, legal, and telecommunications services (including 100% U.S. ownership of telecom operations in Korea within two years of the effective date of *KORUS*, an increase from the 49% cap), and transparency guarantees. Two services sectors are worthy of note.

First, for legal services, before *KORUS*, foreign law firms could not set up an office in Korea. Indeed, under the *Korean Attorney-At-Law Act*, unless an American (or other foreign) attorney passes the Korean Bar Examination (which is administered only in the Korean language) and registers with the Korean Bar Association, that attorney could not provide any counsel in Korea, even on the laws of the jurisdiction in which the attorney is licensed. Consequently, American attorneys work in Korea as "Foreign Legal Consultants," practice the law of their home jurisdictions, but ensure any final transaction is completed and approved by a Korean lawyer. *KORUS* does away with these strictures.

Under *KORUS*, Korea agreed to open its legal market across five years to American lawyers. In Phase I (years 1 and 2), American law firms may open a branch office in Korea and offer legal advisory services on American or international, but not Korean, law. In Phase II (Years 3 and 4), American law firms can work directly with Korean law firms on specific cases, and share profits and fees. In Phase III (Year 5), American firms may establish a partnership or JV with Korean firms, and directly hire local Korean attorneys who have passed the Korean Bar Examination. The ownership stake of an American firm in a partnership or JV may be limited to 49%, thereby ensuring Korean management control.

Second, the AV sector is a curious one. Korea maintains a screen quota requirement. Formerly, all movie theaters had to reserve 40% of their screen time (equivalent to 146 days) for Korean movies. Korea announced in January 2006 it would lower the requirement (as of July 2006) to 20% (73 days), which satisfied the USTR. Korea also agreed to allow (within 3 years of the entry into force of *KORUS*) U.S.

firms to own 100% of program providers. Korean viewers might agree domestic movies are improving—becoming more competitive with Hollywood competitors. Such improvement makes it easier for Korean movie theaters to meet the quota rule profitably—though perhaps not as profitably as a free-trade-in-movies regime.

- **Gains for Korea**

The above discussion is cast in terms of benefits from *KORUS* for the U.S. What did Korea gain? One response is *KORUS* showed how far Korea has come since the end of the 1950–1953 Korean War. When the last shots were fired, the *per capita* GDP of South Korea was roughly $37. South Korean development planners looked up at the figure for the Philippines, about $300, and thought it unattainable. As a more realistic development model, the planners picked Pakistan, the *per capita* GDP of which then was about $150. Sixty years on, South Korea had far surpassed Pakistan and the Philippines, which had descended into the hell of dictatorships and corruption, and nearly caught up with the U.S. During that period, it remained a steadfast American ally in the Cold War, and transitioned to a mature, multi-party democracy.

For Korea, most economic gains arose from improved allocative efficiency, *i.e.*, the deployment of factors of production in a more efficient manner than before. Notably, most of the Korean business community supported the idea of an FTA with the U.S. They included exporters of autos, cell phones, computer chips, and other consumer goods. They advocated coverage of e-commerce, and non-discriminatory, duty-free treatment for digital products. But, they complained of not only American tariff barriers, but also NTBs such as complex technical regulations and sanitary measures, inefficient customs procedures, and of protectionist government procurement practices. The FTA addressed their complaints.

A March 2006 study by the Korea Institute for Economic Policy showed a net gain from an FTA of 2% in Korea's GDP, and a net employment boost of 0.36% (equal to 100,000 jobs). Even less rosy economic studies were optimistic, predicting an annual 0.6% boost in Korea's GDP and 34,000 new jobs owing to increased trade with and investment from the U.S. Korean consumers would face a wider range of imports at reduced prices thanks to the removal of costly tariff and NTBs Korea imposes.

Still, not surprisingly, there was significant opposition within Korea to *KORUS*. The Korean International Trade Association (a business association representing over 90,000 companies) listed 312 tariff lines—or 33.4% of Korea's total imports—as sensitive. Opposition was strong among agricultural constituencies, which virtually ruled out full, immediate, duty free coverage of this sector. For instance, Korea ultimately agreed to eliminate its 40% tariff on beef, but only over 15 years.

The Korean government subsidizes heavily its farm sector. The Korean Rural Economic Institute said in a March 2006 study an FTA would cause a U.S. $1 billion decrease in Korean agricultural production, an increase in imports from $1.9 to $2.3 billion, and a decline from 140,000 to 20,000 jobs. While the farm sector is not globally competitive, it is politically powerful. Over time, that power is likely to wane. The contribution of agriculture to the Korean economy (measured as a percentage of GNP) is shrinking. Korean farmers are aging — over 70% of them are over age 50. In part to address this opposition, the Korean Ministry of Commerce, Industry, and Energy (MOCIE) announced in April 2006 it would implement rules to provide trade adjustment assistance worth $3 billion over the first decade of operation of an FTA with the U.S. The help would include a corporate turnaround fund, job placement, and subsidized loans.

Interestingly, in April 2004 Korea's first FTA — with Chile — took effect. The deal, signed on 15 February 2003, includes agricultural products (albeit non-threatening products). Korea negotiated with Chile, and for coverage of agriculture, as a strategy for developing an FTA with Japan. It hoped the *Korea-Chile FTA* might be a useful precedent for a deal with Japan. However, Korea did not have an easy time in negotiating agricultural trade liberalization with Chile. Among other products, Chile exports apples and grapes. Korea produces a modest volume of apples. Still, Korean apple farmers banded together with other domestic farmers, and joined forces with labor unions. This organized heterogeneity opposed not only the FTA with Chile, but also with Japan. They even opposed an FTA with Singapore, which is not an agricultural exporter.

In brief, the *Korea-Chile FTA* galvanized disparate opponents in Korea, and the FTA did not prove to be an easy entrée into further FTAs. The same phenomenon occurred in Japan, with respect to an FTA with Singapore. Japanese economic reformers focused on an FTA with Singapore, presuming or hoping it would not engender domestic agricultural opposition. In fact, Japanese farmers saw through the Korean-style strategy — that one FTA would be used as leverage for another, and the next one would materially affect their interests. Consequently, they opposed the *Japan-Singapore FTA*. They could not block it. Signed on 13 January 2002, it entered into force on 30 November 2002.

- **American Politics**

Domestic political interests in the U.S. that made *KORUS* politically difficult, even if it is economically rational. One example is the T&A industry, which sought a yarn-forward rule of origin to ensure virtually the entire production process occur in Korea for a T&A product to qualify as originating within the *KORUS* region. Their views were heard, as *KORUS* includes a yarn forward rule (meaning Korean producers must use Korean or U.S. yarn and continue thereafter with originating materials and processes), as well as a special textile safeguard remedy for temporary relief from Korean T&A articles shown to damage U.S. producers.

American steel producers are another example, as are some manufacturers, especially of electronics. They tend to be less competitive than their Korean counterparts, oppose free trade with Korea. They are wont to deploy trade remedies against these competitors. Korea argues the U.S. is too zealous in using AD and CVD remedies, especially against Korean semiconductor and steel producers. For instance, in May 2003 there were 23 American AD and CVD orders against Korea. (Interestingly, about 18 of them were against steel and steel products, suggesting Korea does not have a "trade remedy problem" with the U.S., but rather a "steel problem.") From the Korean perspective, an FTA with the U.S. ought to discipline use of trade remedies. To ask how that perspective would be regarded on Capitol Hill is to intimate the obvious answer.

Overall, there is considerable trade friction between the U.S. and Korea. In its 2003 *National Trade Estimate Report on Foreign Trade Barriers (NTE)*, the USTR published 23 pages of complaints—more than any other country with which the U.S. contemplated an FTA, and behind only Japan, China, and the EU. Moreover, there is significant anti-American sentiment in Korea. In 1989, the U.S. ITC conducted a study on a *KORUS*. The ITC concluded the idea was a bad one, because it would provoke a large increase in anti-American sentiment in Korea. Roughly two decades later, that sentiment has increased. It is a political guess as to whether the FTA might bring exacerbate emotions, or might reduce them by linking the countries closer economically. But, it almost certainly would have been a political and economic miscalculation by the American Congress to reject *KORUS*.

Korea has FTAs with Chile, the EU, and Singapore, and is negotiating one with the EU and Japan. Even without an FTA with Korea, China surpassed (by December 2007) the U.S. as the most important export destination for Korea. A commercially meaningful *ASEAN + 3* accord (an FTA among the *Association of South East Asian Nations* plus China, Japan, and Korea)—one that pointedly excludes the U.S.—is foreseeable. In brief, the U.S. may need *KORUS* simply to keep pace with major trading nations for political and economic influence in East Asia.

This political economy logic, however, did not spell quick passage of *KORUS* in the U.S. Congress. To the contrary, domestic political pressures from (*inter alia*) the beef and auto industries ran counter to the FTA. In April 2008, the USTR and Korea signed the *Beef Import Protocol*, which they followed with an exchange of Side Letters allowing Korea to exclude certain additional cattle parts, and clarifying the right of Korea to protect the health of its citizens. The USDA agreed to monitor a voluntary agreement by American beef exporters that they would ship to Korea only beef from cattle of less than 30 months age. Even this *Protocol* did not satisfy some Congressional officials, who demanded Korea re-open fully its market to all American beef.

Likewise, as of April 2009, certain Congressional, business, and union officials were unconvinced by the *KORUS* auto provisions. The auto industry was not of one mind. In 2001, General Motors acquired Daewoo as a subsidiary, and thus made cars in Korea through "GM Korea." GM and Daewoo were part of the same global supply chain, so *KORUS* made sense for them. In contrast, Ford and Chrysler based their supply chain in the *NAFTA* region, and opposed the deal. Unions also were split: the UAW broke ranks with the AFL-CIO to support *KORUS*.

* **Re-Opening Deal on Autos**

Domestic auto industry opponents prevailed, forcing the U.S. to reopen negotiations. In December 2010, a *Supplemental Agreement* revising the initial *KORUS* terms was reached, and officially initialed in February 2011. This *Agreement* consisted of three documents:

(1) A *Supplemental Auto Agreement*, which took the form of an exchange of letters between the U.S. Trade Representative and the Korean Trade Minister.

(2) An agreement on fuel economy and greenhouse gas (*e.g.*, CO_2) emission standards for motor vehicles, which took the form of *Agreed Minutes*.

(3) An agreement on intra-company transferee (L-1) visas, which extends the period of their validity to 5 years, and which also took the form of *Agreed Minutes*.

The *Supplemental Auto Agreement* did not cover beef trade.

Query whether the U.S. made itself better off through this *Agreement*. Its terms smacked of managed trade.

(1) Under the original deal, the U.S. agreed to phase out over 10 years its 2.5% tariff on cars with small engines, and 25% truck tariff, on Korean vehicles (beginning with small-engine capacity cars). Under the *Supplemental Auto Agreement*, the U.S. agreed to accelerate the phase outs: 5 years for the 2.5% car tariff, and seven years for the 25% truck tariff. This agreement took the form of a modification to *KORUS* Article 2:3(2) and Annex 2-B.

(2) Associated with the 75,000 quota (below) was a 25,000-vehicle cap per company on exports to Korea.[7] The purpose of the cap was to allow American car imports, but also to limit the environmental damage to Korea from those cars. Notably, in 2016, the U.S. auto companies were nowhere close to reaching the cap: the combined exports from Fiat-Chrysler, Ford, and General Motors to Korea that year were 18,289 vehicles.

In exchange for faster American car tariff phase outs, Korea agreed to—

(1) Allow in annually up to 75,000 American cars that meet U.S., rather than Korean, safety standards, and to ensure new environmental standards for cars proposed by Korea in the prior three years would not become *de facto* tariff barriers.

(2) Cut its 8% car tariff not to zero immediately, as under the original deal, but to 4% immediately, and then to zero after five years (*i.e.*, by 1 January 2016). In contrast, under the *Korea-EU FTA*, which took effect in July 2011, Korea phased out its 2%–6% duties on European cars gradually over 4 years.

---

7. *See* Elaine Ramirez, *Ag Is South Korea's "Red Line" in Trade Talks With U.S., Kim Says*, 34 International Trade Reporter (BNA) 1395 (19 October 2017).

Thus, the *Supplemental Agreement* removed what would have been a margin of preference for U.S. vis-à-vis EU cars of zero versus 2%–6% in Years 1 through 4. And, near the end of Year 5, Korean tariffs on American cars were higher than those on European ones (because American cars faced a 4% duty until after year 5). These changes took the form of modifications to *KORUS* Article 2:3(2) and Annex 2-B.

(3) Remove immediately its 10% tariff on trucks.

(4) Establish enhanced rules on transparency.

(5) Create Special procedures for a motor vehicle safeguard under the *KORUS* Chapter 10 bilateral safeguard.

(6) Implement on an accelerated basis the pharmaceutical product provisions in *KORUS* Chapter 18, Article 18:5(b).

(7) Gain a further two-year delay, to 1 January 2016 (instead of 1 January 2014), to eliminate tariffs on pork. Yet, under the *Korea-Chile FTA*, Chilean pork enters the Korean market with lower duties than American pork has under the revised *KORUS* deal.

Notably, under the original *KORUS* terms and the *Supplemental Agreement*, the rule of origin for autos is the same: 35% value added, *i.e.*, 35% American or Korean content. Further, Korea may continue to grant duty drawback to Korean producers on auto parts (*e.g.*, steel, tires) they import from China (or any other countries) and use in the production of cars they export duty-free under *KORUS* to the U.S.

The last above-listed point listed is a clue to how the impasse over *KORUS* finally ended: cars for pork. Essentially, American politicians thought they were getting a better market access deal with the revised provisions on exports of autos to Korea, and were willing to wait longer for Korea to grant duty-free treatment to American pork. American pork producers were willing to accept the deferral, because over the first 10 years of implementation of *KORUS*, they anticipated increases of at least 9,000 jobs and $770 million worth of exports.[8]

Neither *KORUS* nor the *Supplemental Agreement* dealt with another issue that dogged trade relations between the two countries: Was the Korean currency, the *won*, undervalued? As of October 2011, when Congress passed *KORUS* implementing legislation, the IMF thought it was by about 10% relative to the U.S. dollar. For that reason, some in Congress opposed the deal. Opponents argued that Korea, like China, deliberately undervalued—that is, manipulated—its currency. Doing so stimulated exports from Korea (because they are cheaper when American importers convert dollars into *won* to pay for the merchandise) and discourage imports from America (because they are dearer when Korean importers convert *won* into dollars to pay for that merchandise).

---

8. *See* Amy Tsui, *Customs and Border Protection Publishes Interim Regulations for U.S.-Korea Trade Pact*, 29 International Trade Reporter (BNA) 451 (22 March 2012).

More generally, the U.S. may well have damaged its international standing by forcing Korea back to the bargaining table and re-opening *KORUS*. "How reliable is the U.S.?" "When is a deal really a deal with the Americans?" Many trading partners could rightly ask these questions.

- **Re-Opening Deal on Three Issues**

In March 2018, the Administration of President Donald J. Trump (1946–, President, 2017–) announced the conclusion of its first successful trade negotiation — altering terms of *KORUS*. Nearly all of *KORUS* remained the same; *i.e.*, contrary to the President's assertion about "a brand new agreement," the changes were cosmetic, or as South Korean President politely stated, incremental changes that were "improvements and modifications."[9] The new terms covered three areas, autos, pharmaceuticals, and currency manipulation, and they signed the revised deal on 24 September, the first trade agreement cinched by the Trump Administration.[10] The revised deal entered into force on 1 January 2019.[11]

First, on autos, Korea agreed the U.S. would extend by 20 years its 25% tariff on pick-up trucks. (Korean cars continued to receive duty-free treatment; the U.S. agreed not to impose its 2.5% MFN tariff on cars.) That meant the 25% duty would apply to Korean trucks until year-end 2041, instead of 2021, a 30-year phase-out if calculated from 2012, when *KORUS* was implemented — the longest in any U.S. FTA. America hoped this extension would encourage pick-up manufacturers in the U.S. to stay in the U.S., rather than offshore production by shifting to Korea. Conversely, the South Korean labor union that represented Hyundai workers called the 20-year extension of Americas' 25% tariff "humiliating" and a foregone chance to

---

9. *Quoted in* Youkyung Lee, David Tweed & Jenny Leonard, *Trump Clinches His First Trade Deal in Revamped South Korea Pact*, 35 International Trade Reporter (BNA) 1248 (27 September 2018). [Hereinafter, Trump Cinches.]

10. *See Trump Cinches*; David Lawder, *U.S., South Korea to Revise Trade Pact with Currency Side-Deal, Autos Concessions*, REUTERS, 27 March 2018, www.reuters.com/article/us-usa-trade -southkorea/u-s-south-korea-to-revise-trade-pact-with-currency-side-deal-autos-concessions -idUSKBN1H32SI; Toluse Olorunnipa & Andrew Mayeda, *Trump Scores His First Revised Trade Deal, With South Korea*, BLOOMBERG, 27 March 2018, www.bloomberg.com/news/articles/2018 -03-28/trump-scores-his-first-revised-trade-deal-with-south-korea. The revised agreement also memorialized the quotas the U.S. imposed on Korean steel shipments under Section 232 (discussed in a separate Chapter).

The changes to *KORUS* are set forth in *Protocol Between The Government of the United States of America and The Government of the Republic of Korea Amending the Free Trade Agreement Between The United States of America and The Republic of Korea*, and the accompanying documents (a second *Protocol, Interpretation, Agreed Minutes, Attachments*, and *Side Letters*), 3 September 2018, https://ustr.gov/sites/default/files/files/Press/Releases/KORUS%20Texts%20Outcomes.pdf. Note this compilation excludes the MOU between America and Korea on currency manipulation. The revised terms are summarized in Office of the United States Trade Representative, New U.S. Trade Policy and National Security Outcomes with the Republic of Korea, March 2018, https://ustr.gov /about-us/policy-offices/press-office/fact-sheets/2018/march/new-us-trade-policy-and-national.

11. *See* Eunkyung Seo & Jenny Leonard, *South Korean Parliament Passes Revamped Trade Deal With U.S.*, 35 International Trade Reporter (BNA) 1627 (13 December 2018).

what it said was the "U.S. market's blue ocean" and "future bread and butter of the South Korean auto industry."[12]

Korea also agreed to double the quota threshold for car imports from the U.S. that could enter Korea meeting American, but not Korean, environmental, safety, and technical specifications. The new cap was 50,000 per year for each U.S. auto company. Further, Korea would cut NTBs against U.S. vehicles: it would eliminate duplicative environmental testing (*i.e.*, recognize American test results for gasoline engine emissions), ease certain standards (*e.g.*, provide more "eco-credits" for U.S. cars to meet fuel economy and greenhouse gas emissions, and take U.S. standards into account when setting Korean ones), and it would accept U.S. standards for replacement auto parts. Whether these changes would help American manufacturers was unclear. Sales by U.S. car companies in Korea were nowhere near 50,000 vehicles (indeed, no American producer sold more than 10,000 vehicles per year annually), and Korean consumers might be dubious about U.S. testing and standards.

Second, on pharmaceuticals, Korea said it would change its health care laws concerning government payments to its pharmaceutical companies. Those payments, under the Korea's Premium Pricing Policy for Global Initiative Drugs, had been higher to domestic than foreign drug companies. American companies exporting medicines to Korea thus chafed at the national treatment violation. Payments would now be non-discriminatory.

Third, Korea agreed to a *Side Letter* designed to deter competitive currency devaluation. Korea pledged to increase transparency associated with its FX operations, for example, by revealing details of its FX interventions, such as how much its central bank, the BOK, spends (*e.g.*, buying dollars and selling *won*, or *vice versa*) to offset volatility in the currency markets. Korea also promised to eschew competitive devaluation of the *won* relative to the dollar and thereby promote a level playing field for trade and FDI. In other words, what the BOK calls "smoothing operations" against volatility should not be to devalue the *won* and thereby boost Korea's export or investment competitiveness.

The *Letter* did not appear to immunize Korea from the Treasury Department labelling it a "currency manipulator." The Treasury Department had long had Korea on its "Monitoring List," and in October 2017, called on Korea to increase the transparency of its FX operations. The *Side Letter* was not enforceable through any trade sanctions. The *Letter* contained no dispute settlement mechanism, nor did it rely on the mechanisms in the core text of *KORUS*.

As the *Side Letter* was not part of *KORUS*, the Administration felt it did not need Congressional approval. In avoiding Congress, it surely was mindful of opposition

---

12. *Quoted in Hyundai's Union Says Revised Trade Deal with U.S. "Humiliating,"* REUTERS, 26 March 2018, www.reuters.com/article/us-usa-trade-southkorea-hyundai-motor/hyundais-union -says-revised-trade-deal-with-u-s-humiliating-idUSKBN1H30B5.

in 2015–2016 in both the House and Senate to *TPP*, based on the lack of enforceable currency manipulation provisions in that FTA. That said, the Side Letter was the first time in American trade history currency manipulation provisions were included — or associated with — a trade agreement.

Except perhaps for the lack of enforceability of the *Side Letter*, all three changes amounted to concessions by South Korea, thus enabling a swift conclusion to the talks. Only a few rounds were needed. Motivating both sides was their anticipation of direct talks between the President and the North Korean leader, Kim Jong Un, concerning the de-nuclearization of the Korean Peninsula. As a Presidential candidate, and during the first year of his Presidency, the criticisms of *KORUS* Mr. Trump made — including repeated threat to withdraw from the FTA — were an irritant in relations between America and South Korea. Wrapping up talks on new terms was useful so that these two countries could present a united front to the North.

IV. Case Study: *KORUS* and Kaesong

A controversial feature of *KORUS*, which implicates not only economic and political factors of this FTA, but also strengthen the military alliance between Korea and the U.S., is Kaesong. Consider what effect this feature might have on containing North Korea, in particular, on the denuclearization of the Korean Peninsula, and even on reunification of the Korean Peninsula? In May 2006, preparing for the first round of FTA talks with the U.S., held in June, the Korean Ministry of Foreign Affairs and Trade (MOFAT) declared it would call for ROOs that could facilitate reunification. Specifically, it said the U.S. should recognize as of South Korean origin merchandise any goods made in Kaesong.

Kaesong is a city and large inter-Korean industrial zone close to, but on the North Korean side of, the demilitarized zone (DMZ), about six miles on the Northern side. It is about one-hour drive from Seoul, across the DMZ. About 40 South Korean companies (as of August 2006) have built factories in the Kaesong Industrial Complex, which was set up in June 2003 and opened in 2004, and occupies 25 square mile area. Succinctly put, the Complex is a manifestation of the vision of peace-through-trade. The only inter-Korean joint economic project, the Complex is designed to encourage reform in North Korea, with a view to economic integration of the two Koreas, and their eventual peaceful reunification. As the *Financial Times* put it, Kaesong "was intended to pave the way for a broader expansion of economic ties that would ensure lasting stability on the [Korean] peninsula."[13] By April 2013, 123 South Korean companies employed roughly 53,000 North Korean workers in the Complex. However, that goal was tested in 2013 when, for five months, North Korea, amidst a dispute over its nuclear weapons program, shut down Kaesong.

---

13. Simon Mundy, *Kaesong's Woes Reflect Challenge Facing Seoul*, FINANCIAL TIMES, 15 October 2013, at 3. [Hereinafter, *Kaesong's Woes*.]

The Kaesong factories produce consumer goods, including clothing and kitchenware. Labor costs are far cheaper there than in South Korea—a fact prompting the criticism Kaesong is used by "second rate South Korean entrepreneurs to make use of cheap North Korean labor."[14] Guest workers from China also comprise the labor employed at Kaesong.

In June 2006, the South Korean government decided to provide state-backed credit guarantees to firms that invest there. A South Korean firm can get receive a payment guarantee for up to U.S. $10.4 million for establishing production facility in Kaesong. The terms are generous.[15] The guarantee costs between 0.5% and 3% of the amount of the secured loan. The guarantee period is up to seven years for a bank loan that funds up to 70% of an investment expenditure.

In FTA talks during 2006, American negotiators told Korea it would apply any accord only to U.S. and South Korean territory, and not allow products made in North Korea to receive preferential treatment. The prospect of dollars from American consumers fueling nefarious North Korean nuclear ambitions was galling. In an August 2006 C-SPAN television interview, the USTR, Susan Schwab, stridently intoned: "It won't happen, can't happen. That won't change."[16] Following the October 2006 North Korean nuclear test, South Korea indicated flexibility. As Tae-Sik Lee, South Korea's Ambassador to the U.S. said:

> When we started these negotiations, we wanted to include it [Kaesong] in the FTA, but as time goes by we have noticed that the atmosphere has been shifting rather negatively against this idea. That is why we are squeezing our wisdom to find some way out.[17]

Query whether the hardline American position is a cause or consequence, that is, whether it exacerbates or is the effect of differences between the U.S. and North Korea over not only nuclear weapons, but also human rights. Is the "wisdom" to be "squeezed" really about the long-standing theoretical debate over whether to constructively engage an enemy or isolate a country on the axis of evil? Further, is the U.S. position consistent?

Ultimately, Korea and the U.S. reached a compromise for Kaesong, embodied in Annex 22-B to *KORUS*. The *KORUS* rules of origin forbid Kaesong products from entry. However, *KORUS* creates a bilateral commission, the "Committee on Outward Processing Zones," consisting of American and South Korean officials. The Committee meets annually to consider "OPZs." One such zone could be Kaesong.

---

14. *Kaesong's Woes* (describing the skepticism of a former senior South Korean government official).

15. *See* James Lim, *South Korea Plans to Extend Guarantees To Firms in North Korean Industrial Zone*, 23 International Trade Reporter (BNA) 983 (29 June 2006).

16. *Quoted in* Gary G. Yerkey, *U.S. Rejects South Korean Bid to Include North Korean Products in Free Trade Pact*, 23 International Trade Reporter (BNA) 1255 (24 August 2006).

17. *Quoted in* Krishna Guha, *Trade Pact Urged for U.S. and S. Korea*, FINANCIAL TIMES, 23 October 2006, at 2.

However, no good from any OPZ automatically is eligible for duty-free treatment under *KORUS*. Rather, the Committee considers whether conditions on the Korean Peninsula warrant designation of an OPZ to bolster economic development in a particular area, and thus whether preferential treatment ought to be granted to products from such a zone.

The Committee establishes criteria—including progress on de-nuclearization of the Peninsula, respect for environmental and labor rights, and a positive effect on intra-Korean relations—that a product from a zone must meet before qualifying as originating. Then, the Committee recommends to Congress and Korean National Assembly that *KORUS* be amended to include goods from the proposed newly designated OPZ. Only with the approval of both legislatures, and of course signature into law of implementing legislation by the American President as well as the Korean President, can Kaesong-originating goods qualify for *KORUS* duty-free treatment. In brief, final authority as to whether Kaesong goods qualify for this treatment rests with the legislatures, a point made clear in Paragraph 5 of Annex 22-B.

The *U.S.-Singapore FTA* has a precedent for inclusion of SEZs outside the territory of the parties. In that *FTA*, goods made on Batam and Bintam Islands, Indonesia, just off the coast of Singapore, may qualify for preferential treatment. Finally, is the American position politically tenable, given that Korea successfully negotiated an extension of duty-free treatment for Kaesong goods in its FTA with Singapore in 2004, its FTA with the *EFTA* in 2005, and *ASEAN* in 2006?

National security is more than just a criterion for establishing an FTA. It also may be an over-riding exception to all obligations in an FTA. In the 2006 *U.S.-Bahrain* and *U.S.-Oman FTAs*, the following "Essential Security" provision exists:

> [Nothing in the agreement] shall be construed . . . to preclude [either party to the FTA] from applying measures that it considers necessary for the fulfillment of its obligations with respect to the maintenance or restoration of its international peace or security or the protection of its own essential security interests.[18]

This language also exists in the U.S. FTAs with Bahrain, Chile, and Morocco, and in *CAFTA-DR*. The U.S. considers the Essential Security provision to be self-judging, and thus applicable unilaterally. No doubt this provision will be part of any future FTA, for example, with the UAE. Its key terms appear to be self-judging, and thus could apply in a wide range of contexts. Consider the March 2006 dispute over the ultimately unsuccessful takeover by Dubai Ports (DP) World of several port management facilities in several east coast ports. Would the above language immunize from legal action the U.S., were it to block acquisition of its port facilities by a foreign company?

---

18. *See Bahrain FTA*, Chapter 20 (Exceptions), Article 20:2; *Oman FTA*, Chapter 21 (Exceptions), Article 21:2.

- **February 2016 Kaesong Closure, June 2018 Singapore Summit, and Aftermath**

As for Kaesong, it suffered a reversal in February 2016, when South Korea closed it, and brought back across the DMZ all South Korean personnel. The South Korean Ministry of Unification took the decision in protest of what it viewed as provocative North Korean behavior in January, namely, testing a hydrogen bomb and launching a satellite. The North expelled all 280 South Korean workers, and froze South Korea's assets (including factory equipment). As of June 2018, Kaesong remains closed.

No mention was made of Kaesong during the June 2018 Singapore Summit between President Donald J. Trump (1946, President, 2017–) and Chairman Kim Jong Un (1983, in office, 2011–) of North Korea's State Affairs Commission. The Summit yielded a *Joint Statement*:[19]

> President Trump and Chairman Kim Jong Un conducted a comprehensive, in-depth and sincere exchange of opinions on the issues related to the establishment of new US-DPRK relations and the building of a lasting and robust peace regime on the Korean Peninsula. President Trump committed to provide security guarantees to the DPRK, and Chairman Kim Jong Un reaffirmed his firm and unwavering commitment to complete denuclearization of the Korean Peninsula.

> Convinced that the establishment of new US-DPRK relations will contribute to the peace and *prosperity* of the Korean Peninsula and of the world, and recognizing that mutual *confidence building* can promote the denuclearization of the Korean Peninsula, President Trump and Chairman Kim Jong Un state the following:

> 1. The United States and the DPRK commit to establish new US-DPRK relations in accordance with the desire of the peoples of the two countries for peace and prosperity.

> 2. The United States and DPRK will join their efforts to build a lasting and stable peace regime on the Korean Peninsula.

> 3. Reaffirming the April 27, 2018 *Panmunjom Declaration*, the DPRK commits to work toward complete denuclearization of the Korean Peninsula.

> 4. The United States and the DPRK commit to recovering POW/MIA remains, including the immediate repatriation of those already identified.

> Having acknowledged that the US-DPRK summit—the first in history—was an epochal event of great significance in overcoming decades of

---

19. Joint Statement of President Donald J. Trump of the United States of America and Chairman Kim Jong Un of the State Affairs Commission of the Democratic People's Republic of Korea at the Singapore Summit, 12 June 2008, www.bbc.com/news/world-asia-44453330.

tensions and hostilities between the two countries and for the opening up of a new future, President Trump and Chairman Kim Jong Un commit to implement the stipulations in the Joint Statement fully and expeditiously.

The United States and the DPRK commit to hold follow-on negotiations, led by the US Secretary of State, Mike Pompeo, and a relevant high-level DPRK official, at the earliest possible date, to implement the outcomes of the US-DPRK Summit.

President Donald J. Trump of the United States of America and Chairman Kim Jong Un of the State Affairs Commission of the Democratic People's Republic of Korea have committed to cooperate for the development of new US-DPRK relations and for the promotion of peace, *prosperity*, and the security of the Korean Peninsula and of the world.

Manifestly, the *Statement* contained no hard law obligations about denucleariza-tion, as "the North retains its nuclear warheads, the missiles to launch them and has not agreed to any specific process to get rid of them," facts the U.S. implicitly admit-ted the day after the *Statement*, saying it was "hopeful" for "major North Korean disarmament" by the end of 2020.[20] And, despite the two references to "prosperity," there was no suggestion that re-opening Kaesong might be a "confidence building" measure.

V. Case Study: Pakistan, ROZs, and Islamist Extremism

It is difficult to put the national security case for an FTA more directly than did Humayun Akhtar Khan (1955–), Pakistan's Federal Minister for Trade and

---

20. *Trump-Kim Summit, U.S. Wants "Major N. Korea Disarmament" by 2020*, BBC News, 13 June 2018, www.bbc.com/news/world-us-canada-44471419 (*quoting* U.S. Secretary of State Mike Pompeo). Even that admission was a far cry from complete, verifiable, and irreversible disarma-ment (CVID), a point on which the U.S. previously said was essential. When asked why CVID was missing from the Statement, the U.S. (*per* Secretary Pompeo) said such questions were "'insulting' and 'ridiculous.'" *Quoted in id. See also* David Brunstromm, *Trump Says Summit Removed North Korean Nuclear Threat; Democrats Doubtful*, REUTERS, 12 June 2018, www.reuters.com/article /us-northkorea-usa/north-korea-highlights-trump-concessions-on-war-games-after-summit -idUSKBN1J90CA (reporting: "Pompeo bristled at a question about why the words 'verifiable' and 'irreversible' were not in the summit Joint Statement, in the context of denuclearization. 'It's in the statement. You're just wrong about that . . . Because complete encompasses verifiable and irre-versible. I suppose you could argue semantics, but let me assure you that it's in the document,' Pompeo said. Pressed on how the agreement would be verified, he said: 'Of course it will . . . I find that question insulting and ridiculous and frankly ludicrous.'"). Notably, the President declared in a Press Conference following the Summit that the U.S. no longer would conduct joint military exercises with South Korea, as the North deemed them provocative, though sanctions against the North would remain in place until "nukes are no longer a factor." *Quoted in Trump Kim Summit: North Korean Media Celebrate Meeting*, BBC NEWS, 13 June 2018, www.bbc.com/news/world-asia -44464236.

Commerce (2002–2007), to the U.S. authorities in August 2006. A bilateral deal would be

> part of the global "war on terror." [That is because] an agreement with the U.S. would create thousands of jobs in Pakistan, and be a powerful weapon in the "international fight against extremism."[21]

Minister Khan was re-stating a proposal for a *U.S.-Pakistan FTA* first raised by President Pervez Musharraf with President George W. Bush in December 2004. As Minister Khan said in August 2006:

> President Musharraf is very clear that the long-term solution to ending the extremism problem in Pakistan is to economically improve [sic] Pakistan.[22]

In addition to collaborating with Pakistan on traditional infrastructure projects to enhance road networks and energy production in Pakistan, the Administrations of Presidents Bush and Barack H. Obama countered with a different idea: establishing "Reconstruction Opportunity Zones," or "ROZs," on the border between Afghanistan and Pakistan (*i.e.*, the Federally Administered Tribal Areas of Pakistan). ROZs also could be designated for Pakistan's Northwest Frontier Province, Baluchistan (within 100 miles of the Afghan border), and even parts of Kashmir. America would give products originating in an ROZ duty-free treatment. Overall, America also would, in the words of Secretary of State John Kerry in January 2014, support the goal of Pakistani Prime Minister Nawaz Sharif (1949–PM, 1990–1993, 1997–1999, 2013–2017) to make Pakistan "a tiger economy for the 21st century."[23]

Even India might small at that result. A confident, prosperous trading partner on its western flank ought to be less of a security risk than an insecure, impoverished, nearly failed state, and all the better if the Americans footed the bill to help Pakistan make the transition. But, is an ROZ a better, or a distant half-hearted second-best, solution to an FTA with an ally of America on the front lines in the war on terror? How much of a difference can ROZs make?

The same question may be asked of three other American responses to the Pakistani request for an FTA: a "Strategic Dialogue," a *TIFA*, which the countries signed in 2003, and trade preferences. The Dialogue is little else than an agreement to talk about matters of mutual concern. A *TIFA* is a skeletal agreement under which a foreign country the U.S. considers not ready for an FTA commits to trade and investment liberalization, IPR protection and enforcement, labor and the environmental reforms, assistance for SMEs, and legal capacity building. As for preferences, above and beyond benefits under the GSP scheme, Congress has debated

---

21. *Quoted in* Krishna Guha, *Pakistan Hopeful of U.S. Trade Pact*, Financial Times, 7 August 2006.

22. *Quoted in* Christopher S. Rugaber, *Pakistani Commerce Minister Urges U.S. To Consider Pakistan Free Trade Agreement*, 23 International Trade Reporter (BNA) 1195 (10 August 2006).

23. *Quoted in* Brian Flood, *U.S. Wants Pakistan as Center of South Asian Marketplace; Pakistan Seeks GSP Status*, 31 International Trade Reporter (BNA) 230 (30 January 2014).

granting duty-free treatment to certain Pakistani T&A merchandise, along with non-T&A products from ROZs along the Pakistan-Afghan border. The idea was to focus on that conflict-prone border, because if ROZs included industrialized areas of either country, then no job-creation or economic development would occur on the border.

The House of Representatives passed such a measure (the *Pakistan Enduring Assistance and Cooperation Enhancement Act of 2009*, H.R. 1886) in June 2009. That bill would give duty-free treatment to certain T&A, and some non-T&A, items from Pakistani and Afghan ROZs. About 74% of the volume of merchandise shipped by Pakistan to the U.S. would be covered, with duties kept in place on other product categories to protect sensitive sectors in the U.S. But, the Senate version (the *Afghanistan and Pakistan Reconstruction Opportunity Zones Act of 2009*, S. 496) diverged from the House bill, and failed to win passage.

All the while, American T&A and cotton producers expressed concern. Just how much their interests might be hurt would depend on the product. Consider cotton trousers and shirts. They account for over 65% of Pakistan's T&A exports to America (as of September 2010), so duty-free treatment for them would help Pakistan considerably. But, American imports of these products from Pakistan account for just 3.7% of total American imports of cotton trousers and shirts. So, such treatment ought not to affect American T&A producers seriously. To be sure, it was hard to convince the domestic T&A lobby: measured from 2000 to roughly September 2010, the American T&A industry had lost 680,000 jobs. Moreover, Pakistan posed a competitive threat: it is the third largest exporter of T&A items to the U.S. by volume, and seventh largest by value. For cotton products in particular, it is the second and fifth largest exporter to the U.S., by volume and value, respectively.

If the case—which, put succinctly, is the adage "idle hands are the devil's playmate"—is so compelling, then why do FTAs between the U.S., on the one hand, and the likes of Afghanistan, Saudi Arabia, Yemen, as well as Pakistan, not yet exist? One answer is opposition from American producers that make products like or directly competitive with foreign goods. In 2006, Gary C. Hufbauer (1939–) published *Sustaining Reform With a U.S.-Pakistan Free Trade Agreement*, a book on the possible economic effects of a bilateral deal. Each country imposes high tariffs on imports from the other country, and a bilateral deal might boost two-way trade by 40%–50%. The T&A sector in Pakistan would be a key beneficiary—its exports could rise by U.S. $1 billion, and 200,000 new jobs in that sector could be created. Because many Pakistan workers support up to 6 family members, over 1 million Pakistanis might experience positive knock-on effects.

But, opposition from the American T&A industry would be stiff. Should that opposition block a deal that looks to be in America's national security interest? Moreover, is that opposition over-wrought: how many U.S. producers would face stiff, head-to-head competition from Afghani, Saudi, or Yemeni goods? Arguably, the concern would be the reverse: how could infant industries in those countries grow against DFQF American competition?

Might it be said American jobs are the security interest at stake? In May 2014, the USTR signaled that was the case. Announcing a deal under *TIFA* to boost trade and FDI, diversify agricultural production, promote IP protection, help Pakistan accede to the WTO *GPA*, build capacity in state and local governments, and foster entrepreneurship and private sector dialogue, the USTR said: "Trade with Pakistan supports good-paying jobs *in the United States* and is a key part of our effort to unlock opportunity for *American* workers, businesses, farmers, and ranchers."[24] If the *TIFA*, and perhaps an eventual FTA, were instruments in counter-terrorism, *i.e.*, fighting Islamist extremism through meaningful job creation and economic development in Pakistan, as opposed to expressions of American self-interest, that was not apparent from the statement.

VI. Case Study: Turkey

Interestingly, in June 2010, Jordan, Lebanon, and Syria joined with Turkey to agree on establishing an FTA and free travel zone. Frustrated at continued rebuffs by the EU to join that CU, Turkey turned to the Arab world. Since the era of the Ottoman Empire (11th century–1923), Turkey had capitalized on its geography, being a bridge between the west and east. In recent years, it had signed FTAs with Egypt, Jordan, Morocco, Palestine, Syria, and Tunisia. What effect might the shift eastward in Turkish trade policy have on the role of Egypt and Saudi Arabia in the Middle East?

In short, *MEFTA* and certain other RTAs are premised on a new logic for trade liberalization: counter-terrorism. Put differently, they are a manifestation of the vision of Cordell Hull, namely, peace through trade, but in a post-9/11 context in which the threat to peace is not so much from a belligerent nation state, or group thereof, but rather from poverty, and the susceptibility to Islamist and other extremist messages that poverty breeds. President Barack H. Obama evinced his belief in the new logic when, in May 2011, he launched a comprehensive *Trade and Investment Partnership Initiative* (*TIPI*) with the MENA region. *TIPI* was more than just a positive response to the successful democratic reform movements that swept the Arab world, especially in Bahrain, Egypt, Libya, Syria, Tunisia, and Yemen in the spring and summer of 2011. It was an effort to encourage economic reform, in particular and promote integration of Arab economies with that of the U.S. These changes would, the President viewed, end trade and investment protectionism that benefits a few crony elites. In turn, Islamist extremists would have one less rallying cry with which to recruit converts: government corruption exacerbates socioeconomic inequities and denies the poor opportunities for advancement.

---

24. Stephanie Cohen, *U.S.-Pakistan Reach Five-Year Agreement To Expand Bilateral Trade, Investments*, 31 International Trade Reporter (BNA) 915 (15 May 2014) (*quoting* Michael Froman) (emphasis added).

In practice, is the underlying causal nexus on which *MEFTA* and *TIPI* are premised correct? Even if it is, then is it possible for such RTAs to combat terrorism if they do not include certain countries, such as Libya, Syria, or Iran? Can they be effective if they do not include Israel, or without a just, lasting solution to the Palestinian question?

VII. Competitive Imperialism

• **Competition from Europe**

Emphasis in American trade policy on FTAs is more than merely curious. Possibly, it is a watershed shift in American foreign policy. Before the Uruguay Round, the U.S. regarded RTAs as the work of the devil, and the GATT as the exorcist. American leadership guaranteed the multilateral trading system as the foundation of the global economic order, and consistently pushed for non-discriminatory trade relations and progressive lowering and binding of trade barriers. Yet, since that Round, especially since the late 1990s, the U.S. has pursued FTAs with the zeal of a recent convert.

From the U.S. perspective, the EU started the FTA race and continues to sprint. The EU takes the opposite view: it is innocently but necessarily reacting, as it did with respect to Singapore. Competition in the Far East illustrates both views. The American FTA with that city-state entered into force in 2004, and with Korea in March 2012. In December 2012, the EU finished negotiations with Singapore for an FTA, having launched them in March 2010. But, the EU implemented its FTA with Korea in July 2011, whereas the *KORUS* took effect in March 2012.

Consider competition for Latin American markets: which hegemonic trade power is chasing which, or are they chasing each other? In December 2005, the U.S. completed FTA negotiations with Peru, and did so with respect to Colombia in February 2006. (To be sure, the deal with Peru marked a remarkable transformation in the trade policy of that country from hostility toward FTAs to embracing them as a key strategy in economic growth and a springboard to an enhanced international political status. By March 2013, Peru had implemented 12 FTAs, including with Japan, Korea, Panama, and Mexico. As for Colombia, its FTA with America had a security element to it: Colombia was an important partner in the war on drugs.) In March 2006 the *CAFTA-DR* entered (partially) into force. Shortly thereafter, the U.S. finished an FTA with Panama. In February 2009, the Peru FTA took effect.

The EU responded. In May 2006, the EU launched FTA talks with Central America.[25] The EU strengthened trade links with the Andean Community, consisting of

---

25. Jason Gutierrez, *Mandelson Says European Union to Discuss Free Trade Agreement with ASIAN Members*, 23 International Trade Reporter (BNA) 763–64 (18 May 2006); David Haskel, *EU, Central America Agree to Start Talks On Free Trade; Mercosur, Andean Talks Stall*, 23 International Trade Reporter (BNA) 766–67 (18 May 2006).

Bolivia, Colombia, Peru, Ecuador, and (until April 2006, Venezuela). In September 2006, EU Trade Commissioner Peter Mandelson called for a "Global Europe Strategy" that entails a "more 'activist' approach to opening foreign markets by negotiating FTAs, particularly with Asian nations" such as India, Korea, as well as *ASEAN*.[26] French Foreign Trade Minister Christine Lagarde not only echoed his call, urging a "more active, more pragmatic, and better prepared" FTA policy than in the past, but added a key reason for the change: the U.S. is "aggressively pursuing bilateral and regional deals, so France and Europe must join in, or risk being left behind."[27]

The European effort to avoid being shut out of, or losing ground to the Americans in, Latin markets paid off. In June 2012, the EU inked FTAs with Colombia and Peru whereby tariffs would be phased out over 10 years, and NTBs eliminated. The FTA with Peru took effect on 1 March 2013, with immediate elimination of tariffs on 90% of goods, and a nearly-full phase out of tariffs on the remaining 10% of goods (most of which were agricultural) over the next decade. This FTA replaced the preferential treatment Peru had been receiving under the EU GSP+ scheme, which gave duty-free entry to only about 45% of Peruvian goods. Notably, the European FTAs with Colombia and Peru also included commitments to protect human rights and implement international treaties on labor rights and environmental protection. In June 2012 the EU announced it was nearly finished with an association agreement with Costa Rica, El Salvador, Guatemala, Honduras, Nicaragua, and Panama, all of which by then were FTA partners with the U.S.

Put aside the inconvenient chronology in some instances that suggests a reverse causal direction whereby American reacts to perceived European commercial perfidy, and put aside the *de facto* moratorium on bilateral deals the EU implemented after violent anti-free trade protests at the November 1999 WTO Ministerial Conference in Seattle.[28] The fact is in October 2006 EU governments and European businesses expressed concern they were falling behind the U.S. in the race to sign developing countries up to FTAs. They have continued to do so ever since, and so have their counterparts on the other side of the Atlantic Ocean.

In some instances, the EU has done more than kept pace with America's FTAs: it has gained an edge, if temporary. On 1 July 2011, its FTA with Korea entered into force, and was ambitious in scope, with provisions on services, IPRs, government procurement, regulatory barriers, unfair competition, and the promotion and protection of FDI. In the meantime, *KORUS* languished on Capitol Hill, as it was signed

---

26. Gary G. Yerkey, *EU Needs to Take More "Activist" Approach To Trade, Launch New FTAs, Mandelson Says*, 23 International Trade Reporter (BNA) 1366 (21 September 2006).

27. Lawrence J. Speer, *France to Push EU for Bilateral, Regional Trade Deals as WTO Talks Founder*, 23 International Trade Reporter (BNA) 1407 (28 September 2006).

28. *See* Juliane von Reppert-Bismark, *EU Is To Focus on Bilateral Deals After Failed Global Trade Talks*, WALL STREET JOURNAL, 2 October 2006, at A4.

on 30 June 2007, but Congress did not approve it, along with the FTAs with Colombia and Panama, until October 2011.

Indubitably, as to the Korean and Colombian market, America's trade competitors pushed Congress. Along with the *EU-Korea FTA*, Australia and Canada were in advanced stages of negotiating their own bilateral deals. Likewise, with Colombia, Canada signed an FTA that took effect on 15 August 2011. American agricultural and industrial product exporters complained to Congress that they were at a disadvantage relative to their foreign competitors, which enjoyed duty-free access to markets like Korea and Colombia. For instance, Colombia imposed a 35% tariff on auto imports, which affected cars made in Michigan, but not Ontario.

In the words of Venezuelan President Hugo Chavez, the bilateral accords involving Peru and Colombia "mortally wounded" the Andean Community.[29] In one technical sense, he was correct. Those *FTAs* complicated the efforts of the Community to adopt a common tariff. Without a common tariff, it would be unlikely it could negotiate a trade accord with the EU. Had the U.S. effectively blocked EU efforts by dividing and conquering the Andes? In August 2006, the U.S. signed a *TIFA* with the 10-country *ASEAN*.[30] The following month the EU approved exploratory FTA talks with *ASEAN*, launching them formally in May 2007. In June 2012, the EU launched FTA negotiations with Vietnam, and said it was nearing completion of a deal with India.

In sum, it is debatable whether U.S. moves are preemptive or reactive. The best answers probably are "both" and "it depends on the case." Never mind, however, from an official U.S. perspective: the truth is EU behavior justifies, or is used politically to justify, American zeal for FTAs. Moreover, the competitive behavior of both powers is contagious. Many middle-income countries, such as Chile and Mexico, have aggressively pursued FTAs.

For the U.S., then, traditionally, RTAs were a tool of the weak, like the original EC nations. Now, it is a tool in the hands of a large, potent counterweight to the U.S. on the world stage. So, it must also be in the toolkit of the largest and most powerful economy, the U.S. The need to counter preferential inroads of others, particularly major industrial countries, now is a lodestar of American trade policy. The need is all the more pressing given the impotence of the WTO as a forum for ambitious, horizontal multilateral trade liberalization with the death of the Doha Round.

Should "pre-emption" or "rebuttal" (depending on the vantage point) be a criterion for entering into an FTA? That is, should countering the trade strategy of another country be a motive for negotiating an FTA? To put the question provocatively, are

---

29. *Quoted in* Lucien O. Chauvin, *Ecuador Disrupted by Free Trade Talks with United States; Andean Pact Threatened*, 23 International Trade Reporter (BNA) 640 (6 April 2006).

30. *See* Jonathan Hopfner, *ASEAN, U.S. Ink Trade, Investment Pact; Pledge to Work for Breakthrough on Doha*, 23 International Trade Reporter (BNA) 1296–97 (7 September 2006); John Burton, *Washington Signs Pact with ASEAN Nations*, FINANCIAL TIMES, 26–28 August 2006, at 5.

FTAs a tool used by hegemonic trading nations in their race against one another to create neo-colonialist spheres of influence in developing and least developed regions, and thereby vie for economic and political influence with one another? The *Financial Times*, hardly leftist leaning, suggests the possibility, commenting that bilateral trade deals "have tended to be heavily tilted in favor of the powerful and decked out like Christmas trees with provisions for special interests."[31] In brief, do competitive liberalization and economic, political economy, political, and national security criteria explain FTAs? Or, are FTAs really about competition among imperialist powers?

Overall (as of May 2003), the EU has approximately 30 RTAs, with at four additional accords under active negotiations. For example, in the Middle East, EU RTA policy proceeds on three tracks:

First: Euro-Med Agreements

These association agreements are between the EU and individual countries in the Mediterranean region, including Algeria, Egypt, Israel, Jordan, Lebanon, Morocco, the Palestinian Authority, and Tunisia. They are streamlined so as to be similar in substantive content, thereby establishing a template-like arrangement between each country and the EU.

Second: The Agadir Agreement

This *Agreement* is between the EU, on the one hand, and Egypt, Jordan, Morocco, and Tunisia, on the other hand. It bears some resemblance to the *Euro-Med Agreement*, and in effect constitutes a subset of them. However, the *Agadir Agreement* is structured to form the basis of an FTA among the four countries. Whether the EU plans to be part of this FTA is unclear.

Third: GCC FTA

This FTA, which the EU pursues, is a traditional one between the EU and GCC.

Given EU activism in the RTA field, American companies feel disadvantaged, and demand of their government a leveling of the competitive playing field.

Arguably, *MEFTA*, a vision President George W. Bush articulated in May 2003, and U.S. negotiations with the *SACU*, consisting of Botswana, Lesotho, Namibia, South Africa, and Swaziland, launched in 2003, are a response to this call, and thereby an effort to counter European economic (and, in turn, political) influence in the Islamic and developing world. To be sure, official U.S. rhetoric often casts RTAs as in the self-interest of poor countries. Seventy percent of the tariffs paid by developing countries are paid to other developing countries. Surely, then, the USTR does poor countries a favor by pushing a zero-tariff regime.

---

31. *Bilateral Trade Deals: A Dangerous Affair*, Financial Times, 27 July 2006, at 12.

Maybe, depending partly on whether those countries can offset the loss of tariff revenue with other sources of government funding, such as income taxes. Questions of structural reform aside, the fact is the job of the USTR is to promote American economic interests. An FTA with the U.S. is neither an entitlement nor an act of charity. It must (or ought to) be a net benefit to each party. As for American economic interests, they are a component of a larger foreign policy agenda. That is true for the EU. In the Mediterranean region, EU RTAs are motivated strongly by geo-political and economic factors, and EU trade policy has out run and out maneuvered U.S. trade policy.

Notably, the EU has an association agreement with Egypt. Under the EU-Egypt deal, Egypt is phasing out its tariffs on EU products over three, nine, 12, and 15 years (depending on the merchandise). Obviously, if and when fully implemented, this and other such accords will supplement the already considerable economic, and concomitant political, influence of the EU in the Arab world. The U.S. cannot remain idle.

American exporters would be disadvantaged if only their European competitors had duty-free market access to these regions. Likewise, U.S. producers needing inputs from these regions would face higher costs relative to foreign competitors if the competitors, but not them, could import inputs free of duty. One end result would be a diminution of political leverage in the Middle East relative to the EU. Political realists and energy strategists would point out the importance of such leverage, especially as China and India add themselves in the mix with the EU and U.S. as competitors for strategic resources held by some Middle Eastern nations — oil and natural gas.

A similar argument can be made with respect to U.S. negotiations with *SACU*, namely, that they are designed to counter economic (and, in turn, political) influence of the EU in this resource-rich part of the Third World. The EU and Asia heavily dominate the pattern of trade of Southern African countries, with *NAFTA* a distant third. The EU has long-standing preferential arrangements in place with most Sub-Saharan African countries, including the *Lomé* and *Cotonou Conventions*. In 1999, the EU and *SACU*, which is comprised of Botswana, Lesotho, Namibia, South Africa, and Swaziland, entered into an FTA — though the deal is not a comprehensive one.

Here, again, the U.S. cannot stand idly by. Aside from foreign policy benefits of a *SACU FTA*, there are potential economic benefits for the U.S. From *SACU*, the U.S. imports auto parts, diamonds, and platinum for catalytic converters. An FTA would introduce the discipline of rules of origin for such imports. U.S. exports to *SACU* have not grown much. An FTA might help boost exports. To be sure, the margin of preference would decline, because *SACU* members are reducing their tariffs, and incline toward free-trade orientation, as many of their exports are sold outside Southern Africa. The U.S. also might see greater access to services markets and enhanced IP protection. The latter point suggests consumers in *SACU* could be obligated to pay higher prices for IP products that their governments now allow them to buy at cheap prices, or even provide for free. In effect, they would pay the rents to U.S. IP holders, which the U.S. would regard as a condition for increased market access for *SACU* exports (especially T&A), and which would give the U.S. increased economic influence in *SACU*.

How would *SACU* benefit from an FTA with the U.S., especially if the U.S. does not maintain its July 2005 commitment to exercise flexibility in the negotiations? If *SACU* adroitly leverages negotiations with the EU and U.S., then it might win better market access concessions for agricultural and non-agricultural goods, and obtain reasonable provisions on IP protection, from both powers than it would have from isolated talks. An FTA with the U.S. also would be a hedge for *SACU* against expiration of the *AGOA*, the U.S. trade preference program for Sub-Saharan Africa.[32] Finally, *SACU* members would gain duty free access for T&A exports to the U.S. Such access would help them in view of the 31 December 2004 expiration of quotas under the 1974 *MFA*, pursuant to the 1995 WTO *ATC*. T&A exports from *SACU* to the U.S. were not quota-constrained, but MFA expiry meant the loss of guaranteed market access and competition with the likes of China and India.

In practice, however, whether *SACU* realizes the full potential of an FTA depends on two important questions. First, will *SACU* dedicate itself to internal reform, especially expanding its regime to include agriculture, services, and government procurement? American businesses have a keen interest in exporting farm products, and providing services, overseas. Yet, *SACU* provides duty-free treatment only for goods. That is, *SACU* is a common policy on industrial tariffs. If *SACU* as a group does not enlarge its regime, then the undesirable result may be hub-and-spoke arrangements with the U.S., with the U.S. at the hub, and specific spoke arrangements tailored for individual *SACU* members on agriculture and services. Also, American businesses are interested in bidding on government procurement projects abroad. Traditionally, *SACU* has shown a strong preference for doling out contracts to local suppliers in a non-transparent manner.

Second, will *SACU* build the institutional and legal capacity to follow through on its own commitments, and enforce obligations incumbent on the U.S.? Poor capacity is a great constraint on Sub-Saharan African development. Preferential rules of origin are just one illustration in which *SACU* will need an expanded cadre of trade lawyers. With the 1999 *EU-SACU FTA*, an accord between *SACU* and the *SADC*, and an FTA with the U.S., exporters and importers will need sound counsel on three different sets of origin rules to take advantage of duty free treatment.

These two questions are poignant in light of a theme emerging from some economic analyses, including by the World Bank, of the effects of the Uruguay Round on the Third World. That theme is most of the positive economic benefits from

---

32. *See* Gary G. Yerkey, *U.S., SACU Agree to Create "Framework" But Free Trade Agreement Now Longer Term*, 23 International Trade Reporter (BNA) 621–22 (20 April 2006).

the Round came from liberalization entered into by developing and least developed countries. In other words, internal reforms, not gains through greater exports, are the predominant source of benefits from a Round—and, by extension, an FTA.

Consider, too, trade coverage of the U.S. FTAs—with Canada and Mexico through *NAFTA*, most Central American countries via *CAFTA-DR*, and bilaterally with Australia, Bahrain, Chile, Israel, Morocco, Jordan, and Singapore. These FTAs cover roughly one-third of total American trade (mostly accounted for by *NAFTA*). The U.S. has pursued additional FTAs that would push the figure up to about half of its total trade. Query whether the strategy is to develop a two-tier structure whereby MFN rates apply to European products, and preferential rates apply to merchandise from the FTA partners. Lest the question sound preposterous, consider the fact the EU has done just that with respect to the U.S. The number of RTAs and preferential arrangements in which the EU is involved is so large the EU has MFN relations with only seven countries. That is, for imports into the EU, MFN rates apply only to goods from Australia, Canada, China, Japan, New Zealand, Taiwan, and the U.S. Goods from the rest of the world enter under an RTA or an assistance scheme for poor countries.

- **Competition from Canada**

America and Canada are each other's largest trading partners, and undoubtedly the closest of allies. Their healthy economic and security relationship does not prevent them from competing with each other for access to third country markets. Overall (as of October 2014), Canada has FTAs with 10 countries, and pursuing deals with more than 60 additional countries. Consider their respective trade relationships of Canada vis-à-vis the U.S. with Chile, Jordan, and the EU.

- **1997 *Canada-Chile FTA***

As another example of one trade power using an FTA to rebut another, consider competing relationships with Chile. In July 1997, an FTA between Canada and Chile took effect. In February 2003, a comprehensive FTA between the EU and Chile entered into force. The U.S. could not be left out, and in June 2003 signed an FTA with Chile.

Chile has a unified and uniform MFN tariff rate of 6%. U.S. exporters wanted to eliminate this duty on merchandise they shipped to Chile. They were losing market share to European and Canadian exporters. For example, Caterpillar, Inc., complained to the USTR that one of its machines imported into Chile was disadvantaged by about U.S. $13,000–14,000, relative to Canadian like products, because of the Chilean duty. The disadvantage also hurt Idaho potato farmers in their competition with Canadians to export their merchandise—used, of course, in French fries—to Chile.

However, query whether such FTAs may be of diminishing value, as Chile reduces its MFN duties from 6% to zero (akin to Singapore). That would erode the margin of preference enjoyed by its FTA partners. Interestingly, Panama also fits the pattern, but in reverse direction: the U.S. FTA with that country took effect in March 2012, and Canada followed suit. In December 2012, its Parliament approved an FTA with the Central American country.

- **June 2012** *Canada-Jordan FTA*

Jordan offers another example, but in reverse order. Canada followed the U.S. with an FTA with Jordan. The American deal took effect on 17 December 2001. The Canadian Parliament gave final approval to implementing legislation on 29 June 2012, and it entered into force on 1 October 2012, marking Canada's first FTA with an Arab country and second FTA in the Middle East.

The *Canada-Jordan FTA*, which has side agreements on environmental and labor issues, eliminated tariffs on virtually all Canadian exports to Jordan. Canadian agricultural, forestry, and machinery producers, in particular, were delighted not only by the transparent, rules-based framework created by the FTA, but also by the end to over a decade in which their American counterparts, but not them, received preferential treatment from Jordan.

- **September 2017** *Canada-EU FTA*

On 18 October 2013, Canada and the EU completed negotiations they launched in 2009 on an FTA, and after overcoming opposition from Wallonia (the French-speaking part of Belgium), signed it three years later.[33] Their deal, formally called the *"Comprehensive Economic and Trade Agreement,"* or *"CETA,"* took effect on 21 September 2017.[34] On that day, roughly 98% of trade in goods between Canada and the EU became duty free:

> Timber, salmon and maple syrup are now expected to flow from Canada to Europe, and Italian cheese, German machines and Swedish fashion should rush to the Maple Leaf country.

> Canada's duty-free export of goods to the EU will rise from 25 percent to 98 percent of EU tariff lines. One additional percent will be eliminated during a seven-year period. Canada proudly proclaimed its exporters would gain advantages over other exporters, including Americans, on the EU market of 510 million people.

> And similarly, European exporters will save about 590 million euros per year in customs duties as 98 percent of Canada's duties are removed.[35]

---

33. *See* Editorial Board, *Free Trade's Bleak Outlook*, BLOOMBERG, 1 November 2016, https://www.bloomberg.com/view/articles/2016-11-01/free-trade-s-bleak-outlook; Joe Kirwin & Peter Menyasz, *Comprehensive Canada-EU FTA Finalized, May Serve as EU Template for TTIP Talks*, 30 International Trade Reporter (BNA) 1627 (24 October 2013); Joe Kirwin, *EU, Canada Expected to Sign Trade Deal After Breakthrough on Agriculture Issues*, 30 International Trade Reporter (BNA) 1642 (24 October 2013); Joshua Chaffin, *EU and Canada Close to Trade Accord After Compromise on Farm Exports*, FINANCIAL TIMES, 18 October 2013, at 4.

34. Certain provisions, such as ISDS, took effect later after ratification by each EU state.

35. Bengt Ljung, *EU-Canada Deal in Force, Showing World Leadership Role*, 34 International Trade Reporter (BNA) 1288 (28 September 2017).

Unsurprisingly, *CETA* is considered the most ambitious FTA in the world among developed countries. Their 1,600-page accord also was touted as a model for *T-TIP*, an FTA the U.S. and EU began negotiating in summer 2013, but abandoned with the November 2016 election to the Presidency of Donald J. Trump.

That Canada started and finished an accord with Europe before America was a boon to its exporters vis-à-vis their American competitors. For American trade policy, that Canada secured its deal was a strategic political economy defeat. Canada seemed to have a vision, and willingness and ability to implement it, which America lacked. As a result, Canadian—not American—exporters had preferential access to the largest 2 markets in the world, the EU and U.S. Succinctly put, with *NAFTA* alone, Canadian exporters had preferential access to 27.5% of the global economy. With *CETA* plus *NAFTA*, that figure jumped to 53.1%.

The hallmarks of *CETA* are:

(1) Market Access for Industrial Goods—

Effective immediately (*i.e.*, the date of the entry into force of *CETA*), 98% of all tariffs were eliminated. That contrasted with elimination of 29% of all tariffs on the first day *NAFTA* took effect.

In specific, all industrial tariffs were eliminated. For the EU, that meant it dropped previously significant, even prohibitively, high tariffs on certain items to zero. Such items included aluminum and aluminum products, nickel and nickel products, non-ferrous metals, iron, and steel, as well as its 10% duty on cars.

(2) Market Access for Agricultural Goods—

Before *CETA* took effect, only 18% of agricultural products traded between Canada and the EU received duty-free treatment. But, with *CETA*, tariffs on 95% of all agricultural products were eliminated immediately. So, for example, Canada could ship live cattle, or processed beef products, duty free. Here, too, that meant the EU dropped previously prohibitively high tariffs on some goods to zero.

CETA contains special rules to recognize Canada's historic Supply Management Systems for farm products, except for the schemes for eggs, poultry, and certain dairy products (discussed below).

CETA also contains special provisions for agricultural products like chocolates, cat and dog food, and sugar confectionaries, which contain a high percentage of foreign inputs.

(3) Market Access in Fisheries Sector—

Both Canada and the EU have significant seafood producer-exporting industries. The two sides agreed to eliminate 95% of all tariffs on seafood products effective immediately. That meant the EU dropped from 25% to zero the duties it had imposed on seafood imports. For some items, such as cooked and peeled cods and shrimp, *CETA* applied transitional quotas before full liberalization.

CETA also recognized for some products, the Canadian and American seafood industries are integrated. So, on lobster, shrimp, salmon, and certain other items harvested in the U.S. but processed in Canada, *CETA* has flexible ROOs. That represented a concession by the EU, as did its agreement to cease end-use restrictions. Such restrictions had barred come Canadian branded seafood products from retail sale in the EU.

Under *CETA*, the right of Canada and the EU to regulate their seafood industry is protected, and each side cooperates on regulatory matters with a view to avoiding unnecessary TBTs.

(4) Market Access in Automobile Sector—

For automobiles, the 7% Canadian and 10% European tariff is eliminated over seven years.

For automobiles, origin is conferred with 50% Canadian content during the first seven years of *CETA* (matching the tariff phase-out period). Thereafter, the Regional Value Content is 55%. This RVC rule of origin for autos is important, because it means the EU recognizes that the Canadian auto industry is an integrated one, *i.e.*, integrated with Mexico and the U.S. To have insisted on a 100% RVC would have been impossible for Canada, given the integrated North American auto market.

Moreover, the EU agreed to duty-free export of up to 100,000 vehicles annually with a Canadian content of as low as 20%. This quota is large, because when the two sides signed *CETA*, Canadian vehicle exports to the EU were just 8,000–10,000 annually. *CETA* also contains an Annex on 17 automotive standards, in part to ensure these measures do not operate as NTBs.

(5) Preferential ROOs—

The EU agreed Canadian products it requires to be certified could be certified in Canada. Consequently, Canadian exporters could save costs by not having to certify in Europe that their product is of Canadian origin. The Scotch Whisky Association raised a glass: no longer would bulk imports of spirits that are bottled outside Canada need to add a minimum 1% of Canadian content. They would qualify, without the addition, for DFQF treatment in the *CETA* zone.

(6) NTBs (Including TBT and SPS Measures)—

CETA created a Working Group to ensure that regulatory and SPS measures are based on science. Such measures may cover biotechnology and products with small amounts of GMOs. Indeed, the EU maintained its ban on hormone-treated beef. *CETA* Overall, SPS protections are more expansive than those in *NAFTA* and other Canadian FTAs.

(7) Market Access for Services—

Overall, *CETA* liberalized 70% of services trade, including for maritime services. It uses a Negative List approach, a concession by the EU: never before had it agreed to this approach in services. So, unless specifically exempted, a services sector is subject to market access concessions and national treatment disciplines under *CETA*. Those concessions include Mode IV delivery, temporary entry of businesspersons. For example, such migration is permitted for post-sales maintenance services, and for provision of services for mutual recognition of licensing and qualifications. Indeed, under *CETA*, architecture and engineering professional services have nearly joint standards.

CETA also has a ratcheting rule. Under it, any services trade concession Canada or the EU grants to a third party in a post-*CETA* deal automatically is incorporated into *CETA*. That way, services trade liberalization ratchets up, or keeps pace with, the best of market access treatment in new FTAs into which the parties might enter.

(8) Market Access for Government Procurement—

Canadian and European providers of goods to governments enjoy relatively unfettered access to procurement opportunities of each other's central and sub-central governments. So, for example, the EU must treat Canadian firms as it does European ones for procurements by the Union, any of the 28 national governments, or any sub-national bodies. The Canadian Federal and Provincial governments must do the same for European firms.

CETA allows each side to maintain local bidder ("Buy Canadian" or "Buy European") preferences for procurement contracts below specified threshold levels. Arguably, those thresholds are higher than ideal from a free trade perspective. *CETA* also allows each side to set environmental and social criteria for obtaining a contract.

(9) FDI—

FDI rules are liberalized. *CETA* gives investor protections to all Canadian and EU investors, for example, against discrimination and expropriation. That fact represented a concession by the EU, which in no previous trade treaty had granted FDI protections on a Union-wide basis. To hear complaints of investors against host governments, *CETA* also created a dispute settlement mechanism with faster procedures, and better checks against frivolous claims, than *NAFTA* Chapter 11. Known as an Investment Court System (ICS), the mechanism is a permanent adjudicatory body with a supporting secretariat, rather than an *ad hoc* ISDS scheme.[36] While MNCs

---

36. ISDS decisions take four years on average, plus an additional two years if there is an appeal (known as an "annulment"), and considerable time and money is spent by each side trying to

prefer ISDS, because they can choose their arbitrators, the EU argued SMEs support the ICS.

Canada successfully preserved its right to apply the *Investment Canada Act*, including the "Net Benefit to Canada Test" associated with the *Act*, to FDI from Europe. But, the threshold for review under the *Act* for EU investors is Canadian $ 1.5 billion, whereas it is Canadian $1 billion for FDI from other countries. Hence, American investors face a lower threshold trigger for review than do their European competitors.

In specific sectors, *CETA* essentially manages FDI. For example, in energy, the EU can invest in some areas, but others are subject to Canadian reservations. In contrast, in uranium, *CETA* eliminated the JV requirement (which remains for non-EU firms) that a EU firm invest with a Canadian partner. In telecommunications, Canada refused to expand access to foreign carriers, but did agree not to freeze its current restrictions (by moving them from "Annex II" to "Annex I" reservations).

(10) GIs—

CETA protects GIs, but via an interesting compromise. The EU was far keener than Canada to protect GIs, which is unsurprising given its higher profile GI-branded products.

Any product already available on the Canadian market as of the entry into force of *CETA* is exempt from the GI rules. But, any new product must abide by them by using qualifying language for its labels and marketing like "style" or "type." So, for example, a Canadian-made Champagne beverage, or feta cheese, must use a qualifier if it was not grandfathered by virtue of its pre-*CETA* commercial availability.

(11) Labor and Environmental Issues—

Separate Annexes in *CETA* cover labor and the environment. The Environmental Annex, coupled with other provisions, ensure Canada and the EU can issue regulations in the public interest and for environmental protection, and retain control over their natural resource development.

(12) Culture and Values—

CETA contains several provisions that address cultural concerns shared by, or particular to, Canada and the EU. For example, it has an Annex concerning sustainable development. And, via specific provisions, the sides have exempted certain sectors from *CETA* coverage, as Canada did with respect to education and public health care.

---

knock out the arbitrators selected by the other side. *See* Bengt Ljung, *EU, Canada to Launch Investor Protection Court Proposal*, 33 International Trade Reporter (BNA) 1781 (15 December 2016).

(13) Breakthrough on Agriculture—

Negotiations over two sectors, agriculture and IP, caused negotiations to stall for nearly a year across 2012 and 2013. But, the two sides achieved a simple breakthrough on each sensitive topic in October 2013.

On agriculture, Canada agreed to grant European cheese producers greater market access. At issue was whether the EU would agree all Canadian dairy products would remain covered by Canada's long-standing SMS? Both the Canadian and European markets for dairy products are highly protected, and both sides have significant dairy product industries. Canada wanted as full access as possible to the vastly larger European market.

Ultimately, the EU acquiesced, agreeing Canada could keep its SMS for dairy products, except for cheese and dairy protein concentrates. The EU refused to acknowledge the Systems for those items. But, the EU agreed to limit exports to Canada of European cheese to 16,000 tons, and 1,000 tons of industrial cheese, annually. These limits were in addition to the 800-ton country-specific share the EU enjoyed under the Canadian global cheese import quota scheme. (Put differently, the EU got about 17,000 additional tons of market access into Canada for European cheeses, and both sides agreed on what types of cheese qualify as "new entrants" within the 30% cheese quota Canada imposed.[37]) Canada pledged compensation to its cheese producers should they suffer injury from European competition.

---

37. The details of the Canadian concessions to the EU in SMS sectors—specifically milk and cheese—for *CETA* were as follows. Canada agreed to allow 180 million liters of milk and 17,700 tons of cheese (including 16,000 tons of fine cheese), to come from the EU. Further, with respect to milk, Canada agreed to a gradual elimination of tariffs on protein concentrates. And, with respect to cheese, Canada agreed to reserve for the EU additional special access in the annual overall 20,400-ton quota Canada already offered to its trading partners, namely, an increase by 800 tons in the EU-specific access from 13,400 tons that the EU had and was using for its cheese exports to Canada. *See* Les Producteurs de Lait de Québec, *Comprehensive Economic and Trade Agreement (CETA) with the European Union—Impacts and Prospects for the Dairy Sector*, 4 March 2015, http://lait.org/wp-content/uploads/2015/03/4_CETA_Impacts-and-prospects-for-the-dairy-sector.pdf; Stuart Clark, *Food in the Canada-EU Comprehensive Economic Trade Agreement in Principle (CETA)*, November 2013, https://foodsecurecanada.org/sites/foodsecurecanada.org/files/agfoodceta_clark_nov13.pdf.

Canadian dairy farmers anticipated a loss of $150 million in income, equal to the annual output of 365 farms, because of the milk that no longer would be produced or processed in Canada. Thanks to the cheese concession, they anticipated that the percentage of foreign cheese in the Canadian market would rise from 5% to 9% of total Canadian cheese consumption. (Canada had been importing about 21,000 tons of cheese, and with *CETA*, the EU was set to ship Canada an additional 18,500 tons.) Thanks also to the cheese concession, they foresaw capture of up to 30% of the retail fine cheese market (which was 50,000 tons, or 90,000 tons including institutional buyers) by shipments from the EU, with Quebec farmers especially hard hit, as they produce over 50% of Canada's cheese (and over 60% of its fine cheese). Canadian farmers argued the SMS protects them against EU CAP subsidies (discussed in a separate Chapter) that are decoupled from production. *See id.*

In return, the EU agreed to give Canadian beef and pork exports better market access. In specific, the EU established annual quotas for these products: 50,000 tons for beef, in addition to the pre-*CETA* quota of 15,000 tons; and 75,000 tons for pork, in addition to the pre-*CETA* 6,000 tons. The EU also opened its markets to processed pork products.

Essentially, the sides did a cheese-for-beef and pork swap. Canada got better but not unrestricted free trade access to the European market, and got to keep some, but not all, of its supply management protections. In effect, the swap was managed trade in the cheese, beef, and pork markets.

(14) Breakthrough on IP—

IP, the EU wanted Canada to change its policies on prescription pharmaceuticals. It refused, agreeing only to lock them in. But, Canada said it would provide EU pharmaceutical companies with the protection they sought for patents on medicines: they could get an extra two years of patent protection, and would have a right of appeal under procedures more efficient than in patent challenge cases. Canada anticipated this concession (extended patent protection for prescription medication) would cost its provincial-based Canadian health care system after 8 years of *CETA* operation (because the provinces could not switch to generics for an additional two years). Therefore, the Federal government agreed to compensate provinces for the costs.

Additionally, Canada agreed to an EU-style scheme for extending the term of a pharmaceutical patent if there are delays associated with the regulatory approval for that patent. Like the EU, Canada will issue a "Certificate of Supplementary Protection" (CSP) if it takes more than five years from the date of filing a pharmaceutical patent to get regulatory approval to market the pharmaceutical. The extension is calculated by (1) computing the time between the filing date and sale authorization date, and (2) subtracting from that time five years. There is a two-year cap on any extension, though the EU hoped for a five-year cap (*i.e.*, a higher maximum limit, which would have favored drug producers).

Canada and the EU touted *CETA* as a "21st century, gold standard agreement."[38] That was the same phrase America enjoyed applying to both *TPP* and *T-TIP*.

Insofar as *CETA* was a template for *T-TIP*, that meant the EU could use it as leverage against Canada, particularly on issues of importance to Europe, like market access for government procurement (which the U.S. is chary of opening completely) and maritime services (which the U.S. wants to keep closed in respect of cabotage),

---

38. *See* Joe Kirwin & Peter Menyasz, *Comprehensive Canada—EU FTA Finalized, May Serve as EU Template for TTIP Talks*, 30 International Trade Reporter (BNA) 1627 (24 October 2013) (*quoting* the 18 October 2013 joint statement of Canadian Prime Minister Stephen Harper and European Commission President José Manuel Barroso).

and protection for GIs (which the EU seeks). And, so it did: as of October 2016, thanks to EU concerns about *CETA* provisions on FDI, labor and environmental, the EU called on Canada to (at least) enter into "formal clarifications," namely, "interpretative declarations" as to what each side intended, on them. (Re-opening the text to negotiations was out of the question, said Canada.) Might *CETA* be a precursor to *T-TIP*? It is designed as a stand-alone FTA, with no Suspension Clause. But, *CETA* does have Review Clauses to allow for it to be reconsidered if the U.S. and EU agree to a *T-TIP*.

All 28 EU countries, plus the European Parliament, ratified *CETA*, as did all 10 Canadian provincial governments and the Federal Parliament in Ottawa.[39] (No ratification was required of the 3 Canadian territories.) So, *CETA* took effect in 2017.

- **April 2018 Revised *Mexico-EU FTA***

In April 2018, after negotiations that started in May 2016, the EU reached an agreement in principle with Mexico to update expand their 21-year-old FTA beyond coverage of only industrial products.[40] In 1997, Mexico was the first Latin country to sign an FTA with the EU, and that deal took effect in 2000. (The 1997 deal was a "Global Cooperation" accord, the full title of which was the "*Economic Partnership, Political Coordination and Cooperation Agreement*." Mexico and the EU left the *Global Cooperation Agreement* intact, but broadened and deepened its parts that governed trade.) By 2018, Mexico was more than happy to diversify its export destinations away from the U.S. The Administration of President Donald J. Trump catalyzed controversial *NAFTA* renegotiations in August 2017, with threats of withdrawing from the deal if it Mexico (and Canada) failed to acquiesce to its demands. With 80% of its exports destined for the U.S., Mexico sensed its vulnerability, and the EU saw an opportunity: its firms could obtain DFQF access to the Mexican market, and via *CETA* (discussed elsewhere), to the Canadian market, too. That would put American producer-exporters at a competitive disadvantage, as they

---

39. Ratification by the Canadian House of Commons and European Parliament occurred in February 2017.

Note that under the Canadian Constitution, the Federal government has exclusive jurisdiction over international trade. But, some provisions of international trade agreements, like *CETA*, cover matters under provincial jurisdiction. Astutely, Canada included provincial representatives on its negotiating team, giving them access to information, and consulting with them while talking with the EU.

Note also *CETA* Article 20:28 concerns patent linkage, and guarantees "equivalent and effective rights of appeal" to all parties (typically, a drug patent holder versus a firm seeking approval to market a generic version of that drug, with the issue being whether the patent is valid or the generic infringes on the patent) in patent linkage disputes.

40. *See* FratiniVergano European Lawyers, *The EU and Mexico Reach an Agreement in Principle to Update their Existing Trade Agreement*, TRADE PERSPECTIVES, issue 9, 4 May 2018 (hereinafter, FratiniVergano); Philip Blenkinsop, *EU and Mexico Agree New Free Trade Pact*, REUTERS, 21 April 2018, www.reuters.com/article/us-eu-mexico-trade/eu-and-mexico-agree-new-free-trade-pact-idUSKBN1HS0PF. The EU and Mexico pledged to have a final text of their revised FTA by year-end 2018. *See id.*

would have at most *NAFTA* DFQF access, but not to the EU market, whereas Mexican and Canadian firms would enjoy such access to both the U.S. and EU.

The scope of the amended *Global Cooperation Agreement* was ambitious. Nearly all EU-Mexican trade would be DFQF, including Mexican exports like asparagus, chicken, egg white albumin, fruit (*e.g.*, apples and bananas), honey, orange juice, and tuna, and EU exports like dairy and pork products. So, for example, Mexico cut its tariffs, which were 45%, on Gorgonzola and Roquefort cheese, and likewise its 50% tariff on milk powder, 30% tariff on chocolates, and 20% tariff on pasta.[41] Previously, only 62% of total EU-Mexican farm trade was DFQF. Under the new arrangement, just a handful of sensitive sectors carried through from the old version of the FTA—cereals, dairy, meat, sugar, and certain food and processed agricultural products. The old deal had called for even them to be DFQF by 2003, but the two sides settled for TRQs. Under the new deal, over 85% of agricultural tariff lines were DFQF, including dairy and meat, as well as food and processed agricultural products.

Liberalizing trade in beef proved controversial, but again Mexico and the EU agreed on a TRQ:

> Mexico obtained increased market access with partial liberalisation and TRQs for beef and beef offal (10,000 metric tonnes each with a 7.5% duty phased-in over five years). Concessions for Mexican beef have been a key point of disagreement and an important concern for EU producers. *Interbev*, the French National Interprofessional Association of Livestock and Meat, underlined its concerns regarding the concessions offered to Mexican beef to access the EU market. In particular, *Interbev* claimed that Mexican beef is not produced under the same sanitary standards as EU beef, allowing Mexican producers to sell their products at lower prices and leading to unfair competition. . . . [T]he EU European farmers and agri-cooperatives associations *Copa-Cogeca* welcomed the agreement between the EU and Mexico, stating that it was a good and balanced trade agreement. However, *Copa-Cogeca* regrets the increased access offered to Mexican beef to enter the EU market, noting that *"an import quota of 10,000 tonnes of beef is 10,000 tonnes too much."*[42]

Notably, save for ethanol and sugar, which also subject to TRQs, no farm sector was exempt from liberalization. (The EU conceded an ethanol TRQ with DFQF access for 25,000 metric tons, phased in across five years, and a 30,000 metric ton TRQ for

---

41. Jorge Valero, *Mexico Wins "Cheese War" Over Europe in Trade Deal*, EURACTIV, 25 April 2018, http://bilaterals.org/?mexico-wins-cheese-war-over-europe. [Hereinafter, *Mexico Wins*.] For some products, DFQF treatment was subject to a TRQ: fresh cheese was subject to an annual cap of 5,000 tons, and other types of cheese to a cap of 20,000 tons.; milk powder was limited to 30,000 tons upon EIF, rising to 50,000 in five years. *See id.*

42. *Quoted in* FratiniVergano.

raw sugar for refining, at a preferential specific duty rate of € 49.00 per metric ton, phased in over three years.)

Beyond coverage of farm products, the new trade provisions in the *Global Cooperation Agreement* covered ROOs on autos. Up to 45% of the value of a car or other vehicle may come from non-originating materials. The new deal also provided for services, FDI (notably, a pledge to create a Multilateral Investment Court). And, dealt with GIs, which proved contentious on a product-by-product basis:

> The EU succeeded in obtaining exclusive rights for 340 products with a geographical indication, including Comté cheese (France) and Queijo Sao Jorge (Portugal). As a result, only the EU products will be allowed to be sold under the same name.
>
> But Europe did not gain the same protection for Spain's La Mancha [region] farmers to use Manchego [cheese], which has protected geographical status in the EU.
>
> Mexican manchego represents almost 15% of the total cheese sales in Mexico, a precious label to give away.
>
> But while Mexican manchego is produced by using cows' milk, Spain's Manchego uses milk produced by ewes [sheep] of manchega breed. The Mexican cheese takes around one week to produce it, Spain's Manchego could take more than two months.
>
> Farmers in La Mancha argue that this gives a special quality that it is also reflected in the price. In the US, where both products fight tooth and nail to attract consumers, Manchego costs around $14 dollars per pound, double the price of the Mexican product.
>
> As part of the deal, Mexico will have to clearly indicate that their manchego cheese has no relation with the protected EU indication [*i.e.*, the "*manchego*" cheese from Spain's La Mancha region made from sheep milk], and their farmers could use only cows' milk.[43]

The new FTA also facilitated trade by simplifying customs procedures for machinery, pharmaceuticals, and transport equipment. It also opened government goods and services procurement: Mexican companies could bid on EU government contracts (including with respect to utilities), and EU companies could bid on federal-level tenders (such as for the Mexico City international airport).

The new *Global Cooperation Agreement* had Chapters on "Animal Welfare and Antimicrobial Resistance" (with rules on cooperation, exchange of information, and mutual recognition) and "Trade and Sustainable Development" (which the EU made standard in its new trade deals), and pro-labor and pro-environment provisions. The new *Agreement* was the first EU trade deal with anti-corruption obligations, namely, a commitment by the EU and Mexico to adhere to *UNCAC*.

---

43. *Mexico Wins.*

- Taking Aim at China in *NAFTA* 2.0?

Manifestly, an FTA with three Parties cannot be as economically vibrant as another FTA with the same three Parties, containing substantially the same terms, that also has nine other Parties. That first FTA is the *USMCA*. That other FTA is *TPP*, from which America infamously withdrew in January 2017. The trilateral *NAFTA* 2.0 affords fewer production and consumption opportunities than *TPP*, whose Parties include Japan and Vietnam, the world's third largest economy, and one of the biggest emerging markets, respectively. As a strategic matter, *TPP*, the Parties to which also include loyal American allies such as Australia and Singapore, played a role in questioning, if not containing, the rise of a CCP-run China across the Asia-Pacific.

That said, consider Article 32:10 of *NAFTA* 2.0:

Article 32:10: Non-Market Country FTA

1. At least 3 months prior to commencing negotiations, a Party shall inform the other Parties of its intention to commence free trade agreement negotiations with a non-market country. For purposes of this Article, a non-market country is a country that on the date of signature of this agreement at least one Party has determined to be a non-market economy for purposes of its trade remedy laws and is a country with which no Party has a free trade agreement.

2. Upon request, the Party shall provide as much information as possible regarding the objectives for those negotiations.

3. As early as possible, and no later than 30 days before the date of signature, that Party shall provide the other Parties with an opportunity to review the full text of the agreement, including any annexes and side instruments, in order for the Parties to be able to review the agreement and assess its potential impact on this Agreement. If the Party involved requests that the text be treated as confidential, the other Parties shall maintain the confidentiality of the text.

4. Entry by any Party into a free trade agreement with a non-market country, shall allow the other Parties to terminate this Agreement on six-month notice and replace this Agreement with an agreement as between them (bilateral agreement).

5. The bilateral agreement shall be comprised of all the provisions of this Agreement, except those provisions the relevant Parties decide are not applicable as between them.

6. The relevant Parties shall utilize the six-month notice period to review the Agreement and determine whether any amendments should be made in order to ensure the proper operation of the bilateral agreement.

7. The bilateral agreement enter into force 60 days after the date on which the parties to the bilateral agreement have notified each other that they have completed their respective applicable legal procedures.

Consider, first, Article 32:10 from the vantage point of American economic self-interest. Is the provision simply an effort by the U.S. to ensure China does not use Canada or Mexico as a back-door into the American market, by setting up a bilateral FTA with either or both of them, shipping merchandise to them that satisfies the ROOs of that bilateral FTA, and of *NAFTA* 2.0 as well, and thus getting DFQF treatment into the U.S.?[44]

However, consider, second what national security policy might explain Article 32:10? Is it an American effort to isolate (dare it be said, contain) China? This Article, which is without precedent in any of America's FTAs, is a deterrence — but not an outright block — to Canada, Mexico, or the U.S. forging an FTA with China. That America would do so was quite unlikely, particularly in the context of the Section 301 Sino-American Trade War, which raged for much of the period in which the U.S. negotiated *NAFTA* 2.0, and beyond. That Canada and Mexico might do so was improbable, but possible. Canada considered it, starting talks with China in 2016, but apparently was turned off by the refusal of the CCP to incorporate social clauses concerning labor rights, and rights for women and LGBTQ+ persons (discussed in a separate Chapter). To be sure, both Canada and Mexico had an FTA with an NME, namely, *CPTPP*, which includes Vietnam. But, that deal pre-dated *NAFTA* 2.0, so the target of Article 32:10 surely was China.

Does Article 32:10 infringe on the sovereignty of Canada and Mexico to chart their own international economic policies with respect to FTAs, independent of the U.S.? Or, is the provision symbolic, because *NAFTA* 2.0 gives any Party the right to withdraw on six-months' notice? After all, Article 34:6(1) of the *USMCA* says:

> A Party may withdraw from this Agreement by providing written notice of withdrawal to the other Parties. A withdrawal shall take effect six months after a Party provides written notice to the other Parties. If a Party withdraws, the Agreement shall remain in force for the remaining Parties.

No reason need be given for withdrawal, hence (for example), the U.S. could trigger Article 34:6 if Canada or Mexico enters into an FTA with China, notwithstanding Article 32:10. Likewise, is Article 32:10 time-bound, in that it lapses whenever China is recognized as a market economy?

· **Competition from Japan**

Yet another example of competition for FTAs among major trading nations is a dramatic alteration by Japan of its historic and exclusive emphasis on multilateralism. In the late 1990s, Japan began to explore, both informally and formally, FTAs. In 2002, Japan and *ASEAN* signed a "Comprehensive Partnership." Japan has a keen interest building with *ASEAN* an *East Asian FTA* (*EAFTA*), which would link it with China, (including Hong Kong), Korea, and Taiwan — and, possibly, Australia, New

---

44. *See* David Lawder, *Trade Pact Clause Seen Deterring China Trade Deal with Canada, Mexico,* REUTERS, 2 October 2018.

Zealand, and India.[45] Surely, Japan took note of the lack of progress toward an FTA with the U.S., coupled with U.S. pursuit of deals with countries other than Japan. In April 2006, Japan proposed creation of an East Asian economic and trade area that would easily rival the sizes of *NAFTA* and EU by embracing 16 East Asian countries, including all 10 members of *ASEAN*, thereby covering about one half of the global population.[46] These efforts have led to FTAs between Japan and Singapore, Malaysia, the Philippines, and Thailand.

Significantly, in May 2007, Japan reached a basic FTA with *ASEAN*, which the countries signed in November of that year.[47] Under the *ASEAN-Japan EPA*, Japan agreed to eliminate tariffs on 92% of ASEAN goods. However, it excluded rice, sugar, and other sensitive agricultural products. The *ASEAN* nations, except for the four newest and poorest ones—Burma (Myanmar), Cambodia, Laos, and Vietnam— agreed to eliminate tariffs on 90% of imports from Japan within 10 years. Vietnam pledged to do so within 10–15 years, and Burma, Cambodia, and Laos promised to phase out the tariffs on a 15-year schedule. The *EPA* modifies preferential rules of origin to stimulate intra-*ASEAN* trade and investment by qualifying traded components as originating. Suppose a Japanese manufacturer exports and processes an industrial part to Thailand, and then exports the processed product to Malaysia. Before the *EPA*, Malaysia deemed the finished good originating outside *ASEAN*. With the *EPA*, Malaysia counts it as originating in the bloc, subjecting it to the intra-*ASEAN* duty rate of zero to 5%.

Most notably, in respect of competitive imperialism, the *ASEAN-Japan EPA* is an FTA with 650 million people—larger than either *NAFTA* or the EU. The fact Japan excludes intentionally the U.S. is testament to its competition with the U.S., and perhaps also to America's declining influence in East Asia. Indeed, Japan explicitly seeks to enlarge the *EPA* to include China and Korea, which would result in a massive counterweight to the U.S., *NAFTA*, and EU. Interestingly, the *EPA* also spotlights Sino-Japanese competition. In 2006, for the first time since the Second World War, China (excluding Hong Kong) overtook the U.S. as Japan's largest trading partner.[48] (With Hong Kong counted, China did so in 2004.) The trade is diversified, with China exporting to Japan clothes, computers, and certain electronics, and Japan sending China communications equipment, other types of electronics, and organic compounds. But, Japan could not watch China deepen its integration

---

45. *See* Jonathan Hopfner, *ASEAN Ministers Cool to Japanese Proposal To Begin Studying Regional Free Trade Zone*, 23 International Trade Reporter (BNA) 1297–98 (7 September 2006).

46. *See* Toshio Aritake, *Japan to Propose Economic, Trade Area to Rival NAFTA, European Union*, 23 International Trade Reporter (BNA) 572 (13 April 2006).

47. *See* Toshio Aritake, Japan, *ASEAN Strike "Basic" Free Trade Deal to Abolish 90 Percent of Tariffs in 10 Years*, 24 International Trade Reporter (BNA) 650 (10 May 2007).

48. *See* Toshio Aritake, *China Overtakes U.S. as Japan's Top Trade Partner in Fiscal 2006*, 24 International Trade Reporter (BNA) 624 (3 May 2007); Michiyo Nakamoto, *China Overtakes U.S. in Trade with Japan*, FINANCIAL TIMES, 26 April 2007, at 5.

with *ASEAN*, and obtain preferential access through a possible FTA with *ASEAN*, without seeking that same access.

Also significant is the fact Japan's FTA strategy is global. Japan has a bilateral economic partnership agreement with Mexico. In September 2006, Japan and Chile agreed to a framework for an FTA that would eliminate tariffs on most products, covering 92% of bilateral trade (by value), with the notable exception of agriculture, over 10 years.[49] Also that month, Japan commenced FTA negotiations with the GCC.[50] Japan obtains all of its crude oil from abroad, 75% of which comes from the GCC. It also exports a sizeable volume of industrial products, including autos, appliances, and electronics, to the GCC. The outlines of a deal were apparent: Japan could abolish its tariffs on crude oil, as well as refined oil products, and the GCC could eliminate the 5%–10% tariffs it levies on Japanese products.

The Philippine deal, inked in September 2006 after negotiations started in February 2004, is commercially noteworthy for its coverage and treatment of sensitive sectors and immigration. Upon entry into force, the *Japan-Philippines FTA* immediately lifted duties on 97% of Japanese exports to the Philippines, including apples, grapes, pears, and other fruit, and 60% of Japanese steel imports. It cut to zero immediately duties on 92% of Philippine exports to Japan—a significant boon to Japanese companies, for which the Philippines is a manufacturing hub for semifinished goods. Those companies make electrical products and machinery in the Philippines, and then export them to Japan (or third countries) for further work. The *FTA* gave Japan 10 years to phase out tariffs on Philippine bananas, and allowed Japan to set a tariff-free quota for pineapples of 1,000 tons annually (growing to 1,800 tons in 5 years). The *FTA* also gave Japan five years to eliminate duties on tuna and bonito fish, and cut tariffs and set low-tariff quotas on chickens and sugar. The Philippines retained until 2010 its 30% tariff on vehicles with an engine size of 3 liters or less, with renegotiations on the rate in 2009, but had to eliminate duties on larger engine sized-vehicles by 2010. The Philippines can send laborers to Japan, including an initial number of 1,000 nursing care assistants.

Japan also skillfully played both the U.S. and EU in its FTA policy. With the U.S., Japan declared in spring 2012 that it sought to join *TPP* negotiations. From the EU, Japan received an offer in July 2012 to launch FTA talks, which if successful would yield the biggest bilateral trade deal in the world.

- **Competition from China**

The CCP does not like to see China portrayed as an imperialist power. If anything, the historical origins of the CCP, dating to the early 20th century, and its

49. Toshio Aritake, *Japan, Chile Reach Framework For FTA on 92 Percent of Goods*, 23 International Trade Reporter (BNA) 1411–12 (28 September 2006).

50. *See Japan, UAE to Try Speed Up EPA with GCC*, 24 International Trade Reporter (BNA) 632 (3 May 2007); *Japan, GCC To Hold First FTA Meeting This Week*, Khaleej Times (UAE), 20 September 2006, at 49.

record for much of that century, are avowedly anti-imperialistic. Yet, the as a major trading power, China has interests around the globe. One example is its pursuit of trade and investment agreements with resource-rich African countries. Such deals have provoked the accusation of imperialistic behavior.

Might another example be competition for FTAs with the U.S.? By December 2011, China had concluded no less than 15 FTAs, a figure that was up from zero about a decade earlier. Those FTAs included ones with *ASEAN* (2002), Hong Kong (2002), Macau (2003), Thailand (2003), Niger (2005), Chile (2006), Pakistan (2006), New Zealand (2008), Peru (2008), Singapore (2008), and Costa Rica (2010). Manifestly, there is overlap with countries with which the U.S. also has an FTA. Further, in June 2010, China signed a dramatic *ECFA* with a traditional arch-rival, Taiwan.

So, countering China sometimes impels U.S. trade policy proposals. In 1993, China announced its desire to join *ASEAN*, including the *ASEAN FTA*, also called "*AFTA*." Fearing American dominance, *ASEAN* excludes the U.S. In 2002, China came to an accord on *ASEAN* and *AFTA* membership. President George W. Bush reacted with an "Enterprise for *ASEAN* Initiative." Yet, the "EAI" has been ineffectual.

• **Who Divides?**

If competition among imperial powers underlies the drive for FTAs, then is there a danger it becomes enmeshed with, or is perceived as, a "Divide and Conquer" strategy reminiscent of empires past? For example, would *MEFTA*—by design or effect—effectively vitiate the CU envisaged by the GCC? Would a *FTAA* offset the power of *MERCOSUR*, and Brazil in particular? Competition even with Mexico, a *NAFTA* partner, may figure in the calculus. Mexico has a large number of FTAs, covering most of its export markets in Latin America, and is working on an accord with *MERCOSUR*.[51]

Or, to apply the phrase of Sir James Robertson, the British Civil Secretary, who in December 1951 wrote in his diary during the Mahdist-Anti-Mahdist rivalry in Sudan, is it accurate to say: "They divide, and we rule"?[52] If major trading powers use RTAs as an instrument for dominance, then what countries—the ruling or the ruled—do the dividing?

---

51. *See* Michael O'Boyle, *Mexico, Argentina Sign Accord to Expand Limited Free Trade, Will Continue Talks*, 23 International Trade Reporter (BNA) 917 (15 June 2006).

52. *Quoted in* GLEN BALFOUR-PAUL, THE END OF EMPIRE IN THE MIDDLE EAST—BRITAIN'S RELINQUISHMENT OF POWER IN HER LAST THREE ARAB DEPENDENCIES 4 (1991).

Part Two

Common Legal Features of FTAs

Part Two

Commonest Features of RNAs

Chapter 4

GATT-WTO Disciplines on FTAs[1]

I. Poor Countries, *ITO Charter* Article 15, and GATT Article XXIV Origins

The *ITO Charter* and GATT drafters built into their documents a major exception to general trade-liberalizing obligations, namely, for RTAs. Interestingly, during the discussions at the 1946 London and 1947 Geneva Preparatory Conference meetings, the possibility of focusing the exception on less developed countries arose. Syria and some Latin American countries sought provisions tailored to RTAs among Third World countries.[2] They and like-minded developing countries did so to help stimulate trade and industrialization among poor countries. Other delegates rejected provisions that would have allowed less developed countries to enter into RTAs solely or largely to facilitate industrialization. Yet, that rejection was not the end of the effort to tailor RTA rules for developing countries at large.

Later on, at the 1947–1948 Havana Conference, the delegates agreed to a provision in the *ITO Charter*, Article 15, which explicitly acknowledged the link between RTAs and economic development. The Article, entitled "Preferential Agreements for Economic Development and Reconstruction," stated:

1. The Members recognize that special circumstances, *including the need for economic development* or reconstruction, may justify new preferential agreements between two or more countries *in the interest of the programs of economic development* or reconstruction of one or more of them.

2. Any Member contemplating the conclusion of such an agreement shall communicate its intention to the Organization and provide it with the relevant information to enable it to examine the proposed agreement. The Organization shall promptly communicate such information to all Members.

3. The Organization shall examine the proposal and, by a *two-thirds majority of the Members present and voting*, may grant, subject to such conditions as it

---

1. Documents References:
   (1) *Havana (ITO) Charter* Articles 43–45
   (2) GATT Article XXIV
   (3) Relevant provisions in FTAs
2. For treatments of the origins of Article XXIV, see James H. Mathis, *Regional Trade Agreements in the GATT/WTO—Article XXIV and the Internal Trade Agreement* (2002); John H. Jackson, *World Trade and the Law of GATT* § 24.1 at 577–578 (1969) [hereinafter, Jackson 1969].

may impose, an exception to the provisions of Article 16 to permit the proposed agreement to become effective.

4. *Notwithstanding the provisions of paragraph 3, the Organization shall authorize, in accordance with the provisions of paragraphs 5 and 6, the necessary departure from the provisions of Article 16* [*i.e.*, the departure from the general MFN obligation, set forth in Article 16 of the *ITO Charter*, and now contained in Article I:1 of GATT] in respect of a proposed agreement between Members for the establishment of tariff preferences which it determines to fulfill the following conditions and requirements:

   (a) the *territories of the parties to the agreement are contiguous* one with another, or all parties belong to the same economic region;

   (b) any preference provided for in the agreement is *necessary to ensure a sound and adequate market for a particular industry or branch of agriculture which is being, or is to be, created or reconstructed or substantially developed or substantially modernized*;

   (c) the parties to the agreement undertake to grant *free entry* for the products of the industry or branch of agriculture referred to in sub-paragraph (b) or to apply customs duties to such products sufficiently low to ensure that the objectives set forth in that sub-paragraph will be achieved;

   (d) any *compensation* granted to the other parties by the party receiving preferential treatment shall, if it is a preferential concession, conform with the provisions of this paragraph;

   (e) the agreement contains provisions permitting, on terms and conditions to be determined by negotiation with the parties to the agreement, the adherence of other Members, which are able to qualify as parties to the agreement under the provisions of this paragraph, *in the interest of their programs of economic development or reconstruction*. The provisions of Chapter VIII may be invoked by such a Member in this respect only on the ground that it has been unjustifiably excluded from participation in such an agreement;

   (f) the agreement contains *provisions for its termination* within a period necessary for the fulfillment of its purposes but, in any case, not later than at the end of *ten years*; any renewal shall be subject to the approval of the Organization and no renewal shall be for a longer period than five years.

5. *When the Organization*, upon the application of a Member and in accordance with the provisions of paragraph 6, *approves a margin of preference* as an exception to Article 16 in respect of the products covered by the proposed agreement, *it may, as a condition of its approval, require a reduction in an unbound most-favored-nation rate of duty proposed by the Member in respect*

of any product so covered, if in the light of the representations of any affected Member it considers that rate excessive.

6. (a) *If the Organization finds that the proposed agreement fulfills the conditions and requirements set forth in paragraph 4 and that the conclusion of the agreement is not likely to cause substantial injury to the external trade of a Member country not party to the agreement, it shall within two months* authorize the parties to the agreement to depart from the provisions of Article 16, as regards the products covered by the agreement. If the Organization does not give a ruling within the specified period, its authorization shall be regarded as having been *automatically granted.*

   (b) If the Organization finds that the proposed agreement, while fulfilling the conditions and requirements set forth in paragraph 4, is likely to cause substantial injury to the external trade of a Member country not party to the agreement, it shall inform interested Members of its findings and shall require the Members contemplating the conclusion of the agreement to enter into negotiations with that Member. When agreement is reached in the negotiations, the Organization shall authorize the Members contemplating the conclusion of the preferential agreement to depart from the provisions of Article 16 as regards the products covered by the preferential agreement. If, at the end of two months from the date on which the Organization suggested such negotiations, the negotiations have not been completed and the Organization considers that the injured Member is unreasonably preventing the conclusion of the negotiations, it shall authorize the necessary departure from the provisions of Article 16 and at the same time shall fix a fair compensation to be granted by the parties to the agreement to the injured Member or, if this is not possible or reasonable, prescribe such modification of the agreement as will give such Member fair treatment. The provisions of Chapter VIII may be invoked by such Member only if it does not accept the decision of the Organization regarding such compensation.

   (c) If the Organization finds that the proposed agreement, while fulfilling the conditions and requirements set forth in paragraph 4, is likely to jeopardize the economic position of a Member in world trade, it shall not authorize any departure from the provisions of Article 16 unless the parties to the agreement have reached a mutually satisfactory understanding with that Member.

   (d) If the Organization finds that the prospective parties to a regional preferential agreement have, prior to November 21, 1947, obtained from countries representing at least two-thirds of their import trade the right to depart from most-favored-nation treatment in the case envisaged in the agreement, the Organization shall, without prejudice to the conditions governing the recognition of such right, grant the authorization provided for in paragraph 5 and in sub-paragraph (a) of this paragraph, provided that the conditions and requirements set out in sub-paragraphs (a), (e,) and (f) of paragraph 4 are fulfilled. Nevertheless, if the Organization finds that the external trade of one or more Member countries, which have not recognized this right to depart from most-favored-nation treatment, is threatened with substantial injury, it shall invite the parties to the agreement to enter into negotiations with the injured Member, and the provisions of subparagraph (b) of this paragraph shall apply.[3]

In sum, Paragraphs 1 and 3 of the *ITO Charter* would have authorized RTAs among less developed countries upon approval by two-thirds of the ITO members present and voting. The delegates went so far as to say in Paragraphs 4–6 that under certain circumstances, notwithstanding two-thirds approval (or the lack thereof), the ITO would condone creation of an RTA for economic development purposes.

What became of Article 15? It was intended for inclusion in GATT, along with what is now Article XXIV. After the Havana Conference, through a protocol dated 24 March 1948, Article XXIV was added to GATT. Article 15 was not added at that time. Rather, the delegates seem to have believed the provisions on developing countries and RTAs would be inserted into the GATT, once the *ITO Charter* took effect. That expectation never was fulfilled, because of the failure of the *Charter* (owing to the announcement in December 1950 by the Truman Administration that it would not seek Congressional approval for it, given considerable opposition to it in Congress).

Thus, unfortunately for developing countries, Article 15 never entered into force. All that survived of a tailoring effort designed initially for all poor countries was Paragraph 11 of Article XXIV (a special provision for India and Pakistan, discussed later), plus the remainder of this Article.

Why Article 15 was not sewn into the new multilateral trade law, GATT, leaving only a bit of material (Paragraph 11 in Article XXIV) for two poor countries (India and Pakistan) is not clear. Some delegations may have foreseen constitutional and administrative difficulties. Other delegations—namely, those from Syria, the Benelux countries, and Latin America—were satisfied with the exceptions to the Article I:1 MFN obligation for the particular RTAs in which they held membership. (These exceptions are set forth in Article I:2.) In contrast, at a 1954–1955 Review Session of GATT at which the need for Paragraph 11 was debated, both India and Pakistan successfully urged its retention.[4] Their subsequent non-use of the provision is, therefore, all the more ironic.

---

3. Emphasis added.

4. *See* World Trade Organization, Guide to GATT Law and Practice—Analytical Index vol. 2, 829 (Geneva, Switzerland: World Trade Organization, 1995) (entry on Article XXIV, Paragraph 11). [Hereinafter, GATT Analytical Index.]

If these explanations are accurate, then (with the benefit of hindsight) can it be said the delegates from less developed countries gave up too easily? Did they lack sufficient vision and strength to appreciate the role RTAs could play in the future growth of their countries? Perhaps.

But, because neither the GATT nor the WTO Secretariat has stood in the way of RTA creation, it is hard to say inclusion of Article 15 in GATT would have made a material difference. Political rivalries within the Third World (as in the Indo-Pakistani case) have done more to destroy RTA opportunities than even a devilishly obstructionist Geneva-based bureaucrat ever could have imagined. Moreover, given the mixed economic performance of many RTAs (*e.g.*, failing to cover significant volumes of trade, and careening between trade creation and trade diversion), it is not at all clear the aspirations embodied in Article 15 would have been realized in practice.

Finally, with the exclusion from GATT of an Article 15-type provision, a historic opportunity to clarify the distinction between a preferential arrangement, on the one hand, and a regional arrangement (*i.e.*, a CU or FTA) on the other hand, was lost.[5] Nowadays "PTAs" and RTAs are sometimes confused as nearly synonymous, differing only insofar as a PTA includes members not geographically located in the same region, yet in truth, there is a distinction to be made.

Suppose the delegates at the various *ITO Charter* and GATT drafting confer-ences had put the distinction between "PTA" and "RTA" clearly down on paper, and created rigorous legal tests for its enforcement. The answers to the obvious ques-tion "why care?" are counter-factual speculations unsusceptible to definitive proof. Perhaps the drafters might have agreed to a rule on preferential arrangements to benefit more Third World countries than just India and Pakistan. In turn, perhaps a rule for all such countries would have focused even greater attention on developed country policies that create an incentive for a preferential arrangement, particularly of the first form involving non-reciprocal benefits extended by developed to devel-oping countries.

One example would be high prevailing MFN rates (even tariff spikes).[6] Such pol-icies would indicate that a margin of preference for developing country products is large and, therefore, valuable to developing country exports. Another example would be a high rate of effective protection for certain manufacturing industries in developed countries. That could be achieved by an inverted tariff structure, or tariff escalation, whereby a higher tariff is imposed on a finished product than on the raw

---

5. *See* KENNETH W. DAM, THE GATT 275 (1970) (observing "[t]he supposedly self-evident dif-ference between preferences and customs unions proved to be completely misconceived"). [Here-inafter, DAM.]

6. *See* DAM, 249 (explaining a preference granted by a developed country to a developing coun-try product is valuable if the MFN rates on that product are sufficiently high, the effective protec-tion for the developed country industry is significant, and the industry in the developing country is more efficient than the industry in the developed country).

materials and inputs used to make that good.[7] The result is an incentive in favor of processing in the developed country using raw materials and inputs from a developing country. That attention might well have led to yet greater pressure on developed countries to abandon or modify these policies.

The reason to care may be, perhaps, the drafters would have given the world trading community a stronger set of disciplines on RTAs than are contained in Article XXIV. Such provisions might have called even greater attention to the dangers of RTAs, with fewer poor countries eyeing RTAs for their seductive benefits. Perhaps, also, sound RTA rules would have been useful for developing countries interested in seeing their successful preferential arrangements evolve into regional accords. Thereafter, grand multilateral bargains on non-discriminatory trade also could emerge.

II. Purpose of RTAs, Article XXIV:4, and Article XXIV:10 Waiver

The key provision in GATT on RTAs is Article XXIV. It bears the awkward title "Territorial Application—Frontier Traffic—Customs Unions and Free-Trade Areas." Decades ago, Professor Kenneth W. Dam (1932–) offered this assessment of the Article:

> The effort to attain precision and to force future agreements into Article XXIV's mold proved to be . . . a *failure*, if not a *fiasco*. *Ambiguity rather than precision reigned*. The regional agreements that came before the GATT did not conform to the tests of Article XXIV, and in the face of the conflict, *the GATT and not the regional groupings yielded*. As time passed, the agreements that were placed before the GATT for inspection under Article XXIV came to look more and more like outright preferential arrangements, but the fact that they were defended as being within shouting distance of Article XXIV made it politically difficult to treat them as violations of the most-favored-nation clause. . . .
>
> Today it is clear that if a single adjective were to be chosen to describe Article XXIV, that adjective would have to be *"deceptive."* *First*, the standards established are deceptively concrete and precise; any attempt to apply the standards to a specific situation reveals *ambiguities* which, to use an irresistible metaphor, go to the heart of the matter. Second, although the rules appear to be based on economic considerations, the underlying principles make *little economic sense*. Third, the *dismaying experience* of the GATT has been that, with one possible exception [identified by Professor Dam as the United Kingdom–Ireland Free Trade Agreement, see GATT

---

7. *See* Raj Bhala, Dictionary of International Trade Law (New Providence, New Jersey: LexisNexis, 3rd ed., 2015) (entry for "inverted tariff").

B.I.S.D. (14th Supp.) 23, 122 (1966)], no customs-union or free-trade-area agreement thus far presented for review has complied with Article XXIV, yet no such agreement has been disapproved.

. . .

[The GATT] draftsmen thought that it would be possible to impose upon the international legal community a comprehensive set of substantive rules establishing a formal mold into which all regional treaties would have to be forced. *Their essential error was thus in their conception of a legal institution as largely a set of substantive prohibitions rather than as largely a set of procedures.* That the substantive rules eventually adopted were *highly ambiguous* and had *little relation to the freer-trade goals of the General Agreement* as a whole merely exacerbated this error in legal policy.[8]

This blistering critique is not unfair.

The central purpose of the Article is to regulate tension between regionalism and multilateralism, *i.e.,* to ensure GATT contracting parties (now WTO Members), do not enter into RTAs in a way that blocks multilateral trade liberalization. For reasons Professor Dam suggests, the Article itself is not an entirely effective regulator. So, Members probably have entered, and continue to enter, RTAs that are anything but stepping stones to broad-scale trade liberalization. By one account only 6 of 80 RTAs studied complied with GATT rules.[9] Moreover, every Member is Party to at least one, and typically several, RTAs, and that there are more RTAs than WTO Members.[10] There are far more RTAs than there are Members of the WTO, or even countries in the world.

There is another reason to bemoan, if not excoriate, Article XXIV. What is the relationship between (1) Paragraph 4 and (2) Paragraphs 5 through 9? Paragraph 4 says:

[t]he contracting parties *recognize* the *desirability of increasing freedom of trade by the development,* through voluntary agreements, *of closer integration*

---

8. *See* Dam, 275–276, 291 (emphasis added), along with the discussion at 290–291 (arguing the record of applying Article XXIV "is not comforting"). The discussion of the purpose and disciplines of Article XXIV in the present and subsequent Sections draws partly on Raj Bhala, *Trade, Development, and Social Justice* ch. 14 (2003).

9. *See* Raj Bhala & Kevin Kennedy, World Trade Law § 2-2(a) at 163 (1998, with 1999 Supplement) (citing a 1996 study reported by *The Christian Science Monitor*). [Hereinafter, Bhala & Kennedy.] *See also* Gabrielle Marceau & Cornelis Reiman, *When and How is a Regional Trade Agreement Compatible with the WTO?*, 28 Legal Issues of Economic Integration 297–336 (September 2001) (discussing RTAs and GATT obligations).

10. By one estimate, as of October 2004, there were approximately 220 RTAs that had entered into force. If all RTAs then under negotiation were successfully concluded, the number would have increased to roughly 300 by year-end 2007. *See* Report by the Consultative Board to the Director-General Supachai Panitchpakdi, The Future of the WTO—Addressing Institutional Challenges in the New Millennium (2004), www.wto.org. Data updated through December 2012 showed the number of RTAs notified to the WTO approached 400.

between the economies of the countries parties to such agreements. They also *recognize* that the purpose of a customs union or of a free-trade area *should* be to facilitate trade between the constituent territories and *not to raise barriers to the trade of other contracting parties* with such territories.[11]

One approach, based on the aspirational and non-mandatory language, is Paragraph 4 is precatory in nature. The (supposedly) "hard" rules are in the subsequent Paragraphs.

The opposite perspective is Paragraph 4 is a *chapeau* for the subsequent Paragraphs, and itself embodies general rules, particularly a "purpose" test for a proposed RTA.[12] Paragraphs 5–9 elaborate on those rules. Which interpretation is correct? Or, are they both wrong, and is some other intermediate position between the two extremes the best one? Professor Dam's best guess is there are as many ways to view the relationship between Paragraph 4 versus Paragraphs 5–9 as there are ingenious lawyers.[13]

The most important way comes from the 1999 WTO Appellate Body Report in *Turkey Textiles*. In its Report, the Appellate Body clarified the "purpose" test suggested by Paragraph 4 is relevant to interpret the rules of Article XXIV:[14]

> ... the purpose set forth in paragraph 4 informs the other relevant paragraphs of Article XXIV, including the *chapeau* of paragraph 5. For this reason, the *chapeau* of Paragraph 5, and the conditions set forth therein for establishing the availability of a defense under Article XXIV, must be interpreted in the light of the purpose of customs unions [or FTAs] set forth in paragraph 4.[15]

In addition to the possibility of a "purpose" test (based on the second approach to Paragraph 4), Article XXIV lays down 3 basic rules to be followed, or disciplines to be respected, when setting up an RTA. Assuming compliance with them, an RTA may be formed without any further action by the WTO, and the exception to GATT

---

11. Emphasis added.

12. Professor Dam suggests this view, and discusses the relationship between Paragraphs 4 and 5–9. *See* DAM, 276.

13. *See* DAM, 276.

14. *See* Appellate Body Report, *Turkey—Restrictions on Imports of Textile and Clothing Products*, WT/DS34/AB/R (adopted 19 November 1999). [Hereinafter, *Turkey Textiles* Appellate Body Report.]

Critics of the Appellate Body may cite to this decision, in the annals of WTO jurisprudence, as an illustration of "judicial activism." The Appellate Body held Turkey failed to show it was necessary for Turkey to violate Article XI in order to form a CU with the EU. So, the Appellate Body reasoned, Turkey could not defend the violation of the rule against QRs (Article XI:1) by referring to Article XXIV. The problem with this reasoning is Article XXIV does not contain a "necessity" test, at least not in express terms. The Appellate Body imported into Article XXIV some of its jurisprudence from Article XX. *See* Joel P. Trachtman, *Current Developments: Decisions of the Appellate Body of the World Trade Organization*, 12 EUROPEAN JOURNAL OF INTERNATIONAL LAW 793–98 (2001), www.ejil.org.

15. *See Turkey Textiles* Appellate Body Report, ¶ 57.

rules for the RTA in Article XXIV:5 (*e.g.,* from the Article I:1 MFN obligation) is automatic.

The automatic exception assumes Parties in an RTA are GATT contracting parties (*i.e.,* WTO Members).[16] If a proposed RTA has non-Members, then Article XXIV:10 requires a 2/3 majority vote of all Members to approve the deal. This provision states:

> The Contracting Parties *may by a two-thirds majority approve proposals which do not fully comply with the requirements of paragraphs 5 to 9 inclusive,* provided that such proposals lead to the formation of a customs union or a free-trade area in the sense of this Article.[17]

Paragraph 10 provides for the possibility of a waiver from some, or all, RTA disciplines.

Consider the Indian Subcontinent for its application. Of the 7 South Asian countries (Bangladesh, Bhutan, India, Maldives, Nepal, Pakistan, and Sri Lanka), all but 1 (Bhutan, as of March 2015) is a WTO Member. Ceylon (Sri Lanka), India, and Pakistan were founding contracting parties. An FTA or CU involving Bhutan presumably would need a WTO imprimatur, under Paragraph 10, unless those countries got Membership before forming the RTA, and that RTA adhered to the other Article XXIV disciplines.

III. First Discipline: "Substantially All" Test in Article XXIV:8

The first discipline on an RTA concerns its scope. An RTA is supposed to cover "substantially all" the trade among the constituent members.[18] Defining what that means is not easy, but it is highly important. It is not unusual to observe a parade of highly paid attorneys lobby on behalf of an industry for exemption from an RTA under negotiation.

For example, in November 2003, the U.S. announced its intention to negotiate a FTA with Bolivia, Ecuador, Colombia, and Peru, plus a bilateral FTA with Panama. (The first 4 countries were parties to the *ATPA,* until the latter two entered into FTAs with the U.S.) By February 2004, lawyers for the tuna canning industry in American Samoa and Puerto Rico were arguing against exemption from duty-free treatment under these FTAs, predicting devastation for their clients if free trade occurred.[19]

---

16. *See* JACKSON 1969 § 24.3 at 582.
17. Emphasis added.
18. This rule is set out in Article XXIV:8.
19. *See* Rossella Brevetti, *P.R. and American Samoa Officials Urge Canned Tuna Exclusion for FTAs,* 21 International Trade Reporter (BNA) 327, 328 (19 February 2004). Interestingly, America

Likewise, the American sugar industry lobbied for continued tariffs against Panama in respect of the *U.S.-Panama FTA*. The bilateral FTA between the U.S. and Australia, the *CAFTA-DR*, and a large number of association agreements negotiated by the EU, furnish similar illustrations. In all these instances, to varying degrees depending on the accord, the promise of free trade is less than comprehensive in terms of sectoral coverage. *KORUS* intentionally omits, at the insistence of Korea, an entire sector: rice. (Korea would have rejected the entire deal had America not given in on its demands for market access on rice.) Aside from the policy debate of whether these exemptions are a "good idea," the practical issue is whether such exemptions would cause an FTA not to cover "substantially all" trade among the members.

Put succinctly, when is an RTA not an RTA because it does not liberalize a sufficient value or volume of trade? Exactly what percentage of trade constitutes a "substantial" amount has never been defined. Three responses are:

(1) "Substantial" is less than "all," as the work of the Preparatory Conferences indicates.[20]

(2) "Substantial" is more than "zero."

(3) "Substantial" is nearer to "all" than to "zero," *e.g.*, in 1957 a delegate from the EEC suggested 80%.[21]

However these responses are obvious, and hence not that helpful. Professor Dam asks:

Assume . . . the suggestion is correct that "substantially all" means 80[%]. Is the only proper reading of this language that internal tariffs must be eliminated on 80 of all trade? Or can the test also be satisfied by reducing all internal tariffs to 20 of their earlier levels?[22]

Unfortunately, the WTO *Understanding on the Interpretation of Article XXIV*, negotiated during the Uruguay Round, does not add much precision.

Paragraph 4 of the *Preamble* to the *Understanding* states the obvious too:

. . . the contribution [to the expansion of world trade] is increased if the elimination between the constituent territories of duties and other restrictive regulations of commerce extends to all trade, and diminished if any major sector of trade is excluded.[23]

---

imports coffee duty free, but since 1931 Congress has authorized Puerto Rico to maintain a tariff on coffee. Puerto Rico argued in favor of continuing this authorization, and for protection from duty-free treatment for its third key product, low-value rum. *See id.*

20. *See* Jackson 1969, § 24.7 at 608.

21. *See The European Economic Community, Reports Adopted on 29 November 1957*, B.I.S.D. (6th Supp.) 70, 98–99 at ¶ 30 (1958).

22. Dam, 280. Professor Dam opines the latter possibility would derogate from the general purpose test of GATT. *See id.*

23. *Understanding on the Interpretation of Article XXIV, Preamble*, Paragraph 4.

The frustration caused by the ambiguity actually is magnified 4 times.

The term "substantially all" (or "substantially") is used four times in the provision of Article XXIV, namely, Paragraph 8, which contains the discipline. This Paragraph states:

8. For the purposes of this Agreement:

(a) A customs union shall be understood to mean the substitution of a single customs territory for two or more customs territories, so that

(i) duties and other restrictive regulations of commerce (except, where necessary, those permitted under Articles XI, XII, XIII, XIV, XV and XX) are eliminated with respect to *substantially all* the trade between the constituent territories of the union or at least with respect to *substantially all* the trade in products originating in such territories, and,

(ii) subject to the provisions of paragraph 9, *substantially* the same duties and other regulations of commerce are applied by each of the members of the union to the trade of territories not included in the union;

(b) A free-trade area shall be understood to mean a group of two or more customs territories in which the duties and other restrictive regulations of commerce (except, where necessary, those permitted under Articles XI, XII, XIII, XIV, XV and XX) are eliminated on *substantially all* the trade between the constituent territories in products originating in such territories.[24]

It is not even clear whether the term is to be defined the same way in each of the four locations, though it would be risky to eschew any cross-referencing.

Likewise, until the 1999 Appellate Body decision in *Turkey Textiles*, it was not evident whether the judgment was to be based entirely on quantitative criteria, *i.e.*, the volume of trade covered by an RTA, or (as the *EFTA* countries argued in 1960)[25] on qualitative criteria as well. Qualitative benchmarks might allow for the exclusion of certain sectors, including particularly contentious ones like agriculture or steel:

Again, assume that tariffs and other restrictions are totally eliminated on 80[%] of internal trade but that several major industries, comprising, say, the remaining 20 of internal trade, are totally excluded from the scope of the customs union or free-trade area. Is the "substantially all" test met?[26]

---

24. Emphasis added.

25. *See European Free Trade Association, Examination of Stockholm Convention, Report Adopted on 4 June 1960*, B.I.S.D. (9th Supp.) 70, 83–86 at ¶¶ 48–54 (1961). *See also* Jackson 1969 § 24.8 at 610 (detecting "[s]ome agreement . . . for the proposition that no important segment of trade can be omitted from an arrangement and still have that arrangement meet the "substantially all" test).

26. Dam, 280. Professor Dam believes an affirmative answer would result in injury to countries not party to the CU.

In *Turkey Textiles*, the Appellate Body agreed the term "substantially all" embodied both qualitative and quantitative components.[27] Still, the point remains it is sloppy drafting to use such a critical term so many times and leave it undefined—unless, of course, the ambiguity is seen as having some strategic benefit.

That benefit may be the flexibility that typically is the handmaiden of ambiguity. As intimated, presumably, an RTA that eliminates tariffs on just 5% of all products traded between the members would not satisfy the criterion, whereas 95% coverage would. As a real-world example, the 1965 Auto Pact between the U.S. and Canada concerning free trade in autos and auto parts was not eligible for Article XXIV treatment. That agreement covers only one industrial sector, and thus had to be the subject of an explicit waiver from the GATT Contracting Parties.[28]

Technically, the "substantially all" rule applies only to CUs and FTAs.[29] Article XXIV:5(c), which deals with interim agreements, does not contain this phraseology. Rather, it mandates only that the transition period from interim agreement to CU or FTA be reasonable. Of course, once born, the "substantially all" rule does apply. For instance, but for Article XXIV:11 and the accompanying Interpretative Note, were India and Pakistan serious about constructing a meaningful RTA, and were they to begin with an interim agreement, they essentially could ignore the "substantially all" rule only during the transition period. Thereafter, they might be called upon by the WTO Members to explain how their new entity adhered to the rule.

IV. Second Discipline: "Higher or More Restrictive" Test in Article XXIV:5

The second discipline on RTAs imposed by Article XXIV may be colloquially dubbed the "no trade fortress rule." An RTA being created must not impose trade barriers against non-members that, on the whole, are higher than those applicable to the non-members before the RTA was formed. This rule applies to CUs, FTAs, or

---

27. *See* Appellate Body Report, *Turkey—Restrictions on Imports of Textile and Clothing Products*, WT/DS34/AB/R, ¶ 49 (adopted 19 November 1999).

28. *See* JACKSON 1969, § 24.4 at 587. The waiver is published in *United States—Imports of Automotive Products, Decision of 20 December 1965*, GATT B.I.S.D. (14th Supp.) 37 (1966). The GATT Working Party Paper on the American waiver request is published in *United States—Imports of Automotive Products, Report of the Working Party Submitted to the Council of Representatives on 19 November 1965*, B.I.S.D. (14th Supp.) 181 (1966). The Working Party Paper on the pact itself is published in *Canada/United States Agreement on Automotive Products, Report of the Working Party Adopted on 25 March 1965*, B.I.S.D. (13th Supp.) 112 (1965). For a discussion of the *United States—Canada Automotive Products Agreement* and the WTO Appellate Body case about it, see Raj Bhala & David Gantz, *WTO Case Review 2000*, 18 ARIZONA JOURNAL OF INTERNATIONAL AND COMPARATIVE LAW 1, 21–36 (2001).

29. *See* JACKSON, § 24.3 at 584–585.

interim agreements, by virtue of the language of Article XXIV:5 (particularly Sub-Paragraphs (a) and (b)). Paragraph 5 states:

> [T]he provisions of this Agreement shall not prevent, as between the territories of contracting parties, the formation of a customs union or of a free-trade area or the adoption of an interim agreement necessary for the formation of a customs union or of a free-trade area; *Provided* that:
>
> (a) with respect to a *customs union*, or an interim agreement leading to the formation of a customs union, the *duties* and other regulations of commerce imposed at the institution of any such union or interim agreement *in respect of trade with contracting parties not parties to such union* or agreement *shall not on the whole be higher* or more restrictive *than the general incidence of the duties* and regulations of commerce applicable in the constituent territories *prior to the formation of such union* or the adoption of such interim agreement, as the case may be;
>
> (b) with respect to a *free-trade area*, or an interim agreement leading to the formation of a free-trade area, the *duties* and other regulations of commerce *maintained in each of the constituent territories and applicable at the formation of such free-trade area* or the adoption of such interim agreement *to the trade of contracting parties not included in such area* or not parties to such agreement *shall not be higher or more restrictive than the corresponding duties* and other regulations of commerce *existing in the same constituent territories prior to the formation of the free-trade area*, or interim agreement, as the case may be; and
>
> (c) any *interim agreement* referred to in sub-paragraphs (a) and (b) shall include a plan and schedule for the formation of such a customs union or of such a free-trade area within a *reasonable length of time*.[30]

Yet, as with the first discipline, the key language of the second discipline is ambiguous.

With respect to a CU or interim agreement to build one, what does the language in Paragraph 5(a) — "not *on the whole* . . . higher or more restrictive than the *general incidence* of the *duties* and *regulations of commerce applicable* in the constituent territories prior to the formation of such union or the adoption of such interim agreement" — mean in practice? Similarly, with respect to an FTA or interim agreement to build one, what does the language in Paragraph 5(b) — "not . . . higher or more restrictive than the corresponding duties and other regulations of commerce existing in the same constituent territories prior to the formation of the free trade area, or interim agreement" — mean in practice? To be sure, Article XXIV:8(a) allows parties coming together to form an RTA to retain barriers permitted under other Articles (namely, XI–XV and XX). That point aside, about all that is clear from the language of Article XXIV:5 is the lack of an algorithm. Based on the 1957

---

30. Emphasis added.

GATT Working Party Report on the EEC, it can be said there is no generic mathematical formula to be used in every case.[31]

Even if a mathematical formula existed in the annals of GATT-WTO history, by definition it would be helpful only for quantifiable barriers—like duties. What about the other "regulations of commerce" affecting trade? Some of them, like quotas, can be reduced to comparable sets of figures. Others, such as licensing rules, certain technical or sanitary standards, may not be susceptible to a simple quantitative analysis. How, for instance, would the EC Operator Category and Activity Function rules (discussed in a separate Chapter) that were the subject of the infamous 1997 *Bananas* case be quantified?

The problem did not go unnoticed during the Uruguay Round. As the WTO *Understanding on the Interpretation of Article XXIV* from that Round states:

> It is recognized that for the purpose of the overall assessment of the incidence of other regulations of commerce for which quantification and aggregation are difficult, *the examination of individual measures, regulations, products covered and trade flows may be required.*[32]

In other words, the *Understanding* countenances a case-by-case approach.[33]

Yet, there still exists a threshold problem of delineating the "regulations of commerce" contemplated by the language. In a world of increasingly globalized economies, an argument can be made that most commercial regulations bear on cross-border trade. At least they may do so indirectly. But, the drafters of GATT could not have meant to cover every domestic law, regulation, and rule affecting business.

Because the rule is applied on a case-by-case basis and, it tends to be illustrated by way of example. Assume India and Pakistan, before establishing a CU, have bound duties on cotton from third countries like Egypt, of 10% and 20%, respectively. Assume, further, they imported roughly equal volumes of cotton from Egypt, so that in a trade-weighted sense, the split of cotton imports as between them was about 50–50. The pre-union average level of protection is 15% Absent the special provision (discussed later) in Article XXIV:11 and the *Interpretative Note, Ad Article XXIV, Paragraph 11*, once India and Pakistan form the union, the level of protection ought not to rise above 15%.

This discipline poses an obvious difficulty—administration. In reality, India and Pakistan trade far more products with third countries than just cotton. Any increase in a bound duty by a country entering in a CU—*e.g.*, where the Indian

---

31. *See The European Economic Community, Reports Adopted on 29 November 1957*, B.I.S.D. (6th Supp.) 70, 71–72 at ¶ 6 (1958). *See also* DAM, 277 (stating, as regards CUs, "[t]he general intent is clear," namely, "to prevent external barriers from being raised on balance in the process of creating the customs union," but "difficult to state in more specific terms than the treaty language itself").

32. Emphasis added.

33. *See* BHALA & KENNEDY, § 2-2(d) at 168.

tariff rises from 10% to 15%—would necessitate a modification of the Indian Schedule of Concessions in accordance with Article XXVIII. In brief, that provision, expressly referenced in Article XXIV:6 (discussed below), calls for compensatory adjustments in concessions on other products from third countries that are principal suppliers of the good whose tariff is being increased—*e.g.*, Egypt, which is being affected by the increase in the tariff applied to its cotton. This requirement is further stated in the WTO *Understanding on the Interpretation of Article XXIV* (also discussed below).

Thus, the calculation of whether this hypothetical CU on the Indian Subcontinent raises restrictions would be complex. It would involve balancing instances where on some products the tariffs indeed may have risen, whereas on others it may have fallen. That is not surprising, as even the cotton example suggests. In the CU negotiations, Pakistan can be expected to lobby for a higher CET on cotton than India, given its existing tariff of 20%, double that which protects the Indian cotton industry. Yet, in other sectors, it will be India with the higher level of protection, and Pakistan urging a CET below the Indian tariff.

Herein, lies one difficulty in applying the rule: interpreting the terms "on the whole" and "general incidence." The above hypothetical example suggests a before-versus-after-the-RTA examination of tariffs on individual product categories, and computation of an average that is weighted by trade volumes. The WTO *Understanding on the Interpretation of Article XXIV* confirms (more or less) that suggestion:

> The evaluation under paragraph 5(a) of Article XXIV of the general incidence of the duties and other regulations of commerce applicable *before and after* the formation of a customs union shall in respect of duties and charges be based upon an *overall assessment of weighted average tariff rates and of customs duties collected.* This assessment shall be based on import statistics for a previous representative period to be supplied by the customs union, *on a tariff-line basis* and in values and quantities, broken down by WTO country of origin. The [WTO] Secretariat shall compute the weighted average tariff rates and customs duties collected in accordance with the methodology used in the assessment of tariff offers in the Uruguay Round of Multilateral Trade Negotiations.[34] . . .

However, embedded in the suggestion, and in the passage quoted from the *Understanding*, are four significant interpretative issues to be explored.

First, GATT drafting history shows an intentional switch at the 1947–1948 Havana Conference from the phrase "average level" to "general incidence."[35] It also indicates

---

34. *Understanding on the Interpretation of Article XXIV* at ¶ 2 (emphasis added).

35. This history is recounted in Jackson 1969 § 24.8 at 611–612. Professor Dam finds little of use in this history, summarizing it as a call not for a simple mathematical average of CU, but for consideration of volume of trade. He comments: "to concede that no one method of calculation is required is not to state which methods are forbidden." Dam, 279.

that "on the whole" meant not an average tariff for each product category, but a macro-level look at all of the tariffs of a CU in comparison with those of the countries involved before the union took effect. Professor Dam puts it clearly:

> A principal decision to be made is whether the words "on the whole" and "general incidence" refer to *each item* in the common external tariff schedule or to the common external tariff schedule as a *whole*.[36]

In the context of CUs, the above-quoted passage from the *Understanding on the Interpretation of Article XXIV* goes some way to decide the point. It speaks of an "overall assessment" that compares the *status quo ante* (*i.e.,* before the CU) with the proposed *status quo* (*i.e.,* after the union would come into being).

The before-and-after overall assessment hardly is the end of the matter. A second point concerns the methodology for deciding compliance. The goal is to identify the threshold above which the CET of a proposed CU may not rise. What is the proper way to reach that goal? Is the way to start with the existing duty rates of Party countries, or with the existing duties imposed on products?[37]

One methodology might be to calculate the average tariff across all product categories for each Party in a proposed CU, and then establish a union-wide average based on the country averages of each Party. A different methodology might be to disregard country boundaries from the outset, compute an average duty for each product category, and then figure out a union-wide average from the product category averages.

Another route would be to forego efforts at a single number, *i.e.,* to eschew computation of one weighted-average duty for all products and all countries joining the CU. But, there is a fork in this route. First, an effort could be made to calculate a weighted-average tariff for each Party joining the proposed CU, across all product categories. Thus, if three countries proposed to form a CU, then there would be three weighted-averages — one for each Party that encompassed all product categories. Or, second, the effort could be to compute a weighted-average tariff for each product category, across all countries joining the CU. The result would be hundreds (if not thousands) of weighted-average duties, one corresponding to every product category, that encompassed all Parties joining the CU on the eve of that union entering into force.

The WTO *Understanding on the Interpretation of Article XXIV* takes the second fork in the route. It speaks of "weighted average tariff rates" computed on a "tariff-line basis," drawn from "import statistics for a previous representative period . . . broken down by WTO country of origin."[38] It also refers to the methodology used by negotiators during the Uruguay Round. That sounds like a product-specific

---

36. Dam, 277 (emphasis added).
37. *See* Dam, 277.
38. *Understanding on the Interpretation of Article XXIV* at ¶ 2.

computation of tariffs, for each WTO Member that is joining the CU. It also sounds like this calculation requires disaggregating data by the country of origin of each product. Yet, left undefined is the "previous representative period." If there have been changes in the duty structures of the countries coming together in a CU, then choice of that period will be critical in considering whether that union does, or does not, raise barriers to third country imports.

Also left unclear is how to go about the weighting when computing weighted-average duties for the various product categories. That is, there is a problem of weighting duty rates for each product category by trade volume in that category. (If the effort is to average the tariffs of the Parties to a proposed CU, then the problem of weighting still exists—namely, how to weight the country averages into a single, union-wide average?) As both Professors Dam and Jackson rightly suggest,[39] the volume traded of any item always bears an inverse relationship to the magnitude of the duty applied to that item. A lower volume is concomitant with a higher tariff. In turn, if a trade-weighted average tariff is calculated, then a very high tariff probably will get a low volume weight. That is because the weights are the relative trade volumes, and a very high tariff will cut off trade. The result will be a distorted average. The truly restrictive tariff hardly counts, because it is so effective in "killing" imports of the product.

There is a third interpretative matter, also in the context of a CU being established pursuant to Article XXIV:5(a). It arises from the word "applicable."[40] What duties were the "applicable" ones in the constituent territories of the CU before its formation—the bound duties (or, if unbound, the duties authorized by domestic law), or the duties actually being imposed on imported merchandise? This question was not resolved until the Uruguay Round, though it arose as far back as 1957 with the creation of the EEC.

The question is vital. If there is no agreement as to what the "applicable" tariffs are, then there is no benchmark for comparison with the CET of the CU. The *Understanding on the Interpretation of Article XXIV* explains that "the duties and charges to be taken into consideration shall be the *applied* rates of duty."[41] In the 1999 *Turkey Textiles* case, the Appellate Body said this explanation resolved the question.[42]

A fourth point, again one of interpretation with respect to Article XXIV:5(a) and the formation of a CU, is timing. For how long does the rule against imposing higher duties on goods from countries outside the union stay in effect? From the language of the provision, "institution" of a CU, or of an interim agreement leading thereto, triggers the rule. But, after the CU has been in operation for (say)

---

39. *See* DAM 277–278; JACKSON 1969 § 24.8 at 612.

40. This problem and EEC case is recounted in JACKSON 1969, § 24.8 at 612–614.

41. *Understanding on the Interpretation of Article XXIV* at ¶ 2 (emphasis added).

42. *See* Appellate Body Report, *Turkey—Restrictions on Imports of Textile and Clothing Products*, WT/DS34/AB/R, ¶ 53 (adopted 19 November 1999).

a decade, would the Parties ne barred from imposing higher trade barriers on non-originating goods?[43]

If so, then that would amount to a severe restriction on RTAs, and perhaps even deter their establishment in some cases. Likewise, under Article XXIV:5(b), "formation" of an FTA or "adoption" of an interim agreement for an FTA trigger the rule. But, the issue is less pressing in the instance of an FTA than a CU, because— by definition—the FTA does not involve a CET. Consequently, the FTA countries remain free to raise their individual tariff rates against third countries, up to the agreed-upon bindings.

Because of Article XXIV:11 and its Interpretative Note, were India and Pakistan to form a CU, they would not have to worry about any of these 4 interpretative matters. That is no small relief. Consider what Professor Dam writes (albeit before the WTO *Understanding*) as to calculating the pre-existing CU-wide tariff in order to comply with the rule that the CET is not, on the whole, higher than the general incidence of duties before the union: the conundrums (just outlined) "are not merely statistical puzzlers."[44]

The four interpretative points arise in the context of a CU. What if India and Pakistan contemplate an FTA? Suppose they did not have the benefit of Article XXIV:11 and its Interpretative Note. Again, the requirement is trade barriers—duties and other commercial regulations—not be elevated after the FTA comes into being beyond previously-prevailing corresponding levels.

Thus, India and Pakistan could not use formation of an FTA as an excuse to increase their individually-set barriers applicable to third countries. India could not impose a tariff on third country cotton of 11%, nor could Pakistan raise its barrier to 21%. Significantly, the relevant Article XXIV language (in Paragraph 5(b)) does not call for a balancing test. The words "on the whole" do not appear (whereas they do with respect to a CU, in Paragraph 5(c)). That omission is not an accident. There is no need for a judgment about tariff increases in some sectors, and declines in others, because no CET is being established. Each FTA Party retains its pre-FTA schedule vis-à-vis non-members.

---

43. Professor Jackson looks askance at this approach to the language, because it would impose an interminable obligation that would be more onerous than any of the other duties incumbent on a CU. *See* JACKSON 1969, § 24.8 at 616; § 24.9 at 619.

Professor Jackson says the "particularly troublesome problem" of origination occurs only as regards an FTA, but "is not present in the case of a customs union." *See id.*, § 24.9 at 620. That is erroneous. Third-country exporters have an incentive to take advantage of the absence of barriers in an RTA, be it an FTA or CU. Preferential ROOs are needed in both contexts to ensure merchandise from third countries does not get duty-free treatment. Were that not so, then there would be no risk of trade diversion in a CU (because consumers in the CU still could import third-country products free of duty)—a risk Professor Jackson acknowledges, based on the 1950 classic study by Jacob Viner, *The Customs Union Issue. See id.*, § 24.9 at 619. The key part on trade creation versus trade diversion in the Viner book is at pages 41–56.

44. DAM, 278.

V. Compensatory Adjustments, Article XXIV:6, and Case Studies of EU and Gabon

- **EU Enlargement**

In the hypothetical illustration of India, Pakistan, and Egypt discussed above, reference was made to Article XXIV:6. This provision concerns compensatory adjustments, and states:

> If, in fulfilling the requirements of sub-paragraph 5(a), a contracting party proposes to increase any rate of duty inconsistently with the provisions of Article II, the procedure set forth in Article XXVIII shall apply. In providing for compensatory adjustment, due account shall be taken of the compensation already afforded by the reductions brought about in the corresponding duty of the other constituents of the union.

In brief, Paragraph 6 calls for a compensatory adjustment, through a concession on another product, from a third country that supplies the good whose tariff is being increased. It is a "no free lunch" rule to ensure a WTO Member does not join a CU and raise a bound tariff without paying a price for that increase.

Article XXVIII, which concerns modification of Tariff Schedules, lays out the procedure for making a compensatory adjustment, and highlights the importance of third countries with an Initial Negotiating Right (INR) or a principal supplying interest in the good in question. Thus, put together, Articles XXIV:6 and XXVIII mean:

> A WTO Member proposing to increase tariffs as the result of the formation of a customs union or free trade agreement must provide compensatory adjustment in their tariff schedule to any country claiming a substantial trade interest in the products concerned.[45]

The WTO *Understanding on the Interpretation of Article XXIV* both reiterates and amplifies the requirement.

Paragraphs 4, 5, and 6 of the *Understanding* contain the following requirements:

(1) The commencement of negotiations on compensatory adjustments before formation of a customs union or an interim agreement leading to a customs union.

(2) Due account of reductions of duties made on the same tariff line by some countries joining the customs union, along with increases in duties made on that tariff line by other countries joining the union, and

(3) Clarification that compensatory arrangements are not reciprocal, *i.e.,* countries not joining the customs union or interim agreement, but benefiting

---

45. Daniel Pruzin, *EU, Philippines Feud Over Manila Exclusion from Talks on Compensation for Enlargement*, 21 International Trade Reporter (BNA) 1754, 1755 (28 October 2004). [Hereinafter, *EU, Philippines Feud.*]

from a reduction of duties via the union or agreement, are not obligated to provide compensation to the countries joining the union or agreement as "payment" for the benefit.

The principal and most-high profile instance in which Article XXIV:6 and the *Understanding* are potentially applicable is the enlargement of the EU from 15 to 25 countries on 1 May 2004. The 10 new EU member states were Cyprus, the Czech Republic, Estonia, Hungary, Latvia, Lithuania, Malta, Poland, Slovakia, and Slovenia. Because the 10 new EU member states had to discontinue their national tariff regimes and adopt the EU CET, they increased tariffs on various goods.

In connection with the 2004 *Trade Policy Review* of the EU by the WTO, as well as in other venues, the U.S. expressed concern about the trade impact of the EU's enlargement.[46] (The WTO conducts such Reviews every 2 years of Canada, EU, Japan, and U.S., every 4 years of other major trading nations, and every 6 years of the rest of the WTO Membership except for least developed countries.) The U.S. was particularly concerned about tariff hikes in the new EU member states on agricultural products such as poultry and wheat gluten.[47] The U.S. called for adequate compensation for these tariff hikes, as well as for increases in barriers to services.

Along with the U.S., roughly 24 other WTO Members called on the EU for compensatory adjustments due to its enlargement, including Argentina, Australia, Brazil, China, Colombia, Costa Rica, Ecuador, Guatemala, India, Japan, Korea, Malaysia, New Zealand, Pakistan, Panama, Taiwan, Thailand, and Uruguay.[48] One such Member, the Philippines focused on tuna (a major export from the Philippines to the EU), and battled with the EU to be included in negotiations about compensation.[49] All told, the compensation could amount to hundreds of millions of U.S. dollars, and include products such as bananas (exported by Latin American countries to the EU), garlic and mushrooms (exported by China to the EU), and sugar

---

46. *See* Daniel Pruzin, *U.S. Hits Out at EU Trade Barriers at WTO Trade Policy Review Meeting*, 21 International Trade Reporter (BNA) 1753, 1754 (28 October 2004).

47. The initial list of products about which the U.S. claimed compensation covered 260 tariff lines. Separately, the U.S. expressed concern about the EU decision to raise tariffs on imports of brown rice effective 1 September 2004, which the EU did as part of its reform of its CAP. GATT Article XXVIII negotiations occurred on this matter. *See* Daniel Pruzin, *EU Under Pressure on Farm Tariffs in Enlargement Compensation Talks*, 21 International Trade Reporter (BNA) 1714, 1715 (21 October 2004). The EU took the position compensation was due on only about 130 tariff lines. *See* Daniel Pruzin, *EU Gives More Time for Negotiations on Compensation Following Enlargement*, 21 International Trade Reporter (BNA) 1633 (7 October 2004). [Hereinafter, *EU Gives More Time.*]

48. *See EU Gives More Time.*

49. The dispute arose over a 1980 *Understanding*, which sets out procedures for negotiating compensation arrangements, such as a deadline for filing a compensation claim within 90 days of the date a tariff hike is formally notified to the Contracting Parties (*i.e.*, WTO Members). The Philippines argued the 1980 *Understanding* requires a WTO Member raising tariffs to consult with Members on the tariff hikes, and make compensation offers, before the 90-day period begins to run. *See EU, Philippines Feud.*

(exported by several countries to the EU). Compensation adjustments also may be necessary for non-agricultural products, such as television sets and video recorders.

Obviously, an Article XXIV:6 negotiation is a zero-sum game. The country or countries being asked for compensation—such as the EU—argue the tariff increases on some goods are outweighed by the trade benefits from integration, and on average, trade barriers are lower as a result of the RTA. The game is played through product-by-product, country-by-country discussions. If no deal is reached on compensation, then a WTO Member seeking compensation unilaterally can withdraw market access commitments. (However, typically it must do so within six months of the date the tariff increases associated with the RTA take effect, and it must notify the WTO Members at least 30 days in advance of the withdrawal of concessions.) In the EU enlargement case, the EU announced it would not prevent a WTO Member from exercising its right to withdraw concessions if a timely negotiated settlement could not be reached.

- **Gabon and *CEMAC***

A dispute dating back to 1995 when Gabon joined the WTO was whether Gabon should pay compensation for joining *CEMAC*, a CU formed under a 1994 accord among ECCAS states that initially united under the 1964 *Brazzaville Treaty*.[50] Their original CU entered into force in 1966 with five countries: Cameroon; Central African Republic; Chad; Republic of Congo; and Gabon. Equatorial Guinea joined in 1983, and *CEMAC* superseded the original CU in June 1999. The dispute was noted in Gabon's 2001, 2007, and 2013 WTO Trade Policy Reviews.

When Gabon joined *CEMAC*, it adjusted its tariffs on non-agricultural goods to match the *CEMAC* CET. The changes meant Gabon raised duties on 38% (2,131) of its tariff lines in excess of its bound rates set in its WTO Schedule of Concessions. The U.S. and EU, among others, demanded compensation under GATT Articles XXIV:6 and XXVIII. In November 2014, Gabon struck a deal.

Gabon agreed to raise its bound rates on 2,159 tariff lines, but cut them on 2,626 lines. As a result, its average bound rate for non-agricultural imports would be 18.08%. Assume this outcome was technically correct under GATT-WTO law. Was it fair? Was it consistent with social justice? Does insistence on compensation, even where a legal entitlement to it exists, enhance national security?

VI. Third Discipline: Notification under Article XXIV:7

The third discipline on RTAs that GATT Article XXIV sets forth is a rule about notification and, in some instances, modification.[51] Paragraph 7 of this Article states:

---

50. *See* World Trade Organization, *Gabon Announces Final Deal Reached with WTO Members on Tariff Changes*, 17 November 2014, www.wto.org/english/news_e/news14_e/good_17nov14_e.htm.

51. Emphasis added.

(a) Any contracting party deciding to enter into a *customs union* or *free-trade area*, or an *interim agreement* leading to the formation of such a union or area, shall promptly *notify* the Contracting Parties and *shall make available to them such information regarding the proposed union or area as will enable them to make such reports and recommendations to contracting parties as they may deem appropriate.*

(b) If, after having studied the plan and schedule included in an *interim agreement* referred to in paragraph 5 in consultation with the parties to that agreement and taking due account of the information made available in accordance with the provisions of sub-paragraph (a), the Contracting Parties find that such agreement is *not likely to result in the formation of a customs union or a free-trade area within the period contemplated by the parties to the agreement or that such period is not a reasonable one,* the Contracting Parties *shall make recommendations to the parties* to the agreement. The parties shall *not maintain or put into force,* as the case may be, such *agreement if they are not prepared to modify it in accordance with these recommendations.*

As the italicized language indicates, two or more WTO Members contemplating the establishment of a CU, FTA, or interim agreement must notify the WTO of their plan. If these Members are seeking to form a CU or FTA, then they also must provide the WTO with sufficient information to allow it to make appropriate recommendations.

The WTO *Understanding on the Interpretation of Article XXIV* supplements the Article XXIV:7 discipline. The *Understanding* obliges WTO Members contemplating an RTA to engage substantively with the relevant Working Party. That Party reports to the Council on Trade in Goods, which can make recommendations to the Membership.[52]

Suppose two or more WTO Members are entering an interim RTA deal. Suppose, also, the WTO (at its, *i.e.,* the Membership's, initiative[53]) finds the expected date for establishing the CU or FTA is either unreasonable or unlikely. This finding might be based on a sense the transition period is too long, or the Members will not be able to set up the RTA by the end of the period. Then, the Members involved in the interim agreement must hold off creating the RTA.

This scenario is less problematical than it may seem. The lengthy period suggests circumstances in which the Members are not terribly committed to regional trade liberalization. They must await WTO guidance. Only after putting

---

52. *See Understanding on the Interpretation of Article XXIV* at ¶¶ 7–11. *See also* BHALA & KENNEDY, § 2-2(d)(1) at 169–170 (discussing the WTO Committee on Regional Trade Agreements).

53. *See* JACKSON 1969 § 24.6 at 604–605 (emphasizing "[t]he initiative for disapproval must come from the Contracting Parties—there is no prerequisite of 'approval' for an interim agreement," and concluding that "as long as the interim agreement is 'prima facie' in compliance with GATT," contracting parties have "wide latitude" to enter into such agreements without fear of an adverse recommendation from the CONTRACTING PARTIES).

the recommendations of the WTO into effect are they permitted to move forward with the RTA.

The reason for the third discipline is not readily apparent. However, the logic becomes evident when its historical basis is understood. On the one hand, the drafters of the *ITO Charter* and GATT knew that in many instances, an RTA could not be created and operational instantaneously. They appreciated the practical political and economic needs for a transition period. On the other hand, they did not want that period to be abused. They were concerned countries anticipating the entry into force of their RTA might take advantage of an interim period by writing preferences into their forthcoming arrangement that would make the RTA look more like a PTA.[54] Thus, Article XXIV:5(c) tries to minimize this risk by calling for a "plan and schedule."

Quite obviously, that verbal formula is ambiguous. Precisely what must a "plan" consist of? How detailed must it be, particularly given the practical fact that politicians to whom trade negotiators report may want room to maneuver during the interim period? In their 1965 interim agreement toward an FTA, Australia and New Zealand left a great deal unmentioned. They covered only about half of the trade between them, and of that half covered, roughly 90% already qualified for duty-free treatment. Hence, their interim deal eliminated duties on approximately 5% of their bilateral trade.[55]

As for a "schedule" in an interim agreement, what is a reasonable period for implementation? Some less developed countries, as well as developed countries with politically powerful domestic industries feeling threatened by regional trade liberalization, may demand a long transition for adjustment. The period in which Greece associated with the EEC was 22 years. That may seem unreasonable (other than to trade lawyers familiar with Ancient Greek history). There was no consensus about it in the Working Party that examined the terms of association, nor among the Contracting Parties that adopted the Working Party's Report.[56] To mitigate the tension between the need for a transition period, but not too long a one, the drafters of GATT used equivocal phraseologies — *"plan* and *schedule"* and *"reasonable* length of time" in Article XXIV:5(c), and "such period is not a *reasonable* one" in Article XXIV:7(b).

Fortunately, the WTO *Understanding on the Interpretation of Article XXIV* provides some guidance. It explains only in *"exceptional* cases" would a period in excess of a decade be considered "reasonable."[57] Of course, this advice amounts to a trans-

---

54. *See* DAM, 282.

55. *See* DAM, 283.

56. The Working Party discussion of the time period is found at *Association of Greece with the European Economic Community, Report Adopted on 15 November 1962*, B.I.S.D. (11th Supp.) 149, 150 (1963). *See* KENNETH W. DAM, THE GATT 283 (1970) (discussing the Greek association matter).

57. *See Understanding on the Interpretation of Article XXIV* ¶ 3 (emphasis added).

fer of pressure, namely, from defining "reasonable" to defining "exceptional." If the parties to an interim agreement can explain why they need more than 10 years, then they may well get the additional time they want with being given a "hard time."

A final point on this discipline is about what it does not require. Significantly, it does not involve an application to the WTO, nor hold out the prospect of acceptance or rejection by the WTO. RTA creation does not require advance permission from the WTO, and the WTO is not a judge of proposed RTAs. The rule envisions a consultative process whereby Members interested in constructing a CU, FTA, or interim agreement work with the multilateral organization.

At least in theory, that consultative process is more than just a courtesy. It is designed to let the WTO stay abreast of regionalization, and allow for it to influence the process in a positive way that accords with the aspiration for trade liberalization among all WTO Members. Of course, the existence of Article XXIV:11 and its Interpretative Note suggests India and Pakistan are not technically bound by the rule. Should they invoke Paragraph 11, they would be free to consult with the WTO, or not, as they choose.

VII. Are RTA Disciplines Parlous?

GATT Article XXIV contains three vaguely drafted rules about RTAs (both FTAs and CUs, discussed earlier). Given the passive approach historically taken to these rules, and their texts themselves, could it be argued the entire Article is not worth much? The World Bank reported in 2000 that nearly every country in the world was a member of an RTA, or discussing the possibility of joining one, and that over one-half of cross-border trade occurred within actual or prospective RTAs.[58] Decades ago, Professor Jackson identified correctly the "basic problem" of the Article:

> [It contains] criteria that are *so ambiguous* or so unrelated to the goals and policies of GATT Contracting Parties that the international community was not prepared to make compliance with the technicalities of Article XXIV the *sine qua non* of eligibility for the exception from other GATT obligations.[59]

In brief, what difference does Article XXIV really make? If the three rules do not amount to much in the RTA design process, and are not enforced vigorously, then could all WTO Members be said to have a *de facto* waiver from them, while under Article XXIV:11 (discussed later) India and Pakistan just happen to have a *de jure* waiver as well?

---

58. *See* THE WORLD BANK, TRADE BLOCS ix (2000).

59. *See* JACKSON 1969, § 24.4 at 588 (emphasis added). *See also id.*, 591 (stating "[a]lthough the *Havana Charter's* special article for developing countries' regional agreements was not incorporated into GATT, in practice it appears that the essence of its provisions may have been followed in GATT").

That conclusion is harsh. First, the actual and potential relevance of a law "on the books" ought not to be ignored as long as that law remains "on the books." Through Article XXIV:11, India and Pakistan need not worry about the rest of Article XXIV, or other GATT obligations, when thinking about an RTA between them. The legal fact remains the rest of the WTO Members do have to pay some attention—however scant—to these duties. For them, the three Article XXIV rules are law "on the books."

Second, whether the enforcement history of Article XXIV is a reliable guide for future WTO behavior is unclear. The GATT record bespoke a passive approach. Most, if not all, notified RTAs, enjoyed the Article XXIV benefits, regardless of their compliance with it.[60] But, that record was not uniform, in the sense some RTAs attracted more scrutiny than others. The EEC and the EFTA received more stringent examination than RTAs among developing countries.[61] Moreover, the WTO Secretariat and Membership could take the Article more seriously than the GATT Secretariat and contracting parties.

Simply put, not enough time has elapsed since 1 January 1995, when the WTO was born, to know the true value of Article XXIV. What is certain is in other areas of trade law, GATT rules thought nearly dead letter have been resurrected. Safeguards and Article XIX, and Appellate Body decisions in that area (*e.g.*, about the need to show unforeseen circumstances), are an example. What also is evident today is the considerable concern, perhaps more so than existed in the 1950s through 1980s, about regionalism and its possible pernicious effects for the multilateral trading system. That concern is manifest in many academic books, articles, and project reports on the topic.

In practice, the enthusiasm and policies of a country regarding regional trade integration varies according to more than economic, political, security, and cultural variables. What also matters are the geographic neighborhood of that country, and the vision of that country for its future position in its neighborhood, and for the neighborhood itself. And, in respect of vision, few leaders are as visionary as Sir Winston S. Churchill (1874–1965, PM, 1940–1945, 1951–1955), who spoke of a "United States of Europe."

---

60. *See* JACKSON 1969, § 24.4 at 587; Kenneth W. Dam, *Regional Economic Arrangements and the GATT: The Legacy of a Misconception*, 30 UNIVERSITY OF CHICAGO LAW REVIEW 615, 660–661 (1963) (calling the GATT record "a sorry one").

61. *See* JACKSON 1969, § 24.4 at 590.

Chapter 5

Special Disciplines for India and Pakistan[1]

I. Historical Context of Article XXIV:11: August 1947 British Partition of India

For most scholars, students, and practitioners of International Trade Law, Paragraph 11 of GATT Article XXIV is a barely cognizable obscurity.[2] Article XXIV:11 states:

> Taking into account the *exceptional circumstances* arising out of the establishment of *India and Pakistan* as independent States and recognizing the fact that they have long constituted an economic unit, the contracting parties agree that *the provisions of this Agreement shall not prevent the two countries from entering into special arrangements with respect to the trade between them, pending* the establishment of their mutual trade relations on a *definitive* basis.[3]

Lawyers and scholars are not to blame. Blame goes to India and Pakistan. They have not taken advantage of this special exception, which the GATT drafters created for them.[4]

---

1. Documents References:
   (1) *Havana (ITO) Charter* Articles 43–45
   (2) GATT Article XXIV
   (3) Relevant provisions in FTAs

2. This statement is true even with respect to trade law *aficionados*, and despite the fact regionalism and the rest of Article XXIV has, and continues to be, the subject of intense scrutiny. Paragraph 11 attracts essentially no attention in the classic treatises on GATT, namely, DAM and JACKSON 1969. Likewise, there is no recollection of it in contemporary treatises, such as *World Trade Law*, which your Textbook author published with Professor Kevin Kennedy (and for which the former takes the blame). Even books dwelling on legal aspects of Article XXIV, such as James H. Mathis' excellent *Regional Trade Agreements in the GATT/WTO* (2002), do not include it.

3. Emphasis added. The discussion of Article XXIV:11 in this and subsequent Sections draws on Raj Bhala, *The Forgotten Mercy: GATT Article XXIV:11 and Trade on the Subcontinent*, 2002 NEW ZEALAND LAW REVIEW 301–337 (2002).

4. Instead, of taking advantage of Article XXIV:11, there are constant reminders of just how sad the *status quo* on the Subcontinent is. While in Pakistan in February 2001, your Textbook author learned about the roughly 1 trainload per week of goods coming from India to Pakistan across the border of the partitioned state of Punjab. "Why did the Indian potatoes not sell well in Pakistan?"

Rather, since their independence from the British, India and Pakistan have been wildly successful at sabre rattling on their boundary, going to war over Kashmir, and diverting vast resources from economic development toward military armaments, including nuclear weaponry. These South Asian powers have failed miserably to build a meaningful FTA, much less a CU, despite the fact free trade once reigned in their region, and despite the fact many of their peoples (such as the Punjabis of Pakistan and India) share a common culture, language, and tastes and are natural entrepreneurs. They have fallen into the trap of thinking peace and security is to be had through menacing soldiers and their ordnance rather than through wealth-generating traders and investors and their capital. They have not even tried to put Cordell Hull's vision into practice. While mired in that trap, nearly 200 RTAs entered into force.[5]

To be sure, there exists a *SAPTA*, associated with *SAARC*, which entered into force on 8 December 1995 and consists of the seven countries on the Indian Subcontinent (*i.e.*, Bangladesh, Bhutan, India, Maldives, Nepal, Pakistan, and Sri Lanka.) But as yet, *SAPTA* trade liberalizing rules are not ambitious in terms of scope and product coverage. Nothing like the possibility created by the drafters of GATT in Article XXIV:11 exists.

For those outside the Indian Subcontinent, it may be tempting to dismiss the provision. Their counterparts on the Subcontinent have not taken it seriously. The better approach is to examine Paragraph 11. First, there is a hopeful possibility

---

"Because many potential consumers thought the Indians deliberately poisoned the potatoes" was the reply from the hosts in Lahore.

About a year later, religious violence broke out in the Indian state of Gujarat. Muslims attacked a train containing Hindu pilgrims, and 58 people burned to death. *See Shameless*, THE ECONOMIST, 20 April 2002, at 39. Prime Minister Atal Behari Vajpayee (1924–, Prime Minister, 1996, 1998–2004) rightly condemned the initial carnage, but was slow to damn the retaliatory slaughter by Hindus of hundreds of innocent Muslims that resulted in at least 800 deaths. When the condemnation came from the Prime Minister, so too did an echo of anti-Muslim sentiment. *The Economist* quoted his rhetorical question: "but who lit the fire and how did it spread?" *See id. The Financial Times* indicated he (or his Chief Minister in Gujarat, with his tacit acquiescence) said: "Wherever there are Muslims, they do not want to live with others. . . . Instead of living peacefully, they want to propagate their religion by creating terror in the minds of others." *Quoted in Gandhi's Horror*, FINANCIAL TIMES, 16 April 2002, at 14.

Years later, in March 2010 while at the Wagah Border Closing Ceremony on the Indian Punjabi side near Amritsar, not much had changed as to trade value or volume, or mutual suspicion and hostility. There was considerable optimism on the Indian side, a sense that India was a nation moving onward and upward. Pakistan was nearly a failed state, with far less Bollywood cheer on its than on the Indian side. Happily, in 2012 Pakistan agreed to grant India MFN duties, thus rekindling hope for improved trade.

5. Specifically, of the 172 RTAs in force as of July 2000, 148 were FTAs and 24 were CUs. *See* Committee on Regional Trade Agreements, *Mapping of Regional Trade Agreements*, WT/REG/W/41 at 4, Chart 1 (11 October 2000), www.wto.org. Those figures have since increased. Between 1948 and 1994, 106 FTAs and CUs (of which 16 were unions) were notified to the GATT. *See* BHALA & KENNEDY, § 2-2(b) at 165. Of course, that does not imply all of these RTAs became powerful regional economic engines. Obviously, that is not the case.

India and Pakistan might one day use it. Second, from a variety of perspectives, these countries are too important to ignore. They are on the front lines in the war on terrorism, and they confront each other with nuclear armaments. They evince both the promise and difficulties of democracy. With over one billion people, they are home to many of the world's poorest souls, and to some of its most dynamic and creative talents. Simply put, Article XXIV:11 is an under-studied provision of GATT containing hope for a strategically important, unstable, and impoverished but rising area.

Why did the drafters insert into GATT a special provision for India and Pakistan? They put the answer in the first sentence of Article XXIV:11 — namely, the "exceptional circumstances" referenced in that sentence. The circumstances were a cataclysm (some might say a debacle): the creation of the two countries as a result of the British Partition of the Indian Subcontinent, effective at midnight 15 August 1947. Paragraph 11 was inserted in GATT one month after the Partition, on 17 September 1947 at the Geneva session of the Preparatory Committee.[6]

Many histories of the Partition have been written. Doubtless, more will be written, because the subject continues to evoke considerable debate on the Subcontinent — often in the context of discussions about the laggard economic performance of that region in comparison with much of the Far East. A few extant accounts are particularly noteworthy, such as Anita Inder Singh's differentiation of Britain's long- and short-term strategic interests in *The Origins of the Partition of India* (1987), and the eyewitness stories in Sir Penderel Moon's *Divide & Quit* (new ed. 1998). Perhaps no historical work on the subject is more compelling than that by Larry Collins and Dominique Lapierre, *Freedom at Midnight* (1975). But, as is to be expected with writings about a troubled past, few studies of Partition are unbiased. Probably Chapter 27 of Stanley Wolpert's *Nehru* (1996), or the summary at the end of Professor Wolpert's *A New History of India* (5th ed. 1997), are among the most straightforward and brief expositions. Likewise, the Partition has captured the imagination of a few dramatists, who have produced movies and novels (again, not always level) re-creating the events. Notable examples include Sir Richard Attenborough's *Gandhi*, and Khushwant Singh's *Train to Pakistan* (1956).

But, there is a common denominator among these accounts. The idea of post-Partition regional economic integration hardly, if ever, is raised, and Article XXIV:11 is a non-issue. As suggested earlier, trade law *aficionados*, and trade negotiators representing India and Pakistan, forget about, or neglect, this specially-tailored provision. Nevertheless, the drafters of GATT were correct in a literal sense when they called the circumstances "exceptional." Had they selected the adjective "cataclysmic" or "chaotic," they would need no pardon for exaggeration. The movement of Hindus and Sikhs from the newly-created Pakistan to India, and of Muslims from

---

6. *See* GATT ANALYTICAL INDEX, vol. 2 at 829. The INDEX incorrectly dates the Partition as 10 August.

India into Pakistan, was the largest known exodus of peoples in modern history—10 million.[7] In it, about one million perished through violence, disease, deprivation, or some evil combination thereof.

With respect to generating Indo-Pakistani trade, the juxtaposition of events could hardly be more macabre. The drafters of GATT worked to build a multilateral trading system precisely when many parts of the Indian Subcontinent were descending into a living Hell. Surely aware of the horror, and resolute in the belief trade could help India and Pakistan in their long upward climb to prosperity and peace, the drafters must have wanted to liberate the two countries, as far as possible, from the strictures of international trade obligations. That much is evident from the text of Article XXIV:11.

As to setting up a CU or FTA, Paragraph 11 removes otherwise-applicable multilateral rules. It gave the giant figures of the day who led their countries—Muhammad Ali Jinnah (1876–1948, in office, 1947–1948) of Pakistan, and Jawaharlal Nehru (1889–1964, PM, 1947–1964) and Mohandas K. (Mahatma) Gandhi (1869–1948) of India—one less problem to worry about, had they been inclined to focus on regional trade integration.[8] After all, the drafters must have reasoned, India and Pakistan had been a single economic unit—British India. Why not continue it as such, and thereby help heal the wounds of Partition, with a CU or FTA? Article XXIV:11 and the Interpretative Note, *Ad Article XXIV, Paragraph 11*, were the burden-lifting devices.

The drafters of GATT well appreciated trade cannot flourish between two countries that jail themselves in a relationship of mistrust. Buyers will not purchase. Sellers will not ship goods. Financiers will not extend credit. Governments will not lessen obstacles to the flow of goods. Sadly, ever since the British Partition of India on 15 August 1947, "mistrust" is the word that best characterizes Indo-Pakistani relations. Pakistan does not even grant India MFN treatment (though India provides it to Pakistan), in clear violation of its Article I:1 obligation.[9] Small wonder, then, the Subcontinent has been fixated more on monstrosities than special dispensations—like Article XXIV:11—during the last half century.

---

7. *See* Donald C. McKay, *Introduction, in* W. Norman Brown, The United States and India and Pakistan viii (1953) (observing the Partition "precipitated the largest exchange of population in recorded history, and much of it took place amidst violence and bloodshed"). I might add the movement included all of one side of my family, from Multan in Pakistan to Amritsar and (ultimately) Patiala in India, and the families of many friends and students.

8. For a rare favorable biography of Jinnah, showing him in a very different light than the movie *Gandhi*, see Akbar S. Ahmed, *Jinnah, Pakistan and Islamic Identity* (1997). *See also* Stanley Wolpert, *Jinnah of Pakistan* (1999) (an excellent account covering all the complexities of Jinnah and his times). For stimulating biographies of Nehru, see Judith M. Brown, *Nehru* (1999) and Stanley Wolpert, *Nehru* (1996). For a synthesis of Gandhi's life and thought, see Raghavan Iyer ed., *The Essential Writings of Mahatma Gandhi* (1991).

9. *See* Bidanda M. Chengappa, *India-Pakistan Trade Relations*, 23 Strategic Analysis issue 3 (June 1999), *posted on* the website of Columbia International Affairs Online, www.ciaonet.org /olj/sa.

The drafters anticipated the possibility, in Article XXIV:11, India and Pakistan might not adhere to certain general obligations, yet did not want this possibility to damage or destroy prospects for an RTA involving the two countries. Through Paragraph 11, the drafters created a unique dispensation, exempting India and Pakistan from GATT obligations in the context of creating a RTA involving them. Aside from Colonial Preferences (in Article I:2), Article XXIV:11 is the only provision in GATT specifically tailored to less developed countries by name.[10]

II. Applying Article XXIV:11 to Indo-Pakistani Trade

How is Article XXIV:11 to be understood? Judging from the reference in the last clause of Article XXIV:11, about "definitive" trade relations, the paragraph appears designed for an interim RTA. Read broadly, it exempts India and Pakistan from GATT obligations in the formation of an interim agreement leading to a CU or FTA. What would happen thereafter, when the transition period has elapsed?

That is, once a CU or FTA is created, are India and Pakistan subject to GATT obligations as regards their new FTA? The answer seems to be "no." The GATT drafters were careful to leave enough "material in the garment" so that India and Pakistan could expand the size a little, as they grew from an interim agreement to a real RTA. The Interpretative Note, *Ad Article XVIV, Paragraph 11*, is the extra material:

> Measures adopted by India and Pakistan in order to carry out *definitive trade arrangements* between them, once they have been agreed upon, *might depart from particular provisions of this Agreement*, but these measures *would in general be consistent with the objectives of the Agreement*.[11]

The generosity of the tailoring job is quite obvious from the italicized language, specifically, "this Agreement." Should they wish to establish a CU or FTA, India and Pakistan shall not have to adhere to the obligations set forth in Article XXIV, nor to the rest of GATT obligations. It is never too late for India and Pakistan. There is no expiry date—no time boundary—on the Article XXIV:11 and its Interpretative Note.

---

10. To be sure, a provision in the Tokyo Round *Enabling Clause* offers a waiver from the MFN obligation in Article I for less developed countries that enter into a regional arrangement for the mutual reduction or elimination of tariff and non-tariff measures. In this respect, the *Enabling Clause* provides leniency for Third World countries to enter into an RTA. *See Decision on Differential and More Favorable Treatment, Reciprocity and Fuller Participation of Developing Countries*, 28 November 1979, B.I.S.D. (26th Supp.) 203–205 at ¶ 2(c) (1980). However, it must be emphasized that the *Clause* embodies a waiver of the MFN duty alone, not all GATT obligations, and thus is significantly less generous than Article XXIV:11.

11. Emphasis added.

To be sure, if India and Pakistan lacked the benefit of Paragraph 11, then they would not be completely forsaken. Suppose they developed a CU, FTA, or interim agreement that was held widely to run afoul of one or more of the three basic disciplines in Article XXIV (notwithstanding their ambiguities). Absent Paragraph 11, India and Pakistan could seek approval of their proposed RTA under Article XXIV:10. That provision empowers the WTO Members, by a two-thirds majority, to approve a proposal that is not in full compliance with the rules. However, uncertainty, scrutiny, and then more uncertainty are the problems with this solution.

The first uncertainty is whether the hypothetical Indo-Pakistani proposal would qualify for treatment under Article XXIV:10. That Paragraph is invoked when a proposal does "not fully comply" with the rules of Article XXIV. But, how is the textual language—"do not comply fully"—to be interpreted, *i.e.,* how much non-compliance can be tolerated? The European Coal and Steel Community (ECSC) freed trade on only 2 categories of products. Therefore, it was thought ineligible for treatment under Paragraph 10. The approval given to it by GATT was under the general waiver authority of Article XXV:5.[12] Assuming the proposal qualified, no doubt it would be put "under the microscope" before Members decided how they would vote. The outcome of the microscopic examination and the voting would by no means be certain.

As Table 5-1 indicates, understanding the text of Article XXIV:11 and *Ad Article XXIV, Paragraph 11*, requires contemplation.

The language of Article XXIV:11 allows India and Pakistan to set up "special arrangements with respect to the trade between them." Would these "special arrangements" be an interim agreement leading to formation of a CU or FTA? Perhaps, but elision and obfuscation must be avoided here.

The "special arrangements" language is used only in Paragraph 11—nowhere else in Article XXIV—and is not defined. In contrast, "interim agreement" is in Paragraphs 5 and 7, and in each place is articulated as "leading to the formation of" a CU or FTA.

Thus, "special arrangements" seems the broader of the two terms, *i.e.,* these "arrangements" could include an interim agreement leading to a CU or FTA. But, they are not limited to an agreement with that goal. The "arrangements" could be any kind of trade deal between India and Pakistan that is "special" in that the two countries do not have the same exchange of concessions with any other country.

There is another reason why "special arrangements" and "interim agreement" should not be interpreted as interchangeable. If they were, then all of Article XXIV:11 might be redundant with the *chapeau* to Article XXIV:5. A basic principle of treaty construction is not to read words so as to render one provision superfluous with another (at least if an alternate reading is available and permissible). Drafters

---

12. *See* KENNETH W. DAM, THE GATT 290 (1970) (discussing this case).

Table 5-1. India, Pakistan, Article XXIV:11, and Interpretative Note

Text	CArticle XXIV:11	CAd Article XXIV, Paragraph 11
Scope of application (type of RTA)?	"Special arrangements with respect to trade between" India and Pakistan.	"Definitive trade arrangements between" India and Pakistan.
Is Paragraph 11 limited to permission to violate the three disciplines in Article XXIV on RTAs (covering substantially all trade, avoiding higher trade barriers against third countries, and notifying and informing the WTO)?	No.	No.
To what does Paragraph 11 apply?	GATT generally. "The provisions of this Agreement [GATT] shall not prevent" entry into special arrangements.	GATT generally. Departures "from particular provisions of this Agreement [GATT]."
Any limitation on Paragraph 11?	None, other than the pendency of the special arrangements, which are viewed as temporary.	None, if the trade measures India and Pakistan adopt to carry out definitive trade arrangements between them are "in general" "consistent with the objectives of the Agreement [GATT]."

are presumed to have meant something, and not just repeated themselves. As the Appellate Body states in the 1996 *Reformulated Gasoline* case: "one of the corollaries of the 'general rule of interpretation' in the [1969] *Vienna Convention [on the Law of Treaties]* is that interpretation must give meaning and effect to all the terms of a treaty. An interpreter is not free to adopt a reading that would result in reducing whole clauses or paragraphs of a treaty to redundancy or inutility."[13]

In this respect, it is important to recall what Paragraph 11 does. By its terms, it ensures "the provisions of this Agreement [*i.e.*, GATT] shall not prevent the two countries from entering into special arrangements . . ." Recall, too, the effect of the *chapeau* to Paragraph 5: it ensures "the provisions of this Agreement shall not prevent . . . the formation of a customs union or of a free-trade area or the adoption of an interim agreement necessary for the formation of a customs union or of a free-trade area . . . ." If "special arrangements" means "interim agreement," then what is

---

13. Appellate Body Report, *United States — Standards for Reformulated and Conventional Gasoline*, WT/DS2/AB/R, 22 (adopted 20 May 1996).

the point of Paragraph 11? India and Pakistan can form an interim agreement and transgress against Paragraph 5.

Finally, the "special arrangements" are not permanent. The language of Article XXIV:11 indicates the arrangements would not constitute "mutual trade relations on a definitive basis." Rather, they would operate "pending" the conclusion of definitive relations. Just how long the period would last would be up to India and Pakistan. Nothing in Paragraph 11 or the Interpretative Note defines the period. What is clear is given the lack of equivalence between "special arrangements" and "interim agreement," the duration of an Indo-Pakistani special trade arrangement would not be (or ought not to be) restricted (or even influenced) by periods contemplated or deemed reasonable by the WTO Members under Article XXIV:7(b) for interim agreements. In other words, the two passages—Paragraphs 11 and 7(b)—should not be linked.

With these observations in mind, what special dispensation would Article XXIV:11 provide India and Pakistan? With respect to a temporary arrangement, consider—first—the Article XXIV discipline on RTAs:

(1) Coverage of substantially all trade between or among the RTA members.

(2) Avoidance of an increase in trade barriers against products from non-RTA members.

(3) Provision of notice and information to the WTO.

Paragraph 11 essentially waives these obligations for India and Pakistan. Indo-Pakistani special arrangements would not have to embrace substantially all of their trade. The arrangements could entail increased barriers against non-Indian, non-Pakistani goods. India and Pakistan would not have to give the WTO advance notice of, or provide information on, these arrangements. In brief, the special arrangements could skirt the three rules (*i.e.*, the GATT-WTO disciplines discussed in a separate Chapter) for as long as trade officials in New Delhi and Islamabad wanted.

To be sure, the political controversy that would ensue might constrain the trade policy makers in those capital cities. Cynics might laugh at special arrangements that cover a *de minimis* amount of trade. The U.S. and other major trading partners of India and Pakistan might not take kindly to higher duties imposed on their goods by either country. Not presenting the interim agreement to the WTO, or mailing a copy to Geneva *fait accompli*, might undermine other WTO-related projects in which India and Pakistan are engaged. Still, as a legal matter, India and Pakistan would be able to commit these transgressions, just because of GATT Article XXIV:11.

Even after India and Pakistan put their trade relations on a definitive basis, possibly by giving birth to a CU or FTA, but perhaps by a trade deal that is somewhat less ambitious, these countries would not have to adhere strictly to the three disciplines. They could point to the Interpretative Note, *Ad Article XXIV, Paragraph 11*, which allows them to "depart from particular provisions of this Agreement," such provisions including the three rules of Article XXIV. To be sure, trade lawyers in New Delhi and Islamabad would have to be mindful of the last clause of this Note—that their RTA-related measures "would in general be consistent with the objectives of the Agreement."

But, general consistency with GATT objectives does not mean scrupulous adherence to the three rules of Article XXIV. Just how far could India and Pakistan go in departing from the rules? The answer is not clear. The last clause of the *Ad Article XXIV*, Paragraph 11 never has been interpreted. India and Pakistan might be forgiven for an RTA with less-than-impressive product coverage, for raising barriers on some products from certain third countries, or for not telling the WTO everything about their endeavor.

In sum, were they so inclined to establish special trade relations between them, India and Pakistan need not pay any attention to the Article XXIV disciplines. As these arrangements evolved into a permanent *status quo* of some sort, the two countries would not have to pay a great deal of attention to those rules, so long as they could claim the new *status quo* was generally consistent with GATT purposes. Clearly, the special dispensation afforded by Article XXIV:11 is considerable.

Of course, a narrow interpretation is not the only way, or even the correct way, to construe Article XXIV:11. The special dispensation Paragraph 11 offers to India and Pakistan, if they reach an interim agreement, and by the Interpretative Note, if they operate a CU or FTA, would not be limited to the three disciplines of Article XXIV. That limitation would exist if the GATT texts said "this *Article*." However, because the texts say "this *Agreement*," India and Pakistan—unlike every other WTO Member—would have a waiver from all other GATT obligations with respect to any "special arrangements" between them for as long as those arrangements are in place. In other words, the special dispensation seems boundless.[14]

---

14. It is important not to overstate the force of Article XXIV:11, given the *chapeau* to Article XXIV:5. Consider a hypothetical about Article XIII, inspired by an example Professor Dam offers. *See* DAM, 280 (1970). Article XIII contains rules against discrimination in the application of permissible QRs. (In the *Bananas* case, the WTO Panel gave a brief and clear tutorial on these rules.) Suppose an Indo-Pakistani CU or FTA dismantles TRQs, which plainly are covered by Article XIII non-discrimination rules (by virtue of Paragraph 5 of that Article). The problem is TRQs are removed on Indo-Pakistani trade, but not on imports from third countries. Suppose Article XXIV:11 did not exist.

Would the 2 countries be vulnerable to a claim they ran afoul of Article XIII:1, which amounts to an MFN-rule for quantitative measures, as it calls for the same prohibition or restriction to be applied to all like products from all contracting parties? Probably not. India and Pakistan could avail themselves of the *chapeau* to Article XXIV:5. That *chapeau* speaks of GATT not preventing formation of a CU, FTA, or interim agreement. The general reference to "the provisions of this Agreement" includes Article XIII:1.

A distinct question is whether India and Pakistan would be vulnerable to a claim that the QRs they impose against third-country imports do not satisfy the BOP purposes for which such restrictions are allowed, *e.g.*, a claim under Article XVIII:B. Professor Dam seems to think so. *See* DAM, 281, fn. 13. He argues if a member of a CU or FTA faces genuine BOP difficulties, then logically it would impose quantitative restrictions against imports from all sources. He also urges that if only

It is, almost. The only boundary is the last clause of the Interpretative Note. It is triggered by the entry into force of definitive arrangements, such as a CU or RTA, between India and Pakistan. At that juncture, their RTA-related measures would have to stay generally consistent with GATT objectives, which the GATT Preamble sets out:

> Recognizing that their relations in the field of trade and economic endeavor should be conducted with a view to *raising standards of living, ensuring full employment* and a *large and steadily growing volume of real income and effective demand, developing the full use of the resources of the world* and *expanding the production and exchange of goods;*
>
> Being desirous of contributing to *these objectives* by entering into reciprocal and mutually advantageous arrangements directed to the substantial reduction of tariffs and other barriers to trade and to the elimination of discriminatory treatment in international commerce . . . .[15]

Supplementing the above-quoted express statement of objectives would be reasonable inferences drawn about the purposes of GATT from some of its rules. For example, surely enhancing peace and security, through broader and deeper trade ties, is important. It is all the more important in a post-9/11 world in which instability and Islamist extremism, bred in part by poverty and marginalization, is a threat to all nations.

Was that not the vision of Cordell Hull (1871–1955), President Franklin Delano Roosevelt's Secretary of State, for the world trading system?[16] National security concerns resonate in Article XXI, and are detectable in Part IV of GATT, where the plight of developing countries is given special attention. The point is only RTA-related

---

one country in a CU or FTA has *bona fide* BOP difficulties, but the other Party-countries enforce QRs against third-country products, then the other Parties are enforcing these measures to protect the BOP of the first Party. That is an action not countenanced anywhere in GATT. Finally, Professor Dam finds little comfort in Article XXIV:8(a)(i)-(ii) as a basis for an exemption from an Article XVIII:B-type claim. Sub-Paragraph (ii) allows Parties in a CU to apply "substantially the same . . . *other regulations of commerce*" to third country trade, whereas sub-paragraph (i) refers to "other *restrictive* regulations of commerce." (Emphasis added). Professor Dam believes QRs fall within (i) (as "restrictive" regulations of commerce), but not (ii) (as they are not just general regulations of commerce).

The point is that depending on the facts, any WTO Member contemplating formation of an RTA may be able to rely on the *chapeau* of Article XXIV:5. From the perspective of India and Pakistan, they would receive a "double bounty." First, they could obtain special dispensation via Paragraph 11. Second, should they need it, they could obtain "off the rack" (*i.e.,* generally tailored) help via the *chapeau.*

15. Emphasis added.

16. *See* Michael A. Butler, Cautious Visionary: Cordell Hull and Trade Reform, 1933–1937 164–165, 168–169(1998); Raj Bhala, *Poverty, Islam, and Doha*, 36 International Lawyer 159, 174–175 (2002).

measures that egregiously flaunt GATT objectives would put India and Pakistan in legal peril.

It might be difficult to justify discriminatory treatment of a large percentage of trade from all other WTO Members in violation of the MFN and national treatment rules in Articles I:1 and III:4. Similarly, application of AD measures without determining material injury or threat thereof, regardless of the product or exporting country, contrary to Article VI:6(a), could be difficult to rationalize as consistent with GATT objectives. Yet, save for these sorts of blatant transgressions, India and Pakistan could fashion a cogent argument measures associated with their definitive trade arrangements satisfy the criterion of the last clause of the Article XXIV:11 Interpretative Note.

Finally, India and Pakistan need not fret about any single measure. The Interpretative Note speaks of "measures," in the plural, India and Pakistan adopt to carry out their definitive mutual trade arrangements, not one "measure," standing alone. Does avoidance of the singular noun mean a balancing test among the measures is to be used? Perhaps what matters is general consistency of the measures? Then, India and Pakistan have leeway to argue any one offending measure must be seen in the context of the entire mosaic of their trade rules, and the mosaic is harmonious with GATT objectives.

III. Open Questions about Indian Subcontinent and Article XXIV:11

As Article XXIV:11 has not been used, open questions about it exist. Among them, one concerns sectoral coverage, and the other covers country coverage.

First, could Paragraph 11 be read to exempt India and Pakistan from the "other" RTA provision that exists in world trade law, namely, Article V of the *GATS*. That Article contains an exception from the general unconditional MFN principle in *GATS* Article II:1. Arguably, Article XXIV:11 is entirely irrelevant to *GATS*. After all, GATT deals with the cross-border exchange of goods, and the *GATS* covers trade in services. There is a degree of (but not necessarily total) mutual exclusivity.

Second, what implications exist for countries on the Indian Subcontinent other than India and Pakistan. In particular, were India and Pakistan inclined to consider recourse to the Article XXIV:11, would it be (in fact, is it already) too late for Bangladesh, the oft-forgotten South Asian country that is the largest of the roughly 50 least developed countries in the world? That is, could Bangladesh take advantage of Paragraph 11? In turn, might it then be able to start narrowing the large and apparently growing gap between its economic growth and level of development, and the performance and standards of its South Asian neighbors, particularly India and Pakistan?

This hypothetical (which could be posed for Bhutan, Maldives, Nepal, and Sri Lanka) actually is relevant to the Bangladeshi economy. As a leading Bangladeshi scholar, the economist Rehman Sobhan (1935–), points out, the future of that economy:

> lies in trade not aid . . .
>
>   . . .
>
> In order to enhance and develop Bangladesh's production potential we will need to have access to the wider South Asian market particularly to India, through the mechanism of the *South Asian Free Trade Area* . . . .[17]

Yet, insufficient progress has been made. At about 12%, Bangladesh's ratio of merchandise exports to GDP, while rising over the last quarter century, still is only 2/3 that of other low-income countries.[18] Its export base is undiversified, as it depends on one, low value-added sector: RMGs. The majority of Bangladesh's trade, 80%, is with OECD members.[19] Only about 2½% of its trade is with its South Asian neighbors.

Given the lack of geographic diversification, it is unsurprising lawful trade with what ought to be an obvious partner—India—is below potential. There is a huge illegal trade in goods across the Indo-Bangladeshi border, in part because the cost of crossing the border in compliance with tariff and non-tariff rules exceeds the costs associated with risking smuggling.[20] For instance, jute and hides cross from Bangladesh surreptitiously in exchange for consumer goods from India.[21] In brief, the point is lowering barriers might boost legal trade as a percentage of GDP, help in sectoral and geographic diversification, and improve regional integration. Conceivably, it might result in higher tariff revenues actually collected, simply by reducing the incentive to evade customs rules.

Could Article XXIV:11 be a vehicle toward improvement? By its terms, the provision applies only to India and Pakistan. Bangladesh ceased to be a part of Pakistan (namely, East Pakistan) in 1971, declaring independence on 26 March of that year,

---

17. *See* Rehman Sobhan, *Building a Responsible Civil Society: Challenges and Prospects*, in Bangladesh—Promise and Performance 341, 352, 361 (Rounaq Jahan ed. 2000) (emphasis original). This book contains a rare collection of stimulating essays on the development of Bangladesh.

18. *See* Azizur Rahman Khan, *Economic Development: From Independence to the End of the Millennium*, in Bangladesh—Promise and Performance 247, 259 (noting merchandise export to GDP ratios of 2.4%, 5.6%, and 12.2% in 1975, 1980, and 1997, respectively). [Hereinafter, Khan.]

19. *See* Khan, 259–260 (referring to trade with the OECD and India in 1996 and 1993, respectively).

20. *See* Khan, 260–261.

21. *See* Raj Bhala, Dictionary of International Trade Law (3rd ed., 2015) (entry on "SAARC"). Similarly, gold and heroin are traded illegally from Pakistan in exchange for whisky from India. Black-market trade between India and Pakistan is estimated at over $1 billion annually, which is double or quadruple the value of official trade. A number of illustrations of black-market trade are provided in Bidanda M. Chengappa, *India-Pakistan Trade Relations*, 23 Strategic Analysis issue 3 (June 1999), Columbia International Affairs Online, www.ciaonet.org/olj/sa.

and forming a government in exile on 17 April.[22] India recognized Bangladesh as a sovereign state on 6 December 1971, and 10 days later all West Pakistani forces surrendered to combined Indian and Bangladeshi troops. Pakistan recognized the existence of Bangladesh on 22 February 1974. Bangladesh was admitted to the U.N. on 17 September 1974. Thus, a strict application of the textual language would mean Paragraph 11 applied to Bangladesh only so long as it was East Pakistan.

Set against this response is Public International Law, specifically, the law of state succession. Could Bangladesh accede to all the rights and privileges held by the country, Pakistan, of which it once was a part? Furthermore, a humane, and accurate, interpretation would be Article XXIV:11 was designed to help people living in the region that now is known by a different name. The suffering the Bengali people of the former East Pakistan have experienced — the triumvirate of war, economic deprivation, and bad governance — ought to dispose even a hard-hearted trade lawyer or scholar favorably to this interpretation. If the WTO were to extend Paragraph 11 to Bangladesh, then the onus would fall upon leaders in Dhaka, Delhi and Islamabad, to realize its benefits.

---

22. The dates are drawn from the helpful chronology in Rounaq Jahan ed., *Building a Responsible Civil Society: Challenges and Prospects*, *in* Bangladesh — Promise and Performance xxv (2000).

Chapter 6

Preferential ROOs[1]

I. Indispensability

Suppose Countries A, B, C, and D, all WTO Members, form an FTA or CU. As a result, goods from any one of these countries may be imported into any other country in the RTA duty-free. Suppose Country E, but not Country F, is a WTO Member. There are three distinct tariff regimes in Countries A, B, C, and D.

First, preferential duty-free treatment applies to goods originating from within the FTA or CU. Second, MFN rates, negotiated and bound as a result of previous GATT-WTO rounds, apply to goods of E imported into Countries A, B, C, or D. Third, non-MFN rates apply to goods from F imported into Countries A, B, C, or D.

How does a customs official in Countries A, B, C, or D determine whether a good is from (1) the FTA or CU, (2) Country E, or (3) Country F? Customs officials in the *NAFTA* Parties—countries analogous to A, B, C, and D—face this dilemma. Country E is akin to any WTO Member, while Country F is akin to North Korea. Preferential ROOs resolve the dilemma. Such rules establish the country of origin of a good to determine whether it is from the FTA or CU in question. In essence, a "ROO" is a genealogical rule about a category of merchandise. A ROO is "preferential" insofar as DFQF treatment is accorded that article depending on its genealogy. In contrast, non-preferential ROOs determine the correct country of origin label to be affixed to a product or its container, but DFQF treatment is not at stake.

There would be no need for preferential ROOs if all goods from all countries were imported at MFN rates, regardless of the origin of the goods. But, as the above example illustrates, a "true" MFN system does not exist. In practice, the origin of goods matters because the international trade community is divided into customs unions and free trade areas. Because they assign a nationality to a good that is treated differently for tariff purposes according to its country of origin, preferential ROOs are the cornerstone of any customs union or FTA. They ensure that only goods originating from a country in a preferential trading arrangement receive DFQF treatment. After all, the countries that are party to the arrangement have a legitimate interest in seeking to limit the benefits of the arrangement to themselves, *i.e.*, in avoiding free riders. But, the key issue is whether the preferential ROOs

---

1. Documents References:
   (1) *NAFTA* Chapter 4
   (2) Rules of Origin in other FTAs

concocted by the member countries to delineate their goods from the goods of all other countries are unacceptably trade-distorting.

Preferential ROOs also are of paramount importance in resolving the problem of "trade deflection." This term refers to re-routing of products originating in a third country that do not have preferential access to the market of one country. They lack DFQF access because the third country is not a member of the same FTA or CU as the other country. Goods are re-routed through a second country that does have preferential access, because the second country is a member of the relevant FTA or CU. While "trade deflection" is largely synonymous with "trans-shipment," in fact deflection can occur through other than simple trans-shipment, *i.e.*, export from one country and subsequent re-export to another country. In particular, the goods can undergo a basic operation, such as re-packaging, cleaning, or sorting, when they are re-routed in the second country. Preferential ROOs of an FTA or CU are designed to counteract trade deflection by either means, barring preferential treatment for non-originating deflected goods.

For example, suppose Countries R, S, and T are WTO Members, but Country Z is not a Member. Country Z exports basketballs to Country R. In turn, Country R exports the basketballs to Country S. No change is made to them in R. Or, alternatively, they are repackaged, cleaned, or sorted. Thus, the basketballs are deflected from Z to S through R. Assume Country S levies a 20% tariff on the basketballs trans-shipped through Country R, and R protests. Country R points out that as a result of previous negotiations conducted under GATT-WTO auspices, the binding tariff commitment made by Country S with respect to basketballs is 15%. It further points out that S imposes a 12% duty on basketballs imported directly from Country T. Thus, Country R argues it is entitled to either the 15% tariff by virtue of the binding commitment, or the 12% rate by virtue of the MFN clause in GATT Article I. Country R's argument must fail because the basketballs are the product of Country Z.

A slight alteration in the facts may radically change this outcome in Country R's favor. Assume the goods in question are not basketballs but copper. While the copper is in Country R, it is melted down, processed, and made into copper wire. Is the copper wire the product of Z or R? Mere trans-shipment, or even re-packaging, cleaning, and sorting does not result in a change in the country of origin of the good, as the basketball example illustrates. However, transformation of the good into another good may result in a change in the country of origin. Making copper wire out of copper may be a sufficient transformation to justify Country R's argument it is entitled to the bound or MFN rate, because the copper wire truly is a product of R and is categorized differently, and thus a different duty rate applies.

II. Three Generic Categories

In spite of global disharmony, preferential ROOs may be placed in one of three general categories: the (1) Substantial Transformation Test; (2) Value-Added Test;

and (3) Hybrid Approach. These categories are based in part on the work of the 1953 GATT drafting group and the 1974 *Kyoto Convention*.

Note these generic types are the same as those for non-preferential ROOs, even though the purposes served by the preferential versus non-preferential ROOs are different. That means it is not necessarily to re-learn from scratch the concepts underlying preferential ROOs, as those concepts are the same as those for the non-preferential ROOs. But, in practice, it is vital to know whether the context in which a ROO is being applied is country of origin labeling (in which case a non-preferential ROO is used) or DFQF treatment (in which case a preferential ROO is used).

- **Category 1: Substantial Transformation Test and CTC Rule**

   Under the "Substantial Transformation" Test, merchandise becomes the product of the most recent exporting country in which a "substantial" transformation of the input goods imported from another country occurred. For example, transforming copper into copper wire might be considered "substantial."

   This Test still begs the question: what is "substantial"? A reasonably precise, objective answer is a transformation is substantial if it results in a change in the HTS classification of the good, that is, a Change in Tariff Classification (CTC). Specifically, the 4-digit HTS category in which the good is placed is different from the category (categories) of the material(s) used to make the good. That is, if a finished product falls in a tariff classification at the 4-digit level that is different from any of the materials used to make the product, then a shift at the 4-digit level has occurred. This method is sometimes called the "Change in Tariff Heading" (CTH), or simply "tariff shift," rule. If the rule calls for a change at the 6-digit HTS category, *i.e.*, at the level of sub-heading rather than heading, then that rule technically is a "CTSH" rule—a shift in tariff sub-heading.

   Depending on how a tariff shift (whether CTH or CTSH) rule is written, it can allow for less, or more, non-originating material (*i.e.*, inputs) in merchandise. A more flexible tariff shift rule authorizes more inputs from outside the preferential zone to be included in a finished article, and still allow that article to qualify for duty-free treatment. Conversely, a more protectionist tariff shift rule permits fewer inputs from outside FTA, CU, or preference area territory to be in the article if that article is to get duty-free treatment. Notice a more liberal tariff shift rule is analogous to a Regional Value Content (RVC) rule with a lower percentage threshold (*e.g.*, 35%). A more protectionist tariff shift rule is akin to an RVC rule with a higher requisite figure (*e.g.*, 50%).

   For any particular product, a CTH rule may be phrased in positive or negative terms. The positive construction takes the form of saying origin is conferred if there is "a change from any other heading to heading . . . to Chapter ____ . . . ." The negative construction takes the form of saying origin is conferred if there is "a change from any other heading, except for the headings of Chapter ____, to . . . ." Consider the negative construction in relation to specified manufacturing processes (discussed below). Can a negative CTH rule be written to have the same effect as a specified process rule?

Consider the above example involving copper and Countries R, S, T, and Z. Suppose copper appears in one 4-digit HTS classification, while copper wire appears in a different 4-digit heading. The copper is mined in Country Z and exported to Country R, where operations are performed on the copper that result in copper wire. Subsequently, the copper wire is trans-shipped through Country S to Country T. Because of the tariff shift at the 4-digit level, the operations performed in Country R on the copper are "substantial" transformation. Thus, the copper wire is a product of R, not Z.

The CTH rule is particularly helpful in harmonizing ROOs because it relies on the HTS. As of 2014, 207 countries, representing over 98% of world trade, use the HTS. (These figures are up from 1993, the year the Uruguay Round talks concluded, when the HTS covered about 120 countries and 90% of world trade.) In turn, the HTS is structured in a way that facilitates the application of the CTH rule:

> The Harmonized System comprises 21 Sections, 96 Chapters and 1,241 Headings. [More recently, in the U.S. Tariff Schedule, a 22nd Section was introduced for "special classifications." There are now 99 Chapters, with Chapter 77 reserved for future use.] Of these 1,241 headings, 930 are subdivided into 2,449 Sub-Headings, which are further sub-divided into 2,258 two-dash Sub-Headings, thereby providing a total of 5,018 separate categories of classification of goods in the Harmonized System. Classification of goods under these Headings or sub-headings is governed by the Heading or Sub-Heading text, supported by General Rules for the interpretation of the Harmonized System, Section Notes, Chapter Notes and Sub-heading Notes.

> . . .

> The first feature [of the Harmonized System that makes it suitable for use in determining country of origin] is the basic classification division according to industrial sector. [G]oods . . . are first grouped in 21 Sections and then in 96 Chapters which, in principle, are established by industrial sector. This is one of the most important requirements for a nomenclature to qualify for use in the determination of the country of origin, given that the country of origin is determined on the basis of the substantial transformation concept in so far as the goods have been manufactured in two or more countries.

> The second feature is the order of headings within a Chapter. There are 1,241 Headings . . . which constitute the most important level for tariff classification as well as for origin purposes. [H]eadings are placed within a Chapter in the order based upon the degree of processing. For example, Chapter 72 which covers iron and steel begins with pig iron (Heading 72.01) and the heading number increases as a product is further processed; ingot

(Heading 72.04), semi-finished products (Heading 72.06), flat-rolled products (Headings 72.08 to 72.12), bars and rods (Headings 72.13 to 72.15), angles, shapes and sections (Heading 72.16), wire (Heading 72.17). The order of headings within a Chapter generally reflects the degree of processing a product has undergone. This structure makes the Harmonized System a suitable device for applying the concept of substantial transformation in determining the country of origin.[2]

Still, the CTH rule poses some difficulties.

One difficulty is that headings in certain chapters of the HTS do not reflect the degree of processing. For example, there is no processing associated with the live animals listed in Chapter 1. Accordingly, the rule may not always mesh with the HTS. This difficulty reflects the more general fact that the HTS was not designed as a methodology to confer origin. When Product-Specific Rules of Origin (PSROs) are based on the HTS, clever businesses and their attorneys can figure out CTH requirements that best suit their interests, regardless of the underlying economic integrity of those requirements.

A second problem is certain manufacturing or processing operations are deemed insubstantial, even though they result in a change in tariff classification. That is, even a change in tariff classification from one Chapter to another may not result in a substantial transformation. For example, a change to a preparation of vegetables, fruits, or nuts — *i.e.*, items listed in HTS Chapter 20 — from the vegetable products listed in Chapters 6–14 as a result of freezing, canning in water or natural juices, or roasting is not substantial.

Consider HTS Chapter 7, which covers edible vegetables. The first 9 Headings (07.01 to 07.09) list fresh and chilled vegetables. Subsequent headings specify frozen vegetables (Heading 07.10), provisionally preserved vegetables (Heading 07.11) and dried vegetables (Heading 07.12). Have frozen, provisionally preserved, and dried vegetables truly been "substantially" transformed from fresh vegetables? In such cases, countries frequently list exceptions to the CTH rule. Indeed, *NAFTA's* ROOs, which are contained in Section B of Annex 401, contain several dozens of such exceptions. With respect to vegetables, to obtain the status of the country of origin, "a change to heading 07.10 through 07.14 from any other chapter" is required:

> In other words, the change in tariff heading method is not applicable to the classification change within a chapter but is applied only to the classification change from *outside* the chapter. The same is applied in the *NAFTA* in respect to some other chapters, *i.e.*, 1 (animals), 2 (meat), 3 (fish), 5 (animal products, n.e.s. (not elsewhere specified)), 6 (plants), 8 (fruits and nuts), 9 (coffee, tea, spices), 10 (cereals), 11 (milling industry products), 12 (oil seeds), 13 (vegetable saps and extracts), 16 (preparations of meat, fish, etc.),

---

2. Hironori Asakura, *The Harmonized System and Rules of Origin*, 27 JOURNAL OF WORLD TRADE 5–20, at 9, 12 (1993). [Hereinafter, *The Harmonized System.*]

25 (salt, sulphur, etc.), 49 (products of the printing industry), 69 (ceramics), 82 (tools of base metal) and 97 (works of art).[3]

A third concern with the CTH rule follows from the second problem.

Exceptions to the rule necessarily result in protection for certain domestically produced goods. For example, assume Austria exports fresh carrots to Mexico. In Mexico, the carrots are frozen. The frozen carrots are exported to the U.S. Because a change in tariff classification from fresh vegetables to frozen vegetables is deemed not to be a substantial transformation under *NAFTA*, the frozen carrots are a product of Austria, not Mexico. Therefore, they do not qualify for duty-free treatment under *NAFTA*, but rather receive the appropriate MFN rate. This result helps protect U.S. farmers and domestic vegetable processors from competition from non-*NAFTA* agricultural and food producers. The many exceptions to the CTH rule identified in the above-quoted passage suggest protection is afforded to a significant number of industries. To be sure, the result also helps protect *NAFTA* farmers from non-*NAFTA* farmers and food processors who alter slightly their goods to obtain *NAFTA* benefits that the *NAFTA* Parties have not extended to the non-*NAFTA* countries.

A fourth problem is the converse of the second problem. In certain cases, a substantial transformation may occur even though there is no CTC between the inputs and final product. This phenomenon occurs with respect to chemicals, and in classifications that include finished goods and their constituent parts.

Finally, the concepts of "essential character" and substantial transformation must operate in a consistent manner. As one scholar puts it, "one of the fundamental questions when using the Harmonized System to determine the country of origin of goods manufactured or processed in two or more countries is how to ensure the conceptual fusion of essential character and substantial transformation." The HTS GRI rely on the assumption that every good has an essential character. Thus, the doctrine of the entireties set forth in GRI Rule 2(a) states that reference to an article includes reference to the incomplete or unfinished form of the article, as long as that form has the essential character of the complete or finished article.

Consider a car that is made in Japan and exported to Canada without tires. In Canada, tires are placed on the car, and the vehicle is then exported to America. Is the vehicle a product of Japan, in which case the MFN tariff rate applies, or Canada, in which case *NAFTA* duty-free treatment applies? The HTS contains General Explanatory Notes that provide examples of processing that does not alter the essential character of a good. The General Explanatory Note to HTS Chapter 87, which covers vehicles, indicates that a motor vehicle not yet fitted with tires or a battery, or not yet equipped with an engine, still has the essential character of a motor vehicle and is classified as such. Adding tires, a battery or an engine will not result in a change in tariff heading and, therefore, no substantial transformation will occur.

---

3. *The Harmonized System*, 17 (emphasis added).

In spite of these difficulties, the WTO *Agreement on Rules of Origin* advocates the CTH rule as the primary criterion for determining origin. It states origin is to be conferred where the last substantial transformation took place, not where the most significant substantial transformation occurred. By focusing on the last, not the most significant, substantial transformation, the *Agreement* fosters certainty and predictability. That focus also is easier for customs officials, who can disregard previous operations and need not make judgments about which among multiple substantial transformations was the most significant.

The *Agreement* establishes a Technical Committee that must work in conjunction with the CCC to design a specific system of changes in HTS Headings and Sub-Headings that qualify as substantial transformations. The Technical Committee and CCC also must determine what alternative ROOs—such as a Value-Added Test or list of manufacturing and processing operations—should be applied to goods for which a CTH rule is unworkable. The scope of the Agreement is limited: it does not apply to preferential trading arrangements, *i.e.*, FTAs or CUs, nor does it apply to preferential trading policies such as the GSP.

- **Category 2: Value-Added Test**

Under the "Value-Added" test, a good becomes the product of the most recent exporting country only if a specified percentage of value was added to the good in that country. A comparison is made between the ex-factory cost of the product upon exportation, and the cost of all materials used to make the product in the country from which it is exported. To continue with the above example, suppose Country S has a 50% Value-Added Test, and only 49% of the value of materials and processing associated with the manufacture of copper wire is added in Country R. Then, the copper wire would be a product of Country Z, not Country R.

Value-Added Tests are common in U.S. Customs Law (for example, for non-preferential purposes, as discussed in a separate Chapter), and FTAs and PTAs to which America is a Party. An example is the 35% Value-Added Test in the *GSP* program. A second example is the 35% Value-Added test in the *CBI*. A third example is the 35% Value-Added Test in the *Israel FTA*. This test is derived from the *CBI* ROO. Under the *FTA*, a good that is wholly the growth, product, or manufacture of the exporting country (*i.e.*, America or Israel), or that is a new or different article that is grown, produced, or manufactured in the exporting country, qualifies for preferential treatment as a product of the U.S. or Israel if two conditions are met. First, the good is imported directly from Israel into the U.S., or *vice versa*. Second, at least 35% of the appraised value of the good is attributable to the cost of the materials and processing operations performed in the exporting country.

As a practical matter, it is important to know what criteria are used to calculate value. That is, first, what are the elements that enter into the value of the product? Do overhead expenses allocable to different articles qualify, and if so, how are they apportioned among merchandise? Is the calculation an ex-works cost? Second, what valuation method is used? Standard international commercial terms published by the International Chamber of Commerce, *INCOTERMS*, articulate a range of possibilities, including ex-works, f.o.b., c.i.f., ex-factory (which includes cost of production and producer's profit), and so on. The answer to both questions typically is found in the ROOs of the relevant FTA or CU, and implemented by the customs officials in the FTA or CU member countries. Observe that methods such as c.i.f., which are higher-value because they are more inclusive, are thereby more restrictive on the use of non-originating inputs than other methods.

Two other practical points are notable about a value-added preferential ROO. First, an importer of a good for which it seeks preferential treatment, or the producer or exporter of that product, had better keep good records of the production costs. In the event customs authorities seek proof of the costs, or audit relevant facilities, documentary evidence may be dispositive in proving the applicable Value-Added Test was satisfied. This problem afflicts developing countries that make many products using a single input. For instance, crude palm oil from Malaysia is imported by several developing countries, from which they make soap, margarine, and refined cooking oil. Accurate record-keeping and accounting methods are needed to calculate the input cost for each finished good.

Second, exchange rate movements may affect whether a product does, or does not, qualify as originating. Table 6-1 summarizes an example of a product made in Bahrain for which the importer in the U.S. seeks duty-free treatment under the *Bahrain FTA*. The example presumes the good produced in Bahrain requires local and imported inputs, labor, capital goods (*i.e.*, machinery), and allocated factory overhead expenses. The example also presumes the imported inputs are from Japan, and thus non-originating, *i.e.*, the *Bahrain FTA* ROO excludes them from counting in the value-added calculation.

In Scenario 1, the exchange rate is U.S. $1 to 4 Bahraini *dinars*. In Scenario 2, the exchange rate is U.S. $1 to 8 Bahraini *dinars*—a 100% depreciation in the Bahraini currency. Almost certainly, the *dinar* is not static against third country currencies, *i.e.*, if it falls against the dollar, it is likely to tumble against other currencies, too. Suppose the Bahraini producer-exporter relies on inputs from Japan. The *dinar* depreciates not only against the dollar, but also against the Japanese *yen*. Thus, if the producer-exporter spends 2,000 *dinars* for the Japanese inputs before the exchange rate change, and if the *dinar* depreciates by 80% against the *yen*, then the producer-exporter will have to spend 3,600 *dinars* (80% above 2,000 *dinars*) to pay for the inputs. To be sure, 100 and 80% depreciations are enormous, and would put any economy into a crisis were they to occur quickly. Over the long term, however, such movements (for some currencies) are (for some countries) salubrious.

Critically, there is no change in the nature of economic activity in Bahrain. The same inputs and factors of production are used before and after the exchange rate shifts. The example, therefore, highlights how these shifts can affect entitlement to preferential treatment. Might this fact lead the Bahraini producer-exporter to change its source of inputs? For instance, might it source inputs from Bahrain or

Table 6-1. Value-Added Tests, Exchange Rate Fluctuations, and *Bahrain FTA* (Example)

Item *(denominated in dinars unless otherwise noted)*	Cost in Bahraini *dinars* in Scenario #1 *(U.S. $1 = 4 Bahraini dinars)*	Cost in Bahraini *dinars* Scenario #2 *(U.S. $1 = 8 Bahraini dinars)*
Originating inputs (*i.e.*, materials from the U.S. or Bahrain)	600	600
Non-originating inputs (*i.e.*, from third countries)	2,000	3,600 (assumes 80% depreciation in *dinar* against *yen*)
Non-originating inputs (*i.e.*, from third countries) denominated in U.S. dollars	$500	$450
Labor (wages)	500	500
Machinery (depreciation of capital equipment)	400	400
Allocable Factory Overhead Expenses	300	300
Total Cost (ex-factory) in *dinars*	3,800	5,400
Total Cost (ex-factory) in dollars	$950	$675
Value-Added in Bahrain in *dinars*	1,800 (3,800 minus the non-originating inputs)	1,800 (5,400 minus the non-originating inputs)
Value-Added in Bahrain in U.S. dollars	$450 ($950 minus the $500 non-originating inputs)	$225 ($675 minus the $450 non-originating inputs)
Percentage Value-Added in Bahrain (Value-Added in Bahrain divided by Total Cost)	47.37%	33.33%
Would a 35% Value-Added Test for preferential treatment be met?	Yes	No

America—even if they are costlier and of lesser quality than the Japanese inputs? If this sourcing change occurs, then has the operation of the value-added ROO artificially distorted trade patterns?

Finally, suppose non-originating inputs are substantially transformed in Bahrain, under an applicable ROO (such as CTH or CTSH), so that they can be included in the value-added calculation for the finished product. What effect might exchange rate movements of the Bahraini *dinar* against the *yen* have on the value-added calculation?

- **Category 3: Hybrid Test**

The final category of ROOs is a synthesis of the aforementioned approaches. A ROO may be a hybrid of the Substantial Transformation and Value-Added Tests. It may specify both a tariff shift and value-added percentage. *NAFTA* contains hybrid tests for automotive goods.

III. Four Problems

- **Problem 1: Non-Uniformity and Attempts at Harmonization**

In general, the critical issue associated with the application of preferential ROOs is how much must a good be transformed to effect a change in country of origin. The GATT does not resolve this issue. The matter rests with each WTO Member. Consequently, there is no uniform ROO to delineate the threshold transformation needed to alter the country of origin of an article. Moreover, GATT Article XXIV, which permits the creation of FTAs and CUs, says nothing about the ROOs that an area or union may establish. Countries in an FTA or CU have unfettered discretion in establishing preferential ROOs.

Not surprisingly, one observer reports "[t]here exist fourteen different preferential rules [of origin] in the European Communities, six in the United States and one in Japan" and adds that "the number may vary depending on the method of counting used." For example, *AFTA* has made use of a value-added ROO that states that a good is a product of a member country if at least 40% of its content is from any member country. The Andean Community relied on a change in tariff classification ROO, supplemented by a 50% value-added rule. The ROOs used in the *EFTA* consist of specified process lists and a 50% value-added test for certain products.

Non-uniformity also exists within particular countries. A former Deputy Assistant Secretary of the Treasury remarked that:

> [u]nfortunately, courts in the United States have not developed a rational, consistent set of principles for determining the origin of goods. Consequently, case-by-case origin determinations made by both the courts and customs officials have been inconsistent and contradictory, and have offered little guidance on which the international trade community can rely.[4]

The truth of this observation is apparent from case law on non-preferential ROOs.

The lack of uniformity at both the international and domestic level is not a result of a lack of effort at harmonization. Various attempts have been made to develop a harmonized system of ROOs.

---

4. *Quoted in* John P. Simpson, *North American Free Trade Agreement—Rules of Origin*, 28 JOURNAL OF WORLD TRADE 33–41 at 33–34 (1994). [Hereinafter, *North American*.]

For example, in October 1953 the GATT contracting parties studied a resolution submitted by the International Chamber of Commerce that called for uniformity. A drafting group established by the contracting parties prepared a two-part definition of "origin." First, a good resulting exclusively from the materials and labor of a single country was the product of the country where the good was harvested, manufactured, or otherwise brought into being. Second, a good resulting from the materials and labor of two or more countries was the product of the country in which the goods underwent the last "substantial transformation." This term was defined to mean processing that resulted in "a new individuality being conferred on the goods." Eleven countries favored the adoption of the drafting group's definition, but nine (including America) wanted to amend it, and eight opposed adoption. Thus, no action was taken.[5] The heart of the argument against uniformity — one still heard today — is that each country ought to be free to establish ROOs, because these rules are inextricably tied up with national economic policies. In particular, they are a non-neutral tool for those policies, not merely a set of technical, objective, and de-politicized devices.

In September 1974, the CCC adopted the *International Convention on the Simplification and Harmonization of Customs Procedures*, commonly called the "*Kyoto Convention*." (The EC adopted it in 1977. The U.S. did so in 1983, but declined to accept the ROOs provisions. The Convention was amended in June 1999 and February 2006.) Annex D:1 to the *Kyoto Convention* establishes a similar two-part methodology to determine the country of origin. A good "wholly produced" in a country originates in that country. An example is a natural resource product that is extracted from a particular country. Where two or more countries are involved in production, the good is said to originate in the country where "substantial transformation" occurred — that is, the country in which the last substantial manufacturing or processing took place so as to impart the essential character to the good.

All countries agree a simple assembly or cosmetic processing of a product, such as packaging, should not qualify as a substantial transformation. However, most cases are not so obvious. The drafters of the *Kyoto Convention* were aware the second part of the definition would be particularly controversial, because it would be difficult to apply the abstract concept of "substantial transformation" in practice. Accordingly, the *Convention* suggests practical rules indicating a transformation occurs if any of the following three circumstances occurs: (1) there is a CTC; (2) a manufacturing or processing operation identified on an agreed-upon list has been used; or (3) a specific *ad valorem* percentage of materials or value-added is reached.

In general, however, the *Kyoto Convention* delegates substantial discretion to domestic customs authorities. Hence, there is room for material discrepancies among ROOs in different countries. One observer concludes:

> The vagueness of the *Kyoto Convention* and the lack of GATT discipline have allowed countries a great deal of discretion. The consensus appears to be

---

5. *See* GATT B.I.S.D. (2nd Supp) at 56 (1954).

that there is no ideal system of origin, as arguments can be found in the literature in favor and against each rule that is used in practice. Whatever rule is used, transparency and predictability will be maximized if it is applied uniformly and consistently. In practice, however, few countries apply a uniform rule of origin. Indeed, the plethora of existing rules suggests that many countries are not convinced that a uniform rule is preferable.[6]

The Uruguay Round *Agreement on Rules of Origin* does not establish a uniform preferential ROO.

Rather, that *Agreement* focuses on non-preferential rules. The *Agreement* established a three-year plan of action for WTO Members leading toward global harmonization of non-preferential ROOs for roughly 5,500 product tariff lines:

> The *Agreement* applies to rules used in connection with the differential application of commercial policy instruments on the basis of origin, such as tariffs or anti-dumping and countervailing measures or safeguard measures. It aims to establish harmonized rules of origin among Members of the WTO within three years through the completion of a detailed work program, and in the transition period, provides for transparency and procedural rights for exporters. Although the *Agreement* explicitly does not cover the design of rules of origin elaborated under free trade agreements, the fact that rules of origin will be harmonized by WTO Members under the work program, is likely to influence the rules of origin elaborated in future free trade areas, since there will be a multilateral standard against which the free trade area rules of origin may be assessed. While the design of rules of origin for free trade areas is not covered, Annex 11 of the *Agreement* provides for enhanced transparency of such origin rules.[7]

Thus, the aim of the *Agreement* is a universal approach to the challenges of (1) defining when goods originate or are wholly obtained in one country, and (2) identifying what operations or processes do not confer origin, outside of the context of FTAs and CUs.

Unfortunately, the original deadline of July 1998 was missed and pushed back until November 1999, because agreement had been reached on harmonized rules for only 1,300 tariff lines. Controversial sectors, like textiles, barely had been discussed. Significantly, under Section 132 of the *1994 Uruguay Round Agreements Act*, the U.S. may elect not to be bound by the results of the harmonization work.[8] The second and subsequent deadlines also could not be met. Nevertheless, work continues. Even when it is completed, it is likely Members will disagree from time to time

---

6. Bernard Hoekman, *Rules of Origin for Goods and Services—Conceptual Issues and Economic Considerations*, 27 JOURNAL OF WORLD TRADE 81–85, at 85 (1993).

7. WORLD TRADE ORGANIZATION, REGIONALISM AND THE WORLD TRADING SYSTEM 20 (April 1995).

8. *See* 19 U.S.C. § 3552.

on how to interpret and apply the harmonized rules, and on how to classify certain products. Thus, harmonized origin determinations are in some sense an ideal type that never can be realized for all products at one time. The question is really one of minimizing disharmony, and thereby attacking protectionism.

The *Agreement* also imposes certain disciplines Members must observe, before and after such harmonization is achieved, regarding ROOs. Two examples are noteworthy. First, rules must not be used to pursue trade policy objectives, distort trade flows or discriminate against certain Members. Rather, they must be used as a technical device.

Second, all ROOs must be clearly defined, and more generally, they must be highly transparent (*e.g.*, they must be published, new or modified rules must not be applied retroactively, any interested person must have the right to request an advanced, binding assessment of a rule, and the right to independent judicial review of administrative determinations about rules). Relatedly, until harmonized system is in place, Members are not supposed to apply "negative" rules, *i.e.*, rules that state only what does not constitute a substantial transformation (discussed below), but which do not state what does count as a substantial transformation. Negative rules are especially pernicious, because they create uncertainty for exporters, and leave undue discretion in the hands of customs officials in the importing country.

- **Problem 2: Complexity and Compliance Costs**

No RTA can function without preferential ROOs. Such rules determine whether merchandise originates within a member country and, therefore, is eligible to the preferential treatment accorded by the FTA or CU. Such rules also are the playground for protectionist interests in the members. The difficulty in qualifying as an originating good varies directly with the strictness of the rules and their technical complexity, and inversely with the transparency of the rules. In some RTAs, the very articulation of the rules is intimidating. ROOs in the FTA between the EU and Poland take up 81 pages. In *NAFTA*, the origin rules consume about 200 pages.

Consequently, perhaps the most important point about preferential ROOs to appreciate is they can defeat the entire purpose (or purposes) that motivated countries to enter into an RTA. Put simply and generally, in preferential ROOs lurk the devil of protectionism. Armies of lawyers are needed to fight that devil, to counsel exporters and importers how to navigate the rules to qualify merchandise as originating within the RTA. The direct costs associated with ROO compliance are roughly 3%–5% of the value of a shipment in question. If the cost of complying with the ROOs is too high, then why bother claiming duty-free treatment?

For instance, up to 25% of goods eligible for duty-free treatment in the EU and *EFTA* do not receive such treatment. These importers willingly allow their merchandise to be treated as if it came from outside the EU or *EFTA* and, therefore, pay the MFN rate applicable to their goods. The importers simply do not want to struggle with complex ROOs, nor do they wish to bother with the paperwork required by the rules. As another example, less than 5% of exports from Albania to the EU, which are eligible for preferential treatment granted by the Union, actually obtain that treatment. The reason is the high cost of complying with EU preferential ROOs. (Happily, for Albania, as a step toward full Union membership, in September 2006 the European Parliament assented to an FTA between the EU and Albania within 10 years.)

The point is preferential ROOs may be so complex that manufacturers, exporters, and importers simply ignore them. Clearly, when this phenomenon occurs, the efficacy of a PTA diminishes. Further, the development objective of establishing regional production linkages and networks between or among the FTA or CU countries is lost. In any RTA, the specific tipping point is when compliance costs exceed margin of preference benefits. As indicated, compliance costs vary directly with rule complexity. The margin of preference is the difference, for a particular category of merchandise, between the MFN and preferential tariff rates. Suppose legal fees to research the manufacturing process associated with a type of merchandise, and the potentially relevant ROOs, and to prepare certificates of origin amount to 3% of the value of a shipment of that merchandise. If the preference to gain is duty-free treatment, but the MFN rate is 3% or less, then the compliance costs exceed the potential gain.

- **Problem 3: Perverse Incentives, Cumulation, and Tolerance Levels**

Preferential ROOs can create perverse incentives. For example, might a value-added rule discourage a company from investing in new property, plant, and equipment that would increase production efficiency, but drop the cost of manufacturing? Would, and should, the answer depend on that drop in relation to the tariff saved from qualifying for preferential treatment?

Asked differently, do preferential ROOs distort patterns of FDI? Consider the observation of the Chief Executive Officer of BMW North America, Ludwig Willisch: 70% of cars made by BMW at its plant in South Carolina are exported to 140 countries, hence BMW is the largest exporter of vehicles in America.[9] These results are possible because of FTAs. Why not site a BMW facility in the U.S. and thereby take advantage of its FTA network, as well as its lower crash test and emission compliance costs relative to those in Germany?

Equally plausible is a scenario in which a preferential ROO drives the choice of input suppliers. In an era of globalized manufacturing, absent the prospect of preferential treatment under an FTA or CU, producer-exporters are wont to source inputs from the lowest-cost, best-quality supplier. Such rules, however, may be an incentive to purchase inputs from within the FTA or CU. Insofar as the rules are difficult to modify, they cannot possibly accommodate frequent changes in global industrial configurations. In turn, trade diversion away from more efficient input

---

9. *See* Len Bracken, *Trade Deals Seen as Incentive For Companies to Invest in U.S.*, 30 International Trade Reporter (BNA) 1709 (7 November 2013) (reporting on the remarks of Mr. Willisch at the SelectUSA 2013 Investment Summit).

suppliers can vitiate efforts by industries in the FTA or CU region to achieve economies of scale.

NAFTA is a case in point. In 2014 production supply chains were far more integrated across Canada, Mexico, and the U.S. after 20 years of the operation of *NAFTA*. Firms adjusted to the incentive of DFQF treatment created by *NAFTA* by sourcing inputs from within the *NAFTA* region, rather than pay a tariff on an input from outside the region. In turn, by using *NAFTA*-originating inputs to make finished products, firms ensured those products counted as *NAFTA*-originating under the relevant preferential ROO. So, they could ship those products across *NAFTA* on a DFQF basis.

Perhaps, then, the following points from a World Bank publication are both unsurprising and troubling:

> There is no evidence that strict rules of origin over the past 30 years have done anything to stimulate the development of integrated production structures in developing countries. In fact, such arguments have become redundant in the light of technological changes and global trade liberalization, which have led to the fragmentation of production processes and the development of global networks of sourcing. Globalization and the splitting up of the production chain does not allow the luxury of being able to establish integrated production structures within countries. Strict rules of origin act to constrain the ability of firms to integrate into these global and regional production networks and in effect to dampen the location of any value-added activities. In the modern world economy, flexibility in the sourcing of inputs is a key element in international competitiveness. Thus, it is quite feasible that restrictive rules of origin, rather than stimulating economic development, will raise costs of production by constraining access to cheap inputs and undermine the ability of local firms to compete in overseas markets.[10]

That is, ROOs may be injurious to the long-term goal of becoming globally competitive. Why comply with them—save for the short-term benefit of duty-free treatment?

To be sure, there are ways to combat the problem of perverse incentives. In particular, two factors—cumulation rules and *de minimis* thresholds—can help preserve market-based decision making. "Cumulation" refers to the legal ability of a producer to import inputs without altering the origin of the good it makes, and thus without vitiating the entitlement of that good to preferential treatment. Consider, for instance, *CAFTA*. To what extent can a Honduran company incorporate non-*CAFTA* inputs and still obtain duty-free treatment from the U.S. for the finished product it exports to there?

---

10. P. Brenton & H. Imagawa, *Rules of Origin, Trade and Customs, in* CUSTOMS MODERNIZATION: A HANDBOOK 36 (2004, World Bank, L. de Wulf & J. Sokol eds.).

A rule of "bilateral cumulation" allows inputs from only Honduras or the U.S. to qualify as originating inputs. All other imported inputs, whether from El Salvador or India, would not qualify. A "diagonal cumulation" rule allows inputs from any *CAFTA* country to qualify. Obviously, diagonal cumulation is more in keeping with the spirit of an FTA with more than two countries than bilateral cumulation. Significantly, at least four preferential arrangements allow for diagonal cumulation. They are the *ASEAN* FTA (*i.e.*, AFTA), Andean Community, GSP, including the EU's EBA initiative, and SAARC. Thus, for instance, under the EBA, a preferential scheme for least developed countries, the EU allows a least developed country to source inputs from other such countries, and not thereby destroy the ability of a finished product to obtain duty-free or low-tariff treatment upon shipment to the EU.

A rule of "full cumulation" allows inputs from any country, whether or not it belongs to *CAFTA*, to qualify. The inputs themselves need not undergo a substantial transformation in Honduras, though the finished good must satisfy an applicable ROO. Interestingly, the EU ROO under its now-expired *Cotonou Agreement*, a preferential scheme for ACP countries, allowed for full cumulation among ACP countries. That is, one ACP country could source inputs from another ACP country, produce a finished product, export that product, and expect the EU to treat the product as made entirely of parts from the producing-exporting country.

De minimis thresholds also are called "tolerance" levels. They allow a certain percentage of non-originating materials to be incorporated into a good without altering the origin of that good. The obvious purpose is to afford flexibility in the administration of ROOs. The EU permitted a 15% tolerance level in the *Cotonou Agreement*, meaning that up to 15% of the value of a product could originate from a non-ACP country and not disentitle the product from duty-free treatment by the EU. By contrast, in its GPT, Canada sets a 60% *de minimis* threshold for LDC exports, and 40% for developing country exports.

- **Problem 4: Preferential ROOs as NTBs**

The earlier example regarding *NAFTA's* vegetable ROOs and carrots from Australia suggests preferential ROOs can be NTBs. If the definition of "substantial transformation" is sufficiently restrictive, or the percentage value-added requirement is sufficiently high, then imports will not qualify for preferential tariff treatment associated with an FTA or CU, or bound or MFN rates associated with the GATT-WTO regime. In 1974, for example, the U.S. argued ROOs in FTAs between the European Community and certain non-Community European countries were protectionist. The U.S. complained the rules favored parts and partly manufactured goods from non-Community European countries over such goods from the U.S., because of a 95% value-added requirement.

More generally, ROOs can be subtle ways of managing trade in certain goods. As one trade negotiator states:

> The inescapable fact is that rules of origin are tools of discrimination. They have no other purpose. They are used to implement national and

international laws that confer special benefits on goods of some countries and special penalties on goods of other countries.

Those who suggest that rules of origin should be merely technical, and entirely divorced from policy considerations, simply misunderstand why rules of origin exist at all.

. . .

[R]ules of origin are at best a necessary evil. They are needed to allow us to implement, with minimal disruption of trade, national laws that discriminate between goods based on their country of origin. Until the nations of the world achieve a stage of enlightenment that allows non-discriminatory trade, we must work together to ensure that rules of origin required to implement discriminatory laws do not themselves become trade barriers.[11]

Perhaps the response to this stark reality is that as an increasing number of countries realize the benefits of free trade, they will become more vigilant against abuse of ROOs.

IV. Israeli Origin, Occupied Territories, and February 2010 ECJ *Brita* Case

In addition to their legal and economic effects, preferential ROOs can have important political ramifications. That is most apparent when they are drafted to favor merchandise from constituencies in a RTA member country, and discriminate against like products from third countries. For example, as the 2000 WTO Appellate Body case in *Canada Auto Pact—Certain Measures Affecting the Automotive Industry*, suggests, the Pact favored American and Canadian auto and auto parts suppliers, and discriminated against European and Japanese competitors.[12] Other provocative instances are the May 1985 *U.S.-Israel FTA* and November 1995 *EU-Israel Association Agreement*. (The *Association* deal, which effectively is an *EU-Israel FTA*, entered into force on 1 June 2000, and replaces the 1975 *European Community (EC)–Israel Cooperation Agreement*.)

At the time of the U.S. deal, Palestinians did not have a widely recognized state. Effectively, the *U.S.-Israel FTA* discriminated against products made in the Occupied Territories, particularly the West Bank and Gaza Strip (less so the Golan Heights, to which Syria lays claims). Similarly, the EU deal excludes from preferential treatment merchandise made in the Occupied Territories. That exclusion operates to ensure Israeli goods are not from those Territories, though controversies

---

11. *North American*, 40–41.

12. *See* WT/DS139/AB/R (complaint by Japan) and WT/DS142/AB/R (complaint by EC) (adopted 19 June 2000).

between EU and Israel have arisen as to whether some merchandise entered in the EU as "Israeli" actually is.

Indeed, in February 2010, the ECJ ruled products originating in Israeli settlements located in the Occupied Territories are ineligible for preferences under the EU-Israel deal. The case arose when a German customs official refused to grant reduced tariffs on water dispensers and filters made by Brita, as these articles were made in settlements in the West Bank. German authorities asked the precise origin of the merchandise, but were told by Israeli officials the goods came from a location "under their responsibility."[13] The ECJ agreed that generally an exporting country has the right to designate origin, and the importing country is "generally bound" by that declaration. However, in the ECJ case:

> the subsequent verification did not concern the question whether the imported products were wholly obtained in a certain location or whether they had undergone sufficient working and processing there for them to be considered to be products originating in that location. The aim of the subsequent verification was to establish the precise place of manufacture of the imported goods for the purposes of determining whether those products fell within the territorial scope of the EU-Israel Agreement.
>
> Despite a specific request from the German authorities, the Israeli authorities did not reply to the question whether the products had been manufactured in Israeli-occupied settlements in Palestinian territory . . . . [Yet,] under the EC-Israel Agreement, the Israeli authorities are obliged to provide sufficient information to enable the real origin of products to be determined.[14]

Accordingly, the ECJ held:

> 44. Among the relevant rules that may be relied on in the context of the relations between the parties to the EC [European Communities]-Israel Association Agreement is the general international law principle of the relative effect of treaties, according to which treaties do not impose any obligations, or confer any rights, on third States (*"pacta tertiis nec nocent nec prosunt"*). That principle of general international law finds particular expression in Article 34 of the Vienna Convention [on the Law of Treaties], under which a treaty does not create either obligations or rights for a third State without its consent.

---

13. *Quoted in* Joe Kirwin, *EU High Court Rules Israeli-Origin Products from Settlements Ineligible for Low EU Tariffs*, 27 International Trade Reporter (BNA) 361–362 (11 March 2010). [Hereinafter, *EU High Court.*]

14. *EU High Court* (*quoting* in part Judgment of the Court (Fourth Chamber) of 25 February 2010 (reference for a preliminary ruling from the Finanzgericht Hamburg—Germany)—*Brita GmbH v. Hauptzollamt Hamburg-Hafen*, Case Number C-386/08, http://curia.europa.eu/).

45. It follows from those preliminary considerations that Article 83 of the EC-Israel Association Agreement, which defines the territorial scope of that agreement, must be interpreted in a manner that is consistent with the principle "*pacta tertiis nec nocent nec prosunt.*"

46. In this respect, it is common ground that the European Communities concluded two Euro-Mediterranean Association Agreements, first with the State of Israel and then with the PLO [Palestine Liberation Organization] for the benefit of the Palestinian Authority of the West Bank and the Gaza Strip.

47. Each of those two association agreements has its own territorial scope. Under Article 83 thereof, the EC-Israel Association Agreement applies to the "territory of the State of Israel." Under Article 73 thereof, the EC-PLO Association Agreement applies to the "territories of the West Bank and the Gaza Strip."

48. That being so, those two association agreements pursue an identical objective—referred to in Article 6(1) of the EC-Israel Association Agreement and Article 3 of the EC-PLO Association Agreement, respectively—which is to establish and/or reinforce a free trade area between the parties. They also have the same immediate purpose—defined, for industrial products, in Article 8 of the EC-Israel Association Agreement and in Articles 5 and 6 of the EC-PLO Association Agreement, respectively—which is to abolish customs duties, quantitative restrictions and other measures having equivalent effect in relation to trade between the parties to each of those agreements.

49. As regards methods of administrative cooperation, in the case, first, of the EC-Israel Association Agreement, it emerges from Articles 22(1)(a) and 23(1) of the EC-Israel Protocol that the invoice declaration needed in order to be allowed preferential treatment for exports is to be made out by an exporter who has been approved by the "customs authorities of the exporting [State]."

50. Secondly, in the case of the EC-PLO Association Agreement, it emerges from Articles 20(1)(a) and 21(1) of the EC-PLO Protocol that the invoice declaration needed in order to be allowed preferential treatment for exports is to be made out by an exporter approved by the "customs authorities of the exporting [State]." In addition, Article 16(4) of the EC-PLO Protocol implies that, if the products concerned can be regarded as products originating in the West Bank or the Gaza Strip, the "customs authorities of . . . the West Bank and Gaza Strip" have sole competence to issue a movement certificate EUR.1.

51. It follows from the foregoing that the "customs authorities of the exporting [State]," within the meaning of the two protocols mentioned above, have exclusive competence—within their territorial jurisdiction—to issue

movement certificates EUR.1 or to approve exporters based in the territory under their administration.

52. Accordingly, to interpret Article 83 of the EC-Israel Association Agreement as meaning that the Israeli customs authorities enjoy competence in respect of products originating in the West Bank would be tantamount to imposing on the Palestinian customs authorities an obligation to refrain from exercising the competence conferred upon them by virtue of the above-mentioned provisions of the EC-PLO Protocol. Such an interpretation, the effect of which would be to create an obligation for a third party without its consent, would thus be contrary to the principle of general international law, "*pacta tertiis nec nocent nec prosunt*," as consolidated in Article 34 of the Vienna Convention.

53. It follows that Article 83 of the EC-Israel Association Agreement must be interpreted as meaning that products originating in the West Bank do not fall within the territorial scope of that agreement and do not therefore qualify for preferential treatment under that agreement.

54. In those circumstances, the German customs authorities could refuse to grant, in respect of the goods at issue, preferential treatment as provided for under the EC-Israel Association Agreement, on the ground that those goods originated in the West Bank.

Put succinctly:

> Under general international law, an obligation cannot be imposed upon a third party—such as the Palestinian Authority of the West Bank and the Gaza Strip—without its consent. As a consequence, the EC-Israel Agreement may not be interpreted in such a way as to compel the Palestinian Authority to waive their right to exercise the competence conferred upon them by virtue of the EC-PLO Agreement and, in particular, to refrain from exercising their right to issue customs documents providing proof of origin for goods manufactured in the West Bank and Gaza Strip.[15]

Thus, the ECJ reasoned the EU trade treaty with Israel applies only to Israel's internationally recognized boundaries, which exclude the Occupied Territories. Likewise, the ECJ said, the EU deal with the Palestinian Authority has its own territorial scope, which includes the West Bank and Gaza.

In August 2012, the EU confirmed via a Directive that all imports from beyond the Green Line are subject to customs duties. The Green Line, of course, refers to the pre-June 1967 border of Israel with its Arab neighbors. Thus, the Directive made clear that duty-free treatment under the 1995 *EU-Israel FTA* is not available to articles originating in the Occupied Territories.

---

15. *EU High Court.*

Interestingly, on 31 July 2012, Israel and the Palestinian Authority signed an agreement to improve collection of taxes on trade and streamline the transfer of goods in ports, with implementation on 1 January 2013.[16] Tax authorities from each side agreed to improve their IT to monitor passage of goods between Israel and Palestine, and taxing those goods as they cross through Palestinian checkpoints. Until this agreement, under the 1994 *Paris Protocol*, Israeli authorities collected at the Israeli port of entry customs duties, as well as VAT and purchases taxes, on imported goods destined for Palestine. Israel then was obligated to pass on those duties to the Palestinian Authority. Yet, the goods were transferred via road to Palestinian border posts, and en route goods typically were stolen. Consequently, the Palestinians were deprived of goods, and the Israelis lost tax revenues they had to transfer to the Palestinians on the merchandise pilfered in Israel.

Under the July 2012 accord, all imports destined for Palestine are shipped in containers sealed with electronic locks. The locks are monitored from the Israeli port of entry to the Palestinian point of discharge. Tariffs and taxes are collected at a border crossing point that is designated in advance. And, the Palestinian Authority is constructing secure storage facilities, plus a dedicated pipeline in which to ship petroleum from Israel to Palestine (and thereby end shipments of fuel by truck). For all developed and most developing countries, especially in East Asia, the arrangements under the July 2012 agreement would appear unimpressive, if not backward. But, in the near zero-trust environment encompassing much of the Middle East, the accord actually was progress toward trade liberalization.

V. Middle East Politics and QIZs

Suppose merchandise is made in an Occupied Territory. U.S. CBP forbids marking that merchandise with a "Made in Israel" or "Made in Occupied Territories-Israel."[17] Indeed, the name "Israel" cannot be used. Rather, CBP insists on precise marking, such as Made in "Gaza," "Gaza Strip," "West Bank," "West Bank/Gaza," "West Bank/Gaza Strip," "West Bank and Gaza," or "West Bank and Gaza Strip." However, no distinction is made if merchandise is made in a Jewish Settlement in the West Bank, as distinct from an Arab farm or factory.

What are the implications for such marking on duty-free treatment? The answer is, unsurprisingly, American law and policy toward Israel differs from that of the EU. The EU distinguishes between Jewish Settlements and Arab facilities in areas Israel has occupied since the June 1967 War.

---

16. *See* Jenny David, *Israelis, Palestinians Broker Deal to Improve Tax Collections, Transfers of Goods in Ports*, 29 International Trade Reporter 1409 (23 August 2012).

17. *See* United States Customs and Border Protection, West Bank Country of Origin Marking Requirements 23 January 2016, http://www.cbp.gov.

American labeling rules are designed to preserve the integrity of QIZs: a product originating in a QIZ may be designated "Made in Israel," which essentially is an exemption form the general strictures against doing so, because Israeli and foreign firms employ Palestinians in the QIZs. Helping the weak Palestinian economy develop, and encouraging Jews and Arabs to work side-by-side, justifies this exemption.

The entire scheme followed the 1993 and 1995 *Oslo I and II Accords* between Israel and the PLO. On 17 October 1995, the U.S., Israel, and Palestinian Authority exchanged letters agreeing to elimination of duties on articles originating in the West Bank and Gaza Strip. The Palestinian Authority made three pledges: to give American products duty-free access; to prevent illegal transshipment of non-Israeli and non-Palestinian origin goods, which are ineligible for duty-free treatment; and to support every effort at ending the Arab economic boycott of Israel.

In May 1996, America and Israel agreed to amend their *FTA*, whereby they established QIZs between Jordan and Israel. The QIZs are designed to rectify discriminatory effects of the *U.S.-Israel FTA* on Palestinians. To implement the October 1995 side letters and the QIZ arrangement, in October 1996, Congress amended the *United States-Israel Free Trade Implementation Act of 1985 (IFTA Act)* by adding a new section to give the President authority to eliminate tariffs on products from the West Bank or Gaza Strip. The legislation applies to products from areas designated as industrial parks. They are located between the West Bank and Israel, and the Gaza Strip and Israel. It also provides for duty-free treatment for products in QIZs between Israel and Jordan and Israel and Egypt. In November 1996, President Bill Clinton (1946, President, 1993–2001) exercised this authority via Proclamation 6955 (discussed in a separate Chapter). In sum, under the *IFTA Act*, a "QIZ" is defined as an area that (1) covers portions of the territory of Israel and Egypt or Israel and Jordan, (2) local authorities designate as one in which goods can enter duty-free, and (3) the President designates as such.

Thus, the U.S. accords articles originating in designated industrial parks and QIZs the same tariff treatment as Israeli products under the *FTA*. Obviously, these benefits are designed to encourage Arab-Israeli economic and social cooperation. Preferential ROOs are a legal device for this encouragement. The same preferential ROOs as exist in the *Israel FTA* apply to all products from the industrial parks or QIZs. However, there must be a minimum amount of Israeli, Palestinian, Jordanian, or Egyptian content to qualify for duty free treatment. For example (as discussed in an earlier Chapter), in December 2004, QIZs were established in Egypt. The U.S. accords duty-free treatment to an article of merchandise made in an Egyptian QIZ, as long as the article contains at least 10.5% Israeli components.

The prospect of duty-free access is a characteristically American solution to the Arab-Israeli conflict. If enough money is dangled in front of the Palestinians, in the form of duty-free treatment to the consumer market of last resort, the U.S., then surely they will follow rational economic decision-making patterns. They will shift their attention from an *intifada* (uprising) to exports. Sadly, the solution has done little to stem violence throughout Israel and the Occupied Territories. How far can preferential ROOs go to bring about peace? Might they even exacerbate tensions?

Indeed, might those tensions exist in the U.S.? Consider the fact major American retail brands, such as Calvin Klein, Gap, Levi Strauss & Co., and Wal-Mart all have set up operations in the Egyptian QIZs. They are mindful of the comparatively cheaper expense of running a factory in them, including labor costs, than in America. Is it reasonable to inquire whether these operations contribute (albeit modestly) to American job losses—and the corporate "bottom line"—in a quixotic pursuit of peace?

Consider also the fact duty-free treatment for articles from Israeli-Jordanian QIZs created a new problem. Products originating in Jordan did not receive duty-free treatment, and thus were discriminated against relative to like Palestinian merchandise. To address it, and to reward Jordan for signing a peace treaty with Israel in 1994, in 1996 the U.S. and Jordan agreed to a QIZ program whereby companies in American-approved industrial parks may export their goods duty-free to the U.S. The QIZs (as of February 2007) are:

(1) *On the Northern Jordanian-Israeli Border*:

The Gateway QIZ.

(2) *In Amman*:

The Al-Qastal Industrial Zone, Al-Tajamouat Industrial Estate, and Mushatta International Complex.

(3) *In Aqaba*:

The Aqaba Industrial Estate.

(4) *In Irbid*:

The Al-Hassan Industrial Estate and the Jordan Cyber City.

(5) *In Kerak*:

The Kerak Industrial Estate.

(6) *In Zarqa*:

The Ad-Dulayl Industrial Park and the El-Zai Readywear Manufacturing Company.

Even more significantly, the U.S. addressed the problem—and rewarded Jordan for its support of Israeli-Palestinian peace negotiations (especially the 1993 *Oslo Accords*)—by entering into FTA negotiations with Jordan, signing a deal in October 2000.

No less than four questions may be asked about Jordanian QIZs, each one suggesting an irony:[18]

---

18. *See* Sharmilla Devi, *U.S. Trade Pact with Jordan Under A Cloud*, Financial Times, 27 October 2006, at 3.

(1) *Who are the real beneficiaries?*

The QIZs boast 114 companies (as of February 2007). But, most of them are foreign entities, specifically, non-Jordanian and non-Israeli, with a large contingent from China. Of the 54,000–60,000 workers in the QIZs, about 18,000 — a third — are Jordanian. Bluntly put, many Jordanian citizens are unwilling to take a low-paid QIZ job, meaning non-Jordanians, especially from the Indian Sub-Continent, hungrily snap up the jobs.

(2) *Are QIZs in the Middle East a divide-and-conquer strategy by hegemonic powers, or at least is pitting one Arab country against another their effect?*

Egyptian QIZs enjoy two comparative advantages over Jordanian QIZs. Egypt boasts relatively lower labor costs, and the access to its famed cotton is immediate.

(3) *In the short- and medium-term, is a QIZ beneficial if manufacturing continues in sunset industries?*

Jordan, for example, has not provided much governmental support in the form of vocational training, nor created conditions for technology transfer. Thus, products made in the QIZs tend to be low value-added items like T&A, not so-called "new economy" products.

(4) *What long-term value is a QIZ anyway if an FTA exists?*

A QIZ may be an irrelevancy, once duty-free treatment is possible through an FTA. Indeed, when the *Jordan FTA* fully frees up trade between America and Jordan (in 2010), there will be no need to include Israeli components in merchandise to obtain duty-free entry into the U.S.

A final irony is the impact — whatever their intent — of QIZs on Palestinians. Have Palestinians been helped by the various QIZs, and if not, why not? Consider the fact Israeli garment manufacturers generally prefer to outsource work to Jordan, instead of contracting for Palestinian workers in the Occupied Territories. Might it be inferred that the presence of a QIZ in Jordan or Egypt creates an alternative for foreign enterprises to employing Palestinians?

Relations between the U.S. and Central America, and among Central American countries, furnish another example of political ramifications from preferential ROOs. Assume a leading goal of *CAFTA-DR* is broader, deeper linkages among the members. Yet, suppose different ROOs apply to trade between the U.S. and its *CAFTA-DR* partners, depending on the partner. For example, suppose a 50% Value-Added Test is used for wood handicrafts from Costa Rica, but the like product from Guatemala requires only 35% Value-Added to qualify as originating in *CAFTA-DR*. Would genuine trade integration among preferred countries be possible without harmonized preferential origin rules? In turn, would heterogeneity in the rules exacerbate not only economic differences, but also political squabbles, among exporters?

Chapter 7

Preferential ROOs (Continued): *NAFTA* Case Study[1]

I. Overview of Eight Types of Preferential ROOs in *NAFTA* and Other FTAs

It is instructive to consider some of the difficult, real-world problems tackled, or avoided, by negotiators in an FTA such as *NAFTA*. Their bargaining illustrates many of the pros and cons of different types of preferential ROOs. The outcomes indicate the in-the-trenches origin work in which International Trade Law is practiced.

During their negotiations with Mexican trade representatives in 1991–1992, American and Canadian officials were concerned that *NAFTA* would facilitate trans-shipment of third-country goods through Mexico and thereby avoid American and Canadian trade barriers. In particular, they feared Mexico would become an "export platform"—a point of entry into the vast North American market—for Hong Kong, Malaysia, the Philippines, and other Far East countries. At the same time, as *NAFTA* Article 102:1(a) states, the fundamental purpose of the accord is to liberalize trade.

So, the challenge *NAFTA* negotiators faced was to steer a middle course, avoiding both lax preferential ROOs that would cause their fears to be realized and strict rules that were protectionist. Did the negotiators fail in their endeavor? Two critics argue

> ... the main area where the *NAFTA* is open to criticism is its enumeration of restrictive rules of origin. These arcane trade provisions have been aptly labeled "tools of discrimination": they are used to determine which goods qualify for preferential treatment under the *NAFTA* and to deny *NAFTA* benefits to those goods that contain significant foreign-sourced components.
>
> ...
>
> The impact of rules of origin in limiting trade liberalization is suggested by comparing actual and hypothetical duty collections on U.S. imports

---

1. Documents References:
   (1) *NAFTA* Chapter 4
   (2) Rules of Origin in other FTAs

from Canada. Based on 1991 data, duty collections from Canada will eventually drop to about 18 percent of the most-favored-nation (MFN) duty rates rather than the zero level that would occur without rules of origin. In other words, about 18 percent of US imports from Canada will not benefit from the [*Canada-U.S.*] *FTA*.[2]

A third critic predicts:

> In the near future, *NAFTA's* rules of origin will encourage increased foreign investment in North America as foreign multinationals are forced to locate not only "screwdriver" assembly plants but also input manufacturing plants within the region. This re-sourcing of production inputs and assembly plants will be most pronounced in industries whose products face large external tariffs—textiles, for example—or significant non-tariff barriers to trade. On a second level, this forced relocation of production facilities to countries within the free trade area will hamper the economic growth of developing countries that do not have equal terms of access to a large consumer market such as the European Community (EC) or the United States. On a third level, *NAFTA's* restrictive rules of origin threaten to "obliterate" many of the touted benefits of *NAFTA*. Because *NAFTA's* rules of origin only apply to goods that cross borders within *NAFTA*, foreign corporations will have a strong incentive to avoid them by sourcing their assembly plants within the ultimate market (*i.e.*, the U.S.), thereby frustrating the free trade agreement's goal of promoting greater efficiency within North America through the pursuit of comparative advantage.[3]

The merits of the criticism that the negotiators failed to steer a middle course between permissiveness and protectionism must be judged by analyzing carefully the nature and effects of the rules. The devil truly is in the details.

To summarize what follows below, Article 302 of *NAFTA* calls for progressive elimination of tariffs on "originating goods." Under Article 201, a good is "originating" (*i.e.*, it is the product of a *NAFTA* Party) if it satisfies a ROO set forth in Chapter 4 of *NAFTA*. That Chapter indicates the negotiators settled on 8 broad types of ROOs. Subsequent FTA negotiators followed and built on these categories. Thus, many, if not all, of these kinds of preferential ROOs are found in other FTAs to which the U.S. is a party. In all instances—*NAFTA* and the other U.S. FTAs—the rules are set forth in lengthy, complex annexes to the agreements, and rendered effective in the U.S. through the legislation implementing the agreement in question.

---

2. Gary Clyde Hufbauer & Jeffrey J. Schott, NAFTA— An Assessment 5 (rev'd ed. October 1993).

3. Joseph A. LaNasa III, *Rules of Origin Under the North American Free Trade Agreement: A Substantial Transformation into Objectively Transparent Protectionism*, 34 Harvard International Law Journal 381, 401–02 (1993).

Significantly, even if one of the ROOs is satisfied with respect to a particular good, that good can be disqualified from preferential treatment. For example, *NAFTA* Article 411 explains an originating good will be disqualified if it is trans-shipped, that is, "undergoes further production or any other operation outside the territories of the Parties, other than unloading, reloading or any other operation necessary to preserve it in good condition or to transport the good to the territory of a Party." In addition, under Article 412(b), if the purpose of a production process simply is to circumvent *NAFTA's* ROO, then goods subject to that process will be disqualified.

In studying preferential ROOs, whether in *NAFTA* or any FTA or CU, consider whether and how they can function, by design or effect, as "covenants not to compete." Some economists argue the rules distort production decisions in FTAs and CU. There is an incentive for a producer of finished goods in an FTA or CU to select sources of raw materials and intermediate inputs based on eligibility for preferential treatment rather than, or in addition to, efficiency criteria like cost. In turn, the producer may become less efficient, and consumers ultimately may suffer by paying higher prices. This argument suggests that preferential ROO have a detrimental impact not only on third-country suppliers (*i.e.*, those whose raw materials and inputs are ineligible for preferential treatment), but also on certain groups within the preferential trading area.

II. Type 1: Goods Wholly Obtained Rule

The first preferential ROO found in *NAFTA* relies on the concept of "goods wholly obtained." Under *NAFTA* Article 401(a), a good that is wholly obtained or produced in a *NAFTA* Party qualifies for preferential treatment. This rule covers extracted mineral goods, agricultural goods, fish products, and goods from the seabed. (*See NAFTA* Article 415.) This justification for origination is both basic and obvious. Hence, it is found in all FTAs. Thus, for example, Article 4:1(1)(a) of the *Chile FTA* states that a good is originating if it is "wholly obtained or produced entirely in the territory of Chile, the United States, or both." Article 3:1(a) of the *Singapore FTA* contains the same rule, as does Article 5:1(a) of the *Australia FTA* (referring to Singaporean and Australian territory, respectively, of course). Likewise, Article 5:1(a) of the *Morocco FTA* states that a good originates within the territory of Morocco or the U.S. if it is "wholly the growth, product, or manufacture of" either or both countries.

The Goods Wholly Obtained Rule is adapted from Rule 2 of the 1974 *Kyoto Convention*. That Rule lists 10 types of goods that must be considered to be produced wholly within one country. One innovation introduced by *NAFTA* is that a good taken from outer space by a *NAFTA* Party is deemed to be wholly obtained in that Party.

What is not so obvious is that whether an agricultural or fisheries product is "wholly obtained" in one country is not a binomial matter. Rather, there are many possibilities along a continuum of free trade and protectionism. Suppose corn grown in Mexico is from seed imported from Brazil. That seed is genetically modified, using scientific procedures developed at collaborating labs in Australia and Japan. The Mexican farmers use fertilizer from India. Their irrigation equipment is from the U.S., and water services are provided by a partially-privatized company the owners of which include German and Swiss conglomerates. The Goods Wholly Obtained Rule cuts off the inquiry about origin with the soil — the corn is Mexican because it was planted, grown, and harvested in Mexican soil.

The point is, as with the origin of the cosmos, for primary commodities, the origin inquiry can be taken back many steps. The number of steps taken, and the step or steps chosen to confer origin, are policy choices. For example, if a goal of *NAFTA* were to protect domestic corn farmers in each of the Parties, then the goods Wholly Obtained Rule would insist that seed — and maybe the fertilizer, too — come from the U.S., Canada, or Mexico. The only real limits on tracing the origin of a product are practical. Do reliable records exist for each step in the production process? Is it cost-effective, in relation to the benefits of duty-free treatment, to trace back several steps up the commodity chain?

III. Type 2: Originating Materials Rule

Article 401(c) of *NAFTA* is a logical extension of the Goods Wholly Obtained Rule. It indicates a good is originating if produced entirely in a *NAFTA* Party exclusively from originating materials. For example, suppose a pen is made in Canada from plastic, metal, and ink, all of which are from the U.S. or Mexico. Because the materials are originating, the pen is an originating good. Like the Goods Wholly Obtained Rule, the Originating Materials Rule is basic and obvious. It, too, is common to FTAs.

For example, it exists in the *Israel FTA*. To be "Israeli," an article must be grown or manufactured in, or the product of, Israel, which can occur if the product is made in Israel, America, or both, exclusively from originating materials. Likewise, under the *Chile FTA*, a good is considered originating if it is produced entirely in Chilean or American territory, or both, exclusively from originating materials. That also is true, with respect to Singaporean and American territory, under the *Singapore FTA*, and Australian and American territory under the *Australia FTA*.

IV. Type 3: Substantial Transformation Rule

The third rule, set forth in *NAFTA* Article 401(b), relies on the concept of "goods substantially transformed." The Substantial Transformation Rule applies to cases where a good contains non-originating materials. If each non-originating material is transformed by production that occurs entirely within one or more *NAFTA* Parties so that each such material undergoes a change in tariff classification, then the good is an originating good. Consequently, this rule sometimes is called the "Tariff Shift" Rule or "CTH" Rule (for "change in tariff heading or sub-heading"). As noted later with respect to tomato paste and tomato catsup, protectionist impulses may motivate some Tariff Shift Rules.

Globalization demands a Substantial Transformation Rule. Specifically, multi-jurisdictional sourcing and production—sometimes called global commodity or supply chains—mean many articles are not entirely grown or produced in one country. Thus, the first two rules would render them ineligible for preferential treatment. In turn, an FTA would be under-inclusive in coverage, and fail to maximize the potential net gains from trade liberalization. Accordingly, FTAs typically contain a Substantial Transformation Rule. For example, under the *Israel FTA*, if an article is made of foreign materials, then to be "Israeli," it must be substantially transformed into a new or different article that is grown, manufactured, or produced in Israel. Qualifications in the *Israel FTA* ensure a minor pass-through operation is not enough to transform substantially an article.

In fact, FTAs typically contain dozens, even hundreds, of Substantial Transformation Rules. Each is specific to a product category in the HTS, demanding some degree of CTC from one stage of production to another. For example, the *Chile FTA* states a good qualifies as originating, even if the materials used to produce the good are not themselves originating, if those non-originating materials are transformed in such a way as to cause their tariff classification to change (or meet other requirements). The *Singapore* and *Australia FTAs* also contain Tariff Shift Rules.

Typically, a lengthy, detailed annex to an FTA sets out the shift in the HTS categorization required for a transformation of non-originating materials into a new and different article to be considered "substantial." In *NAFTA*, it is Annex 301, in the *Chile FTA*, it is Annex 4.1, in the *Singapore FTA*, it is Annex 3A, and in the Australia FTA is it Annexes 4-A and 5-A. The *Morocco FTA*, too, has product-specific ROOs in Annex 5-A.

As a general proposition, the larger the shift in tariff classification demanded, the more protectionist the rule. For instance, a Substantial Transformation Rule that calls for a CTH at the 4-digit HTS classification level demands a greater degree of economic activity with respect to transformation of an article than a CTH at the 6- or 8-digit level. Not surprisingly, during FTA negotiations lobbyists trying to protect domestic industries vie with free trade advocates for the attention of trade officials.

Protectionist forces tend to seek Substantial Transformation Rules for their clients that require considerable manufacturing activity to qualify a product as originating in the FTA area. That way, most like products will be deemed to originate in third countries, and will receive MFN tariff, not duty-free, treatment. Free traders fight for minimalist CTH obligations, so as to allow their consumer and importer clients access to a wide array of merchandise that qualifies for a zero duty. The battle is fought in the trenches—the 4-, 6-, and 8-digit HTS product categories. The results are published in long, obscure annexes to the FTA that contain product-specific Substantial Transformation Rules referring back to HTS codes.

NAFTA negotiators found the Tariff Shift Rule to be problematical. They sought to differentiate simple from complex assembly operations. For example, the negotiators elected to create new tariff provisions covering major components of products in HTS Chapter 84 and establish a rule to distinguish simple and complex assembly:

> In Chapter 84, in order to develop an origin rule for machine tools that distinguishes between simple and complex assembly, we created new tariff provisions for four major components:
>
> — the main engine;
>
> — hydraulics (that is, the pumps);
>
> — the numerical controller; and
>
> — major weldments or casting (that is, the major structural components of the machine).
>
> Under the rule of origin we created for machine tools, if at least three of these four major components are produced within the *NAFTA* and the final assembly occurs within the free trade area, the machine tool is considered to be eligible for tariff preference.
>
> On the other hand, if two or more of the major components are produced outside the free trade area, mere final assembly of the machine tool from those components is not recognized as resulting in a product eligible for tariff preference.[4]

A related problem the negotiators tackled was how to treat a complex assembly of a good from small parts versus a simple assembly from major components:

> In [HTS] Chapter 85, in order to develop an origin rule for electric ranges and ovens, we created new tariff provisions within Sub-Heading 8516.90, the sub-heading for parts of electric ranges and ovens. In the breakouts we cover the following parts of electric ranges and ovens:
>
> — cooking chambers, whether or not assembled;
>
> — top surface panels, with or without heating elements or controls;
>
> — door assemblies, incorporating at least two of the following: inner panel; outer panel; window; insulation.
>
> Assembly of complete ovens and ranges from smaller parts (regardless of the origin of smaller parts), is recognized as resulting in a product eligible for tariff preference. On the other hand, assembly of final products from the major components, described in the new provisions, does not result in a

---

4. *North American*, 38.

product eligible for preference if those components were produced outside the free trade area.[5]

Similar solutions were devised for other products listed in HTS Chapters 84, 85 and 90 like fax machines, paging devices, and other telecommunications equipment, printers, data processing equipment and radar equipment.

While the *NAFTA* negotiators considered assembly issues, they appear to have avoided the question of whether to adopt a single, general CTH Rule. To be sure, the principle advantage of any CTH Rule is that it provides certainty and predictability to manufacturers, exporters, and importers because it can be articulated clearly and learned quickly. However, the key disadvantage is that different CTH Rules apply to different goods, as the discussion of assembly issues illustrates. In fact, Annex 401 of *NAFTA*, where *NAFTA* ROOs are located, has 148 pages. It is estimated these pages contain over 11,000 ROOs. This estimate suggests a proliferation in CTH ROOs. In *CUFTA*, *NAFTA's* predecessor, 1,498 ROOs were set forth in 20 pages.

Interest group politics — in fancy academic jargon, "Public Choice Theory" — appears to be the leading explanation for this proliferation:

> The case of tomato catsup and tomato paste offers an example. Catsup (*salsa de tomate*) is classified in chapter 21 of the HTS, under item 2103.20, while tomato paste (*pasta de tomate*) is classified in Chapter 20, under HTS item 2002.90. The [*Canada-U.S.*] *FTA* rule of origin provides that the operations necessary to convert a product classified in any chapter other than Chapter 21 into a product classified in that Chapter will confer preferential origin on the chapter 21 product. Thus, when imported tomato paste (Chapter 20) is processed into tomato catsup (Chapter 21), the catsup qualifies for the FTA preference.
>
> Under *NAFTA*, however, the rule is different. Conversion of tomato paste imported from outside *NAFTA* into tomato catsup within *NAFTA* will not confer origin on the catsup for preferential purposes. The formulation of the rule is that a change to item 2103.20 (tomato catsup) from any other Chapter, *except* Sub-Heading 2002.90 (tomato paste), will confer origin. Under *NAFTA*, then, the tomato paste itself must be produced within the territory of a *NAFTA* member if the tomato catsup is to receive preferential treatment.
>
> . . .
>
> This absence of a general rule or principle for determining origin is perhaps the major shortcoming of CTH, one that would be no surprise to political "realists" or to economists of the public choice persuasion. It renders CTH susceptible to capture by industries interested in minimizing their exposure to competition. In *NAFTA*, in the case of tomato catsup,

---

5. *North American*, 39.

it apparently was easy for an industry interested in minimizing competition from tomato paste outside the three-country area to fashion a product-specific rule denying the preference to catsup made from the imported tomato paste. There is no other apparent reason for the change in *NAFTA* from the *FTA* rule. In 1992, it so happens, Chile was the leading foreign supplier of tomato paste to the United States. Thus Chilean tomato paste can be used in catsup that will enjoy preferential treatment under the *FTA*, but none of it will have that privilege under *NAFTA*. It so happens that Mexico was the second leading supplier of tomato paste in the United States in 1992.

These facts would seem to justify the tentative assumption that the rule was changed at the behest of the Mexican producers of tomato paste who presumably would benefit at the expense of their competitors in Chile. . . .

The very fact that we are able only to speculate about the "policy" behind this particular rule illustrates the ease with which CTH may be captured by specific companies or industries. The stated rules are, superficially, comprehensible to all, but their rationale rarely is. . . .

. . . The hundreds of pages and thousands of lines of a tariff schedule offer countless opportunities for similar rules, rules that sometimes may amount to a covenant not to compete.[6]

These sorts of games, which seem to compromise the dignity of International Trade Law, call forth an obvious question: Why not apply one CTH Rule to all items in the HTS?

For example, suppose the policy goal is that only a major manufacturing and processing operation should count as a substantial transformation. Then, the CTH Rule could be that a change in the HTS tariff classification at the 2-digit level is a substantial transformation. Alternatively, if the goal is that a minor operation suffices, then the CTH Rule could be that a change at the 6- (or even 8-) digit level qualifies as a substantial transformation. A uniform rule might de-politicize the process of formulating ROO by barring special rules for industries with lobbying power.

V. Type 4: Value Added Test

Value Added Tests are easy to articulate. A specified percentage of the total value of a product must be added in a country for the product to be considered a product of that country. They are common in FTAs. For example, the *Israel FTA* has a 35% value-added rule for many articles. To qualify as "Israeli," at least 35% of the total

---

6. N. David Palmeter, *Pacific Trade Liberalization and Rules of Origin*, 27 JOURNAL OF WORLD TRADE 49, 51–52 (1993).

value of that article must come from (1) materials produced in Israel plus (2) the direct cost of processing operations performed in Israel.

Typically, the U.S. negotiates for what might be dubbed an American Content Provision. This Provision allows a certain percentage of the materials to come from the U.S. itself, rather than from the partner country, yet still qualify toward the threshold. In the *Israel FTA*, up to 15% of the content of an article may be from the U.S., which means that in calculating whether 35% of the value-added of an article is Israeli, up to 15% of American-origin material will count.

NAFTA contains a Value Added Test. However, *NAFTA* negotiators faced four difficulties with this kind of preferential ROO. First, they "found that value-added ROO are difficult to design, and are unpredictable because of the instability of the cost elements that go into value-added." Suppose a Mexican car manufacturer buys Japanese engines, Indonesian tires, and Thai batteries and exports finished vehicles to America. The manufacturer will pay its suppliers in *yen*, *rupiah*, and *baht*. The exchange rates for *yen-peso*, *rupiah-peso*, and *baht-peso* inevitably fluctuate. The manufacturer will pay its Mexican workforce in *pesos*. The manufacturer's export revenues are denominated in dollars. The dollar-*peso* exchange rate fluctuates, often quickly and dramatically. Thus, the cost of inputs and export revenues, when translated into pesos, will change. Exchange rate fluctuations can affect determinations of origin made on a value-added basis.

Second, suppose in the above example all inputs were denominated in *pesos*. Surely the prices of these inputs will change. Such changes will affect the value-added calculation. Similarly, the Mexican manufacturer is likely to adjust the sale price of the vehicles in response to changes in American market conditions, which in turn may affect the value-added calculation.

Third, the Value-Added Test lacks reciprocity and thereby discriminates against low-wage countries. Suppose athletic shoes are made from Mexican rubber soles, Canadian leather, and American plastic. Consider opposite scenarios.

In Case 1, these parts are transformed into a finished product in Mexico. Subsequently, the shoes are exported to Canada or the U.S. In Case 2, they are transformed into a finished product in either Canada or the U.S., and then exported to the U.S. Because wage rates are lower in Mexico than Canada, the value-added in Mexico is lower than in Canada. As a result, in Case #1, a threshold established in a value-added test may not be satisfied, hence the shoes may fail to qualify for duty-free treatment. In Case 2, because of the higher value-added resulting from higher labor costs in the U.S. or Canada, the shoes are more likely to meet the threshold. More generally, the value-added calculation may be manipulated by altering the location of production processes. In many instances such alterations may be difficult, or any consequent tariff savings may not be offset by other costs.

Finally, enforcing a Value-Added Test is difficult. Customs officials must verify value-added calculations submitted by importers. Such verification requires an examination of the financial records of the manufacturer. These records may be located overseas and based on accounting principles other than GAAP. The foreign manufacturer may not want to divulge the information, particularly in a situation where the importer of the product is not affiliated with the manufacturer. Possibly, the manufacturer simply does not want to assume the burden of such record keeping.

In spite of these difficulties, *NAFTA* makes use of the Value-Added Test for certain products. The Regional Value Content Rule for the automobile industry (discussed below) is a significant example. Other instances are fishing reels, toy electric trains, and certain other products that are placed in the same HTS category as their constituent parts. Because the parts and finished goods are in the same category, even a complex assembly operation cannot cause a change in tariff classification. Thus, a CTH Rule is unhelpful, and a Value-Added Test is used.

Some post-*NAFTA* FTAs rely on Value-Added Tests. For instance, the *Morocco FTA* has a general 35% Test not unlike the Test in the *Israel FTA*. A good qualifies as originating in the territory of Morocco or the U.S. if it is a new or different article, it has been grown, produced, or manufactured in Morocco, America, or both, and the value of the (1) materials produced plus (2) direct cost of processing operations performed in either or both countries is 35% or more of the appraised value of the article. Query when the value is appraised, and by whom?

VI. Type 5: Hybrid Rule

• **Sensitive Sectors**

The *NAFTA* Parties consider certain industries, such as automobiles, chemicals, plastics, machinery, footwear, and electronics, to be sensitive. A subtle phrase in Article 401(b)—"and the good satisfies all other applicable requirements of this Chapter"—is the clue that for these sectors, special hybrid ROO exist. The Hybrid Rules are set forth in Annex 401.1.

For example, to qualify for preferential treatment an automotive product must satisfy two tests. First, it must meet a CTH Rule. Second, the value of the components of the good from *NAFTA* Parties must meet a specified percentage—called the "Regional Value Content" (RVC). The RVC is, therefore, a measure of the value of the content of a good that is added in or derived from one or more *NAFTA* Parties. Put differently, it is a Value Added Test, but with specific respect to a region defined by Parties to an FTA, *i.e.*, "Value Added Test" is a generic term, whereas RVC refers to a particular FTA.

Conceptually, the formula for RVC is:

$$RVC = \frac{(\text{Total Value of the good}) - \left(\begin{array}{c}\text{Value of non-originating} \\ \text{materials in the good}\end{array}\right)}{(\text{Total value of the good})} \times 100$$

(Note that an alternative to the RVC test applies to some goods, namely, they must include specified components.)

- *NAFTA 62.5% RVC for Autos*

The *NAFTA* RVC for cars, light trucks, engines, and transmissions is 62.5%—the highest for such merchandise in any FTA in the world. The RVC is 60% for other vehicles and parts.[7] Thus, to receive duty-free treatment, at least 62.5% of the value of the content of an assembled car exported from one *NAFTA* Party to another must be from a *NAFTA* Party. Under *Canada-U.S. FTA* the RVC was 50%. Thus, *NAFTA* has a stricter—and, therefore, more protectionist—ROO for cars than previously existed for the U.S. and Canada.

The 62.5% ROO applies to any car manufacturer, regardless of national origin. It creates an incentive for non-*NAFTA* companies to "jump" the *NAFTA* tariff walls by investing directly in the *NAFTA* zone. For example, 75% of the content of a Toyota Camry (as of January 2017) is made in the U.S., ensuring that Japanese manufacturer *NAFTA* DFQF treatment. The ROO also helps keep out non-*NAFTA* parts. For instance, no more than 3–6% of the value of a car (as of June 2017) made in the zone comes from Chinese parts. They tend to be electronics and TV screens, the production of which long since migrated to China.

For most goods, manufacturers may calculate RVC using either the "transaction value" or "net cost" method.[8] The basis of the former method is the price actually paid or payable for the good. In contrast, the latter method relies on the total cost of the good with deductions for sales promotion, marketing cost, royalties, and packing and shipping. Thus, in practice the formulas for RVC are:[9]

$$RVC = \frac{(\text{Transaction Value of the good}) - \left(\begin{array}{c}\text{Value of non-originating} \\ \text{materials in the good}\end{array}\right)}{(\text{Transaction value of the good})} \times 100$$

and

$$RVC = \frac{(\text{Net Cost of the good}) - \left(\begin{array}{c}\text{Value of non-originating} \\ \text{materials in the good}\end{array}\right)}{(\text{Net Cost of the good})} \times 100$$

Automobile manufacturers do not have a choice of calculation methodology. They must use the net cost formula.[10] This method may have additional protectionist effects, because it contains a tracing requirement for 69 specified car parts,

---

7. *See NAFTA* Article 403:5. These RVCs were phased in over an 8-year period.
8. *See NAFTA* Article 415.
9. *See NAFTA* Article 402:2-3.
10. *See NAFTA* Article 402:5(d).

including engines, transmissions, bumpers, and mirrors. The make-up of a part is scrutinized to determine whether the part itself is made up of foreign inputs. The value of any foreign content in the part must be subtracted when calculating the net cost of a vehicle, *i.e.*, the foreign content value of a part cannot be included in the RVC calculation.[11]

The tracing requirement is designed to rectify a "roll-up" problem that existed with the *CUFTA*. The problem was that the full value of a good was counted as originating or non-originating even though the good contained a mixture of originating and non-originating materials. For example, assume a car is made in Canada and Thailand. The value-added in Canada is 51%, while 49% of the assembly occurs in Thailand. During the Thai assembly operation, a part whose value is 49% Thai is included in the car. Under the net cost method articulated in the *Canada FTA*, the part was counted as 100% regional (*i.e.*, originating in the U.S. or Canada) on the ground that its domestic value exceeded 50% of its total value. In effect, the foreign contribution to the value of the part was "rolled up" into, or neglected in favor of, the domestic value. Because of the *NAFTA* tracing test, 49% of the value of this part must be deducted in the net cost calculation of RVC. Indeed, the non-originating value remains non-originating through every stage of assembly to the time of calculating the RVC. Annex 403.1 of *NAFTA* contains a list of automotive parts for passenger and light vehicles that are subject to the tracing requirement.

The tracing requirement has a significant adverse consequence. It encourages auto producers to source fully from within *NAFTA*. No producer wants to be audited by a customs authority, and using inputs only from *NAFTA* Parties minimizes the risk of an audit. It also eliminates the necessity of keeping records to satisfy a tracing inquiry from customs officials. In turn, the actual RVC may be raised to over 62.5%, and possibly 100%. More generally, the RVC and tracing requirements may create perverse economic incentives. Producers in *NAFTA* may be compelled to purchase their inputs from less efficient suppliers in *NAFTA* instead of choosing a supplier based strictly on cost and quality considerations. In effect, trade in inputs may be diverted from certain non-*NAFTA* suppliers in favor of *NAFTA* suppliers. The result may be that the global competitiveness of some *NAFTA* producers is undermined.

VII. *NAFTA* Renegotiations on 62.5% Auto RVC

• **Most Controversial of Topics**

No topic proved more controversial in renegotiating *NAFTA* than the 62.5% RVC ROO (though, as discussed below and in a separate Chapter, Canada's SMS for sensitive sectors, and its Class 7 pricing for UF milk, were quite contentious,

---

11. *See NAFTA* Article 403:1-2.

too). These negotiations, commenced in August 2017, and included bitter disputes over U.S. demands for a five-year Sunset Clause (whereby *NAFTA* would terminate automatically after five years, unless the Parties opted otherwise), Chapter 11 ISDS reform, elimination of the Chapter 19 dispute resolution system (for AD-CVD cases), greater access to Canada's dairy market (via liberalizations of the Canadian SMS system, which ironically the U.S. won in *TPP* negotiations, but then abandoned when it withdrew from *TPP* in January 2017), and restrictions on Canadian and Mexican access to America's government procurement market (at Federal and State levels).[12] The ROO negotiations, in particular, were linked to promises during the 2016 Presidential campaign by candidate Donald J. Trump (1946–, President, 2017–) to save American jobs and incomes from *NAFTA*, which he castigated in the September 2016 Presidential Debate at Hofstra University as "the worst trade deal maybe ever signed anywhere, but certainly ever signed in this country."[13] The USTR insisted on raising the threshold to 85%, and also insisted that at least 50% of the steel, aluminum, and other key inputs into a car would have to be sourced specifically from the United States. Never before did an FTA have, embedded in a regional value ROO, a country-specific rule.

Thus, Canada, Mexico, and many groups within the American auto industry fiercely opposed these demands. They feared inefficient disruptions to the North American vehicle manufacturing supply chain that had been entrenched since *NAFTA* entered into force on 1 January 1994, and which would unnecessarily raise the cost of cars by forcing them to comply with a higher RVC by using more high-cost inputs sourced from the region than before (*e.g.*, 22.5% more, the difference between 85% and 62.5%), or not comply and pay MFN duties when shipping across vehicles across the American, Canadian, or Mexican borders (*e.g.*, the 2.5% and 25% car and truck tariffs the U.S. imposed). Finding them so unacceptable, the other two *NAFTA* Parties essentially refused even to table counter-offers. (Canada toyed with allowing intangible assets, like IP, count toward any threshold above 62.5%, but the USTR dismissed that possibility as vague.)

- **Boosting RVC and Adding Minimum Wage Requirement**

By April 2018, the USTR lowered the demand to a 75% RVC, to be phased in across four years for light vehicles and two years for pick-up trucks, provided there were minimum critical component and wage requirements (to assure, respectively, usage of American content, and higher salaries for Mexican workers), and provided there were tiers of U.S.-specific content for auto parts (*e.g.*, core auto parts would

---

12. *See* Raj Bhala, *Lessons About NAFTA Renegotiations from Shakespeare's Othello: From the Three Amigo's to America as Iago?*, 33 Maryland Journal of International Law issue 1, 38-105 (Fall 2018) (Fall 2017 Symposium, *The U.S. Mexico Relationship in International Law and Politics*), https://digitalcommons.law.umaryland.edu/mjil/vol33/iss1/4/

13. *Quoted in* Patrick Gillespie, *Trump Hammers "America's Worst Trade Deal,"* CNN Money, 27 September 2016, http://money.cnn.com/2016/09/27/news/economy/donald-trump-nafta-hillary-clinton-debate/index.html.

have to have 75% American content, complimentary auto parts would be subject to a 70% threshold, with four-year phase-in periods, and still others would have no obligatory American content).[14] The U.S. also demanded that 30% of the value of a car would have to be made with labor paid at least U.S. $15 per hour.[15]

Mexico said "no," because 30% of every car would have to be made in Canada and the U.S. to satisfy that wage rate. Likewise, Mexico rejected the American demand on ROOs for larger vehicles: the U.S. called for 40% of the value of a light-duty passenger vehicle, and 45% of a pick-up truck, to be made in locations where wages are at least $16 per hour.[16] Here again, Mexico said those areas would exclude Mexico, shifting production away from it, northward. Mexico was willing to raise the RVC from 62.5% to 70%, but without any wage targets, and without any mandate as to the value of a vehicle that had to be built at certain wage levels.[17] And, the American demand that 70% of all steel and aluminum in any vehicle originate in the *NAFTA* zone also was unacceptable (even though it was a mild climb down by the Trump Administration from an earlier demand that about 50% of steel and aluminum come from the U.S.).

As talks dragged on, in late May 2018, Mexico offered a compromise: the overall RVC could be 70%, and 20% of the value of a vehicle could be made in a high-wage area.[18] Mexico called on the U.S. to back off certain other demands, such as allowing seasonal agricultural workers to initiate trade cases, and the five-year Sunset Clause.[19] Mexico also insisted that it be exempted from any action the U.S. might take under Section 232 of the *Trade Expansion Act of 1962*, as amended (discussed in a separate Chapter). The U.S. balked, and stuck to its 75% RVC and 40% car and 45% truck thresholds, and its $16 per hour level. In August, the two Parties engaged in bilateral talks, which also covered a possible five-year phase-in period for any new ROO on which they ultimately agreed.[20] Leaving Canada out was a move characterized as sensible, in that Mexico and America needed to sort out their differences

---

14. *See* Rossella Brevetti, *NAFTA Officials Take New Crack at Closing Auto Trade, Other Gaps*, 35 International Trade Reporter 646 (10 May 2018).

15. *See* Josh Wingrove, Andrew Mayeda & Eric Martin, *NAFTA Nations to Meet Again, Mexico Says Deal Possible in Days*, Bloomberg, 26 April 2018, www.bloomberg.com/politics/articles/2018 -04-26/u-s-eyes-nafta-finish-line-before-china-talks-overtake-agenda.

16. *See* Anthony Esposito & David Lawder, *NAFTA Talks Resume Amid Fears of "Zombie" Deal*, Reuters, 7 May 2018, www.reuters.com/article/us-trade-nafta/nafta-talks-resume-amid-fears-of -zombie-deal-idUSKBN1I80BK.

17. *See* Jenny Leonard, Josh Wingrove & Eric Martin, *Mexico Is Said to Offer NAFTA Cars Compromise on Content, Wages*, 35 International Trade Reporter (BNA) 674 (17 May 2018).

18. *See* Daina Beth Solomon & David Lawder, *Mexico's Pena Nieto "Optimistic" on NAFTA as Country Makes New Offer*, Reuters, 24 May 2018, www.reuters.com/article/us-trade-nafta-mexico /mexico-says-will-not-renegotiate-nafta-under-pressure-but-makes-new-offer-idUSKCN1IQ01Y.

19. *See* Rossella Brevetti, *U.S. Push for Mexico Auto Deal Could Force Canada's Hand*, 35 International Trade Reporter (BNA) 1058 (9 August 2018). [Hereinafter, *U.S. Push.*]

20. *See* David Lawder & Sharay Angulo, *U.S. and Mexico Put Off NAFTA Talks until Wednesday, Autos Eyed*, Reuters, 21 August 2018, http://bilaterals.org/?us-and-mexico-put-off-nafta-talks.

and then present a deal to Canada, but also seen as a Trump Administration plot to "divide and conquer" the other two Parties.[21]

The auto industry in the U.S. was itself divided over raising the ROO threshold to qualify for *NAFTA* DFQF treatment. On the one hand, the American Automotive Policy Council, which represents the traditional Big Three Detroit car companies—Chrysler, Ford, and GM—said it was "encouraged by the direction of the discussions" and "share[d] the administration's overall goals of strengthening U.S. auto manufacturing and creating jobs."[22] On the other hand, "Here for America," the members of which include BMW, Daimler, Honda, Hyundai, Kia, Nissan, Subaru, Toyota, Volkswagen, and Volvo, opposed a more stringent ROO than the 62.5% RVC.[23] These foreign-brand automakers account for 50% of vehicle production in the U.S., yet those with modest-sized manufacturing and R&D facilities in the U.S. feared the difficulties, especially higher costs, caused by a higher threshold.

VIII. *NAFTA* 2.0 Hybrid Auto ROO: 75% RVC and Minimum Wage

- **Key Features**

The U.S.-Mexican talks culminated in a deal, on 27 August 2018, with auto sector provisions—the matters that had driven the Trump Administration to renegotiate the deal a year earlier, and which had been the focal point of the talks all year long—essentially along the lines of American demands for PSROs in this sector.[24] In retrospect, that there was a deal at all is surprising in light of how close the

---

21. U.S. Push (*quoting* Bill Reinsch, Senior Advisor, Center for Strategic and International Studies); *see also* Eric Martin & Jenny Leonard, *U.S. and Mexico Are Said to Be Nearing Deal in NAFTA Car Talks*, 35 International Trade Reporter (BNA) 1024 (2 August 2018) (reporting on the talks).

22. David Shepardson & David Lawder, *Foreign Automakers Oppose Trump NAFTA Plan as U.S.-Mexico Talks Resume*, *Reuters*, 20 August 2018, www.reuters.com/article/us-trade-nafta-autos /foreign-automakers-oppose-trump-nafta-plan-as-u-s-mexico-talks-resume-idUSKCN1L6010 (*quoting* Matt Blunt, President, American Automotive Policy Council). [Hereinafter, *Foreign Automakers.*]

23. *See Foreign Automakers* (reporting on a 16 August 2018 letter to Congress from Here for America, signed by John Bozzella, President, Association of Global Automakers).

24. *See Trump Announces "Incredible" Trade Deal with Mexico*, BBC News, 28 August 2018, www.bbc.co.uk/news/business-45323634; Roberta Rampton & Jeff Mason, *U.S., Mexico, Reach NAFTA Deal, Turn Up Pressure on Canada*, REUTERS, 27 August 2018, www.reuters.com/article /us-trade-nafta/u-s-mexico-reach-nafta-deal-turning-up-pressure-on-canada-idUSKCN1LC1E7; Jordan Fabian & Vicki Needham, *Trump Announces Agreement with Mexico on NAFTA Overhaul*, THE HILL, 27 August 2018, http://thehill.com/homenews/administration/403781-trump -announces-deal-with-mexico-on-nafta-overhaul; Eric Martin, Jennifer Jacobs, Josh Wingrove & Andrew Mayeda, *Trump Says He's Agreed on Mexico Trade Deal to Replace NAFTA*, BLOOMBERG, 27 August 2018, www.bloomberg.com/politics/articles/2018-08-27/nafta-breakthrough-seems -imminent-after-year-of-fractious-talks; Sharay Angulo & David Shepardson, *Mexico, U.S. Closing in on NAFTA Deal, Talks to Resume Monday*, REUTERS, 26 August 2018. www.reuters.com

President came to withdrawing America from *NAFTA*. The day after Labor Day 2018, excerpts from a book by veteran investigative reporter and famed Watergate correspondent Bob Woodward (1943–) was published. *Fear: Trump in the White House* was a blockbuster, arguing a "nervous breakdown of Executive power" had occurred in the Trump Administration. With respect to trade:[25]

> According to Woodward, [Gary] Cohn [Director, National Economic Council (1960–)] "stole a letter off Trump's desk" that the president was intending to sign to formally withdraw the United States from a trade agreement with South Korea. Cohn later told an associate that he removed the letter to protect national security and that Trump did not notice that it was missing.
>
> Cohn made a similar play to prevent Trump from pulling the United States out of the North American Free Trade Agreement, something the president has long threatened to do. In spring 2017, Trump was eager to withdraw from *NAFTA* and told [Staff Secretary Robert] Porter [(1977–)]: "Why aren't we getting this done? Do your job. It's tap, tap, tap. You're just tapping me along. I want to do this."
>
> Under orders from the President, Porter drafted a notification letter withdrawing from *NAFTA*. But he and other advisers worried that it could trigger an economic and foreign relations crisis. So Porter consulted Cohn, who told him, according to Woodward: "I can stop this. I'll just take the paper off his desk."[26]

Thanks to the removal of those papers from the Oval Office desk, in what Mr. Woodword described was part of an administrative *coup d'état* on many Presidential matters, negotiations on a *NAFTA* 2.0 proceeded, and the bilateral deal was agreed.

The President also wanted to rename *NAFTA*, thinking *NAFTA* 1.0 was a pejorative acronym that evoked memories of American job losses, income declines, and trade deficits.[27] Options included "*USMC*"—the *United States–Mexico–Canada* pact, assuming Canada joined (a saga discussed below), notwithstanding the long-standing of that acronym for "United States Marine Corps." Rubrics

---

/article/us-trade-nafta-mexico/mexico-u-s-closing-in-on-nafta-deal-talks-to-resume-monday -idUSKCN1LB0J4.

The U.S. and Mexico simultaneously published the text of their bilateral agreement on 28 September 2018. Its language largely excluded Canada.

25. Anthony Zurcher, *Bob Woodward's Book on Trump: The Most Explosive Quotes*, BBC News, 4 September 2018, www.bbc.co.uk/news/world-us-canada-45415151.

26. Philip Rucker & Robert Costa, *Bob Woodward's New Book Reveals a "Nervous Breakdown" of Trump's Presidency*, The Washington Post, 4 September 2018, www.washingtonpost.com/politics /bob-woodwards-new-book-reveals-a-nervous-breakdown-of-trumps-presidency/2018/09/04 /b27a389e-ac60-11e8-a8d7-0f63ab8b1370_story.html?noredirect=on&utm_term=.4d8b3877c879.

27. *See* Jeanna Smialek & Jenny Leonard, *Lighthizer Says U.S. Won't Wait for Canada on New NAFTA Pact (1)*, 35 International Trade Reporter (BNA) 1240 (27 September 2018).

aside, the key elements of the 27 August 2018 U.S.-Mexican bilateral accord were
as follows:

(1) Mexico agreed to an 12.5% increase in the RVC, from 62.5% to 75%.

(2) Mexico also agreed that at least 40% of the value of a car, and 45% of the
value of a truck, would have to be manufactured by high-wage labor, specifically, by workers paid at least U.S. $16 per hour.

(3) Mexico further agreed to enforce ILO labor rights rules (discussed in a separate Chapter), and to eliminate labor contracts signed by employers and
union leaders without the consent of workers.

The first two points amounted to a Hybrid ROO never before seen in any FTA: a
Value Added Test, plus a Minimum Wage Test.

How might the Minimum Wage Test affect the division of labor in the auto
industry across North America? The average hourly pay (as of September 2018) in
the U.S. for auto and auto parts workers is $20.[28] In Canada, the average hourly
wage rate in the auto sector is about $1 higher than in the U.S., and the base pay
range is $20.70–$28.98.[29] In Mexico, the average is about $2, with a base pay range
of $3.41–$7.34 per hour. Mexico is the world's sixth largest automaker, and 112,000
Mexicans work in the auto, auto parts, assembly, and vehicle-related sectors—a
seven-fold increase since *NAFTA 1.0* entered into force on 1 January 1994.[30] Might
the Test shift production of higher-value added parts to Canada and the U.S., and
out of Mexico? Would it lead to rising wages in Mexico, or confine Mexico to low-
end production? Might it encourage more skilled automotive work in Mexico, such
as design and R&D, where the average hourly wage is between $10–$22?[31]

Consider these questions in the context of the overall Mexican economy. The
average Mexican earns $19 per day, 46.2% of Mexicans live below the poverty line
and the Gini coefficient is 0.48 (essentially unchanged between 2008 and 2014).[32]
Yet, Mexico is the 11th largest economy and 13th largest exporting nation in the

---

28. *See* Josh Wingrove & Jenny Leonard, *NAFTA Deal Is Said Unlikely This Week, Raising Tariff
Fears (2)*, International Trade Daily (BNA) (19 September 2018). [Hereinafter, *NAFTA Deal.*] By
another account, the average U.S. auto manufacturing hourly wage rate was well above $22 (as of
June 2018). *See* Jessica Murphy & Natalie Sherman, *USMCA Trade Deal: Who Gets What from "New
NAFTA?,"* BBC News, 1 October 2018, www.bbc.com/news/world-us-canada-45674261. [Herein-
after, *USMCA Trade Deal.*]

29. *See* Maham Abedi, *Why U.S.-Mexico's NAFTA Agreement Could Be Good News for Canada's
Auto Industry*, Global News, 28 August 2018, https://globalnews.ca/news/4413740/nafta-canada
-auto-industry/.

30. Rudolf Traub-Merz, ed., The Automotive Sector in Emerging Economies: Industrial Policies, Market Dynamics, and Trade Unions (Friedrich Ebert Stiftung, 2017), http://
library.fes.de/pdf-files/iez/13154.pdf#page=163; *NAFTA Deal.*

31. *See* Rossella Brevetti, *Tough NAFTA Auto Rules Will Help Spur Investment in Mexico (1)*, 35
International Trade Reporter (BNA) 1357 (18 October 2018).

32. *See* Central Intelligence Agency, The World Factbook, North America: Mexico,
www.cia.gov/library/publications/the-world-factbook/geos/mx.html.

world. The juxtaposition of these two sets of statistics suggests Mexico is a highly unequal society, in terms of income distribution, and the benefits of *NAFTA 1.0* have been captured by elites. Would the Minimum Wage Test help address the socioeconomic disparities?

Office of the United States Trade Representative,

United States–Mexico Trade Fact Sheet: *Rebalancing NAFTA to Support Manufacturing* (28 August 2018)[33]

Key Achievement: Increasing Regional Value Content Rule

This deal encourages United States manufacturing and regional economic growth by requiring that 75 percent of auto content be made in the United States and Mexico.

The rules will:

(1) Incentivize billions annually in additional United States vehicle and auto parts production.

(2) Help to preserve and re-shore vehicle and parts production in the United States.

(3) Transform supply chains to use more United States content, especially content that is key to future automobile production and high-paying jobs.

(4) Close gaps in the current *NAFTA* agreement that incentivized low wages in automobile and parts production.

Key Achievement: Creating New Labor Value Content Rule

This deal uses trade rules to drive higher wages by requiring that 40–45 percent of auto content be made by workers earning at least $16 per hour.

The rules will:

(1) Support better jobs for United States producers and workers by requiring that a significant portion of vehicle content be made with high-wage labor.

(2) Ensure that United States producers and workers are able to compete on an even playing field, and incentivize new vehicle and parts investments in the United States.

(3) Encourage more investment by auto companies in research and development in the region.

Key Achievement: Exceeding NAFTA 1.0 and TPP Standards with Stronger Rules of Origin and Enforcement

The United States and Mexico have agreed to stronger rules of origin that exceed those of both *NAFTA* 1.0 and the *Trans-Pacific Partnership* (*TPP*), including for

---

33. https://ustr.gov/about-us/policy-offices/press-office/press-releases/2018/august/rebalancing-nafta-support.

autos and automobile parts and other industrial products such as chemicals, steel-intensive products, glass, and optical fiber.

This deal exceeds *NAFTA* 1.0 and the *TPP* by establishing procedures that streamline certification and verification of rules of origin and that promote strong enforcement. This includes new cooperation and enforcement provisions that help to prevent duty evasion before it happens.

The new rules will help ensure that only producers using sufficient and significant United States and Mexican parts and materials receive preferential tariff benefits.

- **Lingering Concerns**

The policy goals that each part of the Hybrid Test were designed to serve was clear. Mandating 75% rather than 62.5% RVC would divert trade in auto parts from third countries, and create trade within the Parties. Increasing the threshold by 12.5% made it more difficult for auto manufacturers in North America to source auto parts from China. And, "requiring that 40–45 percent of auto content be made by workers earning at least $16" would "drive higher wages" and thereby "support North American jobs."[34] However, key details about the unprecedented Hybrid ROO were unclear.

For example, would there be a tracing requirement, whereby the origin of sub-components mattered? Suppose a component (such as a low-tech steering wheel, or a high-tech electronic system) is made in North America, but the plastic used in that component is from a petrochemical product made by the Shanghai Petrochemical company in China. Does the value of the plastic sub-component qualify as part of the North American value—is it rolled up into the overall value of the component (as occurred under the 1989 *CUSFTA* roll up rule), or is it deducted from that value (as was required under the *NAFTA* 1.0 tracing requirement).

As another example, would additional resources be devoted to enforcing it? Would the $16 dollar/hour threshold be adjusted for inflation? Likewise, it was unclear exactly which ILO standards Mexico was pledging adherence to—only those relating to minimum wages, or others? Nevertheless, the deal was touted as benefiting American workers, as it supposedly would stem job losses in the auto industry to lower wage Mexican factories (the "giant sucking sound" of which 1992 Independent Presidential Candidate H. Ross Perot (1930–) spoke). Perhaps some auto sector jobs might shift back to America from Mexico, to satisfy the Minimum Wage Test. And, the deal was touted as good for Mexican workers, by setting a partial floor for their wage rates, which could lead to a general lift in those rates.

---

34. United States—Mexico Trade Fact Sheet: *Modernizing NAFTA to be a 21st Century Trade Agreement* (28 August 2018), https://ustr.gov/about-us/policy-offices/press-office/press-releases/2018/august/modernizing-nafta-be-21st-century.

- **U.S.-Mexican Compromise**

In return for the U.S. winning key concessions on auto ROOs, what concessions did the U.S. make, that is, what essential points did Mexico score? The answer is as follows:[35]

(1) The U.S. agreed it would not impose a cap on the number of vehicles shipped from Mexico that would quality for DFQF treatment (*i.e.*, that would be exempt from America's 2.5% and 25% tariffs on cars and trucks, respectively).

(2) In a *Side Letter* to the 27 August 2018 bilateral agreement, the U.S. agreed to lock its 2.5% tariff on cars imported from Mexico, that is, to provide Mexico with certainty and predictability that any potential increase above 2.5% in the American car tariff would not apply to Mexican-origin cars.

(3) In that *Side Letter*, the U.S. preserved its ability to take a Section 232 national security trade remedy against autos and auto parts (a move it was simultaneously contemplating, as discussed in a separate Chapter). But, the U.S. agreed Mexican-made vehicles would benefit from a duty-free quota of 2.4 million car and SUV shipments (a threshold roughly 40%–50% above the 2017 total of such exports from Mexico to the U.S.), before the U.S. imposed any Section 232 remedy. And, the U.S. pledged this cap would be revised upward in keeping with expansion of production in Mexico.

(4) The U.S. agreed to exempt Mexican washing machine and solar panel exports from the Section 201 general safeguard tariffs America had imposed in January 2018 (discussed in a separate Chapter).

(5) The U.S. agreed to drop its demand for a five-year Sunset Rule. It settled on a rule whereby every six-years, *NAFTA* would be reevaluated, and any problems fixed, and then renewed for a further 16 years. That is, the FTA would be in force for 16 years—a baseline 16-year lifespan. But, every six years it would be re-evaluated. The Parties would make any changes they deemed necessary, and then renew the deal for another 16 years.

The Sunset Clause arrangement was problematical. What would happen if the Parties, following a six-year review, were at loggerheads? Would the FTA terminate? These uncertainties suggested businesses could not plan any investment beyond a payback period of 16 years.

---

35. *See* David Ljunggren, *NAFTA Talks Run Up Against Deadline; U.S. Tariffs Remain Tough Issue*, Reuters, 30 September 2018, www.reuters.com/article/us-trade-nafta/nafta-talks-run-up-against-deadline-u-s-tariffs-remain-tough-issue-idUSKCN1MA0UJ; David Ljunggren, *Canada, U.S. Make Progress in Bid to Save NAFTA, No Deal Yet: Sources*, Reuters, 29 September 2018, www.reuters.com/article/us-trade-nafta/canada-u-s-make-progress-in-bid-to-save-nafta-no-deal-yet-sources-idUSKCN1M90RH ; David Lawder & Anthony Esposito, *U.S.–Mexico Trade Deal Text to Exclude Canada, Irritating Lawmakers*, Reuters, 28 September 2018, www.reuters.com/article/us-trade-nafta/u-s-mexico-trade-deal-text-to-exclude-canada-irritating-u-s-lawmakers-idUSKCN1M81OE.

(6) The U.S. also agreed to drop its demand for a special seasonal trade barrier remedy (namely, tariffs) to protect American fruit and vegetable farmers against Mexican competition. Thus, year-round DFQF treatment on all farm products would continue.

Note, however, that the U.S. did not agree to terminate Section 232 steel or aluminum tariffs on Mexico (discussed in a separate Chapter).

IX. From Hybrid Auto ROO to Overall Trilateral Deal

• Fast-Track Timing and Transparency

Auto ROOs (along with dairy market access and dispute settlement) drove *NAFTA* talks, and like all trade negotiations, the ultimate *NAFTA* 2.0 deal depended on a crafted balance of rights and obligations among Canada, Mexico, and the U.S. With the U.S.-Mexican bilateral accord reached on 27 August 2018, the U.S. turned to reach an accord with Canada — that is, to persuade Canada to join the deal it had made with Mexico. The U.S. and Canada aimed to wrap up their arrangement by 31 August, so that the Trump Administration could meet a 90-day notification requirement. For Congress to consider a trilateral FTA by 1 December under fast-track *TPA*, it had to be notified 90-days before that date, hence the negotiating deadline of 31 August. (In effect, the 90-day period meant that the agreement reached on 27 August was one in principle, a handshake deal, which would be signed 90 days hence.) All three Parties saw 1 December as important, because on that date the newly elected Mexican President, Andrés Manuel López Obrador (1953–, President, 2018–), would be sworn into office, taking over from Enrique Peña Nieto (1966–, President, 2012–2018). Whereas the outgoing the conservative Administration was pro-*NAFTA*, the incoming leftist Administration was seen as potentially anti-*NAFTA*, and ratification by Mexico after that date could be problematical. Better, then, that a deal was secure, in terms of American and Mexican ratification, before that date.

To bring Canada into the bilateral U.S.-Mexican accord, Mexico assured Canada it wanted Canada to sign onto the bilateral deal, preserving the three-country status of the pact. America was less reassuring: using a "stick" approach, it said it was willing to terminate *NAFTA* and move forward with a new "*United States — Mexico Trade Agreement*" that would avoid the pejorative conations of the "*NAFTA*" rubric. President Donald J. Trump stated that the deal with Canada would be "totally on our terms."[36] The U.S. also threatened it would apply any Section 232 auto tariffs to Canadian vehicles if Canada did not sign the revised agreement, and reminded

---

36. *Quoted in NAFTA: U.S.-Canada Trade Talks Break Up Without Deal*, BBC News, 31 August 201,www.bbc.co.uk/news/world-us-canada-45375178. [Hereinafter, *U.S.-Canada Trade Talks Break Up.*]

Canada it expected enhanced market access for American dairy exports (ironically a point on which it had made progress in *TPP* negotiations, wherein Canada agreed to modest reforms in its SMS for dairy products). Derek H. Burney (1939–), Canada's Ambassador to the U.S. (1989–1993), and leader of the Canadian team that concluded the 1989 *CUSFTA* negotiations, opined:

> We are witnessing American divide and conquer, might-is-right tactics at their very worst. Mexico has succumbed. Will Canada follow suit accepting salvage as the only option or will we stand firm?
>
> . . .
>
> When we are confronted with schoolyard bully tactics, the choice is clear. Concede and hope that the behavior will improve, or resist in the hope that rational voices in Congress and business will constrain the President's worst impulses.[37]

Objectively, it was difficult to disagree with the Ambassador's assessment. It also was difficult to disagree with the polite but firm observation of Canadian Foreign Affairs and International Trade Minister, Chrystia Freeland (1968–):

> Trade, by definition, is not a one-way street. Of course, trade with the United States is important to Canada. Canada is important to the U.S., too. *We are the largest market for the United States. Larger than China, Japan and the U.K. combined.*[38]

Notably, leaving Canada out of *NAFTA* 2.0 would mean U.S.-Canadian trade relations would revert to the rules set forth in *CUSFTA*. In other words, the U.S. would have not a trilateral, continental FTA, but two bilateral accords.

The U.S. (and Mexico) sought to extend the 27 August 2018 bilateral to Mexico. The terms the U.S. expected of Canada, in addition to all of the aforementioned points, were as follows. By contrast, Canada would not just sign any deal, and had concerns about some of them:

(1) The Parties compromised on a revised mechanism to resolve AD-CVD disputes, abandoning the *NAFTA* Chapter 19 Panel system. The U.S. and Mexico agreed to eliminate Chapter 19 Panels. Canada insisted on retaining the mechanism, which existed in *CUSFTA*, and thus pre-dated *NAFTA* 1.0, and on which Canada had relied to challenge controversial American trade remedies. As Ambassador Burney explained:

> The dispute settlement issue was vital then [during *CUSFTA* negotiations in 1987], and is now because we are dealing with an economic

---

37. Derek Burney, *Canada Must Learn From Our History and Stand Firm on NAFTA*, 2 September 2018, THE GLOBE AND MAIL, www.theglobeandmail.com/opinion/article-canada-must-learn -from-our-history-and-stand-firm-on-nafta/. [Hereinafter, *Canada Must Learn*.]

38. *Quoted in* Jessica Vomiero, *Freeland Says Losing NAFTA Would be a Blow to U.S.: "Canada is Important to the U.S., Too*, Globe News, 9 September 2018, https://globalnews.ca (emphasis added).

giant more than 10 times our size, one that tends to render decisions on trade that are arbitrary, capricious and contravene U.S. trade law. The [Chapter 19] Panels act as a check on such actions obliging each party to adhere strictly to their own trade laws. The mechanism is not fool proof. Canada has won on several issues such as softwood lumber and labelling on meat, but even when we have won, the United States has used every pretext to avoid honouring the result. Significantly, the same mechanism was strengthened in *NAFTA*, emulated by the WTO and in other major trade agreements. It helps temper the raw power imbalance.[39]

Accordingly, Canada was not necessarily willing to trade this mechanism against concessions to the U.S. on access to Canada's dairy market (discussed below).[40]

(2) American dairy farmers chafed under Canada's SMS system, which imposed TRQs with duty rates as high as 300%, but Canada's dairy farmers, concentrated in Ontario and Quebec, were politically powerful lobby, like their American counterparts. They wanted Canada to agree to alter a rule that "effectively blocked American farmers from exporting ultra-filtered milk, an ingredient in cheesemaking, to Canada . . . ."[41] American dairy farmers also wanted at least as good a deal as the U.S. had obtained when it negotiated *TPP* (from which it withdrew in January 2017), and at least as good a deal as the EU obtained from its September 2017 FTA with Canada, *CETA*.

(3) The Parties agreed to new provisions concerning IP protection. The U.S. and Mexico reset the extension of copyright protection from life in being of the author plus 50 years (the *NAFTA* 1.0 rule) to life in being plus 75 years, allowed for 10 years of data exclusivity for biologic medicines (a topic not covered in *NAFTA* 1.0), and wrote a new Chapter in *NAFTA* 2.0 on trade in digital products.[42] Canada was not necessarily supportive of all such changes.

(4) The Parties further compromised on the Chapter 11 ISDS mechanism. It would cover only cases of alleged expropriation or discrimination in favor of domestic firms, and cases concerning state-dominated sectors (*e.g.*,

---

39. *Canada Must Learn.*

40. *See* Julie Gordon & Sharay Angulo, *U.S., Canada Make Late-Night Push for NAFTA; No Deal Yet*, Reuters, 30 August 2018, www.reuters.com/article/us-trade-nafta/as-clock-ticks-canada-and -u-s-seek-ways-to-salvage-nafta-idUSKCN1LF16R; Julie Gordon & Sharay Angulo, *Trump and Trudeau Upbeat About Prospects for NAFTA Deal by Friday*, Reuters, 29 August 2018, www.reuters .com/article/us-trade-nafta/trump-and-trudeau-upbeat-about-prospects-for-nafta-deal-by-friday -idUSKCN1LE179 [hereinafter, *Trump and Trudeau*].

41. *Trump and Trudeau.*

42. *See* Julie Gordon & Sharay Angulo, *Canada Rejoins NAFTA Talks as U.S. Autos Tariff Details Emerge*, Reuters, 28 August 2018, www.reuters.com/article/us-trade-nafta/canada-rejoins-nafta -talks-as-u-s-autos-tariff-details-emerge-idUSKCN1LD1T4.

energy, infrastructure, oil, NG, power, and telecommunications). Canada had its own views of this mechanism, preferring its phase-out.

(5) Canada refused to sign a *NAFTA* 2.0 text that did not exempt it from any Section 232 action the U.S. might take on autos and auto parts.[43] Mexico had won a partial exemption (in a *Side Letter*, discussed above) for its vehicular exports. Canada needed an exemption, too, given the pivotal role auto and auto parts exports played in its economy. Mexico's deal was unsatisfactory to Canada for several reasons — it seemed Mexico had caved into American demands. Why should there be any cap on shipments from a fellow *NAFTA* Party? What was the point of a passive quota (one with a cap well-above prior shipments)? How would a quota be apportioned among automakers?

(6) Canada disagreed with the *de minimis* exemption to which Mexico had agreed, namely, that online retailers (*e.g.*, Amazon) could sell articles of merchandise valued at up to $100 in Mexico free of Mexican sales tax.[44] Canada, which imposes a 15% sales tax, explained that its retailers could not compete with such a low threshold, and insisted on a higher threshold before tax-free allowed.

(7) Canada insisted that any *NAFTA* 2.0 text include language on gender and indigenous peoples rights.[45] (*CPTPP* included the original *TPP* Article 23:4, on promoting women in economic development, and Canada is a Party to both FTAs.)

Notably, the U.S. took pains to tout the terms it had worked out with Mexico as a better deal (at least for America) than *TPP*. Consider the extent to which the key points in the *NAFTA* 2.0 deal truly were *TPP* Plus, as opposed to *TPP* Minus, or simply the same as rules in *TPP*. Consider, too, the position of Canada: why would it make greater compromises on its sensitive SMS for dairy to the U.S. alone than it had made in the context of *TPP* negotiations, when it was negotiating with the U.S. and 10 other Asia-Pacific countries, and likewise than Canada had finalized in the *CPTPP*, with nine other such countries, following the January 2017 U.S. withdrawal from *TPP*.

In any event, Canada would not come into *NAFTA* 2.0 without hard bargaining — despite the pressure on Canada not to hold out or draw red lines

---

43. *See* Adam Button, *NAFTA Negotiations Almost Certainly Can't Meet Sept. 30 Deadline*, FOREXLIVE, 25 September 2018, www.forexlive.com/news/!/nafta-negotiations-almost-certainly-cant-meet-sept-30-deadline-20180925 [hereinafter, *NAFTA Negotiations*] ; David Lunjenggren, *NAFTA Deal Not Yet in Sight, Canada Stands Firm on Auto Tariffs*, REUTERS, 20 September 2018, www.reuters.com/article/us-trade-nafta/nafta-deal-not-yet-in-sight-canada-stands-firm-on-auto-tariffs-idUSKCN1M030Z.

44. *See NAFTA Negotiations*.

45. *See* Josh Wingrove, *Facing U.S. NAFTA Deadline, Canada Digs in on Tariff Protection*, 35 International Trade Reporter (BNA) 1240 (27 September 2018).

following the 27 August 2018 U.S.-Mexican bilateral deal. Indeed, the 31 August 2018 deadline was not met. Canada rejected a simple trade off of preserving the Chapter 19 AD-CVD Panel system in exchange for significant dairy market access enhancements, and knew that deadline was artificially imposed by the Trump Administration. Fast-track *TPA* under which the President sought legislative approval, on an up-or-down, no-amendment, simple majority vote on a new trade deal required that the final text of the deal be submitted 60 days before the vote in the House and Senate.

In other words, Canada understood well the intricacies of the timing of U.S. Presidential trade negotiating authority: the final text of *NAFTA* 2.0 was not due with Congress until 30 days after the Administration notified Congress of its intent to sign a new deal. The Trump Administration notified Congress on 31 August 2018 it intended to enter into *NAFTA* 2.0 with Mexico, based on the 27 August bilateral agreement, and also with Canada, if Canada wished to do so. That meant the key date to which Canada needed to pay attention was 30 September, if Congress was to approve the deal on 1 December.

That also meant the public would have little opportunity to review the final text of the deal. Negotiations were secret, as they had been all along. No draft texts, or even portions thereof, were presented to the public during the talks. Non-transparency was defended by the negotiating governments as necessary for effi-ciency. Query whether that defense was ironic, insofar as governments said they were pursuing "fair" trade. That is, is a non-transparent negotiating process, which arguably is unfair to the common good, legitimate in the pursuit of fair substantive outcomes to support the common good?

- **Making *NAFTA* 2.0 Trilateral**

So, with customary Canadian politeness, Foreign Affairs and International Trade Minister, Chrystia Freeland, stated that "[w]ith good will and flexibility on all sides, we can get there," and that "[f]or Canada, the focus is on getting a good deal, and once we have a good deal for Canada, we'll be done."[46] Neither goodwill nor flex-ibility was on the President's mind. He retorted:

> There is no political necessity to keep Canada in the new *NAFTA* deal. If we don't make a fair deal for the U.S. after decades of abuse, Canada will be out. Congress should not interfere w/ these negotiations or I will simply terminate *NAFTA* entirely & we will be far better off.[47]

This Saturday-of-Labor Day 2018 morning tweet (like so many of the others from Mr. Trump) was false and misleading.

---

46. *Quoted in U.S.-Canada Trade Talks Break Up.*

47. *Quoted in U.S.-Canada Trade Talks Break Up; also quoted in Trump Says Canada Not Needed in NAFTA Deal, Warns Congress Not to Interfere,* REUTERS, 1 September 2018, www.reuters.com /article/us-trade-nafta-trump/trump-says-canada-not-needed-in-nafta-deal-warns-congress-not -to-interfere-idUSKCN1LH3MJ.

For many in Congress, keeping Canada in *NAFTA* was both a political and economic "necessity." Their constituencies relied on Canada as an export destination and/or import source. AFL-CIO President Richard Trumka (1949–) pointed out that "[i]t's pretty hard to see how that [*NAFTA*] would work without having Canada in the deal," because the economies of the three countries are so integrated, and concluded: "[u]nfortunately, to date, the things that he's [President Trump] done to hurt workers outpace what he's done to help workers."[48] Legally, Canada's presence seemed "necessary," too. The President's Congressionally-delegated trade negotiating authority was to present Congress with a trilateral, not bilateral, deal. Suggesting Canada had "abused" the U.S. belied the facts that a quarter century of *NAFTA* experience generated opportunities for Americans. Dislocations in the U.S. labor force were caused by technological change and automation of production. They also were caused by the failure of (some) Americans to invest in their own human capital, coupled with the failure of Federal and State governments to facilitate these investments, the latter failure thanks to relentless, uncompassionate, anti-intellectual ideologies that made it difficult for poor and lower-middle class citizens to keep pace with technology and stay ahead of automation. All such forces, before and after *NAFTA* 1.0, were eminently foreseeable (as per the Stolper-Samuelson Theorem, discussed in a separate Chapter), surely by a graduate of the Wharton School. "Abuse" from America's dearest friend to the North was a red herring to distract voters from political and economic truth.

Rightly so, then, the talks to trilateralize *NAFTA* 2.0 resumed after the Labor Day 2018 holiday. For Canada, a good deal included the following points:[49]

(1) *Dairy*

An allowance for Canada to protect its dairy industry under its SMS regime.

In *TPP* negotiations, Canada agreed to give the then-other 11 *TPP* countries access to the following shares of its domestic market (using 2015 as the base year to measure domestic consumption): 3.25% for dairy products; 2.3% for eggs; 2.1% for chicken; 2% for turkey; and 1.5% for broiler hatching eggs.[50] When, in January 2017, America withdrew from *TPP*, roughly

---

48. *Quoted in* Michelle Price, *On Labor Day, Trump Hits back at Largest Union Leader*, REUTERS, 3 September 2018, www.reuters.com/article/us-usa-trump-labor/on-labor-day-trump-hits-back -at-largest-union-leader-idUSKCN1LJ1H1.

49. *See* Alexander Panetta, *Trump on Cusp of Closing Biggest Trade Deal, in Late-Night NAFTA Marathon*, POLITICO, 30 September 2018, www.politico.com/story/2018/09/30/nafta-trade-canada -819081; Josh Wingrove & Natalie Obiko Pearson, *Trudeau Digs in on Core Issues as NAFTA Talks Poised to Restart*, 35 International Trade Reporter (BNA) 1143 (6 September 2018); Jason Lange & David Ljunggren, *NAFTA Talks Make Progress: U.S., Canadian Officials To Work Into Night*, REUTERS, 5 September 2018, www.reuters.com/article/us-trade-nafta/canada-u-s-resume-talks-to -salvage-nafta-trade-pact-idUSKCN1LL0CM.

50. *See* Kelvin Heppner, *New TPP Deal, Same Concessions for Canada's Supply Managed Sectors*, REAL AGRICULTURE, 23 January 2018, www.realagriculture.com/2018/01/new-tpp-deal-without -the-u-s-same-concessions-for-canadas-supply-managed-sectors/.

60% of the GDP of the original *TPP* market was lost. Canadian farm sectors asked why Canada should continue to grant the same concession in *CPTPP* to fewer Parties (10 instead of 11 other countries), when there was less in return (in respect of export opportunities to the U.S.)?

The answer was that if each *CPTPP* Party withdrew one or more previous concessions, the entire FTA would unravel. The carefully crafted balance of rights and obligations from *TPP* would not carry through to *CPTPP*, thus better for all Parties to agree to keep the market access concessions, across all goods and services sectors, and so they did. Moreover, Canada appreciated that among the *TPP* 11, Japan, Vietnam, and Malaysia were large markets, not only for Canadian farm products, but industrial goods and services, too.

However, that answer did not satisfy the Trump Administration in *NAFTA* 2.0 negotiations. It demanded SMS concessions from Canada that were at least as good as those Canada preserved from *TPP* into *CPTPP* for the remaining Parties. And, the Administration also sought the same concessions from Canada on cheese as Canada had granted to the EU in *CETA* (discussed in a separate Chapter), even though it had abandoned *T-TIP* negotiations.

(2) *UF Milk Classification*

A reasonable accommodation on Canada's Class 7 ultra-filtered milk classification (discussed in a separate Chapter).

(3) *Dispute Settlement*

Continuation of a dispute settlement mechanism by which Canada can challenge, as it had in the past under *NAFTA* Chapter 19, U.S. trade remedies against its exports of softwood lumber, and generally in AD and CVD cases. Canada had brought and won several cases, ironically using Chapter 19, which the U.S. had championed in the original NAFTA negotiations (both to avoid local courts, especially in Mexico, which it perceived as dubious if not corrupt, and as a way to harmonize trade law upwards across the Parties). Eliminating the mechanism was not acceptable to Canada, nor were limits, possibly an expiry clause, on the mechanism.

(4) *Cultural Protections*

Continuation of the *NAFTA* 1.0 exemption (in Article 2106 and Annex 2106, discussed in a separate Chapter) to allow Canada to protect its cultural industries from what it perceived as a threat posed to its sovereignty and identity by the pervasive invasion of U.S. media and entertainment exports, and the prospect of acquisitions by U.S. companies of Canadian broadcasters.

(5) *Section 232 Tariffs*

A commitment from the U.S. to exempt permanently Canada from the existing Section 232 25% steel and 10% aluminum tariffs, and to not impose any Section 232 tariffs on autos or auto parts (discussed in separate Chapters). The latter could include a passive import cap (*e.g.*, 40% above Canadian shipments to the U.S.) that would be flexible (*i.e.*, allow for growth in Canadian auto production and exports).

(6) *Threshold for Sales Tax Exemption*

A *de minimis* level for online retail shopping that would be exempt from sales taxes, up from the $20 in *NAFTA* 1.0 to at least $100 as agreed by Mexico (in its 27 August 2018 bilateral deal with the U.S.), though still lower than the $800 U.S. level.

The talks continued through September 2018.

Tension was high as Canadian and American negotiators tried to trilateralize the U.S.-Mexico Bilateral Agreement before a deadline of midnight (Eastern Time) on 30 September. That deadline (as discussed earlier) was set by the U.S. in view of Congressional fast-track TPA timing, and the change in power in Mexico to a new President on 1 December (discussed above). Canada emphasized that its focus on a deal that was good for Canada, and would not be pressured by an artificial deadline that America imposed. At 11:35 PM (Eastern Time), Canada and the U.S. announced they had reached agreement for a trilateral *NAFTA* 2.0—the *United States–Mexico–Canada Agreement*, or *USMCA*.[51] As Canadian Prime Minister Justin Trudeau (1971–, PM, 2015–) stated: "There wasn't a single ah-ha moment. There was just a series of okay, we got this one settled."[52]

The key points of the deal are outlined below (and, as appropriate, in separate Chapters). Note carefully with respect to all discussions of *NAFTA* 2.0, no text of the U.S.-Mexico Bilateral Agreement ever was produced. That Agreement was one in principle. The need to memorialize it in formal treaty language was obviated when the Agreement became trilateral, with Canada's participation, and was adjusted based on negotiations between Canada and the U.S. between 27 August (when the Bilateral Agreement with Mexico was agreed in principle) and 30 September 2018 (when the three Parties announced their trilateral treaty).

---

51. *See* Chris Anstey, *Live Now: News, Analysis of NAFTA Negotiations*, BLOOMBERG, 30 September 2018, www.bloomberg.com/news/live-blog/2018-10-01/news-analysis-of-nafta-negotiations; Jenny Leonard, Josh Wingrove & Jennifer Jacobs, *U.S. and Canada Reach Trade Deal to Keep NAFTA Trilateral*, BLOOMBERG, 30 September 2018, www.bloomberg.com/news/articles/2018-09 -30/president-trump-s-nafta-deal-with-canada-is-said-to-be-imminent?srnd=premium; David Ljunggren & Roberta Rampton, *Canada, U.S. Reach Deal to Update NAFTA: Canadian Sources*, REUTERS, 30 September 2018, www.reuters.com/article/us-trade-nafta/canada-u-s-reach-deal-to -update-nafta-canadian-sources-idUSKCN1MA0UJ.

52. *Quoted in* Josh Wingrove, Jennifer Jacobs & Eric Martin, *Kushner, Mexico and "Moments of Drama:" How NAFTA Deal Went Down*, 35 International Trade Reporter (BNA) 1312 (11 October 2018).

As to the calculation of RVC, Article 4:5 of the *USMCA* specifies that (in most cases), the importer, exporter, or producer may choose between the Transaction Value or Net Cost Method, but must exclude non-originating materials:

Article 4:5: Regional Value Content

. . .

2. Each Party shall provide that an importer, exporter, or producer may calculate the regional value content of a good on the basis of the following transaction value method:

$$RVC = (TV\text{-}VNM)/TV \times 100$$

where

RVC is the is the regional value content, expressed as a percentage [hence, the entire fraction, not just the denominator, is multiplied by 100 to yield a percentage figure];

TV is the transaction value of the good, adjusted to exclude any costs incurred in the international shipment of the good; and

VNM is the value of non-originating materials including materials of undetermined origin used by the producer in the production of the good.

3. Each Party shall provide that an exporter or producer may calculate the regional value content of a good on the basis of the following net cost method:

$$RVC = (NC\text{-}VNM)/NC \times 100$$

where

RVC is the is the regional value content, expressed as a percentage [again, the entire fraction, not just the denominator, is multiplied by 100 to yield a percentage figure];

NC is the net cost of the good; and

VNM is the value of non-originating materials including materials of undetermined origin used by the producer in the production of the good.

4. Except as provided in Article 10:3 of Appendix 1 to Annex 4-B, for a motor vehicle identified in Article 10.4.2(a) of that Appendix, or a component identified in Table G of that Appendix, the value of non-originating materials used by the producer in the production of a good shall not, for the purposes of calculating the regional value content of the good under paragraph 2 or 3, include the value of non-originating materials used to produce originating materials that are subsequently used in the production of the good.

Manifestly, as per Paragraph 4, there are devilishly detailed rules in the Appendix to be checked in order to apply the RVC test accurately.

Office of the United States Trade Representative,

United States–Mexico–Canada Fact Sheet: *Rebalancing Trade to Support Manufacturing* (1 October 2018)[53]

. . .

Rules of Origin and Origin Procedures

The United States, Mexico, and Canada have concluded substantive discussions on new rules of origin and origin procedures, including product-specific rules for passenger vehicles, light trucks, and auto parts. [These PSROs are set out in Chapter 4, Annex 4-B, and the Appendix to Annex 4-B.] This update to the rules of origin will provide greater incentives to source goods and materials in the United States and North America.

Key Achievement: Increasing Regional Value Content Rule

This deal encourages United States manufacturing and regional economic growth by requiring that 75 percent of auto content be made in North America.

The rules will:

(1) Help to incentivize up to billions annually.

(2) Help to preserve and re-shore vehicle and parts production in the United States.

(3) Transform supply chains to use more United States content, especially content that is key to future automobile production and high-paying jobs.

(4) Close gaps in the current *NAFTA* agreement that incentivized low wages in automobile and parts production.

Key Achievement: Creating New Labor Value Content Rule

This deal uses trade rules to drive higher wages by requiring that 40–45 percent of auto content be made by workers earning at least $16 per hour.

[This obligation—the Minimum Wage Test—must be met by 2023; by 2020, at least 30% of the work on a vehicle must be done with $16 per hour labor. The Test is set out in Article 4-B.7 in Chapter 4 of the Appendix to Annex 4-B. As per Footnote 104 to Paragraph 3(a) of this Article: "The production wage rate is the average hourly base wage rate, not including benefits, of employees directly involved in the production of the part or component used to calculate the LVC, and does not include salaries of management, R&D, engineering, or other workers who are not involved in the direct production of the parts or in the operation of production

---

53. https://ustr.gov/about-us/policy-offices/press-office/fact-sheets/2018/october/united-states–mexico–canada-trade-fa-0.

lines." Moreover, as per Article 4-B.6 in Chapter 4 of the Appendix to Annex 4-B, at least 70% of the steel used in a vehicle must be sourced from North America.]

The rules will:

(1) Support better jobs for United States producers and workers by requiring that a significant portion of vehicle content be made with high-wage labor.

(2) Ensure that United States producers and workers are able to compete on an even playing field, and incentivize new vehicle and parts investments in the United States.

(3) Encourage more investment by auto companies in research and development in the region.

Key Achievement: Exceeding NAFTA 1.0 and TPP Standards with Stronger Rules of Origin and Enforcement

The United States, Mexico, and Canada have agreed to stronger rules of origin that exceed those of both *NAFTA* 1.0 and the *Trans-Pacific Partnership* (*TPP*), including for autos and automobile parts and other industrial products such as chemicals, steel-intensive products, glass, and optical fiber.

This deal exceeds *NAFTA* 1.0 and the *TPP* by establishing procedures that streamline certification and verification of rules of origin and that promote strong enforcement. This includes new cooperation and enforcement provisions that help to prevent duty evasion before it happens.

The new rules will help ensure that only producers using sufficient and significant North American parts and materials receive preferential tariff benefits.

United States–Canada Side Letter, Section 232 (Undated, from United States Trade Representative)[54]

Dear Minister Freeland:

Recognizing that in the negotiations for *United States–Mexico–Canada Agreement* (*USMCA*) the United States and Canada (the "Parties") have made changes to the automotive rules of origin compared to *NAFTA* 1994, and in order to support and enhance the existing manufacturing capacity and mutually beneficial trade of the Parties, if the United States imposes a measure pursuant to Section 232 of the *Trade Expansion Act of 1962*, as amended, with respect to passenger vehicles classified under Sub-Headings 8703.21 through 8703.90, light trucks classified under Sub-Headings 8704.21 and 8704.31, or auto parts, the United States shall exclude from the measure:

(1) 2,600,000 passenger vehicles imported from Canada on an annual basis

(2) light trucks imported from Canada; and

---

54. https://ustr.gov/sites/default/files/files/agreements/FTA/USMCA/US%20Canada%20 232%20Side%20Letter.pdf

(3) such quantity of auto parts amounting to 32.4 billion U.S. dollars in declared customs value in any calendar year.

The Parties will determine how to monitor and allocate or otherwise administer quantities of passenger vehicles and auto parts eligible for this treatment. The Parties may also discuss any modifications to the quantities described above due to changes in production, capacity, or trade.

Canada may have recourse to the dispute settlement procedures in Chapter 20 (Institutional Arrangements and Dispute Settlement Procedures) of the *NAFTA* 1994 or the dispute settlement chapter of *USMCA*, whichever is in effect at the time a dispute arises, only with respect to whether the United States has excluded the number of passenger vehicles and light trucks, and the value of auto parts as set out above, from a measure taken pursuant to Section 232 of the *Trade Expansion Act of 1962*, as amended. Those procedures are incorporated and made part of this agreement *mutatis mutandis.*

I have the honor to propose that this letter and your letter in reply shall constitute an agreement between our two Governments, which shall enter into force on the date of your letter in reply.

[Essentially the same *Side Letter* exists as between Mexico and the U.S., except the threshold for auto parts in point (3) is $108 billion.[55]]

- **Grand Bargain of *NAFTA* 2.0 (*USMCA*)**

Table 7-1 summarizes the structure of *NAFTA* 2.0, and compares that structure with *NAFTA* 1.0 Manifestly, the first iteration of *NAFTA* had 22 Chapters (two of which had Chapter-specific Annexes), plus seven general Annexes. (It also had *Side Letters*, particularly to protect America's long-standing sugar TRQs.) The second iteration has 34 Chapters (two of which had Chapter-specific Annexes, plus general Annexes and 12 *Side Letters*. Looking at the Chapter titles indicates clearly that the larger number of Chapters in the second iteration than the first iteration is thanks in part to splitting Chapters from the first iteration, and in part to coverage of new issues, some of which did not exist in the late 1980s and early 1990s when *NAFTA* 1.0 was negotiated, and/or were not thought proper for inclusion in a trade agreement.

Reviewing the titles of the general Annexes shows that they are structured quite differently in the two agreements. The *NAFTA* 2.0 Annexes reflect what the U.S. did in its other post-*NAFTA* 1.0 FTAs, namely, divide non-conforming measures (so-called "NCMs") in FDI, services, and financial services into two categories: NCMs subject to standstill and rachet commitments, and NCMs not subject to those commitments. A "standstill" commitment is a pledge not to cut-back on market access or national treatment from the current position. (For example, if the U.S. today allows 10 Mexican banks to establish branches anywhere in America, and offer the

---

55. https://ustr.gov/sites/default/files/files/agreements/FTA/USMCA/US%20Mexico%20 232%20Side%20Letter.pdf

Table 7-1. Comparative Structure of *USMCA* (*NAFTA* 2.0) and *NAFTA* 1.0

Chapters		
USMCA Chapter Number	*USMCA* Chapter Title	*NAFTA* 1.0 Analogous Chapter and Chapter Title
Preamble		Preamble
1	Initial Provisions and General Definitions	Chapter 1: Objectives Chapter 2: General Definitions
2	National Treatment and Market Access for Goods Also: U.S. Tariff Schedule and U.S. TRQ Appendix Mexico Tariff Schedule Canada Tariff Schedule and Canada TRQ Appendix	Chapter 3: National Treatment and Market Access for Goods Also: Annex 300-A: Trade and Investment in the Automotive Sector Annex 300-B: Textile and Apparel Goods
3	Agriculture Also: Mexico-U.S. Bilateral Annex Canada-U.S. Bilateral Annex Alcohol Annex Proprietary Food Formulas Annex	Chapter 7: Agriculture and Sanitary and Phytosanitary Measures
4	Rules of Origin with Product Specific Rules	Chapter 4: Rules of Origin Also: Annex 401: Specific Rules of Origin
5	Origin Procedures	Chapter 4: Rules of Origin Also: Annex 401: Specific Rules of Origin Chapter 5: Customs Procedures
6	Textiles and Apparel	Annex 300-B: Textile and Apparel Goods
7	Customs and Trade Facilitation	None

(*continued*)

**Table 7-1. Comparative Structure of *USMCA* (*NAFTA* 2.0) and
NAFTA 1.0 (*continued*)**

Chapters		
USMCA Chapter Number	*USMCA* Chapter Title	*NAFTA* 1.0 Analogous Chapter and Chapter Title
Preamble		Preamble
8	Recognition of the Mexican State's Direct, Inalienable, and Imprescriptible Ownership of Hydrocarbons	Chapter Six: Energy and Basic Petrochemicals
9	Sanitary and Phytosanitary Measures	Chapter 7: Agriculture and Sanitary and Phytosanitary Measures
10	Trade Remedies	Chapter 8: Emergency Action Chapter 19: Review and Dispute Settlement in Antidumping/Countervailing Duties
11	Technical Barriers to Trade	Chapter 9: Standards-Related Measures
12	Sectoral Annexes	
13	Government Procurement	Chapter 10: Government Procurement
14	Investment	Chapter 11: Investment
15	Cross-Border Trade in Services	Chapter 12: Cross-Border Trade in Services
16	Temporary Entry	Chapter 16: Temporary Entry for Business Persons
17	Financial Services	Chapter 14: Financial Services
18	Telecommunications	Chapter 13: Telecommunications
19	Digital Trade	None
20	Intellectual Property	Chapter 17: Intellectual Property
21	Competition Policy	Chapter 15: Competition, Monopolies, and State Enterprises
22	State-Owned Enterprises	Chapter 15: Competition, Monopolies, and State Enterprises

(*continued*)

Table 7-1. Comparative Structure of *USMCA* (*NAFTA* 2.0) and *NAFTA* 1.0 (*continued*)

Chapters		
USMCA Chapter Number	*USMCA* Chapter Title	NAFTA 1.0 Analogous Chapter and Chapter Title
Preamble		Preamble
23	Labor	Labor Side Agreement (not in core text)
24	Environment	Environmental Side Agreement (not in core text)
25	Small and Medium Sized Enterprises	None
26	Competitiveness	None
27	Anticorruption	None
28	Good Regulatory Practices	None
29	Publication and Administration	Chapter 18: Publication, Notification, and Administration of Laws
30	Administrative and Institutional Provisions	Chapter 18: Publication, Notification, and Administration of Laws Chapter 20: Institutional Arrangements and Dispute Settlement Procedures
31	Dispute Settlement	Chapter 19: Review and Dispute Settlement in Antidumping/Countervailing Duties Chapter 20: Institutional Arrangements and Dispute Settlement Procedures
32	Exceptions and General Provisions	Chapter 21: Exceptions
33	Macroeconomic Policies and Exchange Rate Matters	None
34	Final Provisions	Chapter 22: Final Provisions
Annexes		
I	Investment and Services Non-Conforming Measures— Explanatory Note	Annex I: Reservations for Existing Measures and Liberalization Commitments
I	Investment and Services Non-Conforming Measures— Mexico	Annex II: Reservations for Future Measures

(*continued*)

**Table 7-1. Comparative Structure of *USMCA* (*NAFTA* 2.0) and
NAFTA 1.0 (*continued*)**

Chapters		
USMCA Chapter Number	*USMCA* Chapter Title	NAFTA 1.0 Analogous Chapter and Chapter Title
Preamble		Preamble
I	Investment and Services Non-Conforming Measures— United States	Annex III: Activities Reserved to the State
II	Investment and Services— Non-Conforming Measures Explanatory Note	Annex IV: Exceptions from Most-Favored Nation Treatment
II	Investment and Services Non-Conforming Measures— Mexico	Annex V: Quantitative Restrictions
II	Investment and Services Non-Conforming Measures— United States	Annex VI: Miscellaneous Commitments
III	Financial Services Non-Conforming Measures— Explanatory Note	Annex VII: Reservations, Specific Commitments, and Other Items
III	Financial Services Non-Conforming Measures— Mexico	
III	Financial Services Non-Conforming Measures— United States	
III	Financial Services Non-Conforming Measures— Canada	
IV	SOEs Non-Conforming Activities	
Side Letters		
1	United States—Mexico *Side Letter* on Distinctive Products	*Side Letters* on Sugar
2	United States—Mexico *Side Letter* on Auto Safety Standards	
3	United States—Mexico *Side Letter* on Biologics	
4	United States—Mexico *Side Letter* on Prior Users	

(continued)

Table 7-1. Comparative Structure of *USMCA* (*NAFTA* 2.0) and *NAFTA* 1.0 (*continued*)

Chapters		
USMCA Chapter Number	*USMCA* Chapter Title	*NAFTA* 1.0 Analogous Chapter and Chapter Title
Preamble		Preamble
5	United States — Mexico *Side Letter* on Cheese Names	
6	United States — Canada *Side Letter* on Wine	
7	United States — Canada *Side Letter* on Water	
8	United States — Canada *Side Letter* on Guidelines for Research and Development Expenditures, 2004	
9	United States — Canada *Side Letter* on Section 232	
10	United States — Mexico *Side Letter* on Section 232	
11	United States — Canada *Side Letter* on Section 232 Process	
12	United States — Mexico *Side Letter* on Section 232 Process	

same products as U.S. banks, then the U.S. will not subsequently cut the number to five Mexican banks). A "rachet" commitment indicates that if a new liberalization is granted as to market access and/or national treatment, then that new liberalization would become the new benchmark. (To continue that example, if next year the U.S. allows 20 Mexican banks unrestricted branching and level-playing field competition with American banks, then that allowance becomes the new base for market access.) Any NCM (as the term "non-conforming" connotes) is a derogation from free trade obligations (typically in respect of market access and/or national treatment) that are otherwise mandated in the core text of an FTA, *i.e.*, in the appropriate Chapter (*e.g.*, on financial services). NCMs not subject to the standstill or rachet commitments are less-free trade oriented than those that are subject them subject. That is because the former group are akin to unbound tariffs — they could go up, *i.e.*, become more protective, anytime.

But, the Table does not convey what in that structure of the Chapters, Annexes, or *Side Letters* caused the Parties to agree to the *USMCA*. The organization of rules is one matter, but the substantive content of those rules is quite another. In truth, much of the substantive content of *NAFTA* 2.0 looks like *NAFTA* 1.0, with certain ideas or provisions grafted from TPP. Of course, a complete appraisal of what each of them "got" versus "gave" involves a painstaking analysis of not only the provisions in each Chapter, but also the NCMs in the Annexes, and the details of the *Side Letters*. That said, what was the overall balance of rights and obligations that persuaded Canada, Mexico, and the U.S. to agree to *NAFTA* 2.0—the key provisions that led to a "Grand Bargain" of sorts (though not nearly so grand as that of the 1986–1994 Uruguay Round, discussed in a separate Chapter)?

If the rhetoric of President Donald J. Trump on 1 October 2018 (the day after the *USMCA* negotiations concluded), then there was not much of a balance. He declared the pact to be "truly historic," and "the biggest trade deal in the United States history."[56] Yes, revising *NAFTA* 1.0 was historically significant, but no, *NAFTA* 2.0 was not the largest trade agreement. That crown goes to the Uruguay Round Agreements, signed with over 100 countries, which gave birth to the WTO. The President spoke of the "deficiencies and mistakes" in *NAFTA* 1.0, which was "perhaps the worst trade deal ever made," judged the new agreement to be "much more reciprocal," and said it "will support many—hundreds of thousands— American jobs."[57] He saw *NAFTA* 2.0 as an example of his "America First" policy, and declared that "[w]ithout tariffs we wouldn't be talking about a deal," meaning that the actual imposition of Section 232 steel and aluminum tariffs, and the threatened imposition of Section 232 auto and auto parts tariffs, forced Canada and Mexico to the bargaining table with America, and compelled them to submit to American demands.[58]

The reality was more nuanced than the American President bellowed, as Canadian Prime Minister Justin Trudeau explained (politely). *NAFTA* 2.0 was "profoundly beneficial" to Canadians, but the deal was tough to negotiate, and the outcomes were not all one way:

> We had to make compromises, and some were more difficult than others . . . . We never believed that it would be easy, and it wasn't, but today is a good day for Canada.[59]

Ultimately (perhaps) the President agreed with the Prime Minister. After declaring it a "privilege" to trade with the U.S., Mr. Trump added:

> So we have negotiated this new agreement [with Mexico and Canada] based on the principle of fairness and reciprocity—to me it's the most important world in trade, because we've been treated so unfairly by so many nations all over the world.[60]

---

56. *Quoted in Donald Trump Says New Trade Deal is "Most Important Ever,"* BBC News, 1 October 2018, www.bbc.com/news/business-45711595. [Hereinafter, *Donald Trump Says.*]

57. *Quoted in Donald Trump Says.*

58. *Quoted in Donald Trump Says.*

59. *Quoted in Donald Trump Says.*

60. *Quoted in Donald Trump Says.*

He concluded the *USMCA* was "terrific" for all three Parties. What, then, were the terms that caused the Parties to agree to the deal? That is, what was the overall economic "give" and "take" that caused them to see the deal as, on balance, in their self-interests?

First, America achieved its objective of a vastly tighter auto ROO. The 12.5 percentage point increase (from 62.5% to 75%) in required North American value added, and the $16 per hour minimum wage test for 40%–45% of the value, was the strictest ROO found in any FTA in the world.[61] President Trump called the new ROO "the most important thing," and predicted:

> We will be manufacturing many more cars. And our companies won't be leaving the United States, firing their workers and building their cars elsewhere. They no longer have that incentive.[62]

America also won a modest increase in access to Canada's dairy market, essentially from 3.25% of that market (which Canada conceded in *TPP*, and continued in *CPTPP*), to 3.59% (for the benefit solely of American dairy exports). Further, America persuaded Canada to eliminate its Class 7 UF milk classification, which the U.S. said impeded exports of this product. The U.S. did not have to concede its own milk and sugar quota protections. The U.S. also obtained clear MFN and national treatment commitments with respect to financial services, and persuaded Canada and Mexico to prohibit local data storage. And, a copyright protection rule of 70 years, protections for trade secrets, and a commitment to enforce IPRs with civil and criminal penalties.

Alas, the U.S. had to concede that neither Canada nor Mexico would accept a five-year Sunset Rule on *NAFTA* 2.0. As per Article 34:7, the U.S. settled for a 16-year period, with joint review after six years, and renegotiations (if necessary) to extend for a further 16-year term, and so forth:

Article 34:7: Review and Term Extension

1. This Agreement shall terminate 16 years after the date of its entry into force, unless each Party confirms it wishes to continue the Agreement for a new 16-year term, in accordance with the procedures set forth in paragraphs 2 through 6.

2. No later than the sixth anniversary of the entry into force of this Agreement, the Commission shall meet to conduct a "joint review" of the operation of the Agreement, review any recommendations for

---

61. To be sure, the *USMCA* lacks a mechanism for adjusting the $16 for inflation, a point critics noted. *See* David Leonhardt, *Trump's NAFTA is Like a Bacon Sandwich*, New York Times, 2 October 2018, www.nytimes.com/2018/10/02/opinion/trump-nafta-mexico-canada-trade-deal.html. [Hereinafter, *Trump's NAFTA*.]

62. *Quoted in* Shannon Pettypiece & Andrew Mayeda, *Trump Lauds NAFTA Successor Accord, Chides Tariff "Babies" (1)*, 35 International Trade Reporter (BNA) 1283 (4 October 2018).

action submitted by a Party, and decide on any appropriate actions. Each Party may provide recommendations for the Commission to take action at least one month before the Commission's joint review meeting takes place.

3. As part of the Commission's joint review, each Party shall confirm, in writing, through its head of government, if it wishes to extend the term of the Agreement for another 16-year period. If each Party confirms its desire to extend the Agreement, the term of the Agreement shall be automatically extended for another 16 years and the Commission shall conduct a joint review and consider extension of the Agreement term no later than at the end of the next six-year period.

4. If, as part of a six-year review, a Party does not confirm its wish to extend the term of the Agreement for another 16-year period, the Commission shall meet to conduct a joint review every year for the remainder of the term of the Agreement. If one or more Parties did not confirm their desire to extend the Agreement for another 16-year term at the conclusion of a given joint review, at any time between the conclusion of that review and expiry of the Agreement, the Parties may automatically extend the term of the Agreement for another 16 years by confirming in writing, through their respective head of government, their wish to extend the Agreement for another 16-year period.

5. At any point when the Parties decide to extend the term of the Agreement for another 16-year period, the Commission shall conduct joint reviews every six years thereafter, and the Parties shall have the ability to extend the Agreement after each joint review pursuant to the procedures set forth in paragraphs 3 and 4.

6. At any point in which the Parties do not all confirm their wish to extend the term of the Agreement, paragraph 4 shall apply.

The Sunset Clause settlement assured the U.S. that *NAFTA* 2.0 would remain a living document, and potentially an up-to-date, evergreen one, in that the reviews by the Parties would be undertaken at six-year increments, and thereby give the Parties a decade to fix problems before considering whether to approve or terminate the 16-year mark.

Second, Canada saw its three "red lines" respected against severe American onslaughts. The *NAFTA* 1.0 Chapter 19 AD-CVD dispute resolution panel system carried through to *NAFTA* 2.0 (in Chapter 10). So, also, did the *NAFTA* 1.0 cultural industry protections (in Article 32:6 of the *USMCA*). And, via the Section 232 *Side Letter*, the U.S. pledged not to impose national security tariffs on up to 2.6 million vehicles (including cars, and SUVs, but not pick-up trucks) from Canada, and to consider upward revisions of that cap. The initial threshold was passive, set at 40% higher than Canadian shipments.

As for the dairy concessions Canada made were not cosmetic, and the Dairy Farmers of Canada opined that 220,000 Canadians in the dairy sector were "sacrificed."[63] But, in no way did the U.S. succeed in dismantling Canada's long-standing SMS scheme.[64] Canada did not get expanded access to U.S. government procurement markets, nor an easing of immigration rules on *NAFTA* business visas (so-called "TN" visas, via an expansion of the list of eligible occupations eligible for those visas) for its professionals to migrate temporarily to the U.S. (as the visa rules remained largely the same as in *NAFTA* 1.0, though the cap on TN visas for Mexican workers was eliminated).[65]

Finally, Mexico won a clear statement about the sovereignty of its energy resources. Like Canada, Mexico obtained a Section 232 exemption for more vehicles (again, cars and SUVs, but not pick-up trucks) than it historically shipped on an annual basis. Also like Canada, the cap was passive—40% over Mexico's annual shipments. And, Mexico was willing to see labor rates rise in Mexico, with the new auto ROO, to address socioeconomic inequalities that worsened after *NAFTA* 1.0. At the same time, Mexican officials conceded that roughly 32% of the cars made in Mexico (at the time the *USMCA* was agreed) would not qualify for DFQF treatment, because of the new ROO.

Moreover, the drastic reduction of the *NAFTA* 1.0 Chapter 11 ISDS mechanism did not help Mexico in the eyes of foreign direct investors. They enjoyed the certainty of the mechanism with respect to any FDI under *NAFTA* 1.0 (as opposed to adjudicating expropriation and nationalization claims in Mexican courts, which they perceived as less independent than ISDS panels). With *NAFTA* 2.0, the subject matter jurisdiction of ISDS panels was cut down (to the energy, infrastructure, NG, oil, and telecommunications sectors), and only with respect to Mexico (*i.e.*, ISDS mechanism was phased out for Canada). Mexico also conceded less access to American government procurement markets than they had under the old *NAFTA* (though they had not taken advantage of that access).

Aside from their individual, self-interested calculations, the three Parties also came together on shared (or mostly shared) interests. A new Chapter on digital trade, with enforceable consumer protections and limits on liability for third party content posted on internet platforms, and restrictions on the ability of a government to force disclosure of source code, were examples. They agreed to retain the *NAFTA* 1.0 Chapter 20 state-to-state dispute settlement mechanism. They all could take pride in higher and/or more enforceable labor and environmental standards,

---

63. *Quoted in USMCA Trade Deal.*

64. *See* Emily Tamkin, *Trump Has Won The Dairy War With Canada. But Was It Worth It?*, BuzzFeed.News, 1 October 2018, www.buzzfeednews.com/article/emilytamkin/trump-wins-the -dairy-war-with-canada-but-was-it-worth-it#.adBj7Xgykg.

65. *See* Daniel Dale & Tonda Maccharles, *Canada, U.S. Reach New NAFTA Deal*, The Star (Toronto), 30 September 2018, https://www.thestar.com/news/world/2018/09/30/canada-us-reach -nafta-deal.html.

albeit with varying degrees of enthusiasm. Likewise, with respect to the protection period for biologic medicines (*i.e.*, the period of market protection for branded biologics before they faced competition from generics), 10 years reflected a compromise between America's 12-year rule, and Canada's 8-year rule.[66] (Arguably, it was not markedly different from the "5 + 3" rule in *TPP*.)

The Parties also resolved a three-way controversy about the thresholds for cross-border shipments that would be duty-free: the U.S. level remained at $800, while Mexico and Canada raised theirs to $100 and $117, respectively—in effect, a compromise between on-line retailers and local store owners. And, they resolved certain *sui generis* disputes, such as that between the U.S. and Canada on selling wine: the two Parties agreed in a *Side Letter* that Canadian liquor stores (by 1 November 2019) could not prohibit U.S. wine on their shelves. (Stores, particularly in British Columbia, had been doing so via the so-called "store within a store" requirement, whereby imported wines could not be sold on the same shelves as Canadian wine.) But, they left some issues unresolved, most notably, Section 232 steel and aluminum tariffs.[67]

Indubitably, each Party knew it had a shared interest in staying in an integrative, rule-of-law framework that, on balance, had served each of them well for nearly one quarter of a century. They felt the sheer force of historical and political forces in favor of continued North American integration, above and beyond the reciprocal economic concessions they weighed as individually beneficial. Hopefully, they learned the bitter lesson of political history: do not oversell a trade deal to the public, as was done with *NAFTA* 1.0 in the early and mid-1990s.[68] Surely, going forward, they felt the need to repair their relationships after over a year of bitterness.[69]

---

66. *See USMCA Trade Deal*; Heather Long, *U.S., Canada, and Mexico Just Reached a Sweeping New NAFTA New Deal. Here's What's In It*, THE WASHINGTON POST, 1 October 2018, www .washingtonpost.com/business/2018/10/01/us-canada-mexico-just-reached-sweeping-new-nafta -deal-heres-whats-it/?noredirect=on&utm_term=.a7d44482624d.

67. That Canada was willing to sign *NAFTA* 2.0 without a settlement of the Section 232 dispute was notable. Canada relies heavily on the American market for its aluminum and steel exports. Indeed, 84% (as of October 2018) of Canadian aluminum production is shipped to Canada, hence the 10% Section 232 tariff affected most of Canada's output of that commodity. Canada is somewhat less dependent on America as a steel market, but the 25% Section 232 is an even more serious impediment than the 10% duty. *See* Danielle Bochove, Josh Wingrove & Joe Deaux, *With NAFTA Deal, Trump Opens Door to Metal Tariffs Agreement (2)*, 35 International Trade Reporter (BNA) 1284 (4 October 2018).

68. *See Trump's NAFTA* (stating: "The main thing to know about the big new North American trade deal is that it's not actually a new trade deal. It's a set of modest revisions to *NAFTA*—the old deal—and President Trump is exaggerating their significance, so he can claim to have replaced *NAFTA*," and reporting a tweet from historian Kevin Kruse: "I made a wonderful new sandwich by adding Lettuce and Tomato to Bacon and some bread. I'm calling it the LTB!").

69. *See Lessons*; David Ljunggren & Steve Holland, *How Trump's Son-in-law Helped a $1.2 Trillion Trade Zone Stay Intact*, REUTERS, 1 October 2018, www.reuters.com/article/us-trade-nafta-kushner /how-trumps-son-in-law-helped-a-1-2-trillion-trade-zone-stay-intact-idUSKCN1MC04M. At the November 2018 G-20 Summit in Buenos Aires, outgoing Mexican President Enrique Peña Nieto bestowed on President Trump's son-in-law, Jared Kushner, Mexico's highest honor, the Order of the Aztec Eagle for Mr. Kushner's work on the *USMCA*, but his doing so provoked widespread

X. Type 6: Assembled Goods Rule

Suppose as regards an assembled product, the following circumstances exist. First, the product and its constituent parts are listed in the same HTS Sub-Heading. So, the product does not satisfy a CTH Rule. Second, one or more of the constituent parts are non-originating. Hence, the Goods Wholly Obtained Rule is inapplicable. For example, a bicycle assembled in Mexico cannot meet the CTH Rule, because its parts — the tires, handle bar, chain, and seat — are placed in the same HTS category as an assembled bicycle. If any of the parts are non-originating, then the bicycle does not satisfy the Goods Wholly Obtained Rule. Should the bicycle qualify as an originating good?

The answer is provided in *NAFTA* Article 401(d), which calls for the use of an RVC test. Article 401(d) indicates that a finished product that is made of one or more non-originating materials and does not undergo a change in tariff classification because the product and its materials are in the same HTS Heading qualifies as an originating good if it meets an RVC test. That test is a 60% RVC where the transaction value method is used, or a 50% RVC where the net cost method is used. Thus, in the example of the assembled bicycle, if the value of at least 60% of its parts are derived from a *NAFTA* Party, then the bicycle is an originating good.

A major exception to the Assembled Goods Rule, discussed below, is that it does not apply to T&A merchandise.

XI. Type 7: Specified Process Rule

• **T&A Specified Process ROO Options**

One mechanism to determine whether a "substantial transformation" occurs is to agree upon specific manufacturing operations and processes that cause such a transformation. Like the Substantial Transformation Rule and Value-Added Test, a Specified Process Rule for origination can be stated with clarity so that it provides precise guidance for manufacturers, exporters, and importers. However, a key disadvantage stems from the relative knowledge of trade negotiators and industry officials about manufacturing and production. Industry officials will know more than trade negotiators and, therefore, are in a position to influence negotiators because of their knowledge. They may lead negotiators to adopt rules that restrict rather than liberalize trade.

---

criticism, because of Mr. Trump's stance toward, and comments about, Mexican immigrants. *See Mexican Honor for U.S.'s Kushner Sparks Criticism*, BBC News, 28 November 2018, www.bbc.com/news/world-latin-america-46376341; *Mexico to Bestow Top Honor on Trump Son-in-law, Sparking Twitter Outcry*, Reuters, 27 November 2018, www.reuters.com/article/us-mexico-politics-kushner/mexico-to-bestow-top-honor-on-trump-son-in-law-sparking-twitter-outcry-idUSKCN1NX071.

A second disadvantage is it may be costly and time consuming to maintain an up-to-date list of manufacturing operations and production processes. Inevitably, these operations and processes change with technological developments that yield greater efficiency. Finally, Specified Process Rules, unlike CTH Rules, are not based on a uniform foundation like the HTS. Hence, there is room for substantial disharmony across different countries.

In spite of these disadvantages, *NAFTA* negotiators agreed to use Specified Process Rules for certain goods, particularly ones considered sensitive. These Rules are a balance—to put it diplomatically—between free trade and protectionism. A notable class of sensitive goods, indeed of a sensitive sector, is T&A. Thus, T&A are the quintessential context in which specified process rules are used.

The *NAFTA* negotiators devised a special ROO based on manufacturing operations and production processes for the T&A sector. Like the intricate provisions for automobiles, the so-called "Fiber Forward" and "Yarn Forward" ROOs in *NAFTA* for T&A are highly restrictive and less liberal than the *CUFTA* rules. To understand them, it is first necessary to appreciate the basic steps involved in textile and apparel production. Diagram 7-1 shows them.

The *Canada FTA* established a "double transformation" test. A finished garment qualified as originating, and thereby got duty-free treatment under *CUFTA*, if garment parts were cut and sewn into the finished garment in either Canada or the U.S.

Diagram 7-1. Basic Steps in T&A Manufacturing

Fiber	*Yarn*	*Dyeing (Coloring)*
Producing fiber *e.g.*, growing cotton, harvesting silk worms	Spinning fiber threads into yarn, *e.g.*, cotton yarn, silk	Adding color to yarn using dyes

Fabric	*Cutting*	*Sewing*
Producing large pieces of fabric (also called "cloth")	Cutting fabric into pieces or knitting it into shapes, *e.g.*, collars for shirts, pockets for pants	Stitching or weaving cut pieces into articles *e.g.*, shirts or pants

Final Assembly followed by	*Quality Control* +	*Cleaning, Sorting, and Packing*
Putting finishing touches on an article *e.g.*, attaching buttons on shirts or zippers to pants	Checking for defects and discarding defective article	Removing unwanted threads, organizing for delivery, and putting into boxes for shipment

Whether the yarn or other fabric used to make the garment was foreign (*i.e.*, from a non-*CUFTA* country) was irrelevant. Likewise, the country of origin of the fiber, from which the yarn is spun, and in turn from which fabric is made, was irrelevant.

In contrast, *NAFTA* sets forth a triple transformation test. Under this test, a finished garment must be made from (1) yarn spun into fabric in a *NAFTA* Party, (2) fabric cut into pieces in a *NAFTA* Party, and (3) pieces sewn together in a *NAFTA* Party. Thus, the basic ROO for T&A products is called the "Yarn Forward" Rule. It means yarn must be spun in the *NAFTA* region, and all subsequent processing — creating fabric, cutting, sewing, and final assembly — must occur in that region.[70] The only irrelevancy is the origin of the fiber used to spin the yarn.

Similarly, under the *Singapore, Chile, Australia*, and *Morocco FTAs*, for T&A merchandise, the Tariff Shift Rule is a Specified Process Rule, and the basic such Rule is Yarn Forward.[71] For a T&A article to qualify as "Made in Singapore," "Made in Chile," "Made in Australia," or "Made in Morocco," and receive preferential tariff treatment from the U.S., the article must be cut (or knit to shape) and sewn (or otherwise assembled) in Singapore, Chile, Australia, or Morocco from yarn, or fabric made from yarn, which originates in Singapore, Chile, Australia, or Morocco. *CAFTA-DR* contains a similar rule.

The origin of the thread used to assemble a garment can matter, too. Under *CAFTA-DR*, the thread must be wholly formed and finished either in a *CAFTA-DR* country or the U.S. Put generally, a Yarn Forward Rule means using third country yarn (*e.g.*, non-Singaporean, non-Chilean, non-Australian, non-Moroccan, non-*CAFTA-DR*, non-American yarn), in the garment or the thread used to sew together the garment, disqualifies an article from duty-free treatment under the respective *FTA*. When in June 2012 legislation was proposed in Congress to clarify yarn used as sewing thread must be treated the same way as sewing thread, *i.e.*, the yarn to make the thread must come from a *CAFTA-DR* country. Saving American jobs was the justification: about 1,000 of them in Alabama, Florida, and North and South Carolina, as well as in the *CAFTA-DR* countries, were at stake.

To be sure, the impact of a Yarn Forward Rule may be softened by the exemption of certain types of fabrics from the triple transformation test associated with such a rule. For example, *NAFTA* exempts 16 fabrics. The exempted fabrics need not pass through three transformations in order to qualify for preferential treatment:

> Less demanding rules of origin govern certain knitted underwear, brassieres, and shirts made from fabric in short supply in North America, and textile and apparel articles made from fabric not commonly produced in North America. For example, silk and linen apparel articles follow a single-transformation instead of a "yarn-forward" rule. Thus, silk blouses are

---

70. *See NAFTA* Annex 401 Section XI.

71. *See, e.g., Australia FTA*, Chapter 5:1 and Rule 1 in Chapters 61–62 of Annex 4-A, and *Morocco FTA*, Articles 4–5 and Rule 1 in Chapters 61–62 of Annex 4-A.

considered originating even if made from non-originating fabric, provided the fabric is cut and sewn in one or more *NAFTA* countries. [Because the fabric must be cut and sewn in the *NAFTA* region, it might be more precise to call the rule a "double" transformation one.] These exceptions give producers flexibility to import materials not widely produced in North America.[72]

Sometimes, the exemptions reflect consumer preferences, as among Anglophilic Americans for Harris tweed.[73] The general Yarn Forward Rule means a coat is not "Mexican" if it is made from non-*NAFTA* (*e.g.*, Indian) yarn or fabric, or if it is sewn together with thread imported from outside the *NAFTA* region. However, an exception exists for coats made from Harris tweed, where such tweed is hand-woven using a loom less than 76 centimeters wide, and imported from Britain into Mexico.

The protectionist impact of a Yarn Forward Rule is further softened by the fact *NAFTA* establishes Tariff Preference Levels (TPLs) for apparel that fails to satisfy that Rule. Such apparel can receive preferential treatment up to the applicable TPL. That is, the TPL is a TRQ: *NAFTA's* preferential duty applies to imports up to the TPL, and the MFN rate applies to imports in excess of that level. Unfortunately, TPLs are not only a loophole in the ROO, but also create incentives for fraud, transshipment, and other kinds of abuse. Moreover, there are no TPLs established for 14 categories of apparel.[74]

The *Morocco FTA* contains another example of softening the otherwise strict Yarn Forward Rule. Article 4:3:11 of this *FTA* contains an exception to this rule for 30 million square meter equivalents of apparel that does not satisfy the Yarn Forward Rule. ("Square meter equivalents," or "SMEs," are a standard way of measuring quantity of apparel.) However, the exception applies only for the first decade the FTA is in effect, *i.e.*, 1 January 2006 until 31 December 2016. Moreover, the threshold is phased down from 30 million to zero SMEs over this decade. What is the purpose of this time-bound exception? Might it be to give Moroccan garment manufacturers a transition period to adjust their supply sources to meet the Yarn Forward test?

Notably, in some U.S. trade accords, and for certain T&A merchandise, the Specified Process Rule may be stricter than a Yarn Forward Rule. For instance, under *NAFTA*, a "Fiber Forward" Rule is used for products made of fibers that are produced in abundance in the *NAFTA* region. Examples include man-made fiber sweaters and fabrics knitted from cotton. Under the Fiber Forward Rule, it is not sufficient that the yarn (or other material) from which an article is made is from a *NAFTA* Party. The yarn must be spun from fiber that itself is from a *NAFTA* Party. That is, the (1) fiber that is the basic element from which all subsequent operations

---

72. United States Customs Service, NAFTA— Guide to Customs Procedures 17 (January 1994).

73. *See Least Favored Nation*, The Economist, 5 August 2006, at 68.

74. *See NAFTA* Schedule 3:1:2.

occur must originate in a *NAFTA* Party, (2) yarn must be spun from that fiber in a *NAFTA* Party, (3) article must be cut in a *NAFTA* Party, and (4) article must be sewn in a *NAFTA* Party. In effect, the rule is a "quadruple" transformation test.

The restrictive specified process rules for T&A merchandise should not overshadow specified process rules for other industries that clearly result in trade liberalization. For example, a computer qualifies as an originating good if its circuit board is made in a *NAFTA* Party and this board is transformed so that its tariff classification changes (perhaps from a circuit board to a partly-assembled computer). In addition, a low common external tariff exists for computers and related parts. Thus, *NAFTA* essentially establishes a truly free market for computer products.

Not every production process causes an article to become an originating good. For example, *NAFTA* Article 412(a) says merely diluting a good with water, with no material alteration in the good, does not qualify as an operation resulting in an originating good.

- *NAFTA* **2.0 Changes**

What changes to the T&A Specified Process Rule were made under *NAFTA* 2.0? Under the 27 August 2018 U.S.—Mexico bilateral agreement, the two sides agreed to:

> promote greater use of fibers, yarns, and fabrics made in the U.S. . . . . It would do this by limiting rules that allow for use of non-NAFTA inputs in textile and apparel trade.

> Also, it would require that sewing thread, pocketing fabric, narrow elastic bands, and coated fabric, when incorporated in other finished products, be made in the region for those finished products to qualify for duty-free treatment. . . . [75]

Such provisions mimicked those in *CAFTA-DR*, but:

> Among unanswered questions is whether there is an exemption for latex and rubber—both of which are not made in the hemisphere . . . . Also unclear is whether the preliminary deal would fix problems with NAFTA's short-supply process to address the concerns of the apparel and retail industries . . . .

> Other provisions in the new textile chapter would provide additional tools for strengthening customs enforcement and preventing fraud in the sector . . . .[76]

One change provoked sharp criticism:

> The idea that sewing thread lacking sufficient *NAFTA* content would disqualify a garment is "absolutely ridiculous," a Canadian industry source

---

75. Rossella Brevetti, *Details on U.S.-Mexico Textile Deal Seen as Threadbare*, 35 International Trade Reporter (BNA) 1163 (6 September 2018). [Hereinafter, *Details.*]

76. *Details.*

[said] . . . . "The requirement will add an extraordinary level of customs certification." . . . "I don't know whose interest [the sewing thread requirement] would serve."[77]

Whose interests might a ROO about sewing thread serve?

XII. Type 8: *De Minimis* Test

The final type of preferential ROO in *NAFTA* is a *De Minimis* Test. Under Article 405:1, a good that fails to satisfy the applicable ROO nevertheless is an originating good if the value of the non-*NAFTA* materials used to make the good is no more than 7% of the price or total cost of the good. For T&A, the *De Minimis* test is based on the weight of the components of the garment in question. Other FTAs tend to contain *De Minimis* Tests, though the threshold levels may vary from one accord to another.

---

77. *Details.*

Chapter 8

Preferential ROOs (Continued): Additional Issues[1]

I. Tariff Shift and 2006 *Cummins* Case

Cummins Incorporated v. United States,

United States Court of Appeals for the Federal Circuit,
454 F.3d 1361–1366 (2006)

MAYER, CIRCUIT JUDGE:

Cummins Inc. appeals the United States Court of International Trade's grant of summary judgment, which held that the crank shafts imported by Cummins into the United States did not originate in Mexico and were not entitled to preferential treatment under the *North American Free Trade Agreement* ("*NAFTA*"). *Cummins Inc. v. United States*, 377 F. Supp. 2d 1365 (Ct. Int'l Trade 2005). We affirm.

Background

Under the United States' tariff laws, products that "originate in the territory of a *NAFTA* party" are entitled to preferential duty treatment. General Note 12(a)(ii), Harmonized Tariff Schedule of the United States ("HTSUS"); *see also* 19 U.S.C. § 3332 (2000). One way a product may so originate is if it is "transformed in the territory" of a *NAFTA* party. General Notes 12(b)(i)-(iv), HTSUS. One manner in which a good can be transformed, as is relevant to this case, is by undergoing a "change in tariff classification" "to subheading 8483.10 from any other heading." General Notes 12(b)(ii)(A),12(t)/84.243(A), HTSUS. Here, Cummins contends that the crankshafts it imports into the United States undergo such a tariff shift in Mexico from heading 7224 to subheading 8483.10.30, and are thereby entitled to preferential duty treatment.

The facts surrounding the production of the crankshafts are undisputed. Production begins in Brazil, where Krupp Metalurgica Campo Limpo creates a forging having the general shape of a crankshaft. This forging is created from a closed-die forging process, which involves forging alloy steel between matrices. After forging, the excess material that was squeezed out of the matrices, called "flash," is removed

---

1. Documents References:
  (1) *NAFTA* Chapter 4
  (2) Rules of Origin in other FTAs

by a process called trimming. The trimming is done on a separate machine within approximately ten seconds of the forging press operation. Because the process of trimming can distort the forging, the forging is then coined. Coining involves applying pressure to the forging, which is still hot and malleable, in a closed die. After coining, the forging is subjected to shot blasting. Shot blasting uses abrasive particles to strike the surface of the forging to remove dirt and oxide from its surface. The forging is then cooled, and its ends are milled so that it can be securely clamped into machines in Mexico for final machining operations. The last manufacturing process performed in Brazil is mass centering, in which the forging's center of balance is determined and locator center points are machined into each end.

After these processes are performed in Brazil, the forging is imported into Mexico by Cummins de Mexico, S.A. ("CUMMSA"), a wholly owned subsidiary of Cummins. As imported, the forging has the general shape of, but cannot yet function as, a crankshaft. After importation into Mexico, CUMMSA performs at least fourteen different steps on the forging that cover over 95% of its surface area resulting in a useable crankshaft, which Cummins imports into the United States. It is undisputed that the crankshaft imported into the United States is classifiable under subheading 8483.10.30 of the HTSUS, which covers "[t]ransmission shafts (including camshafts and crankshafts) and cranks . . . ."

The Court of International Trade addressed nearly identical facts in an earlier case involving the same crankshafts. *Cummins Engine Co. v. United States*, . . . 83 F. Supp. 2d 1366 (Ct. Int'l Trade 1999) ("*Cummins I*"). The crankshaft manufacturing process there was nearly identical to the one here, except that a grease pocket was milled into the forging in Brazil. The court held that machining the grease pocket in Brazil precluded classification under heading 7224 upon importation in Mexico, because it was further working the product beyond roughly shaping it by forging.

After *Cummins I*, Cummins filed for an amended advance ruling letter from the United States Customs and Border Protection ("Customs"), based on the grease pocket being machined in Mexico instead of Brazil. Despite the change in the manufacturing process, Customs determined that the crankshafts did not originate in Mexico. . . . Prior to issuing its decision, Customs submitted the question to the World Customs Organization ("WCO"), which issued a classification opinion, approved by the member states 31 to 1, determining that the proper classification of the forgings imported into Mexico was under heading 8483, not heading 7224. . . . However, Customs did not expressly rely upon the WCO decision in denying Cummins preferential treatment.

In response to Customs' advance letter ruling, Cummins filed an action in the Court of International Trade under 28 U.S.C. § 1581(h). [Under Section 1581(h), the CIT may review pre-importation Customs' rulings if the party commencing the action demonstrates that "he would be irreparably harmed unless given an opportunity to obtain judicial review prior to such importation."] While that action was pending, Cummins imported into the United States a test shipment of three finished crankshafts marked as originating in Mexico, which Customs classified under subheading 8483.10.30, HTSUS. Cummins protested this classification, arguing that the proper classification was (MX) 8483.10.30. [The prefix "MX" signifies an article is a product of Mexico, and thereby accorded *NAFTA* preferential treatment.] After protesting Customs' classification of the test shipment, Cummins filed an action under 28 U.S.C. § 1581(a). The trial court consolidated the two actions, but later found the section 1581(h) action moot in light of the one under section 1581(a).

The court determined on summary judgment that the articles imported into Mexico were properly classified under subheading 8483.10.30, not heading 7224, and accordingly did not undergo a tariff shift and were not entitled to preferential treatment under *NAFTA*. Cummins appeals the trial court's grant of summary judgment, and we have jurisdiction under 28 U.S.C. § 1295(a)(5).

Discussion

We review the trial court's grant of summary judgment on tariff classifications *de novo*. . . . A classification decision involves two underlying steps: determining the proper meaning of the tariff provisions, which is a question of law; and then determining which heading the disputed goods fall within, which is a question of fact. . . . However, when the nature of the merchandise is undisputed, as it is here, the classification issue collapses entirely into a question of law. . . . Although our review is de novo, we accord deference to a Customs' classification ruling in proportion to its "power to persuade" under the principles of *Skidmore v. Swift & Co.*, 323 U.S. 134, . . . (1944). . . . In addition, "Customs' relative expertise in administering the tariff statute often lends further persuasiveness to a classification ruling, entitling the ruling to a greater measure of deference." . . .

It is undisputed that the crankshafts imported into the United States are properly classified under subheading 8483.10.30. The disputed issue is whether the crankshafts undergo a tariff shift in Mexico. That is, do the crankshafts enter Mexico under a different tariff heading than they leave Mexico? The trial court concluded that the crankshafts do not undergo a tariff shift as they are classified under subheading 8483.10.30 upon import into and export out of Mexico. Cummins contends that this classification was error, and the proper classification of the product upon import into Mexico is under heading 7224, which covers "[o]ther alloy steel in ingots or other primary forms; semifinished products of other alloy steel."

"The General Rules of Interpretation (GRI) govern the classification of goods within the HTSUS." *Hewlett-Packard Co. v. United States*, 189 F.3d 1346, 1348 (Fed. Cir. 1999). Under GRI 1, the classification "shall be determined according to the terms of the headings and any relevant section or chapter notes." As noted above, Cummins contends that the goods imported into Mexico are properly classified as "semifinished products of other alloy steel" under heading 7224. Chapter 72's notes expressly define "semifinished," in pertinent part, as "products of solid section, which have not been further worked than . . . roughly shaped by forging, including blanks for angles, shapes or sections." Chapter 72, Note 1(ij), HTSUS. Thus, if the product imported into Mexico has been further worked beyond being roughly shaped by forging, it does not fall within heading 7224. The parties dispute the meaning of the term "further worked."

Cummins relies on Additional U.S. Note 2 to Chapter 72, which defines "further worked" as subjecting the product to one of several expressly listed surface treatments. [Additional U.S. Note 2 to Chapter 72, HTUS, says that unless the context provides otherwise, "'further worked' refers to products subjected to any of the following surface treatments: polishing and burnishing; artificial oxidation; chemical surface treatments such are [sic] phosphatizing, oxalating and borating; coating with metal; coating with nonmetallic substances (e.g., enameling, varnishing, lacquering, painting, coating with plastics materials); or cladding."] It is undisputed that none of these surface treatments are [sic] performed in Brazil, and Cummins contends that so long as none of these specific operations are performed prior to importation into Mexico, the product has not been "further worked." The trial court rejected this argument in Cummins I, and we do so now.

The definition of "further worked" in Chapter 72 is expressly inapplicable where "the context provides otherwise." Here, to read the term "further worked" as referring to only these specific treatments would lead to a nonsensical result. In particular, this definition would render the phrase "than . . . roughly shaped by forging" meaningless and contravene the well-established principle that a statute should be construed "if at all possible, to give effect and meaning to all the terms." Bausch [v. United States], 148 F.3d [1363] at 1367 [Fed Cir. 1998].

Absent an applicable express definition or contrary legislative intent, we must construe the term "further worked" "according to [its] common and commercial meanings, which are presumed to be the same." Carl Zeiss, Inc. v. United States, 195 F.3d 1375, 1379 (Fed. Cir. 1999) (citing Simod Am. Corp. v. United States, 872 F.2d 1572, 1576 (Fed. Cir. 1989)). Here, the plain meaning of "further worked, "when read in context, means working the product beyond the point of roughly shaping it by forging. The trial court, relying in part on Winter-Wolff, Inc. v. United States, . . . 996 F. Supp. 1258, 1265 (Ct. Int'l Trade 1998) (construing "further worked" in the context of subheading 7607.11.30), defined "further worked" more precisely as "to form, fashion, or shape an existing product to a greater extent." We agree that this definition is suitable in the context before us.

Here, the product was forged and then trimmed, coined, shot blasted, milled, and mass centered in Brazil. Cummins suggests that these are steps within the "forging process." However, the relevant language is not "further worked beyond the forging process" but "further worked than roughly shaped by forging." The government cites evidence that the act of forging is understood in the industry as being distinct from the additional operations performed by Cummins in Brazil. In particular, the Forging Handbook provides that trimming occurs "[u]pon completion of the forging operation." FORGING HANDBOOK FORGING INDUSTRY ASSOCIATION, FORGING HANDBOOK 153 (Thomas G. Byrer 1985). This Handbook also describes coining as a "finishing operation." . . . Significantly, Cummins agreed that trimming (and hence every step thereafter) takes place "after forging." Moreover, milling the ends of the forging product is outside of the forging process and constitutes working the product beyond roughly shaping it by forging, namely forming, fashioning, or shaping it to a greater extent. Thus, the product imported into Mexico from Brazil cannot be classified under heading 7224.

. . .

We agree with the trial court that the forging is properly classified under heading 8483 upon importation into Mexico. GRI 2(a) provides that "[a]ny reference in a heading to an article shall be taken to include a reference to that article incomplete or unfinished, provided that, as entered, the incomplete or unfinished article has the essential character of the complete or finished article." In addition, the Explanatory Notes [II] to GRI 2(a) provide that this rule applies "to blanks unless these are specified in a particular heading. The term 'blank' means an article, not ready for direct use, having the approximate shape or outline of the finished article or part, and which can only be used, other than in exceptional circumstances, for completion into the finished article . . . ." . . . Here, the product imported into Mexico had the general shape of a crankshaft and was intended for use only in producing a finished crankshaft. In fact, certain operations done in Brazil, such as milling the forgings' ends, were done solely to simplify the operations in Mexico in completing the crankshaft. As such, the forged product imported into Mexico was properly classified under subheading 8483.10.30. Accordingly, it did not undergo a tariff shift and was not entitled to preferential treatment under *NAFTA* when imported into the United States.

Finally, Cummins contends that the trial court erred by improperly relying upon the WCO classification opinion. While such an opinion is not given deference by United States courts, it can be consulted for its persuasive value, if any. *Cf. Sanchez-Llamas v. Oregon*, 548 U.S.[___], 126 S. Ct. 2669 . . . (28 June 2006) (rejecting the argument that U.S. courts are obligated to comply with interpretations of the *Vienna Convention* by the International Court of Justice (ICJ)); *Corus Staal BV v. Dep't of Commerce*, 395 F.3d 1343, 1349 (Fed. Cir. 2005) (observing that World Trade Organization decisions are accorded no deference); *Timken Co. v. United States*, 354 F.3d 1334, 1343–44 (Fed. Cir. 2004). The Supreme Court has rejected any notion of deference or obligation to a foreign tribunal's decisions. In so doing, it observed, "If treaties are to be given effect as federal law under our legal system, determining their meaning as a matter of federal law 'is emphatically the province and duty of the judicial department,' . . . ." *Sanchez-Llamas*, 2006 U.S. LEXIS 5177 at*39 (quoting *Marbury v. Madison*, 5 U.S. 137, 1 Cranch 137, 177, 2 L. Ed. 60 (1803)). Like the ICJ's interpretation of the treaty terms in *Sanchez-Llamas*, the WCO opinion is not binding and is entitled, at most, to "respectful consideration." *Id*. It is not a proxy for independent analysis.

Here, the court accorded no deference to either the WCO opinion or the categorization by Mexico's Customs authority. Instead, it independently construed "further worked," based solely on the tariff terms and the principles set forth in the GRIs, and consulted the WCO opinion and Mexican categorization only as persuasive authority. The court properly construed the statutory terms as they are written. *See Corus Staal*, 395 F.3d at 1349; *cf. Suramericana de Aleaciones Laminadas v. United States*, 966 F.2d 660, 668 (Fed. Cir. 1992) ("While we acknowledge Congress's interest in complying with U.S. responsibilities under the GATT, we are bound not by what we think Congress should or perhaps wanted to do, but by what Congress in fact did.").

Conclusion

Accordingly, the judgment of the United States Court of International Trade is affirmed.

II. *NAFTA* Certificate of Origin and 2006 *Corrpro* Case

- **Importance of Certificates**

How does a customs official of the U.S., Canada, or Mexico know an article is an "originating good" as defined in Article 201 and Chapter 4 of *NAFTA* and, therefore, qualifies for preferential treatment under Article 302 of *NAFTA*? The exporter of the article provides the answer.

NAFTA Article 501 obligates every American, Canadian, and Mexican exporter to complete and sign a Certificate of Origin indicating whether the article it is exporting to another *NAFTA* Party is an originating good. The importer is entitled to rely on the Certificate. If the exporter does not manufacture the article, then it is entitled to complete the Certificate based on its knowledge of whether the article qualifies as an originating good, or on information provided by the manufacturer. The exporter, not the manufacturer, is obligated to furnish the Certificate.[2] *NAFTA* establishes a standard Certificate form and obligates exporters to retain all records relating to the origin of their article for 5 years.[3]

The importer claims duty-free treatment by making a written declaration, based on the Certificate, which the importer keeps in its possession and presents to customs officials at the port of entry upon request, specifically, the port director, stating the article is an originating good. This "Traditional Program" filing is due within 1 year of the transaction. The importer must retain a copy of the Certificate for 5 years.[4] If

---

2. *See NAFTA* Article 501:3-4.

3. *See NAFTA* Article 505:(a).

4. *See NAFTA* Article 505:(b). Presentation is required within one year of entry, unless the relevant customs official waives this requirement because the official is satisfied the merchandise originates within *NAFTA*.

the importer has reason to believe the Certificate on which the declaration is based contains incorrect information, then duties (if applicable) must be paid.[5]

• **Reconciliation Program and 2016 *Ford* Case**

What happens if an importer does not have the information to make a timely filing of a Certificate with the port director under the Traditional Program? Perhaps the exporter lacks, or has failed to provide, the necessary data for the Certificate to prove *NAFTA* origination. The importer will have to pay customs duties, but under CBP's "Reconciliation Program" can seek a rebate of any duties it paid. Filing a Certificate under the Reconciliation Program is paperless, *i.e.*, electronic.

Routinely, CBP waives its otherwise strict one-year filing deadline for a paper Certificate under the Traditional Program, and allows rebates under the Reconciliation Program—but not always. In the 2016 case of *Ford Motor Company v. United States*, the Federal Circuit upheld the decision of CBP not to waive this deadline.[6] The Court found CBP's technical distinctions between the Traditional and Reconciliation Program requirements convincing. The latter scheme has special protections for CBP to ensure it can rectify mistakes about claims for duty-free treatment (*e.g.*, a requirement of continuous posting by an importer of a bond).

• **Dubious Certificates**

If customs officials suspect an article is not an originating good in spite of a claim for treatment as such, they may undertake an "origin verification." This procedure entails an extraterritorial investigation. *NAFTA* Article 506:1 authorizes customs officials to send written questionnaires to the exporter or producer of the article, and to visit the premises of the exporter or producer to examine relevant records and observe production facilities. If the exporter or producer does not consent to a verification visit, then customs officials in the importing country may deny preferential treatment to the article in question.[7]

Under what circumstances might customs officials doubt a claim about origin? One instance is where the exporter is a new entrant into the market, one with which the officials are not familiar, and thus has no "track record." A second instance is

---

5. *See NAFTA* Article 502.

6. *See* Number 2014-1581 (6 January 2016); Brian Flood, *Ford Loses Appeal Seeking NAFTA Duty Refund*, 33 International Trade Reporter (BNA) 64 (14 January 2016). Note the Dissent in the case found CBP's explanation unpersuasive, and said the Majority gave CBP excessive deference.

In a different Federal Circuit case, Ford raised the question of whether failure by CBP to respond in a timely fashion to reconciliation entries of an importer (namely, Ford, with respect to 11 entries in 2004–2005 of Jaguar autos from the U.K.) was tantamount to a concession by CBP that the importer overpaid duties and was owed a refund (in the case, $6.2 million). Ford lost, essentially on procedural grounds. *See Ford Motor Co. v. United States*, Number 2014-1726 (3 February 2016); Brian Flood, *Ford Loses Appeal of Jaguar Duties*, 33 International Trade Reporter (BNA) 197 (11 February 2016).

7. *See NAFTA* Article 506:4.

where the exporter "fits a profile" of false claimants. To what degree might use by a new shipper of a customs broker known to customs officials help mitigate any doubts?

Corrpro Companies, Inc. v. United States,

United States Court of Appeals for the Federal Circuit,
433 F.3d 1360–1366 (3 January 2006)

LOURIE, CIRCUIT JUDGE:

The United States appeals from the decision of the United States Court of International Trade denying the government's motion to dismiss for lack of jurisdiction, granting Corrpro Companies, Inc.'s ("Corrpro's") motion for summary judgment, and classifying the subject merchandise under . . . HTSUS MX 8543.40.00, duty-free. *Corrpro Cos. v. United States*, . . . Slip Op. 2004–116 (Ct. Int'l Trade Sept. 10, 2004) ("Decision"). Because Customs did not make a protestable decision as to . . . *NAFTA* eligibility giving rise to jurisdiction in the Court of International Trade under 28 U.S.C. § 1581(a), we reverse.

Background

This case arises from Corrpro's attempt to claim preferential treatment under *NAFTA* for certain entries of sacrificial magnesium anodes. Enacted on December 8, 1993, *NAFTA* is an agreement between the United States, Canada, and Mexico to promote the free flow of goods through a reduction or phased elimination of tariffs and non-tariff barriers to trade. 19 U.S.C. § 3312 (1994) (approving and implementing *NAFTA*). *See Xerox v. United States*, 423 F.3d 1356, 1359 (Fed. Cir. 2005). Preferential tariff treatment under *NAFTA* allows importers to enter qualified goods into the United States free of duty.

Under *NAFTA*, an importer's right to preferential tariff treatment for qualifying goods does not vest automatically on entry. . . . As provided in Articles 501(1) and 503(1) of NAFTA, implemented in 19 C.F.R. § 181.21(a), an importer seeking preferential tariff treatment under *NAFTA* must make a written declaration that the goods qualify for *NAFTA* treatment and must base that declaration on a properly executed *NAFTA* "Certificate of Origin" that covers the goods being imported. 19 C.F.R. §§ 181.11(a), 181.21(a) (2005) ("A Certificate of Origin shall be employed to certify that a good being exported either from the United States into Canada or Mexico or from Canada or Mexico into the United States qualifies as an originating good for purposes of preferential tariff treatment under the *NAFTA*.").

However, an importer is not required to submit a written declaration and the appropriate *NAFTA* Certificates of Origin immediately upon entry of the subject goods. *Xerox*, 423 F.3d at 1361. Under Article 502(3) of *NAFTA*, codified at 19 U.S.C. § 1520(d), an importer who does not make a *NAFTA* claim at the time of entry may nevertheless apply for a "refund of any excess duties paid" on a good qualifying for *NAFTA* treatment by submitting a written declaration and the appropriate Certificates of Origin "within 1 year after the date of importation." 19 U.S.C. § 1520(d) (2000). In this case, Corrpro claims that its imported goods are entitled to *NAFTA* treatment even though it did not make a *NAFTA* claim at the time of entry or within one year of entry.

On August 16, 1999, Corrpro began importing magnesium anodes into the United States.... The United States Bureau of Customs and Border Protection ("Customs") classified the goods under HTSUS 8104.19.00 as "magnesium and articles thereof, including waste and scrap: Unwrought magnesium: Other" at the rate of 6.5 percent *ad valorem*. ... Corrpro did not make a claim for *NAFTA* treatment at the time of entry under 19 C.F.R. § 181.21(a). ... On June 30, 2000, Customs liquidated the subject merchandise under 19 U.S.C. § 1500. Customs did not accord the goods any preferential treatment under *NAFTA* because Corrpro had not yet raised the issue. ...

Corrpro also did not claim preferential treatment under *NAFTA* within one year of the date of importation under 19 U.S.C. § 1520(d). However, on September 12, 2000, Corrpro filed protests to Customs' liquidation under 19 U.S.C. § 1514(a), arguing that the goods were classifiable as HTSUS MX 8543.30.00, free of duty under *NAFTA*. ... Section 1514(a) is a procedural mechanism by which an importer may protest Customs' decision pertaining to the classification, rate, and amount of duties, but it does not specifically relate to *NAFTA* eligibility. ...

Corrpro claimed preferential treatment under *NAFTA* in its 19 U.S.C. § 1514(a) protest without filing a written declaration or Certificates of Origin substantiating its assertion of *NAFTA* eligibility. On August 13, 2001, Customs denied Corrpro's protests in full.... Later in 2002, for the first time, Corrpro submitted to Customs Certificates of Origin covering the goods, after it had filed a complaint in the Court of International Trade.... [The parties dispute whether the Certificates of Origin were filed on February 4, 2002, as stated in the affidavit attached to the Certificates, or on June 27, 2002, the date indicated on the certificates themselves.]

Corrpro had filed its complaint in the Court of International Trade seeking preferential duty treatment for the imported goods on September 6, 2001. In its complaint, Corrpro asserted that the trial court had jurisdiction under 28 U.S.C. § 1581(a) because of its 19 U.S.C. § 1514(a) protest challenging the "classification and the rate and amount of duties chargeable." ... Corrpro then moved for summary judgment that the subject merchandise was entitled to preferential duty treatment under *NAFTA*. ... On September 10, 2004, the Court of International Trade held that it had jurisdiction to entertain the action and granted Corrpro's motion for summary judgment.

In determining whether Customs had made a protestable decision that conferred-jurisdiction over Corrpro's *NAFTA* claims, the trial court first held that Customs' initial classification of the goods was a decision on *NAFTA* eligibility that could be protested, even though Customs had not expressly considered the question of preferential treatment under NAFTA at that time. ... The trial court reasoned that this inference was warranted because Corrpro had been precluded by Customs Head-quarters Ruling Letter ("HQ") 557046 from making a *NAFTA* claim at the time of entry. . . . HQ 557046, which provides that anodes classifiable in HTSUS 8104.19.00 are not eligible for duty-free treatment under the Generalized System of Prefer-ences, was issued on May 17, 1993, prior to the enactment of *NAFTA* (although it was retracted on October 10, 2001). The trial court therefore concluded that Cor-rpro had acted properly under a standard of reasonable care in not seeking *NAFTA* treatment at the time of entry or within one year of entry. . . . Second, the trial court held that Corrpro's post-importation submission of *NAFTA* Certificates of Origin met the procedural requirements of 19 C.F.R. § 10.112 because Corrpro's delay in submission had resulted from its adherence to Customs' classification ruling. . . . Third, the trial court held that the subject merchandise satisfied *NAFTA's* rules of origin and thus was eligible for preferential treatment under *NAFTA* as a matter of law. . . .

The government timely appealed. . . .

Discussion

We review the Court of International Trade's jurisdictional ruling based on its interpretation of 19 U.S.C. §§ 1514 and 1520(d) *de novo. Xerox v. United States,* 423 F.3d 1356, 1359 (Fed. Cir. 2005). We also review that court's grant of summary judgment *de novo. Int'l Trading Co. v. United States,* 412 F.3d 1303, 1307 (Fed. Cir. 2005).

. . .

We agree with the government that the Court of International Trade lacked jurisdiction over the complaint for lack of a protestable decision by Customs. 28 U.S.C. § 1581(a) establishes jurisdiction over protestable decisions, providing that the "Court of International Trade shall have exclusive jurisdiction of any civil action commenced to contest the denial of a protest, in whole or in part, under section 515 of the *Tariff Act of 1930*." However, we recently held in Xerox that Cus-toms' liquidation of an importer's entries was not a protestable decision with respect to preferential treatment under *NAFTA* because "Customs at no time considered the merits of *NAFTA* eligibility, nor could it [have] without a valid claim by [the importer] for such eligibility." 423 F.3d at 1363 (emphasis added). We observed, "in the absence of a proper claim for *NAFTA* treatment, either at entry or within a year of entry . . . Customs cannot make a protestable decision to deny an importer preferential *NAFTA* treatment." *Id.* at 1365. We concluded that because "the exis-tence of a protestable decision of the type enumerated in 19 U.S.C. § 1514(a) is a condition precedent for jurisdiction to lie in the Court of International Trade under section 1581(a)," Xerox's appeal of an invalid protest was properly dismissed for lack of jurisdiction. *Id.* Accordingly, under our precedent, there is a protestable decision as to *NAFTA* eligibility that confers jurisdiction in the Court of Interna-tional Trade under 28 U.S.C. § 1581(a) only when the importer has made a valid claim for *NAFTA* treatment, either at entry or within a year of entry, with a written declaration and Certificates of Origin presented in a timely fashion, and Customs has engaged in "some sort of decision-making process" expressly considering the merits of that claim. *Id.* at 1363 (*quoting U.S. Shoe Corp. v. United States*, 114 F.3d 1564, 1569 (Fed. Cir. 1997)).

Corrpro concedes that it did not make a post-importation *NAFTA* claim within a year of entry under 19 U.S.C. § 1520(d). Corrpro argues, however, that its late submission is excused because, under a standard of reasonable care, it could not make a *NAFTA* claim until after HQ 557046 was revoked. We will not decide that question; even assuming that Corrpro could have made a valid claim after the expiration of the one-year time limit, Corrpro cannot establish that Customs engaged in some sort of decision-making on the merits of a valid *NAFTA* claim. In order to make a valid *NAFTA* claim, an importer must submit a written declaration and the appropriate Certificates of Origin. 19 C.F.R. §§ 181.11(a), 181.32. An importer may not circumvent these statutory and regulatory requirements. Corrpro did not submit the appropriate Certificates of Origin until 2002. Thus, neither Customs' initial classification decision, made in 1999, nor its liquidation of goods, made in 2000, could have been a decision on the merits of a valid *NAFTA* claim, as no valid *NAFTA* claim existed at that time. As we held in Xerox, "there is simply no basis for attributing to Customs a decision denying [a *NAFTA*] claim that did not exist." 423 F.3d at 1363. Moreover, there is no evidence that Customs in fact considered Corrpro's *NAFTA* claim after the Certificates of Origin were submitted in 2002, while Corrpro's action was pending in the Court of International Trade. Therefore, Customs did not make a protestable decision establishing jurisdiction under 28 USC § 1581(a).

In holding that it had jurisdiction over Corrpro's claim, the Court of International Trade erred in concluding that the initial classification decision by Customs in 1999 was a protestable decision. We recognize, of course, that Xerox was decided after the trial court rendered its decision in this case. In any event, the trial court's reasoning assumed that Corrpro had made a valid *NAFTA* claim at the time of entry, even though Corrpo had not yet raised that issue. But we cannot attribute to Customs a decision on a *NAFTA* claim that did not yet exist. Because Customs could not have considered and did not consider the merits of *NAFTA* eligibility in the initial classification decision, it did not make a protestable decision at that time. For the same reason, we disagree with Corrpro's argument that Customs' liquidation of the goods is a protestable decision. Customs could not have engaged in any sort of decision-making as to *NAFTA* eligibility in liquidating the goods because Corrpro had not yet raised the *NAFTA* issue.

. . .

Conclusion

Because Corrpro did not satisfy the statutory requirements in order to make a valid *NAFTA* claim until 2002, Customs could not have and did not consider the merits of that claim in its initial classification decision or liquidation. Accordingly, there was no protestable decision conferring jurisdiction on the Court of International Trade under 28 U.S.C. § 1581(a). The decision of that court denying the government's motion to dismiss and granting summary judgment for Corrpro is therefore *reversed*.

III. Trans-Shipment and *Singapore FTA*

Generally, trans-shipment of a good through a party to an FTA does not confer origin on that good. To the contrary, preferential ROOs help screen out trans-shipped goods. These rules differentiate them from products that underwent meaningful economic activity in the territory of one or more FTA parties. Further, FTAs tend to contain a "direct shipment" requirement as a complement to preferential ROOs, meaning the product for which duty-free treatment is sought must move directly from 1 FTA party to another. However, is there any instance of an FTA that permits trans-shipment to confer origin and, therefore, authorize duty-free treatment?

The answer is "yes." The *Singapore FTA*, in Annex 3B, contains a list of goods that are deemed to originate in Singapore. To qualify for the list and thus duty-free entry into the U.S., these goods, as finished, must be imported from Singaporean to American territory. Annex 3B uses the term "itself, as imported," with respect to a good shipped from Singapore to America. This term means a good is deemed to originate in Singapore only if that good is trans-shipped through Singapore. If a good is incorporated into another product as a component thereof, then that good is not considered "originating" in Singapore, and does not qualify for Annex 3B.

There is an unsurprising exception: a component not trans-shipped through Singapore, and incorporated in another product there, originates in Singapore if that component is shipped first from America to Singapore. In other words, components count if they come from America, but non-American components do not qualify for Annex 3B. Note the effect of this exception on RVC Rules in the *Singapore FTA*.[8] A component does not qualify as "originating" in the RVC calculation, unless shipped from the U.S. to Singapore, and then in Singapore incorporated in a final product.

What kinds of goods does Annex 3B of the *Singapore FTA* contain? This Annex covers the "Integrated Sourcing Initiative" (ISI), and the listed goods—called ISI goods—are, for the most part, IT goods. As a member of the WTO *ITA*, the U.S. accords duty-free MFN treatment to such products. Thus, from the American perspective, accepting trans-shipped IT products from Singapore for duty-free treatment was no major concession in the FTA negotiations. Why might Annex 3B be in the interests of Singapore? Might the reasons lie in Singapore's interest in being both a leading center for high technology and obtaining trans-shipment business for its famed Port of Singapore Authority (PSA)?

---

8. Section 202(d) of the *United States-Singapore Free Trade Implementation Act* sets out these Rules.

Part Three

Legal Commitments in FTAs

Chapter 9

Typical FTA Market Access Obligations[1]

I. Check List

An RTA, be it an FTA or CU, is most obviously an economic entity, central to which are market access opportunities. No less evidently, however, an RTA is borne of and sustained by political and national security factors, and even cultural affiliations. And, for scholars, students, and practitioners of International Trade Law, every RTA is a legal phenomenon.

That is so in two senses. First, any FTA or CU exists within the multilateral trading system, specifically, within the framework of GATT Article XXIV and various WTO provisions (assuming any of the FTA or CU countries is a WTO Member). Second, an FTA or CU creates legal rights and duties for the members. In effect, it is a contract among a subset of the world's trading nations designed to work to the mutual advantage of the contracting states. This second sense is the present subject.

The most legally correct way to study RTAs is to read them carefully. That means starting with definitional provisions, which often appear early on in the FTA. For instance, Chapter 1 of the *Korea-U.S. FTA* has initial provisions and definitions. Thereafter, as in many FTAs, in *KORUS* the key provisions designed to liberalize trade, albeit in a controlled fashion, appear: Chapter 2 of *KORUS* covers national treatment and market access; Chapter 6 deals with ROOs; and Chapter 7 is about customs administration and facilitation.

For now, that kind of thorough, "bottom-up" review is impossible. Only a dedicated work, with several volumes, can do justice to all of America's FTAs, much less the FTAs and CUs of other countries. Perhaps the second-best solution is a conceptual, "top-down" approach. Rather than chronicle the details of what each and

---

1. Documents References:
   (1) *Havana (ITO) Charter* Article 44
   (2) GATT Article XXIV
   (3) *NAFTA* Chapters 1–3
   (4) Relevant provisions in other FTAs

every FTA and CUs says, consider the essential features common to all of them, and the typical variations observed among those features. Put differently, what framework ought to be in mind when opening up an RTA? What is to be expected in the text? What is new?

The obvious starting point is to appreciate what countries are party to the RTA in question. Instances in which borders are in controversy, and merchandise might originate in a disputed territory, can pose legal issues. An example is Israel and the Occupied Territories. Another, albeit hypothetical, illustration would be an FTA between India and Pakistan in which neither side agreed to admit duty-free products from Kashmir, the borders of which have been hotly contested since the British Partition of 15 August 1947.

Sometimes, a country not included in a particular RTA may have preferential treatment under an accord with one (or more) of the members of that RTA. The Dominican Republic is an illustration. In the initial *CAFTA-DR* negotiations, it was excluded from coverage. However, its merchandise was eligible for preferential treatment under the *CBI*, a manifestation of special and differential treatment for poor countries. During *CAFTA-DR* talks, concerns arose that its benefits should not exceed those the *CBI* provides. An integrated market in Central America and the Caribbean, especially in the agriculture and T&A sectors, with harmonized rules, was thought desirable. Eventually, the Dominican Republic was added to *CAFTA-DR*, hence the acronym *CAFTA-DR*.

Similarly, FTAs may be crafted to allow "docking on" (to use a Science Fiction metaphor) of new countries. The *U.S.-Australia FTA* is an illustration, as its drafters anticipated one day, New Zealand might join this FTA or a subsequent iteration and enlargement of it, like *TPP*. This example—and plenty of others, including enlargement of the EU CU, associate memberships in *MERCOSUR*, and new countries in the FTA of *ASEAN*, called *AFTA*—suggests membership of an RTA is not immutable.

Generally, Parties to an RTA, and their geopolitical boundaries, are self evident and uncontroversial. What is germane is the political economy mixture among members. *NAFTA* is the first FTA major developed countries (the U.S. and Canada) signed with a developing country (Mexico). *CAFTA-DR* is the first FTA the U.S. negotiated with least developed countries. Members such as Honduras, Nicaragua, and Guatemala qualify for this status, and among *CAFTA-DR* members about 65% of the population in each country is engaged in agriculture. How might the diversity in levels of economic development affect trade liberalization rules of the RTA? Is an RTA with poor countries inherently more about development than commerce, as least in the short and medium term? Is such an RTA likely to prove contentious, because these countries typically specialize in products developed countries regard as sensitive? As for political systems represented in the RTA, they may range from democracies to kingdoms. Is one form of government an easier type for negotiation and implementation? Are there differences as to building legitimacy among a populace for trade liberalization?

To these questions, consider the interactive effects of economics and politics. Trade policy, especially its economic dimensions, can affect trade politics. If the policies underlying an RTA are sound, and if they are formulated transparently and explained honestly to the public, then can political polarization be avoided? If so, then perhaps the make-up of RTA members matters less than how the government of each RTA Party manages—and sometimes leads—its domestic constituencies.

Indubitably, in an FTA or CU there are market access obligations, and exceptions to them for sensitive sectors. These obligations include goods. How ambitious they are depends on the agreement, and particularly the (1) number of tariff lines covered, (2) rapidity with which barriers are phased out, and (3) number of sensitive product exceptions. An FTA or CU that covers only such obligations is a "first generation" one. A "second generation" FTA covers a far broader subject matter, and sometimes is called a "deep FTA," because it involves deeper integration between or among the parties.

So, depending on the RTA, it may include services and electronic commerce (e-commerce) as well. Also present are process-type duties, notably transparency rules. The FTA likely creates new institutions, or adds to or modifies the responsibilities of existing institutions, and establishes one or more dispute settlement mechanisms. In addition, there will be Chapters on special sectors, like agriculture and IP, on special concerns, like environmental and labor rights. Trade remedies—special rules on AD, CVD, and safeguards cases—also are likely to appear in an RTA text.

Should coverage of broad and fundamental social matters also be expected? The answer depends on the FTA. The U.S. FTAs tend to eschew these topics. In contrast, all newer association agreements and RTAs of the EU contain language on sustainable development and human rights. That language may be in the geopolitical interests of the EU, but undoubtedly also embodies European social values.

The aforementioned issues might be grouped under the rubric of a "Check List." Below, issues on the List are discussed. No Check List is failsafe, however. Some RTAs cover topics not dealt with by WTO agreements. *NAFTA*, for example, has provisions (in Chapter 15) on trade and competition policy. That fact suggests that, as a compliment to the Check List, it is useful to consider whether obligations created by an RTA are "WTO Plus." That is, does the RTA go beyond what a WTO text covers or requires? To take an example, *NAFTA* Chapter 17, on IP, has a reciprocity rule on secondary broadcasting rights.[2] There is no analogous provision in the WTO *TRIPs Agreement*.

Legal aspects of RTAs is as rapidly evolving an area of international trade law as any other specialty in the field. Mastery of an FTA or CU comes from the intimate knowledge gained, in part, through perusal of the primary source text. Yet, a new RTA subsequently is signed, the features of which are not entirely taken from the

---

2. *See NAFTA* Article 1703.

template of previous deals. To illustrate the point, an attorney could not be satisfied with a sound knowledge of the IP rules of *NAFTA*. Within a decade of that deal, the U.S. negotiated FTAs with Singapore and Chile. These accords contain innovative methods for protecting digital IP rights. Evidently, RTA law is a stimulating area of practice and scholarship.

II. "Ambitious" Elimination of Trade Barriers?

• Four "Ambition" Variables

Perhaps the first and most obvious legal question about an FTA (or CU), other than the identity of the members and the effective date, is how ambitious the deal is. "Ambition" depends on four variables, summarized in Table 9-1, namely, the: (1) number of parties; (2) comprehensiveness (scope) of coverage; (3) timing of liberalization; and novelty of commitments.

Table 9-1. Gauging "Ambition" of FTA

Variable	Question	An FTA Is More "Ambitious" . . .
Parties?	How many Parties are in the FTA?	. . . the larger the number of Parties
Comprehensiveness?	For goods, how many tariff lines does the FTA cover? Conversely, how many sensitive product categories does the FTA exempt?	. . . the larger the number of tariff lines and the fewer the number of exemptions.
	For services, on how many sectors, sub-sectors, and sub-sub sectors, and how many Modes of service supply, are commitments made? Is a Positive or Negative List approach used for scheduling commitments?	. . . the larger the number of commitments, and the greater the number of Modes covered by those commitments. . . . if it uses a Negative List.
Timing?	How fast does the FTA bring down tariffs and NTBs? How quickly does the FTA eliminate barriers to services trade?	. . . if it provides for DFQF treatment immediately upon its entry into force for nearly 100% of goods.
Novelty?	Does the FTA cover "behind the border" barriers such as SPS and TBT measures, open up government procurement markets to foreign bidding, put disciplines on the commercial activities of SOEs and STEs, address antitrust matters, advance IPR protection, and harmonize regulations?	. . . if it covers non-obvious, difficult-to-root-out barriers to trade.

There is an implicit free trade bias here: "ambitious" is "positive" based on the Laws of Absolute and Comparative Advantage from Adam Smith and David Ricardo. The ideology is that the more and faster an FTA liberalizes trade, the better.

Consider a paradigm other than Classical and Neo-Classical Economics. What ideology would underlie that paradigm? What would the criteria for an "ambitious" trade deal be in that other paradigm?

- **Judgment Calls and "Market Access" Issues**

Rarely does an FTA admit to a clear "yes-or-no" answer on "ambition." Politicians often simplify matters. But, International Trade Lawyers know better than to evaluate the quality of trade liberalization commitments. The "devil is in the details," so the correct answer often is "yes-and-no."

For example, in August 2006, Chile signed an FTA with China. The match is literally natural: China needs copper and other natural resources to fuel its growth, and Chile is a major supplier of these resources. The *Chile-China FTA* frees 92% of Chile's exports to China from Chinese tariffs, eliminates Chilean tariffs on 50% of China's exports to Chile, and phases out over five-to-10 years certain other tariffs. Is this deal "comprehensive"?

The starting point to address the question is to think about market access. "Market access" has the same meaning in the context of trade liberalization negotiations at the multilateral, regional, and bilateral level. The term connotes the extent to which, and under what conditions, goods and services from one country may enter into the commercial stream of another country. While the negotiating dynamics differ among the three levels, the negotiating issues are similar.

The preeminent such issues, endemic in the provisions of any existing or potential FTA, are below. Essentially, these issues elaborate the Four "Ambition" variables. Depending on the answers, an FTA is more or less economically ambitious, that is, comprehensive, in terms of its breadth and depth of economic coverage, and its anticipation of hidden barriers to trade.

- **Tariff Barriers**

Scope?

To what extent does the FTA eliminate tariffs on trade among the member countries?

Speed?

How fast does the FTA eliminate tariffs, *i.e.*, what is the phase-out period?

Sensitivities?

If the FTA does not accord duty-free treatment to all goods, then how many exceptions from tariff elimination for so-called "sensitive" products does it contain? Despite the large number of FTAs around the world, only 16% of global merchandise trade (as of October 2011) is eligible for preferential treatment. That is partly because many agreements exclude sensitive sectors.

Phase Out Periods?

If the FTA does not provide duty-free treatment immediately to all products, then how fast are tariffs cut, and on how many products? Does the FTA establish a large number of "staging categories," into which goods are placed and on which barriers are reduced slowly over time?

E-Commerce?

Does the FTA extend (sooner or later) duty-free treatment to e-commerce, or is it restricted to traditional physical commerce?

Overall Benefits?

Does the FTA yield a significant margin of preference? The "margin of preferences" is the difference between the normal MFN tariff applied to a good from a non-FTA member, and the duty rate applied to a like product from a member. Most FTAs offer limited benefits. Hence, only 2% of global trade is eligible for a margin of preference equal to or in excess of 10%. That is because, first, in the post–Second World War era, through multilateral GATT rounds, MFN rates fell considerably. They average 4% (as of December 2009), and half of global trade receives duty-free treatment. Second, FTAs tend to avoid cutting tariff peaks on sensitive products. FTAs (as of October 2011) have failed to reduce 66% of tariff lines that have duty rates above 15%.

- NTBs

Scope?

To what extent does the FTA eliminate or reduce NTBs, such as quotas, import licenses, other QRs, customs procedures, and non-transparency in trade rules or administration? If many FTAs do not produce major tariff benefits, then their economic *raison d'être* must lie elsewhere, such as in the reduction of NTBs.

SPS and TBT Measures?

Does the FTA impose strict disciplines against the abuse of SPS and TBT measures for protectionist purposes?

Competition Policy?

Does the FTA consider how antitrust law may be used to promote competition, vis-à-vis abused against foreign companies to protect the market position of domestic firms?

Speed?

How fast does the FTA eliminate or reduce NTBs?

- Services

Scope?

Does the FTA reduce or eliminate barriers to all services trade, or does it cover only some service sectors and sub-sectors? For example, are service sector commitments made using a "Negative List" approach, whereby all sectors are presumed covered unless specifically protected by exemption, or a "Positive List" approach, which implies the reverse presumption, and is relatively less trade-liberalizing? With a Negative List, trade liberalization occurs in all service sectors (and government procurement), except for areas excluded by putting them on the list. The presumption is in favor of open markets, unless otherwise said. With a Positive List, trade liberalization occurs only in service sectors (and likewise for government procurement) specifically stated on the list. The presumption is against open markets, unless otherwise indicated.

Modes?

Will there be any restrictions in the four modes of service supply—Mode I (cross border trade), Mode II (consumption abroad), Mode III (establishment, *i.e.*, FDI), and Mode IV (temporary migration)? (These Modes are set out in *GATS.*) Embracing Modes I, II, III, and IV of supplying services across borders means that access through one Mode will not be offset by restrictions in another Mode. If so, then what restrictions will apply, and to what specific service sectors and sub-sectors?

• **Government Procurement**

Scope?

To what extent does the FTA open government procurement markets to cross-border goods and services? For example, does the FTA cover sub-central as well as central government entities? Does it cover quasi-governmental entities? Does the FTA use a Negative List approach or a Positive List approach?

Thresholds?

What monetary value must a prospective contract have for it to be subject to government procurement disciplines in the FTA?

• **Non-Discriminatory Treatment**

Coverage?

Does the FTA mandate that each party accord non-discriminatory treatment to all goods, services, and government procurement from all other member countries? Does it harmonize regulations on topics such as packaging and labeling of goods, food safety and the use of GMOs, auto safety and emissions, safety and soundness of financial institutions, and other matters that impede market access of foreign products?

Exceptions?

In what, if any, instances does the FTA permit a Party to discriminate in favor of its own businesses or industries? Does the FTA permit discrimination for its SOEs and STEs, or does the FTA obligate the Party to privatize those entities, or at least subject them to commercial disciplines when they operate in the market place?

III. Case Studies on Ambition: *Singapore* and *Chile FTAs*

The *U.S.-Singapore* and *U.S.-Chile FTAs*, both implemented on 1 January 2004, are examples of deals more comprehensive than even *NAFTA*. All three accords cover agricultural and industrial products, and services, insist on phased reductions in tariff and NTBs depending on the product category, and mandate considerable opening of many service sectors and sub-sectors. But, the *Chile FTA* eliminated immediately (as of the date of entry into force, 1 January 2004), tariffs on 85% of U.S. tariff lines. That is, it created truly free trade overnight on 85% of the product categories listed in the U.S. HTS. The extended liberalization period applied to agriculture and wine.

The *Singapore* and *Chile FTAs* contain preferential ROOs that are easier to administer—at least in their design—than the *NAFTA* origin rules. This generalization must be qualified with the remarks that rules on specific categories of merchandise may be complex, and *NAFTA* itself is a high benchmark for complexity. Nonetheless, unlike *NAFTA*, the *Singapore* and *Chile FTAs* contain obligations covering the following areas:

(1) E-commerce.

(2) Customs procedures.

(3) Services using a "Negative List" approach, whereas *NAFTA* employs a "Positive List" method, and all 4 "Modes" of supply. (These approaches and Modes are discussed in a separate Chapter.)

(4) Government procurement, using a "Negative List" approach, whereas *NAFTA* employs a "Positive List" method.

The *Chile FTA* also terminates Chile's status as a GSP beneficiary, which makes sense because the FTA effectively makes permanent duty-free treatment that would otherwise occur under the GSP. Each of the above obligations is significant.

Internet shoppers appreciate the burgeoning value and volume of e-commerce. Similarly, any shopper who has crossed an international boundary lawfully can appreciate the potential NTB posed by customs procedures, and is aided in advance of the border crossing by transparency in customs rules (*e.g.,* publication on the Internet, which the *Singapore FTA* mandates).

Notably, in May 2012, Chile announced it was joining Singapore and Hong Kong as one of the few jurisdictions that do not tax imports. Chile cut its general MFN tariff from 6% to 4% in 2013, 2% in 2014, and zero in 2015. Thanks to its FTAs with the U.S., China, EU, Japan, and Korea, the move to duty free status did not affect a large percentage of imports. Under those deals, most imports already entered Chile duty free.

IV. Case Study on Negotiating Objectives: *Australia FTA*

Australia FTA, which took effect on 1 January 2005, is a comprehensive bargain. Data pre-dating the deal (as of 2003) showed an FTA would help an already strong commercial relationship flourish. There was about $21 billion in 2-way goods trade between the U.S. and Australia, and $6.6 billion in their services trade, with Australia having a bilateral trade deficit. Roughly 11% of Australian exports went to the U.S., but less than 2% of U.S. exports were shipped to Australia. Bilateral FDI mattered to each country. American FDI in Australia approximated $141.5 billion (with U.S. affiliates located Down Under selling $65 billion), and Australian investment in the U.S. was $70.4 billion (with Aussie affiliates in the U.S. generating $56 billion in sales revenues).

So, negotiators sought a comprehensive deal. Save for sugar, they achieved that result, in part because of their similar open economy dispositions. For example, before the *FTA* took effect, their levels of goods protection were similar. The average applied Australian MFN tariff was 4.3%. Australia had an average bound rate of 10.5%, but unilaterally decided to drop this rate. The average U.S. MFN rate was 5.4%.

What were the key negotiating objectives on each side? Each country had sectors in which they had a keen export interest, or, a particular sensitivity. The American and Australian objectives concerning market access for goods and services included:

- **American Negotiating Objectives**

    (1) Agricultural Single Desks

    The "single desk" refers to a government body, *i.e.*, an SOE or STE, which has a monopoly on importation of the product in question, and from which domestic buyers must purchase the product. Australia operated single desks for barley, sugar, and wheat. With a keen export interest in these products—Kansas, for instance, typically is the largest wheat producing American state—the U.S. wanted Australia to end this import monopoly and allow its wheat farmers to sell directly to Australian buyers. Australia resisted reforms, recalling that after it had eliminated its single desk for wool imports, its domestic wool market collapsed.

    (2) Entertainment

    The U.S. urged Australia to eliminate its screen quotas, which apply to TV (in contrast to Korea's quotas, which apply to movies). The issue was not too contentious. Australian news and cultural programs easily fill up the quota time.

    (3) Government Procurement

    The U.S. hoped to pry open Australian government procurement markets.

    (4) Mode IV Services Supply

    The U.S. sought business visa facilitation, *i.e.*, eased requirements and procedures concerning business visas.

- **Australian Negotiating Objectives**

    (1) Light Trucks

    Australia sought elimination of the 25% MFN tariff imposed by the U.S. on light trucks, which could occur immediately through an FTA.

    (2) Beef

    Australia desired meaningful access to the U.S. market for exports of beef, dairy, and sugar. Whether the U.S. would treat these farm products alike was dubious. In FTA negotiations with Chile, the U.S. agreed to treat Chilean beef exports more favorably than Chilean dairy or sugar exports. In the *Chile FTA*, the U.S. agreed to liberalize its TRQs (and phase in tariffs in lieu of them) across five years on beef, but across 12 years for dairy and sugar.

    (3) Dairy Products

    Australia held only a small share of the U.S. dairy products market. Australia hoped to export high-value added products (such as cheese), rather than low value added products (such as milk powder). So, Australia believed its negotiating objectives were not averse to the U.S. dairy support program, but rather there was "trade complementarity."

    (4) Sugar

    Australia sought a quick end to American TRQs on sugar. Yet, whether Australia could benefit from free trade in sugar was unclear. Queensland produces sugar, but less efficiently than Brazilian competitors. Brazilian sugar exports might still fare well against Queensland products, even if the latter were not subject to a TRQ. The issue never came to fruition, as sugar was excluded in the *Australia FTA*. Aside from the exclusion in *NAFTA* of dairy products and eggs (in that Canada was permitted to maintain its Supply Management System (SMS) of import limits via TRQs, and production controls via licensing) and poultry (in that Canada kept its TRQs), sugar was the first time an American FTA entirely exempted a product from coverage. It was not the last, as in 2007 *KORUS* left out rice, a sensitive product for Korea.

Two points pertinent to any FTA negotiation emerge from these bargaining objectives.

First, where the Parties end up, *i.e.*, what kind of RTA they get, depends on what they seek. The more ambitious their aims, and the more hesitant they are to carve out protections, the broader and deeper their results. Second, how contentious negotiations become is not always predictable from initial stated positions. If one Party opposes protective measures that the other Party does not, in fact, administer strictly, then the Party maintaining those measures may not cling to them in the face of this opposition.

V. Sensitive Products and Sectors

- ## How Many Sensitivities, and Why?

Doha Round negotiations involved hard bargaining over the number of tariff lines in the HTS a WTO Member could designate as "sensitive" and, therefore, exempt the product category represented by that line from tariff cuts. Typically, FTA (or CU) negotiations also involve intricate, give-and-take on how many, and which, products each prospective Party can protect, what protective methods can be used, and for how long these methods are available. That is no surprise.

Every country has sensitivities, in respect of goods, services, and/or FDI. When countries negotiate, their sensitivities are not typically aligned, *i.e.*, the countries do not share the same sectors in which they are sensitive. What one country considers sensitive and seeks to block or impede imports is a sector to which another country seeks market access for its exports. Thus, a lot of trade negotiating time is spent on a small number of sensitive sectors, and the analysis of proposals for even modest liberalizations in those sectors entails cross-sectoral evaluation of all the give-and-take that has occurred.

The reasons for a sensitivity may vary, from sector to sector within a country, and across countries. In some instances, sheer economic and/or political muscle may explain the sensitivity. Sugar in the U.S. is an example. In other instances, a sector may be deemed sensitive because of national security concerns. For most countries, steel illustrates this rationale. In still other instances, culture (including historical tradition) may be the determinant. Beef in Japan and Korea are showcases. Some sectors are sensitive for multiple reasons, such as media and entertainment.

Several existing FTAs to which the U.S. is a Party provide illustrations of sensitive products and sectors. They are as follows, arranged chronologically according to the date of entry into force.

Of what legal moment is identification of a product or sector as "sensitive"? The mere designation results in placement of a sensitive product into a special, or "staging," category. That category is special, because products in it do not receive duty free treatment immediately upon the entry into force of the FTA. The key questions are the date when such products do receive duty-free treatment, and the formula for phasing out tariffs on those products.

The longer the phase out period, the more extended the period of protection. But, the impact of the tariff reduction methodology matters, too. Often, tariffs are phased out in equal annual installments. For instance, if the sensitive product is corn, the Mexican tariff is 30%, and *NAFTA* calls for a 15-year phase out, then the reduction methodology would be to cut two points off the tariff in each of the 15 years. At the end of the first year, the Mexican tariff would be 28%, and at the end of the 15th year, it would be zero. An accelerated schedule would call for bigger cuts up front, perhaps 20 percentage points cut in the first five years. In contrast, a back-ended methodology would be protectionist. It would permit the steepest cuts to occur toward the end of the phase-out period (*e.g.*, cutting 20 points from the 30% tariff in the last five years of the 15-year period).

VI. Case Studies on Sensitive Products: Agricultural Products and T&A

The best guess for designation of a sensitive product, and for establishment of a special remedy, is a primary or processed agricultural product. Virtually every FTA into which the U.S. has entered designates multiple such products, and includes some kind of special remedial provision. T&A are the next best guess.

• **30 August 1985** *Israel FTA*

When originally signed on 22 April 1985, this *FTA* did not cover either agriculture or services. A side agreement, signed on 4 November 1996, was added to cover agriculture. It lapsed in 2002, but then was extended twice, through 31 December 2002 and 31 December 2003. Renewal of the side agreement was negotiated, and signed on 27 July 2004, effective through 31 December 2008.

The *U.S.-Israel FTA* allows for emergency relief for perishable agricultural products. The provision is modeled after the *CBI*, and contained in Section 404 of the *Trade and Tariff Act of 1984*. A U.S. petitioner may file with the Secretary of Agriculture for relief against perishable imports from Israel. The criteria are that the product is being imported in such increased quantities as to be a substantial cause of serious injury, or threat thereof, to a U.S. industry. The Secretary of Agriculture has 14 days to render a determination and report to the President, who then has seven days to decide whether to take emergency action. That action could consist of re-imposition of the original (*i.e.*, pre-*FTA*) MFN rate on the product in question.

• **1 January 1994** *NAFTA*

While this accord is one of America's most comprehensive RTAs, *NAFTA* did not liberalize trade in all sectors with equal alacrity. Rather, goods were divided into three categories, and tariff and non-tariff barriers phased out immediately, or over five-, 10-, or 15-year periods. Trade in the most sensitive goods—in the "C+" category, noted in *NAFTA* Annex 302:2—was not freed up for 15 years after *NAFTA* entered into force. Specifically, duties on these goods were removed in 15 annual stages commencing on 1 January 1994, with duty free treatment effective 1 January 2008.

A, if not the, quintessential example, particularly for the U.S., is sugar. It is subject to special protections, in effect for 14 years after *NAFTA* entered into force. They are in Chapter 7, entitled Agriculture and Sanitary and Phytosanitary Measures, specifically Paragraphs 13–22 of Section A of Annex 703:2. Observe the obscurity of the placement of these protections, not to mention their complexity, which becomes apparent upon even a glance at them. Reputedly, there exist one or more side letters on sugar restrictions. Yet, they are difficult to obtain.[3]

Is protecting the sugar growing and harvesting industry (both cane and beet) in the U.S. through *NAFTA* and other FTAs, or by simply excluding it from coverage, as in the *Australia FTA*, a dubious policy? That policy is reinforced by agricultural legislation, such as the *2002 Farm Bill*, which:

(1) Continued a quota system on imported sugar limiting foreign sugar to 15% of the U.S. market share,

(2) Required the USDA to operate a loan program (whereby producers receive loans at minimum price levels) at no cost to the taxpayer,

(3) Set minimum domestic prices for sugar at prices substantially higher than the world market level, and

(4) Had marketing allotments for sugar produced domestically.

When the effects of protection on sugar-consuming product businesses are considered, the answer is "yes." These businesses are called "sugar-containing product (SCP) manufacturers," and the three most significant of them are chocolate and chocolate confectionary, non-chocolate confectionary, and breakfast cereal. In February 2006, the DOC published *Employment Changes in U.S. Food Manufacturing: The Impact of Sugar Pricing.*[4] This study points out:

(1) Over the last quarter century (1980–2005), the wholesale price of refined sugar in the U.S. has been two-to-three times higher than the world price. In 2004, the U.S. price was 23.5 cents per pound, but the world price was 10.9 cents per pound.

(2) Over 10,000 American jobs were lost in the SCP manufacturing sector between 1997–2002 because of the high cost of sugar.

(3) The job loss occurred through SCP manufacturers closing facilities in the U.S. and relocating their plants to Canada, where sugar prices average less than half of U.S. prices, or Mexico, where the prices average two-thirds of U.S. prices.

(4) In 1997, the SCP manufacturers employed 987,210 people, whereas 61,000 worked in growing and harvesting sugar cane and beet, hence the protectionist policy benefits a group less than 10% of the size of the group it injures.

---

3. As one *NAFTA* attorney put it to your Textbook author, "good luck if the Side Letters ever see the light of day."

4. *See* http://ita.doc.gov/media/Publications/pdf/sugar06.pdf; Rossella Brevetti, *Commerce Study Says 10,000 Jobs Lost Because of High U.S. Sugar Prices*, 23 International Trade Reporter (BNA) 266–267 (23 February 2006). *See also* Competitive Enterprise Institute, *Is the U.S. Sugar Problem Solvable?* (April 2006) (arguing sugar protection has a negative impact on the environment), www.cei.org/pdf/5263.pdf.

(5) For every job in the growing and harvesting sector the protectionist policy saves, it costs about three jobs in the confectionary producing area.

What was the counter-argument of sugar growers and harvesters, led by the American Sugar Alliance (ASA)?

First, the world market prices the Commerce Department examined were artificially depressed, because of sugar dumping by foreign countries, and excluded transportation and storage costs. Second, without support like the loan program, the industry would be in a sour position. Sugar producer prices have fallen 30% since 1996. Third, plants leave the U.S. because of high wages, taxes, rental, and health care costs. Concerned about the persuasiveness of their rebuttal, the ASA welcomed creation of a Sugar Caucus in the House of Representatives, dedicated to their protection.

From Mexico's perspective, two examples in the C+ category are beans and white corn. They are staples in the Mexican diet. Following *NAFTA*, Mexican bean and corn farmers lobbied their government not only for this delay, but also for help in competing with subsidized U.S. farm products. In March 2006, Mexico sought approval from the USTR to delay opening the Mexican market for these products. In June 2006, the USTR rejected Mexico's request, and also ruled out direct American assistance to small Mexican bean and corn farmers, whose output risked being displaced by U.S. products.

- **17 December 2001 *Jordan FTA***

The general origin rule in the *Jordan FTA* for T&A merchandise is yarn forward. This *FTA* is concerned with all T&A articles, but has notably restrictive special origin rules for certain products that effectively deny them preferential treatment. Wool scarves are an illustration, to which the yarn forward rule does not apply. Wool sweaters also appear to be a case in point. The abstruse prose used to cover these sweaters is in Paragraph 9(b)(iii) of the ROOs in Annex 2:2:

> ... except for goods classified under such headings as of cotton or of wool or consisting of fiber blends containing 16 percent or more by weight of cotton, if the fabric in the goods is dyed and printed, when such dyeing and printing is accompanied by 2 or more of the following finishing operations: bleaching, shrinking, fulling, napping, decating, permanent stiffening, weighting, permanent embossing, or moireing.

To what does this refer? The answer is articles within this description — such as wool sweaters — are not subject to the general yarn forward rule. Rather, these articles are entirely outside of the *Jordan FTA*, because this "except clause" takes them out of otherwise applicable rules that would confer origin on them. Hence, they are not accorded duty-free treatment. Put bluntly, they remain protected, and thus an example — albeit obscure, of how an FTA does not create true free trade in all goods.

- **1 January 2005 *Singapore FTA***

Is "protectionist" too strong a label to affix to T&A market access rules in the *Singapore FTA*? This merchandise receives duty-free treatment, but, only if it meets applicable preferential ROOs. Such treatment applied immediately, upon entry into force of the FTA. Of course, Singapore is neither a major T&A exporter, nor an important source of components for T&A articles. Not surprisingly, then, the FTA permits a limited amount of T&A to be admitted duty free each year, even if they contain third country (*i.e.*, non-U.S., non-Singaporean) yarns, fibers, or fabrics. In other words, given the nature of the Singaporean economy, a generous third-country T&A provision in the FTA almost was a necessity.

That said, the *FTA* contains tough monitoring and anti-circumvention rules. They include reporting requirements, licensing rules, and allowance for unscheduled factory checks. From an American perspective, they ensure only Singaporean T&A receive tariff preferences. The President authorized to exclude from entry any T&A merchandise from any enterprise in Singapore that does not permit a site visit requested by U.S. Customs officials, or that engages intentionally in circumvention. From a Singaporean vantage, these rules help minimize the instances in which the major port facility in Singapore, the PSA, is a conduit for illegal T&A trans-shipment.

- **1 January 2004 *Chile FTA***

This *FTA* includes agricultural products and wine, in which Chile has a significant export interest. However, this merchandise receives duty-free treatment not immediately, but over an extended period. As a southern hemispheric country, Chile supplies grapes, plums, and other produce to the U.S. and other countries in the northern hemisphere from roughly November to May. During the "out-of-season," farmers in these countries are not harvesting and selling their crop. Thus, Chilean farmers do not compete head-to-head with their U.S. counterparts. This complementary, counter-cycle suggests free trade "over night" in agricultural products ought to be easy to negotiate.

Not so, as the *Chile FTA* liberalizes agricultural trade with lags of eight and 12 years, depending on the product. Specifically, horticultural products obtained immediate duty free treatment. But, the *FTA* phases out tariffs on dairy and meat across eight years. For grain, livestock, processed products, and sugar, it phases out tariffs across 12 years. What factors explain these product-specific tariff deferments?

One point about American tariffs on Chilean farm products is the semi-transparency of the duty rates. Chapter 7 of the HTS covers unprocessed vegetables and fruit, while Chapter 20 of the HTS covers processed vegetables and fruit. Tariffs on such products ought to be listed in these Chapters, as they are—for example—for spinach (Chapter 7) and tomato paste (Chapter 20) imported from Canada and Mexico under *NAFTA*. However, for the *Chile FTA*, tariffs on many unprocessed and processed vegetables and fruit are in Chapter 99 of the HTS. Thus, for instance, the American tariff on Chilean tomato paste, listed in Chapter 99, is 11.6%. In contrast, it is duty-free for Mexican tomato paste. But, this contrast is hard to see without flipping through the HTS Chapters. The clue to connecting the Chapters is to read the footnotes within the duty schedule in Chapters 7 and 20. Observe that seasonally counter-cyclical farm products are listed (based on products) in the HTS, and tomato paste is not one of them. Who, then, might the 11.6% tariff protect? Might Mexican tomato paste producers be the answer, given that they are largest exporter of this product to the U.S. (as of 2005)? In turn, might it then be said that one FTA (*Chile FTA*) is used to protect third country interests under another FTA (*NAFTA*)?

As for T&A, they qualify for immediate duty-free treatment if they satisfy the applicable ROO. Like the Singapore FTA, the Chile FTA contains a third country source provision. A limited amount of T&A containing fiber, yarn, or fabric that is not from the U.S. or Chile may be admitted duty free.

- **1 January 2005 *Australia FTA***

Impressively from a free trade perspective, Australia agreed to wipe out duties on all U.S. agricultural exports immediately upon entry into force of the *Australia FTA*. Less impressively from that perspective, the U.S. agreed to phase out duties on Aussie agricultural imports over a four-to-18-year period. Still less impressively, each country preserved protections on a limited number of sensitive farm products.

The U.S. kept TRQs on beef, dairy products, and sugar. (The TRQs are preferential, implying higher in-quota thresholds, lower above-quota tariffs, or both.) Indeed, the *FTA* excludes sugar entirely. The American side gave its beef sector the most extended protection, a TRQ regime lasting 18 years. The quota grows by 18.5% over 18 years, and the tariff on over-quota shipments is phased out starting in the eighth year (2013) through the 18th year (2023). So, not until 2023 did Australian beef enter the U.S. on DFQF terms. Throughout, and thereafter, special safeguards apply to beef.

Australia maintained TRQs on cheese and tobacco. Special safeguards also apply to these products. Further examples of sensitive products, to which TRQs or special safeguards apply, are cotton, peanuts, and other horticultural products.

The Parties also restrict FDI and certain kinds of transactions. For example, the U.S. applies the *Jones Act* restrictions against foreign vessels engaging in cabotage (carriage of goods between U.S. ports). Because Australia makes "fast ferries," it is not pleased by this ban. For its part, Australia maintains restrictions on media ownership, and local content requirements for broadcasting—neither of which appeal to the U.S. entertainment industry. Because Australia is not a member of the WTO *GPA*, it refused to open its government procurement market to the U.S.

- **1 March 2006 *CAFTA-DR***

Not surprisingly, as with *NAFTA*, treatment of agricultural products—especially sugar—proved to be the most controversial market access issue in *CAFTA-DR* negotiations. The agricultural sector (as of May 2003) employs 30–40% of the Central American labor force, but about 1% of American workers. This sector accounts for about 17% of the GDP of Central America, but about 1%–2% of U.S. national income. There is a dualism in Central American agriculture. One part of the sector is traditional, highly protected, and domestically oriented. For it, *CAFTA-DR* was more of a threat than opportunity. The other part, comprised of major, internationally competitive farms, is modern. For it, *CAFTA-DR* was less of a threat and more of an opportunity. This kind of dualism also exists in U.S. agriculture. Sugar was the bitter battleground, with American producers lobbying ferociously to defeat the deal entirely.

In brief, *CAFTA-DR* regulates sugar imports into the U.S. by a TRQ system. During the first year of operation, it allows a maximum additional 107,000 metric tons of sugar. The figure rises to 151,000 tons over 15 years. The latter figure is just 1.2% of sugar consumption in the U.S. (as of 2006), and in 15 years is projected to be only 1.7%.

Not surprisingly, *CAFTA-DR* also regulates T&A imports into the U.S. It does so in part through the use of "Tariff Preference Levels," or "TPLs."[5] For example, the TPL for Nicaragua is 100 million square meters of apparel. This amount entered the U.S. duty free for the first five years during which *CAFTA-DR* is operative, even though the apparel could be made of yarn or fabric from third countries, *i.e.*, ones not members of *CAFTA-DR*. Up to 100 million meters of apparel made of Chinese fabric could qualify. However, after five years, this TPL was eliminated. Further, to get the benefit of the TPL, Nicaragua had to agree to purchase trouser fabric from the U.S. in an amount equal to its use of the TPL. Hypothetically, if Nicaragua used two million square meters of such fabric from India, then it had better purchase this amount from an American source, too.

The technique of regulating T&A imports through TPLs reflects a tug-of-war between foreign manufacturers and domestic producers of a like or directly competitive product. Manufacturers located in a *CAFTA-DR*, which may be American, Canadian, European, Chinese, or other non-*CAFTA-DR* firms operating in production facilities in Central American, seek the freedom to source inputs like yarn and fabric from the cheapest price, highest quality source. China and India are obvious candidates.

Conversely, domestic producers seek to limit duty-free treatment only to products containing components from *CAFTA-DR* members. They—and their industry association, the National Council of Textile Organizations—point out the *CAFTA-DR* region is the second largest market in the world for American-made yarns and fabrics. The NCTO also explains that whereas the content of clothing imported into the U.S. from Central American is about 70% "Made in the U.S.A.," for Chinese apparel it is just 1% U.S. content. Query, then, whether for the NCTO and its members, *CAFTA-DR* may not be so much about free trade in T&A, but fair trade— "fair" in the sense of protecting the input relationships with Central America.

---

5. *See* Christopher S. Rugaber, *Senate Approves Promised Textile Changes To CAFTA–DR as Part of Pension Legislation*, 23 International Trade Reporter (BNA) 1198 (10 August 2006).

VII. Case Study on Enhanced Market Access for Agricultural Goods and T&A: *NAFTA* 2.0

How can Parties to an FTA operating under a DFQF environment thanks to that already-fully implemented FTA liberalize trade further? This was addressed by the *NAFTA* Parties in their 2017–2018 renegotiation of rules affecting trade in primary and processed agricultural goods, T&A and (as discussed later) manufactured items. The Parties focused on behind-the-border barriers, that is, NTBs, SPS measures, that affect farmers, ranchers, and economic agents in special sectors, and promoted *TRIPs* Plus IP standards.

- **27 August 2018 U.S.-Mexico Bilateral FTA**

Office of the United States Trade Representative,

United States–Mexico Trade Fact Sheet: *Strengthening NAFTA for Agriculture* (28 August 2018)[6]

Key Achievement: Maintaining Zero Tariffs on Agricultural Products

Under a modernized agreement, tariffs on agricultural products traded between the United States and Mexico will remain at zero.

. . .

Key Achievements: Significant Commitments to Reduce Trade Distorting Policies, Improve Transparency, and Ensure Non-Discriminatory Treatment for Agricultural Product Standards

Building on *NAFTA*, the United States and Mexico agree to work together in other fora on agriculture matters, improve transparency and consultations on matters affecting trade between the two countries, and provide for non-discriminatory treatment in grading of agricultural products.

The United States and Mexico agreed to several provisions to reduce the use of trade distorting policies, including:

(1) To not use export subsidies or . . . WTO special agricultural safeguards [set out in the *Agreement on Agriculture*] for products exported to each other's market.

(2) Improved commitments to increase transparency and consultation regarding the use of export restrictions for food security purposes.

(3) If supporting producers, to consider using domestic support measures that have minimal or no trade distorting or production effects and ensure transparency of domestic support and supply management programs.

---

6. https://ustr.gov/about-us/policy-offices/press-office/press-releases/2018/august/strengthening-nafta-agriculture.

To facilitate the marketing of food and agricultural products, Mexico and the United States agree that grading standards and services will be non-discriminatory, including for grains and that grading will operate independently from domestic registration systems for grain and oilseed varietals. In addition, Mexico and the United States agreed to disciplines related to cheese compositional standards.

Key Achievement: Enhanced Rules for Science-Based Sanitary and Phytosanitary Measures

In the . . . SPS Chapter, the United States and Mexico have agreed to strengthen disciplines for science-based SPS measures, while ensuring Parties maintain their sovereign right to protect human, animal, and plant life or health. Provisions include increasing transparency on the development and implementation of SPS measures; advancing science-based decision making; improving processes for certification, regionalization and equivalency determinations; conducting systems-based audits; improving transparency for import checks; and working together to enhance compatibility of measures. The new agreement would establish a new mechanism for technical consultations to resolve issues between the Parties.

. . .

Office of the United States Trade Representative,

United States–Mexico Trade Fact Sheet: *Rebalancing NAFTA to Support Manufacturing* (28 August 2018)[7]

. . .

Textiles

The new provisions on textiles incentivize greater United States and Mexican production in textiles and apparel trade, strengthen customs enforcement, and facilitate broader consultation and cooperation among the Parties on issues related to textiles and apparel trade.

Key Achievement: Strengthening Supply Chains to Provide New Market Opportunities for the Textile and Apparel Sector

The provisions will:

(1) Promote greater use of Made-in-the-USA fibers, yarns, and fabrics by:

    (a) Limiting rules that allow for some use of non-*NAFTA* inputs in textile and apparel trade.

    (b) Requiring that sewing thread, pocketing fabric, narrow elastic bands, and coated fabric, when incorporated in apparel and other finished products, be made in the region for those finished products to qualify for trade benefits.

---

7. https://ustr.gov/about-us/policy-offices/press-office/press-releases/2018/august/rebalancing-nafta-support.

(2) Establish a Textiles Chapter for United States-Mexico trade, including textile-specific verification and customs cooperation provisions that provide new tools for strengthening customs enforcement and preventing fraud and circumvention in this important sector.

The new Textiles chapter provisions are stronger than those *in NAFTA* 1.0 with respect to both enforcement and incentivizing North American production of textiles.

- **Background on Canada's Class 7 Ultra-filtered Milk Category**

The complex UF milk dispute between Canada and the U.S. started in February 2017.[8] Until February 2017, Canada had six categories, or Classes of milk, with items in Class 1 being the most expensive products. Those six categories operate under the SMS, with price supports to ensure Canadian dairy farmers receive prices that are above both international and U.S. price levels. Under the National Ingredient Strategy, Canada authorizes Provincial Marketing Boards to set the price of at or below international levels. (Under Canada's Federalist system, agriculture is an area of responsibility shared by the Central government and Provincial governments. Each Province has a Marketing Board for each of the SMS sectors, including dairy. The Boards do not fix retail prices. Rather, the Boards set prices that producers, *i.e.*, farmers, are paid for their output, based on the demand for and end uses of that output. The CDC, a national organization, coordinates Federal and Provincial policy formulation and implementation, and identifies annually reference prices for "industrial" or "raw" milk that Provincial Boards use in setting prices for producers.)

In February 2017, Canada added a seventh category for certain dairy product ingredients, the lowest (cheapest) level. Ingredients in Class 7 are high-protein items such as edible and rennet casein, milk protein concentrates and isolates, skim milk, skim and whole milk powder, and UF milk. As to UF milk:

> Diafiltered milk, or ultrafiltered milk as the Americans call it, is milk that has been finely filtered through a membrane in order to target its protein content. It has a similar consistency to coconut milk and typically has a

---

8. *See New Canadian Dairy Pricing Regime Proves Disruptive for U.S. Milk Producers*, EVERYSRSREPORT.COM, 20 April 2017, www.everycrsreport.com/reports/IN10692.html; David Lawder, *U.S. Agriculture Chief Says NAFTA Deal Must End Canada's Milk Protein Scheme*, REUTERS, 9 September 2018, www.reuters.com/article/us-trade-nafta-dairy/u-s-agriculture-chief-says-nafta -deal-must-end-canadas-milk-protein-scheme-idUSKCN1LP0JQ; John Grieg, *The New World of Canadian Dairy Pricing*, FARMTARIO, 9 August 2018, https://farmtario.com/news/the-new-world -of-canadian-dairy-pricing/; Wyatt Bechtel, *Dairy Report: Canada's Class 7 Pricing a Focus of U.S. Policy Makers*, DAIRY HERD MANAGEMENT, 9 May 2018, www.dairyherd.com/article/dairy -report-canadas-class-7-pricing-focus-us-policy-makers; Rod Nickel, *U.S. Asks Canada to End "Underhanded" Dairy Pricing Class*, REUTERS, 5 June 2017, https://ca.reuters.com/article/topNews /idCAKBN18W2L0-OCATP; Kelsey Johnson, *Dairy 101: The Canada–U.S. Milk Spat Explained*, IPOLITICS, 22 April 2017, https://ipolitics.ca/2017/04/22/dairy-101-the-canada-u-s-milk-spat -explained/.

very high protein content (greater than 40 per cent). When raw milk is processed for butterfat (necessary for making butter) it is separated into two parts: butterfat and what's called "non-fat solids," commonly referred to as milk ingredients. Diafiltered milk is non-fat solids that have been processed one step further.[9]

Interestingly, it was American producers that invented UF milk.

The fact the Class 7 UF milk price in Canada is cheaper than the international or U.S. price for UF milk creates an incentive for Canadian dairy product companies to source UF milk from Canadian, not American, dairy farmers. The U.S. argues Canada—specifically, the CDC—is not transparent in explaining the factors used to price Class 7 milk, making it difficult for the U.S. to assess whether Canada violates GATT-WTO or *NAFTA* 1.0 rules. Canada argues no trade agreements are implicated, because Category 7 pricing pertains only to domestic items, not imports. That is, says Canada, the Class 7 pricing program is an agreement among Canadian dairy producers (*i.e.*, farmers) and processers (*e.g.*, Saputo, Inc. and Parmalat Canada), not in the U.S. or any other country. Canadian processers remain free to choose their suppliers, whether Canadian or American, for UF milk and other Class 7 items; Class 7 is not an import restriction. And, about 29% of the price Canadian farmers receive is based on world market prices (*i.e.*, pricing is not entirely fixed by the CDC).

The transparency concern aside, the core of the dispute concerns pricing. UF milk is a high-protein liquid used to produce cheese, yoghurt, and other products sought by consumers for their protein content, *i.e.*, UF milk and other Class 7 items are ingredients to boost the protein in those products, and they produce high yields with less waste than alternatives. UF milk itself is made from separating and concentrating certain milk proteins (as intimated above). Given the increased interest in high-protein dairy items, the demand for UF milk has risen. That contrasts with the decline in demand for regular milk, thanks to competition from almond, cashew, and soya milk, and to over-production in both Canada and the U.S. Over-production is due in part to the increased demand for butter, and thus butterfat, which comes from milk. Canada raised its production quotas—by over 20% in 2015–2017—to allow for more milk, and thereby more butterfat needed to produce butter and meet the increased demand, thanks to popularity, for butter. The result was surplus production of skim milk and skim milk powder, *i.e.*, non-fat solids. In 2016, Canada created a Class 6 category for certain dairy ingredients to allow them to be sold at lower international prices, rather than higher SMS prices. In 2018, to address the oversupply, Canada trimmed the output quotas, by 1.5% in Ontario, and 3.5% in the other Provinces. Indeed, Canada argues the SMS is designed to adjust supply and demand levels, and cope with uncertainties created by price volatility, *i.e.*, to stabilize prices.

---

9. *Dairy 101.*

The Class 7 policy is essentially similar to that of Class 6, namely, it allows for lower-than-SMS prices so as to adjust for the excess of supply over demand. When in 2008 Canada revised its standards for the composition of dairy products, it reduced the requisite content of various milk products that American dairy processors had been supplying to Canadian food companies, thus allowing for increased use of UF milk. American suppliers thus boosted shipments to Canada of UF milk.

The CBSA took the position that UF milk is not subject to SMS TRQs, because it and other Class 7 items are a protein ingredient, not a milk or other dairy product. That customs classification decision meant UF milk did not receive the support pricing, through the application by CBSA at the border of SMS quotas and tariffs to American-originating UF milk, which otherwise would have assured UF milk price levels in Canada above world market or U.S. prices. Moreover, because UF milk was invented after *NAFTA* 1.0 entered into force on 1 January 1994, Canada could not impose TRQs on them, as such trade barriers were eliminated by the FTA. So, low-priced American shipments of UF milk and milk protein isolates to Canada increased substantially after 2008, and especially in 2016, with Canada being the largest UF milk market for American suppliers in the world in 2016. The "American dairy industry has had complete and unfettered access to the Canadian market place for diafiltered milk for several years." *Dairy 101*. Hence, Canada introduced Class 7 in February 2017.

American UF milk producer-exporters (for example, from Minnesota, New York, Pennsylvania, and Wisconsin) viewed Class 7 categorization, in which UF milk falls, as a way to discourage Canadian companies from importing their UF milk. That was because the price of Class 7 items, like UF milk, was set at below international and U.S. levels. In other words, the price differential between Canadian-produced Class 7 items (lower) and American-produced ones (higher) creates an incentive for Canadian processors to substitute American imports for domestically-made ingredients. Indeed:

> Led by a strong push from Ontario, the Canadian dairy sector responded in 2016 to rising imports of milk protein isolates, dried milk powders high in protein that could be imported free of tariffs, by creating Class 7, a special class of milk that was priced competitively with imported protein isolates.

> The result has been hundreds of millions of dollars of investment in dairy processing across the country as processors here committed to replacing imported ingredients with Canadian-sourced milk.[10]

Ironically, UF milk is not used by American dairy processors, so American UF milk farmers had no readily available home market to substitute for the decline in their shipments to Canada. Still, despite the Class 7 scheme, the U.S. is the top source of dairy imports into Canada, and has enjoyed dairy trade surpluses with Canada.

---

10. *The New World*.

American suppliers also feared the Class 7 pricing program facilitated dumping in the U.S. or world markets of milk proteins and skim milk from Canada (because it encouraged overproduction of milk that Canada protected with quotas and support pricing). Canada pointed out that American dairy producers benefit from a variety of price support measures, which incentivize overproduction and facilitate dumping.

• **30 September 2018 Trilateral *NAFTA* 2.0 (*USMCA*)**

Office of the United States Trade Representative,

United States–Mexico–Canada Trade Fact Sheet: *Strengthening North American Trade in Agriculture* (1 October 2018)[11]

Key Achievement: Expanded Market Access for American Food and Agricultural Products

America's dairy farmers will have new export opportunities to sell dairy products into Canada. Canada will provide new access for United States products including fluid milk, cream, butter, skim milk powder, cheese, and other dairy products. It will also eliminate its tariffs on whey and margarine. For poultry, Canada will provide new access for United States chicken and eggs and increase its access for turkey. Under a modernized agreement, all other tariffs on agricultural products traded between the United States and Mexico will remain at zero.

Key Achievement: Canada's Milk Classes 6 and 7 to Be Eliminated

The top priority for America's dairy industry in this negotiation has been for Canada to eliminate its program that allows low priced dairy ingredients to undersell United States dairy sales in Canada and in third country markets. As a result of the negotiation, Canada will eliminate what is known as its milk classes 6 and 7. In addition, Canada will apply export charges to its exports of skim milk powder, milk protein concentrates and infant formula at volumes over agreed threshold, which will allow United States producers to expand sales overseas.

. . .

Key Achievements: Significant Commitments to Reduce Trade Distorting Policies, Improve Transparency, and Ensure Non-Discriminatory Treatment for Agricultural Product Standards

Building on *NAFTA*, the United States, Mexico, and Canada agreed to work together in other fora on agriculture matters, improve transparency and consultations on matters affecting trade among the countries.

The United States, Mexico, and Canada agreed to several provisions to reduce the use of trade distorting policies, including:

(1) To not use export subsidies or World Trade Organization (WTO) special agricultural safeguards for products exported to each other's market.

---

11. https://ustr.gov/about-us/policy-offices/press-office/fact-sheets/2018/october/united -states-mexico-canada-trade-fa-2.

(2) Improved commitments to increase transparency and consultation regarding the use of export restrictions for food security purposes.

(3) If supporting producers, to consider using domestic support measures that have minimal or no trade distorting or production effects and ensure transparency of domestic support and supply management programs.

Canada and the United States also agreed to strong rules to ensure tariff-rate quotas are administered fairly and transparently to ensure the ability of traders to fully use them.

Key Achievement: Fair Treatment for Quality Requirements for Wheat and Other Agricultural Products

Canada has agreed to grade imports of United States wheat in a manner no less favorable than it accords Canadian wheat, and to not require a country of origin statement on its quality grade or inspection certificate. Canada and the United States also agreed to discuss issues related to seed regulatory systems.

To facilitate the marketing of food and agricultural products, Mexico and the United States agreed that grading standards and services will be non-discriminatory for all agricultural goods and will establish a dialogue to discuss grading and quality trade related matters.

Key Achievement: Enhanced Rules for Science-Based Sanitary and Phytosanitary Measures

In the Sanitary and Phytosanitary (SPS) Measures chapter, the United States, Mexico, and Canada have agreed to strengthen disciplines for science-based SPS measures, while ensuring Parties maintain their sovereign right to protect human, animal, and plant life or health. Provisions include increasing transparency on the development and implementation of SPS measures; advancing science-based decision making; improving processes for certification, regionalization and equivalency determinations; conducting systems-based audits; improving transparency for import checks; and working together to enhance compatibility of measures. The new agreement would establish a new mechanism for technical consultations to resolve issues between the Parties.

Office of the United States Trade Representative,

United States–Mexico–Canada Trade Fact Sheet: *Agriculture: Market Access and Dairy Outcomes of the USMC Agreement* (1 October 2018)[12]

. . .

Canada and Mexico are our first and third largest exports markets for United States food and agricultural products, making up 28 percent of total food and agricultural exports in 2017. These exports support more than 325,000 American jobs.

---

12. https://ustr.gov/about-us/policy-offices/press-office/fact-sheets/2018/october/united-states-mexico-canada-trade-fact

All food and agricultural products that have zero tariffs under the *North American Free Trade Agreement* (*NAFTA*) will remain at zero tariffs. Since the original *NAFTA* did not eliminate all tariffs on agricultural trade between the United States and Canada, the USMCA will create new market access opportunities for United States exports to Canada of dairy, poultry, and eggs, and in exchange the United States will provide new access to Canada for dairy, peanuts, processed peanut products, and a limited amount of sugar and sugar containing products.

Key Achievement: Increasing Dairy Market Access

In addition to the current exports of dairy products that the United States makes to Canada of $619 million in 2017, Canada will provide new tariff rate quotas exclusively for the United States. The agreement includes market access gains for the following American products:

Fluid Milk:

50,000 metric tons (MT) by year six of the agreement, growing one percent for an additional 13 years. Eighty-five percent of the quota will be reserved for further processing.

Cheese:

12,500 MT by year six of the agreement, growing one percent for an additional 13 years. Fifty percent of that amount will be available for any kind of cheese, while the remainder will be for industrial cheeses.

Cream:

10,500 MT by year six of the agreement, growing one percent for an additional 13 years. Eighty-five percent of the volume in year one will be reserved for further processing.

Skim Milk Powder:

7,500 MT by year six of the agreement, growing one percent for an additional 13 years.

Butter and Cream Powder:

4,500 MT by year six of the agreement, growing one percent for an additional 13 years. Eighty-five percent of the volume in year one will be reserved for further processing, which will be reduced to 50 percent by year five.

Concentrated and Condensed Milk:

1,380 MT by year six of the agreement, growing one percent for an additional 13 years.

Yogurt and Buttermilk:

4,135 MT by year six of the agreement, growing one percent for an additional 13 years.

Powdered Buttermilk:

520 MT by year six of the agreement, growing one percent for an additional 13 years.

Products of Natural Milk Constituents:

2,760 MT by year six of the agreement, growing one percent for an additional 13 years.

Ice Cream and Ice Cream Mixes:

690 MT by year six of the agreement, growing one percent for an additional 13 years.

Other Dairy:

690 MT by year six of the agreement, growing one percent for an additional 13 years.

Whey:

4,134 MT by year six of the agreement, growing one percent for an additional 4 years. Whey will have its over quota tariff eliminated in 10 years.

Margarine:

Tariff elimination in five years. The margarine rule of origin for use in trade between the United States and Canada will allow the use of non-originating palm oil in the manufacture of margarine.

The United States will provide reciprocal access on a ton-for-ton basis for imports of Canada dairy products through first-come, first-served tariff rate quotas.

Key Achievement: Canada's Milk Class Pricing System

Six months after entry into force of the USMCA, Canada will eliminate milk price classes 6 and 7. Canada will ensure that the price for skim milk solids used to produce nonfat dry milk, milk protein concentrates, and infant formula will be set no lower than a level based on the United States price for nonfat dry milk. Canada has also committed to adopt measures designed to limit the impact of any surplus skim milk production on external markets. These measures include resumption of its program to use skim milk domestically as animal feed and a new commitment to cap its exports of skim milk powder, milk protein concentrates, and infant formula. For skim milk powder and milk protein concentrates, the aggregate export cap will be 55,000 MT in the first year after the agreement enters into force, falling to 35,000 MT in the second year. Exports that exceed this threshold will face an export surcharge of C$0.54 per kilogram. For infant formula, the export cap will be 13,333 MT in the first year, increasing to 40,000 MT in the second and subsequent years. Exports that exceed this threshold will face a surcharge of C$4.25 per kilogram. Both caps will be increased by 1.2 percent a year, an amount equivalent to Canada's historical population growth. To assist with monitoring implementation of this new program, Canada has agreed to discuss any matter related to this mechanism upon request of the United States, and both countries will review the agreement five years after entry into force and every two years thereafter.

Key Achievement: Expanding Poultry and Eggs Market Access

In addition to the $600 million worth of poultry and egg products that the United States exported to Canada in 2017, Canada will provide new tariff rate quotas for the United States as follows:

Chicken:

57,000 MT by year 6 of the agreement, growing one percent for an additional 10 years. The United States will still be eligible to export up to 39,844 MT under Canada's World Trade Organization (WTO) tariff rate quota regime.

Egg and Egg Products:

Ten million dozen eggs and egg-equivalent products in year one of the agreement, growing one percent for an additional 10 years. Canada has agreed to allow 30 percent of import licenses for shell egg imports to be granted to new entrants as well. As with chicken, the United States will still be eligible to export up to 21.37 million dozen egg and egg-equivalent products under Canada's WTO tariff rate quota regime.

Turkey:

Canada has agreed to provide the United States and other country members of the World Trade Organization access equivalent to no less than 3.5 percent of the previous year's total Canadian turkey production. This will allow the United States to export additionally up to 1,000 MT of turkey products each year for the next 10 years than the current access and potentially more thereafter.

Broiler Hatching Eggs:

The United States continues to maintain current access as agreed to under [the 1989] *Canada-US Free Trade Agreement (CUSFTA)* of 21.1 percent of Canada's domestic production.

Office of the United States Trade Representative,

United States–Mexico–Canada Fact Sheet: *Rebalancing Trade to Support Manufacturing* (1 October 2018)[13]

Textiles

The new provisions on textiles incentivize greater North American production in textiles and apparel trade, strengthen customs enforcement, and facilitate broader consultation and cooperation among the Parties on issues related to textiles and apparel trade.

Key Achievement: Strengthening Supply Chains to Provide New Market Opportunities for the Textile and Apparel Sector

The provisions will:

(1) Promote greater use of Made-in-the-USA fibers, yarns, and fabrics by:

— Limiting rules that allow for some use of non-*NAFTA* inputs in textile and apparel trade.

---

13. https://ustr.gov/about-us/policy-offices/press-office/fact-sheets/2018/october/united-states-mexico-canada-trade-fa-0.

— Requiring that sewing thread, pocketing fabric, narrow elastic bands, and coated fabric, when incorporated in most apparel and other finished products, be made in the region for those finished products to qualify for trade benefits.

(2) Establish a Textiles Chapter for North American trade, including textile-specific verification and customs cooperation provisions that provide new tools for strengthening customs enforcement and preventing fraud and circumvention in this important sector.

The new Textiles Chapter provisions are stronger than those in *NAFTA* 1.0 with respect to both enforcement and incentivizing North American production of textiles.

• **Lingering Concerns**

Query whether it is reasonable to call the maintenance of DFQF treatment for farm products, from *NAFTA* 1.0 into *NAFTA* 2.0, a "key achievement." Likewise, it is reasonable to brand as a "key achievement" a commitment not to provide agricultural export subsidies, when all WTO Members made that pledge in the December 2015 Nairobi Ministerial Conference *Decision*? Conversely, in respect of promises of the Canadian government to compensate dairy farmers for concessions made to the U.S., would the assistance they receive be sufficient?

VIII. Sensitivities and Bilateral and Special Safeguards

Beyond separate (or non-existent) phase-out periods for trade barriers on "sensitive" products and sectors, the possibility of a special remedy is a second legal ramification of the label "sensitive." An FTA may establish a remedy for action against imports of sensitive products. But, this protective possibility is not necessarily limited to sensitive products. It could apply just to designated products, or to any imported article.

The special action is legally distinct from an AD, CVD, or general safeguard remedy, and it is one of the surest challenges to market access, and strongest tools for managing trade. Conceptually, and sometimes by title, safeguard provisions in FTAs are dubbed "bilateral safeguards" or "emergency action," if they apply to all product types, or "special safeguards" or "product-specific safeguards," if they apply only to designated types. Whatever the label, the remedy allows an importing country that is an FTA member to put back—or snap back—the pre-FTA MFN tariff on a sensitive product, or to suspend any further scheduled tariff reductions on the product.

For any FTA safeguard, the key question concerns the legal criteria for imposing relief. Under what conditions may one FTA partner "hit" a category of imports from another partner? The first option is to use trigger price and trigger volume criteria fixed by an arithmetic formula. The second, and possibly more frequently used option, is to articulate elastic textual criteria modeled after global safeguard relief pursuant to GATT Article XIX and the WTO *Agreement on Safeguards*.

As a general pattern, the first option is used for special agricultural safeguards. The second option is used for bilateral safeguards, and T&A safeguards. For example, Article 4:1 of *KORUS* creates a special safeguard to T&A products. Under this provision, an American T&A producer can seek safeguard relief against Korean T&A merchandise that is being imported into the U.S. in quantities that could damage the American industry producing a like or directly competitive article. However, this pattern is not invariant. The *CAFTA-DR* T&A safeguard is based on a trigger threshold (which for the first time, in July 2006, the U.S. threatened to use against Honduran socks). What explains this pattern and deviations?

Thus, for example, the *Jordan FTA* permits the U.S. to impose a bilateral safeguard under criteria akin to the global safeguard remedy in the GATT-WTO regime. The ITC must decide whether, as a result of the reduction or elimination of a duty, a Jordanian article is being imported into the U.S. in such increased quantities, and under such conditions, that the imports alone are a substantial cause of serious injury or threat thereof to a domestic industry producing an article that is like or directly competitive with the Jordanian import. Upon an affirmative ITC determination, the President must provide necessary import relief. The relief could include suspension of any further duty reduction, or an increase in the rate of duty.

The *Chile FTA* has a special safeguard provision, designed for certain agricultural products, known as "agricultural safeguard goods." It calls for automatic assessment of a duty on such a good if the unit import price of that good upon entry to the U.S. is less than the trigger price for that good set out in the FTA. The *Australia FTA* has an elaborate special agricultural safeguard remedy, which is contained in Article 3:4 and Annex 3-A. Article 3:4 authorizes the U.S. to impose a safeguard, namely, an additional duty, on Australian agricultural imports listed in Annex 3-A. There are three categories of potentially targeted goods:

(1) Horticulture Safeguard:

   For certain horticultural goods.

(2) Quantity-Based Beef Safeguard:

   For certain beef imports imported into the U.S. above specified quantities between 1 January 2013 and 31 December 2022.

(3) Price-Based Beef Safeguard:

   For the same categories of beef as the Quantity-Based remedy, but applicable to beef imported into the U.S. after 31 December 2022, above a specified quantity, if the monthly average index price in the U.S. falls below a specified trigger price.

Note the legal criteria for the beef safeguard are trigger volume and trigger price, not GATT-WTO type language. The remedy under any special safeguard is an additional duty. But, the sum of that additional duty and the applied rate in the U.S. Tariff Schedule may not exceed the lesser of the MFN rate imposed by the U.S. when the Australia *FTA* entered into force. In other words, the tariff cannot snap back to a level higher than what existed when the two countries commenced "free" trade on 1 January 2005.

Redolent of the *Australia FTA*, the *Morocco FTA* has a price-based safeguard for some horticultural products. Under Article 3:5 and Annex 3-A of the *Morocco FTA*, the U.S. can impose an agricultural safeguard, namely, an additional duty, on certain Moroccan horticultural goods. The U.S. Schedule to Annex 3-A of the *FTA* lists these goods. The *Singapore, Chile, Australia,* and *Morocco FTAs* also have a T&A safeguard.[14] So, too, does *CAFTA-DR.* In the U.S., CITA has authority over these special safeguards.

An interested party may ask the President to determine whether, because of duty elimination under the relevant FTA, a Singaporean, Chilean, Australian, Moroccan, or *CAFTA-DR* T&A article, is being imported into the U.S. in such increased quantities and under such conditions as to cause serious damage, or actual threat thereof, to a domestic industry. The *Singapore FTA* requires causation to be substantial. Evidence CITA requires to show injury includes data on imports, market share, and production. The increase in imports may be absolute, or relative to the domestic market for that article. The domestic industry must produce a product that is either like, or directly competitive with, the imported article. The second possibility broadens considerably the range of potentially interested parties. The petitioner—an "interested party"—could be any entity, whether a firm, certified union, group of workers, or trade association, which represents a domestic producer of a like or directly competitive article, or which represents a domestic producer of a component used in the production of a like or directly competitive article. This second possibility—to include upstream, or input, producers—further broadens the range. CITA also may self-initiate a petition.

The relief under the *Singapore* and *Chile FTAs* is to suspend duty reduction on T&A merchandise (if the tariff is not already zero), or re-impose the MFN rate for the article at the time relief is granted. Under the *Australia* and *Morocco FTAs,* the relief appears different: suspension of any remaining duty reduction, or imposition of the lesser of the MFN rate (1) extant at the time of the remedy or (2) rate when the *FTA* entered into force. That also is the rule under Article 3:23 of *CAFTA-DR.* What explains the distinction from the *Singapore* and *Chile FTAs,* and is it a material difference?

If an FTA creates a safeguard—be it bilateral (*i.e.,* general, as most FTAs do) or special (as is common in FTAs for agricultural goods, T&A)—then how does

---

14. *See* §322(a) of the *United States-Singapore Free Trade Implementation Act,* §322(a) of the *United States-Chile Free Trade Implementation Act,* and §322(a) of the *United States-Australia Free Trade Implementation Act,* §322(a) of the *United States-Morocco Free Trade Implementation Act.*

that remedy relate to global safeguard actions under GATT-WTO law? Theoretically, multilateral rules ought to be pre-eminent, and perhaps even pre-empt any regional action. That is not the position U.S. FTAs take. They allow exemption from a global safeguard for imports from an FTA Party, if the ITC determines those imports are not the substantial cause of serious injury or threat to a U.S. industry. This exemption is a kind of rule against double jeopardy that ensures the U.S. does not impose both a global and FTA safeguard against the same merchandise from the same country.

Suppose the U.S. imposes safeguard relief under GATT Article XIX, the WTO *Safeguards Agreement*, and Section 201 of the *Trade Act of 1974*, as amended, to protect certain phosphate products. The *Jordan FTA* requires the ITC to consider whether phosphate articles of Jordanian origin are responsible for damage to American producers of a like or directly competitive product. Following a negative ITC determination, the President may exclude the Jordanian merchandise from the global safeguard action. Consider the interaction of the global and regional safeguard provisions. Does the "no double jeopardy" protection found in FTAs violate GATT-WTO Rules?

Similarly, the *Singapore, Chile, Australia*, and *Morocco FTAs* contain a bilateral safeguard. The rules authorize the President, after an investigation and affirmative determination by the ITC, to impose import relief. The legal criteria to provide relief track GATT Article XIX and the WTO *Safeguards Agreement*. It must be the case that a Singaporean, Chilean, Australian, or Moroccan product is imported into the U.S. in such increased quantities, and under such conditions, as to be the substantial cause of serious injury, or threat thereof, to the domestic industry.[15] If these criteria are satisfied, then the ITC renders an affirmative determination and recommends to the President relief necessary to remedy or prevent serious injury, and facilitate the efforts of the petitioning domestic industry to make a positive adjustment to competition posed by the target foreign good. The relief is to increase the applicable duty to the lesser of the existing MFN rate, or the MFN rate imposed when the relevant *FTA* entered into force, or to suspend duty reductions if they have not yet been fully implemented.

Significantly, FTAs contain grounds for exempting merchandise from a safeguard action. The question is whether the grounds are pre- or post-investigation. Pre-investigation exemption means an imported article is not subject to investigation — in effect, a "no double jeopardy" rule. Generally, under the *Chile, Singapore*, and *Australia FTAs*, any article already subject to import relief under a global (*i.e.*, GATT-WTO) safeguard, or under the bilateral safeguard created by the *FTA*, is immune from a special safeguard investigation under the *FTA*. Further, any article subject to

---

15. *See* §§ 311–316 of the *United States-Singapore Free Trade Agreement Implementation Act*, Sections 311–316 of the *United States-Chile Free Trade Agreement Implementation Act*, §§ 311–316 of the *United States–Australia Free Trade Agreement Implementation Act*, §§ 311–316 of the *United States–Morocco Free Trade Agreement Implementation Act*.

a bilateral safeguard once is exempt from another investigation, meaning relief cannot be provided twice in respect of the same article. The exemption also covers T&A merchandise targeted for relief under the special safeguard provisions in the *FTA*, or an agricultural product subject to special safeguard relief under Article 5 of the WTO *Agreement on Agriculture.*

As for post-investigation exemptions, FTAs typically provide for Presidential discretion in remedy decisions. First, under the *Singapore, Chile,* and *Australia FTAs,* the President need provide import relief only to the extent he determines necessary to remedy or prevent injury and facilitate positive adjustment by the relevant domestic industry. Accordingly, the President could depart from an ITC recommendation, in particular, by imposing a less potent remedy than urged by the ITC.

Second, FTA general and special safeguards contain outright waiver authority. Under the *Jordan FTA,* the President can waive the otherwise mandatory imposition of a bilateral safeguard if it is not in the U.S. national interest to block imports, or if extraordinary circumstances exist and providing relief would cause serious harm to U.S. national security. The paragon context for waiver is if the imported product is in short supply in the U.S. and needed for defense purposes. The *Singapore, Chile, Australia,* and *Morocco FTAs* authorize the President not to provide bilateral safeguard relief, even if the legal criteria for it are satisfied, if relief would not provide greater economic or social benefits than costs. This standard gives the President considerable discretion, and affords plenty of room for political factors to enter into the calculus. The *Australia FTA* permits the USTR to waive application of the quantity- or price-based beef safeguard if extraordinary market conditions indicate a waiver would be in the American national interest. Exercise of this waiver requires prior notice and consultation with the House Ways & Means and Senate Finance Committees, and private sector advisory bodies.

FTAs also are likely to place a cap on the period of safeguard relief. For the bilateral and T&A safeguard, the *Chile FTA* limits relief to three years. A three-year limit exists for the bilateral and T&A safeguard under the *Morocco FTA.* However, the relief period may be extended, up to an aggregate maximum duration of five years. The *CAFTA-DR* limit is a maximum of three years. But, if the initial relief period is less than three years, then CITA may extend it to three years if needed to (1) remedy or prevent serious injury, or actual threat of serious injury, and (2) facilitate adjustment to import competition by the domestic industry. The industry must show it is making positive adjustment. Under the *Singapore* and *Australia FTAs,* relief under the bilateral or T&A safeguard may not exceed two years. But, this period may be extended once under certain circumstances, yielding a maximum aggregate relief period of four years. The *Australia* and *Morocco FTAs* specify that any bilateral safeguard relief lasting longer than one year must be subject to progressive liberalization over the course of its application.

Query why a limit of three years (or less) is common in safeguards? Might the reason relate to Article 8:3 of the *WTO Agreement on Safeguards?* This provision defers for three years the right of one WTO Member to suspend substantially equivalent concessions granted to another Member, where the latter has adopted a safeguard measure based on an absolute increase in imports from the former Member. In other words, does a three-year cap on safeguard relief under an FTA help ensure a "Three Year Pass" (discussed in a separate Chapter) under the WTO *DSU*?

Three further notable features of special safeguards in U.S. FTAs are critical circumstances, compensation arrangements, and sunset dates. First, the *Singapore* and *Chile FTAs* allow for provisional relief and critical circumstances in respect of bilateral safeguards. What are they and how do they work? Does the bilateral safeguard in the *Australia FTA* have an analogous provision? The T&A safeguard in the *Australia FTA* permits provisional relief for up to 200 days in the event clear evidence is adduced to show critical circumstances exist. What circumstances might be "critical"? Do T&A safeguards in the other accords have this provision?

Second, FTAs tend to authorize the President to compensate an FTA party against which the U.S. takes a safeguard action. Both the bilateral and T&A safeguards of the *Singapore* and *Chile FTAs* contain this authority. Similarly, Article 9:4 of the *Australia FTA* and Article 8:5 of the *Morocco FTA* call for compensation to a target country for a safeguard imposed against one of its exports. Article 2:23:6 of *CAFTA-DR* requires "mutually agreed trade liberalizing compensation" to a target country, *i.e.*, the country whose T&A article is subject to a safeguard.

The compensation takes the form of concessions by the country imposing the safeguard that have substantially equivalent trade effects, or are equivalent in value, to the additional customs duties expected from remedial action. These provisions are consistent with the compensation principle in GATT Article XIX and Article 8 of the WTO *Agreement on Safeguards*. The multilateral disciplines call for the safeguard-imposing country to provide the target country with concessions substantially equivalent to the adverse effects of the relief. Of course, there may be considerable debate as to whether concessions are substantially equivalent. That is especially true when, as often occurs, compensation is in a different sector from the targeted article. What if the safeguard-imposing and target countries cannot agree on the value of trade-liberalizing compensation? Then, the FTAs tend to provide the target with the right to increase customs duties on imports from the imposing country.

Third, bilateral and special FTA safeguard provisions tend to have a sunset rule. The *Singapore FTA* discontinues any safeguard relief 10 years from the date of entry into force of the *FTA*, unless Singapore consents. The *Chile FTA* states no bilateral safeguard relief may be given after 10 years from the date of entry into force (or 12 years if that is the relevant period for tariff elimination). For the T&A safeguard, the sunset date is eight years after entry into force. The *CAFTA-DR* sunset date for the T&A safeguard is five years from the date on which the accord takes effect.

Sunset rules are not as trade liberalizing as they appear. The *Australia and Morocco FTA* sunset rules are less free-trade oriented than analogs in the other *FTAs*. That is because of the date on which the clock for the sunset starts to tick.

Whenever that date is after the entry into force, the sunset is postponed. For the bilateral safeguard, the *Australia FTA* specifies 10 years: the remedy ceased to exist on 1 January 2015, unless tariff elimination for the article in question exceeded a decade, in which case the remedy terminates as soon as zero duty treatment starts. For the special T&A safeguard, the sunset period is 10 years, but measured from the date on which duties on the merchandise in question are eliminated. Thus, hypothetically, if duties on 100% cotton sleeveless dresses are eliminated on 1 July 2012, then the safeguard remedy is available to protect a domestic industry making a like or directly competitive article until 30 June 2022.

The *Morocco FTA* employs the same deferred sunset rule for its bilateral and T&A safeguards. No safeguard action may be taken after 5 years (for the bilateral safeguard) or 10 years (for the T&A safeguard) from the date on which duties on the good in question were eliminated. For the special agricultural safeguard in the *Australia FTA*, the sunset date depends on the product. The horticulture safeguard ends when duty-free treatment on the horticultural good in question is phased in. That also is the rule for the quantity-based beef safeguard. But, the price-based beef safeguard never terminates, meaning the free-trade value of the agreement in the beef sector always is in peril.

As a final note about bilateral and special safeguards, what must not be lost amidst technical legal criteria is the role politics associated with specific products can play in a case. Pockets for apparel are one illustration. To get support for *CAFTA-DR* from legislators representing textile producing states, the administration of President George W. Bush promised to change ROOs on pockets.[16] It did just that, with the Senate passing legislation (H.R. 4) by a vote of 93–5 in August 2006. The change ensures that material used to make pockets must be made in the U.S., or in another *CAFTA-DR* country, for the apparel product to receive duty-free treatment. That is, using third-country material in pockets vitiates trade benefits.

Honduran socks are another example of writing product-specific rules to get votes.[17] To help secure passage of *CAFTA-DR*, the Bush Administration, in a July 2005 letter, told Representative Robert Aderholt (Republican, Alabama) it would enforce aggressively the T&A safeguard under *CAFTA-DR* (as well as the China-specific remedy in China's terms of WTO accession). The Administration also promised to renegotiate a *CAFTA-DR* rule eliminating immediately U.S. tariffs on socks, and substitute a decade-long phase out of tariffs, or at least tighten the rule of origin for socks to require they be finished in the U.S. to receive duty free treatment. Significant sock manufacturers are located in Congressman Aderholt's Alabama district. With these promises, he voted for *CAFTA-DR*, which passed the House of Representatives by the narrowest of margins.

---

16. Christopher S. Rugaber, *Senate Approves Promised Textile Changes to CAFTA-DR as Part of Pension Legislation*, 23 International Trade Reporter (BNA) 1198 (10 August 2006).

17. *See* Christopher S. Rugaber, *U.S. Preparing to Use CAFTA Safeguard to Restrict Sock Imports from Honduras*, 23 International Trade Reporter (BNA) 1139 (27 July 2006).

In July 2006, before *CAFTA-DR* was implemented in all members, the Administration threatened Honduras with the first use of the safeguard. After all, sock imports from the tiny country had increased 49.9% in June 2006, and a Canadian company was constructing a sizeable new sock production facility there. Was the threat pressure on Honduras to change its stance against lengthening the phase-out of sock tariffs, and against tightening the rule of origin? What implications would there be, including for *NAFTA*, of action against socks made in the Canadian company's facility?

IX. Case Study on Safeguards: 1998 *NAFTA Corn Brooms* Case

A safeguard remedy created by an FTA need not be restricted to a sensitive sector. *NAFTA* Chapter 8 is a case in point, providing for emergency action in any sector. A key case brought under it is the *"Broom Corn Brooms"* dispute. According to *NAFTA* Article 801:1 and the definition of "domestic industry" in Article 805, the "domestic industry" must produce a "like or directly competitive good." This prerequisite is the same as the elements of GATT Article XIX and Section 201 of the *Trade Act of 1974*, as amended. It is the prerequisite at issue in the 1996–1998 *Corn Brooms* dispute. The U.S. and Mexico hotly contested application of the phrase "like or directly competitive product." In its determinations, the ITC excluded straw brooms and plastic brooms from its definition of the U.S. corn broom industry. Mexico contended straw and plastic brooms are like or directly competitive with corn brooms.

Four aspects of the *Corn Brooms* case are noteworthy. First, the case is a leading one on the prerequisite a competitive industry produce a "like or directly competitive good." Second, the case is of historical interest in its own right because it was the first significant dispute between *NAFTA* Parties. As the *International Herald Tribune* put it, it was "the first case since the trade agreement began that has resulted in one of the three nations taking economic revenge against another."[18] Third, the case highlights the perils of an FTA for marginal industries, and the propensity of these industries to seek escape clause relief when threatened by such a deal. Fourth, the case illustrates the tandem operation of the *NAFTA* bilateral escape clause and Section 201.

The *Corn Brooms* dispute was a direct result of *NAFTA* tariff elimination. The U.S. offered duty-free treatment to imports of most categories of corn brooms from Mexico, and slashed tariffs from 33% to 22% on certain other corn broom categories. In March 1996, the U.S. Cornbroom Task Force filed a petition against Mexican producers and exporters of corn brooms under both *NAFTA* Chapter Eight and implementing American law, and Section 201, the conventional escape

---

18. Molly Moore, *Fight Sweeps Through NAFTA*, Iɴᴛᴇʀɴᴀᴛɪᴏɴᴀʟ Hᴇʀᴀʟᴅ Tʀɪʙᴜɴᴇ (London ed.), 14–15 December 1996, at 12. [Hereinafter, *Fight Sweeps.*]

clause. (American law authorizes submission of a petition under *NAFTA* Chapter Eight, Section 201, or both laws.)[19] Imported corn brooms account for about 60% of the American market, with Mexican brooms capturing the single biggest share.

The *NAFTA* complaint was directed at corn broom imports from Mexico, *i.e.*, it called for a bilateral escape clause action. The Section 201 complaint was directed at imports from all sources, including Mexico. To be sure, "[j]ust 382 [American] jobs and less than $10 m[illion] of imports are involved [in the corn brooms dispute] out of two-way [U.S.-Mexican] trade totaling $140 b[illio]n."[20] However, the employees in these jobs make the case heart-rending: "because corn brooms are so labor intensive, broom-weaving has been a popular product for American companies founded to employ the blind."[21] The American employees felt that "Mexican brooms, which sold for less than their U.S. counterparts, threatened to put them out of business."[22]

Where complaints are brought under both laws, the ITC conducts the investigation jointly, but renders separate determinations in accordance with the differences in the prerequisites for remedial action, and the more limited duration and nature of remedial measures under Chapter Eight. Following the *NAFTA* investigation, in August 1996, the ITC rendered a 5–1 affirmative determination that because of a *NAFTA* duty elimination or reduction, corn brooms from Mexico are being imported into the U.S. in increased quantities such that the imports alone are a substantial cause of serious injury or threat thereof to the domestic industry. The ITC (specifically, the Chairman and two commissioners) recommended that President Clinton increase the duty on Mexican corn brooms to the prevailing MFN rate for three years, which is the maximum relief allowable under Chapter Eight.

Following the Section 201 investigation, the ITC rendered a 4–2 affirmative determination in August 1996 that corn brooms are being imported into the U.S. in such increased quantities as to be a substantial cause of serious injury or threat thereof to the domestic industry. In this investigation, the ITC Chairman and one Commissioner recommended a four-year tariff increase encompassing Mexico, and products from the *CBI* and Andean Pact countries (but not against Canadian or Israeli products). They called for a duty increase to the MFN rate, plus 12% *ad valorem* in Year 1, 9% in Year 2, 6% in Year 3, and 3% in Year 4. Their recommendation encompassed the relief indicated in the *NAFTA* investigation, so they pointed out that there would be no need to engage in a separate *NAFTA* remedy if the duty increase plus a surcharge were implemented. Two other Commissioners called for a four-year tariff increase on corn brooms other than whisk brooms to, in general, 40% *ad valorem* in Year 1, 32% in Year 2, 24% in Year 3, and 16% in Year 4.

---

19. *See* § 19 U.S.C. § 3357.

20. Leslie Crawford & Nancy Dunne, *Spirit of NAFTA Is Swept Under the Carpet*, Financial Times, 19 December 1996, at 8. [Hereinafter, *Spirit of NAFTA.*] Roughly 600 jobs at small plants in various states were at stake. *See Fight Sweeps.*

21. *Spirit of NAFTA.*

22. *Fight Sweeps.*

In September 1996, President Bill Clinton (1946–, President, 1993–2000) elected to seek a negotiated settlement in lieu of adopting the various remedial measures recommended by the ITC. The President correctly observed that a broader range of remedies is available under Section 201 than *NAFTA* Chapter Eight, and that the period in which remedies may remain in effect is longer under Section 201 than Chapter Eight. (Section 201 permits non-tariff as well as tariff remedies, whereas Chapter Eight focuses only on tariff measures. Section 201 remedies may remain in effect for up to eight years, whereas Chapter Eight measures generally are limited to three years.) Therefore, he reserved the ability to raise tariffs in an amount equal to or greater than the ITC recommendations.

When negotiations between the USTR and Mexican officials failed after several months, President Clinton announced in December 1996 increased tariffs under Section 201. For one tariff classification of corn brooms (HTS Sub-Heading 9603.10.60), he raised tariffs from 22.4% to 33%. For another tariff classification of corn brooms (HTS Sub-Heading 9603.10.50), he raised tariffs from zero to 33 cents per broom. These increases in tariffs were phased out by 2000, at which time the applicable rate was at or below the 1996 rates. For a third category of corn brooms (HTS Sub-Heading 9603.10.40, which encompasses brooms with a value of less than 96 cents), the President continued duty-free treatment, but imposed a global tariff rate quota of 121,478 dozen per year. Imports in excess of this amount were subject to a tariff.

Not surprisingly, the Mexican government and broom makers were angry. The Mexican corn broom industry employs about 2,000 workers, and 60% of its brooms are exported to the U.S. The Mexicans argued President Clinton's action:

> devastated the small town of Cadereyta, capital of the Mexican corn broom industry, which lies just outside the northern city of Monterrey, on the road to Texas.
>
> . . .
>
> Mr. Jorge Trevino, president of the Mexican Corn Broom Manufacturers' Association, believes the U.S. protectionist measures have imperiled thousands of jobs in and around Cadereyta.[23]

In essence, the U.S. action led to sorrow in the Mexican industry. It also led to retaliation.

In December 1996, Mexico imposed tariff increases on almost two dozen American imports. For example, Mexico imposed a tariff increase of 20% on brandy and bourbon whiskey, wine and wine products (*e.g.,* wine coolers), and flat glass, a tariff increase of 12–14% on wood office and bedroom furniture, a 12.5% tariff increase on all chemically-pure sugar, fructose, and syrup products, and a 10% tariff increase on certain notebooks (*e.g.,* telephone agendas). Mexico valued its retaliation at

---

23. *Spirit of NAFTA.*

about $1 million, the amount raised by the American safeguard action, and thereby argued it was substantially equivalent to that action. The Mexican authorities expressly invoked *NAFTA* Article 802:6 as authority to take the retaliatory action.

In January 1997, these authorities also requested a dispute resolution panel pursuant to *NAFTA* Chapter 20. They alleged President Clinton's action was not in conformity with *NAFTA*, and that the ITC investigation misapplied the *NAFTA* Article 805 definition of a "domestic industry" as one that produces a like or directly competitive product. The U.S. could have argued *NAFTA* is inapplicable, because the American action ultimately was taken pursuant to Section 201. Of course, this argument would suggest the U.S. is insincere about Chapter Eight, and will resort to Section 201 whenever convenient. Interestingly, this suggestion might not be entirely inaccurate. Are there certain limitations on Chapter Eight bilateral actions that (at least from a petitioner's perspective) are worrisome?

In February 1998, the *NAFTA* Chapter 20 Panel issued a ruling in favor of Mexico.[24] The Panel found the American safeguard measure against corn brooms was inconsistent with *NAFTA* Article 803 Annex 803:3(12). That provision mandates the administering authority (the ITC), in making a determination, provide reasoned conclusions on all pertinent issues of law and fact. The Panel concluded the ITC failed to explain how it defined "directly competitive" in finding that plastic brooms were not part of the domestic industry. Accordingly, the Panel recommended the U.S. bring its conduct into compliance with *NAFTA*. American and Mexican officials met to plan a course of action. What did they decide?

Presumably, one option would have been for the ITC to re-open its investigation and render a new decision that satisfies *NAFTA* Article 803 Annex 803:3(12). On 3 December 1998, President Clinton announced the removal of the safeguard measure against Mexican corn brooms. He emphasized the removal was because of an August 1998 ITC report that the U.S. corn broom industry had not made adequate efforts to make a positive adjustment to import competition.[25] Conspicuously absent from the justification was the fact compliance with the Panel Report demanded removal. Indeed, perhaps removal, and the reasons for it, were disingenuous. Recall the safeguard measure had been in place for a full two years (December 1996–December 1998), the Panel had issued its Report in January 1998, and the ITC report came in August 1998. Had the U.S. dragged out the case so as to afford protection as long as possible?

---

24. See *U.S. Safeguard Action Taken on Broomcorn Brooms from Mexico*, U.S.A.-97-2008-01, available on the U.S. *NAFTA* Secretariat website, www.nafta-sec-alena.org. (The report actually was issued on 30 January 1998.)

25. See *Broom Corn Brooms: Efforts of Workers and Firms in the Industry to Make a Positive Adjustment to Import Competition*, Inv. No. 332-394, U.S. ITC Pub. 3122 (August 1998).

X. Case Study on Enhanced Market Access for Industrial Goods: *NAFTA* 2.0

How can Parties to an FTA operating under a DFQF environment thanks to that already-fully implemented FTA liberalize trade further? This question (asked earlier in the context of trade in farm and T&A products) was addressed by the *NAFTA* Parties in their 2017–2018 renegotiation of rules affecting trade in industrial products. They focused on behind-the-border barriers, that is, NTBs. They also raised the minimum threshold for shipment values, regardless of the merchandise shipped, that qualifies for duty-free treatment.

- **27 August 2018 U.S.-Mexico Bilateral FTA**

With respect to the 27 August 2018 U.S.-Mexico bilateral FTA, the two Parties agreed as follows:

Office of the United States Trade Representative,
United States–Mexico Trade Fact Sheet: *Rebalancing NAFTA to Support Manufacturing* (28 August 2018)[26]

New commitments [for the renegotiated *NAFTA*] have been included in the Market Access Chapter to reflect developments in United States trade agreements that address non-tariff barriers related to trade in remanufactured goods, import licensing, and export licensing.

Key Achievement: Exceeding NAFTA 1.0 and TPP Standards to More Effectively Support Trade in Manufactured Goods

The new Market Access Chapter will more effectively support trade in manufactured goods between the United States and Mexico by removing provisions that are no longer relevant, updating key references, and affirming commitments that have phased in from the original agreement.

Specifically, the Market Access Chapter:

(1) Maintains duty-free treatment for originating goods.

(2) Maintains the prohibition on export duties, taxes, and other charges and the waiver of specific customs processing fees.

(3) Adds new provisions for transparency in import licensing and export licensing procedures.

(4) Prohibits Parties from applying: (a) requirements to use local distributors for importation; (b) restrictions on the importation of commercial goods that contain cryptography; (c) import restrictions on used goods to

---

26. https://ustr.gov/about-us/policy-offices/press-office/press-releases/2018/august/rebalancing-nafta-support.

remanufactured goods; and (d) requirements for consular transactions and their associated fees and charges.

(5) Updates provisions for duty-free temporary admission of goods to cover shipping containers or other substantial holders used in the shipment of goods.

. . .

Sectoral Annexes

The United States and Mexico have also reached agreement on new provisions covering trade in specific manufacturing sectors, including Information and Communication Technology, Pharmaceuticals, Medical Devices, Cosmetic Products, and Chemical Substances. Each of the Annexes includes provisions that exceed *NAFTA* 1.0 and *TPP* that promote enhanced regulatory compatibility, best regulatory practices, and increased trade between both countries.

Office of the United States Trade Representative,

United States–Mexico Trade Fact Sheet: *Modernizing NAFTA to Be a 21st Century Trade Agreement* (28 August 2018)[27]

Key Achievement: Increased De Minimis Shipment Value Level

To facilitate greater cross-border trade, the United States has reached an agreement for Mexico to raise its *de minimis* shipment value level to $100 USD, up from $50 USD. Shipment values up to this level would enter Mexico without customs duties or taxes, and with minimal formal entry procedures, making it easier for more businesses, especially small- and medium-sized ones, to be a part of cross-border trade.

Increasing the *de minimis* level with a key trading partner like Mexico is a critical outcome for United States . . . SMEs. These SMEs often lack resources to pay customs duties and taxes, and bear the increased compliance costs that low, trade-restrictive *de minimis* levels place on lower-value shipments, which SMEs often have due to their smaller trade volumes.

New traders, just entering Mexico's market, will also benefit from lower costs to reach consumers. United States express delivery carriers, who carry many low-value shipments for these traders, also stand to benefit through lower costs and improved efficiency.

• **30 September 2018 Trilateral *NAFTA* 2.0 (*USMCA*)**

Canada agreed with the U.S. and Mexico as follows, hours before the midnight deadline of 30 September 2018, to trilateralize *NAFTA* 2.0, as follows:

---

27. https://ustr.gov/about-us/policy-offices/press-office/press-releases/2018/august/modernizing-nafta-be-21st-century.

Office of the United States Trade Representative,

United States–Mexico–Canada Fact Sheet: *Rebalancing Trade to Support Manufacturing* (1 October 2018)[28]

. . .

Goods Market Access

New commitments have been included in the Market Access Chapter to reflect developments in United States trade agreements that address non-tariff barriers related to trade in remanufactured goods, import licensing, and export licensing.

Key Achievement: Exceeding NAFTA 1.0 and TPP Standards to More Effectively Support Trade in Manufactured Goods

The new Market Access chapter will more effectively support trade in manufactured goods between the United States, Mexico, and Canada by removing provisions that are no longer relevant, updating key references, and affirming commitments that have phased in from the original agreement.

Specifically, the Market Access Chapter:

(1) Maintains duty-free treatment for originating goods.

(2) Maintains the prohibition on export duties, taxes, and other charges and the waiver of specific customs processing fees.

(3) Adds new provisions for transparency in import licensing and export licensing procedures.

(4) Prohibits Parties from applying: (a) requirements to use local distributors for importation; (b) restrictions on the importation of commercial goods that contain cryptography; (c) import restrictions on used goods to remanufactured goods; and (d) requirements for consular transactions and their associated fees and charges.

(5) Updates provisions for duty-free temporary admission of goods to cover shipping containers or other substantial holders used in the shipment of goods.

. . .

Sectoral Annexes

The United States, Mexico, and Canada have also reached agreement on new provisions covering trade in specific manufacturing sectors, including Information and Communication Technology, Pharmaceuticals, Medical Devices, Cosmetic Products, and Chemical Substances. Each of the annexes includes provisions that exceed *NAFTA* 1.0 and *TPP* that promote enhanced regulatory compatibility, best regulatory practices, and increased trade among the countries.

---

28. https://ustr.gov/about-us/policy-offices/press-office/fact-sheets/2018/october/united-states-mexico-canada-trade-fa-0.

Office of the United States Trade Representative,

United States–Mexico–Canada Fact Sheet: *Modernizing NAFTA into a 21st Century Agreement* (1 October 2018)[29]

. . .

De Minimis

Key Achievement: Increased De Minimis Shipment Value Level

To facilitate greater cross-border trade, the United States has reached an agreement with Mexico and Canada to raise their *de minimis* shipment value levels. Canada will raise its *de minimis* level for the first time in decades, from C$20 to C$40 for taxes. Canada will also provide for duty free shipments up to C$150. Mexico will continue to provide USD $50 tax free *de minimis* and also provide duty free shipments up to the equivalent level of USD $117. Shipment values up to these levels would enter with minimal formal entry procedures, making it easier for more businesses, especially small- and medium-sized ones, to be a part of cross-border trade. Canada will also allow a period of 90 days after entry for the importer to make payment of taxes.

Increasing the *de minimis* level with key trading partners like Mexico and Canada is a significant outcome for United States small- and medium-sized enterprises (SMEs). These SMEs often lack resources to pay customs duties and taxes, and bear the increased compliance costs that low, trade-restrictive *de minimis* levels place on lower-value shipments, which SMEs often have due to their smaller trade volumes.

New traders, just entering Mexico's and Canada's markets, will also benefit from lower costs to reach consumers. United States express delivery carriers, who carry many low-value shipments for these traders, also stand to benefit through lower costs and improved efficiency.

XI. Managed Trade in Goods?

It is possible to infer four general points about RTAs, be they FTAs or CUs.[30] First, in any RTA negotiation, both sides are likely to count agriculture, or at least certain agricultural products, as sensitive. T&A merchandise are classic examples. For example, Chapter 4 of *KORUS* covers T&A. Article 4-B-1 grants preferential treatment to imports of T&A products, but only up to 100 million square meters annually. CITA is charged with the responsibility for determining whether fiber, yarn, or textile items are in short supply in the U.S. and, therefore, how to address any shortfalls.

---

29. https://ustr.gov/about-us/policy-offices/press-office/fact-sheets/2018/october/united -states-mexico-canada-trade-fa-1.

30. *See* Raj Bhala, Dictionary of International Trade Law (3rd ed. 2015) (adducing these points in Annexed Tables).

Beef, rice, and sugar also are quintessential instances in which FTAs manage rather than create pure free trade. Only when negotiating an RTA with a city-state (and there are few of them aside from Singapore and the Holy See), or with a country that lacks an export interest in agriculture, is agriculture not an issue. The negotiating points include (1) the number of primary and processed agricultural commodities is each country allowed to designate as sensitive, (2) the precise identification of which products qualify as sensitive, and perhaps why, (3) the extent to which tariff and non-tariff barriers will be reduced on sensitive products. The third point concedes freer trade will come later rather than sooner on sensitive products. How much deviation will be permitted from the trade liberalization rules that apply to non-sensitive sectors?

A temptation to avoid is a monolithic stereotype of the agricultural sector in any country. Not all farmers are protectionists, nor are all free traders. At the risk of simplification, in the U.S. there are two broad groups: (1) big field crop farmers, and (2) small crop farmers. The first category includes corn, cotton, soybean, and wheat. Many of them—including Great Plains wheat farmers in Kansas—have been ardent free traders. They rely on export markets to take their surplus production. But, they tend to receive USDA subsidies. It is not easy for this first group to give up their subsidy payments in a multilateral trade round, such as the Doha Round, unless they obtain at least an equivalent guaranteed value in market access to developing country markets and the EU.

Similarly, they may be skeptical of an RTA, if its rules fail to mandate accelerated reductions in barriers to their commodities. The second group includes farmers producing dairy products, peanuts, and sugar. Their domestic market—particularly dairy and sugar—is regulated, putting them in a privileged position. Indeed, their political clout puts them there, and they can wring promises from political candidates to preserve barrier and subsidy levels. Like the first group, the second group insists on equivalency in WTO talks, *i.e.*, equivalent levels of protection to ensure equivalent market access, and equivalent subsidy levels to ensure equivalent support. But, dairy, peanut, and sugar producers may be relatively less enthusiastic about a multilateral or RTA deal that provides equivalence. That is, they may be especially prepared to use trade remedies such as AD, if equivalence actually occurs and threatens their position.

Two other issues are important: safeguard mechanisms and SPS measures. Does a special safeguard remedy exist for agricultural products? If so, then what legal criteria must be satisfied to trigger the safeguard? Does the safeguard have a sunset date (*i.e.*, does the remedy terminate after a certain number of years)? What should the date be? As for SPS measures, how are they defined and disputes about them resolved?

Second, in most RTA negotiations, T&A is important—but, not necessarily for the same reasons. That is especially true if the RTA involves economies at different stages of economic development. The sector is not contested if the prospective members do not produce or export this merchandise. Developed countries with declining T&A sectors are wont to have as many protections against competing imports as possible. Developing countries and LDCs take the opposite position. Thus, hard bargaining is foreseeable over the following topics: (1) tariff rates, (2) quota thresholds, (3) both tariff rates and quota thresholds if TRQs are relevant, (4) periods for phasing in tariff rate reductions or quota growth, and (5) periods for phasing out tariffs, quotas, and TRQs.

Also, ROOs for T&A merchandise will be contested. Developed countries generally prefer more restrictive rules, which call for origination based on activity as early as possible in the production chain (*e.g.*, Fiber Forward or Yarn Forward rules, which mandate, respectively, that the fiber — such as cotton — or yarn come from within the RTA, and all subsequent activity occur within the RTA). Developing countries and LDCs push for rules that allow more inputs to be sourced from, and processing to be done, outside the RTA (*e.g.*, a Sewing Forward rule, which allows all inputs to come from third countries, including fiber, yarn spun from the fiber, fabric made from the yarn, and allows cutting of pieces to occur in a third country). Further, as with agriculture, assuredly T&A products raise a debate about whether to insert in an RTA a special safeguard mechanism for them. If one is inserted, then the debate shifts to the technical criteria for applying the remedy. And, the matter of a sunset date must be considered.

The third general point is about the rubric "FTA," and is an inference from the first three points. Ought the "F" word in this acronym to be "freer," not "free"? A truly "free trade agreement" would state all tariff and NTBs on all merchandise traded are eliminated as of the date of entry into force. That never happens. Duty elimination invariably occurs on less than 100% of the trade between or among FTA Parties. Always there are a few product categories, or even entire sectors, scheduled for deferred duty elimination. The deferral periods typically are cast in terms of "staging categories," such as "A," "B," "C," "D," and so forth. Products in the first category receive immediate duty-free treatment as of the date of entry into force of the FTA. But, products in remaining categories are not subject to free trade for years from that date — such as five years for Category B, 10 years for Category C, 15 years for Category D, and so on.

Each derogation from the simple but quixotic obligation — "all tariff and NTBs are eliminated effective on the date of entry into force" — is a step away from comprehensive free trade. Given the large number of derogations in practice, it may be asked not only whether the term "free" trade agreement is accurate, but also, and more fundamentally, whether there is any such thing as "free trade" outside of the minds of some economists.

Finally, if "FTAs" are really "MTAs" — Managed Trade Agreements — then why are they so, and what are the implications for politics and society? Consider the conclusion of Professor Dani Rodrik (1957–):

> Th[e] tendency to view trade agreements as an example of efficiency-enhancing policies that may nevertheless leave some people behind would

be more justifiable if recent trade agreements were simply about eliminating restrictions on trade such as import tariffs and quotas. In fact, the label "free trade agreements" does not do a very good job of describing what recent proposed agreements like the *Trans-Pacific Partnership (TPP)*, the *Trans-Atlantic Trade and Investment Partnership (TTIP)*, and numerous other regional and bilateral trade agreements actually do. Contemporary trade agreements go much beyond traditional trade restrictions at the border. They cover regulatory standards, health and safety rules, investment, banking and finance, intellectual property, labor, the environment, and many other subjects. They reach well beyond national borders and seek deep integration among nations rather than shallow integration . . . . According to one tabulation, 76 percent of existing preferential trade agreements covered at least some aspect of investment (such as free capital mobility) by 2011; 61 percent covered intellectual property rights protection; and 46 percent covered environmental regulations . . . .

To illustrate the changing nature of trade agreements, compare US trade agreements with two small nations, Israel and Singapore, signed two decades apart. The *U.S.-Israel Free Trade Agreement*, which went into force in 1985, was the first bilateral trade agreement the U.S. concluded in the postwar period. It is quite a short agreement — less than 8,000 words in length. It contains 22 articles and three annexes, the bulk of which are devoted to free-trade issues such as tariffs, agricultural restrictions, import licensing, and rules of origin. The *U.S.-Singapore Free Trade Agreement* went into effect in 2004 and is nearly ten times as long, taking up 70,000 words. It contains 20 chapters (each with many articles), more than a dozen annexes, and multiple side letters. Of its 20 chapters, only seven cover conventional trade topics. Other chapters deal with behind-the-border topics such anti-competitive business conduct, electronic commerce, labor, the environment, investment rules, financial services, and intellectual property rights. Intellectual property rights take up a third of a page (and 81 words) in the *U.S.-Israel Agreement*. They occupy 23 pages (and 8,737 words) plus two side letters in the *U.S.-Singapore agreement*.

Taking these new features into account requires economists to rethink their default attitudes toward trade agreements, and the politics behind them. . . . I . . . argue that economists' conflation of free trade with trade agreements is rooted in an implicit political economy perspective that views import-competing interests as the most powerful and dominant architect of trade policy. Under this perspective, protectionists on the import side are the main villain of the story. Trade agreements, when successfully ratified, serve to counter their influence and get us closer to a welfare optimum by reducing the protectionism (or harmful regulations) that these special interests desire. In particular, they prevent beggar-thy-neighbor and beggar-thyself policies that would result in the absence of trade agreements.

In achieving these ends, governments may be assisted by *other* special interests—those with a stake in expanding exports and market access abroad. But the latter play an essentially useful role, since they are merely a counterweight to the protectionist lobbies.

There is an alternative political economy perspective, one that reverses the presumption about which set of special interests hold the upper hand in trade policy. In this view, trade agreements are shaped largely by rent-seeking, self-interested behavior on the export side. Rather than reining in protectionists, trade agreements empower another set of special interests and politically well-connected firms, such as international banks, pharmaceutical companies, and multinational corporations. Such agreements may result in freer, mutually beneficial trade, through exchange of market access. But they are as likely to produce welfare-reducing, or purely redistributive outcomes under the guise of free trade.

When trade agreements were largely about import tariffs and quotas—that is before the 1980s—the second scenario may not have been particularly likely. But with trade agreements increasingly focusing on domestic rules and regulations, we can no longer say the same. Taking these new features into account requires us to cast trade agreements, and the politics behind them, in quite a different light.[31]

Simply put, the question is whether FTAs have morphed from net social welfare enhancing, agreements that open opportunities to illiberal MTAs that redistribute wealth in favor of plutocratic interests with respect to goods, services, IP, and government procurement.

---

31. Dani Rodrik, *What Do Trade Agreements Really Do?*, 32 Journal of Economic Perspectives number 2, 73–90, at 74–76 (Spring 2018), https://drodrik.scholar.harvard.edu/files/dani -rodrik/files/what_do_trade_agreements_really_do.pdf.

Chapter 10

Liberalizing Trade in Services through FTAs[1]

I. Financial Services and Capital Controls

The *U.S.-Chile FTA* contains special rules on capital controls, a non-trade issue not dealt with in most other RTAs, but which raises important international financial policy questions. Most U.S. FTAs contain "capital transfer" provisions that require governments to permit all transfers relating to a covered investment to be made "freely and without delay into and out of" the relevant territory. A capital control by a host government potentially contravenes this requirement, triggering the right of a private foreign direct investor to sue the host government.

Before the 1997–1999 Asian Economic Crisis, the IMF strongly encouraged developing countries to liberalize fully their capital accounts. Its free market economists argued opening the Capital Account: (1) allows a poor country to access more easily foreign funds (*e.g.*, investment in local equity and debt instruments); (2) makes capital allocation more efficient by subjecting it to market forces (*i.e.*, decisions of international investors); and (3) expands the sharing of risks in poor countries by enlarging financing sources. Unsurprisingly, MNCs favor freedom of capital movement, arguing restrictions on capital transfers not only retard development in poor countries, but also are an unfair NTB to imports of goods and services, and invite politicized decision-making on access to and allocation of funds.

One lesson from Asian countries in that Crisis is developing countries cannot benefit from full Capital Account liberalization unless they have in place sound institutions and mature domestic financial markets. They need a well-functioning legal system, strong corporate governance, macroeconomic discipline, and appropriate exchange rate policies before opening the capital account. Another lesson, especially from countries like Malaysia, which rejected IMF assistance during the Crisis, is Capital Account liberalization renders a country vulnerable to speculative financial flows that, if large and fast enough, can wreak havoc on an economy.

Chile paid careful attention to the debate about how quickly, and under what conditions, to open a capital account, and to the Asian experience. In its negotiations

---

1. Documents References:
   (1) *NAFTA* Chapters 10–14
   (2) Relevant provisions in other FTAs

with the U.S., it sought a mechanism to insulate itself from volatile movements in financial flows and the untoward knock-on effects of such flows in the real economy. The result was a compromise. The *Chile FTA* makes controls on the flow of financial capital illegal. Concerned Chile might be tempted to restrict capital, the U.S. insisted upon this obligation. But, Chile won an exception to the obligation.

Peru followed the example of Chile. Annex 10-E to the *U.S.-Peru* FTA, implemented on 1 February 2009, imposes a cooling off period before a foreign direct investor can file a claim arising out of a capital control. It also limits the amount of damages the investor can collect as compensation for certain capital control measures.

Similarly, Article 13:10(1) of *KORUS* permits capital controls. It allows for their imposition for prudential reasons, namely, assisting an individual financial institution or cross-border financial service supplier. Footnote 5 to Article 13:10(1) clarifies a "prudential reason" justifying a capital control includes maintaining the safety, soundness, integrity, or financial responsibility of an individual institution or supplier. In May 2012, in response to Congressional concern about this provision, and its replication in *TPP*, the Administration of President Barack H. Obama said it did not object to capital controls as long as they were not implemented for the purpose of trade discrimination.

Moreover, despite Article 13:10(1), *KORUS* is widely recognized as the best bilateral free trade agreement in terms of services commitments generally, including financial services. In respect of financial services, *KORUS* prohibits market access limitations, such as caps on the number of service providers, total value or quantity of services provided, or total number of persons that can be employed by service providers, and restrictions on the type of business entity through which a service must be provided.

As for capital controls, the compromise in the *Chile* and *Peru FTAs*, and the language in *KORUS*, was a harbinger of a shift in the consensus among economists. In January 2011, over 250 economists, many of whom were inclined to free trade or had worked at the IMF, signed a letter to senior American government officials. Their letter argued U.S. FTAs should permit governments to implement capital controls without being liable to suits by investors. Such controls are a legitimate tool to manage short-term flows of "hot money" in and out of a country, and thereby prevent or mitigate a financial crisis. Therefore, FTAs should protect the right of a host country government to enact capital controls by immunizing it to some degree from lawsuits.

Are controls in an FTA the best way to deal with a surge in financial capital afflicting a country? Arguably, governments and central banks have at their disposal better tools to respond to large, fast inflows or outflows of funds. Such tools include sound monetary and fiscal policy, FX rate adjustment (*i.e.*, appreciation in response to an inflow, depreciation in the event of an outflow), and non-discriminatory bank regulatory measures such as adjustments to reserve and capital adequacy ratios and limits on exposure to currency risk.

II. Freer Trade or Safer Roads? *NAFTA* Cross Border Trucking Case

Trucking is big business in *NAFTA*. About 80% of trade between the U.S. and Mexico, and 70% of all *NAFTA* trade, occurs over roads. The roots of the *Mexican Cross Border Trucking Services* date to the early 1980s. In 1982, Congress passed the *Business Regulatory Reform Act*, which (*inter alia*) imposed a two-year moratorium issuing new licenses to foreign carriers operating in the U.S. By Executive Order on 20 September 1982, President Ronald Reagan lifted the moratorium for Canada, but preserved it for Mexico. This Order was extended in 1984, 1986, 1988, 1990, 1992, and 1995.

NAFTA entered into force on 1 January 1994. *NAFTA* Annex I, entitled "Reservations for Existing Measures and Liberalization Commitments, which covers cross border services, took effect on 18 December 1995. In this Annex (specifically, I-U-21), Mexican commercial trucks were to have full access to 4 U.S. border states in 1995, and access throughout the U.S. in 2000. Likewise, U.S. trucks were to be allowed to deliver goods into Mexico. Instead, the Administration of President Bill Clinton, pointing to concerns about the safety of Mexican trucks and drivers, suspended these provisions. U.S. trucks were shut out of Mexico. As had been true since 1982, Mexican trucks were restricted to making deliveries only into a 20–25 mile commercial zone on the U.S. side of the border between the two countries, adjacent to border crossings. Then, they had to transfer their cargo to a U.S. entity within the post-border buffer zone.

The *NAFTA* Annex 1 provisions also allow for applications for new licenses, from Mexico and Canada, to operate a truck or other vehicle to carry freight across the U.S. border in the same truck or vehicle. However, since 1982, the U.S. issued no licenses to Mexican applicants. On the day the Annex took effect, Mexico's Secretary of Commerce and Industry (formerly called "SECOFI," and now called the *Secretaría de Economía*, *i.e.*, the *Ministry of the Economy*, or "*Economía*"), Herminio Blanco, wrote a letter to then USTR Mickey Kantor, requesting consultations. Consultations were held on 19 January 1996, but with no resolution to the basic Mexican complaint against the U.S. refusal to issue licenses to Mexican trucking firms. Two years later, on 24 July 1998, Secretary Blanco wrote again to USTR Charlene Barshefsky asking for a *NAFTA* Free Trade Commission (FTC) meeting. He expanded the claim: not only did the U.S. reject cross-border trucking licenses for Mexican firms, but also it denied Mexican investors the right to invest in American trucking enterprises. On 19 August 1998, the FTC met, but failed to resolve either issue. On 22 September 1998, the Mexican government called for formation of an arbitral panel to decide both issues. Over a year later (on 10 December 1999), the U.S. asked for consultations with Mexico over its reciprocal decision to refuse to allow American trucking companies into the Mexican market.

The two countries were in a classic tit-for-tat spat, and a *NAFTA* Chapter 20 Panel was formed on 2 February 2000, with a final decision issued a year later. The Final Report in the case, *Cross Border Trucking Services*, was issued 6 February 2001.[2] The principal legal issue before the Panel was whether the U.S. violated *NAFTA* by failing to phase out restrictions on cross border trucking services and Mexican investment in the U.S. trucking industry. The U.S. defense was its interpretation of "in like circumstances" in *NAFTA* Article 1202. This Article concerns national treatment, while Article 1203 concerns MFN treatment. Article 1202 mandates that each Party "accord to service providers of another Party treatment no less favorable than that it accords, *in like circumstances*, to its own service providers" (emphasis added). The U.S. used the italicized language to justify a "blanket ban," because Mexico lacked the same rigorous truck safety rules as the U.S. or Canada. Interestingly, Article 1204 requires the *NAFTA* Parties to accord each other the better of MFN or national treatment, in the event there is a distinction between the two standards. That is, Article 1204 prevents them from choosing what standard to apply.

Siding with Mexico, the Panel held the American concerns about safety were unwarranted. The Panel found the U.S. violated *NAFTA* (specifically Annex 1) obligations, and said the defective regulatory environment in Mexico was an insufficient defense. The "blanket ban" was at issue, not the pursuit of legitimate regulatory objections, hence the Panel advised the U.S. to bring their practices into compliance. Furthermore, regulatory issues should not affect investment recommendations, as the Parties agreed investment does not affect safety. The Panel did not mean to say the U.S. must ignore safety regulations in considering licenses for cross border services. The U.S. could impose safety standards, and restrict access, with respect to specific Mexican trucking companies — but not slap on a prophylactic ban. Moreover, the Panel insisted the U.S. must afford Mexican (and Canadian) service providers equal treatment in their application review process. In effect, the Panel ruled the U.S. discriminated against Mexican applicants, violating both the national treatment obligation (based on differential treatment of Mexican and American trucking companies), and MFN obligation (based on differential treatment of Mexican and Canadian providers).

Throughout the remainder of 2001, obstinacy was the American response to the adverse Chapter 20 Panel decision. It was no secret the International Brotherhood of Teamsters Union did not want competition from cheap Mexican truckers. Worse yet for the Mexican side, the 11 September terrorist attacks galvanized Congress to pass legislation heightening border security. Only after midterm elections in late

---

2. *See* File No. USA-MEX-98-2008-1, www.nafta-sec-alena.org.

November 2002 did President George W. Bush issue an Executive Order implementing the Panel decision, and thereby lift the ban.

Unfortunately for Mexican trucking interests, that Executive Order engendered another controversy. Environmental groups sued the U.S. government. They argued the President lacked the right to issue the Order without an environmental impact study on the effect of Mexican trucking on the U.S. environment. In June 2004, the Supreme Court ruled the President had authority to issue the Order, holding the Federal Motor Carrier Safety Administration was not under any obligation to evaluate the environmental effects of cross-border trucking, because FMCSA lacks the power to prevent cross-border trucking services.[3] This narrow holding is based on the general presumption the President has the right (delegated by Congress) to regulate foreign trade.

The ban, then, on issuing licenses to Mexican trucking companies to carry freight into the U.S., and on Mexican investment in U.S. trucking interests, is over. Yet, difficulties remain. The U.S. is concerned about terrorism infiltrating any borders, illegal immigration and narcotics flows across its southern border, and the effect on the environment of Mexican trucks hauling freight around the U.S. Conversely, Mexico has wondered whether the victory in the Chapter 20 case might be Pyrrhic. If there is a *bona fide* cross-border trucking services market in the *NAFTA* region, then can its companies compete with more efficient, better financed American firms? The U.S. often implements new customs regulations, including requiring the electronic filing of cargo manifests (which list the contents of a shipment, and serves as a security check, and which differs from an entry summary, which is used for tariff purposes). Some Mexican companies cannot meet the new rules as easily as their U.S. and Canadian counterparts—or at all.

Not surprisingly, under a system known as "drayage," freight still is transferred at the border between American- and Mexican-owned trucks in the 20–25 mile commercial zone. Literally, near the border, a Mexican cargo truck stops at a drayage yard and hands off its cargo to a drayage truck. The drayage truck is designed for short haulage, but typically is aged, in poor condition, and in need of maintenance. Nevertheless, this truck carries the cargo across the border, makes multiple stops and goes through various inspections, and then transfers the cargo to an American truck. The American truck then proceeds north. The reverse also is true—cargo is physically moved from a U.S. to a Mexican truck via a drayage truck, and the recipient Mexican cargo truck heads south.

In this inefficient transaction, repeated thousands of times daily, the real winners are drayage companies that perform the work of transferring cargo from truck to truck. Who are the losers in this relay? They include *maquiladoras*, which compete with low- or lower-cost companies making like products in China, and border trade hubs like San Antonio, which do not realize the benefits of expanded trade

---

3. *See Department of Transportation v. Public Citizen*, 541 U.S. 752 (2004).

NAFTA should bring. The largest loser may be *NAFTA* itself, and the faith of each Party in the Chapter 20 dispute resolution process. When studying Chapter 20, consider whether, following a favorable adjudicatory outcome, Mexico or Canada can enforce a judgment against the U.S.?

To be sure, in September 2004, Congress passed legislation giving Mexican trucking companies and their drivers two years to meet American safety standards. Those standards included:

(1) Possessing a valid commercial driving license.

(2) Showing medical fitness.

(3) Complying with maximum hours-of-service rules.

(4) Proving the ability to understand questions and directions in English.

(5) Carrying insurance with a U.S.-licensed insurer.

(6) Passing in-person audits and safety inspections.

In February 2007, the U.S. DOT Secretary, Mary E. Peters, announced creation of a one-year pilot program. Ironically, under *NAFTA*, U.S.-domiciled carriers were free to apply for and operate throughout Mexico starting in 2007. It would be another eight years before Mexican carriers would get that same treatment.

Under it, effective September 2007, a select group of 100 Mexican trucking companies would be allowed to make deliveries beyond existing restricted commercial zones, which vary in size from 3–25 miles inland on the U.S. side of the border. There was no cap on the number of trucks each company could operate. However, the anointed companies could make only international deliveries. They could not deliver goods between U.S. cities, nor carry hazardous materials or passengers. Mexico agreed to grant reciprocal access to the same number of American carriers. The essential purpose of the program would be to give the U.S. and Mexico time to figure out precisely what safety hazards and environmental problems existed, and the most efficient, least trade-distorting way to deal with them. By limiting the size of the program, the two sides could evaluate matters carefully on a small scale, and contain risks.

Evidence from the DOT suggested American trucks are more likely than Mexican trucks to be cited for safety violations in the U.S. and thereby removed from the road. Early signs from the operation of the pilot program suggested most Mexican trucks met U.S. safety standards. Nevertheless, by April 2007, opposition to the pilot program in Congress, as well as by the Teamsters Union and environmental groups, was so fierce the DOT had to suspend it. There is no way, opponents complained, to be sure a Mexican truck driver complies with U.S. safety regulations on hours of service (*i.e.*, that the driver has not been operating for longer than a safe, reasonable period). After all, only 5% of Mexican trucks entering the U.S. are inspected. Mexican trucks lack safety features, like anti-lock brakes, which are standard on American trucks.

Moreover, the zone serves a law enforcement purpose. As long as Mexican trucks are kept within a 25 mile zone, and required to offload cargo to U.S. carriers, then any illicit items—such as narcotics or weapons—may be detected at that point. Thus, Congress tried to restrict the pilot program by inserting a provision in a supplemental spending measure for the Iraq War (Public Law No. 110-28), signed by President George W. Bush (1946, President, 2001–2009) on 25 May 2007. That provision stated the DOT must operate the program as a "pilot" as that term was defined in the DOT spending bill for FY 2002 (Public Law Number 107-87)—which meant the program could be extended for at most up to three years.

On its side, Mexico said it would consider license applications from U.S. firms seeking to operate in Mexico, but would license only about 100 of them. In May 2007, whether, and when, there might be free trade in trucking services became even more dubious. The House of Representatives approved (by a 411–3 vote) the *Safe American Road Act* (H.R. 1773). The *Act* not only limits participation in any pilot program to 100 Mexican motor carriers and 1,000 commercial motor vehicles, but also has stricter parameters than the DOT envisaged.

In its omnibus appropriations bill for FY 2008, signed by President Bush on 26 December 2007, Congress shut off funding for, and thereby banned, the pilot program. In that bill, Congress forbade the DOT from "establishing" the program. While only 25 Mexican companies (with 52 trucks total), and 10 American companies, had participated in the program, the Bush Administration said the program already had been "established," and felt justified in continuing to expend funds on it. The two branches of government thus quarreled over the difference in meaning between "establish" and "implement." The Congressional ban ended at the end of FY 2008. But, in March 2009 President Barack H. Obama signed a new $410 billion omnibus spending bill (H.R. 1105), which again prohibited funding to any program that would allow Mexican trucks to operate beyond 25 miles of the border. The language in this bill clearly forbade expenditures on the program, even to satisfy a *NAFTA* obligation. The "trucking amendment" in the bill was sponsored by Senator Byron Dorgan, a Democrat from North Dakota. The American side justified the action by saying only three Mexican trucks per day traveled beyond the zone.

Mexico was furious. It countered that under the pilot program, 46,000 Mexican trucks had entered the U.S. without a single major incident. Striking back, Mexico invoked *NAFTA* Article 2019:1. This provision allows an aggrieved *NAFTA* Party to suspend benefits vis-à-vis an accused Party, if the latter does not reach a mutually satisfactory agreement in a dispute. In particular, if the disputants fail to resolve their conflict within 30 days after a *NAFTA* Panel issues its final report, then the winning side can engage in cross-sectoral retaliation against the losing side. Following its 2001 *NAFTA* Panel victory, Mexico was eligible to implement trade sanctions. It held off, because of the pilot program, hoping that through it the U.S. would comply with its obligations as defined by the Panel. Mexico viewed the U.S. cancellation of the program not only as tantamount to a rejection of the Panel report, but also as disrespectful of the *NAFTA* dispute resolution process.

Its termination meant that once again, Mexican trucks had to offload their cargo at the border region for re-loading onto American trucks. With 4.5 million northbound truck crossings annually (as of April 2009), there was a lot of re-loading. As indicated above, nearly every shipment from Mexico to the U.S., involved 3 trucks: a Mexican truck from the factory at which the exported merchandise is produced to a storage depot in Mexico; a second Mexican drayage truck from that depot to a depot on the U.S. side of the border, and a third, but American, truck from the American depot to their final destination. In reverse, three trucks typically were needed for exports from the U.S. to Mexico, too. Ironically, even if only one truck could be used, another logistical problem had not been solved: congestion at U.S. customs facilities on the border with Mexico caused delays of up to five hours.

Effective 19 March 2009, Mexico said it would increase tariffs on 89 American products (some of which were perishable), or 1.5% of U.S. exports to Mexico, the total import value of which (as of 2007) was $2.4 billion. (That figure was a fraction of total U.S.-Mexican trade, which was $368 billion in 2008.) Mexico said it would boost tariffs to between 10% and 45% on the merchandise, which ranged from Christmas trees and deodorant to strawberries and sunglasses—all of which had been entering Mexico duty-free under *NAFTA*. For example, Mexico would slap a 10% tariff on carbonless paper, a 15% tariff on pencils and shaving cream, and a 20% duty on chewing gum, chocolate, mineral water, potatoes and processed potatoes (including frozen French fries), and red and white wine. Mexico deliberately targeted a broad spectrum of American producers, in the hope they might lobby the Obama Administration to change policy, while at the same time avoiding products essential to poor Mexicans. At risk were over four million American jobs that depended on exports to Mexico and Canada.

In August 2010, Mexico revised the list, adding 26 newly tariffed products and eliminating 16 others (*e.g.*, battery waste, copy paper, dental floss, metal furniture, precious metal articles, shelled peanuts, and textile carpeting), for a total of 99 American products with a similar export value of $2.6 billion. The revised list included cheeses (with duties between 20%–25%), frozen sweet corn (15%), pork and ham products (with a 5% duty), and pork rind pellets (20%). It also covered apples, chewing gum, chocolate, grapefruits, ketchup, oranges, and pistachios (all 20%), car polish and heavy machinery (*e.g.*, trenchers) (both 15%), and vulcanized rubber goods.

Effectively, Mexico applied to the U.S. the strategy of carousel (rotational) retaliation, which was designed to deepen the pressure on the Obama Administration by broadening the pain felt in the American export sector. The strategy worked. Between March 2009 and March 2010, exports to Mexico of items subject to retaliatory tariffs plunged by 81%. Before the tariffs, Mexico had been the second largest importer of American pork, obtaining over 90% of its pork, as well as over 90% of its apples, cheese, and certain aluminum products from the U.S.

The State of Washington felt the pain of the Mexican retaliation.[4] In 2008, it was the top exporter to Mexico of frozen potato products, with French fry exports totaling $40 million. When Mexico imposed a 20% tariff, Washington state potatoes and French fries lost market share in Mexico to Canadian like products. So, in 2009, the value of French fry exports from Washington to Mexico fell to $19 million. (It later rebounded modestly to $22 million when Mexico cut the tariff to 5%.) Acreage in Washington dedicated to potatoes dropped from 160,000 to 135,000 (shifting to corn and wheat, which were fetching high world market prices), one potato processor shut down, and another reduced hours. The Washington state apple industry lost $44 million because of the 20% Mexican tariff, though increased sales to India cushioned the blow. The negative effect on apricot, cherry, and pear exports from Washington and Oregon to Mexico was over $30 million.

In September 2009, the U.S. Chamber of Commerce published a study arguing America paid a steep price for failing to implement fully the *NAFTA* cross-border trucking provisions. Mexico's retaliatory tariffs cost America 25,600 jobs. Because the tariffs impeded the ability of American farm and industrial goods to enter the Mexican market, the U.S. lost $2.6 billion worth of exports. The National Association of Manufacturers (NAM) agreed, saying the central problem created by Mexico's retaliatory tariffs was the loss of American jobs. But, the Teamsters disputed the Chamber study.[5] The key issue was *NAFTA* itself had cost the U.S. over 1 million jobs.

Retaliatory tariffs were one of two official Mexican responses. In June 2010, Mexico pointed out it had increased truck safety, driver training standards, and licensing requirements, and its truck safety officials inspected over 1,500 commercial vehicles as part of their yearly participation in "Roadcheck Week" with their Canadian and American counterparts. In addition to these official measures, a private trade association of Mexican truckers—*Camara Nacional del Autotransporte de Carga (CANACAR)*—launched a case under *NAFTA* Chapter 11, which contains the investment provisions of the FTA, against the U.S. By singling out Mexican carriers as the only cohort in the world barred from getting authorization to offer trucking services in the U.S., the U.S. breached two key provisions of *NAFTA* Chapter 11: Article 1102, the national treatment rule; and Article 1103, the MFN rule. The U.S. also violated Article 1105, which provides for a minimum standard of treatment under international law, by failing to comply with the 2001 *NAFTA* Chapter 20 arbitral award.

The considerable pressure of tariff retaliation and Chapter 11 case appeared to work. In December 2009, Congress unblocked funding for a new cross-border trucking pilot program. The Obama Administration called on Congress for legislation to

---

4. *See* Paul Shukovsky, *Pacific Northwest Agricultural Sector Poised to Benefit from Mexico's Cuts of Tariffs*, 28 International Trade Reporter (BNA) 1180 (14 July 2011).

5. *See* Rossella Brevetti, *Teamsters Union Takes Issue with Estimate of Job Losses Due to NAFTA Trucking Dispute*, 26 International Trade Reporter (BNA) 1292 (24 September 2009).

establish a new program. Was that the right response? On the one hand, the Owner-Operator Independent Drivers Association, which is the largest association representing small-business trucking professionals, urged the USTR to sue Mexico on the ground Mexico lacked the necessary highway safety and security apparatus to implement the *NAFTA* trucking provisions, hence the retaliatory tariffs were illegal. Said OOIDA, Mexico lacked regulatory schemes to deal with criminal activity in its trucking industry, resulting in routine findings by American customs officials of narcotics and illicit cargo in truckloads crossing the border. OOIDA and its supporters in Congress went so far as to call for the deletion from *NAFTA* Annex I (I-U-21) of the commitment by the U.S. to liberalize cross-border trucking.

On the other hand, arguably, Mexican sanctions were disproportionate in violation of *NAFTA*. The maximum degree of retaliation *NAFTA* permits against a product is for the tariff on that product to snap back to the level at which it stood before *NAFTA* was implemented (*i.e.*, as of 31 December 1993). Article 2019(3) allows for the *NAFTA* Free Trade Commission to establish a panel (upon written request by either disputing Party) to determine whether retaliation is "manifestly excessive." Mexico said the tariff revenue it garnered from the sanctions was roughly $427 million, which offset the $500 million income Mexican truckers lost from the U.S. violation. Public Citizen, an NGO led by activist Ralph Nader (1934–), said Mexican losses were between $69 and $227.6 million, *i.e.*, 16%–53% less than the monies Mexico collected from the sanctions. Likewise, the Teamsters argued Mexican tariffs were "manifestly excessive." Citing a report by the Inspector General of the DOT, the Teamsters said in the 18 month life of the pilot program, only 118 trucks, making 1,442 trips beyond the restricted border zone, participated in the program. How could such low totals account for $427 million in trade?

In a bid to resolve the dispute, in January 2011, U.S. Transportation Secretary Ray LaHood issued a "Concept Paper" to Congress and the Mexican government. Mexico replied it would not lift the retaliatory tariffs until the dispute in fact was over. But, as a gesture of good will, Mexico ended the carousel retaliation it had started in August 2010, and pledged not to take aim at any additional products. Now, at least, the list of targeted American products would remain the same. The essence of the Concept Paper was that Mexican long-haul trucks could enter the U.S. after meticulous security checks. Their entry would not be part of a pilot program, but rather an initial stage involving several thousand trucks, though the exact number of carrier and truck participants would be managed to ensure effective oversight. Eventually, the number would rise to the level needed to carry cargo into the U.S. The security checks would be conducted under a new inspection and monitoring regime, and Mexican carriers would have to apply for authority to engage in long-haul operations, providing carrier- and driver-specific data the U.S. DHS and DOJ would verify. Neither hazardous materials nor passenger carriers would be eligible for entry.

The new security regime, "Pre-Authorization Safety Audits" (PASA), would include vehicle maintenance checks, drug and alcohol testing, and driver record reviews. Once a PASA audit was completed successfully, an applicant would have to prove it was insured to FMCSA. This body would monitor the required insurance filings.

Further, each vehicle would be tested for compliance with U.S. Federal Motor Vehicle Safety Standards (FMVSS) and EPA emission standards. A Mexican vehicle meeting all the American regulations would be inspected by FMCSA each time it crossed the border headed north for an agreed-upon period. Each Mexican trucking company with participating trucks would undergo a follow-up review. Its trucks would be subject to inspection not only at FMCSA border stations, but also in the U.S. and would have to display a valid safety inspection sticker — just like American trucks. If a Mexican company passed a second compliance review, then FMCSA would grant it full authority to operate in the U.S. Additionally, the Mexican government would have to construct and maintain a database of federal and state traffic infractions for each driver.

In effect, the Concept Paper proposed to export American trucking standards to Mexico. Mexican trucks could haul cargo across the border and in the U.S., if the American and Mexican governments applied to them the same safety standards as the American government applies to American trucks. Notwithstanding what *NAFTA* said, or might say, the price of doing business in America was to accept a regulatory bar set at a height determined by the U.S.

Predictably, the Teamsters Union opposed the Concept Paper. It reiterated its contention Mexican trucks do not meet the same safety standards as American trucks, and the physical and medical standards for Mexican trucking firms and drivers are beneath those applied to their American counterparts. As for foisting the higher American safety standards on Mexico, the Teamsters questioned the enforcement ability of the Mexican government, pointing out drug cartels run rampant in parts of Mexico. The Teamsters, along with OOIDA, predicted allowing Mexican truckers would threaten American jobs and wages. Conversely, and equally predictably, the American Chamber of Commerce, NAM, and the Emergency Committee for Foreign Trade (ECAT) all welcomed the Concept Paper. As a result of the retaliatory tariffs, American companies had lost market share in Mexico to competitors from Canada, China, and Latin America.

Finally, in March 2011, the U.S. and Mexico reached a deal to settle the 20-year old dispute, in April 2011, the DOT announced a three-year pilot program to implement the deal, and in July 2011 they finalized the deal via an MOU. Under the MOU:

(1) Mexico suspended 50% of its retaliatory tariffs in July 2011 (*i.e.*, cut the retaliatory tariffs in half) and across the board (*i.e.*, horizontally), and suspended the remaining half of the retaliatory tariffs in October 2011, when the U.S. granted operating authority to the first tractor-trailer from a Mexican long-haul trucking company (*i.e.*, within five days of that first Mexican truck crossing the border), which was a 20-year old vehicle from Grupo Behr in Tijuana.

(2) Overall, the trucks and drivers of Mexican carrier companies had to comply with all relevant American laws, including rules on customs, fuel taxation, immigration, motor carrier safety, vehicle registration, and vehicle taxation.

(3) The U.S. granted qualified Mexican trucks and their drivers expanded access north of the border, beyond the 25-mile border commercial zone. This operating authority was provisional for 18 months, and irrevocable thereafter if there are no adverse incidents.

(4) More specifically, Mexican trucks had to comply with American safety standards, proceeding through a three-staged registration process, leading from a provisional permit to a permanent pass.

In Stage 1, lasting for at least the first three months during which Mexican trucks were permitted to cross the border, all of the trucks and drivers of a particular Mexican-domiciled motor carrier company, and the carrier itself, were subject to rigorous document checks and inspections by FMSCA. The purpose of these PASAs was to ensure compliance with environmental, security, and technical standards, cargo, driver, and vehicular insurance rules, as well as international license requirements. In this stage, FMCSA did roughly 4,100 inspections, half of them in Mexico, and calculate violation rates and other statistics and compare them with metrics of American carriers. Thus, for example, in August 2012 FMCSA announced GCC Transportes SA de CV, a Mexico-domiciled motor carrier that had been approved to operate in the U.S. beyond the border, passed the PASA and was granted operating authority. It progressed to Stage 2.

In Stage 2, FMCSA inspected the trucks and drivers of that carrier in the same way it inspected carriers that cross the border but stay within the border commercial zone. FMCSA monitored the safety data of that carrier, to ensure compliance with safety rules, and issue it provisional operating authority. There were two key reviews, within three months of operation, and then within 15 months. Border checks of trucks and drivers also occurred.

Within 18 months of issuing provisional authority, the FMCSA conducted a compliance review of the carrier. Assuming the carrier passed this review, and had no enforcement or safety actions against it for at least 18 months, then the authority would become permanent, putting that carrier into Stage 3. The total time from entry into Stage 1 to graduating to Stage 3 is three years.

(5) Through PASAs, Mexican truck drivers also were subject to personnel inspections and driver accreditation, as the FMCSA scrutinizes the driving records and drug test samples of Mexican drivers, and gauges their ability to comprehend American traffic laws in English.

(6) There was no limit to the number of Mexican carrier companies that could participate.

(7) Mexican trucks had to be equipped with electronic monitoring devices, known as Electronic On Board Recorders, which have a GPS, to track trucks and ensure no driver operates one for too many hours without a rest. The U.S. might fund EBORs for Mexican trucks (pending legislation in Congress in summer 2011, which could use of the Highway Trust Fund would be limited), but American drivers must pay for their EBORs.

(8) American carriers, trucks, and truck drivers had to follow the same regulations as Mexican ones to obtain the status of an authorized cargo carrier. Assuming they do, then Mexico grants them reciprocal rights to operate in Mexico.

Predictably, the Teamsters and OOIDA remained adamantly opposed. They argued the MOU failed to resolve highway safety and border security issues, violated U.S. law on environmental assessments (EAs), and jeopardized American warehouse and trucking jobs.[6] For its part, Mexico argued America still did not comply fully with its *NAFTA* obligations that Mexican exporters be allowed to take cargo on the same truck from the point of origin to destination.[7]

Nevertheless, the FMCSA proceeded with publication of data for carriers receiving operating authority, and giving notice for public comment on granting clearance under PASA. Such publication and notice is mandated under the 2007 *U.S. Troops Readiness, Veterans' Care, Katrina Recovery, and Iraq Accountability Appropriations Act.* And, by August 2013, border crossings had become far more efficient than before: inspection times had been cut from an average of three hours to just 25 minutes, and there was no need for cargo to be transferred to another truck once it crossed the border.[8]

Interestingly, at the same time as the America and Mexico announced the deal—a period in which much of the Arab Middle East was undergoing revolution and oil prices were skyrocketing on fears of supply disruptions—they also announced the U.S. would work with Mexico to find new energy sources in the Gulf of Mexico.

---

6. In April 2013, the U.S. Court of Appeals for the District of Columbia Circuit rejected petitions by the Teamsters and OOIDA (in which they made six and seven objections respectively) to the FMCSA pilot program that allows Mexican-domiciled trucking companies to operate across America if those companies satisfy federal safety standards. *See Int'l Bhd. Of Teamsters v. Dep't. of Transp.*, D.C. Cir., No. 11-1444, 19 April 2013. The D.C. Circuit concluded the program does not unlawfully allow Mexican drivers to use their Mexican commercial driver's licenses on American roads; rather, Congress agreed those licenses "would be considered the essential equivalent of a state commercial driver's license for purposes of this statutory scheme." *Id.* Interestingly, among the arguments the Court rejected was one put by the Teamsters: Mexican vision tests require only that a truck driver recognize the color red, while American drivers also must be able to spot green and yellow. The Court sided with FMCSA, which said the overall degree of safety provided by Mexican standards was at least equivalent to American ones.

7. *See* Maja Wallengren, *Mexico Says U.S. Continues to Block Full Implementation of Truck Pilot Program*, 30 International Trade Reporter (BNA) 1292 (15 August 2013). [Hereinafter, *Mexico Says.*]

8. *See Mexico Says.*

The pilot program established by the MOU on 14 October 2010 ended on 10 October 2014. OOIDA attacked it as a failure. Only 15 out of 132,000 Mexican-domiciled carriers participated in it, and 83% of the miles the participants travelled were in the border zone. With such a low participation rate, how could the FMCSA claim it had enough data to declare the program a success and make it a permanent one?

The FMCSA answered by declaring the 15 Mexican trucking companies for which it had converted their operating authority from provisional to standard under the pilot program would continue to operate, and thus could travel beyond the commercial zone along the border. These 15 companies had crossed the U.S.-Mexican border over 28,000 times, travelled over 1.5 million miles on American roads, and undergone over 5,500 U.S. inspections. They and their drivers satisfied U.S. and Canadian-level safety standards. So, Mexico dropped its retaliatory tariffs.[9]

Under permanent rules, for Mexican carriers to obtain long-haul operating authority from the U.S., they had to (1) pass a PASA audit to ensure they met safety standards; (2) had a U.S. commercial driver's license (or a Mexican *licencia federal de conductor*); (3) satisfied DOT English-language proficiency standards; and (4) comply with all relevant laws, including border and random roadside inspections.[10] If a carrier met these requirements, then its vehicles would be subject to a 37-point "North American Standard Level 1 Inspection" every 90 days for at least four years. FMCSA data in 2016 indicated "roadside inspections of Mexican-owned trucks resulted in 0.86 percent of driver violations serious enough to halt their trips immediately, compared with a 4.8 percent of such driver violations for all motor carriers on U.S. highways."[11] But, the Teamsters objected, saying those data came from short hauls in the border area, not long haul trips from Guadalajara to Minneapolis, which would produce a higher violation rate. They called upon President Donald J. Trump (1946–, President, 2017–) to cut the trucking services provision in any *NAFTA* re-negotiation.

Free trade in trucking services finally arrived, but subject to significant regulatory oversight. Was each element in this oversight legitimate, or did protectionism still lurk?

---

9. Efforts by OOIDA and the Teamsters to challenge the pilot program results, arguing (inter alia), the DOT failed to include a large enough sample of carriers to yield statistically significant results, failed. *See International Brotherhood of Teamsters v. U.S. Department of Transportation*, Number 15-70754 (9th Cir.) (*rehearing denied*, 20 December 2017); Brian Flood, *Court Won't Reconsider Truckers' Challenge to Program*, 35 International Trade Reporter (BNA) 18 (4 January 2018). In a June 2017 decision in this case, Judge Kim McLane Wardlaw chided the American truckers for opposing their Mexican counterparts on grounds of "highway safety," when in fact "their real concern appears to be preventing the increased competition threatened by the entrance of Mexico-domiciled carriers."

10. *See* Rossella Brevetti, *Transportation Department Clears Way Of Roadblocks for Mexican Carriers*, 32 International Trade Reporter (BNA) 129 (15 January 2015).

11. Stephanie Beasley, *Teamsters Press Trump to Drop NAFTA's Mexican Trucker Provision*, 34 International Trade Reporter (BNA) 220 (2 February 2017).

• *NAFTA* 2.0 Annex II

The answer to that question came on 30 September 2018, with *NAFTA* 2.0. In Annex II to the Schedule of the U.S., America adopted an NCM with respect to Land Transportation:

> . . . the United States reserves the right to adopt or maintain limitations on grants of authority for persons of Mexico to provide cross-border long-haul truck services in the territory of the United States outside the border commercial zones if the United States determines that limitations are required to address material harm or the threat of material harm to U.S. suppliers, operators, or drivers.[1] The United States may only adopt such limitations on existing grants of authority if it determines that a change in circumstances warrants the limitation[2] and if the limitation is required to address material harm.[3] The Parties shall meet no later than five years after the entry into force of this agreement to exchange views on the operation of this entry.

---

[1] For purposes of this entry, "material harm" means a significant loss in the share of the U.S. market for long-haul truck services held by persons of the United States caused by or attributable to persons of Mexico.

[2] For greater certainty, a substantial increase in services supplied by the grantee may constitute a change in circumstances.

[3] The Parties confirm their shared understanding that current operations under existing grants of authority as of the date of entry into force of this Agreement are not causing material harm.

In other words, the U.S. "reserve[d] the right" to limit "grants of authority" for Mexican carriers to supply cross-border, long-haul trucking services beyond the border zones, if doing so was "required to address material harm or the threat of material harm to U.S. suppliers, operators, or drivers," where "material harm" was defined in terms of the economic self-interest of American carriers—a "significant loss in the share of the U.S. market" for them, caused by Mexicans.[12] The commercial zones were defined northward from the Mexican border as 25 miles from municipalities in California, New Mexico, and Texas, and 75 miles from ones in Arizona.

The Annex II restriction was "a victory for the International Brotherhood of Teamsters and . . . OOIDA, which had worked for over 20 years to block *NAFTA* cross-border trucking provisions," and could "disfavor Mexican carriers that have not been granted authority to operate in areas beyond the U.S. commercial zones."[13] There was no reciprocal provision in *NAFTA* 2.0 for Mexico, with respect to American carriers hauling cargo southward across the border. How much comfort could Mexico take from footnote 3, which exempted Mexican carriers that already

---

12. Rossella Brevetti, *U.S. Could Put Brakes on Mexican Trucks Under Trade Deal*, 35 International Trade Reporter (BNA) 1353 (18 October 2018). [Hereinafter, *U.S. Could.*]

13. *U.S. Could.*

operated in the border zones from a finding of "material harm." Depending on whether and how Congress applied the Annex through *NAFTA* 2.0 implementing legislation, they and prospective new Mexican carriers could be barred.

III. Case Study on Non-Discrimination and Data Localization: *NAFTA* 2.0

- 27 August 2018 U.S.-Mexico Bilateral Agreement

Office of the United States Trade Representative,

United States–Mexico Trade Fact Sheet, *Modernizing NAFTA to Be a 21st Century Trade Agreement* (28 August 2018)[14]

. . .

U.S. financial services firms provide services critical to every sector of the economy, including small- and medium-sized businesses. The United States exported about $115 billion in financial services in 2016, generating around a $41 billion surplus in trade in financial services.

The updated Financial Services Chapter includes commitments to liberalize financial services markets and facilitate a level playing field for U.S. financial institutions, investors and investments in financial institutions, and cross-border trade in financial services. The Chapter also preserves the discretion of financial regulators to ensure financial stability.

Key Achievement: Core Obligations to Prevent Discrimination Against U.S. Financial Services Suppliers

The Chapter includes core obligations, such as:

(1) National treatment, to ensure that U.S. financial service suppliers receive the same treatment as local suppliers.

(2) Most-favored-nation treatment, to ensure that U.S. financial service suppliers receive the same treatment as those from other countries.

(3) Market access, which prohibits imposition of certain quantitative and numerical restrictions that would limit the business of U.S. financial services suppliers.

Key Achievement: First Provision Against Local Data Storage Requirements

For the first time in any U.S. trade agreement, this deal includes a prohibition on local data storage requirements in circumstances where a financial regulator has the access to data that it needs to fulfill its regulatory and supervisory mandate.

---

14. https://ustr.gov/about-us/policy-offices/press-office/press-releases/2018/august /modernizing-nafta-be-21st-century (emphasis original).

Key Highlights Supporting Financial Services

The new Financial Services Chapter will include:

(1) Updated provisions to allow for the cross-border transfer of data and an updated market access obligation.

(2) The most robust transparency obligations of any U.S. trade agreement, to ensure good regulatory practices in government licensing and other market access authorizations.

(3) A separate Annex on commitments relating to cross-border trade, including application of the national treatment and market access obligation to an expanded list of cross-border services, such as portfolio management, investment advice, and electronic payment services.

(4) Specific procedures related to Investor-State Dispute Settlement claims with Mexico, including provisions regarding expertise of arbitrators and a special procedural mechanism to facilitate the application of the prudential exception and the other exceptions.

- **30 September 2018 Trilateral *NAFTA* 2.0 (*USMCA*)**

Office of the United States Trade Representative,

United States–Mexico–Canada Fact Sheet: *Modernizing NAFTA into a 21st Century Agreement* (1 October 2018)[15]

Financial Services

U.S. financial services firms provide services critical to every sector of the economy, including small- and medium-sized businesses. The United States exported about $115 billion in financial services in 2016, generating around a $41 billion surplus in trade in financial services.

The updated Financial Services Chapter [*USMCA* Chapter 17] includes commitments to liberalize financial services markets and facilitate a level playing field for U.S. financial institutions, investors and investments in financial institutions, and cross-border trade in financial services. The Chapter also preserves the discretion of financial regulators to ensure financial stability.

[Note that also in respect of liberalizing services trade, *USMCA* Chapter 18 covers telecommunications services, providing "reasonable and non-discriminatory access" for telecommunications providers of one Party to the public telecom infrastructure network of another Party. Thus, a foreign telecom provider cannot be barred from reselling its services over the network of another Party. The Parties also are barred from favoring a state-owned telecom provider over a private company.]

---

15. https://ustr.gov/about-us/policy-offices/press-office/fact-sheets/2018/october/united
-states–mexico–canada-trade-fa-1.

Key Achievement: Core Obligations to Prevent Discrimination Against U.S. Financial Services Suppliers

The Chapter includes core obligations, such as:

(1) National treatment [in Article 17:3], to ensure that U.S. financial service suppliers receive the same treatment as local suppliers.

(2) Most-favored-nation treatment [in Article 17:4], to ensure that U.S. financial service suppliers receive the same treatment as those from other countries.

(3) Market access [in Articles 17:5–17:7], which prohibits imposition of certain quantitative and numerical restrictions that would limit the business of U.S. financial services suppliers.

Key Achievement: First Provision Against Local Data Storage Requirements

For the first time in any U.S. trade agreement, this deal includes [in Article 17:20] a prohibition on local data storage requirements in circumstances where a financial regulator has the access to data that it needs to fulfill its regulatory and supervisory mandate.

Key Highlights Supporting Financial Services

The new Financial Services Chapter will include:

(1) Updated provisions [in Articles 17:5–17:7, and 17:19] to allow for the cross-border transfer of data and an updated market access obligation.

(2) The most robust transparency obligations [in Article 17:13] of any U.S. trade agreement, to ensure good regulatory practices in government licensing and other market access authorizations.

(3) A separate Annex on commitments relating to cross-border trade, including application of the national treatment and market access obligation to an expanded list of cross-border services, such as portfolio management, investment advice, and electronic payment services.

(3) Specific procedures [set out in Article 17:23] related to Investor-State Dispute Settlement claims with Mexico, including provisions regarding expertise of arbitrators and a special procedural mechanism to facilitate the application of the prudential exception and other exceptions.

Currency

Key Achievements: High-Standard Policy and Transparency Commitments, with Robust Accountability Mechanisms

The renegotiated agreement includes a Chapter on Macroeconomic Policies and Exchange Rate Matters [Chapter 33], with new policy and transparency commitments on currency issues. The Chapter will address unfair currency practices by requiring high-standard commitments to refrain from competitive devaluations and targeting exchange rates, while significantly increasing transparency and providing mechanisms for accountability. This approach is unprecedented in the context of a trade agreement, and will help reinforce macroeconomic and exchange rate stability.

- **Lingering Concerns**

Juxtapose the financial services provisions of *NAFTA* 2.0 against those of *NAFTA* 1.0 and *TPP*. Are there significant differences with respect to MFN and national treatment? As between *NAFTA* 2.0 and *TPP*, are the data localization rules better for both financial services suppliers and consumers in one deal versus the other? Likewise, in any of these agreements, are the definitions of wrongful currency behavior harmonized? Are any of the provisions on currency manipulation enforceable?

IV. Managed Trade in Services?

Market access rules on services suggest the same or similar general points as for goods. Is free trade the regime, or is it really managed trade?[16] Evident are the sensitivities in services areas. To be sure, as a September 2006 WTO Working Paper, highlights, the general pattern on Modes I and III (cross-border supply and temporary migration of persons) is that FTA pledges go beyond scheduled *GATS* commitments.[17]

The U.S., in particular, obtains better service market access through FTAs—largely because of its use of a Negative List approach—than under *GATS*. In the U.S. FTAs with Bahrain, the *CAFTA* countries and Dominican Republic, Chile, Colombia, Morocco, Oman, Peru, and Singapore, over 80% of all services sub-sectors are covered by trade-liberalizing commitments in Modes I and III. Under *GATS*, the figure is less than 50%. Through its FTAs, the U.S. is able to focus on access in areas in which it has a keen interest, such as audiovisual, educational, express delivery, and financial, and telecommunications services.

That said, even FTAs involving the U.S. do not reflect full free trade in services. Manifest in the details of the market access commitments on services in every FTA is that no FTA accords across-the-board free trade in services. Were the FTAs to do so, then the rules would occupy just a page or two. As with goods, there are sensitivities in services—and, for that matter, government procurement. Market access rules may obligate FTA members to give MFN and national treatment to service providers and government contractors. In practice, though, these rules may

---

16. *See* Raj Bhala, Dictionary of International Trade Law (3rd ed. 2015) (containing Annexed Tables detailing obligations for each FTA to which the U.S. is a Party).

17. *See* Martin Roy, Juan Marchetti & Hoe Lim, *Services Liberalization in the New Generation of Preferential Trade Agreements (PTAs): How Much Further than the GATS?* (ERSD-2006-07) (September 2006, www.wto.org).

be undermined by corollary concerns, such as environmental degradation, labor rights, and national security.

Accordingly, it must be asked, is the term "Free Trade Agreement" a misnomer for services as well as goods? To be sure, Adam Smith and David Ricardo studied trade in goods. Yet, inspired by their paradigm, may it be said every services deal is about managed trade?

Chapter 11

Liberalizing and Protecting FDI through FTAs

I. Overview of FTA Investment Chapters

- **Trade-FDI Link**

Cross-border investment flows are a major feature of globalization. These flows typically dwarf in value cross-border trade in goods, and are concomitants—indeed, catalysts—for trade in both goods and services. A sizeable percentage of trade in goods and services occurs between or among business affiliates, such as between a Japanese parent corporation and its Chinese subsidiary. In a historical sense, the world in which the Classical Economists Adam Smith (1723–1790) and David Ricardo (1772–1823) hypothesized about one enterprise producing goods in one country and exporting it to consumers in another country no longer exists. Global production and inter-affiliate trading are predominant modern realities. Of course, even in bygone eras, there were multinational enterprises such as the British East India Company. In brief, trade and investment are integrally linked.

- **Sources of FDI Law and U.S. FTAs**

Because there is no comprehensive MAI, FDI is governed through BITs, regional investment treaties, and investment chapters in FTAs. These accords are the primary source of the specialty known as International Investment Law, or FDI Law, as they are the primary mechanisms for promoting and protecting global investment of investors of a home state in the territory of a host state. Table 11-1 summarizes Investment and Competition Policy Chapters in U.S. FTAs.

For example, Chapter 11 of *NAFTA* both liberalizes restrictions on FDI and affords protections to investors. The *NAFTA* negotiators appreciated that securing the right to invest, protecting all forms of investment—such as concessions, contracts, debt, enterprises, and IP—and ensuring regulatory transparency is essential to attracting overseas capital. So, too, is giving foreign investors the right to establish, acquire, and operate investments on an equal footing with domestic entities. Chapter 11 covers these topics. While less ambitious, the later-in-time WTO *TRIMs Agreement* affords certain investor protections, namely, national treatment. Consider the extent to which *NAFTA* Chapter 11, and FDI sections in other FTAs, contain obligations that go beyond *TRIMs* mandates—*i.e.*, that are "*TRIMs* Plus."

To be sure, whether FDI rules are necessary in an FTA depends on the parties and the rules vary on the needs and sensitivities of contracting parties. For example,

Table 11-1. Overview of FDI and Competition Policy Chapters in U.S. FTAs

FTA	Date FTA Entered Into Force	Name and Location of FDI Chapter	Name and Location of Competition Policy Chapter
Israel	1 September 1985	None (Limited treatment, only in context of trade-related performance requirements)	None
NAFTA	1 January 1994	Chapter 11: Investment	Chapter 15: Competition Policy, Monopolies and State Enterprises
Jordan	17 December 2001	None	None
Singapore	1 January 2004	Chapter 15: Investment	Chapter 12: Anticompetitive Business Conduct, Designated Monopolies and Government Enterprises
Chile	1 January 2004	Chapter 10: Investment	Chapter 16: Competition Policy, Designated Monopolies, and State Enterprises
Australia	1 January 2005	Chapter 11: Investment—absence of investor-state arbitration provisions	Chapter 14: Competition-Related Matters
Morocco	*1 January 2006*	*Chapter 10: Investment*	*None*
CAFTA-DR (Dominican Republic-Central America)	*1 March 2006 (El Salvador); 1 April 2006 (Honduras and Nicaragua); 1 July 2006 (Guatemala); 1 March 2007 (Dominican Republic); and 1 January 2009 (Costa Rica)*	*Chapter 10: Investment*	*None*
Bahrain	1 August 2006	None (U.S.-Bahrain BIT is in place)	None
Oman	1 January 2009	Chapter 10: Investment	None

(*continued*)

Table 11-1. Overview of FDI and Competition Policy Chapters in
U.S. FTAs (*continued*)

FTA	Date FTA Entered Into Force	Name and Location of FDI Chapter	Name and Location of Competition Policy Chapter
Peru	1 February 2009	Chapter Ten: Investment	Chapter Thirteen: Competition Policy
KORUS (Republic of South Korea)	15 March 2012	Chapter Eleven: Investment	Chapter Sixteen: Competition-Related Matters
Colombia	15 May 2012	Chapter Ten: Investment	Chapter Thirteen: Competition Policy
Panama	31 October 2012	Chapter Ten: Investment	None

if the parties have a BIT in place, then additional FDI rules may be unnecessary. Both the *Bahrain* and *Jordan FTAs* do not include Investment Chapters, because BITs have been in force between the countries since 2001 and 2003 respectively.

However, the majority of U.S. FTAs contain rules to liberalize FDI, and thereby complement trade-liberalizing rules. For example, under the *Singapore FTA*, Singapore protects all forms of investment, unless specifically exempted, offers national treatment to American investors, and—like *NAFTA*—uses a Negative List approach to FDI access. This generosity to foreign investors is unsurprising, given Singapore's desire and need to attract FDI. The scope of the *Morocco FTA* stands rather in between the two extremes of zero and full coverage of FDI in the *Jordan* and *Singapore FTAs*, respectively. The *Morocco FTA* provisions protect all American investment in Morocco, except investment covered by an existing agreement, of which there are two kinds—agreements on natural resources, and agreements on assets controlled by the Moroccan government.

- Special Case of *Australia FTA*

Negotiations for the *Australia FTA* yielded another example of FDI treatment. America opposed Australia's foreign investment review process. In practice, the issue proved not to be too controversial. Few U.S. businesses complained about the process, as Australia routinely granted FDI approval. What result did the negotiators achieve?

The answer is all American investment in new businesses is exempt from screening by Australia's Foreign Investment Review Board. The *Australia FTA* also raised significantly thresholds imposed by Australian law for acquisitions in almost all sectors by American investors. Why do countries like Australia—and Canada—reserve the right to review foreign investments? Candidly, is it to ensure their economies are not dominated by investment from one country, such as the U.S.? Is national security, either through overall dominance or a single investment in a sensitive area, a factor?

The U.S. does not have a completely open or transparent investment regime. CFIUS, and the *Exon-Florio Amendment*, provide the means to block foreign acquisitions of American companies. Acquisitions of firms that export military or dual-use goods, or that engage in significant classified government contracting, pose particular concerns. In addition to these devices, loud, unwelcome Congressional attention, not to mention prejudice, can make prospective acquirers go away, as happened in spring 2006, when Dubai Ports World (DPW) dropped its bid to acquire port son the Eastern Seaboard. As it happens, DPW operates an important container terminal at the Jawaharlal Nehru Port Trust (JNPT) in Mumbai. India certainly is no stranger to being victimized by terrorism

- **Negative versus Positive List Approach**

The Negative List approach has the potential to provide greater liberalization of markets than those based on a Positive List approach. Many countries pursue this method in their negotiations of bilateral agreements including not only with America, but also with counter-parties like Canada and Japan. A benefit of this approach is that because every sector is presumed to be included, but for specific reservations, investors in future investments or the development of new industries can be assured of their protection.

As a general matter, the Negative List approach provides greater clarity for investors and lawmakers alike as all sectors are presumed to fall within the FTA's provisions unless there is an express provision otherwise. This allows investors to assess whether their specific industry is covered and what protective rights they might have under an FTA. Optically, pursuing a Negative List approach shows a country is more willing to pursue free trade and welcome global competition as opposed to a Positive List approach, which can be more protectionist than its opposite.

- **Underlying Rationales**

Rationales for negotiation of Investment Chapters vary depending on a country's economic status. For advanced economies, investment rules provide a legal framework of rights to protect an investor's investment in the host State. Often time, the promotion of investment is considered a secondary benefit. In contrast, for developing and least developed economies, negotiating investment regulations serves as a vital method of attracting FDI. By agreeing to include investment provisions in FTAs, it signals to foreign investors that the country is willing to do what it takes to protect foreign property rights and offers a stable investment climate.

FDI often is the largest source of external financing for developing economies. An abundance of FDI from MNCs can transform host State economies into exporters of manufactured goods at a faster rate than a national market may be able to on its own. New investments into an economy may create jobs for citizens of the host state and also provide additional tax revenue. Welcoming competition from foreign investors has the potential to spur greater productivity levels of locally owned firms and the increased competition could translate into lower consumer prices. Some have considered the benefits of FDI and investment rules as critical in fostering rule of law, decreasing local corruption, developing institutions, protecting private property and contract rights, streamlining administrative and legal procedures, and developing a regulatory environment conducive towards capital formation.

- **Labor and Environmental Issues**

FDI can also represent a double-edged sword for developing countries and LDCs. With benefits, come risks of opening one's economy to outside investment. Domestic industries may falter under the additional competition from foreign investors. Investment by large MNCs raises potential for abuses of market power by foreign investors.

Consider the buying power Wal-Mart. Not only would Wal-Mart have the ability to undercut domestic competitors in terms of pricing but could also lead to declining working conditions for local employees as companies seeking to do business with Wal-Mart often need to provide the lowest costs for the company. An increasing worry surrounding FDI are the rights afforded to local workers. Advocates for poor countries often (with good reason) are concerned MNCs may exploit their local workforce. There is also the risk of environmental damage as a result of exploitation of natural resources.

- **Sovereignty**

The greatest risk of entering into a FDI agreement is the loss of sovereignty. By agreeing to the terms of Investment Chapters and FTAs in general, countries no longer have the complete power to govern as they see fit. After an FTA enters into force, domestic governments must now take into considerations the obligations imposed by investment provisions when considering certain measures on behalf of the state's citizens. This point is particularly poignant for host States subject to ISDS schemes.

- **Types of Limits**

To prevent foreign investors from dominating a local economy, host-countries historically have imposed restrictions on the entry of FDI. Such limits include limitations on investment in sensitive sectors, limiting foreign investment through company formation, restrictions on land ownership or entity management, performance requirements, and restrictions on currency transactions. To counter these issues, BITs and Investment Chapters address potential problems by providing framework protections for market access, non-discrimination, rules against nationalization and expropriation, and the ability to settle disputes that may arise between an investor and the host State.

Investment Chapters in U.S. FTAs generally consist of two parts. The first section details substantive obligations for the home and host country governments aimed towards investors of member countries and their investments in the host country. The second section provides investors with the right to seek compensation for violations of the first section through an investor-state dispute resolution mechanism.[1] Key substantive obligations commonly found in the Chapters include national and MFN treatment for foreign investors in the host country, the right to transfer profits in hard currency to the home country, the prohibition against the use of performance requirements, and the right to compensation in the event of direct and indirect expropriation.[2]

- Post-*NAFTA* Language Changes

Owing to Congressional concerns, the language of Investment Chapters in America's FTAs has evolved in conjunction with American BITS since *NAFTA*. It was believed that the protections afforded to foreign investors in *NAFTA* were broadly phrased and may have granted more favorable treatment for claims by foreign investors than American investors would have had access to under U.S. law. In response, Congress mandated negotiating objectives in the *Trade Act of 2002* to clarify the scope of investment protection in FTAs.[3] The principal negotiating objectives for foreign investment aimed to reduce or eliminate trade-distorting barriers "while ensuring that foreign investors in the United States are not accorded greater substantive rights with respect to investment protections that United States investors in the United States, and to secure for investors important rights comparable to those that would be available under United States legal principles and practice."[4]

As a result, following 2002 and the release of the 2004 Model BIT, the language used in FTAs and bilateral investment treaties included narrower definitions of covered investments, narrower minimum standards of treatment, more detailed provisions investor state disputes, and provisions to increase transparency of national laws and proceedings as well as increasing language involving environmental and labor standards. The objectives and language of future Investment Chapters in U.S. FTAs are more than likely to flow from the Obama Administration's 2012 Model BIT.[5]

Building on the foundation of the 2004 Model, the updated Model addressed changes to the global commercial landscape. For example, investment obligations were expanded to include application against SOEs, performance requirements involving technology, environment and labor interests, financial services and the prudential exception, increased transparency, standard setting organizations, and

---

1. The *Australia FTA* does not include a Section B detailing an ISDS mechanism.

2. For example, see Articles 10:3 (National Treatment), 10:4 (Most-Favored-Nation Treatment), 10:7 (Expropriation and Compensation), 10:8 (Transfers), and 10:9 (Performance Requirements) of the *Peru FTA*. The majority of the FTAs have Articles addressing each of these topics, but the Article numbers vary depending on the placement of the Investment Chapter in the FTA. The *Singapore FTA*, for example, has corresponding provisions in Article 15.

3. Public Law Number 107-210.

4. Section 2102 (b)(3).

5. *See* 2012 U.S. Model BIT, U.S. Department of State, Bureau of Economic and Business Affairs, Bilateral Investment Treaties and Related Agreements, www.state.gov/e/eb/ifd/bit/index.htm.

further details on dispute resolution. Countries seeking investment agreements with the U.S. can be assured of the baseline American negotiating position as evidenced in the 2012 Model BIT.

II. FDI Market Access Rules

- **Performance Requirements**

A major barrier against foreign investors entering domestic markets is the use of national laws and regulations that restrict access by foreign investors to the domestic market. A typical barrier against FDI is the imposition of performance requirements by the host State. Such requirements may require investors to utilize a certain level of local content in their goods, hire local workers, and place ownership restrictions on companies.

Host countries impose such barriers for various reasons. One reason is to protect domestic industries from being hard hit by the foreign competition. Another could be the fear that foreign investors may leave the country in the event of economic instability and take its profits out of the local economy. Market access rules strike a balance between foreign investors and host States, offering the former some freedoms but saving policy space for the latter.

- **Negative List Approach in U.S. FTAs**

In American FTAs, market access rules in Investment Chapters follow the Negative List approach. All industries are eligible for foreign investment unless specific exemptions are included in the FTA, typically listed in a corresponding annex. Under *NAFTA*, Canada made various reservations including the right to review direct acquisitions of $150 million or greater, restrictions in the oil and gas sectors, and limitations in connection with the ownership and privatization of certain state enterprises.[6] Similarly, Mexico took reservations on the ownership of land, for cable television, air and land transportation, and retail sales of certain petrochemical while the U.S. input reservations for existing, nonconforming legislation in respect to nuclear power, broadcasting, mining, customs brokers, and air transportation.

Certain excluded sectors under an FTA may also be constitutionally mandated. An example is Panama's right to appoint the Panama Canal Authority as the entity

---

6. Addressing reservations and exceptions under *NAFTA,* Article 1108:1 provides that the obligations under Articles 1102 (National Treatment), 1103 (Most-Favored-Nation Treatment), 1106 (Performance Requirements) and 1107 (Senior Management and Boards of Directors) "do not apply to: (a) any existing non-conforming measure that is maintained by (i) a Party at the federal level, as set out in its Schedule to Annex I or III . . . ." Annex I is comprised of each countries' reservations for existing measures and schedule of liberalization commitments and Annex III includes Activities Reserved to the State of Mexico. Article 1108.3 excludes "any measure that a Party adopts or maintains with respect to sectors, subsectors, or activities, as set out in its Schedule to Annex II (Reservations for Future Measures)" from Articles 1102, 1103, 1106 and 1107.

exclusively responsible for the activities of the Panama Canal as provided under Panama's 1972 Constitution.[7] The Annex protects measures adopted by the Panama Canal Authority within its outlined responsibilities investor state dispute settlement.

While a host State may contract with investors of another Party for services or goods relating to the authority, it does not mean that the host State has surrendered its exemption for that economic sector. Depending on the Annex, certain timelines are set forth for liberalizing investment restrictions or to phase out a Party's performance requirements over time. A prospective investor must pay close attention to the Annexes to Investment Chapters as they may provide clues as to whether investment in a particular sector is prohibited and whether it eventually will be liberalized.

- Scope of Application

Investment Chapter provisions apply to all measures adopted or maintained by a Party relating to investors, covered investments as defined in the FTA, and all investments in the host State with regard to performance requirements and investment and the environment.[8] It should be noted that if there is a conflict or inconsistency between the provisions of the Investment Chapter and another Chapter in the FTA such as cross-border trade in services, then the other Chapter's provisions must prevail.[9] Parties may also adopt special formality measures on covered investments like the requirement that investors be residents of the Party or that covered investments be incorporated under the laws of the host Party. These formalities must still comply with the protections afforded to investors of the other Party.

- Restricting Performance Requirements

One method to increase market access is to prevent parties from imposing certain performance requirements in connection with the life span of an investment in its territory. Parties are obligated to avoid imposing the following performance requirements on investors that would result in trade distortion:

(a) to export a given level or percentage of goods or services;

(b) to achieve a given level or percentage of domestic content;

---

7. Addressing Panama Canal Authority, Annex 10-F (1) provides: "For greater certainty, nothing in this Chapter or Chapter Eleven (Cross-Border Trade in Services) shall be construed to derogate from Panama's right to appoint the Panama Canal Authority as the entity exclusively responsible for the use, administration, functioning, conservation, maintenance, modernization, and related activities of the Panama Canal, as provided under Panama's 1972 Constitution . . . ."

8. Each Investment Chapter begins with an article outlining the scope and coverage of the chapter that is identical in each FTA. For example, Article 11:1:1 of the *KORUS FTA* states: "This Chapter applies to measures adopted or maintained by a Party relating to: (a) investors of the other Party; (b) covered investments; and (c) with respect to Articles 11:8 and 11:10, all investments in the territory of the Party."

9. Article 10:2:1 of *Colombia FTA* provides: "In the event of any inconsistency between this Chapter and another Chapter, the other Chapter shall prevail to the extent of the inconsistency."

(c) to purchase, use, or accord a preference to goods produced in its territory, or to purchase goods from persons in its territory;

(d) to relate in any way the volume or value of imports to the volume or value of exports or to the amount of foreign exchange inflows associated with such investment;

(e) to restrict sales of goods or services in its territory that such investment produces or supplies by relating such sales in a way to the volume or value of its exports or foreign exchange earnings;

(f) to transfer a particular technology, a production process, or other proprietary knowledge to a person in its territory; or

(g) to supply exclusively from the territory of the Party the goods that such investment produces or the services that it supplies to a specific regional market or to the world market.[10]

Similarly, host States may not make potential receipt of an advantage in connection with the establishment, acquisition, expansion, management, conduct, operation or sale of the investment contingent on compliance with performance requirements.[11]

A host State may condition advantages to investors if they locate production, supply a service, train employees, construct facilities, or carry out R&D in its territory.[12] This practice is common for States seeking to attract FDI. They offer benefits such as tax subsidies or other corporate perks in exchange for investors infusing their cash flow into the local community with jobs. Government procurement, qualifications requirements related to export promotion and foreign aid programs, as well as content requirements relating to qualifying goods for preferential tariffs or quotas are exempt from some of the performance requirements. It should be noted that the ban against these specific performance requirements applies equally to both Parties to the FTA and non-Parties.

Market access rules address employment and management requirements by including a provision addressing senior management and composition of Boards of Directors. Parties are barred from requiring investors to award senior management

---

10. Article 10:9:1 of the *Colombia FTA* states "[n]o Party may, in connection with the establishment, acquisition, expansion, management, conduct, operation, or sale or other disposition of an investment of an investor of a Party or of a non-Party in its territory, impose or enforce any requirement or enforce any commitment or undertaking," and explicitly lists the performance requirements referenced above.

11. *See* Article 10:9:2 of the *Colombia FTA*.

12. Article 10:9:3(a) of the *Colombia FTA* states: "Nothing in paragraph 2 shall be construed to prevent a Party from conditioning the receipt or continued receipt of an advantage, n connection with an investment in its territory of an investor of a Party or of a non-Party, on compliance with a requirement to locate production, supply a service, train or employ workers, construct or expand particular facilities, or carry out research and development, in its territory."

positions based on nationality.[13] But, in a compromise to host States, a host State "may require that a majority of the board of directors, or any committee thereof, of an enterprise of that Party that is a covered investment, be of a particular nationality, or a resident in the territory, provided that the requirement does not materially impair the ability of the investor to exercise control over its investment."[14] The caveat on the composition of a Board suggests designation of a local national would be in name only as the decision making power would remain with the investor.

Investment rules also attempt to reserve sovereign power for host States via provisions on the environment and the denial of benefits. Parties may pursue measures to ensure investment activities take into consideration environmental protection when pursuing certain activities.[15] A host State could hold an investor for environmental clean up costs, or limit the amount of an activity in relation to an environmental concern, as long as the measure comports with MFN and national treatment.

For enterprises a non-Party owns or controls within the covered FTA territory, a host State is not obligated to provide the same benefits of investors of an FTA Party, if that State has no diplomatic relations with the non-Party, or if it maintains measures against the non-Party or an investor of the non-Party that prohibit transactions with the enterprise.[16] Measures under this provision could be trade controls and export sanctions. Enforcing this provision, which allows for discriminatory investment practices, can become difficult with respect to subsidiaries and individuals. Identifying controlling investors of an enterprise is necessary. For example, American sanctions imposed on a Russian investor could impact the benefits a Dominican Republic business receives under *CAFTA-DR*, it that investor holds controlling share of the covered investment.

• **Non-Conforming Measures**

Non-conforming measures are important to consider as regards market access. During FTA negotiations, countries consult with their domestic industries to consider existing regulations that may hinder access to their domestic market. A

---

13. Article 10:10:1 of the *Panama FTA* states: "Neither Party may require that an enterprise of that Party that is a covered investment appoint to senior management positions natural persons of any particular nationality."

14. Article 10:10:2 of the *Panama FTA*.

15. Since *NAFTA,* the FTAs have included an article specifically addressing investment and the environment. For example, Article 15:10 of the *Singapore FTA* provides: "Nothing in this Chapter shall be construed to prevent a Party from adopting, maintaining, or enforcing any measure otherwise consistent with this Chapter that it considers appropriate to ensure that investment activity in its territory is undertaken in a manner sensitive to environmental concerns."

16. Addressing the denial of benefits, Article 11:11:1 of the *KORUS FTA* states: "A Party may deny the benefits of this Chapter to an investor of the other Party that is an enterprise of such other Party and to investments of that investor if persons of a non-Party own or control the enterprise and the denying Party: (a) does not maintain normal economic relations with the non-Party; or (b) adopts or maintains measures with respect to the non-Party or a person of the non-Party that prohibit transactions with the enterprise or that would be violated or circumvented if the benefits of this Chapter were accorded to the enterprise or to its investments."

country might try to create a reservation for an existing, inconsistent measure. That is, it might seek to "grandfathered" a measure that the FTA otherwise would not allow, and thereby give federal and state governments time to review the measure and decide whether to include it as a permanent reservation in an Annex to the relevant Chapter.

This reservation process applies to state and federal regulations but inconsistent regulations at a local level are automatically grandfathered on a permanent basis. Once a regulation has been "grandfathered" in or is listed as a reservation, the party is protected from dispute challenges regarding non-discrimination, performance requirements, and senior management, as long is it is not altered or renewed in a manner that makes it more inconsistent with the FTA. As with the Negative List approach, if a Party decides not to take a reservation, or liberalizes the measure in a way to allow for greater market access, it may not be reversed, and the regulation will stand as amended and foreign investors may invest in that particular sector.[17]

III. FDI Non-Discrimination Rules

- **National Treatment Generally**

The cornerstone of FDI Chapters is to protect investors from discriminatory practices in the host State that would undermine the benefits of their investment. Consider a prospective investor studying a country with growth potential in the sector of that investor. The investor observes that if it makes the FDI in that country, it will be charged twice the rate of similar domestic companies when seeking business permits, or will be obliged to satisfy additional regulatory steps if it wants to sell its business. Non-discrimination rules address these potential pitfalls for investors through national treatment, MFN status, and providing for a minimum standard of treatment.

- **GATT Article III:4 Standard**

National treatment protection in Investment Chapters apply the same standard as in GATT Article III:4.[18] Host States must accord investors of the other Party "treatment no less favorable" than given towards its own investors in like circumstances. National treatment must be given to investors and covered investments for the entire duration of an investment, including the establishment period, acquisition, expansion, management, conduct, operation, and sale or disposition of

---

17. *See* Article 10:13 (Non-Conforming Measures) of the *Peru FTA* and accompanying Schedules to Annex I and Annex II.

18. Article 10:3:1 of the *Peru FTA* states: "Each Party shall accord to investors of another Party treatment no less favorable than that it accords, in like circumstances, to its own investors with respect of the establishment, acquisition, expansion, management, conduct, operation, and sale or other disposition of investments in its territory." Article 10:3:2 similarly obligates national treatment for covered investments.

investments. By protecting the entire life span of an investment, this prevents a host government from agreeing to terms when attracting FDI from investors but then raising additional barriers to investors or requiring investors to sell, because of their nationality, once the company has been established.

This level of treatment applies to all levels of government regulation, including that of states, territories, and other possessions. Similarly, host states are obligated to accord MFN status to investors of the other Party during the life cycle of the investment.[19] That is, host states should not treat investors or investments of non-Parties to the agreement better than an investor from a nation party to the agreement. Further, some, but not all, FTAs have included a provision requiring host countries to provide the better of national treatment or MFN status to investors and their investments.

- **Luring Foreign Automobile Investment**

Consider for example, the subsidies and treatment by certain American states seeking to lure FDI from European automotive companies like BMW and Volkswagen and Japan's Toyota. Viewed in this manner, states hope to benefit from the creation of local manufacturing jobs and the influx of money spent on facilities and working employees with disposable income. Foreign companies also benefit from being guaranteed equal if not better treatment by investing in American auto manufacturing, gaining a foothold in American auto sales and decreasing the supply chain and transportation time to manufacture vehicles for American consumption that had been produced outside of the U.S. This is not to say there are no negatives to such a relationship like states competing to offer greater investment packages to foreign investors through the use of tax subsidies and other corporate advantages, often at the expense of local taxpayers. However, for purposes of explaining the potential benefit of investment rules, this example illustrates the case.

- **Minimum Standards of Protection**

In addition to national and MFN treatment, American Investment Chapters include provisions on the minimum standard of treatment to be applied.[20] The minimum standard of protection for covered investments must be in accordance with customary international law, specifically the minimum standard of treatment of aliens. The host State "shall accord to covered investments treatment in accordance with customary international law, including fair and equitable treatment and full protection with security."[21] "Fair and equitable treatment" refers to due process, as host States must not deny an investor access to justice in criminal, civil, or

---

19. Article 10:4:1 of the *Peru FTA* addresses MFN treatment by requiring each Party accord to investors of another Party "treatment no less favorable than that it accords, in like circumstances, to investors of any other Party or of any non-Party with respect to the establishment, acquisition, expansion, management, conduct, operation, and sale or disposition of investments in its territory."

20. *See* Article 10:4 (Minimum Standard of Treatment) of the *Chile FTA*.

21. *Chile FTA* Article 10:4:1.

administrative adjudicatory proceedings. Host States must provide parties the level of police protection required under customary international law. This standard does not create additional substantive rights for covered investments nor require treatment beyond this minimum standard.

These three basic non-discriminatory rules are present in all of the American FTAs. There is some variance as to additional terms on conditions affecting a particular country. For example, measures adopted relating to investment loses as a result of armed conflict or civil strife should be non-discriminatory. However, the *Colombia, Peru, KORUS* and *Panama FTAs* provide detailed provisions imposing greater scrutiny on the host State and an additional layer of protection for investors. Each includes an article addressing treatment in cases of strife. If the investor's loss is a result of the host state's requisitioning of the covered investment or the host state's forces cause unnecessary destruction of a covered investment, then the investor must be made whole by the host state in the form of restitution, compensation, or both. Such compensation must be prompt, adequate, and effective.[22] Beyond armed conflict or civil strife, *KORUS* includes measures adopted as a result of revolt, insurrection, and riot. Such provisions are likely to be included in future FTAs, especially given the increase globally of domestic conflicts.

IV. Rules on Compensation for Expropriation

• **Expropriation and Nationalization Risk**

For investors, FDI presents risks of (*inter alia*) expropriation and nationalization of their investment. In terms of expropriation, a foreign investor may fear that in the event of a dispute with the host Party or in the event of political unstableness or a coup in the host country, the investor may see its investments confiscated by the host country, leaving it with little recourse. The risk of expropriation is exacerbated in economically and/or politically unstable environments, and where security is deteriorating. Governments facing such pressures may look to foreign investments as a remedy, however modest or temporary, and may be tempted to blame (rightly or wrongly) those pressures on foreign interests.

Consider Argentina's 2012 expropriation of the majority stake in the Argentinean energy firm YPF that was held by a Spanish oil company, Repsol. After two years of litigation between the company and the Argentinean government, a $5 billion settlement agreement was struck between the parties in 2014. To assuage the fears

---

22. Specifically, Article 10:6:2 of the *Peru FTA* provides that if an investor of a Party, in situations of armed conflict or civil strife, "suffers a loss in the territory of another Party resulting from: (a) requisitioning of its covered investment or part thereof by the latter's forces or authorities; or (b) destruction of its covered investment or part thereof by the latter's forces or authorities, which was not required by the necessity of the situation, the latter Party shall provide the investor restitution, compensation, or both, as appropriate, for such loss. Any compensation shall be prompt, adequate, and effective in accordance with Article 10:7:2 through 10:7:4, *mutatis mutandis*."

of investors losing the value of money spent on an investment in a host State, one of the main protections sought for investors sought during negotiations of investment chapters and BITs is the right to compensation for expropriation of their investment property or interests.

- **Protection: Compensation Formulas for Expropriation**

Investment rules in American FTA Investment Chapters aim to prevent governments from nationalizing or expropriating an investment of a foreign investor either directly or indirectly through measures that are tantamount to nationalization or expropriation of the investment. In the event of expropriation of an investment by a host Party, the investor must be compensated the equivalent to the fair market value of the expropriated investment *immediately before* the expropriation ("date of expropriation"), plus interest from the date of expropriation until the date of payment. The compensation must not reflect any change in value occurring because the intended expropriation had become known earlier.

Consider a hotel owner in a foreign country where it was foreseeable the hotel would be expropriated in coming months. The fair market value on the date of expropriation is likely to be less than the property's actual worth prior to the potential expropriation. As a result, fair compensation would be the price prior to the news of the potential for expropriation.

Compensation must be paid without delay and fully realizable and transferable. Article 1110:4 of *NAFTA* outlined the amount of payment based on G7 currency and required that compensation be freely transferable. However, to simplify the process, all later FTAs removed the reference to G7 currency and replaced it was "freely usable currency," *i.e.*, hard currency.

- **Lawful Expropriations**

Note that expropriation by a host State may be lawful under particular circumstances. In order for expropriation to avoid running afoul of investment provisions, it must have been for a "public purpose" and accomplished in a non-discriminatory manner. Additionally, the host State must provide "prompt, adequate, and effective" compensation to the investor. The expropriation of the investment must be in accordance with due process of law, including fair and equitable treatment and full protection and security. Investment provisions negotiated after *NAFTA* equated due process of law to treatment in accordance with customary international law. The minimum standard of treatment under customary international law refers to all customary international law principles protecting the economic rights and interests of aliens.

What constitutes a "public purpose" has seemingly been left to the interpretation of the host government as only the *Peru FTA* attempted relate the term to customary international law and likened it to "public necessity," "public interest," or "public use" in domestic laws. Because of this lack of definitive principle as to what expropriation would be considered a "public purpose," it is a low bar for an expropriating host State to provide some type of justification for its actions so long as it can meet the second prong of having acted in a non-discriminatory matter and not against a particular person or government. The second prong is not without its own grey areas. Consider a scenario where nationals of one foreign state exclusively control a particular sector, like energy for example, and that industry becomes nationalized. Under these facts, it would be difficult to conclude whether the expropriation was based on nationality or rather the specific industry sector.

- **Additional Guidance in FTA Annexes and 3 Considerations on Defining "Expropriation"**

Since *NAFTA*, the majority of Investment Chapters have Annexes specifically addressing expropriation in an attempt to provide more guidance beyond the general principles previously discussed. An action or series of actions by a host State is not considered expropriation unless it interferes with a tangible or intangible property right or interest. Additionally, the direct method of expropriation or nationalization occurs when there is a formal transfer of title or an outright seizure of the property interest.

The more difficult aspect is determining whether an indirect expropriation has occurred. This determination requires a case-by-case, fact-based inquire taking into consideration the following:

(1) Economic impact of the government action, which would not establish an indirect expropriation when viewed in isolation;

(2) Extent to which the government action interferes with distinct, reasonable investment-backed expectations; and

(3) Character of the government action.

The *KORUS FTA,* in particular, has specific additions to be taken into consideration when evaluating the government's action that were not present in any of the other American FTAs.[23]

A footnote to the second consideration indicated that the reasonableness of an investor's investment-backed expectations was dependent in part on the nature and extent of government regulation in the relevant sector. If a sector is already heavily regulated by the host State, then an investor's expectations that additional regulatory changes may occur are less likely to be reasonable, as opposed to a sector that generally receives little regulatory attention. It also mandated that when considering the character of the government action, parties should take into consideration the government's objectives and the particular context for the action, for example, whether that action imposes a special sacrifice on a particular investor or investment beyond what an investor should have expected to endure on behalf of the public interest. Additionally, non-discriminatory regulatory actions designed to protect legitimate public welfare objectives like safety, public health, and real estate price stabilization are not indirect expropriations. The *KORUS* Investment

---

23. *See KORUS Annex 11-B* (Expropriation).

Chapter also includes an Annex addressing whether a taxation measure, in a specific factual situation, might constitute an expropriation and designates factors to take into consideration.

The majority of FTAs also exempt nondiscriminatory regulatory actions pursued by host States with legitimate public welfare objectives in mind from constituting indirect expropriation, except in rare circumstances. Enumerated public welfare objectives included public health, safety, and the environment. The *Peru, KORUS, and Colombia FTAs* provided additional certainty that the list of "legitimate public welfare objectives" was not to be considered exhaustive.[24] This provision attempts to carve out and protect sovereign initiatives that a host State might pursue for the benefit of its citizens. (A claim of indirect expropriation as a result of a host State's tobacco restriction in relation to public health initiatives is discussed in the Investor State section below.)

Additional expropriation rules have excluded the issuance of compulsory licenses granted in relation to intellectual property rights in accordance with the *TRIPS Agreement* and the revocation, limitation, or creation of intellectual property rights to the extent that such action is consistent with the corresponding IP Chapters as beyond the purview of the expropriation obligations. Other FTAs have provided other specific exemptions from expropriation provisions.

For example, *NAFTA* makes clear the general applicable non-discriminatory measures are not considered expropriation of a debt security or loan if it was solely on the ground that the measure imposes costs on the debtor that cause it to default on the debt.[25] The *Singapore FTA* took a unique approach as it addressed expropriation through two *Side Letters*, rather than being within the body of the FTA.[26]

In the *Side Letters* submitted to the USTR, Singapore confirmed its agreement to the general terms governing expropriation. Singapore also distinguished land expropriation based on negotiations with the U.S. and compared to the government's land acquisition law already in place in Singapore. Specifically, Singapore indicated it had no plans to expropriate investor land or a covered investment and agreed to withhold from expropriating land or investments for three years after the FTA entered into force. Failure to satisfy this three year moratorium would allow

---

24. Article 3(b) of Annex 10-B of the *Peru TPA* and *Colombia FTA* provide: "Except in rare circumstances, non-discriminatory regulatory actions by a Party that are designed and applied to protect legitimate public welfare objectives, such as public health, safety, and the environment do not constitute indirect expropriations."

Article 3(b) of Annex 11-B of the *KORUS* excludes legitimate public welfare objectives such as "public health, safety, the environment, and real estate price stabilization (through, for example, measures to improve the housing conditions for low-income households)" from constituting indirect expropriations.

25. *See NAFTA* Article 1110:8.

26. *See* 6 May 2003 letters between Ambassador Robert B. Zoellick, U.S. Trade Representative, and Minister George Yeo, Minister for Trade and Industry Singapore referred to as the "Exchange of Letters on Expropriation" and the "Exchange of Letters on Land Expropriation."

investors to pursue Singapore through both investor-state disputes as well as the overall FTA dispute settlement mechanism. If found in violation, then Singapore agreed it would pay the fair market value of the expropriated land as enumerated in the expropriation provisions.

Save for a few particularities, overall, the U.S. position on rules governing expropriation and compensation has remained the same following *NAFTA*. This continuity indicates foreign governments are satisfied with the terms, provides a guideline for new negotiations.

V. Overview of Institutions and Dispute Resolution Mechanisms

• **Transparency**

Of the most notable commitments concerning the process by which trade is liberalized and institutions consider, promulgate, and enforce trade rules, surely transparency ranks at the top. Not surprisingly, therefore, RTAs are likely to contain some rules on the topic. The easiest such rule is to insist on application of GATT Article X and WTO standards on transparency. That rule effectively "piggy backs" on the multilateral system. It may be the safest such rule, too, for an RTA partner that is not a democracy and whose regime is reluctant to go beyond international standards.

There are, however, RTAs with WTO-Plus commitments on transparency. Two examples are the *U.S.-Singapore* and *Chile FTAs*. Their provisions go beyond both GATT-WTO and *NAFTA* rules. For instance, the *Singapore FTA* demands transparency in dispute settlement through open public hearings and public access to submissions. It also creates opportunities for participation, allowing third parties to make submissions.

• **Categories of Mechanisms**

Dispute resolution procedures in RTAs share common points and boast distinctive features. To approach these similarities and differences, it is useful to start by identifying what the mechanisms are. They can be divided into 2 broad categories:

(1) *General Dispute Resolution*

   Does the RTA contain a general mechanism to resolve disputes among the member countries about the meaning an interpretation of the terms of the accord?

(2) *Topical Dispute Resolution*

   Does the RTA contain a special mechanism applicable to a specific subject matter?

In most FTAs, the answer to both questions is "yes." That answer leads to two follow up questions.

First, does the RTA in question create private rights of action, and private remedies? Traditionally, the answer was "no." Older American FTAs, such as the *Israel FTA*, create no such rights. That answer also is true for some dispute settlement schemes in other FTAs. But, newer FTAs tend to create room for private rights and remedies, albeit in limited subject matter contexts. The quintessential example is *NAFTA* Chapter 11, which allows private investors to sue host governments. Another example is *CAFTA-DR* Chapter 10, which lets them seek arbitration against host governments.

Typically under such Chapters, benefits for foreign direct investors, such as pursuing an action directly against the host government, are limited by a kind of "minimum contacts" test. Under *CAFTA-DR* Article 10:12(2), a host government can deny an investor of another *CAFTA-DR* Party the benefits of Chapter 10, if that investor has "no substantial business activities in the territory of any Party, other than the denying Party and persons of a non-denying Party, or of the denying Party, own or control the enterprise . . . ." In June 2012, El Salvador successfully invoked this provision against a claim brought against it by the American subsidiary of a Canadian firm Pacific Rim Mining Corporation.

That claim was the first-ever environmental dispute under *CAFTA-DR*. It concerned the health and environmental effects of gold and silver mining activities. Pac Rim claimed damages from a *de facto* ban on such mining announced in March 2008 by the El Salvadorian government. Without ruling on the merits of the claim, the three-member tribunal of ICSID hearing the case ruled the claim could not proceed under *CAFTA-DR*. Canada is not a *CAFTA-DR* Party, and the tribunal ruled the American subsidiary, Pac Rim Cayman LLC, did not have sufficiently "substantial" business activities in America to support its claim under Article 10:12(2).

The second follow up question concerns the infrastructure for dispute resolution. What institutions does an FTA create to perform dispute resolution, and possibly other, functions? It is possible to write an entire book (or multi-volume series) in response to this question. Indeed, some such works exist. While there is no substitute for examining individually each FTA, case studies may be instructive. Consider *NAFTA*, which has six different dispute settlement mechanisms.

NAFTA Chapter 20 is the general mechanism. The most prominent case brought under this procedure involved the right of Mexican truckers to carry freight on U.S. roadways (discussed in a separate Chapter). *NAFTA* has five topical dispute resolution mechanisms. Chapter 11 deals with investor-state disputes over FDI. The number of Chapter 11 cases is large, and most opinions are considered well-reasoned. Chapter 14 deals with financial services, though there have been few if any cases. Chapter 19 covers AD and CVD issues. Effectively, *NAFTA* Chapter 19 extends the bi-national panel system created by the *Canada FTA*. In addition, *NAFTA* has rules on safeguards, contained in Chapter 8. They distinguish regional (*i.e.*, *NAFTA*-based) from global (*i.e.*, WTO-based) safeguards. Finally, the *Environmental* and *Labor Side Agreements* each have mechanisms to deal with the central obligation in each *Side Agreement*, namely, to enforce effectively existing environmental or labor laws. Many observers feel the *Side Agreement* mechanisms have been a disappointment. Similarly, Chapter 22 of *KORUS* contains a general dispute settlement mechanism, and Chapter 11 sets out an ISDS mechanism.

- *NAFTA* **Chapter 19 and Examples of 2004** *Softwood Lumber* **and 2017** *Supercalendered Paper* **CVD Cases**

NAFTA Chapter 19 is particularly noteworthy. It provides for review of national determinations in AD or CVD cases, in lieu of judicial review in the domestic court system of the relevant *NAFTA* Party (though constitutional issues may be appealed back to that system). A Chapter 19 Panel must apply the law of the importing country. A politically charged example is the March 2006 Chapter 19 Panel decision in *Softwood Lumber*.[27] President George Washington (1732–1799, President 1789–1797) complained about imports from Canada of British lumber.

Softwood lumber comes from coniferous trees, such as pine and spruce trees, and is used in building construction and box spring manufacturing. Canada is the world's largest producer-exporter of this wood, and America is its biggest market. Its colder climate yields wood with finer grains, which resists squeaking and warping. Modern origins of the dispute date to the 1980s. Generally, the Parties settled their dispute through managed trade agreements of varying duration, but when a bilateral accord lapsed (as it did in 2015), they renewed their trade litigation (as when the U.S. imposed ADs and CVDs in 2001).

In America, timber is harvested from private land, or public land that is auctioned off by the Federal government. The auction system is used in Ontario and Quebec, but in other Canadian Provinces, most notably British Columbia, the Provincial government owns the forests. The U.S. long alleged that unlike timbering activity in America, where prices incorporate the cost of private ownership and maintenance of tree forests, British Columbia charges a "Stumpage Fee" to Canadian companies for felling a tree. Originally, the Fee was per stump (hence the name), but was revised based on the cubic meters (or board feet) of wood a stump yields. The U.S. claimed the Fee was set at below-market rates, thus giving softwood lumber producer-exporters in Canada a subsidy vis-à-vis their American competitors. The Chapter 19 Panel applied U.S. CVD law, and ruled in favor or Canada, finding (*inter alia*) that the Ontario subsidy was *de minimis* (*e.g.*, 0.8%). After the case, British Columbia phased in an auction system, which it applied to timber on public lands along its coast, and explained that auction prices tend to track world market prices.

Nevertheless, in April 2017, the DOC announced a preliminary affirmative subsidization determination, and imposed CVDs ranging from 3.0% to 24.12%

---

27. *See* Article 1904 Binational Panel Review under the North American Free Trade Agreement, *In the Matter of Certain Softwood Lumber Products from Canada (Final Affirmative Countervailing Duty Determination and Final Negative Critical Circumstances Determination)*, USA-CDA-2002-1904-03, Decision of the Panel on the Fifth Remand Determination (17 March 2006), www.nafta-sec-alena.org/Home/Dispute-Settlement/Decisions-and-Reports.

(depending on the respondent Canadian lumber company), totaling $1 billion annually. That translated into an increase of 1.4% in the average cost to build a home in America.

As another illustration, in the 100-page 2017 decision in *Supercalendered Paper*, in which Canada challenged 17.87%–20.18% CVDs imposed in 2015 by the DOC on Canadian exports of glossy paper (used for catalogs, coupons, corporate brochures, direct mailings, directories, flyers, magazines, and retail inserts), the Panel applied U.S. law.[28] The Panel ordered the DOC to re-compute the CVDs, based on flaws in the DOC's calculation, as well as its view the DOC erred (*inter alia*) in (1) concluding the provincial government of Nova Scotia directed Nova Scotia Power to bestow a financial contribution, namely, discounted electricity, to the Port Hawkesbury Paper LP company, and (2) valuing direct transfer payments from the central government of Canada to a mill Port Hawkesbury sold to the Pacific West Commercial Corp. to ensure equipment in the mill remained operable and efficient (so-called "hot idle" status).

The Chapter 19 case volume is large, and includes highly contested disputes over softwood lumber, sugar, and wheat, and many cases have been settled. The quality of decisions appears reasonably high, but the process can be slow. For instance, a dispute between the U.S. and Mexico over cement dumping took 16 years to resolve. There have been few "extraordinary challenges," which are made to an Extraordinary Challenge Committee (ECC) — also a mechanism that existed in the *Canada FTA*.

- **Other FTA Dispute Resolution Mechanisms**

Likewise, the *Chile FTA* has a general dispute resolution mechanism in Chapter 22. This *FTA* also contains three major topical mechanisms: Chapter 12 on Financial Services, Chapter 18 on Labor, and Chapter 19 on Environment. Unlike *NAFTA*, the *Chile FTA* does not speak about AD or CVD issues, nor contain a special dispute settlement mechanism for them. Rather, the *Chile FTA* states only that each member country reserves the right to apply its own AD or CVD rules. A different pattern exists in the *Singapore* and *Australia FTAs*, which set out a general prohibition from taking any trade remedy, except in accordance with GATT rules.

Of course, America did not take a leap of faith regarding AD or CVD rules in its FTA partner countries. As all the partners are WTO Members, those rules are (or should be) certain and predictable, in the sense they conform to GATT Article VI, the WTO *Antidumping Agreement*, and the WTO *SCM Agreement*. The *Chile, Singapore, Australia,* and *Morocco FTAs* dispute settlement mechanisms promote

---

28. *See* Article 1904 Binational Panel Review under the North American Free Trade Agreement, *In the Matter of Supercalendered Paper from Canada: Final Affirmative Countervailing Duty Determination*, Memorandum Opinion and Order, USA-CDA 2015-1904-1 (17 April 2017), www .nafta-sec-alena.org/Home/Dispute-Settlement/Decisions-and-Reports; Brian Flood, *NAFTA Panel Sides With Canada In U.S. Paper Duty Dispute*, 34 International Trade Reporter (BNA) 634 (20 April 2017).

compliance through consultation and remedies that enhance trade, instead of a conventional sanctions-based approach. Thus, these *FTAs* allow for "equivalent" remedies in commercial, as well as labor and environmental, disputes, and allow a winning party to opt for a monetary assessment to enforce obligations.

- *NAFTA* Chapter 11

NAFTA Chapter 11 both liberalizes restrictions on FDI and affords protections to investors. The *NAFTA* negotiators appreciated that securing the right to invest, protecting all forms of investment—such as concessions, contracts, debt, enterprises, and IP—and ensuring regulatory transparency is essential to attracting overseas capital. So, too, is giving foreign investors the right to establish, acquire, and operate investments on an equal footing with domestic entities. Chapter 11 covers these topics. While less ambitious, the later-in-time WTO *TRIMs Agreement* affords certain investor protections, namely, national treatment. Consider the extent to which *NAFTA* Chapter 11, and FDI sections in other FTAs, contain obligations that go beyond *TRIMs* mandates—*i.e.*, that are "*TRIMs* Plus."

NAFTA Chapter 11 also contains an ISDS mechanism. That is, it authorizes investor-state legal action, *i.e.*, the *NAFTA* Parties essentially waive sovereign immunity and allow themselves to be sued by private parties on a claim relating to Chapter 11. A three-member panel of independent arbitrators, not the domestic court system of the host country, handles the claim using procedures set out in Chapter 11. A number of Chapter 11 disputes have been adjudicated, yielding both written opinions and a robust body of scholarship about the cases.

Not all constituencies are fans of ISDS mechanisms. Consider the AFL-CIO. Its March 2014 study, *NAFTA at 20*, decries *NAFTA* for focusing "on creating privileges and protections for investors," at the expense of workers and the environment.[29] The study faults Chapter 11 for "allow[ing] investors to directly challenge government regulations that interfere with actual or potential profits before international panels that are unaccountable to the public." Coming from a different perspective than trade unions, the Securities Industry and Financial Markets Association (SIFMA) opposes the exclusion of financial services from ISDS; SIFMA thinks the mechanism to be pro-investor, and an incentive to engage in FDI, and thus wants financial market investors to enjoy the right to bring cases directly against a host *NAFTA* Party.

To be sure, whether FDI rules are necessary in an FTA depends on the parties. For example, if the parties have in place a BIT, then they may be unnecessary. The *Jordan FTA* does not have an investment chapter, given the 1997 BIT between the two countries. Still, following *NAFTA*, a number of American FTAs contain rules to liberalize FDI, and thereby complement trade-liberalizing rules. For example, under the *Singapore FTA*, Singapore protects all forms of investment, unless specifically

---

29. AFL-CIO, *NAFTA at 20* (March 2014), www.aflcio.org/content/download/121921/3393031 /March2014_NAFTA20_nb.pdf; Michael Rose, *AFL-CIO Report Denounces NAFTA, Argues for New Approach to Trade Pacts*, 31 International Trade Reporter (BNA) 621 (3 April 2014).

exempted, offers national treatment to U.S. investors, and—like *NAFTA*—uses a Negative List approach to FDI access. This generosity to foreign investors is unsurprising, given Singapore's need—as a city-state—to attract FDI, coupled with its economic ambitions in the Asia-Pacific region.

The scope of the *Morocco FTA* stands rather in between the two extremes of zero and full coverage of FDI in the *Jordan* and *Singapore FTAs*, respectively. The *Morocco FTA* provisions protect all American investment in Morocco, except investment covered by an existing agreement, of which there are two kinds— agreements on natural resources, and agreements on assets controlled by the Moroccan government.

• *Australia FTA* **Counterexample**

Interestingly, the *Australia FTA* has no analog to *NAFTA* Chapter 11. There are no provisions for allowing investors to arbitrate disputes with host countries. That is because of the trust each side has in the security and predictability of the legal framework of the other side, and the long-standing economic relations between the two countries. Put indelicately, in the *NAFTA* context, many American (and Canadian) investors recoil at the prospect of suing the Mexican government in Mexican court. They are dubious as to the ability of the Mexican court system to afford them procedural and substantive protections. But, suing the Australian government in an Australian court is acceptable (though the *Australia FTA* permits re-visitation of the topic, should circumstances warrant). Again, bluntly, investor protection concerns probably explain why the *Morocco FTA* has an investor-state dispute settlement provision.

Also of note is that a Negative List approach to liberalizing FDI is not used by the EU its trade agreements. Europe prefers a progressive strategy. Under it, restrictions on the entry, establishment, and operation of investments are removed over time. What might explain the European preference, and what are the pros and cons of the two methods?

• **Similarities and Differences**

Most RTA dispute settlement mechanisms use arbitration-style procedures. They call for the establishment of a Panel of experts. The complainant and respondent present oral and written arguments to the Panel. The Panel is supposed to render a reasoned decision. Time deadlines are set for each step, or at least each phase, of a case. How effective these deadlines are in practice varies.

One complaint is the arbitral-style procedures in the *NAFTA* mechanism take too long and cost too much, and thus are of less value than had been hoped when *NAFTA* entered into force on 1 January 1994. Moreover, whether the decision may be appealed depends on the FTA and mechanism. For instance, as alluded to above, *NAFTA* contains an "extraordinary challenge" procedure, which has been used thrice, once in a Chapter 19 case involving alleged conflicts of interest by a panelist.

A second complaint about arbitration procedures—indeed, any type of dispute settlement mechanism in an FTA—is that it may be abused for protectionist purposes. Bringing a case can itself be a trade barrier. Addressing this concern is partly a matter of legal culture: if FTA partners tend toward litigiousness in their domestic arenas, then they shall have to adjust their approach to each other in trade disputes. Precisely that pledge was made on 23 July 2001, when America and Jordan exchanged official letters stating the intention of each side not to apply formal dispute settlement mechanisms in a way that would block trade.

The Americans and Jordanians stated a preference for informal mechanisms, specifically bilateral consultations, to secure compliance with obligations in the *Jordan FTA*, lieu of seeking formal trade sanctions. Only if the sides fail to resolve a dispute after consultations is recourse made to a dispute settlement panel. The Panel may issue legal interpretations of the FTA. Notably, as with decisions by a Panel under the *Israel FTA*, decisions by a *Jordan FTA* panel are not binding. A similar arrangement exists under the *Morocco FTA*, namely, anticipation that most interpretative questions would be resolved by informal or formal government-to-government contacts, and recourse to a dispute settlement panel, which could issue legal interpretations, only if consultations fail.

How, then, if decisions of an FTA arbitral Panel are recommendations, are obligations enforced in the event of non-compliance? Any dispute resolution mechanism holds little value if it does not contain a rigorous enforcement device in the event of non-compliance by the losing party. The conventional device is retaliation, which must be appropriate and proportional. That device exists, for instance, in the *Jordan FTA*. Generally, retaliation preferably occurs in the same sector as the dispute. If same-sector sanctions are not feasible, then cross-sectoral retaliation may be authorized. Significantly, in recent U.S. FTAs, there is a choice offered between retaliation and monetary damages.

VI. Critique of ISDS Mechanisms

- **Controversy**

One of the most contentious aspects surrounding FTAs is the inclusion of an ISDS in Investment Chapters. Both *CPPP* and *T-TIP* are examples. Indeed, ISDS provisions are in 50 BITs and FTAs in force to which America is a Party, and 3,000 agreements around the world.[30]

Generally, ISDS is a mechanism for foreign investors to pursue legal action against the host State by initiating binding arbitration proceedings. A tribunal of three independent arbitrators, not the domestic court system of the host State, adjudicates the claim consistent with internationally accepted arbitration rules outlined

---

30. *See* Patrick Gillespie, *The NAFTA Teardown: Here's Where Trump Could Start*, CNN BUSI-NESS, 1 December 2016, https://money.cnn.com/2016/12/01/news/economy/nafta-trump-chapter-11/index.html (citing USTR data). [Hereinafter, *NAFTA Teardown*.]

in the relevant Chapter. The existence of this right means host State governments that are Party to the FTA have waived sovereign immunity as a defense to FDI claims brought against them by foreign private parties.

ISDS contrasts with a dispute settlement mechanism provided in an FTA allowing States to bring claims against each other for violations under the FTA in its entirety. Each Investment Chapter provides a detailed outline for the procedures for initiating a claim, what claims may be brought, selecting a tribunal, applying governing rule, and the grant of a final award. The ISDS mechanism procedures in investment chapters of American FTAs are modeled from the dispute settlement policies in U.S. BITs.

- **Eligible Claims**

Potential claims eligible for submission to arbitration include allegations of direct or indirect injury to an investor or his investment in violation of the host State's substantive obligations provided in the first section of its respective investment chapter. Additional grounds for claims vary depending on the language of the particular FTA. For example, the *NAFTA* provides additional claims arising from Article 1503:2 regarding State Enterprises and Article 1502:3(a) in circumstances when a monopoly has acted inconsistently with the Party's substantive obligations causing the investor to incur loss or damages from the breach.

In contrast, ISDS provisions under *CAFTA-DR* and the *Chile FTA* expanded potential claims to include breaches of an "investment authorization." That term refers to authorization by the foreign investment authority of the host State granted to a covered investment or investor. These provisions also cover an "investment agreement," meaning written agreements, effective after the date of entry into force, between the host State and a foreign investor granting investor rights to natural resources or other assets controlled by the State which the foreign investor relies on.

Four of the most recently concluded FTAs involving America—with Peru, Panama, Colombia, and Korea—give greater detail on the rights granted by an investment agreement between a national authority of the host State in the areas of national resources, public services, and infrastructure.[31] Rights to natural resources include those right controlled by a national authority such as extraction, refining, transportation, distribution, or sale. Public service rights include power generation or distribution, water treatment or distribution, or telecommunications.

Lastly, rights to undertake infrastructure projects relate to the construction of roads, bridges, canals, dams, or pipelines, which are not solely for the use and benefit of the government. Since *NAFTA*, the trend in language for potential claims has increasingly become more detailed and effectively narrowing the potential claims that may be brought under ISDS procedures.

---

31. The rights are elaborated in detail through the specific definition of the term "investment agreement" in Article 10:28 of the *Peru FTA* and *Colombia FTA*, Article 10:29 of the *Panama FTA*, and Article 11:28 of *KORUS*.

• **Procedures**

Each Investment Chapter provides specific details regarding the dispute settlement procedures. Common amongst all agreements is the requirement that disputing parties first attempt to settle claims via private consultation and negotiations.[32] Additionally, a three-year statute of limitations is imposed on potential claims.[33] The clock begins running based on the date the investor first acquired or *should have* acquired knowledge of the alleged breach and incurred loss or damage. Investors may bring forth claims on its own personal behalf, or on behalf an enterprise owned or controlled directly or indirectly by the investor.[34]

If settlement negotiations fail between the conflicting parties, the disputing investor must provide written notice to the disputing host State of its intention to submit a claim to arbitration at least 90 days prior to the actual submission.[35] Similar to a complaint in the American legal system, the written notice must detail the allegedly breached provision, issues and the facts surrounding the claim, and the relief sought and approximate damages claimed.

After at least six months have passed since the triggering event giving rise to the claim, the investor may submit the claim for arbitration under either the arbitration rules provided by the *ICSID Convention*, the *Additional Facility Rules* of ICSID, or the *Arbitration Rules* of UNCITRAL.[36] The *ICSID Convention* requires the disputing host State and the home State of the foreign investor to be parties to the convention. If one of the countries is not a party to the convention, then the disputing investor may elect to proceed under ICSID's "Additional Facility" Rules. Since *NAFTA*, Investment Chapters have expanded to allow for disputing parties to mutually agree to submit the claim to any other arbitration institution or apply other arbitration rules however the majority of arbitration disputes continue to be settled at ICSID.[37]

Once each party has properly consented to the submission of a claim to arbitration, parties will move towards establishing the three-person tribunal.[38] Each party may appoint an arbitrator and the presiding arbitrator will be appointed by agreement between the disputing parties. If after a certain amount of days (depending on the provision in the FTA) from the date the claim was submitted to arbitration a tribunal has not yet formed, the Secretary-General will appoint the remaining position(s). Under *NAFTA*, Parties were required to establish and maintain a roster of 45 presiding arbitrators experienced in international law and investment to

---

32. *See* Article 10:15 of the *Colombia FTA*.

33. *See* Article 10:18:1 of the *Colombia FTA*.

34. *See* Article 10:16:1(a) and (b) of the *Colombia FTA*.

35. *See* Article 10:16:2 of the *Peru TPA*.

36. *See* Article 10:16:3 of the *Peru TPA*.

37. Article 10:16:3(d) of the *Peru TPA* allows for the filing of arbitration claims under alternative methods "if the claimant and respondent agree, to any other arbitration institution or under any other arbitration rules."

38. *See Panama FTA* Article 10:19 (Selection of Arbitrators).

choose from.[39] In post-*NAFTA* FTA Investment Chapters, the roster was no longer explicitly required.

The specific conduct of tribunals then varies according to particular FTA. A *NAFTA* tribunal then decides the issues in dispute with the Investment Chapter and the applicable rules of international law with the potential to request binding interpretations as to whether an alleged breach is within the scope of a reservation or exception of the Investment Chapter Annexes.[40] The tribunal could also request export reports on factual issues like environmental, health, safety, or other scientific matters raised by a disputing party.[41] The tribunal was then able to issue a final award providing either monetary damages including interest or the restitution of property with the option to pay monetary damages in lieu of restitution.[42]

In contrast, the ISDS provisions in FTAs following *NAFTA* are more akin to the American justice system. These provisions, in respect of the conduct of arbitration, allow for non-disputing Parties to make oral and written submissions to the tribunal regarding the interpretation of the FTA, grant the ability of a tribunal to consider *amicus curiae* submissions from non-parties, and set a process with which a tribunal would rule on objections made by parties.[43] Such provisions allow for NGOs and other interested non-parties to voice their opinions through these "friend of the court" submissions. Interestingly, prior to issuing a decision or award, the tribunal is required to submit its proposed decision to the disputing parties and to non-disputing parties. The disputing parties are then provided with an opportunity to submit additional written comments for the tribunal's consideration prior to the final award. In both circumstances, tribunals are forbidden from ordering punitive damages.

• Transparency

Post-*NAFTA* FTAs also placed great emphasis on the inclusion of provisions regarding the transparency of arbitral proceedings.[44] This is in large part a response to the redefined FDI objectives imposed by Congress in the *Trade Act of 2002*. While *NAFTA* did not highlight transparency in relation to ISDS procedures, all FTAs published after 2002 equipped ISDS procedures with transparency provision. The transparency provisions required the respondent party to promptly transmit and make available to the public documents associated with the arbitral proceedings including the notice of arbitration, pleadings, briefs and written submissions to the tribunal, transcripts of the tribunal where available, as well as orders, awards, and decisions of the tribunal.

---

39. *See NAFTA* Article 1124:4 (Constitution of a Tribunal When A Party Fails to Appoint an Arbitrator or the Disputing Parties are Unable to Agree on a Presiding Arbitrator).

40. *See NAFTA* Article 1131 (Governing Law) and Article 1132 (Interpretation of Annexes).

41. *See NAFTA* Article 1133 (Expert Reports).

42. *See NAFTA* Article 1135 (Final Award).

43. *See Panama FTA* Article 10:20 (Conduct of the Arbitration).

44. *See Chile FTA* Article 10:20 (Transparency of Arbitral Proceedings).

Additionally, the tribunal hearings must be open to the public. The provisions protect a respondent from having to disclose confidential business information or privileged information and allowed parties to withhold information in accordance with articles addressing Essential Security and the Disclosure of Information. Akin to the American litigation procedures, disputing parties were allowed to designate information as protected against non-disputing parties and provide redacted versions to the general public. Similar to judges, the tribunal retains the power to accept or reject the designation of information as protected.

• **Exclusions**

Annexes to Investment Chapters often highlight individual reservations central to particular negotiating parties. For example, Article 1138 of *NAFTA* excludes from investor-state claims government action prohibiting or restricting FDI for national security reasons, and exempts from ISDS and the overall dispute settlement mechanism decisions by Canada or Mexico to review potential acquisitions and decide whether or not to permit the acquisition similar to the American review process by CFIUS.

CAFTA-DR excludes investor claims in cases of strife as a result of an armed movement or civil disturbance.[45] The *Peru* FTA excludes investors from submitting a claim to arbitrations if the investor or the enterprise has already alleged that breach in proceedings before a court or administrative tribunal of that Party.[46] To be sure, this provision exists to prevent investors from having "two bites at the apple" by pursuing a claim through both the court system and the ISDS. The *Panama FTA* exempts measures adopted or maintained by the Panama Canal Authority in pursuant of its responsibilities associated with the administration, maintenance, use, and conservation of the Panama Canal.[47] Many of the Investment Chapters with Latin America trading partners also include provisions on public debt with respect to defaults and non-payment of debt.

Additionally, many FTAs, especially the post-2008 global recession FTAs, all have special provisions relating to the imposition of restrictive measures regarding the payment and transfers by a party other than the U.S. Investor-state claims will not be accepted until one year after the event giving rise to the claim and loses arising form the restrictive measure on capital inflows are limited to the reduction in value of the transfer and exclude the consequential loss of profits or business. However, the one-year waiting period requirement is inapplicable if the claim arises from restrictions based on current transactions, equity investments, or loan or bond conditions.

---

45. Annex 10-D specifically excludes from arbitration claims alleging that Guatemala breached Article 10:6:2 as a result of an armed movement or civil disturbance.

46. *See Peru TPA* Annex 10-G.

47. *See Panama FTA* Annex 10-F.

- **Underlying Purposes**

The purpose of ISDS provisions as pursued by the U.S. is to provide Americans investing abroad with the similar legal protections that would be available to domestic and foreign investors in the U.S. The provisions seek to prevent discrimination against American investors, unfair expropriation without due process, and the nullification of investment contracts. The ISDS process is designed to provide a fair process to both the foreign investor and the host State by utilizing established international legal principles to resolve investment disputes and requiring independent and impartial behavior from arbitrators. The rules also allow for either party to request the disqualification of an arbitrator if necessary.

Moreover, the strict definitions provided in American FTAs raise the standard of claims and offer the opportunity to expedite claims leading to the dismissal of frivolous claims. Instituting investor state provisions in its investment chapters and bilateral investment treaties has had the result of replicating certain aspect American legal tradition on its trading partners as referenced above. This can be viewed as potentially strengthening the legal institutions and rule of law of the host countries or as imposing American rule over its trading partners.

- **Criticisms**

ISDS is not without its criticisms and is often cast in a negative light. For example:

Take the case of ExxonMobil . . . versus Canada. Exxon argued against Canada's requirement that it invest in local research and development, such as education, job training and innovation. It's meant to ensure oil drillers provide an economic benefit to the local province where they're drilling.

Exxon said the regulation was too onerous. It took the case to a *NAFTA* Panel in 2012 and won. Canada was forced to pay Exxon about $14 million. Canada didn't repeal the law, so Exxon has filed a second case seeking more cash.

. . . On one hand, it [ISDS] gives companies assurance that they can invest abroad and won't get crushed by foreign regulations.

On the other hand, it allows a company to go head-to-head with a foreign country—an idea that bothers some.

"It goes way too far in giving corporations a power against foreign governments that they don't have against their own government," says Alan Deardorff, a trade expert at the University of Michigan. . . .

Canada and Mexico have paid dearly in *NAFTA* cases while the U.S. government has won all its cases.

Canada has paid $160 million to corporations, almost entirely American, since *NAFTA* was implemented in 1994. Mexico has paid $204 million . . . .

[As of December 2016,] Canada has received 39 claims against it, while Mexico has had 24. The U.S. has received 21 claims against it and it's never lost one . . . .

Of course, past need not be prologue in terms of claim filings or winning cases.[48]

Critics of ISDS often point to the lack of transparency of the forum in contrast to domestic courts. A common point made about ISDS proceedings before an arbitration tribunal is it is the preferred approach for dispute settlement, because America and other advanced nations do not trust the local courts of developing countries to provide investors with a fair hearing and due process under the law. The system effectively allows investors to bypass the domestic court process and seemingly allows corporations to act above the domestic laws of a country. Others view the mechanism as a loss of sovereignty by limiting a State's ability to regulate its financial stability, environmental protection, or public health.

Consider that of all the FTAs to which the U.S. is a Party (14 as of August 2018), only the *Australia FTA* does not contain ISDS provisions. *TPP* does, but the U.S. withdrew from that deal—notwithstanding its successful negotiation of an ISDS mechanism generally to its liking. *CPTPP* continues with that mechanism, albeit with certain aspects of it suspended on account of the American withdrawal. As for the *Australia FTA*, there are no provisions allowing investors to arbitrate disputes in that deal. That is because of the trust each side has in the security and predictability of the legal framework of the other side, and the long-standing economic relations between the two countries. During negotiations, Australia argued ISDS procedures were unnecessary due to the similar legal traditions regulating investment in both countries and promised American investors would receive fair treatment before Australian courts.

In contrast, put indelicately, in the *NAFTA* context, many American (and Canadian) investors recoil at the prospect of suing the Mexican government in Mexican court. They are dubious as to the ability of the Mexican court system to afford them procedural and substantive protections. But, suing the Australian government in an Australian court is considered acceptable. To be fair, the *Australia FTA* does include a provision that if there has been a change in circumstances affecting dispute settlements relating to investment, a Party may request consultations with the other Party on the subject to consider the development of appropriate procedures.

However, this method does not provide the investor with direct recourse of approaching the host State but the investor may still pursue claims in the domestic courts of Australia. A lingering issue surrounding Australia's aversion towards ISDS is how negotiations will proceed as the trend amongst bilateral and regional free trade agreements has included ISDS provisions. While the *Australia FTA* did not include ISDS provisions, the *TPP* is more likely to have them, particularly in light of the fact five of the current members with which the U.S. has an FTA all include ISDS provisions.

The loss of sovereignty associated with investor-state policies can also constitute a great social and economic risk to countries, particularly in the age of multi-level

---

48. *NAFTA Teardown.*

corporations often valued at valued greater than the GDP of some nations. The high cost imposed on host states defending claims as well as the risk of paying multi-million dollar compensation to multi-national corporations has the potential to chill a country's social policies like public health and the environment.

- **Tobacco Regulations and Plain Packaging**

Consider the challenges by tobacco titan, Phillip Morris against the tobacco regulations of Uruguay and Australia under investment treaties, albeit not American FTAs or BITs. In February 2010, Phillip Morris requested arbitration against Uruguay under the Switzerland-Uruguay BIT challenging Uruguay's newly enacted tobacco regulations. The regulations sought to impose (1) a "single presentation" requirement prohibiting marketing more than one tobacco product under each brand; (2) the use of graphic images showcasing the consequences of smoking to health; and (3) the imposition of health warnings covering 80% of cigarette packages.

Phillip Morris argued the regulations were overbroad and imposed "unreasonable measures" lacking a rational relation to the regulation's public health objectives. It claimed its trademarks were unjustly expropriated because their use on multiple brands was prohibited. Similarly, under the Hong Kong BIT with Australia, Phillip Morris challenged Australia's plain packaging law for tobacco products. The plain packaging law required all tobacco products in Australia to be a certain color and contain no logo or brand features on the packaging except for the brand name in a standardized form and font. The company argued the regulation violated free speech, expropriated the value of the trademarks, violated FTA obligations, and lacked a rational relationship to its regulatory purpose.

The fight against Australia's tobacco regulations have gone beyond investor-state dispute and led to challenges against Australia at the WTO by tobacco producing countries like the Dominican Republic and Honduras. Nations seeking similar tobacco policies are waiting to see how Australia's fight will pan out prior to acting on their own accord. (The WTO litigation is discussed in a separate Chapter.)

Such challenges—through ISDS mechanisms in FTAs, and under the WTO *DSU*—motivate third parties to assist countries defend or bring claims. Tobacco companies helped pay legal expenses of Honduras and the Dominican Republic against Australia at the WTO, while American billionaire Michael R. Bloomberg has helped to fund the legal defense of Uruguay in its tobacco packaging rules.

- **2015 Canadian Study on *NAFTA* ISDS**

In January 2015, the Canadian Center on Policy Alternatives in Ottawa published an empirical analysis of the *NAFTA* Chapter 11 ISDS from 1 January 1994, when *NAFTA* entered into force, through 31 December 2014.[49] This analysis argued:

---

49. *See* Scott Sinclair, Canadian Center for Policy Alternatives, *Democracy Under Challenge Canada and Two Decades of NAFTA's Investor-State Dispute Settlement Mechanism* (January 2015), www.policyalternatives.ca/sites/default/files/uploads/publications/National Office/2015/01/NAFTA _Chapter11_Investor_State_Disputes_2015.pdf. [Hereinafter, Sinclair.]

When *NAFTA* came into force 21 years ago, there was plenty of debate about its impact on jobs, energy and sovereignty. Unfortunately, little attention was paid to an obscure provision in the treaty that allowed foreign investors to invoke binding investor-state arbitration to challenge government measures that allegedly diminish the value of their investments. The dubious rationale for granting this extraordinarily sweeping right to foreign investors was that the Mexican courts of the day were prone to corruption and political interference.

Over two decades later, *NAFTA's* Chapter 11 and its . . . ISDS system have become notorious. Of the 77 investor-state claims filed to date under *NAFTA*, only a handful pertain to the administration of justice in the Mexican courts. Instead, foreign investors have used Chapter 11 to target a broad range of government measures, especially in the areas of environmental protection and natural resource management, which allegedly impaired corporate profits . . . .

. . .

Claimants can challenge government measures that are allegedly unfair or inequitable (*NAFTA* Article 1105), discriminatory (*NAFTA* Articles 1102 and 1103), constitute direct or indirect expropriation (*NAFTA* Article 1110) or apply performance requirements such as local development benefits (*NAFTA* Article 1106). While tribunals cannot force a government to change *NAFTA*-inconsistent measures, they can award monetary damages to investors. These damage awards are fully enforceable in the domestic courts.

. . .

Canada has been the target of 35 investor-state claims, significantly more than either Mexico (22 claims) or the U.S. (20 claims), despite the fact that the latter's economy is 10 times larger than Canada's.

. . .

Of decided cases—those which ended either in an award by the tribunal or a negotiated settlement—governments have won 24 (69%) and lost 11 (31%). But, breaking these down by countries is revealing. Canada has won seven and lost six decided cases [resulting in damage pay-outs of Canadian $172 million]. Mexico has won six and lost five of decided cases. Only the U.S. has an unbroken winning record, having won 11 decided cases and lost none.

. . .

NAFTA's investor rights system has been used repeatedly to attack regulations in all three countries. . . . All of Canada's losses concerned important public policy issues or regulatory matters. . . . Canada's six losses . . . [show] how profoundly *NAFTA* Chapter 11 impinges on sovereign regulatory authority.

Two decades ago, when *NAFTA's* Chapter 11 was put in place, neither governments nor the public grasped that it would be used to successfully attack the regulation of harmful chemicals or toxic waste exports, to second-guess routine bureaucratic and administrative decisions, to expand private property rights to encompass publicly-owned water and timber, to compensate investors when governments refuse to approve contentious proposals, or to restrict the ability of local governments to enforce local economic development requirements in return for an investor's access to resources. . . .

. . .

Canada has been sued more times and faces more active claims than any other *NAFTA* Party. . . . Canada is now the most sued developed country in the world. This dubious distinction is entirely due to lawsuits under *NAFTA* Chapter 11.

. . .

The success rate of foreign investors in cases against Canada has been fairly high, with claimants being successful in 46% of decided claims. When looking at all concluded ISDS cases on a global basis, . . . approximately 31% were decided in favour of the investor, 43% in favour of the state, and the remaining 26% of cases were settled.

. . .

ISDS can no longer be rationalized as simply a mechanism to protect foreign investors in developing countries with spotty investment protection records or unreliable court systems. In truth, it is a coercive tool with which multinational corporations can assail and frustrate government regulation in both developing and developed countries. ISDS has truly evolved into a private, parallel system of justice for foreign investors . . . .[50]

The report concluded by warning about a "chilling effect" of ISDS on public policy formation and regulatory enforcement. Does it make governments wary of exercising these functions, even on legitimate matters, for fear of lawsuits by foreign MNCs?

VII. *NAFTA* 2.0 ISDS Cut Back

Chapter 14 of *NAFTA* 2.0 substantially limits the availability of what had been the ISDS mechanism in Chapter 11 of *NAFTA* 1.0. The U.S. generally opposed ISDS, arguing the mechanism undercut its sovereignty, and was a form of political risk insurance that encouraged American companies to investors overseas. America argued in the *NAFTA* 2.0 negotiations that it was not America's responsibility to

---

50. Sinclair, 30–31, 34, 36–37.

mollify concerns of foreign direct investors about the judiciary systems in other countries, by allowing ISDS so that investors could bypass local courts. That would facilitate FDI in other countries, but America's first interest was to encourage investment inflows into the U.S.

So, under the *USMCA*, ISDS is phased out as between the U.S. and Canada (across three years following the termination of *NAFTA* 1.0, and allowable during the phase out period then only for legacy claims, *i.e.*, ones brought by investors already present in the U.S. or Canada). ISDS is available as between the U.S. and Mexico (thanks to Chapter 14, Annex 14-D). But (as per Annexes 14-D and 14-E), claims by investors under ISDS are limited to alleged breaches of obligations concerning non-discrimination (*USMCA* Articles 14:4 and 14:5) or expropriation (Article 14:8 and Annex 14-B). Hence, claims about denial of minimum standards of treatment (MST), such as fair and equitable treatment (Article 14:6), are not allowable. Also, aggrieved investors cannot use ISDS as a first resort; rather (as per Article 5:1 of Annex 14-D), they must press their case in local courts, and only after issuance of a final ruling, or passage of 30 months, can they seek recourse through ISDS.

So, for example, financial services providers cannot use ISDS to press claims concerning the full array of FDI protections afforded in *USMCA* Chapter 14.[51] They cannot, for instance, bring a claim "to enforce commitments on the minimum standard of treatment (MST) [under *USMCA* Article 14:6], armed conflict and civil strife [under Article 14:7], indirect or regulatory appropriations, and transfers."[52] For such claims, banks and other financial institutions would need to access local courts, or rely on government-to-government dispute settlement (under Chapter 31).[53] But, like other foreign direct investors, financial services firms can use ISDS for claims about breaches of national or MFN treatment (under *USMCA* Articles 14:4 and 14:5, respectively), or direct expropriation (under Article 14:8 and Annex 14-B).

That said, select sectors—namely, energy, infrastructure (specifically, the management of ownership of infrastructure), oil, NG, power generation, telecommunication services, transportation services, plus government procurement—are given special treatment under *USMCA* Annex 14-E. Annex 14-E modifies the general U.S.-Mexican ISDS rules of Annex 14-D for these select sectors. They are identified in Paragraph 6 of Annex 14-E as "covered sector[s]" and "covered government contract[s]." For investors in these areas, as between the U.S. and Mexico,

---

51. *See* Report of the International Trade Advisory Committee on Services, *A Trade Agreement with Mexico and Potentially Canada*, 27 September 2018, https://ustr.gov/sites/default/files/files/agreements/FTA/AdvisoryCommitteeReports/ITAC%2010%20REPORT%20-%20Services.pdf [hereinafter, *ITAC Services Report*]; Len Bracken, *NAFTA 2.0 Limits Financial Services Investment Protections (1)*, 35 International Trade Reporter (BNA) 1192 (4 October 2018).

52. *ITAC Services Report*, 20.

53. *USMCA* Article 17:23 sets out additional rules on dispute settlement in financial services cases.

controversies about most of the protections afforded by the *USMCA* for FDI (under Chapter 14), including ISDS, may be resolved through ISDS.

One aspect of the *NAFTA* 2.0 ISDS rules is targeted at China. It is the definition of "claimant" in Article 1 of Annex 14-D:

> **claimant** means an investor of an Annex Party, excluding an investor that is owned or controlled by a person of a non-Annex Party that the other Annex Party considers to be a non-market economy, that is a party to a qualifying investment dispute;

Suppose a Chinese investor owns or controls a Mexican company that, in turn, invests in the U.S. The Mexican company is excluded from the definition of "claimant," and thus cannot use ISDS to bring an action against the U.S. government. Rather, that company would be restricted to litigating in U.S. courts.

VIII. FDI and Competition Policy, and SOEs

- **Why Cover Antitrust Issues?**

Suppose an FTA liberalizes trade and FDI regimes, so businesses have open access to markets of the Parties. What is the next concern of a businessperson? It is that market access, while existing on paper, is undermined in practice by anti-competitive behavior in the host country. So, if one FTA Party has a strong (or, indeed, any) antitrust regime, then provisions in the FTA against anti-competitive practices may be needed. *NAFTA* negotiators anticipated this concern, and agreed upon provisions — in Chapter 15 — concerning competition policy, and the behavior of lawful monopolies and SOEs.

In the FTAs America negotiated following *NAFTA*, six of the 12 deals included provisions addressing competition policy. Interestingly, no American FTA with a Middle Eastern country includes such provisions. Singapore, Chile, and Australia furnish progressive counter-examples.

Before the *Singapore FTA*, Singapore lacked an antitrust regime. In the *FTA*, Singapore committed to enact a law regulating anticompetitive practices, and create a competition policy, by January 2005. Similarly, the *Chile FTA* contains competition policy provisions obligating Chile to maintain laws enforcing antitrust rules, including laws prohibiting anti-competitive business conduct, and controlling SOEs and officially designated monopolies. The *Australia FTA* forbids anticompetitive business conduct and mandates enforcement against it. This *FTA* contains rules against harmful conduct by government-designated monopolies, and against abuse by SOEs of their official position that would harm the interests of American companies or discriminate against them in the sale of goods or services. The *Australia FTA* also calls for cooperation between the two countries on consumer protection and mutual recognition and enforcement of certain monetary judgments to provide restitution to consumers or investors who suffered economic injury due from deceitful, fraudulent, or misleading practices.

- **Underlying Rationales**

It is vital to appreciate the distinction between the justifications for AD law and antitrust law. The purpose of AD law is to protect individual domestic producers of a like product from unfairly priced foreign competition. The purpose of anti-trust law is not to protect any one producer, but rather the competitive process — in effect, the "freedom" and "openness" of the capitalist market system. Accordingly, the underlying reasoning behind including antitrust rules in Competition Policy Chapters of FTAs is that if such rules exist and are regularly enforced by host States, then prospective foreign direct investors will have the legal means to combat local cartels or monopolies that abuse their position through anti-competitive behavior. Further, a transparent and effective competition law and policy enhances the attractiveness of an economy for FDI.

- **Basic Obligations**

American FTAs addressing antitrust issues continue to evolve since *NAFTA*. But, all share the same foundational principals. Each FTA with competition policy pro-visions addresses competition law, monopolies and state enterprises. For example, Parties must adopt or maintain competition laws addressing anticompetitive busi-ness conduct and enforce their laws through an enforcement authority. Borrowing from the American legal system, parties subject to sanctions for violating anti-competitive measures must be afforded their due process by having the opportunity to be heard and to present evidence in their defense before a domestic court or inde-pendent tribunal if requested.[54]

The *KORUS FTA* outlines specific provisions ensuring the respondent an admin-istrative hearing, the ability to cross-examine potential witnesses, and to review and rebut any collected evidence.[55] Charging different prices for goods or services alone does not run afoul of the provisions addressing designated monopolies and state enterprises when accounting for normal commercial considerations like supply and demand. However, charging difference prices on a discriminatory basis because of

---

54. Article 13:2:3 of the *Peru TPA* provides:
Each Party shall ensure that: (a) before it imposes a sanction or remedy against any per-son for violating its competition law, it affords the person the right to be heard and to present evidence, except tat it may provide for the person to be heard and present evi-dence within a reasonable time after it imposes an interim sanction or remedy; and (b) a court or other independent tribunal established under that Party's laws imposes or, at the person's request, reviews any such sanction or remedy.
55. Article 16:1:3 of *KORUS* states:
Each Party shall ensure that a respondent in an administrative hearing convened to determine whether conduct violates its competition laws or what administrative sanc-tions or remedies should be ordered for violation of such laws is afforded the opportunity to present that evidence in its defense and to be heard in the hearing. In particular, each Party shall ensure that the respondent has a reasonable opportunity to cross-examine any witnesses or other persons who testify in the hearing and to review and rebut the evidence and any other collected information on which the determination may be based.

one's nationality would violate the Chapter and be subject to dispute settlement procedures.[56]

• **Transparency Provisions**

Competition Policy Chapters in FTAs stress the importance of transparency and cooperation amongst parties. Recognizing the importance of cooperation and coordination for effective competition purposes, parties have agreed to cooperate on issues and consult and share info relating to the enforcement competition laws. Parties agreed to share a breadth of information, at the request of the other Party, to make public information concerning aspects relating to its enforcement of antitrust laws, government enterprises and designated monopolies, as well as exemptions available under its competition laws.

The requesting party cannot simply submit a blanket request for information but rather must submit a detailed request indicating indicia of bad faith practices by indicating entities involved, particular products or markets concerned, and the practice or exemption suspected of hindering trade. The *Peru and Colombia FTAs* also allow for requests for information relating to export associations registered to the central government as well as any conditions imposed on them by the party. Realizing that new issues not addressed at the time of negotiation may arise in the future, the FTAs have also allowed for parties to request consultations to raise its concerns on matters affecting trade or investment. Dispute settlement procedures governing the FTA are available under the Competition Chapters for obligations addressing transparency, differences in pricing, state enterprises, and designated monopolies.

---

56. *See* Article 16:4 (Differences in Pricing) of *KORUS*.

Chapter 12

Additional Commitments in "Deep" FTAs[1]

I. "Deep," "Second Generation," or "21st Century" FTAs

"Deep" FTAs, which sometimes are called "Second Generation" or "21st century" FTAs, go beyond expanding market access through cutting tariffs and NTBs, and covering agricultural and industrial products, and services. They endeavor to deepen the economic integration of the participating countries. They do so because of increased interdependence, which follows from increased trade liberalization, across a range of issues. Multi-jurisdictional supply chains are an example. A unilateral behind-the-border measure adopted by one country in the chain can disrupt the entire chain, notwithstanding DFQF treatment that already exists between the relevant countries.

Accordingly, a deep FTA establish enduring institutions, and include disciplines (or harmonization) of regulatory measures, opens up and makes more transparent the market for government procurement, has provisions about enforcing IPRs, liberalizes FDI rules, discusses competition policy, calls for privatization of SOEs and STEs, and establishes minimum standards for the treatment of labor and the environment.

II. *NAFTA* Chapter 20 Case Study

- FTC and Secretariat

NAFTA is not typically considered a "second generation" FTA, and it was a product of the 20th century. But, it has produced some measure of "deep" integration, and set a standard to be matched or excelled in some respects. One example is its institutions. Chapter 20 establishes two of them, the Free Trade Commission (FTC)

---

1. Document References:
   (1) *Havana (ITO) Charter* Articles 3, 7, 46–54, 87
   (2) *NAFTA* Chapters 7A, 10–17, 19–22
   (3) Relevant provisions in other FTAs

and the Secretariat. They are charged with administering *NAFTA* and settling disputes among *NAFTA* Parties.

The FTC is the central institution of *NAFTA* and is loosely akin in structure and function to a hybrid between the WTO Ministerial Conference and General Council (discussed in a separate Chapter). Like the Ministerial Conference, the FTC is comprised of cabinet-level representatives — namely, the trade ministers — from each *NAFTA* Party. As Article 2001:2 explains, the FTC supervises the implementation of *NAFTA*, resolves disputes about its interpretation and application, and oversees the work of committees and working groups established under *NAFTA*. At the WTO level, the General Council performs these day-to-day tasks, with ultimate authority lying in the Conference. The FTC's interpretive rulings about *NAFTA* are binding on *NAFTA* dispute resolution panels, though not on the courts of the *NAFTA* Parties. The FTC meets at least once a year, and the *NAFTA* Parties alternate as chairperson of these meetings. Article 2001:4 specifies that unless the FTC opts otherwise, it takes decisions by consensus.

The Secretariat is staffed and supported by the Parties and has three national Sections, one for each *NAFTA* Party.[2] It provides administrative assistance to the FTC and committees and working groups established by the FTC. It also provides administrative assistance to *NAFTA* dispute resolution panels, panels and committees established under *NAFTA* Chapter 19 for the resolution of AD and CVD disputes.

- **Two Scenarios for Use**

In general, the *NAFTA* Chapter 20 dispute settlement mechanism is used in two instances. The first scenario is where a *NAFTA* Party disagrees with another Party's interpretation or application of *NAFTA*. That is, in this scenario one Party has taken, or proposes to take, an action potentially inconsistent with *NAFTA*. The second scenario is when a Party challenges a measure (which is defined in Article 2001 to include any "law, regulation, procedure, requirement or practice") that is inconsistent with *NAFTA*, or nullifies or impairs a benefit that the complaining Party reasonably could expect to accrue to it under *NAFTA*.

The "nullification or impairment of benefits" standard in *NAFTA* Article 2004 plainly is lifted from GATT Article XXIII:1. How is a nullification or impairment complaint proven? The complainant Party must show that (1) an otherwise *NAFTA*-consistent measure adopted by the respondent Party has resulted in the impairment of an expected *NAFTA* benefit, and (2) at the time *NAFTA* was negotiated, it was not reasonably foreseeable the respondent would adopt the measure. In contrast to the first scenario, the second scenario covers instances where there is no *prima facie* violation of a *NAFTA* obligation.

---

2. *See NAFTA* Article 2002.

The Chapter 20 dispute resolution mechanism is mandatory in that a Party cannot enforce a provision of *NAFTA* against another Party in a domestic court. Rather, *NAFTA's* provisions are enforced by the dispute mechanism *NAFTA* itself creates.

• **Procedural Steps**

There are three broad steps in a *NAFTA* Chapter 20 adjudication: consultation, review by the FTC, and arbitration. To promote efficiency and ensure a result is obtained, there are strict time limits associated with each step. The steps are designed so that a dispute can be resolved within eight months.

Only *NAFTA* Parties—*i.e.*, governments, not private parties—have standing to use the dispute settlement mechanism. Further, Article 2021 bars the Parties from creating a private cause of action under *NAFTA*. Thus, as is true with respect to the *DSU*, a private business or individual can bring an action only indirectly, by petitioning or otherwise inveighing upon its government to file suit. No doubt this restriction is a source of concern for "Kantian-minded" international trade lawyers. They would like to see the normative status of individuals as the primary focus of trade law, if the trade law regime is to be judged "legitimate." In turn, they would favor direct access for individuals to an adjudicatory mechanism, because that is likely to be the best way to ensure claimed wrongs about the normative status of individuals are heard.

The first step, consultation, is intended to be the primary way to resolve disputes. Consultation may entail inter-governmental meetings.[3] Special consultative devices exist under Chapter 7B for disputes about SPS measures and Chapter 9 for disputes about standards. These devices are procedurally similar to, but a substitute for, Chapter 20 consultation and involve technical expert advice.

If a dispute remains unresolved after 30–45 days of consultation (or, in the case of perishable agricultural products, 15 days), then either the complaining or responding Party may request a meeting of the FTC. Interestingly, because the FTC acts by consensus, it is effective at resolving a dispute only when all three governments agree on a course of action. Thus, *NAFTA* gives the FTC broad latitude in fashioning an appropriate dispute resolution strategy. For example, the FTC may rely on experts and technical advisors, convene a working group, or make use of an alternative dispute resolution technique such as conciliation or mediation.

If the FTC is unable to resolve the dispute within 30 days, then any consulting Party may request the establishment of a five-member arbitral Panel.[4] (The Parties may agree to extend the period for the second step.) A third party with a substantial interest in the dispute can join as a complaining party. *NAFTA* Article 2006:5 makes clear Panel proceedings cannot be commenced until the FTC has unsuccessfully attempted to resolve the dispute through conciliation.

---

3. *See NAFTA* Article 2006.
4. *See NAFTA* Articles 2008:1 and 2011.

The operation of the *NAFTA* arbitral Panel is similar to that of a WTO Panel. For example, panel members are chosen from a long roster comprised of experienced experts; there is at least one hearing; each Party may offer written initial and rebuttal statements; the panel may rely on experts for advice on environmental, health, safety, and scientific matters; and the panel must issue initial and final reports within a specific time frame.[5]

Once a Panel issues its report, the disputing Parties must agree on the way to resolve the dispute in conformity with the panel's determinations and recommendations. The preferred means of conformity is to remove any measure that the panel finds inconsistent with that Party's *NAFTA* obligations or impairs another Party's benefits under *NAFTA*. An alternative means is payment of compensation to the aggrieved Party.

If the violating Party fails to conform to a Panel's determination or report, then the aggrieved Party—and only it—is entitled to retaliate. Retaliation entails suspension of the application of benefits under *NAFTA* that were previously extended to the violating Party.[6] For example, suppose the U.S. establishes a quota on imports of lumber from Canada, which a panel finds violate *NAFTA*, and the U.S. does not comply with the panel's report. Canada, but not Mexico, could retaliate by limiting the same value of U.S. exports of a different product, perhaps beer. The violating Party that is the target of retaliation can seek panel review of the retaliatory measures if it believes they are manifestly excessive.[7] What is the justification for this right? It is simply to serve as a check against potential excesses that inhere in any instance when international law condones unilateral retaliation.

Plainly, retaliation involves a trade-distorting action that is otherwise inconsistent with *NAFTA* obligations to offset a *NAFTA* violation. Does this reflect an "eye for an eye" approach? Could retaliation be criticized by saying that "two wrongs don't make a right"? Observe that retaliation is supposed to occur in a sector that is closely related to the one in which the violation occurred, yet cross-retaliation (*i.e.*, retaliation against a different sector) is permissible. Observe also the violating Party may apply to the FTC to establish a panel to determine whether the suspension of benefits is manifestly excessive.

Many obligations established by *NAFTA* resemble or are identical to GATT-WTO obligations. If a complaining Party alleges another Party has violated both sets of obligations, then the complainant can choose to bring its action in either the *NAFTA* or GATT forum. Under certain circumstances, the responding Party, or an affected third Party, can insist a *NAFTA* panel resolve the dispute.

---

5. *See NAFTA* Articles 2009, 2012, and 2016-1017.
6. *See NAFTA* Article 2019:1.
7. *See NAFTA* Article 2019.

• **Modifications**

In three types of cases, the paradigmatic *NAFTA* dispute resolution mechanism may be modified: ISDS brought under Chapter 11 before an arbitral panel; financial services disputes brought under Chapter 14; and reviews of AD and CVD actions conducted under Chapter 19. *NAFTA* Chapter 11 concerns FDI. Such investment is broadly defined to include an equity, debt security, loan, profit-sharing, asset-sharing, real estate acquisition, capital commitment or other interest taken by an investor in one *NAFTA* Party in the territory of another *NAFTA* Party. An example is the purchase or construction by an individual or firm in one *NAFTA* Party of a factory in another Party. In general, Chapter 11 obliges a *NAFTA* Party that hosts FDI to accord foreign investors and their investments MFN and national treatment, and to comply with certain minimum standards regarding treatment.[8] Failure to do so may trigger a Chapter 11 dispute.

Significantly, only private parties have standing to bring an investor-state claim against a *NAFTA* Party government. In this regard, Chapter 11 is a break with international legal tradition, which accords only to sovereign states the right to bring an action against another state. The "Kantian-minded" lawyer can take some satisfaction in this departure. Individuals have the opportunity to shape jurisprudence to a greater extent under Chapter 11 than provisions in most other international agreement.

NAFTA Chapter 14 modifies the paradigmatic Chapter 20 dispute resolution mechanism outlined above in three respects. First, disputes may be resolved not only by the FTC or an arbitral panel, but also by an investor-state tribunal under Chapter 11 with the permission of the Financial Services Committee.[9] The Committee's critical task is to determine whether the exception for prudential measures set forth in *NAFTA* Article 1410 provides a defense against the investor's claim. (That Article enshrines the right of a *NAFTA* Party to adopt prudential measures—for example, regulations related to the safety and soundness of commercial banks—in order to safeguard its financial system.) The Committee must make its decision within 60 days. If the Committee decides the disputed measure, in whole or in part, falls outside the prudential capacity of government, then it will convene an investor-state tribunal. Second, the roster from which an arbitral panel is chosen is comprised of experts in financial services.[10] Third, there are restrictions on cross-retaliation (*i.e.*, on an aggrieved party's right to retaliate outside of the financial services sector).[11]

Chapter 19 establishes binational review panels as an alternative to domestic judicial review of AD and CVD determinations made by administrative agencies like the DOC and ITC. It also establishes an extraordinary challenge procedure to

---

8. *See NAFTA* Articles 1102–1104.
9. *See NAFTA* Articles 1412 and 1415.
10. *See NAFTA* Article 1414:3.
11. *See NAFTA* Article 1414:5.

ensure a binational panel review is handled properly. Finally, under Chapter 19 a special committee may be established to determine whether a Party's domestic law hinders operation of the panel or implementation of one of the panel's decision.

III. Economic Significance of Government Procurement

Roughly 20% of world trade consists of government procurement, and private companies poised to compete successfully in cross-border sales of goods and services to foreign governments would like to see this figure increase. At all levels — federal (central), sub-central (state or provincial), or local — governments around the world must buy goods and services to function, and to provide goods and services themselves. Frequently, the vendors are private companies. Whether they are domestic or foreign businesses, however, depends on a complex array of legal and business considerations.

However, procurement from non-local companies — though often economically efficient, in terms of low costs and high quality — raises two major difficulties. First, should local companies get preference in selling goods and services to a government? GATT Article III:8(a) allows for derogation from the national treatment obligation for government procurement. Second, is it in the national security interest of a government to rely on a foreign company for a particular good or service? The answer to depends in part on the availability of domestic substitutes (*e.g.*, how quickly, and in what quantities, and with what quality, can they be produced?), the home country of the foreign company (*i.e.*, is it a friend, foe, or neutral nation?), and the good or service in question (*e.g.*, is it a guidance system for an advanced fighter jet, or generic paint for the jet?).

On a multilateral level, a multilateral *GPA* exists. It was produced during the Uruguay Round. However, not all Uruguay Round negotiators agreed to commit their countries to government procurement liberalization. Hence, the WTO *GPA* is a plurilateral agreement, set forth in Annex 4 to the *WTO Agreement*. To be sure, there are an impressive number of signatories to the *GPA*, including the U.S., EU, Korea, Hong Kong, and Israel. Moreover, that number is rising. China, for example, agreed to join the *GPA* in connection with its accession to the WTO. However, the number of WTO Members that have signed on to the *GPA* is a minority of the total Membership. Further, the *GPA* uses a Positive List approach to government procurement liberalization, which is inherently less ambitious than a Negative List method.

Thus, much of the action in government procurement liberalization occurs at the level of an FTA or CU. The U.S. places considerable importance on government procurement provisions in its FTAs, which is not surprising given the competitive position of many American businesses to offer goods and services to foreign governments.

IV. Managed Trade in Government Procurement

Not surprisingly, the higher the monetary threshold for coverage by FTA rules, the greater the degree of protection conferred on local government procurement providers.[12] That is because government procurement contracts valued at below the threshold are exempt from the market access rules of the FTA in question. Further, the extent to which market access in government procurement is liberalized depends not only on the contract thresholds, but also on two other factors—use of a Negative List (which is inherently more liberalizing than a Positive List), and the number and prominence of government entities subject to the market access rules.

Consider, then, consider what, if any, patterns appear? Would it be accurate or fair to say that America proposes, if not imposes, a template on other countries with which it negotiates FTAs? Or, are the variations in procurement thresholds sufficient to suggest real bargaining? Overall, is the story in the government procurement area—as with private goods and services—managed trade? Would an even better characterization be "micro-managed trade"?

V. Malaysian Social Engineering through Government Procurement

Emphasis on liberalized government procurement sometimes conflicts with another reason government procurement is significant. In some countries, it is an instrument of social policy. Malaysia is a case in point.

Following ethnic and race riots in 1969, in which Malays protested against economic dominance by Chinese and Indians, the Malaysian government implemented a New Economic Policy. Essentially, the NEP is affirmative action for the majority Malays (who account for about 60% of the population). The NEP creates special privileges—such as job preferences, equity share distribution rights, low-interest mortgages, reserved seats universities and study-abroad scholarships—for Malays. In FTA negotiations with Malaysia during 2006–2007, America called for a Negative List approach to government procurement. Malaysia not only insisted on a Positive List, but also on the reservation for Malays of certain Malaysian government contracts.

Social engineering through government procurement is not unknown in the U.S., which has reservations for small and minority owned businesses. How many concessions ought the U.S. to make to Malaysia for ethnic- and race-based reservations? What were the negotiating positions of the two countries with respect to *TPP* rules on government procurement, and what were the outcomes?

---

12. *See* Raj Bhala, *Dictionary of International Trade Law*, Annex A (3rd ed., 2015) (detailed Table on market access rules on government procurement and services in U.S. FTAs).

VI. Exporting American IP Standards and Pushing *TRIPs* Plus Commitments

• **Minimum Protection and Enforcement Commitments**

Even America's first FTA, with Israel in 1985, spoke of IP rights. That accord reaffirmed the commitment of the two countries to existing bilateral obligations on IP rights. It did not advance the cause of IP protection, in the sense of establishing new or higher-than-extant duties. But, it provided a minimum, or floor, ensuring neither country would tolerate a lowering of commitments. In *NAFTA* Chapter 17, the U.S., Canada, and Mexico committed themselves to IP protection at the level provided by the leading world conventions and treaties on patents, trademarks, and copyrights. Strong, comprehensive rules in this Chapter served as a basis, even template, for the WTO *TRIPs Agreement*.

Invariably, the minimum commitment in an FTA with America allows for the creation, maintenance, and enforcement of patents, trademarks, and copyrights. Typically, the FTA partner must agree not to promulgate such laws, or to make amendments where necessary—it must have done so already before the FTA is implemented. A promise of future legislative or regulatory reforms will not do, because once the negotiations are over, the U.S. loses considerable leverage to influence legal reform in the FTA partner. Additionally, enforcement is essential to secure the interests of the American IP sector—and, therefore, to American trade negotiators. Put bluntly, whining from developing or least developed countries about a lack of judicial or law enforcement resources will fall on deaf ears.[13] It may be met with an argument that IP piracy in those countries benefits a corrupt elite.

• **Post-Uruguay Round IP Commitments in U.S. FTAs**

Many of America's newer FTAs, especially if negotiated after the Uruguay Round, call upon partner countries to go beyond IP protection and enforcement measures set out in the *TRIPs Agreement*. In part, that reflects America's bitter experience with lax IP enforcement in major markets like China. American trade negotiators relied, to the detriment of the American IP sector, on promises made by China of future implementation and enforcement during talks for China's WTO accession, which culminated in a November 1999 Sino-American bilateral agreement, and entry effective 11 December 2001. The subsequent history, from the American vantage point, was one of failure to adhere to the promises. One lesson learned by American trade negotiators was to insist on results—actual implementation and enforcement—before accession. They drilled the point in WTO accession talks

---

13. *See generally* Margaret Chon, *Intellectual Property and the Development Divide*, 27 Cardozo Law Review 2821–2912 (2006) (articulating developing country perspectives); Sue Ann Mota, *TRIPs: Ten Years of Disputes at the WTO*, 9 Computer Law Review and Technology Journal 455–478 (2005) (discussing WTO adjudications on IP matters).

with Saudi Arabia, which culminated with a bilateral accord in the fall of 2005, and accession on 11 December 2005.

A second lesson from the adverse experience with China was to use FTAs as a vehicle to go beyond the *TRIPs Agreement, i.e.*, to demand *TRIPs* Plus commitments from a would-be FTA partner. Consider the following examples:

(1) In the *Jordan FTA*, Jordan agreed to ratify and implement within two years two IP agreements that are not part of its *TRIPs* obligations: the WIPO *Copyright Treaty*, and the WIPO *Performances and Phonograms Treaty*. The aim of these agreements, which are known as "Internet Treaties," is to protect copyrighted works in a digital network environment. Thus, for example, they provide a creator with the exclusive right to make its creative works available online. The same *TRIPs* Plus provisions, incorporating the most up-to-date international copyright protection standards, exist in the *Morocco FTA*.

(2) In America's FTAs with Chile and Singapore, the partner countries agreed to *TRIPs* Plus commitments not only for patents, trademarks, and copyrights, but also for trade secrets. The two countries also accepted the obligation of ensuring its legal system contains meaningful penalties for piracy and counterfeiting.

(3) In negotiations with Australia for an FTA, the U.S. had two key objectives concerning IP. First, it sought better IP protection, especially with respect to grey (parallel) market products. America achieved this objective through provisions in the FTA that not only complement, but also enhance, existing international standards for both protection and enforcement of IP rights. These *TRIPs* Plus provisions include strong penalties for counterfeiting and piracy. Second, the U.S. opposed the Australian pharmaceutical benefits scheme of pricing. Here, agreement proved difficult and the end result— though *TRIPs* Plus—was nebulous.

The two countries affirmed their shared objectives of (1) maintaining high quality healthcare and (2) improving public health standards. They agreed on three principles in pursuit of these objectives: (1) the importance of innovative pharmaceuticals, (2) the significance of research and development in the pharmaceutical industry, with appropriate governmental support including IP protection, and (3) the need for timely and affordable access to innovative pharmaceuticals through procedures that value objectively pharmaceuticals based on their therapeutic relevance. The sticking point was the procedures by which a federal health care program lists and prices new pharmaceuticals for reimbursement. Both sides agreed the procedures should demand transparency and accountability. But, how could the U.S. be certain Australia would not discriminate against drugs from American pharmaceutical companies when listing and pricing medicines in its Pharmaceutical Benefits Scheme? From Australia's perspective, how could its consumers be assured they would have access to effective American drugs at non-astronomical prices?

The *FTA* establishes a Medicines Working Group to continue the conversation between the two countries on pharmaceutical issues, and creates in Australia an independent review process for listing decisions. The conversation indeed continues on this and other controversies. For example, when approving the FTA, the Australian Parliament added an "Anti-Evergreening" amendment to Australian law. This change blocks a pharmaceutical company from evergreening a patent or using the judicial process to preclude introduction of a generic medicine. The U.S. opposed the amendment.

(4) In June 2006, NGOs—416 of them, including the AFL-CIO, Citizens Trade Campaign, Communications Workers of America, Friends of the Earth, National Farmers Union, Sierra Club, and United Steel Workers—signed a letter urging Congress to reject the *Oman FTA* (which Congress ultimately passed that summer). They argued the accord not only lacked meaningful labor and environmental protections, but also would hurt poor and sick Omanis. The *FTA* IP provisions benefited large pharmaceutical companies by protecting their "unprecedented monopoly rights" of large pharmaceutical companies, forbidding for extended periods competition from generic products, and limiting access to affordable medicines.[14]

(5) In the *Colombia TPA*, Colombia agreed to join the WTO *ITA*. The *ITA*, an outgrowth of the Uruguay Round, lists a large number of computer and computer-related products subject to DFQF treatment. However, it is a plurilateral accord. Hence, joining is required neither by *TRIPs* nor any other WTO accord. The *Colombia FTA* also calls for promotion of innovation and technology through collaboration.

(6) The FTA between Korea and the U.S., *KORUS*, calls on Korea to adhere to patent, trademark, and copyright protection and enforcement consistent with American I.P. standards, including a 70-year period for copyright protection (rather than the 50-year *TRIPs* mandate), and strong protections for data and digital products (*e.g.*, music text, software, and videos). That is, American law, not *TRIPs*, is the benchmark. Interestingly, as the *Colombia* and *Panama FTAs*, the patent provisions of *KORUS* begin with the statement:

> Each Party shall make patents available for any invention, whether a product or process, in all fields of technology, provided that the invention is new, involves an inventive step, and is capable of industrial application.

But, these FTAs differ on exclusions, *i.e.*, on items ineligible for patents. The *Colombia FTA* excludes only items in *TRIPs*, plus the following:

---

14. Christopher S. Rugaber, *Baucus Slams Administration for Omission of Forced Labor Amendment from Oman FTA*, 23 International Trade Reporter (BNA) 1034 (6 July 2006).

Each Party may provide limited exceptions to the exclusive rights conferred by a patent, provided that such exceptions do not unreasonably conflict with a normal exploitation of the patent and do not unreasonably prejudice the legitimate interests of the patent owner, taking account of the legitimate interests of third parties.

In contrast, *KORUS* says Korea and the U.S.:

. . . may only exclude inventions from patentability when it is necessary to protect public order or morality; or when the invention is a diagnostic, therapeutic, and surgical procedure for the treatment of humans or animals.

Both exclusions are *TRIPs* Plus, but they are not harmonious.

- **Thailand Says "No"**

In January 2006, America and Thailand were engaged in FTA negotiations, which commenced in June 2004. American insistence on *TRIPs* Plus IP commitments contributed to large-scale protests in Chiang Mai, Thailand, against an FTA, and brought talks to a halt. (In January 2006, your Textbook author and his family personally witnessed their peaceful demonstration while on holiday staying at the Sheraton Chiang Mai, where a round of the FTA negotiations happened to be held.) Four specific *TRIPs* Plus controversies arose:

(1) The U.S. insisted on 25-year span for patent protection, beyond the *TRIPs Agreement* norm of 20 years.

(2) The U.S. called for compensatory patent extensions by the Thai government to pharmaceutical companies, if the government "unreasonably" delayed either the grant of a drug patent, or approval of a drug for market use. The *TRIPs Agreement* does not contain this mandate.

(3) The U.S. sought a data exclusivity provision not found in the *TRIPS Agreement*. This provision would preclude manufacturers of generic drugs (which, of course, tended to be Thai companies) from using clinical trial data, or other scientific information, from any other company (*e.g.*, an American pharmaceutical giant), to prove its generic product was safe and effective after the product had entered the market. Thailand's Government Pharmaceutical Organization objected. The GPO provides "first line" antiretroviral medicines (*i.e.*, older ones, some of which the patent had lapsed) to 80,000 AIDS patients (as of 2006), and sought to expand this program to 150,000 patients (by 2008). The GPO planned to offer generic "second line" drugs (*i.e.*, newer, more sophisticated medicines still subject to a patent). Data exclusivity would inhibit its ability to do so. Further, data exclusivity would apply even to an unpatented drug, where no patent had been sought because the market for the drug was thought to be too small.

(4) The U.S. required tight language that would limit the terms and conditions under which the GPO could effect a compulsory license of a new drug.

> The U.S. offered a *Side Letter* assurance that the language would be consistent with the November 2001 Doha Ministerial Conference *Declaration on TRIPs and Public Health*. Again, the GPO replied the language would adversely affect its ability to provide drugs to Thai AIDS patients.

Thousands of Thai health care workers, AIDS victims, and activists—fearful of high-priced medicines should their government "cave" to the demands, demonstrated noisily, but peacefully (in front of the Sheraton Chiang Mai!) for about two days. Farmers, who were upset at U.S. demands concerning agricultural trade (*e.g.*, that Thailand reduce rice tariff barriers), joined them.

The U.S. team left the Sheraton as inconspicuously as possible, through a side door behind the concierge desk, into an unmarked van, and down a side street. The USTR blamed the ensuing stall in negotiations on Thai political unrest.[15]

- *TPP* and *CPTPP* IP Provisions

In *TPP* negotiations, there were no more contentious issues than American demands for significantly *TRIPs* Plus provisions. What were those demands? Were they met? To what degree? What IP provisions in the text of *TPP* were suspended in *CPTPP* after the January 2017 withdrawal from *TPP*?

- Patent Linkage

"Patent linkage" is yet another example of a *TRIPs* Plus requirement championed by the U.S. This term refers to a legal requirement, which is not mandated under the *TRIPs Agreement*, and which ties the granting of approval to market (distribute and sell) a pharmaceutical medicine with the status of the patent on that or related medication.

The requirement operates to defer entry into a market of a generic pharmaceutical, if a valid patent still exists on the equivalent branded medication. The U.S. is an ardent advocate of patent linkage, whereas the EU forbids it. America's position stirred controversy with respect to *KORUS* and *TPP*.

Fratini Vergano European Lawyers, Brussels, Belgium,

Trade Perspectives, Issue Number 10, May 2015, www.fratinivergano.eu

The implementation of the provisions relating to patent linkage in the . . . *KORUS* FTA . . . has recently triggered a controversy between the two trading partners. At the heart of the exchange between the two administrations is whether the patent linkage requirement included in Chapter 18 of the agreement (on Intellectual Property Rights, hereinafter, IPRs) covers biopharmaceutical products (also referred to as "*biological*" or "*biologics*"). Patent linkage requirements, which some jurisdictions maintain as an incentive to stimulate innovation and attract investments in the pharmaceutical sector, have an impact on the marketing and trade of generic

---

15. *See* Christopher S. Rugaber, *U.S.–Thailand FTA Talks On Hold, But U.S. Not "Giving Up,"* 23 International Trade Reporter (BNA) 801–02 (25 May 2006).

pharmaceutical products and, where applicable, on biosimilars (*i.e.*, non-originator biologic pharmaceutical products). As a consequence, they affect the accessibility and availability of medicines and competition in the pharmaceutical products sector.

"Patent linkage" refers to the requirements linking regulatory approval of pharmaceutical products to the patent status of the products. Patents on pharmaceutical inventions and regulatory approval for pharmaceutical products are normally granted by separate agencies (patent offices and health regulators, respectively). However, certain jurisdictions' domestic laws link regulatory approval (which is based on an evaluation of safety and efficacy of the pharmaceutical product) to the patent status of the pharmaceutical product. Therefore, under a patent linkage mechanism, the marketing authorization will not be granted to a generic medicinal product until the patent has expired or is found to be invalid. This has the consequence of considerably delaying market entry of generic products. In countries where patent linkage is recognized, the regulatory authority effectively acts as a patent enforcement agency, as patent linkage prevents that authority from granting marketing authorization to a generic medicine where it appears that there is a valid patent still in existence.

Patent linkage requirements are present, in relevant part, in Canada, the U.S. and Japan, as well as in few other jurisdictions as a result of the conclusion of FTAs, notwithstanding the fact that patent linkage is not a requirement of the . . . the *TRIPs Agreement* . . . . The U.S. incorporated patent linkage into the *Drug Price Competition and Patent Term Restoration Act of 1984* (which is usually, and hereinafter, referred to as the *"Hatch-Waxman Act"*) [Public Law Number 98-417, 98 Stat. 1585, 24 September 1984, codified in scattered Sections of 21 and 35 U.S.C.]

In relevant part, under the *Hatch-Waxman Act*, a manufacturer that is seeking marketing approval for a generic pharmaceutical product must inform the holder of the relevant patent. If the holder of the relevant patent objects, such as when it believes that its patent is still valid, the U.S. Food and Drug Administration grants an automatic stay of 30 months to allow for legal challenges. To encourage patents' challenges, the *Act* also provides that the first company that files a generic application containing a patent challenge certification may be rewarded with 180 days of generic market exclusivity. The *Hatch-Waxman Act* does not apply to biologics. Instead, relevant requirements for manufacturers of biosimilars are found in the *Biologics Price Competition and Innovation Act* [*BPCIA*], which does not foresee patent linkage. [The *Biologics Price Competition and Innovation Act of 2009* is Title VII, Sub-Title A, Sections 7001 through 7003 of the *Patient Protection and Affordable Care Act*, Public Law Number 111-148, 124 Stat. 804, 30 March 2010. The *Affordable Care Act* (sometimes referred to as "Obama Care") and *BPCIA* are codified in scattered Sections of 21 and 42 U.S.C.]

. . . [P]atent linkage requirements are not allowed in the EU. As recognized by the EU Commission in its Pharmaceutical Sector Inquiry of 2008, the EU's regulatory framework for approval of pharmaceutical products does not allow authorities to take the patent status of the originator medicine into account when deciding on marketing authorizations of generic medicines. Therefore, patent linkage is considered by the EU Commission an anti-competitive instrument to delay generic and biosimilar medicines entry into the market and, as such, subject to EU competition rules. As result, EU trade agreements do not contain patent linkage requirements.

As it is common for international trade agreements to which the U.S. is a party, the *KORUS* FTA provides a patent linkage obligation. Under Article 18:9:5 thereof, when a non-originator manufacturer of a "*pharmaceutical product*" applies for marketing approval, the relevant patent owner must be notified of the identity of the person making such request, and the government must have measures implemented "*to prevent such other persons from marketing a product without the consent or acquiescence of the patent owner during the term of a patent notified to the approving authority as covering that product or its approved method of use.*" Chapter 18 of the *KORUS* FTA does not define "*pharmaceutical product.*" The concept of "*new pharmaceutical product*" is found in other provisions (*i.e.,* Article 18:8:6) as "*a product that at least contains a new chemical entity that has not been previously approved as a pharmaceutical product in the territory of the Party.*" A definition of "*pharmaceutical product*" which explicitly covers biologics (*i.e.,* "*pharmaceutical product or medical device means a pharmaceutical, biologic, medical device, or diagnostic product*") is included in Chapter 5 of the *KORUS* FTA, which pertains to pharmaceuticals and medical devices. However, as clarified by Article 5:8 thereof, this definition is valid only for the purposes of Chapter 5, and is therefore not applicable to the provisions contained in Chapter 18, including the patent linkage requirement. The wording employed in the two definitions, and the fact that the latter distinguishes clearly between "*pharmaceutical*" and "*biologic*" arguably suggests that patent linkage for biologics is not a requirement under the *KORUS* FTA.

This apparent ambiguity of the *KORUS* FTA has fuelled a debate between South Korea and the U.S. on whether patent linkage under the *KORUS* FTA covers biologics.

Under the terms of the *KORUS* FTA, South Korea was required to fully implement patent linkage by 15 March 2015 (*i.e.,* at least three years from entry into force of the agreement). In order to do so, South Korea had to amend its patent laws and introduce patent linkage requirements. In response to proposals in South Korea's National Assembly aimed at carving out biologics from the government's draft, the U.S. Ambassador to South Korea issued a letter in which he sought to "*assure . . . that KORUS patent linkage obligations cover all pharmaceutical products, including biologics, as set forth in the agreement.*" The Ambassador also stated that the U.S. "*meets its obligation through the Hatch Waxman Act and the Biologics Price Competition and Innovation Act.*" South Korea's implementing act, an amendment of the *Pharmaceutical Affairs Act,* ultimately introduced a "*Hatch-Waxman*" style patent linkage requirement for both generic and biosimilar medicines.

Therefore, while South Korea applies the same notification requirements to manufacturers of generics and biosimilars, the U.S. framework distinguishes between generics and biosimilars, insofar as patent linkage is concerned. In the U.S., under the . . . *BPCIA*, a non-originator applying for marketing approval of a biologic must simply *"provide notice to the reference product sponsor not later than 180 days before the date of the first commercial marketing"* of the biosimilar. This obligation is a requirement to notify the marketing of the product, not the kind of notification requirement that exists under the *Hatch-Waxman Act* for generics, where the applicant for authorization of a generic medicine must notify of its intent to seek approval for a generic version of the reference product, and which may ultimately trigger the authority to grant an automatic stay in case of objections from the patent holder. In addition, the *"reference product sponsor,"* which is the addressee of the notification requirement, is not necessarily the patent holder. The sponsor, who would receive such notice, can be different from the patent holder. In simple terms, marketing authorization for biosimilars under the *BPCIA* is not linked to the status of the patent.

As a result of the apparent ambiguity of the language in the *KORUS* FTA and the related exchange between the two administrations, South Korea has effectively implemented more burdensome requirements on manufacturers of South Korean biosimilars than those that would arguably be required under the agreement and that apply to manufacturers of biosimilars in the U.S. The U.S. Ambassador indicated that the U.S. is advocating for similar provisions to be included in the . . . *TPP* . . . , which is currently [as of May 2015] being negotiated by 12 countries (*i.e.*, Australia, Brunei, Canada, Chile, Japan, Malaysia, Mexico, New Zealand, Peru, Singapore, the U.S. and Vietnam). To avoid the type of ambiguity that has affected South Korea's implementation of the *KORUS* FTA, future trade agreements should at least clarify that patent linkage does not apply to biologics.

In fact, the inclusion of patent linkage requirements in trade agreements should be avoided altogether. Inasmuch as it prevents the registration and authorization of generic medicines until after a finding of invalidity or expiry of a patent pending marketing approval, patent linkage has the effect of delaying generic market entry and affecting competition in pharmaceutical products. The degree of investment and innovation that patent linkage requirements are supposed to stimulate is outweighed by the burdens caused by the implementation of such requirements, which often result in onerous procedures and instances of patent abuse, especially where appropriate safeguards to prevent this are not put in place.

Patent linkage requirements stand to be particularly problematic in a context such as the *TPP* negotiating framework, which involves countries with little IPR enforcement *"experience"* and no patent linkage requirements in place. Inasmuch as the functioning of the patent linkage mechanism relies on the ability of domestic systems to quickly assess the existence or the validity of a patent, pending the grant of regulatory approval, patent linkage requirements imposed on countries whose systems do not currently meet such standard are likely to pose significant challenges and to result in additional burdens and further delays and impediments on trade in pharmaceutical products. In the context of these negotiations, certain countries are reportedly accepting the inclusion of patent linkage requirements in exchange for concessions in other sectors or areas of the agreement, without properly considering the impact that patent linkage requirements stand to have on their domestic framework. With respect to biologics, the further consideration to be made is that, given the early stage of competition in the biologic industry and the constantly evolving scientific and regulatory landscape surrounding biologics, the establishment of complex and layered IP protection for biologics (including patent linkage requirements) is largely premature. Instead, proposals tabled in the various stages of the *TPP* negotiations included suggestions to broaden the scope of patent linkage, while avoiding the "*check and balances*" that such systems should include (such as requirements to provide for incentives to encourage patent challenge).

Therefore, it is important that all factors be appropriately considered and reflected in the negotiation of IPR Chapters of trade agreements. Negotiators and affected constituencies must ensure that the appropriate balance, between encouraging investment and ensuring competition and technology transfer in the pharmaceutical sector, is achieved. Where present, patent linkage requirements add to a number of other, WTO "*TRIPs Plus*", protections (*e.g.*, data exclusivity requirements and patent term extensions) that are routinely included in bilateral or plurilateral trade agreements by the US and other countries or blocks, such as the EU, EFTA (*i.e.*, Iceland, Liechtenstein, Norway and Switzerland) and Switzerland, all of which result in delayed generic and biosimilar entry, less competition, higher costs for medicines and loss of significant savings for national healthcare systems and the economy.

With respect to patent linkage requirements, the simplest way of achieving such balance is to avoid including such requirements, just as the EU does. Where included in the negotiations, it must be clear that patent linkage must not apply to biologics, and, with respect to generics, that such requirements be limited as to the scope of the patents that are covered and be balanced by appropriate "*safeguards*" to prevent abuse. On the other hand, stakeholders must also ensure that domestic implementation of such requirements does not in itself result in unnecessary and unwarranted stricter frameworks.

VII. El Said Argument on *TRIPs* Plus Commitments

Is "*TRIPs* Plus" actually "*TRIPs* Minus" for poor countries? Scholars such as Professor Mohammed El Said of the University of Central Lancashire think so. Professor El Said argues *TRIPs* Plus commitments in deals like the *U.S.-Jordan* and *Bahrain FTAs* end up doing greater harm than good to the American partners, hence rendering those countries worse off than under WTO disciplines.

He has at least three good reasons to make this argument. First, many countries are utterly unaware that there is no provision in *TRIPs* akin to GATT Article XXIV.

Therefore, when a country makes a *TRIPs* Plus commitment in an FTA (such as extending patent protection to 25 years, instead of the *TRIPs* standard of 20 years), then by virtue of the MFN rule in *TRIPs* Articles 4, that country must extend the commitment to all WTO Members. Jordan made this blunder in its FTA with America.

Second, many countries forget that there is no provision in *TRIPs* that is as comprehensive as GATT Article XX. Thus, they have only limited bases to derogate from *TRIPs* or *TRIPs* Plus obligations. For example, suppose in an FTA an Islamic country seeks not to grant trademark protection to alcoholic beverage products. It must ensure that it writes the exception into the FTA, because Article 15:4 of *TRIPs* does not give it a basis for limiting the scope of protectable subject matter.

Third, in many FTAs, the U.S.s effectively extends the provision of patent protection not only from the *TRIPs* standard of 20 years to the *TRIPs Plus* standard of 25, but also tacks on an additional eight years. It does so by requiring that its FTA partner agree that data used to justify the grant of an original patent must be protected for eight years after the expiry of the patent. Therefore, a new patent applicant cannot the original data to support its application for a patent. Rather, the applicant must redo all of the scientific testing needed to support its case. That puts a tremendous expense burden on the applicant, which may be a company from a developing country. If the applicant ends up waiting for eight years, then the original holder essentially retains its patent rights for that period, thus enjoying protection from competition for up to 32 years (25 plus eight years).

To be sure, arguments about *TRIPs* Plus commitments are not all one way. As a general matter, to the extent a country is an actual or potential producer of goods and services embodying patents, trademarks, and copyrights, such commitments may redound to the benefit of its economy. IP protection is necessary to ensure inventors make sufficient returns on their investment in research and development, without which the financial incentive for creativity would be gone. Innovation, in turn, is a healthy dynamic influence on economic growth and competitiveness. Moreover, generic manufacturers may produce drugs sub-par in quality, and may lack the capacity to meet market demand. There also is the harsh truth that in some developing and least developed countries, the real enemy to efficacious delivery of medicines is not high prices charged by American pharmaceutical companies, but decrepit infrastructure and rampant corruption.

What is the empirical record? American trade negotiators insist there is no proof *TRIPs Plus* commitments either injure the pharmaceutical industry of an FTA partner or limit access to medicines in that partner. They point to Jordan, claiming that since the *Jordan FTA* took effect, the number of new innovative pharmaceuticals launched has increased, and Jordanian generic manufacturers have thrived. Of course, the Jordanian market is small, relative to Thailand, not to mention China or India. Indeed, when confronted with a compulsory license threat in a large country, is the official American reaction noticeably stronger?

Consider the 2005 case of the AIDS drug Kaletra, invented by Abbott Laboratories of the U.S.[16] To ensure low-cost provision of Kaletra to patients, Brazil nearly issued a compulsory license. It backed off, allegedly because of phone calls from the White House and Congress, and threats of retaliation. Brazilian President Luiz Inácio da Silva compromised on a deal in which Abbott would keep its patent but offer Kaletra for 6 years at a reduced price.

Another example where pressing for *TRIPs* Plus commitments engenders heated debate arose in the *KORUS* negotiations. In June 2006, the Korean Ministry of Health and Welfare announced it would adopt a "Positive List" system for reimbursement of pharmaceuticals. Only medicines explicitly put on the List would be eligible for reimbursement. With a Negative List, reimbursement is provided for all medicines, except those drugs not on the List. It is inherently a more free-trade policy than a Positive List approach, which potentially discriminates against foreign pharmaceuticals. Fixated on market access for its big drug companies, the U.S. expressed "grave concern" at the announcement.[17] Surely the Ministry had in mind its responsibility, and Korea's sovereign right, to design a system that would avoid sending Koreans needlessly to their graves, and would control costs to ensure their access to affordable medicines. Yet, when Korean negotiators stuck to their position in July 2006, American negotiators simply walked out of the pharmaceutical talks. Fortunately, the next month the two sides agreed to discussions on the basis of a Positive List, but with coverage of transparency, non-discriminatory pricing, and reimbursement.

Equally touchy is the subject of the rate at which Korea's National Health Insurance (NHI) reimburses generic pharmaceuticals. Roughly 73% of reimbursement expenses are on generics. The reimbursement rate is about 70% of the price of the original brand-name medicine, in contrast to the rate in the U.S. for generics — 20–30% of the original drug.[18] American lobbyists, notably the Pharmaceutical Research and Manufacturers of America (PhRMA), say the high rate paid to firms that imitate, not innovate, is disguised industrial policy to hinder foreign firms seeking to expand business, investment, and R&D in Korea. These lobbyists called for the same WTO-Plus provision on independent board review that exists in the *Australia FTA* to prevent systematic over-valuation of generics and undervaluation of new medicines. They were successful, as *KORUS* establishes a Medicines and Medical Devices Committee to monitor relevant commitments.

---

16. *See* Amy Kazmin, Andrew Jack & Alan Beattie, *Patent or Patient? How Washington Uses Trade Deals To Protect Drugs*, Financial Times, 22 August 2006, at 9.

17. Rossella Brevetti, *Early Progress in U.S.-Korea FTA Talks Bodes Well for Completion, U.S. Official Says*, 23 International Trade Reporter (BNA) 907 (15 June 2006). *See also* Christopher S. Rugaber, *U.S.-Korea FTA Talks Remain On Track, U.S. Trade Official Says*, 23 International Trade Reporter (BNA) 1134 (27 July 2006).

18. *See* Christopher S. Rugaber, *U.S., South Korea Aim for Quick Start To FTA Talks; Will Exchange Text in May*, 23 International Trade Reporter (BNA) 411–12 (16 March 2006).

Traditional knowledge is another IP-related topic that can generate debate about *TRIPs* Plus commitments. In the *Peru TPA*, Peru agreed to provisions on the protection of pharmaceutical products. From the American perspective, there were concerned about the strength of those commitments. From the Peruvian vantage point, the issue was whether those commitments would weaken Peru's legislation—Law 27811, which had been in force since August 2002—that protects collective knowledge of indigenous communities about biological resources.[19] That Law allows a native community to register knowledge it has of a biological resource, and use it makes of the resource, with Peru's IP agency (known in Spanish by the acronym "INDECOPI"). The registration is done the same way as a patent is recorded. The *TRIPs Agreement* says little about the topic of traditional knowledge. Might the IP rules of the *FTA* blunt this Law?

VIII. Case Study on *TRIPs* Plus Commitments: *NAFTA* 2.0

- **27 August 2018 U.S.-Mexico Bilateral Agreement**

Office of the United States Trade Representative,

United States–Mexico Trade Fact Sheet: *Modernizing NAFTA to Be a 21st Century Trade Agreement* (28 August 2018)[20]

. . .

Key Achievement: Most Comprehensive Enforcement Provisions of Any Trade Agreement

For the first time, a trade agreement will require <u>all</u> of the following:

(1) Enforcement authorities must be able to stop goods that are suspected of being pirated or counterfeited at all areas of entry and exit.

(2) Enforcement against counterfeits and piracy occurring on a commercial scale.

(3) Meaningful criminal procedures and penalties for camcording of movies.

(4) Civil and criminal penalties for satellite and cable signal theft.

(5) Broad protection against trade secret theft, including against state-owned enterprises.

---

19. *See* Lucien O. Chauvin, *U.S.-Peru Free Trade Accord on Schedule Despite Last Minute Concerns, Engel Says*, 25 International Trade Reporter (BNA) 1620–1621 (13 November 2008).

20. https://ustr.gov/about-us/policy-offices/press-office/press-releases/2018/august/modernizing-nafta-be-21st-century (emphasis original).

Key Achievement: Strongest Standards for
Trade Secrets of Any United States FTA

This deal, . . . will be the first FTA to require all of the following to protect United States rightsholders from theft of trade secrets, including by state-owned enterprises: civil remedies, criminal remedies, prohibition on impeding licensing of trade secrets, protections for trade secrets during the litigation process, and penalties for government officials who wrongfully disclose trade secrets.

Key Highlights: Protections for Innovators

The new IP Chapter will:

(1) Require at least 10 years of data protection for biologic drugs [*i.e.*, a 10-year data exclusivity period] and include an expanded scope of products eligible for protection from previous FTAs. [A "biologic" medicine is one made from living organisms.]

(2) Require full national treatment for copyright and related rights so United States creators are not deprived of rights in foreign markets that domestic creators receive.

(3) Provide strong patent protection for innovators by enshrining patentability standards and patent office best practices to ensure that United States innovators, including small- and medium-sized businesses, are able to protect their inventions with patents.

(4) Include strong protection for pharmaceutical and agricultural innovators.

(5) Set a minimum standard of 75 years of copyright term for sound recordings and other works calculated by date of publication, and life plus 70 years for works calculated based on the life of the author.

(6) Ensure that works such as digital music, movies, and books can be protected through current technologies such as technological protection measures and rights management information tools.

(7) Establish a notice-and-takedown system for copyright safe harbors for Internet service providers (ISPs) that provides protection for IP and predictability for legitimate technology enterprises that do not directly benefit from the infringement [*i.e.*, safe harbors for ISPs that inadvertently post pirated material], consistent with United States law.

(8) Provide important procedural safeguards for recognition of new geographical indications (GIs), including strong and comprehensive standards for protection against issuances of GIs that would prevent United States producers from using common names.

(9) Enhance provisions for protecting trademarks, including well-known marks, to help companies that have invested effort and resources into establishing goodwill for their brands.

Office of the United States Trade Representative,

United States–Mexico Trade Fact Sheet: *Strengthening NAFTA for Agriculture* (28 August 2018)[21]

. . .

Key Achievement: Setting Unprecedented Standards for Agricultural Biotechnology

For the first time, the Agreement specifically addresses agricultural biotechnology to support 21st century innovations in agriculture. The text covers all biotechnologies, including new technologies such as gene editing, whereas the *Trans-Pacific Partnership* text covered only traditional rDNA technology. Specifically, the United States and Mexico have agreed to provisions to enhance information exchange and cooperation on agricultural biotechnology trade-related matters.

. . .

Key Achievement: New Disciplines on Geographic Indications and Common Names for Cheeses

For the first time in *NAFTA*, the United States and Mexico have agreed to geographical indication standards that: enhance transparency for opposition and cancellation proceedings for . . . GIs; establish a mechanism to consult on GIs pursuant to international agreements; and allow for additional factors that may be taken into account in determining whether a term is a common name instead of a GI. In addition, for the first time in a United States trade agreement, Mexico and the United States agreed to not restrict market access in Mexico for U.S. cheeses labeled with certain names.

Key Achievement: Prohibiting Barriers for Alcoholic Beverages

The United States and Mexico agreed to labeling and certification provisions that will help the countries avoid barriers to trade in wine and distilled spirits. Mexico agreed to continue recognition of Bourbon Whiskey and Tennessee Whiskey as distinctive products of the United States. The United States agreed to continue recognition of Tequila and Mezcal as distinctive products of Mexico.

Key Achievement: New Protections for Proprietary Food Formulas

The United States and Mexico agreed on the first ever Annex on Proprietary Food Formulas, which requires each Party to protect the confidentiality of proprietary formulas for food products in the same manner for domestic and imported products. It also limits such information requirements to what is necessary to achieve legitimate objectives.

---

21. https://ustr.gov/about-us/policy-offices/press-office/press-releases/2018/august/strengthening-nafta-agriculture.

- **30 September 2018 Trilateral *NAFTA* 2.0 (*USMCA*)**

Office of the United States Trade Representative,

United States–Mexico–Canada Fact Sheet: *Modernizing NAFTA
into a 21st Century Agreement* (1 October 2018)[22]

. . .

Key Highlights: Protections for United States Innovators and Creators

The new IP Chapter [*i.e.*, Chapter 20, which, at 63 pages, is the longest in the *USMCA*] will:

(1) Include [in *USMCA* Article 20:F:14(1)] 10 years of data protection for biologic drugs and a robust scope of products eligible for protection. [Note that Mexico had no special data exclusivity period for biologic medicines, but owing to its participation in *CPTPP*, was obliged to follow the minimum "5 + 3" rule in Article 18:52 of that FTA, *i.e.*, 5 years of outright data exclusivity plus 3 years of other measures that provide comparable marketing exclusivity, or 8 years of outright protection. Canada, also a *CPTPP* Party, was obliged to follow that rule, but went further with an 8-year period of protection. Thus, the 10-year *USMCA* rule is two years longer than the *CPTPP* minimum period.]

(2) Require [in Article 20:A:8] full national treatment for copyright and related rights so United States creators are not deprived of the same protections that domestic creators receive in a foreign market.

(3) Continue [through Articles 20:F-1–20:F-9] to provide strong patent protection for innovators by enshrining patentability standards and patent office best practices to ensure that United States innovators, including small- and medium-sized businesses, are able to protect their inventions with patents. [Note that Article 20:F:1(3) empowers a Party to refuse to grant a patent in order (1) "to protect "human, animal, or plant life or health" or (2) "to avoid serious prejudice to nature or the environment," and also to exclude from patentability a grant for "diagnostic, therapeutic and surgical methods for the treatment of humans or animals,"]

(4) Include [in Article 20:F:10] strong protection for pharmaceutical and agricultural innovators.

(5) Require [in Article 20:H:7] a minimum copyright term of life of the author plus 70 years, and for those works with a copyright term that is not based on the life of a person, a minimum of 75 years after first authorized publication.

---

22. https://ustr.gov/about-us/policy-offices/press-office/fact-sheets/2018/october/united-states-mexico-canada-trade-fa-1.

(6) Require [in Article 20:H:11] strong standards against the circumvention of technological protection measures [also called "TPMs"] that often protect works such as digital music, movies, and books.

(7) Establish [in Articles 20:J:10–20:J:11] appropriate copyright safe harbors to provide protection for IP and predictability for legitimate enterprises that do not directly benefit from the infringement, consistent with United States law. [That is, these safe harbors are for the benefit of websites against liability for user-posted content, though under U.S. law—Section 230 of the *Communications Decency Act*—such immunity from liability does not extend to the intentional, knowing promotion of prostitution or facilitation of online sex trafficking.]

(8) Provide [through *USMCA* Articles 20:E:1–20:E:7] important procedural safeguards for recognition of new geographical indications (GIs), including strong standards for protection against issuances of GIs that would prevent United States producers from using common names, as well as establish a mechanism for consultation between the Parties on future GIs pursuant to international agreements.

[That is, Chapter 20 of *NAFTA* 2.0:

> . . . allows the three countries to set up a system to protect geographical indications, which link a product's reputation to where it is traditionally produced. For example, European law requires that only sparkling wine from the Champagne region of France be labeled as "champagne."

> U.S. law doesn't specifically protect geographical indications, but it does allow for a type of trademark protection to cover terms like "Idaho Potato" or "Napa Valley Wine." The American agricultural industry, particularly dairy producers, has complained to the U.S. Trade Representative that European-based geographical indications unfairly restrict uses of names like Parmesan or Gruyere.

> In Europe, those terms are protected as geographical indications, but in the U.S., dairy producers say that they are the common names for types of cheese. American cheesemakers say that requiring them to use a term like "Alpine-style cheese" instead of "Gruyere" hurts their sales.

> A country would need to create procedures for objecting to geographical indication restrictions for companies seeking to use a word like Gruyere for its product, under the . . . [*USMCA*]. One basis for such an objection is that the geographical term is typically used as the common name for a product in that country.

> A footnote [specifically, Footnote 19 to Article 20:E:3(a)(c)] . . . says that in the case of wine or spirits, a signatory country doesn't have to recognize a term as a restricted geographical indication if

"the relevant indication is identical with the customary name of a grape variety."

The . . . [IP Chapter] sets forth guidelines [in Article 20:E:4] for determining whether a word is a customary name for a product, as opposed to an indication of the goods' geographic origin.[23]]

(9) Enhance provisions for protecting trademarks, including well-known marks [discussed in *USMCA* Article 20:C:5], to help companies that have invested effort and resources into establishing goodwill for their brands. [For instance, recognition of a well-known mark may help a company prevent the confusing use of its mark in a country in which it does not use business. Additionally, Article 20:C:1 allows for a non-visual mark, such as a sound or a scent, to be trademarked.]

Key Achievement: Most Comprehensive Enforcement Provisions of Any Trade Agreement

For the first time, a trade agreement [*i.e.*, the *USMCA*] will require [in Articles 20:J:1–20:J:11] all of the following:

(1) *Ex officio* authority for law enforcement officials to stop suspected counterfeit or pirated goods at every phase of entering, exiting, and transiting through the territory of any Party.

(2) Express recognition that IP enforcement procedures must be available for the digital environment for trademark and copyright or related rights infringement.

(3) Meaningful criminal procedures and penalties for unauthorized camcording of movies, which is a significant source of pirated movies online.

(4) Civil and criminal penalties for satellite and cable signal theft.

(5) Broad protection against trade secret theft, including against state-owned enterprises.

Key Achievement: Strongest Standards of Protection for Trade Secrets of Any Prior FTA

In particular, the Chapter [on IP, Chapter 20, in Articles 20:I:1–20:I:8] has the most robust protection for trade secrets of any prior United States trade agreement. It includes all of the following protections against misappropriation of trade secrets, including by state-owned enterprises: civil procedures and remedies, criminal procedures and penalties, prohibitions against impeding licensing of trade secrets, judicial procedures to prevent disclosure of trade secrets during the litigation process, and penalties for government officials for the unauthorized disclosure of trade secrets.

---

23. Anandashankar Mazumdar, *U.S-Mexico-Canada Pact Seeks to Protect Intellectual Property*, 35 International Trade Reportrer (BNA) 1286 (4 October 2018).

Office of the United States Trade Representative,

United States–Mexico–Canada Trade Fact Sheet: *Strengthening North American Trade in Agriculture* (1 October 2018)[24]

. . .

Key Achievement: Setting Unprecedented Standards for Agricultural Biotechnology

For the first time, the agreement specifically addresses agricultural biotechnology to support 21st century innovations in agriculture. The text covers all biotechnologies, including new technologies such as gene editing, whereas the *Trans-Pacific Partnership* text covered only traditional rDNA technology. Specifically, the United States, Mexico, and Canada have agreed to provisions to enhance information exchange and cooperation on agricultural biotechnology trade-related matters.

. . .

Key Achievement: New Disciplines on Geographic Indications

For the first time in *NAFTA*, the United States and Mexico have agreed to geographical indication standards that: enhance transparency for opposition and cancellation proceedings for geographical indications (GIs); establish a mechanism to consult on GIs pursuant to international agreements; and allow for additional factors that may be taken into account in determining whether a term is a common name instead of a GI.

Key Achievement: Market Access for Certain Cheese Names

In addition, for the first time in a United States trade agreement, Mexico and the United States agreed [via a *Side Letter*] to not restrict market access in Mexico for U.S. cheeses labeled with certain names.

Key Achievement: Prohibiting Barriers for Alcohol Beverages

The United States, Mexico, and Canada agreed [via *Side Letters*] to non-discrimination and transparency commitments regarding sale and distribution, and labeling and certification provisions to avoid technical barriers to trade in wine and distilled spirits. They agreed to continue recognition of Bourbon Whiskey, Tennessee Whiskey, Tequila, Mezcal, and Canadian Whisky as distinctive products.

Key Achievement: New Protections for Proprietary Food Formulas

The United States, Mexico, and Canada agreed on the Annex on Proprietary Food Formulas, which requires each Party to protect the confidentiality of proprietary formulas for food products in the same manner for domestic and imported products. It also limits such information requirements to what is necessary to achieve legitimate objectives.

---

24. https://ustr.gov/about-us/policy-offices/press-office/fact-sheets/2018/october/united-states-mexico-canada-trade-fa-2.

- **Lingering Concerns**

Query whether it is reasonable to call a "key achievement" a commitment concerning GIs and guaranteed market access for luxury items, such as fine cheese and hard liquor. Is it, rather, a pay-off to get political support from officials in the affected geographic areas?

IX. Securitization and Relationship between *TRIPs* Plus and Other FTA Obligations

Consider how IP commitments might relate to other obligations in an FTA. Securitization of IP could be one context. "Securitization" refers to the issuance of financial instruments, typically bonds, based on revenue streams expected from an underlying financial asset of the issuer, like mortgages held, credit card receivables, or car loan payments. Roughly two-thirds of the total value of the balance sheets of American companies is the implied value of intangible assets, like patents, trademarks, and copyrights. Seeing this value, ingenious Wall Street investment bankers created bonds backed by IP royalty payments. Trademarks are a good example. In May 2006, Dunkin' Donuts issued $1.7 billion in bonds secured (*inter alia*) by royalties it expects from its franchisees. Earlier, in 1997, the British rock star David Bowie issued $55 million in "Bowie Bonds." They were backed by future sales of his music.

Obviously, if IP rights are not enforced, then the revenue streams needed to repay securitized bonds could be compromised. Less obvious is the ability of investment banking, accounting, and legal services to provide securitization products. An FTA can assist on both counts. It not only can mandate IP enforcement, but also open services markets so the bankers, accountants, and lawyers can devise and offer innovative financial instruments the underlying value of which depends on IP.

X. Cultural Industries Exceptions and 1997 *Canada Magazines* Case

- **Cultural Protection versus Free Trade?**

Of English language magazines circulating in Canada, half are foreign. Eighty percent of magazines sold at Canadian news stands are foreign, mostly American. Of the 1,400 magazines Canadian publishers produce, over half have no operating profit. Do these data bespeak a threat to Canadian culture, or a triumph of a free market for ideas?

To be sure, many of American magazines are split-run editions, *i.e.*, an edition is produced for the Canadian market containing advertisements directed at this market and extra pages for local editorial content. But, most of the editorial content remains American. Moreover, the parent publisher is an American company with the advantage of vast economies of scale.

Worst of all from the Canadian perspective is that split-run editions siphon off scarce advertising revenues. Every dollar of an advertising budget spent on placing an ad in an American or other foreign magazine directed at the Canadian market is one less dollar available for expenditure on an ad in a Canadian magazine. The result is that Canadian magazines are starved for advertising revenues. Indeed, the foreign parents find split-run editions to be effective ways to raise advertising revenues in local markets. In brief, to many in the Canadian magazine industry, a split-run edition is an essentially American product paid for by Canadian advertisers.

• Canada's Protective Measures

To preserve its domestic magazine market, on 15 December 1995 Canada enacted legislation—"Part V.I of the *Excise Tax Act*," the "Tax on Split-run Periodicals"—slapping an 80% excise tax on advertising revenues of split-run editions of foreign magazines. That is, Part V.I required imposition, levy, and collection of a tax equal to 80% of the value of all the advertisements in a split-run edition of a periodical. Tax liability lay with the publisher, or person connected with the publisher (*e.g.*, through an equity interest of 50% or more), or the distributor, printer, or wholesaler. To ensure collection, Canada imposed the tax on whichever of these persons resided in Canada, with joint and several liability for the tax operating between publisher and person connected with it, and also operating among distributor, printer, and wholesaler.

Clearly, a key term in Part V.I was "split run." Under Part V.I, a "split run" edition was defined as one (1) distributed in Canada, (2) in which more than 20% of the editorial material is the same or substantially the same as the editorial material that appears in one or more excluded editions of the periodical, and (3) contains an advertisement that does not appear in identical form in the excluded editions. There was an exemption for grandfathered periodicals, essentially those distributed in Canada before 26 March 1993. Part V.I also contained an exemption from the meaning of "split run" for any edition that is primarily circulated outside of Canada. Finally, it exempted from the definition any edition with identical advertisements in the Canadian and non-Canadian issues, so long as the circulation outside Canada exceeded the circulation within Canada. (Canada also excluded from the definition of "periodical" any catalog made up substantially of advertisements.)

Part V.I defined the value of all advertisements in a split-edition to be the total of all the gross fees for all the advertisements contained in the edition, and it applied the tax on a per-issue basis. Canada added an anti-avoidance provision to its tax code to make sure advertising expenses in a split-run edition of a foreign-owned magazine were not deductible from taxable income. These measures did not affect regular editions of foreign magazines distributed in Canada.

The U.S., which initiated both a Section 301 investigation and WTO case, argued the periodicals tax amounted to a virtual ban on the entry of split-run magazines into the Canadian market: 80% is so high, it makes operation economically unfeasible. It also argued the tax was discriminatory.

Canada pointed out the tax would apply equally to a domestic publisher with a split run edition containing foreign content and Canadian advertising. Moreover, the tax closed a loophole created by electronic publishing. Time-Warner, Inc. had declared its intention to produce a Canadian edition, with mostly American editorial content, of *Sports Illustrated* that would be transmitted electronically into Canada for printing. This transmission would circumvent Tariff Code 9958, a special restriction blocking importation into Canada of split-run periodicals.

Canada enacted Tariff Code 9958 in 1965. It applied to any special edition periodical (including a split-run edition or regional edition) containing an advertisement "primarily directed" to a market in Canada that did not also appear in identical form in all editions of that issue of the periodical distributed in the country of origin of the periodical. Tariff Code 9958 prohibited imports of these editions. To determine whether an advertisement was "primarily directed" at the Canadian market, the Canadian government took a number of factors into consideration.

These factors included (1) specific invitations to Canadian consumers only, (2) listing of Canadian addresses as opposed to foreign addresses, (3) whether there were enticements to the Canadian market, and (4) references to Canada's goods and services tax. In addition, Tariff Code 9958 applied to any edition of a periodical in which more than 5% of the advertising content consisted of advertisements "directed" at the Canadian market. Advertisements were considered "directed" to the Canadian market if they indicated specific sources of product or service availability in Canada, or if they had specific terms or conditions relating to the sale of goods or services in Canada. Naturally, the U.S. argued Tariff Code 9958 violated the GATT XI:1 rule against prophylactic restrictions on imports.

The U.S. also was irked by Canadian postal subsidies to its domestic publishing sector. These subsidies took the form of low rates charged by Canada Post Corporation, a crown corporation, to magazines produced in Canada by Canadian-owned companies. (In 1989, the value of the subsidy peaked at $ 172 million; by 1998 it had fallen to about $ 35 million.) Specifically, Canada had three categories of postal rates for publications:

(1) "funded" rates, which were subsidized by the Canadian government, and which were available only to periodicals edited, printed, and published in Canada that were Canadian-owned and controlled, and which met certain editorial and advertising requirements (*e.g.*, the subject of the periodical had to be news, commentary, religion, science, agriculture, literature or the arts, criticism, health, or academic/scholarly matters, and no more than 70% of the space in the periodical could be devoted to advertising);

(2) "Canadian" rates, which were available to Canadian-owned and controlled periodicals that were edited, printed, and published in Canada, and which to such periodicals that did not qualify for a funded rate; and

(3) "international" rates, which applied to all foreign publications mailed in Canada.

The funded rates program aimed to promote Canadian culture by reducing distribution costs for Canadian periodicals. Canada said this "subsidy" was the most efficient way to provide assistance. The U.S. retorted that because it was not provided directly by the Canadian government, it violated WTO rules.

- **WTO Panel and Appellate Body Reports**

Curiously, Canada did not invoke the cultural industry exemption provisions of *NAFTA* (Article 2106 and Annex 2106), in spite of American provocation to do so. Indeed, neither side availed itself of the *NAFTA* Chapter 20 forum. The U.S. urged that as a cultural product, a magazine should be considered in the same way as any merchandise. It accused Canada of using "culture" as an excuse to favor domestic firms. Canada said the matter was purely domestic, hence *NAFTA* was irrelevant. At bottom, Canada knew that invoking the *NAFTA* exemption would create the possibility of U.S. retaliation, which the exemption specifically authorizes.

In March 1997, a WTO panel ruled against Canada, upholding most of the American arguments. In *Canada—Measures Prohibiting or Restricting Importation of Certain Periodicals*, the Panel said the periodicals tax violated the GATT Article III:2 national treatment obligation, and the 1965 tariff prohibiting imports of split-run editions violated the Article XI rule against import bans. The preferential postal rates did accord less favorable treatment to imported magazines than to like Canadian magazines, thus violating the national treatment provision of GATT Article III:4. But, said the panel, the preference was a subsidy under GATT Article III:8(b), hence the violation was excused.

Canada appealed the ruling, arguing the controversial measures were directed at a service—advertising in foreign magazines—not the magazines *per se*. In July 1997, the WTO Appellate Body rejected this argument. Its Report is excerpted below. Essentially, the Appellate Body upheld the findings of the Panel, though it reversed the panel's conclusion on the postal subsidy issue, concluding postal rates did not constitute a subsidy under GATT Article III:8(b). Presumably, therefore, they violated Article III:4.

- **1997 *Canada Magazines* Findings**

WTO Appellate Body Report,

Canada—Certain Measures Concerning Periodicals,
WT/DS31/AB/R (Adopted 30 July 1997)

V. Article III:2, First Sentence, of the GATT 1994

With respect to the application of Article III:2, first sentence, we agree with the Panel that:

> ... the following two questions need to be answered to determine whether there is a violation of Article III:2 of GATT 1994: *(a)* Are imported "split-run" periodicals and domestic non "split-run" periodicals like products?; and *(b)* Are imported "split-run" periodicals subject to an internal tax in excess of that applied to domestic non "split-run" periodicals? If the answers

to both questions are affirmative, there is a violation of Article III:2, first sentence. If the answer to the first question is negative, we need to examine further whether there is a violation of Article III:2, second sentence.

[Citing its Report in *Japan—Alcoholic Beverages*, the Appellate Body observed in a footnote that it:

> need not examine the applicability of Article III:1 separately, because, as the Appellate Body noted in its recent report, the first sentence of Article III:2 *is*, in effect, an application of the general principle embodied in Article III:1. Therefore, if the imported and domestic products are "like products," and if the taxes applied to the imported products are "in excess of" those applied to the like domestic products, then the measure is inconsistent with Article III:2, first sentence. (emphasis original)]

A. Like Products

We agree with the legal findings and conclusions in ... the Panel Report [concerning the "like produce" analysis]. In particular, the Panel correctly enunciated, in theory, the legal test for determining "like products" in the context of Article III:2, first sentence, as established in the Appellate Body Report in *Japan—Alcoholic Beverages*. We also agree with the second point made by the Panel. As Article III:2, first sentence, normally requires a comparison between imported products and like domestic products, and as there were no imports of split-run editions of periodicals because of the import prohibition in Tariff Code 9958, which the Panel found (and Canada did not contest on appeal) to be inconsistent with the provisions of Article XI of the GATT 1994, hypothetical imports of split-run periodicals have to be considered. As the Panel recognized, the proper test is that a determination of "like products" for the purposes of Article III:2, first sentence, must be construed narrowly, on a case-by-case basis, by examining relevant factors including:

(i) the product's end-uses in a given market;

(ii) consumers' tastes and habits; and

(iii) the product's properties, nature and quality.

However, the Panel failed to analyze these criteria in relation to imported split-run periodicals and domestic non-split-run periodicals. Firstly, we note that the Panel did not base its findings on the exhibits and evidence before it, in particular, the copies of *TIME*, *TIME Canada* and *Maclean's* magazines, presented by Canada, and the magazines, *Pulp & Paper* and *Pulp & Paper Canada*, presented by the United States, or the *Report of the Task Force on the Canadian Magazine Industry* (the "*Task Force Report*").

Secondly, we observe that the Panel based its findings that imported split-run periodicals and domestic non-split-run periodicals "can" be like products, on a single hypothetical example constructed using a Canadian-owned magazine, *Harrowsmith Country Life*. However, this example involves a comparison between two editions of the same magazine, both imported products, which could not have been in the Canadian market at the same time. Thus, the discussion . . . [in] the Panel Report is inapposite, because the example is incorrect.

> The Panel leapt from its discussion of an incorrect hypothetical example to . . . conclude that imported "split-run" periodicals and domestic non "split-run" periodicals *can* be like products within the meaning of Article III:2 of GATT 1994. In our view, this provides sufficient grounds to answer in the affirmative the question as to whether the two products at issue *are* like because, . . . the purpose of Article III is to protect expectations of the Members as to the competitive relationship between their products and those of other Members, not to protect actual trade volumes. (Emphasis added)

It is not obvious to us how the Panel came to the conclusion that it had "sufficient grounds" to find the two products at issue *are* like products from an examination of an incorrect example which led to a conclusion that imported split-run periodicals and domestic non-split-run periodicals *can be* "like."

We therefore conclude that, as a result of the lack of proper legal reasoning based on inadequate factual analysis, . . . the Panel could not logically arrive at the conclusion that imported split-run periodicals and domestic non-split-run periodicals are like products.

We are mindful of the limitation of our mandate in Articles 17:6 and 17:13 of the *DSU*. According to Article 17:6, an appeal shall be limited to issues of law covered in the Panel Report and legal interpretations developed by the Panel. The determination of whether imported and domestic products are "like products" is a process by which legal rules have to be applied to facts. In any analysis of Article III:2, first sentence, this process is particularly delicate, since "likeness" must be construed narrowly and on a case-by-case basis. We note that, due to the absence of adequate analysis in the Panel Report in this respect, it is not possible to proceed to a determination of like products.

We feel constrained, therefore, to reverse the legal findings and conclusions of the Panel on "like products." As the Panel itself stated, there are two questions which need to be answered to determine whether there is a violation of Article III:2 of the GATT 1994: (a) whether imported and domestic products are like products; and (b) whether the imported products are taxed in excess of the domestic products. If the answers to both questions are affirmative, there is a violation of Article III:2, first sentence. If the answer to one question is negative, there is a need to examine further whether the measure is consistent with Article III:2, second sentence.

Having reversed the Panel's findings on "like products," we cannot answer both questions in the first sentence of Article III:2 in the affirmative as is required to demonstrate a violation of that sentence. Therefore, we need to examine the consistency of the measure with the second sentence of Article III:2 of the GATT 1994.

B. Non-Discrimination

In light of our conclusions on the question of "like products" in Article III:2, first sentence, we do not find it necessary to address Canada's claim of "non-discrimination" in relation to that sentence.

VI. Article III:2, Second Sentence, of the GATT 1994

We will proceed to examine the consistency of Part V.1 of the *Excise Tax Act* with the second sentence of Article III:2 of the GATT 1994.

A. Jurisdiction

Canada asserts that the Appellate Body does not have the jurisdiction to examine a claim under Article III:2, second sentence, as no party has appealed the findings of the Panel on this provision. [The Appellate Body rejected this argument, essentially because (1) the legal obligations in the first and second sentences of Article II:2 are closely linked, (2) the Panel made findings legal findings concerning the first sentence, one of which the Appellate Body reversed, and (3) it would be remiss of the Appellate Body not to complete the analysis of Article III:2.]

. . .

B. The Issues Under Article III:2, Second Sentence

In our Report in *Japan—Alcoholic Beverages*, we held that:

> . . . three separate issues must be addressed to determine whether an internal tax measure is inconsistent with Article III:2, second sentence. These three issues are whether:
>
> (1) the imported products and the domestic products *are "directly competitive or substitutable products" which are in competition with each other*;
>
> (2) the directly competitive or substitutable imported and domestic products are *"not similarly taxed"*; and
>
> (3) the dissimilar taxation of the directly competitive or substitutable imported domestic products *is "applied . . . so as to afford protection to domestic production."*

1. Directly Competitive or Substitutable Products

In *Japan—Alcoholic Beverages*, the Appellate Body stated that as with "like products" under the first sentence of Article III:2, the determination of the appropriate range of "directly competitive or substitutable products" under the second sentence must be made on a case-by-case basis. The Appellate Body also found it appropriate to look at competition in the relevant markets as one among a number of means of identifying the broader category of products that might be described as "directly competitive or substitutable," as the GATT is a commercial agreement, and the WTO is concerned, after all, with markets.

According to the Panel Report, Canada considers that split-run periodicals are not "directly competitive or substitutable" for periodicals with editorial content developed for the Canadian market. Although they may be substitutable advertising vehicles, they are not competitive or substitutable information vehicles. Substitution implies interchangeability. Once the content is accepted as relevant, it seems obvious that magazines created for different markets are not interchangeable. They serve different end-uses. Canada draws attention to a study by the economist, Leigh Anderson, on which the *Task Force Report* was at least partially-based, which notes:

> U.S. magazines can probably provide a reasonable substitute for Canadian magazines in their capacity as an advertising medium, although some advertisers may be better served by a Canadian vehicle. In many instances however, they would provide a very poor substitute as an entertainment and communication medium.

Canada submits that the *Task Force Report* characterizes the relationship as one of "imperfect substitutability"—far from the direct substitutability required by this provision. The market share of imported and domestic magazines in Canada has remained remarkably constant over the last 30-plus years. If competitive forces had been in play to the degree necessary to meet the standard of "directly competitive" goods, one would have expected some variations. All this casts serious doubt on whether the competition or substitutability between imported split-run periodicals and domestic non-split-run periodicals is sufficiently "direct" to meet the standard of *Ad* Article III.

According to the United States, the very existence of the tax is itself proof of competition between split-run periodicals and non-split-run periodicals in the Canadian market. As Canada itself has acknowledged, split-run periodicals compete with wholly domestically-produced periodicals for advertising revenue, which demonstrates that they compete for the same readers. The only reason firms place advertisements in magazines is to reach readers. A firm would consider split-run periodicals to be an acceptable advertising alternative to non-split-run periodicals only if that firm had reason to believe that the split-run periodicals themselves would be an acceptable alternative to non-split-run periodicals in the eyes of consumers. According to the United States, Canada acknowledges that "[r]eaders attract advertisers" and that, ". . . Canadian publishers are ready to compete with magazines published all over the world in order to keep their readers, but the competition is fierce."

According to the United States, the *Task Force Report* together with statements made by the Minister of Canadian Heritage and Canadian officials, provide further acknowledgment of the substitutability of imported split-run periodicals and domestic non-split-run periodicals in the Canadian market.

We find the United States' position convincing, while Canada's assertions do not seem to us to be compatible with its own description of the Canadian market for periodicals.

. . .

The statement by the economist, Leigh Anderson, quoted by Canada and the *Task Force Report*'s description of the relationship as one of "imperfect substitutability" does not modify our appreciation. A case of perfect substitutability would fall within Article III:2, first sentence, while we are examining the broader prohibition of the second sentence. We are not impressed either by Canada's argument that the market share of imported and domestic magazines has remained remarkably constant over the last 30-plus years, and that one would have expected some variation if competitive forces had been in play to the degree necessary to meet the standard of "directly competitive" goods. This argument would have weight only if Canada had not protected the domestic market of Canadian periodicals through, among other measures, the import prohibition of Tariff Code 9958 and the excise tax of Part V.1 of the *Excise Tax Act*.

Our conclusion that imported split-run periodicals and domestic non-split-run periodicals are "directly competitive or substitutable" does not mean that all periodicals belong to the same relevant market, whatever their editorial content. A periodical containing mainly current news is not directly competitive or substitutable with a periodical dedicated to gardening, chess, sports, music or cuisine. But news magazines, like *TIME*, *TIME Canada* and *Maclean's*, are directly competitive or substitutable in spite of the "Canadian" content of *Maclean's*. The competitive relationship is even closer in the case of more specialized magazines, like *Pulp & Paper* as compared with *Pulp & Paper Canada*, two trade magazines presented to the Panel by the United States.

The fact that, among these examples, only *TIME Canada* is a split-run periodical, and that it is not imported but is produced in Canada, does not affect at all our appreciation of the competitive relationship. The competitive relationship of imported split-run periodicals destined for the Canadian market is even closer to domestic non-split-run periodicals than the competitive relationship between imported non-split-run periodicals and domestic non-split-run periodicals. Imported split-run periodicals contain advertisements targeted specifically at the Canadian market, while imported non-split-run periodicals do not carry such advertisements.

We, therefore, conclude that imported split-run periodicals and domestic non-split-run periodicals are directly competitive or substitutable products in so far as they are part of the same segment of the Canadian market for periodicals.

2. Not Similarly Taxed

Having found that imported split-run and domestic non-split-run periodicals of the same type are directly competitive or substitutable, we must examine whether the imported products and the directly competitive or substitutable domestic products are not similarly taxed. Part V.1 of the *Excise Tax Act* taxes split-run editions of periodicals in an amount equivalent to 80 per cent of the value of all advertisements in a split-run edition. In contrast, domestic non-split-run periodicals are not subject to Part V.1 of the *Excise Tax Act*. Following the reasoning of the Appellate Body in *Japan—Alcoholic Beverages*, dissimilar taxation of even some imported products as compared to directly competitive or substitutable domestic products is inconsistent with the provisions of the second sentence of Article III:2. In *United States—Section 337*, the panel found:

> . . . that the "no less favorable" treatment requirement of Article III:4 has to be understood as applicable to each individual case of imported products. The Panel rejected any notion of balancing more favorable treatment of some imported products against less favorable treatment of other imported products. [GATT B.I.S.D. (36th Supp.) at 345 ¶ 5.14 (adopted 7 November 1989).]

With respect to Part V.1 of the *Excise Tax Act*, we find that the amount of the taxation is far above the *de minimis* threshold required by the Appellate Body Report in *Japan—Alcoholic Beverages*. The magnitude of this tax is sufficient to prevent the production and sale of split-run periodicals in Canada.

3. So as to Afford Protection

The Appellate Body established the following approach in *Japan—Alcoholic Beverages* for determining whether dissimilar taxation of directly competitive or substitutable products has been applied so as to afford protection:

> . . . we believe that an examination in any case of whether dissimilar taxation has been applied so as to afford protection requires a comprehensive and objective analysis of the structure and application of the measure in question on domestic as compared to imported products. We believe it is possible to examine objectively the underlying criteria used in a particular tax measure, its structure, and its overall application to ascertain whether it is applied in a way that affords protection to domestic products.

> Although it is true that the aim of a measure may not be easily ascertained, nevertheless its protective application can most often be discerned from the design, the architecture, and the revealing structure of a measure. The very magnitude of the dissimilar taxation in a particular case may be evidence of such a protective application, . . . Most often, there will be other factors to be considered as well. In conducting this inquiry, panels should give full consideration to all the relevant facts and all the relevant circumstances in any given case.

With respect to Part V.1 of the *Excise Tax Act*, we note that the magnitude of the dissimilar taxation between imported split-run periodicals and domestic non-split-run periodicals is beyond excessive, indeed, it is prohibitive. There is also ample evidence that the very design and structure of the measure is such as to afford protection to domestic periodicals.

The Canadian policy which led to the enactment of Part V.1 of the *Excise Tax Act* had its origins in the *Task Force Report*. It is clear from reading the *Task Force Report* that the design and structure of Part V.1 of the *Excise Tax Act* are to prevent the establishment of split-run periodicals in Canada, thereby ensuring that Canadian advertising revenues flow to Canadian magazines. Madame Monique Landry, Minister Designate of Canadian Heritage at the time the *Task Force Report* was released, issued the following statement summarizing the Government of Canada's policy objectives for the Canadian periodical industry:

> The Government reaffirms its commitment to protect the economic foundations of the Canadian periodical industry, which is a vital element of Canadian cultural expression. To achieve this objective, the Government will continue to use policy instruments that encourage the flow of advertising revenues to Canadian magazines and discourage the establishment of split-run or "Canadian" regional editions with advertising aimed at the Canadian market. We are committed to ensuring that Canadians have access to Canadian ideas and information through genuinely Canadian magazines, while not restricting the sale of foreign magazines in Canada.

Furthermore, the Government of Canada issued the following response to the *Task Force Report*:

> The Government reaffirms its commitment to the long-standing policy of protecting the economic foundations of the Canadian periodical industry. To achieve this objective, the Government uses policy instruments that encourage the flow of advertising revenues to Canadian periodicals, since a viable Canadian periodical industry must have a secure financial base.

During the debate of Bill C-103, *An Act to Amend the Excise Tax Act and the Income Tax Act*, the Minister of Canadian Heritage, the Honorable Michel Dupuy, stated the following:

> ... the reality of the situation is that we must protect ourselves against split-runs coming from foreign countries and, in particular, from the United States.

Canada also admitted that the objective and structure of the tax is to insulate Canadian magazines from competition in the advertising sector, thus leaving significant Canadian advertising revenues for the production of editorial material created for the Canadian market. With respect to the actual application of the tax to date, it has resulted in one split-run magazine, *Sports Illustrated*, to move its production for the Canadian market out of Canada and back to the United States. Also, *Harrowsmith Country Life*, a Canadian-owned split-run periodical, has ceased production of its United States' edition as a consequence of the imposition of the tax.

We therefore conclude on the basis of the above reasons, including the magnitude of the differential taxation, the several statements of the Government of Canada's explicit policy objectives in introducing the measure and the demonstrated actual protective effect of the measure, that the design and structure of Part V.1 of the *Excise Tax Act* is clearly to afford protection to the production of Canadian periodicals.

VII. Article III:8(b) of the GATT 1994

. . .

Both participants agree that Canada's "funded" postal rates involve "a payment of subsidies." The appellant, the United States, argues, however, that the "funded" postal rates program involves a transfer of funds from one government entity to another, *i.e.*, from Canadian Heritage to Canada Post, and not from the Canadian government to domestic producers as required by Article III:8(b).

As we understand it, through the PAP, Canadian Heritage provides Canada Post, a wholly-owned Crown corporation, with financial assistance to support special rates of postage for eligible publications, including certain designated domestic periodicals mailed and distributed in Canada. This program has been implemented through a series of agreements, the MOA [*i.e.*, the Memorandum of Agreement Concerning the Publications Assistance Program Between the Department of Communications and Canada Post Corporation], between Canadian Heritage and Canada Post, which provide that in consideration of the payments made to it by Canadian Heritage, Canada Post will accept for distribution, at special "funded" rates, all publications designated by Canadian Heritage to be eligible under the PAP. The MOA provides that while Canadian Heritage will administer the eligibility requirements for the PAP based on criteria specified in the MOA, Canada Post will accept for distribution all publications that are eligible under the PAP at the "funded" rates.

[The appellant, the U.S., cited four GATT Panel reports for its interpretation of Article III:8(b). But, these Reports were not directly on point. In the 1958 *Italian Agricultural Machinery* case,[25] and 1990 *EEC—Oilseeds* case,[26] the Panels held subsidies paid to purchasers of agricultural machinery and processors of oilseeds were not made "exclusively to domestic producers" of agricultural machinery and oilseeds, respectively. In the 1992 *United States—Malt Beverages* case,[27] and 1990 *United States—Tobacco* case,[28] at issue was whether a reduction in a federal excise tax on beer or a remission of a product tax on tobacco constituted a "payment of subsidies" under GATT Article III:8(b). The *Malt Beverages* Panel found a reduction of taxes on a good does not qualify as a "payment of subsidies" for the purposes of Article III:8(b). In *United States—Tobacco*, having found that the measure at issue was not a tax remission, the Panel concluded that it was a payment which qualified under Article III:8(b) of the GATT 1994.]

In *EEC—Oilseeds*, the Panel stated that "it can reasonably be assumed that a payment not made directly to producers is not made 'exclusively' to them." This statement of the panel is *obiter dicta*, as the panel found in that report that subsidies

---

25. *See* GATT B.I.S.D. (7th Supp.) at 60 (adopted 23 October 1958).
26. *See* GATT B.I.S.D. (37th Supp.) at 86 (adopted 25 January 1990).
27. *See* GATT B.I.S.D. (39th Supp.) at 206 (adopted 19 June 1992).
28. *See* GATT B.I.S.D. (37th Supp.) at 86 (adopted 25 January 1990).

paid to oilseeds processors were not made "exclusively to domestic producers," and therefore, the EEC payments of subsidies to processors and producers of oilseeds and related animal feed proteins did not qualify under the provisions of Article III:8(b).

A proper interpretation of Article III:8(b) needs careful examination of the text, context and object and purpose of that provision. In examining the text of Article III:8(b), we believe that the phrase, "including payments to domestic producers derived from the proceeds of internal taxes or charges applied consistently with the provisions of this Article and subsidies effected through governmental purchases of domestic products" helps to elucidate the types of subsidies covered by Article III:8(b) of the GATT 1994. It is not an exhaustive list of the kinds of programs that would qualify as "the payment of subsidies exclusively to domestic producers," but those words exemplify the kinds of programs that are exempt from the obligations of GATT Articles III:2 and III:4.

Our textual interpretation is supported by the context of Article III:8(b) examined in relation to Articles III:2 and III:4 of the GATT 1994. Furthermore, the object and purpose of Article III:8(b) is confirmed by the drafting history of Article III. In this context, we refer to the following discussion in the Reports of the Committees and Principal Sub-Committees of the Interim Commission for the International Trade Organization concerning the provision of the Havana Charter for an International Trade Organization that corresponds to Article III:8(b) of the GATT 1994:

> This sub-paragraph was redrafted in order to make it clear that nothing in Article 18 could be construed to sanction the exemption of domestic products from internal taxes imposed on like imported products or the remission of such taxes. At the same time the Sub-Committee recorded its view that nothing in this sub-paragraph or elsewhere in Article 18 would override the provisions of Section C of Chapter IV. [Interim Commission for the International Trade Organization, Reports of the Committees and Principal Sub-Committees: ICITO I/8, Geneva, September 1948, p. 66. As the Appellate Body stated in footnote 73 of its Report, Article 18 and Section C of Chapter IV of the Havana Charter for an International Trade Organization correspond, respectively, to Article III and Article XVI of the GATT 1947.]

We do not see a reason to distinguish a reduction of tax rates on a product from a reduction in transportation or postal rates. Indeed, an examination of the text, context, and object and purpose of Article III:8(b) suggests that it was intended to exempt from the obligations of Article III only the payment of subsidies which involves the expenditure of revenue by a government.

We agree with the panel in *United States — Malt Beverages* that:

> Article III:8(b) limits, therefore, the permissible producer subsidies to "payments" after taxes have been collected or payments otherwise consistent with Article III. This separation of tax rules, *e.g.*, on tax exemptions or reductions, and subsidy rules makes sense economically and politically. Even if the proceeds from non-discriminatory product taxes may be used

for subsequent subsidies, the domestic producer, like his foreign competitors, must pay the product taxes due. The separation of tax and subsidy rules contributes to greater transparency. It also may render abuses of tax policies for protectionist purposes more difficult, as in the case where producer aids require additional legislative or governmental decisions in which the different interests involved can be balanced.

As a result of our analysis of the text, context, and object and purpose of Article III:8(b), we conclude that the Panel incorrectly interpreted this provision. For these reasons, we reverse the Panel's findings and conclusions that Canada's "funded" postal rates scheme for periodicals is justified under Article III:8(b) of the GATT 1994.

XI. International Digital Trade

Negotiations on the single undertaking package of Uruguay Round agreements were completed on 15 December 1993, well before the Internet had been widely commercialized.[29] Less than two decades thereafter, in the five-year period 2009–2013, Internet commerce accounted for almost 21% of the growth in GDP of developed countries. GATT-WTO texts had not kept pace with cross-border electronic trade, though WTO Members periodically extended a moratorium on taxation of e-commerce. They failed to address the topic in the Doha Round, so by the mid-2000s, America and other countries keen on Internet commerce pursued their objectives through FTA talks. The U.S. first did so in *TPP* and *T-TIP* negotiations.

To begin, international "Internet commerce," "e commerce," or more generally "digital trade" as "the cross-border transmission of goods and services by electronic means." Admittedly, that definition is circular, and technically the transmission may occur by means other than the Internet. There are five categories of digital trade, summarized with examples in Table 12-1.

Consider, then, what exactly are the barriers to digital trade on which America and like-minded countries seek to impose disciplines through FTAs? The answer is that there are five barriers (or categories of barriers), which affect all categories of digital trade:

(1) localization requirements;

(2) censorship;

(3) privacy and security;

(4) border measures; and

(5) IP infringement.

---

29. This discussion draws on Duane W. Layton & Kelsey M. Rule, *Debugging Digital Trade: Challenges for the Global Trade Regime*, 31 International Trade Reporter (BNA) 516 (13 March 2014). Unless otherwise noted, quotations are from this source.

Table 12-1. Five Categories of Digital Trade

Category	Examples
Digital Content	Electronic books, electronic news media, electronic images, and music or videos that are streamed
Social Media	Online dating, social and professional networking sites such as Linked In, and user-created content platforms
Search Engines	Database or web search engines, such as Google
Data Storage	Cloud computing, hosted servers, or managed servers

First, as the term intimates, "localization" is a requirement of physical presence in an importing country. That is, it is a rule demanding "a domestic nexus of the supply-side of digital transactions." A quintessential example is that a company providing Internet services (*e.g.*, data storage) use local servers, for example, in Brazil (the "importing" country), rather than the U.S. (the "exporting" country). Other illustrations are rules that a company use locally sourced software or programming services. Still another example is a mandate that on-demand and streamed media, such as movies or radio programs, satisfy local content quotas. All such rules sometimes appear in the context of government procurement.

Localization requirements cut off the opportunity for global competition for digital services, so what justifications are offered for them by Brazil, China, and other prominent proponents of them? One rationale is to counter American espionage. Following the revelations in 2013–2014 by former NSA employee Edward Snowden of NSA data collection, such countries prefer that including Internet servers, not be located in the U.S., where data stored in them concerning their citizens is relatively more vulnerable to American eavesdropping, and subject to U.S. territorial jurisdiction, than if it is within Brazilian or Chinese territory. A second rationale is that those countries have their own national security interests. Localization measures are especially likely in banking, energy, telecommunications, and other strategically sensitive sectors the networks of which are essential to national infrastructure. Note, however, the admixture of motives and touch of hypocrisy: America hardly is alone in seek to monitor communications in pursuit of perceived interests, and in in the case of the CCP, preserving socioeconomic order and morality in support of Party is the prime directive.

Second, as reference to the CCP intimates, censorship is a barrier to digital trade. Along with China, Iran, Saudi Arabia, and Vietnam are notorious for "systematic and pervasive censorship" of the free flow of information across the Internet. Critics charge their measures are more than just counter-terrorist operations against Islamist extremist groups, or efforts to fight immoral and exploitative content pornography. They extend to blocking or filtering political information, information, and discourse that challenges ruling elites, and "disrupt[ing] the operations of foreign digital providers . . . ," for example, by routing those providers through domestic gateways, or slowing up the delivery of their content.

Third, privacy and security concerns are at stake with respect to personal, payment, or controlled data. Personal data include not only basic census information such as name, physical and email address, and telephone number, but also statistics about behavior, like web pages viewed, time spent on each page, posting of "likes" and "sharing," consumption spending patterns, plus biometric facts concerning body size and type, caloric intake, and physical and mental fitness. From an American corporate perspective, mass personal databases are key to identifying profitable marketing opportunities. Hence, collection, storage, sharing, and sale are unobjectionable, with each company free to set its own privacy policies. Conversely, the EU takes the view gathering and downstream use of such data is permissible only with the *a priori* consent of the individual, otherwise capitalist greed trumps respect for privacy. So, any American company operating in Europe must certify it complies with EU data privacy measures.

Korea, too, restricts offshore data processing. Foreign financial institutions operating in Korea, such as asset management companies, are barred from transmitting detailed data on their portfolio positions to colleagues in other countries. Foreign banks must process customer transaction data in Korea. The Korean Financial Services Commission justifies these limits "to protect sensitive consumer information, and ensure the ability of financial regulators to have access to records of financial service suppliers relating to the handling of such information."[30] In their FTAs with Korea, both the U.S. and EU would prefer a relaxed standard that would allow foreign banks to transfer data out of Korea when required in the "ordinary course of business."[31]

Fourth, though digital products flow across borders at mouse click, there are barriers at geopolitical boundaries to such flows. These barriers take the form of tariffs that might be insignificant to large vendors, but which are costly to SMEs. That is because the *de minimis* threshold, below which tariffs are not imposed, is a low price point that covers SME merchandise. Raising that threshold to exempt their goods, would liberalize so called digitally-enabled micro exports.

Finally, IP infringement remains a concern in respect of digital trade, notwithstanding the *TRIPs Agreement* protections for patents, trademarks, copyrights, semiconductor mask works, and trade secrets. Producers of software and other digital content worry about infringement via illegal downloading or bootlegging. Indeed, it is said that in India, once a hardcopy book is provided in e book form, pirated copies become immediately and freely available across the Subcontinent. WTO Members do not have harmonized rules on IP protection for digital content

---

30. Simon Mundy, *S. Korea Pressed on Trade Deals*, FINANCIAL TIMES, 23 May 2013, at 3. [Hereinafter, *S. Korea Pressed.*]

31. *S. Korea Pressed.*

or intermediary liability for infringement, and there are multiple regulatory agencies across them. So, there is uncertainty and confusion for producers.

To illustrate, Internet sites like YouTube based on user-created (*i.e.*, user-posted) content are subject to liability for IP infringement in some, but not other, Members. To be sure, the U.S. has implemented the WIPO *"Internet Treaties,"* formally known as the *Copyright and Performances and Phonograms Treaties*. But, not all of its trading partners have. Pressing them to do so through FTAs to rectify divergences over online IP protection regimes is logical.

Finally, consider whether and to what extent *TPP*, and *CPTPP* with the certain IP provisions suspended, address those barriers through appropriate disciplines.

XII. Case Study on Digital Trade: *NAFTA* 2.0

- **27 August 2018 U.S.-Mexico Bilateral Agreement**

Office of the United States Trade Representative,

United States–Mexico Trade Fact Sheet: *Modernizing NAFTA to Be a 21st Century Trade Agreement* (28 August 2018)[32]

Key Highlights of the Digital Trade Chapter

The new Digital Trade Chapter will:

(1) Prohibit customs duties and other discriminatory measures from being applied to digital products distributed electronically (e-books, videos, music, software, games, etc.).

(2) Ensure that data can be transferred cross-border, and that limits on where data can be stored and processed are minimized, thereby enhancing and protecting the global digital ecosystem.

(3) Ensure that suppliers are not restricted in their use of electronic authentication or electronic signatures, thereby facilitating digital transactions.

(4) Guarantee that enforceable consumer protections, including for privacy and unsolicited communications, apply to the digital marketplace.

(5) Limit governments' ability to require disclosure of proprietary computer source code and algorithms, to better protect the competitiveness of digital suppliers.

(6) Promote collaboration in tackling cybersecurity challenges while seeking to promote industry best practices to keep networks and services secure.

(7) Promote open access to government-generated public data, to enhance innovative use in commercial applications and services.

---

32. https://ustr.gov/about-us/policy-offices/press-office/press-releases/2018/august/modernizing-nafta-be-21st-century.

(8) Limit the civil liability of Internet platforms for third-party content that such platforms host or process, outside of the realm intellectual property enforcement, thereby enhancing the economic viability of these engines of growth that depend on user interaction and user content.

- **30 September 2018 Trilateral *NAFTA* 2.0 (*USMCA*)**

Office of the United States Trade Representative,

United States–Mexico–Canada Fact Sheet: *Modernizing NAFTA into a 21st Century Agreement* (1 October 2018)[33]

. . .

The new Digital Trade Chapter [*USMCA* Chapter 19] contains the strongest disciplines on digital trade of any international agreement, providing a firm foundation for the expansion of trade and investment in the innovative products and services where the United States has a competitive advantage.

Key Highlights of the Digital Trade Chapter

The new Digital Trade Chapter will:

(1) Prohibit [in Article 19:3] customs duties and other discriminatory measures from being applied to digital products distributed electronically (e-books, videos, music, software, games, etc.).

(2) Ensure that data can be transferred cross-border, and that limits on where data can be stored and processed are minimized, thereby enhancing and protecting the global digital ecosystem.

[In respect of data transfer, Article 19:11 contains a near-blanket prohibition:

1. No Party shall prohibit or restrict the cross-border transfer of information, including personal information, by electronic means if this activity is for the conduct of the business of a covered person.

2. Nothing in this Article shall prevent a Party from adopting or maintaining a measure inconsistent with paragraph 1 necessary to achieve a legitimate public policy objective, provided that the measure:

  (a) is not applied in a manner which would constitute a means of arbitrary or unjustifiable discrimination or a disguised restriction on trade; and

  (b) does not impose restrictions on transfers of information greater than are necessary to achieve the objective.

Article 19:12 imposes a blanket prohibition against data localization: "No Party shall require a covered person to use or locate computing facilities

---

33. https://ustr.gov/about-us/policy-offices/press-office/fact-sheets/2018/october/united -states-mexico-canada-trade-fa-1.

in that Party's territory as a condition for conducting business in that territory."]

(3) Ensure [in Article 19:6] that suppliers are not restricted in their use of electronic authentication or electronic signatures, thereby facilitating digital transactions.

(4) Guarantee [in Articles 19:7–19:8] that enforceable consumer protections, including for privacy and unsolicited communications [*e.g.*, spam emails, as per Article 19:13], apply to the digital marketplace.

(5) Limit [via Article 19:16] governments' ability to require disclosure of proprietary computer source code and algorithms, to better protect the competitiveness of digital suppliers.

(6) Promote collaboration [via Articles 19:14–19:15] in tackling cybersecurity challenges while seeking to promote industry best practices to keep networks and services secure.

(7) Promote [in Article 19:18] open access to government-generated public data, to enhance innovative use in commercial applications and services.

(8) Limit [in Article 19:17] the civil liability of Internet platforms for third-party content that such platforms host or process, outside of the realm of intellectual property enforcement, thereby enhancing the economic viability of these engines of growth that depend on user interaction and user content.

Part Four

Preferences for Poor Countries: Development Economics

Chapter 13

Measuring Growth, Development, and Poverty[1]

I. What Is "Growth"?

- **GNP**

GNP is the broadest measure of income earned by nationals of a country. GNP is the total value of all finished output of goods and services produced by nationals of a country. *Per capita* GNP is the final value of all finished goods and services produced by nationals of a country in one year, divided by the number of nationals (*i.e.*, citizens) of that country.

It does not matter whether or where the output is consumed, invested, or if it used by a government. The value of the output is income to its producer. Therefore, GNP is defined equivalently as all income earned by nationals — but only nationals, *i.e.*, citizens, of a country — regardless of where the nationals earn the income. The letter "N" in "GNP" emphasizes nationals of the country earned the income being measured. GNP may be computed in terms of current (also called "nominal") price levels in the country.

However, the prices of income-generating output (*e.g.*, agricultural commodities, manufactured goods, services) change over time. Consequently, a more reliable measurement than current GNP is "constant" GNP. "Constant" GNP is current GNP, corrected for price inflation (or deflation) using a numerical factor that sets a specific year as the base year from which to define a price index (*e.g.*, prices in 2005 equal 100).

For example, the income of a Filipino receptionist working at the Sheraton Hotel in Bahrain would be included in the GNP of the Philippines, but not of Bahrain, because the receptionist is a national of the Philippines. To the extent the receptionist repatriates the earnings, the economy of the Philippines directly benefits. In addition to the Philippines, Bangladesh, India, Sri Lanka, and various other poor countries send workers to Persian Gulf countries to earn income, which then is repatriated to the home countries.

---

1. Documents References:
   (1) *Havana (ITO) Charter* Preamble
   (2) GATT Preamble
   (3) *WTO Agreement* Preamble

Consider the income earned by the Sheraton Hotel in Bahrain. It would be included in the GNP of the U.S., but not of Bahrain. That is because, as an American-based MNC, Sheraton Hotels are a national of the U.S. Many such corporations rely for a large percentage of their revenues on foreign-generated income. Yet, for purposes of computing GNP, the location in which income is produced is irrelevant. What matters is the nationality of the owner of the asset producing the activities.

As for the letter "G," standing for "Gross," it indicates the calculation is an aggregate one, with no subtraction for items like consumption of capital. ("Capital consumption" refers to the decline in value of equipment, which occurs because as equipment ages, becomes obsolete, or is used, and because of technological enhancements.) The letter "P," standing for "Product," suggests only the value of real output produced is included in GNP. The value of output absorbed in the manufacturing process—namely, intermediate or semi-finished goods—is excluded.

As a practical matter, there are three ways to compute national income—the GNP or GDP—of a country: income approach; expenditure approach; and output approach. Under the income approach, the incomes derived from each type of economic activity, that is, the income accruing to all owners of factors of production, is summed. Thus, income from self-employment, trading profits, rent, and property income from abroad are added together. Only the incomes and profits of residents of the country are included in the calculation. Transfer payments (*e.g.*, welfare), that is, payments that are not made to factors of production for current services, also are excluded.

Under the expenditure approach, spending on final goods and services is aggregated. The principal categories of spending are consumption (C), investment (I) (*i.e.*, expenditures that add to the capital stock, as distinct from consumption), government purchases (G), and net exports (*i.e.*, exports less imports, or X–M). These categories give rise to the familiar macroeconomic equation

$$GNP = C + I + G + (X - M),$$

or, using "Y" to symbolize GNP,

$$Y = C + I + G + (X - M)$$

Under the output approach, the values of products of each of the various sectors in the economy are summed. Thus, the value added by agricultural and extractive industries, manufacturing industries, construction, and services, along with net property income from abroad, are aggregated. GDP is reported both in "nominal" or "current" terms (*i.e.*, uncorrected for inflation), and in "real" or "constant" terms (*i.e.*, corrected for inflation).

· **GDP**

GDP is a slightly narrower measure of income earned than GNP. GDP is the total value of all finished output of goods and services produced in an economy. *Per capita* GDP is the final value of finished goods and services produced in the territory of a country in one year, divided by the number of persons (whether or not nationals) in that country.

It does not matter whether or where the output is consumed, invested, or used by a government. The value of the output is income to its producer. Therefore, GDP is defined equivalently as all income earned within the territory of a country, whether or not produced by nationals (*i.e.,* citizens) or non-nationals of that country. Like GNP, GDP may be measured at current price levels in a country, or at constant prices.

The letter "D" in GDP serves to emphasize the income measured is earned within the territorial jurisdiction of the country. That is, GDP measures economic activity within the domestic territory of a country. For example, income earned by a Filipino receptionist working at the Sheraton Hotel in Bahrain would be included in the GDP of Bahrain, but not in the GDP of the Philippines. That is true even if the receptionist repatriates all or some of the income. Likewise, income earned by Sheraton Hotel in Bahrain would be included in the GDP of Bahrain, not the U.S., even though Sheraton is an American-based multinational corporation. That is because the facility in question is located in Bahrain. In brief, for GDP, the owner of the asset producing income is irrelevant. Rather, the location of the income-generating activities matters.

As with GDP, the letter "G" in GNP indicates the calculation is an aggregate one. No subtraction is made for consumption of capital. Also, as with GNP, the letter "P" in GDP suggests the value of output absorbed in the manufacturing process—namely, intermediate or semi-finished goods—is excluded.

- **PPP**

PPP is a method of comparing national income—either GNP or GDP—and other economic growth statistics that accounts for different price levels across countries. There is an obvious problem when relying on any one of these measurements of "growth" in a country to make comparisons and contrasts across countries. Price levels differ across countries. The price of identical, like, similar, or substitutable merchandise—whether the good is a baseball, protein bar, or textbook—often differs across countries. The reasons for the variance include market conditions, such as competition among suppliers, demand and income levels among consumers, inflation, protection, and taxation. Such variations also exist for the same or comparable services, be they banking, dental, or legal.

Consequently, comparisons of growth—and, as a closely related matter, income levels—among countries using raw GNP or GDP data are misleading, insofar as cross-country differences may be explained in part by price variations. Typically, the raw data overstates the true extent of growth and income differences. The correction economists make is to put the data on PPP terms. That is, economists measure and compare growth and income using:

(1) GNP (PPP terms)

(2) *Per Capita* GNP (PPP terms)

(3) GDP (PPP terms)

(4) *Per Capita* GDP (PPP terms)

Measuring income at market prices means valuing the quantity of goods and services in a country at the price levels for those goods and services prevailing in that country during a particular point or period in time. To make cross-country comparisons, the resulting figures must be converted from local currency (*e.g.,* Chinese *yuan*) into a common currency (*e.g.,* U.S. dollars). In contrast, PPP terms means valuing the quantity of goods and services at price levels prevailing in a chosen country during a particular year—say the U.S. in the year 2005.

With income statistics put on a PPP basis, no exchange conversion is necessary, because from the outset goods and services from all countries are valued in terms of a common currency. Typically, that currency is the U.S. dollar. Essentially, PPP is a way to correct for differences in prices across countries, and for the possibility exchange rate fluctuations undermine the reliability of cross-country GNP comparisons. The device eliminates the need to convert valuation of goods and services in a foreign currency to valuation in a standard set of prices denominated in a major currency.

There is a second, subtle, advantage to measuring GNP and GDP in PPP terms. PPP helps correct for the fact not every type of good or service is traded across borders. For example, childcare services are not traded among countries, and in general, water is not traded across international boundaries either (though countries share boundary waters pursuant to treaties). Indeed, in many Third World countries, a large portion of national income is comprised of goods and services that are not traded internationally. That creates a problem if cross-country comparisons are made using GNP at market prices.

In each country, the ratio of the price of goods and services that are traded internationally to the price of goods and services that are not traded internationally will differ. The differences will depend in part on the importance of non-traded goods and services in each the economy of a country. Yet, at the same time, exchange rates are determined in part by the flow of goods and services that are traded internationally. That is to say, exchange rates do not embody economic activity in non-traded sectors.

As a result, when a GNP statistic measured at market prices (such as Chinese *yuan*) is converted to a major currency (such as U.S. dollars), the exchange rate used for the conversion is "incomplete." In turn, the comparison of GNP statistics across countries is misleading. The PPP measure circumvents the problem by valuing goods and services produced in each country on the basis of prices prevailing in one country. Thus, the fact the ratio of prices in traded versus non-traded sectors differs from one country to the next does not matter, because the prices in only one country are used for valuation.

To understand how income-based measures of growth are calculated and compared in PPP terms, consider the following example involving the GDP of China and America. To simplify, suppose the output of the U.S. consists of rice (to represent all agricultural products), navigational equipment for long-haul commercial aircraft (to represent advanced manufactured products), and pediatric dental services for children age 5 or under (to represent the service sector). Suppose further the output of China consists of rice and dental services, but not navigational equipment. Chinese manufacturing, at a less advanced stage, consists of H-shaped steel beams (used, for example, in building construction).

Table 13-1 presents the volume of output for each category and country in a given year. It also specifies the price of each good or service in the American market, measured in U.S. dollars, in a specified base year (2005). Using the PPP method, the output of each country is valued in dollars.

Table 13-1. Example of PPP GDP — China and U.S.

Output (Good or Service) → Country and Measurement ↓	Rice	H-Shaped Steel Beams	Navigational Equipment for Long-Haul Commercial Civil Aircraft	Pediatric Dental Services for Children Age 5 Or Under
Volume of Output in China	100 kilos	500 tons	China does not make this good, it relies on imports	1 million dental visits (*i.e.*, the number of dental visits in China by kids age 5 or under was 10 million)
Volume of Output in U.S.	200 kilos	The U.S. does not make this good, it relies on imports	100 units	5 million dental visits (*i.e.*, the number of dental visits in the U.S. by kids age 5 or under was 50 million)
Price of Output in U.S., in 2005, in U.S. dollars	$10 per kilo	$100 per beam (price of imported H-beams)	$1,000 per unit	$50 per visit
PPP Value of Output in China	100 × $10 = $1,000	500 × $100 = $50,000	Zero, because no domestic (Chinese) production	1 million × $50 = $50 million
PPP Value of Output in U.S.	200 × $10 = $2,000	Zero, because no domestic (American) production	100 × $1,000 = $100,000	5 million × $50 = $250 million

PPP GDP of China (Total PPP Value of Output): $50,051,000

PPP GDP of U.S. (Total PPP Value of Output): $250,102,000

If the comparison of the value of the output of each country is in U.S. dollars, and if China's output initially is measured in local currency at price levels prevailing in China, then the Chinese currency—the *yuan*—needs to be converted into dollars. No doubt that exchange rate, at any point in time, reflects only the goods and services China and the U.S. trade internationally. No doubt the exchange rate selected today might be different from the one tomorrow.

What if the *yuan* depreciates relative to the dollar after the conversion is made? Then, China's GNP—in dollar terms—will be overstated. It will have been valued at the exchange rate just before the depreciation. Conversely, if the *yuan* appreciates after the conversion, then China's dollar-denominated GNP will be understated. That output will have been valued at the lower rate, the one prevailing before the appreciation. Thus, when the comparison of China and the U.S. is done the next time, the results will differ—in part because of the exchange rate fluctuation that occurred since the last comparison.

Using PPP not only avoids the problem of traded versus non-traded sectors in different countries, but also helps ensure GNP comparisons are not adulterated by exchange rate fluctuations. After all, these fluctuations do not necessarily mean the real quality of life in the countries being compared has changed. At market prices, GNP, or *per capita* GNP, figures not measured in PPP terms can present a misleading picture of growth. But, getting the truest possible picture of the quality of life is what we must have if we are to draw reliable inferences about problems in less developed countries, and how (if at all) international trade law and policy can be altered to remedy the problems.

Accordingly, a PPP comparison is premised on a common set of prices in one currency. The common standard typically used by economists is dollar-denominated prices prevailing in America during a reference year. In the Table, the reference year is 2005. The Table sets forth the hypothesized prices prevailing in the U.S. during 2005, in U.S. dollars. The cells in the last row of the Table show the value of the good or service produced in the U.S. at those prices. The cells in the penultimate row show the value of the good or service produced in China, but the valuation is computed at those same prices. By using the common set of prices in one currency, the near-certainty that the prices of those goods and services in China, denominated in *yuan*, in 2005 were different, is immaterial. Likewise, any *yuan*-dollar exchange rate fluctuations have no effect on the valuation. The PPP GDP of each country, set forth at the bottom of the Table, simply is the sum of the cells in the row pertaining to each country.

To emphasize, because prices change from year to year with inflation or deflation, it is critical to select a particular year, such as 2005, as a basis for measurement. Comparisons of GDP (or GNP) over time would be distorted by inflation or deflation if the prices used to measure goods and services were those prevailing in the year of measurement. Thus, to measure "real" (as distinct from "nominal") GDP (either at market prices or in PPP terms), economists typically select a "base" year and stick with it. That is, they calculate the value of goods and services produced in various countries on the basis of prices from only one year.

It should not come as a surprise that when GDP and *per capita* GDP are measured in PPP terms, the differences between low- and high-income countries are compressed. After all, the output volumes of poor countries measured at price levels prevailing in America. Almost certainly, those levels are higher than the prices for the same goods and services in poor countries. In turn, critics of the multilateral trading system should take heed. The lot of poor people anywhere is horrific, and in least developed countries, by definition, they earn less than a dollar a day. Yet, the actual statistical gap between low- and high-income countries should not be exaggerated, and exaggerations ought not to be a basis for criticizing the trading system.

II. What Is "Development"?

· HDI

If development is a far broader concept than growth, then it is appropriate to construct an index of development that takes into account more than just the hallmark of growth, which is income. In 1990, the UNDP began publishing just such an index—the HDI. In 1994, it revised the way it constructs the index to allow for comparison of countries over time, instead of static relative rankings, in part by defining a possible range of minimum and maximum values for each variable in the index.

The essential theory of the HDI is a country with a higher income is not necessarily more developed than one with a lower income. For example, in 1998 the U.S. sat atop the world in terms of *per capita* GDP ($29,605), but scored second to Canada on the HDI (0.929 for America, and 0.935 for Canada). Comparing the relative levels of development of countries depends on a mix of factors.

There are three variables on which the HDI focuses, as follows. Observe the HDI is not a complete break from orthodox measures of growth, as the third variable is income.

(1) *Health*: To measure the level of health of people in a country, the HDI examines average life expectancy at birth. A longer life expectancy indicates better health. The possible range is from 25 to 85 years.

(2) *Knowledge*: To gauge the level of education of people in a country, the HDI covers two factors: literacy rates and average number of years of schooling. The higher the literacy rate and average number of years of schooling, the higher level of education. Literacy rates may range from zero to 100%. Average years of schooling may range from zero to 15 years. They are measured using the combined primary, secondary, and tertiary enrollment ratios (in effect, the percentage of children in school at these levels). As between these

two factors, literacy is given a two-thirds weight, and enrollment a one-third weight.

(3) *Income*: Income matters, of course, and the HDI incorporates *per capita* GDP using the PPP method, with a deflator to account for price inflation (putting the income figure in real, as opposed to nominal, terms). The range is from U.S. $100 to $40,000. However, as explained below, an adjustment is made to take account of the law of diminishing marginal utility to income. The average world real *per capita* income, in PPP terms, establishes a threshold level. The actual income level of a country is not adjusted if it is below that threshold. If the actual income level is above the threshold, then it is discounted according to a formula (known among economists as "Atkinson's formula for the utility of income"). The maximum figure of $40,000 requires discounting, and the discounted amount is $6,154.

Arithmetically, the UNDP calculates the value for each variable using a formula.

In the formula, X_A is the actual value of the variable for a particular country, X_{MAX} is the maximum value possible, and X_{MIN} is the minimum value possible:

$$\text{Value of Variable} = \frac{X_A - X_{MIN}}{X_{MAX} - X_{MIN}}$$

For example, in 1994, life expectancy in Egypt was 64.3 years, the adult literacy rate was 50.5%, the combined enrollment ratio at the first, second, and third levels was 69%, and adjusted real *per capita* GDP on PPP terms was U.S. $3,846. (The world average real *per capita* income in PPP terms that year was $5,835. The actual figure for Egypt is below this threshold, so no adjustment is needed.) Using the formula, and the aforementioned minimum and maximum values, the variable scores are:

For Life Expectancy:

$$\text{Egyptian Score} = \frac{64.3 - 25}{85 - 25} = 0.66$$

For Adult Literacy:

$$\text{Egyptian Score} = \frac{50.5 - 0}{100 - 0} = 0.51$$

For Enrollment:

$$\text{Egyptian Score} = \frac{69 - 0}{100 - 0} = 0.69$$

For Education (combining Adult literacy and Enrollment):

$$\text{Egyptian Score} = (66.66\% \text{ weight}) \times (0.51)$$
$$+ (33.33\% \text{ weight}) \times (0.69)$$
$$= 0.57$$

For Income:

$$\text{Egyptian Score} = \frac{3,846 - 0}{6,154 - 0} = 0.62$$

Then, to compute the HDI for a country, the UNDP takes the average of the three variables. In the example of Egypt, the result would be:

$$\text{HDI for Egypt} = \frac{0.66 + 0.57 + 0.62}{3} = 0.62$$

Significantly, especially for the poor living in places like the Cairo slums (known as the "City of the Dead"), this HDI put Egypt at number 109 of 175 countries the UNDP ranked in 1994. Comparing the HDI against Egypt's performance on real *per capita* GDP (PPP terms), the result was—22. The negative sign means Egypt's HDI score was 22 notches worse than its ranking solely on income (which was 87 out of 175). Many countries in the Middle East, especially oil-exporting ones, score well on income charts, but lowly on indexes of social development like the HDI. Have they improved since the Arab Spring, which commenced in January 2011?

A key aspect of how the UNDP constructs the HDI is its weighting of the 3 factors, particularly income. In the jargon of economics, there is diminishing marginal utility of income. Accruing income (like consuming most goods or services) is subject to the law of diminishing returns. A person—or country—derives a great deal of satisfaction—or utility—from the first dollar of income earned. Levels of utility from incremental—or marginal—amounts of income are positive—but not forever. Each additional dollar of income brings a little less satisfaction than the previous one. At some point, a person (or country) has more than enough income needed or desired, and additional amounts do not confer much satisfaction at all. Indeed, after a large amount of income, the increments may cause more trouble than they are worth (*e.g.*, because of time and energy consumed in managing the additional money and protecting it from theft and fraud). To a poor person, one dollar brings huge satisfaction, but to a billionaire, it means virtually nothing.

Thus, recognizing the phenomenon of diminishing marginal utility of income, the UNDP incorporates it by adjusting statistics on income. If a country has a high *per capita* income, the UNDP discounts that income. Conversely, it assigns a greater weight to the *per capita* income of poor countries. The higher the *per capita* income, the less the weight the UNDP gives it, in proportion to health and knowledge, in the HDI.

Despite that adjustment, the HDI has failed to impress many economists. Indeed, that adjustment is a source of criticism. The maximum real *per capita* income figure of $40,000, discounted to $6,154, effectively puts a cap on the contribution income can make to development in the HDI. Suppose a country moves from the income level of Laos to that of Singapore, and the upward trend continues. The HDI disregards increases beyond the maximum. Yet, surely those increases, to Singapore-style levels and beyond, matter, albeit with diminishing returns.

Among other deficiencies they cite are the weighting of the variables and positive correlation among the variables. Assigning coefficients to weigh health, education, and income ultimately depends on subjective preferences. Those preferences differ depending on a range of factors — time, culture, and so forth. For example, perhaps Americans do not experience diminishing returns to income to the same degree that Scandinavians do. Nonetheless, the UNDP essentially imposes its preferences when weighing variables. As for the variables themselves, health, knowledge, and income are not statistically independent of one another. People with higher incomes tend to be healthier and better educated than those with lower incomes, precisely because they can afford to spend on gym memberships and law school tuition. Consequently, the addition of two other variables may say little beyond what income data reveal.

• Sen and Development as Freedom

Amartya Sen (1933–) sets out a theory of development in his 1999 book bearing the rubric "development as freedom." Professor Sen, winner of the 1998 Nobel Prize in Economics, accepts the risk of an expansive definition of "development," and possible dilution of progress on basic human rights. Indeed, in *Development as Freedom*, he eagerly embraces the risk — or, perhaps better put, he rejects entirely that such a risk exists.[2] As the book title suggests, he defines "development" as expansion of freedom.

---

2. *See also* Richard Pomfret, The Age of Equality: The Twentieth Century in Economic Perspective (Cambridge, Massachusetts: Belknap Press, 2011) and the review of this book, Richard N. Cooper, *Economic, Social, and Environmental*, 90 Foreign Affairs 179 (November/December 2011).

Sen's paradigm-shifting work correlates with decisions by a handful of governments to supplement conventional measures of economic growth, namely, GDP and *per capita* GDP, with metrics that gauge the welfare of their people. For example, Bhutan (the last Buddhist Kingdom on earth) uses a "Gross National Happiness" index. *See* Haoqian Chen, *An Analysis of Bhutan's Gross National Happiness*, 4 Moral Cents issue 2 (Summer/Fall 2015), https://sevenpillarsinstitute.org/wp-content/uploads/2017/11/Bhutan-GNH-EDITED.pdf. Similarly, New Zealand (thanks to the leadership of Prime Minister Jacinda Ardern (1980-, PM, 2017-)) considers the expectations of its citizens on matters like child poverty and mental health, and sets budgets based on kindness and empathy. *See "Beginning of Doing Things Differently": Ardern Pitches NZ Budget Based on Wellbeing*, The Sydney Morning Herald, 24 January 2019, www.smh.com.au/world/oceania/beginning-of-doing-things-differently-ardern-pitches-nz-budget-based-on-wellbeing-20190124-p50tdf.html;

Sen argues the expansion of freedom is not only the pre-eminent end of development, but also the principal means by which development occurs. That is, freedom is both constitutive of development and the instrument of development. As a goal, to develop is to remove different kinds of "unfreedoms" from the lives of people. The main unfreedoms are:

(1) Poverty, and more generally poor economic opportunities, which robs a person of the freedom to satisfy hunger (sometimes because of famine) or achieve sufficient nutrition, remedy a treatable illness, obtain adequate clothing and shelter, have access to clean water and sanitation, and enter into gainful employment.

(2) Tyrannical or authoritarian regimes, or overly active repressive states, which rob a person of political and civil liberties (such as participation and uncensored speech), and thereby of the freedom to participate in the economic, political, and social life of a community.

(3) Systematic social deprivation, including the neglect of public facilities, which robs a person of the freedom to enjoy organized arrangements for functional education (leading to literacy and numeracy), health care (including epidemiological programs), and law and order, and forces a person to spend life fighting unnecessary morbidity.

(4) Intolerance, which may be based on ethnic, gender, linguistic, racial, or religious grounds, and which robs a person of the ability to enjoy many kinds of freedom.

Why is the removal of unfreedoms the primary goal of development? The answer is the lack of substantive freedoms means the lack of choice and opportunity to exercise the reasoned agency inherent in each person.

Sen uses the term "agency" not in the economic or legal sense of one person employed to act on behalf of another (whether a disclosed or undisclosed principal). Rather, he harkens to the traditional sense of an "agent" as an individual who acts and brings about economic, political, or social change, and whose behavior in the spheres of economics, politics, and society may be judged either by the values and goals of that individual, or by an external set of criteria.

As for the term "freedom," Sen focuses on five specific types of freedom:

(1) *Economic facilities*, *i.e.*, the opportunity to use economic resources for exchange, production, and consumption, including the freedom to make and exchange goods and services (*i.e.*, to participate in economic production and interchange), made possible through opportunities created by the market mechanism, the freeing of labor from explicit or implicit bondage, made

Ceri Parker, *New Zealand Will Have A New "Well-Being Budget," Says Jacinda Ardern*, World Economic Forum Annual Meeting, 23 January 2019, www.weforum.org/agenda/2019/01/new -zealand-s-new-well-being-budget-will-fix-broken-politics-says-jacinda-ardern/.

possible through an open labor market, the freedom of access to product markets to obtain inputs into production, and the availability and access to finance, whether the agent is a large enterprise or small establishment.

(2) *Political freedom*, in the sense of the civil liberty to participate in public discussions and scrutinize policy decisions, to exercise free speech and dissent, and enjoy an uncensored press, to engage in elections among competing candidates and parties to select legislative and executive leaders, to critique leaders, and to choose principles of governance.

(3) *Social opportunities*, in the sense of facilities like education and health care, which enhance the ability to make use of the other freedoms and thus allow for a better quality of life.

(4) *Transparency guarantees*, namely, the need for openness so that individuals can deal with each other, and their government, in a lucid manner in confidence all relevant material is disclosed, and so that irresponsible or corrupt behavior is prevented.

(5) *Protective securities*, which create a safety net to ensure an individual is not vulnerable to abject misery, such as starvation, and which typically consist of income supplements to indigent persons, unemployment benefits, emergency public works projects (to generate income and employment for indigents), and episodic relief programs.

These "real" freedoms, as Sen calls them, are crucial as ends in themselves.

Each real freedom advances human freedom in general, and the overall capability of an individual. Sen is not naïve about the need for appropriate public regulation, particularly of markets, to ensure some equity in the enjoyment of economic freedom. He emphasizes "development" is the process of expanding each type of real freedom enjoyed by people. This definition contrasts with orthodox approaches to development, which focus on growth, define growth in terms of increases in GNP or *per capita* GNP, and model the process of industrialization and technological change, is obvious.

To illustrate, Sen recounts the example of African-Americans, who enjoy a higher *per capita* income than people in many Third World countries. Yet, they suffer from a lower likelihood of reaching a mature age than people in many such countries, including China, Sri Lanka, and parts of India, such as the southern state of Kerala. Likewise, a rich person who is prevented from participating in public debates and decisions, and from speaking freely, is deprived of something she has reason to value. The process of development ought to include removal of that deprivation. Some illustrations are both shameful and stunning—for example, the fact a black male in Harlem has less of a chance of living beyond 40 years of age than a man in Bangladesh.

The real freedoms, Sen asserts, also are crucial as instruments of development. Hence, Sen also dubs them "instrumental" freedoms. The expansion of one kind of freedom promotes freedom of other types. That is because different freedoms are linked in a causal way that is empirically demonstrable. For example, social freedoms, such as the opportunity for education and health care, complement individual economic and political freedoms. These opportunities help an individual to overcome economic and political deprivations. The point is simply that instrumental freedoms are interactive.

As another instance of interaction among instrumental freedoms, Sen urges economic and political freedoms are complementary, not competing—contrary to the so-called "Lee Thesis" (named after Singaporean Prime Minister Lee Kuan Yew (1923–, PM, 1959–1990)), which alleges harsher political conditions, meaning denial of certain civil liberties, stimulate rapid economic growth. Political freedom helps promote economic security. Sen—an expert on famines—observes that in world history, no famine has occurred in a functioning democracy. Famines plague colonial territories governed by distant rulers (*e.g.*, in India and Ireland, when they were ruled by the British), in one-party states (like the Ukraine in the 1930s, China during the 1958–1962 "Great Leap Forward," and Cambodia under the Khmer Rouge led by Pol Pot (Saloth Sâr, 1925–1998, in office, 1976–1979)), or in military dictatorships (*e.g.*, in Ethiopia, North Korea, and Somalia across various decades). Rarely if ever are the political leaders in famine-stricken countries the victim of hunger. Political freedom means rulers are held accountable through elections and public criticisms, and thus have a strong incentive to take measures to avert potential economic catastrophes before they occur. In effect, political freedoms offer security for economic facilities.

Still another illustration is economic facilities can generate personal and public wealth to help fund social facilities, such as better schools and health care delivery. Interestingly, life expectancy increases with *per capita* GNP, but the causal chain is not direct. Rather, additional income, if spent on health care and poverty alleviation, helps boost life expectancy. This nexus—from greater income to higher life expectancy through spending on health care and poverty alleviation—explains why Korea and Taiwan, but not Brazil experienced increased life expectancy as *per capita* income grew.

What matters is not the fruits of economic growth *per se*, but how those fruits are used. Brazil—in contrast to the East Asian Tigers—largely neglected its public health care system. Brazil tolerated severe social inequalities and high levels of unemployment. In this area, the records of India (especially outside the Southern state of Kerala, which embarked on support-led strategies for education and health care, rather than on growth-mediated processes, *i.e.*, waiting for the effects of fast growth to redound to social programs) and Pakistan, resemble that of Brazil.

A final example of the interactive effects of promoting instrumental freedoms concerns social opportunities and economic facilities. Adequate health care reduces mortality rates, which in turn can help reduce birth rates (as there is less necessity to have more children in the hope that some of them reach maturity). In turn, with lower birth rates women can take more full advantage of educational opportunities, enhancing their literacy and numeracy skills. With a stronger skill base, their fertility rate may drop, and they can enter and stay longer in the labor force, thereby earning income and improving their material well-being.

Is income important to development? Indeed, Sen acknowledges, but not as a narrow end in itself. Rather, income matters as a means to expanding substantive freedoms and the ability to enjoy them. The idea is not new. At the start of *Nicomachean Ethics*, which Sen quotes, Aristotle writes "wealth is evidently not the good we are seeking; for it is merely useful and for the sake of something else." That "something else" is to exercise individual volitions, become fuller social persons, and influence the world.

Moreover, as the connections among instrumental freedoms indicate, these freedoms are not a hierarchy with economic facilities at the top. It is commonly believed, but flat wrong, Sen says, that social opportunities can wait until income has grown significantly. Japan raised social standards before it got rich. During the Meiji Era (1868–1911), Japan had a higher literacy rate than Europe, even though industrialization was more advanced in Europe than Japan at the time. Japan developed economically at a rapid pace, and reduced poverty, in part because it had skilled human resources—related to positive social opportunities. He adds a rebuttal to the oft-made argument poor countries cannot afford to spend on education and health care because of their low income: relative cost. In such countries, education and health care are low-cost and labor-intensive. Thus, a poor country—while it has less money—also needs less money to provide these services than a rich country.

Similarly, China in 1979, when economic reform began under Premier Deng Xiaoping (1904–1997, in office, 1978–1990), was better prepared, in a social sense, than India, when economic liberalization began there in 1991. After the Communist Revolution of 1949, China—while denying political as well as economic freedoms—improved basic education and health care. By 1979, its people were literate and in respectable health, and good educational and health care facilities existed in most parts of the country. In contrast, following Independence in August 1947, India failed to raise the educational or health care standards of its masses. By 1991, only half of the adult population was literate, and dreaded diseases plagued parts of the country. With elites well-educated and in good health, India in 1991—in contrast to China in 1979—was poorly positioned for broadly-based economic growth.

To be fair, denial of political freedoms in pre-reform China was a handicap both to avoidance and response to economic crises. The largest recorded famine in history occurred in China, when at least 30 million died in the Great Leap Forward. In contrast, following Independence, democratic India has not had a famine. Nonetheless, Sen's encapsulation of the point—"The lesson of opening of the economy and the importance of trade has been more easily learned in India than the rest of the message from the same direction of the rising sun"—is a powerful reminder of the importance of non-economic variables like education and health care in ready-ing a population to take advantage of economic liberalization.[3]

Why is the expansion of freedom an instrument of development? Sen offers two justifications—the "evaluative" reason and the "effectiveness" reason. First, the extent to which freedom is advanced is a gauge by which to measure development progress. In a normative sense, the extent to which individuals in a society enjoy substantive freedoms determines the success of that society. Traditional economists give primacy to income, not to the characteristics of human life. Utilitarian philos-ophers focus on mental satisfaction, on discontent that is creative or dissatisfaction that is constructive. Libertarians are preoccupied with procedures, but forget about the consequences of procedures. Sen, however, urges the enhancement of freedom is (or the) an evaluative criterion for development. In effect, the process of develop-ment resembles the history of overcoming unfreedom.

Second, the enhancement of freedom translates directly into the enhancement of the ability of an individual to help herself and influence her society and the world. The fewer the arbitrary governmental hindrances on the exercise of substantive free-doms, the more able a person is to gain not only in income, but also in the comple-mentary spheres of education and health. In a sense, the effectiveness justification emphasizes the favorable consequences of enhanced substantive freedoms.

For instance, the exercise of economic freedom, though individual transactions, can lead to higher income and greater efficiency. Also, the exercise of political free-dom can lead to better public policy choices through robust debate. In this respect, Sen singles out for criticism ayatollahs and other religious authorities (acting in the name of Islam or another faith), governmental dictators (acting in the name of so-called Asian or other values), and cultural experts (acting as elitist guard-ians of culture). They insist on adhering to established traditions and obedience to their decisions about these traditions, thus choking off the participatory freedom to which individuals have a right.

The concept of "poverty," as Sen sets out in *Development as Freedom*, follows logi-cally from his definition of "development." If "development" is about the expansion of freedom, then "poverty" is about "unfreedom." In turn, "unfreedom" arises for either of two reasons: inadequate processes, or inadequate opportunities. To violate a political freedom, such as voting rights, is to create an inadequate process. To vio-late an economic freedom, like the right to be free from hunger, is to foster an inad-equate opportunity. When these violations occur, it is not possible for an individual to achieve all, or any, of her capabilities.

Accordingly, Sen eschews a focus only on the adequacy of procedures, saying that libertarians (who focus only on appropriate procedures) forget about whether a dis-advantaged person is systematically deprived of substantive opportunities. He also

---

3. AMARTYA SEN, DEVELOPMENT AS FREEDOM 91 (1999).

eschews a focus only on the adequacy of opportunities, saying consequentialists (who focus only on outcomes) neglect whether an individual has adequate opportunities or freedom of choice. "Poverty," to Sen, has both a process and opportunity aspect. Inadequate processes and opportunities afflict the poor.

So, Sen defines "poverty" not as income deprivation, but as capability deprivation. To be "poor" is to lack more than just a high income, though lowness of income is both a handicap for the poor, as it is a leading cause of capability deprivation. To be poor is to lack basic capabilities, such as employment skills (leading to undernourishment), functional education (resulting in illiteracy), or health care (resulting in premature mortality). To inquire into "capability" is to inquire into whether a person can lead the kind of life she values, and has reason to value. Aggregating persons in a society, it is for each society to determine the capability most important to that society.

Sen's definition of "poverty" as capability deprivation, like his definition of "development" as "freedom," runs counter to modern orthodoxies in development economics (though, as he points out, classical economists like Adam Smith took the more expansive view he does). Much of the development economics literature focuses on, or assumes, low income is intrinsically important. Yet, capabilities matter more than income, as Adam Smith (1723–1790) suggested in *The Wealth of Nations* (1776). To have a relatively low income in a rich country can be a serious impediment to participation in the life of that country, and immediate community, even though the income level is high in comparison with poor countries. The lack of means makes it impossible to buy consumer electronics and other consumption items, join clubs, go to schools, and pursue ends common in the rich country. Thus, low income is only instrumentally important, whereas deprivations in certain basic capabilities have intrinsic importance.

Moreover, a number of factors call for attention to capability, not income. First, the relationship between low income and capability deprivation differs across individuals, communities, and countries. For instance, parametric variations (*e.g.*, age, gender, proneness to natural disaster, proximity to civil unrest, and disease environment) can affect the relationship between income and capability (*e.g.*, the relationship may be weaker for older people, women, individuals near flood, war-torn, or disease areas, because these parameters themselves affect capability). Some parameters (like age, gender, or illness) may be coupled, and thereby affect the relationship between income and capability. Second, there may be intra-family biases that affect this link. Such biases tend to afflict young girls in various poor countries, who may suffer from smaller food allocation, limited education, extra labor, and bodily degradations (*e.g.*, sexual abuse and female genital mutilation). Third, factors other than low income cause capability deprivation. Instrumental freedoms—political freedoms, social opportunities, transparency guarantees, and protective security—are examples. Fourth, the causal link between income and capability goes in both directions. Enhanced capabilities can lead to higher income, as well as *vice versa*.

European countries, for instance, tend to select a social safety net over high unemployment. In contrast, the U.S. prefers low unemployment over social security and, more generally, a welfare system. Development "as freedom," therefore, means each country is or ought to be free to order its priorities as to the capabilities. It does not mean freedom in the sense of individuals having maximum ability to pursue liberties in an American-style sense. Rather, the provision of basic capabilities provides for individual freedom. For instance, education helps a person find a job, prosper in it, and build a career. Health care helps a person live well, and recover should illness strike. Significantly, Sen also argues only through a well functioning democracy is it possible to make such choices properly and wisely. That is because only democracy allows for a discourse among different members of society as to what the choices are, the criteria for selection, and the ultimate outcomes.

III. Absolute Poverty

There is no single definition of "poverty." It is both an absolute and relative concept. And, it is measured in a variety of ways, some narrow, some broad. The leading such gauges are as follows.

Following the poverty-as-income deprivation approach (*i.e.*, that "poverty" is simply a lack of income), development economists measure poverty using three principal methodologies.[4] The first methodology, dubbed the "Poverty Line," is to set a minimum income threshold. Then, a "poverty headcount" is taken, *i.e.*, the number of people below the Poverty Line are counted and defined as "impoverished."

The most commonly cited threshold is "a dollar a day," meaning a person earning less than U.S. $1.00 per day lives in "absolute" poverty, and thereby is counted among the poorest of the poor. The second method (discussed below) is to calculate a Top/Bottom ratio. The third methodology (also discussed below) is a Gini Coefficient, which is derived from a Lorenz Curve.

As for the first measure, the World Bank introduced the dollar-a-day metric to gauge "absolute" (or "extreme") poverty. It set the figure at U.S. $1.08 per day, at 1993 PPP terms, or one third of the average consumption level of a country, if that consumption level is above $1.08. (It defines "poverty" as living on less than $2.00 per day.) The World Bank first published the absolute poverty threshold of $1.08 per day in its 1990 *World Development Report*. The threshold is based on the work of

---

4. For stimulating discussions of poverty and poverty-alleviating policies, see, e.g., Paul Collier, *The Bottom Billion—Why the Poorest Countries Are Failing and What Can Be Done About It* (2007) and Richard Pomfret, *The Age of Equality: The Twentieth Century in Economic Perspective* (Cambridge, Massachusetts: Belknap Press, 2011). *See also* the review of the Pomfret book, Richard N. Cooper, *Economic, Social, and Environmental*, 90 FOREIGN AFFAIRS 179 (November/ December 2011).

Bank economists, specifically, Martin Ravallion and his co-authors, who observed the national poverty levels—lines established by six governments in developing countries for their particular societies—tended to cluster around $1.08. By using PPP terms instead of market exchange rates, the poverty line threshold accurately takes into account the fact that lower prices prevail in poor countries.

This Poverty Line reflects minimum levels of basic human needs, namely, staple foods, clothing, shelter, health and sanitation facilities (including access to safe drinking water), and primary education needed to earn an adequate income. The number of people living below the Line can be expressed as a percentage of a total population, or as an absolute figure. Of course, the percentage changes with the Line, but the results remain grim. For instance (as of August 2018), if the Line is set at $2.50 per day, then about one-half of the population of the world, *i.e.*, 3.3 billion, are below that Line, and about 17%, *i.e.*, over 1.3 billion, are below $1.25 per day. Of the people below any threshold drawn, the majority are in Asia, with India accounting for large numbers in that majority.

The latter fact bespeaks a weakness in Asia's generally strong economic record in the post-Second World War era.[5] Most Asian countries have experienced rapid growth in GDP, and *per capita* GDP, over the last several decades, and the rates of growth have exceeded the rates in Africa, Latin America and the Caribbean, and the Middle East. The relatively faster growth in Asia has helped to eliminate extreme poverty in the region. Further, Asia was projected, between 2008 and 2015, to cut poverty by half, achieve universal primary education, and reach gender parity in education. It did not meet that projection. Indeed, Asia still has an absolute poverty rate of approximately 17%—higher than in, for example, Latin America and the Caribbean. Consequently, in Asia, hunger remains widespread, and infant mortality unacceptably high.

Gauging income poverty using an Absolute Poverty threshold like $1 per day, while simple, also is simplistic. First, because of inflation in the U.S., the original 1993 figure of $1.08 is (as of 2005) $1.45.

Second, governments tend to focus more on their own poverty lines—the national poverty lines developed for their own societies. Within a society, relative deprivation matters. Thus, notably, the original developer of the $1.08 threshold, Martin Ravallion, along with co-researchers, suggested in a 2008 World Bank Working Paper that a new line of $1.25 be established:[6]

> They gather 75 national poverty lines, ranging from Senegal's severe $0.63 a day to Uruguay's more generous measure of just over $9. From this collection, they pick the 15 lowest (Nepal, Tajikistan, and 13 Sub-Saharan

---

5. *See* Roel Landingin, *Asia Better Off But Still Hungry*, FINANCIAL TIMES, 8 October 2007, at 7.

6. *See* Martin Ravallion, Shaohua Chen & Prem Sangraula, *Dollar A Day Revisited*, WORLD BANK WORKING PAPER 4620 (2008).

countries) and split the difference between them. The result is a new international poverty line of $1.25 a day.

Why those 15? The answer is philosophical, as well as practical. In setting their poverty lines, most developing countries aim to count people who are poor in an absolute sense. The line is supposed to mark the minimum a person needs to feed, clothe, and shelter himself. In Zambia, say, a poor person is defined as someone who cannot afford to buy at least two to three plates of *nshima* (a kind of porridge), a sweet potato, a few spoonful's of oil, a handful of groundnuts and a couple of teaspoons of sugar each day, plus a banana and a chicken twice a week.

But even in quite poor countries, a different concept of poverty also seems to creep in . . . It begins to matter whether a person is poor relative to his countrymen; whether he can appear in public without shame, as Adam Smith put it.

This notion of relative deprivation seems to carry weight in countries once they grow past a consumption of $1.95 per person a day. Beyond this threshold, a country that is $1 richer will tend to have a poverty line that is $0.33 higher. . . . The authors thus base their absolute poverty line on the 15 countries in their sample below this threshold.[7]

Changing the absolute poverty line from $1.08 to $1.25 affects the estimate of the number of people lifted out of poverty in recent decades, particularly in China.[8] The higher the threshold, the larger the number of people falling below it.

Subsequently, the World Bank adopted the $1.25 threshold as the global standard for absolute poverty in August 2008.[9] Again, that standard is based not on market exchange rates, but rather on PPP rates. The percentage of people in the world living below $1.25 per day in 1990 was 43%, and in 2012 was 22%.[10] Moreover, applying this threshold, for the first time in recorded history, in 2012 less than half of Africans were below the poverty line.

Globally, the number of people beneath the old yardstick dropped by over 270 million between 1990 and 2004, to 969 million in 2004. The majority of that decrease—about 250 of the 270 million—occurred in China. With the new yardstick, in 2005 there were 204 million Chinese people subsisting in absolute poverty. Though the number fell between 1990 and 2004 (by 407 million instead of

7. *On the Poverty Line*, THE ECONOMIST, 24 May 2008, at 100.

8. *See* Martin Ravallion, Shaohua Chen & Prem Sangraula, *China is Poorer than We Thought, but No Less Successful in the Fight Against Poverty*, WORLD BANK WORKING PAPER 4621 (2008); *On the Poverty Line*, THE ECONOMIST, 24 May 2008, at 100.

9. *New Data Show 1.4 Billion Live On Less Than US$1.25 A Day, But Progress Against Poverty Remains Strong*, www.worldbank.org.

10. "Trade Improves the Lives of People," Speech of Pascal Lamy, WTO Director General, to Minnesota Economic Club, Minneapolis, 17 April 2012, www.wto.org.

250 million), the actual number of absolutely poor people in 2005 was roughly 130 million more than estimated earlier.

China is a key case. As *The Economist* reported in December 2011:

> Since 1978, China has liberated more people from poverty than any other country in history, partly because China before 1978 consigned more people to poverty than anywhere in history.[11]

In December 2011, the CCP adopted a new absolute poverty line near to that of the World Bank threshold of $1.25 per day. The result was that 128 million Chinese in rural areas were deemed poor, as they earned less than 2,300 *yuan* (about $361) annually.[12] Until the revision, the CCP classified 26.9 million rural Chinese as poor, under the previous threshold of 1,196 *yuan* annually.

Third, even if a person is at or above the line, it does not mean he or she has access to the infrastructure and institutions to lead a full life. There may be no schools for that person to attend, or the quality of the instruction may be dreadful. Health care may not be readily accessible, and when provided, may be substandard. Food, while available, may not have the right balance of proteins and carbohydrates to support normal physical and cognitive growth. The environment may be stressed, as in urban slums, drought-stricken rural areas, or famine-prone regions. In brief, an Absolute Poverty threshold says nothing about capability or empowerment.

Given these concerns about an absolute poverty threshold, *The Economist* wisely observed in May 2008 any number was statistically arbitrary:

> Give or take a dime or two, it matters little where a poverty line is drawn. Like a line in the sand, an absolute poverty standard shows whether the economic tide is moving in or out. It does not matter too much where on the beach it is drawn.[13]

Nonetheless, in October 2015, the World Bank updated the definition of "extreme poverty" to approximately $1.90 per day. Doing so added 148 million to its ranks, with 136 million of the increase in Asia and 8 million in Africa.[14]

IV. Top-Bottom Ratio

The second of three major methods to measure income poverty, the others being an absolute poverty threshold and a Gini coefficient, is the "Top/Bottom Ratio." As its name suggests, the "Top/Bottom Ratio" is the ratio of the share of income the

---

11. *Poor by Definition*, THE ECONOMIST, 3 December 2011, at 56. [Hereinafter, *Poor.*]
12. *See Poor.*
13. *On the Poverty Line*, THE ECONOMIST, 24 May 2008, at 100.
14. *See* Shawn Donnan, *Rise in World Bank Poverty Threshold Set to Push Millions More Below the Line*, FINANCIAL TIMES, 24 September 2015, at 1.

top 20% of the population in a country receives to the share of income the bottom 20% gets:

$$\text{Top/Bottom Ratio} = \frac{\text{Income received by Top 20\%}}{\text{Income received by Bottom 20\%}}$$

Clearly, a higher ratio connotes more severe inequality than a lower ratio. While 20% is the typical benchmark, others—such as 10% or 25%—can be used.

The poorest 10% of people in China control only 1.4% of total income (as of May 2008).[15] In contrast, the top 10% own 45% of all assets. On the absolute poverty scale of $1 per day, between 130 and 200 million (according to different World Bank estimates) fall below the threshold. As of late 2006, 19 of China's top 100 business tycoons (gauged by a Chinese publication akin to *Forbes*) were deputies to the National People's Congress (NPC), double that number in one year. What do these data suggest?

The advantage of using a Top/Bottom Ratio over an absolute threshold is it comports with an important psychological fact about poverty. Poverty is not just about living below a minimum acceptable standard. Rather, it is a relational concept. To be "poor" has meaning in part because someone else is "rich." Consequently there is a sense of deprivation in relation to a reference group. Accordingly, the Ratio in China is helpful in gauging poverty in this sense. But, the sheer number of people still below an absolute threshold is itself staggering. And, the number of tycoons in, or with easy access to, high office, may indicate stronger efforts are needed to ensure poor people are not excluded from the political process.

The Top/Bottom Ratio, like an absolute poverty threshold and Gini coefficient, are measures of income poverty. But, again, as Sen points out in *Development as Freedom* (1999), poverty may be conceptualized in terms broader than just income. Poverty may be thought of as capability deprivation.

V. Gini Coefficient

The third of three major methods of measuring poverty in terms of income deprivation, along with Absolute Poverty (*i.e.*, a Poverty Line) and a Top/Bottom Ratio, is the Gini coefficient, named after the early 20th century Italian statistician, Corrado Gini. A Gini coefficient (also called a "Gini Concentration Ratio") is the most sophisticated tool for measuring income-based poverty. The coefficient:

ranges between 0 (signifying "perfect" or maximum equality), and 1 (signifying maximum inequality).

---

15. *See* Dorothy J. Solinger, *Inequality's Specter Haunts China*, 171 Far Eastern Economic Review 19, 20, 22 (June 2008).

The coefficient indicates the gap between two percentages: the percentage of the population, and the percentage of income received by each percentage of the population. If, say, 1% of the population receives one percent of total income, and all subsequent percentages of the population receive the corresponding percentages of total income, the Gini coefficient is 0—there is no gap between the income and the population percentages. If, at the other extreme, all of the economy's income were acquired by a single recipient, the gap would be maximized, and the coefficient would be 1.[16]

The amount (and changes) in a Gini coefficient can have major social and political, as well as economic, consequences for a society.

If the coefficient approximates 0, income received by each individual (or family, or household) would be exactly the same—each percentage of the population would receive the corresponding percentage of income; the system's survival would be jeopardized by an absence of pecuniary incentives for entrepreneurship, innovation and productivity. If . . . the coefficient approximates 1, all of the economy's income would be acquired by a single recipient. The system's survival would depend precariously on the altruism of that single recipient, with the risk of revolution if altruism is insufficient![17]

(The multifarious implications of a Gini coefficient are considered below.)

Mathematically, a Gini coefficient is derived from a Lorenz Curve. A Lorenz Curve, shown in the Graph 13-1, is plotted in a square box where the left-hand vertical side measures the cumulative percentage of income in a country, and the lower-horizontal side gauges the cumulative percentage of recipients of income (*i.e.*, population percentiles). In the lower left-hand corner of the square, the zero point, there is no income and there are no recipients of income. At the upper right-hand corner of the square, 100% of the income, and 100% of the people, in a country are accounted for. The 45-degree "Equality Line" connecting the lower-left hand and upper-right hand corner shows perfect equality.

On the Equality Line, at each cumulative percentage of income, the same percentage of the population receives that income. For example, in the center of the square, on the 45-degree line, 50% of the income generated in the country is received by 50% of the people. Below the "50/50 Center Point," 25% of the income is received by 25% of the people. Above that Center Point, 75% of the people get 75% of the income.

Not surprisingly, therefore, the 45-degree line is the benchmark against which to measure inequality of income distribution. In brief, plotting data on a country, the

---

16. Arthur C. Brooks & Charles Wolf, Jr., *All Inequality is Not Equal*, 171 Far Eastern Economic Review 23–24 (June 2008). [Hereinafter, *All Inequality.*]

17. *All Inequality.*

Graph 13-1. Lorenz Curve

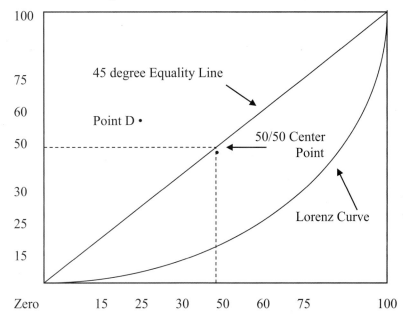

Cumulative Percentage of Population

larger a curve is away (to the right) from this line, the greater the income inequality in that country. (What about points above, *i.e.*, to the left, of the 45-degree line? They are not observed in reality. For instance, Point D would mean the bottom 25% of the population gets 50% of the income, suggesting an extreme redistribution that renders them no longer at the bottom.)

Graph 13-2 shows an example, with hypothetical data from Bangladesh (where income is stratified) and Sweden (where it is not). The curve LC_B is the Lorenz Curve for Bangladesh, and LC_S is the Lorenz Curve for Sweden.

Using this example, LC_B represents greater income inequality than LC_S, because LC_B deviates further from the 45-degree equality benchmark than LC_S.

To read these curves, consider and contrast specific points on them, such as A_B and A_S. At A_B, 50% of the population in Bangladesh receives less than 15% of the income. But, at A_S, 50% of the Swedish population receives over 25% of the income. Or, contrast points C_B and C_S. At point C_B, 50% of the income in Bangladesh goes to well over 75% of the population, implying the other 50% of income is shared by far less than 25% of the population. At point C_S, however, 50% of the income in Sweden goes to about 70% of the population, indicating the remaining 50% of income accrues to about 30% of the people. Neither society is perfectly egalitarian, but poverty—in terms of the unequal distribution of income—is worse in Bangladesh than Sweden.

Graph 13-2. Hypothetical Lorenz Curves for Sweden and Bangladesh

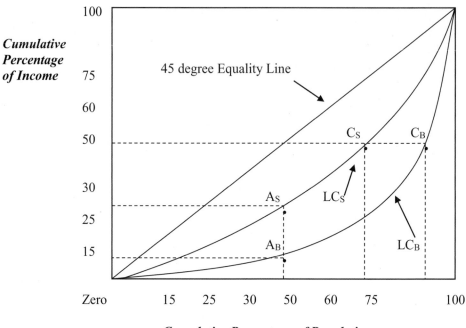

Cumulative Percentage of Population

Gini coefficients are derived from a Lorenz Curve. Essentially, they are the area between the Lorenz Curve for a country and the 45-degree equality line, divided by the total area underneath (to the right and bottom of) that line.

Arithmetically, the formula is:

$$\text{Gini Coefficient} = \frac{\begin{array}{c}\text{Extent of Deviation} \\ \text{from Perfect Equality}\end{array} \left(\begin{array}{c}\text{Area between Lorenz Curve} \\ \text{and 45-degree line}\end{array} \right)}{\text{Total Income (Area underneath 45-degree line)}}$$

$$= \frac{A}{A+B}$$

where the areas "A" and "B" are shown in Graph 13-3, the Lorenz Curve.

A Gini coefficient of zero represents perfect equality. Every person (or family) earns the same amount of income. There is no gap between the Lorenz Curve and the 45-degree line, hence the numerator in the ratio is zero. A Gini coefficient of one bespeaks complete inequality—in effect, all income is controlled by one person (or family). Thus, the lower the Gini coefficient, which is associated with a less "bloated" Lorenz Curve, the more equal the distribution of income in a country.

Depending on the country, Gini coefficients range from roughly 0.25 (in Japan and Scandinavia) to 0.60 (in some Latin American and Sub-Saharan African countries).

Graph 13-3. Calculation of Gini Coefficient from Lorenz Curve

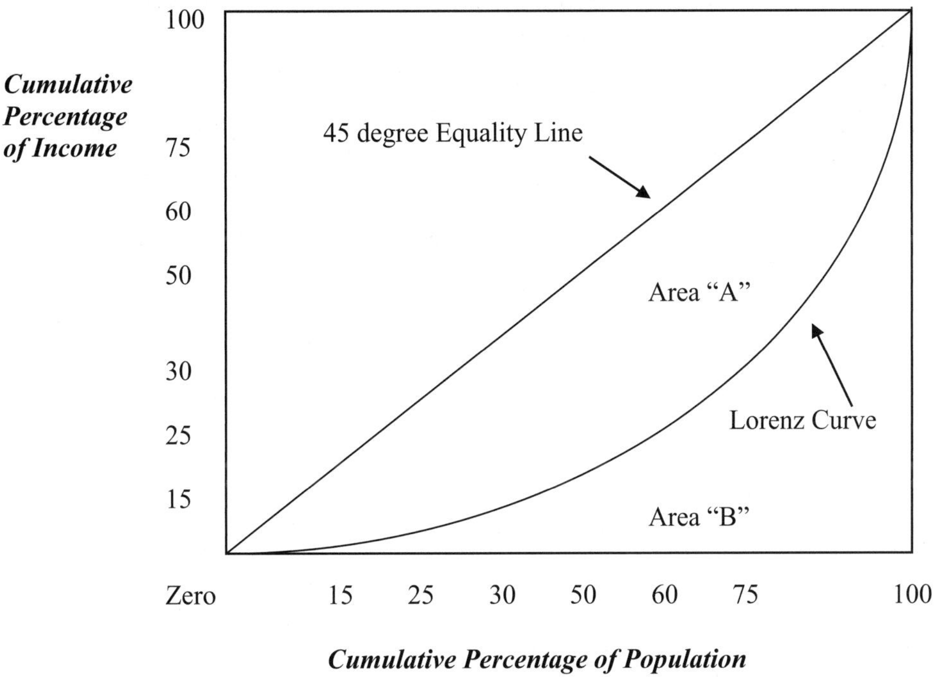

Cumulative Percentage of Income

Cumulative Percentage of Population

Generally speaking, higher income countries have lower Gini coefficients—an observation consistent with the Kuznets Curve. But, among middle- and low-income countries, it is hard to render a general statement, as some have more, and some less, income inequality. Also as a general matter, there is a high degree of correlation between the Gini coefficient for a country and the Top/Bottom ratio for that country.

When studying Lorenz Curves and Gini coefficients, four caveats should be observed. First, equality and equity are not synonymous, at least not to economists. Equality suggests every person earns the same income, but equity is a normative concept that distinguishes right from wrong using some philosophical or theological paradigm. Income equality may be—indeed, is—regarded in some paradigms as inequitable.

Second, Gini coefficients of zero or one are extreme referential standards. Neither perfect equality (zero) nor inequality (one) is observed in reality. However, seemingly modest changes—from, say, 0.42 to 0.36—can indicate fairly important changes in a country in terms of increased income equality. Conversely, a modest redistribution of income, say 1%, from the top to the bottom 20% of the population might not change the Gini Coefficient by a large amount. But, the redistribution could mean a lot to poor people, in terms of the marginal difference it makes to their income. It is important not to focus on the extremes and thereby become insensitive to actual changes in distribution.

Third, the Lorenz Curves from which Gini coefficients are derived can intersect, *i.e.*, cross over one another. In turn, the different income distributions evinced by the Curves can generate the same Gini Coefficient.

Graph 13-4 shows a hypothetical example of India and Canada. LC^{India}, for India, exhibits a steep slope at the top (upper right hand), but a gentle slope at the bottom (lower left hand). The steep portion indicates more extreme income inequality at the higher income range, but more equality at the lower income end. Poor people in India are poor, with few gradations among them. But, among the rich in India, there is considerable stratification. LC^{Canada}, for Canada, shows the opposite pattern. There is plenty of inequality at the lower range, but at the upper end, there is less inequality among rich people. Thus, the caveat is two different Lorenz Curves can generate the same value for a Gini coefficient when each has different degrees of inequality along the Curve.

Fourth, an increase in the value of the Gini coefficient indicates worsening income inequality, but making a judgment as to whether that movement is "good" or "bad" requires some caution:

> ... [The] judgment [as to whether a shift in a Gini Coefficient closer to, or further from, equality is "good" or "bad"] depends on whether the strengthened incentives toward higher productivity that might be associated with a

Graph 13-4. Different Hypothetical Lorenz Curves Generating Same Gini Coefficient

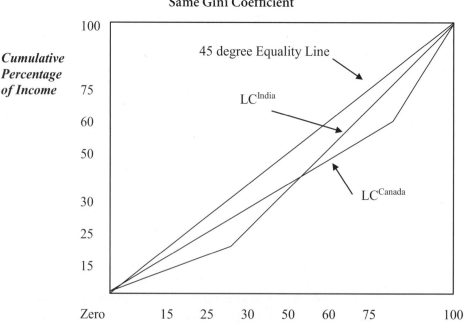

Cumulative Percentage of Population

movement toward higher inequality are offset by the aggravation of social tensions that might be associated with the same movement.

In turn, such a judgment is likely to depend critically on how and why the change in inequality has occurred, rather than on the magnitude of the change. For example, whether the coefficient's change is (or is perceived to be) due to favoritism, nepotism, and corruption, or instead to innovation, productivity and entrepreneurship; whether the change is viewed as earned, fair and legitimate, or instead as connived, unfair and illegitimate.[18]

To be sure, the general presumption is an upward movement in the value of a Gini coefficient is likely to have adverse economic, social, and political ramifications. But, more than just the math must be checked. The degree of the change, and the reasons for it, must be examined.

---

18. *All Inequality.*

Chapter 14

Economic Growth Models: Stages of Growth and Sources of Growth

I. 1960 Rostow Stages of Growth Theory

- Five Stages

Is there a pattern to the process of economic growth through which most poor countries proceed as they gain in riches? Economist Walt Whitman Rostow (1916–2003) answered "yes" in a famous book initially published in 1960, *The Stages of Economic Growth*.[1] To be sure, the idea of modeling economic growth to highlight the progressive movement of a country through different levels and kinds of economic activity did not originate with Rostow. Karl Marx (1818–1883) and Vladimir Lenin (1870–1924) developed and refined, respectively, a deterministic model of economic development in which they categorized stages of production, namely, primitive, feudalism, capitalism, socialism, and communism.[2] Rostow, however, was no communist—indeed, the sub-title of his book is "A Non-Communist Manifesto."

Rostow marshaled a massive amount of historical evidence and found five stages characterize economic growth. Graph 14-1 summarizes them, and they are as follows:

Stage I: Traditional Society

Poor countries have traditional societies stuck in a vicious cycle of poverty. Earnings are at a subsistence level, so saving is low or non-existent. With no sizeable savings pool, there is no investment. With no investment, there is no growth.

Stage II: Pre-Conditions for Take Off

To break the vicious cycle of poverty, poor countries must create the pre-conditions for a takeoff. These pre-conditions, when in place, will lead to self-sustained growth. There are 4 key pre-conditions. First, a class of entrepreneurs must develop. By definition, an entrepreneur is willing to take risks

---

1. *See* W.W. Rostow, The Stages of Economic Growth—A Non-Communist Manifesto 1960 (3rd ed. 1990); Lynn, Stuart R., Economic Development: Theory and Practice for a Divided World 33, 47–49 (2003) (including Figure 3-2).
2. *See* Lenin, V.I., Imperialism: The Highest Stage of Capitalism (1917, 1969 ed.).

Graph 14-1. Rostow Stages of Growth Theory

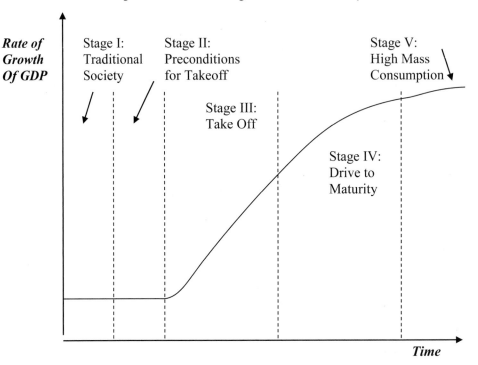

in business. Second, people must accumulate savings, and their savings must be channeled into investments. These investments are in productive methods, in both the agricultural and manufacturing sectors. Entrepreneurs play the key role here, as they draw on the savings pool to make investments. Third, people work diligently, whether for themselves or as employees of others. In effect, there is a strong work ethic dedicated to growth. Fourth, there is national unity. The fourth pre-condition allows for enlarged markets for output and specialization of production.

Stage III: Take Off

Given the pre-conditions, at some point there is an increase in investment from less than 5% of total output to more than 10% of total output. When this 10% threshold is crossed, a country enters the Take Off stage. With higher investment, the growth rate of output accelerates. To be sure, growth may not be even across all sectors. It may be unbalanced (as discussed later), but leading sectors would grow rapidly. Improved technology leads to yet greater productivity and output, and profits are reinvested, as well as allow for new sectors. The financial system improves, in order to mobilize savings and channel them into investments more efficiently than before. The demand for output rises, so as to absorb increased production.

Stage IV: Drive to Maturity

In this stage, the ratio of investment to income increases to between 10% and 20%, and the savings rate correspondingly grows to that range. Output *per capita* rises, and the leading sectors of the economy change.

Stage V: High Mass Consumption

The final stage results from sustained high investment activity and savings rates. While income growth rates taper off, as the name of this Stage connotes, most people enjoy a high degree of material comfort. In comparison with the earlier Stages, especially the first 3 Stages, it is easy to see the change in the mix of employment and output.

To summarize, the concept of the "Take Off" signifies the point at which a traditional society begins the process of growth. Thereafter, a less developed country would drive toward maturity, and eventually experience high mass consumption. In a general sense, these stages correlate with a less developed country evolving from an agricultural economy and rural society, to a low-value added manufacturing economy with larger cities, to a high-value added manufacturing economy with major metropolises, and ultimately to a service-based economy.

There is a relationship between sources of national income and employment, on the one hand, and the stage at which a country is in, on the other hand. Among low-income countries (which are at earlier Stages in the Rostow Model), agriculture accounts for roughly 25% of total output, and two-thirds of employment. As these countries grow (*i.e.*, move through the last two Stages), agriculture becomes a less significant source of income and employment in relation to manufacturing. Eventually, both agriculture and manufacturing account for a smaller proportionate share of aggregate income and employment than services.

- **Historical Examples**

Looking at the historical evidence for major developed countries, Rostow argued they hit the Take Off and Drive to Maturity Stages at slightly different periods. Table 14-1 summarizes these periods.

Table 14-1. Major Developed Countries, Take Off, and Drive to Maturity

Country	Take Off Stage	Drive to Maturity Stage
Great Britain	1783–1802	By 1850
Japan	1878–1900	By 1940
Russia/Soviet Union	1890–1914	By 1950
U.S.	1843–60	By 1900

- **Three Critiques**

As conceptually appealing as Rostow's Stages of Growth Model may be, it is important to appreciate the critical questions that have been asked of the Model. First, is the Model too simplistic? Rostow paints with a broad brush. Not every country goes through the five stages in lock step. There is no single path of development that all less developed countries must tread. The more nuanced the review of the economic history of one country in comparison with that of another, the more likely differences will emerge. Another way to put this question is what level of generalization of comparative economic development history is too general?

Indubitably, the Stages of Growth Model is a helpful intellectual framework for considering the relative position of less developed countries, both against each other and vis-à-vis developed countries. Yet, the Model is taken as determinism, it becomes an intellectual straightjacket. That is equally true for the Marxian stages — the Asiatic mode of production, feudalism, capitalism, socialism, and communism. They do not accurately capture the economic history of every country. Germany, China, and Russia are cases in point. Development does not proceed at a uniform pace for all countries, nor in a uniform manner.[3] The precise nature of structural changes in Mexico is not the same as those in China. Indeed, the pace and nature of the changes often differ within a country. Some classes of people (not infrequently delineated by race or ethnicity), and some regions of a country, benefit more from the development process than others.

Moreover, in some countries, like Malaysia and Indonesia, there are periods in which the process seems to stall. Such countries are in the infamous "middle income trap," stagnating at one Stage, unsure of how to vault themselves into the ranks of rich countries. In other countries, like Egypt and Pakistan, there are regressions. In fact, such examples highlight another limitation of stage theory: the impact of exogenous factors or internal instability.

The 1997–1999 Asian economic crisis struck all South East Asian countries hard, but its effects — and even more so the responses to it — were somewhat varied in different countries. Malaysia reacted with controls on flows of financial capital, and experienced a decline in FDI. Indonesia imploded with political unrest and violent secessionist movements in some islands, though by the mid-2000s it emerged with robust growth. For all its democratic and human rights benefits, the Arab Spring, which began in January 2011 in Tunisia and spread quickly to Egypt and across the Middle East, created internal economic uncertainty, the effects of which will be felt for years and mitigated only with responsible governance. As for Pakistan, it has

---

3. As one observer notes:

> Despite all the works on this subject, a general theory of capitalist development, valid across widely different cultures, remains a distant dream. There is also no clear-cut or universal relationship between democracy and development, or for that matter between dictatorship and development.

Anatol Lieven, *The Road to Riches Discredited*, Financial Times, 12 August 2002, at 11.

been cursed and cursed itself with a War on Terror following 11 September 2001 that it did not seek, and monstrously irresponsible and corrupt internal governance which it cannot seem to cure.

Second, how does a country get from one stage to another? The Model provides an exposition of the internal dynamics of capitalist economic development. It does not explain how the transition is made from one developmental stage to another. Is the story one of channeling increased savings into investment in capital equipment? Or, are other factors important, such as good governance? Are the transition mechanisms different from one country to another, or one region to the next? Is it possible to skip a stage?

Third, what role does international trade play in each Stage, and in the transition from one stage to another? The Model is largely silent as to imports and exports. Yet, in reality, imports are necessary for most countries to industrialize. Exports of surpluses are needed to generate revenues to pay for needed imports. In brief, a closer inspection of the link between trade and stages of income growth than the Model affords is desirable.

Oil exporters, particularly in the Arab Middle East, are an example of a group of countries that implicates all three critiques of Stages of Growth Theory. A cursory view of cities like Abu Dhabi and Dubai in the UAE, Doha in Qatar, Manama in Bahrain, and Riyadh in the Kingdom of Saudi Arabia suggests these countries are in the High Mass Consumption stage. They bear all the indicia of that stage, and more (including, for example, health problems like high obesity rates). A closer inspection of these countries reveals features of Traditional Society. There is little in the way of industrialization. Virtually all exports are energy or energy-related, and almost all other items are imported. There are large, poor rural and semi-rural areas where subsistence herding and farming occurs. Dependence on state subsidies, generated from oil and gas exports, means education and health care costs are covered. But, government nannying also creates disincentives to entrepreneurship.

Such countries, members of the OPEC have not passed through Rostow-type Stages the way Great Britain, Japan, or the U.S. did. Might the Arab OPEC countries be able to jump from Traditional Society to High Mass Consumption, *i.e.*, skip industrialization and move straight to reliance on services? That surely is the aspiration of some of them, including Bahrain and the Emirates, which seek to be regional financial hubs and look to Singapore as a model of development.

II. Essential Growth Model Concepts

- ## Role of Trade in Growth

No right-minded economist would contend trade is a panacea for growth. Trade can be—and, in practice, often is—an engine of growth for a country. But, in neither theory nor practice is trade the only engine. Other engines, such as domestic consumption, are critical. Put simply, in the capitalist economic theory that underpins International Trade Law, trade matters, but not completely so, in Third World economic growth.

The compelling theory of growth emanates from grand modeling efforts of classic development economists like Sir Roy Harrod (1900–1978), Evsey Domar (1914–1997), Sir William Arthur Lewis (1915–1991), Robert Solow (1924–), John C.H. Fei (1923–1996), and Gustav Ranis (1929–). These great scholars explain how the economic structure of a Third World country changes, or would change, as the country grows, and what drives that growth.[4] Their stories are captured in a few simple arithmetic and graphic models. Sadly, these theories receive less attention among International Trade Law scholars, students, and practitioners than they deserve, and many academic and practicing economists are unaware of them.

The models of economic growth are venerable monuments to a key fact: in the history of development economics, growth always has been about more than just trade. In the single-sector growth models of Lewis and Solow, and of Harrod and Domar, and the dual-sector labor surplus models of Fei and Ranis, growth is a multi-variable process. Therefore, enthusiastic proponents and diehard opponents of trade liberalization system should take heed. Trade neither can solve all growth problems of a poor country, nor should be blamed for such problems.

In brief, what these classic models teach is growth never was just a trade story. Even the most widely cited example of trade as an engine of growth—East Asia—has been shown to be a story of more than just trade. That insight alone is a strong platform on which to reform International Trade Law as it relates to poor countries. The models highlight where trade can help the cause of developing and least developed countries, and in so doing, point the way to a more prudent and generous type of S&D treatment for them than generally exists.

• Crude Specification of Aggregate Production Function

The starting point for any model of growth is necessarily the concept of a "Production Function."[5] A Production Function is a mathematical relationship between the total output of a firm and the factors of production used to produce that output. If that relationship pertains to the economy of an entire country, then it is called an "Aggregate Production Function."

Output is symbolized with the letter "Y." At the level of a firm, Y is measured in appropriate units of the commodity in question, such as the number of cars (for an automobile company) or metric tons of rice (for a rice paddy). At the economy-wide level, Y is GNP or GDP. The inputs are likewise symbolized logically as follows:

L = labor (*e.g.*, number of workers)

N = land (*e.g.*, hectares or acres) and natural resources (*e.g.*, oil)

---

4. *See* MALCOLM GILLIS, DWIGHT H. PERKINS, MICHAEL ROEMER & DONALD R. SNODGRASS, ECONOMICS OF DEVELOPMENT 8 (4th ed. 1996). [Hereinafter, GILLIS ET AL.]

5. *See* GILLIS ET AL., 41–51.

K   =   capital (*i.e.,* the stock of capital, such as machine tools)

H   =   human capital (*e.g.,* educational attainment)

T   =   technology (*e.g.,* computer hardware and software)

Thus, the Aggregate Production Function is:

$$Y = L + N + K + H + T$$

"Y" is the "dependent variable" in this equation, because it is dependent on the factors of production. Logically, the factors are dubbed "independent variables." Distinguishing separate independent variables, rather than focusing on one, and identifying their relative causal contributions to growth, are essential in identifying sources of growth. Yet, this Function is crude, hence development economists prefer a more refined version.

- **Aggregate Production Function with Coefficients (Ratios)**

Not all factors of production contribute to total output to the same extent. Consider an analogy to eating. Proteins, carbohydrates, and fats are the building blocks of food necessary for energy. But, these building blocks do not translate into energy to the same extent. The contribution of each differs, depending on the nature of the protein, carbohydrate, and fat, and depending on the type of energy in question. The precise mathematical formula is learned from nutritional science. So it is with economic output.

Each input contributes to total output, but not all inputs are helpful to the same degree. Based on engineering specifications (akin to the studies of nutritional scientists in the food example above) that differ from one commodity to another, the contribution of each input to "Y" differs. These contributions are expressed in terms of coefficients, that is, fixed numbers. Engineering specifications are needed in order to know the value of these coefficients. The coefficients are fixed numbers, though over time with developments in production engineering, they change.

In the abstract, the coefficients are symbolized by a small letter corresponding to each of the capital letters that stand for the inputs. So:

l   =   contribution made by a unit of labor to total output, known as the "labor-output ratio"

n   =   contribution made by a unit of land (or natural resource) to total output, known as the "land-output ratio"

k   =   contribution made by a unit of capital to total output, known as the "capital-output ratio"

h   =   contribution made by a unit of human capital (training) to total output, known as the "human capital-output ratio"

t   =   contribution made by a unit of technology to total output, known as the "technology-output ratio"

With these coefficients, a less crude mathematical version of an Aggregate Production Function is:

$$Y = \frac{1}{1} \cdot L + \frac{1}{n} \cdot N + \frac{1}{k} \cdot K + \frac{1}{h} \cdot H + \frac{1}{t} \cdot T$$

(In the labor input term, the fraction is the number "1" divided by the letter "l." Likewise, each of the other coefficients is a denominator, with the "1" in the numerator.)

This Aggregate Production Function expresses for a country the relationship between, on the one hand, GNP (or GDP) and, on the other hand, the size of the labor force, its productive land mass, its stock of physical and human capital, and its level of technological sophistication. (The concept of human capital was developed by economist Gary Becker (1930–), who won the 1992 Nobel Prize in Economics. It is the sum total of education and on-the-job training that gives a person greater command over knowledge, and thus allows the person to be more productive.[6]) Moreover, the Function tells us the contribution that each factor of production makes to total output.

It is not evident why the reciprocal of the coefficients is used. That is, why do they express the coefficients as a ratio (a quotient), such as 1/n or 1/k? Why not express the coefficient directly as "n," "k," and so on. Why not express the aggregate production function in the following simple manner?

$$Y = 1 \cdot L + n \cdot N + k \cdot K + h \cdot H + t \cdot T$$

In truth, there is no conceptual difference between this expression and the formula first laid out.

What matters in both is the basic insight of the direct dependence of total output on various factors of production, with each factor of production contributing to that output in a different amount in accordance with engineering specifications. These specifications are exogenously determined. Forces outside of the model determine their magnitudes; the model does not explain them, i.e., they are "independent" variables. (In contrast, an "endogenous" variable is one whose value is determined by the model in question, such as "Y" in the Production Function. It is the "dependent" variable, as it depends on the independent ones.)

• **Why Ratios Matter**

These coefficients in the Aggregate Production Function are known in development economics jargon as "ratios." They include capital-output ratios, labor-output ratios, and so forth. For instance, "l" is the labor-output ratio, and "k" is

---

6. *See* Andy Rosenfield, *The Internet Learning Dream*, 12 LSE Magazine 4, 5 (winter 2000).

the capital-output ratio.[7] Of course, it is technically more precise to say 1/l is the labor-output ratio, 1/k is the capital-output ratio, and so on. There is an advantage to expressing each coefficient as a ratio. That advantage is arithmetic.

The reason for this terminology is straightforward: if all factors of production but one are held constant, and thus just one factor — say capital — is the focus, then "k" represents the contribution a unit of capital makes to total output.

$$k = \frac{K}{Y}$$

The assumption of holding all other variables constant is known in Latin as "*ceteris paribus.*" Likewise, under the *ceteris paribus* assumption, the labor-output ratio is:

$$l = \frac{L}{Y}$$

By expressing the ratios in this manner, it also is possible to see that the higher the value of the coefficient ("k," "l," etc.), the greater the contribution of the corresponding input to total output.

Thus, for a capital-intensive commodity (*i.e.,* one that uses capital relatively more in its production than other inputs) the value for "k" would be higher than the other coefficients. For example, suppose the stock of capital is 40 units, and total output is 100. That suggests a capital-output ratio of 0.3 (assuming other inputs held constant):

$$0.4 = \frac{40}{100}$$

If the capital stock were just 25 units, then the capital-output ratio would be 0.25. A 0.4 capital-output ratio indicates a more capital-intensive commodity than a 0.25 ratio. In contrast, for a labor-intensive commodity (*i.e.,* one whose production uses labor to a greater extent than the other factors of production) the value for "l" would be higher for the other coefficients.

- **Input-Output Relationships and Law of Diminishing Returns**

There is another point to observe: There is a direct relationship between the size of the input and the volume of output. That is, an increase in any one of the factors should result in an increase in total output. This direct relationship in the Aggregate Production Function rests on two hidden assumptions.

First, whether an increase in output actually occurs with an increase in a particular input depends on whether the coefficient associated with that input is a positive

---

7. Development economists happily invert variables whenever the inversion helps facilitate a discussion, sometimes at the risk of perverting rules of mathematics. In the context of the Fei-Ranis Labor Surplus Model (discussed in a separate Chapter), they also are wont to invert graphs to advance an argument.

number. In most instances, that should be true. More laborers, for example, should result in more production. If engineering specifications indicate a particular input is counterproductive, then obviously that input would not be employed in the production process.

Second, in the input-output relationship, there is a point of "diminishing returns," which is to say adding more factors of production just will not help coax out more output. The direct relationship between each input and total output, based on the ratio pertaining to that input, cannot go on forever, anymore than a student can study forever. At some point, adding more of an input does little to increase output, just as a student who is too sleepy cannot benefit much from yet another hour spent in the library studying.

This point is precisely where the famous Law of Diminishing Returns takes hold. Adding more inputs actually becomes counter-productive. It stands to reason that adding more farmers cannot increase agricultural yields in perpetuity, nor can putting more workers on an assembly line increase industrial output in perpetuity. Eventually, the farmers bump into each other, and the line workers are in each other's way.

The Law of Diminishing Returns helps explain the shape of a Production Function when plotted on a graph. In theory, at early stages of development, an economy is learning how to organize all of its inputs in an efficient manner to yield the maximum amount of output. In these stages, the input-output ratios are low. But, as the factors become more productive, and the overall economy becomes more efficient, the values of the coefficients increase. Adding more units of each input has a significant, positive effect on output, hence economic growth is strong. But, eventually, the Law of Diminishing Returns must operate (*i.e.*, increasing or constant returns cannot be had in perpetuity). Adding more labor, capital, etc. does little to boost output. If inputs continue to be added—and, in effect, thrown together on a farm or in a factory—then returns become negative, meaning that the additional factors of production actually produce less output than before they were added.

- **Graph of Aggregate Production Function**

This growth pattern suggests that the shape of a Production Function, at least conceptually, is a gentle (or elongated) curve that loosely resembles the letter "S." Graph 14-2 shows this Function. The vertical (or *y*-) axis measures "Y" (that is, output). The horizontal (or *x*-) axis measures time. The horizontal axis indirectly measures inputs (that is, all inputs), which are added over time. (While most input quantities are fixed in the short-term, they may be varied in the medium- and long-term. Sometimes, the "short-term" is defined as a period of six-to-12 months.) Where the axes intersect, no inputs are used, and no output is produced. Movement to the right on the horizontal axis corresponds to ever-increasing amounts of inputs. This movement correlates to an upward movement on the vertical axis, which indicates increases in aggregate output.

Changes in the slope of the Production Function relate to the different stages of economic development of the economy. The first (*i.e.*, left-hand most) section

Graph 14-2. Aggregate Production Function

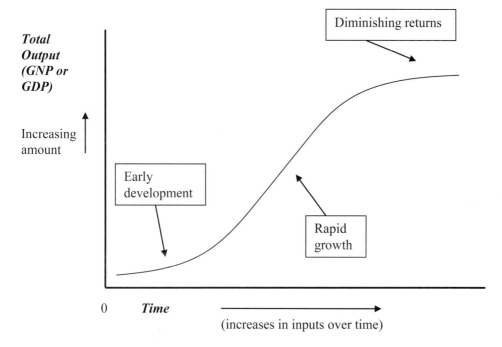

corresponds to a relatively earlier stage in development. The second (*i.e.,* middle) section captures events when the economy has organized its factors of production efficiently and, therefore, is growing rapidly. The final (*i.e.,* right-hand most) section depicts the economy afflicted by diminishing returns. These generic phases correspond, respectively, to an agrarian society, a society in the throes of industrialization, and a modern industrial and post-industrial society. Emphasis should be placed on the word "generic." The picture is not a deterministic model of how the growth process invariably must proceed.

- **Krugman Total Factor Productivity Argument about East Asian "Miracle"**

As intuitive and seductive as this Production Function model of growth is, it has been the source of great controversy among development economics. Consider the debate about the sources of post–Second World War growth in the Far East. Professor Paul Krugman (1953–) argued East and South East Asian growth actually was less remarkable than most admirers thought.[8] It was based simply on adding factors of production—in particular, more labor through population growth, more land through land reclamation projects, and more physical capital through investment. He said the growth of the Asian tigers was bound to reach a plateau—that is, eventually, the Law of Diminishing Returns was sure to take effect.

---

8. *See* Paul Krugman, *The Myth of Asia's Miracle*, 73 FOREIGN AFFAIRS 62–78 (November/December 1994).

Professor Krugman's analysis ran against the conventional wisdom that the growth of the Asian Tigers was an economic "miracle."

His analysis did not sit well with some of the Far East's most respected leaders. They had boasted of the "Miracle" over which they had presided, and presented their leadership as a model to the rest of the developing (and even developed) world, along with their purportedly "Asian" values. Professor Krugman was telling them their ostensible miracle was nothing more than adding factor inputs. If the Tigers were to sustain their growth, then they would have to increase productivity.

That is, the Tigers would have to get more output out of each additional input, and thus boost Total Factor Productivity. Professor Krugman argued the Tigers no longer could keep adding farmers or line workers and expect impressive growth rates. They would have to focus on TFP, *i.e.*, the residual (or portion) of growth not explained by increases in factors of production. Thus, for example, they would have to increase their input-output ratios, so that each farmer and each line worker contributed more to output than before. In turn, the Tigers would have to find more efficient ways of producing—a far harder task than simply adding units of input. As any law or economics student knows, it is one thing to study for longer hours, but quite another to develop a plan of study that ensures each hour is well spent.

III. Harrod-Domar One-Sector Growth Model

Understanding the Aggregate Production Function makes it easy to comprehend the famous Harrod-Domar Model. Two economists conceived of the Model independently, publishing separate classic articles.[9] Roy Harrod worked in England, Evsey Domar in the U.S., and their publications appeared in 1939 and 1945, respectively. They sought to explain the relationship between growth and unemployment in developed countries during the Second World War era, knowing full well the global Great Depression and German Weimar Republic hyper-inflation that preceded the War. There is no better testament to the potency of the Harrod-Domar Model than its extension to the Third World context to highlight the relationship between growth and capital.

At bottom, the Harrod-Domar Model is the simplest of Production Functions. It is a one-sector Model. The critical, indeed only, input into the production process is physical capital. Professors Harrod and Domar argued the key to economic growth is capital. Whether the unit of analysis is an individual firm or a macro-economy,

---

9. *See* Evsey Domar, *Expansion and Employment*, 37 AMERICAN ECONOMIC REVIEW 34–55 (1947); Evsey Domar, *Capital Expansion, Rate of Growth, and Employment*, ECONMETRICA 137–147 (1946); Roy F. Harrod, *An Essay in Dynamic Theory*, ECONOMIC JOURNAL 14–33 (1939).

the greater the investment in capital, the greater the output generated. Thus, the Model is expressed by the following equation:

$$Y = \frac{1}{k} \cdot K$$

where "Y" stands for "Output" or "Income," "K" stands for "capital,"

Or, because 1 multiplied by K is still K (by virtue of the mathematical Identity Field Axiom), the Model is

$$Y = \frac{K}{k}$$

This equation can be expressed in the way set forth earlier that highlights "k" as the capital-output ratio:

$$k = \frac{K}{Y}$$

Earlier, examples for possible values of "k" were given—0.4 and 0.25—depending on the contribution capital made to total output, which in turn depended on exogenously determined engineering specifications.

The earlier examples were static: a capital stock of 40 and total output of 100 led to a capital-output ratio of 0.4. Because the picture was a static one, it is more accurate to call "k" the "average" capital-output ratio. Likewise, the other ratios were average ones (*e.g.*, the average labor-output ratio, and so forth.

The ratio can be put in dynamic terms, *i.e.*, the change in total output associated with a change in the capital stock, is called the "Incremental Capital Output Ratio," or ICOR. That is, the arithmetic definition of ICOR is:

$$ICOR = \frac{\Delta K}{\Delta k} = \frac{I}{\Delta Y}$$

where "Δ" means "change in" whatever variable this small triangle appears in front of.

Through mathematical manipulation, it can be shown that the Harrod-Domar Model can be re-expressed as:[10]

$$g = \frac{\Delta s}{\Delta k} = \frac{MPS}{ICOR}$$

---

10. For a full treatment of this Model, including the mathematical derivation of the above expression, see Raj Bhala, *Dictionary of International Trade Law* (entry for "Harrod-Domar Model").

where "g" stands for the growth rate of total output, Δs is the savings rate, *i.e.*, the "Marginal Propensity to Save," that is

$$MPS = \frac{\Delta s}{\Delta k}$$

where "S" stands for "Saving," ΔS is the change in Saving, and Δk is the change in the capital stock in relation to the change in total output, *i.e.*, ICOR. Note carefully a high MPS indicates the marginal propensity to save an additional dollar of income is greater than does a low MPS. (For example, an MPS of 0.3 versus 0.1 means 30 cents versus 10 cents of an additional dollar earned is saved.) A low ICOR indicates a smaller amount of additional capital leads to a larger amount of output. (Consider an illustration.)

This expression embodies the powerful idea at the heart of the Harrod-Domar Model: the rate of growth of output (g) depends directly on the savings rate (MPS), and inversely on ICOR.

Intuitively, the higher the savings rate, the greater the output, because more funds are available for investment in productive capital. The lower ICOR, the more efficient capital is, that is, the greater the contribution an incremental unit of capital makes to output. So, growth in the Harrod-Domar Model depends directly on a generous savings rate, and inversely on inefficient use of capital (in effect, directly on efficient use of capital).

IV. Sources of Growth Accounting

- **Limitation of Harrod-Domar Model**

The most obvious conceptual limitation of the Harrod-Domar Model is it dwells on capital as the key stimulant of economic growth. There are far more factors of production, and thus various sources of growth in addition to industrial plants and machine tools. Many great development economists—such as Robert Solow (1924–), Edward F. Denison (1915–1992), Dale W. Jorgenson (1933), Hollis B. Chenery (1918–1994), and Moises Syrquin (1944–)—tried to improve on the Harrod-Domar Model by using a more complex Production Function.

Their aim has been to identify with greater precision than is possible using that Model the different sources of growth, and the relative contributions of each source to growth. This inquiry is known as "Sources of Growth Analysis," or "Growth Accounting." It requires the more complex Aggregate Production Function presented earlier:

$$Y = \frac{1}{1} \cdot L + \frac{1}{n} \cdot N + \frac{1}{k} \cdot K + \frac{1}{h} \cdot H + \frac{1}{t} \cdot T$$

This Function is the first step in building any Sources of Growth Model. It embodies a relationship between aggregate output (Y) and various factors of production, namely, labor (L), land and natural resources (N), capital (K), human capital (H), and technology (T). However, even this specification is rather generic.

Each of the factors can be broken down into different categories. For example, within "L," there is skilled labor and unskilled labor. Within "N," there is arable land versus natural resources. Within "K" there are factories, and there are assembly lines within factories. Within "H," there are different levels of human capital development: primary school; secondary (high school); tertiary (college); graduate and professional; adult education; and on-the-job training. Within "T," there are a large variety of technologies that increase the efficiency with which inputs are used, from computers to lasers. Thus, in separating out the contributions different factor inputs make to growth, the conceptual design of the Production Function matters. Some designs are more precise than others, and the more precise the design, the more precise the possible delineations.

- **Contributions to Growth of Factor Inputs**

Relying on the Aggregate Production Function with several factor inputs, the next step in constructing a Sources of Growth Model is to convert that Function into one that captures the respective contributions of the various factors to economic growth. The dependent variable, economic growth, is measured in terms of increases in *per capita* GNP or *per capita* GDP. In the Harrod-Domar Model, this variable is "g."

But, how are shares of the various factor inputs denoted? Development economists seek to measure the extent to which growth in a particular factor input results in growth in output. In the Harrod-Domar Model, increases in one factor, capital, is denoted by ΔK. So, too, it is with the other factor inputs:

ΔL = increases in the supply of labor

ΔN = increases in the availability of land and/or in the amount of natural resources

ΔH = increases in human capital

ΔT = improvements in technology

These variables are almost certain to differ in value from one another, and to differ over time. For example, in a particular less developed economy in a given year, labor supply may grow at 4% a year, while arable land grows at 0.5%. The next year, labor supply may increase by 5.5%, and arable land may increase at 0.3%.

Also, the contribution each input makes to growth differs from one input to the next, and differs over time. Indeed, that is the whole point of the exercise: to build a model that can be used to distinguish among sources of growth, but also highlights and measures their differing contributions. As a crude example, in a particular less developed economy in a given year, the growth in *per capita* GDP will have resulted in part from increases in labor, land, and capital. The question is what is meant by "in part"?

The answer might be 50% labor, 10% land, and 40% capital. That is, 50% of the increase in *per capita* GDP can be explained by growth in the labor supply, 10% of output growth due to the increase in arable land, and 40% of growth from new capital equipment. That is the kind of insight all Sources of Growth Models seek to obtain.

Here, then, it is necessary to define the variables of keen interest—the shares of each factor input in growth as measured by aggregate income (GNP or GDP). Development economists define these shares associated with each factor input as follows.

s_l = share of labor in aggregate income, *i.e.*, the share of wages

s_n = share of land and natural resources in aggregate income, *i.e.*, share of rents

s_k = share of capital in aggregate income, *i.e.*, returns to capital

s_h = share of human capital in aggregate income, *i.e.*, returns to human capital

Development economists also point out technology is a variable that affects all factors of production. Depending on the nature of the technology, it makes any one of the factors more productive. The variable in question is productivity.

For instance, a computer makes labor more efficient, genetically-modified (GM) agricultural seeds make land more efficient, and better drilling technology makes the process of extracting natural resources more efficient. In all such instances, the effect of technology is to shift the entire Production Function upward, because technology allows for greater output from a given input.

Accordingly, in constructing a Sources of Growth Model, development economists specify a variable to represent potential shifts in the Production Function that result from new technologies. They include a variable for "productivity."

p = shifts in the Production Function due to technology that allows one or more factor inputs to be used more efficiently, *i.e.*, improvements in productivity.

- **Expression and Use of Model**

A classic Sources of Growth Model is expressed algebraically as follows:

$$g = s_l \cdot \Delta L + s_n \cdot \Delta N + s_k \cdot \Delta K + s_h \cdot \Delta H + p$$

What does this expression say in common sense terms? It says to explain output growth, it is necessary to look at the growth rates of four factors of production, along with the potential impact of new technologies on these factors. Each input contributes to growth to a different extent. Those differing contributions, or shares, are represented by the coefficients attached to each input.

How do development economists put this theoretical Sources of Growth Model to practical, empirical use? They gather data on as many variables as they can, and use the equation to solve for a missing variable. Alternatively, they might use the equation to estimate the value for a variable based on a target growth rate.

Consider a hypothetical case. Suppose India has a 10% growth rate in *per capita* GNP (or, alternatively, that this rate is the target). (The same example could be used for China, though it must be kept in mind that many economic statistics published by the CCP are dubious, and many have been found to be erroneous.) Suppose further the following data (on an annual basis) are available about the Indian economy:

ΔL = the size of the labor force increases by 6%

ΔN = the amount of arable land, through land reclamation projects around Madras (Chennai), increases by 1%

ΔK = the stock of capital increases by 9%

ΔH = literacy rates, primary education enrolment, post-secondary education enrolment, and other measures of human capital are (taken together) improving at 7% per year

s_l = the share of labor in aggregate income, *i.e.*, the share of wages, is 40%

s_n = share of land and natural resources in aggregate income, *i.e.*, share of rents, is 10%

s_k = share of capital in aggregate income, *i.e.*, returns to capital, is 30%

s_h = share of human capital in aggregate income, *i.e.*, returns to human capital, is 20%

Armed with these data, the Sources of Growth Model can tell Indian economic officials the productivity increases necessary to sustain (or achieve) a 10% growth rate. In the abstract, the Model is:

$$g = s_l \cdot \Delta L + s_n \cdot \Delta N + s_k \cdot \Delta K + s_h \cdot \Delta H + p$$

Using the Model empirically (*i.e.*, plugging in the data, and remembering the data are percentages, hence they need to be expressed in decimal form) results in the following:

0.10 = $(0.40) \cdot (0.06) + (0.10) \cdot (0.01) + (0.30) \cdot (0.09) + (0.20) \cdot (0.07) + p$

Clearly, the exercise is to solve the equation for p:

0.10 = $0.024 + 0.001 + 0.027 + 0.014 + p$

The result is:

0.10 = $0.066 + p$

Hence:

p = 0.034, or 3.4%.

This result means India must achieve a 3.4% increase in productivity to continue (or reach the target of) 10% growth.

Another way to look at this result is to see productivity as a source of growth. With an achieved or targeted growth rate of 10%, productivity is 3.4%. That means productivity accounts for about ⅓ of Indian growth.

To be sure, the example is a hypothetical one. Nevertheless, it illustrates an important fact about empirical results from Sources of Growth Analysis. Before "running the numbers," it sometimes is thought that the principal contributors to aggregate income growth in a Third World country would be a factor like capital. This view reflects what we might call a "capital bias," that is, a bias among development planners in favor of capital. Mao's China during the monstrously misnamed "Great Leap Forward" of 1958–1961 is a hideous example of this bias. Chinese planners focused all of their efforts on rapid industrialization, partly through increases in plant and equipment. The result was mass starvation and the death of anywhere from 18 to 45 million people.[11]

In fact, the consensus among development economists based on repeated empirical testing is increases in capital stock tend to account for less than one-half of the increase in output in Third World countries with rapid growth rates.[12] By no means is this amount insignificant. Rather, the point is that a priori, what is sometimes underestimated is the impact of productivity. The consensus is increases in efficiency account for a much higher proportion of growth than is sometimes realized. Put simply, empirical tests suggest that in the growth story, productivity as well as capital play large roles.

· **Reliability and Importance of Model Design**

The reliability of Growth Accounting depends on the conceptual design of the mathematical model, and the quality of the data plugged into that model. If the model is poorly specified, or the data are inaccurate, then little confidence can be put in the results. The point about the importance of productivity is a good example.[13]

Productivity can be tied into new capital, or better-trained workers. How is it possible to separate out productivity in a generic sense from productivity embodied in this capital or these workers? That is, how is it possible to delineate a broad-based increase in efficiency from technological improvements that already are measured by increases in a factor of production? Without a precise model and data that are sufficiently disaggregated, the answer is that it will be difficult to make this delineation.

So, for example, in trying to account for the sources of American economic growth, economists such as Edward Denison and Dale Jorgenson have built into their models the difference between workers with a high-school education and those with just a primary-school education, counting 1 high-school educated worker as

---

11. *See Great Leap Forward*, Wikipedia, http://en.wikipedia.org/wiki/Great_Leap_Forward.
12. *See* Gillis et al., 46–47. The summary of these empirical tests draws on the discussion therein.
13. This example is mentioned in Gillis et al., 47.

equal to two primary-school educated workers.[14] In still other models, the contribution to productivity of workers is counted differently depending on whether the worker is employed in a low-productivity job in the agricultural sector, or in a high-productivity job in the manufacturing sector.

- **Again, Role of Trade and International Trade Law in Perspective**

From a trade perspective, the remarkable aspect of Growth Accounting is how little trade seems to matter, at least in a direct sense. Sources of Growth Models do not ascribe an explicit role for imports and exports in the process of economic growth. In that respect, they are no different from the Harrod-Domar Model. Sources of Growth Models tell a story of economic growth in which trade does not play a prominent role, and hardly that of the protagonist. In turn, that puts the role of GATT-WTO agreements, FTAs, and CUs in a humbling light: their legal provisions can at best assist poor countries to grow, but they hardly can "cause" that growth in any significant sense.

To be sure, the failure to incorporate expressly in the Models a role for trade does not mean trade plays no role whatsoever, or that GATT and the WTO texts are utterly irrelevant. Sources of Growth Models (as with the Harrod-Domar Model) do not exclude the possibility of international trade, and by extension, International Trade Law, playing some role. For example, what might stimulate increases in productivity? Exposure to international competition could be one answer. What might be the origin of increases in capital? Imports could be one answer. The point is simply that whatever role trade does play in the Growth Accounting paradigm, it is an indirect one. The trade variable operates through other, expressly modelled, variables.

---

14. *See* Dale Jorgenson et al., Productivity and U.S. Economic Growth (1987); Edward F. Denison, Accounting for United States Economic Growth, 1929–1969 (1974); Gillis et al., 47.

Chapter 15

Economic Growth Models: Industrialization and Labor Surplus

I. Transformation from Agriculture to Industry

- **Modern Economic Growth and Industrialization**

The Harrod-Domar Model (discussed in a separate Chapter) is a simple Production Function approach to economic growth that emphasizes two variables, the savings rate and ICOR.[1] Sources of Growth Models (also discussed in a separate Chapter) can provide insights into the catalysts for economic growth by distinguishing among the contributions of various factor inputs to productivity. But, what about the composition of aggregate output—the "stuff" being produced and measured as "growth"? Neither paradigm speaks directly about the constituents of GNP (or GDP). Put simply, neither paradigm tells much about different sectors of the economy.

This inquiry—which is a natural one—calls for a different kind of development theory, one that leads to Labor Surplus Models, principally the Fei-Ranis Model. Rather than proceed apace to these Models, it is better to appreciate their intellectual underpinning. That underpinning is, in brief, a theory about structural change in the composition of output during the development process of many, if not most, poor countries.

It is dramatic to say no country in human history has become wealthy and yet remained a purely agrarian society. That statement may be historically dubious, if grand civilizations of ancient times are included. Defending the statement (or not) is for economic historians. Mesopotamia, Egypt, Persia, Greece, and Rome were, at their peak, rich and powerful empires. But, even these Ancient civilizations were not purely agrarian: they traded internationally, and they produced a variety of simple manufactured items. Carthage is a quintessential ancient example of a great trading empire.

It is not necessary to begin in Ancient times. It is defensible to assert no country has experienced modern economic growth and remained purely agrarian. Since the Industrial Revolution, countries have distinguished themselves (or not) partly on their *per capita* economic growth performance. That performance, in turn, is linked

---

1. This discussion draws on GILLIS ET AL., 47–51.

447

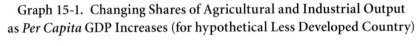

Graph 15-1. Changing Shares of Agricultural and Industrial Output
as *Per Capita* GDP Increases (for hypothetical Less Developed Country)

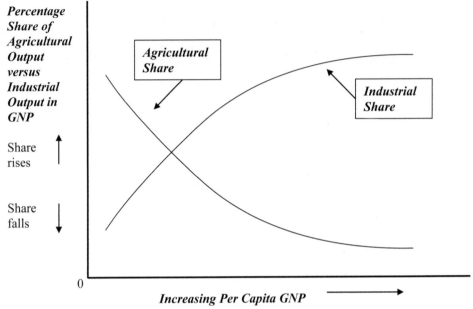

critically to the changing share in aggregate output of the agricultural versus industrial sectors. The hallmark of growth, of membership in the First World club, is the
increasing share of industry in GNP, the concomitant decreasing share of agriculture, and the attendant shift of labor from rural to urban areas. Graph 15-2 depicts
this change in shares.

Modern economic growth is about structural transformation from agriculture to
industry. That is the intellectual underpinning of Labor Surplus Models. They tell
a story of:

(1) mobilizing excess, unproductive labor, known as "surplus labor," in the
agricultural sector,

(2) shifting surplus labor from its rural homelands to the industrial sector,
which tends to be concentrated around cities,

(3) using that surplus labor taken from the agricultural sector for manufacturing, and

(4) experiencing greater industrial relative to agricultural output in GNP.

Labor Surplus Models depict the story through simple graphs (presented below).

In the story, international trade plays no explicit role. Rather, the story is based
on how the giants of development economics perceive the modern history of First
and Third World nations. They look at Britain versus China, Germany versus India,

and later at China versus India, and they seek an explanation for the patterns of growth. The heart of the explanation they offer is the agriculture-to-industry transformation: some countries had achieved it, albeit at different rates, while others had not yet made the change.

In this classic of development economics modeling, as with the Harrod-Domar and Sources of Growth Models, the growth story is not primarily a story about trade. That is not to say Labor Surplus models exclude trade entirely. That would be a libelous remark. The accurate inference to draw from the Labor Surplus Models is that to the extent they grant trade a role, it is a limited and rather indirect one. By extension, so, too, is the role of GATT and the WTO agreements.

- **Engel's Law**

Also by way background, it is worth contemplating why proponents of Labor Surplus Models see modern economic history in the way they do? That is, why are builders of these Models comfortable resting on the intellectual underpinning of an agriculture-to-industry transformation? There are two reasons, both of which are essentially empirical observations about economic behavior.

The first reason is an economic law developed in the 19th century by Ernst Engel (1821–1896) (not to be confused with Friedrich Engels (1820–1895), the colleague of Karl Marx (1818–1883)). "Engel's Law" holds that as the income of a family increases, the proportion of its income that it spends on food declines. After all, an individual can (or should) eat only so much, and after an average threshold of about 2,000 to 2,500 calories per day has been reached, additional calories are stored as fat. Income growth does not necessitate an increase in caloric intake, although it may lead people to consume "richer" food and beverages (organic fruit and vegetables, high-quality meat, champagne, etc.). Engel observed that as family income grows, the family tends to spend more of its budget on non-food items, such as housing, education, durable goods (*e.g.*, cars and appliances) and leisure activities (*e.g.*, vacations, clubs, etc.). So invariable is this observation that it is dubbed a "Law" of economics. In every country that has experienced modern economic growth, Engel's Law has operated.

The implication of Engel's Law for the composition of aggregate output is clear. As *per capita* GNP (or GDP) rises, each person spends a smaller proportion of her income on food, and a larger proportion on non-food goods and services. The sector from which food comes is agriculture, and the sectors from which non-food items come are the manufacturing and service sectors. Thus, as *per capita* GNP rises, the proportion of that income spent on agricultural commodities falls, while the proportion spent on manufactured products and services rises. Stated differently, demand for agricultural output does not rise as quickly as demand for manufactured items and services. In brief, the rise in *per capita* GNP results in a transition from a largely agrarian-based economy to a modern, industrial and ultimately post-industrial economy.

The empirical reason pertains to productivity in the agricultural sector associated with GNP growth. While Engel's Law mandates an increase in demand for output from that sector that grows more slowly than the demand for industrial products, another phenomenon also takes place during modern economic growth that catalyzes a transition from agriculture to industry. The agricultural sector becomes more productive than it was before. Farmers no longer operate at subsistence level on inefficiently small patches of land that are left entirely vulnerable to natural disasters.

Rather, the farmers concentrate their holdings, planting on larger properties than before. They use new machinery. They take advantage of better seed, that is, seed that is resistant to various pests and that produces higher yields. They protect their crops with fertilizer. They benefit from large-scale public works projects, such as dams that prevent flooding (Egypt's Aswan Dam is a prime example), power stations that provide electricity (Thailand's Ratchaburi power plant is one illustration), and road networks that make transportation of fresh produce to urban markets and ports faster and safer than before (China's Shenzhen Expressway, India's Grand Trunk (GT) Roads, and Malaysia's North-South Highway, have helped in this regard). Still another factor would be improvements in communication networks that enable farmers to arrange, in a quick and low-cost manner, for sales of their product. Cell phone technology (which, of course, obviates the need for laying land lines) that is common throughout Asia is a good example.

To be sure, some of the developments that benefit farmers are criticized by NGO for having negative externalities. High-technology crops that are GM may be adverse to human or animal health, or to the health of other plants, or may render farmers dependent on multinational corporations from rich countries for expensive, patented seed and fertilizer. Public works projects may threaten certain animal or plant species. Some of these projects may require the involuntary (even forced) relocation of tens of thousands of people, and wipe out traditional local cultures in the process. Controversies as different as growth-stimulant beef hormones used in the U.S. and the Three Gorges Dam project in China illustrate a common point: the productivity gains in the agricultural sector, which are associated with strides in aggregate output, are not necessarily an unmitigated blessing. There are trade-offs to be made if these gains are to be had.

As with Engel's Law, the implication of increased productivity in the agricultural sector is evident. Fewer and fewer workers are needed in this sector. By definition, each farmer is able to grow more, given the technology and machinery she has, and the benefits that flow from improved power, transportation, and communication infrastructures. Each farmer can support—that is, produce enough food for—a much larger number of people who live and work in the cities than before. Put differently, one farmer now can do the work of two, or perhaps of several. The other farmers become under- or unemployed. They are, to use the development economics jargon, "surplus" labor. Removing them from the farm sector would have no effect on the output of that sector.

II. Concept of Labor Surplus and Its Shift

Labor surplus and its shift is the heart of the story of transformation from agriculture to industry. This surplus of labor in the agricultural sector can be shifted from rural to urban areas, put to gainful employment in manufacturing (and, ultimately perhaps, service) industries, and yet be fed by the increasingly productive agricultural sector. The growth experience of the U.S. is a case in point: the average farmer supports at least 70–80 non-farm workers, hence only 3% of America's work force is employed in farming.[2] But, it is not just the mere movement of workers from one sector in which they are not needed to another sector in which they can be productively employed that matters. It is the expectation that this movement can occur without affecting wage rates in either the agricultural or industrial sectors, at least for the short- and medium-term.

That is, in the Labor Surplus paradigm, wage rates need not rise in either sector. A common-sense reason exists for each sector. In the agricultural sector, the surplus workers are under- or unemployed. Their withdrawal from that sector does not affect the wages of farmers who are gainfully employed. Only if those farmers leave would the agricultural sector begin to face a labor shortfall. In that case, wage rates would have to rise to attract farmers back to the rural areas.

In certain contexts, withdrawal of surplus labor from the agricultural sector actually helps improve productivity in that sector. Suppose all arable land in a less developed country is under cultivation, and farmers face diminishing returns. Marginal increases in an input, such as adding more farmers to work the land, results in ever-smaller harvest yields. Farms are crowded enough, and farmers get in each other's way.

In this environment, marginal costs of production—the cost of producing an extra unit of output—are rising. Only by bringing new, fertile land into cultivation could farmers increase production efficiently. Unfortunately, the only land available in the country is desert or mountain terrain. Trying to settle farmers on that land, and have them cultivate it, would be expensive. Marginal costs of production would be high. In this context, moving redundant farmers out of the sector would enable the remaining farmers to use good quality land more efficiently. This land would not be "over-farmed," and could lie fallow to allow for its restoration. No longer would farmers trip over each other in the fields. The net result might well be constant or even increasing returns.

As for the industrial sector, wage rates are sufficiently high to entice under- and unemployed workers off the farms and into the factories. They need not necessarily be high, because these workers face poor prospects if they stay in their traditional rural communities. But, industrial wages must be above subsistence level, and they must cover the costs of shifting from these communities to the cities.

---

2. *See* GILLIS ET AL., 48.

Certainly, in the long term, assuming industrialization continues apace, for two reasons industrial wages are likely to rise. First, owners of capital may seek to expand their existing factories, and to open new factories. They will need to hire still more laborers to staff these factories. So, the demand for industrial labor will increase.

Second, the set of surplus agricultural workers is not infinite. That is, the supply of surplus labor will decline. Even allowing for population growth in rural areas, if factory expansion and creation is rapid enough, the owners of capital will have to compete with one another to attract laborers to their factories. Ultimately, these demand and supply forces are likely to conspire to cause an increase in industrial wage rates. At that juncture, the country may well be an industrialized one, or nearly so, and its legal system may contain a number of worker rights. Consequently, workers in both sectors may be sufficiently well organized to reinforce the demand and supply trends through political lobbying and, if necessary, protests and strikes.

Nevertheless, by definition, the "bottom line" result of the agriculture-to-industry transformation is that the proportion of GDP accounted for by agriculture falls relative to that of industry. Why? Because more and more of a country's labor force works in the industrial sector, and industrial sector output starts growing at a more rapid rate than that of agricultural output. The differential growth rate is not just a supply phenomenon (*i.e.,* not just a result of more output being supplied in one sector versus another). It also is a result of the changes in the pattern of demand that Engel's Law addresses.

• Rural-Urban Migration and Its Causes

To say surplus labor is shifted, or shifts itself, from the agricultural to the industrial sector is another way of putting the point that there is rural-urban migration. More and more people — a higher percentage of the country's population — live in cities. The obvious result, as any traveler to a Third World city knows, is congestion, pollution, and squalid shanty-towns. Mel Gibson toured the squalid parts of Jakarta in *The Year of Living Dangerously* (1982), which is just one of many movies — *Salaam Bombay* (1988), *City of Joy* (1992) and *Slumdog Millionaire* (2009) are others — in which the monstrous plight of hundreds of millions is recounted. Why is life like this in major cities of less developed countries?

A full answer to this question calls upon not only economics, but also most other social sciences, and probably theology too. It is possible to highlight 2 aspects of the economic dimension, namely, internal and external economies of scale. In general, an "economy of scale" exists whenever output per unit of input rises. In other words, there are increasing returns to scale. In the industrial sector, the search for economies of scale leads to larger firm sizes. As an enterprise grows, it hopes that for each dollar spent on production costs (that is, on factor inputs), it can realize a larger amount of output. This phenomenon is an "internal" economy of scale, one that is specific to an enterprise.

There also is the possibility of "external" economy of scale. Output per unit of input might rise for reasons exogenous to the enterprise itself, namely, because of where the enterprise is located. Imagine several firms in the same industry situating themselves near one another, such as the congregation of computer firms in Bangalore, as well as Hyderabad, India. The firms may benefit from this closeness by availing themselves of common infrastructure support—power, communication and transportation networks, port facilities, security, and the like. There is no need for separate infrastructure facilities, one for each firm.

Hence, no firm is haunted by the specter of absorbing some or all of the costs (either directly, or indirectly through higher taxes) of constructing and operating a facility for itself. Rather, all of the firms can use the same infrastructure, and share the costs associated with construction and operation. In addition, the physical proximity might cause the neighboring firms to learn new production techniques from one another, and spur them to innovate given the constant reminder of the competition.

What are the results? Greater efficiency, no doubt, and thus a greater share of industrial output in GNP relative to the share of agricultural output. To realize internal economies of scale, industrial behemoths that employ large numbers of workers evolve in urban areas. To realize external economies of scale, these behemoths tend to congregate in the same urban areas. Sometimes, government policy encourages this congregation. Pudong, in Shanghai, is one example. More and more surplus agricultural workers pack up and head for jobs in the big city. The industrial sector expands, and so too do the cities along with it.

But, in the long run, the Law of Diminishing Returns will take hold (imagine clogged communications and transportation networks due to excess traffic), and absent product innovation, comparative advantages will be lost to new market entrants. Even before then, there will be downturns in the business cycle, meaning layoffs and plant closures. In brief, the result is a transfer of surplus labor from agriculture to industry, with all the attendant benefits and costs.

• **Pace of Transformation**

The results discussed above are observed throughout the developing world, from Chile to China, Peru to Pakistan, with the caveat there is great diversity in the actual patterns from one country to another. They are the story of growth, and it must be stressed again that international trade, and by extension the law of GATT and the WTO—while having a role in that story—is not cast as the protagonist. What also must be stressed is that the transformation from an economy dependent on agricultural output to one relying on industrial output does not occur at the same rate in every country. The pace at which the story unfolds differs from one country to the next.

In fact, a central issue is the pace at which the story ought to unfold. Put differently, to what extent ought the government of a less developed country encourage an acceleration of the transformation, and how ought it to do so? A spectacular example with dreadful consequences is the 1958–1962 Great Leap Forward in China. The government of Mao Zedong (1893–1976, in office, 1949–1976) looked to emulate Soviet efforts at a rapid transformation. The Chinese government invested heavily in the industrial sector, particularly in industries such as steel and machinery. Simultaneously, the government raised production quotas for the agricultural sector, and ordered a transfer of a large percentage of the harvest to support urban workers and thereby the industrialization process.

In brief, Chairman Mao's government sought to take a "Great Leap Forward" in the sense of turning China into an industrialized nation fast. The plan was simple: demand more and more of collective farms, and take a larger and larger chunk of farm output to feed the ever-growing number of laborers who toiled in factories concentrated in urban areas. That way, more workers could be hired, so factories could expand and multiply, and industrial output could increase. The example in Table 15-1, which is based on hypothetical data for rice, illustrates the plan and the reality of its implementation. (All of the amounts are in tons, and the data pertain to total rice production in China.)

The fatal flaw with the plan was Chinese communes could not possibly meet the production targets set for them by the Communist Party. (The example assumes they could meet only 70% of the targets.) However, it was not possible to "just say no." Local Communist Party cadres responsible for production on the communes were under enormous pressure to meet the quotas and supply the urban sector with the requisite amounts. When the farms could not meet unrealistically high quotas, the cadres concealed this failure. Yet, they still made sure the urban sector received the share demanded for it to support industrialization—in the hypothetical example, 60% of the production quota.

Clearly, if the amount to be siphoned off for the benefit of urban workers had been set on the basis of actual output, or on the basis of realistic targets, the shortfall in the last (right-hand most) column would not have existed. But, it was a formula for disaster to demand a fixed percentage of a quixotic target in a political environment where revising targets was impossible. The result was a Great Leap Backward in the agricultural sector: the sector languished, and tens of millions of Chinese peasants starved to death.

Judging from Column (4) alone, it may seem that the results could not have been too dreadful. After all, there was rice left in rural areas for the farmers to eat, and the amount of the balance grew from one year to the next. However, it must be remembered at the time, China's population was expanding rapidly. Hence, there were more mouths to be fed each year. Furthermore, it is rather evil to require farmers to work harder and not improve the quantity and quality of their caloric intake. Thus, the last 2 (right-hand most) Columns illustrate why the results indeed were dreadful. The actual amount of rice left in the agricultural sector was less than the theoretical amount (compare Columns (7) and (4)), and the shortfall increased each year (Column (8)).

In fact, while aggregate food production grew during the Great Leap Forward, because China's population grew at a rate of 2% per annum, *per capita* food

Table 15-1. Hypothetical Example of China's Great Leap Forward, Plan Versus Reality (Rice Market, in tons)

(1) Target and Harvest Year	(2) Rice Production Quota (Target for Total Rice Output)	(3) Amount of Rice to be Transferred to Cities to Support Industrial Workers (60% of Target)	(4) Amount of Rice Supposed to Remain to Support Farmers	(5) Actual Rice Production Achieved (Assume 70% of Target)	(6) Amount of Rice Actually Transferred to Cities (Same as Column 3)	(7) Actual Amount of Rice Left to Support Farmers (Difference between Columns 5 and 6)	(8) Shortfall of Rice in Agricultural Sector (Difference between Columns 7 and 4)
1959	1,000	600	400	700	600	100	−300
1960	2,000	1,200	800	1,400	1,200	200	−600
1961	3,000	1,800	1,200	2,100	1,800	300	−900

consumption remained flat.[3] Following the death of Mao in 1976, and the market reforms championed by Deng Xiaoping in the late 1970s and early 1980s, the Chinese government took major steps to re-invest in the agricultural sector. Most importantly, it abolished centralized planning and setting of production quotas, eliminated communes, and allowed farmers to own their own plots (sometimes as individuals, and sometimes in small groups through "Town and Village Enterprises" or "TVEs"), and sell their output for profit. So, agricultural output not only increased, but increased at an accelerated rate.

III. Background to Labor Surplus Models

• **Two Preliminary Points**

Aside from their intellectual underpinning, the first point to appreciate about 2-sector Labor Surplus Models is their rich intellectual heritage.[4] John C.H. Fei (1923–1996) and Gustav Ranis (1929–) were not the first scholars to develop such a Model. The classic book in which they lay out their Model, *Development of the Labor Surplus Economy*, published in 1964, was preceded by another classic, *The Theory of Economic Growth*. In this 1955 publication, Sir William Arthur Lewis (1915–1991) conceived of a Labor Surplus Model.

Their Models are somewhat different. Fei and Ranis focused on the connection between the agricultural and industrials sectors, while Lewis highlighted the distribution of income between these sectors. However, even Lewis owed a great debt to a predecessor, namely, the classical economist David Ricardo (1772–1823). More than 200 years earlier, in 1817, Ricardo published *The Principles of Political Economy and Taxation*. It was Ricardo who pioneered the concept of surplus labor in the agricultural sector and developed a two-sector model of the economy.

The second point to appreciate about Labor Surplus Models is that neither of the two sectors is international trade. Imports and exports are not expressly incorporated into these Models. The two sectors are, of course, agriculture and industry. The story these Models tell is transformation from the former to the latter sector. Neither cross-border transactions nor International Trade Law is not banished from the story. But, they simply are not given a prominent (much less leading) role. The two-sector Labor Surplus Models seek to show how surplus labor from an agricultural sector experiencing diminishing returns can be redeployed to the industrial sector, leading to a change in the shares of agricultural and industrial output in GNP. That is, Labor Surplus Models tell a story of modern economic growth through industrialization.

---

3. *See* GILLIS ET AL., 49.
4. This discussion draws on GILLIS, 51–57.

Therefore, one lesson to be drawn from a Labor Surplus Model is about the role international trade and law, in theory and practice, can play in economic growth. The lesson is to take a balanced perspective about that role. Unfortunately, critics of the modern multilateral trading system and its rules who espouse the claim that GATT and the WTO are "anti-Third World" tend not to have learned this lesson. Few of them even bother to examine development through Labor Surplus Models.

Rather, hidden under the "anti-Third World claim" is an assumption about the contribution of trade (and by extension, GATT and the WTO agreements) to growth, and to development in general: the contribution — at least potentially — is great, even to the degree trade can be an engine of growth. That is why critics of GATT and the WTO find it easy to "blame" international trade and international trade law for many of the sufferings of less developed countries. The logic implicit in that claim is that trade plays a (if not the) leading role in growth and development, therefore it also is a (if not the) villain causing many problems in poor countries. This logic, such as it is, and the consequent ascription of blame, exaggerates the role of trade in growth and development.

As the Fei-Ranis Labor Surplus Model suggests, importing and exporting are not the protagonists in the story of growth or development. They are supporting actors. Whether they can play their supporting roles, namely, whether they are able to facilitate growth through industrialization, depends on a range of other factors a country (such as good governance, sound macroeconomic fiscal and tax management, appropriate monetary policies, the rule of law, and a strong physical infrastructure) are in place. But, in all instances, the story is about transformation away from an economy excessively dependent on agriculture for its income. The protagonist in that story, according to Labor Surplus Models, is industrialization itself. One reason Labor Surplus Models are appealing is their use to explain this role of trade, and thus to keep a fair perspective on what trade can and cannot do, and what trade can and cannot be blamed for.

That use is as true for pro- as for anti-globalization assertions. The intellectual dynamic of over-estimating the role of trade is not confined to the "anti-Third World claim." Proponents of globalization, including enthusiastic advocates of GATT and the WTO sometimes err in giving trade more credit than is fair. If trade is not a villain for all the Third World's woes, then it surely is not a panacea for them either. Put differently, care is needed to avoid over-selling the potential salubrious effects of trade. Both sides of the debate about the GATT-WTO system can learn from Labor Surplus Models.

- **Elements of Fei-Ranis Labor Surplus Model**

The Fei-Ranis Model is neatly expressed in a three-paneled picture, Graph 15-2. To understand that Graph, it is essential to be familiar with their elements, namely, (1) the Agricultural Production Function, (2) the concept of the marginal productivity of labor, and (3) supply and demand curves for the agricultural and industrial labor markets through which the wage rates of workers in those markets are established. Accordingly, it is necessary to spend a moment on 3 elements.

First: Agricultural Production Function

A Production Function for any sector, or for the economy as a whole, relates the amount of output that can be expected from a specified amount of inputs into the production process. The Production Function for the agricultural sector, or "agricultural production function," is no different. It reveals the expected output of agricultural commodities from a particular combination of land, labor, physical capital, human capital, and technology.

Thus, conceptually the equation used for the aggregate production function is similar to that for the agricultural production function. Recall the Aggregate Production Function specified earlier is:

$$Y = \frac{1}{1} \cdot L + \frac{1}{n} \cdot N + \frac{1}{k} \cdot K + \frac{1}{h} \cdot H + \frac{1}{t} \cdot T$$

The dependent variable, Y, stands for GNP (or GDP).

To derive the Agricultural Production Function, the key change is in the dependent variable, *i.e.,* the variable on the left-hand side of the equation whose value depends on the values of the independent (right-hand side) variables. Instead of goods and services produced by the entire economy, the focus narrows to commodities produced in the agricultural sector, or Agricultural Output (AO):

$$AO = \frac{1}{1} \cdot L + \frac{1}{n} \cdot N + \frac{1}{k} \cdot K + \frac{1}{h} \cdot H + \frac{1}{t} \cdot T$$

AO is comprised of all commodities produced in the non-urban, non-industrial, non-service sector. Thus, it would include everything from apples to wheat, from chicken to veal, but would exclude the production of irrigation pipes or tractors. These latter items would be counted as industrial output.

Second: Marginal Productivity of Labor

It is an axiom of economic theory that the marginal productivity of labor ultimately must diminish. Development economists do not use the term "marginal" in the sense of making a value judgment. They do not mean that the workers are of poor quality, or that their output is slipshod. Rather, for development economists, "marginal" and "additional" are synonymous. That is, "marginal labor" is the addition of one more unit of labor — one more worker — to the production process. The next worker who toils on a rice paddy farm in Laos, or the next worker who harvests wheat in the Pakistani Punjab — they are the "marginal" workers.

With time, it is quite possible that the size of the paddy farm, or the wheat-growing area, will expand. The landlord may acquire new lands, or bring lands lying fallow into cultivation. However, that sort of transformation is done in the long term, *i.e.*, over a period of longer than (at the very least). In the short and medium term, the marginal farm worker must plant, cultivate, and harvest crops on a piece of land that is fixed in size. Similarly, in the long term, the farmer may obtain (directly by purchase or through rural credit financing, or via a landlord) new technology and capital with which to work. For example, better seeds that are resistant to disease and produce high yields, better irrigation systems, and better machinery are possibilities for the future. But, for now, the farmer works with a given level of technology. The same is true with his human capital. In time, he may take classes on better farming techniques. But, in the short and medium term, he is limited to the education he already has received.

In sum, the stocks of land, technology, physical machinery, and human capital with which the farmer has to help him in his work are fixed in the short and medium run. Only with time, and money to cover the investment costs, can the size of these independent variables change.

Imagine what would happen if this worker were not the last person added to work on the rice paddy or cotton farm. Assuming the worker had been working alone, or one of just two or three people, then no doubt she would welcome the help. She could not possibly manage, say, a 500 acre paddy field or cotton farm without perhaps 10 workers total. At 10 workers, for example, let us suppose that the paddy or farm operates at its optimum efficiency. It produces the largest amount of output, for the lowest amount of labor input. Stated differently, labor is at its maximum productivity. But, what would happen if marginal labor went beyond this optimum point? What if an 11th, and then a 12th, and then a 13th, and so on, all the way to a 50th worker were added to the paddy or farm?

Surely, the land would be akin to a kitchen in which there are too many chefs. No single farmer would have the room to do her work properly. Moreover, there would be an insufficient number of other factors of production—tractors, for instance—to go around. Finally, the land itself would become over-cultivated. In the end, the output of rice and cotton would suffer, in the same way that the food from an over-crowded kitchen ultimately would diminish in quantity and quality.

To imagine this scenario (which can occur because of rapid population grown, through high fertility or immigration rates, recession in the industrial sector, or a variety of other causes) is to understand why the marginal product of labor must fall. In brief, it is a manifestation of the law of diminishing returns: after a certain optimality point, adding extra workers actually detracts from output. Each additional unit of farm labor produces less and less output, and eventually, total output levels off and even drops. This scenario is plotted in Graph 15-2.

The Graph shows the Agricultural Production Function, coupled with diminishing marginal productivity of labor. Total output in the agricultural sector is measured on the *y*- (vertical) axis, and the quantity of labor is measured on the *x*- (horizontal) axis. Initially, as workers are added to the agricultural sector (starting from zero workers, and rising), output increase. These workers make productive

Graph 15-2. Agricultural Production Function with Diminishing Marginal Productivity of Labor

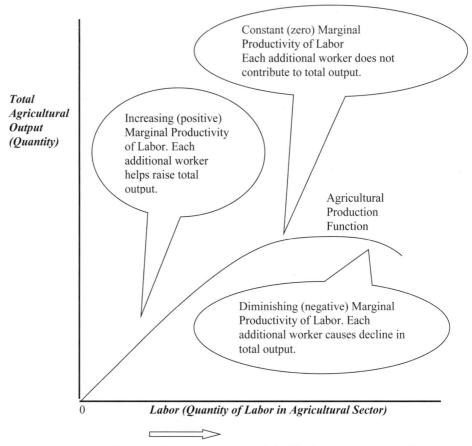

Horizontal movement rightward signifies increase in number of workers employed in agricultural sector.

Upward movement (bottom to top) signifies increase in total agricultural output.

contributions to the farms. In particular, each additional worker contributes more and more to total output. Put in the terms of development economics, the marginal product of labor—the increment to total output associated with an additional worker—rises.

However, eventually the extra workers are not able to contribute as much to total output as their colleagues who had come to work on the farms earlier. The Law of Diminishing Returns is beginning to set in, as outlined above. Hence, the Agricultural Production Function levels off—equal increases in labor lead to smaller increases in output. As workers continue to stream into the agricultural sector, output in that sector fails to increase at all. At that point (as explained below), the marginal product of labor is zero, or even negative, which is to say the increment to total output contributed by an additional worker is nothing, or that worker even causes total output to fall.

Third: Wage Rates, Supply and Demand for Labor, and Essence of Growth

The third and final building block in Labor Surplus Models concerns the labor market. Actually, because these Models are dualistic (*i.e.,* because they emphasize two sectors), rural and urban, there are two labor markets at issue: the agricultural and industrial labor markets. The key points about these markets are to see how wage rates in each sector are determined, and to understand how changes in the supply of labor to each sector affect (or do not affect) wage levels.

David Ricardo (1772–1823) assumed rural wage rates never would fall below a basic minimum level. That level is, of course, the minimum wage rate needed for a farm worker to maintain herself, not in luxury, but at subsistence. The assumption is not arbitrary. Rather, it is predicated on the view that a farm worker will entertain a rational calculation: "how much can I earn from working on the land in comparison with what I could earn in alternative pursuits?" It is assumed the farm worker would not take up a different occupation unless she could earn more than the wage rate she gets in the agricultural sector. (In truth, she also would include in the calculation the cost of moving to a new occupation, and establishing herself in a new place.) At the same time, it is assumed that there are wage levels in the farm sector that certainly would drive her off the land, namely, any level below subsistence. Thus, the subsistence wage rate is the minimum needed to keep her engaged in farming.

This assumption of a minimum wage rate in the agricultural sector has been retained in all Labor Surplus Models developed since Ricardo's time. In the language of development economics, that minimum level is called an "institutionally fixed wage,"[5] because the market forces of supply and demand for labor do not determine it. Exactly what level is this minimum? Again using the development economics terminology, it is "the average product of farm labor in households with a labor surplus."[6] Those terms embody 2 vital concepts—average product, and labor surplus.

The "average product" of labor is the total output in the agricultural sector, divided by the total number of workers in that sector. The contrast with marginal product should be clear: whereas the average product is precisely what its name suggests, the marginal product is (as defined earlier) the addition to total output resulting from the work of one more worker. The marginal product may be above, below, or equal to the average product, depending on the number of workers in the sector, and their output.

Eventually, the marginal product of labor becomes zero if too many people migrate into the agricultural sector in relation to the amounts of other factor inputs available for them to use in farming. However, even when the marginal product of labor falls to zero, the average product is not zero. After all, farms still are producing some

---

5. GILLIS ET AL., 53 (emphasis omitted).
6. GILLIS ET AL., 52–53 (emphasis omitted).

commodities. The problem is that additional workers are not boosting output. The point is that while the subsistence wage rate is assumed to be at the level of the average product of farm labor, the marginal product could be below that average level.

Consider this assumption in light of what happens in a free labor market in which there is perfect competition. In that scenario, the wage rate a worker earns equals the marginal product that worker contributes, *i.e.*, he is paid in accordance with the additional to total output for which she is responsible. But, if the marginal product were zero (for the reasons discussed above), then the worker would receive nothing. Obviously, he could not live on a zero wage rate—hence the need for an assumption about a minimum wage rate. The assumption means that a worker whose marginal product is below the average, or zero, still receives a wage equal to the average product.

What about the words "labor surplus," which impart the name to the class of development models like the Fei-Ranis Model? As the words suggest, at bottom they mean that there are extra workers in the agricultural sector who are under-employed and/or un-employed. Stated differently, there is an excess supply of labor—too many chefs in the kitchen, to recall the metaphor used earlier.

This metaphor suggests the time is ripe to get some chefs out of the kitchen. That is, why not shift the under- and un-employed workers from the agricultural sector, to which they are making no meaningful contribution, and have them work in the industrial sector? (In considering this question, the vexing negative externalities transition can cause, such as excess rural-urban migration, congestion, pollution, disease, and slums in cities, and family dysfunctions, are set aside.) Indeed, if these under- and un-employed workers could be taken off of the farms, the agricultural wage rate would not rise immediately. There are so many of them, that by assumption this rate has been driven down to a subsistence level. Only when all of them have been shifted out of the farm sector, and the remaining farmers are contributing meaningfully to total production, will wage rates in the farm sector begin to climb.

To put the scenario in the terms of development economics, only when the marginal productivity of agricultural workers rises will the agricultural wage rate start to increase. All of the surplus labor from the farm sector shall have to be shifted into the industrial sector first. At that point, the workers left on the farms will be able to cultivate the land without over-taxing it, and they will be able to use their tractors effectively. In other words, the remaining farmers will be able to work effectively on the land with the other factors of production at their disposal. Each will add to total output, *i.e.*, the marginal product of each will start rising. This scenario is set forth in Graph 15-3.

In that Graph, the marginal product of labor is plotted on the y- (vertical) axis, and the quantity of labor is plotted on the x- (horizontal) axis. The origin of the Graph, where the axes meet, is defined as the point at which all of the laborers in the economy are engaged in farming. That is, all of them are in the agricultural sector, and none is in the industrial (or service) sector. To understand Graph 15-3, think

Graph 15-3. Marginal Product of Labor and Subsistence Wage in Agricultural Sector, as Labor Surplus is Withdrawn from that Sector

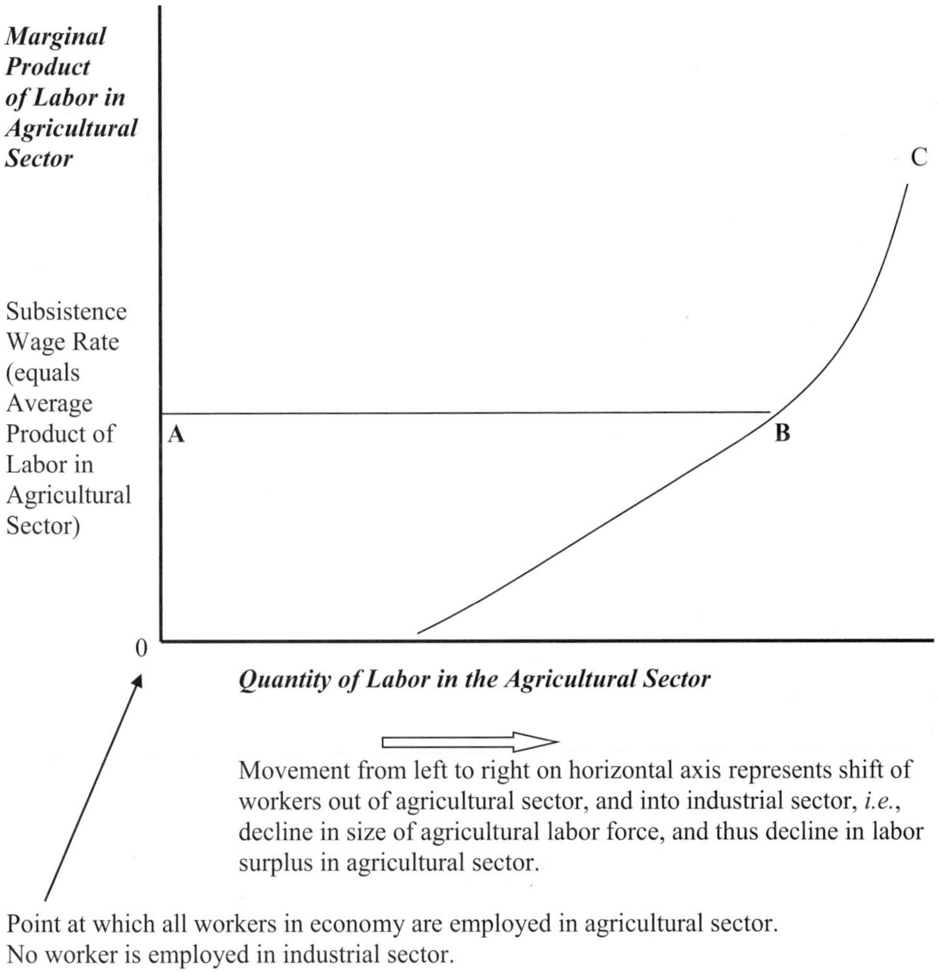

Marginal Product of Labor in Agricultural Sector

Subsistence Wage Rate (equals Average Product of Labor in Agricultural Sector)

A   B

C

0

Quantity of Labor in the Agricultural Sector

Movement from left to right on horizontal axis represents shift of workers out of agricultural sector, and into industrial sector, *i.e.*, decline in size of agricultural labor force, and thus decline in labor surplus in agricultural sector.

Point at which all workers in economy are employed in agricultural sector. No worker is employed in industrial sector.

of the analogy to chefs in a kitchen. With the excess chefs gone, the remaining chefs can do what they do best, resulting in a higher quantity, better quality, meals for the patrons of the restaurant.

In sum, the scenario is one of decreasing the quantity of labor in the agricultural sector in order to realize increases in the marginal productivity of labor. Indeed, it is not merely a "scenario." It is also a policy prescription for Third World economies plagued with labor surplus in rural areas.

But, how exactly will the industrial sector—specifically, the capitalists who own the factories in the urban areas—attract workers from farms to leave their rural homes and come to work on an assembly line? The answer lies in the wage rate. Farmers are assumed to make a rational calculation about the wages they can earn. They will not leave what they are doing, unless (on the one hand) their circumstances become so desperate that they cannot reach subsistence, or (on the other hand) they are paid above what they could earn on the farm. In brief, the captains of industry shall have to pay the surplus agricultural laborers a wage that makes it worth the while of those laborers to shift sectors.

What would that industrial wage rate be? As long as subsistence wages prevail in the agricultural sector, then it will be the subsistence wage (or, in fact, a bit above it to compensate for the transition costs of moving). But, as surplus laborers continue to move off the farms, and into the cities, the agricultural wage rate will increase, because (as discussed above) the marginal product in the farm sector of the remaining workers rises. Consequently, the captains of industry will have to raise wages to attract workers from rural areas.

After all, the remaining farmers are doing quite nicely, earning a higher wage rate that is commensurate with their increased productivity. Their plots of land are not over-farmed, and they do not have to share tractors. Why leave for a factory in the big city, unless the job pays better than the current rural wage rate? Again, consider the kitchen metaphor. The first few chefs come cheaply, but once the remaining chefs are happy and productive, they will need to be paid more to entice them to stay, or to leave.

Not surprisingly, this point can be put in the language of development economics: the supply curve of labor to the industrial sector is the same as the marginal product curve, coupled with the subsistence level, associated with the agricultural sector. This scenario/prescription of extracting workers from the agricultural sector without affecting wage rates until marginal productivity in that sector rises is depicted in Graph 15-4. As in previous Graphs, the marginal product of labor is plotted on the y- (vertical) axis, and the quantity of labor is plotted on the x- (horizontal) axis. The origin of the Graph, where the axes meet, is defined as the point at which all of the laborers in the economy are engaged in farming. That is, all of them are in the agricultural sector, and none is in the industrial (or service) sector.

To be precise in the terminology associated with Graph 15-4, what is depicted is the Labor Supply curve to the industrial sector. It represents the workers who are able and willing to offer their labor to capitalists at alternative wage rates. The curve slopes upward, above subsistence wage level, for obvious reasons: the higher the wage rate, the larger the number of workers who are able and willing to leave their farms and go to work in urban factories. So, the Labor Supply curve is demarcated by the letters "ABC."

Because it is not possible for an industrial to attract labor surplus from the agricultural sector at a wage level below the subsistence rate prevailing in that sector, the portion of the marginal product curve below the subsistence level is not viable. In other words, that portion is irrelevant as a practical matter. Thus, the Labor Supply curve is bounded by the flat line representing existence at subsistence level. Then,

Graph 15-4. Supply of Labor to Industrial Sector as Labor Surplus is withdrawn from Agricultural Sector

Wage Rate in Industrial Sector

Industrialists must offer at least subsistence wage rate prevailing in agricultural sector to recruit surplus agricultural labor

Point at which all labor surplus is withdrawn from agricultural sector

To continue to recruit, industrialists must increase wages in line with marginal product of labor

C

Subsistence Wage Rate in Agricultural Sector

A

B

Impossible to attract workers to industrial sector at sub-subsistence wage levels

0

Quantity of Labor in Industrial Sector

Movement from left to right on horizontal axis represents shift of workers out of agricultural sector, and into industrial sector, *i.e.*, decline in size of agricultural labor force, and thus decline in labor surplus in agricultural sector, but corresponding increase in industrial labor force.

Point at which all workers in economy are employed in agricultural sector. No worker is employed in industrial sector.

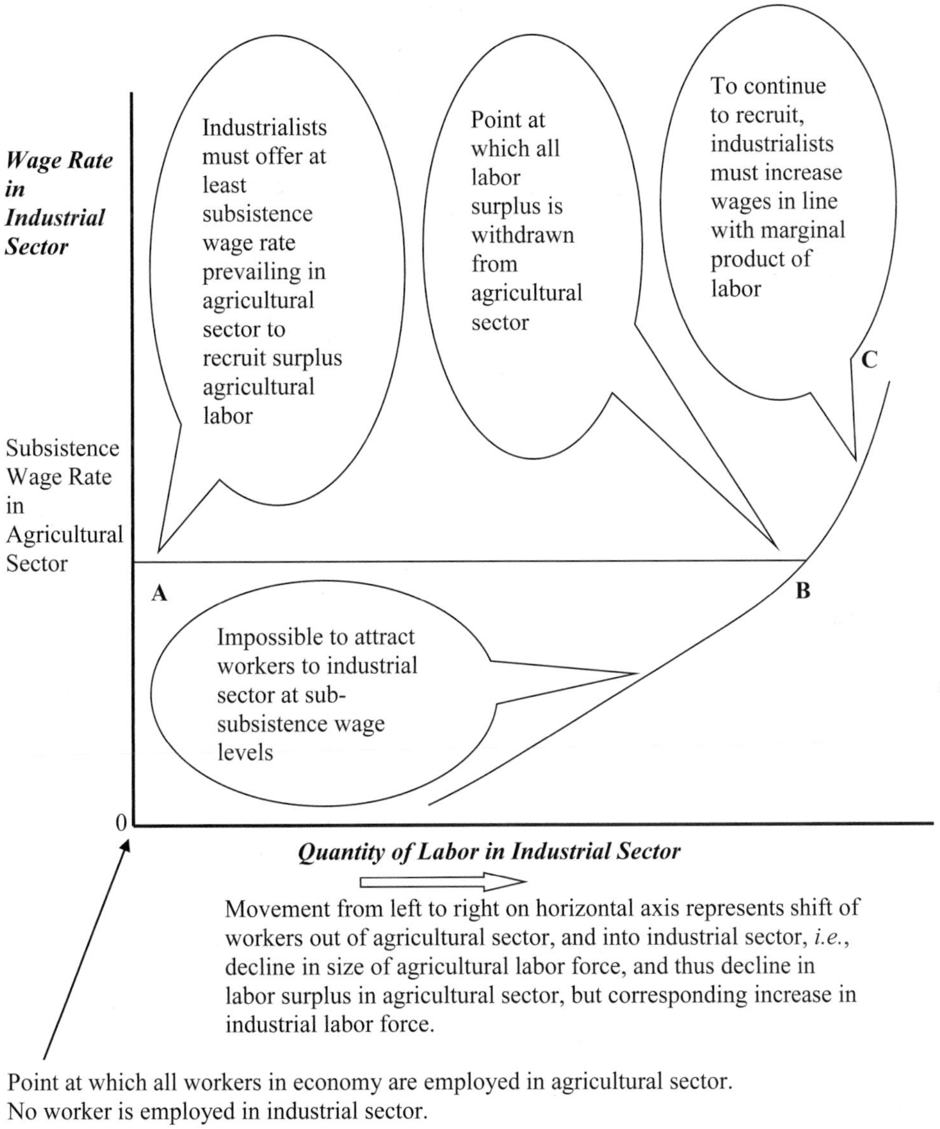

the curve rises once all labor surplus is withdrawn and marginal productivity in the agricultural sector.

Also to be accurate with terminology, industrial wage levels equal the "marginal revenue product" of the workers. That is, in a competitive labor market, an employer such as a factory owner will pay an additional worker the value of the product that worker contributes to the total output of the factory. The words "marginal product" encapsulate the concept of the increment to factory output that the newly hired worker contributes. The additional word "revenue" encapsulates the value of that incremental output. Thus, the entire phrase "marginal revenue product" connotes the additional value to total output for which the new worker is responsible.

So, for example, suppose the capitalist owns a shoe factory. The question is what wage rate will the capitalist offer to lure labor surplus off of the farm? The answer — again, assuming a competitive labor market — is the marginal revenue product of an extra worker. If a new worker adds 350 shoes per year to the factory output (*i.e.*, roughly a pair of shoes per day), then the worker's marginal product is 350 shoes. If those shoes are worth $3,500 (based on a per unit price of $10 per pair), then the capitalist would offer the worker $3,500. To be sure, the capitalist would sell the shoes for as much as possible, and in particular look to fetch a price that would earn a profit (revenue over and above labor and other costs).

A key point about Labor Surplus Models is the flat part of the Labor Supply curve, *i.e.*, from points A to B on the ABC curve in Graph 15-4. Because the context of this curve is a Third World country at which subsistence wage rates are a sad reality (or, at the very least, a "threat"), the A-to-B portion is relevant. If the context were the U.S., EU, Australia, Canada, or Japan, then there would be no need to depict that portion of the Labor Supply curve, because it would be a highly unlikely contingency. In the language of development economics, the flat part of the Labor Supply curve (indeed, of any supply or demand curve) is called a "perfectly elastic" portion.

In general, "elasticity" is a measure of the percent change in quantity that results from a percent change in price.

$$\text{Elasticity of Supply or Demand} = \frac{\text{Percent change in Quantity Supplied or Demanded}}{\text{Percent change in Price offered to supplier or in price of product offered for sale}}$$

Put broadly, "elasticity" gauges responsiveness, *i.e.*, the responsiveness of one variable to changes in another. Any two variables can be measured in terms of the responsiveness of one to changes in the magnitude of the other. For example, the ability and willingness of a lawyer to supply labor to a law firm might increase by 10% — there might be 10% more lawyers seeking law firm jobs — if law firm salaries rise by 5%. That would suggest an elasticity of 2 (10% divided by 5%).

In Labor Surplus Models, elasticity reveals the responsiveness of labor supply, meaning labor surplus in the agricultural sector that potentially could shift to the industrial sector, to changes in wage rates in the industrial sector.

$$\text{Elasticity of Labor Supply To Industry} = \frac{\text{Percent change in Quantity of labor supplied to industry}}{\text{Percent change in Wage Rate offered to surplus laborers in agricultural sector}}$$

Certainly, there are variables to which workers respond other than wages—quality of work, distance in commuting time, collegiality of the working environment, and so on. Elasticity captures only one such variable, but it is a highly important one.

To say that a portion of a line or curve is "perfectly elastic" is to say it has an elasticity of infinity. This value results from a zero value in the denominator (reflecting no percentage change in the wage rate), coupled with very large changes in the numerator (representing sizeable percentage increases in the supply of labor). (Conversely, perfect inelasticity would have a zero value—an infinitely large denominator, with no change in the numerator.) In the present context, the infinite value means that factory owners can hire surplus laborers off of the farm, thereby increasing the industrial labor force, but need not increase wage rates. Depicted graphically in Graph 15-4, on the perfectly elastic portion of the Labor Supply curve, no matter what the change in quantity of labor, there is no need to raise wages to entice workers.

This phenomenon is highly significant. It means industrialists can continue to expand output, by increasing their labor force, and yet not face increasing wage rates. That is, they need not worry about a rise in wage rates. That freedom is a relief to them. It means they will not be compelled by rising wage rates to increase the price of their products. In turn, their product will not become less price competitive than rival goods. Rather, the industrialists can increase the supply of their product to consumers at competitive prices, and thereby increase sales.

By hiring more workers, the overall wage bill the industrialists must foot will rise. But, it will not go up on account of an increase in the wage rate. Instead, it will rise only because of the increase in the number of employees. Likewise, to manufacture more output, factory owners will need more raw materials and intermediate goods consumed in the production process. But, what is possibly the most important variable in the overall cost of production—the wage rate—holds constant. It will remain flat in the industrial sector as long as there exists a pool of surplus workers in the agricultural sector on which to draw. Thus, industrial product prices need not rise on account of the wage rate.

Herein lies the essence of the growth story told by Labor Surplus Models: extract the labor surplus from the agricultural sector, put it to work in industry, and thereby take advantage of the constancy of industrial wages to expand industrial production while remaining price competitive. In a nutshell, that is the industrialization process captured by the Fei-Ranis Model.

The very fact industrial wages remain flat on the elastic portion of the Labor Supply curve is an invitation for capitalists to increase output by hiring more workers off of the farm at the same wage. The fact that wages stay the same assures the price competitiveness of industrial output vis-à-vis other sectors, both domestically and overseas. In sum, the perfect elasticity of labor supply caused by surplus labor in the agricultural sector is the great economic incentive to industrialize.

One point implicit in the discussion of the Labor Supply curve is that it is limited by the population size of the country in question. A labor surplus economy is presumed to begin, at its initial stage of development, with all of its population in the agricultural sector. Obviously, not every person living in the rural areas of the country is a farmer. There are children and elderly, and there are family members who stay to care for these dependents. Fortunately, it is not particularly significant to distinguish between the (1) total labor supply available in the agricultural sector, and thus to the industrial sector, and (2) the total population size. The reason is that in most instances, these numbers are closely correlated — a large population size would suggest a large agricultural labor force and, therefore, a large pool of surplus labor.

It is evident from the above discussion that industrialization requires an increase in demand for labor on the part of factory owners. This increase can, and is, depicted graphically in the Fei-Ranis Model through a Labor Demand curve. That curve, along with the Labor Supply curve, is shown in Graph 15-5. As the captains of industry expand their demand for labor, the Demand curve shifts outward, to the right. Thus, four Labor Demand curves are shown. The outward movement represents successive increases in demand for labor by employers in the industrial sector.

Graph 15-5 builds on the earlier Graphs. Graph 15-5 shows the familiar Labor Supply curve developed in Graph 15-3 and depicted in Graph 15-4. Graph 15-5 extends the earlier ones by picturing the Labor Demand curve, and outward shifts in that curve.

In general, a demand curve represents the number of units of a good or service that consumers of that good or service are able and willing to buy at alternative prices. For any normal good or service, the demand curve slopes downward. The downward slope reflects the common sense rationale that the lower the price, the larger the quantity of the good or service that consumers are able and willing to consume. Implicitly, this rationale assumes consumer preferences are governed by prices, which is to say that it abstracts from non-price determinants of demand like quality or snob appeal. In this respect, there is symmetry in assumptions underlying supply and demand curves. Supply curves dwell on price (in the labor context, the wage rate) as the critical determinant of the quantity of the good or service owners are able and willing to offer.

Here, there is no difference from the general case. In the market for labor in the industrial sector of a less developed country, factory owners are able and willing to hire more workers as the wage rate falls. That rationale explains the downward slope of each of the Labor Demand curves depicted in Graph 15-5.[7]

---

7. As a technical matter, it is possible to derive the Labor Demand curve from the Production Function for the industrial sector. That curve is based on the marginal productivity of labor in the industrial sector. This sort of derivation for the Labor Supply curve is provided earlier herein. The derivation is similar for the Labor Demand curve. However, these details are not needed for the discussion of the Fei-Ranis Model. *See* Gillis et al., 54–55.

Graph 15-5. Demand for, and Supply of, Labor in Industrial Sector as Labor Surplus is Withdrawn from Agricultural Sector

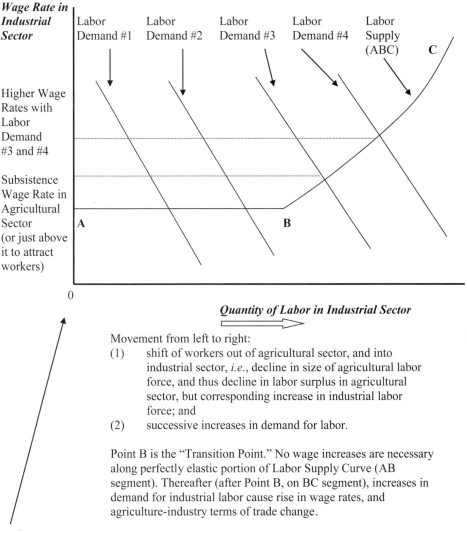

Movement from left to right:

(1) shift of workers out of agricultural sector, and into industrial sector, *i.e.*, decline in size of agricultural labor force, and thus decline in labor surplus in agricultural sector, but corresponding increase in industrial labor force; and

(2) successive increases in demand for labor.

Point B is the "Transition Point." No wage increases are necessary along perfectly elastic portion of Labor Supply Curve (AB segment). Thereafter (after Point B, on BC segment), increases in demand for industrial labor cause rise in wage rates, and agriculture-industry terms of trade change.

Point at which all workers in economy are employed in agricultural sector.
No worker is employed in industrial sector.

Also in general, the intersection of a demand and supply curve sets the market equilibrium price at which the good or service is offered for sale, and sold. Again, Graph 15-5 is no different from the general case; rather, it is a specific instance—the industrial labor market in a less developed country. Thus, in Graph 15-5, the equilibrium wage rate—the price at which surplus workers from the agricultural sector offer their services in the industrial sector, and the price they receive for their services from industrialists—is set at the intersection points of the Labor Demand and Labor Supply curves.

• **Transition Point**

What is critical in the Fei-Ranis Model, and other Labor Surplus Models, is the fact the demand for labor in the industrial sector can expand to a considerable degree without driving up wage rates. That fact results from the large pool of surplus labor in the agricultural sector that is available for work in the industrial sector. It is assumed that before modern economic growth commences, the entire population of the less developed country lives and works in agriculture. Hence, the large pool of surplus labor assures the perfect elasticity of the Labor Supply curve during the initial phases of industrialization (associated with the AB segment of that curve).

Yet, the set of workers considered labor surplus is not infinite. At some point—in particular, at Point B and after—industrialists must pay more if they are to continue expanding their labor force. The dashed lines in Graph 15-5, associated with increases in demand for labor shown by the third and fourth Labor Demand curves, trace out the higher wage levels industrialists must pay.

So, in the Fei-Ranis Model (and other Labor Surplus Models), Point B is critical for a less developed country. At that point, it is impossible to withdraw labor surplus from the agricultural sector without offering higher wages in the industrial sector. Why?

The answer is at Point B, the supply of surplus labor is exhausted. After point B, the marginal productivity of labor in the agricultural sector rises, which means agricultural workers—who are assumed to earn their marginal revenue product after this point—receive higher wages. With less crowded farms and more efficient use of factor inputs, the workers still on the farms are more productive. So, it is only natural that they begin to command higher earnings. But, of course, higher earnings in the agricultural sector is a deterrent to moving to a factory job—unless the factory job pays more than what can be had from farm work.

The exhaustion of labor surplus at Point B has a significant implication for the less developed country in its growth process. After this Point, withdrawal of workers from the agricultural sector causes total output in that sector begins to fall. Industrialization cannot proceed by taking more workers off of the farm without causing a reduction in agricultural output. In other words, industrialization cannot continue without placing demands on the agricultural sector. Why?

As just indicated, simply because workers who are taken off of farms after Point B are productive, in the sense of making a meaningful contribution to total output. Losing them "hurts." Until Point B, the marginal productivity of labor is negative or zero. Therefore, workers can be withdrawn from the agricultural sector without any loss in total farm output. The workers that are being withdrawn, represented by the segment AB on the Labor Supply curve in Graph 15-5, had no impact on this output in the first place.

But, after Point B, the economic climate changes. After this Point, the marginal product of labor no longer is negative or zero. Rather, it is positive and rising. Every additional worker removed leads to a decline in total output, because all the surplus workers—those whose marginal product was negative or zero—have been with-drawn. Put bluntly, if more workers are lost from the agricultural sector, that sector begins to "feel the pinch" in terms of a "hit" to its output.

How would the remaining farmers respond to further labor losses from their sec-tor? They would raise the price of their output, and thus earn more for themselves. As productive workers leave the agricultural sector, lured by higher wages in the industrial sector, the remaining farmers are in a position (assuming no government price controls or market distortions) to increase their wages by charging more for their product. That increase means the captains of industry shall have to boost what they offer to prospective workers if they hope to get any more of them off of the farm and into the factory.

Thus, Point B is when the TOT of agriculture relative to industry change. By "terms of trade," development economists mean the price of the goods from one sector relative to the price of goods from another sector. Expressed as a ratio:

$$\text{TOT of agriculture relative to industry} = \frac{\text{Price of agricultural goods}}{\text{Price of industrial goods}}$$

These agriculture-industry TOT measures the price of agricultural output relative to the price of industrial output. If they "deteriorate" from the perspective of indus-trial workers, the price of agricultural goods rises relative to the price of industrial goods. (Conversely, that change would be an "improvement for agricultural work-ers.) After Point B, these terms rise, because the cost of labor in the agricultural sector (*i.e.,* the farm wage rate) rises. In sum, Point B is called the "Turning Point."

There is another common sense explanation for what happens after the Turn-ing Point, one which helps explain the link between rising industrial wages and the change in the terms of trade against industry. After Point B, the price of farm output rises. The price increase occurs because removal of productive workers from the agricultural sector after the pool of surplus labor has been exhausted leads to a fall in agricultural output. (Plainly, as in any market, with less agricultural output, the price of each product rises, *ceteris paribus*.)

How will the formerly surplus agricultural workers, who now work in the indus-trial sector, pay for the higher-priced food? They require higher wages from their factory jobs to do so. In brief, to compensate industrial workers for the decline in the terms of trade (*i.e.,* in the rise in the price of food relative to industrial goods), capitalists who employee the workers shall have to pay them more than before. If they do not, then they hardly can expect their workers to be efficient on the assem-bly lines. But, capitalists suffer higher labor costs, which mean lower profits (again, *ceteris paribus*).

This explanation sounds gloomy, but it need not be. With farm workers getting paid better, they have an incentive to increase output. Because of higher agricul-tural commodity prices, they are eager to produce, sell, and hence earn more. If this scenario materializes (that is, if the farm sector is more productive), then the terms of trade need not shift dramatically against industry. With more food coming to market, the price increases need not be so dramatic. Depending on how much comes to market, these prices may even hold steady or decline. In sum, if the agricultural sector is more productive after the withdrawal of surplus labor, then total output from that sector may expand rapidly enough to support industrialization without a dramatic rise in food prices.

· **Size of Labor Surplus**

An interesting question that naturally arises from the Fei-Ranis Model is the availability of labor surplus. How big is the pool, or in terms of Graph 15-5, how long is that perfectly elastic segment AB? The answer depends on population growth in the rural areas of the less developed country in question. Assuming a close correlation between the country's population size and its labor supply, then a larger population size suggests a larger pool of surplus labor.

This presumed correlation does not mean rapid population growth in rural areas is a "good" idea for poor countries.[8] A clear implication of the Fei-Ranis Model is adding more surplus labor will not increase agricultural output, because surplus labor—by definition—has a zero or negative marginal productivity. In turn, with a larger population to feed, but no corresponding rise in commodity production, food consumption *per capita* would fall. Only imports of food, or use of other factors of production (say, technology, or land reclamation), would prevent this unhappy scenario. Moreover, David Ricardo worried that population growth would dampen food supply because it would result in over-farming and necessitate the use of poor quality land.[9]

Nevertheless, the overall repercussions of population growth are complex. They demand careful study beyond merely the effect on the pool of surplus labor. Indeed, not only are the repercussions a subject of inquiry, but so too are the factors that result in faster population growth (*e.g.,* the average age at first marriage of women, and the education and income levels of women). Such studies often yield an eclectic position, revealing differences in causes and consequences that depend on the particular circumstances of the less developed country in question.[10]

---

8. For an engaging and well-reasoned argument that population growth is "good" in a normative sense, see JULIAN L. SIMON, THE ULTIMATE RESOURCE 2 (Princeton, New Jersey: Princeton University Press, rev'd ed., 1996).

9. Like Thomas R. Malthus (1766–1834), Ricardo also worried that higher urban wages would cause workers to have more children, thus not only exacerbating population pressures, but also diminishing profitability in the industrial sector. The consequence of the latter effect, reasoned Ricardo, could be a reduction in investible funds necessary to continue industrialization. *See* GILLIS ET AL., 57.

10. *See, e.g.,* Allen C. Kelley, *Review of National Research Council "Population Growth and Economic Development: Policy Questions,"* 12 POPULATION AND DEVELOPMENT REVIEW 563–68 (1986); ALLEN C. KELLEY ET AL., POPULATION AND DEVELOPMENT IN RURAL EGYPT (1982). *See generally,*

What can be said is a large pool of surplus labor, based on a large population size, will postpone the Transition Point. Industrial wages will remain low (and, correspondingly, profits high) — hardly a happy event for the surplus workers who have moved to the cities. That is, the existence of a large pool will put off further into the future the moment when industrialization would cause agricultural output to decline and wages to rise. Industry can continue to expand, by absorbing the labor surplus, without putting demands on agriculture in terms of output. Put simply, as long as that pool is not exhausted, the productivity and overall output of the agricultural sector are not a concern. A less developed country operating at points before the Transition Point can focus on industrialization.

- **Transfer of Food from Rural to Urban Areas**

One aspect of the withdrawal of labor surplus that is not expressly dealt with in the Fei-Ranis Model should be highlighted — namely, food distribution. In shifting surplus workers represented by the segment AB on the Labor Supply curve in Graph 15-5 from farms to factories, what matters (in an economic sense) is that the food produced in the agricultural sector by the remaining workers is transferred to the cities in which the factories are located. Labor surplus that has shifted from village to city can be fed.

Whether food is distributed efficiently throughout the country is largely a question of whether the wholesale and retail markets for agricultural commodities function efficiently. If these markets do not function properly, and thus food does not get distributed properly to urban areas, then the industrialization process will be retarded. Worse yet, serious problems of malnutrition and even street-level anarchy can develop.

IV. 1964 Fei-Ranis Labor Surplus Model

- **Three-Panel Fei-Ranis Labor Surplus Model**

The Fei-Ranis Labor Surplus Model consists of the elements laid out above.[11] Quite literally, the Model is depicted with three graphs, or panels, each of which has been explained earlier. These graphs are the Agricultural Production Function, the

---

RICHARD A. EASTERLIN, GROWTH TRIUMPHANT (1998) (discussing the linkages among modern economic growth, population growth, and political upheaval).

11. A different graphical presentation of the Fei-Ranis Model, which appears in Raj Bhala, *Trade, Development, and Social Justice* (2003) at page 113, is possible. The difference is Panel I is inverted, *i.e.*, flipped over upside down. The advantage of that presentation is then there is an inconsistency in what a rightward shift means across all three Panels: an outward horizontal movement represents a shift in workers from the agricultural to the industrial sector. (In depictions of Agricultural and Industrial Labor markets, a movement from left to right often signifies a diminution in the quantity of labor in the agricultural sector, a corresponding transfer of labor to the industrial market, and thus an increase in labor employed in the industrial sector. In Graph 60-6, that is true for Panel III, but the opposite, *i.e.*, increasing labor employed in the agricultural sector, for Panels I and II.) Thus, in the top left-hand corner of an inverted Agricultural Production

Agricultural Labor Market (specifically, the Marginal Productivity curve), and the Industrial Labor Market (specifically, the Labor Supply and Demand curves).

In other words, the three panels are a composite of Graphs 15-3, 15-4, and 15-5. In its complete expression, the Fei-Ranis Model simply is the placement of the three Graphs—one on top of the other—on the same page. That placement is set forth in Graph 15-6.

- **Understanding Three-Panel Fei-Ranis Labor Surplus Model**

Taken together, all three panels in Graph 15-6 portray the industrialization process made possible by a pool of surplus labor. The Agricultural Production Function, set forth in Panel One, shows initial increases in total agricultural output as labor increases in the farm sector, but also shows the Law of Diminishing Returns begins to operate as more and more farm workers are added to that sector. The marginal productivity of each additional agricultural worker declines, hence increases in total farm output level off.

Farm output actually decreases after the Transition Point, when all farm workers are surplus labor, with zero productivity or worse. Adding more such workers compounds the problem, leading to further declines in farm output, as the labor surplus has negative marginal productivity and detracts from total output.

Conversely, reading the Agricultural Production Function backward, from right to left, indicates the salubrious economic benefits of withdrawing labor surplus from the agricultural sector and re-allocating it to the industrial sector. By definition, labor surplus that is withdrawn from the agricultural sector has a zero or negative marginal product—hence, the label "labor surplus." So, withdrawing them from farm work does not harm total agricultural output. To the contrary, getting these workers off of the farm helps the remaining farmers plant, fertilize, cultivate, and harvest more efficiently than when the plots of land were over-worked, over-crowded, and thereby subject to diminishing, zero, and negative returns. Yet, once all surplus workers have moved out, and workers with positive marginal productivity are siphoned off, total farm output begins to suffer. It must, because the workers now shifting to industry had contributed positively to agricultural output.

As for the middle panel (Panel II), what is shown is the familiar marginal productivity of labor curve. At the bottom left-hand corner, all workers are assumed to

---

Function, it is assumed all workers are employed in farming. The marginal productivity of each worker is nil or negative.

However, the disadvantage of this presentation is it can be confusing. For example, flipping the Agricultural Production Function in Panel I means the vertical (y-) axis must be read with care. A movement upward (from the zero point to the top of the axis) signified an increase in farm production. When this Panel is inverted in, moving from the bottom to the top of the page still represents an increase in total agricultural output. Conversely, by moving along the curve from the top to the bottom of the page, it is evident total agricultural output declines. This decline results from industrialization after the Transition Point, *i.e.*, the successive withdrawal of workers from the agricultural sector who are productive (as measured by a positive marginal productivity), and signifies a change in the terms of trade (the relative price) of industry to agriculture.

Graph 15-6. Fei-Ranis Labor Surplus Model

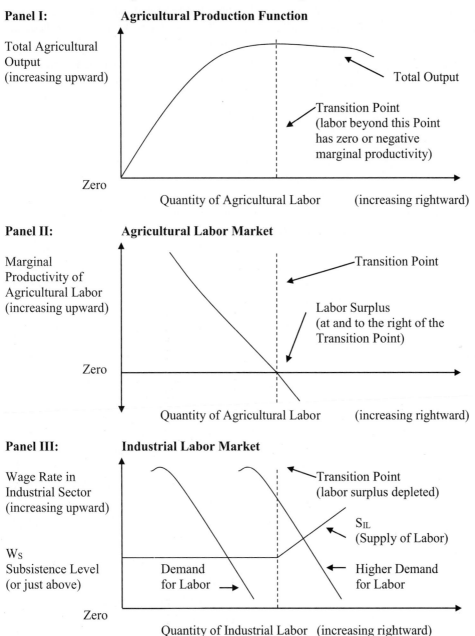

Panel I: **Agricultural Production Function**

Total Agricultural
Output
(increasing upward)

Total Output

Transition Point
(labor beyond this Point
has zero or negative
marginal productivity)

Zero

Quantity of Agricultural Labor   (increasing rightward)

Panel II: **Agricultural Labor Market**

Marginal
Productivity of
Agricultural Labor
(increasing upward)

Transition Point

Labor Surplus
(at and to the right of the
Transition Point)

Zero

Quantity of Agricultural Labor   (increasing rightward)

Panel III: **Industrial Labor Market**

Wage Rate in
Industrial Sector
(increasing upward)

Transition Point
(labor surplus depleted)

S_{IL}
(Supply of Labor)

W_S
Subsistence Level
(or just above)

Demand
for Labor →

Higher Demand
for Labor

Zero

Quantity of Industrial Labor   (increasing rightward)

be engaged in industry, and none in agriculture. A rightward movement signifies an increase in the quantity of workers in the farm sector. Predictably, as more farmers are added, the marginal productivity of each additional farmer declines. At the Transition Point, agricultural workers have zero marginal productivity, and thereafter, a negative marginal productivity. Conversely, moving backwards (from right to left) on the Marginal Productivity line indicates that withdrawing labor surplus from the agricultural sector, and redeploying it to the industrial sector, boosts marginal productivity in the agricultural sector. That is worth doing until industrialists have exhausted the pool of surplus farm labor, when the economy reaches the Transition Point. After this critical point, marginal productivity in the agricultural sector begins to rise, because the remaining farmers can do their jobs unfettered by workers who are essentially under-and un-employed, and make better use of the other factor inputs (land, technology, and so on).

Marginal productivity in the agricultural sector is the basis for the Labor Supply curve to the industrial sector (because workers are willing and able to sell their labor for the value of their marginal product, *i.e.,* for their marginal revenue product). The Labor Supply and Labor Demand curves are portrayed at the bottom of Graph 15-6 (Panel III). For as long as the Labor Supply curve is perfectly elastic (the AB segment in Graphs 15-3 and 15-5), workers can be enticed away by the captains of industry for subsistence wages (or just above that level). When all labor surplus is gone, farm workers need a higher wage if they are to leave the idyllic countryside for an urban factory job. Hence, the industrial wage rate must rise if the demand on the part of capitalists for labor continues to increase.

Corresponding to this increase in wage rates in the industrial sector is an ineluctable decline in total agricultural output (a shift from right to left in Panel I). Recall that once past the Transition Point (Point B in Graphs 15-3 and 15-4), all labor surplus has been exhausted. Any more workers who shift from farms to factories are, by definition, productive farmers (in the sense of having a positive marginal productivity). Enticing these farmers to pack their bags for the bright lights and big city causes total agricultural output to fall (again, reflected in a shift from right to left on Panel I). In turn, that fall necessitates a rise in the price of farm goods. As in any market, if agricultural commodity output declines, then (*ceteris paribus*) agricultural prices rise. Hence, the terms of trade of industry relative to agriculture (*i.e.,* the price of industrial versus farm goods) deteriorate. Put equivalently, urban factory workers must pay more for their food, which is all the more reason why they need higher wages.

Here, therefore, is why the Transition Point (Point B in Graphs 15-3 and 15-4) is so critical. Industrialization before the Point can continue apace on the backs of labor surplus transferred from the agricultural sector. After the Point, steady agricultural output no longer can be taken for granted. Continued industrialization will impose demands on the agricultural sector that shall have to be addressed if modern economic growth is to continue without straining that sector beyond its limits.

In sum, with respect to Panel I, the Agricultural Production Function indicates the total output in the agricultural sector. The vertical axis measures total output. An upward movement indicates increased output. The horizontal axis depicts the quantity of workers in the agricultural sector, *i.e.,* in effect, the number of workers on farms. A rightward movement on this axis is an increase in the quantity of those workers. The Production Function indicates total output falls as the quantity of labor in that sector rises. The reason, of course, is the declining marginal productivity of labor, which in turn is based on the Law of Diminishing Returns. The Transition Point indicates the point at which the marginal productivity of agricultural workers is zero. Therefore, output increases as labor is withdrawn from the agricultural sector, *i.e.*, a leftward movement on the horizontal axis.

Thus, the Three-Panel Fei-Ranis Labor Surplus Model tells a visual story of growth through industrialization, which in turn is fueled by movement of labor surplus from the agricultural to industrial sector. Panel I shows the effect of industrialization on agricultural output, illustrating a rise (moving from right to left in the segment after the Transition Point) in total agricultural output as this surplus leaves agrarian lands for factory shop floors. Panel II depicts the rise (moving right to left) in marginal productivity of agricultural workers as labor surplus shifts to the industry. Panel III highlights the ability of capitalists to pay a subsistence wage (or just above that level) to attract labor surplus off the farm, but the necessity to increase wages (after the Transition Point) once that pool of workers is depleted.

- **Yet Again, Role of Trade and International Trade Law in Perspective**

What role exists for international trade in the Fei-Ranis Labor Surplus Model? The short answer is there is no explicit role. Industrialization through labor surplus takes the lead role. However, trade can play a supporting role. First, as industrial output expands, where do capitalists sell the output? They look to their domestic market. However, if and when this market becomes saturated, and profit margins thereby shrink, they look overseas. In other words, export markets may absorb increased industrial production. Second, exports of that production generate revenue that capitalists may use to import capital equipment. Indeed, as their labor costs rise after the transition point, they have an incentive to shift away from labor-intensive, and toward labor-saving, production processes.

In addition to exporting industrial products and importing capital equipment, trade may enter into the labor surplus growth story in two other ways. In the agricultural sector, as Panel I exhibits, output rises before the transition point, *i.e.*, until additional farm workers become surplus labor and for as long as they are not withdrawn from farms and reallocated to factories. Who consumes the additional primary and processed farm goods?

One answer is factory workers. Typically, this group expands in size and is based in and around urban areas, such as Bombay, Jakarta, Mexico City, and Shanghai. To the extent surplus agricultural output exists, *i.e.*, to the extent a country produces enough food for its own people, it may become a net exporter of agricultural products. That is, increased agricultural output, made possible by increased marginal productivity, enables the country to generate and export excess production. Naturally, it earns revenues from these exports. It might save these revenues, and channel them into capital investments in the industrial sector. It also might spend some of the revenues on agricultural commodities, in which it does not specialize, *i.e.*, in which it lacks a comparative advantage. For example, Vietnam might export rice to Kansas in exchange for beef.

In sum, in the process of industrialization in a labor surplus economy, exports and imports are not the principal catalyst. Can this process, made possible through the use of labor surplus, be enhanced (*i.e.*, accelerated) by international trade? The answer is "of course." They can support that process. By extension, so too can S&D treatment provisions in GATT-WTO law, FTAs, or CUs.

In particular, if the captains of industry have overseas markets to which they can export the output from their factories, then no doubt they will have all the more incentive to expand production. To do so, they will hire the labor surplus from the agricultural sector more quickly, and thus the transition from agriculture to industry will be hastened. However, this trade-enhancing effect on industrialization is not a predominant feature of Labor Surplus Models such as the Fei-Ranis Model. It is rarely mentioned. In other words, these Models neither highlight it, nor rule it out. They simply leave open the question of where industrial output is sold, *i.e.*, they tend not to specify whether the consumers are at home or abroad.

Another potential role for trade is in mitigating the demands placed by industrialization on the agricultural sector after the Transition Point is reached. Domestic agricultural output falls after this point (*i.e.*, moving leftward on Panel I in Graph 15-6), because of the enticement of non-surplus workers away from farming through higher industrial wages. How can this decline be addressed?

One answer is to provide the remaining farmers with better technology, in the form of high-yielding and disease-resistant seeds (some of which are likely to be genetically modified, which raises a separate set of concerns). A second answer is to make available better physical capital, in the form of mechanized tools (such as tractors). A third answer is to train the remaining farmers—raise their level of human capital through appropriate courses that will enable to farm in more intelligent ways. That expansion may occur through land reclamation (from the seas), or steppe farming (in mountainous areas). A fourth answer is to expand the land available for cultivation, so the remaining farmers can realize economies of scale.

All 4 answers involve changing the mix of factor inputs, so that farm labor is rendered more productive by virtue of better technology, physical capital, human capital, and more land. But, there exists still another answer—trade. The less developed country that has passed the Transition Point can export its excess industrial output, which results from continued expansion of the industrial sector. In exchange, it can import agricultural commodities. Indeed, that sort of bargain may enhance the process of industrial product specialization, thus hastening the agriculture-to-industry transformation.

Indeed, China adopted precisely this policy in the late 1970s.[12] Faced with a labor surplus economy, Chinese economic planners sought to hasten the

---

12. *See* Gillis et al., 59.

agriculture-to-industry transformation. Yet, they did not want to repeat the disastrous mistakes of the Great Leap Forward (1958–1962), where tens of millions died from starvation during an industrialization effort that all but neglected domestic food production. Thus, China increased food imports to cover the needs of its expanding urban factory labor force.

To be sure, such a policy may rub against the wishes of some politicians — for example, in India — who prefer self-sufficiency in food production. For them, it is a matter not only of national pride, but also national security. Happily, the policy options are not necessarily mutually exclusive. In some parts of the Third World, finding a better mix of factor inputs, and formulating an appropriate trade strategy that eschews excessive dependence on food imports, may occur simultaneously in order to satisfy political and economic criteria.

V. Critique of Labor Surplus Models

- **First: Does Labor Surplus Exist?**

At the heart of the Fei-Ranis Model — or, for that matter, any Labor Surplus Model — is the assumption that there is surplus labor whose marginal productivity is at, near, or even below zero in the agricultural sector. This assumption would seem to be quite safe for China[13] or India. But, what about Laos or Kenya?[14] Any traveler to less developed countries knows they are not all over-populated.

That is, China and India are candidates for the label "labor surplus economy." Each has several hundred million people living in rural areas. However, China's population is rapidly ageing one, and by no means do Labor Surplus Models capture reality in every developing country or LDC. Not all such countries evince labor surplus. Some are under-populated, albeit with fast-growing populations, and rely heavily on foreign workers. While not necessarily developing countries, the six GCC members — Bahrain, Oman, Qatar, Kuwait, Saudi Arabia, and UAE — illustrate the point. Even if a country has a large supply of labor, it does not mean that country has labor surplus at all times. Some farm workers may be needed, and have a positive marginal productivity, on a seasonal basis — e.g., when crops are planted or harvested. In the off-season, their productivity may be zero. Still, as a generalization, in varying degrees, several African, Asian, and Latin American poor countries demonstrate labor surplus features.

These observational insights suggest a shortcoming in the zero-marginal-productivity assumption underlying the Fei-Ranis Model. Maybe, for a particular

---

13. For the argument China has been a labor surplus country since (at least) the 1950s, and that the labor surplus was not falling in absolute numbers during the 1980s or 1990s because of population growth, see GILLIS ET AL., 59–60.

14. For the argument Kenya was not a labor surplus country from the 1950s until the late 1970s, see GILLIS ET AL., 60.

Third World country, the assumption needs to be relaxed. The Neo-Classical Two-Sector Model (discussed below) does precisely this. Before entertaining a discussion of that Model, however, care should be taken not to abandon the assumption too quickly. While, indeed, there are under-populated parts of developing world, there is an unmistakable trend in that world of urbanization. Between 1980 and roughly 2000, more than a dozen new "mega-cities" have arrived.[15] These cities are defined as urban areas with more than 10 million people, and there were no less than 20 of them—such as Buenos Aires, Lagos, Karachi, Dhaka, Manila, and Jakarta. More of them have and will come.

What relevance does the trend of mega-cities have for Labor Surplus Models? That question is answered by another inquiry: what explains the trend? One answer, suggested by the U.K. Department for International Development, is labor surplus in agricultural areas.[16] The argument is that rural areas of many less developed countries have reached their so-called "carrying capacity," which means they no longer can support the population living in those areas. Improvements in medical care have extended life expectancies, and thereby contributed to population growth. Technological improvements in agriculture have meant each productively-employed farmer can produce more output with fewer factor inputs.

Therefore, some of the new population in rural areas is surplus. These surplus workers, who typically are young, can find no employment that is, in numerically positive terms, productive. The end result is a lower carrying capacity of rural areas. Where are those surplus workers to go for gainful employment but to cities, thus fueling the urbanization trend? In sum, the relevance of the trend for Labor Surplus Models is that from this trend, the existence of surplus labor in rapidly urbanizing countries can be inferred. Put more colloquially, perhaps the Fei-Ranis characterization of less developed countries as being labor surplus economies is not so widely off the mark after all.

• **Second: Is Agriculture Ignored?**

The Fei-Ranis Model has a rather uncomfortable implication. It suggests the agricultural sector can be ignored for as long as the labor surplus remains unexhausted. Maybe so, but is there not a possibility for a great deal of suffering in that neglected sector? The disastrous Great Leap Forward in China from 1958–1961 is a case in point.

In a relentless drive to industrialize, the Communist Party demanded more and more output from the agricultural sector to support the expanding urban factory populations that had been transferred from rural areas. Farm output could not keep pace with central planning directives, yet local Party cadres were reluctant to admit

---

15. *See The Brown Revolution,* THE ECONOMIST, 11 May 2002, at 73. [Hereinafter, *The Brown.*]
16. *See The Brown Revolution,* at 73, 74 (discussing the work of Michael Mutter, an urban planning advisor to the Department).

their agricultural communes had not met output quotas. Accordingly, to cover up the failures, they had food output transferred from rural areas to support the factory workers as called for by the Party-dictated targets—even when that transfer meant leaving less and less food for the farmers themselves.

So, for example, suppose the output target was 500 tons for a commune, of which 50% was to be transferred to a city for factory workers, but only 300 tons actually were produced. Rural Party bosses would transfer 250 tons (50% of the quota amount), thus indicating (falsely) the quota was met, rather than 150 tons (50% of actual output), which would signal failure. In so doing, the amount left over was only 50 tons (the difference between 300 tons of actual output and 250 tons) sent to the city. The result was a human tragedy. Tens of millions of Chinese peasants died from starvation.

To be sure, the cause was not the Fei-Ranis Model. Rather, it was unrealistic agricultural output targets set by central government planners, coupled with a political structure in which admitting failure to meet those targets hardly was encouraged. Still, the Model dwells on industrialization and conveys a high degree of comfort with the *status quo* in the agricultural sector until the Transition Point.

Travel observations, coupled with the concern about ignoring an entire economic sector, have led to the development of a variation of the Labor Surplus Model. The variation is not radical, in the sense that the story remains the same—the transformation from an economy predicated on agriculture to one driven by industry. Hence, the focus remains on two sectors. The variation is called the "Neo-Classical Two Sector Model" (discussed below).

- **Third: Should International Trade Be Highlighted?**

Another less-than-realistic aspect of Labor Surplus Models concerns international trade. As highlighted earlier, these Models do not ascribe any explicit role to exports or imports in the industrialization process. Most developing and least developed countries engage in some trade, however small. In fact, the need to do so can be seen even within a Labor Surplus framework. These Models ascribe the most important role in the story of growth to industrialization, not trade.

As workers are pulled out of the agricultural sector, their consumption level may rise, because they are paid slightly higher wages in industry than the subsistence wage they got as farmers. Domestic production might not satisfy entirely their consumption demand. Some consumer goods may need to be imported to meet the wants of the burgeoning urban population. Were agricultural output to fall because industrialization proceeds beyond the point of extracting surplus labor, then it may be necessary to import food items. As for exports, they may result from higher industrial output. If not all output of a particular kind of merchandise can be consumed directly, then the excess may be exported abroad in exchange for needed imports. In brief, while trade is not the protagonist in a Labor Surplus Model, it could well be an important supporting actor.

VI. Neo-Classical Two-Sector Model[17]

• Different Assumptions, Different Perspectives

In the Neo-Classical Two-Sector Model, the marginal product of labor never is zero. It cannot be, because by assumption there are no surplus workers. Every worker contributes something positive to total farm output. Thus, if the size of a less developed country's population increases, and consequently the size of its agricultural labor force increases, then total farm output will rise. Conversely, if any workers are taken off of farms and put into factories, farm output will fall. No surplus labor exists for transfer to the industrial sector without diminishing agricultural output. In terms of Graph 15-5, and Panel III of Graph 15-6, no portion of the Labor Supply curve is perfectly elastic.

This assumption means that wages paid to industrial workers equal the marginal product of those workers, and there is no "breathing space" for the captains of industry to pay a wage rate that equals (or is just above) the subsistence wage in agriculture.

The distinction between the Fei-Ranis and Neo-Classical Two-Sector Models can be put in terms of population growth and its impact on the quantity of labor in rural areas and *per capita* food consumption. In the Fei-Ranis Model, an increase in farm labor adds to the pool of surplus labor. Because that pool does not add to total agricultural output, the difficulty is one of having more mouths to feed without an increase in output. In the Neo-Classical Two-Sector Model, the increased population and agricultural labor force means more mouths to feed. But, the added agricultural workers are productive. Hence, there is more food to go around. In the first Model, the risk of population growth is that *per capita* food consumption will fall. In the variant Model, this risk does not exist.

The difference between the two Models also can be seen on the Transition Point. In the Fei-Ranis Model, an increase in the pool of labor resulting from population growth means an extension further into the future of the Transition Point. That is, the Point at which industrial wages must rise to attract workers off of the farms is deferred. In the Neo-Classical Two-Sector Model, there is no Transition Point at such. All farm workers are productive, hence industrialists must offer ever-higher wages if they are to attract these workers into their factories. Put simply, the Fei-Ranis Model gives industrialists a perfectly elastic segment of the Labor Supply give during early phases of the transition. The Neo-Classical Model does not give industrialists that luxury.

Still another way to see the difference between the Models is to consider the terms of trade. Because there is a Transition Point in the Fei-Ranis Model, there is room to industrialize without affecting the terms of trade of agricultural relative to industrial products. That is not the case with the Neo-Classical Two-Sector Model.

---

17. This discussion draws on GILLIS ET AL., 57–59.

Because all workers have a positive marginal productivity and output falls when they are transferred to the industrial sector, agricultural commodity prices begin to rise immediately (*ceteris paribus*) with the transfer of these workers.

The only way industrialization can proceed is to prevent a dramatic deterioration in the terms of trade for industry by finding ways to maintain or increase agricultural output. (An increase in other factor inputs, such as capital and technology, a better mix of factor inputs, and food imports in exchange for industrial output, are the principal policy tools.) Put bluntly, the gravest threat to industrialization in the Neo-Classical Two-Sector Model is a stagnant or declining agricultural sector (owing to the transfer of workers from farms to factories), coupled with rising industrial wage rates (owing to the need to attract productive workers off of the farms). The end results can be too little to eat for a large number of people, a decline in industrial profitability, a lack of funds for new capital investments, and even widespread civil unrest.

• **Model Depiction**

The Two-Sector Neo-Classical Model is depicted in Graph 15-7. Like the Fei-Ranis Labor Surplus Model in Graph 15-6, there are three panels. Panel One is the Agricultural Production Function, Panel II is the Marginal Productivity of Labor in the Agricultural Sector, and Panel III is the Industrial Labor Market (*i.e.*, the Supply and Demand Curves for Labor). Also like the Fei-Ranis Model, a movement horizontally (along the x-axis) of any of the Panels represents an increase in the quantity of labor in the industrial sector, and a concomitant decrease in the quantity of labor in the agricultural sector.

In Panel I of the Two-Sector Neo-Classical Model, the Agricultural Production Function indicates a steady diminution in total farm output as workers are withdrawn from the agricultural sector (*i.e.*, moving rightward away from the origin (O) on the horizontal (x-) axis corresponds to withdrawing workers from agriculture, and putting them into the industry, so the Function declines). Recall that, as with the Fei-Ranis Model in Graph 15-6, an upward movement along the vertical (y-) axis represents an increase in total output. The Agricultural Production Function slopes downward, thus indicating an output decline.

This decline in Panel I is a direct result of the trend in marginal productivity depicted in Panel II. By assumption, in the agricultural sector, there is no surplus labor. Hence, marginal productivity never falls to subsistence levels, much less zero or negative ranges. Every worker "matters" in the sense of contributing positively toward total farm output. As workers are withdrawn from the agricultural sector, the marginal productivity of the remaining workers rises. The reasons are the same as those in the Fei-Ranis context: less crowded farms, less over-farming, and more efficient use of inputs.

The key departure from the Fei-Ranis context is that marginal productivity rises steadily and never is zero or negative. That departure has obvious implications for the industrial labor market, which is depicted in Panel III. There is no portion of

Graph 15-7. Neo-Classical Two-Sector Model

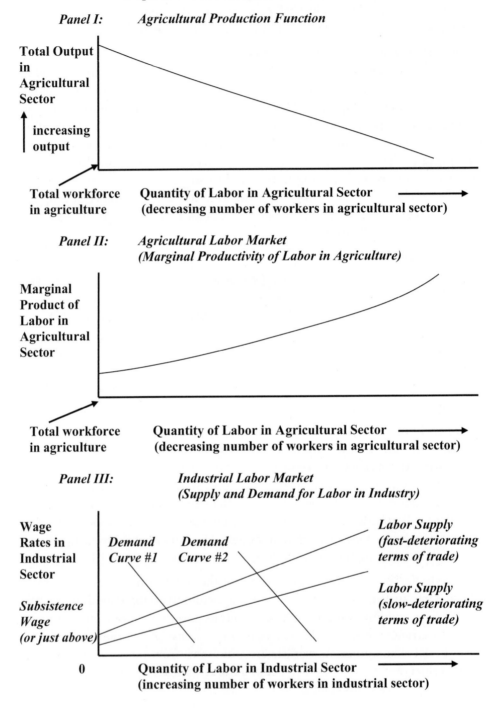

Panel I: ***Agricultural Production Function***

Total Output in Agricultural Sector

increasing output

Total workforce in agriculture

Quantity of Labor in Agricultural Sector ⟶
(decreasing number of workers in agricultural sector)

Panel II: ***Agricultural Labor Market***
(Marginal Productivity of Labor in Agriculture)

Marginal Product of Labor in Agricultural Sector

Total workforce in agriculture

Quantity of Labor in Agricultural Sector ⟶
(decreasing number of workers in agricultural sector)

Panel III: ***Industrial Labor Market***
(Supply and Demand for Labor in Industry)

Wage Rates in Industrial Sector

Subsistence Wage (or just above)

Demand Curve #1   *Demand Curve #2*

Labor Supply (fast-deteriorating terms of trade)

Labor Supply (slow-deteriorating terms of trade)

0   **Quantity of Labor in Industrial Sector** ⟶
(increasing number of workers in industrial sector)

the Labor Supply curve that is perfectly elastic. Because that curve is, in effect, the marginal productivity curve of Panel II, and because marginal productivity never is flat, it follows that the Labor Supply curve must slope upwards from the outset.

Likewise, there is no minimum subsistence wage in effect at any point. The wage rate in the industrial sector depends on the marginal productivity of workers in the agricultural sector, because it is those workers who must be attracted to urban factories if industrialization is to proceed. In common sense terms, Panel III highlights the implications of the assumption of no surplus agricultural labor.

Farm workers earn their marginal product, which is above subsistence. To entice them off of the farm, they must be paid a higher wage than what they are earning in the agricultural sector. They would be indifferent if paid exactly the same wage rate in both sectors. To coax them to move, they will need to receive a premium over the farm wage rate, which in turn depends on their marginal productivity in farming. At a minimum, that premium should cover the costs of moving to, and re-establishing in, the city.

The larger the number of farmers who leave for factories, and thus the smaller the quantity of labor in the agricultural sector, the higher the marginal product of the remaining farm workers. Moreover, because total farm output falls owing to the withdrawal of productive workers, agricultural commodity prices rise (*ceteris paribus*). In other words, the remaining farmers are both more productive and able to earn more for their output. These remaining farmers rationally ask themselves: "Why leave farming for a factory job unless it pays better, particularly when I am earning more because the food I grow is fetching higher prices than before given the overall decline in farm output?"

The "bottom line" result is that industrial wages must rise as demand for labor on the part of industrialists rise. This result is reinforced by the rise in agricultural commodity prices. Workers know they face these rising prices, hence they will require more from their factory jobs so as to ensure they can pay for food. In other words, the Labor Supply curve to industry rises for two reasons: rising marginal productivity, and hence rising wage rates, in the agricultural sector; and the worsening terms of trade of agriculture to industry (*i.e.*, rising food costs relative to industrial products).

The second reason explains why two Labor Supply curves are depicted in Panel III. If food prices rise fast with industrialization, then urban factory workers require higher wages than if they rise slowly. That is, the more quickly the terms of trade of agriculture to industry deteriorate, the more quickly wages must rise. The upper Labor Supply curve reflects rapidly rising wages in consequence of fast-deteriorating terms of trade.

To be sure, it is important not to exaggerate the differences between the Fei-Ranis Labor Surplus and Neo-Classical Two-Sector Models. Both Models lead to the same end result: to continue industrialization, capitalists must pay more for workers to attract them away from the agricultural sector. In the Neo-Classical Model, capitalists face this problem from the outset, because they do not have a pool of surplus labor on which to draw, and hence cannot "get away with" paying subsistence wages (or just above them) during the early phases of industrialization. In the Fei-Ranis Model, capitalists do have this pool. They draw upon it and, ultimately, exhaust it. When it is used up, then the capitalist in the Fei-Ranis world is in the same position in the Neo-Classical world.

VII. Patterns of Development and 1975 Chenery-Syrquin Study

Labor Surplus Models teach that transformation from agriculture to industry is the story of modern economic growth told for, and by, all countries. So, it is tempting to inquire whether there are quantitative patterns of growth true for all countries. For example, might it be the case that the share of agriculture in GNP remains at or above X% until *per capita* GNP rises above $Y, and that once the $Y *per capita* GNP threshold is reached, the share begins to fall below X%? This inquiry is precisely the one pursued by the great development economists, Hollis B. Chenery and Moises Syrquin.[18]

They answered the question in the negative. No pattern held true for all countries, though patterns could be discerned within three categories of countries: large countries (those whose population in 1960 exceeded 15 million), small countries that emphasized the export of primary commodities (*i.e.*, agricultural and mining products), and small countries that focused on industrial exports. Since Chenery and Syrquin published their results, other development economists have pursued the same inquiry using similar methodologies. But, no constant, enduring quantitative relationship linking agricultural and industrial shares of GNP with *per capita* GNP levels exists. While the shares to change with *per capita* GNP growth, the precise transformation points are diverse.

To be sure, in any diverse pattern, an average can be calculated, and development economists have done just that.[19] The average *per capita* GNP thresholds of note are $600 and $1,600 (in 1983 prices). At a *per capita* GNP level of $600, the share of primary commodities in GNP in large developing countries (those with a population of roughly 15–50 million) begins to fall below 32%. At a *per capita* GNP level of $1,600, that share averages 19%.

---

18. Their classic work on this question is *Hollis B. Chenery & Moises Syrquin, Patterns of Development, 1950–1970* (1975). *See also* Hollis B. Chenery & Lance J. Taylor, *Development Patterns: Among Countries and Over Time*, REVIEW OF ECONOMICS AND STATISTICS 391–416 (November 1968).

19. *See* GILLIS ET AL., 51.

There is a considerable risk in the calculation of an average. The average is what a country might expect, on the understanding that there is a large variance possible. But, it is not at all designed as a target that embodies an efficient allocation of productive resources. A height-weight chart on the wall in the office of a physician contains broad ranges for acceptable individual health. Averages in patterns of growth across countries and over time must be viewed with the same flexible attitude.

Chapter 16

Trade, Growth, and Poverty:
Export Orientation[1]

I. Industrialization and Unbalanced Growth

Models of economic growth — including labor Surplus Models, such as the Fei-Ranis Model or of any other ilk (discussed in a different Chapter) — presume a clear understanding of what "industrialization" means. In a vague sense, the casual observer typically thinks of building factories and "making stuff." But, it is important to be precise. What, exactly, is involved in the process of industrialization? The details of the answer vary from among less developed countries. And, the question raises the matter of emphasis — of balanced versus unbalanced growth, which is worth considering now.

Yet, there is a key question: "what economic benefit is there for a small, impoverished country to join, or participate in, the GATT-WTO system?" Typically, behind this question lies a hidden presumption: the country does not yet have a diversified economy. At best, it may be competent at exporting one or two products. WTO entry means relaxing tariff and NTBs, not only on those products, but also on a large number of other items. Participation means subjecting the country to the possibility of being named as a respondent in a remedial action — an AD, CVD, or safeguard suit — brought by a complainant. Often, the complainant will be a major export market for producers in the respondent — otherwise why bring the case in the first place?

The most obvious answer is membership in the WTO not only will help the small, impoverished country realize comparative advantages (because of existing and planned commitments of the Members to trade liberalization), but also will ensure rich, powerful countries are bound by the same set of rules for resolving disputes (namely, the Uruguay Round *DSU*). That is the answer that has been sold to SVEs, such as Tonga, which have acceded to the WTO. However, this answer rarely is persuasive, and it even may be naïve. As for the idea of a level playing field created

---

1. Documents References:
   (1) *Havana (ITO) Charter* Preamble
   (2) GATT Preamble
   (3) *WTO Agreement* Preamble

by the *DSU* in dispute resolution, the questioner advocating developing country interests is sure to rebut with two points.

First, the hegemonic powers do not always "play by the rules," particularly as regards compliance—witness the 1997 *Bananas*, 1998 *Beef Hormones*, and 2000 *Foreign Sales Corporations* cases (discussed in separate Chapters) in the first five years of experience with the *DSU*. Second, Third World countries do not yet, for the most part, have the resources—finances or human capital—to prosecute or defend cases.

More fundamentally, the answer is wanting because of a fear (sometimes unstated) in the mind of the questioner that the less developed country will lose its few comparative advantages, and never be able to develop any more advantages. Reciting the virtues of free trade based on the comparative advantage model actually can exacerbate these fears. In the Smith-Ricardo world, the focus is on development of a sector in which a less developed country has a comparative advantage, based on cost. But, what if making decisions based solely on relative cost advantages reinforces the country's position of dependence on just one or a few sectors?

Neither the Fei-Ranis Labor Surplus Model, nor the Two-Sector Neo-Classical Model (discussed in a separate Chapter), explains what industrial sectors ought to be encouraged. Precisely on what manufactured goods should a poor country concentrate its resources as it moves toward, and beyond, the Transition Point? One of the most famous development economists, Hollis B. Chenery (1918–1994), worked on this problem in the 1960s through 1980s.[2] Among his classic publications are *Patterns of Development: 1950–1970*, published in 1975,[3] and *Industrialization and Growth: A Comparative Study*, published in 1986.[4]

Among many leaders of less developed countries, the conventional wisdom is industrialization mandates a certain growth pattern, and that pattern typically requires emphasis on heavy industries like cars, steel, and petrochemicals. The consequent policy prescription is support for nurturing these infant domestic industries with subsidies and trade barriers. In a word, Chenery says "no" to this conventional wisdom.

Perhaps the most important insight from his studies is that no single pattern of industrialization exists that "must" be followed by a less developed country as it

---

2. The discussion of Chenery's work draws in part on Malcolm Gillis, Dwight H. Perkins, Michael Roemer & Donald R. Snodgrass, Economics of Development 61-62 (4th ed. 1996). [Hereinafter, Gillis et al.]

3. At the time, Mr. Chenery was Vice President for Development Policy at the World Bank, and co-authored *Patterns of Development* with another famous development economist, Moises Syrquin, then a Senior Lecturer in Economics at Bar-Ilan University in Israel.

4. Mr. Chenery co-authored *Industrialization and Growth* with Professor Syrquin, and another acclaimed development economist, Sherman Robinson. *See also* Hollis B. Chenery & Lance J. Taylor, *Development Patterns: Among Countries and Over Time*, 50 Review of Economics and Statistics 391-416 (November 1968).

tries to climb out of poverty. Indeed, his work is a testament to the impossibility of identifying a handful of patterns of transformation from an agrarian economy to an industrial economy to which a poor country "must" adhere. To say that industrialization necessarily requires domestic car, steel, petrochemical industries, and therefore support and trade policies to ensure their success against potential foreign competition, simply is untrue. (It might be remembered here that Belgium, Denmark, Finland, Holland, Norway, and Switzerland have no domestic car, steel, or petrochemical industries, yet they are highly developed countries.) There are "horses for courses." Each country can industrialize in a manner that best suits its circumstances.

Chenery's work is not a tribute to unplanned industrialization. As just intimated, there are certain factor endowments that might lead a country to stress growth in a particular industry early on. For example, the existence of a large pool of unskilled surplus agricultural workers, coupled with a lack of sophisticated machine tools, would suggest focusing on low-value added products. Garments made with foot-pedal sewing machines might be an example; civilian aircraft ought to be avoided for the time being.

Footwear might be another example. But, these sorts of examples bring us back to the problem of diversification. A less developed country that produces only garments or shoes surely will make more than it needs for domestic consumption.[5] Worse yet, if farm incomes have not risen during this early phase of industrialization—because labor surplus still exists in the agricultural sector, hence in terms of the Fei-Ranis Labor Surplus Model, owners of the garment and shoe factories still face a perfectly elastic labour supply curve—then farmers might not be able to afford the domestically-made shoes. The result might be the garment and shoe factories go bankrupt, because there is insufficient domestic demand for their product. Inventories pile up in the factory warehouses.

There are two ways out of this problem. The first strategy is "balanced growth," which may be coupled with an open economy. The second strategy is "unbalanced growth," coupled with an economy open to international trade. The distinction between them is seen in Graph 16-1. The line representing a balanced growth strategy suggests that a Third World country produces output in different sectors simultaneously, such as T&A and consumer electronics. Neither sector is emphasized at the expense of the other. The line representing an unbalanced growth strategy is a path of focusing on the output of one sector at one phase of industrialization, and another sector at a later phase.

First, why not attempt a balanced growth strategy, which as its name suggests, means that more than just one or two industrial products are produced? It directly

---

5. This discussion of the balanced growth strategy draws on GILLIS ET AL., 62. The discussion of the unbalanced growth strategy draws on *id.* at 63. Graph 60-5, comparing the strategies, is found on *id.* at 64.

Graph 16-1. Balanced versus Unbalanced Growth Strategies

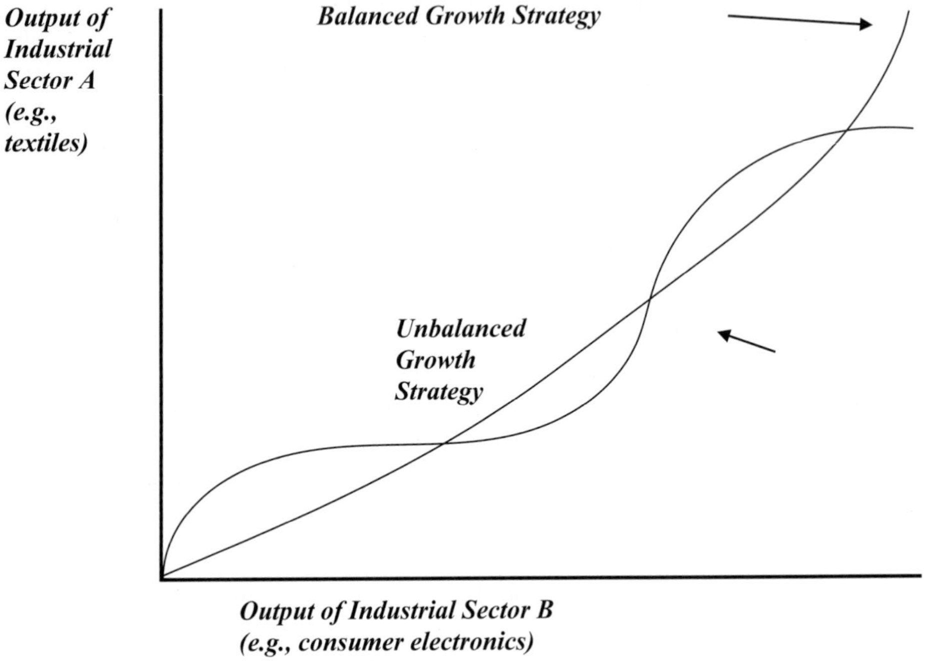

Output of Industrial Sector A (e.g., textiles)

Balanced Growth Strategy

Unbalanced Growth Strategy

Output of Industrial Sector B (e.g., consumer electronics)

addresses the problem of a non-diversified economy. Advocates of this strategy include Ragnar Nurkse (1907–1959) and Paul Rosenstein-Rodan (1902–1985), who wrote about it in the 1940s and 1950s.[6] Factories to produce other low-value added industrial products—say bicycles and calculators—could be built. Workers in the garment and shoe factories buy the domestically-made bicycles and calculators, and conversely the bicycle and calculator workers buy garments and shoes. Each sector supports the other, and industrialization proceeds in a balanced way.

In addition, if the economy is open to international trade, industrial surpluses could be exported in exchange for agricultural commodities, or for industrial products the country is not yet producing. Note there also is balance on both the demand and supply side. The factories that are built respond to consumption patterns (the demand side), and also help alleviate shortages of necessary products (the supply side).

While it seems to be straightforward common sense, balanced growth strategy is not without critics. In the words of some development economists, it is "a counsel of despair."[7] It tells a Third World country that if it is not successful in starting

---

6. *See* RAGNAR NURKSE, PROBLEMS OF CAPITAL FORMATION IN UNDERDEVELOPED COUNTRIES (1953); Paul N. Rosenstein-Rodan, *Problems of Industrialization of Eastern and Southeastern Europe,* ECONOMIC JOURNAL (June-September 1943), *reprinted in* THE ECONOMICS OF UNDERDEVELOPMENT (A.N. Agarwala & S.P. Singh eds., 1963).

7. GILLIS ET AL., 62.

up several industries simultaneously, then it is condemned to its status. That is a difficult task for less developed countries, which by definition face factor resource constraints and limited funding. When these problems are compounded by political instability, corruption, and a breakdown in law and order, balanced growth is a quixotic prescription. The balanced growth strategy demands a "big push," or "critical minimum effort."[8] That "push" or "effort" must be sustained for years. Many countries cannot possibly meet this challenge.

Why not, then, fall back on the second strategy? This alternative also seems to accord with common sense economic ideas, namely, comparative advantage. A less developed country can specialize in the production of one or a few industrial products, and then export the surplus of industrial goods in exchange for agricultural commodities. That way, any slack in domestic demand can be offset through export demand (assuming, of course, the export markets are open and not suffering from recession or depression). Overseas consumers recognize the comparative advantage of the less developed country in garments and shoes, and begin buying them. Inventory levels fall, and the incomes of the factory workers rise, because of an open economy, *i.e.,* one that participates in the multilateral (or at least regional) trading system.

Clearly, the second strategy is one of unbalanced growth, because industrialization proceeds for one or a few goods, but not for several goods simultaneously. One of the greats in the theory of development economics, Albert O. Hirschman (1915–2013), argues in favor of it in his 1958 book, *The Strategy of Economic Development*. He calls forth several historical examples to make the case that many countries have specialized in a select few industrial sectors at the early stages of economic growth.

Contrary to the fears of balanced growth advocates like Nurkse and Rosenstein-Rodan, his work indicates that in most instances, Hirschman's work suggests concentration has not led to over-production and under-consumption of industrial output. After all, in a Third World country in early stages of development, the problem is one of too few factories, not too many. Hence, excess production ought to be less of a worry than an inability to meet demand.

During early phases of industrialization, the difficulties are setting factories up fast, accelerating the shift of surplus labor from the agricultural to industrial sector, training that surplus labor for factory jobs, positioning them in those jobs, ensuring a steady flow of output of satisfactory quality, and getting that output to market. These difficulties are made all the more poignant by the fact that the output produced—say, garments and shoes—has millions of ready, willing, and able buyers, both domestically and overseas. That output tends to be simple, low-priced manufactured necessity items. Failure to meet demand in a timely fashion could mean that another less developed country will capture the market. Consider competition between Bangladesh and Vietnam in textiles, or Brazil and India in shoes.

---

8. GILLIS ET AL., 63.

Suppose this forecast proves wrong for a Third World country. It could be wrong for a variety of reasons. First, export demand might not materialize, or might slacken after a period of robustness.

Second, the industry in which the Third World country seeks a comparative advantage faces competition from imports. This competition might not be severe enough to undermine the possibility of gaining a comparative advantage in the future. But, it might be serious enough to give credence to calls for protection for a few years until the industry grows out of its infancy.

Third, to take a more politicized example, the leadership in a Third World country might seek to avoid depending on foreign markets in wealthy countries for industrial product demand? Following a school of thought in development economics called "Dependency Theory" (discussed later), which warns of excess reliance by peripheral (*i.e.*, Third World) countries on "center" (*i.e.*, First World) countries through trade, the leaders may attempt to eschew export-import links with developed countries. The mixed political and economic aim is to avoid reliance for export earnings and, thereby, industrialization, on the center. To fall into dependence is to surrender to neo-colonialism, whereby modern economic growth in the developed country is held hostage to the interests of politicians and corporate chieftains in the First World.

One problem with both balanced and unbalanced growth is that they do not tell us what to do about the agricultural sector. Balance between this sector and the industrial sector is important too. The Fei-Ranis Labor Surplus Model teaches us that those incomes in the agricultural sector will remain flat, at subsistence level, until the Transition Point. Thereafter, it predicts the terms of trade of industry to agriculture will shift against the industrial sector. Exactly how to manage this transition, and deal with the shift in the terms of trade, is not immediately obvious from either strategy.

Possibly in the long run, most countries end up with a balanced growth strategy. Some countries might use this strategy throughout the course of modern economic growth. A large number of Third World countries might not, for the reasons mentioned above—namely, the reality of one or a few comparative advantages, coupled with an inability to mount a big push or critical minimum effort. In the end, however, even the countries that pursue unbalanced growth early on in the industrialization process will move towards a more balanced strategy. Why?

Because, to borrow Hirschman's concept, there are "backward" and "forward" linkages in every economy. In brief, because of his confidence that linkages ultimately would compel balance in the industrialization process, Hirschman was not overly troubled with unbalanced growth early on in this process.

Suppose a country concentrates on the development of a steel industry. As steel output increases, economic actors—namely, entrepreneurs—will take note of this ability and set up factories producing goods that take advantage of the domestic steel output. So, for instance, they might set up factories making chain-link fences, pipes, and cars. The linkage is a forward one—forward from the steel sector to the steel-using sector. What about backward linkages? To make steel, the key inputs are iron, coke, and blast furnaces. Iron and coke must be mined, and blast furnaces must be produced. Thus, entrepreneurs will step into to provide the necessary inputs for the nascent steel industry—iron and coke mines will open up, as will blast furnace factories.

When, exactly, the linkages are made and balanced economic growth proceeds will vary from one less developed country to the next. Where there is unbalanced growth, international trade may play a role: steel output will be exported; and iron, coke, and blast furnaces will be imported. Where there is balanced growth, there may be less reliance on exports and imports, simply by virtue of domestic demand for steel output and domestic supplies of steel inputs. The point is that with unbalanced growth, entrepreneurial opportunities created by linkage pressures (the availability of steel output and the need for steel inputs) will serve as a check against long-run imbalances. To be sure, if entrepreneurs are not free to seize these opportunities—for political or economic reasons—then the imbalances can remain.

II. Growth, Poverty, and Kuznets Inverted U Theory

Before addressing the relationship between trade and poverty, consider the relationship between growth and poverty. Here, two preliminary points are relevant. The first point concerns the relationship between growth rates and income levels. It is sometimes handy to know two mathematical relationships. One relationship is that if *per capita* GNP grows at 2% annually, then average *per capita* GNP will double in 35 years. A second relationship is that if *per capita* GNP grows at 4% annually, then average *per capita* GNP will double in less than one generation (which is roughly 20 years).

These relationships highlight the relevance of the rate of growth to rises in income levels. They also reinforce common sense, namely, faster growth means reaching a higher level of income faster. And, the relationships help us understand some of the tremendous gaps within the Third World. Since 1965, virtually all of less developed countries with annual *per capita* GNP growth rates in excess of 4% have been in Asia. In contrast, nearly all of the countries with declining average *per capita* GNP levels, which reflect declining growth rates, have been in Sub-Saharan Africa.

The second point is about the relationship between growth and poverty. As my brief account of *Trade Liberalization and Poverty* implies, during the last several decades, both academic and practicing development economists have devoted increasing attention not only to the relationship between growth and income, but

Graph 16-2. Kuznets Inverted U Theory (Kuznets Curve)

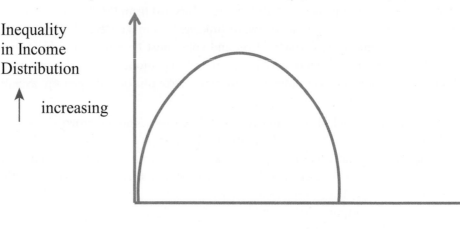

also to the closely related subject of the relationship between growth and poverty. Thus, Professor Simon Kuznets (1901–1985) did far more than develop the title "modern economic growth." He also invented the so-called "Inverted U Theory."[9] Graph 16-2 depicts this Theory, and the curve depicted therein is widely known as the "Kuznets Curve."

As its name suggests, the Inverted U Theory states that the relationship between (1) growth in *per capita* GNP and (2) inequality in the distribution of income resembles the letter "U," but upside down. In other words, as *per capita* GNP rises, with industrialization, inequality in the distribution of income also rises — at least initially, and for a while. This state of affairs is found in many growing less developed countries. However, the increases in inequality tend to level off over time, with continued and advanced industrialization, as *per capita* GNP continues to rise to intermediate levels. Thereafter, further advances in *per capita* GNP lead to declines in inequality. That state of affairs, in which income inequality is reduced with increases in *per capita* GNP, characterizes many developed countries.

A discussion of empirical tests of Kuznets Inverted U Theory is beyond the present scope. But, it is worth pointing out that the Theory has received considerable support.[10]

That support comes from cross-sectional data, especially drawn from Latin American countries. To be sure, the Theory remains controversial, and some time-series analyses do not reveal a discernible inverted U. Moreover, country case studies are not always consistent with the Theory. Consider Sri Lanka, a poor country with relatively equal income distribution. It can be contrasted with Korea and

---

9. This discussion draws on GILLIS ET AL., 80-81.

10. *See* GILLIS ET AL., 81, and the studies cited therein.

Taiwan, which have been able to achieve rapid economic growth without excessively unequal income distribution.

III. Piketty Critique of Kuznets Curve

By no means is the Kuznets Inverted U Theory universally accepted. French economist Thomas Piketty (1971–), for example, takes issue with the argument of Kuznets that long-term inequality levels off thanks to structural economic changes, namely, the transformation of the labor force from low-productivity agriculture to high-productivity industry, and technological progress associated with that transformation. Piketty argues that wage inequality does not, in fact, decrease — only the values of estates do, if there are deliberate policy interventions such as progressive income taxation — and points to a bevy of data showing how (for example) inequality in late 20th and early 21st century America has returned to the level of the 1930s. His data, of course, are more up to date than those of Kuznets, who worked in the 1950s.

Thus, in *Capital in the Twenty-First Century* (2013), Piketty argues that inequality is endemic to Capitalism, and specifically that in developed countries, the rate of return to capital consistently exceed the rate of economic growth, resulting in ever-greater wealth inequality. He calls for appropriate interventions, including a progressive, global tax on wealth, without which this inequality not only will it persist, but also will undermine political stability.

IV. Terms of Trade

Does participation in the international trading system help or hinder a country's economic growth? This question obviously concerns the trade-growth linkage. One statistic often examined is the TOT, or more technically, the "Net Barter TOT."

International trade and development economists define the Net Barter TOT as the ratio of export to import prices. That is:

$$\text{TOT} = \frac{\text{Index of prices of merchandise exported by a country}}{\text{Index of prices of merchandise imported by a country}}$$
$$= \frac{P_{EX}}{P_{IM}}$$

The TOT measures the purchasing power of a country, in the sense of how much it can buy (import) from what it sells (exports). Thus, the TOT as defined above also are known as the "net barter terms of trade."

The TOT of a country are "unfavorable" or "deteriorating" if prices of imported merchandise rise, prices of exported merchandise fall, or both. The intuition is readily apparent. Import prices are akin to expenditures, and export prices are akin to revenue, whether of a household or firm. High or rising expenses, low or falling revenues, or both can imperil a family or business. So, too, it is for a country. One ill effect of unfavorable TOT is a decline in the share of world trade accounted for by a country.

Advocates of Export Orientation policy (discussed below) argue the TOT of a country rise through trade. In contrast, advocates of Import Substitution (also discussed below), being export pessimists, point out instances in which increased trade led to deteriorating TOT of a country. Notwithstanding this policy debate, TOT are a useful tool to explore the effects of trade on an economy.

Occasionally, international trade and development economists sometimes rely on a statistic known as the "Income TOT," which is closely related to the Net Barter TOT. The arithmetic formula for Income TOT is:

$$\frac{P_{EX} \times Q_{EX}}{P_{IM}}$$

where Q_{EX} = quantity of goods exported

Hence, the numerator represents export revenues (the price of exports multiplied by the volume of those exports). Studying Income TOT is it reveals export revenues generated by a country, which the country can use to pay for imports. That is, it gives a more direct sense than Net Barter TOT of what a country earns from trade and, thereby, what it can afford to spend.

V. Export Orientation versus Import Substitution

In their struggle to boost growth and cut poverty, developing and least developed countries have two basic choices about trade policy: Export Orientation or Import Substitution. That was true before the advent of GATT, and remains true with GATT and the WTO agreements. But, as the GATT-WTO system is predicated on free trade principles, they incline toward Export Orientation, while disciplining Import Substitution. The choices are radically different, in both underlying theory and practical implications.

Export Orientation is premised on Ricardo's Law of Comparative Advantage, and on a presumed causal link between trade and growth. This policy calls for openness to trade, not only to implement the Law and thereby realize the net gains of which Ricardo wrote, but also to boost national income. Through free (or freer) trade, a country specializes in production of goods in which it has a comparative cost advantage, leading to an efficient division of labor and allocation of resources. It attains higher levels of social utility from a wider range of consumption choices at cheaper prices than would exist without trade.

Advocates of this policy generally agree with the proposition "the more trade, the better." For them, trade is an engine of growth, a key stimulant for output. Their paragon is the East Asian "Tigers"—Hong Kong, Korea, Singapore, and Taiwan.[11] Their policy is to expand overseas markets, and dismantle domestic trade barriers. They look for toward FTAs or CUs, and multilateral deals, and look askance at protectionist constituencies.

In contrast, Import Substitution is premised on a Marxist-oriented view trade with rich nations is inherently exploitative. Such trade reinforces an international division of labor that confines poor countries in agricultural. They plant, grow, and harvest primary products, and extract natural resources, the world market prices of which tend to be low and gyrate. Rich countries benefit from cheap food and natural resources coming from poor countries, and specialize in high-value added manufactured merchandise, as well as services. Whereas Export Orientation advocates agree trade is an engine of growth, Import Substitution proponents are "export pessimists." Export pessimism means trade cannot propel a country to higher levels of growth.

Import Substitution advocates argue that for the Third World, "the more trade, the worse," because it traps poor countries in the role of sending raw materials to the mighty industrial and service economies of the First World. Consequently, they call for tariff and non-tariff barriers against imports, and favor local production over foreign-made goods. That way, infant industries in poor countries have the chance to grow, and the risk of dependence on manufactured items and services from rich nations is minimized. They tout as successful exemplars India and some Latin American countries.

VI. Market-Based Theory for Export Orientation

Export Orientation calls for reliance on international markets to stimulate growth. In contrast to the interventionist role of a government in implementing Import Substitution, with Export Orientation a government takes a neutral stance. Its primary focus is creation and maintenance of an environment favorable to the free market, with key features of this environment being the rule of law and transparency to create as level a playing field as possible for all economic actors (large or small, foreign or domestic).

In particular, a government does not encourage domestic industries to source inputs from in-country suppliers, nor does it promote (*e.g.*, through protection, subsidies, or tax breaks) export-oriented over other industries. It minimizes trade barriers, ensuring tariffs and quotas are low or zero on inputs needed for finished

11. The list of Tigers varies somewhat depending on the study. In a 1993 publication, the World Bank identified seven Tigers, and used yet another acronym, HPAEs, for "High Performing Asian Economies."

products, and eliminates artificial disincentives to exportation (*e.g.*, export licenses or taxes). The government relies on market forces—particularly world market price signals—to determine the most efficient, profitable allocation of factors of production (capital, human capital, labor, land, and technology). The result is the manufacture of goods in which a comparative advantage exists, or reasonably can be expected through private capital investment.

Export Orientation draws on the intellectual heritage of the Classical economist, David Ricardo (1772–1823), and Neo-Classical economists. Net gains to a country from trade liberalization matter. Specialization of production leads to an efficient allocation of factor resources based on comparative cost advantage. The source of relative cost advantages is relative endowments of factor resources among countries. Labor-rich countries focus on labor-intensive goods, land-abundant countries on land-intensive goods, and so on.

Initially, many developing countries find their comparative advantage in labor-intensive, low-value added manufactured products, along with primary agricultural products. As the skill level of the labor force develops, and as technology is imported, the country should be able to move into higher-value added manufacturing that relies more intensively on human capital than before. Overall, this focus contrasts with Import Substitution, which typically involves production of capital-intensive goods even if a country is not relatively well endowed with capital.

Moreover, Export Orientation takes advantage of a scale effect. The world market for virtually every product is by definition larger than the market in any one country (the rare exceptions being where a product is produced and consumed in only one country). Producers can, therefore, build productive capacity, employ more factors of production, become efficient and develop economies of scale, all with a view to serving a larger world, rather than a smaller domestic, market. In turn, production of an exportable surplus may be traded for products in which a comparative advantage is lacking.

Through exportation, an economy advances from an agrarian-based to a modern industrial one. Complementing it is FDI, which is attracted to a country in part by the neutral stance of its government, and flows in response to market forces. In keeping with the Product Life Cycle Hypothesis, put forth by a leading scholar of MNCs, Professor Raymond Vernon (1913–1999), FDI may lead to shifts in the locus of production. After a product is invented and marketed in a developed country, and the manufacturing process becomes standardized, production moves to developing countries. IP the product embodies is transferred to local companies (or the original periods of protection expire). Then, developing countries move through, at a phase behind developed countries, the Cycle.

As for consumers, they have before them a wider array of alternatives from which to choose, at lower prices, than without trade. The gains from production specialization and higher consumption outweigh losses from tariff revenue or quota rents, which are no longer reaped with free trade, plus losses to producers whose enterprises are shut down or downsized because of a lack of comparative advantage. In principle, the "winners" from trade can compensate the "losers" by agreeing to share some of their gain.

Another point in favor of Export Orientation concerns TOT. In theory trade liberalization should improve the TOT of a country. In respect of import prices, P_{IM}, as well domestic like and substitute product prices, they should fall for two reasons. (Recall P_{IM} is the denominator of the TOT ratio.) First, trade liberalization means a drop in tariff and non-tariff barriers. Second, this liberalization leads to increased competition. As regards export prices, P_{EX}, they should rise with freer trade. (Recall P_{EX} is the numerator of the TOT ratio.) The demand of foreign consumers supplements demand by local consumers for the merchandise in question. With more consumers after the same products, the price of the products should rise (assuming all other factors are held constant, *i.e.*, *ceteris paribus*, most notably, product supply). Thus, Export Orientation proponents argue greater openness should improve the TOT of a country.

Not surprisingly, the theory of Export Orientation also relies on the classical and neo-classical economic critique of tariff and non-tariff barriers. To recap, this theory demonstrates such barriers impose a net welfare cost on a country in comparison with the free-trade equilibrium. Tariffs and quotas provide the protected sector with more producer surplus than before (*i.e.*, producer's earn more than the marginal cost of production), and offer the government tariff revenue or the protected sector quota rents. These benefits are outweighed by the loss of consumer surplus, which means there is a decline in the number of consumers willing and able to pay a higher price for the protected product than is charged. Protection raises that price, and consequently cuts into consumer surplus. The net negative effect counsels against increasing trade barriers, and indicates dismantling such barriers, even unilaterally, is economically rationale.

Export Orientation also is backed by the promise of dynamic gains from trade. When a country imports goods, it also imports ideas and IP the goods embody. Domestic entrepreneurs may be encouraged to enter the market and make a like product. Existing producers may be spurred by the competition from overseas. Foreign investors may enter the market to make the product. The result is higher output, which generates surplus income, and thereby savings to be channeled into investment. That new investment can improve production techniques and quality, leading to further output and innovation.

VII. Risk of Immiserizing Growth

To be sure, export orientation entails a risk of immiserizing growth, especially as regards primary commodities, if a country is a large enough supplier of a particular commodity (because increased exports of the product could drive down world market prices). Professors Harry G. Johnson (1923–1977), in 1955, and working independently, Jagdish Bhagwati (1934–), in 1958, developed the concept of "immiserizing growth."[12] They meant a scenario in which an exporting country becomes worse off after economic growth than before economic growth.

That scenario could occur from export-oriented growth that causes a fall in the TOT of the exporting country. Of course, TOT deterioration could happen only if that exporting country is sufficiently influential in one or more export markets to cause the TOT deterioration, in particular, it is such a large supplier of a commodity that its exports cause an outward shift in the world supply curve of that commodity, and thus a fall in the price of that commodity (*ceteris paribus*). Any benefit from GDP growth associated with that country's exports is more than offset by the decline in the TOT. In effect, the country is a victim of its own success—its growth immiserates (*i.e.*, impoverishes, or makes miserable) itself.

Nevertheless, the remedy for immiserizing growth is not import substitution. Rather, it is export diversification. That is, the country should diversify away from exports of the commodities that cause immiserizing growth, and into manufactured goods.

VIII. Evidence for Export Orientation

To what extent does empirical evidence support Export Orientation? The famously cited examples of success are the East Asian Tigers. Within each Tiger, the general cultural, economic, and political environment is favorable to Export Orientation. In particular, the Tigers benefit from a mix of factors:

(1) *Sound Macroeconomic Management*

Fiscal expenditures are sensible (not profligate or grossly imbalanced), taxation simple and reasonably low (sometimes involving a flat tax), and monetary policy stable to ensure low levels of inflation. Government commitment to these policies is credible, hence businesses can rely on certainty and predictability in macroeconomic management.

(2) *Strong Infrastructure*

Communication networks, port facilities, transportation links, and utilities support economic growth. The government attends to needed upgrades.

(3) *Free Labor Markets*

Markets for factors of production, particularly labor, are flexible. Government do not impose minimum wages or working conditions, nor employment requirements, on businesses, and discourages (even fights)

---

12. *See* Harry G. Johnson, *Economic Expansion and International Trade*, 23 MANCHESTER SCHOOL 95–112 (1955); Jagdish Bhagwati, *Immiserizing Growth: A Geometrical Note*, 25 REVIEW OF ECONOMIC STUDIES 201-205 (June 1958).

unionization. Consequently, labor can move fairly quickly to adjust to new incentives associated with changed economic conditions.

(4) *Strong Work Ethic*

Hard work, dedication, and sacrifice of personal interest for group and national benefits are long-standing cultural values.

(5) *Memories of Suffering*

Memories of devastation of the Second World War are poignant. No one wants a repeat of that suffering.

(6) *Anti-Communism*

The post–Second World War generation does not want to fall victim to communism, and a strong national economy is consistent with a strong defense. Former Singaporean Prime Minister Lee Kuan Yew (1923–2015, PM, 1959–1990) adds the American defense umbrella, including keeping communism at bay in North Korea and Vietnam, gave the Tigers the breathing space they needed to develop.

(7) *Pragmatism*

With few exceptions (*e.g.*, rice), people do not hold a sentimental attachment to goods or industries. As their country moves up the value-added production chain, they know jobs are lost in one sector, but look forward to new opportunities in others.

(8) *Relatively Low Corruption*

While not free from corruption, and in many instances plagued by so-called "crony capitalism," the Tigers have not inflicted the damage on themselves that the countries of the Indian Subcontinent and Sub-Saharan Africa have through monstrous levels of corruption.

Add to these factors a strong scaffolding of the rule of law, and it is hardly surprising the Tigers are "Exhibit A" for successful implementation of Export Orientation.

Also, not surprising is the large number of empirical studies about the Tigers, and Export Orientation more generally. Had the Tigers "figured it out"? Is Export Orientation "the way to go"? Among the near-classic studies, which tend to corroborate each other and support Tiger-style Export Orientation are the following:

(1) ***1983 Krueger Study on Employment***

In 1983, renowned development economist Anne O. Krueger (1934–) examined data on 10 countries for 1960–1973.[13] Her focus was the relationship between trade policy and jobs: does Export Orientation generate more jobs than Import Substitution? She studied the ratio of (1) labor per unit of

---

13. ANNE O. KRUEGER ET AL., TRADE AND EMPLOYMENT IN DEVELOPING COUNTRIES—SYNTHESIS AND CONCLUSIONS (VOL. 3) (1983).

value added to a good that is exported to (2) labor per unit of value added to a good that competes with imports, *i.e.*:

$$\frac{\text{Labor Used per unit of Value Added to Exportable Good}}{\text{Labor Used per unit of Value Added to Import-Competing Good}}$$

In theory, if Export Orientation generates more jobs than Import Substitution, then the ratio should exceed one, *i.e.*, there is more labor per dollar's worth of exports than labor per dollar's worth of import substitutes. This result should occur for two reasons.

First, export-oriented industries use a greater quantity of labor than import-competing industries. Second, export-oriented industries grow faster than import-substituting industries. To be sure, these ratios do not reveal the occupant profile or nature of the jobs. Happily, there is evidence to suggest in some countries the job-growth associated with Export Orientation benefits women. Unhappily, there is evidence to indicate in some countries the job growth is in low-pay, low-skill work. These shortcomings aside, Krueger's 1983 results are clear: in 9 of the 10 countries studied, the average ratio was 1.57. Moreover, only 1 country had a ratio below 1 (0.8).

(2) *1985 Krueger Study*

In 1985, Professor Krueger studied the overall economic performance of the East Asian Tigers — Hong Kong, Korea, Singapore, and Taiwan, against that of all countries also considered to be "middle income."[14] Does growth through industrialization and exportation "work"? The answer is clear. The Tigers grew more rapidly than the others in their income cohort. Despite 2 kinds of difficulties in the 1970s — a change in the TOT against middle income countries, and the oil price shocks of 1973 and 1979 — the Tigers boasted high growth rates and proved more resilient than the other countries. Moreover, income distribution remained fairly equitable in the Tigers.

However, Krueger offers an important caveat. The Tigers commenced their Export Orientation policies in the 1960s, but their success was made possible by more than just these policies. A combination of contributing factors mattered, including — significantly — the international economic climate.

First, for most of the 1960s and after, this climate was favorable to Export Orientation, because international trade in general expanded during this period. In part through successive GATT rounds, such as the Dillon, Kennedy, and Tokyo Rounds, tariffs and NTBs fell, especially in the markets

---

14. Anne O. Krueger, *The Experience and Lessons of Asia's Super Exporters, in* EXPORT-ORIENTED DEVELOPMENT STRATEGIES: THE SUCCESS OF FIVE NEWLY INDUSTRIALIZING COUNTRIES 210 (Vittorio Corbo, Anne O. Krueger & Fernando Ossa eds., 1985).

of major countries. Conversely, when countries with large populations and purchasing power, like the U.S., EU, and Japan, adopt protectionism policies, particularly in certain product markets through trade remedies like safeguards in response to import surges, export-oriented developing countries may be vulnerable—particularly if their consumer markets are too small to pick up any slack in demand. In other words, the Tigers had access to key markets. This access existed when the Tigers most needed it, namely, when they were developing a comparative advantage—initially, low-value added, labor-intensive products (*e.g.*, shoes and T&A), and later higher-value added, sophisticated products (*e.g.*, cars, consumer electronics, semi-conductors, steel).

Second, the Tigers did not face much competition for most manufactured items in which they sought to develop an international comparative advantage. The world market for such items was not saturated. Dozens of other countries did not simultaneously set up factories to build and export radios, TVs, and other consumer electronic products. Hence, prices were robust, and demand in developed countries was strong. Many countries in the Caribbean, Latin America, and Sub-Saharan Africa remain largely dependent on primary goods for export revenues. Consequently, their revenues and TOT are vulnerable to commodity price movements. Asked about diversifying into manufactured goods, a response they offer is the market for such goods now is crowded.

Third, international banking and securities markets developed, so that the Tigers (and particularly businesses within them) could obtain financial capital from overseas quicker and more cheaply than ever before. While these businesses drew on extended family savings in their early stages, as they grew they benefited from the flows of funds from developed countries channeled by the international capital markets. The former Merrill Lynch Dragon Fund was one of many examples of investing savings and retirement funds—at one point, roughly $1.5 billion—from developed countries in equities of approximately 120 East Asian companies.

Fourth, MNCs from developed countries became increasingly prominent actors in developing countries. The MNCs invested directly in countries like the Tigers. These countries had low trade barriers to inputs MNCs needed for production. They encouraged MNCs to source their inputs from them with a generally pro-business climate. As they established production facilities, they boosted local employment and transferred (to some degree) technology.

In sum, Krueger cautioned, the Tigers implemented the right policy at the right time. Their experience of the Tigers might well have been different had they tried Export Orientation during an era of declining values and volumes of trade.

(3) *1989 Balassa Study on Outward Orientation*

Béla Balassa (1928–1991), another highly regarded development economist, examined data on a large number of developing countries, classifying them as (1) outward-oriented economies, (2) inward-oriented economies, or (3) nearly closed economies.[15] In the first category are East Asian Tigers, namely, Korea, Singapore, and Taiwan. In the second category are major Latin American countries, including Argentina, Brazil, and Mexico. The third category included Chile, India, and Uruguay. His data covers two periods, 1960–1973, and 1973–1983. The first oil price shock, engineered by OPEC, occurred at the break point, 1973, and a second OPEC shock occurred in the middle of the second period, 1979. Balassa asked two questions: (1) which kind of economy grew faster, and (2) how did the different kinds of economies react to the oil price shocks?

The answer to both questions was unambiguous. In both periods, countries with outward-oriented economies grew faster than countries with economies in the other two categories. Moreover, outward-oriented economies were able to generate more employment and needed less capital per unit of output (in effect, their ICORs were lower) than the other kinds of economies.

To be sure, the oil price shock caused greater economic damage to outward-oriented economies than to other kinds of economies. That result was unsurprising, as an outward-oriented economy by definition is more vulnerable to changes in the prices of energy and major commodities than economies insulated from world markets. But, Balassa found the outward-oriented economies are more resilient than inward-oriented or essentially closed economies. They rebounded from the 1973 and 1979 shocks relatively quickly, and regained growth rates that were higher than the other types of economies. In fact, they also generated relatively higher savings rates, were less dependent on external borrowing, and had lower inflation rates.

(4) *1987 World Bank Study*

The World Bank published a study in 1987 of 41 developing countries.[16] Using Balassa-type categorization, the World Bank slotted them on a continuum depicted in Graph 16-3.

Consistent with the 1985 Krueger and 1987 Balassa studies, the World Bank found outward orientation associated with better economic performance than inward orientation. It concluded the evidence on this point is convincing. Similar follow-up studies show specific positive correlations between, on the one hand, openness to trade and FDI, and, on the other hand, growth

---

15. Bela Balassa, *Outward Orientation*, *in* Handbook of Development Economics vol. 2 1645-90 (H.B. Chenery & T.N. Srinivasan eds. 1989).

16. World Bank, World Development Report 1987 ch. 5 (1987).

Graph 16-3. Continuum of Openness

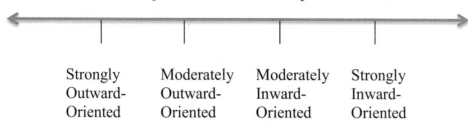

| Strongly Outward-Oriented | Moderately Outward-Oriented | Moderately Inward-Oriented | Strongly Inward-Oriented |

in income, growth in productivity, investment in human capital, investment in physical capital, and technology transfer.

(5) *1992 Dollar Study*

In 1992, David Dollar published his analysis of data from 1976–1985.[17] He compared Latin American and African countries against Asian countries. His question is counter-factual: if the Latin American and African countries had pursued Export Orientation and other policies similar to the policies implemented in Asia, what would their performance have been?

Professor Dollar estimated Latin America would have grown 1.5% faster, and Africa 2.1% faster, than they actually did. These countries would have been better off by mimicking pro-trade, Asian-style development strategy.

(6) *1995 Sachs-Warner Study*

Jeffrey Sachs (1954–), a high-profile, controversial economist in his own right, and Andrew Warner teamed up to publish a study in 1995 in which they developed criteria for the "openness" of an economy.[18] They asked whether open economies grew faster than closed economies.

Their answer was unambiguously affirmative. Almost all open countries grew faster than closed economies. They found annual *per capita* GDP growth rate in open economies exceeded that in closed economies by between 2.2% and 2.5%. Sachs and Warner also considered whether the timing, or extent, of remaining closed made a difference. The answer, again, was affirmative. Countries that maintained closed economies up until the mid-1970s, or later, were considerably more likely to suffer from serious macroeconomic problems, even crises, in the 1980s, than countries that were open or abandoned their closed policies by the mid-1970s.

Arguably, Sachs and Warner defined "openness" and "closed" in too rigid a manner. They constructed a "dummy" variable (*i.e.*, and on-off indicator,

17. *See* David Dollar, *Outward-Oriented Developing Economies Really Do Grow More Rapidly: Evidence from 95 LDCs, 1976-85*, 40 ECONOMIC DEVELOPMENT AND CULTURAL CHANGE 523-44 (April 1992).

18. *See* Jeffrey D. Sachs & Andrew Warner, *Economic Reform and the Process of Global Integration*, BROOKINGS PAPERS ON ECONOMIC ACTIVITY 1995(1) 1-95 (1995).

whose value is 1 when a condition such as openness, is true, and 0 when it is false) for "openness." To determine if an economy is "open," they looked at tariffs and quotas on intermediate and capital goods, the foreign exchange rate premium in the black (unofficial) market, the existence of export marketing boards, and whether a country was "socialist." They considered "closed" any economy that was not open for 20 years, from 1970 through 1989.

Similarly, their data set started in 1970. Therefore, by definition they exclude countries that benefited from Import Substitution in the 1950s and 1960s, and countries that opened up thereafter. (For instance, South Korea had been open since 1968, but Brazil did not open up until 1991, and India not until 1994.) These concerns led to a more general one, namely, the lack of standardized definitions of "openness" and "closed." In a June 1996 paper, Lant Pritchett pointed out there was no correlation among criteria for categorizing economies as outward- or inward-oriented.[19]

(7) *2012 International Collaborative Initiative on Trade and Employment (ICITE) Report*

Ten international organizations teamed up to study whether countries that keep their markets open to trade boost their economic growth by doing so.[20] Their 450-page *Report*, which drew on 14 studies conducted since 2000 in regions and countries across the globe, gave a resounding affirmative answer. Free trade, said the *Report*, can play a powerful role in driving growth and increasing employment. In particular, free trade improves labor productivity and, therefore, enhances average wage levels.

Between 1970 and 2000 manufacturing workers in countries with economies open to trade earned wages 3 to 9 times higher than their industrial counterparts in closed economies. This empirical evidence matches Neo-Classical Labor Economic Theory: wages should equal the marginal revenue product of labor, so, the greater the marginal contribution of a worker to the total revenue of a firm, the greater the wages of that worker, and this enhanced contribution reflects higher productivity stimulated by trade. The Report even argued that offshoring and outsourcing of jobs from developed to developing countries actually complement jobs in developed countries, and create new, higher-wage opportunities in developing one. Conversely, protectionist and discriminatory measures thwart growth and clog up labor markets.

---

19. Lant Pritchett, *Measuring Outward Orientation in LDCs: Can It Be Done?*, 49 Journal of Development Economics 307-336 (June 1996).

20. *See* International Collaborative Initiative on Trade and Employment, Policy Priorities for International Trade and Jobs (ICITE), May 2012, www.oecd.org; Rick Mitchell, *Report Says Free Trade Conducive to Creation of Jobs, Higher Wages*, 29 International Trade Reporter (BNA) 867-868 (31 May 2012).

Arguably, this result was predictable given the authors: AfDB, ADB, ECLAC, IADB, ILO, OAS, OECD, UNCTAD, World Bank, and WTO. In the wake of the 2008 global economic slump, these organizations were eager to promote a free trade agenda.

(8) *2012 Interagency Report on Agricultural Productivity Growth*

Also in 2012 came an *Interagency Report* to the G-20 nations on the positive effects of free trade on productivity in the agricultural sector.[21] This *Report* argued (1) substantial reductions in farm subsidies that distort patterns of production and trade, (2) eliminating export subsidies, and (3) strengthening disciplines on export restrictions boost growth in agricultural productivity, and do so in a sustainable way. This direct relationship is particularly pronounced for small, family farms.

Of course, as with the *ICITE Report*, given the authors of the research, perhaps the results were unsurprising. The research was coordinated by the OECD and FAO, was a collaborative effort among various non-governmental and international organizations, including the World Bank and WTO.

To be sure, the evidence is not all one way, as explained below.

IX. Evidence Questioning Export Orientation

• **1986 Bradford Critique**

Impressive as it is, the large volume of empirical data for openness is not unchallenged. A clever line of argument against it is historical revisionism. Were the East Asian Tigers as free trade oriented as their advocates and evidence suggests?

Among others, Colin Bradford, whose study appeared in 1986, tries to discern fact from fiction.[22] A closer inspection of the policies of the Four Tigers shows that only one of them—Hong Kong—followed Export Orientation in its pure form. The other three Tigers intervened to help their export industries, suggesting implementation of Export Orientation does not mean a *laissez-faire* approach to the economy.

Among the sins of these three are the following:

(1) Korea pursued some Import Substitution policies, and extended preferential, subsidized credit to export industries.

(2) Singapore gave tax incentives to certain industries engaged in exportation.

(3) Taiwan also gave tax incentives to certain export industries, controlled imports in a way to encourage exportation, and used government enterprises to provide one-third of all fixed investment.

---

21. *See Sustainable Agricultural Productivity Growth and Bridging the Gap for Small-Family Farms*, www.wto.org.

22. *See* Colin I. Bradford, Jr., *East Asian "Models:" Myths and Lessons, in* Development Strategies Reconsidered 115-128 (John P. Lewis & Valerina Kallab eds. 1986).

Bradford concludes it is erroneous to give all the credit for the success of the Tigers to Export Orientation. A fuller, more accurate rendition of their history reveals effective public- private partnerships to create conditions in which Export Orientation could be successful. In some instances, such as Korea, trade policy evolved, or switched, from Import Substitution in early stages of growth to Export Orientation in more advanced states. In other instances, trade policy involved a mix of the two policies, with Export Orientation predominating, but Import Substitution used to protect a one or a few infant industries. In sum, the Tigers benefited from good governance focused on economic growth, plus a national consensus in favor of making sacrifices to achieve growth.

A second significant thrust at the Export Orientation evidence is methodological and quantitative in nature. Critics point out much of the evidence is correlative, not causal, in nature. Because growth and other favorable macroeconomic trends accompany trade does not mean trade causes them. In turn, it is unclear exactly how strong the relationship between trade and growth is. That is, it is not easy to attribute a specified percentage of growth to trade, as distinct from other pro-growth factors (like, as in the Harrod-Domar and Solow Models, capital investment).

In fact, the causal direction is not clear. Perhaps growth is associated with, or causes trade. Empirical evidence about Israel and Mexico shows a causal relationship from trade to growth, but from growth to trade in Pakistan. To add to the confusion, evidence concerning some countries (*e.g.,* Colombia and Morocco) shows causation in each direction. Concerning other countries (*e.g.,* Brazil and Korea), data point to the importance of exogenous factors, and industrialization, in boosting trade and growth.

Even if growth causes trade, the precise causal path is not yet certain. A leading hypothesis is "trade causes growth," because trade means any or all of the following:

(1) Competition from imports.

(2) Greater FDI.

(3) Improved productivity.

(4) More learning (and, therefore, higher human capital).

(5) More efficient allocation of resources.

However, the relative importance of these causal chains is not clear. Of course, if the arrow runs in the opposite direction, then these factors, which occur with growth, could generate trade. Ultimately, there may be no single answer for all developing countries.

· **2014 Abbas Study**

Trade liberalization can distort economic growth, depending on the relative share of imports and exports. For example, a 2014 study by Shujaat Abbas of the University of Karachi, Pakistan examined the impact between 1990–2011 of trade liberalization on economic growth of developing countries (including Indonesia, Pakistan, Philippines, and Turkey) and LDCs (including Bangladesh, Botswana, Mauritius, and Morocco).[23] Abbas used a standard production function model, wherein growth of GDP, the dependent variable, depends on (*i.e.*, is a function of, f) 4 independent macroeconomic variables: the real capital stock (K), labor force (L), exports (X), and trade liberalization (TL). Abbas measured TL with a proxy, the ratio of total trade to GDP:

$$GDP = f[K, L, X, TL],$$

or in terms of a multivariable regression equation

$$GDP = \text{ß}i + \text{ß}_1 \cdot K + \text{ß}_2 \cdot L + \text{ß}_3 \cdot X + \text{ß}_4 \cdot TL + e$$

where the first ß term is the intercept, the remaining ß are coefficients on the respective macroeconomic variables and capture the significance, if any, of the causal effect of those variables on GDP, and e is the error term.

Using World Development Indicators data published by the World Bank, Abbas found a significant positive effect of the macroeconomic variables on GDP, except for TL. Indeed, TL had contradictory negative impacts, which Abbas said were consistent with economic theory: exports boosted GDP, whereas imports entailed an outflow of national income. So, if a higher degree of TL is due to exports over imports, then economic growth increases. Conversely, if TL rises because of an excess of imports over exports—that is, a balance of trade deficit—then economic growth deteriorates. For his sample of developing countries and LDCs, Abbas found TL adversely affected economic growth, because of increased imports and sluggish exports.

What policy advice does Abbas give? Developing countries need to correct their trade deficits by accelerating exports. To do so, they must reform domestic constraints on exports, and allocate scarce capital to labor-intensive production sectors based on their comparative advantages. Vitally, foreign trade barriers to their products must be reduced. "Let the market freely work," he concludes.

---

23. *See* Shujaat Abbas, *Trade Liberalization and Its Economic Impact on Developing and Least Developed Countries*, 13 Journal of International Trade Law and Policy number 3, 215–221 (2014). Abbas' review of the literature reveals that while most empirical studies show trade liberalization stimulates economic growth, that result depends on the country or regions studied (with greater positive effects for Asia and Latin America than for Africa), the ability of a country or region to take advantage of the benefit of openness (*e.g.*, by aligning the allocation of resources with social marginal cots and benefits, providing access to technology, utilizing economies of scale, and responding to competitive stimuli). Overall, he finds the causal nexus between trade liberalization and economic growth is not simple, straightforward, or invariant. *See id.*, 217.

• **Export Orientation and Poverty Alleviation?**

Perhaps most importantly of all to the issue of poverty alleviation is that the aforementioned studies do not focus on the link between trade and poverty. As impressive as they may be in showing trade generates growth, they do not resolve the question of whether that growth leads to a reduction in poverty.[24] Yet, whether economic growth, and increased trade in particular, contribute to decreases in poverty rates is an extraordinarily important question — as the example of Mexico suggests.

This question is ably discussed in a large number of sources. One is the excellent book *Trade Liberalization and Poverty: A Handbook* (2001), by Neil McCulloch, L. Alan Winters, and Xavier Cirera of the University of Sussex. *Trade Liberalization and Poverty* argues trade liberalization ultimately assists in poverty alleviation, and that it does so by stimulating growth. However, *Trade, Liberalization and Poverty* also explains poverty alleviation through trade is more effective if complimented by policies aimed directly at poverty reduction, *i.e.,* by policies that target the poor as beneficiaries. Such policies relate to education, infrastructure development (*e.g.,* transportation), financial services, prices of goods, wage levels, and employment opportunities.

Especially since roughly the 1990s, there is mounting evidence that growth associated with trade has led to greater socioeconomic stratification, particularly in terms of higher Gini coefficients. In other words, the belief "the rich get richer while the poor get poorer" has not been put to rest. Quite the contrary.

Even if that belief is true, trade *per se* is not necessarily to blame. A host of other variables influence whether gains from trade are captured by a cabal of elites, or distributed widely across a society. As *Trade Liberalization and Poverty* suggests, they include good governance, low corruption, and prudent policies on government infrastructure and social welfare spending, and appropriate taxation. Indeed, a 2016 internal World Bank briefing document illustrates these points.[25]

The World Bank admitted global free trade exacerbates inequality: "the effects of globalization on advanced economies is 'often uneven' and 'may have led to rising wage inequality.'" To address "adjustment costs" associated with trade, and avoid downward intra- and inter-generational socioeconomic mobility, the World Bank called for robust social security mechanisms and appropriate skills training to prepare for the jobs of the future. Yet, the Bank did not put all the blame for rising inequality in high-income countries on trade. The Bank linked about 20% of jobs

---

24. For a more direct study of the trade-poverty link, see, e.g., Matthew Kofi Ocran & Charles K.D. Adjasi, *Trade Liberalisation and Poverty: Empirical Evidence from Household Surveys in Ghana*, 8 JOURNAL OF INTERNATIONAL TRADE LAW & POLICY number 1, 40–59 (2009).

25. *See* Kamal Ahmed, *World Bank Admits Some Have Lost Out from Free Trade*, BBC NEWS, 6 October 2016, www.bbc.com/news/business-37580844.

lost in advanced economies to trade (especially, in the U.S., positions exposed to import competition from China), and the other 80% to technological change, automation, and the weakening of unions and worker groups that traditionally represent labor interests.

- **EPZs**

An important qualification to the theory of Export Orientation is how this policy is implemented in practice. It would be naïve to think every government takes a wholly laissez-faire approach to building export industries. In fact, many governments adopt modest measures of support. A common example is the creation of FTZs or EPZs. Led by Premier Deng Xiaoping (1904–1997), China commenced its movement away from strict socialism in the late 1970s by establishing 4 "special economic zones" in which market-oriented liberalizations took place.

Generally speaking, an FTZ or EPZ is a geographic location, or a firm or group of enterprises with acknowledged legal standing, to which special governmental treatment applies. This treatment consists of some or all of the following measures:

(1) *Lower Taxes*

Tax rates and/or valuations of assets to which tax rates are applied may be reduced or even eliminated. In the alternative, or in addition, tax holidays may be declared whereby no taxes are paid for a certain period (the holiday). Tax deductions from gross income, tax credits against tax liability, and/or accelerated tax write-offs (*e.g.*, depreciation schedules) may be offered.

(2) *Lower Trade Barriers*

Tariffs may be reduced or eliminated for goods imported for use as inputs in the production of exported products. Quotas, import licenses, and other non-tariff barriers may be liberalized or eliminated.

(3) *Rebates*

Refunds may be offered on all or a portion of certain taxes or tariffs paid, particularly for finished products that are exported.

(4) *Subsidies*

Certain infrastructure facilities, such as buildings, and utilities like power and water, as well as training programs for workers, may be subsidized.

The *quid pro quo* for special treatment is, of course, exportation of goods produced in the FTZ or EPZ. In effect, an FTZ or EPZ is a bargain between the public and private sectors. The government hopes to grow the economy and, in the process, create backward linkages and enhance the level of technology in the country. Businesses hope to grow in size and profitability, and gain market access overseas.

Whether this bargain—or, perhaps better put, partnership—between public and private sectors works depends on the overall political, economic, and legal environment of the FTZ or EPZ. In addition to China, Korea and Taiwan are cited as successful examples. However, in certain countries, exploitative working conditions (*e.g.*, long hours, low pay, and occupational health and safety risks), environmental damage, and gender discrimination (namely, excessive reliance on young female workers) have been concomitant with FTZ or EPZs. Moreover, preferences granted can create resentment within a country, and generate concerns about differential, or dualistic, economic development and widening domestic income gaps, as the Indian experiment with SEZs under reformist Prime Minister Manmohan Singh (1932–, PM, 2004–2014) suggested.

Chapter 17

Trade, Growth, and Poverty (Continued): Import Substitution[1]

I. Marxist Intellectual Heritage of Import Substitution

Like Export Orientation, Import Substitution has a powerful (if flawed) intellectual tradition. The inspiration is Marxist theory, and its various incarnations, which offer a radically different perspective on international trade from Capitalist models.

Few better articulated the Marxist maxim that trade is needed by capitalists to obtain inputs for finished goods, and as an outlet for over-production, than Cecil Rhodes (1853–1902), namesake of both Rhodesia (now Zimbabwe) and the Rhodes Scholarship. He declared:

> We must find new lands from which we can easily obtain raw materials and at the same time exploit the cheap slave labor that is available from the natives of the colonies. The colonies would also provide a dumping ground for the surplus goods produced in our factories.[2]

Similarly, in March 1899, a delegate to the French Association of Industry and Agriculture intoned that colonial power must be exercised

> to discourage in advance any signs of industrial development in our colonies, to oblige our overseas possessions to look exclusively to the mother country for manufactured products and to fulfill, by force if necessary, their natural function, that of a market reserved by right to the mother country's industry.[3]

The term "development," urge Marxists, is a euphemism for imperialism and colonialism.

---

1. Documents References:
   (1) *Havana (ITO) Charter* Preamble
   (2) GATT Preamble
   (3) *WTO Agreement* Preamble
   2. *Quoted in* Edward Goldsmith, *Development as Colonialism, in* THE CASE AGAINST THE GLOBAL ECONOMY 253–66 (Jerry Mander & Edward Goldsmith eds. 1996). [Hereinafter, *Development as Colonialism*.]
   3. *Quoted in Development as Colonialism*.

Marxists see continuity between the colonial era of the 1600s through 1960s, and the era of development following the independence of former colonies. For example, the Asian colonial experience included Britain bullying Siam, and France bullying Annam, into signing treaties in 1855 and 1862, respectively, and European powers and Japan carving China up into spheres of influence. Through such arrangements, the colonial powers had access to markets of most Asian coastal regions, special rights for their expatriates working in Asia, and the freedom to build transportation networks and extend their enterprises inland. The renowned English Marxist historian, Eric Hobsbawm (1917–2012), reports that in the 1800s, Britain held direct imperial control over one-fourth of the world's surface, the Royal Navy controlled sea lanes to protect trade routes, and London was the financial capital of the world. Britain made one-third of all manufactured goods in the world, and produced two-thirds of the world's coal, half its iron, half of the world's factory-made cotton, 40% of the world's hardware, and five-sevenths of the world's steel.

What has changed, other than the identities of some bullies and the form of the bullying? MNCs act in lieu of (or as if they were) sovereigns, rely not so much on official "gun boat diplomacy" as on playing off small countries against one another, and if need be bribing officials to extract trade and investment concessions. Exhausted by two world wars, Britain's economic might has declined—but America's has risen. Significantly, like Britain before her, the U.S. preaches the virtues of free trade to achieve commercial goals. These hegemonic powers contend free trade ensures competitiveness.

Marxists also deride free trade for strangling infant industries in the Third World. The European colonial powers made industrial organization among local populations difficult, partly by taxing products consumed by locals, such as alcohol, animals, opium, or salt. To get income to meet their tax obligations, colonized peoples had little choice but to work on plantations or in mines owned by colonial masters. When the colonies gained independence, they lacked diversified economies. With few goods to export, other than primary products, their export revenues were vulnerable to market vicissitudes. They also were not hedged against First World protectionism. Sugar is one example. Poor countries sought to market access for sugar exports, yet America maintained since the late 1940s tight QRs on sugar imports, which generally are controversial if not illegal under GATT Article XI, and encouraged sugar substitutes like artificial sweeteners. The EU subsidized sugar beet production.

Countries throughout Latin America, as well as India, resorted to Import Substitution policies in the 1950s through 1980s. Mainstream economists criticized them for doing so. Efforts to prefer local raw materials and intermediate goods, and local production, to imports were inconsistent with the national treatment obligation found in GATT, and their abandonment was a condition for receiving funds from the World Bank.

Yet, critics like Walden Bello, in his 1994 study *Dark Victory*, argue a poor country receiving a structural adjustment program loan experiences an increase in commodity exports, but not always an increase in GNP. Why not? Because abandoning Import Substitution led to a net contraction in the domestic economy.

More generally, such critics see lending as a technique of colonialist control. In the mid-1800s, France lent money to the *bey* of Tunis, particularly through bonds, to help the *bey* develop an army and loosen ties with Turkey. ("*Bey*" is a Turkish word for the governor of a province in the Ottoman Empire.) The French bondholders obtained the help of the French Foreign Office to supervise finances in the *bey's* economy. In the great game against the Ottoman Empire for control in the Middle East, the Foreign Office was happy to oblige. In 1869, a Franco-Tunisian Commission imposed stringent conditions on the *bey*, and took the right to collect and distribute state revenues to ensure bondholders were preferred over other creditors. With public finance under foreign control, Tunisia slid into colonial status. When the *bey* needed to raise taxes to pay interest on the bonds and other loans, popular unrest ensured. France responded in predictable fashion. In 1881, to secure its interests, it annexed Tunisia.

Critics charge the formalities of lending are different in contemporary times, but not the underlying control relationships. In exchange for emergency lending to Mexico during the *peso* crisis in 1995, President Bill Clinton imposed similar terms on the Government of Mexico as the French had on the *bey* over a century earlier, namely, conditions to ensure the priority of Wall Street creditors. The IMF and World Bank, through their lending programs, effectively takes over management of the economy of a borrower to ensure timely repayment of principal and interest. The result now is *de facto* colonial control. Conversely, countries such as Singapore and Taiwan, which have been able to minimize external debt, have performed well. Korea, which did take on debt, resisted pressures from the IMF and World Bank to eliminate trade barriers and capital controls until it, essentially, had exported its way out of the debt.

Furthermore, say Marxists, it is hypocritical for the U.S. to advocate free trade given its early history. No less than Alexander Hamilton, in his famous 1791 *Report on Manufacturers*, called for protectionism in the service of economic nationalism. The U.S. maintained high duty rates through 1832, gradually reducing them between 1832 and 1860. To this day, America resorts to protectionist measures to serve powerful domestic constituencies, as the sugar example indicates.

Even temporary, episodic retreats from free trade did not stop colonialism. Marxists point out that whenever a colonial power implemented protectionist measures, capitalist entrepreneurs simply relied on FDI, and the overt colonial control by their home-country governments, to secure new markets. This process occurred in Africa, Asia, Latin America, and the Pacific in the 1870s and 1890s, when economic depression led some European countries (other than Belgium, the Netherlands, and Britain) to raise tariffs. By 1878, Europeans had colonized 67% of the land surface of the planet. By 1914, Europeans colonized 84.4%.

Within individual poor countries, some scholars surmise this process has resulted in dualistic economic growth. Dualism, or the creation of a dual economy, refers to a phenomenon in which there are two different sectors. Typically, one sector is capital-intensive and relatively wealthy, and the other sector is labor-intensive and relatively poor. The sectors are not integrated with one another. Writing in the 1950s, the Burmese economist, Hla Myint (1920–2017), argued colonialism led to dualism. He finds the theory explaining exports from developing countries is not Ricardo's Law of Comparative Advantage, but rather a pre-Adam Smith theory known as "Vent for Surplus." As the rubric suggests, export markets are a "vent" for "surplus" production.

To be sure, at early stages of growth, poor countries have little if any surplus production to export. They lack an integrated national market that would generate sizeable demand for products. But, as foreign businesses enter a country, often as part of a colonial linkage or legacy, they build an infrastructure to support expanded production. They do so because foreign demand would support output growth, *i.e.*, overseas buyers (especially in colonial countries) would consume the surplus. Yet, Myint observes the infrastructure they built does not serve to integrate a labor-intensive agricultural sector with a capital-intensive industrial sector in the host country.

To the contrary, the infrastructure served to integrate one or the other sector directly to the home, *i.e.*, colonial, country (*e.g.*, in Europe, or the U.S.). Specifically, road networks and railway lines, plus attendant communication lines, led directly from farm areas or mines to port facilities to facilitate shipment of crops and natural resources to the home country. The routes were not designed to link these input sources with emerging industrial producers in other parts of the host country. Consequently, the agricultural and natural resource sector generated an exportable surplus, and became the export sector. Products from this sector were land-intensive, and in some instances even capital-intensive. In contrast, industrial production stagnated, hence so too did demand for skilled labor. The end result was 2 different, non-integrated sectors.

Likewise, the economist Karl Gunnar Myrdal (1898–1987) wrote in his classic *Asian Drama* (1968) and in other works, about dualism. Myrdal, who shared the 1974 Nobel Prize in Economics with Friedrich A. Hayek (1899–1992), pointed out dualism results in increased income inequality within a poor country, as owners of factors of production in the export sector become wealthier, but factor resources in the rest of the economy see no real increases in demand for their services.

Classic examples are tea plantation owners in Ceylon (Sri Lanka) and India, palm oil, rubber and tin plantation owners in Indonesia and Malaysia, and mine owners in Sub-Saharan African countries. The large supply of labor in agriculture and mining ensures wage rates are low, and thus profits to owners high. The emphasis on this sector leads to dualistic development, as no integrated national market develops and local industries are neglected, even deliberately suppressed. In turn, dualism means the economy and export base of the poor country remain undiversified—a problem plaguing virtually all least developed countries.

Marxist-oriented scholars view international trade law as part of an overall free-trade framework that creates optimum conditions for First World businesses. From their perspective, this law is a control device in favor of capitalist enterprise, not an empowerment mechanism for the Third World. In most Third World countries, raw power exercised from major trading nations is not necessary to enforce the laws in the framework. The political influence of the hegemons, felt through free-trade oriented rules articulated in and enforced through WTO agreements and FTAs, does the job. Indeed, this legal network is far more extensive than the British Empire ever was.

Ostensibly, this framework is palatable because the field on which trading nations compete is said to be level. Even if it were, the imbalance in political and economic might render the result of any competition unfair. In fact, the field is anything but level. Marxist-oriented critics argue the rules of the GATT-WTO game are designed to create favorable conditions for MNCs. The rights of MNC entry and establishment, removal of restrictions on repatriating earnings, abolition of tariff and non-tariff barriers (particularly for components used by MNCs in production), liberalization of the labor market (to ensure cheap labor unprotected by unions), and national treatment are oft-cited examples of such rules. The favorable conditions are low costs of production, docile laborers, un-enforced environmental standards, and little if any competition. Consequently, roughly 20% to 30% of world trade occurs within MNCs (*i.e.*, between different parts of a vertically integrated MNC, such as a parent and one of its subsidiaries). Many world commodity markets are characterized by monopoly or oligopoly conditions, with 40% or more of a particular market being controlled by less than five companies.

Official American and European trade delegations consistently advocate for these rules. They do so behind a self-serving veil that the rules are needed to attract trade and FDI, which, in turn, will propel development in poor countries. If and when a poor country resists, the response from representatives of the major powers is "fine, our businesses will go elsewhere." They play poor countries off against one another to tilt the field in their favor. As few such countries are large or powerful enough to continue resisting, the result is global corporate colonialism protected by International Trade Law.

Aside from this corpus of law, another feature of the free-trade framework—one that also bespeaks continuity between colonial and post-independence eras—concerns elites. For a capitalist in the First World, what better way to safeguard long-term market access than to have allies in the private and public sectors of the Third World? The British understood the point clearly after the 1857 Indian (or Seapoy) Mutiny, thereafter focusing on the creation of an Anglicized Indian elite that would keep the Indian populace under control and thereby support British commercial interests.

To what extent are the interests of elites in developing countries and LDCs any more aligned with the needs of the majority of their countrymen than in the 1800s?

Marxists argue the elites of today are akin to the colonial administrators of yester-year. The large percentage of foreign aid that consists of security assistance of one kind or another (*e.g.*, military training, weapons) is designed to promote the rule of law, not as goal in its own right, but as a means to the aim of advancing neo-colonial interests. When a Third World leader threatens this aim, the First World—led by America, Britain, continental European countries, or some coalition of the interested—takes action.

Examples involving the U.S. to which Marxists point include:

(1) The American military intervention in Guatemala in 1954, which resulted in the overthrow of a government that nationalized American-owned banana plantations.

(2) The American-inspired military *coup d'etat* in Brazil in the 1960s, which led to the overthrow of a government that tried to limit the amount of currency a foreign corporation could withdraw from Brazil, initiate a land-reform program that would have returned control of mineral resources from such corporations to locals, and raise wages (leading to higher labor costs for these corporations).

(3) Efforts throughout the 1960s and 1970s to remove Fidel Castro from power in Cuba, as he had not only nationalized American business property, but also had agreed to the positioning of Soviet nuclear weapons on Cuban soil.

(4) Overt and covert military engagements in Latin America and the Caribbean in the 1980s, including El Salvador, Grenada, and Nicaragua, all of which had Marxist-oriented governments threatening American business interests.

(5) High- and low-intensity conflicts in the Middle East, including the 1991 Gulf War and the 2003 Iraq invasion, which at bottom were at least as much about securing oil supplies as fighting terrorism.

Indubitably, each one of these examples, and perhaps any illustration Marxists trot out, is open to considerable debate.

To reduce every instance of the use of force as motivated by a search for new markets, cheap labor, raw materials, or the need to shore up faltering elites is simplistic. Neither the Korean nor Vietnam War is well explained by those rationales, as neither Korea nor Vietnam was a major market or input source at the time of the conflicts. The Marxist perspective also implicitly degrades the contribution of military personnel from the U.S. and its partners. They might be surprised to learn they are helpless, gullible soldiers in the service of an international capitalist conspiracy manipulated by misguided patriotism and rhetoric about spreading peace and democracy abroad.

Nonetheless, the perspective matters, because it resonates in contemporary trade debates. For instance, Marxist-oriented critics fault FTAs, especially for poor countries (*e.g.*, in Latin America) or countries with natural resources (*e.g.*, in the Middle

East), as being more about neo-colonialism and less about development. Similarly, FTAs between countries like America and Australia, or America and Singapore, are rewards to countries that act as deputy sheriffs to enforce American commercial interests.

II. Frank and Dependency Theory

One of the most provocative schools of thought in development economics to emerge in the 20th century is known as "Dependency Theory." Dependency Theory (in one form or another) resonates in many contemporary debates about trade liberalization and its purportedly salubrious implications. This intellectual debt, however, sometimes goes unrecognized or ignored by economists. For example, while one prominent Textbook (*Economic Development* (2003) by Professor Stuart Lynn of Assumption College) covers the theory, another higher-profile text (*Economics of Development* (4th ed. 1996) by Professor Malcolm Gillis of Rice and Professors Dwight H. Perkins, Michael Roemer, and Donald R. Snodgrass of Harvard) devotes not a word to it.

The father of Dependency Theory is Andre Gunder Frank (1929–2005). Writing in the 1960s, Frank's target was a large one: world capitalist development from the 1400s onwards. Frank did not believe in Marxian historical stages of economic growth. Ironically, his dissertation supervisor at the University of Chicago was none other than the free-market champion and 1976 Nobel Economic Prize Winner Milton Friedman (1912–2006).[4]

But, the studies by Frank, along with the work of Immanuel Wallerstein, drew on Marxian ideas, and showed a division of the world into two categories:

(1) A small number of developed or "metropolitan" countries, collectively called the "center" or "core." The G7 (or G8) countries would be considered the center.

(2) A large number of un- or under-developed, or "satellite" countries, collectively called the "periphery." Most developing and all least developed countries would be considered the periphery.

This division draws on Marxist-Leninist theory. Karl Marx (1818–1883) saw capitalist growth occurring through the accumulation of capital at home and, later, abroad. Vladimir Lenin (1870–1924) argued as capitalists produce ever-increasing amounts of goods and thereby drive down profit rates in their domestic markets, they force themselves to search overseas for new markets.

Frank and other Dependency Theorists elaborate on and extend these ideas. The center drives the development process in the periphery, and that process is a capitalist one. The center uses military power, directly or indirectly, to secure supplies of

---

4. *See Andre Gunder Frank*, WIKIPEDIA, http://en.wikipedia.org/wiki/Andre_Gunder_Frank.

raw materials and cheap labor for its enterprises. Typically, those enterprises export raw materials back to the center for use in manufacturing, or if engaged in production in the periphery, use labor-intensive methods of production. The enterprises repatriate their profits, or leave them in the hands of local business elites. These elites become a capitalist class in the periphery reliant on the enterprises for their wealth and privileges. Over time, the center gets relatively more developed, taking resources from the periphery, and the periphery relatively less-developed, being drained of those resources. The capitalist class in the periphery facilitates the disparate development.

Frank devised a memorable caption for the process: the "development of underdevelopment." The caption embodies the hallmark of Dependency Theory: a peripheral country can develop economically, but only in inverse relation to the strength of its ties to the center. The stronger the ties that bind a peripheral country to the center, the harder it is for that country to develop.

Frank argued the world's least developed regions are the ones with the closest historical ties to Europe and the U.S. Only a large dose of autonomy from the center allows for real development. Hence, Dependency Theory holds that expanded trade is orthogonal to the development interests of poor countries, because it is innately exploitative in favor of rich countries. By implication, the Theory (in contrast to Marxist-Leninist ideology) does not stress class struggle as the force driving historical progress.

This conclusion is entirely contrary to the pro-globalization, pro-free trade tide that has dominated mainstream legal, business, policy, and academic circles in most countries since the end of the Cold War. It suggests developing and least developed countries are foolish to enter FTAs or CUs with developed countries. Yet, the conclusion resonates favorably among an influential group of thinkers and activists in various IOs and NGOs, and in parts of the academy. To be sure, they are not all so radical as to counsel a complete break of economic linkages with the major powers, as ardent Dependency Theorists would. But, they advise a re-balancing of the interactive relationships, and are more patient with Import Substitution, infant industry protection, and trade policies that carve out space for poor countries.

Frank's conclusion, in particular, is based on historical and empirical research focusing on Brazil and Chile. Until the late 1920s, the center-periphery pattern existed, meaning the center countries established the conditions under which peripheral countries developed, or better put, remained underdeveloped. The break from this pattern came when two cataclysmic events distracted the major powers. Between 1929 and 1945, Europe and the U.S. could not dictate the conditions of development, because of the Great Depression and Second World War. During this period, Frank said, the likes of Brazil and Chile were able to develop autonomously. But, when the War ended, dominance by the major powers resumed. Interestingly, Frank also observed in some regions, there were small center-periphery patterns, for example Brazil and its neighbors.

III. Prebisch-Singer Thesis

Along with the work of Dependency Theorists, the scholarship of the Argentine economist Raúl Prebisch (1901–1986) provides critical theoretical footing for Import Substitution.[5] Prebisch—sometimes called "Latin America's Keynes"—was a major figure in international trade and development economics from the 1940s through 1970s. He served with the U.N. Economic Commission for Latin America, and was the first Secretary General for the UNCTAD, and coined the term "NIEO."

Some observers in America and Europe regarded Prebisch as a dangerous radical. In fact, he was a moderate, preferring reform to revolution, advocating a mixed economy in which the private sector played a leading role, central bank independence, fiscal stability, and vigilance against inflation. He was of 2 minds about Dependency Theory, and never put himself in the camp of Latin American Marxists. Rather, he was pro-American, inspiring President John F. Kennedy's Alliance for Progress aid program for Latin America.

Writing in the 1950s, Prebisch argued trade causes deterioration in the price of primary products exported by poor countries. In contrast, prices of manufactured goods—the main exports from rich to poor countries—are stable or rising over time. After all, manufactured goods embody higher productivity than do primary products. Therefore, the TOT of poor countries deteriorate.

Faced with lower export earnings and higher import costs, they are unable to generate savings necessary for capital investment, and thus to industrialize. Participation in trade actually reinforces the international division of labor in which they are trapped in a pattern of producing and exporting primary commodities and natural resources. The solution? Structural change of the international trading system, and industrialization in poor countries through inward development, import substitution, and regional integration.

The research of another great scholar, the British economist Sir Hans Wolfgang Singer (1910–2006), echoed these conclusions. Together, their argument about declining TOT and entrapment in the trading system is called the "Prebisch-Singer Thesis," or "Singer-Prebisch Thesis." (Regrettably, Prebisch himself never systematized his theories into a major book.) Succinctly put, the Thesis states the TOT move against producers and exporters of primary products.

This Thesis runs counter to a standard classical and neo-classical prediction in favor of free trade. That prediction is free trade ought to lead to an improvement in the TOT of a country. Increased demand in several other countries for the exports of one country should result in higher prices for those exports. At the same time,

---

5. For an excellent biography of this important development and trade economist, see Edgar J. Dosman, *The Life and Times of Raúl Prebisch 1901–1986* (Montreal, Canada: McGill-Queen's University Press, 2008). *See also* the review of this book, *Misunderstood Moderate*, THE ECONOMIST, 7 March 2009, at 90.

lower trade barriers (*i.e.*, a fall in tariffs and quotas) in that country should mean a drop in prices of imported merchandise, as well as in the price of like or directly competitive domestically-made goods. Thus, the ratio of export prices, P_{EX}, to import prices, P_{IM}, which is the definition of the TOT, should rise. However, when Prebisch examined data from 1870 to 1936, he found the TOT rose for developed countries, but not developing countries. Singer's findings supported the conclusions Prebisch reached.

Empirical evidence from the 20th century concerning primary product exports, in which developing countries tend to specialize, indicates long-term price declines. Overall, during the First World War (1914–1918) and Great Depression (1929 through the early 1930s), prices of primary commodities fell. They recovered during the Second World War. During the 1950s and 1960s, there was no general trend. In the mid-1970s, these prices spiked, and thereafter remained constant at higher levels during the 1980s and 1990s. In 1997, Peruvian economist Hernando De Soto (1941–) published a study of prices of 24 different major commodities from 1900 to 1992. He found the prices trended downward for 17 commodities, increased for four commodities, and exhibited no pattern (downward or upward) for three commodities. In the same period, prices of merchandise imported by developing countries rose steadily, indicating a TOT decline for many such countries.

Naturally, Prebisch asked why the TOT of developing countries deteriorate as a result of trade. One answer is known as "immiserizing growth." As discussed earlier, if a country exports a product in sufficiently large volumes, and if those exports account for a substantial share of total world supply of the product, then the exports may cause a fall in the world market price of the product. The country is a large player in the market — such as, for instance, Brazil in the coffee market — and this size redounds to its detriment. The more it exports, the greater the downward pressure on the price of the product, which in turn means P_{EX} deteriorates. Put in graphical terms, the world market supply curve for the product shifts outward, and assuming all other factors are unchanged (*ceteris paribus*), the price falls.

Is it possible to apply the immiserizing growth answer to small developing countries? The response depends on the product in question. Suppose several small developing countries make the same or a substitutable product, and their cumulated exports account for a sizeable portion of world supply. Primary commodities, like banana, cocoa, rubber, and tea provide classic examples. Then, should they increase their exports, the world supply by definition increases substantially, and the product price falls.

Prebisch offered four other possible reasons for the decline in developing country TOT associated with trade:

(1) *Engel's Law*

   A well-known microeconomic principle, which empirical evidence bears out, is as income rises, the portion of income spent on necessities — particularly food — falls. This principle is "Engel's Law." Simply put, as people become richer, they spend a smaller percentage of their overall budget on food than they did in the past. Engel's Law is based on a behavioral tendency to consume different goods in different proportions as income rises—in particular, as consumers obtain higher levels of income, their spending patterns shift toward luxury items. Stated in economic terms, there are differences in the income elasticity of demand for products. The income elasticity of demand is the percent change in the quantity demanded of a product that is associated with a given percent change in income.

Expressed arithmetically, it is:

$$\text{Income Elasticity of Demand} = \frac{\text{Percentage Change in Quantity Demanded of a Product}}{\text{Percentage Change in Income of a Consumer}}$$

Income inelasticity occurs if the ratio is less than 1, and income elasticity exists if the ratio exceeds 1. Thus, if income rises by 10%, and demand increases by more than 10%, then the product is said to be "income elastic." If a 10% rise in income leads to an increase in demand of less than 10%, then it is "income inelastic."

Primary commodities, which are and go into food products, and which are necessity items, tend to be income inelastic. Manufactured goods, which typically are not necessities, tend to be income elastic. Thus, Prebisch argued, as income rises, the demand for products in which developing countries specialize (primary commodities) rises less rapidly than the demand for products in which developed countries specialize (manufactured goods). Increases in income may occur in developed countries (as they get richer), in developing countries (as segments of their society grow richer), or both.

(2) *Asymmetric Benefits from Technology*

Prebisch alleged technological gains do not have the same impact in developed and developing countries. In developed countries, improved technology helps bolster labor productivity. Wage rates tend to be "sticky downward" for structural reasons, including organized worker groups (*e.g.*, unions). Likewise, product prices tend to remain strong, because of imperfect competition among suppliers (*i.e.*, monopolistic or oligopolistic product markets).

In contrast, in developing countries, technological enhancements do more than increase productivity. They also replace labor, and result in lower product prices. Structural features in place to keep wages from sliding do not exist in most poor countries. Some product markets in those countries may be characterized by monopoly or oligopoly, yet the world market for the product is competitive, thereby allowing for price declines with increased exports of the product.

Therefore, urged Prebisch, the net effect of technological enhancement on relative TOT is asymmetric. For developing countries, technological improvements lead to a fall in export prices and, hence, falling TOT. For developed countries, these improvements do not put downward pressure on the price of their exports, so there is no adverse effect on their TOT.

(3) *Substitution Effects*

Prebisch pointed out substitutes have been invented for several products in which developing countries specialize. Examples include petrochemicals (*e.g.*, plastics), which substitute for rubber, and synthetic fibers (*e.g.*, nylon and rayon), which substitute for natural fibers (like cotton). Consequently, the demand in developed countries for the specialty of developing countries has slowed or fallen. In turn, from the perspective of developing countries, the price of that product, P_{EX}, has not increased, and possibly declined. This price is P_{IM} from the perspective of developed countries. The effect on relative TOT is apparent—the TOT of developing countries (where P_{EX} is the numerator of the TOT ratio) is stagnant or drops, and the TOT of developed countries (where P_{IM} is the denominator) stays the same or rises.

(4) *Protectionism*

Prebisch argued the trade policies of developed countries are to blame, in part, for the failure of the TOT of developing countries to improve with international trade. These policies tend to work against trade liberalization on products of keen export interest to developing countries. Tariff and non-tariff barriers remain high, and tariff escalation exists, on such products. Demand for these products does not increase markedly. Hence, P_{EX}, as viewed by developing countries, does not rise.

The Prebisch-Singer Thesis has not gone without challenge. Three basic categories of questions are put to it.

First, as a conceptual matter, is it appropriate to focus on the Net Barter TOT (*i.e.*, the ratio of P_{EX} to P_{IM}) rather than Income TOT (*i.e.*, the ratio of $P_{EX} \times Q_{EX}$ to P_{IM}, where Q_{EX} is the quantity of goods exported, hence the numerator represents export revenues, the price of exports multiplied by the volume of those exports)? Focusing on income TOT reveals export revenues a country generates, which it can use to pay for imports.

Second, how good are the data Prebisch used? A number of problems existed with these data. For example, the period examined, 1870 to 1936, ended during the Great Depression, before world agricultural process recovered. Had the period been different (either shorter, ending before the Depression, or longer, ending after it), prices of developing country exports, P_{EX}, might not have been so low. Further, the price data included transportation costs (*e.g.*, shipping charges), which may have distorted the underlying values for P_{EX} and P_{IM}. Indeed, between 1870 and 1936, transportation costs fell considerably. During this period, the quality of certain goods improved, but these improvements were not necessarily reflected in increased prices.

Still another illustration of data problems concerns missing data. Prebisch did not have statistics on exports from Argentina to Great Britain, so he had to infer the value and volume of these exports by examining British statistics on imports from Argentina. Additionally, there are periods of boom in commodity prices, such as the early part of the new millennium. Thus, the choice of the period of investigation can support, or undermine, the Prebisch-Singer Thesis.

Third, is it insightful to speak of the TOT of developing countries generally? When data are disaggregated by region, not every developing region shows declining TOT. For example, the TOT for Asia are stable or improve. For Latin America, the trend is improvement in the mid-1970s, followed by long-term decline. The TOT for Middle East countries, particularly oil exporters, depends heavily on oil prices. The point is developing countries are heterogeneous in what they export, and to where. Measuring TOT for this diverse group risks obfuscating success stories with problem cases.

IV. Policy Implications of Prebisch-Singer Thesis

Notwithstanding the challenges to the Prebisch-Singer Thesis, the policy implications of the Thesis are clear: developing countries should diversify their export base by industrialization. That is, rather than rely on exports of agricultural products, they should move into markets for manufactured products—and, by extension of the Thesis, into services. Once they establish a position in certain finished goods markets, these countries can "work backwards" and develop industries in intermediate goods. That is, they can build linkages in their economy, with the end results being vertically integrated industries, improved human capital and technology through industrial development, and less dependence on certain imports from major countries.

Exactly what manufactured products (and services) a particular developing country specializes in depends on its comparative advantages. The Heckscher-Ohlin Theorem lends help on this matter. The Theorem predicts a country will specialize in the production and export of a product that uses intensively in its production the factor (capital equipment, human capital, labor, land, or technology) with which the country is relatively well endowed. Still, answering "what to export?" is a challenge for many countries. This question relates directly to market access in developed countries. Suppose a developing country aspires to specialize in refined chocolates (and thereby lessen its dependence on cocoa exports) and dress shoes (and thereby lessen its dependence on leather exports). But, suppose also the tariffs on these products in major markets are high (*e.g.*, there are tariff spikes), or there is tariff escalation (*i.e.*, the tariff on a finished product exceeds that on inputs). The developing country will have little luck in penetrating these markets, unless it can orchestrate barrier reduction through multilateral trade negotiations under WTO auspices, or through talks to form an FTA or CU.

Not surprisingly, in considering "what to export?" a closely related question arises, namely, "how to diversify?" Might it be better for a developing country to eschew trade liberalization temporarily? The logic is that of the infant industry: new industries in a developing country cannot withstand international competition at early stages. In contrast with established industries in developed countries, infant industries in developing countries have not yet achieved low-cost production methods or realized economies of scale (*i.e.*, declining long-run average costs of production), and their output is not of high quality. If faced with direct competition from developed country industries, the infants will not survive, as consumers in developing countries would prefer cheaper, better imports rather than domestically-made like or directly competitive products. Private sector financiers would be unwilling to lend funds to the infant industries, because their high costs and low profits render them risky borrowers. In this scenario, a period of protection from import competition will allow the infants to mature, at which point they can compete globally. Financing from development banks, and the government (of the developing country), either directly through grants or "soft" (*i.e.*, low-interest, long-term) loans, or indirectly through guarantees, may be needed.

To be sure, after the American Revolution, no less than Alexander Hamilton (1755–1804), in *Report on Manufactures* (1791), offered this logic for high tariffs. A developing country at the time, America needed to establish an industrial base. Hamilton said it should do so through such protection. In the process, it could gain economic independence from Europe, an aspiration dubbed "economic nationalism." However, free-trade oriented economists point out problems with the infant industry-economic nationalism argument.

First, protection tends not to be removed after its economic purpose is served. Political lobbying from leaders in the protected industry results in mollycoddling long after the infant has matured. The end result of protection may be the creation of a domestic monopoly. Relatedly, the initial imposition of protection, as well as its continuation, presumes the government of the developing country is astute at picking an industry with strong potential to develop an international comparative advantage. Not all such governments, and not all such planners, are skilled at this strategic thinking.

Second, if developing country officials furnish information to private financiers about the long-term viability of infant industries, then they may adjust the tenor of loans. Specifically, lenders may permit long maturity dates sufficient to encompass the time needed to realize economies of scale. Also, a government can subsidize either interest rates or production, and either policy is more efficient than protection.

Third, the challenge infant industries face in some developing countries is not production cost or quality, but infrastructure in a country. Most of the Indian

Subcontinent, in contrast to China, is a case in point. Throughout much of the Subcontinent, roads, utilities, and port facilities range from mediocre to decrepit. (Not surprisingly, the Subcontinent attracts service-based businesses like call centers, which rely less on infrastructure than traditional manufacturing.) Protection will not address this challenge. Only government-led initiatives will make a difference. Dismantling trade barriers may facilitate infrastructure improvement, as foreign-based providers of heavy equipment and expertise needed to build roads, utilities, and ports flow in.

V. Evidence for Import Substitution

Export pessimism, Dependency Theory, and the Prebisch-Singer Thesis have been important rationales used by many developing countries to justify Import Substitution. They imposed high tariffs and non-tariff barriers (especially quotas and import licenses) to make imports more expensive or restrict the availability of imports, and thereby gave preference to domestic producers.

Brazil is a notable example. It opted for Import Substitution in response to the Great Depression and Second World War. Table 17-1 shows its consequent shift to domestically-made goods.[6] Arguably, because of that strategy, Brazil advanced from reliance on primary products and T&A to intermediate goods.

Likewise, Korea employed Import Substitution in the 1950s and 1960s. Eschewing dependence on foreign firms for technology, Korea honed its own know-how. Table 17-2 shows the impact of the strategy on industrial output and industrial exports. Both statistics rose considerably. Import Substitution proponents point to the strategy as a, if not the, key reason.

Obviously, Import Substitution is one strategy in an overall policy mix. A developing country implements it along with policies on exchange rates, interest rates, wages, prices in various markets, and the balance of payments. For example, it may make little sense for a country with a large population, indeed labor surplus, to embark on an Import Substitution strategy that favors capital-intensive production, without further policies to employ the large labor pool and develop its skills. Yet, this result can occur, by design or effect, through exchange rate policies (*e.g.*, keeping them artificially high to facilitate imports of capital equipment) or interest rates (*e.g.*, keeping them artificially low, or subsidizing them, to encourage borrowing for capital equipment purchases). Proper policy coordination, and adaptation of policies to changing economic circumstances, both of which imply a sound policy

---

6. Tables 17-1 and 17-2 are constructed from data presented in Stuart R. Lynn, *Economic Development: Theory and Practice for a Divided World* 342–344 (Upper Saddle River, New Jersey: Prentice Hall, 2003).

Table 17-1. Brazil and Import Substitution, 1939–1958

Sector and Year	1939 Percent of Total Industrial Output Accounted for by Sector	1958 Percent of Total Industrial Output Accounted for by Sector
Food and T&A	63%	18%
Intermediate Goods (*e.g.*, equipment, metal goods, machinery, and minerals)	44%	33%

Table 17-2. Korea and Import Substitution, 1950s and 1960s

Statistic and Year	1960	1965
Share of Industrial Output in GDP	19%	24%
Share of Manufactured Goods in Total Exports	13%	61%

formation process, are necessary for the right integration of Import Substitution and supporting initiatives.

India is a case in point of good and bad results from Import Substitution. From its Independence on 15 August 1947 to approximately 1991, it pursued this strategy in many sectors. Protection of domestic industries took the form of high tariff rates and the requirement of a license to import. On the one hand, India achieved some degree of independence from imports of certain chemicals, fertilizer, iron, some machinery, petroleum, and steel. Indians are proud (sometimes excessively so) of their innovative and self-reliant economy. On the other hand, corruption abounded with the so-called "License Raj" system, as would-be importers offered bribes to obtain a precious license to import and thereby, in effect, become a monopolist.

Moreover, protection led to diversification into product lines in which India lacked a strong potential for comparative advantage, and dependence on some kinds of foreign technology. A domestic producer, once it obtained a license to import technology, was safe from foreign competition for the product in which it incorporated the technology — it had no incentive to innovate.

Nevertheless, for most mainstream economists, the success stories do not amount to persuasive evidence for Import Substitution. They reiterate the well-known classical and neo-classical arguments about the net costs associated with tariffs and quotas: the protection necessary for Import Substitution imposes a dead weight loss caused by inefficient allocation of factors to producing the protected good, and by diminished consumption opportunities. Further, the economic consensus points to counter-evidence on failures in specific countries, and to repeated mistakes associated with this strategy.

As for failed cases, Ghana, Mexico, Pakistan, Tanzania, and Uruguay are among the examples. They experimented with Import Substitution, but implementation

Table 17-3. Near-Term Effects of Import Substitution in Ghana

Statistic and Year	1962	1966
Composition of Imports	Over 50% of imports are consumer goods	30% of imports are consumer goods 65% of imports are capital goods and materials
Growth in Manufacturing	Growth of 10% per year between 1962–1966	Growth of 10% per year between 1962–1966

Table 17-4. Long Term Effects of Import Substitution in Ghana

Statistic and Year	1950s	1980
Per capita GNP	20 year decline starting in 1950s	20 year decline starting in 1950s
Investment Rate (Investment as a percent of GDP)	20%	5%
Exports (Exports as a percent of GDP)	30%	12%

was poor and accompanied by inappropriate policies that distorted exchange rates, interest rates and wages, as well as the prices of various imported and domestic goods. Ghana, Mexico, and Pakistan are particularly worthy of note.

Ghana gained independence from Britain in 1957. In 1961, it adopted Import Substitution. The average tariff rate jumped from 17% to 25%, and import licenses were mandatory. Table 17-3 shows some near-term results, through 1966.[7] The long-term effects of Import Substitution, which Table 17-4 shows, were unequivocally negative.

A *coup d'état* in 1966 changed political leadership. It also ushered in modest trade policy changes, though not until the 1980s did Ghana abandon Import Substitution. Its roughly 20 million people remain poor by any measure—low *per capita* GNP (U.S. $400, ranking it 166 in the world), low life expectancy (57 for men and 59 for women), and low literacy rates with a large gender gap (79% and 61% for men and women, respectively).

Why did Ghana fail to grow through Import Substitution? There are at least four reasons. First, tariff rates were not coordinated. Consequently, the Effective Rate of Protection (ERP) was over 200% for some domestic industries, but negative for export industries. Some export industries were faced with the ridiculous situation of having to pay an amount for imported raw materials and components greater than the value of the exported finished product they made.

---

7. Tables 16-3 and 16-4 are constructed from data presented in Stuart R. Lynn, *Economic Development: Theory and Practice for a Divided World* 342–344 (Upper Saddle River, New Jersey: Prentice Hall, 2003).

Second, obtaining an import license depended on arbitrary and capricious behavior by government officials. Worse yet, officials solicited—and got—bribes in exchange for licenses. Corruption in license administration, and the trade regime generally, became rampant.

Third, the local currency was fixed against foreign currencies. It could not depreciate when Ghana experienced inflation (as market forces would require, because of the increase in supply of local currency that contributed to inflation). With an over-valued exchange rate, exports other than cocoa did not rise. Cocoa export revenues slumped as world market prices for cocoa fell. This environment discouraged entrepreneurs from investing in businesses that could help diversify the export base of the country.

Fourth, on manufacturing, two policies encouraged capital-intensive production: minimum wages and interest rate ceilings. Minimum wages raised the cost of labor relative to capital. Credit cost caps encouraged borrowing for capital equipment expenditures. Yet, with a growing population, Ghana needed labor-intensive investments.

Mexico is an important case of policy change. Following Import Substitution for decades, in the early 1980s, Mexico reversed course. It began liberalizing its restrictive trade and investment regime, and withdrawing from state intervention in the economy. In 1986, Mexico acceded to GATT. Commencing free trade negotiations with Canada and the U.S. in the early 1990s, Mexico impressed its partners with its commitment to reform, manifest in new IP protection laws. It became a Party to *NAFTA* as soon as *NAFTA* took effect (1 January 1994).

Mexico has well over 50 FTAs. They cover its key export markets, including Japan. These accords evince Mexico's dedication to trade liberalization. They entail international legal commitments to openness and reform. Not surprisingly given their experience and sophistication, Mexican trade officials and practitioners assist countries in Central America in their trade negotiations, such as for with the U.S. on *CAFTA-DR*.

As for Pakistan, Dorosh and Valdes construct a model of its economy.[8] They apply data from 1983–1987 to the model, not only on Import Substitution, but also agricultural price and exchange rate policies. They conclude the combined effects of these policies lowered wheat production by 24%, and rice production by 52%. Posing the counterfactual, if Pakistan had not adhered to Import Substitution and the other policies, then incomes of farmers from five major crops would have been 40% higher. Another interesting counterfactual is whether and how better economic performance might have altered subsequent history, including the October 1998 military *coup d'état* by General Pervez Musharraf (1943–), and internal battles

---

8. *See* Paul Dorosh & Alberto Valdes, *Effects of Exchange Rate and Trade Policies on Agriculture in Pakistan*, INTERNATIONAL FOOD POLICY RESEARCH INSTITUTE RESEARCH REPORT No. 84 (December 1990).

against Islamic extremism (especially in the North West Frontier Province (NWFP, renamed Khyber Pakhtunkhwa in 2010), Baluchistan, and Karachi).

As for often-repeated mistakes with Import Substitution, critics point first and foremost to the political difficulty of removing trade barriers and subjecting domestic industries in developing countries to import competition. The period of protection is one in which captans of the domestic industry become adept at rent-seeking behavior, leading them to lobby for continued protection rather than enhance the competitiveness of their businesses. Insofar as these businesses produce consumer goods, consumers in the developing country are stuck with high-priced, low quality goods. If a developing country has a small market, then it may not be able to support a large number of producers, which reinforces the tendency toward monopoly (or oligopoly).

Yet, at the same time, the country remains dependent on imports for capital equipment. To finance such imports, the country may need to borrow from official or private sources, especially if its performance in export markets for consumer goods is lackluster, leading to an increase in foreign debt. In brief, Import Substitution often is a recipe for inefficient, even corrupt, imperfect competition in consumer goods markets, plus increased dependence on foreign physical and financial capital.

A second set of mistakes concerns the relationship of the agricultural to industrial sector. Import Substitution raises the cost of imported seeds, fertilizers, and equipment used by farmers in a developing country. Moreover, this approach sometimes is coupled with maintenance of an overvalued exchange rate. A higher-than-market exchange rate allows a developing country to reduce the cost of imports of approved items, such as capital goods needed for industrialization (because at the higher rate, the country can convert a unit of its currency into more units of foreign currency than the market would justify, and then use the foreign currency to buy needed items). But, the overvalued exchange rate makes agricultural exports less attractive to foreign buyers (because they get less units of the developing country currency per unit of their currency than a free currency market otherwise would allow, and thus their purchasing power is reduced).

The result is TOT deterioration, not internationally, but domestically, namely, between the rural and urban sectors within a country. That is, farmers are worse off because their costs are higher, and sales lower, relative to the industrial sector. This situation, if pronounced or prolonged, can lead to social unrest in rural areas. Economically, it can cause a decline in the balance of trade, and create dependence on borrowing from overseas, thereby leading to (or exacerbating) debt problems.

What, then, is the "bottom line" about Import Substitution versus Export Orientation? The debate is highly contentious, yet it may be said the consensus of economists favor Export Orientation. "Consensus" here does not mean essential unanimity, as it does in WTO decision-making. Rather, it means the majority of economists, and perhaps the caveat should be added that the pool of economists involved is trained in Neo Classical Economic Theory. The consensus would agree trade is not the only engine of growth, but it can be an engine of growth, if other complementary factors exist, not the least of which is good governance and a strong rule-of-law framework.

VI. 1981 Lord Bauer Rebuttal

One of the most provocative economists to comment on development issues is England's Lord Peter T. Bauer, a long-time professor at the London School of Economics and Cambridge University.[9] Born in Budapest in 1915, Lord Bauer wrote in the mid-and latter half of the 20th century and was a fellow of the British Academy. (He passed away in 2002.) Lord Bauer's research, while not all directly bearing on trade, both raises and attempts to rebut criticisms often made about the world trading system, and more generally, of globalization. His perspectives demonstrate the charges and counter-charges heard today are not new.

In *Equality, The Third World and Economic Delusion* (1981), Lord Bauer considered the accusation the First World (*i.e.*, developed nations), manipulate international trade to the detriment of the Third World (*i.e.*, developing and least developed nations). In specific, the First World stood accused of inflicting unfavorable and deteriorating TOT. That is, following the accusation, the First World was charged with orchestrating a decline in the share of international trade held by the Third World. The obvious policy implication from this accusation is Export Orientation is not a viable growth strategy. However, Lord Bauer offered five arguments in rebuttal to this accusation.

First, the poorest areas of the Third World have little or no external trade. It makes little sense to blame the First World for manipulating trade against largely autarkic countries. They are poor for domestic reasons, not because of First World manipulation. Virtually any external commercial contracts would be beneficial, *i.e.*, expanded trade would benefit such countries. Indubitably, Lord Bauer would agree with the proposition espoused by former U.N. Secretary General, Kofi Annan, and others, namely, the poor are poor not because of too much globalization, but because of too little.

Second, most countries are developing or least developed, *i.e.*, the bulk of the world is the Third World. Roughly 80% of the WTO Membership consists of such countries. Accordingly, said Lord Bauer, it is not possible to consider the TOT of the Third World in the aggregate. The TOT for any one such country may move favorably during one period, but may deteriorate in another period. Much depends on the period selection for measurement. OPEC countries enjoyed high export prices for their key commodity, oil, in the 1970s, but had to reassess lavish government spending programs in the late 1990s as those prices—and the revenues from them

---

9. This discussion draws on Raj Bhala, *International Trade Law: Interdisciplinary Theory and Practice* 1248-1252 (Newark, New Jersey: LexisNexis, 3rd ed. 2008).

to fund expenditures—shrank. The point is that TOT for the entire Third World makes little sense.

Third, it is simplistic to draw inferences from the TOT alone. Many factors affect the economic performance of Third World countries. For example:

(1) *Cost of Production*

   The TOT cannot be inferred simply from the ratio of import and export prices. This ratio does not take into account the cost of production of exports. The higher the cost of production of exports, the more expensive it is for a Third World country to engage in international trade. High costs of production are based on the cost of factors of production, *i.e.,* land, labor, physical capital, human capital, and technology.

(2) *Export Diversification*

   The diversity of the export base of a country, and quality of its imports, are critical determinants of economic success.

(3) *Trade Volume*

   The volume of trade in which a country is engaged affects its success.

(4) *Import Purchasing Power*

   The amount of imports a country can purchase with a unit of domestic resources also affects its success.

Moreover, Bauer argued, Third World countries contribute significantly to their own dismal performance. Corruption, war and conflict, and economic mismanagement are self-inflicted wounds readily apparent in many poor countries. It is difficult to blame developed countries in every instance.

For example, the U.S. has had since 1977 the *Foreign Corrupt Practices Act and Antibribery Provisions,* which bars bribery of foreign government officials.[10] On 21 November 1997, the OECD agreed to an *Anti-Bribery Convention* (formally, the *Convention Combating Bribery of Foreign Public Officials in International Business Transactions*). (Both regimes are discussed in a separate Chapter.) Neither the U.S. nor any other OECD country plausibly can be blamed for every war, conflict, or poor policy choice. There is far more to the problem than TOT.

Fourth, in the vast majority of markets, it is naïve to believe major trading countries can manipulate international prices. Most markets are too broad and deep for price cartels or other anti-competitive practices to work. Prices are the outcome of innumerable individual decisions of market participants. The result is what economists chart as supply and demand curves, not conspiracies to distort TOT.

Fifth, the accusation major powers inflict bad and worsening TOT on the Third World wrongly presumes the share of a country in world trade is, by itself, a gauge

---

10. *See* 15 U.S.C. §§ 78dd-1 *et seq.*

of its prosperity or wealth. That share is just one such indicator. Some high-income countries like Brunei, Singapore, Switzerland, and the UAE have small shares. Still, as a general trend, the Third World share of world trade has increased. By 2004, it approximated 31%, the highest figure since 1950, and continues to grow.

A second accusation leveled not directly at the GATT-WTO system, but rather at the related international financial order, concerns external debt. Many developing and least developed countries owe staggering amounts of debt to official creditors (*e.g.*, governments of developed countries), private lending institutions (*e.g.*, commercial banks), and international organizations like the World Bank and IMF. The accusation is this debt reflects exploitation by hegemonic powers of poor countries (if the debtors are sovereign) and businesses in those countries (if the debtors are private enterprises).

The loans, it is said, were thrust on the Third World (particularly in the 1970s, to re-cycle petrodollars deposited by oil exporting countries in western and Japanese financial institutions). The loans help ensure debtor countries buy products from the creditor countries, and thereby remain dependent on them. Many debtors cannot hope to emerge from the burden in a reasonable period of time, and need new funds to repay previously-contracted debt. The link to the trade regime is these debtors are forced to use a large portion of their export revenues to repay principal and interest, rather than for reinvestment in productive assets. Not surprisingly, many scholars, governments, think tanks, and so forth have offered proposals since the 1970s, when the debt problem emerged, to alleviate the burden. Serious talk of canceling African debt began in 1987.

Debt forgiveness, advocated by (*inter alia*) the Holy See and Her Majesty's Government, is the most dramatic proposal. In the summer 2005, British Prime Minister Tony Blair and Chancellor of the Exchequer Gordon Brown persuaded the Group of 8 (G-8, *i.e.*, the rich countries, the G-7, plus Russia) to endorse a plan to cancel all debts of 18 highly indebted poor countries (HIPCs) owed to the World Bank, IMF, and AfDB. The face value of the debt is $40 billion, on which average service payments are $1 to $1.5 billion. The intended beneficiaries were Bolivia, Guyana, Honduras, Nicaragua, and 14 African countries. Nine other debtor-countries could become eligible for relief, and a further 11 countries would be if they reduced ineptitude and corruption.

There were two "catches" to the G-8 plan. First, the amount of loans or grants a debtor-country receives from the World Bank or ADB is "adjusted" (*i.e.*, cut) by the amount of money the country saves in debt servicing. For example, in 2006, Rwanda was supposed to pay $4.5 million to the World Bank and AfDB, and $2.9 million to the IMF. The G-8 proposal eliminates these repayment obligations. But, it also cuts World Bank and AfDB (but not IMF) funding to Rwanda by $4.5 million. The net saving to Rwanda, then, is $2.9 million it does not have to repay the IMF. Second, the G-8 (or any member thereof) could cut funding to the World Bank and AfDB, or their bilateral aid budgets. It is not apparent they all will allocate taxpayer funds to multilateral lenders, as opposed to setting off amounts they might have given against forgiven debt.

Lord Bauer addressed head on the accusation the external debt of the Third World is the result of exploitation by the West. First, he counters this debt represents resources supplied, namely financial capital from commercial and investment banks, and ultimately saver-investors in the U.S. and other wealthy countries, to the Third World. It is the responsibility of the debtors to channel the funds into productive investments. If they make poor investment choices, or if they allow some of the funds to be skimmed off to corrupt ends, then the creditors hardly are to blame.

To be fair, a country receiving $100 million in aid and paying $50 million in debt service is not necessarily as well off as a country receiving $50 million in aid. Former IMF Chief Economist and RBI Governor, Raghuram Rajan (1963–), pointed out the stock of liabilities matters, not just the amount of net inflow of funds. The stock of debt, in particular, can deter FDI. Would-be private investors may be concerned the debtor-government will over-tax their profits to cover debt service obligations. If they elect not to invest, and the investment rate in the debtor-country falls, then growth in the country will fall. In turn, the country will be less able to service its debt than a debt-free country.

Second, Lord Bauer explained the difficulties Third World countries have in servicing their debt do not reflect external exploitation generally, nor unfavorable TOT in particular. Rather, the causes lie in:

(1) Wasteful use of the funds supplied (*i.e.*, living beyond the country's means).

(2) Corruption.

(3) Inappropriate fiscal or monetary policies (*e.g.*, maintaining overvalued exchange rates).

(4) The need to import raw materials, intermediate goods, and capital goods (machine tools) to support industrialization.

Regarding the last-listed cause, Lord Bauer pointed out as Third World countries industrialize, they typically run large overall BOP deficits (though certain bilateral relationships may be in surplus). Malaysia and China are examples (though, for instance, China has had large trade surpluses with the U.S.). In brief, Lord Bauer's response is to differentiate an exploitative lending relationship from the normal process of economic development, and from bad choices by borrowers.

Finally, Lord Bauer dubbed condescending an aspect of the allegation about debt, namely, that imports from major countries ultimately damage people in the Third World. These people exercise free choice to import goods, based on their economic wants. If they did not want the imports, then the goods could not be sold. Yet, they are, and people are willing to produce goods to export and thereby pay for the imports. To allege otherwise is to take no account of the preferences of people in the Third World, and how they organize their economic lives in expressing their preferences.

To these points it is worth adding most poor countries receive many times more in multilateral, regional, and bilateral aid than they pay in external debt servicing. In the 1990s, reports the World Bank, HIPCs received roughly twice as much aid as they paid to service their debts. Mozambique, an extreme example, paid $71.8 million to service its debts in 2003, but got 14 times that amount in aid.

Chapter 18

Modern Indian Trade Policy[1]

I. 15 August 1947 Partition

An ancient civilization, the modern Indian nation was born at the stroke of midnight on 15 August 1947. At that moment, the British Partition took effect, creating "India" in Hindu-majority areas, and "Pakistan" in Muslim-majority areas. The Partition hardly was perfect. Hindus and Sikhs on the Pakistan side of the line streamed into the Indian Punjab, while some Muslims on the Indian side shifted to Pakistan. Ten million people moved, the largest exodus in human history. One million were killed in communal violence, Hindus and Sikhs on Muslims, and vice

---

1. The literature on Indian economic reforms is sizeable and growing. In addition to references cited later, excellent sources include:

Books —

1. Chambers, Michael R., ed., South Asia in 2020: Future Strategic Balances and Alliances (November 2002).
2. Cohen, Stephen P., India — Emerging Power (2001).
3. Das, Tarun, Colette Mathur & Frank-Jürgen Richter, India Rising — Emergence of a New World Power (2005).
4. Ganguly, Sumit & Neil DeVotta eds., Understanding Contemporary India (2003).
5. Gulati, Ashok & Tim Kelley, Trade Liberalization & Indian Agriculture (1999).
6. Hossain, Moazzem, Iyanatul Islam & Reza Kibria, South Asian Economic Development — Transformation, Opportunities and Challenges (1999).
7. Husain, Ishrat, Pakistan — The Economy of an Elitist State (1999).
8. Khan, Shahrukh Rafi, ed, 50 Years of Pakistan's Economy — Traditional Topics and Contemporary Concerns (1999).
9. Krueger, Anne O. & Sajjid Z. Chinoy eds., Reforming India's External, Financial, and Fiscal Policies (2003).
10. Lal, Deepak, Unfinished Business — India in the World Economy (1999).
11. Myrdal, Gunnar, Asian Drama — An Inquiry into the Poverty of Nations (abridged ed., 1971).
12. Pal, Izzud-Din, Pakistan, Islam & Economics — Failure of Modernity (1999).
13. Singh, Inderjit, The Great Ascent — The Rural Poor in South Asia (1990).
14. Srinivasan, T.N., Eight Lectures on India's Economic Reforms (2000).
15. Srinivasan, T.N. & Suresh D. Tendulkar, Reintegrating India with the World Economy (March 2003).
16. Zaidi, S. Akbar, Issues in Pakistan's Economy (1999).

Articles —

1. Buckley, Ross P., *The Economic Policies of China and India, and of the Washington Consensus: An Enlightening Comparison*, 27 Wisconsin International Law Journal 707–726 (2010).

versa. Ghost trains pulled into Amritsar and Multan, the occupants having been slaughtered.

Visually, Partition scenes are depicted in the epic film *Gandhi* (1982), which won 8 of the 11 Academy Awards for which it was nominated, including Best Picture, Best Director (Sir Richard Attenborough (1923–2014)), and Best Actor (Ben Kingsley (1943–) as the Mahatma). Many writers have chronicled the Partition: Sir Penderel Moon (1905–1987), the former Chief Commissioner for Himachal Pradesh, in *Divide and Quit—An Eyewitness Account of the Partition of India* (1961); Anita Inder Singh, an international affairs scholar, in *The Origins of the Partition of India: 1936–1947* (1987); and, Yasmin Khan (1977–), a historian, *The Great Partition—The Making of India and Pakistan* (2007). But no book on the Partition bests *Freedom at Midnight* (1975), by journalists Larry Collins (1951–) and Dominique Lapierre (1931–).

The debate strewn across thousands of pages about the cataclysmic events and repercussions of the Partition continues. Why did it occur? Was it necessary? And, the debate about the giant figures of Partition continues: Jawaharlal Nehru (1889–1964), the first Indian Prime Minister (1947–1964) and an intellectual giant; Muhammad Ali Jinnah (1876–1948), the first Pakistani leader (1947–1948), its *Quaid-i-Azam* (Great Leader) and Baba-i-Qaum (Father of the Nation); Lord Mountbatten (1900–1979), the last British Viceroy of India (1947) and first Governor-General of the Independent Union of India (1947–1948, from which the Republic of India emerged in 1950); and, of course, the *Mahatma*, Mohandas Karamchand Gandhi (1869–1948) or *Bapu* (Father of the Nation). What were their motives, their strokes of genius, and their tragic mistakes? The legacy of Partition lives on in the children (such as your author) and grandchildren of the parents who lived and died in that era through countless family stories, mementos, and novels like *Train to Pakistan* (1956), by Khushwant Singh (1915–2014), and *Midnight's Children*, (1980) winner of the 1981 Booker Prize, by Salman Rushdie (1947–).

The legacy of Partition also lives on in International Trade Law.[2] GATT provided a *sui generis* provision, Article XXIV:11, for India and Pakistan, in light of

---

2. Hochberg, Shari B., Student Article, *United States—India Relations: Reconciling the H-1B Visa Hike and Framework for Cooperation on Trade and Investment*, 24 PACE INTERNATIONAL LAW REVIEW 233–257 (2012).

3. Jain, Sumeet, *"You Say Nano, We Say No-No": Getting a "Yes" Instead for Special Economic Zones in India*, 32 NORTHWESTERN JOURNAL OF INTERNATIONAL LAW & BUSINESS 1–35 (2011).

4. Ranjan, Prabhash, *Treaties in Trade and Investment and the Indian Legal Regime: Should We Mind the Gap?*, 11 AUSTRALIAN JOURNAL OF ASIAN LAW 56–81 (2009).

5. Singhania, Monica & Akshay Gupta, *Determinants of foreign Direct Investment in India*, 10 JOURNAL OF INTERNATIONAL TRADE LAW AND POLICY 64–81 (2011).

6. Viswanathan, K.G., *The Global Financial Crisis and Its Impact on India*, 9 JOURNAL OF INTERNATIONAL BUSINESS & LAW 41–62 (2010).

2. *See* Raj Bhala, *The Forgotten Mercy: GATT Article XXIV:11 and Trade on the Subcontinent*, 2002 NEW ZEALAND LAW REVIEW 301–337 (2002).

the "*exceptional* circumstances arising out of" their creation.[3] Seeing the two newly independent countries had "long constituted *an* economic unit," the GATT contracting parties granted India and Pakistan special dispensation from multilateral trade disciplines to enter into "*special arrangements* with respect to the trade between them, pending the establishment of their mutual trade relations on a *definitive* basis."[4] They forgot this special mercy, this permission naming only them to "depart from particular provisions of" GATT as long as they fulfilled its objectives.[5] Never taking advantage of it, never establishing definitive trade arrangements, they instead fought 3 wars. India won them all: in 1965; 1971, resulting in the split of West and East Pakistan, the latter becoming the new nation of Bangladesh; and 1999, an undeclared war fought in the icy climbs of the Himalayas in Kashmir, the key Muslim-majority area the British left to India.[6] To this day, mutual suspicion over-rides what obviously is a geographically and culturally free trade region. Though original contracting parties to GATT, only recently did each side even grant MFN treatment to the other.

II. Socialism, Nationalism, and Anti-Colonialism

In 1949, Prime Minister Nehru spent several weeks travelling across the U.S., giving lectures at universities, and meeting Albert Einstein. "[S]hocked by the commercialism he saw,"[7] the Prime Minister quipped: "one should never visit America for the first time."[8] Speaking at Columbia University, he worried about unsustainable inequities: if the hopes of poor people remain unmet, "then there is the apathy of despair or the destructive rage of the revolutionary."[9]

Given the *Pandit Ji's* observations, coupled with the intellectual influences from his student days in England, it is unsurprising that he and his economic leadership team were enamored with Socialism.[10] This romance became deeply "embedded in the Indian freedom struggle":[11]

> [S]ince the British had come to trade and stayed on to rule, Nehruvian nationalists were deeply suspicious of foreigners approaching them for commercial motives.

---

3. GATT Article XXIV:11 (emphasis added).

4. GATT Article XXIV:11 (emphasis added).

5. GATT Article XXIV:11, *Ad Article XXIV, Paragraph 11*.

6. For a primer on the nearly 7 decades of conflict between the rivals, see Stanley Wolpert, *India and Pakistan — Continued Conflict or Cooperation?* (Berkeley, California: University of California Press, 2010).

7. *Charming, Disarming*, THE ECONOMIST, 4 October 2014, at 48. [Hereinafter, *Charming*.]

8. *Quoted in Charming*.

9. *Charming*.

10. *See* SHASHI THAROOR, NEHRU — THE INVENTION OF INDIA 240 (New York, New York: Arcade Publishing, Inc., 2003). [Hereinafter, THAROOR.]

11. THAROOR, 239.

Nehru, like many Third World nationalists, saw the imperialism that had subjugated his people as the logical extension of international capitalism, for which he therefore felt a deep mistrust. As an idealist profoundly moved by the poverty and suffering of the vast majority of his countrymen under colonial capitalism, Nehru was attracted to non-capitalist solutions for their problems. . . . As a democrat, he saw the economic well-being of the poor as indispensable for their political empowerment, and he could not entrust its attainment to the rich.[12]

The February 1927 Brussels International Congress Against Colonial Oppression and Imperialism, at which Jawaharlal Nehru represented the Indian National Congress Party, is said to have "confirmed his conversion to Socialism."[13]

He, like many leaders in the Quit India Movement seeking independence from Britain, had been schooled in England. Fabian Socialism was popular in the early 20th century, the way *laissez-faire* economics was in the 1980s, and continues to be in some ideological circles. And, though from a supremely privileged background, Nehru was acutely aware of the desperate poverty of India. Nehru was well aware that Colonialism had much to do with that impoverishment. As Shashi Tharoor (1956–), an Indian MP, former U.N. Under Secretary General, and author of *Inglorious Empire: What the British Did to India* (2017), said in a July 2015 speech to the Oxford Union:

India's share of the world economy when Britain arrived on it shores was 23 per cent. By the time the British left it was down to below four per cent. Why? Simply because India had been governed for the benefit of Britain. Britain's rise for 200 years was financed by its depredations in India.

In fact, Britain's industrial revolution was actually premised upon the deindustrialisation of India.[14]

So, searching for a development path in a post-Colonial India, Nehru, at the 1936 annual Congress Party meeting in Lucknow, confessed:

I am convinced that the only key to the solution of the world's problems and of India's problems lies in Socialism . . . . I see no way of ending the poverty, the vast unemployment, the degradation and the subjection of the Indian people except through Socialism. That involves vast and revolutionary changes in our political and social structure, . . . a new civilization radically different from the present capitalist order. Some glimpse we can have of this new civilization in the territories of the USSR [Union of Soviet

---

12. THAROOR, 239–240.

13. THAROOR, 55.

14. *Quoted in* Maya Oppenheim, *"Winston Churchill is No Better than Adolf Hitler," Says Indian Politician Dr. Shashi Tharoor*, Independent, 21 March 2017, www.independent.co.uk/news/world/world-history/winston-churchill-adolf-hitler-no-better-shashi-tharoor-indian-politician-post-colonialist-author-a7641681.html (emphasis added).

Socialist Republics].... if the future is full of hope it is largely because of Soviet Russia.[15]

So:

> [l]ike many others of his generation, Nehru thought that central planning, state control of the "commanding heights" of the economy, and government-directed development were the "scientific" and "rational" means of creating social prosperity and ensuring equitable distribution.[16]

Yet, Nehru was nothing if not independent of mind, and nothing if not an Indian above a Socialist.

He declared after the 1927 Brussels International Congress Against Colonial Oppression and Imperialism, at which he represented the Indian National Congress Party, that "[p]ersonally I have the strongest objection to being led by the nose by the Russians or anyone else."[17] He wrote in 1919 that:

> Present-day democracy, manipulated by the unholy alliance of capital, property, militarism and an overgrown bureaucracy, and assisted by a capitalist press, has proved a delusion and a snare. [But,] Orthodox Socialism does not give us much hope .... [A]n all-powerful state is no lover of individual liberty .... Life under Socialism would be a joyless and soulless thing, regulated to the minutest detail by rules and orders.[18]

Thus, when confronted with a tradeoff between Nationalism and Socialism, he chose the former, indeed being the glamorous face of Indian nationalism and modernity to complement the other-worldly, deific status of the Mahatma.[19]

Not surprisingly, when their quarters changed from the jails of Colonial India to government offices, and their work changed from challenging the British Empire through non-violent means to running a nation, Nehru and his Independence movement colleagues put into practice economic strategies that were *de rigueur* in their era, but refused the political step of entering the Soviet or Chinese Communist orbit. For his entire tenure as Prime Minister, Nehru would strive for a middle path, picking the best of Socialist economic strategies fort the Indian context and avoiding capitalist extremes, but equally avoiding the excesses of Socialism. In that effort, he was *avant garde*: how many critics of global economic order and the world trading system understand the failures of Socialism, but are repulsed by American Capitalism and its current crop of ignorant and petty champions?

---

15. *Quoted in* THAROOR, 174.
16. THAROOR, 240.
17. *Quoted in* THAROOR, 57.
18. *Quoted in* THAROOR, 174.
19. THAROOR, 100–101, 175.

III. Three Hallmarks of Post-Partition Socialist Style Planning

In respect of international trade, steering a middle course did not mean autarky, or free trade. It meant self-sufficiency and self-reliance, "twin mantras" that disallowed western corporations from entering India to exploit its resources and oppress its people.[20] In turn, self-sufficiency and self-reliance translated into a trade strategy of import substitution, a preference for the use of domestic inputs into finished manufactured goods, rather than imports.[21] To implement import substitution, India set up a system that came to be known as the "License *Raj*," a term coined in 1959 by statesman and scholar Chakravati Rajagopalachari (1878–1972), or "Rajaji," a lawyer, veteran of the Quit India Movement, and the last Governor-General of India (1948–1950).[22]

Tariffs were levied at high rates to impede importation, and QRs were imposed. Licenses and quotas, anathema to free market economists as being inefficient, were the key QRs used. To import or export most categories of merchandise, a government-granted license was needed, and the government fixed by quota quantities of imports or exports. Only private enterprises favored by the government were granted such licenses, and favoritism often resulted from historic pre-Partition relations between political officials in the Indian National Congress, on the one hand, and agricultural landowners and capitalist industrialists, on the other hand. Corruption and nepotism characterized many such linkages. Indeed, corruption, plus a decrepit physical infrastructure, remain India's greatest barrier to robust growth and sustained poverty alleviation.

Import substitution, however sorry its effects in historical and Neo-Classical economic perspective, was not a fanciful Fabian or economically irrational strategy. In agriculture, reflected concerns about food security, which given the country's history of famines, and its dependence on Britain even for salt—an injustice Gandhi poignantly laid bare with his famous 12 March–6 April 1930 Salt March—was understandable. India pursued self-sufficiency in food. To feed its growing population, India did not want to be a "peripheral" country reliant on food imports from "center" countries like Great Britain, much less food aid from the U.S. or Soviet Union that those donor countries could use to pressure India to support one or the

---

20. THAROOR, 240.

21. *See* Anne O. Krueger & Sajjid Z. Chinoy, *Introduction*, 1 *in* REFORMING INDIA'S EXTERNAL, FINANCIAL, AND FISCAL POLICIES (ANNE O. KRUEGER & SAJJID CHINOY EDS., Stanford, California: Stanford University Press, 2003). [Hereinafter, Krueger & Chinoy.]

22. *See* Ramachandra Guha, *The Delhi Dilemma*, FINANCIAL TIMES, 13–14 July 2013, at 10 (reviewing Amartya Sen & Jean Drèze, *An Uncertain Glory: India and its Contradictions* (London, England: Allen Lane, 2013), www.ft.com. [Hereinafter, *The Delhi Dilemma*.]

other side in the Cold War.[23] Indeed, it did grow from 361.1 million in 1951, just four years after Partition to 447.8 million in 1960 to 1.241 billion in 2011.[24]

In industry, how else could India industrialize, develop vertically integrated manufacturing, mature to developed country status, and thereby avoid dependence as a "peripheral" country on "center," but through import-substituting production? India had just endured over a century of dependence on England for manufactured garments, being confined to the role of providing British T&A mills with cotton. Here again, the Mahatma had poignantly demonstrated the injustice with his *khadi* (homespun) campaign.

Import substitution was one of three hallmarks of Socialist-style economic planning that characterized India in its first four decades of independence. The second was widespread use of SOEs. The government reserved large swathes of the economy—such as airlines, banking, electricity, insurance, oil and gas, shipping, telephones—entirely for SOEs.[25] There they held monopoly positions. SOEs even had monopoly positions on importation of bulk consumer goods. In other sectors, SOEs played a significant, sometimes pre-eminent, role: bakeries, fertilizers, heavy chemicals, hotels, infrastructure, machine tools, and steel.[26] Across all sectors, the government imposed strict investment licensing requirements, akin to its QRs in international trade. These licenses, too, were part of the License Raj system: to engage in private direct investment or technological development, a private enterprise needed a license.[27] Via them, the government directed private economic activity toward its overall aims of food self-sufficiency and industrialization.

Conservatism in fiscal and monetary policies was the third hallmark of post-Partition Indian economic strategy. For the first 35 years of Independence, *i.e.*, from 1947 to 1982, these policies were less expansionary than in other developing countries.[28] Only in the mid-1980s did Indian fiscal policy turn expansionary, contributing to annual economic growth of over 5%. Yet, having been too conservative for too long, that policy became too liberal. Inflation rose above 13%, foreign debt increased dramatically, and in 1991 India faced a BOP crisis, with FX reserves

---

23. The references to "center" and "peripheral" countries, and "dependency" or "reliance," are of course to Dependency Theory and World Systems Theory. *See* DUDLEY SEERS ED., DEPENDENCY THEORY—A CRITICAL REASSESSMENT (London, England: Francis Pinter Publishers, 1981), and IMMANUEL WALLERSTEIN, THE ESSENTIAL WALLERSTEIN (New York, New York: The New Press, 2000). These Marxist-tinged Theories are out of favor in the present era of free market economics and global supply chains. Yet, query whether such chains, which link low-valued added operations in poor countries with higher value-added activities in rich ones, actually are evidence in favor of these Theories.

24. *See Demographics of India*, WIKIPEDIA, http://en.wikipedia.org/wiki/Demographics_of _India.

25. *See* Krueger & Chinoy, 1.

26. *See* Krueger & Chinoy, 1.

27. *See* Krueger & Chinoy, 1.

28. *See* Krueger & Chinoy, 1.

covering less than two weeks' worth of imports.[29] This unsustainable course had to be reversed. Therein was a catalyst for the 1991 reforms.

Underlying these hallmarks was fear. India was afraid of world markets and foreign and portfolio investors. To rely on their markets for export revenues from sales of Indian agricultural or industrial output, or for inputs into Indian goods, was to be vulnerable to their exploitation. Emerging from centuries of foreign control, why should Indians risk neo-colonial dependence, "neo" in the sense that such dependence was via the so-called "free" market?

In sum, "[f]or more than four decades after India attained independence in 1947, Indian economic policy was governed by a philosophy that emphasized inward-oriented, state-led development."[30] Yet, notwithstanding the prominence of Communist parties in a few states, especially Kerala and West Bengal, India rejected Communism, that is, full public ownership of the means of production, in contrast to the China of Mao Zedong (1893–1976). "Red" China, which became independent under the CCP on 1 January 1949, and the Soviet Union, which fell under Bolshevik control in November 1917. Indians would never accept the human rights cost incurred by Communist central planning (and never will), nor would they agree to unbridled Capitalism with its excesses. India sought a third way, and championed the Non-Aligned Movement (NAM), a highpoint of which was the April 1955 Bandung Conference, attended by India and 28 other newly independent Asian and African countries representing roughly 25% of the surface of the earth and 1.5 billion people.[31]

During the Cold War, India became adept at balance of power politics. In August 1971, Prime Minister Indira Gandhi (1917–1984) signed the 20-year Indo-Soviet Treaty of Peace, Friendship, and Cooperation with Soviet General Secretary Leonid Brezhnev (1906–1982), which helped India offset the American alliance with Pakistan. Yet, as a democracy with a large NRI population in the U.S. and its former colonial master, the U.K., Indians—while not wanting to be a proxy for either the American or Soviet superpower—had no strong hostility towards, but rather warm links to, the non-Communist west.

IV. 1970s: Inefficiencies

Indian economic policy in the first few decades after Partition achieved some successes. India became self-sufficient in food, and even a net exporter of certain farm products. That was thanks to the Green Revolution, particularly in Punjab.

---

29. *See* Krueger & Chinoy, 1.

30. *See* Krueger & Chinoy, 1.

31. *See Asian-African Conference*, WIKIPEDIA, http://en.wikipedia.org/wiki/Asian-African_Conference.

However, by the 1970s, it was clear Indian economic growth and development lagged that of its East Asian counterparts. India was anything but an international trade powerhouse under the License *Raj* system:

> The result [of the system and its drive for self-sufficiency and self-reliance] was a state that ensured political freedom but presided over economic stagnation; that regulated entrepreneurial activity through a system of licenses, permits, and quotas that promoted both corruption and inefficiency but did little to promote growth; that enshrined bureaucratic power at the expense of individual enterprise. *For most of the first five decades since Independence, India pursued an economic policy of subsidizing unproductivity, regulating stagnation, and distributing poverty.* Nehru called this socialism.[32]

Indeed, the contrast between its performance, and the export-oriented growth of East Asian countries, especially the Four Tigers (or Dragons), Hong Kong, Korea, Singapore, and Taiwan, was vivid. Bloated with underemployed, low-human capital workers, and plagued by politicized decision-making, Indian SOEs were infamously inefficient. During the Thatcher-Reagan Era (1979–1991), as other Asian countries began liberating their SOEs from government controls and converting them into private enterprises operating on commercial principles, India stood out as a laggard in privatization.

So, for all its fascinating ancient ethnic, culinary, linguistic, and religious traditions and pluralism, for all its lively post-Partition democratic elections, in the first 40 years after Partition, India had marginalized itself in the world economy.[33] Between 1950 and 1973, world exports grew at an annual average rate of 7.9%. Exports from India rose only 2.7% in that period.[34] The ratio of Indian exports to GDP fell from its high of 7.3% in 1951 to its low of 3% in 1965, and stayed under 4% until 1973.[35] In that respect, at least, import substitution was working. Among its neighbors to the east, India had fallen behind economically the likes of the Four Tigers, and indeed most of East Asia. The gap between the Elephant and Tigers seemed to be widening as the decades after the Second World War and Partition passed. To be sure, Bollywood churned out movies and songs, but with poor quality, and only to the Sub-Continent, Middle East, and Africa.

---

32. Tharoor, 241 (emphasis added).

33. *See* T.N. Srinivasan, *Integrating India with the World Economy: Progress, Problems, and Prospects, in* Reforming India's External, Financial, and Fiscal Policies 17–19 (Anne O. Krueger & Sajjid Chinoy eds., Stanford, California: Stanford University Press, 2003). [Hereinafter, Srinivasan.]

34. *See* Srinivasan, 17. The year 1973 was a watershed, because of the Arab oil embargo and its adverse effects on the world economy.

35. *See* Srinivasan, 17.

While major MNCs like Honda, Toyota, and Sony emerged from Japan, and Hyundai and Samsung from Korea, no household name or brand emerged from India:

> The mantra of self-sufficiency might have made some sense if, behind these protectionist walls, Indian business had been encouraged to thrive. Despite the difficulties placed in their way by the British Raj, Indian corporate houses like those of the Birlas, Tatas, and Kirloskars had built impressive business establishments by the time of Independence, and could conceivably have taken on the world. Instead they found themselves being hobbled by regulations and restrictions, inspired by Nehru's socialist mistrust of the profit motive, on every conceivable aspect of economic activity: whether they could invest in a new product or a new capacity, where they could invest, how many people they could hire, whether they could fire them, what sort of expansion or diversification they could undertake, where they could sell and for how much. Initiative was stifled, government permission was mandatory before any expansion or diversification, and a mind-boggling array of permits and licenses were required before the slightest new undertaking.[36]

Conversely, none of the foreign household names thought much of investing in India: at the start of the 1990s, of all FDI attracted by developing countries around the world, India got less than 1% of it.[37]

India fared no better as a destination for portfolio investment, attracting just 3% of all investment funds obtained by developing countries at the start of that decade.[38] The lack of financial capital flows into India, coupled with socialist-style central government planning, doomed prospects for most would-be Indian private sector entrepreneurs. With foreign capital going to the likes of the Tigers, and with the Indian government taking loans from state-run banks, unless an entrepreneur had a pool of personal savings or family capital on which to draw, how could she establish and build a business? Even if she could, her company would have to navigate decrepit physical infrastructure and a stultifying, corrupt political bureaucracy. Small wonder millions of Indians left the country, a major brain drain in the first 40 years after Independence.

Most tellingly, but unsurprisingly, was the bottom line statistic on economic growth: from the late 1940s to 1980, Indian GDP at a pathetically low 2% *per annum*, nowhere close to the rates in East Asia:[39]

> The combination of internal controls and international protectionism gave India a distorted economy, underproductive and grossly inefficient,

---

36. THAROOR, 242–243.
37. *See* Srinivasan, 17–59.
38. *See* Srinivasan, 17–59.
39. *See* Krueger & Chinoy, 1.

making too few goods of too low a quality at too high a price. Exports of manufactured goods grew at an annual rate of 0.1 percent until 1985; India's share of world trade fell by four-fifths. Per capita income, with a burgeoning population and a modest increase in GDP, anchored India firmly to the bottom third of the world rankings. The public sector, however, grew in size though not in production, to become the largest in the world outside the Communist bloc. Meanwhile, income disparities persisted, the poor remained mired in a poverty all the more wretched for the lack of means of escape from it in a controlled economy, the public sector sat entrenched at the "commanding heights" and looked down upon the toiling, overtaxed middle class, and only bureaucrats, politicians, and a small elite of protected businessmen flourished from the management of scarcity.[40]

As intimated, under the License Raj system, well-connected families prospered. Names like "Ambani," "Birla," and "Tata" were household ones in India. But, few Americans would have recognized them as akin to the Carnegies or Rockefellers. India had proved itself a power on the Subcontinent in its victories over Pakistan, and even shown its scientific and military potential with its 1974 successful nuclear test. However, it was no match for China, which it found out in a brief 1962 border war. In sum, in a haunting phrase purportedly heard among the U.S. State Department, India was "the biggest country that didn't matter."

V. 1991 First Generation Reforms

• **Overview**

Dr. Manmohan Singh (1932–, PM, 2004–2014), whose party, the Indian National Congress had led the Quit India Movement and governed India for most of the post-Independence period, understood the need for reform. Coming to the position of Finance Minister in 1991 under Prime Minister P.V. Narasimha Rao (1921–2004, PM, 1991–1996), and became Prime Minister in 2004. As Finance Minister, he faced the 1991 BOP crisis. He was well prepared. He had trained as an economist, culminating with a dissertation he wrote at Oxford entitled "India's Export Performance, 1951–1960," under the supervision of renowned development economist I.M.D. Little (1919–2012). (The dissertation became a book in 1964, *India's Export Trends and Prospects for Self-Sustained Growth.*)

In 1991, Singh ushered in the dramatic, first generation economic reforms. They were dramatic in that they were "structural," dismantling many post-Partition socialist-style policies.[41] The changes aimed to unshackle Indian firms and entrepreneurs from red tape, foster competition, and open India to the global economy.

---

40. Tharoor, 243–244.
41. Krueger & Chinoy, 2.

The reforms may be put into three broad categories: External Sector Reforms, FDI Reforms, and Financial Sector Reforms. Each is discussed in turn below, with greatest emphasis on the first category. Across these categories were three common denominators: de-regulation; privatization; and, rationalization.

- **External Sector Reforms**

The "external sector" refers not only to international trade (imports and exports), but also to exchange rates and capital flows. Indian reforms on trade were particularly impressive, even dramatic:

> Some of the most far-reaching reforms were focused on restoring the health of the external sector. They included the transition to a market-determined exchange rate, major reductions in customs tariffs, phased elimination of quantitative restrictions on imports, decisive opening up to foreign direct and portfolio investment, strict controls on external debt, and the deliberate buildup of foreign exchange reserves.[42]

More precisely, with respect to traditional international trade law matters, there were five dimensions to the 1991 reforms: (1) cutting the average level of tariffs; (2) reducing maximum tariff levels (peaks) in a phased manner; (3) attacking tariff dispersion and tariff escalation; (4) simplifying the tariff schedule; and (5) dismantling the License Raj. A sixth dimension, closely related to trade but not conventionally considered within the boundaries of multilateral trade rules, concerned exchange rate liberalization.

First: Average Tariff Levels

So, India cut its applied (as distinct from bound) MFN tariffs on industrial goods from an overall average of 15% to an average of 12.5%. In 1990–1991, across all merchandise categories, the average Indian import-weighted tariff was 87%, and 164% on consumer goods.[43] But, by 1996–1997, the average imported-weighted tariff tumbled to 24.6%.

Second: Tariff Peaks

In these reductions, India addressed its tariff peaks (extremely high tariffs on particular products). In 1990–1991, the highest duty level hit 355%.[44] In 1997–1998, the highest duty level was 45%.

Third: Tariff Dispersion and Escalation

India also dealt with its problem of tariff dispersion (the spread of tariffs across large wide numerical ranges), which created a bias against the use of imports in domestic agriculture and manufacturing, distorted incentives in resource allocation,

---

42. Shankar Acharya, *Comment—Opening the Economy: Further Reforms, in* REFORMING INDIA'S EXTERNAL, FINANCIAL, AND FISCAL POLICIES 57 (ANNE O. KRUEGER & SAJJID CHINOY EDS., Stanford, California: Stanford University Press, 2003). [Hereinafter, Acharya.]

43. *See* Krueger & Chinoy, 2; Srinivasan, 18–20.

44. *See* Srinivasan, 20.

and ultimately discouraged exports. India did so by slashing the standard deviation of tariff levels to one-quarter of their 1990–1991 levels on intermediate and capital goods, and one third of those levels on agricultural goods.[45]

In so doing, India also began to address the problem of tariff escalation, whereby tariffs on merchandise increase with the degree of processing, with lower tariffs on raw materials, higher tariffs on intermediate items, and the highest tariffs on finished goods. (Escalation is designed to promote vertically integrated manufacturing, and higher value-added production, domestically. It provides a higher level of effective protection for finished manufactured goods in comparison with the simple tariff on those goods, because of the tariffs at each earlier stage of processing.)

Fourth: Simplification

By 2000–2001, India had simplified its tariff schedules, and narrowed the duty levels, to just 4 categories: 35%; 25%; 15%; and 5%.[46] To be sure, most merchandise fell into the 35% and 25% categories. Nevertheless, after decades of protectionism, the change was remarkable—and, it may be added, one for which American trade negotiators in the Doha Round rarely if ever publicly credited India, choosing instead to castigate it for not doing enough.[47] All the more remarkable was the price tag: In 1990–1991, government revenue from import tariffs equaled 3.6% of Indian GDP, and total tax revenue accounted for 9.5% of GDP.[48] India had taken the difficult step of starting to wean itself off customs duties as a key source of government financing.

Fifth: License Raj

As part of its first-generation reforms, India also began to dismantle the License *Raj* system and expose the country not to complete free trade, but freer trade. For most categories of merchandise, India abolished many import licensing requirements.[49] By 1998, seven years after the launch of the first-generation reforms,

---

45. *See* Srinivasan, 18–21.

46. Srinivasan, 20. India also cut the number of exemptions, also called use-based concessions, on tariff rates. *See id.*

47. *See* The Doha Round Trilogy, Raj Bhala, *Poverty, Islamist Extremism, and the Debacle of Doha Round Counter-Terrorism: Part One of a Trilogy—Agricultural Tariffs and Subsidies*, 9 University of Saint Thomas Law Journal issue 1, 5–160 (2011, Annual Law Journal Lecture); Raj Bhala, *Poverty, Islamist Extremism, and the Debacle of Doha Round Counter-Terrorism: Part Two of a Trilogy—Non-Agricultural Market Access and Services Trade*, 44 Case Western Reserve Journal of International Law issues 1 & 2, 1–81 (2011, War Crimes Research Symposium on International Law in Crisis); and, Raj Bhala, *Poverty, Islamist Extremism, and the Debacle of Doha Round Counter-Terrorism: Part Three of a Trilogy—Trade Remedies and Facilitation*, 40 Denver Journal of International Law and Policy issues 1–3, 237–320 (2012, 40th Anniversary Symposium Festschrift in Honor of Professor Ved P. Nanda, "Perspectives on International Law in an Era of Change"), *posted on* various databases and websites, including Gateway House—The Indian Council on Global Relations, www.gatewayhouse.in/poverty-islamist-extremism-and-the-debacle -of-doha-round-counter-terrorism-a-trilogy/. [Hereinafter, Doha Round Trilogy.]

48. *See* Srinivasan, 19.

49. *See* Krueger & Chinoy, 3; Srinivasan, 18–21.

roughly 32% of all Indian tariff lines were subject to import licensing.[50] That figure, while still too high, was significant, because Indian import licensing had functioned in practice as an import ban.

Just before commencing the reforms, in 1988–1989, 95% of all products imported into India, and 80% of all manufactured products (excluding basic metals and certain miscellaneous items), were subject to one type of NTB or another.[51] More specifically, consider the percentage of internationally tradable goods India protected by QRs or NTBs in terms of total tradable GDP: at the end of the 1980s, it was 93% overall, and 90% for manufactured goods.[52] By May 1995, it fell to 66% overall, and by May 1996, to 36% for manufactured items. These staggering facts bespeak how pervasive the License Raj system had become in the decades following Partition: QRs had become the "dominant means for control of imports."[53] They also show how dramatic the 1991 reforms to the License *Raj* system were.

To be sure, they could have been yet more dramatic. Most remaining QRs were on consumer goods, and the reforms still left the agricultural sector protected: the pre-1991 share of tradable agricultural goods as a percentage of total tradable GDP was 94%, and in May 1994 it was down only to 84%.[54] Under GATT Article XI:1 and Uruguay Round agreements, India was obliged to eliminate all QRs. Regrettably, it sought to retain many of them under the BOP exceptions of GATT Article XVIII. On 1 April 1999, India still had QRs on 1,200 tariff lines. It fought to keep them, but lost the 1999 *India Quantitative Restrictions* case (discussed in a separate Chapter) at the WTO Appellate Body.[55] So, on 1 April 2000, it cut QR-protected tariff lines to 600, and on 1 April 2001 eliminated all QRs. In brief, India phased out its QRs—albeit with external WTO adjudicatory pressure—across 10 years following the 1991 reforms.

Still another type of NTB India addressed in its 1991 reforms were government import monopolies. On 50 categories of commodities, Indian government agencies long had held import monopolies: save for agricultural products and petroleum, India eliminated them.[56] Concomitantly, in government procurement, India eliminated preferences (stated in terms of partial purchases or prices) for domestic suppliers of goods, thus opening opportunities for foreign bidders.[57]

---

50. *See* World Trade Organization, Trade Policy Review Body, *Trade Policy Review for India, 1998*, www.wto.org.

51. *See* Srinivasan, 19.

52. *See* Srinivasan, 20–21.

53. Srinivasan, 19.

54. *See* Srinivasan, 21.

55. *See* WTO Appellate Body Report, *India—Quantitative Restrictions on Imports of Agricultural, Textile, and Industrial Products*, WT/DS90/AB/R (adopted 22 September 1999).

56. *See* Srinivasan, 20.

57. *See* Srinivasan, 20.

The 1991 reforms dealt not only with QRs on imports, but also on exports. India (as of 1 April 2001) eliminated them (*e.g.*, quotas) on agricultural exports, and dropped minimum export price requirements.[58] It also reduced the size of the list of merchandise subject to export restrictions or bans.

Sixth: Market-Determined Exchange Rate

Finally, as for the *rupee*, the Indian government had allowed it to depreciate against hard currencies (such as the U.S. dollar and British pound sterling) ever since the Bretton Woods fixed exchange rate system ended in 1971.[59] Official devaluation was part of the 1991 reforms: in July of that year, India reduced its value by 22.8% against a basket of currencies where each currency was weighted by Indian exports to the country of that currency.[60] India also dismantled the dual exchange rate system it had created to cope with the 1991 BOP crisis, eliminated foreign exchange licensing, and requirements concerning export-based imports and import compression.[61]

By 1993, and since then, the *rupee* was freely convertible for all current account transactions (*i.e.*, for purposes of Article VIII of the *Articles of Agreement of the International Monetary Fund*).[62] To be sure, the float is a managed one, but that hardly is peculiar to India. And, full capital account liberalization has yet to occur, which again is not an expectation unique to India.

Still, the result of exchange rate regime changes was predictably positive. Indian exports (in terms of volume) grew faster than the world average after 1973, though (as explained below) were insignificant in overall world trade.[63]

Notably, the aforementioned external sector reforms did not occur all at once, in 1991.[64] India did not choose the shock therapy treatment that Poland used in 1989. Rather, it deferred tariff cuts and QR elimination on consumer goods until the mid-1990s. Also, of significance, India sought to build up its reserves of hard foreign currency.[65] It did so with difficulty, particularly in the late 1990s and the rounds of nuclear tests vis-à-vis Pakistan, and the imposition by the U.S. of sanctions against both India and Pakistan in response to those tests.

- **FDI Reforms**

Amidst the first-generation reforms were legal and policy changes to encourage FDI. Egregious regulations were wiped away in favor of aggressive inducements to

---

58. *See* Srinivasan, 20.
59. *See* Srinivasan, 17–20.
60. *See* Srinivasan, 19–20. India also withdrew most of its subsidies to exports, so the devaluation of the real effective exchange rate for exporters was 16.3 percent. *See id.* at 20.
61. *See* Srinivasan, 20.
62. *See* Srinivasan, 20.
63. *See* Srinivasan, 17.
64. *See* Srinivasan, 19.
65. *See* Acharya, 57.

attract MNCs to open, expand, and operate production facilities in India, and hire Indian workers. Three such clusters of measures stood out.[66]

First, India relaxed investment (equity share ownership) limits on FDI in certain (albeit not all) sectors, such as telecommunications. In particular, reversing pre-1991 strictures, India dropped its insistence on restricting FDI entry to government-determined priority sectors, and eliminated its 40% cap on foreign equity participation in JVs.[67]

Second, India eliminated trade-related FDI restrictions. No longer was a foreign direct investor obligated to export a certain percentage of its production. That obligation had been as high as 100% in some sectors, and manifestly was designed to protect Indian producers of like products. India also dropped domestic production content obligations, so foreign investors could source inputs and intermediate items from the most efficient suppliers, be they Indian or not. Again, that pre-1991 rule had been designed to protect domestic suppliers.

Third, India created Special Economic Zones (SEZs). They were modeled loosely after the famous SEZs in China inaugurated in the late 1970s in the Deng Xiaoping era.

Fourth, India began improving its IP regime. Foreign direct investors (as well as exporters) look carefully at the state of IPRs as a factor in deciding where to place an investment: they expect not only protection at least at internationally-acceptable levels, but also actual IPR enforcement by legal and judicial authorities. And, they do not want to be forced to transfer patents, trademarks, copyrights, or trade secrets to local firms. As the 1998 WTO Appellate Body Report in the *India Patent* case (discussed in a separate Chapter) intimates, India emerged from the Uruguay Round (1986–1994) of MTNs with a sub-par record on enactment and enforcement of IP laws.[68] So, with the 1991 reforms, India loosened requirements about technology transfer. It extended patent protection to pharmaceuticals, agricultural chemicals, and certain food products.

• **Financial Sector Reforms**

Financial sector reforms aimed to liberalize commercial and investment banking markets and institutions operating in India. Three market reforms were key: partial freeing of interest rates; promotion of competition among commercial and investment banks; and creation of a new securities exchange for equities trading.[69] The reforms also included technological innovations, such as electronic trading and un-certificated (*i.e.*, paperless) securities, and greater efficiencies in clearing and settlement.

---

66. In this respect, the observation that "[t]he 1991 reforms did not significantly liberalize FDI" is arguable. Srinivasan, 23.

67. *See* Srinivasan, 18–19.

68. *See* WTO Appellate Body Report, *India — Patent Protection for Pharmaceutical and Agricultural Chemical Products*, WT/DS50/AB/R (adopted 16 January 1998).

69. *See* Krueger & Chinoy, 2.

Of these three reform categories, the "centerpiece" and "focal point" of Indian economic reforms was the first.[70] That was for good reason. One clear result emerging from economic development research is the direct relationship between the outward orientation and growth: economies that are more open to trade (and FDI) experience faster gains in GDP than those pursuing protectionist policies like import substitution, or worse yet, autarky.

Underlying all categories was a shift in economic ideology from the era of Prime Minister Nehru and his daughter, Prime Minister Indira Gandhi (1917–1984, PM, 1966–1977, 1980–1984): away from central planning, and toward the market. Trade was not to be discouraged, but promoted. Foreign investment was not to be regarded with suspicion, much less hostility, but to be pursued. Finance was not to be a backward and inefficient sector, but rather a dynamic, innovative link between savings and investment. Among many indicators of the paradigmatic shift was the shrinkage in the size of the Indian government. The central government fiscal deficit as a percentage of GDP dropped from 7.7% to 5.5% between 1990–1991 and 1992–1993.[71]

The reforms worked quickly. Spurred by a private sector unshackled from government strictures, real annual growth in Indian GDP exceeded 6% in the mid-1990s.[72] In 1996, the share of exports in Indian GDP rose to 9.2%, and between 1993 and 1996, Indian merchandise exports and imports (measured in U.S. dollar value terms) grew at an average rate of 20% per annum.[73] The share of India in the growth of world exports increased. So:

> Together with deregulation of industry and fiscal stabilization, these external sector reforms yielded exceptionally good results by the mid-1990s. Export growth soared to 20 percent in three successive years, inward remittances quadrupled to $8 billion by 1994–95, foreign investment rose from negligible amounts to over $6 billion by 1996–97, foreign exchange reserves climbed steeply from the precarious levels of 1991 to over $26 billion by the end of 1996–97, and the debt-service ratio was halved over the decade.[74]

But, the good news was not to last.

VI. 1990s and Early 2000s: Reforms Sputter

· Backsliding on Tariff Cuts

By the late 1990s, first generation reforms sputtered, with predictable adverse consequences. Consider the external sector. A lurking problem with the impressive

---

70. Acharya, 57; Krueger & Chinoy, 3.
71. *See* Krueger & Chinoy, 2.
72. *See* Krueger & Chinoy, 2.
73. *See* Krueger & Chinoy, 3.
74. Acharya, 57.

reductions in tariffs is they were cuts to applied, not bound, MFN rates. Put in legal terms, the 1990–1991 tariff cuts were not locked in under the tariff binding princi-ple of GATT Article II. Thus, India could post its applied rates back up again, up to its bound levels—and so it did, taking advantage of considerable "water" (*i.e.*, gaps between lower applied and higher bound rates) in its tariff schedules.

After 1996, Indian import-weighted average applied tariffs crept back up from its 1996–1997 low of 24.6% to 30.2% in 1999–2000.[75] For intermediate goods, the import-weighted average jumped nearly 10 percentage points in the same three-year period, from 21.0% to 31.9%. The zenith of the economy-wide simple average tariff rates was 1997–1998, at 34.4%, after falling steadily from 128% in 1990–1991.[76] It rose to 40.2% in 1989–1999, and stayed essentially unchanged at 39.6% the next year.

Not surprisingly, backsliding on tariff cuts meant India compared unfavor-ably with other countries. Consider 1993, just two years into the first generation of reforms, and the end of Uruguay Round negotiations. A 1996 World Bank study examined 26 developing countries, asking what the post-Uruguay Round bound and applied tariff rates, as of 1993, were for 13 product categories.[77] It drew two key conclusions.

First, India had the highest or second highest applied rates for all product cat-egories. Indeed, its average applied tariff rate for all categories was nearly thrice the average of all other countries: India had an exceptionally high average applied rate of 51.6%, whereas the average for the other developing countries was 19.2%. Second, the patterns for applied rates existed for bound tariff rates: Indian post-Uruguay Round bound levels were higher than all other countries, across all prod-uct groupings, and for some groupings, they were significantly higher.

Further research shows India's first generation of tariff cuts were unimpressive relative to other poor or emerging countries.[78] In 1994, among 13 developing coun-tries, India had the highest average tariff level, 55%. Save for Egypt, India had the highest maximum tariff level, 65%. Six years on, India still compared unfavorably: of all large countries (ones with over 20 million people), the average Indian tariff rate was second only to that of Argentina, and well above averages in the rest of Asia and Latin America.

Perhaps most disappointing is that the first generation of external sector reforms failed to enhance the relative status of India across the decade of the 1990s. That decade, of course, was a crucial one for free market-oriented reform across much of the developing and developed world after the November 1989 fall of the Berlin Wall

---

75. *See* Srinivasan, 20.

76. *See* Srinivasan, 20–21.

77. This World Bank study, G. Pursell & A. Sharma, *Indian Trade Policies Since the 1991/92 Reforms*, is discussed in Srinivasan, 22.

78. *See* Srinivasan, 23 (*citing* a 1994 study for the IMF by A. Chopra, *et al.*, and a 2000 study by the World Bank).

and collapse of Communism. For India, however, though not a lost decade, it was a disappointing one.

Unsurprisingly, India fared poorly in respect of openness as measured by low tariffs when compared with East Asian countries. Table 18-1 shows India against them across approximately 1989 to 2000.[79] To be sure, in terms of percentage cuts to simple mean tariffs, India was in line with the other countries: all of them cut their average applied tariffs by at least 41.9% (Korea) and as much as 72.9% (Philippines). Likewise, on imported-weighted mean tariffs, India was in between the low of 36.2% (Malaysia) and 83% (Philippines), albeit at the low end of this range. But, the key is the final tariff rate: after the cuts, the Indian average (both simple and import-weighted) was still the most protectionist. Moreover, the Indian record on chopping tariff peaks manifestly was execrable: it cut by just 4.1% the share of lines in its Schedule with duty rates above 15%, whereas all other countries made large double-digit cuts. These points are true, even though India showed the most significant decrease in the degree of dispersion in its tariff Schedules, and two other countries (Korea and Malaysia) actually injected additional dispersion into their Schedules.

Surprisingly, the Indian record was undistinguished even against its Sub-Continental neighbors, except for Pakistan. Table 18-2 records tariff cuts on the Sub-Continent, again across the decade of the 1990s. At first glance, India looks to compare well: India cut its simple mean tariff by 58.9%, amidst a range from 8.4% (Pakistan) to 80% (Bangladesh); and, India dropped its average imported weighted tariff by 42.5%, while one country (Nepal) actually raised its average by 11.3%, and another country (Bangladesh) lowered its average by 76.5%. But, as intimated, it is Bangladesh and Sri Lanka that outshine India in respect of aggressive tariff reductions: after the cuts, India's simple and imported weighted average tariff levels were the highest, save for Pakistan. Similarly, India yielded the lowest percentage reduction in tariff peaks, though it did relatively well in reducing tariff dispersion.

In sum, the economic evidence is clear: neither the 1991 reforms nor the 1986–1994 Uruguay Round catalyzed dramatic applied or bound tariff reductions in India relative to other countries. India did cut them in the early 1990s. But, India failed to stay the course, and thus failed to liberalize to the extent of its competitors.

Note the East Asian Financial Crisis is not a plausible explanation for these Indian failures. That largely unanticipated (but in retrospect, foreseeable) Crisis occurred between 1997–1999. So, it would be chronologically inaccurate to argue Indian external sector reforms intentionally were at a slower pace than those of East Asia, so as to avoid adverse contagion effects of rapid trade liberalization. If anything, then it is the admixture of a legacy of post-Partition protection and domestic

---

79. Except for the calculations on percentage reductions (columns 4, 6, 8, and 10), data in Tables 20-1 and 20-2 are drawn from the 2002 World Bank *World Development Indicators*, which is discussed in Srinivasan, Table 1.3 at 23.

Table 18-1. Indian versus East Asian Tariffs in 1990s

Country	Year	Simple Average Tariff (%)	Percentage Reduction in Simple Average Tariff	Tariff Dispersion: Standard Deviation of Simple Average Tariff	Percentage Reduction in Tariff Dispersion (Percentage Cut in Standard Deviation of Simple Average Tariff)	Import-Weighted Average Tariff (%)	Percentage Reduction in Imported Weighted Average Tariff	Tariff Peaks: Percentage of Tariff Lines with Tariff Peaks (Tariffs Above 15%)	Percentage Reduction in Tariff Peaks (Percentage Decrease in Number of Tariff Lines with Tariffs Above 15%)
India	1990	79.0		43.6		49.6		97.0	
	1999	32.5	−58.9%	12.3	−71.8%	28.5	−42.5%	93.1	−4.1%
China	1992	41.0		30.6		33.2		77.6	
	2000	16.3	−60.2%	10.7	−65.0%	14.7	−55.7%	4.2	−94.6%
Indonesia	1989	21.9		19.7		13.0		50.3	
	2000	8.4	−61.6%	10.8	−45.2%	5.2	−60.0%	11.2	−77.7%
Korea	1988	14.8		5.3		10.5		12.5	
	1999	8.6	−41.9%	5.9	+10.2% (increased tariff dispersion)	5.9	−43.8%	0.7	−94.4%
Malaysia	1988	17.0		15.1		9.4		46.7	
	1997	9.3	−45.3%	33.3	+120.5% (increased tariff dispersion)	6.0	−36.2%	24.7	−47.3%
Philippines	1989	28.0		14.2		22.4		77.2	
	2000	7.6	−72.9%	7.7	−45.8%	3.8	−83.0%	8.8	−88.6%
Thailand	1989	38.5		19.6		33.0		72.8	
	2000	16.6	−56.9%	14.1	−28.1%	10.1	−69.4%	45.9	−37.0%

Table 18-2. Indian versus Other Sub-Continental Tariffs in 1990s

Country	Year	Simple Average Tariff (%)	Percentage Reduction in Simple Average Tariff	Tariff Dispersion: Standard Deviation of Simple Average Tariff	Percentage Reduction in Tariff Dispersion (Percentage Cut in Standard Deviation of Simple Average Tariff)	Import-Weighted Average Tariff (%)	Percentage Reduction in Imported Weighted Average Tariff	Tariff Peaks: Percentage of Tariff Lines with Tariff Peaks (Tariffs Above 15%)	Percentage Reduction in Tariff Peaks (Percentage Decrease in Number of Tariff Lines with Tariffs Above 15%)
India	1990	79.0		43.6		49.6		97.0	
	1999	32.5	−58.9%	12.3	−71.8%	28.5	−42.5%	93.1	−4.1%
Bangladesh	1989	106.6		79.3		88.4		98.2	
	2000	21.3	−80.0%	13.6	−82.8%	21.0	−76.2%	51.8	−47.2%
Nepal	1993	21.9		17.8		15.9		58.9	
	2000	17.9	−18.3%	20.9	+17.4% (increased tariff dispersion)	17.7	+11.3% (increased imported weighted average tariff)	18.7	−68.3%
Pakistan	1995	50.9		21.5		46.4		91.4	
	1998	46.6	−8.4%	21.2	−1.4%	41.7	−10.1%	86.3	−5.6%
Sri Lanka	1990	28.3		24.5		26.9		51.7	
	2000	9.9	−65.0%	9.3	−62.0%	7.4	−72.5%	22.0	−57.4%

political problems that accounts for deceleration and reversals in the 1990s of first-generation reforms.

· Persistence of Tariff Escalation

Concomitantly, India had yet to rid itself of tariff escalation.[80] In 1997–1998, its lowest tariff duties, averaging 25%, were on unprocessed items. Semi-processed goods attracted a higher tariff, averaging 35%. The steepest tariff was on processed merchandise, 37%. Manifestly, India still concocted its tariff schedules to promote domestic industry as per its history of import substitution.

No less troubling than the aforementioned points was the unwinding of the depreciation of the *rupee*:

> India's trade reforms of the early 1990s were characterized by a significant nominal depreciation of the exchange rate, which translated into a substantial real devaluation in the early 1990s. . . . India's export-weighted multilateral real exchange rate in relation to the country's five largest export markets (the United States, Japan, Germany, the United Kingdom, and Hong Kong) depreciated by almost 60 percent by 1993 relative to its level in 1990. From that point, however, there seems to have been a persistent— albeit gradual—real appreciation vis-à-vis these currencies—thus eroding some of the early gains. This pattern is also evident in India's real exchange rate in relation to the labor-abundant Asian countries—which constitute India's major competition in export markets. India's real exchange rate vis-à-vis these countries depreciated significantly (relative to its level in 1990) until the mid-1990s. With the onset of the [1997–1999] Asian crisis and the subsequent depreciation of most East Asian currencies, however, the *rupee* began to appreciate significantly in relation to these currencies. Indeed, as of September 2000, India's real exchange rate had appreciated almost 20 percent vis-à-vis the East Asian countries—relative to its value just before the crisis—thus offsetting much of the real depreciation that India had experienced in the early 1990s.[81]

In short, as with tariff reforms, on exchange rate reforms, the benefits of *rupee* depreciation in the early 1990s, which helped fuel high growth rates, were "undone" by *rupee* appreciation by the end of that decade.[82] Export growth, in particular, slumped, especially in relation to other Asian emerging countries, like Korea, and even Latin American ones, like Chile. Thus, Indian exchange rate policy failed to provide the stimulus exporters needed to sustain their growth, and concomitantly to ensure a healthy balance between foreign exchange revenues they generate as against foreign exchange expenditures incurred by importers.[83]

---

80. *See* World Trade Organization, Trade Policy Review Body, *Trade Policy Review for India, 1998*, www.wto.org.

81. *See* Krueger & Chinoy, 5.

82. *See* Krueger & Chinoy, 5.

83. *See* Krueger & Chinoy, 5.

· **Almost Standing Still**

Export growth slowed. Perhaps most tellingly, India—an original contracting party to the 30 October 1947 GATT and founding Member of the 1 January 1995 WTO—stood in the same position in world trade for over half a century. In 1948, the share of Indian exports in world merchandise exports (in value terms) was 2.2%. It fell to 0.5% by 1983. It grew back to just 0.7% in 2000.[84] Not only had its post-Partition trade policy failed, but also its 1991 reforms had yet to bear full fruit.

Indeed, its status as a founding member of the modern multilateral trading system belied its commitment to open markets. At the 1948 Havana Conference, throughout much of GATT history, and all of the Doha Round of WTO negotiations, India championed S&D treatment for developing countries.[85] That is, India argued for asymmetric obligations on developed countries, once again fearful that dramatic opening by developing countries would "retard industrialization," and thereby lead to neocolonialist exploitation.

· **FDI and Banking Sector Difficulties**

As regards FDI, the twin devils of decrepit physical infrastructure and rampant top-down corruption highlighted the disadvantages of establishing or expanding production facilities in India vis-à-vis China. The share of FDI to developing countries for which India accounted reached a highpoint of 2% in the 1990s—a paltry figure for a country the size of India.[86]

In the financial sector, the Indian government deficit jumped to 10.8%.[87] Financing government expenditures crowded out bank lending to the private sector, throttling its rapid growth. Indian banks were saddled with NPLs and other poor quality assets at levels in excess of in, international standards. Banking and securities regulation proved inadequate, even corrupt, and scandals struck equities trading on the BSE.

· **Reasons**

Why did Indian economic reforms decelerate after a promising start? India faced (again) domestic political uncertainty and international turmoil. Domestically, enthusiasm for reforms among Indian leaders declined amidst concerns that of rising socioeconomic inequality. Liberating the economy to boost growth was welcome, but that growth should alleviate, not exacerbate, poverty. After all, governments can and do rise and fall when citizens find "reforms" injure their interests. The Congress Party came to power in 2004, defeating the Bharatiya Janata Party, with the support of hundreds of millions of poor, minority, lower-caste, and rural voters who had not benefitted economically as had the upper and middle classes from BJP policies.

---

84. *See* Srinivasan, 18.
85. *See* The Doha Round Trilogy; Srinivasan, 18.
86. *See* Krueger & Chinoy, 4.
87. *See* Krueger & Chinoy, 2, 6.

Additionally, within India, the reforms had not operated long enough to root out entirely the mindset of post-Partition socialist-style policies. For instance, some Indian industrialists failed to push for a more depreciated *rupee*, even though the producer-exporters among them would benefited from a weaker currency, and non-exporters would see opportunities in foreign markets:

> A significantly cheaper *rupee* would at a stroke neutralize all the arguments about India's lack of competitiveness coming from electricity tariffs, poor infrastructure, and high interest rates, and provide . . . [a] level playing field . . . .

In short, many Bombay Club captains of Indian Industry still thought in terms of a strong *rupee* to (1) make raw materials and intermediate goods they used to produce finished goods cheaper, and (2) function as a protective tariff against foreign finished goods.[88]

Internationally, there was an undeclared war with Pakistan centered on Kargil, in which India triumphed at great cost, plus (another) military *coup d'état* in Pakistan, this one led by General Pervez Musharraf (1943–, President, 2001–2008) against the elected Prime Minister, Nawaz Sharif (1949–, PM, 1997–1999, 2013–2017). There were pressures associated with the American invasions of Afghanistan and Iraq. Indian Muslims numbered in the range of 200 million, and the possibility of Islamist extremism lurked — and manifested itself in the horrific Bombay bombings of November 2008, which were perpetrated by Lashkar-e-Taiba, a militant organization based in Pakistan

Exogenous threats to Indian stability were not the only reason India lost focus on domestic economic reforms. There was a loss of faith in reforms, which to some Indians seemed like a neo-colonialist trick. Some Indian constituencies were wary about more integration into the global economy.[89] After all, the Grand Bargain of the Uruguay Round (1986–1994) was disappointing. Via this promising trade-off, developing countries like India would gain improved market access for T&A and agricultural products into developed country markets, and developed countries would cut their farm subsidies. In return, developing countries would grant access to their markets for service suppliers from developed countries, and strengthen protection for IP of developed country firms.

But, in phasing out the global quota system for T&A that had been in place under the 1974 *Multi-Fiber Arrangement*, the WTO *ATC* created a near-*laissez faire* regime. T&A companies from the U.S. and EU consolidated their production facilities in a handful of cheap-labor countries, as they no longer had to spread operations across

---

88. *See* Naushad Forbes, *Comment—Indian Exports and Exchange Rate Policy*, in Reforming India's External, Financial, and Fiscal Policies, 90 (Anne O. Krueger & Sajjid Chinoy eds., Stanford, California: Stanford University Press, 2003).

89. *See* Anne O. Krueger & Sajjid Chinoy eds., Reforming India's External, Financial, and Fiscal Policies, *Preface* at xvii (Stanford, California: Stanford University Press, 2003).

dozens of countries to stay within quota limits. Here, then, from an Indian perspective was divide and conquer: pitting India, China, Vietnam, Sri Lanka, Indonesia, and other countries with T&A plants against one another to avoid local shutdowns. As for farm product exports from poor to rich countries, the international competitive playing field hardly had leveled. Tariff spikes and non-tariff barriers remained. Spending by rich countries on domestic agricultural support measures and agricultural export subsidies did not fall dramatically.

Conversely, developed countries — again, from an Indian perspective — seemed to be the primary beneficiaries of the WTO *GATS* and *TRIPs Agreement*. Many of their services suppliers, across sectors such as banking, construction, engineering, finance, insurance, and telecommunications, expanded into the markets of emerging countries in what seemed to be a one-way trade flow. Developed countries insisted developing countries do more to protect corporate patents, trade and service marks, copyrights, and semiconductor mask works, and opposed efforts to liberalize *TRIPs* Article 31 in respect of compulsory licensing in situations when a country lacks capacity to manufacture pharmaceuticals.

VII. Path Ahead

• **Challenges and Complementarity**

The first-generation reforms and their aftermath have borne some fruit. Perhaps most impressively, India has recorded high growth rates and cut into poverty. In the first term of Prime Minister Singh (2004–2009), Indian GDP grew roughly 8%–9% annually, and hit a historical high of 9% in 2007, then the second fastest growing major economy in the world.[90] In 2010, the Indian economy grew at an even faster clip than that of China.[91] The poverty rate (*i.e.*, the percentage of the total population falling below the absolute poverty line) in 2004–2005 was 27.5%, down from 44.5% in 1983.[92]

---

90. *See Manmohan Singh*, Wikipedia, http://en.wikipedia.org/wiki/Manmohan_Singh (*citing* CIA *World Factbook* and *The India Report* by Astaire Research).

91. *See What a Waste*, The Economist, 11 May 2013, at 12. This comparison presumes the measurements used for each country are consistent. *See id.* (also reporting that from 2005 to 2007, the Indian economy grew by roughly 9% annually).

92. *See* Jagdish Bhagwati & Arvind Panagariya, Why Growth Matters: How Economic Growth in India Reduced Poverty and the Lessons for Other Developing Countries (New York, New York: PublicAffairs, 2013). The poverty statistics are from the Indian Planning Commission, and the figure for 1983 obviously pre-dates the first-generation reforms. *See also* James Crabtree, *A Robust Defense of India's Growth Story*, Financial Times, 20 May 2013, at 8 (reviewing *Why Growth Matters*).

But, in a number of serious respects, the first generation of Indian reforms proved inchoate.[93] Growth has fallen off to half its peak level, at about 4.5% *per annum*.[94] Unacceptable still is not only the poverty rate, but also the facts that:

(1) 43% of Indian children go hungry, which is twice the rate of Sub-Saharan Africa;

(2) 50% of all Indians defecate in the open, leading to deaths from diarrhea and encephalitis;

(3) India spends just U.S. $39 per person annually on public health, as against $203 in China and $483 in China, or 1.2% of Indian GDP, as against a global average of 6.5%;

(4) 400 million Indians, about one-third of the population, have no electricity; and

(5) Roughly 600,000 babies are aborted every year because they are girls.[95]

Manifestly, then, the 1991 reforms left many challenges unaddressed. They include:

(1) Upgrading and expanding physical infrastructure needed to support economic growth, such as roads, railroads, air and sea ports, energy (especially electricity) generation, sanitation facilities, and telecommunication systems.

(2) Opening certain sectors to FDI, including retail stores (especially large, multi-brand retailers).[96]

(3) Continuing privatization of SOEs, which (as of October 2007) still accounted for 38% of total output in the formal non-farm sector, are one-third less productive than private firms, and grow less rapidly than firms benefiting from privatization (*e.g.*, in the IT sector).

---

93. *See A Himalayan Challenge*, THE ECONOMIST, 13 October 2007, at 84–85; Gary G. Yerkey, *U.S. Expects India to Play Greater Role in Coming Months to Help Revive WTO Talks*, 24 International Trade Reporter (BNA) 10 (4 January 2007).

94. *See Wasting Time*, THE ECONOMIST, 11 May 2013, at 23.

95. *See Beyond Bootstraps*, THE ECONOMIST, 29 June 2013, at 74–74 (reviewing Amartya Sen & Jean Drèze, *An Uncertain Glory: India and its Contradictions* (London, England, Allen Lane, 2013)).

96. In September 2012, the government of Prime Minister Manmohan Singh pushed through long-stalled reforms on FDI in the retailing sector, allowing foreign companies to own up to 51% of local supermarkets. *See* Avantika Chilkoti & Barney Jopson, *Wal-Mart's India Chief in Sudden Departure*, FINANCIAL TIMES, 27 June 2013, at 13. Their doing so posed a threat to the millions of mom-and-pop stores in India's "vast but fragmented retail market." *Id.* But, foreign retailers could do so only if they fulfilled local infrastructure investment requirements, so by June 2013, no foreign retailer had taken a controlling stake. *See id.* By then Wal-Mart had opened only 20 wholesale stores through a 50-50 JV with Bharti Enterprises (controlled by Indian billionaire Sunil Mittal). In June 2013, the head since 2007 of Wal-Mart India, Raj Jain, abruptly resigned. Wal-Mart India had complained about the investment restrictions against its expansion.

(4) Eliminating investment (equity) caps on foreign ownership of local financial service providers, especially in banking and insurance, and in other key sectors, such as agriculture, civil aviation, and telecommunications.

In this respect, the July 2013 announcement that India would scrap its 74% cap on foreign holdings in mobile phone operations was welcome.[97] So, too, was the Indian pledge to foreign investors in defense production: if they had state-of-the-art technology, then they could exceed the 26% equity cap limit, subject to the approval of a Cabinet Committee on National Security. But, the reforms with respect to other sectors, including commodity exchanges, oil refining, and single-brand retailing, was less impressive: the foreign equity caps would stay, but a larger percentage would be permissible without requiring government approval (*i.e.*, via the so-called "automatic route"). Likewise, a commitment to ease or abolish restrictions on outside investment in other sectors, such as insurance and tea plantations, seemed vague, as well as disappointing absent lifting equity cap limits.

(5) Cutting tariffs further, which (as of October 2007) average about 20%, among the highest figures in the world, continuing to compress tariffs so as to reduce tariff dispersion, and reduce tariff peaks.

(6) Continue the movement to a fully and freely convertible *rupee* for current and capital account purposes, local foreign exchange markets, and even internationalization of the *rupee* (*i.e.*, its hardening as an internationally tradable and acceptable means of payment), even if such developments entail greater volatility in exchange rates for the *rupee*.[98]

(7) Drastically reducing government subsidies, which (as measured as a percentage of GDP) are the second highest in the world among countries surveyed by the OECD.

(8) Reforming the labor market, specifically to make it more flexible by eliminating (1) restrictive employment protection laws against collective dismissals, and (2) the requirement manufacturing firms obtain government permission to lay off workers at any factory with more than 100 employees.

(9) Modernizing and strengthening copyright and patent laws.

(10) Enforcing IP laws, especially with respect to pharmaceuticals (India is a leading center for counterfeit medicines), software (74% of which in India is pirated), and entertainment (notably, movies and music, the pirating of which damages Bollywood).

---

97. *See* Victor Mallet, *India to Loosen Curbs on Foreign Holdings*, Financial Times, 17 July 2013, at 4.

98. *See* Acharya, 57–58.

(11) Reducing social stigmas based on gender, caste, religion, and ethnicity, which aside from being against both secular and natural law, inhibit the full realization of India's tremendous human capital potential.

The complementarity of these 11 reforms to changes in international trade rules cannot be over-emphasized.

Nor can the need for urgency be over-emphasized. Foreign (and domestic) portfolio and direct investors have lost considerable confidence in India, and shown their displeasure at the stymied reforms by pushing down the value of the *rupee* relative to the dollar. In August 2013, it hit a record low of roughly 65 *rupees* to the dollar, a decline of about 12% theretofore in 2013.[99] The crash of the *rupee* raised the prospect of import-driven inflation (reinforced by ambitious Indian government plans to provide subsidized rice, wheat and other essential to 67%, roughly 800 million Indians[100]), which if manifest would disproportionately injury the poor.

The full fruits of external sector changes cannot be realized simply because they are made. Those changes operate in tandem—or not—with other reforms. So, sclerosis caused by an unresponsive and overweening state, stifling labor laws, strictures on SMEs, a backward financial sector, a crumbling infrastructure, disrespect for IP rights, and segregating women or minorities away from education and jobs must be tackled. Until they are, external sector reforms—however good—will operate sub-optimally.

It is worth commenting that the difficulties India faces with its reform project contrast in some respects with the experience of China. For instance, in respect of economics, because Indian labor laws make hiring and firing so difficult, 87% (as of October 2007) of employment in the manufacturing sector is with firms that employ less than 10 workers. In China, only 5% of industrial jobs are at firms with fewer than 10 workers. Consequently, Chinese firms can develop and maximize economies of scale, absorb new technology, and enjoy higher labor productivity, than Indian companies.

- **Importance of REER**

Also, of importance to sustaining an outward-oriented international trade regime is continued reform of the exchange rate, with particular attention to the Real Effective Exchange Rate.[101] The REER is:

---

99. *See Amy Kazmin & Victor Mallet, New Delhi's Critics Call for Longer-term Thinking to Tackle Problems*, Financial Times, 21 August 2013, at 3; Amy Kazmin, Robin Wigglesworth & James Crabtree, *Rupee Blow As Emerging Markets Hit By Turmoil*, Financial Times, Aug. 20, 2013, at 1; James Crabtree, *Q&A—Low Growth and Rising Deficit Leave Rupee on the Ropes*, Financial Times, Aug. 20, 2013, at 3.

100. *See* Andy Mukherjee, *Breaking News—India Grain Subsidy May Only Outsource Hunger*, Reuters, 10 July 2013, www.reuters.com.

101. *See* Krueger & Chinoy, 4.

The weighted average of a country's currency relative to an index or basket of other major currencies adjusted for the effects of inflation. The weights are determined by comparing the relative trade balances, in terms of one country's currency, with each other country within the index.[102]

Simply put, the REER is the value of the currency of one country (*e.g.,* the Indian *rupee*) against the value of other major (*i.e.,* hard) currencies in an index (namely, the U.S. dollar, Japanese *yen*, EU *euro*, and a few others), with adjustments for the effects of inflation. Gauging the currency against others makes the REER "effective" (as distinct from a value against just one other currency, *i.e.,* a bilateral rate), while correcting for inflation makes the REER "real" (as distinct from nominal). Using a basket is more realistic in a globalized world in which any one country, (*e.g.,* India) trades with many countries, with payment often made in a major currency.[103] Correcting for inflation obviously makes the REER unadulterated by price level changes in any one country.

Economists teach that the REER ought to be judged by a two-pronged test: (1) Does the REER keep foreign exchange earnings and expenditures roughly in balance over the intermediate term?; and (2) Does the REER give exporters a sufficient incentive such that exports grow at a satisfactory pace?[104]

As a country seeks to grow through export-orientation, and does so by dismantling tariff and non-tariff barriers, passing the test is particularly important: the level and path of the REER must not undermine the salubrious effects of eliminating trade barriers.[105] The exchange rate must not operate orthogonally to trade law reform. So, the exchange rate must be devalued in real terms to an appropriate degree.[106] That way, domestic factors of production (land, labor, physical capital, human capital, and technology) will respond by shifting into export-oriented production. Those devaluations, by making imports more expensive, also will offset (at least in part) increased competition from imports to domestic producers that comes with lower trade barriers.

---

102. *Definition of "Real Effective Exchange Rate—REER,"* Investopedia, www.investopedia.com/terms/r/reer.asp.

103. Note that the basket of currencies selected may be weighted according to trade between the other countries (U.S., Japan, EU, etc.), on the one hand, and the country of the currency being valued, on the other hand (India). That weighting may be based on exports, imports, or exports plus imports (total trade). If so, then the full and proper term is "trade weighted effective exchange rate." *See Trade-Weighted Effective Exchange Rate,* Wikipedia, http://en.wikipedia.org/wiki/Trade-weighted_effective_exchange_rate_index. A trade-weighted rate, such as for the *rupee,* gives a more accurate picture of the prices Indian exporters receive for their exports, and the prices Indian importers pay for their imports.

104. *See* Krueger & Chinoy, 4.

105. *See* Krueger & Chinoy, 4.

106. *See* Krueger & Chinoy, 4.

• Three Economic Options

Going forward, in theory India has 3 economic options. These are ably discussed by Amartya Sen (1933–), winner of the 1998 Nobel Prize in Economics, and his co-author, Jean Drèze (1959–), in their 2013 book, *An Uncertain Glory: India and its Contradictions*. The first option is to go back to post-Partition policies: turn again to the Indian government to re-occupy the commanding heights of the economy, this time with the benefit of experience from the 1947 to 1991. The idea here is India committed a fatal blunder departing from its leftist policies, as only "[h]igh rates of taxation, expropriation of large holdings [including land, which is essential for industrialization], and nationalization of large companies" can "redistribute wealth to the backward regions and poorer parts of the population."[107] This option, the darling of unreconstructed Marxists, is seductive: it seems to be a panacea for the excesses concomitant with the first generation reforms, and the persistence of mass poverty.

The second option is to accelerate the pace of free-market reforms: drive India as quickly as possible to a deregulated, *laissez-faire* economy. The idea here is India did not go far enough down the free market path, and its problem is not too much capitalism, but too little. Stop regulating the conditions under which businesses fire and fire, and the wage rates they pay, and continue to dispose of state-owned land so that private businesses can use those plots to industrialize. Indeed, "[i]f labor laws were liberalized, and companies allowed to buy land directly from peasants at the prevailing market rate, then . . . more jobs and more wealth would be created."[108] This option, the darling of Neo-Classical fundamentalists, is seductive: ostensibly, the failure to follow through after 1991 on reforms, and to tolerate backsliding, are the source of India's woes.

But, as Sen and Drèze astutely argue, both options are extreme, and neither jogging back to the past nor sprinting straight ahead is satisfactory, or even realistic. What is needed is a third way, a course that continues privatization, bolsters entrepreneurship, rewards innovation, and welcomes openness to globalization, but also reduces the absolute poverty rates and enhances broader human development indicators, including access to and enhancement of education and health care, and the empowerment of women. Growth rates matter, but so also do real wage rates (which have been stagnant), levels of malnutrition (which are high), gender ratios (which are unequal), sanitation (which is monstrous), and social stigmas (like caste and region, which persist). The private sector should take the lead in activism, but the state must be activistic, at least in a supervisory role, and the latter is not destined to be corrupt or subject to politicization, as the examples of Canada and Sweden illustrate.

Ironically, that is what Prime Minister Nehru sought—a third way between American capitalism and Soviet communism that would yield sustainable GDP *per*

---

107. *See The Delhi Dilemma.*
108. *See The Delhi Dilemma.*

capita growth rates with distributional equity and social justice. Renowned Indian economist Jagdish Bhagwati (1934–) remarked India is cursed by the affliction of having brilliant economists.[109] They have debated endlessly about trade and other economic policies, yet few appreciate the legal dimensions of their various proposals, and none has yet devised a third way that is theoretically robust and practically appealing. That may take a grand lawyer-*cum*-politician, as Nehru was, updated to the new millennium.

A simple example adduces the point. Tariff collections account for nearly 30% of all central government tax revenues.[110] Free trade-oriented economists clamor for a reduction in applied duties, but that cannot happen without structural change in the composition of government funding. In turn, that cannot occur without fundamental tax reform, especially in respect of income tax rules and enforcement. All such changes are far beyond the narrow ken of economists. Good lawyers and skillful politicians, guided by sound economic thinking, are indispensable.

- **Getting Politics and Law Straight**

At bottom, however, India's challenges are not economic. They are legal and political. Why did the first-generation reforms peter out? Why has growth slowed? Why is the export sector and underachiever? Why do hundreds of millions of Indians remain poor? A typical answer is population, but the one-word answer is: "government," or "governance." It is the government, by its obstructionist action, maddening paralysis, and rampant corruption, that has held, and continues to hold, India back from achieving the successes enjoyed by other developing countries, particularly in East Asia. It is not the lack of rule of law on statute books or in cases, but in implementation in villages, towns, and cities, that holds India back from these successes.

As regards political and legal reform, Communist or other extremist parties in India have blocked or impeded change or implementation, partly out of understandable concerns the changes benefit the rich and widen income disparities. Yet, reform-minded governments, such as the Congress Party-led coalition headed by Prime Minister Singh, sometimes rely on the Communist parties for support. Conversely, with a monopoly on political power, the Communist Party of China can push through necessary reforms — albeit after internal consultations, negotiations, and debate. Yet, as has been widely reported for several years, large and growing socioeconomic disparities in China, plus many cases of cadres and their families benefitting corruptly from their Party positions, are frequent sources of protest (sometimes violent) against Party rule and policies.

As modern India is a young country atop an ancient civilization, as is modern China, debates about their relative systems and performance are only just beginning. Born in 1947 and 1949 respectively, their economic records are short as against a timeline many Americans can hardly understand. But, in the end, it is hard not

---

109. *See* THAROOR, 244.
110. *See* Acharya, 57–58.

to be sanguine about India, its economic future, and its status in the global trading system. Over 40% of Indians were not born in 1991, when the first generation of reforms transpired.[111] As any traveller to India knows, the young are full of optimism and hope. Besides, Indians are survivors—and joyful ones at that.

VIII. New Era with Prime Minister Modi?

In May 2014, Indian voters handed the opposition BJP the most lop-sided victory in the history of the world's largest free market democracy since 1984. Then, the spoils went to the Congress Party in a wave of sympathy following the assassination of Prime Minister Indira Gandhi. Three decades later, after being in office since 1991, the electorate had enough of the Congress Party: with corruption rampant, the national infrastructure decrepit, and the economy performing sub-optimally, the BJP seemed to be the answer. The voter turnout was nearly 67% of the eligible 815 million voters—the largest election in human history.

The BJP leader, Narendra Damodardas Modi (1950–), promised to write large across the country what he had done as Chief Minister of Gujarat from 2001–2014, the same western coastal home state of Mahatma Gandhi (1869–1948):

(1) Pro-growth, pro-business, pro-manufacturing, pro-FDI economic reforms;

(2) Better governance, especially less corruption;

(3) Less government, with streamlined procedures and decisive outcomes;

(4) More emphasis on renewable energy; and

(5) Linking clearly India's Foreign Service and pragmatic commercial diplomacy, and encouraging states to forge trade and commercial relations abroad (*e.g.*, in Africa, where there is a large Indian diaspora).

With the first clear majority in the *Lok Sabha* since 1984, the BJP was on course to put through Parliament the necessary legislation.

With 282 of 543 seats, boosted to 336 by allied parties in its National Democratic Alliance (NDA), the BJP easily cleared the key figure of half plus one, or 272 seats.[112] Congress and its United Progressive Alliance (UPA) scored just 44 and 58 seats, respectively—their words drubbing in Indian history. So, the BJP was liberated from the "divisive and regressive coalition politics" that plagued Congress Party-led governments in the 1990s and early 2000s.[113] It also was emboldened by the electorate's rejection of Congress Party populist entitlement programs.

---

111. *See What a Waste*, The Economist, 11 May 2013, at 12.

112. *See Indian General Election, 2014*, Wikipedia, http://en.wikipedia.org/wiki/Indian_general_election,_2014.

113. Madhur Singh, *India's Opposition Party Given Historic Mandate; Business Eager for Change*, 31 International Trade Reporter (BNA) 950 (22 May 2014).

But, the new government had to proceed mindful of suspicions among Indian minorities that it was chauvinistically Hindu, partly because during the spring 2014 campaign the Mr. Modi failed to allay concerns that as Gujarat Chief Minister he was implicated in February 2002 riots in which 900–2,000 mainly Muslims were massacred—though in May 2010 a Special Investigation Team of the Supreme Court found no substantial incriminating evidence that Modi willfully allowed the communal violence.[114]

One point was clear: what William Dalrymple (1965–), the astute British historian of India, called a "sexually transmitted democracy," *i.e.*, dominance by the Nehru-Gandhi family of the Congress Party and Indian government, was over.[115] "Modi *Ji*" came from a family of grocers and was a *chai wallah* (tea seller) helping his father sell tea at the Varnagar Railway Station, the humblest of origins of any Indian Prime Minister to date.

The new Prime Minister wasted no time boosting trade and investment relations with America. He visited the U.S. in September, saw President Barack H. Obama at an APEC forum in November, and hosted President Obama in India in January 2015—the first time a sitting American President visited India twice, and the first time an American President was named Chief Guest at the Indian Republic Day celebrations (which commemorate the 26 January 1950 entry into force of the Indian Constitution). The sides also revived their bilateral "Trade Policy Forum," with a view to resolving market access and IP disputes.

However, the new Prime Minister was not above taking protectionist steps if he thought there were good economic or political reasons to do so. Indeed, in 2018, his budget included across-the-board tariff hikes—the first such move since the 1990s:

> [R]eversing a 20-year trend, Union Budget 2018–19 substantially raises tariffs across a range of sectors: Thus, on imported mobile phones, the applicable rate jumps from 15% to 20%, in addition to a 15% tariff on certain components of mobile phones and television sets.[116]

Aside from revenue generation, the justification was classic economic nationalism: the Prime Minister sponsored a *"Make In India"* initiative to promote manufacturing and thereby industrialization in India. The tariff hikes were criticized:

> the policy choice reflects an erroneously mercantilist mindset, that one can cut back on imports while boosting exports, not realizing that a reduction in imports, induced by an increase in tariffs, is generally expected to lead to a decrease in exports of a corresponding value—a proposition known

---

114. *See Narendra Modi*, Wikipedia, en.wikipedia.org/wiki/Narendra_Modi.

115. *See* William Dalyrmple, *Narendra Modi: Man of the Masses*, New Statesman, 14 May 2014, www.newstatesman.com/politics/2014/05/narendra-modi-man-masses.

116. *See* Vivek Dehejia, *India's Protectionist Folly*, Livemint, 12 February 2018, www.livemint.com/Opinion/TjhwiyIuWRAjVma8IsneKI/Indias-protectionist-folly.html. [Hereinafter, *India's Protectionist Folly.*]

in jargon as the Lerner's Symmetry Theorem [discussed in a separate Chapter].

As an illustration, note that more expensive imported inputs, due to higher tariffs, make for more expensive domestic production and thus less, not more, competitive exports. One cannot have one's cake and eat it too![117]

Still, that same year, Mr. Modi agreed to "a populist and counter-productive set of restrictions on the sale of cardiac stents and knee implants in India."[118] Though a small sector, medical equipment is an "influential" one.[119]

---

117. *India's Protectionist Folly.*

118. *See* Mihir Sharma, *Who Doesn't Love a Trade War?*, Bloomberg Quint (India), 21 June 2018, www.bloombergquint.com/opinion/2018/06/22/who-doesn-t-love-a-trade-war?utm _campaign=website&utm_source=sendgrid&utm_medium=newsletter. Yet, the statutory exclusions from product eligibility (discussed below) disqualify leather goods, such as wallets and purses.

119. *Who Doesn't.*

Part Five

Preferences for Poor Countries (Continued): Trade Laws

Chapter 19

Special and Differential Treatment[1]

I. Prebisch, Baran, and Intellectual Background for Non-Reciprocal Trade Preferences and GATT Part IV

From 30 October 1947, when the original contracting parties signed GATT, until 1966, there were no specific rules in multilateral trade law designed for the benefit of poor countries. Part IV of GATT, which was added to GATT in 1966, bears the rubric "Trade and Development." This Part consists of the final three Articles in GATT—XXXVI, XXXVII, and XXXVIII (along with *Ad Articles*). These Articles grew out of concern for development challenges facing Third World countries after the Second World War. The challenges prompted calls to re-balance the trading system to help poor countries.

Specifically, Third World countries called for a complete overhaul of the rules governing world trade. They wanted rules to construct a system that took account of their interests. The unfettered free-flow of goods across borders, prescribed by Adam Smith's (1723–1790) logic of Absolute Advantage and David Ricardo's (1772–1823) Law of Comparative advantage, was unacceptable. Free trade seemed somehow to reinforce inequality between rich and poor countries, and to facilitate neo-colonization, through economic rather than political or military might, of the Third World by the First World.

Leading the calls on behalf of the Third World were the renowned economists, Raúl Prebisch (1901–1986) and Paul Baran (1909–1964). In the 1950s and 1960s, Prebisch spoke from two influential positions, Executive Secretary of ECLAC, and Secretary General of the UNCTAD. In 1964, during Prebisch's tenure (which lasted until 1968) as the first UNCTAD Secretary General, UNCTAD published a highly influential document—*Towards a New Trade Policy for Development*, more commonly known as the "Prebisch Report." Baran was a Stanford University economist

---

1. Documents References:
   (1) *Havana (ITO) Charter* Articles 1, 8–15, 24, 55–70
   (2) GATT *Preamble* and Articles XXXVI–XXXVIII
   (3) Tokyo Round *Enabling Clause*
   (4) *WTO Agreement Preamble*
   (5) Provisions in GATT-WTO texts referenced in Tables herein.

and renowned exponent of Marxist-Leninist thinking. Baran issued the call most impressively in writing, publishing *The Political Economy of Growth* in 1957. Now largely forgotten in the American economic academy, at the time it probably was the most widely read book on development in the world.

The likes of Prebisch and Baran argued Third World countries could not compete in the great game of cross-border trade on an equal basis with developed countries. Poor countries needed tariff preferences to ensure access for its goods to developed country markets. Through special market access, poor countries could increase their exports and FX earnings. In turn, they could use those earnings, and the opportunities, linkages, and know-how from increased exports, to diversify their economies. The consequence would be reduced dependence on foreign trade, specifically, on imports from the developed countries of the western world.

In a highly-charged debate, the Prebisch-Baran side called for six specific reforms to world trade rules, designed as a package to help Third World countries achieve an "attainable minimum" level of participation in the trading system, and thereby of development through that participation:

- **First: Market Access for Primary Commodities**

Primary commodities should be given easier access to the markets of major industrial countries. True, some developed countries, such as the U.S., Canada, and Australia, are big exporters of primary commodities. However, many less developed countries are major producers and net exporters of primary commodities.

- **Second: Purchasing Power and Price Stabilization**

The purchasing power generated from export earnings of less developed countries should be higher, and it should be stabilized. Stabilization should occur through two devices: commodity agreements designed to influence prices; and compensatory financing mechanisms. (The first device implicates the exception in GATT Article XX(h) for international commodity agreements.) The rationale behind this proposal was many less developed countries rely for FX earnings on one or a few commodities. The earnings of such countries are adversely affected by swings in the prices of their exports. But, commodity price pacts can be fragile, and break apart. (Cases in point are the near-constant controversies in OPEC over production quotas.)

- **Third: Preferences for Industrial Products**

There should be preferences for industrial products from less developed countries, particularly from infant industries in these countries. Preferences would assist emerging industries in less developed countries find external markets for their output, and thereby facilitate the industrialization process in these countries. The early rounds of multilateral trade negotiations under GATT auspices succeeded in reducing tariffs on goods produced by developed countries, particularly advanced manufacturers such as cars, machine tools, and computers.

However, for lower-value added manufactured items (*e.g.,* textiles, shoes, etc.) trade barriers did not fall so dramatically or rapidly. Developed countries produced these items, but the industries making them were marginally profitable. These industries successfully lobbied for protection from relatively low-cost manufacturers in less developed countries. Put bluntly, rich countries were reluctant to lower barriers to overseas low-value added manufacturing industries, and sought to protect themselves from low-wage competition. And, in spite of the non-reciprocity rule in Article XXXVI:8, rich countries observed most poor countries had little of value to offer in return for expanded market access for exports from less developed countries.

- **Fourth: Import Substitution**

Less developed countries should be allowed to protect their industries from foreign competition. Again, the rationale was to assist new industries in those countries, particularly ones that make components, in securing a customer base among domestic producers of finished products. Moreover, producers of intermediate goods in less developed countries might benefit from protection from foreign competition in the sense of being able to find external markets for their products.

- **Fifth: Trade with Socialist Countries**

Trade with socialist countries should be expanded under long-term accords. Clearly, this proposal is outdated. It reflected the era in which it was made, when a large number of Third World development thinkers had faith in state planning.

- **Trade in "Invisibles" and Debt Servicing**

More attention should be paid to trade in intangible items, and the burden of servicing external debt should be reduced by re-adjusting loan periods and terms. Given the importance of IP and services, and the continued (indeed worsened) Third World debt problem, this proposal is as relevant today as when offered.

Few of these proposals found their way into "hard law." Developed countries and their advocates rejected (or diluted to the point of meaninglessness) some (cynics would say most) of the proposed reforms. Viewing matters in the context of Cold War politics, they tended to dismiss UNCTAD as a polemical forum for attacking the U.S. and Europe, and to condemn the economic ideology of Prebisch and Baran as leftist and anti-free market.

Still, Prebish, Baran, and their supporters could point to two "hard law" victories. First, in the 1970s, some developed countries implemented preferential tariff schemes for imports from less developed countries. The GSP is the leading example. Second, in 1966, GATT contracting parties elevated S&D treatment to a new level, adding Part IV to their constitutional document.

II. 1958 *Haberler Report*

More than the work of Baran and Prebisch was behind the second achievement. In November 1957, the CONTRACTING PARTIES created a three-person group of experts, and appointed Dr. Gottfried Haberler as chair of this Panel. The terms of reference of the Haberler Panel were to examine "past and current international trade trends and their implications." The Panel was to make "special reference" to:

> certain trends in international trade, in particular the failure of the trade of less developed countries to develop as rapidly as that of industrialized countries, excessive short-term fluctuations in prices of primary products, and widespread resort to agricultural protection.

The Panel issued a document in October 1958, formally entitled *Trends in International Trade*, but colloquially known as the "*Haberler Report.*"

The *Haberler Report* "galvanized" the GATT community "to examine ways in which developing countries could achieve greater access for their exports in world markets." During the next few years, discussions about trade and development intensified, as did negotiations about ways to adjust GATT obligations to ensure trade could realize its full potential in contributing to the economic growth of poor countries. The tangible result of this activity of the late 1950s and early 1960s was Part IV, *i.e.*, Articles XXXVI, XXXVII, and XXXVIII.

On 8 February 1965, in Geneva, the GATT Contracting Parties agreed to the "Protocol Amending the General Agreement on Tariffs and Trade to Introduce a Part IV on Trade and Development." By that Protocol, Part IV was enshrined in GATT, and it entered into force in 1966. (For the U.S., Part IV took effect on 17 June 1966.[2]) In GATT history, it was the largest, most significant, and last amendment.

Neither the GATT Contracting Parties nor WTO Membership has resolved the problem of subjectivity in self-proclamations of "developing" country status. While relatively objective metrics (discussed in a separate Chapter) define the contemporary term "least developed," designation as "developing"—and, therefore, entitlement to the S&D treatment that comes with this status—is up to each Member. Tired of what it perceives as abusive invocations of this status by large emerging countries, notably, Brazil and China, the USTR, Ambassador Robert Lighthizer (1947–) told Members at the 11th WTO Ministerial Conference in Buenos Aires, Argentina in December 2017:

> [W]e need to clarify our understanding of development within the WTO. We cannot sustain a situation in which new rules can only apply to the few, and that others will be given a pass in the name of self-proclaimed development status. There is something wrong, in our view, when five of the six richest countries [including Qatar and Singapore] in the world presently claim developing country status. Indeed, we should all be troubled that so many Members appear to believe that they would be better off with exemptions to the rules. If in the opinion of a vast majority of Members

---

2. *See* 17 U.S.T. 1977, 572 U.N.T.S. 320.

playing by current WTO rules makes it harder to achieve economic growth, then clearly serious reflection is needed.

We need to clarify our understanding of development within the WTO. We cannot sustain a situation in which new rules can only apply to a few and that others will be given a pass in the name of self-proclaimed development status.[3]

Is the underlying problem a legal one, namely that GATT-WTO rules are ill-equipped to deal with the real-world complexities in some countries wherein there are pockets of jaw-dropping wealth amidst swaths of heart-rending poverty?[4]

Mumbai is a case in point of the juxtaposition of developed and developing in close proximity within a single WTO Member. Malabar Hill is the city's exclusive residential neighborhood, with Hanging Gardens and Arabian Sea views, but 14 kilometers away is Dharavi, depicted in the 2008 hit British drama film, *Slumdog Millionaire*, one of the world's five largest slums, and one of the world's most densely populated areas. Multilateral trade rules do not allow for intra-country distinctions (other than in the *SPS Agreement*, as discussed in a separate Chapter, which considers regions within a Member afflicted by disease or disease-bearing pests versus ones that are certified free of such infestations, as discussed in a separate Chapter).

Perhaps India's case for "developing" country status is more obvious than China's, insofar as its poverty is both more widespread and deeper than that of China. But, what is the "line" to say that one WTO Member is, and the other Member is not, "developing"? And, who should draw that line?

III. Substantive Content of Article XXXVI:8

• Overview

Is Part IV of GATT a set of meaningless platitudes? Arguably, "no." There is substantive "hard law" content in its three Articles. Broadly speaking, Articles XXXVI, XXXVII, and XXVIII call for exceptional—or "special and differential"—treatment for "less developed countries." When, in 1966, the Articles were added to GATT, the

---

3. Office of the United States Trade Representative, Opening Plenary Statement of USTR Robert Lighthizer at the WTO Ministerial Conference, 11 December 2017, https://ustr.gov/about-us/policy-offices/press-office/press-releases/2017/december/opening-plenary-statement-ustr. *See also* Luc Cohen, *WTO Losing Trade Focus, Too Easy on Some Developing Nations: U.S.*, REUTERS, 11 December 2017, www.reuters.com/article/us-trade-wto/wto-losing-trade-focus-too-easy-on-some-developing-nations-u-s-idUSKBN1E51MG (reporting on this speech).

4. *See generally* Andrew D. Mitchell, *A Legal Principle of Special and Differential Treatment for WTO Disputes*, 5 WORLD TRADE REVIEW issue 3, 445–469 (November 2006) (arguing the principle of S&D treatment ultimately is incoherent, and "developing" countries are an amorphous group, hence it is of limited value in dispute settlement).

distinction between "developing" and "least developed" countries was not made. The 1979 *Enabling Clause* formally introduced this distinction into multilateral trade law. So, the term "less developed countries" is understood as an umbrella one, to refer to both types of poor countries—developing and least developed.

What kind of S&D treatment for less developed countries does Part IV envision? In brief, Article XXXVI identifies objectives concerning the link between trade and development, distinguishes between earnings generated by primary product exports and market access for industrial products, and establishes the important principle of non-reciprocity. Article XXXVII lays out commitments of developed contracting parties (WTO Members) to less developed contracting parties (Members), and even establishes a skeletal framework for resolving disputes about whether a country in the first category meets its obligations. Article XXXVIII links the objectives set forth in Article XXXVI with by the CONTRACTING PARTIES (*i.e.*, joint action by the Members), calling for collective action to further those objectives.

- **Non-Reciprocity and GATT Article XXXVI:8**

Perhaps the most famous, and likely the most abused, provision in all of Part IV of GATT, which concerns Trade and Development, is Article XXXVI:8. This Paragraph contains a "non-reciprocity rule," or more accurately, a "non-expectation of reciprocity rule." The mandate (and, it is a mandate) is that developed contracting parties *do not expect reciprocity* in trade negotiations to reduce or remove tariffs and other barriers to the trade of less-developed contracting parties. An Interpretative Note, *Ad Article XXXVI Paragraph 8*, reinforces the language of the Paragraph itself, and clarifies the context for the rule is trade negotiations.

The rule is forgotten or neglected in the public pronouncements of plenty of trade policy officials from developed countries, when they opine about what impoverished countries should do. The rule has been forgotten or neglected for so long, some less developed country officials seem either unaware of it, or no longer put any hope in it. The tendency in practice is to adhere to the tradition of conducting and evaluating trade negotiations on the basis of reciprocity. Yet, to forget about Paragraph 8 is to forget about the most significant substantive provision of Part IV, because it is a hard law commitment vis-à-vis less developed countries.

Paragraph 8 is a quintessential example of a rule embodying an unconditional benefit for poor countries. In exchange for whatever a developed country offers, nothing is to be expected. Money is given, though in an indirect manner. Developed countries are obligated not to ask for a reciprocal reduction, or for elimination, in a tariff or NTB. When a rich country offers concessions on protectionist measures, Paragraph 8 tells it not to ask for equivalent concessions from poor countries.

Accordingly, rich countries give up a customary and legal right to ask—indeed, to demand or else withdraw their concession offers—for reciprocity. That right is inherent in any kind of negotiations, other than (perhaps) a pure charitable donation. Yet, the fact of legal history is they held onto that right until the 1964–67

Kennedy Round. At that juncture, they took the major step of codifying a new practice through Article XXXVI:8.

Article XXXVI:8 is more than just a rule by which developing countries are obligated to forgo a legal right to insist on reciprocity. It is a rule mandating they acquiesce in continued protectionism by poor countries. To be sure, according to standard capitalist economic theory, including Ricardo's principle of comparative advantage, it is almost never in the interest of a less developed country to maintain high tariff or non-tariff barriers. There are net gains from increased trade, even if the increases result from unilateral dismantling of barriers. Still, Paragraph 8 allows a less developed country to maintain these measures, while developed countries tear down their barriers. Consequently, a less developed country can continue to accrue revenue from tariffs, and reap rents from quotas and other NTBs (*e.g.,* import licensing requirements). The permitted revenue and rents are a financial transfer from rich to poor countries.

Specifically, they are a transfer of funds from exporters in developed countries (on whose goods tariffs are imposed, or whose goods are affected by quotas or licensing requirements) to the governments of less developed countries. It cannot be assumed these funds will be managed properly or put to good use. Quite possibly, a certain percentage (in some Third World contexts, 10%) is vulnerable to misappropriation by unscrupulous behavior. Corruption aside, accrued revenues and rents are available to the governments to help their countries industrialize. For example, they can be deployed for industry-enhancing infrastructure, like roads, power plants, ports, and schools.

Moreover, it may be argued the protection afforded by the permitted tariffs and NTBs gives time to "infant" industries in the Third World for growth and maturation. During the period of protection, the infants may mature into strong, profitable, job-generating industries. Absent the protection, the infants might die from premature exposure to foreign competition. In effect, foreign competitors incur not only the direct costs of protection (*e.g.,* higher tariff liabilities on their exports to Third World countries), but also an opportunity cost. Lost profits (*i.e.,* potential profits foregone in favor of the infant industries as a result of the protection) are the opportunity cost. Here, then, is another financial transfer.

Significantly, Paragraph 5 of the 1979 Tokyo Round *Enabling Clause* relates closely to Article XXXVI:8. Paragraph 1 of the *Clause* contains the waiver from the Article I:1 MFN principle for contracting parties (*i.e.,* WTO Members) to grant "differential and more favorable treatment to developing countries." Paragraph 2 defines such treatment to include tariff preferences, and specifically mentions GSP programs, and non-tariff preferences. Tariff and non-tariff preferences are a form of assistance to poor countries. Paragraph 5 of the *Enabling Clause* is a reaffirmation — indeed, reincarnation — of Article XXXVI:8.

Are financial benefits transferred via practice of Article XXXVI:8 obtained by poor countries without any condition whatsoever? The question is rather difficult.

A careful reading of Paragraph 8 reveals no condition put upon less developed countries. They are to benefit from "no expectation of reciprocity," regardless of their existing array of tariffs and NTBs, and regardless of their offers (or lack thereof) to reduce these barriers. Simply put, rich countries are not to demand reciprocity, period.

An Interpretative Note to Article XXXVI:8. *Ad Article XXXVI, Paragraph 8* elaborates on what "do not expect reciprocity" means. This *Ad Article* says:

> "do not expect reciprocity" means, in accordance with the objectives set forth in this Article, that the less-developed contracting parties *should* not be expected, in the course of trade negotiations, to make contributions which are *inconsistent* with their individual development, financial and trade needs, *taking into consideration* past trade developments. (Emphasis added.)

The use of the very "should" is sloppy drafting. The main Paragraph uses an imperative construction that creates an obligation (namely, that developed countries "do not expect reciprocity"). Careful drafting of the *Ad Article* would have conveyed the same obligatory sense as the main Paragraph.

Consequently, the *Ad Article* suggests a developed country could expect a less developed country to offer some reciprocal trade concession. Does this suggestion mean the rule in the main Paragraph is conditional? No.

The suggestion is carefully limited. The *Ad Article* is not an unrestricted license for a developed country to demand concessions of poor countries. It merely allows a developed country to take into account the specific economic circumstances—the "individual development, financial and trade needs"—of the poor country with which it is negotiating. It also allows it to consider past trade developments. In some circumstances, it may be fair for the rich country to ask of the poor country some modest reduction in tariffs or NTBs, subject to the highly significant caveat the reduction is consistent with the specific circumstances and trade trends relevant to that poor country.

Suppose, then, a poor country maintains prohibitive barriers in a particular product market. In a recent three-year period, that country has gained a large share in many foreign markets for the product. Suppose, further, a drop in the barriers to imports of that product from a "prohibitive" level to a "stiff" level (*e.g.*, from a 100% tariff to a 20% tariff) would not affect adversely the performance of producers and exporters. Would it be reasonable for a developed country to ask for that kind of drop? *Ad Article XXXVI, Paragraph 8* says "yes." Put differently, this Interpretative Note provides some guidance as to when the "do not expect reciprocity" rule of the main Paragraph terminates. It does not make the rule conditional. Rather, it helps identify the outer limits of the scope of application of the rule.

IV. Collaboration, GATT Article XXXIII, and 1980 *Sugar Refunds* Case

Among adopted GATT panel reports attracting little attention, one concerns Part IV, and deals specifically with Paragraph 1 of Article XXXVIII. It is the 1980 case of *EC—Refunds on Exports of Sugar* (*Sugar Refunds*). A complaint Brazil lodged in November 1978 against subsidization by EC of sugar exports triggered the *Sugar Refunds* case. Australia, Cuba, India, and Peru supported the complaint. Australia had brought a case against the EC on essentially the same facts, and Brazil cited that case in its favor (though the result of that case was somewhat inconclusive). The thrust of Brazil's complaint did not involve Part IV. Brazil focused on Article XVI:3, arguing refunds on sugar exports granted by the EC resulted in European exporters obtaining more than an equitable share of world export trade in sugar.

Brazil decried the EC's substantial sugar subsidies, which consistently exceeded international prices of the product. These subsidies were one part of the CAP. Brazil alleged the EC was "unrestrained" in its "use of massive subsidies."[5] The EC "had turned from a net importer into a sizeable net exporter of sugar by displacing more efficient producers, mostly less developed countries, at a time of world over-production."[6] (The EC retorted such a change was irrelevant under Article XVI.)

After its six findings under Article XVI, the Panel came to its final conclusion:

> The Panel recognized the efforts made by the European Communities in complying with the provisions of Articles XXXVI and XXXVIII. It nevertheless felt that increased Community exports of sugar through the use of subsidies in the particular market situation in 1978 and 1979, and where developing contracting parties had taken steps within the framework of the *ISA* [*International Sugar Agreement*] to improve the conditions in the world sugar market, inevitably reduced the effects of the efforts made by these countries. For this time-period and for this particular field, *the European Communities had therefore not collaborated jointly with other contracting parties to further the principles and objectives set forth in Article XXXVI, in conformity with the guidelines given in Article XXXVIII.*[7]

What constitutes joint collaboration? Might it be said that while Article XXXVIII is rarely invoked, when it is used, it can have real significance?

---

5. GATT Panel Report, *EC—Refunds on Exports of Sugar*, B.I.S.D. (27th Supp.) 69–98 (March 1981) (adopted 10 November 1980), ¶ 2.6 at 72. [Hereinafter, GATT *Sugar Refunds* Panel Report.]

6. GATT *Sugar Refunds* Panel Report, ¶ 2.6 at 72.

7. GATT *Sugar Refunds* Panel Report, conclusion (h) at 97–98 (emphasis added).

V. Summary Tables of S&D Treatment in GATT-WTO Texts

- **Typology**

Special and differential treatment is not limited to Part IV of GATT. In June 2013, the WTO reported there were nearly 150 provisions on S&D treatment for developing countries and LDCs in GATT and the many other WTO agreements.[8] Table 19-1 summarizes them. Under Column 1, each row of the Table identifies a particular GATT-WTO text contained in Annex 1 (including 1A, 1B, and 1C), 2, 3, or 4 to the *WTO Agreement*. The columns categorize S&D provisions into one of six types.

The typology distinguishes the nature, purpose, and design of the different provisions:

Column 2:   Trade Enhancement—

Boost trade opportunities of developing countries and LDCs.

Column 3:   Special Interests—

Encourage or obligate developed countries to take account of the special interests of developing countries and LDCs.

Column 4:   Flexibility—

Give flexibility to developing countries and LDCs to implement and enforce their commitments and pursue policies.

Column 5:   Extra Time—

Grant additional time to developing countries and LDCs to implement and enforce their commitments.

Column 6:   Technical Assistance—

Call for or offer technical aid by developed countries to developing countries and LDCs.

Column 7:   LDCs Only—

Help for LDCs exclusively (not developing countries).

The 8th (right-hand most) column tallies the number of S&D provisions in each text.

---

8. Table 19-1 is adapted from World Trade Organization, Committee on Trade and Development, Note by the Secretariat, *Special and Differential Treatment Provisions in WTO Agreements and Decisions*, WT/COMTD/W/196, Table on Special and Differential Treatment Provisions by Type and Agreement, at 5 (14 June 2013), www.wto.org.

Table 19-1. Types of S&D Treatment Provisions in GATT-WTO Agreements

Text[9]	Increase Trade Opportunities for Developing Countries and LDCs	Exhort or Require Developed Countries to Account for Developing Country and LDC Interests	Provide Developing Countries and LDCs Flexibility in Their Commitments, Actions, and Policies	Transitional Time Periods	Technical Assistance	For LDCs Only	Total Number of Provisions in Text
GATT	8	13	4	0	0	0	25
Uruguay Round Understanding on BOP	0	0	1	0	1	0	2
Agriculture Agreement	1	0	9	1	0	3	13
SPS Agreement	0	2	0	2	2	0	6
TBT Agreement	0	8	1	1	8	1	19
TRIMs Agreement	0	0	1	2	0	1	3
Antidumping Agreement	0	1	0	0	0	0	1
Customs Valuation Agreement	0	1	2	4	1	0	8
Import Licensing Procedures Agreement	0	3	0	1	0	0	4

(continued)

9. There are no S&D provisions in the WTO *Agreement on Rules of Origin*. At the December 2013 Bali Ministerial Conference, WTO Members agreed to a *Decision on Preferential Rules of Origin for Least Developed Countries*. See WT/MIN(13)/42 or WT/L/917, www.wto.org. This *Decision* sets out guidelines (such as simplicity, ease of compliance by LDCs, and transparency) for Members to adopt their own preferential ROOs (*e.g.*, for GSP schemes), and calls on the WTO Committee on Rules of Origin to review developments annually. At the December 2015 Nairobi Ministerial Conference, Members urged each other to base their preferential ROOs on common guidelines, and notify the WTO of their ROOs. They also called on preference-granting Members to consider allowing LDCs to use non-originating materials up to 75% of the final value of the product, and still qualify for a preference. *See* World Trade Organization, Ministerial Conference, Tenth Session, Nairobi, 15–18 December 2015, *Preferential Rules of Origin for Least-Developed Countries—Ministerial Decision of 19 December 2015*, WT/MIN(15)/W/38, www.wto.org.

Table 19-1. Types of S&D Treatment Provisions in GATT-WTO Agreements (*continued*)

Text	Increase Trade Opportunities for Developing Countries and LDCs	Exhort or Require Developed Countries to Account for Developing Country and LDC Interests	Provide Developing Countries and LDCs Flexibility in Their Commitments, Actions, and Policies	Transitional Time Periods	Technical Assistance	For LDCs Only	Total Number of Provisions in Text
SCM Agreement	0	2	10	7	0	0	19
Safeguards Agreement	0	1	1	0	0	0	2
GATS	3	4	4	0	2	2	13
TRIPs Agreement	0	0	0	2	1	3	6
DSU	0	7	1	0	1	2	11
GPA	0	3	6	0	1	2	10
TOTAL	12	45	40	20	17	14	148/139[10]

At an April 2015 WTO meeting, Bangladesh spoke for the "LDCs Group" and pointed out there was no one system of preferential ROOs that preference-granting Members used, and no single system was better than all others. Rather, "unequivocal evidence" showed ROOs need to "reflect current global value chains and commercial realities" so as to benefit LDCs by allowing them to make increased use of preferences, attracting factories to relocate to LDCs, and increase manufacturing capacity and generate skilled jobs in LDCs. *See* World Trade Organization, *LDCs Urge Movement on Implementing Bali Decision on Preferential Rules of Origin*, 30 April 2015, www.wto.org/english/news_e/news15_e/roi_01may15_e.htm.

10. There are 9 provisions classified in more than 1 category: 1 provision in the *Agreement on Agriculture*; 1 in the *TRIMs Agreement*; 3 in the *SCM Agreement*; 2 in *GATS*; and 2 in the *GPA* (the details can be found in the relevant sections). The total of 139 over all the Agreements counts these provisions only once, while the total of 148 is the total of all listed provisions.

• **Questions**

In reviewing Table 19-1 and consulting the textual provisions it references, consider whether the 1986–1994 Uruguay Round heralded a change in the substantive nature—the generosity—of S&D treatment? That is, what patterns emerge from the S&D treatment afforded by the WTO texts? Does it appear that much of that treatment consists of the length of time a developing country or LDC has to phase in an obligation, or phase out a trade barrier? How does this kind of treatment compare with the treatment GATT Part IV affords? Might it be argued persuasively that GATT, dating from 1947, provides more generous S&D treatment than the WTO texts that emerged from the Uruguay Round? What would be the basis for such an argument—non-reciprocity, and the relief from obligations, perhaps?

A few WTO texts afford no, or hardly any, S&D treatment. One example is the *Antidumping Agreement*. Essentially, aside from a higher negligible volume threshold for poor countries, it treats all WTO Members alike.

Other WTO texts were intended to help poor countries. The *ATC* is an example. It removed (effective 1 January 2005) all quotas on T&A. These quotas, set forth under the 1974 *MFA*, had regulated global T&A trade, and thereby constrained growth in T&A exports from any one country. Producers sourced merchandise in many countries, so that if the quota for a T&A article (*e.g.*, the U.S. quota on ties from China) were filled, they could ship from another country (*e.g.*, ties from Thailand). Most Third World countries lobbied for, and heralded, the opening of markets—particularly developed country markets—to their T&A articles. Exporters could compete in developed country markets based on price and quality, without worrying whether shipments of their merchandise were subject to a quota, and if so, whether the applicable quota had been filled. Finally, as of 1 January 2005, when all *MFA* quotas were abolished, the playing field in the T&A market appeared level.

As that date neared, small players like Lesotho and Sri Lanka realized large players, like China, India, and Vietnam would dominate the playing field. No longer needing to spread manufacturing operations across dozens of countries to meet quota limitations, T&A producers responded to the *ATC* by consolidating operations in the large countries. The decision where to open or maintain operations was driven by business concerns (*e.g.*, input sources and transportation costs) and legal risks (*e.g.*, rule of law and the risk of expropriation), not artificial distortions of trade (aside from occasional special safeguard actions, or the threat thereof, particularly against Chinese T&A exports). Had the smaller less developed countries sought and obtained an agreement during the Uruguay Round that now haunted them? Or, had they simply failed to use the decade-long transition period (1 January 1995, when the *ATC* took effect, until 21 December 2004, the last day of *MFA* quotas) wisely by enhancing their attractiveness to multinational producers as a place in which to operate facilities?

• **Text-Specific Tables**

Tables 19-2 through 19-16 identify the specific provisions in each GATT-WTO text, on an agreement-by-agreement basis, based on the type of those provisions as categorized in Table 19-1.[11] Table 19-2 also provides a brief comment on the specific provisions.

None of these Tables is to be memorized (a nearly impossible task). Rather, as indicated earlier, the goal is to study them for the patterns (or lack thereof) that emerge across time, and across texts, in respect of the legal treatment afforded to poor countries, and the generosity of that treatment, under the multilateral trade regime. Moreover, as a practical matter, understanding these Tables helps identify opportunities and constraints with respect to importation and exportation trans-actions between developed countries, on the one hand, and developing and least developed countries, on the other hand.

So, work through the Tables carefully, to get a lawyer-like understanding of what the law "is" and what it "should be." Consider not only how the S&D provisions are designed to work, but also whether they actually work at all. How many of them are useless, in the sense of not being used? Why are they not used? How might they be improved?

---

11. Tables 19-2 through 19-16 are adapted from World Trade Organization, Committee on Trade and Development, Note by the Secretariat, *Special and Differential Treatment Provisions in WTO Agreements and Decisions*, WT/COMTD/W/196, Sections 2–6, at 6–83 (14 June 2013), www .wto.org. Documents referenced in the Tables indicate their WTO Document Number, and are posted on the WTO website, www.wto.org.

None of the Tables cover three other instances of S&D treatment: (1) amendments to Article 31 of the *TRIPs Agreement* concerning compulsory licensing approved at the December 2005 Hong Kong Ministerial, (2) *Trade Facilitation Agreement* approved at the December 2013 Bali Ministe-rial Conference, or (3) *Decision on Monitoring Mechanism on Special and Differential Treatment* approved at the Bali Conference. The first two texts are discussed in separate Chapters, and the third is discussed later in this Chapter. The Tables do include other pertinent *Decisions* taken at the Bali Ministerial Conference.

Table 19-2. 25 Specific S&D Treatment Provisions in GATT

Article	Content	Comment
	8 Provisions to Increase Trade Opportunities for Developing Countries and LDCs	
XXXVI:2	There is need for a rapid and sustained expansion of the earnings of the less-developed contracting parties.	
XXXVI:3	There is need for positive efforts designed to ensure that less-developed contracting parties secure a share in the growth in international trade commensurate with the needs of their economic development.	Thanks to implementation of Uruguay Round industrial tariff cuts, the average trade weighted tariff imposed on industrial goods exported by developing countries fell by 37%.
XXXVI:4	Given the continued dependence of many less-developed contracting parties on the exportation of a limited range of primary products, there is need to provide in the largest possible measure more favorable and acceptable conditions of access to world markets for these products, and wherever appropriate to devise measures designed to stabilize and improve conditions of world markets in these products, including in particular measures designed to attain stable, equitable and remunerative prices, thus permitting an expansion of world trade and demand and a dynamic and steady growth of the real export earnings of these countries so as to provide them with expanding resources for their economic development.	
XXXVI:5	The rapid expansion of the economies of the less-developed contracting parties will be facilitated by a diversification of the structure of their economies and the avoidance of an excessive dependence on the export of primary products. There is, therefore, need for increased access in the largest possible measure to markets under favorable conditions for processed and manufactured products currently or potentially of particular export interest to less-developed contracting parties.	The GSP schemes maintained by some WTO Members may be viewed as their response to Article XXXVI:3–5.

(continued)

Table 19-2. 25 Specific S&D Treatment Provisions in GATT (*continued*)

Article	Content	Comment
XXXVII:1(a)	The developed contracting parties shall to the fullest extent possible — that is, except when compelling reasons, which may include legal reasons, make it impossible give effect to the following provisions: (a) Accord high priority to the reduction and elimination of barriers to products currently or potentially of particular export interest to less-developed contracting parties, including customs duties and other restrictions which differentiate unreasonably between such products in their primary and in their processed forms;	Some WTO Members attempted to apply this provision in the Doha Round negotiations in agriculture and NAMA, as regards goods in which developing countries and LDCs have a keen export interest, for example, cutting tariffs on tropical products.
XXXVII:4	Less-developed contracting parties agree to take appropriate action in implementation of the provisions of Part IV for the benefit of the trade of other less-developed contracting parties, in so far as such action is consistent with their individual present and future development, financial and trade needs taking into account past trade developments as well as the trade interests of less-developed contracting parties as a whole.	
XXXVIII:2(c)	. . . collaborate in analyzing the development plans and policies of individual less-developed contracting parties and in examining trade and aid relationships with a view to devising concrete measures to promote the development of export potential and to facilitate access to export markets for the products of the industries thus developed and, in this connection, seek appropriate collaboration with governments and international organizations, and in particular with organizations having competence in relation to financial assistance for economic development, in systematic studies of trade and aid relationships in individual less-developed contracting parties aimed at obtaining a clear analysis of export potential, market prospects and any further action that may be required; . . .	The Aid-For-Trade Initiative of the WTO, launched at the December 2005 Hong Kong Ministerial Conference, aims to boost production and exports of goods and services from developing countries and LDCs. In collaboration with the IMF, World Bank, and regional development banks, the WTO helps poor countries implement their WTO commitments, and build trade-related infrastructure, a lack of which is a key supply-side, or capacity-side, constraint on increasing production and exportation. Aid-For-Trade is not supposed to substitute for bilateral ODA from individual countries. The WTO General Council regularly reviews the Initiative.

XXXVIII:2(e)	. . . collaborate in seeking feasible methods to expand trade for the purpose of economic development, through international harmonization and adjustment of national policies and regulations, through technical and commercial standards affecting production, transportation and marketing, and through export promotion by the establishment of facilities for the increased flow of trade information and the development of market research; . . .	The joint WTO-UNCTAD International Trade Center seeks to implement this provision.

13 Provisions Exhorting or Requiring Developed Countries to Account for Developing Country and LDC Interests

XXXVI:6	Because of the chronic deficiency in the export proceeds and other foreign exchange earnings of less-developed contracting parties, there are important inter-relationships between trade and financial assistance to development. There is, therefore, need for close and continuing collaboration between the CONTRACTING PARTIES and the international lending agencies so that they can contribute most effectively to alleviating the burdens these less-developed contracting parties assume in the interest of their economic development.	Several *Decisions* calling for greater coherence in global economic policymaking emerged from the Uruguay Round and are included in the *Final Act* from that Round, such as the *Decision on Relationship of the WTO with the International Monetary Fund*, which essentially maintains their pre-WTO, GATT era relationship. Topics in these *Decisions* include FX rate stability to contribute to trade expansion and sustainable growth and development.

Likewise, the *Final Act* includes a *Declaration on the Contribution of the World Trade Organization to Achieving Greater Coherence in Global Economic Policy Making*, which admits that the WTO cannot address problems arising from non-trade causes.

In November 1996, the WTO General Council approved stronger inter-agency ties with the IMF and World Bank. (*See* WT/L/194.)

The Enhanced Integrated Framework (EIF), initially established in 1997 as the "IF," illustrates collaboration among these 3 IOs, plus UNCTAD and UNDP, for LDCs. So, too, does Aid-For-Trade. |

(*continued*)

Table 19-2. 25 Specific S&D Treatment Provisions in GATT (*continued*)

Article	Content	Comment
XXXVI:7	There is need for appropriate collaboration between the CONTRACTING PARTIES, other intergovernmental bodies and the organs and agencies of the United Nations system, whose activities relate to the trade and economic development of less-developed countries.	In September 1995, the WTO exchanged letters with the UN on cooperation. (*See* WT/GC/W/10.)
XXXVI:9	The adoption of measures to give effect to these principles and objectives shall be a matter of conscious and purposeful effort on the part of the contracting parties both individually and jointly.	
XXXVII:1(b)	. . . refrain from introducing, or increasing the incidence of, customs duties or non-tariff import barriers on products currently or potentially of particular export interest to less-developed contracting parties; and . . .	
XXXVII:1(c)	. . .(i) refrain from imposing new fiscal measures, and (ii) in any adjustments of fiscal policy accord high priority to the reduction and elimination of fiscal measures, which would hamper, or which hamper, significantly the growth of consumption of primary products, in raw or processed form, wholly or mainly produced in the territories of less-developed contracting parties, and which are applied specifically to those products.	
XXXVII:2	(a) Whenever it is considered that effect is not being given to any of the provisions of subparagraph (a), (b) or (c) of paragraph 1, the matter shall be reported to the CONTRACTING PARTIES either by the contracting party not so giving effect to the relevant provisions or by any other interested contracting party. (b)(i) The CONTRACTING PARTIES shall, if requested so to do by any interested contracting party, and without prejudice to any bilateral consultations that may be undertaken, consult with the contracting party concerned and all interested contracting parties with respect to the matter with a view to reaching solutions satisfactory to all contracting parties concerned in order to further the objectives set forth in Article XXXVI. In the course of these consultations, the reasons given in cases where effect was not being given to the provisions of subparagraph (a), (b) or (c) of paragraph 1 shall be examined.	

	(ii) As the implementation of the provisions of subparagraph (a), (b) or (c) of paragraph 1 by individual contracting parties may in some cases be more readily achieved where action is taken jointly with other developed contracting parties, such consultation might, where appropriate, be directed towards this end. (iii) The consultations by the CONTRACTING PARTIES might also, in appropriate cases, be directed towards agreement on joint action designed to further the objectives of this Agreement as envisaged in paragraph 1 of Article XXV.	
XXXVII:3	The developed contracting parties shall: (a) make every effort, in cases where a government directly or indirectly determines the resale price of products wholly or mainly produced in the territories of less-developed contracting parties, to maintain trade margins at equitable levels. (b) give active consideration to the adoption of other measures designed to provide greater scope for the development of imports from less-developed contracting parties and collaborate in appropriate international action to this end. (c) have special regard to the trade interests of less-developed contracting parties when considering the application of other measures permitted under this Agreement to meet particular problems and explore all possibilities of constructive remedies before applying such measures where they would affect essential interests of those contracting parties.	The *Antidumping Agreement* incorporates Article XXXVIII:3(c).
XXXVII:5	In the implementation of the commitments set forth in paragraph 1 to 4 each contracting party shall afford to any other interested contracting party or contracting parties full and prompt opportunity for consultations under the normal procedures of this Agreement with respect to any matter or difficulty which may arise.	
XXXVIII:1	The contracting parties shall collaborate jointly, with the framework of this Agreement and elsewhere, as appropriate, to further the objectives set forth in Article XXXVI.	

(*continued*)

Table 19-2. 25 Specific S&D Treatment Provisions in GATT (*continued*)

Article	Content	Comment
XXXVIII:2(a)	In particular, the CONTRACTING PARTIES shall: . . . where appropriate, take action, including action through international arrangements, to provide improved and acceptable conditions of access to world markets for primary products of particular interest to less-developed contracting parties and to devise measures designed to stabilize and improve conditions of world markets in these products including measures designed to attain stable, equitable and remunerative prices for exports of such products;	Some WTO Members attempted to raise the problem of declining primary commodity prices in the context of the Doha Round agriculture and NAMA negotiations.
XXXVIII:2(b)	seek appropriate collaboration in matters of trade and development policy with the United Nations and its organs and agencies, including any institutions that may be created on the basis of recommendations by the United Nations Conference on Trade and Development;	Same Comment as for Article XXXVI:7.
XXXVIII:2(d)	keep under continuous review the development of world trade with special reference to the rate of growth of the trade of less-developed contracting parties and make such recommendations to contracting parties as may, in the circumstances, be deemed appropriate;	The WTO CTD regularly reviews the performance of developing countries in world trade, the results of which are published on the WTO website.
XXXVIII:2(f)	establish such institutional arrangements as may be necessary to further the objectives set forth in Article XXXVI and to give effect to the provision of this Part.	The CTD is the key WTO body dealing with Trade and Development. Established in 1995 when the WTO was born, its terms of references are in WT/L/46.
4 Provisions Providing Developing Countries and LDCs Flexibility in Commitments, Actions, and Policy		
Section A, XVIII:7(a)	If a contracting party coming within the scope of paragraph 4 (a) of this Article considers it desirable, in order to promote the establishment of a particular industry with a view to raising the general standard of living of its people, to modify or withdraw a concession included in the appropriate Schedule annexed to this Agreement, it shall notify the CONTRACTING PARTIES to this effect and enter into negotiations with any contracting party with which such concession was initially negotiated, and with any other contracting party determined by the	Since 1 January 1995 when *WTO Agreement* entered into force and the WTO was born, this provision has never been invoked.

	CONTRACTING PARTIES to have a substantial interest therein. If agreement is reached between such contracting parties concerned, they shall be free to modify or withdraw concessions under the appropriate Schedules to this Agreement in order to give effect to such agreement, including any compensatory adjustments involved.	
Section B, XVIII:8	The contracting parties recognize that contracting parties coming within the scope of paragraph 4(a) of this Article tend, when they are in rapid process of development, to experience balance-of-payments difficulties arising mainly from efforts to expand their internal markets as well as from the instability in their terms of trade.	Before the birth of the WTO, developing countries invoked Section B over 20 times. Since that birth, 14 developing countries have invoked Section B. In the 1989 *Korea Beef* case, the GATT Panel looked askance at Korea's argument that its import restrictions on beef were justified as necessary to secure an adequate level of FX reserves. Economic data showed Korea's development was robust, so the Panel said Korea should phase out its BOP restrictions on beef. In the 1999 *India Quantitative Restrictions* case, the Appellate Body rejected India's that its BOP restrictions satisfied the Article XVIII, Section B criteria, and held they were not justified by Article XIII.
Section C, XVIII:13	If a contracting party coming within the scope of paragraph 4(a) of this Article finds that governmental assistance is required to promote the establishment of a particular industry with a view to raising the general standard of living of its people, but that no measure consistent with the other provisions of this Agreement is practicable to achieve that objective, it may have recourse to the provisions and procedures set out in this Section.	Before the birth of the WTO, Section C was invoked 14 times. Since that birth, through July 2002, Bangladesh, Colombia, and Malaysia have invoked it. Malaysia cited it in its defense to the first complaint ever brought under the *DSU*, Singapore's claim against a Malaysian import prohibition on polyethylene and polypropylene. Singapore withdrew its complaint, perhaps accepting the Malaysian Section C defense.

(continued)

Table 19-2. 25 Specific S&D Treatment Provisions in GATT (*continued*)

Article	Content	Comment
XXXVI:8	The developed contracting parties do not expect reciprocity for commitments made by them in trade negotiations to reduce or remove tariffs and other barriers to the trade of less-developed contracting parties.	This non-reciprocity expectation is provision is discussed earlier in the Chapter. To what extent, if any, was it taken into account during the Uruguay and Doha Rounds? Consider average tariff levels in developing countries and LDCs, and the extent of their bindings on agricultural and industrial goods.

At the 9th WTO Ministerial Conference in December 2013 in Bali, Indonesia, WTO Members adopted a *Decision on Duty-Free and Quota-Free Market Access for Least Developed Countries* (WT/MIN(13)/44 or WT/L/919). This *Decision* repeats calls for developed countries to grant DFQF treatment to at least 97% of the exports of LDCs, with a target date of the 10th Ministerial Conference in December 2015. Not all developed countries met the target. |

Table 19-3. 2 Specific S&D Treatment Provisions in Uruguay Round *Understanding on BOP*

Paragraph	Content	Comment
	1 Provision to Increase Trade Opportunities for Developing Countries and LDCs	
8	Members, Recognizing the provisions of Articles XII and XVIII:B of GATT 1994 and of the *Declaration on Trade Measures Taken for Balance-of-Payments Purposes* adopted on 28 November 1979 (B.I.S.D. 26S/205-209, referred to in this *Understanding* as the "1979 *Declaration*") and in order to clarify such provisions; Hereby agree as follows: . . . Procedures for balance-of-payments consultations: Consultations may be held under the simplified procedures approved on 19 December 1972 (B.I.S.D. 20S/47-49, referred to in this *Understanding* as "simplified consultation procedures") in the case of least-developed country Members or in the case of developing country Members which are pursuing liberalization efforts in conformity with the schedule presented to the Committee in previous consultations. Simplified consultation procedures may also be used when the Trade Policy Review of a developing country Member is scheduled for the same calendar year as the date fixed for the consultations. In such cases the decision as to whether full consultation procedures should be used will be made on the basis of the factors enumerated in paragraph 8 of the 1979 *Declaration*. Except in the case of least-developed country Members, no more than two successive consultations may be held under simplified consultation procedures	
	1 Provision on Technical Assistance	
12	Notification and documentation: The Secretariat shall, with a view to facilitating the consultations in the Committee, prepare a factual background paper dealing with the different aspects of the plan for consultations. In the case of developing country Members, the Secretariat document shall include relevant background and analytical material on the incidence of the external trading environment on the balance-of-payments situation and prospects of the consulting Member. The technical assistance services of the Secretariat shall, at the request of a developing country Member, assist in preparing the documentation for the consultations.	

Table 19-4. 13 Specific S&D Treatment Provisions in *Agriculture Agreement*

Article	Content	Comment
1 Provision Designed to Increase Trade Opportunities for Developing Countries and LDCs		
Preamble	Having agreed that in implementing their commitments on market access, developed country Members would take fully into account the particular needs and conditions of developing country Members by providing for a greater improvement of opportunities and terms of access for agricultural products of particular interest to these Members, including the fullest liberalization of trade in tropical agricultural products as agreed at the Mid-Term Review, and for products of particular importance to the diversification of production from the growing of illicit narcotic crops; . . .	The WTO says Schedules of developed countries show reductions in tariffs on various goods of keen export interest to developing countries that are greater than average, as well as accelerated implementation of commitments on those cuts. Their average tariff cut of 43% on tropical agricultural goods is an example. But, most rich countries are not in the tropics, whereas most poor ones are. So, steep cuts in such tariffs tend not to threaten domestic producers of a like product.
9 Provisions Providing Developing Countries and LDCs Flexibility in Commitments, Actions, and Policies		
6:2	Domestic Support Commitments: In accordance with the Mid-Term Review Agreement that government measures of assistance, whether direct or indirect, to encourage agricultural and rural development are an integral part of the development programs of developing countries, investment subsidies which are generally available to agriculture in developing country Members and agricultural input subsidies generally available to low-income or resource-poor producers in developing country Members shall be exempt from domestic support reduction commitments that would otherwise be applicable to such measures, as shall domestic support to producers in developing country Members to encourage diversification from growing illicit narcotic crops. Domestic support meeting the criteria of this paragraph shall not be required to be included in a Member's calculation of its Current Total AMS.	Several developing countries invoked Article 6:2 when providing data for computation of their Current Total AMS for their Schedules. Examples include: Bahrain; Bangladesh; Barbados; Botswana; Brazil; Burundi; Chile; Colombia; Costa Rica; Cuba; Ecuador; Egypt; Fiji; Gambia; Honduras; India; Indonesia; Jordan; Korea; Malawi; Malaysia; Maldives; Mauritius; Mexico; Morocco; Namibia; Nepal; Oman; Panama; Paraguay; Peru; Philippines; Qatar; Sri Lanka; Thailand; Tunisia; Turkey; UAE; Uruguay; and Venezuela. Such Members are listed in WTO documents in the G/AG/N/. . . series.
6:4(b)	Domestic Support Commitments — Calculation of Total AMS: For developing country Members, the *de minimis* percentage under this paragraph shall be 10%.	Several developing countries have invoked this *de minimis* clause when computing their Base Total AMS (for both product- and non-product specific support) so as to schedule their domestic support reduction commitments.

Article	Provision	Examples / Notes
		Examples include: Bangladesh; Barbados; Brazil; Chile; India; Israel; Jordan; Korea; Mexico; Pakistan; Panama; Peru; Philippines; Saudi Arabia; Thailand; Tunisia; Turkey; and Uruguay. Such Members are listed in the WTO GA/AG/N/ . . . series.
9:2(b)(iv)	The Member's budgetary outlays for export subsidies and the quantities benefiting from such subsidies, at the conclusion of the implementation period, are no greater than 64% and 79% of the 1986–1990 base period levels, respectively. For developing country Members these percentages shall be 76 and 86%, respectively.	Every developing country that has scheduled an export subsidy reduction commitment has invoked this flexibility to apply a lower rate of reduction. Examples include: Brazil; Colombia; Indonesia; Israel; Mexico; Romania; Turkey; Uruguay; and Venezuela. Such Members are listed in the WTO GA/AG/N/ . . . series.
9:4	During the implementation period, developing country Members shall not be required to undertake commitments in respect of the export subsidies listed in subparagraphs (d) [i.e., for costs of marketing exports] and (e) [i.e., for internal transport and freight charges for exports] of paragraph 1 above, provided that these are not applied in a manner that would circumvent reduction commitments:	Several developing countries (e.g., Barbados, India, Korea, Mauritius, Mexico, Morocco, Pakistan, Sri Lanka, Thailand, and Tunisia, all of which, and others, are listed in the WTO GA/AG/N . . . series), have notified the WTO they provide Article 9:1(d) and/or (e) subsidies.
12:2	The provisions of [Article 12.1] shall not apply to any developing country Member, unless the measure is taken by a developing country Member which is a net-food exporter of the specific foodstuff concerned.	No developing country has ever notified the WTO that it has used export restrictions and prohibitions. So, there are no formal invocations of this provision.
15:1	In keeping with the recognition that differential and more favorable treatment for developing country Members is an integral part of the negotiation, S&D in respect of commitments shall be provided as set out in the relevant provisions of this *Agreement* and embodied in the Schedules of concessions and commitments.	Schedules of developing countries and LDCs indicate recourse to flexibilities on ceiling bindings, extended implementation periods, and lower reduction commitments on market access, domestic support, and export subsidies.

(continued)

Table 19-4. 13 Specific S&D Treatment Provisions in *Agriculture Agreement (continued)*

Article	Content	Comment
Annex 2, Paragraph 3 and Footnote 5	Public Stock Holding for Food Security Purposes: For the purposes of paragraph 3 of Annex 2, governmental stockholding programs for food security purposes in developing countries whose operation is transparent and conducted in accordance with officially published objective criteria or guidelines shall be considered to be in conformity with the provisions of this paragraph, including programs under which stocks of foodstuffs for food security purposes are acquired and released at administered prices, provided that the difference between the acquisition price and the external reference price is accounted for in the AMS.	Developing countries (listed in the WTO GA/AG/N . . . series) have utilized this provision. At the December 2013 Bali Ministerial Conference, WTO Members adopted the *Decision on Public Stockholding for Food Security Purposes.* (WT/MIN(13)/38 or WT/L/913.) This *Decision,* and possible Green Box reform under it, is a major issue between India and the U.S., and other poor and rich countries, respectively. In July 2014, the U.S. agreed it would not sue India for alleged breach of Indian domestic farm support limits caused by India's food security purchases and stockpiling until final resolution of the issue.
Annex 2, Paragraph 4, Footnotes 5–6	Domestic Food Aid: For the purposes of paragraphs 3 and 4 of Annex 2, the provision of foodstuffs at subsidized prices with the objective of meeting food requirement of urban and rural poor in developing countries on a regular basis at reasonable prices shall be considered to be in conformity with the provisions of this paragraph.	Developing countries (listed in the WTO GA/AG/N . . . series) have utilized this provision.
Annex 5, Section B, Paragraphs 7, 10	7. The provisions of paragraph 2 of Article 4 shall also not apply with effect from the entry into force of the *WTO Agreement* to a primary agricultural product that is the predominant staple in the traditional diet of a developing country Member and in respect of which the following conditions, in addition to those specified in paragraph 1(a) through 1(d), as they apply to the products concerned, are complied with: (a) minimum access opportunities in respect of the products concerned, as specified in Section I-B of Part I of the Schedule of the developing country Member concerned, correspond to 1% of base period domestic consumption of the products concerned from the beginning of the first year of the implementation period and are increased in equal annual installments to 2% of corresponding domestic consumption in the base period at the beginning of the fifth year of the implementation period. From the beginning of the sixth year of the implementation	Korea, Philippines, and Taiwan have made recourse to this flexibility, as manifest in their Schedules.

period, minimum access opportunities in respect of the products concerned correspond to 2% of corresponding domestic consumption in the base period and are increased in equal annual installments to 4% of corresponding domestic consumption in the base period until the beginning of the 10th year. Thereafter, the level of minimum access opportunities resulting from this formula in the 10th year shall be maintained in the Schedule of the developing country Member concerned;

(b) appropriate market access opportunities have been provided for in other products under this *Agreement*.

. . .

10. In the event that special treatment under paragraph 7 is not to be continued beyond the 10th year following the beginning of the implementation period, the products concerned shall be subject to ordinary customs duties, established on the basis of a tariff equivalent to be calculated in accordance with the guidelines prescribed in the attachment hereto, which shall be bound in the Schedule of the Member concerned. In other respects, the provisions of paragraph 6 shall apply as modified by the relevant S&D accorded to developing country Members under this *Agreement*.

1 Transitional Time Period

15:2	Developing country Members shall have the flexibility to implement reduction commitments over a period of up to 10 years. Least-developed country Members shall not be required to undertake reduction commitments.	Article 15:2 is listed twice, as it also is under provisions for LDCs only. But, it is counted just once as to the total number of S&D Treatment provisions in the *Agriculture Agreement*.

3 Provisions for LDCs Only

15:2	As above.	
16:1	Developed country Members shall take such action as is provided for within the framework of the *Decision on Measures Concerning the Possible Negative Effects of the Reform Program on Least-Developed and Net Food-Importing Developing Countries*.	This provision also applies to NFIDCs.
16:2	The Committee on Agriculture shall monitor, as appropriate, the follow-up to this *Decision*.	This provision also applies to NFIDCs.

Table 19-5. 6 Specific S&D Treatment Provisions in *SPS Agreement*

Article	Content	Comment
2 Provisions Exhorting or Requiring Developed Countries to Account for Developing Country and LDC Interests		
10:1	In the preparation and application of sanitary or phytosanitary measures, Members shall take account of the special needs of developing country Members, and in particular of the least-developed country Members.	Poor countries have difficulty managing information on changes in the SPS measures of other WTO Members (which may not always be transparent), often resulting in shipments of their exports held up at ports in those other Members. They also struggle with basis *SPS Agreement* obligations (owing partly to a lack of legal capacity). In March 2011, the WTO Secretariat launched the SPS Notification Submission System (NSS), to address these concerns. NSS is a centralized, online database into which authorities in WTO Member countries can input notifications of their SPS measures. The Secretariat also has a Standards and Trade Development Facility (STDF).
10:4	Members should encourage and facilitate the active participation of developing country Members in the relevant international organizations.	Increasing the active engagement of poor countries in IOs such as the FAO, OIE, and WHO was a topic at the margins of the Doha Round. A key barrier is the lack of finances in those countries to enhance their capacity to participate.
2 Transitional Time Periods		
10:2	Where the appropriate level of sanitary or phytosanitary protection allows scope for the phased introduction of new sanitary or phytosanitary measures, longer time-frames for compliance should be accorded on products of interest to developing country Members so as to maintain opportunities for their exports.	The November 2001 Doha Ministerial Conference *Decision on Implementation-Related Issues* clarified that "longer time frame for compliance" normally means at least 6 months. The Decision set the same 6-month period for the gap between publication and entry into force of an SPS measure under Annex B, Paragraph 2, of the *SPS Agreement*.

10:3	With a view to ensuring that developing country Members are able to comply with the provisions of this *Agreement*, the Committee is enabled to grant to such countries, upon request, specified, time-limited exception in whole or in part from obligations under this *Agreement*, taking into account their financial, trade and development needs.	No developing country has made a request under this provision.

2 Provisions on Technical Assistance

9:1	Members agree to facilitate the provision of technical assistance to other Members, especially developing country Members, either bilaterally or through the appropriate international organizations. Such assistance may be, inter alia, in the areas of processing technologies, research and infrastructure, including in the establishment of national regulatory bodies, and may take the form of advice, credits, donations and grants, including for the purpose of seeking technical expertise, training and equipment to allow such countries to adjust to, and comply with, sanitary or phytosanitary measures necessary to achieve the appropriate level of sanitary or phytosanitary protection in their export markets.	
9:2	Where substantial investments are required in order for an exporting developing country Member to fulfill the sanitary or phytosanitary requirements of an importing Member, the latter shall consider providing such technical assistance as will permit the developing country Member to maintain and expand its market access opportunities for the product involved.	*See* comment concerning Article 10:1. Among the key scientific and technical matters with which poor countries need assistance are laboratory facilities and technologies to provide proper risk assessments in compliance with the *SPS Agreement*.

Table 19-6. 19 Specific S&D Treatment Provisions in *TBT Agreement*

Article	Content	Comment
	8 Provisions Exhorting or Requiring Developed Countries to Account for Developing Country and LDC Interests	
10:6	The Secretariat shall, when it receives notifications in accordance with the provisions of this *Agreement*, circulate copies of the notifications to all Members and interested international standardizing and conformity assessment bodies, and draw the attention of developing country Members to any notifications relating to products of particular interest to them.	
12:1	Members shall provide differential and more favorable treatment to developing country Members, through the provisions of this Article, as well as through the relevant provisions of other Articles of this *Agreement*.	Article 2:12 obligates Members to allow a "reasonable internal" between publishing and enforcing a TBT measure so as to allow exporters, especially in developing countries, time to adapt their products or production methods. The November 2001 Doha Ministerial Conference *Decision on Implementation-Related Issues and Concerns* defines "reasonable interval" to mean normally no less than 6 months, unless that period would be ineffective to fulfill the objectives of the measure.
12:2	Members shall give particular attention to the provisions of this *Agreement* concerning developing country Members' rights and obligations and shall take into account the special development, financial and trade needs of developing country Members in the implementation of this Agreement, both nationally and in the operation of this *Agreement's* institutional arrangements.	
12:3	Members shall, in the preparation and application of technical regulations, standards and conformity assessment procedures, take account of the special development, financial and trade needs of developing country Members, with a view to ensuring that such technical regulations, standards and conformity assessment procedures do not create unnecessary obstacles to exports from developing country Members.	It is unclear whether and how developed countries actually account for the needs of developing countries and LDCs when they draft, implement, and enforce TBT measures. In November 2003, the WTO TBT Committee encouraged developed countries to provide more than a 60-day comment period developing countries and LDCs on proposed TBT measures. (*See* G/TBT/13, ¶ 26.)

12:5	Members shall take such reasonable measures as may be available to them to ensure that international standardizing bodies and international systems for conformity assessment are organized and operated in a way which facilitates active and representative participation of relevant bodies in all Members, taking into account the special problems of developing country Members.	
12:6	Members shall take such reasonable measures as may be available to them to ensure that international standardizing bodies, upon request of developing country Members, examine the possibility of, and, if practicable, prepare international standards concerning products of special interest to developing country Members.	As the WTO TBT Committee stated in Section F of its November 2000 *Decision*, international standard-setting bodies need to operate in a transparent, impartial manner, on the basis of consensus, if they are to account for the interests of poor countries. Otherwise, those countries are *de facto* excluded from the decision making process. (*See* G/TBT/1/Rev.9; November 2001 Doha *Decision on Implementation-Related Issues and Concerns*.) Devising international standards that account for the interests of poor countries also is important for goods in which those countries are likely to gain a keen export interest as they ascend the value-added chain.
12:9	During consultations, developed country Members shall bear in mind the special difficulties experienced by developing country Members in formulating and implementing standards and technical regulations and conformity assessment procedures, and in their desire to assist developing country Members with their efforts in this direction, developed country Members shall take account of the special needs of the former in regard to financing, trade and development.	
12:10	The Committee shall examine periodically the Special and Differential Treatment, as laid down in this *Agreement*, granted to developing country Members on national and international levels.	No developing country or LDC has made a request under Article 12:8 for a "specified, time-limited exception."

(*continued*)

Table 19-6. 19 Specific S&D Treatment Provisions in *TBT Agreement* (*continued*)

Article	Content	Comment
	1 Provision Providing Developing Countries and LDCs Flexibility in Their Commitments, Actions, and Policies	
12:4	Members recognize that, although international standards, guides or recommendations may exist, in their particular technological and socio-economic conditions, developing country Members adopt certain technical regulations, standards or conformity assessment procedures aimed at preserving indigenous technology and production methods and processes compatible with their development needs. Members therefore recognize that developing country Members should not be expected to use international standards as a basis for their technical regulations or standards, including test methods, which are not appropriate to their development, financial and trade needs.	
	1 Transitional Time Period Only	
12:8	Accordingly, with a view to ensuring that developing country Members are able to comply with this *Agreement*, the Committee on Technical Barriers to Trade provided for in Article 13 is enabled to grant, upon request, specified, time-limited exceptions in whole or in part from obligations under this Agreement. When considering such requests the Committee shall take into account the special problems, in the field of preparation and application of technical regulations, standards and conformity assessment procedures, and the special development and trade needs of the developing country Member, as well as its stage of technological development, which may hinder its ability to discharge fully its obligations under this Agreement. The Committee shall, in particular, take into account the special problems of the least-developed country Members.	This provision has never been invoked.
	8 Provisions on Technical Assistance	
11:1	Members shall, if requested, advise other Members, especially the developing country Members, on the preparation of technical regulations.	

11:2	Members shall, if requested, advise other Members, especially the developing country Members, and shall grant them technical assistance on mutually agreed terms and conditions regarding the establishment of national standardizing bodies, and participation in the international standardizing bodies, and shall encourage their national standardizing bodies to do likewise.	
11:3	Members shall, if requested, take such reasonable measures as may be available to them to arrange for the regulatory bodies within their territories to advise other Members, especially the developing country Members, and shall grant them technical assistance on mutually agreed terms and conditions regarding: (i) the establishment of regulatory bodies, or bodies for the assessment of conformity with technical regulations; and (ii) the methods by which their technical regulations can best be met.	WTO Members have acknowledged that technical assistance must be provided in a timely, predictable, and sustainable manner if it is to be efficient and effective. (*See* G/TBT/19, ¶ 74.)
11:4	Members shall, if requested, take such reasonable measures as may be available to them to arrange for advice to be given to other Members, especially the developing country Members, and shall grant them technical assistance on mutually agreed terms and conditions regarding the establishment of bodies for the assessment of conformity with standards adopted within the territory of the requesting Member.	
11:5	Members shall, if requested, advise other Members, especially the developing country Members, and shall grant them technical assistance on mutually agreed terms and conditions regarding the steps that should be taken by their producers if they wish to have access to systems for conformity assessment operated by governmental or non-governmental bodies within the territory of the Member receiving the request.	
11:6	Members which are members or participants of international or regional systems for conformity assessment shall, if requested, advise other Members, especially the developing country Members, and shall grant them technical assistance on mutually agreed terms and conditions regarding the establishment of the institutions and legal framework which would enable them to fulfill the obligations of membership or participation in such systems	

(continued)

Table 19-6. 19 Specific S&D Treatment Provisions in *TBT Agreement* (*continued*)

Article	Content	Comment
11:7	Members shall, if so requested, encourage bodies within their territories which are members or participants of international or regional systems for conformity assessment to advise other Members, especially the developing country Members, and should consider requests for technical assistance from them regarding the establishment of the institutions which would enable the relevant bodies within their territories to fulfill the obligations of membership or participation.	
12:7	Members shall, in accordance with the provisions of Article 11, provide technical assistance to developing country Members to ensure that the preparation and application of technical regulations, standards and conformity assessment procedures do not create unnecessary obstacles to the expansion and diversification of exports from developing country Members. In determining the terms and conditions of the technical assistance, account shall be taken of the stage of development of the requesting Members and in particular of the least-developed country Members.	
1 Provision for LDCs Only		
11:8	In providing advice and technical assistance to other Members in terms of Article 11:1 to 11:7, Members shall give priority to the needs of the least-developed country Members.	

Table 19-7. 3 Specific S&D Treatment Provisions in *TRIMs Agreement*

Article	Content	Comment
	1 Provision Providing Developing Countries and LDCs Flexibility in Their Commitments, Actions, or Policies	
4	A developing country Member shall be free to deviate temporarily from the provisions of Article 2 to the extent and in such a manner as Article XVIII of GATT 1994, the *Understanding on the Balance-of-Payments Provisions of GATT 1994*, and the *Declaration on Trade Measures Taken for Balance-of-Payments Purposes* adopted on 28 November 1979 (B.I.S.D. 26S/205–209) permit the Member to deviate from the provisions of Articles III and XI of GATT 1994.	1 developing country cited this provision in a TRIMs Committee meeting, but other Members cast doubt on its invocation. (*See* G/TRIMS/M/9 ¶¶ 30–37, G/TRIMS/M/10 ¶¶ 16–22.)
	2 Transitional Time Periods	
5:2	*Each Member shall eliminate all TRIMs which are notified under Article 5:1, within two years of the date of entry into force of the WTO Agreement in the case of a developed country Member, within five years in the case of a developing country Member, and within seven years in the case of a least-developed country Member.*	This provision is categorized also as for LDCs only, but is counted only once in the aggregate number of S&D treatment provisions in the *TRIMs Agreement*. 47 Members have submitted notifications under Article 5:1. For most of them, the Article 5:2 transition period to eliminate the TRIMs they notified on 1 January 2000. (*See* G/L/860.) Members remain uncertain as to (1) what TRIMs should be notified under Article 5:1, and (2) whether a TRIM notified after the deadline still may benefit from the transition period. (*See* WT/G/TRIMS/M/2-7.)
5:3	On request, the Council for Trade in Goods may extend the transition period for the elimination of TRIMs notified under Article 5:1 for a developing country Member, including a least-developed country Member, which demonstrates particular difficulties in implementing the provisions of this Agreement. In considering such a request, the Council for Trade in Goods shall take into account the individual development, financial and trade needs of the Member in question.	10 developing countries asked for extensions of the transition period in which to eliminate TRIMs. On 31 July 2001, the WTO Council for Trade in Goods gave 8 developing countries transition period extensions through year-end 2003, 7 of them via Article 5:3 (*see* G/L/460–466 and G/L/497–504), and 1 of them via a waiver under *WTO Agreement* Article IX (*see* W/L/410).
	1 Provision for LDCs Only	
5:2	As above.	Only 1 LDC has notified TRIMs under Article 1, and no LDC has requested an extension.

Table 19-8. 1 Specific S&D Treatment Provision in *Antidumping Agreement*

Article	Content	Comment
	1 Provision Exhorting or Requiring Developed Countries to Account for Developing Country and LDCs Interests	
15	It is recognized that special regard must be given by developed country Members to the special situation of developing country Members when considering the application of anti-dumping measures under this Agreement. Possibilities of constructive remedies provided for by this Agreement shall be explored before applying anti-dumping duties where they would affect the essential interests of developing country Members.	In some AD cases, such as *Bed Linens* (DS 141) *Steel Plates* (DS 206) and *Tube or Pipe Fittings* (DS 216) developing country respondents have invoked this provision. Panels, but not the Appellate Body, have examined (1) when and to which Member "special regard" must be given, (2) what "explore" means, and (3) what "before applying anti-dumping duties" means.

Paragraph 7:2 of the November 2001 Doha *Ministerial Decision on Implementation-Related Issues and Concerns* called this provision mandatory, and noted the need for its clarification. |

Table 19-9. 8 Specific S&D Treatment Provisions in *Customs Valuation Agreement*

Article	Content	Comment
	1 Provision Exhorting or Requiring Developed Countries to Account for Developing Country and LDC Interests	
Annex III:5	Certain developing countries may have problems in the implementation of Article 1 of the *Agreement* in so far as it relates to importations into their countries by sole agents, sole distributors and sole concessionaires. If such problems arise in practice in developing country Members applying the *Agreement*, a study of this question shall be made, at the request of such Members, with a view to finding appropriate solutions.	No request for this study has ever been made.
	2 Provisions Providing Developing Countries and LDCs Flexibility in Their Commitments, Actions, or Policies	
Annex III:3	Developing countries which consider that the reversal of the sequential order at the request of the importer provided for in Article 4 of the *Agreement* may give rise to real difficulties for them may wish to make a reservation to Article 4 in the following terms: "The Government of . . . . . reserves the right to provide that the relevant provision of Article 4 of the *Agreement* shall apply only when the customs authorities agree to the request to reverse the order of Articles 5 and 6." If developing countries make such a reservation, the Members shall consent to it under Article 21 of the *Agreement*.	40 developing countries and 13 LDCs have invoked this provision. (*See* G/VAL/W/70, G/VAL/70/Corr.1.)
Annex III:4	Developing countries may wish to make a reservation with respect to Article 5:2 of the *Agreement* in the following terms: "The Government of . . . . reserves the right to provide that Article 5:2 of the Agreement shall be applied in accordance with the provisions of the relevant note thereto whether or not the importer so requests." If developing countries make such a reservation, the Members shall consent to it under Article 21 of the *Agreement*.	40 developing countries and 11 LDCs have invoked this provision. (*See* G/VAL/2/Rev.10/Corr.2, G/VAL/2/Rev.24.)
	4 Transitional Time Periods	
20:1	Developing country Members not party to the *Agreement on Implementation of Article VII of the GATT* (Tokyo Round), may delay application of the provisions of this *Agreement* for a period not exceeding five years from the date of entry into force of the *WTO Agreement* for such Members. Developing country Members who choose to delay application of this *Agreement* shall notify the Director-General of the WTO accordingly.	44 developing countries and 12 LDCs have invoked this provision. (*See* G/VAL/2, G/VAL/2/Rev.1-24.) The provision expired on 1 January 2000 for 29 of these WTO Members, and between July 2000–July 2001 for another 24 of them. In March 2009, this provision expired.

(*continued*)

Table 19-9. 8 Specific S&D Treatment Provisions in *Customs Valuation Agreement* (*continued*)

Article	Content	Comment
20:2	In addition to paragraph 1, developing country Members not party to the *Agreement on Implementation of Article VII of the GATT* (Tokyo Round), may delay application of paragraph 2(b)(iii) of Article 1 and Article 6 for a period not exceeding three years following their application of all other provisions of this *Agreement*. Developing country Members that choose to delay application of the provisions specified in this paragraph shall notify the Director-General of the WTO accordingly.	37 developing countries and 11 LDCs invoked this provision. In March 2009, this provision expired.
Annex III:1	The five-year delay in the application of the provision of the *Agreement* by developing country Members provided for in paragraph 1 of Article 20 may, in practice, be insufficient for certain developing country Members. In such cases a developing country Member may request before the end of the period referred to in paragraph 1 of Article 20 an extension of such period, it being understood that the Members will give sympathetic consideration to such a request in cases where the developing country Member in question can show good cause.	20 Members requested extensions, 1 Member asked for a second extension, and 13 of the requests were granted. (*See* G/VAL/2, G/VAL/2/Rev.1-24.) In March 2009, this provision expired.
Annex III:2	Developing countries which currently value goods on the basis of officially established minimum values may wish to make a reservation to enable them to retain such values on a limited and transitional basis under such terms and conditions as may be agreed to by the Members. (*See also Decision* on texts relating to minimum values and imports by sole agents, sole distributors and sole concessionaires.)	17 developing countries reserved the right to retain minimum values. (*See* G/VAL/2, G/VAL/2/Rev.1-24.) The WTO Customs Valuation Committee authorized 4 Members to use minimum values.
1 Provision on Technical Assistance		
20:3	Developed country Members shall furnish, on mutually agreed terms, technical assistance to developing country Members that so request. On this basis developed country Members shall draw up programs of technical assistance which may include, inter alia, training of personnel, assistance in preparing implementation measures, access to sources of information regarding customs valuation methodology, and advice on the application of the provisions of this *Agreement*.	

Table 19-10. 4 Specific S&D Treatment Provisions in *Import Licensing Procedures Agreement*

Article	Content	Comment
	3 Provisions Exhorting or Requiring Developed Countries to Account for Developing Country and LDC Interests	
1:2	General Provisions: Members shall ensure that the administrative procedures used to implement import licensing regimes are in conformity with the relevant provisions of GATT 1994 including its annexes and protocols, as interpreted by this *Agreement*, with a view to preventing trade distortions that may arise from an inappropriate operation of those procedures, taking into account the economic development purposes and financial and trade needs of developing country Members.	This provision has been invoked in 3 cases. (*See* WT/DS/27, WT/DSI69/R, and WT/DS/334.) It has not been the subject of an Appellate Body Report.
3:5(a)(iv)	Non-Automatic Import Licensing: (a) Members shall provide, upon the request of any Member having an interest in the trade in the product concerned, all relevant information concerning: (iv) where practicable, import statistics (*i.e.*, value and/or volume) with respect to the products subject to import licensing. Developing country Members would not be expected to take additional administrative or financial burdens on this account.	
3:5(j)	Non-Automatic Import Licensing: In allocating licenses, the Member should consider the import performance of the applicant. In this regard, consideration should be given as to whether licenses issued to applicants in the past have been fully utilized during a recent representative period. In cases where licenses have not been fully utilized, the Member shall examine the reasons for this and take these reasons into consideration when allocating new licenses. Consideration shall also be given to ensuring a reasonable distribution of licenses to new importers, taking into account the desirability of issuing licenses for products in economic quantities. In this regard, special consideration should be given to those importers importing products originating in developing country Members and, in particular, the least-developed country Members.	This provision has been invoked in 7 cases. (*See* WT/DS/27, WT/DS/69, WT/DS/90, WT/DS/113, WT/DS/161, WT/DSI69, and WT/DS/334.) It has not been the subject of an Appellate Body Report.
	1 Transitional Time Period	
2:2, Footnote 5	Automatic Import Licensing: A developing country Member, other than a developing country Member which was a Party to the [Tokyo Round] *Agreement on Import Licensing Procedures* done on 12 April 1979, which has specific difficulties with the requirements of Article 2:2 subparagraphs (a)(ii) and (a)(iii) may, upon notification to the Committee, delay the application of these subparagraphs by not more than two years from the date of entry into force of the WTO Agreement for such Member.	24 developing countries invoked this provision to delay application of Articles 2:2(a)(ii)–(iii). (*See* WT/LT/Rev. 2, 14, 19, 24, 41, 48, and 72.) Their 2-year delay period has expired. During that period, they were obligated to provide notifications under Articles 1:4(a), 7:3, and 8:2(b).

Table 19-11. 16 Specific S&D Treatment Provisions in *SCM Agreement*

Article	Content	Comment
	2 Provisions Exhorting or Requiring Developed Countries to Account for Developing Country and LDC Interests	
27:1	Members recognize that subsidies may play an important role in economic development programs of developing country Members.	
27:15	The Committee shall, upon request by an interested developing country Member, undertake a review of a specific countervailing measure to examine whether it is consistent with the provisions of 27:10 and 27:11 as applicable to the developing country Member in question.	The SCM Committee has never received such a request.
	10 Provisions Providing Developing Countries and LDCs Flexibility in Their Commitments, Actions, and Policies	
27:2(a)	The prohibition of paragraph 1(a) of Article 3 shall not apply to: (a) developing country Members referred to in Annex VII.	This provision is applicable only to a subset of developing countries. On 15 December 2000, the General Council decided, through the Director General, to include Honduras on the Annex VII(b), as it was omitted even though it was the only founding WTO Member with a GNP of less than $1,000.
Annex VII	Developing Country Members Referred to in Article 27.2(a): (a) Least-developed countries designate as such by the United Nations which are Members of the WTO. (b) Each of the following developing countries which are Members of the WTO shall be subject to the provisions which are applicable to other developing country Members according to Article 27.2(b) when GNP per capita has reached $1,000 per annum; Bolivia, Cameroon, Congo, Côte d'Ivoire, Dominican Republic, Egypt, Ghana, Guatemala, Guyana, India, Indonesia, Kenya, Morocco, Nicaragua, Nigeria, Pakistan, Philippines, Senegal, Sri Lanka and Zimbabwe.	In the November 2001 Doha Ministerial Conference *Decision on Implementation-Related Issues and Concerns*, WTO Members agreed a Member can remain on the Annex VIII(b) list until its GNP *per capita* reaches $1,000 in constant 1990 dollars for 3 consecutive years. A Member may be re-included on that list, if its GNP *per capita* falls back below $1,000. (*See* WT/MIN(01)/17.)

27:4	Any developing country Member referred to in Article 27:2(b) shall phase out its export subsidies within the eight-year period, preferably in a progressive manner. However, a developing country Member shall not increase the level of its export subsidies, and shall eliminate them within a period shorter than that provided for in this paragraph when the use of such export subsidies is inconsistent with its development needs. If a developing country Member deems it necessary to apply such subsidies beyond the eight-year period, it shall not later than one year before the expiry of this period enter into consultation with the Committee, which will determine whether an extension of this period is justified, after examining all the relevant economic, financial and development needs of the developing country Member in question. If the Committee determines that the extension is justified, the developing country Member concerned shall hold annual consultations with the Committee to determine the necessity of maintaining the subsidies. If no such determination is made by the Committee, the developing country Member shall phase out the remaining export subsidies within two years from the end of the last authorized period.	*See* comment under Transitional Time Periods.
27:6	Export competitiveness in a product exists if a developing country Member's exports of that product have reached a share of at least 3.25% in world trade of that product for two consecutive calendar years. Export competitiveness shall exist either (a) on the basis of notification by the developing country Member having reached export competitiveness or (b) on the basis of a computation undertaken by the Secretariat at the request of any Member. For the purposes of this paragraph, a product is defined as a section heading of the Harmonized System Nomenclature. The Committee shall review the operation of this provision five years from the date of the entry into force of the *WTO Agreement.*	*See* comment to Article 27:5.
27:7	The provisions of Article 4 shall not apply to a developing country Member in the case of export subsidies which are in conformity with the provisions of Article 27:2 through 27:5. The relevant provisions in such a case shall be those of Article 7.	This provision was invoked in 1 case. (*See* WT/DS/46/R.)

(continued)

Table 19-11. 16 Specific S&D Treatment Provisions in SCM Agreement *(continued)*

Article	Content	Comment
27:8	There shall be no presumption in terms of Article 6:1 that a subsidy granted by a developing country Member results in serious prejudice, as defined in this *Agreement*. Such serious prejudice, where applicable under the terms of Article 27:9, shall be demonstrated by positive evidence, in accordance with the provisions of Article 6:3 through 6:8.	Article 31 limited the application of Article 6:1 to 5 years from the entry into force of the *WTO Agreement*, unless the SCM Committee by consensus extended that period. No such consensus was reached, so Article 6:1 lapsed on 31 December 1999. In a case lodged by 2 developed countries, a Panel found that subsidies granted by a developing country exceeded the 5% threshold allowed under Article 6:1, so a claim of serious prejudice could be brought against that country. The Panel found those subsidies caused serious prejudice in the form of significant price undercutting. (*See* WT/DS54/R, WT/DS55/R, WT/DS59/R, and WT/DS64/R.)
27:9	Regarding actionable subsidies granted or maintained by a developing country Member other than those referred to in Article 6:1, action may not be authorized or taken under Article 7 unless nullification or impairment of tariff concessions or other obligations under GATT 1994 is found to exist as a result of such a subsidy, in such a way as to displace or impede imports of a like product of another Member into the market of the subsidizing developing country Member or unless injury to a domestic industry in the market of an importing Member occurs.	
27:10	Any countervailing duty investigation of a product originating in a developing country Member shall be terminated as soon as the authorities concerned determine that: (a) the overall level of subsidies granted upon the product in question does not exceed 2% of its value calculated on a per unit basis; or (b) the volume of the subsidized imports represents less than 4% of the total imports of the like product in the importing Member, unless imports from developing country Members whose individual shares of total imports represent less than 4% collectively account for more than 9% of the total imports of the like product in the importing Member.	

27:11	For those developing country Members within the scope of Article 27:2(b) which have eliminated export subsidies prior to the expiry of the period of eight years from the date of entry into force of the *WTO Agreement*, and for those developing country Members referred to in Annex VII, the number in Article 27:10(a) shall be 3% rather than 2%. This provision shall apply from the date that the elimination of export subsidies is notified to the Committee, and for so long as export subsidies are not granted by the notifying developing country Member. This provision shall expire eight years from the date of entry into force of the *WTO Agreement*. (Article 27:10 (a): Any countervailing duty investigation of a product originating in a developing country Member shall be terminated as soon as the authorities concerned determine that: the overall level of subsidies granted upon the product in question does not exceed 2% of its value calculated on a per unit basis.)	This higher *de minimis* subsidization threshold provision expired on 31 December 2002.
27:12	The provisions of Article 27:10 and 27:11 shall govern any determination of *de minimis* under Article 15:3.	
27:13	The provisions of Part III (Actionable Subsidies) shall not apply to direct forgiveness of debts, subsidies to cover social costs, in whatever form, including relinquishment of government revenue and other transfer of liabilities when such subsidies are granted within and directly linked to a privatization program of a developing country Member, provided that both such program and the subsidies involved are granted for a limited period and notified to the Committee and that the program results in eventual privatization of the enterprise concerned.	The SCM Committee has ever received and discussed only 1 notification, from Brazil. (*See* G/SCM/N/13/BRA and G/SCM/N/13/BRA/Corr.1.)
7 Transitional Time Periods		
27:2(b)	The prohibition of Article 3:1(a) shall not apply to: (b) other developing country Members for a period of eight years from the date of entry into force of the *WTO Agreement*, subject to compliance with the provisions in Article 27:4.	*See* Comment to Article 27:4 In addition to the 7 Article 27 transitional time periods, Article 29 contains rules for Members in transition from a centrally-planned to free market-oriented economy.
27:3	The prohibition of Article 3.1(b) shall not apply to developing country Members for a period of five years, and shall not apply to least developed country Members for a period of eight years, from the date of entry into force of the *WTO Agreement*.	The 5- and 8-year transition periods expired on 31 December 1999 and 2002, respectively.

(*continued*)

Table 19-11. 16 Specific S&D Treatment Provisions in SCM Agreement (*continued*)

Article	Content	Comment
27:4	Any developing country Member referred to in Article 27:2(b) shall phase out its export subsidies within the eight-year period, preferably in a progressive manner. However, a developing country Member shall not increase the level of its export subsidies, and shall eliminate them within a period shorter than that provided for in this paragraph when the use of such export subsidies is inconsistent with its development needs. If a developing country Member deems it necessary to apply such subsidies beyond the eight-year period, it shall not later than one year before the expiry of this period enter into consultation with the Committee, which will determine whether an extension of this period is justified, after examining all the relevant economic, financial and development needs of the developing country Member in question. If the Committee determines that the extension is justified, the developing country Member concerned shall hold annual consultations with the Committee to determine the necessity of maintaining the subsidies. If no such determination is made by the Committee, the developing country Member shall phase out the remaining export subsidies within two years from the end of the last authorized period.	The 8-year phase out period expired on 31 December 2002. However, some WTO Members obtained extensions of this transition period. Article 27:4 is discussed in detail in a separate Chapter.
27:14	The Committee shall, upon request by an interested Member, undertake a review of a specific export subsidy practice of a developing country Member to examine whether the practice is in conformity with its development needs.	The SCM Committee has never received such a request.
27:5	A developing country Member which has reached export competitiveness in any given product shall phase out its export subsidies for such product(s) over a period of two years. However, for a developing country Member which is referred to in Annex VII and which has reached export competitiveness in one or more products, export subsidies on such products shall be gradually phased out over a period of eight years.	No developing country ever notified that it had reached export competitiveness. However, other Members requested calculations that certain developing countries had reached that threshold. (*See* G/SCM/Q3/COL/12, G/SCM/46, G/SCM/103, G/SCM/103/Add.1 and Add.2, G/SCM/47 —G/SCM/Q3/THA/16, G/SCM/48, G/SCM/132 and G/SCM/132/Add.1/Rev.1.)
27:6	*See above.*	*See* comment for Article 27:5.
27:11	*See above.*	*See* comment for Article 27:11.

Table 19-12. 2 Specific S&D Treatment Provisions in *Safeguards Agreement*

Article	Content	Comment
	1 Provision Exhorting or Requiring Developed Countries to Account for Developing Country and LDC Interests	
9:1, and Footnote 2	Safeguard measures shall not be applied against a product originating in a developing country Member as long as its share of imports of the product concerned in the importing Member does not exceed 3%, provided that developing country Members with less than 3% import share collectively account for not more than 9% of total imports of the product concerned. Footnote 2: A Member shall immediately notify an action taken under Article 9.1 to the Committee on Safeguards.	One GSP-granting Member excluded a developing country from eligibility under Article 9:1, arguing that country was not on the list of GSP beneficiaries of the granting Member. This exclusion triggered opposition. (*See* G/SG/M/9, G/SG/M/14.)
	1 Provision Providing Developing Countries and LDCs Flexibility in Their Commitments, Actions, and Policies	
9:2	A developing country Member shall have the right to extend the period of application of a safeguard measure for a period of up to two years beyond the maximum period provided for in Article 7:5. Notwithstanding the provisions of Article 7:3, a developing country Member shall have the right to apply a safeguard measure again to the import of a product which has been subject to such a measure, taken after the date of entry into force of the *WTO Agreement*, after a period of time equal to half that during which such a measure has been previously applied, provided that the period of non-application is at least two years.	Brazil and Philippines invoked this provision to extend their safeguard measures for up to 10 years. (*See* G/SG/N/10/BRA1 and 2, and G/SG/N/10/PHL/1 and G/SG/N/14/PHL, and supplements thereto.)

Table 19-13. 13 Specific S&D Treatment Provisions in GATS

Article	Content	Comment
3 Provisions to Increase Trade Opportunities for Developing Countries and LDCs		
Preamble	Wishing to establish a multilateral framework of principles and rules for trade in services with a view to the expansion of such trade under conditions of transparency and progressive liberalization and as a means of promoting the economic growth of all trading partners and the development of developing countries; Desiring to facilitate the increasing participation of developing countries in trade in services and the expansion of their services exports including, *inter alia*, through the strengthening of their domestic services capacity and its efficiency and competitiveness. . . .	Section I of the Doha Round *Guidelines and Procedures for the Negotiations on Trade in Services* (S/L/93) reflects this provision.
VI:1	The increasing participation of developing country Members in world trade shall be facilitated through negotiated specific commitments, by different Members pursuant to Parts III and IV of this *Agreement*, relating to: (a) the strengthening of their domestic services capacity and its efficiency and competitiveness, *inter alia* through access to technology on a commercial basis; (b) the improvement of their access to distribution channels and information networks; and (c) the liberalization of market access in sectors and modes of supply of export interest to them.	Section I, Paragraphs 1-4, and Section II, Paragraph 5, of the Doha Round *Guidelines and Procedures for the Negotiations on Trade in Services* (S/L/93) reflect this provision.
VI:2	Developed country Members, and to the extent possible other Members, shall establish contact points within two years from the date of entry into force of the WTO Agreement to facilitate the access of developing country Members' service suppliers to information, related to their respective markets, concerning:	Every developed country, and many developing ones, have established contact points, and notified them to the Council for Trade in Services. The Council periodically publishes the list of contact points. (*See, e.g.*, S/ENQ/78/Rev. 13 (4 December 2012).)

(a) commercial and technical aspects of the supply of services;

(b) registration, recognition and obtaining of professional qualifications; and

(c) the availability of services technology.

4 Provisions Exhorting or Requiring Developed Countries to Account for Developing Country and LDC Interests

Preamble	Recognizing the right of Members to regulate, and to introduce new regulations, on the supply of services within their territories in order to meet national policy objectives and, given asymmetries existing with respect to the degree of development of services regulations in different countries, the particular needs of developing countries to exercise this right. . . .	Section I, Paragraphs 1-2, of the Doha Round *Guidelines and Procedures for the Negotiations on Trade in Services* (S/L/93) reflect this provision.
XII:1	. . . It is recognized that particular pressures on the balance of payments of a Member in the process of economic development or economic transition may necessitate the use of restrictions to ensures, *inter alia*, the maintenance of a level of financial reserves adequate for the implementation of its program of economic development or economic transition.	
XV:1	. . . Such negotiations [on subsidies] shall recognize the role of subsidies in relation to the development programs of developing countries and take into account the needs of Members, particularly developing country Members, for flexibility in this area . . .	
XIX:3	For each round, negotiating guidelines and procedures shall be established. For purposes of establishing such guidelines, the Council for Trade in Services shall carry out an assessment of trade in services in overall terms and on a sectoral basis with reference to the objectives of this Agreement, including those set out in paragraph 1 of Article IV. Negotiating guidelines shall establish modalities for the treatment of liberalization undertaken autonomously by Members since previous negotiations, as well as for the special treatment for least-developed country Members under the provisions of paragraph 3 of Article IV.	Section I, Paragraph 2, and Section III, Paragraph 13-15, of the Doha Round *Guidelines and Procedures for the Negotiations on Trade in Services* (S/L/93) reflect this provision.

(continued)

Table 19-13. 13 Specific S&D Treatment Provisions in GATS (*continued*)

Article	Content	Comment
	4 Provisions Providing Developing Countries and LDCs Flexibility in Their Commitments, Actions, and Policies	
III:4	Each Member shall also establish one or more enquiry points to provide specific information to other Members, upon request, on all such matters as well as those subject to the notification requirement in paragraph 3. Such enquiry points shall be established within two years from the date of entry into force of the *Agreement Establishing the WTO* (referred to in this *Agreement* as the "*WTO Agreement*"). Appropriate flexibility with respect to the time-limit within which such enquiry points are to be established may be agreed upon for individual developing country Members. Enquiry points need not be depositories of laws and regulations.	
V:3	(a) Where developing countries are parties to an agreement of the type referred to in Article V:1, flexibility shall be provided for regarding the conditions set out in Article V:1, particularly with reference to Article V:1(b) thereof, in accordance with the level of development of the countries concerned, both overall and in individual sectors and sub-sectors. (b) Notwithstanding Article V:6, in the case of an agreement of the type referred to in Article V:1 involving only developing countries, more favorable treatment may be granted to juridical persons owned or controlled by natural persons of the parties to such an agreement.	Members have never clarified what S&D treatment in the context of RTAs means.
XIX:2	The process of liberalization shall take place with due respect for national policy objectives and the level of development of individual Members, both overall and in individual sectors. There shall be appropriate flexibility for individual developing country Members for opening fewer sectors, liberalizing fewer types of transactions, progressively extending market access in line with their development situation and, when making access to their markets available to	Section I, Paragraphs 2–3, and Section III, Paragraph 12 and 14–15, of the Doha Round *Guidelines and Procedures for the Negotiations on Trade in Services* (S/L/93) reflect this provision.

Annex on Telecommunications, Paragraph 5(g)	foreign service suppliers, attaching to such access conditions aimed at achieving the objectives referred to in Article IV. Notwithstanding the preceding paragraphs of this section, a developing country Member may, consistent with its level of development, place reasonable conditions on access to and use of public telecommunications transport networks and services necessary to strengthen its domestic telecommunications infrastructure and service capacity and to increase its participation in international trade in telecommunications services. Such conditions shall be specified in the Member's Schedule.	No developing country has ever invoked this provision by including in its Services Schedule a reservation or condition on the obligations the Annex imposes.
2 Provisions on Technical Assistance		
XXV:2	Technical assistance to developing countries shall be provided at the multilateral level by the Secretariat and shall be decided upon by the Council for Trade in Services.	The Doha Round *Guidelines and Procedures for the Negotiations on Trade in Services* (S/L/93) reflect this provision.
Annex on Telecommunications, Paragraph 6	In cooperation with relevant international organizations, Members shall make available, where practicable, to developing countries information with respect to telecommunications services and developments in telecommunications and information technology to assist in strengthening their domestic telecommunications services sector.	In May and July 2000, respectively, the WTO Council for Trade in Services and ITU adopted an accord to collaborate on technical assistance.
2 Provisions for LDCs Only		
IV:3	Special priority shall be given to the least-developed country Members in the implementation of Article IV:1 and 2. Particular account shall be taken of the serious difficulty of the least-developed countries in accepting negotiated specific commitments in view of their special economic situation and their development, trade and financial needs.	Section I, Paragraph 2, of the Doha Round *Guidelines and Procedures for the Negotiations on Trade in Services* (S/L/93) reflect this provision. WTO Members adopted a *Decision of 17 December 2011 on Preferential Treatment to Services and Service Suppliers of Least Developed Countries* (also called the "2011 Waiver Accord"), and at the December 2013 Bali Ministerial Conference adopted a *Decision for the Operationalization of the Waiver Concerning Preferential treatment to Services and Service Suppliers of Least Developed Countries* (referred to as "operationalizing the LDC Services Waiver," WT/MIN(13)/W15, WT/L/918).

(*continued*)

Table 19-13. 13 Specific S&D Treatment Provisions in GATS (*continued*)

Article	Content	Comment
		Under these *Decisions*, a Member may grant special priority to LDC services and service suppliers that otherwise would violate the MFN rule in *GATS* Article II. That is, they can give non-MFN (*i.e.*, preferential) access to their markets to services and service suppliers from LDCs. The non-reciprocal preferences would last for as long as a Member remains on the U.N. list of LDCs.

In February 2014, over 24 Members (but not the U.S.) agreed to do so, covering Modes I, II, and III in the following sectors or sub-sectors: professional; IT and computer; other business; construction; distribution; financial; transportation and logistics; tourism; recreational and sporting. These developed countries also agreed to expand LDC services access on Mode IV, waive fees for business and employment visas for LDC service persons, waive economic needs and labor market tests for LDCs services, and extend the duration of stay in their (developed) countries permitted to LDC professionals.

Yet, by the 31 July 2015 deadline, just 11 developed countries (Australia, Canada, China, Japan, Hong Kong, Korea, New Zealand, Norway, Singapore, Taiwan, Switzerland), notified the WTO of specific services preferences for LDCs. Whether they responded in a commercially meaningful manner to the July 2014 collective request from LDCs was uncertain, insofar as LDCs were not players in the sectors in which they were granted preference. For example, Australia pledged to provide preferential access for business (computer, professional and others), tourism, and transport (maritime, air, rail, road and auxiliary) services from LDCs. |

In September 2015, the U.S. agreed to a waiver, offering preferential access to LDC service providers in the following sub-sectors: accounting, auditing and bookkeeping; engineering; environmental services; foreign legal consulting; higher education; motion picture and video home entertainment; physical well-being; radio and television; road freight transport and cargo handling; research and development; technical testing and analysis; and telecommunications.

But, the American offer did not cover Mode IV, and query whether LDCs did or could provide these services to America in a commercially meaningful sense.

At the December 2015 Nairobi Ministerial Conference, Members adopted a *Decision on LDC Trade in Services*, WT/MIN(15)/W/39, and a *Decision on Implementation of Preferential Treatment in Favor of Services and Service Suppliers of Least Developed Countries and Increasing LDC Participation in Services Trade*, WT/MN(15)/48–WT/L/982, in which they urged non-LDC Members that had not offered preferential access to LDC service suppliers to do so. This *Decision* extended the Waiver period from 2026 to 2030.

By February 2018, the WTO received 24 notifications, representing 51 Members, granting preferences under the Waiver.

| XIX:3 | … Negotiating guidelines shall establish modalities for the treatment of liberalization undertaken autonomously by Members since previous negotiations, as well as for the special treatment for least-developed country Members under the provisions of paragraph 3 of Article 4. | Section III, Paragraph 13 of the Doha Round *Guidelines and Procedures for the Negotiations on Trade in Services* (S/L/93) reflect this provision. Members adopted services negotiation modalities for developing countries and LDCs on 3 September 2003 (TN/S/13). |

Table 19-14. 6 Specific S&D Treatment Provisions in *TRIPs Agreement*

Article	Content	Comment
		2 Transitional Time Periods
65:2	A developing country Member is entitled to delay for a further period of four years the date of application, as defined in paragraph 1, of the provisions of this *Agreement* other than Articles 3, 4 and 5.	Developing countries extensively use of this transition period. This period expired on 1 January 2000.
65:4	To the extent that a developing country Member is obliged by this *Agreement* to extend product patent protection to areas of technology not so protectable in its territory on the general date of application of this *Agreement* for that Member, as defined in paragraph 2, it may delay the application of the provisions on product patents of Section 5 of Part II to such areas of technology for an additional period of five years.	Some developing countries used this transition period for technology fields not subject to product patent protection. This period ended on 1 January 2005.
		1 Provision on Technical Assistance
67	In order to facilitate the implementation of this *Agreement*, developed country Members shall provide, on request and on mutually agreed terms and conditions, technical and financial cooperation in favor of developing and least-developed country Members. Such cooperation shall include assistance in the preparation of laws and regulations on the protection and enforcement of intellectual property rights as well as on the prevention of their abuse, and shall include support regarding the establishment or reinforcement of domestic offices and agencies relevant to these matters, including the training of personnel.	The WTO Council on TRIPs dedicates considerable attention to technical cooperation, particularly on issues of information sharing, monitoring compliance, and needs of poor countries.

3 Provisions for LDCs Only

Preamble	Recognizing also the special needs of the least-developed country Members in respect of maximum flexibility in the domestic implementation of laws and regulations in order to enable them to create a sound and viable technological base.
66:1	In view of the special needs and requirements of least-developed country Members, their economic, financial and administrative constraints, and their need for flexibility to create a viable technological base, such Members shall not be required to apply the provisions of this *Agreement*, other than Articles 3, 4 and 5, for a period of 10 years from the date of application as defined under Article 65:1. The Council for TRIPS shall, upon duly motivated request by a least-developed country Member, accord extensions of this period.	1 January 2006 was the initial expiry date for the Article 66:1 transition period for LDCs. On 29 November 2005, the TRIPs Council extended it until 1 July 2013 (*see* IP/C/40), and further extended it on 11 June 2013 to 1 July 2021 (*see* IP/C/64), because of the special needs of LDCs. Via a 1 July 2002 *Decision* to implement Paragraph 7 of the Doha *Declaration on the TRIPs Agreement and Public Health* (WT/MIN(01)/DEC/2), the TRIPs Council extended until 1 January 2016 the LDC transition period to protect and enforce patents and undisclosed information. On protecting and enforcing patents and undisclosed information, the General Council on 19 July 2002 waived Article 70:9 obligations of LDCs as to exclusive marketing rights for pharmaceutical products until 1 January 2016. (*See* WT/L/478.)
66:2	Developed country Members shall provide incentives to enterprises and institutions in their territories for the purpose of promoting and encouraging technology transfer to least developed country Members in order to enable them to create a sound and viable technological base.	Under the *Decision of the TRIPs Council of 20 February 2003*, there is a monitoring mechanism for implementation of Article 66:2 obligations, whereby developing countries submit annual reports the Council reviews. Under the *Decision of the General Council on the Implementation of Paragraph 6 of the Doha Declaration on the TRIPS Agreement and Public Health* (*see* WT/L/540 and WT/L/540/Corr.1) and the *Protocol Amending the TRIPS Agreement* (*see* WT/L/641), Members pledged to pay special attention to technology transfer and capacity building in the pharmaceutical sector pursuant to Article 66:2.

Table 19-15. 11 Specific S&D Treatment Provisions in *DSU*

Article	Content	Comment
	7 Provisions Exhorting or Requiring Developed Countries to Account for Developing Country and LDC Interests	
4:10	During consultations Members should give special attention to developing country Members' particular problems and interests.	Among the problems developing countries and LDCs face in respect of *DSU* participation are: (1) reasonable timeframes for proceedings in light of their legal capacity; (2) adjustment of remedies to induce effective compliance by developed countries when developing countries or LDCs win a case; (3) costs of litigation; and (4) regulating access to proceedings to ensure positive outcomes.
		In one case, a developing country alleged a developed country disregarded its request for consultations, thereby discriminating against it and impairing its interests in violation of Article 4:10. (*See* WT/DSB/M/7, at 2.)
8:10	When a dispute is between a developing country Member and a developed country Member the panel shall, if the developing country Member so requests, include at least one panelist from a developing country Member.	There have been 249 different individuals serving as Panelists, of whom 118 are from developing countries, but just 2 from LDCs.
		Panelists from developing countries are common in cases between developing and developed countries. (*See, e.g.,* WT/DS248/R; WT/DS249/R; WT/DS251/R; WT/DS252/R; WT/DS253/R; WT/DS254/R; WT/DS258/R; WT/DS259/R.)
		In the 2003 *Steel Safeguards* case, the Director General was asked to compose the Panel with Article 8:10 in mind.
		In several cases, Panels have taken into account the status of a respondent as a developing country when setting and revising the schedule for the proceedings. (*See, e.g., EC–Bananas III (Article 21:5–Ecuador II)*, WT/DS27/RW2/ECU, ¶¶ 2.74–2.76; 2007 *Turkey— Rice*, WT/DS344/R, ¶ 7.305; *Philippines—Distilled Spirits*, WT/DS396/R, WT/DS403/R, ¶ 7.190; *Dominican Republic—Safeguard Measures*, WT/DS417/R, WT/DS418/R, ¶ 7.443.) India invoked Article 12:10 in the 1999 *India Quantitative Restrictions* case for extra time to review the interim Panel Report.

In one case, the developing country respondent argued the process raised 3 fundamental *DSU* S&D treatment issues: (1) difficulties developing countries face when a developed country insists consultations be held only in Geneva; (2) the meaning and significance of the consultations stage; (3) whether a developed country may decide unilaterally consultations are finished, in light of the Article 12:10 statement that "in the context of consultations involving a measure taken by a developing country Member, the parties may agree to extend the period established in paragraphs 7 and 8 of Article 4." (*See* WT/DSB/M/21, at 4.)

In the 2007 *Turkey—Rice* case (WT/DS334), Turkey invoked Article 12:10 for a longer consultation period. At the 22 October 2007 meeting at which the DSB adopted the Panel Report, the U.S, with Australia and Canada, argued against inclusion in the Report of Part VII.G, on S&D treatment, because neither Party had requested a finding on the topic or had a chance to review it in the interim Report. They said inclusion by the Panel of a new, unrequested finding after it issued its interim Report raised systemic concerns.

| 12:10 | In the context of consultations involving and measures taken by a developing country Member, the parties may agree to extend the periods established in paragraphs 7 and 8 of Article 4. If, after the period has elapsed, the consulting parties cannot agree that the consultations have concluded, the Chairman of the DSB shall decide, after consultation with the parties, whether to extend the relevant period and, if so, for how long. In addition, in examining a complaint against a developing country Member, the panel shall allow sufficient time for the developing country Member to prepare and present its argumentation. The provisions of paragraph 1 of Article 20 and paragraph 4 of Article 21 are not affected by any action pursuant to this paragraph. | |
| 12:11 | Where one or more of the parties is a developing country Member, the panel's report shall explicitly indicate the form in which account has been taken of relevant provisions on differential and more-favorable treatment for developing country Members that form part of the covered agreements which have been raised by the developing country Member in the course of the dispute settlement procedures. | Several Panel Reports contain an Article 12:11 statement. (*See, e.g.,* WT/DS27/R; WT/DS27/RW2/ECU; WT/DS46/R; WT/DS90/R; WT/DS204/R; WT/DS217; WT/DS234/R; WT/DS248/R; WT/DS249/R; WT/DS251/R; WT/DS252/R; WT/DS253/R; WT/DS254/R; WT/DS258/R; WT/DS259/R; WT/DS308/R; WT/DS334/R; WT/DS396/R; WT/DS403/R; WT/DS417/R; WT/DS418/R.) |

(*continued*)

Table 19-15. 11 Specific S&D Treatment Provisions in DSU (continued)

Article	Content	Comment
21:2	Particular attention should be paid to matters affecting the interests of developing country Members with respect to measures which have been subject to dispute settlement.	Several arbitration awards under Article 21:2. (*See, e.g.,* WT/DS54/15; WT/DS55/14; WT/DS59/13; WT/DS64/12; WT/DS87/15; WT/DS110/14; WT/DS207/13; WT/DS217/14; WT/DS234/22; WT/DS246/14; WT/DS265/33; WT/DS266/33; WT/DS283/14; WT/DS268/12; WT/DS269/13; WT/DS285/13; WT/DS286/15; WT/DS366/13; WT/DS384/24; WT/DS386/23.)
21:7	If the matter is one which has been raised by a developing country Member, the DSB shall consider what further action it might take which would be appropriate to the circumstances.	
21:8	If the case is one brought by a developing country Member, in considering what appropriate action might be taken, the DSB shall take into account not only the trade coverage of measures complained of, but also their impact on the economy of developing country Members concerned.	In one arbitral decision in the 1997 Bananas case, this provision was invoked. (*See EC-Bananas III (Article 21:5-Ecuador II)*, WT/DS27/RW2/ECU.)
1 Provision Providing Developing Countries and LDCs Flexibility in Their Commitments, Actions, and Policies		
3:12	Notwithstanding Article 3:11, if a complaint based on any of the covered agreements is brought by a developing country Member against a developed country Member, the complaining party shall have the right to invoke, as an alternative to the provisions contained in Articles 4, 5, 6 and 12 of this Understanding, the corresponding provisions of the Decision of 5 April 1966 (BISD 14S/18), except that where the Panel considers that the time-frame provided for in paragraph 7 of that Decision is insufficient to provide its report and with the agreement of the complaining party, that time-frame may be extended. To the extent that there is a difference between the rules and procedures of Articles 4, 5, 6 and 12 and the corresponding rules and procedures of the Decision, the latter shall prevail.	In the 1997 *Bananas* case, in 2007, Colombia and Panama invoked Article 3:12 in their consultation request, reserving the right to ask the Director General to use his good offices to facilitate a solution to their compliance dispute with the EU. (*See* WT/DS361/1 and 2.) They did so. Through those offices on 15 December 2009 they, with 8 other Latin American countries, announced a comprehensive solution, the *General Agreement on Trade in Bananas* (GATB). (*See* WT/L/784.) On 8 November 2012, the EU and 10 Latin American companies reached a final settlement, encompassing the *GATB*.

1 Provision on Technical Assistance

27:2	While the Secretariat assists Members in respect of dispute settlement at their request, there may also be a need to provide additional legal advice and assistance in respect of dispute settlement to developing country Members. To this end, the Secretariat shall make available a qualified legal expert from the WTO technical cooperation services to any developing country Member which so requests. This expert shall assist the developing country Member in a manner ensuring the continued impartiality of the Secretariat.	The WTO Secretariat provides 2 consultants to offer legal aid to developing countries and LDCs.

2 Provisions for LDCs Only

24:1	At all stages of the determination of the causes of a dispute and of dispute settlement procedures involving a least-developed country Member, particular consideration shall be given to the special situation of least-developed country Members. In this regard, Members shall exercise due restraint in raising matters under these procedures involving a least-developed country Member. If nullification or impairment is found to result from a measure taken by a least-developed country Member, complaining parties shall exercise due restraint in asking for compensation or seeking authorization to suspend the application of concessions or other obligations pursuant to these procedures.	Only 1 LDC, Bangladesh, has initiated a dispute settlement proceeding. (*See India Antidumping Measure on Batteries from Bangladesh, WT/DS306.*) 8 LDCs have participated in *DSU* proceedings as a third party: Bangladesh, (DS243) Benin, (DS267) Chad, (DS267) Madagascar, (DS27, DS265, DS266, DS283) Malawi, (DS265, DS266, DS283, DS434) Senegal, (DS27, DS58) Tanzania, (DS265, DS266, DS283) Zambia, (DS434) Of the above-listed cases, 6 were appealed, hence LDCs participated as third parties in 6 Appellate Body cases.
24:2	In dispute settlement cases involving a least-developed country Member, where a satisfactory solution has not been found in the course of consultations the Director-General or the Chairman of the DSB shall, upon request by a least-developed country Member offer their good offices, conciliation and mediation with a view to assisting the parties to settle the dispute, before a request for a panel is made. The Director-General or the Chairman of the DSB, in providing the above assistance, may consult any source which either deems appropriate.	The Director General has suggested procedural steps to operationalize the *DSU* Article 5 provision on use of his good offices, conciliation, and mediation. (See WT/DSB/25.)

Table 19-16. 10 Specific S&D Treatment Provisions in GPA

Article	Content	Comment
	3 Provisions Exhorting or Requiring Developed Countries to Account for Developing Country and LDC Interests	
V:1	In negotiations on accession to, and in the implementation and administration of, this *Agreement*, the Parties shall give special consideration to the development, financial and trade needs and circumstances of developing countries and least developed countries (collectively referred to hereinafter as "developing countries," unless specifically identified otherwise), recognizing that these may differ significantly from country to country. As provided for in this Article and on request, the Parties shall accord S&D to: (a) least developed countries; and (b) any other developing country, where and to the extent that this S&D meets its development needs.	The thrust of *GPA* S&D treatment provisions is to give poor countries more flexibility to negotiate for *sui generis* exclusions from and exceptions to the *GPA* when scheduling commitments. That flexibility is an inducement to join this plurilateral accord. On 30 March 2012, *GPA* Members adopted revisions to the accord, including its S&D provisions, pursuant to *GPA* Article XXIV:7.
V:2	Upon accession by a developing country to this *Agreement*, each Party shall provide immediately to the goods, services and suppliers of that country the most favourable coverage that the Party provides under its annexes to Appendix I to any other Party to this *Agreement*, subject to any terms negotiated between the Party and the developing country in order to maintain an appropriate balance of opportunities under this *Agreement*.	
V:10	The Committee shall review the operation and effectiveness of this Article every five years.	
	6 Provisions Providing Developing Countries and LDCs Flexibility in Their Commitments, Actions, and Policies	
V:3	Based on its development needs, and with the agreement of the Parties, a developing country may adopt or maintain one or more of the following transitional measures, during a transition period and in accordance with a schedule, set out in its relevant annexes to Appendix I, and applied in a manner that does not discriminate among the other Parties:	This provision identifies specific kinds of flexibilities, and requires that flexibilities used by developing countries or LDCs, *i.e.*, specific measures be (1) negotiated individually by them to suit their particular developmental needs, (2) limited in duration, (3) non-discriminatory, and (4) set out in an Annex.

	(a) a price preference program, provided that the program: (i) provides a preference only for the part of the tender incorporating goods or services originating in the developing country applying the preference or goods or services originating in other developing countries in respect of which the developing country applying the preference has an obligation to provide national treatment under a preferential agreement, provided that where the other developing country is a Party to this *Agreement*, such treatment would be subject to any conditions set by the Committee; and (ii) is transparent, and the preference and its application in the procurement are clearly described in the notice of intended procurement; (b) an offset, provided that any requirement for, or consideration of, the imposition of the offset is clearly stated in the notice of intended procurement; (c) the phased-in addition of specific entities or sectors; and a threshold that is higher than its permanent threshold.
V:4	In negotiations on accession to this *Agreement*, the Parties may agree to the delayed application of any specific obligation in this *Agreement*, other than Article IV:1(b), by the acceding developing country while that country implements the obligation. The implementation period shall be: (a) for a least developed country, five years after its accession to this *Agreement*; (b) for any other developing country, only the period necessary to implement the specific obligation and not to exceed three years.
V:5	Any developing country that has negotiated an implementation period for an obligation under paragraph 4 shall list in its Annex 7 to Appendix I the agreed implementation period, the specific obligation subject to the implementation period and any interim obligation with which it has agreed to comply during the implementation period.

(continued)

Table 19-16. 10 Specific S&D Treatment Provisions in GPA (*continued*)

Article	Content	Comment
V:6	After this *Agreement* has entered into force for a developing country, the Committee, on request of the developing country, may: (a) extend the transition period for a measure adopted or maintained under paragraph 3 or any implementation period negotiated under paragraph 4; or (b) approve the adoption of a new transitional measure under paragraph 3, in special circumstances that were unforeseen during the accession process.	
V:7	A developing country that has negotiated a transitional measure under paragraph 3 or 6, an implementation period under paragraph 4 or any extension under paragraph 6 shall take such steps during the transition period or implementation period as may be necessary to ensure that it is in compliance with this *Agreement* at the end of any such period. The developing country shall promptly notify the Committee of each step.	
V:9	The Committee may develop procedures for the implementation of this Article. Such procedures may include provisions for voting on decisions relating to requests under paragraph 6.	
1 Provision on Technical Assistance		
V:8	The Parties shall give due consideration to any request by a developing country for technical cooperation and capacity building in relation to that country's accession to, or implementation of, this *Agreement*.	Arguably to provide maximum freedom, this provision specifies no specific type of technical assistance, and allows WTO Members that have acceded to the *GPA* to help poor countries that have not acceded to it. The Secretariat also sponsors regional and national *GPA* seminars for such countries.
2 Provisions for LDCs Only		
V:1(a)	*See above.*	Article V:1 also is categorized as a provision exhorting or requiring rich countries to account for the interests of poor ones, but is not counted twice in tallying *GPA* S&D treatment provisions.
V:4(a)	*See above.*	Article V:4 also is counted as a provision affording flexibility to poor countries and LDCs, but is not counted twice in tallying *GPA* S&D treatment provisions.

(4) Property Rights

A country is ineligible if it has nationalized or expropriated American property, including IP, or has taken action that is similar in effect to a nationalization or expropriation (namely, nullifying or repudiating an existing contract, or imposing or enforcing taxes or restrictive maintenance or operational conditions). There are three exceptions: the country has provided adequate and effective compensation to the property owner, is in negotiations to provide compensation, or is engaged in arbitration over compensation.

The "property rights" limit on eligibility protects not only individual American citizens, but also any corporations, partnerships, or association that is 50% or more owned by a citizen.[17] This constraint is redolent of the behavior against which Title III of the *Helms-Burton Act* was aimed, namely, trafficking in American assets confiscated by Fidel Castro's regime in Cuba. That *Act* created a secondary boycott against, and called for treble damage liability for, such trafficking. (Of course, in December 2014, the U.S. announced an end to its trade embargo of Cuba.)

(5) Enforcement

A country is ineligible if it fails to recognize as binding, or enforce, an arbitral award in favor of the U.S. This "arbitration" limit protects individual American citizens, and also any corporation, partnership, or association that is 50% or more owned by an American citizen.[18] For example, in 2012, the U.S. suspended Argentina because it failed to pay several long-standing international arbitration awards to American firms. The U.S. restored the benefits effective 1 January 2018, after Argentina resolved those arbitration award disputes, plus agreed to enhanced market access for American farm products and IP protection.

(6) Terrorism

A country is ineligible if it aids or abets international terrorism (*e.g.*, by granting sanctuary from prosecution for an alleged act), or fails to support the efforts of the U.S. to combat terrorism.[19] This limitation is consistent with the *Iran and Libya Sanctions Act of 1996*, as amended, which takes aim at terrorist sponsorship, and at the proliferation of nuclear, biological, and chemical weapons.

(7) Worker Rights

A country is ineligible if it fails to afford "internationally recognized worker rights."[20] These rights track the five most important ones set forth by the

---

17. *See* 19 U.S.C. § 2462(b)(2)(D).
18. *See* 19 U.S.C. § 2462(b)(2)(E).
19. *See* 19 U.S.C. § 2462(b)(2)(F).
20. 19 U.S.C. § 2462(b)(2)(G).

ILO: the right of association; the right to organize and bargain collectively; a prohibition on forced or compulsory labor; a minimum age for the employment of children (as well as a prohibition on the worst forms of child labor); and acceptable conditions of work (specifically, as to minimum wages, work hours, and safety and health standards).[21] In the *GSP* context, however, this list is not exclusive. The President must report annually to Congress on the status of internationally recognized worker rights in each BDC.[22]

(8) Child Labor

A country is ineligible if it "has not implemented its commitments to eliminate the worst forms of child labor."[23] There are four "worst forms": slavery in any form (*e.g.*, sale, trafficking, debt bondage, forced or compulsory labor generally or for the armed forces); prostitution and pornography; illicit activities (*e.g.*, narcotics production and trafficking); and work that by its nature "is likely to harm the health, safety, or morals of children."[24] The President's annual report on the status of internationally recognized worker rights in each BDC must include discussion of efforts to eliminate the worst forms of child labor in that country.[25]

Not all political limitations on the President's discretion are equally severe.

The President cannot waive the first three limits. However, the President can designate a country as a BDC if it is not in full compliance with any one of the last five restrictions, if that designation "will be in the national economic interest of the United States."[26] While the President must report to Congress on what would amount to a waiver of one or more of these eligibility criteria, the words "national economic interest" seem intended to give the President flexibility to escape a restriction. Further, the President must withdraw or suspend designation (by Executive Order or Presidential Proclamation) of any country as a BDC under "changed circumstances," *i.e.*, a country no longer satisfies the political considerations.[27]

Interestingly, the list of political considerations has grown longer over time. For instance, Section 412 of the *Trade and Development Act of 2000* added the eighth restriction. Section 4102(a) of the *Trade Act of 2002* prohibited designation of beneficiary status to any country that has not supported the U.S. in combating terrorism. Section 4102(b) of the *Act* added "prohibition on the worst forms of child labor" to the definition of "internationally recognized worker rights." As a general proposition, to what extent is it accurate to say *GSP* benefits have become more, not less, conditional?

---

21. *See* 19 U.S.C. § 2467(4).
22. *See* 19 U.S.C. § 2464.
23. 19 U.S.C. § 2462(b)(2)(H).
24. 19 U.S.C. § 2467(6).
25. *See* 19 U.S.C. § 2464.
26. 19 U.S.C. § 2462(b).
27. 19 U.S.C. § 2462(d)(2).

Demands from politicians to add yet more considerations continue. For example, in September 2013, Representative Lee R. Terry (Republican-Nebraska) introduced the *Playing Fair on Trade and Innovation Act* (H.R. 3167).[28] He was particularly vexed at India for engaging in what he claimed was unfair and discriminatory treatment that hurt American companies and workers. So, his bill called for two amendments to the *GSP* consideration: a country would not be treated as a BDC if it (1) fails to provide adequate and effective IPR protection, or (2) maintains local content requirements (other than for government procurement for non-commercial purposes).[29]

- **Seven Additional Factors**

There are seven further requirements the President must consider in deciding whether to grant BDC status to a particular country. That is, even if a country is not a developed one, and even if it satisfies the aforementioned political considerations, the President must consider the following factors:

(1) Desire?

Has the country expressed a desire to be designated a BDC?[30] In most instances, this factor ought to be a mere formality.

(2) Development Level?

Does the level of economic development of the country, measured by *per capita* GNP, living standards, and other economic factors the President deems appropriate, make it an appropriate designee for BDC status?[31] This factor leaves some room for discretion, as it essentially calls for a decision by the President as to whether the country "is poor enough" for the *GSP* program.

(3) Other Countries?

Do other major developed countries extend *GSP* treatment to the country?[32] Arguably, this factor can be used in favor or against a designation of eligibility.

On the one hand, getting benefits from other developed countries helps the case of a country for BDC status. It shows other wealthy countries judge the country worthy for such benefits. On the other hand, it hurts the case, because it supports a conclusion that the burden of giving is appropriately shared, or that others have done enough.

(4) Market Access?

To what extent has the country assured the U.S. "it will provide equitable and reasonable access to the markets and basic commodity resources" of the

28. *See* Anandashankar Mazumdar, *Rep. Terry Seeks to Bar GSP Status If Protection of U.S. IP Rights Inadequate*, 30 International Trade Reporter (BNA) 1474 (26 September 2013).
29. In 19 U.S.C. § 2462(b)(2).
30. *See* 19 U.S.C. § 2462(c)(1).
31. *See* 19 U.S.C. § 2462(c)(2).
32. *See* 19 U.S.C. § 2462(c)(3).

country, and also assured the U.S. "it will refrain from engaging in unreasonable export practices."[33] It is difficult to see this factor as other than an expression of American self-interest, *i.e.*, a kind of *quid pro quo*, contrary to the letter and spirit of GATT Article XXXVI:8, calling for "something in return" for a designation of BDC status.

America applied this criterion against India in March 2019, with President Donald J. Trump (1946–, President, 2017–) announcing he would withdraw GSP treatment to India, because India failed to provide U.S. companies with equitable and reasonable access to Indian markets. Petitions from America's dairy industry (the U.S. Dairy Export Council and National Milk Producers Federation) and medical device manufactures (the Advanced Medical Technology Association) had triggered the GSP review of India. The petitioners argued Indian trade barriers impeded (e.g., high tariffs and onerous safety checks on dairy products, and price controls on medical devices) their exports. Also upsetting the U.S. was India's new e-commerce legislation mandating data localization for credit card payment companies (e.g., MasterCard and Visa), restrictions on e-commerce businesses (e.g., Amazon and Flipkart, disallowing them from selling goods made by companies in which they have an equity interest), plus higher tariffs on electronic items and smartphones. India argued such measures were necessary to protect data privacy, provide health care products at affordable prices, and ensure a level playing field for Indian SMEs. Though India was the largest GSP beneficiary, the tariff savings amounted only to about $250 million. In other words, withdrawing GSP benefits from India was of limited commercial significance. Yet, is it appropriate to use the threat of withdrawal as leverage to force changes in trade laws that may not be in the interests of a BDC?

(5) IP?

To what extent does the country provide "adequate and effective" IP rights?[34] Once again, query the extent to which American self-interest is at play? Query, also, whether this is necessary given the WTO *TRIPs Agreement* and Special 301 in U.S. trade law? Notably, there are lobbying groups carefully monitoring which countries are designated BDCs.

For instance, the Coalition for *GSP* (based in Washington, D.C., and on line at www.tradepartnership.com), is comprised of businesses, trade associations, and consumer organizations. It lobbies for the longest possible extension of the *GSP* program. However, some of its members have a particular interest in the IP sector (*e.g.*, entertainment and pharmaceutical companies). For them, *GSP* renewal may be an opportunity to pressure actual or

---

33. 19 U.S.C. § 2462(c)(4).
34. 19 U.S.C. § 2462(c)(5).

prospective BDCs to tighten enforcement of IPs, by conditioning their support for renewal on such action.

(6) Investment and Services?

To what extent has the country reduced trade distorting investment practices (*e.g.*, export performance requirements) and barriers to trade in services?[35] The strong American interest in FDI and market access for services again raises the questions of self-interested conditions and insertion of reciprocity into the *GSP* program.

For instance, this factor empowers the President to deny designation of BDC status to a country that offers service schedule liberalization commitments that the President judges insufficient to meet the interests of U.S. financial institutions, telecommunications firms, and other service providers.

(7) Worker Rights?

To what extent is the country taking steps to afford its workers internationally recognized worker rights?[36] While not to be read as such under basic statutory construction rules, this factor appears superfluous in light of the seventh political consideration above. Still, it is used. For instance, Belarus lost *GSP* benefits because of its failure to afford its workers internationally recognized worker rights (declared by President Clinton (1946, President, 1993–2000) on 6 July 2000). So, too, did Burma in 1989, but effective November 2016 they were restored thanks to what the U.S. said were improvements by Burma's government (which was democratically elected in November 2015) in fighting child and forced labor, and human trafficking.

The President may designate particularly poor countries as "least developed beneficiary developing countries" (LDBDCs). To receive this status, a country must be a BDC, and thus must meet all eligibility requirements.[37] General Note 4(b) of the HTSUS lists these countries. For example, on 10 January 2003, President George W. Bush (1946, President, 2001–2009) designated Afghanistan a BDC (with retroactive effect to 29 January 2001), and an LDBDC (effective 13 February 2003). The benefit (as it were) of LDBDC status is a modestly expanded eligible product list applies to that country.

Summing the limitations above, there are 17 in total—two income criteria, eight political considerations, and seven additional factors. Are these limitations justifiable, and by what rationale? If the aim of the *GSP* program is, or ought to be, assistance to poor countries and the promotion of them into healthy trading partners,

---

35. *See* 19 U.S.C. § 2462(c)(6).
36. *See* 19 U.S.C. § 2462(c)(7).
37. *See* 19 U.S.C. §§ 2462(a)(2), 2467(5).

then what sort of limitations, if any, are justifiable, and why? Should least developed countries have fewer eligibility requirements?

III. Case Study of Bangladeshi Worker Rights

Is it appropriate to base *GSP* eligibility on worker rights criteria? One argument is such rights naturally accrue, or trickle down, as a country grows in prosperity. Oxfam International, however, counters that "[t]he trickle-down discourse of trade incorrectly sees good labor standards as an outcome of economic development, rather than a contributing factor towards it."[38] So, Oxfam urges "workers' rights and the enforcement of these rights should be seen as crucial determinants of poverty alleviation."[39]

Is Bangladesh a case in point for both arguments? That country has been in trouble for allegedly not demonstrating progress on affording internationally recognized worker rights. In 2007, the AFL-CIO petitioned the USTR to review compliance by Bangladesh with labor laws. The union was concerned about systemic problems, such as the Bangladeshi government thwarting efforts by workers in that country to unionize, putting up baseless criminal charges against labor activists, and failing to enforce laws on election of worker representatives, minimum wages, mandatory employer contributions to social security funds, and safety. The USTR still had not completed the review by October 2012, when the AFL-CIO filed a petition with the Administration of President Barack H. Obama (1961, President, 2009–2017) calling for removal of the BDC status because of concerns about the failure of Bangladeshi authorities to enforce labor laws, and fire safety.

Those concerns proved tragically prescient. In November 2012, there was a fire at the Tarzeen Fashions clothing factory in Dhaka in which 112 workers were killed. That factory made apparel for the American market, including Marine Corps-branded clothes. It also made clothes for Wal Mart on an unauthorized basis, as Wal Mart had de-authorized it as a supplier. In December 2012, 12 Democratic Members of the House of Representatives joined the AFL-CIO, urging the USTR to finish its review of the BDC status of Bangladesh. Then, in April 2013, the collapse of the Rana Plaza garment factory on the outskirts of Dhaka took the lives of 1,129 workers. Pressure from Congress, including a letter from 9 Democratic Senators, increased: *GSP* benefits from Bangladesh should be suspended because of its failure to satisfy the statutory worker rights criteria.

---

38. Oxfam International, *Stitched Up: How Rich-Country Protectionism in Textiles and Clothing Trade Prevents Poverty Alleviation* 24 (Oxfam Briefing Paper 60, March 2004). [Hereinafter, Oxfam International.]

39. Oxfam International.

And, so they were, by President Barack H. Obama in June 2013. But, query whether the move was wrong-headed. T&A merchandise accounts for 96% of Bangladeshi exports to America (as of 2012), none of which receives *GSP* treatment. Most T&A items are excluded from the *GSP* product eligibility list. Indeed, less than 1% of Bangladeshi merchandise shipped to America gets *GSP* treatment. Specifically, 0.5% of Bangladeshi exports got that treatment, whereas T&A merchandise were subject to duty rates of 15–32%. So, the suspension penalized that tiny fraction of Bangladeshi exporters, and they likely had little if anything to do with the RMG factory disasters. Conversely, the suspension did not target the guilty T&A producers.

In July 2013, the U.S. and Bangladesh signed an "Action Plan" to bolster worker rights and safety, with a view to reinstatement of *GSP* benefits. One year on, Bangladesh remained ineligible.

The EU took a different, two-pronged approach. First, rather than annul Bangladeshi *GSP* treatment under its scheme, it issued a caution in the form of a "compact." The compact took a form of a July 2013 trilateral deal to enhance workers' safety among the EU, Bangladesh, and ILO. Pointedly, the EU said it was not willing to strike Bangladesh from DFQF treatment, partly out of concern for Bangladesh: shipping 60% of its clothing exports to the EU, it is dependent on that market, and its RMGs get duty-free treatment under the European EBA scheme. Rendering millions of Bangladeshis in the RMG sector was not on for the Europeans, and counterproductive for both sides.

Second, in May, EU retailers signed with Bangladesh an "Accord on Fire and Building Safety in Bangladesh" to improve workplace safety and enhance labor rights in the RMG sector, including EPZs. Under it, Bangladesh agreed to address structural building and fire safety schemes by June 2014, recruit 200 additional inspectors by the end of 2013, and strengthen rights of freedom of association and collective bargaining. Notably, no less than 72 large clothing retailers, most of them European (*e.g.*, Carrefour and Marks and Spencer), signed the Accord. Other signatories included fashion brands (*e.g.*, Benetton), labor unions (*e.g.*, Industriall, UNI union), and non-governmental organizations (NGOs, *e.g.*, Clean Clothes Campaign and Worker's Rights Consortium).

Under the Accord, all factories used by the retailers are inspected, with the results published. Any facility with a failing grade is ordered to cease operations, and devise remedial plans. The workers therein are informed of their right to refuse to enter that facility, but while it is closed, to be paid for up to 6 months. If a company owning the facility does not make the necessary repairs, thus remaining in breach of its commitments under the Accord, then the other signatories to the Accord can lodge a complaint against it. (Of course, they also can boycott the violator and its facility.) The complaint initially is heard by a steering committee, and then (failing resolution) by an arbitration panel. The outcome of the arbitral process is enforceable in a court of law in the home country of the relevant company. However, the Accord does not contain any penalties.

So, the Accord is legally binding under Bangladeshi law, meaning foreign retailers are responsible for safety lapses in the Bangladeshi factories from which they source, even if those facilities are owned and managed by Bangladeshis. It also is binding under the law of the home country of the company owning a factory in question. The binding nature of the Accord and specter of legal accountability proved too much for many North American retailers, like Gap and Wal-Mart, which refused to sign the Accord. They developed their own action plan, the provisions of which resembled those in the Accord, but which were unenforceable. Wal-Mart argued that "[i]f you have to find $10 m[illion] for factory safety, and put aside another $10 m for lawyers, you will really start to suck the energy out of this."[40]

To be sure, the increase in well-being of Bangladeshi RMG workers, especially women, and the multiplier effects thereof, is undeniable. Robbing Bangladesh of its comparative advantage by increasing its costs prematurely will help only other countries, such as China and Vietnam, with substantial RMG industries. Disney said it would shift production out of Bangladesh.

But, query whether an unenforceable obligation will compel foreign multinationals to deal with dangerous conditions in their Bangladeshi suppliers. They have promised to reduce the high human cost of cheap garments since 1993, but the sanction of reputational integrity seems not to have made much difference.

IV. Eligible Articles and Extensive Ineligibility List

Under authority delegated by Congress to the President, the President may designate articles—*i.e.*, a category of merchandise—as eligible for *GSP* preferences, namely, duty-free treatment. The designation occurs by Executive Order or Presidential Proclamation.[41] The USTR announces both designations and denials of eligibility in the *Federal Register*. An article denied designation may not be reconsidered for at least 3 years after the denial.[42] The President also is authorized to designate eligible articles from LDBDCs.

Procedurally, before any designation of eligibility with respect to articles, public hearings must be held, and advice must be obtained from the ITC (and other Executive Branch agencies) on the probable domestic economic impact of granting eligibility to a particular category of merchandise. This process is an opportunity

---

40. *Accord, Alliance, or Disunity?*, THE ECONOMIST, 13 July 2013 at 57 (*quoting* Wal-Mart executive Jay Jorgensen).

41. *See* 19 U.S.C. § 2463(a)(1)(A).

42. *See* 19 U.S.C. § 2463(a)(1)(C).

for lawyers representing exporting countries, importers, domestic producers, and consumers to make arguments in favor or, or against, an eligibility designation.[43]

By no means is a petition for eligibility accepted without controversy, at least not unless there is no American producer of a like product that could fear competition from the foreign merchandise if it received eligibility. In December 2012, the Administration of President Barack H. Obama denied a petition to add pinch-seal plastic bags to the *GSP* product eligibility list. Might there have been a good environmental reason for this denial?

For some kinds of merchandise, the room for argument is focused. The *GSP* statute renders seven categories of "import sensitive" merchandise as ineligible for duty-free treatment—the "Ineligible List," outlined below. Arguments about eligibility, then, focus on as a factual and legal matter an article is properly classified within an ineligibility category.[44]

Arguments also may focus on whether an article is, in fact, "import sensitive." That is because it is not clear from the statutory language whether an article properly classified in one of the categories on the Ineligible List is deemed, by virtue of that classification, to be import sensitive. On the one hand, the *chapeau* to the List says "The President may not designate any article as an eligible article . . . if such article is within one of the following categories of import-sensitive articles." That text appears to presume an article within a category is import-sensitive. On the other hand, some of the categories on the List (identified below) repeat the adjective "import-sensitive," which suggests room for an argument about import sensitivity.

Obviously, advocates for preferential treatment (typically, counsel for exporters and importers, and some consumer groups) will argue against a finding of import sensitivity and a classification of ineligibility, and advocates against preferential treatment (typically, counsel for domestic producers) will argue the contrary positions.

The Ineligible List is as follows. Consider the extent to which a BDC may have a keen export interest in articles on the list. (Consider, too, the List in relation to the development model Walt Rostow presents in *The Stages of Economic Growth* (1960), discussed in a separate Chapter.) Is it likely a BDC may have an export interest in ineligible articles as it proceeds from lower- to higher-value added manufacturing? Finally, is production of any of these articles in an advanced, services-based economy worth protecting? Is the American comparative advantage in these articles all but lost? If so, then is adjustment assistance for dislocated American workers, rather than protection against the products made by workers and poor countries, a better policy choice?

(1) T&A Articles

---

43. *See* 19 U.S.C. § 2463(a)(1)(A), (e).
44. *See* 19 U.S.C. § 2463(b)(1).

All T&A articles are ineligible for *GSP* treatment.[45] There are two minor exceptions. First, articles are eligible if they were eligible before a specific date (1 January 1994). In other words, the date operates as a closure—if an article was not eligible as of the date, then it remains ineligible. Second, certain carpets, based on their method of production, are eligible. They are ones that are hand-loomed, hand-woven, hand-hooked, hand-tufted, or hand-knotted and classified under specific 8-digit categories in Chapter 57 of the HTSUS.

(2) Watches[46]

All watches are ineligible for *GSP* treatment, with one exception. A watch entered into the U.S. after a specific date (30 June 1989) is eligible, but only if the President determines it will not cause "material injury" to U.S. manufacturing and assembly operation of watches, watch bands, straps, or bracelets.

(3) Import-Sensitive Electronic Articles[47]

Any electronic article that is "import sensitive" is ineligible for *GSP* treatment. The reference to import sensitivity creates the possibility of arguing a class of electronic merchandise does not affect domestic producers, and thus ought to receive *GSP* treatment.

(4) Import-Sensitive Steel Articles[48]

Any steel article that is "import sensitive" is ineligible for *GSP* treatment. Again, reference to import sensitivity creates the possibility of arguing no adverse effect on, or threat to affect adversely, domestic producers exists.

(5) Import-Sensitive Glass Products[49]

Any glass (whether semi-manufactured or finished) article that is "import sensitive" is ineligible for *GSP* treatment. Once again, the reference to import sensitivity creates the possibility of arguing there is no adverse effect on domestic producers or threat thereof, and thus ought to receive *GSP* treatment.

(6) Other Import-Sensitive Articles

Any other article the President determines is "import sensitive" in the context of the *GSP* program is ineligible.[50] This "catch all" category of the Ineligible List is a potentially large, as it is unrestricted to the type of merchandise, the production process, or its classification in the HTSUS.

---

45. *See* 19 U.S.C. § 2463(b)(1)(A), (4).
46. *See* 19 U.S.C. § 2463(b)(1)(B).
47. *See* 19 U.S.C. § 2463(b)(1)(C).
48. *See* 19 U.S.C. § 2463(b)(1)(D).
49. *See* 19 U.S.C. § 2463(b)(1)(F).
50. *See* 19 U.S.C. § 2463(b)(1)(G).

(7) Footwear[51]

All shoes and other footwear are ineligible for *GSP* treatment. There is a minor exception, namely, for footwear that was eligible on or before a specific date (1 January 1995). That is, footwear ineligible as of that date remain ineligible.

(8) Leather Goods[52]

All leather goods are ineligible for *GSP* treatment. Such goods include handbags, luggage, flat goods (*e.g.*, change purses, eyeglass cases, and wallets), and work gloves, as well as apparel and shoes. The same minor exception exists for these goods as for footwear, namely leather goods are eligible if they were eligible on or before a specific date (1 January 1995).

(9) Articles Subject to a Safeguard[53]

An otherwise eligible article subject to a safeguard action under Section 201 of the *Trade Act of 1974* (*i.e.*, the Escape Clause[54]) is ineligible. During the Tokyo Round, less developed countries worried developed countries would use GATT Article XIX to protect their domestic industries. The U.S. ensures *GSP* benefits do not undermine safeguard relief by putting articles targeted for this relief on the Ineligible List.

(10) Articles Subject to a National Security Sanction[55]

Any otherwise eligible article subject to a national security action under Section 232 or 351 of the *Trade Expansion Act of 1962*, as amended is ineligible.[56] This exception came into play in the Section 232 actions of the Administration of President Donald J. Trump (1946–, President, 2017–) (discussed in a separate Chapter).

(11) Agricultural Products[57]

There is no prophylactic ban on agricultural commodities (either primary or processed) from *GSP* treatment. However, there are two considerations. First, appropriate governmental agencies are required to assist BDCs to ensure their agricultural sectors are not oriented to export markets to the detriment of producing foodstuffs for their own people. Second, if an agricultural product is subject to a TRQ, then any shipment of that product above the in-quota threshold is ineligible for *GSP* treatment. In other words, over-quota shipments do not get a preference.

---

51. *See* 19 U.S.C. § 2463(b)(1)(E).
52. *See* 19 U.S.C. § 2463(b)(1)(E).
53. *See* 19 U.S.C. § 2463(b)(2).
54. *See* 19 U.S.C. §§ 2251–2254.
55. *See* 19 U.S.C. § 2463(b)(2).
56. *See* 19 U.S.C. §§ 1862, 1981.
57. *See* 19 U.S.C. § 2466.

The limit on agricultural products affects sugar. Sugar is subject to a TRQ set by the Secretary of Agriculture. Once the Agriculture Secretary establishes the quota quantity that can be entered at a lower-tier duty, the USTR allocates the quantity among sugar exporting countries. These countries get a "Certificate of Quota Eligibility" (CQE), which must be returned with a sugar shipment to receive in-quota treatment. Under the *GSP*, a sugar-exporting BDC gets duty-free treatment for the in-quota quantity allocated to it, but not for any above-quota shipments. Of course, sugar is a product in which many developing countries and LDCs have a keen export interest, and for which (thanks to U.S. quotas) Americans pay a far-higher than world market price (resulting in considerable use of high fructose corn syrup (HFCS) as a substitute, yet HFCS is of dubious health value).

The fact there are 11 broad categories on the Ineligible List illustrates the proposition that *GSP* treatment is not about duty-free entry of all merchandise from every poor country. Preference is only for certain products originating in eligible countries.

Significantly, even if an article is on the Ineligible List, it might be eligible for *GSP* treatment if the country of origin is a LDBDC. Specifically, six categories of otherwise ineligible merchandise remain ineligible even if they are from a least-developed beneficiary, namely: (1) T&A; (2) watches; (3) footwear; (4) leather goods; (5) articles subject to a safeguard remedy, national security sanction, or emergency tariff adjustment, or (6) agricultural products.[58] That leaves a few categories from the Ineligible List as eligible if they are from a LDDC: (1) import-sensitive electronics, (2) import-sensitive steel, (3) import-sensitive glass, and (4) other import-sensitive articles. There is a "catch": the ITC must advise the President that the article in question is "not import sensitive in the context of imports from least-developed beneficiary developing countries."[59] So, even as to the poorest of countries, product eligibility is conditional.

V. Sleeping Bags, Import Sensitivity, and Politics

Manifestly, the more extensive the list of *GSP*-ineligible products, the less generous the *GSP* program is. A longer list adduces the exaltation of the self-interest of the rich over the needs of the poor. Yet, is there an argument for caution?

Consider the debate that raged over whether to designate sleeping bags as an import-sensitive article and, therefore, ineligible for *GSP* treatment. Following the 1989 fall of the Berlin Wall, in 1992, to help the textile industry of the former Czechoslovakia, sleeping bags, the U.S. designated sleeping bags as not being import sensitive. So, they became eligible for duty free treatment, though ironically, Czechoslovakia never manufactured them. Subsequently, one of the world's

---

58. *See* 19 U.S.C. § 2463(a)(1)(B).
59. *See* 19 U.S.C. § 2463(a)(1)(B).

poorest countries, Bangladesh, began exporting this product to the U.S. Because of *GSP* treatment, Bangladeshi sleeping bags were not subject to the U.S. MFN duty rate of 9%.

In 2010, when the *GSP* program required another Congressional renewal, Senator Jeff Sessions (Republican-Alabama) vigorously opposed such action unless President Barack H. Obama agreed to designate non-down sleeping bags as import sensitive, and thereby remove them from *GSP* eligibility. Why? Because in Alabama was a sleeping bag manufacturer that purportedly prospered once the *GSP* scheme lapsed and its Bangladeshi competitors had to pay a 9% tariff. The Senator responded that those competitors were not Bangladeshi, but Chinese. That is, a Chinese company established manufacturing and export operations in Bangladesh to avoid the 9% rate.

Ultimately, to secure renewal of not only the *GSP* program, but also of *TAA*, and to obtain passage of implementing legislation for FTAs with Colombia, Korea, and Panama, President Obama did as Senator Sessions asked. To critics, the President appeased the Senator, setting an adverse precedent that could prompt other legislators to hold hostage trade bills unless their protectionist demands were met. The legal reality is *GSP* eligibility depends on the country of origin of merchandise, based on rules of origin. It does not depend on the country of origin of the owners of the production and export facilities located overseas in a BDC. Hence, the fact the owners of the sleeping bag facility in Bangladesh are Chinese (or American, or of any other nationality) is irrelevant; what matters is the value added to the product in Bangladesh.

VI. *GSP* Preferential ROOs

- **First: Statutory Value-Added Test**

Even if a country qualifies as a BDC, and even if a merchandise category is eligible, it does not follow automatically a shipment of that merchandise will receive *GSP* duty-free treatment. The shipment must satisfy a rule of origin to ensure the article is "the growth, product, or manufacture" of a BDC.[60] This preferential ROO has two prongs.

First, there must be no transshipment.[61] The shipment of merchandise at issue must be imported directly from a BDC into the customs territory of the U.S. Thus, for example, assuming Mauritania is eligible for *GSP* treatment, Toyota cannot make cars in Japan, ship them to Mauritania, and thereby qualify those cars for *GSP* treatment. After all, the benefits of the treatment supposedly are directed at a poor country, and designed to encourage meaningful economic activity in that country.

---

60. 19 U.S.C. § 2463(a)(2)(A).
61. *See* 19 U.S.C. § 2463(a)(2)(A)(i).

Second, a Value-Added Test must be met. This test is designed to answer the question: "How much economic activity is 'meaningful'?" The answer is 35%. The value added to merchandise in a BDC must be 35% or more of the appraised value of the article when it enters the U.S.[62] The formula for the *GSP* Minimum Value-Added Test is:

If   (1)   Cost or value of materials produced in the BDC

+

(2)   Direct costs of processing operations in the BDC

= or >35% of total value as appraised by the CBP at time of entry,

then merchandise satisfies the Test. If < 35%, then fails.

The extreme cases are easy ones. If all inputs used to produce merchandise are from a BDC, and all processing occurs in the BDC, then the Test is met. Conversely, the *GSP* statute expressly excludes (1) simple combining or packaging operations, and (2) mere dilution with water or another substance that does not materially alter the characteristics of an article. These operations alone do not qualify an article for originating in a BDC.[63] However, difficulties and disputes arise when sourcing and production is multinational. Then, meaningful economic activity, in the sense of value added to merchandise, occurs both within and outside the BDC.

Should the location in which value is added matter? On the one hand, conferring a *GSP* preference on merchandise made largely outside of a BDC undermines country eligibility criteria. The 35% Value Added Test works in tandem with those criteria. On the other hand, as long as a BDC is not a mere transshipment platform, then at least some useful activity is undertaken there, and at least a few people are employed, even if all they do is minor assembly. By denying *GSP* treatment because less than 35% of the value is added in a BDC, is there a risk no work will be performed in the BDC, and no jobs will be created? Or, does the Test operate to shift—even distort—sourcing and production patterns to take advantage of *GSP* benefits?

Observe the 35% Test does not inquire into the nationality of the workers. It does not matter whether they are legal or illegal residents, or permanent or migrant workers. In theory, a group of American law students could be the employees on a farm, or in a factory, in a BDC producing *GSP* eligible merchandise. Put simply, what is done where, but not who does what, matters.

What happens if materials are imported into a BDC, and then incorporated into the production of an eligible article? Do imported materials qualify toward the 35% Test? This question is treated in the 1985 *Torrington* case. In brief, the answer is "yes, but only if the materials imported into a BDC are substantially transformed into a new and different article in that BDC before they are incorporated into the eligible article." Stated differently, there must be (at least) two substantial

---

62. *See* 19 U.S.C. § 2463(a)(2)(A)(ii).
63. *See* 19 U.S.C. § 2463(a)(2)(B).

transformations—of the imported materials into some intermediate product, and then of that product into the finished article, which is eligible for *GSP* treatment. This requirement is known as the "Dual Substantial Transformation" requirement, and it arises out of the *Torrington* case.

What, then, constitutes "substantial transformation"? Further, what difference should the number of substantial transformations make? Is the rationale, once again, that the U.S. seeks to ensure real economic activity takes place in a BDC, that the BDC is not a mere assembly operation? If so, consider a poor country in which, depending on the type of merchandise, even an assembly operation is a substantial activity.

Suppose two or more BDCs are members of a FTA or CU. An example might be Indonesia and Vietnam, which are in *ASEAN*, and *ASEAN* has an FTA, called "*AFTA*." Assume an eligible article comes from Vietnam, but components come from Indonesia. Can the Indonesian components qualify in calculating the 35% minimum local content requirement? The answer is "yes." Two or more BDCs that are members of the same FTA or CU may be treated as one BDC and cumulated to meet this requirement.

• **Second: Dual Substantial Transformation and 1985 *Torrington* Case**

Torrington Company v. United States,

United States Court of Appeals for the Federal Circuit,
764 F.2d 1563, 1565–1572 (1985)

DAVIS, CIRCUIT JUDGE:

The Government appeals from a decision of the United States Court of International Trade . . . holding that certain industrial sewing-machine needles imported from Portugal by appellee (Torrington) are entitled to enter the United States duty free under the Generalized System of Preferences (*GSP*). . . . Agreeing that the imported articles meet the prerequisite for duty free entry under the *GSP* statute, . . . we affirm.

I.

Background.

The *GSP* statute . . . represents the United States' participation in a multinational effort to encourage industrialization in lesser developed countries through international trade. The [1974] *Act* authorizes the President (subject to certain restrictions) to prepare a list of beneficiary developing countries (BDCs), and to designate products of those countries which are eligible for *GSP* treatment. . . . A designated product imported from a listed country may enter the United States duty free. . . . One problem with this general program is that it could be used to allow a non-eligible country to conduct minimal finishing operations in a BDC, thereby reaping the benefits of the *GSP* at the expense of American manufacturers, but without the salutary effect of fostering industrialization in the designated country. Congress therefore provided that products from BDCs must meet certain minimum content requirements in order to qualify for duty-free treatment. To this end, 19 U.S.C. § 2463 [re-worded and re-codified at § 2463(a)(2)(A) as a result of amendments in 1996] provides:

> (b) The duty-free treatment provided under section 2461 of this title with respect to any eligible article shall apply only—
>
> . . .
>
> (2) If the sum of (A) the cost or value of the materials produced in the beneficiary developing country . . . plus (B) the direct cost of processing operations performed in such beneficiary developing country . . . is not less than 35 percent of the appraised value of such article at the time of its entry in the customs territory of the United States.
>
> . . .

. . . [T]he Customs Service has promulgated regulations interpreting the operative phrase . . . "materials produced in the beneficiary developing country." 19 C.F.R. § 10.177(a) (1984) states that

> the words produced in the beneficiary developing "country" . . . refer to constituent materials of which the eligible article is composed which are either:
>
> (1) Wholly the growth, product or manufacture of the beneficiary developing country; or
>
> (2) Substantially transformed in the beneficiary developing country into a new and different article of commerce.

Thus, if the value of the materials described in § 10.177(a)(1) and (2) plus the direct cost of processing operations performed in the BDC account for 35% of the appraised value of the merchandise, the merchandise is entitled to enter duty-free. . . .

The question in this case is whether industrial sewing-machine needles which Torrington imported met these minimum content requirements. . . .

The sewing machine needles at issue were exported from Portugal to the United States by Torrington *Portuguesa*, a manufacturing subsidiary of Torrington. The needles are classifiable under item 672.20 of the Tariff Schedules of the United States (TSUS), "Sewing machines and parts thereof." At the time of the exports, Portugal was designated as a BDC and articles classifiable under item 672.20 were eligible products.

Torrington *Portuguesa* produced the needles from wire manufactured in a non-BDC and brought into Portugal. On this ground the Customs Service denied duty-free treatment to the needles because they did not incorporate any "materials produced" in Portugal, and the direct cost of producing the needles does not account for 35% of their appraised value. In Customs' view the needles failed to meet the minimum content requirements of 19 U.S.C. § 2463(b). Torrington agrees that if Customs' decision not to include the non-BDC wire in the calculation is correct, then the needles do not satisfy the 35% BDC content requirement. On the other hand, if the other requirements are met, then the 35% BDC content prerequisite is also satisfied.

. . . Initially, the wire runs through a swaging machine, which straightens the wire, cuts it to a particular length, bevels one end of the wire segment and draws out the straightened wire to alter its length and circumference at various points. The result is known in the needle industry as a "swaged needle blank," a "needle blank," or merely a "swage." In an exhibit before the trial court, the parties included a linear drawing of a swage. The first quarter of a swage has roughly the same circumference as the wire segment from which it was made; the second quarter narrows from that size down to roughly half that circumference; the other half then extends straight out from the second quarter. At this point, the swage is useful solely in the production of sewing-machine needles with a predetermined blade diameter, though the resulting needle may vary in other respects (*e.g.,* eye placement, eye size, and needle length).

The next process in the production of needles is "striking." Striking involves pressing an eye into the swage, forming a spot to provide clearance for the thread, and bending the swage at a particular point. At this stage, the articles are known as struck blanks. The struck blank enters a mill flash machine which removes excess material around the eye and forms a groove along the length of the needle which carries the thread while the needle is in use. The merchandise is then pointed (*i.e.,* sharpened) and stamped with a logo or other information. Finally, the needles are hardened, tempered, straightened, buffed, polished, cleaned and plated. Upon completion, the needle has a sharp point at the narrow end, a long groove running down three-quarters of its body ending near the point, and an eye somewhere in the groove with an indentation in the groove near the eye.

. . . In 1973–74, Torrington *Portuguesa* twice shipped large amounts of swages to Torrington to correct production imbalances between the two companies. Torrington *Portuguesa* realized no profit on the exchange, and the transfer was accounted for through appropriate entries in the two companies' inventory and receivables accounts. These are the only transactions in swages in which Torrington (now the only U.S. manufacturer of these needles) has participated.

Based on these facts, the Court of International Trade held the needles to be entitled to duty-free entry under the *GSP*. . . . [T]he Court ruled that, under Customs' regulations, the non-BDC wire must undergo *two* substantial transformations when it is manufactured into a needle if the value of the wire is to be included in the 35% calculation, and that each of these transformations under 19 C.F.R. § 10.177(a)(2) must result in an "article of commerce." The court stated:

> It is not enough to transform substantially the non-BDC constituent materials into the final article, as the material utilized to produce the final article would remain non-BDC material. There must first be a substantial transformation of the non-BDC material into a new and different article of

commerce which becomes "materials produced," and these materials produced in the BDC must then be substantially transformed into a new and different article of commerce.

... The court noted that the Customs Service and Treasury Department have consistently interpreted the regulations to require a dual transformation (*i.e.*, two successive substantial transformations) in order to be eligible for *GSP* treatment, and that the requirement of a dual transformation advances the *GSP's* goals by requiring greater work in the BDC and by thwarting manipulation of the *GSP* (which the content requirements were designed to avoid).

The court then turned to the question of whether the production of needles in Portugal satisfied the dual transformation requirement. The court determined that a substantial transformation occurs if a manufacturing process results in an article of commerce which has a distinctive name, character, or use. ... Here, the court held, the swaging process constitutes an initial transformation, and the succeeding processes constitute the second. The swage blanks, the court said, have a distinctive name, a different character from the wire segments from which they are made, and a specific use. Moreover, the swages are "articles of commerce" because, on the two documented occasions set forth in the stipulations, they have been the object of large transactions. Thus, the court concluded that the swaged needle blanks are constituent materials of which the needles are made, and their value (which includes the value of the non-BDC wire) should be included in the 35% value added calculation.

II.

The dual transformation requirement.

The parties disagree whether the *GSP* statute and regulations mandate a dual transformation between raw material and finished product if the latter is to be granted duty-free entry. Torrington contends that its transformation of the non-BDC wire into sewing machine needles—even if considered only a single transformation—was in itself sufficient. The Government counters that a single transformation is insufficient to change the non-BDC wire into a material "produced in the developing country" which, if used in the BDC, may then be considered in the BDC-content evaluation.

Like the CIT, we think that the statutory language of 19 U.S.C. § 2463(b) leads to the Government's position. Congress authorized the Customs Service to consider the "cost or value of *materials produced*" in the BDC. (Emphasis added.) [*See* 19 U.S.C. § 2463(a)(2)(A)(ii)(I).] The parties agree that the wire clearly was not a BDC product. As wire, therefore, it may not be considered a BDC material. However, if Torrington Portuguesa transformed the wire into an intermediate article of commerce, then the intermediate product would be an article produced in the BDC, and the value of *that* product (including the contribution of the wire to the value of that intermediate product) would be included.

The legislative history of § 2463 supports this reading. Congress used the content requirement to protect the *GSP* program from untoward manipulation:

> The percentage . . . assure[s] that, to the maximum extent possible, the preferences provide benefits to developing countries without stimulating the development of "pass-through" operations the major benefit of which accrues to enterprises in developed countries.

. . . In the absence of a dual transformation requirement, developed countries could establish a BDC as a base to complete manufacture of goods which have already undergone extensive processing. The single substantial transformation would qualify the resulting article for *GSP* treatment, with the non-BDC country reaping the benefit of duty-free treatment for goods which it essentially produced. his flouts Congress' expressed intention to confer the benefits of the *GSP* fully on the BDC and to avoid conferring duty-free status on the products of a "pass-through" operation.

Moreover, Torrington's contentions, if accepted, would tend to render the 35% requirement a nullity. If only a single transformation were necessary, then the "material produced" in the BDC as a result of this transformation would be the imported product itself. Customs would then face the problem of determining how much of the appraised value of the import resulted from materials produced in the BDC, when the only material produced was the import. The result would always be 100% since the product would always be a constituent material of itself. Congress clearly envisaged some way of separating the final product from its constituent materials, and the dual transformation requirement achieves this end.

. . .

III.

The swages — substantial transformation into a new and different article of commerce.

A. In *Texas Instruments* [*v. United States*, 681 F.2d 778 (CCPA 1982)] . . . the Court of Customs and Patent Appeals adopted the rule, well-established in other areas of customs jurisprudence, that a substantial transformation occurs when an article emerges from a manufacturing process with a name, character, or use which differs from those of the original material subjected to the process. . . . *Anheuser-Busch Brewing Assn. v. United States*, 207 U.S. 556 (1908) . . . . The CIT determined here that this substantial transformation test was satisfied when Torrington *Portuguesa* manufactured needle swages from the wire.

. . . Two critical manufacturing steps separate three items (wire, swage and needle) each of which is markedly different from the others. The initial wire is a raw material and possesses nothing in its character which indicates either the swages or the final product. The intermediate articles — the swages — have a definite size and shape which renders them suitable for further manufacturing into needles with various capabilities. At that phase of the production process the material which emerges is more refined, possesses attributes more specifically applicable to a given use, and has lost the identifying characteristics of its constituent material. It is a new and different article.

... Manufacturing processes often differ in detail, but we must consider these differences in light of the *GSP's* fundamental purpose of promoting industrialization in lesser developed countries. Trivial differences in manufacturing processes or techniques will not affect the overall benefit conferred upon the BDCs from the manufacturing conducted in those countries.

. . .

B. The CIT also concluded correctly that the swages were "articles of commerce." The Government attacks this determination principally by arguing that the two incidents in which Torrington *Portuguesa* transferred swages to Torrington in this country should not count in deciding whether swages are articles of commerce. We note initially that the phrase "article of commerce" is found only in the regulation, not in the *GSP* statute, and therefore we interpret the "of commerce" requirement of the regulation in light of the statute's purpose to further BDC industrialization. By emphasizing that the article must be "of commerce," the Customs regulation imposes the requirement that the "new and different" product be commercially recognizable as a different article, *i.e.*, that the "new and different" article be readily susceptible of trade, and be an item that persons might well wish to buy and acquire for their own purposes of consumption or production.

. . .

Our conclusion is that an "article of commerce"—for the purposes of the pertinent Customs regulation—is one that is ready to be put into a stream of commerce, but need not have actually been bought-and-sold, or actually traded, in the past. Indeed, by requiring proof of actual arms-length transactions by unrelated parties, the Government implies that a new article (never before produced) can never be an article of commerce entitled to *GSP* treatment—a result not envisaged by Congress. In this instance, we agree with the CIT that the transfer of over four million swaged needle blanks from Torrington *Portuguesa* to Torrington is an adequate showing that swaged needle blanks are articles of commerce. There is no reason to believe that those articles could and would not be sold to other manufacturers of needles who wanted to purchase them for further manufacture into the final product.

IV.

The needles—substantial transformation into a new and different article.

The Government urges that, even if the production of swages from wire constitutes a substantial transformation, the manufacture of the needles from the swages does not. We are referred to ... the parties' stipulations, in which they note that swages "are dedicated for use solely as sewing machine needles with a predetermined blade diameter.... In the majority of cases, a particular type of swaged needle blank becomes only a single particular type of needle." The Government concludes from this that the swages are actually unfinished needles, and do not undergo a substantial transformation into a new article in order to reach their final form. Torrington, also reading from the stipulations, notes that the swages lack the key characteristics of a needle since they have no points or eyes, and that a given swage can be processed into needles with different properties, *e.g.*, eye size.

The Government relies for its position that swages are merely unfinished needles on cases such as *Avins Industrial Products Co. v. United States*, 515 F.2d 782 (1975) . . . and *Lee Enterprises, Inc. v. United States*, 84 Cust. Ct. 208 (1980). These decisions concern the proper classification of imports under the rule that an item in the TSUS covers the article mentioned in finished or unfinished form. The courts ruled that a product is an unfinished form of an article if the product has been manufactured to the point where it is dedicated solely to the manufacture of that article. . . . However, the Government's reliance on these cases is not pertinent. The proper tariff classification is not dispositive of whether the manufacturing process necessary to complete an article constitutes a substantial transformation from the original material to the final product. . . . Instead, we look — keeping in mind the *GSP's* fundamental purpose of fostering industrialization in BDCs — to the actual manufacturing process by which the intermediate article becomes the final product.

In *Midwood Industries v. United States*, 313 F. Supp. 951 (1970), . . . the Customs Court (now the CIT) determined that forgings for flanges could enter the United States without permanent country-of-origin markings because the importer substantially transformed the forgings in the United States into pipe. In one case, the importer cut the edges; tapered, beveled and bored the ends; and removed die lines and other imperfections from the surface of the final article. . . . The court also heard testimony that, in their imported state, the forgings are useless unless processed into the final flange. . . . The decision in that case was that the importer's efforts resulted in a substantial transformation from the rough forgings into "different articles having a new name, character and use." . . . The court noted that the "imports were *producers'* goods, and the flanges are *consumers'* goods," and held: "While it may be true, as some of the testimony of record indicates, that some of the imported forgings are made as close to the dimensions of the ultimate finished form as possible, they, nevertheless, remain forgings unless and until converted by some manufacturer into *consumers'* goods." . . .

The production of needles from swages is a similar process. The swages are bored (to form an eye), the ridge is carved, and the needle is pointed, cleaned, hardened, plated, etc. The swage is also the approximate size necessary to create the final needle, but, like the forgings in *Midwood*, they are producers' goods. The final needles are consumers' goods. The production of needles from swages is clearly a significant manufacturing process, and not a mere "pass-through" operation as the Government apparently contends. Portugal certainly reaps the benefit of this manufacturing process; indeed, short of manufacturing the wire itself, Torrington *Portuguesa* could do no more than it already does in the production of needles. In these circumstances, we think that Congress intended the *GSP* statute to apply.

For these reasons, we conclude: (1) that a dual substantial transformation in a BDC is a prerequisite for *GSP* treatment under the *GSP* statute and Customs regulations, (2) that the swages which Torrington Portuguesa produced are a separate, intermediate "article of commerce," and (3) that the industrial sewing-machine needles imported by Torrington are entitled to duty-free entry. The decision appealed from is therefore affirmed.

VII. Discretionary Graduation and CNLs

- **Presidential Authority to Exercise Discretionary Graduation**

The President may withdraw, suspend, or limit the application of duty-free treatment as regards a particular article, or indeed all articles from a country (in effect, the entire country). This process is known as "discretionary graduation," and it has occurred annually since 1981 after an inter-agency review. Under amendments to the discretionary graduation rules in the *Trade and Tariff Act of 1984*, the President is required to engage in an annual review of all *GSP*-eligible products to determine whether they are sufficiently competitive to graduate. For any individual BDC, the outcome can be graduation of just one product (with the other products remaining eligible), or graduation of all products (meaning the country loses its status as a BDC).

So, discretionary graduation can apply to a product, several products, or a whole country. The central question in the review is whether the article still needs *GSP* treatment, *i.e.*, does it need duty-free treatment to stay competitive in the American market? After all, there may be more worthy products and BDCs to which preferences should be shifted or focused. Technically, the President must take into account the general factors for *GSP* treatment, and the 7 additional factors for country-eligibility criteria.[64] In practice, discretionary graduation occurs for certain products from particular BDCs that demonstrate competitiveness, and thus allows a shift of preferences to lesser developed countries.

- **Instances of Discretionary Graduation of Countries**

Examples of discretionary graduation of entire countries are Hong Kong, Korea, Singapore, and Taiwan. President George H.W. Bush (1924–, President, 1989–1993) graduated these countries (on 29 January 1988, effective 2 January 1989), because of their impressive level of economic development and competitiveness. (In October 2018, Taiwan self-declared for WTO purposes that it was a "developed" country.) He decided they could sustain their performance without *GSP* treatment. President Clinton graduated Malaysia (on 17 October 1996, effective 1 January 1997) because

---

64. *See* 19 U.S.C. § 2463(c)(1).

of its sufficient advancements in economic development and improved trade competitiveness.

Discretionary graduation does not impact only NICs in East Asia. President Clinton also graduated (effective 1 January 1998) Aruba, Cayman Islands, Cyprus, Greenland, Macau, and Netherlands Antilles, as they met the definition of "high income" country set by the World Bank. For the same reason, he also graduated (on 6 July 2000, effective 1 January 2002) French Polynesia, Malta, New Caledonia, and Slovenia. Likewise, President Barak H. Obama graduated Saint Kitts and Nevis (effective 1 January 2014), because this country had attained "high income" status.

- **Russia and Appearance versus Reality**

President Obama did the same (on 7 May 2014) with respect to Russia, removing it entirely from the list of countries eligible for American *GSP* treatment. With a *per capita* GNP (in 2012) of $12,700, Russia satisfied World Bank criteria for being a "high income" country, and, as the President put it to Congress, Russia is "sufficiently advanced in economic development and improved trade competitiveness."[65] But, reality and appearance in Washington, D.C., often differ: was that the reason, or was it an "economic power play against Russia," because of its actions in the Ukraine?

Consider the fact the only other high-income BDC, Uruguay, with a higher *per capita* income ($13,580) than Russia, stayed on the BDC list of 123 countries and territories. Could Russia complain against the U.S. in the WTO that America discriminated against it in withdrawing *GSP* benefits? What might be the American defenses: that the EU, too, excluded Russia from its *GSP* scheme; that there was no discrimination against high-income countries, because only Russia and Uruguay from that cohort were BDCs; and, that among high-income countries, only Russia was among the top 10 beneficiaries of the U.S. *GSP*?

- **MFN Snap Back**

In every instance, the result of withdrawal or suspension of duty-free treatment is re-imposition of the duty otherwise applicable, which in most instances is the MFN rate. That is because Congress—not the President—has the Constitutional authority (under the Foreign Commerce Clause, Article I, Section 8, Clause 3) to regulate foreign commerce, and thus establish tariff rates.

- **CNLs**

A major constraint on product eligibility for *GSP* treatment is known as "competitive need," or a competitive need limitation (CNL).[66] If (in any year beginning after 31 December 1995) a BDC exports to the U.S. (directly or indirectly) a product receiving duty-free benefits under the *GSP* program, and that product becomes competitive in the American market, then the President must terminate duty-free

---

65. *Quoted in* Ken Monahan, *Russia First GSP BRIC to Fall; Brazil, India Next? BGOV Insight*, 31 International Trade Reporter (BNA) 934 (22 May 2014).

66. *See* 19 U.S.C. § 2463(c)(2).

treatment. Here again, termination results in imposition of the normally-applied duty, which in most cases is the MFN rate. So, for example, in June 2013, President Barack H. Obama eliminated *GSP* benefits based on the breach of CNLs for a corn product from Brazil, and tires from Indonesia.

CNLs support the same policy goals served by discretionary graduation. First, they establish a benchmark for determining when products are successful in the American market against domestic and other foreign products and, therefore, no longer warrant preferential tariff treatment. Second, they ensure *GSP* benefits are allocated, or re-allocated, to less competitive articles and less well-off countries. Of course, from the perspective of a BDC, the concern is punishment for market success. Do both discretionary graduation and competitive need limitations serve an ulterior third goal, namely, to provide import protection to domestic producers of like or directly competitive products?

• **Defining "Competitive Need"**

A critical practical question is how the *GSP* statute defines "competitive needs." Not surprisingly, it calls for an examination of the quantity, value, and relative import penetration of the eligible article shipped to the U.S.:

First: Value Limitation

The quantity of an eligible article has an appraised value in excess of the applicable amount for the calendar year in which the article is exported. In 1996, the threshold was $75 million. Each year thereafter, the threshold rises by $5 million. Thus, for example, in 2012 the threshold was $155 million, indicating it took 15 years (from 1996 to 2010) for the threshold to double.[67] By 2016, the CNL was $175 million. No adjustment is permitted for the nature of the article. That is, the same threshold applies, whether the merchandise is a low-value added product like woven baskets, or a higher-value added product like batteries. Interestingly, earlier versions of the *GSP* statute used a different value benchmark, namely, an absolute level (which in 1994 was $114.1 million) adjusted annually in relation to changes in the U.S. GNP.

Second: Import Percentage Limitation

The quantity of an eligible article equals or exceeds 50% of the appraised value of total imports (from all countries) of that article into the U.S. in any calendar year.[68] No adjustment is permitted for the number of other foreign countries exporting the product into the U.S., or for the size of foreign competitors. From the perspective of a BDC avoiding this competitive need limitation, it is better to be one of many small exporters to the U.S. However, the long-term economic interests of the BDC may be to be a major player in the world market for the product.

---

67. *See* 19 U.S.C. § 2463(c)(2)(A)(i)(I), (ii).
68. *See* 19 U.S.C. § 2463(c)(2)(A)(i)(II).

The two restrictions are simultaneously applicable. Suppose a BDC ships eligible merchandise below the value threshold, but exceeds 50% of the total value of imported merchandise. In that scenario, the BDC is not necessarily a large player in the American market, but it is successful in competing in this market against other foreign countries. The consequence is removal of *GSP* treatment. Termination also is the consequence of the opposite scenario, where the BDC accounts for less than half of American imports of the article, but individually exceeds the value threshold.

Termination under the competitive need limitations occurs no later than 1 July of the year after the BDC breached a limitation. Is termination permanent? The answer is "no." Eligibility can be reinstated to a product if in a later year the competitive need ceilings are not reached.[69] That is, a BDC that loses *GSP* eligibility for a particular article can apply for re-designation of benefits. The same eligibility criteria apply as on an initial designation, plus the BDC must have stayed within the competitive need limits in the calendar year preceding re-designation.

Are there exceptions to the competitive need limitations? In other words, is there no choice but to terminate *GSP* benefits for an eligible product from a BDC that exceeds these limitations? The answer is there is room for maneuver. Indeed, there are two "full" exceptions, and one "partial" exception.

First, neither of the competitive need limitations applies to a LDBDC.[70] Second, neither limitation applies to a beneficiary Sub-Saharan African country (BSSAC), *i.e.*, a country eligible under the *African Growth and Opportunity Act* for *AGOA* benefits, which also meets the *GSP* country-eligibility criteria.[71] There also is a "partial" exception, namely, an exception known as "short supply" to the import percentage limitation. This limitation does not apply to an article if there is no like or directly competitive good produced in the U.S. (as of 1 January 1995).[72] It would be against the self-interest of the U.S. to deny *GSP* treatment based on competitive need for an eligible article that not only poses no competitive threat to an American producer, but also is in short supply in the American economy.

- **CNL Waivers**

A follow-up matter is how much room there is for maneuver? Are there circumstances under which the President may waive CNLs? The answer is "yes."

The ITC reviews the *GSP* Program annually, and issues a public report. A portion of that review is dedicated to the probable economic effects of the prospective addition of merchandise to the *GSP* eligibility list by granting a waiver of the relevant CNL. The President, of course, is free to accept or reject the ITC advice. Indubitably, political calculations may enter into consideration.

---

69. *See* 19 U.S.C. § 2463(c)(2)(C).
70. *See* 19 U.S.C. § 2463(c)(2)(D).
71. *See* 19 U.S.C. § 2463(c)(2)(D).
72. *See* 19 U.S.C. § 2463(c)(2)(E).

Specifically, there are three waiver possibilities. First, the President may issue a *de minimis* waiver of the import percentage (but not value) limitation.[73] Waiver is based on the aggregate appraised value of imports into the U.S. of an eligible article during the preceding calendar year not exceeding a *de minimis* threshold for that year. In 1996, the threshold was $13 million, and for each calendar year thereafter the threshold has been raised by $500,000. Thus, in 2012 the *de minimis* threshold was $21 million. (Earlier versions of the *GSP* statute implied adjusting the threshold annually with changes in U.S. GNP.)

It takes more than 15 years for the *de minimis* threshold to double to $26 million, and that the absolute dollar value ($500,000) by which the threshold grows is 10% of the amount by which the value limit rises ($5 million). Are these facts a basis to claim the threshold is not generous to BDCs? The answer is "probably not."

It is important to consider the size of the threshold in relation to the value limitation. In 1996, the threshold was 3.85% of the value limitation ($500,000 divided into $13 million). In 2012, the threshold is 13.5% of the value limit ($21 million divided into $155 million). In other words, the *de minimis* threshold rises as a percentage of the value limitation. Is this rise consistent over time?

Second, there is what might be called a "self-interest waiver" of the competitive need limitations.[74] This waiver involves a two-pronged test:

(1) The ITC advises the President (under Section 332 of the *Tariff Act of 1930*, as amended) that an industry in the U.S. would be adversely affected by loss of *GSP* benefits. For example, short supply induced by loss of the benefits would be relevant. As another example, an industry may rely on duty-free access to an article it uses as an input into production, and would be damaged by the higher cost associated with an MFN tariff imposed on the article.

(2) The President must also determine that a waiver of the limitations "is in the national economic interest of the United States." Here again, short supply considerations would be relevant. In making this determination, the President must examine (or reexamine) the country-eligibility criteria, and consider the advice of the ITC. The President also must "give great weight" to two factors: the extent to which the BDC assures the U.S. it "will provide equitable and reasonable access to the markets and basic commodity resources" of that country and "provides adequate and effective protection of intellectual property rights."

These waiver criteria authorize the President to ensure continuous flow of duty-free imports to support domestic needs, and provide leverage on BDCs seeking a waiver to provide American (and other foreign) business interests market access and IP protection.

---

73. *See* 19 U.S.C. § 2463(c)(2)(F).
74. *See* 19 U.S.C. § 2463(d)(1)-(2).

Third, the President can waive the CNL if there is a special preferential relationship, and formal agreement, between the U.S. and a BDC. This waiver is designed for possible use with respect to the Philippines. It mandates the Philippines neither "discriminate" against American commerce, nor impose any "unjustifiable" or "unreasonable" barriers to American commerce.[75] No President has used this waiver.

In sum, there exists considerable room for maneuver in the authority delegated by Congress to the President to waive the competitive need limitations. But, the room is restricted. The President cannot exercise the waiver "too much," and cannot concentrate waivers on just one or a few BDCs. "Too much" and "concentration" are defined according to two quantitative tests:

First: 30% Restriction:

> There is an overall limit on the total value of waivers granted to all BDCs.[76] In any calendar year (after 1995), total waivers for all BDCs above existing competitive need limitations cannot exceed 30% of the aggregate appraised value of all articles imported into the U.S. duty-free under the *GSP* program in the previous calendar year.

> Thus, to establish the dollar value of this restriction, it is necessary to calculate the aggregate appraised value in a calendar year of eligible merchandise imported into the U.S., and compute 30% of the aggregate appraised value for articles entered duty-free in the previous year. The 30% figure from the previous calendar year sets the threshold against which the current calendar year value is measured. The President cannot grant a waiver on an article if doing so would mean the value of articles for which the competitive need limitation is waived crosses the overall 30% threshold.

Second: 15% Restriction:

> There also is a restriction to ensure waivers of competitive need limitations are distributed among BDCs, rather than being focused on just one or a few beneficiaries.[77] The President may not grant waivers to more than 15% of the aggregate appraised value of all articles imported into the U.S. entered duty-free under the *GSP* program from BDCs with a *per capita* GNP of $5,000 or more, or from BDCs that account for at least a 10% share of total *GSP* imports.

> Thus, to establish the dollar value of this restriction, it is necessary to identify these 2 categories of BDCs, calculate the aggregate appraised value in a calendar year of eligible merchandise imported into the U.S., and compute 15% of the aggregate appraised value of articles entered duty-free in the previous calendar year. The 15% figure from the prior year sets the benchmark

---

75. *See* 19 U.S.C. § 2463(d)(3).
76. *See* 19 U.S.C. § 2463(d)(4)(A).
77. *See* 19 U.S.C. § 2463(d)(4)(B).

for measuring current *GSP* imports. The President cannot grant a waiver on an article if doing so would mean the value of articles for which the CNL is waived exceeds 15% of the value of imports from the two types of BDCs.

Calculating the 30 and 15% boundaries can be tricky.[78]

Recall that a CNL, if imposed, applies prospectively, specifically, as of 1 July of the following calendar year. Waiver of a CNL is based on the 30 and 15% thresholds, which are calculated using data from the previous calendar year. In that previous calendar year, the article in question received duty-free treatment under the *GSP* program, and the issue is whether that treatment must be withdrawn in the next year because the CNL is exceeded — and, if so, whether a waiver is appropriate.

To calculate the waiver thresholds, it is necessary to add three figures:

(1) the amount of the article that actually entered the U.S. duty-free in the previous year, when the CNL was inapplicable;

(2) the amount of the article that would have entered the U.S., had the CNL applied, and thus the MFN rate imposed; and

(3) the difference between figures (1) and (2).

In calculating the waiver threshold, the first and third figures — that is, the amount actually entered duty-free, and the extent to which the amount actually entered exceeds what would have been entered had the competitive need limitation been imposed — are both included. The "bottom line" is that it is somewhat easier to reach the waiver threshold because both the first and third figures are included.

There is no time limit on a waiver of a CNL. A waiver lasts until the President determines it is no longer warranted because of "changed circumstances."[79] What might constitute such circumstances, and thereby call for removal of a waiver?

VIII. Non-Discriminatory Discrimination or Divide and Rule? 1979 Tokyo Round *Enabling Clause* Paragraph 2(a) Defense and 2004 *EU GSP* Case

- European *GSP* Scheme and War on Drugs

---

78. *See* 19 U.S.C. § 2463(d)(4)(C).
79. 19 U.S.C. § 2463(d)(5).

WTO Appellate Body Report,

European Communities—Conditions for the Granting of Tariff
Preferences to Developing Countries,
WT/DS246/AB/R (Adopted 20 April 2004)

I. Introduction

1. . . . The Panel was established to consider a complaint by India against the European Communities regarding the conditions under which the European Communities accords tariff preferences to developing countries pursuant to Council Regulation (EC) No. 2501/2001 of 10 December 2001 "applying a scheme of generalized tariff preferences for the period from 1 January 2002 to 31 December 2004" (the "Regulation").

2. The Regulation provides for five preferential tariff "arrangements," namely:

  (a) general arrangements described in Article 7 of the Regulation (the "General Arrangements");

  (b) special incentive arrangements for the protection of labor rights;

  (c) special incentive arrangements for the protection of the environment;

  (d) special arrangements for least-developed countries; and

  (e) special arrangements to combat drug production and trafficking (the "Drug Arrangements").

3. All the countries listed in Annex I to the Regulation are eligible to receive tariff preferences under the General Arrangements, which provide, broadly, for suspension of Common Customs Tariff duties on products listed as "non-sensitive" and for reduction of Common Customs Tariff *ad valorem* duties on products listed as "sensitive." . . . The four other arrangements in the Regulation provide tariff preferences *in addition* to those granted under the General Arrangements. [For instance, the tariff preferences include further reductions in the duties imposed on certain "sensitive" products.] However, only some of the country beneficiaries of the General Arrangements are also beneficiaries of the other arrangements. Specifically, preferences under the special incentive arrangements for the protection of labor rights and the special incentive arrangements for the protection of the environment are restricted to those countries that "are determined by the European Communities to comply with certain labor [or] environmental policy standards," respectively. Preferences under the special arrangements for least-developed countries are restricted to certain specified countries. Finally, preferences under the Drug Arrangements are provided only to 12 predetermined countries, namely Bolivia, Colombia, Costa Rica, Ecuador, El Salvador, Guatemala, Honduras, Nicaragua, Pakistan, Panama, Peru, and Venezuela.

4. India is a beneficiary of the General Arrangements but not of the Drug Arrangements, or of any of the other arrangements established by the Regulation. In its request for the establishment of a Panel, India challenged the Drug Arrangements as

well as the special incentive arrangements for the protection of labor rights and the environment. However, in a subsequent meeting with the Director-General regarding the composition of the Panel—and later in writing to the European Communities—India indicated its decision to limit its complaint to the Drug Arrangements, while reserving its right to bring additional complaints regarding the two "special incentive arrangements." Accordingly, this dispute concerns only the Drug Arrangements.

5. The Panel summarized the effect of the Drug Arrangements as follows:

> The result of the Regulation is that the tariff reductions accorded under the Drug Arrangements to the 12 beneficiary countries are greater than the tariff reductions granted under the General Arrangements to other developing countries. In respect of products that are included in the Drug Arrangements but not in the General Arrangements, the 12 beneficiary countries are granted *duty free* access to the European Communities' market, while all other developing countries must pay the *full duties applicable under the Common Customs Tariff*. In respect of products that are included in both the Drug Arrangements and the General Arrangements and that are deemed "sensitive" under column G of Annex IV to the Regulation with the exception for products of CN codes 0306 13, 1704 10 91 and 1704 10 99, the 12 beneficiary countries are granted *duty-free* access to the European Communities' market, while all other developing countries are entitled only to *reductions in the duties applicable under the Common Customs Tariff*. (original italics)

6. India requested the Panel to find that "the Drug Arrangements set out in Article 10" of the Regulation are inconsistent with Article I:1 of the *General Agreement on Tariffs and Trade 1994* (the "GATT 1994") and are not justified by the *Decision on Differential and More Favorable Treatment, Reciprocity, and Fuller Participation of Developing Countries* (the "*Enabling Clause*") [GATT Document L/4903, 28 November 1979, BISD 26S/203.] . . .

• **Holdings and Rationales**

WTO Appellate Body Report,

European Communities—Conditions for the Granting of Tariff Preferences to Developing Countries,
WT/DS246/AB/R (Adopted 20 April 2004)

[Omitted is the finding of the Appellate Body, upholding that of the Panel, on the relationship between the MFN obligation of GATT Article I:1 and the *Enabling Clause*. The Appellate Body, agreeing with the Panel, concluded the *Clause* is an exception to the obligation.

Omitted, too, is the Appellate Body's modification of the finding of the Panel that the EC bears the burden of invoking the *Enabling Clause* and justifying the Drug Arrangements under the *Clause*. The Appellate Body said it was incumbent on

India to raise the *Enabling Clause* in forging its claim of inconsistency under the GATT Article I:1 MFN provision. Then, the EC had the burden of proving the Drug Arrangement satisfied the *Clause*. The Appellate Body said India did, to a sufficient extent, invoke the *Clause*, specifically, Paragraph 2(a) thereof.]

V. Whether the Drug Arrangements Are Justified Under the *Enabling Clause*

. . .

B. *Interpretation of the Term "Non-Discriminatory" in Footnote 3 to Paragraph 2(a) of the Enabling Clause*

. . .

143. . . . Paragraph 1 of the *Enabling Clause* authorizes WTO Members to provide "differential and more favorable treatment to developing countries, without according such treatment to other WTO Members." [S]uch differential treatment is permitted "notwithstanding" the provisions of Article I of the GATT 1994. Paragraph 2(a) and footnote 3 thereto clarify that Paragraph 1 applies to "[p]referential tariff treatment accorded by developed contracting parties to products originating in developing countries in accordance with the Generalized System of Preferences," "[a]s described in the [*1971 Waiver Decision*], relating to the establishment of 'generalized, non-reciprocal and non-discriminatory preferences beneficial to the developing countries.'"

144. The *Preamble* to the *1971 Waiver Decision* in turn refers to "preferential tariff treatment" in the following terms:

> *Recalling* that at the Second UNCTAD, unanimous agreement was reached in favour of the early establishment of a mutually acceptable system of generalized, non-reciprocal and non-discriminatory preferences beneficial to the developing countries in order to increase the export earnings, to promote the industrialization, and to accelerate the rates of economic growth of these countries;
>
> *Considering* that mutually acceptable arrangements have been drawn up in the UNCTAD concerning the establishment of *generalized, non-discriminatory, non-reciprocal preferential tariff treatment* in the markets of developed countries for products originating in developing countries[.] (original italics; underlining added)

145. Paragraph 2(a) of the *Enabling Clause* provides, therefore, that, to be justified under that provision, preferential tariff treatment must be "in accordance" with the *GSP* "as described" in the *Preamble* to the *1971 Waiver Decision*. "Accordance" being defined in the dictionary as "conformity," only preferential tariff treatment that is in conformity with the description "generalized, non-reciprocal and non-discriminatory" treatment can be justified under Paragraph 2(a). [Again, the Appellate Body cited to the *Shorter Oxford English Dictionary*.]

146. In the light of the above, we do not agree with European Communities' assertion that the Panel's interpretation of the word "non-discriminatory" in footnote 3

of the *Enabling Clause* is erroneous because the phrase "generalized, non-reciprocal and non-discriminatory" in footnote 3 merely refers to the description of the *GSP* in the *1971 Waiver Decision* and, of itself, does not impose any legal obligation on preference-granting countries. . . .

. . .

148. Having found that the qualification of the *GSP* as "generalized, non-reciprocal and non-discriminatory" imposes obligations that must be fulfilled for preferential tariff treatment to be justified under Paragraph 2(a), we turn to address the Panel's finding that:

> . . . the term "non-discriminatory" in footnote 3 requires that *identical* tariff preferences under *GSP* schemes be provided to *all* developing countries without differentiation, except for the implementation of *a priori* limitations. (emphasis added)

149. The European Communities maintains that "'non-discrimination' is not synonymous with formally equal treatment" and that "[t]reating differently situations which are objectively different is not discriminatory." The European Communities asserts that "[t]he objective of the *Enabling Clause* is different from that of Article I:1 of the GATT." In its view, the latter is concerned with "providing equal conditions of competition for imports of like products originating in all Members," whereas "the *Enabling Clause* is a form of Special and Differential Treatment for developing countries, which seeks the opposite result: to create unequal competitive opportunities in order to respond to the special needs of developing countries." The European Communities derives contextual support from Paragraph 3(c), which states that the treatment provided under the *Enabling Clause* "shall . . . be designed and, if necessary, modified, to respond positively to the development, financial and trade needs of developing countries." The European Communities concludes that the term "non-discriminatory" in footnote 3 "does not prevent the preference-giving countries from differentiating between developing countries which have different development needs, where tariff differentiation constitutes an adequate response to such differences."

150. India, in contrast, asserts that "non-discrimination in respect of tariff measures refers to formally equal[] treatment" and that Paragraph 2(a) of the *Enabling Clause* requires that "preferential tariff treatment [be] applied equally" among developing countries. In support of its argument, India submits that an interpretation of paragraph 2(a) of the *Enabling Clause* that authorizes developed countries to provide "discriminatory tariff treatment *in favor of the developing countries* but not *between the developing countries* gives full effect to both Article I of the GATT and Paragraph 2(a) of the *Enabling Clause* and minimizes the conflict between them." India emphasizes that, by consenting to the adoption of the *Enabling Clause*, developing countries did not "relinquish[] their MFN rights [under Article I of the GATT 1994] as between themselves, thus permitting developed countries to discriminate between them."

151. We examine now the ordinary meaning of the term "non-discriminatory" in footnote 3 to Paragraph 2(a) of the *Enabling Clause*. As we observed, footnote 3 requires that *GSP* schemes under the Enabling Clause be "generalized, non-reciprocal and non-discriminatory." Before the Panel, the participants offered competing definitions of the word "discriminate." India suggested that this word means "'to make or constitute a difference in or between; distinguish' and 'to make a distinction in the treatment of different categories of peoples or things.'" The European Communities, however, understood this word to mean "'to make a distinction in the treatment of different categories of people or things, esp. *unjustly* or *prejudicially* against people on grounds of race, color, sex, social status, age, etc.'" [In both instances, the Panel quoted from (quoting *The New Shorter Oxford English Dictionary*, L. Brown (ed.) (Clarendon Press, 1993), Vol. 1, p. 689.]

152. Both definitions can be considered as reflecting ordinary meanings of the term "discriminate" and essentially exhaust the relevant ordinary meanings. [The Appellate Body, again, pointed to the *Shorter Oxford English Dictionary*.] The principal distinction between these definitions, as the Panel noted, is that India's conveys a "*neutral* meaning of making a distinction," whereas the European Communities' conveys a "*negative* meaning carrying the connotation of a distinction that is unjust or prejudicial." Accordingly, the ordinary meanings of "discriminate" point in conflicting directions with respect to the propriety of according differential treatment. Under India's reading, any differential treatment of *GSP* beneficiaries would be prohibited, because such treatment necessarily makes a distinction between beneficiaries. In contrast, under the European Communities' reading, differential treatment of *GSP* beneficiaries would not be prohibited *per se*. Rather, distinctions would be impermissible only where the basis for such distinctions was improper. Given these divergent meanings, we do not regard the term "non-discriminatory," on its own, as determinative of the permissibility of a preference-granting country according different tariff preferences to different beneficiaries of its *GSP* scheme.

153. Nevertheless, . . . we are able to discern some of the content of the "non-discrimination" obligation based on the ordinary meanings of that term. Whether the drawing of distinctions is *per se* discriminatory, or whether it is discriminatory only if done on an improper basis, the ordinary meanings of discriminate" converge in one important respect: they both suggest that distinguishing among similarly-situated beneficiaries is discriminatory. For example, India suggests that all beneficiaries of a particular Member's *GSP* scheme are similarly-situated, implicitly arguing that any differential treatment of such beneficiaries constitutes discrimination. The European Communities, however, appears to regard *GSP* beneficiaries as similarly-situated when they have "similar development needs." Although the European Communities acknowledges that differentiating between similarly-situated *GSP* beneficiaries would be inconsistent with footnote 3 of the *Enabling Clause*, it submits that there is no inconsistency in differentiating between *GSP* beneficiaries with "different development needs." Thus, based on the ordinary meanings of "discriminate," India and the European Communities effectively appear to agree that,

pursuant to the term "non-discriminatory" in footnote 3, similarly-situated *GSP* beneficiaries should not be treated differently. The participants disagree only as to the basis for determining whether beneficiaries are similarly-situated.

[In an edifying footnote following the penultimate sentence of Paragraph 153, the Appellate Body observed:

> We note that the contrasting definitions proffered by the participants, as well as the convergence of those definitions on the fact that similarly-situated entities should not be treated differently, find reflection in the use of the term "discrimination" in general international law. In this respect, we note, as an example, the definitions of "discrimination" provided by the European Communities, in footnotes 56 and 57 of its appellant's submission:

> > [56] . . . Mere differences of treatment do not necessarily constitute discrimination . . . discrimination may in general be said to arise where those who are in all material respects the same are treated differently, or where those who are in material respects different are treated in the same way.

> (*quoting* R. Jennings and A. Watts (eds.), *Oppenheim's International Law*, 9th ed. (Longman, 1992), Vol. I, p. 378)

> > [57] . . . Discrimination occurs when in a legal system an inequality is introduced in the enjoyment of a certain right, or in a duty, while there is no sufficient connection between the inequality upon which the legal inequality is based, and the right or the duty in which this inequality is made.

> (*quoting* E.W. Vierdag, *The Concept of Discrimination in International Law*, (Martinus Nijhoff, 1973), p. 61).]

154. Paragraph 2(a), on its face, does not explicitly authorize or prohibit the granting of different tariff preferences to different *GSP* beneficiaries. It is clear from the ordinary meanings of "non-discriminatory," however, that preference-granting countries must make available identical tariff preferences to all similarly-situated beneficiaries.

155. We continue our interpretive analysis by turning to the immediate context of the term "non-discriminatory." We note first that footnote 3 to Paragraph 2(a) stipulates that, in addition to being "non-discriminatory," tariff preferences provided under *GSP* schemes must be "generalized." According to the ordinary meaning of that term, tariff preferences provided under *GSP* schemes must be "generalized" in the sense that they "apply more generally; [or] become extended in application." [The Appellate Body, here too, cited the *Shorter Oxford English Dictionary*.] However, this ordinary meaning alone may not reflect the entire significance of the word "generalized" in the context of footnote 3 of the *Enabling Clause*, particularly because that word resulted from lengthy negotiations leading to the *GSP*. In this regard, we note the Panel's finding that, by requiring tariff preferences under

the *GSP* to be "generalized," developed and developing countries together sought to eliminate existing "special" preferences that were granted only to certain designated developing countries. Similarly, in response to our questioning at the oral hearing, the participants agreed that one of the objectives of the *1971 Waiver Decision* and the *Enabling Clause* was to eliminate the fragmented system of special preferences that were, in general, based on historical and political ties between developed countries and their former colonies.

156. It does not necessarily follow, however, that "non-discriminatory" should be interpreted to require that preference-granting countries provide "identical" tariff preferences under *GSP* schemes to "all" developing countries. In concluding otherwise, the Panel assumed that allowing tariff preferences such as the Drug Arrangements would necessarily "result [in] the collapse of the whole *GSP* system and a return back to special preferences favoring selected developing countries." To us, this conclusion is unwarranted. We observe that the term "generalized" requires that the *GSP* schemes of preference-granting countries remain generally applicable. Moreover, unlike the Panel, we believe that the *Enabling Clause* sets out sufficient conditions on the granting of preferences to protect against such an outcome. . . . [P]rovisions such as Paragraphs 3(a) and 3(c) of the *Enabling Clause* impose specific conditions on the granting of different tariff preferences among *GSP* beneficiaries.

157. As further context for the term "non-discriminatory" in footnote 3, we turn next to Paragraph 3(c) of the *Enabling Clause*, which specifies that "differential and more favorable treatment" provided under the *Enabling Clause*:

> . . . shall in the case of such treatment accorded by developed contracting parties to developing countries be designed and, if necessary, modified, to respond positively to the development, financial and trade needs of developing countries.

158. . . . [U]se of the word "shall" in Paragraph 3(c) suggests that Paragraph 3(c) sets out an obligation for developed-country Members in providing preferential treatment under a *GSP* scheme to "respond positively" to the "needs of developing countries." Having said this, we turn to consider whether the "development, financial and trade needs of developing countries" to which preference-granting countries are required to respond when granting preferences must be understood to cover the "needs" of developing countries *collectively*.

159. The Panel found that "the only appropriate way [under Paragraph 3(c) of the *Enabling Clause*] of responding to the differing development needs of developing countries is for preference-giving countries to ensure that their [*GSP*] schemes have sufficient breadth of product coverage and depth of tariff cuts to respond positively to those differing needs." In reaching this conclusion, the Panel appears to have placed a great deal of significance on the fact that Paragraph 3(c) does not refer to needs of "*individual*" developing countries. The Panel thus understood that Paragraph 3(c) does not permit the granting of preferential tariff treatment exclusively to a sub-category of developing countries on the basis of needs that are common

to or shared by only those developing countries. We see no basis for such a conclusion in the text of Paragraph 3(c). Paragraph 3(c) refers generally to "the development, financial and trade needs of developing countries." The absence of an explicit requirement in the text of Paragraph 3(c) to respond to the needs of "all" developing countries, or to the needs of "each and every" developing country, suggests to us that, in fact, that provision imposes no such obligation.

160. Furthermore, . . . the participants in this case agree that developing countries may have "development, financial and trade needs" that are subject to change and that certain development needs may be common to only a certain number of developing countries. We see no reason to disagree. Indeed, Paragraph 3(c) contemplates that "differential and more favorable treatment" accorded by developed to developing countries may need to be "modified" in order to "respond positively" to the needs of developing countries. Paragraph 7 of the *Enabling Clause* supports this view by recording the expectation of "less-developed contracting parties" that their capacity to make contributions or concessions under the GATT will "improve with the progressive development of their economies and improvement in their trade situation." Moreover, the very purpose of the special and differential treatment permitted under the *Enabling Clause* is to foster economic development of developing countries. It is simply unrealistic to assume that such development will be in lock-step for all developing countries at once, now and for the future.

161. In addition, the *Preamble* to the *WTO Agreement*, which informs all the covered agreements including the GATT 1994 (and, hence, the *Enabling Clause*), explicitly recognizes the "need for positive efforts designed to ensure that developing countries, and especially the least developed among them, secure a share in the growth in international trade commensurate with the needs of their economic development." The word "commensurate" in this phrase appears to leave open the possibility that developing countries may have different needs according to their levels of development and particular circumstances. The *Preamble* to the *WTO Agreement* further recognizes that Members' "respective needs and concerns at different levels of economic development" may vary according to the different stages of development of different Members.

162. In sum, we read Paragraph 3(c) as authorizing preference-granting countries to "respond positively" to "needs" that are *not* necessarily common or shared by all developing countries. Responding to the "needs of developing countries" may thus entail treating different developing-country beneficiaries differently.

163. However, Paragraph 3(c) does not authorize *any* kind of response to *any* claimed need of developing countries. First, we observe that the types of needs to which a response is envisaged are limited to "development, financial and trade needs." In our view, a "need" cannot be characterized as one of the specified "needs of developing countries" in the sense of Paragraph 3(c) based merely on an assertion to that effect by, for instance, a preference-granting country or a beneficiary country. Rather, when a claim of inconsistency with Paragraph 3(c) is made, the existence of a "development, financial [or] trade need" must be assessed according

to an *objective* standard. Broad-based recognition of a particular need, set out in the *WTO Agreement* or in multilateral instruments adopted by international organizations, could serve as such a standard.

164. Secondly, Paragraph 3(c) mandates that the response provided to the needs of developing countries be "positive." "Positive" is defined as "consisting in or characterized by constructive action or attitudes." [The Appellate Body relied again on the *Shorter Oxford English Dictionary*.] This suggests that the response of a preference-granting country must be taken with a view to *improving* the development, financial or trade situation of a beneficiary country, based on the particular need at issue. As such, in our view, the expectation that developed countries will "respond positively" to the "needs of developing countries" suggests that a sufficient nexus should exist between, on the one hand, the preferential treatment provided under the respective measure authorized by paragraph 2, and, on the other hand, the likelihood of alleviating the relevant "development, financial [or] trade need". In the context of a *GSP* scheme, the particular need at issue must, by its nature, be such that it can be effectively addressed through tariff preferences. Therefore, only if a preference-granting country acts in the "positive" manner suggested, in "respon[se]" to a widely-recognized "development, financial [or] trade need," can such action satisfy the requirements of Paragraph 3(c).

165. . . . [B]y requiring developed countries to "respond positively" to the "needs of developing countries," which are varied and not homogeneous, Paragraph 3(c) indicates that a *GSP* scheme may be "non-discriminatory" even if "identical" tariff treatment is not accorded to "all" *GSP* beneficiaries. Moreover, Paragraph 3(c) suggests that tariff preferences under *GSP* schemes may be "non-discriminatory" when the relevant tariff preferences are addressed to a particular "development, financial [or] trade need" and are made available to all beneficiaries that share that need.

166. India submits that developing countries should not be presumed to have waived their MFN rights under Article I:1 of the GATT 1994 *vis-à-vis* other developing countries, and we make no such presumption. In fact, we note that the *Enabling Clause specifically* allows developed countries to provide differential and more favorable treatment to developing countries "notwithstanding" the provisions of Article I. With this in mind, and given that Paragraph 3(c) of the *Enabling Clause* contemplates, in certain circumstances, differentiation among *GSP* beneficiaries, we cannot agree with India that the right to MFN treatment can be invoked by a *GSP* beneficiary *vis-à-vis* other *GSP* beneficiaries in the context of *GSP* schemes that meet the conditions set out in the *Enabling Clause*.

167. Finally, . . . pursuant to Paragraph 3(a) of the *Enabling Clause*, any "differential and more favorable treatment . . . shall be designed to facilitate and promote the trade of developing countries and not to raise barriers to or create undue difficulties for the trade of any other contracting parties." This requirement applies, *a fortiori*, to any preferential treatment granted to one *GSP* beneficiary that is not

granted to another. Thus, although Paragraph 2(a) does not prohibit *per se* the granting of different tariff preferences to different *GSP* beneficiaries, and Paragraph 3(c) even contemplates such differentiation under certain circumstances, Paragraph 3(a) requires that any positive response of a preference-granting country to the varying needs of developing countries not impose unjustifiable burdens on other Members.

168. Having examined the context of Paragraph 2(a), we turn next to examine the object and purpose of the *WTO Agreement*. We note first that Paragraph 7 of the *Enabling Clause* provides that "[t]he concessions and contributions made and the obligations assumed by developed and less-developed contracting parties under the provisions of the [GATT 1994] should promote the basic objectives of the [GATT 1994], including those embodied in the *Preamble*." . . . [T]he *Preamble* to the *WTO Agreement* provides that there is "need for positive efforts designed to ensure that developing countries, and especially the least developed among them, secure a share in the growth in international trade commensurate with the needs of their economic development." Similarly, the *Preamble* to the *1971 Waiver Decision* provides that "a principal aim of the CONTRACTING PARTIES is promotion of the trade and export earnings of developing countries for the furtherance of their economic development." These objectives are also reflected in Paragraph 3(c) of the *Enabling Clause*, which states that the treatment provided under the *Enabling Clause* "shall . . . be designed and, if necessary, modified, to respond positively to the development, financial and trade needs of developing countries."

169. Although enhanced market access will contribute to responding to the needs of developing countries *collectively*, we have also recognized that the needs of developing countries may vary over time. . . . [T]he objective of improving developing countries' "share in the growth in international trade," and their "trade and export earnings," can be fulfilled by promoting preferential policies aimed at those interests that developing countries have in common, *as well as* at those interests shared by sub-categories of developing countries based on their particular needs. An interpretation of "non-discriminatory" that does not require the granting of "identical tariff preferences" allows not only for *GSP* schemes providing preferential market access to all beneficiaries, but also the possibility of additional preferences for developing countries with particular needs, provided that such additional preferences are not inconsistent with other provisions of the *Enabling Clause*, including the requirements that such preferences be "generalized" and "non-reciprocal." We therefore consider such an interpretation to be consistent with the object and purpose of the *WTO Agreement* and the *Enabling Clause*.

170. The Panel took the view, however, that the objective of "elimination of discriminatory treatment in international commerce, found in the *Preamble* to the GATT 1994, "contributes more to guiding the interpretation of 'non-discriminatory'" than does the objective of ensuring that developing countries "secure . . . a share

in the growth in international trade commensurate with their development needs."
We fail to see on what basis the Panel drew this conclusion.

. . .

[The Appellate Body considered the relevance of Paragraph 2(d) of the *Enabling Clause* to the interpretation of the term "non-discriminatory." This Paragraph deals with special treatment of LDCs. The Panel characterized Paragraph 2(d) as an exception to Paragraph 2(a), and used Paragraph 2(d) to support its view that paragraph 2(a) requires "formally identical treatment." The Appellate Body found otherwise, stating Paragraph 2(d) is not an exception to Paragraph 2(a), and the reliance of the Panel on Paragraph 2(d) was misplaced. The Paragraphs of the *Escape Clause* are not mutually exclusive, and no one of them is an exception to the other. The critical, independent function of Paragraph 2(d) is to highlight least developed countries as a sub-category of developing countries, and authorize distinct preferences for these poorest-of-the poor countries. Thus, because of Paragraph 2(d), a preference-granting country need not establish that differentiating between developing and least-developed countries is "non-discriminatory."]

173. Having examined the text and context of footnote 3 to Paragraph 2(a) of the *Enabling Clause*, and the object and purpose of the *WTO Agreement* and the *Enabling Clause*, we conclude that the term "non-discriminatory" in footnote 3 does not prohibit developed-country Members from granting different tariffs to products originating in different *GSP* beneficiaries, provided that such differential tariff treatment meets the remaining conditions in the *Enabling Clause*. In granting such differential tariff treatment, however, preference-granting countries are required, by virtue of the term "non-discriminatory," to ensure that identical treatment is available to all similarly-situated *GSP* beneficiaries, that is, to all *GSP* beneficiaries that have the "development, financial and trade needs" to which the treatment in question is intended to respond.

174. For all of these reasons, we *reverse* the Panel's finding . . . that "the term 'non-discriminatory' in footnote 3 [to paragraph 2(a) of the *Enabling Clause*] requires that identical tariff preferences under *GSP* schemes be provided to all developing countries without differentiation, except for the implementation of *a priori* limitations."

. . .

[The Appellate Body also reversed the Panel holding that the term "developing countries" in Paragraph 2(a) means "all developing countries, except as regards *a priori* limitations." The Appellate Body reasoned that because footnote 3 and Paragraph 3(c) do not ban granting of differential tariffs to different sub-categories of *GSP* beneficiaries, as long as the remaining conditions of the *Escape Clause* are met, the term "developing countries" should not be read to mean "all." In effect, the Appellate Body held "developing countries" can mean less than all of them.]

D. *Consistency of the Drug Arrangements with the Enabling Clause*

. . .

180. We found above that the term "non-discriminatory" in footnote 3 to paragraph 2(a) of the *Enabling Clause* does not prohibit the granting of different tariffs to products originating in different sub-categories of *GSP* beneficiaries, but that identical tariff treatment must be available to all *GSP* beneficiaries with the "development, financial [or] trade need" to which the differential treatment is intended to respond. The need alleged to be addressed by the European Communities' differential tariff treatment is the problem of illicit drug production and trafficking in certain *GSP* beneficiaries. . . . [T]herefore, the Drug Arrangements may be found consistent with the "non-discriminatory" requirement in footnote 3 only if the European Communities proves, at a minimum, that the preferences granted under the Drug Arrangements are available to all *GSP* beneficiaries that are similarly affected by the drug problem. [In the case, the EU argued the Drug Arrangements are *non-discriminatory* because designation of beneficiary countries depends only and exclusively on their development needs, and all developing countries that are similarly affected by the drug problem have been included in the Drug Arrangements.] We do not believe this to be the case.

181. By their very terms, the Drug Arrangements are limited to the 12 developing countries designated as beneficiaries in Annex I to the Regulation. Specifically, Article 10:1 of the Regulation states:

> Common Customs Tariff *ad valorem* duties on [covered products] which originate in a country that according to Column I of Annex I benefits from [the Drug Arrangements] shall be entirely suspended.

182. Articles 10 and 25 of the Regulation, which relate specifically to the Drug Arrangements, provide no mechanism under which additional beneficiaries may be added to the list of beneficiaries under the Drug Arrangements as designated in Annex I. Nor does any of the other Articles of the Regulation point to the existence of such a mechanism with respect to the Drug Arrangements. . . . This contrasts with the position under the "special incentive arrangements for the protection of labour rights" and the "special incentive arrangements for the protection of the environment," which are described in Article 8 of the Regulation. The Regulation includes detailed provisions setting out the procedure and substantive criteria that apply to a request by a beneficiary under the general arrangements described in Article 7 of the Regulation (the "General Arrangements") to become a beneficiary under either of those special incentive arrangements.

183. . . . [T]he Drug Arrangements themselves do *not* set out any clear prerequisites—or "objective criteria"—that, if met, would allow for other developing countries "that are similarly affected by the drug problem" to be *included* as beneficiaries under the Drug Arrangements. . . . Similarly, the Regulation offers no criteria according to which a beneficiary could be *removed* specifically from the Drug Arrangements on the basis that it is no longer "similarly affected by the drug

problem." . . . [E]ven if the European Commission found that the Drug Arrangements were having no effect whatsoever on a beneficiary's "efforts in combating
drug production and trafficking," or that a beneficiary was no longer suffering from
the drug problem, beneficiary status would continue. Therefore, even if the Regulation allowed for the list of beneficiaries under the Drug Arrangements to be modified, the Regulation itself gives no indication as to how the beneficiaries under the
Drug Arrangements were chosen or what kind of considerations would or could be
used to determine the effect of the "drug problem" on a particular country. . . .

     . . .

186. Against this background, we fail to see how the Drug Arrangements can be distinguished from other schemes that the European Communities describes as "confined *ab initio* and permanently to a limited number of developing countries." As
we understand it, the European Communities' position is that such schemes would
be discriminatory, whereas the Drug Arrangements are not because "all developing
countries are potentially beneficiaries" thereof. In seeking a waiver from its obligations under Article I:1 of the GATT 1994 to implement the Drug Arrangements,
the European Communities explicitly acknowledged, however, that "[b]ecause the
special arrangements *are only available* to imports originating in [the 12 beneficiaries of the Drug Arrangements], a waiver . . . appears necessary." This statement
appears to undermine the European Communities' argument that "all developing
countries are potentially beneficiaries of the Drug Arrangements" and, therefore,
that the Drug Arrangements are "non-discriminatory."

187. We recall our conclusion that the term "non-discriminatory" in footnote 3
of the *Enabling Clause* requires that identical tariff treatment be available to all
similarly-situated *GSP* beneficiaries. We find that the measure at issue fails to meet
this requirement for the following reasons. First, as the European Communities
itself acknowledges, according benefits under the Drug Arrangements to countries
other than the 12 identified beneficiaries would require an amendment to the Regulation. Such a "closed list" of beneficiaries cannot ensure that the preferences under
the Drug Arrangements are available to all *GSP* beneficiaries suffering from illicit
drug production and trafficking.

188. Secondly, the Regulation contains no criteria or standards to provide a basis for
distinguishing beneficiaries under the Drug Arrangements from other *GSP* beneficiaries. . . . As such, the European Communities cannot justify the Regulation under
Paragraph 2(a), because it does not provide a basis for establishing whether or not a
developing country qualifies for preferences under the Drug Arrangements. Thus,
although the European Communities claims that the Drug Arrangements are available to all developing countries that are "similarly affected by the drug problem,"
because the Regulation does not define the criteria or standards that a developing
country must meet to qualify for preferences under the Drug Arrangements, there is
no basis to determine whether those criteria or standards are discriminatory or not.

189. For all these reasons, we find that the European Communities has failed to prove that the Drug Arrangements meet the requirement in footnote 3 that they be "non-discriminatory." Accordingly, we *uphold*, for different reasons, the Panel's conclusion . . . that the European Communities "failed to demonstrate that the Drug Arrangements are justified under Paragraph 2(a) of the *Enabling Clause*."

IX. NTMs and RTAs: 1979 Tokyo Round *Enabling Clause* Paragraphs 2(b)–(c) Defenses and 2019 *Brazil Tax* Case

The 2019 *Brazil Tax* case was a major challenge by the EU and Japan on a complex array of preferences Brazil granted to domestic economic agents. Taken together, the controversial measures summed to a broad, deep import substitution policy.

• **Brazil's Controversial Tax Preferences**

WTO Appellate Body Report,

Brazil — Certain Measures Concerning Taxation and Charges, WT/DS472/AB/R, WT/DS497/AB/R (Adopted 11 January 2019)

1. Introduction

. . .

1.5. The taxes and contributions relevant for the purposes of the present appeals are: (i) the Tax on Industrialized Products (IPI tax); (ii) the Social Integration Program/Civil Service Asset Formation Program (PIS/PASEP) contribution and the Contribution to Social Security Financing (COFINS); (iii) the Social Integration and Civil Service Asset Formation Programs contribution applicable to Imports of Foreign Goods or Services (PIS/PASEP-Importation) and the Contribution to Social Security Financing applicable to Imports of Goods or Services (COFINS-Importation); and (iv) the Contribution of Intervention in the Economic Domain (CIDE).

1.6. The measures at issue can be divided into three groups of measures through which Brazil provides exemptions, reductions, or suspensions of the federal taxes and contributions mentioned above. The first group of measures concerns the ICT [Information and Communications Technology] sector and comprises tax treatment granted under: (i) the Informatics program; (ii) the program of Incentives for the Semiconductors Sector (PADIS program); (iii) the program of Support for the Technological Development of the Industry of Digital TV Equipment (PATVD program); and (iv) the program for Digital Inclusion (Digital Inclusion program). [The Appellate Body refers to this first group of measures collectively as the "ICT programs."] The second group comprises tax treatment granted under the program of Incentive to the Technological Innovation and Densification of the Automotive Supply Chain (INOVAR-AUTO program), which targets the automotive sector. The third group of measures comprises tax treatment granted under: (i) the regime for

Predominantly Exporting Companies (PEC program); and (ii) the Special Regime for the Purchase of Capital Goods for Exporting Enterprises (RECAP program).

1.7. The Informatics program provides for exemptions and reductions on the IPI tax on the sale of information technology goods. It also provides for suspensions of the IPI tax on the purchase or import of raw materials, intermediate goods, and packaging materials used in the production of information technology, and automation goods incentivized under the program. In order to benefit from the tax treatment, companies must obtain an accreditation. The eligible companies under the Informatics program are companies that: (i) develop or produce information technology and automation goods and services in compliance with the relevant Basic Productive Processes (PPBs); and (ii) invest in information technology research and development (R&D) activities in Brazil. Moreover, under this program, products that have obtained the status of "developed in Brazil" are subject to additional tax reductions.

1.8. The PADIS program exempts, through zero rates, accredited companies from paying certain taxes with respect to semiconductors and information displays, as well as inputs, tools, equipment, machinery, and software for the production of semiconductors and displays. In order to obtain accreditation, legal persons must: (i) invest in R&D in Brazil; and (ii) engage in certain activities in Brazil with respect to semiconductor electronic devices, information displays, and inputs and equipment intended for the manufacture of electronic semiconductor devices and information displays.

1.9. The PATVD program exempts accredited companies from paying certain taxes with respect to radio frequency signal transmitting equipment for digital television (digital television transmission equipment), as well as machinery, apparatus, instruments, equipment, inputs, and software for the production of digital television transmission equipment (production goods). In order to obtain accreditation, legal persons must: (i) invest in R&D in Brazil; (ii) engage in developing and manufacturing activities of digital television transmission equipment; and (iii) either comply with the relevant PPB or, alternatively, meet the criteria for a product to be considered "developed in Brazil."

1.10. The Digital Inclusion program exempts, through zero rates, Brazilian retailers from paying PIS/PASEP and COFINS contributions with respect to the sale of certain digital consumer goods produced in Brazil in accordance with the relevant PPBs.

1.11. The INOVAR-AUTO program provides for reduction of the IPI tax burden on certain motor vehicles either: (i) through presumed IPI tax credits granted to accredited companies; or (ii) through reduced IPI tax rates on the importation of vehicles originating in certain countries, as well as on certain domestic vehicles. All companies using presumed IPI tax credits, and certain companies using reduced IPI tax rates, must obtain one of three forms of accreditation: (i) domestic manufacturer; (ii) importer/distributor; or (iii) investor. In order to obtain accreditation, a company must comply with certain requirements of both a general and specific nature. All such companies must comply with the same two general requirements and also with certain additional specific requirements that vary by the type of accreditation. A company applying for accreditation as a domestic manufacturer shall comply with the two general requirements as well as "three out of four specific requirements, one of which must be the performance of a minimum number of defined manufacturing and engineering infrastructure activities in Brazil." A company applying for accreditation as importer/distributor shall comply with the two general requirements and "the following three specific requirements: (i) investments in R&D in Brazil; (ii) expenditure on engineering, basic industrial technology and capacity-building of suppliers in Brazil; and, (iii) participation in the vehicle labelling program by [the] National Institute of Metrology, Quality and Technology (INMETRO)." A company applying for accreditation as an investor shall submit to the Ministry of Development, Industry and Trade (MDIC) an investment project containing a description and the technical features of the vehicles to be imported and manufactured. Accreditation shall be granted once the investment project is approved by that Ministry. An investor shall be required to apply for a specific accreditation for every factory, plant, or industrial project that it plans to establish.

1.12. Under the PEC program, the IPI tax and the PIS/PASEP, COFINS, PIS/PASEP-Importation, and COFINS-Importation contributions are suspended with respect to raw materials, intermediate goods, and packaging materials purchased by predominantly exporting companies. Similarly, under the RECAP program, the PIS/PASEP, COFINS, PIS/PASEP-Importation, and COFINS-Importation contributions are suspended with respect to purchases of new machinery, tools, apparatus, instruments, and equipment by predominantly exporting companies.

- **National Treatment Violations**

The Appellate Body upheld all of the substantive rulings against Brazil, including multiple national treatment violations identified by the claimants, the EU and Japan. Brazil lost on all issues concerning national treatment for fiscal measures under GATT Article III:2, national treatment for non-fiscal measures under GATT Article III:4, and correspondingly under *TRIMs Agreement* Article 2:1.

In brief:

(1) Brazil violated GATT Article III:2, first sentence, because it taxed imported finished ICT products in excess of like domestic finished ICT products. In particular:

6.2. Imported finished ICT products are not eligible for either tax reductions or exemptions because foreign producers cannot be accredited under the ICT programs and, consequently, bear the full tax burden, as opposed to like domestic finished ICT products. In the case of an imported finished ICT product, when an importer sells the imported finished ICT product to a wholesaler, retailer, or distributor, the importer will charge the IPI tax to the wholesaler, retailer, or distributor and remit the tax to the Brazilian Government. In contrast, in the case of a like domestic finished ICT product that is subject to IPI tax exemption or reduction under the ICT programs, the seller does not charge any tax or charges a reduced tax, as the case may be, to the wholesaler, retailer, or distributor. At this last stage, the tax rate is thus higher for imported finished ICT products than for like domestic finished ICT products, and the tax burden on the former is necessarily in excess of that on the latter.

(2) Brazil violated GATT Article III:2, first sentence, because it taxed imported intermediate ICT products in excess of like domestic intermediate ICT products. In particular:

6.4. Under the credit-debit system, purchases of non-incentivized imported intermediate ICT products involve the payment of a tax upfront that is not faced by companies that purchase incentivized like domestic intermediate ICT products, which are exempted from the relevant taxes. Even in the case of tax reductions, companies purchasing incentivized like domestic intermediate ICT products have to pay a lower tax compared to companies purchasing non-incentivized imported intermediate ICT products. We fail to see how these situations do not have the effect of limiting the availability of cash flow for companies purchasing non-incentivized imported intermediate ICT products. The fact that purchasers of imported intermediate ICT products have to pay the relevant taxes under the ICT programs, irrespective of the point in time, in comparison to purchasers of incentivized like domestic intermediate ICT products, who do not have to pay the relevant tax or pay a reduced amount, "limit[s] the availability of cash flow," resulting in a higher effective tax burden on imported intermediate ICT products. Moreover, the value of the tax credit that is generated upon the payment of the relevant tax on the sale of a non-incentivized imported intermediate ICT product will depreciate over time until it is used or adjusted. To that extent, in as much as there is a time lag between the accrual of the tax credit and the adjustment or use thereof, it necessarily results in the value of money (in the form of accrued tax credits) depreciating over time. Therefore, imported intermediate ICT products, the purchase of which is subject to a payment of tax upfront, bear a higher tax burden than that faced by the incentivized like domestic intermediate ICT products, which benefit from tax exemption or reduction.

(3) Brazil violated GATT Article III:4, because its accreditation requirements under the ICT programs accord treatment less favorable to imported products than that accorded to like domestic products inconsistently. In particular:

6.6. The aspect of the ICT programs challenged by the complaining parties as being inconsistent with Article III:4 of the GATT 1994 concerned the accreditation requirements, the fulfilment of which enabled the obtaining of the relevant tax exemption, reduction, or suspension on the sales or purchases of ICT products. It is undisputed that in order to be eligible for the tax exemption, reduction, or suspension under the ICT programs, companies must fulfil the accreditation requirements. The accreditation requirements under the ICT programs therefore result in less favorable treatment for imported ICT products in the form of the differential tax burden that imported ICT products are subjected to by virtue of the fact that foreign producers cannot be accredited under the ICT programs. The consequence being, as the Panel also noted, that foreign producers "can never qualify for the tax exemptions, reductions or suspensions." We note that the aspects of the ICT programs found to be inconsistent with Article III:2, first sentence, and Article III:4 are distinct. In the case of Article III:2, first sentence, the aspect of the ICT program found to be inconsistent is the differential tax treatment that results in a higher tax burden on imported ICT products, *i.e.*, imported ICT products are taxed in excess of like domestic ICT products. Whereas, for the purposes of Article III:4, the aspect of the ICT programs found to be inconsistent is the accreditation requirements that result in less favorable treatment in the form of the differential tax treatment for imported ICT products.

(4) Brazil violated GATT Article III:4, because its ICT programs resulted in a lower administrative burden on companies purchasing incentivized domestic intermediate products. In particular:

6.8. Under the credit-debit system, purchasers of imported intermediate ICT products that are not incentivized under the ICT programs will have to anticipate and pay the full amount of tax due on such imported intermediate ICT products. Although any such tax paid on the purchase of imported intermediate ICT products will generate a corresponding tax credit in favor of the purchaser, nonetheless, offsetting this tax credit entails an *administrative burden* that is not faced, or faced to a lesser extent, by a purchaser of domestic intermediate ICT products that are incentivized. This is the case because under the credit-debit system, "if the tax credit cannot be offset by debits after three taxation periods," the process of compensating the tax credit with other federal taxes, or reimbursement thereof can "be burdensome for companies, and can take years."

(5) Brazil violated GATT Article III:4, because its PPBs and other production-step requirements under the ICT programs are contingent upon the use of domestic goods. In particular:

6.10. ... [T[he PPBs and other production-step requirements under the Informatics, PATVD, PADIS, and Digital Inclusion programs provide an incentive to use domestic ICT products. ... [T]he the Informatics,

PATVD, PADIS, and Digital Inclusion programs accord less favorable treatment to imported intermediate ICT products than that accorded to like domestic products.

(6) Brazil violated GATT Article III:4, because the accreditation requirements under the INOVAR-AUTO program are more burdensome for companies seeking accreditation as importers/distributors as opposed to domestic manufacturers. In particular:

6.13. ... [I]n order for companies to obtain any sort of accreditation under the INOVAR-AUTO program, which entitles them to accruing and using presumed IPI tax credits, they must either be located and operate in Brazil, in the case of domestic manufacturers and importers/distributors, or be in the process of establishing in the country as domestic manufacturers, in the case of investors. The only viable way for foreign manufacturers to be able to enjoy the benefit of the presumed IPI tax credits in reducing their IPI tax liability under the INOVAR-AUTO program is to become accredited as importers/distributors. However, in order to do so, foreign manufacturers must, first and foremost, be located and operate in Brazil. This indicates that foreign manufacturers seeking accreditation as importers/distributors face a corresponding burden that necessarily comes with having to operate in, or establish themselves in, Brazil, unlike domestic manufacturers, who already operate or are established in Brazil. Moreover, we note that in order to become accredited as importers/distributors, a company shall comply with the following three specific requirements: (i) investments in R&D in Brazil; (ii) expenditure on engineering, basic industrial technology, and capacity-building of suppliers in Brazil; and (iii) participation in the vehicle-labelling program by INMETRO. A fourth requirement also exists, which calls for the performance in Brazil of certain manufacturing steps. These activities cannot be considered to be typical for foreign manufacturers seeking to import motor vehicles into Brazil. The fact that foreign manufacturers have to undertake these activities to get accredited as importers/distributors implies that foreign manufacturers face a burden that domestic manufacturers do not face. Almost all of these requirements can be considered to be typical of the nature of activity carried out by a domestic manufacturer. Indeed, any domestic manufacturer will carry out and perform a minimum number of manufacturing activities in Brazil, and, in that process, it is likely to make investments in R&D in Brazil and make expenditures in the categories indicated in the INOVAR-AUTO program. The INOVAR-AUTO program is thus designed in such a manner that the accreditation requirements thereunder adversely modify the competitive conditions for imported products in comparison to like domestic products.

(7) Brazil violated the national treatment rule in *TRIMs Agreement* Article 2:1, by virtue of its violations of GATT Article III:4.

- **Unsuccessful GATT Article III:8 Defense**

The Appellate Body also found Brazil could not justify its GATT Article III:2 and 4 national treatment violations as domestic subsidies exempted under Article III:8. Essentially, Brazil was incorrect in characterizing its tax preferences as "subsidies to domestic producers," as that phrase is used in the Article III:8(b) limitation on national treatment.

WTO Appellate Body Report,

Brazil—Certain Measures Concerning Taxation and Charges,
WT/DS472/AB/R, WT/DS497/AB/R (Adopted 11 January 2019)

6.17. Insofar as the payment of subsidies exclusively to domestic producers of a given product affects the conditions of competition between such a product and the like imported product, the resulting inconsistency with the national treatment obligation under Article III is justified under Article III:8(b), provided that the conditions thereunder are met. Moreover, conditions for eligibility for the payment of subsidies that define the class of eligible "domestic producers" by reference to their activities in the subsidized products' markets are also justified under Article III:8(b). By contrast, a requirement to use domestic over imported goods in order to have access to the subsidy is not covered by the exception in Article III:8(b) and would therefore continue to be subject to the national treatment obligation in Article III. Furthermore, an examination of the text and context of Article III:8(b), in light of its object and purpose and as confirmed by the negotiating history, suggests that the term "payment of subsidies" in Article III:8(b) does not include within its scope the exemption or reduction of internal taxes affecting the conditions of competition between like products. Instead, as noted by the Appellate Body in [its 1997 Report in] *Canada—Periodicals* [discussed in a separate Chapter], Article III:8(b) "was intended to exempt from the obligations of Article III only the payment of subsidies which involves the expenditure of revenue by a government."

6.18. The Panel's interpretation and application of Article III:8(b) to the measures at issue obfuscate the distinction between the effects of the payment of a subsidy to a domestic producer on the conditions of competition in the relevant product markets and the conditions for eligibility attaching thereto, on the one hand, and any other effects arising from requirements to use domestic over imported inputs in the production process, on the other hand. Moreover, at no stage did the Panel undertake an assessment of whether the measures at issue constitutes the "payment of subsidies exclusively to domestic producers" within the meaning of Article III:8(b).

6.19. Because of these shortcomings in the Panel's reasoning, we reverse the Panel's overly broad and unqualified findings . . . that "subsidies that are provided exclusively to domestic producers pursuant to Article III:8(b) . . . are not *per se* exempted from the disciplines of Article III" and that "aspects of a subsidy resulting in product discrimination (including requirements to use domestic goods, as prohibited by Article 3:1 of the *SCM Agreement*) are not exempted from the disciplines of Article III pursuant to Article III:8(b)." Under a proper interpretation of Article III:8(b), none of the measures at issue in this dispute are capable of being justified under that provision because they all involve the exemption or reduction of internal taxes affecting the conditions of competition between like products and therefore cannot constitute the "payment of subsidies" within the meaning of Article III:8(b).

[Additionally, the Appellate Body ruled against Brazil in respect of claims under Article 3:1(b) of the *SCM Agreement*.]

- **Brazil's GATT Article I:1 MFN Violation and Failed *Enabling Clause* Paragraph 2(b) Defense Concerning Non-Tariff Measures**

The Appellate Body determined that the MFN claim the EU and Japan raised (namely, that Brazil violated GATT Article I:1) was within the terms of reference of the Panel. Likewise, the Appellate Body ruled the defense Brazil offered for the differential and more favorable treatment (in the form of internal tax reductions under the INOVAR-AUTO program) Brazil accorded to imports from Argentina, Mexico, and Uruguay (namely, Paragraphs 2(b) and 2(c) of the *Enabling Clause*) was within the Panel's terms of reference. These essentially procedural portions of the Appellate Body Report are dilated and dull, but they set up the Appellate Body holdings on the key substantive issues concerning the *Enabling Clause*.

WTO Appellate Body Report,

Brazil—Certain Measures Concerning Taxation and Charges,
WT/DS472/AB/R, WT/DS497/AB/R (Adopted 11 January 2019)

5.5.2 Whether the Panel erred in its interpretation of Paragraph 2(b) of the *Enabling Clause* and in finding that the differential tax treatment under the INOVAR-AUTO program was not justified under that provision

. . .

5.399. Before the Panel, Brazil argued that "the tax reductions challenged by the complaining parties fall within the scope of Paragraph 2(b)." Brazil submitted that the internal tax reductions at issue "are non-tariff measures (NTMs) because they constitute internal taxes subject to Article III of the GATT 1994 and, consequently, are subject to the [most-favored nation] MFN obligation under Article I:1 of the GATT 1994." Brazil further submitted that "internal taxes are NTMs 'governed by the provisions of instruments multilaterally negotiated under the auspices of the GATT' because the GATT 1947 (and subsequently the GATT 1994) are relevant multilaterally-negotiated instruments covering internal taxation, and there is no specific agreement covering internal taxes."

5.400. The Panel noted that the issue before it included "whether internal taxes are 'non-tariff measures governed by the provisions of instruments multilaterally negotiated under the auspices of the GATT.'" The Panel, however, did not consider it necessary to define the term "non-tariff measures" in isolation from the rest of

Paragraph 2(b), and considered instead the question of "[w]hether the alleged non-tariff measures at issue . . . have been demonstrated to be within the scope of [Paragraph] 2(b)." Accordingly, the Panel proceeded to assess whether Paragraph 2(b) applies to non-tariff measures governed exclusively by those provisions of the GATT 1994 that were incorporated from the GATT 1947.

5.401. The Panel considered that Paragraph 2(b), in referring to "[d]ifferential and more favorable treatment with respect to the provisions of the General Agreement concerning *non-tariff measures governed by the provisions of instruments multilaterally negotiated under the auspices of the GATT{}*" at the time the *Enabling Clause* was adopted, "meant non-tariff measures *other than* those non-tariff measures governed exclusively by the provisions of the GATT 1947." [Emphasis original.] Recalling that the *Enabling Clause* was adopted by the GATT CONTRACTING PARTIES during the Tokyo Round when a number of plurilateral agreements covering certain non-tariff measures were concluded, the Panel considered that "the intended application of Paragraph 2(b) must have been limited to the discrimination explicitly provided for in specific [special and differential (S&D)] provisions of the Tokyo Round *Codes*." The Panel noted that the provisions of the GATT 1994 that Brazil relied on, namely Articles III:2 and III:4, "do not introduce any special and differential treatment for taxes in the form of non-tariff measures" and "are substantively identical to provisions in the GATT 1947." Accordingly, the Panel concluded that "a non-tariff measure within the scope of Paragraph 2(b) must be governed by specific provisions on special and differential treatment[] that are distinct from the provisions of the GATT 1994 incorporating the GATT 1947."

5.402. For these reasons, the Panel found that "the tax reductions accorded to imported products from Argentina, Mexico and Uruguay and found to be inconsistent under Article I:1 of the GATT 1994 are not justified under Paragraph 2(b) of the *Enabling Clause*."

5.403. On appeal, Brazil disagrees that "instruments multilaterally negotiated under the auspices of the GATT" must be "'distinct from the provisions of the GATT 1994 incorporating the GATT 1947' because the GATT 1994 itself is an instrument which was multilaterally negotiated under the auspices of the GATT (institution)." Brazil argues that "[t]he GATT 1994 is the covered agreement that governs internal taxation, in Article III" and the *Enabling Clause* itself "as it was incorporated to the WTO as part of the GATT 1994, is, therefore, an 'instrument multilaterally negotiated under the auspices of the GATT.'" Brazil contends that the Panel interpreted Paragraph 2(b) to apply "only to specific Special and Differential (S&D) provisions present in the covered agreements other than the GATT itself." Brazil submits that, according to the Panel's reasoning, if the *Enabling Clause* is incorporated in the GATT 1994 but only applies to provisions outside of the GATT, "it also follows that the S&D provisions prevail over the GATT and therefore the *Enabling Clause* itself, according to [the general interpretative note to] Annex 1A of the *Marrakesh Agreement*." Brazil therefore asserts that "[t]he Panel's interpretation renders the text of Paragraph 2(b) of the *Enabling Clause inutile*." Brazil therefore seeks reversal of the Panel's conclusion that a non-tariff measure within the scope of Paragraph 2(b) must be governed by specific provisions on S&D treatment that are distinct from the provisions of the GATT 1994 incorporating the GATT 1947. Brazil also seeks reversal of the Panel's "consequential finding" that the internal tax reductions accorded to imported products from Argentina, Mexico, and Uruguay and found to be inconsistent under Article I:1 of the GATT 1994 are not justified under Paragraph 2(b) of the *Enabling Clause*, and requests the Appellate Body to complete the analysis and find that "the differential tax treatment is justified under Paragraph 2(b) and complies with the requirements of Paragraph 3 of the *Enabling Clause*."

5.404. In response, the European Union asserts that "Brazil's over-creative reading," according to which Paragraph 2(b) refers to "all the provisions of the GATT relating to non-tariff measures as being negotiated under the auspices of the GATT (or of the WTO), does not find any support in the text, context or the object and purpose of the *Enabling Clause*." The European Union points to the Panel's explanation that the *Enabling Clause* was adopted by the GATT CONTRACTING PARTIES during the Tokyo Round in the context of which a number of plurilateral agreements governing certain non-tariff measures were concluded. The European Union submits that it is in this context that the reference in Paragraph 2(b) to "instruments multilaterally negotiated under the auspices of the GATT" should be understood.

5.405. Japan submits that Paragraph 2(b) "does not endorse exceptions to the MFN principle with respect to 'non-tariff measures' themselves," but instead "pertains to differential and more favorable treatment with respect to '*the provisions of the General Agreement concerning* non-tariff measures *governed by the provisions of instruments multilaterally negotiated under the auspices of the GATT*.'" According to Japan, the Panel carefully interpreted those terms and confirmed that they mean "since 'Article III:2 and III:4 of the GATT 1994 [] do not introduce any special and differential treatment for taxes in the form of non-tariff measures,'" and "there is no specific WTO Agreement dealing with internal taxation, Brazil's measures cannot be substantially covered by Paragraph 2(b)."

5.406. We begin by analyzing the scope of the phrase "non-tariff measures governed by the provisions of instruments multilaterally negotiated under the auspices of the GATT" as it appears in Paragraph 2(b) of the *Enabling Clause*. This Paragraph provides, in relevant part:

> 2. The provisions of Paragraph 1 apply to the following:
>
>   . . .
>
>   (b) Differential and more favorable treatment with respect to the provisions of the General Agreement concerning non-tariff measures governed by the provisions of instruments multilaterally negotiated under the auspices of the GATT[.]

5.407. Paragraph 2(b) thus identifies a certain form of differential and more favorable treatment to which the authorization of Paragraph 1 of the *Enabling Clause* applies. In other words, a measure that a Member claims to be excepted from a finding of inconsistency with Article I of the "General Agreement" "must fit within" the meaning of Paragraph 2(b). To this effect, Paragraph 2(b) provides for the adoption of a limited category of differential and more favorable treatment, namely treatment that concerns "non-tariff measures governed by the provisions of instruments multilaterally negotiated under the auspices of the GATT [as an institution]." The text of Paragraph 2(b) does not, however, support a reading of that provision as extending to the adoption of differential and more favorable treatment concerning non-tariff measures governed by "provisions of the General Agreement" itself. Indeed, had it been so, the latter part of Paragraph 2(b) in referring to "provisions of instruments multilaterally negotiated under the auspices of the GATT" would be deprived of any meaning.

5.408. We find support for this reading from the contextual history surrounding the adoption of the *Enabling Clause*. . . . [T]he *Enabling Clause* was adopted in 1979 during the Tokyo Round of multilateral trade negotiations, which also witnessed the conclusion of a number of plurilateral agreements governing various non-tariff measures, *i.e.*, the Tokyo Round *Codes*. The Tokyo Round *Codes* were "negotiated under the auspices of the GATT [as an institution]." . . . [A] number of these plurilateral agreements sought to further the objectives of and/or build upon existing provisions of the GATT 1947, and contained provisions on S&D treatment for developing countries. The reference in Paragraph 2(b) to differential and more favorable treatment "with respect to the provisions of the General Agreement concerning non-tariff measures governed by the provisions of instruments multilaterally negotiated under the auspices of the GATT" was in relation to these plurilateral agreements that were negotiated under the auspices of the GATT, as an institution and furthered the objectives of and/or built upon existing provisions of the GATT 1947. Moreover, in using the phrase "provisions of instruments multilaterally negotiated under the auspices of the GATT," as opposed to "instruments multilaterally negotiated under the auspices of the GATT," Paragraph 2(b) referred to specific provisions of these plurilateral agreements, in particular, the S&D treatment provisions, and not the entire agreements themselves.

5.409. We find additional support from contemporaneous decisions adopted during the Tokyo Round of multilateral trade negotiations. In particular, we recall the *Decision* entitled "Action by the CONTRACTING PARTIES on the Multilateral Trade Negotiations," which recognized in Paragraph 2 thereof that "as a result of the Multilateral Trade Negotiations, a number of Agreements covering certain non-tariff measures . . . have been drawn up." We observe that Paragraph 1 of that *Decision* provided that the CONTRACTING PARTIES "reaffirm their intention to ensure the unity and consistency of the GATT system, and to this end they shall oversee the operation of the system as a whole and take action as appropriate." Paragraph 3, in particular, stated that "[t]he CONTRACTING PARTIES also note that existing rights and benefits under the GATT of contracting parties not being parties to these Agreements, including those derived from Article I, are not affected by these Agreements."

5.410. In other words, the GATT CONTRACTING PARTIES addressed the issue of MFN treatment arising out of Article I of the GATT 1947 by reaffirming "their intention to ensure the unity and consistency of the GATT system" and expressly confirming that the benefits of the Tokyo Round plurilateral agreements were to accrue to all the contracting parties to the GATT, even those that were not parties to the plurilateral agreements, insofar as the subject matter of those agreements were covered by Article I of the GATT 1947. Therefore, at the time of the conclusion of the Tokyo Round *Codes*, absent the *Enabling Clause*, a Contracting Party who was not a party to a Tokyo Round plurilateral agreement could have challenged a measure taken by a party to that plurilateral agreement pursuant to a S&D treatment provision thereof in favor of a developing country as being inconsistent with Article I of the GATT 1947.

5.411. The adoption of the *Enabling Clause*, particularly Paragraph 2(b), addressed this situation. Paragraph 2(b) provided an umbrella by excepting differential and more favorable treatment concerning non-tariff measures governed by the provisions of instruments multilaterally negotiated under the auspices of the GATT, *i.e.*, differential and more favorable treatment accorded pursuant to the S&D treatment provisions of the Tokyo Round *Codes*, from the purview of a challenge under Article I of the GATT 1947.

5.412. The foregoing considerations therefore suggest that the phrase "non-tariff measures governed by the provisions of instruments multilaterally negotiated under the auspices of the GATT" in Paragraph 2(b), at the time of the adoption of the *Enabling Clause*, concerned non-tariff measures taken pursuant to the S&D treatment provisions of the Tokyo Round *Codes* and not the provisions of the GATT 1947.

5.413. . . . [W]ith the entry into effect of the *WTO Agreement* [on 1 January 1995], the Tokyo Round *Codes* are no longer in force. The *Enabling Clause*, however, stands incorporated as an "integral part" of the GATT 1994. The Appellate Body considered in *EC—Tariff Preferences* [*i.e.*, the 2004 *EU GSP* case, excerpted above] that "Members reaffirmed the significance of the *Enabling Clause* . . . with [its] incorporation . . . into the GATT 1994." The Uruguay Round of multilateral trade negotiations culminated in the establishment of the WTO, following which GATT as an institution was replaced by the WTO. Article II:1 of the *WTO Agreement* expressly recognizes that "[t]he WTO shall provide the common institutional framework for the conduct of trade relations among its Members in matters related to the agreements and associated legal instruments included in the Annexes to [the WTO] Agreement." The *Enabling Clause* as an "integral part" of the GATT 1994 falls within the scope of Article II:1 of the *WTO Agreement*. Therefore, while at the time of its adoption, Paragraph 2(b) of the *Enabling Clause* speaks of "instruments multilaterally negotiated under the auspices of the GATT" as an institution, following the entry into force of the *WTO Agreement*, Paragraph 2(b) refers to "instruments multilaterally negotiated under the auspices of the [WTO]" as an institution. Paragraph 2(b) of the *Enabling Clause*, following the entry into force of the *WTO Agreement*, thus provides for the adoption of a limited category of differential and more favorable treatment, namely treatment that concerns non-tariff measures governed by provisions of instruments multilaterally negotiated under the auspices of the WTO. The GATT 1994, while an integral part of the *WTO Agreement*, was not negotiated under the auspices of the WTO as an institution.

5.414. These considerations, read in light of the text, context, and circumstances surrounding the adoption of the *Enabling Clause* and thereafter the establishment of the WTO, indicate that Paragraph 2(b) does not concern non-tariff measures governed by the provisions of the GATT 1994. Instead, Paragraph 2(b) speaks to non-tariff measures taken pursuant to S&D treatment provisions of "instruments multilaterally negotiated under the auspices of the [WTO]." Brazil's contention that Paragraph 2(b) applies to non-tariff measures taken pursuant to the provisions of the GATT 1994 incorporating the GATT 1947, in our view, calls for Paragraph 2(b) to be given a meaning that was not ascribed to it either at the time of its adoption or thereafter with the establishment of the WTO. We therefore uphold the Panel's finding . . . that "a non-tariff measure within the scope of Paragraph 2(b) must be governed by specific provisions on special and differential treatment, that are distinct from the provisions of the GATT 1994 incorporating the GATT 1947."

5.415. Turning to the Panel's application of Paragraph 2(b) of the *Enabling Clause*, we recall that the Panel found that the provisions of the GATT 1994 relied on by Brazil, namely Articles III:2 and III:4, "do not introduce any special and differential treatment for taxes in the form of non-tariff measures." We have considered above that Paragraph 2(b) of the *Enabling Clause* did not apply, at the time of its adoption, with respect to Articles III:2 and III:4 of the GATT 1947, and following the entry into force of the *WTO Agreement*, does not apply with respect to Articles III:2 and III:4 of the GATT 1994. Thus, subjecting like products of different WTO Members to different internal taxes inconsistently with Article I:1 of the GATT 1994 cannot be justified under Paragraph 2(b) of the *Enabling Clause*. We therefore uphold the Panel's finding . . . that the internal tax reductions under the INOVAR-AUTO program accorded to imported products from Argentina, Mexico, and Uruguay and found to be inconsistent under Article I:1 of the GATT 1994 are not justified under Paragraph 2(b) of the *Enabling Clause*.

- **Brazil's GATT Article I:1 MFN Violation and Failed *Enabling Clause* Paragraph 2(c) Defense Concerning RTA Preferences**

WTO Appellate Body Report,

Brazil—Certain Measures Concerning Taxation and Charges,
WT/DS472/AB/R, WT/DS497/AB/R (Adopted 11 January 2019)

5.5.3 Whether the Panel erred in its interpretation of Paragraph 2(c) of the ***Enabling Clause*** and in finding that the differential tax treatment under the INOVAR-AUTO program was not justified under that provision

5.416. We now turn to Paragraph 2(c) of the *Enabling Clause*. We recall that we have agreed with the Panel to the extent the Panel found that there is no genuine link or a rational connection between differential tax treatment under the INOVAR-AUTO program and the notified arrangements adopted under Paragraph 2(c). Consequently, we have upheld the Panel's finding that the differential and favorable treatment (*i.e.*, the differential tax treatment in the form of internal tax reductions accorded to some but not other Members) under the INOVAR-AUTO program was not notified as adopted under Paragraph 2(c), as required pursuant to paragraph 4(a) of the *Enabling Clause*. In this section, we review whether the Panel erred in finding that the differential tax treatment under the INOVAR-AUTO program was not substantively justified under Paragraph 2(c).

5.417. The Panel recalled that, to satisfy the notification requirement in Paragraph 4(a), any differential and more favorable treatment adopted under Paragraph 2(c) must have "a close and genuine link to an RTA sufficient to alert other WTO Members to the adoption of such differential and more favorable treatment pursuant to the *Enabling Clause*." The Panel considered that a "similar standard" applies with respect to the substantive justification under Paragraph 2(c) itself. Thus, the Panel found that, "[i]n order for any differential and more favorable treatment to be justified under Paragraph 2(c) of the *Enabling Clause*, there must exist a close and genuine link to a 'regional arrangement entered into amongst less-developed contracting parties.'" In this case, the Panel found that Brazil had not identified an RTA with a close and genuine link to the internal tax reductions at issue. The Panel stated that, while "Brazil has made assertions regarding the [1980] *Treaty of Montevideo* and the *ECAs*," Brazil has not pointed to a provision providing for tax preferences in those RTAs nor "demonstrated how the tax reductions at issue are related to those RTAs," and therefore how the relevant differential and more favorable treatment could be justified under Paragraph 2(c). The Panel therefore found that "Brazil has not met its burden of proof in respect of the substantive requirements of Paragraph 2(c)."

5.418. For these reasons, the Panel concluded that "the tax reductions accorded to imported products from Argentina, Mexico and Uruguay and found to be inconsistent under Article I:1 of the GATT 1994 are not justified under Paragraph 2(c) of the *Enabling Clause*."

5.419. On appeal, Brazil contends that the Panel's substantive evaluation of Paragraph 2(c) "is essentially indistinguishable from its evaluation of whether the notification was sufficient under Paragraph 4(a)." Brazil submits that the Panel rested its finding on its "flawed conclusion that because the [1980] *Treaty of Montevideo* and the provisions of the relevant *ECAs* do not expressly make reference to internal taxation, they did not have a genuine link with Paragraph 2(c)" and therefore "WTO Members could not have been expected to be informed that Brazil intended to accord internal tax reductions to motor vehicles from Argentina, Mexico and Uruguay." Brazil further submits that the Panel's finding that "Brazil has not demonstrated 'how the tax reductions at issue are related to [the] RTAs'" is "directly contradicted by the facts on the record." Brazil asserts that the 1980 *Treaty of Montevideo*, the relevant *ECAs*, and *LAIA* [the *Latin American Integration Association*, established by the *Montevideo Treaty*, and also known by the acronym "ALADI," after its Spanish and Portuguese names, *Asociación Latinoamericana de Integración* and *Associação Latino-Americana de Integração*, respectively; any Latin American country may join, and (as of December 2018) 13 of them have done so] have "an ample scope comprising internal tax reduction measures." Accordingly, Brazil requests the Appellate Body to reverse the Panel's conclusion that Brazil did not meet its burden of proof with respect to the substantive requirements of Paragraph 2(c), and to complete the analysis and find that "the differential tax treatment is justified under Paragraph 2(c) and complies with the requirements of Paragraph 3 of the *Enabling Clause*."

. . .

5.422. Paragraph 2 of the *Enabling Clause* provides, in relevant part:

The provisions of Paragraph 1 apply to the following:

. . .

(c) Regional or global arrangements entered into amongst developing country Members for the mutual reduction or elimination of tariffs and, in accordance with criteria or conditions which may be prescribed by the [WTO Members], for the mutual reduction or elimination of non-tariff measures, on products imported from one another[.]

5.423. Paragraph 2(c) excepts differential and more favorable treatment accorded pursuant to "[r]egional or global arrangements entered into amongst" developing country Members from a finding of inconsistency with Article I of the GATT 1994. Paragraph 2(c) limits the kind of differential and more favorable treatment to the: (i) mutual reduction or elimination of tariffs; and (ii) mutual reduction or elimination of non-tariff measures. In case of the latter, Paragraph 2(c) adds that the "mutual reduction or elimination of non-tariff measures" have to be "in accordance with criteria or conditions which may be prescribed" by the WTO Members. Paragraph 2(c) does not exclude the possibility that developing country Members that are parties to regional or global arrangements may adopt such instruments that they may deem appropriate for the mutual reduction or elimination of tariffs and non-tariff measures. However, it suffices that the instrument adopted that way, to be justified under Paragraph 2(c) for the differential and more favorable treatment it accords, has a "genuine" link or a rational connection with the regional or global arrangement adopted and notified to the WTO. Therefore, we disagree with the Panel to the extent it considered that, in order for any differential and more favorable treatment to be justified under Paragraph 2(c), there must exist *both* a "close" and "genuine" link to a "regional arrangement entered into amongst" developing country Members.

5.424. . . . Brazil submits that the Panel rested its finding on its "flawed conclusion that because the [1980] *Treaty of Montevideo* and the provisions of the relevant *ECAs* do not expressly make reference to internal taxation, they did not have a genuine link with Paragraph 2(c)." . . . Brazil mischaracterizes the Panel's finding. The Panel did not find, as Brazil contends, that the 1980 *Treaty of Montevideo* and the relevant *ECAs* do not bear a genuine link with the requirements of Paragraph 2(c). Instead, the Panel found that "Brazil has not demonstrated how *the relevant tax reductions* [under the INOVAR-AUTO program] found to be inconsistent under Article I:1 of the GATT 1994 are *related* to the RTA that Brazil has notified to the WTO (the *Treaty of Montevideo*) or the *ECAs* allegedly implementing that RTA." Consequently, the Panel was not satisfied "how the relevant differential and more favorable treatment could be justified under Paragraph 2(c)." In reaching this conclusion, the Panel examined the provisions of the 1980 *Treaty of Montevideo* and found that "none of the provisions cited to in the [1980] *Treaty of Montevideo*" had any relation "in and of themselves" to the differential tax treatment under the INOVAR-AUTO program (in the form of internal tax reductions accorded to some but not other Members) found to be inconsistent with Article I:1 of the GATT 1994. Turning to the relevant *ECAs* referred to in Articles 21 and 22(I) of Decree 7,819/2012, the Panel noted that it "could not discern any . . . relationship" that would attest to "the fundamental premise of Brazil's argument, namely that the INOVAR-AUTO program is implementing the objectives of the ECAs."

5.425. The Panel was required to undertake this analytical exercise given that, as Brazil explains on appeal, it contended before the Panel that "the tax treatment accorded within the framework of [the] INOVAR-AUTO [program] . . . is inscribed in the context of the implementation process of the . . . [*ECAs*] negotiated . . . under the umbrella of the 1980 *Treaty of Montevideo*." Consequently, as Brazil further explains, the differential tax treatment was not only justified under Paragraph 2(c)1140 but also "did not require additional notification."

5.426. We have considered above the question whether or not the differential tax treatment under the INOVAR-AUTO program was notified pursuant to Paragraph 4(a) of the *Enabling Clause* as having been adopted under Paragraph 2(c) by virtue of the notification of the 1980 *Treaty of Montevideo* and the relevant *ECAs* under Paragraph 2(c). In so doing, we have noted that Articles 21 and 22(I) of Decree 7,819/2012 do not refer to the 1980 *Treaty of Montevideo* and that the 1980 *Treaty of Montevideo* does not itself specify any rules regarding internal tax reductions. We have also considered that, while Articles 21 and 22(I) of Decree 7,819/2012 refer to the relevant *ECAs*, those *ECAs* provide for the adoption of tariff preferences in the automotive sector and do not refer to internal taxation. Accordingly, in the absence of a genuine link between the differential tax treatment under the INOVAR-AUTO program, on the one hand, and the 1980 *Treaty of Montevideo* and the relevant *ECAs*, on the other hand, we have agreed with the Panel's finding that "Brazil has not demonstrated how the . . . tax reductions found to be inconsistent under Article I:1 of the GATT 1994 are related to the RTA that Brazil has notified to the WTO (the [1980] *Treaty of Montevideo*) or the *ECAs* allegedly implementing that RTA." Therefore, to the extent that the Panel relied on its earlier analysis concerning whether or not the INOVAR-AUTO program, which accords the differential and more favorable treatment (*i.e.*, the differential tax treatment in the form of internal tax reductions accorded to some but not other Members), had a genuine link to "the arrangement notified to the WTO" in determining if the differential and more favorable tax treatment was substantively justified under Paragraph 2(c), we find no error in the Panel's approach. The considerations outlined by the Panel in that part of its analysis were bound to have a substantial bearing on whether or not the differential and more favorable treatment under the INOVAR-AUTO program was substantively justified under Paragraph 2(c), given the manner in which Brazil framed its arguments before the Panel. Indeed, if there is no genuine link between the measure at issue according the differential and more favorable treatment and the arrangements notified to the WTO, it is difficult to see how the measure at issue could be substantively justified under paragraph 2(c).

5.427. . . . [W]e <u>uphold</u> the Panel's finding . . . to the extent that the Panel found that Brazil has not identified any arrangement with a genuine link to the differential tax treatment envisaged under the INOVAR-AUTO program. [Emphasis original.] Consequently, we also <u>uphold</u> the Panel's finding . . . that the internal tax reductions accorded under the INOVAR-AUTO program to imported products from Argentina, Mexico, and Uruguay and found to be inconsistent under Article I:1 of the GATT 1994 are not justified under Paragraph 2(c) of the *Enabling Clause*. [Emphasis original.]

5.5.4 Conclusion with respect to the *Enabling Clause*

. . .

5.432. . . . [P]aragraph 2(b) provides for the granting of "[d]ifferential and more favorable treatment with respect to the provisions of the General Agreement concerning non-tariff measures governed by the provisions of instruments multilaterally negotiated under the auspices of the GATT." Paragraph 2(b) provides for the adoption of a limited category of differential and more favorable treatment, namely treatment that concerns "non-tariff measures governed by the provisions of instruments multilaterally negotiated under the auspices of the GATT" as an institution. The phrase "non-tariff measures governed by the provisions of instruments multilaterally negotiated under the auspices of the GATT," at the time of the adoption of the *Enabling Clause*, concerned non-tariff measures taken pursuant to the S&D treatment provisions of the Tokyo Round *Codes*, and not the provisions of the GATT 1947. Following the entry into force of the *WTO Agreement*, Paragraph 2(b) of the *Enabling Clause* provides for the adoption of a limited category of differential and more favorable treatment, namely treatment that concerns non-tariff measures governed by the provisions of instruments multilaterally negotiated under the auspices of the WTO. The GATT 1994, while an integral part of the *WTO Agreement*, was not negotiated under the auspices of the WTO. These considerations read in light of the text, context, and circumstances surrounding the adoption of the *Enabling Clause* and thereafter the establishment of the WTO indicates that Paragraph 2(b) does not concern non-tariff measures governed by the provisions of the GATT 1994. Instead, Paragraph 2(b) speaks to non-tariff measures taken pursuant to S&D treatment provisions of "instruments multilaterally negotiated under the auspices of the [WTO]."

5.433. We therefore <u>uphold</u> the Panel's finding . . . that "a non-tariff measure within the scope of Paragraph 2(b) must be governed by specific provisions on special and differential treatment, that are distinct from the provisions of the GATT 1994 incorporating the GATT 1947." [Emphasis original.] We also <u>uphold</u> the Panel's findings . . . that the tax reductions accorded under the INOVAR-AUTO program to imported products from Argentina, Mexico, and Uruguay and found to be inconsistent under Article I:1 of the GATT 1994 are not justified under Paragraph 2(b) of the *Enabling Clause*. [Emphasis original.]

5.434. . . . [P]aragraph 2(c) excepts differential and more favorable treatment accorded pursuant to "[r]egional or global arrangements entered into amongst" developing country Members from a finding of inconsistency with Article I of the GATT 1994. Paragraph 2(c) does not exclude the possibility that developing country Members that are parties to regional or global arrangements may adopt such instruments that they may deem appropriate for the mutual reduction or elimination of tariffs and non-tariff measures. However, it suffices that the instrument adopted that way, to be justified under Paragraph 2(c) for the differential and more favorable treatment it accords, has a "genuine" link or a rational connection with the regional or global arrangement adopted and notified to the WTO.

5.435. . . . [T]he Panel did not find, as Brazil contends, that the 1980 *Treaty of Montevideo* and the relevant *ECAs* do not bear a genuine link with the requirements of Paragraph 2(c). Instead, the Panel found that Brazil has not demonstrated how the internal tax reductions under the INOVAR-AUTO program found to be inconsistent under Article I:1 of the GATT 1994 are related to the RTA (the 1980 *Treaty of Montevideo*) that Brazil has notified to the WTO or the *ECAs* allegedly implementing that RTA. Consequently, the Panel was not satisfied how the relevant differential and more favorable treatment under the INOVAR-AUTO program could be justified under Paragraph 2(c). Therefore, to the extent that the Panel relied on its earlier analysis concerning whether or not the INOVAR-AUTO program, according the differential and more favorable treatment (*i.e.*, the differential tax treatment in the form of internal tax reductions accorded to some but not other Members), had a genuine link to "the arrangement notified to the WTO" in determining if the differential and more favorable treatment was substantively justified under paragraph 2(c), we find no error in the Panel's approach. Indeed, if there is no genuine link between the measure at issue according the differential and more favorable treatment and the arrangements notified to the WTO, we find it difficult to see how the measure at issue could be substantively justified under Paragraph 2(c).

5.436. We therefore <u>uphold</u> the Panel's finding . . . to the extent that the Panel found that Brazil has not identified any arrangement with a genuine link to the differential tax treatment envisaged under the INOVAR-AUTO program. [Emphasis original.] Consequently, we also <u>uphold</u> the Panel's findings . . . that the tax reductions accorded under the INOVAR-AUTO program to imported products from Argentina, Mexico, and Uruguay and found to be inconsistent under Article I:1 of the GATT 1994 are not justified under Paragraph 2(c) of the *Enabling Clause*. [Emphasis original.]

Chapter 21

Special Help for Africa[1]

<hr>

I. Background on *AGOA*

On 18 May 2000, Congress passed the *"Trade and Development Act of 2000."*[2] Signed by President Bill Clinton (1946–, President, 1993–2001) on that date, the legislation took effect on 1 October 2000. Title I is the *"African Growth and Opportunity Act,"* or *"AGOA."*[3] The function of *AGOA* is to provide preferential trade treatment for certain products originating in eligible SSACs for a limited period. But, the protectionist devil is in the details.

Thanks to *AGOA*, exports from SSACs that qualify as Beneficiaries qualify for DFQF treatment. That treatment extends to 97.5% of all tariff lines in the HTSUS, meaning just 316 out of 10,700 lines are dutiable (as of August 2014). Eligible products and SSACs include cashews and cocoa from Ghana, petrochemicals from Angola, and textiles from Mauritius. In that respect, *AGOA* is more generous than any other American preference scheme for poor countries.

Yet, *AGOA* is anything but an unconditional grant of assistance for Africa. The devilish statutory details reveal the limits of American generosity. *AGOA* is not social justice in action, or put metaphorically, not an International Trade Law expression of the Parable of the Good Samaritan. Consider the positive fact that over 6,000 products (as of December 2018) are eligible for DFQF treatment under *AGOA*.[4] The flip side is that about 4,000 are not, given that the HTSUS lists about 10,000 product lines. So, for example, several farm and fisheries products of keen export interest to SSACs, like groundnuts, sugar, tobacco, and tuna, are subject to TRQs with low in-quota limits and high tariffs on above-quota shipments.

Moreover, at any time, an SSAC can lose its status as a Beneficiary, or a product it ships can be stricken from the roster of eligible merchandise, to suit U.S.

<hr>

1. Documents References:
   (1) *Havana (ITO) Charter* Articles 1, 8–15, 24, 55–70 1–12
   (2) GATT Preamble and Articles XXXVI–XXXVIII
   (3) Tokyo Round *Enabling Clause*
   (4) *WTO Agreement* Preamble
2. Public Law 106-200, 114 Stat. 251.
3. *See* 19 U.S.C. §§3701–3741, with the provisions on trade policy and SSAC benefits in §§3701–3724.
4. *See* Prinesha Naidoo, *U.S. in Talks for First Free-Trade Deal in Sub-Saharan Africa*, 35 International Trade Reporter (BNA) (13 December 2018).

interests. For instance, in June 2017, the USTR investigated the status of Rwanda, Tanzania, and Uganda. (The USTR agreed not to investigate Kenya, after Kenya agreed not to forbid importation of used clothing and reversed its tariff hikes on that merchandise.) Their sin was to ban imports of, or raise tariffs on, used clothing and footwear from the U.S. under a March 2016 EAC decision. They did so to protect their local garment industries, which they hoped would help elevate them to middle-income countries. Local producers could not compete with cheap second-hand clothes imports from America and Europe. An American lobbying group, Secondary Materials and Recycled Textiles Association (SMART), petitioned the USTR for it to conduct an Out-of-Cycle Review of those countries. SMART argued the ban imposed significant economic hardship on the U.S. used clothing industry, and said 40,000 American jobs were jeopardized by that decision, adversely affecting charitable organizations (*e.g.*, Goodwill and Saint Vincent de Paul) that rely on selling donated used clothing. Yet whether the significance of that hardship had to be weighed against the sufferings of those three countries:

> Representatives of the African countries under review said that their new policies on used clothing did not amount to a ban but rather a phase out of used clothing that will allow domestic textile manufacturing to increase and improve quality of life. The phase out did not target the U.S. and remained in line with *AGOA* obligations by aiming to reduce poverty, witnesses at the hearing said.
>
> Uganda Minister of Trade, Industry, and Cooperatives Amelia Kyambadde said during the hearing that secondhand clothing raised sanitary concerns and kept individuals impoverished by necessitating the frequent purchasing of clothes because of used clothing's shorter lifespan and decreased quality.
>
> "If we're talking about poor people, we're actually impoverishing them with these second-hand clothes," Kyambadde said.[5]

Thus, the questions posed above seem to answer themselves. Yet, as a legal matter under *AGOA*, are those questions relevant?

As another example, in July 2018, the U.S. suspended the eligibility of Rwanda for DFQF treatment of T&A merchandise under *AGOA*. The U.S. said Rwanda failed to eliminate duties on a sufficient number of American exports to that country.[6] Said the USTR:

> When Congress first passed *AGOA* in 2000, it imposed certain eligibility criteria to encourage recipient countries to adopt free market-oriented

---

5. *Quoted in* Andrew Wallender, *Hand-Me-Down Clothing Dispute Prompts Pushback*, 34 International Trade Reporter (BNA) 29 (20 July 2017).

6. *See* Office of the United States Trade Representative, *President Donald J. Trump Upholds AGOA Trade Preference Eligibility Criteria with Rwanda*, 30 July 2018, https://ustr.gov/about-us/policy-offices/press-office/press-releases/2018/july/president-donald-j-trump-upholds-agoa. [Hereinafter, July 2018 USTR Rwanda Suspension Notice.]

development models and to ensure fair market access for United States firms. The *AGOA* eligibility requirements include: "making continual progress toward establishing . . . a market-based economy . . . [and] the elimination of barriers to United States trade and investment." 19 U.S.C. 3703(1)(A), (C). The . . . USTR is charged with enforcing *AGOA's* requirements.

An *AGOA* issue relating to new barriers to United States trade and investment first arose in 2015 when the East African Community (EAC) established a plan to ban imports of used clothing and footwear. The USTR's engagement on this issue intensified in 2016 when the EAC announced it would phase in the ban by 2019. Thereafter, three EAC *AGOA* beneficiaries— Kenya, Tanzania, and Uganda—worked with the United States and took actions to revise their policies. As a result, they continue to receive full benefits under *AGOA*. Unfortunately, Rwanda has insisted on keeping in place a policy that has raised tariffs on imports of used apparel and footwear by more than one thousand percent, effectively banning imports of these products.

United States efforts over the past two years to address this issue with the Government of Rwanda have been unsuccessful. As a result, on March 29, 2018, the President determined that Rwanda was not making sufficient progress toward the elimination of barriers to United States trade and investment and was, therefore, out of compliance with *AGOA's* eligibility requirements. The President informed the Government of Rwanda of his decision in March, giving Rwanda an additional 60 days to engage with the United States to resolve this problem before the suspension of its apparel benefits under *AGOA*. Rwanda has, however, continued to insist on retaining its tariffs. The President, therefore, has decided to suspend Rwanda's duty-free access to the United States for apparel products until Rwanda comes back into compliance with *AGOA's* eligibility requirements.

The President believes suspension of *AGOA's* benefits, instead of termination of Rwanda's status as an *AGOA* beneficiary, is the appropriate remedy in this instance. The Administration supports continued engagement with the aim of restoring market access for used apparel and bringing Rwanda into compliance with *AGOA's* eligibility requirements. The President can reinstate full *AGOA* benefits for Rwanda once he has determined that Rwanda is meeting the eligibility criteria laid out by Congress.[7]

The suspension followed from the same SMART OCR petition.

Conversely, the extent to which an SSAC can enjoy the full benefits of *AGOA* depends on itself: however generous a giver America may be, not all recipients can absorb that generosity, *i.e.*, in economic terms, there are supply-side constraints. Does the SSAC suffer from decrepit infrastructure, especially in energy and

---

7. July 2018 USTR Rwanda Suspension Notice.

transportation, thus adding to the cost of import-export transactions? Does the SSAC lack a robust supply of skilled, productive, competitive labor, thus inhibiting the establishment and operation of quality export operations? Does the SSAC impose burdensome customs procedures, thereby impeding its integration into its regional, must less the world, trading system? Does the merchandise the SSAC seeks to export meet high SPS and TBT standards that developed countries impose?

As intimated, the President must designate an SSAC as eligible for *AGOA* duty-free benefits, and the article of merchandise must be eligible for such benefits. There are eligibility requirements for both designations. Neither is automatic.

For instance, with respect to the first designation, in December 2012, President Barack H. Obama (1961–, President, 2009–2017) designated South Sudan (which became independent in July 2012) as an eligible country. But, he terminated the *AGOA* beneficiary status of Guinea-Bissau and Mali, because they failed to make continual progress to satisfy *AGOA* criteria. Likewise, in November 2015, he terminated that status for Burundi. Home to 6% of the world's nickel reserves, Burundi did not show good governance: violence erupted after its President (Pierre Nkurunziza (1963–, President, 2005–)) declared in April he wanted to be re-elected for a third term, notwithstanding a July 2005 peace agreement to the contrary, plus criticisms elections were neither free nor fair.

As regards the second designation, both the USTR and ITC must agree an article at issue is not import-sensitive. Essentially, that means if DFQF treatment for exports of that article from a Beneficiary SSAC would cause economic or political problems in the U.S., because of domestic production of a like product, then the article will not be given a preference.

To be sure, the GSP and *AGOA* are not the only scheme of trade preferences the U.S. offers to developing countries and LDCs. In 1983, the U.S. enacted the *Caribbean Basin Economic Recovery Act*, commonly known as the "*CBI*."[8] The *CBI* provides zero- or low-duty treatment to certain merchandise originating in a beneficiary country. But, the GSP provides the broadest array of benefits (in terms of beneficiary countries and commodities), and *AGOA* concerns the poorest of the poor countries. So, they merit special attention.

AGOA details concern the words "certain," "originating," "eligible," and "limited." The legislation authorizes the President to grant unilateral preferential trade benefits to an SSAC, but only if it pursues economic and political reform, and satisfies other criteria, only with respect to its exports that satisfy an array of technical requirements, and only up through a sunset date. Thus, certain — but not all — T&A merchandise from a SSAC may receive duty-free, quota-free treatment from the U.S. (In addition, eligible SSACs may receive enhanced GSP benefits, such as the waiver of CNLs.)

---

8. *See* 19 U.S.C. §§ 2702–2707.

II. Devilishly Protectionist Details

- **Specified Processes in T&A Production**

A key set of requirements a Beneficiary SSAC must satisfy under AGOA to receive duty-free treatment from the U.S. on T&A shipments are a dizzying array of preferential ROOs of origin. (There are four additional sets of requirements, concerning documentation, visas, "findings and trimmings," and "interlinings." What are the details of, and justifications for, each of these requirements?) There is little doubt the rationale for such rules is protection of T&A interests in the U.S. producing articles that are like or directly competitive with merchandise from a T&A Beneficiary.

To understand the different *AGOA* categories of rules of origin for apparel articles, it is important to recall the six basic steps in making T&A. That is because the *AGOA* T&A ROOs are specified process rules, not value added rules. In other words, in order for the finished merchandise to qualify for preferential treatment, these rules demand that particular production activity occur in a T&A Beneficiary:

Step 1:
Growing cotton or other fiber as raw materials, or manufacturing synthetic fibers, such as nylon or rayon

A rule of origin demanding all production activity from this Step onward occur in one location is called a "*Fiber Forward Rule.*" This kind of Rule is the most restrictive of all T&A specified process requirements. All economic activity must occur in one country, otherwise the finished article is considered not to originate in that country and, therefore, is disqualified from preferential treatment. In turn, the more restrictive a preferential ROO, the more protectionist it is. By making it difficult to obtain DFQF treatment, a tighter rule confers greater protection on domestic (*e.g.*, American) producers of like merchandise.

In theory, a "Seed Forward" or "Fertilizer Forward" Rule could be devised to afford even greater protection than a Fiber Forward Rule. The idea would be to require the seeds used to plant cotton (or other fiber), or the fertilizer used to help the crop grow, to originate in the same country in which all further activity occurs. Failure would mean the finished article would not qualify as originating in that country, hence DFQF treatment would be devised. In practice such a Rule does not exist.

Step 2:
Spinning yarn from fiber

A requirement that all activity from this Step onward occur in a particular country is a "*Yarn Forward Rule.*" A Yarn Forward Rule is the second most restrictive — and thereby protectionist — type of specified process requirement. In effect, it is used in *AGOA*, for instance, in the 1st or 2nd of the Preference (*i.e.*, Preferential Treatment) Categories, in combination with Assembly Rules (discussed below).

Step 3:
Making fabric (also called cloth) from yarn

A mandate that all activity from this Step onward occur in a particular country is a *"Fabric Forward Rule."* A cursory glance at the 1st, 2nd, 3rd, 7th, and 8th *AGOA* Preferential Treatment Categories suggests they rely (to varying degrees) on Fabric Forward Rules. However, in fact the categories are constructed in a protectionist manner, because of requirements about yarn.

A garment that is knit does not technically go through the fabric stage. The original *AGOA* legislation did not specify knit-to-shape garments as eligible for duty-free treatment, and the CBP issued draft regulations stipulating they were ineligible. *AGOA II* contained a "knit-to-shape amendment" clarifying knit-to-shape apparel is eligible.

Step 4:
Cutting fabric into pieces (or knitting to shape)

A rule calling for all activity from this Step onward to occur in a particular country is called *"Cutting Forward."* Generally, a Cutting Forward origin rule is more liberal than Fiber, Yarn, or Fabric Forward Rules, because it allows activity in the early stages of the chain of production to occur in countries other than the potential beneficiary of preferential treatment. The 2nd and 6th *AGOA* Preference Categories use a variant of a Cutting Forward Rule. However (as discussed below), in *AGOA*, the variants are protectionist because of requirements concerning yarn. The 4th *AGOA* Preference Category also uses a Cutting Forward Rule, albeit for knitting to shape sweaters.

Depending on the garment, cutting may occur in more than one country— so-called "hybrid cutting." The original *AGOA* legislation, did not specify that apparel made in a hybrid cutting process was eligible for duty-free treatment. The CBP issued draft regulations that would have denied eligibility. *AGOA II* contained amendments allowing for preferential treatment for apparel cut both in the U.S. a Beneficiary SSAC.

Step 5:
Sewing pieces of cut fabric together

An obligation that all activity from this Step onward to occur in a particular country is a *"Sewing Forward Rule."* This kind of rule is relatively liberal, *i.e.*, not as protectionist as the previous rules, as it permits all previous Steps to occur in other countries. Sometimes, cutting and sewing are considered parts of the same operation, and the attendant rule is "Cutting and Sewing Forward."

A variation of the Sewing Forward Rule exists in *AGOA*, namely, in the 2nd and 6th Preference Categories. However, the variations are protectionist. In the 2nd Preferential Category, the sewing thread must come from the U.S., and in the 6th Category, non-American fabric or yarn may be used only if it is in short supply in the U.S.

Step 6:
Assembling pieces into a finished article (i.e., final assembly)

A rule calling only for assembly to occur in a particular country—an *"Assembly Rule"*—is the most liberal of all specified process rules, in that it requires the least amount of economic activity to occur in the country seeking preferential treatment. The 4th *AGOA* Preference Category essentially fits this type. Ostensibly, the 1st and 3rd Categories are Assembly Rules. However (as explained below), strictures embedded in these categories concerning where fabric is from and cutting occurs render them considerably more restrictive than a simple Assembly Rule.

Overall, the *AGOA* preference categories are not pure in the sense of relying entirely on one kind of process forward occurring in a T&A Beneficiary. Rather, the categories are hybrids, blending different specified process rules.

- **Eight *AGOA* Preferential ROOs**

There are eight groupings of apparel articles potentially eligible for DFQF treatment under *AGOA*.[9] (The italicized titles below are unofficial. They are mnemonic aids to summarize the gist of the Category.) Apparel from a T&A producer/exporter in a Beneficiary SSAC must fit within a Category if, upon entry into the U.S., its apparel exports are to benefit from DFQF treatment. Examining each Category reveals how the devil operates, and why the rules are properly characterized—from the perspective of T&A Beneficiary SSACs—as a "devil."

Briefly, of the 8 Preferential Treatment Categories, the first 4 of them, and the 8th one, call for some activity to occur in a T&A Beneficiary using inputs from the U.S. (or, in the 3rd and 7th Category, from a Beneficiary). The 6th Category obviates the need for American inputs only if they are in short supply. The 5th and 7th Categories, dealing respectively with sweaters and cultural products, are not as commercially important as the other categories. While the rules of origin are highly technical, the theme emerging from them is evident enough: generosity. Query how generous the U.S. is toward Sub-Saharan Africa. Consider also whether generosity should matter in U.S. trade policy, and if so, why.

In the details of the origin rules of the 1st, 2nd, 3rd, 4th, 6th, and 8th *AGOA* Preference Categories, lives (indeed, thrives) the protectionist devil—and, in turn, is manifest America's generosity, or lack thereof, toward T&A Beneficiaries. A donor shows most poignantly its generous spirit in areas in which it faces the largest potential sacrifice, as does America in these categories. Generosity in a preferential trading program does not demand economic martyrdom. But, generosity is greater when it is not convenient or easy for a donor, and when it does not put undue strictures on a beneficiary to suit the commercial self-interest of the donor. Yet, again, the 1st, 2nd, 3rd, 4th and 6th Categories bear the most restrictive origin rules. Might the explanation lie in the prospect U.S. producers are considerably less

---

9. *See* 19 U.S.C. § 3721(b)(1)-(6).

likely to produce merchandise that is like or directly competitive with articles in the 5th and 7th Categories?

After all, as the examination below reveals, at least *prima facie*, the 5th Category appears drafted in a way to exclude sweaters made in a T&A Beneficiary that could substitute for American-made sweaters. Possibly, a rule about using American cashmere or wool whose diameter is 21.5 microns or less does not exist in *AGOA*, because it would be unnecessary, as few (if any) such inputs are made in the U.S. As for the 7th Category, while there no doubt are American-made hand-loomed, hand-made, or folklore articles, and ethnic printed fabrics, such production is of small volume and not substitutable with African-made handicraft items. In contrast, precisely where American producers are most likely to be challenged—in the 1st, 2nd, 3rd, 4th, 6th, and 8th Categories, which have the broadest potential array of merchandise—the origin rules are crafted to confer not generosity toward African producer/exporters, but protection for American producers of like or directly competitive products.

It is important to appreciate the relevance of the 1st, 2nd, 3rd, 4th, and 6th Categories. Their relevance is evident in terms of commercial potential. These categories may contain the broadest array of T&A merchandise. By definition, the 5th Category is limited not just to sweaters, but specifically to sweaters of a certain weight of cashmere, or of a certain weight and diameter of wool. By definition, the 7th Category is restricted to handicraft type articles. In contrast, the 1st, 2nd, 3rd, 4th, and 6th Categories may contain articles as diverse as sleepwear for babies and neckties for men. Yet, it is in the categories of greatest potential commercial significance where the ROOs are tightest.

First Preference Category:
U.S. Yarn Forward with Beneficiary Assembly

Essentially, this Category is for apparel articles sewn together in a T&A Beneficiary SSAC using American fabric, which is from American yarn.[10] Specifically, to qualify for duty-free treatment under this Category, an article must meet five requirements:

(1) The article must be sewn (or otherwise assembled) wholly in a T&A Beneficiary (or in multiple such Beneficiaries).

(2) The article must be made from fabric (cloth) wholly formed in the U.S. (or, if knit, must be from components knit-to-shape in the U.S.). (The article could be made from both fabric and knit-to-shape components.)

(3) The article must be wholly cut in the U.S. (or, if knit, the components knit-to-shape in the U.S.).

(4) The fabric itself must be from yarns wholly formed in the U.S. (or, if knit, the components must be from yarns wholly formed in the U.S.).

---

10. *See* 19 U.S.C. § 3721(b)(1); HTSUS Chapter 98, U.S. Note 7(a) at 98-II-3.

(5) Upon entry, the apparel must be classified in either 1 of 2 categories in the HTSUS. The 1st Category is Sub-Heading 9802.00.80. This Sub-Heading appears in Chapter 98, which consists of special classifications for articles exported and returned, having been advanced or improved abroad. Items covered by this Chapter may enter the U.S. duty-free, or partially duty-free, under certain circumstances. These circumstances include re-importation of an article that was exported from the U.S. (without improvement in the condition of the article), articles subject to a personal exemption brought back to the U.S. by a citizen or permanent resident who traveled overseas, government importations, goods used for religious, educational, or scientific institutions, samples, and articles admitted under bond. As for Sub-Heading 9802.00.80, it covers articles exported from and returned to the U.S., having been advanced or improved abroad. The 2nd Category is Chapter 61, which covers "Articles of Apparel and Clothing Accessories, Knitted or Crocheted," and Chapter 62, which covers "Articles of Apparel and Clothing Accessories, Not Knitted or Crocheted." The 2nd Category applies only to apparel that would have been classified in the 1st Category, but for the fact they were embroidered, or subjected to a particular process. The processes include acid washing, enzyme washing, or stone washing, perma-pressing, oven baking, bleaching, garment dyeing, and screen printing.[11]

This Category also includes apparel articles made from fabrics that are not from yarns, as long as the fabrics are wholly formed and cut in the U.S., and the fabrics are classified under Heading 5602 or 5603 of the HTSUS. Chapter 56 of the HTSUS deals with T&A articles from "wadding," "felt," "non-wovens," and "special yarns." Heading 5602 contains "felt articles" ("whether or not impregnated, coated, covered, or laminated"). Heading 5603 consists of non-woven articles ("whether or not impregnated, coated, covered, or laminated").

An understandable immediate reaction to this Category is to ask why the U.S. insists on a T&A Beneficiary SSAC using American fabric that itself is made of American yarn? One answer is some Beneficiaries do not have the spinning and weaving capacity to produce enough fabric to supply their domestic apparel industry. This scenario is true, for instance, in Bangladesh (in which T&A exports accounted in 2001 for 85.8% of merchandise exports, the highest figure in the world). But, even if the same supply constraint exists in a Beneficiary SSAC, it does not follow that *AGOA* must mandate use of American fabric and yarn. Indeed, as Oxfam International points out:

> Rich countries try to justify these heavy requirements [preferential rules of origin for T&A] by saying that they encourage poor countries to develop textile production to supply their clothing sector. However, historical experience and contemporary production patterns undermine this argument.

---

11. *See* HTSUS Chapter 98, Sub-Heading 9819.11.03 at 98-XIX-4 (concerning these articles).

No small, poor country with a significant clothing industry has ever succeeded in developing a matching supply-capacity in textiles.[12]

Why not, then, let apparel producers in the Beneficiary choose input sources based on market considerations like price and quality? Does this query suggest there are deep economic and social justice concerns about the ROO?

Second Preference Category:
U.S. Yarn-Forward with Beneficiary Cutting and Sewing Forward Using American Thread

Essentially, this Category is for apparel articles cut in a T&A Beneficiary SSAC from American-made fabric. The fabric must be made of American yarn, and then sewn together in the Beneficiary with American thread.[13] Specifically, to qualify for duty-free treatment under this Category, an article must satisfy five requirements.

(1) The article must be sewn (or otherwise assembled) entirely in a T&A Beneficiary SSAC (or in multiple such Beneficiaries).

(2) The article must be made from fabric (cloth) wholly formed in the U.S. (or, if knit, must be from components knit-to-shape in the U.S.). (The article could be made from both fabric and knit-to-shape components.)

(3) The fabric itself must be from yarns wholly formed in the U.S. (or, if knit, the components must be from yarns wholly formed in the U.S.).

(4) The fabric must be cut in the T&A Beneficiary SSAC (or in multiple such Beneficiaries).

(5) After cutting, the article must be sewn (or otherwise assembled) using sewing thread from the U.S.

The 2nd Preference Category also includes apparel articles made from fabrics that are not from yarns, as long as the fabrics are wholly formed (but not cut) in the U.S., and the fabrics are classified under Heading 5602 or 5603 of the HTSUS (explained above).

The first three requirements are the same as in the 1st Preference Category. But, the latter two requirements distinguish the categories. In brief, the 2nd Preference Category is a cutting forward rule, whereas the 1st Category is an Assembly (Sewing) Forward Rule.

In both categories, American fabric made of American yarn must be imported into the T&A Beneficiary SSAC. In the 1st Preference Category, the items imported already are cut in the U.S. They can be sewn with or without U.S. thread, but this flexibility comes at a cost: they must satisfy enter into particular HTSUS

---

12. Oxfam International, *Stitched Up: How Rich-Country Protectionism in Textiles and Clothing Trade Prevents Poverty Alleviation* 19 (Oxfam Briefing Paper 60, March 2004) [Hereinafter, Oxfam Briefing Paper.]

13. *See* 19 U.S.C. § 3721(b)(2); HTSUS Chapter 98, Sub-Heading 9819.11.06 at 98-XIX-4.

classifications. In the 2nd Preference Category, fabric is imported, and cutting goes on in the T&A Beneficiary SSAC. That is advantageous to the Beneficiary, as more goes on there than sewing. But, when it is time to sew the cut fabric pieces, the thread must be American. The trade-off for using U.S. thread is no HTSUS classification is mandated for the finished article.

Third Preference Category:
Regional or Other Fabric

The first two Preference Categories mandate use of American fabric, which in turn is made of American yarn. The 3rd Category affords flexibility on the origin of the fabric and yarn, essentially providing duty-free treatment for apparel articles from regional fabric and yarn, but subject to quantitative limits, and only for a limited period.[14] In particular, to qualify, an apparel article must satisfy three requirements:

(1) The article must be assembled wholly in a T&A Beneficiary SSAC (or multiple such Beneficiaries).

(2) The article must be made of fabric (cloth) wholly formed in a T&A Beneficiary SSAC (or multiple such Beneficiaries). The T&A Beneficiary in which assembly occurs need not be the same one as the Beneficiary in which fabric is made.

(3) The fabric (cloth) must be from yarn originating either in the U.S. or a T&A Beneficiary SSAC (or multiple such Beneficiaries, or a former Beneficiary, *i.e.*, one that is party to an FTA with the U.S.). If the fabric originates in a T&A Beneficiary, then it need not be the same Beneficiary as the one in which the yarn originates.

This Preference Category also is called "Apparel assembled from regional and other fabric." A more accurate rubric would be "U.S. Yarn Forward or Beneficiary Yarn Forward with Beneficiary Fabric Forward." With the words "regional" and "other fabric," this appellation obfuscates the requirement that not all other fabric qualifies.

"Regional" refers only to fabric from yarn spun in a T&A Beneficiary SSAC, and "other" is restricted to fabric from American yarn. For example, men's dress shirts assembled in Kenya from cotton cloth derived from cotton yarn spun either in the same or another Beneficiary, or in the U.S., would qualify. The shirts would not qualify if the cotton cloth came from Egypt or Pakistan, or if the cloth came from a Beneficiary or the U.S., but the yarn came from Egypt or Pakistan.

Significantly, duty-free treatment of articles in this Category is subject to an annual quota. In effect, this Category is a TRQ, which subjects over-quota shipments to the MFN rate. To what is the cap—the specific percentage figure for a particular year—applied? The answer is "square meter equivalents" (SMEs), a

---

14. *See* 19 U.S.C. § 3721(b)(3); HTSUS Chapter 98, Sub-Heading 9819.11.09 at 98-XIX-4 (concerning these articles).

denomination that allows for comparison among different kinds of apparel articles, as diverse (for example) as wool sweaters and nylon tights. Thus, for instance, the initial cap, for the 12 months commencing 1 October 2000, was 246,500,393 SMEs. In that year, no more than this amount of apparel from T&A Beneficiary SSACs could obtain preferential treatment in the form of a zero tariff.

The "bottom line," then, is the 3rd Preference Category is not as generous as it first appears. It promises flexibility to T&A Beneficiary SSACs by allowing them to use fabric made of yarn from either the U.S. or a Beneficiary. But, it imposes serious limits on the volume of apparel made from such fabric, in the form of a TRQ with caps allowed to grow modestly to low ceiling levels. Lest there be any doubt about this verdict, consider the fact that a special safeguard remedy applies to this Category.

In particular, if imports from Beneficiaries surge, then the U.S. can remove duty-free treatment. The Secretary of Commerce is authorized to determine whether "there has been a surge in imports of an article [qualifying under the regional fabric Preference Category] . . . from a" Beneficiary SSAC.[15] Specifically, under this provision, the Secretary must decide whether the article

> is being imported in such increased quantities as to cause serious damage, or threat thereof, to the domestic industry producing a like or directly competitive article.

The list of factors the Secretary considers in making an injury determination is open-ended, and includes any economic variable with an effect on imports, such as capacity utilization, domestic production, employment, exports, inventories, investment, market share, prices, profits, and sales. If the answer is affirmative, then the President must suspend duty-free treatment.

Any "interested party" can request a ruling from the Secretary. The definition of this term includes not only producers (including workers, unions, and worker groups, as well as trade or business associations) of a like or directly competitive product, but also anyone (producers, workers, unions, and worker groups, and trade or business associations) "engaged in the manufacture, production, or sale of essential inputs for the like or directly competitive article." In other words, the universe of potential claimants with standing to bring a surge mechanism case includes most of the commercial chain, upstream and downstream.

The surge mechanism might be dubbed (diplomatically) "noteworthy." It is a weapon against exports containing regional fabric, yet the weapon targets the apparel sectors of desperately poor countries. The legal aspects of this weapon make it all the more "noteworthy." That is evident by contrasting this mechanism with the legal criteria for an escape clause action under Section 201 of the *Trade Act of 1974*.[16] These criteria accord (though not completely) with the general safeguard

---

15. 19 U.S.C. §3721(b)(3)(C)(ii).
16. *See* 19 U.S.C. §§2251–2254.

remedy in Article XIX of GATT. The contrast shows the criteria associated with an *AGOA* surge mechanism are less rigorous than the requirements for an Escape Clause action, meaning it appears comparatively easier to get relief against African apparel.

To invoke the escape clause, increased imports must be "a substantial cause of *serious* injury, or the threat thereof, to the domestic industry producing an article like or directly competitive with the imported article. . . ." The investigation is conducted not by one executive branch official, but rather by an independent agency—the ITC. An affirmative determination results in a recommendation to the President for relief, but the President may choose not to raise trade barriers, because such action is "appropriate and feasible." As indicated, the causation test in the surge mechanism is unmodified, *i.e.*, it does not have the descriptive adjective "substantial." Any causal contribution is enough to justify relief. In contrast to a Section 201 case, in a surge mechanism case, it is not necessary to show there is no cause more important than the imports from a Beneficiary.

Also in contrast to a Section 201 case, in a surge mechanism case, one member of the President's cabinet makes the decision. The President has no choice but to suspend duty-free treatment if the decision is positive. Finally, the universe of potential petitioners in a Section 201 case does not expressly include upstream producers, workers, or associations. Rather, the petitioner must be "an entity, including a trade association, firm, certified or organized union, or group of workers, which is representative of an industry." In turn, the industry must be the one subject to actual or threatened serious injury.

Fourth Preference Category:
Third Country Fabric

One dimension of the regional fabric grouping is, in effect, a separate ROO category. There is a special rule for a T&A Beneficiary SSAC designated as "lesser developed," sometimes called the "Third Country Fabric Provision," or "Third Country Fabric Exception for Apparel."[17] The basic rule for qualifying as "lesser developed" is a *per capita* GNP of less than $1,500 (as of 1998, measured by the World Bank). However, *AGOA* identifies three countries by name as "lesser developed"—Botswana, Namibia, and Mauritius—that have higher *per capita* incomes. Indeed, the *per capita* income of Mauritius, at $10,186 (in 2017), is considerably higher (indeed, it is 81% of the global average per capita GDP), and that country sometimes is cited as a success story.[18]

The special rule is an apparel article wholly assembled (or knit-to-shape) in a lesser developed Beneficiary (or multiple such Beneficiaries) may qualify for duty

---

17. *See* 19 U.S.C. §3721(b)(3)(B); HTSUS Chapter 98, Sub-Heading 9819.11.12 at 98-XIX-4 (concerning these articles).

18. *See* Trading Economics, Mauritius GDP Per Capita, https://tradingeconomics.com /mauritius/gdp-per-capita.

free treatment, regardless of the country or origin of the fabric or yarn used to make the articles. In effect, the lesser developed Beneficiary can source inputs from anywhere in the world: its apparel can qualify for an *AGOA* preference regardless of the origin of the fabric it uses to make the apparel. However, this special rule is subject to two limitations.

First, the special rule initially applied only through 30 September 2007, which is just half the length of extension of other *AGOA* benefits.[19] The special rule was extended to September 2012, and then again through 30 September 2015. Uncertainty created by whether and when Congress might extent this rule is difficult for T&A businesses. They are part of a global supply chain and operate on thin margins. Typically, they make decisions about sourcing fabric six-to-nine months before actual importation and use of the fabric. When Congress fails to extend the third-country fabric provision in a timely fashion, they plan on moving T&A factories out of *AGOA* beneficiary countries, thus threatening jobs and incomes in those countries.

Second, there is a cap on third-country fabric imports. It is defined in terms of an "applicable percentage" of SMEs of all apparel articles imported into the U.S. in the previous 12-month period for which data are available.[20] The cap rises, then falls. For example, initially under *AGOA*, in the first year (1 October 2003 through 30 September 2004), the applicable percentage was 2.3571%. In the second year, (1 October 2004 through 30 September 2005), it was 2.6428%. In the third year (1 October 2005 through 30 September 2006), it peaked at 2.9285%. In the final year (1 October 2006 through 30 September 2007), the cap dropped to just 1.6071%.

Fifth Preference Category:
Beneficiary Knit to Shape-Forward for Certain Sweaters

Certain kinds of sweaters potentially qualify for duty-free treatment.[21] To qualify, the sweaters must satisfy two requirements:

(1) The sweaters are knit-to-shape in a T&A Beneficiary SSAC.

(2) The sweaters are made either of cashmere or fine merino wool.

If the sweaters are cashmere, then their chief weight must consist of cashmere. They also must be classified under Sub-Heading 6110.10 of the HTSUS, which covers sweaters, pullovers, sweatshirts, waistcoats (*i.e.*, vests), and other similar articles that are knitted or crocheted. If the sweaters are wool, then they must contain 50% or more merino wool, and the diameter of that wool must be no finer (*i.e.*, not exceed) 21.5 microns. As indicated earlier, this Preference Category is narrow and not of great commercial significance.

---

19. *See* 19 U.S.C. § 3721(b)(3)(B)(i).

20. *See* 19 U.S.C. § 3721(b)(3)(B)(ii).

21. *See* 19 U.S.C. § 3721(b)(4); HTSUS Chapter 98, Sub-Headings 9819.11.15, 9819.11.18 at 98-XIX-5.

Sixth Preference Category:
Short Supply and NAFTA Parity

Are there any circumstances in which the U.S. will accord duty-free treatment to apparel from a T&A Beneficiary SSAC, which is not a lesser developed country, even though the fabric, or the yarn making up the fabric, is from neither America nor a Beneficiary? That is, can apparel made of third country fabric or yarn qualify? Yes, under the 6th Preference Category, the origin or fabric or yarn is irrelevant.[22]

The usual rubric for this Category is the "Third Country Fabric" provision. A full (but cumbersome) title for this Category might be "Beneficiary Cutting and Sewing Forward with a *NAFTA* Rule of Origin or with Short-Supply Fabric or Yarn." That is because to qualify, the apparel must be cut (or knit to shape), sewn, and further assembled in a Beneficiary. But, duty-free treatment depends on satisfaction of a short-supply test, plus the applicable *NAFTA* rule of origin. (Generally, *NAFTA* sets out a yarn-forward rule of origin for garments to obtain DFQF treatment.)

The short supply test is that the fabric, or the yarn used in the fabric, is "not available in commercial quantities in the United States."[23] The exact *NAFTA* rule of origin depends on the customs classification of the apparel article. They are (for the most part) CTH rules, also known as "tariff shift" rules. In theory at least, this kind of rule of origin determines whether a sufficient amount of economic activity occurred in a country to justify conferral of origin in that country. Generally, the greater the shift (*e.g.,* at the 4-digit HTS classification level), the greater the economic activity in a country. Conversely, the smaller the shift (*e.g.,* at the 8-digit level), the more modest the activity.

To apply a CTH rule, two sets of records must be available to answer two questions. First, what HTS classification applied to the imported components before they were manufactured into a finished apparel article? Second, what HTS classification applied to the finished apparel article?

The first question concerns customs classification by a Beneficiary (*i.e.,* when the materials imported were imported into the Beneficiary). The second question concerns classification upon entry of the finished article into the U.S. Of course, applying the rule also presumes an exporter in a T&A Beneficiary SSAC has access directly, or through counsel, to *NAFTA.* Annex 401 of *NAFTA* contains the rules of origin (including for Chapters 50–63 of the HTS, which cover T&A merchandise), and they are reproduced in the General Notes to the HTSUS. While this may be true for prominent, well-connected exporters, it is difficult to imagine either *NAFTA* or the HTSUS is a bestseller anywhere on the African continent. Put simply, aside from the complexity of the CTH rules, access to them is difficult, and both problems raise the cost of compliance with *AGOA* to qualify for duty-free treatment.

---

22. *See* 19 U.S.C. § 3721(b)(5); HTSUS Chapter 98, Sub-Headings 9819.11.21 and 9819.11.24 at 98-XIX-5.

23. 19 U.S.C. § 3721(b)(5)(A).

No less important significant a concern is the oddity of *AGOA* incorporating by reference the Annex 401 origin rules. True, it may be preferable to creating a whole new set of origin rules. But, why give the relatively poorer countries of SSA the same treatment as Mexican apparel exporters? The origin requirement creates a kind of legal parity between two patently unequal categories of exporters whenever fabric or yarn is neither American nor African, subjecting the poorer ones to the same origin strictures as the comparatively better-off ones. Evidently, the scale of relative deprivation plays no role in this Preference Category.

Implicit in the short-supply test is permanence, *i.e.*, that the fabric or yarn in question is unavailable in commercial quantities in the U.S. now and in the long run. Silk is an example of such a fabric. However, what if the fabric or yarn is available, but not immediately, nor in the short or medium term? In that instance, if an "interested party" requests, the President may proclaim duty-free treatment for yarns or fabrics that "cannot be supplied by the domestic industry in commercial quantities in a *timely* manner."[24]

To qualify, such apparel must come from fabric or yarn not available in commercial quantities in the U.S. (the first prong), and that American producers cannot supply in commercial quantities in a timely manner (the second prong). In brief, the apparel qualifies, despite consisting of non-American fabric or yarn, if the inputs are in short supply in the U.S. The President makes the short-supply determination, though in practice the President delegates this authority to the DOC Office of Textiles and Apparel (OTEXA). The criteria applied are the fabric or yarn in question "cannot be supplied by the domestic [American] industry in commercial quantities in a timely manner."[25]

Seventh Preference Category:
Cultural T&A

Certain T&A goods, specifically, ones that are hand-loomed, handmade, or folklore articles, or ethnic printed fabrics, potentially qualify for preferential treatment. (*See* 19 U.S.C. §3721(b)(6); HTSUS Chapter 98, Sub-Heading 9819.11.27 at 98-XIX-5.) Conceptually, there are three stages for qualification.

First, the prospective T&A Beneficiary SSAC must consult with the U.S. as to the eligibility of the good. Second, the U.S. must decide whether the good indeed qualifies as a hand-loomed, handmade, or folklore article, or an ethnic printed fabric. Third, if the U.S. renders an affirmative determination in the second step, then a competent authority in the beneficiary country must certify the good as an eligible hand-loomed, hand-made, or folklore article, or ethnic printed fabric.

This Preference Category poses virtually no competitive threat to any American producer. Almost by definition, African cultural T&A articles do not have like or directly competitive products. Generosity through duty-free treatment in this

---

24. 19 U.S.C. §3721(b)(5)(B)(i) (emphasis added).
25. 19 U.S.C. §3721(b)(5)(B)(i).

Category hardly is self-giving. The practical benefit from this generosity, for exporters, depends on the value and volume of exports in this Category. Once again, by definition, small, cottage-industry-like producers, are among the likeliest of beneficiaries. How significant they are in a national economy, and the role they play in boosting growth, is dubious. Few if any countries reached developed country status through a handicrafts industry.

Eighth Preference Category:
Multi-Jurisdictional Apparel

The final *AGOA* Preference Category covers apparel assembled in a T&A Beneficiary SSAC from components originating in both a Beneficiary and the U.S.[26] Accordingly, the Category might be called "Beneficiary Assembly Forward with Beneficiary or American Components." In specific, sewing may occur in a Beneficiary using American thread, where the components stitched together come from, and are cut in, the U.S. and a Beneficiary (or former Beneficiary) SSAC. The fabric must be American. This fabric must consist of American yarn (or components knit-to-shape in the U.S. and one or more Beneficiary or former Beneficiary, or both).

So, suppose the apparel article in question is a 100% cotton men's dress shirt. The pockets and sleeves are cut in the U.S., while the body is cut in one Beneficiary. In a second Beneficiary, with U.S. thread, the pockets, sleeves, and body, are stitched together (along with other components, like collars and cuffs, which may come from any country). The pockets, sleeves, and body are from cotton fabric made of cotton spun in the U.S. The article would qualify for duty-free treatment under this Category.

This Category gives a T&A Beneficiary SSAC a modicum of flexibility in sourcing components. It can choose from multiple jurisdictions, without sourcing all components from one jurisdiction. But, it is constrained to choose from the U.S., a fellow Beneficiary, or a domestic source. Insistence on American fabric made of American yarn is a familiar stricture. A similar one exists in the 1st and 2nd Preference Category. Thus, the flavor of all three categories is — put colloquially — "you (the Beneficiary) can have duty-free treatment, but only if you use our (American) fabric and yarn."

- *AGOA* **Amendments and Ford Kansas City Case Study**

Congress amended *AGOA* often, most notably with the 2004 *AGOA Acceleration Act* and 2006 *Africa Investment Incentive Act*, generally with a view to expanding preferential access for merchandise from Beneficiary SSACs. The 2004 legislation extended *AGOA* until 30 September 2015. The 2006 legislation added over 700 HTSUS tariff lines eligible for *AGOA* preferences, especially for T&A articles, and granted greater DFQF treatment to T&A articles originating entirely in one or more lesser developed Beneficiary SSACs. The 2006 changes had special rules for fabrics

---

26. *See* 19 U.S.C. § 3721(b)(7); HTSUS Chapter 98, Sub-Heading 9819.11.30 at 98-XIX-5.

or yarns a Beneficiary SSAC country makes in commercial quantities as inputs for T&A articles.

Have these changes helped African countries develop vertically integrated T&A industries? Have they resulted in increased exports from them to America? Have they caused American companies to outsource jobs and use SSACs as an export platform?

Consider the following case study: thanks to *AGOA*, Ford Motor Company invested over $300 million in its South African engine manufacturing plants. From them, Ford exports engines world-wide, including DFQF to America. Secretary of State John Kerry (1943–) declared to the August 2014 *AGOA* Forum at the World Bank that: "the efficiencies of the South African operation have allowed Ford to create 800 new jobs at its Kansas City, Missouri, plant as part of the global production line."[27]

III. Trade Distortion?

Apparel articles are quintessential examples of low-value added manufactured items economists such as Walt Whitman Rostow (1916–2003) in his *The Stages of Economic Growth* (1960) identify as significant to countries advancing to and beyond the "take off" for industrialization. For a poor country, these products tend to be ones in which they have a keen export interest, and thus ones for which preferential rules of origin matter greatly.

Trade in T&A constitutes roughly 8% of all trade in manufactured goods. The leading example of "high dependence" on T&A (defined as earning more than 50% of export revenue from one sector) is Bangladesh, for which T&A account for 85.8% of the merchandise export revenue. In India, 20% of industrial production comes from T&A, and this sector employs 15 million people. Exports in this sector play prominent roles in many SSACs and North African countries. In all such economies, there are multiplier effects from T&A production and exports. Businesses develop around this activity, from fruit and newsagents to haircutting and pharmacies. There also are externalities, including the employment and potential empowerment (as well as exploitation) of women.

To pick up the question of "why?," why is it appropriate to characterize the preferential ROOs for these articles as "devilish," from the vantage of a prospective Beneficiary SSAC? Surely, the rules are defensible on the ground many SSACs lack the capacity to weave, cut, or assemble fabric, and indeed do not even have significant domestic yarn production. In brief, inputs into apparel articles are not readily available anyway, so what is wrong with ROOs requiring use of U.S. inputs?

---

27. *Quoted in* Len Bracken, *Froman Launches AGOA Renewal Campaign, Says Product Coverage Could Be Expanded*, 31 International Trade Reporter (BNA) 1447 (7 August 2014).

One answer, in brief, is distortion. This response arises out of conventional Neo-Classical economic theory. These rules create an artificial distortion about sourcing inputs. Consider the reality of global T&A production as seen by Victor Fung, the Chairman of Li & Fung, the major garment supplier in Hong Kong to American and European clothing brands:

> We might decide to buy yarn from a Korean producer but have it woven and dyed in Taiwan. So we pick the yarn and ship it to Taiwan. The Japanese have the best zippers and buttons, but they manufacture them mostly in China. Okay, so we go to YKK, a big Japanese manufacturer, and we order the right zippers from their Chinese plants. Then we determine that . . . the best place to make the garments is Thailand. So we ship everything there. . . . We're not asking which country can do the best job overall. Instead, we're pulling apart the value chain and optimizing each step—and we're doing it globally. . . . If you talk to the big global consumer-products companies, they are all moving in this direction—toward being best on a global scale.[28]

Yet, the *AGOA* preferential ROOs seem either oblivious to, or flout deliberately, this free market logic.

It will not do to criticize an SSA for lacking globally-minded entrepreneurs like Victor Fung, or to castigate African rulers for bad governance and corruption, without also engaging in introspection. What technical American trade rules impede the likes of Victor Fung in SSA? In *AGOA*, the 1st and 3rd Preference Categories are not based on pure assembly rules. Rather, they combine assembly operations in an SSA T&A beneficiary with Yarn Forward requirements. Likewise, the 2nd Preference Category is not a pure Cutting Forward Rule. Rather, it contains a yarn-forward requirement. The 8th Category suffers from the same problem.

These strictures discourage would-be African entrepreneurs in a T&A SSAC Beneficiary from obtaining fabric from the cheapest cost or highest quality sources, and creating an efficient, vertically integrated, global production chain like that of Li & Fung. Rather, under the 1st and 3rd Categories, they must pay attention to the country of origin of yarn, not its price or quality. Under the 2nd Category, they must focus on the source of the thread, not its price and quality. Under the 8th Category, they most focus on the source of fabric, yarn, and thread. If fabric, yarn, or thread is not American, then any hope of duty-free, quota free treatment from the U.S. is lost. The economic fact substitute material from a third country, such as Egypt or Pakistan, may be cheaper or better quality than the American inputs, is legally irrelevant.

One response to the trade distortion critique is the *AGOA* preferential ROOs encourage regional development. Some of them allow for use of fabric or yarn from more than one Beneficiary. The 3rd and 8th Preference Categories are illustrations. Such allowance is known as "regional cumulation," indicating via a mathematical

---

28. *Quoted in* Oxfam Briefing Paper, 20.

RVC rule that a proportion of the inputs into a finished garment may come from other countries in the region of the beneficiary, yet not vitiate eligibility for preferential treatment.

However, Oxfam International dubs regional cumulation a "flawed trade instrument," stating "there is no development rationale for promoting *regional* rather than *global* cumulation." It adds:

> The USA's *African Growth and Opportunity Act (AGOA)* . . . contains imperfect rules on cumulation. The *Act* stipulates that apparel exported from African countries to the USA must use either US or African fabrics to qualify for *AGOA* benefits, *notably discriminating against fabrics produced in Asia*. One recent study [by the World Bank] estimates that Mauritius *would have* seen its total exports increase by 36 percent between 2001 and 2004 under *AGOA*, rather than 5 percent, had restrictive rules of origin *not* been in place.[29]

Whether the points Oxfam makes are true generally, or depend on the industry and regional in question, is a matter best left to development economists.

For now, five points should be emphasized. First, not all *AGOA* rules encourage regional development. If they did, then why are they (as Oxfam International puts it) "unreasonably demanding"? Second, the rules are inconsistent, if not disingenuous, in helping SSA. They address development in the American T&A industry as much as in SSA. Arguably because of fears of competition from Asian suppliers, there is no analog to *AGOA* for developing or least developed countries in Asia. Third, whether a ROO is an appropriate tool to encourage regional development is questionable. Surely there are more direct, efficient legal instruments. Fourth, the *AGOA* cumulation rules are not unconditionally generous. They are subject to limits, specifically, on the cumulation of labor costs. So, the degree to which labor inputs from one Beneficiary can count toward satisfying the pertinent ROO are limited. Moreover, for certain products, satisfying the ROO depends on having a specified percentage of American content. Fifth, and most fundamentally, there may well be strong arguments against promoting regional versus global development.

IV. Economic Dependency?

Applying Dependency Theory, *AGOA* preferential ROOs tie a T&A Beneficiary SSAC to the U.S., or at least encourage that outcome. As Oxfam International observes, "agreements [like *AGOA* and the European 'Everything But Arms' (EBA) program] that are supposed to benefit poor countries actually serve to promote the production of textiles in rich countries, to the detriment of the developing world as a whole." In *AGOA*, this tying is patent in all but the 5th and 7th Preference

---

29. Oxfam Briefing Paper, 22.

Categories. It is operationalized through hybrid specified process rules of origin. Rather than, for example, a pure assembly rule in the 1st and 3rd Categories, or a pure cutting forward rule in the 2nd and 8th Categories, there are added mandates about the American origin of fabric, yarn, or thread. Such mandates encourage a Beneficiary to become dependent on the U.S. for inputs.

This encouragement is ironic. In the aftermath of the Second World War, when the U.S. actively engaged in the drafting of GATT at the 1946 London Preparatory Conference and the 1947 Geneva Preparatory Conference, it argued strongly against the preferential trading arrangements of the European colonial powers. Tying peripheral countries in Africa, Asia, and the Caribbean to the center countries like the U.K. and France was incongruous with free trade and the development interests of the poor countries. The American argument was not entirely successful. But, it did at least limit the schemes to the parameters set forth in Article I:2 of GATT, a restricted exception to the MFN obligation in Article I:1.

Does *AGOA* bespeak an historic reversal of American efforts to resist center-periphery type links? Does it reveal a neo-colonial tolerance (indeed, support) for vertical integration of the T&A production through such links? Why does *AGOA* confer no meaningful reward for economic integration among poor countries, for instance, where a Beneficiary SSAC seeks high-quality, low-cost cotton from Egypt or Pakistan? Is it too cynical a response to say *AGOA* is about divide and rule? These questions are not pleasant to pose, nor should an ideologically-driven answer be presumed. But, *AGOA* is not pleasant reading for an international trade lawyer or scholar who believes, perhaps mistakenly or foolishly, that International Trade Law can be about more than politically-motivated protection, that it can be a policy instrument to assist poor countries.

Another irony about *AGOA* is the first and second rationales may be practically inconsequential. From a legal standpoint, the rules of origin are complex. The cost of understanding and complying with them surely are high, all the more so for an African producer/exporter with limited resources to spend on competent trade counsel (if it even exists nearby). The cost may approach the margin of preference, cut into that margin, or even dwarf it. If compliance costs discourage use of *AGOA* benefits, then neither trade distortion nor dependency occurs. The consequence is "missing preferences"—a poor country does not develop a T&A industry capable of meeting the requirements for duty-free access to the markets of rich countries. Missing preferences is the heart of the irony. The ostensible purpose of *AGOA*—to provide a preference—is unfulfilled.

The problem of missing preferences may be even more likely to arise when an African producer-exporter seeks to ship merchandise to multiple importing countries. Suppose the producer/exporter aspires to gain a foothold not only in the American market, but also the EU market. To gain preferential access, it will be necessary to satisfy *AGOA* origin rules for the American market, and EU origin rules for the European market. To the extent the rules differ, the problem of understanding and applying them increases. If the producer-exporter seeks entry for its merchandise into still more markets, and the importing countries have non-harmonized rules, then the problem is yet worse. Heterogeneous rules of origin are dubbed the "spaghetti-bowl effect." The point is to see the interaction between this effect and missing preferences, as producer-exporters simply — and rationally, from a cost-benefit perspective — elect not to seek preferential access.

V. Social Justice?

To analyze preferential programs like *AGOA* in terms of trade distortion or Dependency Theory is to employ Development Economics. There also is a non-economic basis to brand as "devilish" *AGOA* ROOs for apparel articles. That reason is moral, indeed, religious: these rules are at variance with the preferential option for the poor, which is a tenet of Catholic social justice theory (and of justice criteria in other faiths). This tenet is grounded in Gospel teaching and articulated and elaborated, for example, in the Magisterium of the Roman Catholic Church through (*inter alia*) Papal encyclicals starting in 1891 with *Rerum Novarum* (On the Condition of the Working Classes), by Pope Leo XIII (1810–1903, 256th Pope, 1878–1903), and emphasized by Pope Saint John Paul II (1920–2005, 264th Pope, 1978–2005) in encyclicals such as *Labourem Exercens* (On Human Work) (1981), *Sollicitudo Rei Socialis* (On Social Concern) (1987), and *Centesimus Annus* (On the Hundredth Anniversary of *Rerum Novarum*) (1991).

In brief, it demands primacy in public policy choices be given to the interests of the poor over the well-to-do. America has moved from a generic 35% Value Added Test in its GSP program to product-specific rules of origin namely specified processes. Is that move selfish? Is it the case each U.S.-based company can insert into what is or ought to be a charitable program its own special device to make sure generosity stops where its self-interest, however real or remote, begins?

In contrast, Canada adopted in 2003 an "Initiative for Least Developed Countries," making it the only major developed country to fulfill its promise at the Doha Ministerial Conference in November 2001 to provide DFQF treatment on T&A articles from LDCs This Initiative imposes a two-pronged test to qualify for such treatment, and only one prong need be satisfied. Either:

(1) An article is made in a LDC, regardless of value added at the final stage of production (*i.e.*, there is no value-added threshold at that stage), or

(2) At least 25% of the value added to an article occurs in the final stage in a least developed country, but inputs may come from any other country in the world, and there is no dual substantial transformation requirement concerning yarn-to-fabric and fabric-to clothing.

Yet, under *AGOA*, the keen export interest in T&A of Beneficiary SSACs is subordinated to producers of T&A producing like merchandise made in the U.S.

Understandably, the American T&A sector feels besieged by cheaper imports. Hundreds of thousands of jobs have been lost in recent years, as some politicians, especially from the Southeast (the epicenter of the sector), intone. From their vantage, to give GSP treatment to T&A imports exacerbates decline, or at least complicates orderly contraction. The GSP statutory product exemptions are right to calculate generosity to poor countries. The 4th Preference Category, for the poorest SSA countries, with early its sunset rule and TRQ thresholds, is a good balance. American willingness to give DFQF treatment should extend only to the line of potential threat to U.S. producers.

However, is the socially just response to cut back on generosity toward the poorest countries? Is it better to help the shrinking American T&A sector through more generous *TAA*? Ought not generosity to be a positive sum game?

Part Six

Trade and Labor

Chapter 22

International Labor Law and Trade Restrictions

I. ILO Overview

The ILO is a U.N. agency that creates labor policies and standards, but which lacks stringent enforcement authority. Based in Geneva Switzerland, the ILO initially was located in a building now occupied (and subsequently refurbished) by the GATT and WTO Secretariats.

The ILO has 185 member countries, and also counts employer and worker organizations among its active participants. The term "Member" refers to a country in the ILO, as does "Member" in the context of the WTO. In contrast, the terms "Employer Representative" and "Worker Representative" are used for employer and worker organizations, respectively, that hold membership in the ILO. This unique framework makes the ILO the only U.N. organ comprised of government and NGO actors of equal standing.

- **History**

The ILO was founded in 1919 with the signing on 28 June of the *Treaty of Versailles*. This *Treaty* ended the First World War. Part XIII of the *Treaty*, titled "Labour," established the ILO, and this Part to this day is the Constitution of the ILO, which has 40 Articles.[1] The drafters of the *Treaty* believed peace could not exist in the world without social justice and, therefore, created a permanent organization to fight against labor conditions that produced injustice and hardship. The broader political context in which the ILO was borne was one of struggle between capitalism and communism. Bolsheviks had overthrown the Russian Czar just two years earlier, and communist movements were afoot in many capitalist countries. They were fueled in part by oppressive conditions faced by workers. Perhaps if the ILO could succeed in its mission, capitalism — sporting a kinder, gentler face — might be saved.

There were 42 founding Members of the ILO. They were the 29 signatories of the *Treaty of Versailles*, plus 13 other nations that were invited and signed on to adhere to the Covenants of the League of Nations. Table 21-1 presents those founding

---

1. P. Bollé, *The International Labor Review and the ILO: Milestones in a Shared History*, 152 INTERNATIONAL LABOR REVIEW 1–12 (2013).

Table 21-1. Initial ILO Members and GATT Contracting Parties

Name of Country (Alphabetical)	Founding and Invited ILO Members (*Treaty of Versailles,* 28 June 1919)	Original GATT Contracting Parties (GATT, 30 October 1947)
Argentina	Yes	No (Joined 11 October 1967)
Australia	Yes	Yes
Belgium	Yes	Yes
Bolivia	Yes	No (Joined 8 September 1990)
Brazil	Yes	Yes
British Empire	Yes	Yes
Burma (Myanmar)	No (Joined 18 May 1948)	Yes
Canada	Yes	Yes
Ceylon (Sri Lanka)	No (Joined 28 June 1948)	Yes
Chile	Yes	Yes
China	Yes	Yes
Columbia	Yes	No (Joined 3 October 1981)
Cuba	Yes	Yes
Czechoslovakia	Yes	Yes
Denmark	Yes	No (Joined 28 May 1950)
France	Yes	Yes
Guatemala	Yes	No (Joined 10 October 1991)
Haiti	Yes	No (Joined 1 January 1950)
Honduras	Yes	No (Joined 10 April 1994)
India	Yes	Yes
Italy	Yes	No (Joined 30 May 1950)
Japan	Yes	No (Joined 10 September 1955)
Lebanon	No (Joined 23 December 1948)	Yes (subsequently withdrew from GATT)
Liberia	Yes	No
Luxemburg	No (Joined 16 December 1920)	Yes
Netherlands	Yes	Yes
New Zealand	Yes	Yes
Nicaragua	Yes	No (Joined 28 May 1950)
Norway	Yes	Yes

(continued)

Table 21-1. Initial ILO Members and GATT Contracting Parties (*continued*)

Name of Country (Alphabetical)	Founding and Invited ILO Members (*Treaty of Versailles*, 28 June 1919)	Original GATT Contracting Parties (GATT, 30 October 1947)
Pakistan	No (Joined 31 October 1947)	Yes
Panama	Yes	No (Joined 6 September 1997)
Paraguay	Yes	No (Joined 6 January 1994)
Persia	Yes	No
Peru	Yes (invited)	No (Joined 7 October 1951)
Poland	Yes (invited)	No (Joined 18 October 1967)
Portugal	Yes (invited)	No (Joined 6 May 1962)
Romania	Yes (invited)	No (Joined 14 November 1971)
Salvador	Yes (invited)	No (Joined 22 May 1991)
Serbo-Croatian-Slovene State	Yes (invited)	No (Serbia joined 22 November 2000, Croatia joined 30 June 1991, Slovenia joined 29 May 1992)
Siam (Thailand)	Yes (invited)	No (Joined 20 November 1982)
South Africa	Yes (invited)	Yes
Southern Rhodesia (Zimbabwe)	No (Joined 6 June 1980)	Yes
Spain	Yes (invited)	No (Joined 29 August 1963)
Switzerland	Yes (invited)	No (Joined 1 August 1966)
U.S.	No (Joined 18 February 1980)	Yes
Uruguay	Yes (invited)	No (Joined 6 December 1953)
Venezuela	Yes (invited)	No (Joined 31 August 1990)

Members, and also states whether they went on to become original contracting parties to the 30 October 1947 GATT.

A few points from this Table are noteworthy. First, the U.S. was not a founding Member of the ILO.

Second, a small number of countries that were founding Members did not go onto become original GATT contracting parties. For a variety of reasons, some idiosyncratic, their interest in international worker rights did not extend to trade liberalization.

Third, an even smaller number of countries—Burma and the U.S., for instance—declined to join the ILO initially, but were original GATT contracting parties. Perhaps their interest in trade liberalization in 1947 was not matched by an interest in worker rights in 1919.

Fourth, consider the extent to which there is a balance of power between manufacturing and buyer countries. Labor standards apply to manufacturers to protect workers. Buyers (setting aside individual consumer preferences) are keen on maximizing consumption opportunities at low prices. The balance of power among nations that are buyers, such as the U.S., are different from the manufacturing nations, such as China, creates a tug of war within the ILO for competing interests.

- **Evolution in Mission**

Since 1919, the mission of the ILO has evolved. For its initial decades, and through much of the Cold War, the Organization focused on general labor policy. Specifically, in the 1920s, the ILO engaged in legislative efforts to promote minimum labor standards across Members. In the 1930s, the ILO understandably focused on economic strategies to generate jobs and incomes in the face of the Great Depression.

As public concerns grew about international labor rights with globalization in the 1980s and 1990s, the ILO shifted to emphasizing monitoring and enforcement of labor rights in Member. Accordingly, it established offices in the field: it has offices in 52 different locations, excluding its headquarters (as of 2008).

- **Tripartite Constituents**

The ILO is comprised of three categories of membership, with all three categories relatively equal: (1) Governments (*i.e.*, countries), again, called "Members," (2) Worker Representatives, and (3) Employer Representatives. In Category (1) are countries that have agreed to comply by the ILO Constitution.

Worker Representatives are in Category (2). They consist of trade unions and groups that promote the rights of workers. Workers Organizations link to the ILO through the Bureau for Workers' Activities (ACTRAV), which is a unit of the ILO Secretariat. That is, the Organizations bring to ACTRAV their concerns, and they along with ACTRAV work collaboratively to advance their cause at the ILO. ACTRAV is helpful to smaller organizations by providing a kind of strength in numbers.

Category (3) is Employer Representatives They advocate for the advancement of employer interests. This tripartite system allows the ILO to get the perspectives of all major players in the global capitalist labor model. The ILO serves as a forum for the three categories of members to collaborate in drafting policies and standards in pursuit of social justice.

- **Governing Body**

The Governing Body is the administrative arm of the ILO, which is composed of 56 titular members (28 Members, 14 Employer Representatives and 14 Worker Representatives) and 66 deputy members (28 Members, 19 Employers and 19 Workers). Industrial powerhouses permanently hold 10 of the titular government seats, which are Brazil, China, France, Germany, India, Italy, Japan, Russia, U.K., and U.S. The other Members are elected by the ILO Conference every three years. Employer and Worker Representatives are elected in their individual capacity.

- **Conference**

The ILO Conference is held once a year in Geneva, Switzerland. Individuals from Governments, Employer Representatives, and Worker Representatives meet to make decisions on a mutually agreed-upon agenda. Each has a delegation, which consists of two Government delegates, one Employer Representative Organization delegate, and one Worker Representative delegate. All delegates have equal rights and may vote, as they desire. So, for example, the voting positions of the U.S. government and a Worker Representative (*e.g.*, a union) from America could be different.

- **Membership**

Article 1 of the ILO Constitution set membership for countries in the ILO. Article 1:3 says any country that is part of the United Nations can join the ILO by accepting unconditionally the ILO Constitution. Article 1:4 allows non-U.N. members to become part of the ILO, but under more rigorous requirements. Under them, the ILO Conference admits countries by a vote of two-thirds of the delegates attending the session, including a quorum whereby two-thirds of the Government delegates must be present and voting.

- **Implementation**

All countries in the ILO must ratify the ILO Constitution. That is not true of ILO *Conventions*. A policy or standard ratified by the ILO Conference creates a legal obligation for a Member to enact that policy or standard—but, only if the country ratifies the policy or standard. ILO *Conventions*, which the Conference enacts, embody policies or standards. So, a sovereign country must implement the rules of that *Convention*, if that Member ratifies the *Convention*. Assuming it does, then that Member has a grace period, typically two years, to enact implementing legislation in its domestic system.

- **Enforcement Mechanism 1: Self-Reporting**

The ILO has four principal ways to supervise application and implementation of ILO policies within Members. The first technique is self-reporting, a duty the Constitution imposes on each Member. Specifically, there is a:

(1) Duty to report on ratified *Conventions*: Article 22 says each Member agrees to make an annual report to the International Labor Office on measures it has taken to give effect to the provisions of *Conventions* to which it is a party.

(2) Duty to report on unratified *Conventions*: Article 19 says that a Member that does not ratify a particular *Convention* has an obligation to report on the problems causing delayed ratification, and progress toward ultimate passage.

- **Enforcement Mechanism 2: Expert Committee Annual Report**

ILO Members must submit reports on ILO *Conventions* they have ratified. They do so to an Expert Committee, and Employer and Worker Representatives that are ILO members. Employer and worker Representatives, which typically are "on the ground" with officers and advisers in pertinent countries, can comment on a government report for the Expert Committee to weigh.

The Expert Committee is comprised of 20 jurists who are not officials of the ILO. These judges come from different geographic areas across the world to provide a balanced view. These impartial individuals provide an objective view on the application of labor standards, memorialized in a published annual report. As a Committee, they can make direct requests to a government to answer further questions, which they list in their report. Additionally they offer observations in their report.

- **Enforcement Mechanism #3: Complaint and Representation System**

The systems of complaint and representations within the ILO allows for Members, Employer Representatives, and Worker Representatives to file a complaint against a Member. The key distinction between a "complaint" and "representation" is the former is lodged by an ILO Member, while the latter is made by an employer or worker. The pertinent Articles governing them are Articles 24 and 26 of the ILO Constitution:

Article 24
Representations of non-observance of Conventions
[For Worker and Employer Representatives]

1. In the event of any representation being made to the International Labor Office by an industrial association of employers or of workers that any of the Members has failed to secure in any respect the effective observance within its jurisdiction of any Convention to which it is a party, the Governing Body may communicate this representation to the government against which it is made, and may invite that government to make such statement on the subject as it may think fit.

Article 26
Complaints of non-observance
[For ILO Members, i.e., countries]

1. Any of the Members shall have the right to file a complaint with the International Labor Office if it is not satisfied that any other Member is securing the effective observance of any Convention which both have ratified in accordance with the foregoing articles.

2. The Governing Body may, if it thinks fit, before referring such a complaint to a Commission of Inquiry, as hereinafter provided for, communicate with the government in question in the manner described in Article 24.

3. If the Governing Body does not think it necessary to communicate the complaint to the government in question, or if, when it has made such communication, no statement in reply has been received within a reasonable time which the Governing Body considers to be satisfactory, the Governing Body may appoint a Commission of Inquiry to consider the complaint and to report thereon.

4. The Governing Body may adopt the same procedure either of its own motion or on receipt of a complaint from a delegate to the Conference.

5. When any matter arising out of Article 25 or 26 is being considered by the Governing Body, the government in question shall, if not already represented thereon, be entitled to send a representative to take part in the proceedings of the Governing Body while the matter is under consideration. Adequate notice of the date on which the matter will be considered shall be given to the government in question.

Note an Employer or Worker Representative may or may not be a trade union. The founding ILO Members carefully avoided restricting representations to trade unions. There are many smaller groups of workers that could not themselves mount a successful representation, but can do so by working through larger associations.

Generally, the complaint system is governed by Articles 26 and 34 of the ILO Constitution. These Articles allows for Member to file a complaint against another Member that is following a particular ILO *Convention* in dispute. Upon receiving a complaint, the Governing Body may appoint a Commission of Inquiry to investigate. Upon completion of the investigation, the Commission generates a report with recommendations, which the ILO publishes. The respondent may accept the recommendations, or appeal to the ICJ. The Governing Body has the option to pass the case on to the Committee of Experts to follow up on the recommendations, or take actions under Article 33 of the Constitution. Note the fact of publication can encourage the respondent to implement the recommendations to avoid further reputational damage. Bluntly put, publication of the report can shame a country into compliance.

- **Enforcement Mechanism 4: Conference Action**

Article 33 of the Constitution allows the Governing Body to take "such action as it may deem wise and expedient to secure compliance therewith." Article 33 has only been invoked once in the history of the ILO. In 2000, the Body asked the Conference to take actions against Myanmar for widespread forced labor. For over 30 years, there were forced labor issues from the dictatorial Burmese government. That military *junta* showed no signs of compliance, even after a published 1998 report, which documented government involvement in child labor and forced.[2]

---

2. Kari Tapiola & Lee Swepston, *The ILO and the Impact of Labor Standards: Working on the Ground after an ILO Commission of Inquiry*, 21 STANFORD LAW AND POLICY REVIEW 513–526 (2010).

In 2000, the Conference agreed, invoking Article 33. Since 2001, the ILO has had a uniquely strong presence in Burma. It has a Liaison office in Rangoon, enabling it to create a complaint system whereby individuals who are forced into working can file complaints. Forced labor still exists, but appears to be diminishing.

As for Employer and Worker Representatives, they may file a complaint—called a "representation"—against a Member. The ILO receives representations and informs a respondent Member and the Governing Body. The Body may decide to establish a Tripartite Committee comprised of individuals from Members and Employer and Worker Representatives to investigate the alleged violations. The Committee produces a report for the Governing Body. Then, the Body may render findings, accept the report, and create an Expert Committee to follow up on the recommendations or it can create a Commission of inquiry to investigate further the complaint.

II. Defining "Internationally Recognized Worker Rights" Based on ILO *Conventions*

Eliding for the moment the problem of defining "worker rights," why do these rights get violated? Oxfam International offers the following 5 reasons:

   (1) National governments, desperate to attract much-needed foreign investment, offer incentives, including increased labor-market "flexibility"—that is, the denial of fundamental labor rights such as freedom of association, along with the failure to enforce existing legislation.

   (2) Powerful global buyers, whose business model is based on short-term profit maximization, squeeze the players lower down the supply chain.

   (3) Producers use cheap labor as their primary competitive advantage, actively discouraging workers from organizing.

   (4) Lending agencies such as the IMF and World Bank insist on labor-market flexibility as a part of their lending policy.

   (5) Young women and migrants, who constitute a majority of the "flexible, obedient, pliant" workforce, are often not aware of their rights and are highly vulnerable to exploitation (notably including sexual exploitation).[3]

These reasons bespeak the reality of working conditions in the agricultural and industrial sectors of many countries. This reality is not limited to poor countries, nor to those sectors. Service sector workers (including American lawyers!) complain not unreasonably of dreadful working conditions.

These reasons also intimate the parameters of a definition of "worker rights." There are, in fact, an internationally agreed-upon set of such rights.

---

3. Oxfam International, *Stitched Up: How Rich-Country Protectionism in Textiles and Clothing Trade Prevents Poverty Alleviation* 25 (Oxfam Briefing Paper 60, March 2004).

United States International Trade Commission,

Trade Issues of the 1990s—Part II,
International Economic Review 18, 19 (December 1994)

Trade, Employment, and Labor Standards

... [B]etween the December 1993 conclusion and the April 1994 signing of the Uruguay Round agreements, the United States sought to have labor standards—also referred to as worker rights—included in discussions of factors affecting trade under the forthcoming WTO regime. However, developing countries were deeply suspicious that such multilateral discussions were likely, at best, to undermine their comparative trade advantage arising out of lower labor costs; at worst, to afford developed countries an issue that could be abused for patently protectionist purposes. [The U.S. tried to have labor topics included on the DDA, but many WTO Members from the developing countries and LDCs.]

U.S. Focus on Worker Rights

The ... U.S. effort to bring labor standards under multilateral discussion in the trade arena has both a longstanding and a more immediate stimulus. Congressional mandates to pursue "worker rights" have been common as part of the legislative renewal of Presidential trade-negotiating authority since the Eisenhower administration. This mandate was reiterated most recently in Congressional instructions to U.S. negotiators in the *Omnibus Trade and Competitiveness Act of 1988*. Of the 16 negotiating objectives set out in section 101 of the act, no. 14 reads—

(14) Worker Rights.—The principal negotiating objectives of the United States regarding worker rights are—

(A) To promote respect for worker rights;

(B) To secure a review of the relationship of worker rights to GATT articles, objectives, and related instruments with a view to ensuring that the benefits of the trading system are available to all workers; and

(C) To adopt, as a principle of the GATT, that the denial of worker rights should not be a means for a country or its industries to gain competitive advantage in international trade.

... The United States has said it supports ... [labor] rights as a means to raise the living standards of all citizens, including workers.... The United States has stated repeatedly that it in no way seeks to use new labor standards to erect new trade barriers for protectionist purposes.

Although unsuccessful in inserting language concerning worker rights into the *Marrakesh Declaration* in April 1994, the United States did succeed in having trade and labor standards acknowledged by other Round participants as a legitimate subject for consideration ... [in future WTO projects.]

...

Labor Standards Precursors

In its efforts to raise worker rights as a multilateral issue, the United States pointed out that the *Havana Charter* of 1948 and, subsequently, the GATT, addressed these rights. The *Havana Charter* specified—

> The Members recognize that . . . all countries have a common interest in the achievement and maintenance of fair labor standards related to productivity, and thus in the improvement of wages and working conditions as productivity may permit. The Members recognize that unfair labor conditions, particularly in production for export, create difficulties in international trade and accordingly each Member shall take whatever action may be appropriate and feasible to eliminate such conditions within the territory.

The *Havana Charter* . . . never came into existence as the ITO was never ratified by national legislatures. Although the later preamble to the GATT states that members are joining the General Agreement "Recognizing that their relations in the field of trade . . . should be conducted with a view to raising standards of living," the more specific labor standards of the Havana Charter serve now only as guidelines for present-day negotiators, taken from the collective history of the original negotiation of the General Agreement.

ILO Labor Standards

The United States' campaign to discuss labor standards in relation to trade concentrates largely on five of the most widely recognized labor standards. These five standards are—

1. The freedom of association;
2. The right to organize and bargain collectively;
3. The freedom from forced or compulsory labor;
4. A minimum age for the employment of children; and
5. Measures that set forth minimum standards for work conditions.

These standards, as well as others, are internationally recognized by the International Labor Organization (ILO) of the United Nations in its conventions and endorsed by a number of countries.

[The four most significant ILO *Conventions* are: (1) Number 87, on *Freedom of Association and Protection of the Right to Organize*; (2) Number 98, on the *Right to Organize and Collectively Bargain*; (3) Number 105, on *Abolition of Forced Labor*; and (4) Number 138, on *Minimum Age*. Consider which countries (including the U.S.) have not ratified these and other *Conventions* noted below, as well as which ones ratified by later denounced a *Convention*, and why.[4]]

---

4. *See* International Labor Organization, Table, Ratifications of Fundamental Conventions by Country, www.ilo.org/dyn/normlex/en/f?p=NORMLEXPUB:10011:0::NO::P10011_DISPLAY _BY,P10011_CONVENTION_TYPE_CODE:1,F.

[On 17 June 1999, the ILO unanimously adopted *Convention* 182 on the *Prohibition and Immediate Action for the Elimination of the Worst Forms of Child Labor*. *See* 38 INTERNATIONAL LEGAL MATERIALS 1215 (1999). *Convention* 182 defines "child" as anyone less than 18 years old, and identifies the "worst forms" as slavery, debt bondage, forced or compulsory labor (including the use of children in armed conflict), prostitution, pornography, the use of children for illicit activities (*e.g.*, narcotics production and trafficking), and work that is likely to harm the health, safety, or morals of children. ILO Members are obligated to take immediate and effective measures to eliminate these practices. Article 10 of the *Convention* states the *Convention* enters into force one year after the date on which two ILO Members have ratified it. The Seychelles ratified it on 28 September 1999, and Malawi ratified it on 19 November 1999. Thus, the *Convention* took effect on 19 November 2000. In August 1999, President Bill Clinton (1946–, President, 1992–2001) sought the advice and consent of the Senate for ratification, and the Senate acted favorably on 2 December 1999. Note, however, the *Convention* can be viewed as a pragmatic, if not depressing, compromise. Rather than trying to outlaw all forms of child labor, a possibly hopeless effort, it seeks only to rid the globe of the worst forms.]

[The ILO's Governing Body identifies 8 "Fundamental *Conventions*," which cover:

> subjects that are considered as fundamental principles and rights at work: freedom of association and the effective recognition of the right to collective bargaining; the elimination of all forms of forced or compulsory labor; the effective abolition of child labor; and the elimination of discrimination in respect of employment and occupation. These principles are also covered in the ILO's *Declaration on Fundamental Principles and Rights at Work* (1998). There are [as of September 2017] over 1,367 ratifications of these *Conventions*, representing 91,4% of the possible number of ratifications. A further 129 ratifications are still required to meet the objective of universal ratification of all the fundamental.

The eight Fundamental *Conventions* are:

(1) 1948 *Freedom of Association and Protection of the Right to Organize Convention* (Number 87)

(2) 1949 *Right to Organize and Collective Bargaining Convention* (Number 98)

(3) 1930 *Forced Labor Convention* (Number 29)

(4) 1957 *Abolition of Forced Labor Convention* (Number 105)

(5) 1973 *Minimum Age Convention* (Number 138)

(6) 1999 *Worst Forms of Child Labor Convention* (Number 182)

(7) 1951 *Equal Remuneration Convention*, 1951 (Number 100)

(8) 1958 *Discrimination (Employment and Occupation) Convention* (Number 111).]

... The United States incorporates these five standards as conditions for affording trade preferences to developing countries under such programs as the Generalized System of Preferences (GSP). In a review of existing trade and labor provisions, prepared for the November 1994 meeting of its governing body, the ILO found that virtually all trade liberalizing agreements lack a "social dimension" or a "labor dimension," particularly concerning the areas covered by the ILO conventions on freedom of association, collective bargaining, prison labor, and forced and child labor. Although the idea is adamantly opposed by developing countries, the paper suggests incorporating some ILO conventions into the WTO rules where the WTO could make decisions concerning trade sanctions following ILO judgment about whether violations had occurred.

III. EU *Social Charter*

Organization for Economic Co-Operation and Development,
Trade and Labor Standards 9–17, 19, 21 (1995)

I. Introduction

...

Trade and labor market policies are continuously being discussed and reformulated. . . . When does "free trade" give way to "fair trade"? When does the pursuit of one labor standard (*e.g.*, free collective bargaining) take precedence over another (*e.g.*, full employment)?

...

[Below, the following] five questions are raised for consideration:

1. On what basis should labor standards be chosen?

2. Is there such a thing as basic labor rights? If so, should they be harmonized internationally?

3. What labor standards are appropriate beyond the basic level and how might they be achieved?

4. Based on countries' experiences, is it better to promote labor standards directly or indirectly?

5. Are labor standards and international trade substitutes or complements?

II. The Basis for Deciding on "Appropriate" Labor Standards

... [T]wo extreme positions on labor standards have to be rejected. One is "the more the better." The other is "the fewer the better."

...

How, then, are we to decide which labor standards are appropriate? While it is argued by some that international labor standards are needed in order to prevent countries from competing with one another on the basis of "illegitimate advantages," a different basis for evaluation could be suggested, namely, *basic human rights in the workplace*. The distinguishing criterion one could propose *is whether it is better to have no production at all than to have production using "illegitimate means."*

If this criterion is adopted, it would imply that labor rights would be set at a minimum level appropriate to all working people in rich and poor countries alike and guaranteed by appropriate international agreements. They would be taken out of the realm of benefit-cost comparisons with tradeoffs among desirable goals and would instead be treated as *inviolable* rights.

What are the basic human rights in the workplace for men, women, and children everywhere? Would it be desirable to go beyond these basic labor rights to other labor standards?

III. Basic Labor Rights and Harmonization of Labor Standards

It is useful at the outset to distinguish between a "labor standard" and a "labor right"; a "labor standard" is something we would aim towards and rather have than not have, whereas a "labor right" is something that is not to be violated except under the most extreme circumstances. "Labor standards" thus include "labor rights" but go beyond them.

The U.S. Department of Labor has repeatedly upheld the desirability of the following list of labor standards:

1. Freedom of association.

2. The right to organize and bargain collectively.

3. Prohibition on forced or compulsory labor.

4. A minimum age for the employment of children.

5. Guarantee of acceptable working conditions (possibly including maximum hours of work per week, a weekly rest period, limits to work by young persons, a minimum wage, minimum workplace safety and health standards, and elimination of employment discrimination).

Section 502 (b)(8) of the 1984 *Trade and Tariff Act* authorizes the President to withhold recognition under the GSP to a country that "has not taken or is not taking steps to afford internationally recognized worker rights to workers in the country (including any designated zone in that country)."

The EU's "Social Charter," approved by all of the EC Member countries except for the U.K., specifies an even broader list of worker "rights" (which, because they are voluntary, might better be viewed as "targets"):

— Freedom of movement.

— The right to employment and remuneration.

— The improvement of living and working conditions.

— The right to social protection.

— The right to freedom of association and collective bargaining.

— The right to vocational training.

— The right of men and women to equal treatment.

— The right of information, consultation, and participation.

— The right to health and safety in the workplace.

— The protection of children and adolescents in employment.

— The protection of elderly persons.

— The protection of persons with disabilities.

It is sad but true that standards like these are unattainable for most of the world's people. The reason is very basic: most of the world's economies are too poor to assure these standards for the majority of their people, and even in the rich countries, these standards are not guaranteed to everyone. For example, when rural parents in the developing countries must decide between employing their children on the family farm during planting and harvesting season or sending them to school, the children are often made to work long and hard, even though not going to school is known to have potentially negative effects on the children's future opportunities. Or, to take another example of a clash of priorities, when people receive extremely low hourly earnings from wage jobs or self-employment, they will want to work very long work weeks in order to meet their basic subsistence needs; in these circumstances, it would be heartless to limit the work week or compel a weekly rest period. However, the preceding lists are too ambitious and unrealistic for the majority of the world's workers.

Even leading labor officials now recognize the impossibility of guaranteeing "acceptable working conditions" at an internationally uniform level.... [T]he United States' Secretary of Labor [in the Clinton Administration], Robert Reich, said . . . :

> It is inappropriate to dictate uniform levels of working hours, minimum wages, benefits, or health and safety standards. The developing countries' insistence that they must grow richer in order to afford American or European labor standards—and that they must trade if they are to grow richer—is essentially correct.

Along similar lines, the General Secretary of the International Confederation of Free Trade Unions (ICFTU), one of the strongest advocacy groups for labor, wrote:

> The ICFTU-APRO does not think that is possible or desirable to set a world-wide minimum wage. Negotiations between employers, unions, and governments within countries, which take into account productivity and other factors, are the best way to ensure that as trade and development progress, wages and other conditions of work improve.

These statements suggest that a "guarantee of acceptable working conditions" has effectively been removed from current policy debate.

In the spirit of aiming for something that is both attainable and enforceable in *every* country, a set of *basic labor rights for workers throughout the world* can be proposed:

   (i) No person has the right to enslave another or to cause another to enter into indentured servitude, and every person has the right to freedom from such conditions.

   (ii) No person has the right to expose another to unsafe or unhealthy working conditions without the fullest possible information.

   (iii) Children have the right not to work long hours whenever their families' financial circumstances allow.

   (iv) Every person has the right to freedom of association in the workplace and the right to organize and bargain collectively with employers.

Such labor rights are essential for assuring fundamental human rights and that they should, therefore, be adopted around the world as soon as possible. Viewed in this way, the question of whether this four-point program should be harmonized internationally can be answered easily. Yes, it should be: basic labor rights should be "taken out of competition" and guaranteed everywhere precisely because these rights are basic to all people.

IV. International Pressure for Additional Labor Standards

Should international pressure be brought to bear in the pursuit of additional labor standards that go beyond the four basic labor rights just proposed? Here, one would argue that such standards should not be harmonized under the aegis of international organizations even if "deep integration" were possible, which it probably is not. Labor standards should, rather, be left to the individual countries. The reasons for concluding this are several:

1. Although developed countries' concerns for developing countries' labor standards are motivated in part by a humanitarian desire to improve the conditions of work in other countries, they nonetheless strike many in the developing world as unwarranted intrusion into their internal affairs and affronts to their national sovereignty. People in the developing world are offended when they are treated as being incapable of deciding what would be appropriate for themselves, and they rightly regard developing countries' advice as patronizing. A remarkable unanimity of views against imposed international labor standards has been expressed by the leaders of developing countries around the world, including the Member states of the Association of South-East Asian Nations and the "Rio Group" of Latin American nations.

2. To many in the Third World, the First World's call for labor standards is protectionism of a badly-disguised sort. Protestations about benevolent

motives are regarded with considerable skepticism and, anyhow, motives are not observable. What is observable is that most of the support for labor standards comes from labor unions and labor ministries in some of the developed countries. Not surprisingly, the developing countries often react with anger. Consider this from the Prime Minister of Malaysia [Mahathir Bin Mohamed (1925–, PM, 1981–2003, 2018–)]:

> Western governments openly propose to eliminate the competitive edge of East Asia. The recent proposal for a world-wide minimum wage is a blatant example. Westerners know that this is the sole comparative advantage of the developing countries. All other comparative advantages (technology, capital, rich domestic markets, legal frameworks, management and marketing networks) are with the developed states. It is obvious that the professed concern about workers' welfare is motivated by selfish interest. Sanctimonious pronouncements on humanitarian, democratic and environmental issues are likely to be motivated by a similar selfish desire to put as many obstacles as possible in the way of anyone attempting to catch up and compete with the West.

3. International standards designed with one problem in mind may make little sense in other contexts. Take the widely-urged standard of prohibiting production by forced or convict-labor and banning the trade in such goods. This standard is motivated by abuses in countries which have been found to use political prisoners who are given only meager subsistence and no wages to produce low-cost goods for export. This is indeed outrageous. But would it be any less outrageous if the goods were sold only within those countries? Anyhow, most convicts around the world are imprisoned not for political reasons but because they have been convicted of crimes. To the extent that those who have committed violent or antisocial acts are made to work in prison for their living, why should not the goods they produced be sold abroad, with the proceeds to be used as partial compensation to the home societies (by, for example, defraying the social cost of maintaining prisons)? The case for banning the export of goods made by prison labor is unconvincing.

4. It is unlikely that an enforcement mechanism can be found that would be acceptable to all sides, but let us suppose for the moment that one could be. For instance, one of the world's leading advocates for free trade. Professor Jagdish Bhagwati [(1934–)] . . . has proposed that U.S. labor laws be applied to subsidiaries of U.S. firms producing in Mexico. Assuming that international labor standards could be enforced in this way, one can reasonably ask whether they should be. Would it be good to apply the U.S. minimum wage to subsidiaries of U.S. firms operating in Mexico, considering the likely adverse employment effects? Should the labor of Mexican children be outlawed even when families rely on that labor for their livelihoods? Would it be

right to impose an eight-hour day or a forty-hour week on people who want to work longer? If Mexico were to agree to these standards, how many jobs would move to other countries where these standards are not imposed? How many non-U.S. companies who would not have to meet U.S. labor standards would move into Mexico and replace U.S. companies which would have to meet those standards? It is not obvious what would be good for Mexico: that is not for us to decide, but for them.

. . .

6. Finally, it is interesting to note that the ILO itself has *opposed* sanctions against countries that have failed to comply with conventions they have ratified or with the ILO's universal principles. Why? "In addition to implementing sanctions, the mere prospect of sanctions is capable of discouraging ratification, or even membership in the Organization." And: "[To] link trade concessions (such as access to their markets) to compliance with certain labor standards with a view to combating what they refer to as 'social dumping' . . . [could cause our supervisory machinery to suffer] if the conclusions that result from it are used in a context of coercion."

IV. Push versus Pull Debate on Labor Rights in Poor Countries

Organization for Economic Co-Operation and Development,

Trade And Labor Standards 9–17, 19, 21 (1995)

V. *How to Raise Labor Standards: Push or Pull?*

Assuming that it is left to individual countries to decide when and how to raise labor standards, what lessons might they find helpful from comparative analysis of other countries' experiences? First, it is necessary to be explicit about what is meant by "improved labor standards." Above, it was suggested that higher labor standards might be conceived as enabling workers to achieve higher real earnings at the fullest possible level of employment, and that is the objective that is taken here as given.

Two broad approaches toward raising labor standards can be found:

— Governments often take direct action aimed at raising labor standards: directly increasing employment, directly raising wages by means of government pay policy for the public sector and minimum wages for the private sector, encouraging and facilitating strong trade unions, instituting ambitious labor codes.

— Labor standards are also promoted indirectly, *via* actions to accelerate economic growth so that improvements in wage and employment opportunities can be afforded. Among the developing countries, the direct approach of pushing up wages and employment has been the dominant one in Latin America and the Caribbean, Africa, and South Asia; by contrast, some Far Eastern economies (Singapore, Hong Kong, Korea, and Taiwan) are noteworthy for their reliance on indirect methods and the virtual absence of direct ones. In the developed world, the European countries might appropriately be classified in an intermediate position.

Setting labor standards directly is a tricky business. . . . [D]ue account must be taken of such predictable consequences as informalization, partial coverage, and international movement of companies and jobs. . . .

Modern economic theory seeks to justify government intervention in the economy as a response to market failure, but the literature on the labor standards question has not gone very far toward specifying what market failure is being corrected. There are some apparent failures—asymmetric information on the health and safety risks associated with particular jobs (which motivates proposed basic labor standard number (ii) "No person has the right to expose another to unsafe or unhealthy working conditions without the fullest impossible information") and severe limits on international migration as a response to poor labor conditions—but discussion of these is conspicuously missing from the labor standards literature. On the other hand, one "failure" that is sometimes alleged in the literature is the failure of companies to do what is in their own interest, leading some economists and other social scientists to argue that the imposition of labor standards could lead to improved industrial relations practices, more and better worker training, greater purchasing power of labor, and the like, all of which are presumed to be better for firms. This line of reasoning implicitly assumes that firms are not now maximizing profits and furthermore that the deviations from profit-maximizing behavior in the absence of enforced labor standards are systematic—too little labor-management co-operation, for example. Neoclassically-oriented economists are not likely to be convinced by such claims, implicit or otherwise.

A more convincing argument might be the following: there exist multiple equilibria, the world's economies have somehow got locked into an inferior one because of coordination failures, and the imposition of labor standards on a world-wide scale would cause a shift to a superior equilibrium. This would, however, have to be demonstrated to be applicable to current conditions.

Consider now the alternative of waiting for labor standards to be pulled up by the forces of supply and demand. Have the indirect methods worked? . . . [D]ata [from 1948–1990 concerning four East Asian economies, Hong Kong, Korea, Singapore, and Taiwan] show two distinct phases . . . . In the first phase, when these economies were labor-abundant, real labor earnings stayed roughly constant while unemployment fell. In the second phase, once essentially-full employment was attained, real labor earnings rose rapidly while full or nearly-full employment was maintained. The results are astounding: in Taiwan, real wages are eight times higher than they were a generation ago, and in Korea, they are more than six times higher.

The extent to which workers in the Far East shared in their economies' economic growth can be demonstrated in another way.... [I]n all four economies in the 1980s, real labor earnings grew at least as fast as real *per capita* GNP. The four Far Eastern economies have had very low rates of unemployment and very low levels of income inequality by international standards. This means that people at the bottom end of the income distribution have benefited proportionately from economic growth, and in this way, growth raised labor standards: real minimum wages were increased, unemployment insurance systems were instituted, social protection systems were created, and collective bargaining grew in importance.

. . .

These international data suggest that there may be an effective alternative to pushing up wages and other labor standards directly: promoting labor standards indirectly through measures that foster economic growth. This is a call not for inattention to basic labor rights, which have not always been fully honored in the Far East. It is, rather, a call for careful analysis of which mechanisms would best promote improved labor standards in particular country contexts.

V. GATT Article XX(e) Prison Labor Exception

Given the increased attention galvanized by the anti-globalization movement to the effects of trade liberalization on labor rights, item (e) is perhaps the most notable of the 10 general exceptions to GATT obligations listed in GATT Article XX. Yet, this exception is not a broad one for all kinds of workers' rights. It is narrowly crafted for "prison" labor. The drafters of GATT had a precedent for their work. A provision in the U.S. *Tariff Act of 1930*, as amended, bans importation of prison-made goods.

Why single out prison labor? One justification is economic. Setting aside questions of product comparability or quality, if prison workers are maintained at subsistence level, then their product is akin to unfairly subsidized merchandise. Workers in other countries, who are not imprisoned, cannot compete against goods made by prisoners kept barely alive. The price of their output will be higher, in reflection of their higher wages. (That higher price also may suggest higher marginal productivity.)

Is this justification persuasive? All too many workers around the world are paid a bare subsistence wage (or less). About one billion people earn one U.S. dollar per day or less, and another one billion people earn two dollars or less per day. Obviously, they are not all in prison. If the rationale for Article XX(e) is to combat an unfair form of competition, then the language of this exception is under-inclusive. Ought it not also cover merchandise for which a worker, jailed or not, is paid less than an agreed-upon threshold? Of course, agreeing on that threshold is nearly impossible, with wealthy WTO Members advocating a high level and poorer Members fearing the higher the level, the greater their loss of comparative advantage.

GATT Article XX(e) is not always easy to implement. For instance, is it possible to determine whether a particular facility in a WTO Member is, in fact, a prison? The Member may be willing to disclose many, even most, of its prisons. For reasons (however dubious) of internal security, it may keep one or a few facilities secret. The 1994 *China Diesel* case raises these matters.

VI. U.S. Section 307 Ban on Merchandise from Convict, Forced, or Indentured Labor

- **Operation of Section 307**

Section 307 of the *Tariff Act of 1930*, as amended, authorizes the U.S. Secretary of Labor to ban importation of merchandise produced through convict labor, forced labor, or indentured labor.[5] Pursuant to regulations of CBP, members of the public (*inter alia*) can petition CBP to investigate a case. This authorization, while pre-dating GATT, falls within GATT Article XX(e), at least with respect to prison labor.

So, for example, in May 2013, the International Labor Rights Forum, an American NGO, petitioned CBP to deny entry at U.S. ports of goods made from cotton yarn and fabric from Uzbekistan. Such goods were made by Daewoo International, Indorma Kokand, and other manufacturers. ILRF alleged the Uzbek government forced millions of Uzbekis, including children, to pick cotton under unforgiving circumstances, in pursuit of its state order system for cotton production. Those circumstances were physical abuse, fines, loss of job and farmland, school expulsion, and denial of welfare benefits for refusal to pick cotton.

- **Limits of Section 307 and Construction Services in Dubai and Qatar**

It is critical to appreciate the limits of Section 307. It applies only to imports of goods into the U.S. It does not apply to exports of goods from America, which presumably would be produced under the protections of federal and state labor laws. Section 307 also does not apply to exports or imports of services. Consider the implications of this latter point.

In 2012, the UAE surpassed Saudi Arabia as the largest market for construction in the Gulf region (as measured by contracts awarded, which in that year were U.S. $16.2 billion).[6] Labor rights groups have criticized labor conditions in the construction services sector in the Gulf. Migrant workers from Bangladesh, India, and Pakistan, and other countries toil for long hours yet low pay (in the UAE, about $160–$200 a month as of May 2013), which sometimes is deferred, only to return to congested labor camps out of sight from the gleaming tours, five-star hotels, and

---

5. *See* 19 U.S.C. § 1307.

6. *See* Simeon Kerr, *Site Workers Defy Law in Dubai Strike*, FINANCIAL TIMES, 21 May 2013, at 3. [Hereinafter, *Site Workers*.]

designer stores. Such camps are shown on the fringe of Dubai in *Syriana*, and in that 2005 movie were a recruiting ground for Islamist extremists.

It is said in the UAE the construction workers may call it a day, as it were, if the officially declared temperature rises above 50 degrees Celsius, so such declarations are rare—even when the thermometers on car dashboards of passersby registers such extremes. Migrant workers sometimes are "plunged into debt by unscrupulous middlemen used to secure jobs,"[7] *i.e.*, they have to pay large sums to employment agencies in their home countries to get a job in the first place, which they covet because the promised salaries exceed those in their home countries, and they hope to repatriate a majority of their Gulf earnings to their families at home to support elderly parents and school-age children.

For instance, in May 2014, Gulf Labor, an international group of artists pushing since 2011 for stronger migrant labor protections, explained most workers from the Indian Sub-Continent recruited for projects in the Abu Dhabi cultural district pay fees between U.S. $1,000–$3,900 to an agent in their home country.[8] If they borrow funds to pay those fees, then typically they pledge collateral such as family land. Gulf Labor called on Abu Dhabi to give $2,000 to migrants working in that Emirate on museums, including branches of the Guggenheim and Louvre on Saadiyat Island, to pay their recruitment fee debts. The Tourism Development and Investment Company (TDIC), a government-owned developer of those museums, as well as a branch of New York University (NYU) on the Island, agreed to provide accommodations for the workers. Gulf Labor said TDIC was willing to "engage in worker welfare 'seriously.'"[9] Whether that meant fee reimbursement was unclear. As a matter of UAE law, strikes are illegal, though in May 2013, thousands of migrant workers struck for at least three days against Arabtec (a contractor that helped build the *Burj Khalifa* in Dubai, the tallest building in the world). Dubai has introduced reforms to ensure "prompt payment of salaries and minimi[ze] exploitation."[10]

So, suppose a construction services firm provides services for a skyscraper in the Emirates, but does not afford basic labor rights to the migrant workers it hires through an employment agency. Suppose further such workers might be considered "indentured labor," given their debt burdens. Whether or not this firm is American, Section 307 does not provide a cause of action against that firm. It is subject to local law.

A similar problem arises with respect to construction services in Qatar. A burst of building activity followed the awarding by the *Fédération Internationale de Football Association (FIFA)* to Qatar to host the 2022 World Cup. Qatar has 1.39 million migrant workers, or 94% of its workforce. The *Financial Times* stated "[h]undreds

---

7. *Site Workers.*

8. *See* Simeon Kerr, *Artists Press Abu Dhabi on Workers' Debts*, Financial Times, 3–4 May 2014, at 4. [Hereinafter, *Artists Press.*]

9. *Quoted in Artists Press.*

10. *Site Workers.*

of workers have died in the state, amid reports—denied by the government—that they were caused by poor working conditions."[11] In May 2015, Qatar reformed its labor laws by abolishing the *kafala* (sponsorship) system, whereby employers exercised "excessive control over their staff, and which critics . . . [said] effectively creates a system of bonded labor." Workers could be held in criminal detention for breach of contract.[12]

The key changes were to eliminate the condition that an expatriate worker could get an exit permit to return home only if the employer agreed, and assure employers they were not liable for debts of their workers. Under the new rule, the Ministry of Labor grants an exit permit automatically, subject to a 72-hour period in which the employer could object.[13] Did the new rule eliminate the risk of exploitation, or were migrants still vulnerable during that three-day window?

The Emirati and Qatari cases illustrate the limited reach of Section 307. It may help remedy labor exploitation overseas only in instances of importation of goods. If the context of abusive treatment is provision of an in-country service, then Section 307 is useless. Local labor law is the recourse.

VII. Section 307 Cases

- **Standing and 1986 *McKinney* Case**[14]

Facts:

During the Cold War, three years before the November 1989 fall of the Berlin Wall, a lawsuit was brought against the U.S. Department of the Treasury alleging it should have prohibited importation of goods from the (former) Soviet Union goods, because those goods may have been produced by forced labor. Multiple parties sued the Department, including members of Congress, labor unions, public interest organizations, and shareholders of domestic companies that produced products competing with the Soviet-made merchandise.

Issue:

At issue was whether any, much less all, of the diverse array of plaintiffs had standing under Section 307 of the 1930 *Tariff Act* to bring an action in Federal court.

Holding:

The Federal Circuit held the plaintiffs seeking standing failed to satisfy the two step test used to determine whether a litigant has standing in a federal court.

---

11. Simeon Kerr, *Qatar Labor Move Fails to Allay Fears*, FINANCIAL TIMES, 15 May 2014, at 3. [Hereinafter, *Qatar Labor*.]
12. *Qatar Labor*.
13. *See Qatar Labor*.
14. *See McKinney v. U.S. Dept. of Treasury*, 799 F.2D 1544, 1547–1558 (Fed. Cir. 1986).

Rationale:

Whether a litigant has standing depends on the outcome of a two-step test (or process) that involves examination of American Constitutional and prudential limitations. First, under Article III of the Constitution, a litigant must show:

(1) It personally has suffered an actual injury, or is threatened with one, as a result of the putatively illegal conduct of the defendant;

(2) A casual connection between the litigant's injury and the putatively illegal conduct; and

(3) The injury is likely to be redressed should the Court grant the relief requested.

In the second step a Court examines prudential limitations, according to which a litigant must:

(1) Assert its own legal rights or interests, as it cannot rest its claim to relief on the legal rights or interest of third parties;

(2) Identify an injury peculiar to itself or a distinct group of which it is a part; and

(3) Show its complaint falls within the "zone of interests" to be protected or regulated by the statute or constitutional guarantee in question.

Commentary:

The test for standing is difficult for litigants to pass, because they have the burden to prove that they satisfy all of its parts, including what amounts to substantial injury. Thus, as here, a general contention under Section 307 against alleged prison or other forced labor, or political antipathy toward an exporting country, will not suffice as bases for standing.

- **Consumptive Demand Exception and 1994 *China Diesel* Case**[15]

Facts:

Certain diesel engines purportedly were made by convict or prison labor in China. Applying Section 307, the U.S. Customs Service banned importation of those engines. The importer, China Diesel Imports, Inc., sued to overturn the ban.

China has multiple types of penal institutions, including traditional style prison facilities, "reform through labor" facilities, and "education through labor" facilities. The engines at issue were made in the JINMA Diesel Engine Factory, which American authorities considered a "reform through labour" institution.

Representatives for the plaintiffs, along with officials from the Department of State, visited the JINMA Factory to observe whether it was a prison labor camp. Despite multiple visits, the Factory failed to provide documentation about its

---

15. *See China Diesel Imports, Inc. v. United States*, 870 F.Supp. 347, 348–352 (CIT 1994) (Judgment Entered).

personnel (*e.g.*, the demographic profiles of the workers) and the production of the engines (*e.g.*, the volume and value of output). Additionally, the American team observed (1) a prison truck leaving from the direction of the JINMA Factory gate, (2) a worker hiding her face from a video camera used by the plaintiff during one visit, (3) hesitancy about showing the State Department observers the location of the wall of the Yunnan Number 1 Prison, and (4) blank space on a city map for both the Prison and factory grounds.

Issue:

The case raised two issues. First, were the diesel engines manufactured by convict or other forced labor? Second, if they were so manufactured, then did the Consumptive Demand Exception in Section 307 apply, that is, was there sufficient domestic production of a substitute product to meet domestic demand?

Holding:

The CIT concluded the JINMA Factory diesel engines were made in whole or in part with convict labor. The Consumptive Demand Exception to the prison labor import prohibition did not apply to convict made goods. Therefore, the CIT excluded from entry into the U.S. engines made in the JINMA Factory.

Rationale:

The Consumptive Demand Exception allows prohibited goods to be imported if they are not produced in sufficient quantities in the U.S. The CIT found this Exception was potentially applicable, because there are no diesel engines manufactured in the U.S. that were comparable.

The CIT said that but for the fact the engines were made by prison labor, the Exception would have applied, and the engines could have been imported under the Exception. However, unfortunately for the plaintiff, the Exception does not apply to convict labor merchandise. The Exception can be invoked only if merchandise at issue is made by labor that is not convict labor, *i.e.*, non-convict labor. Rather confusingly, the CIT stated: "The Consumptive Demand Exception does not apply to convict made goods, and its applicability is unaffected by non-convict or non-forced labor foreign production." The CIT's reference to "non-forced labor" seems rather confusing, but clearly the Exception applies to merchandise made by any non-convict labor.

The CIT reached this conclusion by examining the legislative history during the *1930 Act* debates about Section 307. The CIT observed the Consumptive Demand Exception in the statute as proposed was amended to exclude convict labor from the Exception, and limit the Exception to forced and indentured labor. In other words, Congress rejected a broader Exception—one that would have covered short supply merchandise, whether it was made by convict or non-convict labor.

Congress did so because of concerns about the rubber industry. It wanted to be sure America had a steady source of supply of rubber, even if it was from foreign indentured labor, so it was willing to allow rubber from foreign indentured labor to enter the U.S. under the Exception to 307. But, Congress was unwilling to go so far as to allow convict-made rubber to qualify for the Exception.

Observations:

The Consumptive Demand Exception is intended to benefit consumers of foreign-origin merchandise made by (for lack of a better word) "dubious" foreign labor. The Exception creates a distinction between "convict" and non-convict "forced" labor, with goods made by the latter, but not the former, qualifying for the Exception. So, the Exception allows Americans to gain the benefit of consuming goods that are not manufactured in the U.S. in sufficient quantities.

Consider the implication of the underlying distinction: all "convict" labor surely is "forced," (unless the convicted person genuinely is volunteering for work), but not all "forced" labor is "convict" (as there are many instances of human rights violations wherein a person is compelled to work, but has not been convicted of an offence). The CIT decision means that under no circumstances—not even short supply—will America import convict-made merchandise. Is this decision hypo-critical, in light of the fact many state and local governments in the U.S. purchase goods, and use services, of convicted criminals?

- **Standing, Consumptive Demand Exception, and 2005 *International Labor Rights Fund* Case**[16]

Facts:

The International Labor Rights Fund, Global Exchange and Fair Trade Federation, which are all non-governmental human rights organizations, collectively filed suit against President George W. Bush, the Secretary of DHS, DHS itself, and the Commissioner of CBP. The plaintiffs filed suit because of the refusal by the defendants to (1) investigate credible allegations that cocoa imported to the U.S. from Côte d'Ivoire was produced by forced child labor, (2) require cocoa importers to show their imports are not the product of forced child labor, and (3) prohibit importation of merchandise shown to be the product of forced child labor as required by Section 307 of the *Tariff Act of 1930*.

Issue:

At issue was whether the plaintiffs had standing to file a Section 307 action.

Holding:

The CIT ruled the plaintiffs failed to satisfy the minimum Article III criterion of showing they had a redressable injury, which was necessary for them to do to establish standing.

Rationale:

Article III requires a litigant to establish a causal connection between its injury and the conduct of the defendant, and show this injury is likely to be redressed if

---

16. *See International Labor Rights Fund v. United States*, 391 F.Supp.2d 1370 (CIT 2005).

relief is granted. The CIT recognized the inactions of the defendant, which alleg-edly caused injury to the plaintiffs, yet dismissed their complaint for lack of lack of standing.

Significantly, their lack of standing stemmed from the Consumptive Demand Exception. It applied in the case. Both sides agreed there was no domestic pro-duction of cocoa in the U.S. to meet domestic consumption needs. There was no allegation the imported cocoa was made by convict labor. The plaintiffs could not show injury as producers of cocoa — they did not make cocoa at all. They said their injury was due to the money they had to spend attempting to enforce prohibitions on forced labor in Côte d'Ivoire, because the U.S. government did not do so. That, said the CIT, was not the kind of injury that gave rise to standing under Section 307. Moreover, even if the plaintiffs could have shown standing, the Consumptive Demand Exception applied, thus permitting the cocoa imports.

Comment:

Essentially, the CIT ruling means that when the Consumptive Demand Excep-tion applies, a plaintiff cannot establish standing, even if the merchandise at issue is produced by non-convict forced labor and otherwise would be subject to a Sec-tion 307 import ban. Put bluntly, if the Exception applies, there is no point bringing a Section 307 complaint. Further, that Exception protects Federal regulators from any potential liability.

VIII. End of 85-Year-Old Consumptive Demand Exception[17]

There is a monstrously negative externality associated with the Consumptive Demand Exception: American customs officials cannot block from entry merchan-dise made by child or slave labor, if the amount of that merchandise made in the United States is insufficient to meet domestic demand. For example, suppose cocoa from West Africa is imported into the United States for refining into chocolate and candies, and CBP knows the cocoa plantation workers are children or slaves. The Exception entitles chocolate and candy companies to import the raw mate-rial, because America does not make enough cocoa to fulfil their manufacturing demand. This instance is actually one of several documented global supply chains in which child and slave labor is used, with Hershey Co., Mars Inc., and Nestle SA being implicated. Likewise, Costco Wholesale Corp. was alleged to ignore the use of slaves on boats in Thailand that provide it with frozen shrimp and fish for pet food.

---

17. *See* Erik Larson, *Slave-Labor Loophole Closed by U.S. Senate After 85 Years*, BLOOMBERG BUSINESS, 11 February 2016, www.bloomberg.com/news/articles/2016-02-11/slavery-loophole-is -closed-by-u-s-senate-after-85-years.

The U.N. estimates 21 million people were slaves (as of 2015), producing $150 billion annually in revenue for their captors.

Fortunately, in February 2016, the Senate voted 75–20 to eliminate the Exception, via an amendment to the 2015 *TFTEA* (H.R. 644) that it passed, and which the House already had approved. CBP got the message. Customs authorities had not imposed any restrictions on imports under the Section 307 forced labor provision since 2001. But, in March 2016, they took action against a Chinese chemical supplier, Tangshan Sanyou Group Co. Ltd., of soda ash (sodium bicarbonate).[18]

The action—detention of the suspicious merchandise at the U.S. port of entry—imperilled certain T&A imports. That was because Section 307 allows CBP to bar from merchandise "manufactured wholly or in part in any foreign country" by forced. America's Wal Mart, Sweden's Hennes & Mauritz AB (H&M), Japan's Uniqlo Co. Ltd., and Spain's Industria de Diseno Textil SA (Inditex, known popularly by its store name, Zara) imported clothing made from fabric and viscose rayon that was cleaned and dyed using soda ash. They obtained merchandise from an Indonesian textile supplier, PT Sri Rejeki Isman Tbk, or Sritex, which got its soda ash from Tangshan.

What are the evidentiary barriers to CBP enforcement of the ban on forced labor products? On the one hand, cases in which merchandise is from a foreign government-run prison camp or farm are "easy" to prove. All such merchandise is derived from convict labor. On the other hand, cases in which merchandise is produced by a private entity, or ones in which inputs into the merchandise are of mixed origin (some from prison camps or farms mixed in the supply chain with others from private businesses), and ones in which forced and non-forced merchandise are commingled, are "hard" to prove. What is the right evidentiary burden ("reasonable doubt"? "preponderance"?) to impose, and on what side (CBP or the importer)?

---

18. *See* U.S. Customs and Border Protection, *CBP Commissioner Issues Detention Order on Chemical, Fiber Products Produced by Forced Labor in China*, 29 March 2016, http://www.cbp.gov /newsroom/national-media-release/2016-03-29-000000/cbp-commissioner-issues-detention -order-chemical; Llewellyn Hinkes-Jones, *Clothing Makers at Risk From Forced-Labor Import Ban*, 33 International Trade Reporter (BNA) 558 (21 April 2016); Rossella Brevetti, *Customs Detains Imports From China*, 33 International Trade Reporter (BNA) (7 April 2016). The detention order also covered calcium chloride, caustic soda, and viscose/rayon fiber (which is made from purified cellulose).

In a 2nd detention action within a month, CBP held potassium, potassium hydroxide, and potassium nitrate manufactured or mined by Tangshan. *See* Rossella Brevetti, *Customs Detains Potassium Products From China*, 33 International Trade Reporter (BNA) 563 (21 April 2016).

Chapter 23

Substantive Labor Rules in FTAs[1]

I. Controversy

In all of America's FTA negotiations with developing countries and LDC, no topics are more controversial, and stir more passion, than labor and the environment. The GATT-WTO framework for these matters is inchoate, hence there is creates considerable policy space for parties in FTA negotiations. Put simply, if simplistically, urged by labor and environmental NGOs, the U.S. is wont to demand rigorous obligations and meaningful enforcement mechanisms.

Poor countries often see such demands as an effort to rob them of a comparative advantage: cheap labor. They also decry efforts to infringe on their sovereign right to fashion rules suitable to their level of development. The invariable response is an FTA creates opportunities to move their denizens out of poverty and into the middle class, at which point inevitably they will seek enhanced labor and environmental protections.

The practical consequence of the heated debates, in terms of legal texts, is there are semblances among FTAs. But, there is no single pattern, no iron template, used in every instance on labor and the environmental. Rather, there exists an evolving menu of options. Not surprisingly, then, with respect to virtually any FTA, there is a robust debate as to whether it contains substantively meaningful obligations, whether disputes about those obligations are susceptible to fair and efficient adjudication, whether dispute resolution outcomes are enforceable in an effective manner, and whether any transition periods to phase in or phase out rules are reasonable.

II. November 2013 ILO Study on Significance

• **Increasing Use**

In November 2013 the ILO published *Social Dimensions of Free Trade Agreements*, an empirical study on the use of labor provisions in FTAs the results of which it

---

1. Documents References:
   (1) *NAFTA Labor Side Agreement*
   (2) Labor provisions in other FTAs

found, by its own admission, "somewhat surprising and largely unexpected."[2] It anticipated that the controversial nature of such provisions would mean they are not widely incorporated into FTAs. In fact, they are.

In 1995, the year after the *NAFTA* entered into force, only three FTAs had labor provisions. A decade later, in 2005, 21 accords did. By 30 June 2013, 58 FTAs contained labor provisions. Over all, of then 190 countries that were party to one or more FTAs, 120 of them were in an FTA an arrangement that contained labor provisions. And, of course, with both the original *TPP* and *CPTPP*, labor provisions are in the core text (Chapter 19), supplemented by a bevy of *Side Letters*. (That is the same pattern with respect to environmental provisions, which are in *TPP* and *CPTPP* Chapter 20, and in *Side Letters*.)

- **Developed-Developing Country FTAs and South-South FTAs**

Most of those 58 FTAs referenced in the 2013 *ILO Report* were between developed and developing countries. That was for good reason, as the former group had concerns about labor rights in the latter lot. Thus, all of America's FTAs, starting with *NAFTA*, had provisions in or annexed to them.

Yet, 16 of the 58 FTA that had labor provisions were between or among developing countries, *i.e.*, South-South FTAs. Thus, the stereotype that such countries did not care about labor rights seemed inaccurate. They seemed to be increasingly interested in the topic, as half of the South-South deals with labor provisions were struck after 2005. This acceleration also was a change in direction: at the 1999 WTO Ministerial Conference in Seattle, developing countries were angered at the call by President Bill Clinton for enforceable, sanctionable minimum labor provisions in the core text of trade agreements.[3] They feared a plot to rob them of their comparative advantages derived from cheap labor.

- **Pre-Ratification Conditionality versus Promotional Strategy**

In its FTAs, the U.S. demanded pre-ratification conditionality, meaning it would not grant the economic benefits of the FTA to its FTA partner unless that partner adhered to the labor provisions in the FTA. For example, in its *Oman FTA*, Oman was required to grant the right to forge and participate in unions. In the *Bahrain FTA* and Morocco FTA, Bahrain and Morocco had to strengthen their rules against union discrimination. In the *Peru FTA*, Peru had to implement rules against fraudulent use of temporary workers and outsourcing. In the *Panama FTA*, Panama had to strengthen its laws on freedom of association and protections for short-term contract workers.

---

2. *Quoted in* Daniel Pruzin, *ILO Report Surveys Proliferation Of Labor Provisions in Trade Pacts*, 30 International Trade Reporter (BNA) 1755 (14 November 2013). [Hereinafter, *ILO Report*.] The *ILO Report* is available at www.ilo.org.

3. *See ILO Report*.

Only after these countries made the changes America sought did the U.S. approve the *FTAs*, and thereby liberalize trade with those countries. Canada, too, used the pre-ratification conditionality strategy. Indeed, the ILO reported that 40% of all FTAs made FTA benefits contingent on respect for labor provisions.

The other 60% of the FTAs with labor provisions were promotional in nature. In these deals, there was no link between trade liberalization benefits and compliance with labor provisions. Instead, the labor provisions emphasized cooperation and monitoring. This promotional strategy was used by the EU and New Zealand, and in many South-South FTAs. Rarely did this strategy include a mechanism for dispute settlement, with economic sanctions, thought the FTAs between Chile and Turkey, and between Nicaragua and Taiwan, were exceptions.

III. Four Models

With nearly 20 FTAs in effect between the U.S. and foreign countries, and hundreds of other FTAs around the world to which America is not a party, it is impractical to pour through each one of them in detail, in respect of their labor provisions (or lack thereof). Fortunately, the CRS identified four distinct paradigms for dealing with the link between trade and labor.[4] The CRS calls them "Models," in the sense they are ways the U.S. uses to address labor issues.

Table 23-1 summarizes these Models. Aside from their distinctive features, note the years in which America employed each Model. Manifestly, American trade policy with respect to labor has evolved. Query the directions and reasons for this evolution.

From this Table, at least four shifts are evident. First, the placement of labor provisions has moved from outside to within the core text of the FTA. This shift is politically, if not legally, strategic. Second, the key substantive obligations have expanded beyond effective enforcement of existing rules to respecting internationally recognized worker rights. This shift reflects dissatisfaction by many in Congress with poor quality labor laws in some FTA partner countries, and a desire by them to use ILO standards as a metric (not merely an aspiration) to raise that quality. Third, the dispute settlement mechanism for labor issues has become mainstreamed, that is, the same mechanism is used for any dispute. At least in theory, this shift reflects the seriousness with which a trade-related labor dispute is taken: it is as important as, say, a dispute about national treatment. Fourth, caps on penalties for labor violations are removed. This shift also reflects the seriousness with which labor issues are taken.

---

4. Mary Jane Bolle, *Overview of Labor Enforcement Issues in Free Trade Agreements*, CONGRESSIONAL RESEARCH SERVICE (31 January 2013), www.fas.org/sgp/crs/misc/RS22823.pdf. [Hereinafter, January 2013 CRS *Overview.*]

Table 23-1. Four Models of Labor Provisions in U.S. FTAs

Model	Approximate Number of Years Model Was Used?	FTAs Covered by Model?	Distinctive Features of Labor Provisions Under Model?
1	8 years (1994–2001)	1994 *NAFTA*	*Placement:* Labor provisions not in core text of the *FTA*, but rather in a *Side Agreement*. *Obligations:* The only enforceable labor provision with a sanction is Article 29, which concerns "persistent pattern of failure . . . to effectively enforce its occupational safety and health, child labor or minimum wage technical standards" by a Party. The offense also must be related to trade, and covered by mutually recognized labor laws. Lack of resources is an excuse for failure by a Party to enforce its labor laws. *Procedures and Remedies:* Dispute resolution procedures for labor are separate and distinct from those for commercial provisions. Limits are placed on monetary enforcement assessment and suspension of benefits for non-compliance.
2	3 years (2001–2004)	2001 *Jordan FTA*	*Placement:* Labor provisions are moved into the core text of the FTA. *Obligations:* The key obligation, which is in Article 6:4, remains to "not fail to effectively enforce its labor laws in a manner affecting trade." But, "labor laws" are defined as five specifically listed internationally recognized worker rights: (1) right of association; (2) right to organize and bargain collectively; (3) prohibition on forced or compulsory labor; (4) minimum age for child labor; and (5) acceptable working conditions (*e.g.*, minimum wages, maximum hours, and occupational health and safety). All labor provisions are made equally enforceable.

#	Years	Placement	
			Lack of resources remains an excuse for failure by a Party to enforce labor laws. (Article 6:4(b).)
			Procedures and Remedies:
			Dispute resolution procedures for labor issues are the same as those for commercial provisions, with no caps on penalties for violations.
			If a labor dispute is not resolved under the procedures, then the affected Party is entitled to take "any appropriate and commensurate measure" (Article 17:2(b)).
			Based on *Side Letters* exchanged between USTR Robert Zoellick and Jordanian Ambassador Marwan Muasher prior to implementation legislation in 2001, "governments would not expect or intend to apply the Agreement's dispute settlement enforcement procedures . . . in a manner that results in blocking trade."[5]
3	4 Years (2004–2007)	2004 *Singapore*, 2004 *Chile*, 2005 *Australia*, 2006 *Morocco*, 2006 *CAFTA-DR*, 2006 *Bahrain*, and 2009 *Oman FTAs*[6]	*Placement:* Labor provisions remain in the core text of the *FTA*.
			Obligations:
			The lone enforceable labor provision (typically the second one in the Labor Chapter of the FTA) is that each Party "shall not fail to effectively enforce its labor laws . . . in a manner affecting trade between Parties."
			But, "labor laws" are slightly redefined to mean "a Party's statutes or regulations . . . that are directly related to . . . internationally recognized labor rights."
			The same five such rights as in Model 2 are listed, except for the fourth right, which is expanded to conform to ILO standards to include not only a minimum age for child labor, but also a prohibition and elimination of worst forms of child labor.
			Lack of resources remains an excuse for failure by a Party to enforce labor laws.

(continued)

5. January 2013 CRS Overview, fn. 7 (*citing Jordan Free Trade Agreement Approved by Finance and Ways and Means*, INSIDE U.S. TRADE, 27 July 2001).
6. While the *Oman FTA* entered into force in 2009, it was negotiated during the period in which Model 3 was operative.

Table 22-1. Four Models of Labor Provisions in U.S. FTAs (*continued*)

Model	Approximate Number of Years Model Was Used?	FTAs Covered by Model?	Distinctive Features of Labor Provisions Under Model?
			Procedures and Remedies: Dispute settlement mechanism and sanctions for labor matters are separate and distinct from those for commercial disputes. Monetary assessments for labor violations are limited to $15 million, although commercial violations are not limited.
4	3 years and counting (2007–present)	2009 *Peru*, 2012 *Panama*, 2012 *KORUS*, 2012 *Colombia* *FTAs* Also: *CPTPP*	The May 2007 Bipartisan Trade Deal is incorporated. ***Placement:*** Labor provisions remain in the core text of the *FTA*. ***Obligations:*** The entire Labor Chapter is fully enforceable. The key obligation is that each Party must "adopt and maintain" in its laws and practices the 1998 *ILO Declaration on Fundamental Principles and Rights at Work and its Follow-Up.* This *Declaration* covers the fundamental labor rights, namely: (1) freedom of association; (2) right to collective bargaining; (3) prohibition on compulsory or forced labor; (4) abolition of child labor and prohibition on the worst forms of child labor; (5) elimination of discrimination in respect of employment and occupation. Note the change in the fifth of these rights from Models 2 and 3. Lack of resources is not an excuse for failure by a Party to enforce labor laws. ***Procedures and Remedies:*** The dispute settlement mechanism and penalties for labor issues are the same as those for commercial matters, with no monetary cap.

IV. Special Importance of Model 4

Special attention should be given to Model 4. It is the Model currently in effect, but only after it was developed amidst bitter political controversy. The context for the 2007 controversy was Presidential fast track negotiating authority. Due to growing concerns over a lack of enforceable labor standards in FTAs and a sagging economy, the *TPA* granted under the *Trade Act of 2002*, expired on 30 June 2007. The newly Democratic-controlled Congress insisted it would not renew the authority unless they were confident the president would include labor standards in future trade deals.[7] Before its expiration, America had negotiated and signed free trade agreements with Colombia, Peru, Panama, and Korea but Congress had only approved implementing legislation for the agreement with Peru prior to the expiration of fast track.

To improve the prospect of passage of the stalled FTAs, a deal was struck when the Bush Administration agreed to amend the deals to include more stringent labor provisions than initially negotiated.[8] The 10 May 2007 Bipartisan Trade Deal (BTD) between the White House and Congress required the Bush administration to modify pending trade pacts that had been negotiated with Peru, Panama, Colombia, and Korea.[9] The labor provisions were modified to incorporate internationally-recognized labor principles into FTAs by including enforceable reciprocal obligation for countries to adopt and maintain in their laws and practice the five labor principles stated in the ILO *Declaration on Fundamental Principles and Rights at Work*, including the:

(1) freedom of association;

(2) effective recognition of the right to collective bargaining;

(3) elimination of all forms of forced or compulsory labor;

(4) effective abolition of child labor and a prohibition on the worst forms of child labor; and

(5) elimination of discrimination in respect of employment and occupation.[10]

The deal created an enforceable obligation to effectively enforce labor laws and the *ILO Declaration*. A violation of the FTA requires showing that non-enforcement

---

7. Lee Hudson Teslik, *Fast-Track Trade Promotion Authority and Its Impact on U.S. Trade Policy*, COUNCIL ON FOREIGN RELATIONS, 25 June 2007, www.cfr.org/trade/fast-track-trade-promotion -authority-its-impact-us-trade-policy/p13663. [Hereinafter, *Fast-Track Trade.*]

8. *Fast-Track Trade.*

9. Doug Palmer, *Top U.S. Labor Group Wary of Bipartisan Trade Deal*, REUTERS, 11 May 2007, www.reuters.com/article/2007/05/11/us-usa-trade-labor-idUSN1117298020070511. [Hereinafter, *Top U.S. Labor.*]

10. Trade Facts, OFFICE OF THE UNITED STATES TRADE REPRESENTATIVE, Bipartisan Trade Deal www.ustr.gov/sites/default/files/uploads/factsheets/2007/asset_upload_file127_11319.pdf. [Hereinafter, Trade Facts.]

of labor obligations occurred through a sustained or recurring course of action or inaction by a party in a manner affecting trade or investment between the parties.[11]

However a footnote provided in the Model 4 agreements limit the scope of the obligations, as they relate to the ILO, refer only to the *ILO Declaration*. The footnote indicates Partners are obliged to follow the principles of the *ILO Declaration*, but (arguably) not the specific details of the *Conventions* and the *Follow-Up Procedures*.[12] That is likely, because America has ratified only two of the relevant ILO *Conventions*.

Labor obligations now are subject to the same dispute settlement procedures and remedies as commercial obligations and possible remedies include fines and trade sanctions, based on the amount of trade injury. Only a government can invoke dispute settlement against the other government for the labor violation. The BTD was considered to have strengthened the labor and environmental protections in FTAs, although some skeptics criticized whether the White House would be willing to enforce the provisions.[13]

As a result of the trade deal, negotiators for USTR have gone forth with a new "bottom line" standard for labor chapters of future trade deals. After the deal was established, the four deals listed above as Model 4 were renegotiated to incorporate the concepts agreed to in the BTD.

Model 4 FTAs are have increased the standard of obligation enforcement from where a country was obligated to "enforce its labor laws" to now where countries must "adopt and maintain in their laws and practices of the *ILO Declaration*" in addition to any laws and regulations currently existing within a country. Parties also are prohibited from lowering their labor standards. All obligations within the agreements can seek recourse within the dispute settlement mechanism of the agreement and are able to seek remedies in monetary assessments, with no cap on the amount, and the suspension of benefits if the monetary assessment is not paid. Plus, enforcement discretion in terms of a country's resource is no longer a viable excuse for non-compliance with the terms of the FTAs. Model 4 FTAs are much stronger in enforcement power for labor provisions. Will, and should, they be the standard for future trade deals?

V. Case Study of Collective Bargaining and ILO Implementation: *NAFTA 2.0*

NAFTA 2.0 repositions the *NAFTA 1.0 Labor Side Agreement*, putting it into the core text of the FTA and making them enforceable therein. It also recasts ILO standards from the status of aspirational to mandatory. (And, as discussed in a separate

---

11. Trade Facts.
12. January 2013 CRS *Overview*, 8.
13. *Top U.S. Labor.*

Chapter, it significantly tightens the Hybrid Auto ROO.) Yet, is it ironic that "Right to Work" laws remain in the U.S.?

- 27 August 2018 U.S.-Mexico Bilateral Agreement

Office of the United States Trade Representative,

United States–Mexico Trade Fact Sheet, *Modernizing NAFTA to Be a 21st Century Trade Agreement* (28 August 2018)[14]

. . .

One of President Trump's principal objectives in the renegotiation is to ensure the agreement benefits American workers. The United States and Mexico have agreed to a Labor chapter that brings labor obligations into the core of the agreement, makes them fully enforceable, and represents the strongest provisions of any trade agreement.

Key Achievement: Worker Representation in Collective Bargaining

The Labor Chapter includes an *Annex on Worker Representation in Collective Bargaining in Mexico*, under which Mexico commits to specific legislative actions to provide for the effective recognition of the right to collective bargaining.

Key Achievement: Labor Rights Recognized by the International Labor Organization

The Labor Chapter requires the Parties to adopt and maintain in law and practice labor rights as recognized by the International Labor Organization, to effectively enforce their labor laws, and not to waive or derogate from their labor laws.

Additionally, the Chapter includes new provisions to take measures to prohibit the importation of goods produced by forced labor, to address violence against workers exercising their labor rights, and to ensure that migrant workers are protected under labor laws.

- 30 September 2018 Trilateral *NAFTA 2.0 (USMCA)*

Office of the United States Trade Representative,

United States–Mexico–Canada Fact Sheet: *Modernizing NAFTA into a 21st Century Agreement* (1 October 2018)[15]

. . .

. . . The United States, Mexico, and Canada have agreed to a Labor Chapter that brings labor obligations into the core of the agreement [as distinct from a *Side*

---

14. https://ustr.gov/about-us/policy-offices/press-office/press-releases/2018/august /modernizing-nafta-be-21st-century (emphasis original).

15. https://ustr.gov/about-us/policy-offices/press-office/fact-sheets/2018/october/united -states-mexico-canada-trade-fa-1.

Agreement, where labor provisions were located in *NAFTA* 1.0], makes them fully enforceable, and represents the strongest provisions of any trade agreement.

Key Achievement: Worker Representation in Collective Bargaining

The Labor Chapter includes an Annex on Worker Representation in Collective Bargaining in Mexico, under which Mexico commits to specific legislative actions to provide for the effective recognition of the right to collective bargaining.

Key Achievement: Labor Rights Recognized by the International Labor Organization

The Labor Chapter requires the Parties to adopt and maintain in law and practice labor rights as recognized by the International Labor Organization, to effectively enforce their labor laws, and not to waive or derogate from their labor laws.

Additionally, the chapter includes new provisions to take measures to prohibit the importation of goods produced by forced labor, to address violence against workers exercising their labor rights, and to ensure that migrant workers are protected under labor laws.

Key Achievement: New Labor Value Content Rule

To support North American jobs, the deal contains new trade rules of origin [discussed in a separate Chapter] to drive higher wages by requiring that 40–45 percent of auto content be made by workers earning at least USD $16 per hour.

VI. Provisions for Women and LGBTQ+ Persons

TPP and *CPTPP* Article 23:4 contain a special rule concerning women. *NAFTA* 2.0 Article 29:2 contains a special rule for women and LGBTQ+ communities—a rule championed by Canada throughout the negotiations. Both are set forth below. Consider how the similarities and differences between the rules. How, for example, do they compare on scope of application, and with respect to benchmarks (metrics) of performance? Consider, too, whether these rules are enforceable. Are they both "hard" law, "soft" law, or a hybrid of "hard" and "soft" law?

TPP and *CPTPP*, Article 23:4:
Women and Economic Growth

1. The Parties recognize that enhancing opportunities in their territories for women, including workers and business owners, to participate in the domestic and global economy contributes to economic development. The Parties further recognize the benefit of sharing their diverse experiences in designing, implementing and strengthening programs to encourage this participation.

2. Accordingly, the Parties shall consider undertaking cooperative activities aimed at enhancing the ability of women, including workers

and business owners, to fully access and benefit from the opportunities created by this Agreement. These activities may include providing advice or training, such as through the exchange of officials, and exchanging information and experience on:

(a) programs aimed at helping women build their skills and capacity, and enhance their access to markets, technology and financing;

(b) developing women's leadership networks; and

(c) identifying best practices related to workplace flexibility.

NAFTA 2.0 (USMCA), Article 23:9:
Sex-Based Discrimination in the Workplace

The Parties recognize the goal of eliminating sex-based discrimination in employment and occupation, and support the goal of promoting equality of women in the workplace. Accordingly, each Party shall implement policies that protect workers against employment discrimination on the basis of sex, including with regard to pregnancy, sexual harassment, sexual orientation, gender identity, and caregiving responsibilities, provide job-protected leave for birth or adoption of a child and care of family members, and protect against wage discrimination.

In November 2018, nearly 50 Republican members of the House of Representatives urged removal of the sexual orientation and gender identity provisions in USMCA (Article 23:9, as above, and Article 23:12(5)(l)(i)), which calls upon the NAFTA 2.0 Parties to cooperate to promote equality and remove employment discrimination on the basis of SOGI. They asserted "[a] trade agreement is no place for the adoption of social policy," and that it was "inappropriate and insulting to our sovereignty to needlessly [sic] submit to social policies which [sic] the United States Congress has so far explicitly refused to accept."[16] Not coincidentally, perhaps, a new footnote (numbered 13) appeared in the text (following the word "policies") stating:

The United States' existing federal agency policies regarding the hiring of federal workers are sufficient to fulfill the obligations set forth in this Article. The Article thus requires no additional action on the part of the United States, including any amendments to Title VII of the Civil Rights Act of 1964, in order for the United States to be in compliance, with the obligations set forth in this Article.

This footnote limits the effect of Article 23:9 with respect to LGBTQ+ protections in America. It does not explicitly strip these persons of protections they may have under applicable federal or state law, but it does not oblige the U.S. to do any

---

16. Letter to President Donald J. Trump from Doug Lamborn, Member of Congress *et al.*, 16 November 2018, https://lamborn.house.gov/uploadedfiles/final_letter.pdf.

more on their behalf, and does not guarantee that any protections they do have will remain in place.

However, did their assertion rest on the dubious assumptions that (1) a hard line could be drawn between "economic" and "social" policy in international trade agreements, and (2) even if such a line could be drawn, other countries would do so?

Finally, consider that footnote 13 to Article 23:9 raises two serious problems. First, substantively, as of 30 November, when the Parties signed the USMCA, there was no U.S. federal law concerning protection on the basis of sexual orientation and gender identity.[17] At the State level, it is legal to discriminate on the basis of sexual orientation in 29 States, and legal to discriminate against transgender workers in 34 States.[18] By contrast, both Canadian and Mexican law have protections for LGBTQ+ workers. In 1996, Canada banned discrimination based on sexual orientation, and in 2003, Mexico did so; in 2017, Canada banned discrimination based on gender identity or expression, but Mexico has not done so.[19] Second, procedurally, the footnote was inserted in a non-transparent manner. The introduction of footnote 13 to the text of Article 23:9 may well have occurred because of the above-referenced Republican letter to the President.[20] There was no advance discussion or notice of it, nor any official mention of it once it was inserted. Indeed, the entire episode was scarcely reported. Simply put, footnote 13 is demonstrably false in asserting that the U.S. is in compliance with the Article 23:9, and its insertion was oddly if not eerily secretive.

---

17. *See* Rebecca Joseph, *Footnote in CUSMA Text Allows U.S. to Avoid LGBTQ Rights Clause*, Global News (Canada), 5 December 2018, https://globalnews.ca/news/4732591/cusma-lgtbq-footnote/ (hereinafter, *Footnote in CUSMA*); Grace Dobush, *Republicans Win Rollback Of Sex Discrimination Protections In New Free Trade Deal*, Fortune, 4 December 2018, http://fortune.com/2018/12/04/new-nafta-usmca-lgtbq-rights/ (hereinafter, *Republicans Win*).

18. *See Footnote in CUSMA*.

19. *See Footnote in CUSMA*.

20. *See Republicans Win*.

Chapter 24

Resolving Labor Disputes under FTAs[1]

I. Procedures under 1994 *NAFTA*
Labor Side Agreement

• Origins of *Labor Side Agreement*

It is commonly thought the origins of the *NAFTA Labor Side Agreement*—officially entitled the *North American Agreement on Labor Cooperation*—lie in Bill Clinton's (1946–, President, 1993–2000) 1992 Presidential campaign. Candidate Clinton was hesitant to endorse *NAFTA*, which the incumbent President, George H.W. Bush (1924–2018, President, 1989–1993), and his USTR, Carla Hills (1934–), had negotiated. After all, he was running against the President, and he needed to court the traditional Democratic labor vote. In truth, the genesis of the *Labor Side Agreement* was a "May 1 Plan" offered by President Bush on 1 May 1991 to respond to the labor and environmental activists who were campaigning against extending *CUFTA* to Mexico.

President George H.W. Bush sought an extension of fast track negotiating authority under the *Omnibus Trade and Competitiveness Act of 1988* until 1 June 1993 to complete a deal with Mexico and Canada.

> Labor and environmental organizations were among the most vocal of these groups [opposing President Bush's request for an extension of fast track authority]. During the fast track debate, labor groups argued that a free trade agreement with Mexico would erode U.S. wages and encourage industrial flight to Mexico, thereby costing U.S. jobs. Environmental and consumer organizations argued that a free trade agreement would increase unsustainable growth in Mexico, and compromise the ability of the United States to enact and maintain adequate environmental, health, and safety laws. Together, these two communities joined to advance a regulatory competitiveness argument against the fast track extension, arguing that Mexico's failure to enact and enforce a host of labor, worker protection,

---

1. Documents References:
   (1) *NAFTA Labor Side Agreement*
   (2) Labor provisions in other FTAs

environmental, health, and safety laws would provide companies operating in Mexico with a competitive advantage over U.S. industries. Relying upon these arguments, many groups formed coalitions to petition Congress to reject fast track and to further consider [*sic*] the ramifications of a trade agreement that fast track would allow.[2]

---

2. Robert F. Housman & Paul Orbuch, *Integrating Labor and Environmental Concerns into the North American Free Trade Agreement: A Look Back and A Look Ahead*, 8 AMERICAN UNIVERSITY JOURNAL OF INTERNATIONAL LAW & POLICY 719, 724–725 (1993). [Hereinafter, *Integrating Labor.*]

As the discussion below makes clear, a persistent problem associated with America's FTAs is a lack of systematic monitoring and vigorous enforcement by foreign countries that are Parties to an FTA with the U.S. *See* U.S. Government Accountability Office, *Free Trade Agreements: U.S. Partners Are Addressing Labor Commitments, but More Monitoring and Enforcement Are Needed*, GAO-15-160 (6 November 2014), www.gao.gov. The problem also exists on the American side. As this GAO Report revealed, between 2008 and November 2014, the DOL had accepted only five labor submissions under the 14 U.S. FTAs with 20 countries. They involved the following allegations:

(1) In 2008 under *CAFTA-DR*, against Guatemala for violations of the rights to freedom of association, and to organize and bargain collectively, and for unacceptable working conditions.

(2) In 2011 under the *Peru TPA* (the first FTA sealed under the May 2007 BTD) against Peru for failure to comply with laws on collective bargaining.

(3) In 2011 under the *Bahrain FTA*, against Bahrain for violation of the right to freedom of association, and discrimination.

(4) In 2012 under *CAFTA-DR*, against the Dominican Republic for human trafficking, forced labor, and retaliatory firing of workers for union activities.

(5) In 2012 under *CAFTA-DR*, against Honduras for violations of the rights to freedom of association, and to organize and bargain collectively, and use of child labor.

For each submission, the DOL exceeded by an average of 9 months the FTA time limit of 6 months for investigation. *See id.* The Bahrain and Guatemala cases are discussed below.

In July 2015, the ILRF and Peruvian unions complained *Decree Laws 22342* and *27360* violate the requirement that Peru comply with ILO minimum standard on freedom of association. Unlimited short-term contracts could be used in any "non-traditional" export (NTE) sector. *Decree Law 22342*, which dates from 1978, defined NTEs broadly to encompass all significant Peruvian export sectors, save for minerals, oil and gas, and a few farm products (*e.g.*, coffee, cotton, and sugar). Employers in them could use short-term contracts on an unlimited basis, or (for certain other sectors, such as T&A) up to 5 years. Workers on such contracts were vulnerable to threats, intimidation, and exploitation, and unlikely to receive training and benefits. In September 2015, DOL agreed to investigate allegations by the Forum, *Perú Equidad*, a Lima-based NGO, and 7 Peruvian workers' organizations, that the Peruvian government "failed to effectively enforce its labor laws in the non-traditional export and agricultural sectors with respect to freedom of association, the effective recognition of the right to collective bargaining and acceptable conditions of work," and also that "Peru's Non-Traditional Export Promotion Law—which allows employers to hire workers for short-term, renewable contracts—fails to comply with . . . ILO minimum standards for freedom of association. The DOL issued a report in March 2016 indicating "significant concerns." Rossella Brevetti, *Peru Faces Claims of Violating Trade Pact Labor Rules*, 32 International Trade Reporter (BNA) 1712 (1 October 2015).

In November 2016, USTR discussed the controversy with Peru, hoping dialogue could push Peru to improve, and in December extended by 6 months the time for Peru to finish the transition to permanent employment for certain temporary workers in the agriculture and T&A export sectors, and boost the number of labor inspectors and courts to address violations. In April 2018, pledged to work with DOL to limit the use of consecutive short-term contracts in the NTE sectors.

President Bush aimed to keep *NAFTA* negotiations focused on what he viewed as singularly trade matters, and to avoid cluttering the accord. Not surprisingly, except for the Preamble to *NAFTA*—which states the Parties are resolved to create new employment opportunities and improve working conditions, and to protect, enhance, and enforce workers' rights—the agreement is silent on labor rights issues. *NAFTA* contains no mechanisms to implement, monitor, or enforce the goals set forth in the Preamble.

President George H. W. Bush responded by dividing the opposition. In his May 1 Plan, he proposed labor and environmental concerns should be dealt not in the text of an FTA, but rather, separately on a "parallel track." Some opponents agreed, while others did not, and President Bush's request for fast track extension was approved by Congress.[3] Thus was born the idea for a side deal on labor matters.

The President implemented the idea by negotiating three separate MOUs with Mexico. First, on 13 May 1991, the American Labor Secretary and Mexican Labor Minister signed a five-year MOU on labor that called for increased cooperation (*e.g.*, information sharing on child labor, worker health and safety, and employment statistics) and joint action (*e.g.*, procedures for resolving labor conflicts). On 14 September 1992, the U.S. and Mexico supplemented this MOU with a bilateral agreement that extended the term of the MOU beyond five years and established a consultative commission on labor matters to provide a forum for discussing labor matters. Second, in October 1991, the Office of Management and Budget entered into an MOU with its Mexican counterpart on cooperation in generating statistical data on labor matters. Third, on 7 February 1992, the Occupational Safety and Health Administration entered into an MOU with its Mexican counterpart on the monitoring and enforcement of workplace safety laws.

The fact these MOUs were in place was lost amidst the 1992 presidential campaign rhetoric. Hence, there was little discussion about their substantive merits, and the debate that did occur about the need for a further side agreement on labor was artificial. Yet, the fact was the MOUs helped nurture a culture of social justice as regards in Mexican in employment practices. True, the MOUs did not deal with adversarial labor-management relations in Mexico. But, it is hard to expect this nearly intractable problem could be solved through an MOU, and in any event the *Labor Side Agreement* also glosses over the problem. Candidate Clinton merely capitalized on the possibility of a new side deal to justify his ultimate lukewarm endorsement of *NAFTA*.

> *NAFTA* did, in fact, put . . . Clinton in a difficult position. Although Clinton had said that he was in favor of free trade, he also wanted the support of both organized labor and the environmental community, and *NAFTA* was

---

See Lucien O. Chauvin, *Peru Says It Will Work With U.S. to Address Labor Concerns*, 35 International Trade Reporter (BNA) 620 (3 May 2018).

3. *See* 137 Congressional Record H3588 (daily ed., 23 May 1991); 137 Congressional Record S6829 (daily ed., 24 May 1991).

a critical issue for securing their support. . . . Clinton did not want to adopt a campaign position that might . . . endanger a *NAFTA*. In an attempt to balance these interests, Clinton-Gore campaign representatives consulted with both Mexican officials and members of the environmental and labor communities in developing Clinton's position. Ultimately, Clinton adopted a compromise position in his October 4, 1992 speech given in Raleigh, North Carolina. . . . Candidate Clinton's compromise approach sought to differentiate from the Bush approach by focusing additional attention on the environmental and labor concerns with *NAFTA*. . . . Rather than renegotiate the *NAFTA*, the Clinton plan entailed substantial use of certain unilateral measures [such as adjustment assistance for U.S. workers adversely impacted by *NAFTA*] and "supplemental agreements" to address the perceived environmental and labor flaws.[4]

Accordingly, when Clinton became President, it fell upon his USTR, Mickey Kantor (1939–), to negotiate a side deal somewhat more elaborate than the three earlier MOUs that might fulfill a campaign promise to labor voters.

• Cross-Border Harmonization of Labor Laws

How one appraises the outcome of the Clinton Administration's labor negotiations with Mexico and Canada depends very much on one's initial expectations. In brief, if cross-border harmonization of labor law is expected, then one is sure to be disappointed. But, if one is looking for better enforcement of the existing labor laws of each *NAFTA* Party, then perhaps the dispute resolution procedures set forth in the *Labor Side Agreement* offer some comfort.

The *Labor Side Agreement* sets forth lofty goals for worker rights. The Preamble states the *NAFTA* Parties are committed to raising the standard of living of workers, promoting investment that is consistent with labor laws, and maintaining workplace health and safety standards. However, given the different stages of economic development of the U.S. and Canada, on the one hand, and Mexico, on the other hand, it is not surprising that labor laws are not harmonized among the Parties. Indeed, the incongruity between the lofty goals stated in the *Labor Side Agreement* and the actual accomplishments of the *Agreement* is stark.

To say the *Labor Side Agreement* does not harmonize labor laws among the *NAFTA* Parties is not much of an overstatement. There is no commitment in *NAFTA* toward upward harmonization, nor is there even an obligation to make labor standards compatible. There is only an agreement to cooperate on labor standards.

To be sure, the *Agreement* makes a half-hearted attempt to encourage harmonization. In Article 1(b) and Annex 1, the *NAFTA* Parties committed themselves to promoting 11 guiding principles:

---

4. *Integrating Labor*, 793–794.

(1) protecting freedom of association and the right to organize;

(2) protecting the right to freely engage in collective bargaining on matters concerning the terms and conditions of employment;

(3) protecting the right to strike so that workers may defend their collective interest;

(4) prohibiting and suppressing all forms of forced labor, except those forms that are generally considered acceptable, such as compulsory military service;

(5) placing restrictions on the employment of children and young persons to safeguard their physical, mental, and moral development;

(6) establishing minimum employment standards, such as minimum wages and overtime pay;

(7) eliminating employment discrimination "on such grounds as race, religion, age, sex, or other grounds, subject to certain reasonable exceptions";

(8) providing equal pay for women and men for equal work in the same establishment;

(9) establishing standards to prevent occupational injuries and illnesses;

(10) compensating workers and their dependents in cases of occupational injuries, accidents, or fatalities that arise during the course of employment; and

(11) providing the same protection to migrant workers as domestic workers with respect to working conditions.

However, Annex 1 makes plain that the extent to which these principles are implemented depends on each Party's domestic law, and each Party "in its own way" will have developed an appropriate legal framework. Thus, the principles "do not establish common minimum standards for their domestic law."

Moreover, a careful review of the 11 principles suggests both ambiguity and controversy. For example, with respect to the seventh principle, should discrimination on the basis of a worker's sexual orientation be outlawed? How is "equal work" to be defined in the eighth principle? With respect to the tenth principle, should compensation be provided for repetitive motion injuries, such as carpal tunnel syndrome? Furthermore, while Article 2 calls on the Parties to adopt "high labor standards, consistent with high quality and productivity workplaces," it also affirms the right of each Party to "establish its own domestic labor standards." In sum, there are no legal obligations in the *Labor Side Agreement* to compel harmonization of labor laws among the *NAFTA* Parties.

Perhaps Articles 3–7 provide the greatest hope for cross-border harmonization. Article 3:1 obligates each *NAFTA* Party to "promote compliance with and effectively enforce its labor law through appropriate government action." What is noteworthy about this obligation is its specificity. Article 3:1-2 suggests to Parties how they might enforce their laws, namely, by appointing and training inspectors, requiring record keeping, monitoring compliance, investigating suspected violations including on-site inspections, initiating proceedings to seek appropriate sanctions to remedy violations, and giving due consideration to a request for an investigation of an alleged violation made by private parties. This obligation is directed particularly at Mexico, in part to placate its labor critics who fear American job losses if the Mexican government entices American companies to relocate to Mexico through lax enforcement of Mexican labor laws.

Article 4 requires that the private parties have "appropriate access to administrative, quasi-judicial, judicial or labor tribunals for the enforcement" of labor laws. Again, this provision is aimed especially at Mexico. Traditionally, its legal system has been more restrictive with respect to private party access than that in the other *NAFTA* Parties. The thrust of Articles 5–7 is the harmonization of administrative law at the national level. Under Article 5, the *NAFTA* Parties guarantee procedural rights in labor law proceedings. These rights involve due process, public access, presentation of evidence, and publication of adjudicatory decisions. Articles 6 and 7 are aimed at improving the transparency of labor laws.

Not too much should be made of Articles 3–7. It is clear from Article 5:8 that decisions of judicial, quasi-judicial, or administrative tribunals of the *NAFTA* Parties on labor matters are not subject to review under the *Labor Side Agreement*. Therefore, while there may be some procedural harmonization in labor adjudication, there is no supra-national body to ensure consistency in substantive adjudicatory outcomes in like cases arising in different *NAFTA* Parties. The rationale for Article 5:8 is the "greater certainty" afforded when labor decisions in the U.S. or any other Party are not subject to review at a supra-national level. This rationale is ironic. No doubt it was evaluated and rejected by the Parties with respect to Chapter 19 dispute resolution procedures in AD and CVD cases, and more generally with respect to the WTO dispute settlement mechanism.

- **Background on Dispute Resolution**

Right to Complain About Lax Enforcement:

What does the *Labor Side Agreement* accomplish? The answer is it primarily serves to establish a dispute resolution mechanism for cases where it is alleged a *NAFTA* Party is not enforcing its own labor laws. Suppose one *NAFTA* Party feels another Party has failed to enforce the provisions of the *Side Agreement*. Articles 27–29 specify the complaining Party has the right to bring an enforcement proceeding against any other Party that allegedly exhibits a "persistent pattern of failure" to enforce its "occupational safety and health, child labor or minimum wage technical labor standards."

In two respects, this right is remarkable. First, exercise of the right implies a sort of "extraterritorial" enforcement. To be sure, exercise of the right does not entail any loss of sovereignty. For example, no *NAFTA* Party or body created by the *Labor*

Side Agreement can force the U.S. to change its labor laws. Only Congress and the President can effect such a change. Nonetheless, it is hardly commonplace in international trade law to witness one sovereign state obtaining a "judgment" from an international tribunal that another sovereign state has been lax in enforcing its domestic laws. Yet, the theory underlying the *Side Agreement* is each *NAFTA* Party has a vested interest in labor law enforcement in the other Parties, and that such enforcement is integrally related to trade among the Parties. There are 2 bases for that interest: a humanitarian concern that workers not be exploited; and a pragmatic concern that worker exploitation not be used as a means of maximizing a comparative advantage or securing direct foreign investment.

Second, the *Labor Side Agreement* allows for the use of trade sanctions — namely, retaliation in the form of suspension of *NAFTA* benefits — against a Party that fails to enforce effectively its labor laws.[5] Here too, it is relatively rare to observe trade law remedies used to combat labor law problems. Traditionally, such problems were not viewed as related to trade and, therefore, were said to be outside the ambit of trade remedies. Indeed, the *Side Agreement* is the first deal on labor issues crafted specifically in the context of, and designed to join, a trade accord.

Yet, in three other respects, the importance of the right of one *NAFTA* Party to complain about labor law enforcement in another *NAFTA* Party is inflated. First, the *Labor Side Agreement's* dispute resolution mechanism is intricate, and the time deadlines overly generous. It can take three and one-half years before a complaining Party can retaliate against a Party that has exhibited a persistent pattern of failure to enforce effectively its labor laws.

Second, there is no private right of action against another Party.[6] For instance, American trade unions cannot sue directly the Mexican government. As the *GE* and *Honeywell* cases suggest, the access of private parties is limited to their National Administrative Office (NAO). It does not extend to the dispute resolution mechanism.

Third, an individual labor case decided under the law of a *NAFTA* Party cannot be reviewed under the *Labor Side Agreement*. And, with the exception of ministerial consultations, the dispute resolution mechanism of the *Side Agreement* may not be used to resolve disputes about the rights to associate, organize, or bargain collectively.[7] These facts intimate the scope of application of the *Agreement* is rather narrow.

Some Critical Terminology:

The definitions of key terms set forth in Article 49 are critical to understanding the enforcement provisions of the *Labor Side Agreement*. However, there are uncertainties associated with some of these terms.

---

5. *See* Article 41.
6. *See* Article 43.
7. *See* Articles 23:2, 27:1, 33:3, and 49.

First, a "persistent pattern of practice" means one that is "sustained or recurring," and "does not include a single instance or case."

> The term "persistent pattern" was not chosen lightly. The U.S. initially proposed that a "persistent and unjustifiable pattern" of non-enforcement would trigger sanctions. The U.S. proposal did not define these terms. Canada proposed that a "consistent pattern" of non-enforcement would trigger consultations and evaluation by a Panel that could issue non-binding recommendations. Although the Canadian proposal did not define the operative terms "a consistent pattern of violations," the same terms were used in the Canadian proposal for the environmental side agreement and were defined in that proposal by stating that a "consistent pattern of violations does not mean a single violation of this agreement but a pattern of reliably documented violations." . . . Thus, the Parties combined the U.S. and Canadian proposals by first defining a pattern of practice in a manner reflective of the Canadian proposal for a "consistent pattern" and then requiring that the violations also be "persistent." By adopting this framework the Parties have ensured that only the most egregious and continuing violations will ever raise the possibility of binding arbitration and sanctions.[8]

In spite of insights provided by the definition of and history behind the language, there are unresolved questions. For example, can it be inferred that a single, recent, major domestic enforcement action is sufficient to rebut a claim that a persistent pattern of failure exists? There is no numerical test—such as failure to investigate more than 50% of complaints submitted during a specified period—to resolve this dilemma.

Second, "technical labor standards" are a subset of those items listed in the Article 49 definition of "labor law." Yet, this subset corresponds to the last eight of the eleven general principles set forth in Annex 1. (Freedom of association and protection of the right to organize, the right to bargain collectively, the right to strike, and the prohibition of forced labor are the first four principles not included as "technical labor standards.") In effect, Articles 27:1, 28, 29, and 49 convert eight general principles into "technical" labor standards. Accordingly, the scope of the dispute settlement mechanism may be not only rather narrow, but also unclear. Quite obviously, there are ambiguities inherent in many of these standards.

Third, Article 49 provides the respondent in an enforcement action with a defense. A *NAFTA* Party has not failed to enforce effectively its standards if its action or inaction reflects a reasonable exercise of official governmental discretion, or a *bona fide* decision to allocate resources to enforcement of other labor matters to which a higher priority is given. Without this defense, one Party could invoke the

---

8. Stanley M. Spracker & Gregory M. Brown, *Labor Issues Under the NAFTA: Options and Resolutions, in* THE NORTH AMERICAN FREE TRADE AGREEMENT 351, 370 (Judith H. Bello et al., eds. 1994). *See also* BARRY APPLETON, NAVIGATING NAFTA 181, 186 (1994); LESLIE ALAN GLICK, UNDERSTANDING THE NORTH AMERICAN FREE TRADE AGREEMENT 121 (2d ed. 1994).

Labor Side Agreement to challenge the failure of another Party to take action simply as a consequence of limited resources and discretionary choices of appropriate authorities.

Institutional Infrastructure:

What are the mechanics of an enforcement proceeding brought under the *Labor Side Agreement*? To answer this question, it is first necessary to comprehend the institutional infrastructure created by the *Agreement*. Article 8 establishes a Commission for Labor Cooperation, which has three components: a (1) ministerial Council, comprised of the labor ministers of the *NAFTA* Parties; (2) 15 member permanent Secretariat, which is located in Dallas, Texas; and (3) National Administrative Office (NAO) in each Party, which is funded by the respective Parties.[9] While the Council is the governing body of the Commission, the Council's day-to-day work is performed by the Secretariat. The NAOs play a significant early role in resolving disputes.

> These Offices specifically serve as points of contact and sources of information for the Council and Secretariat. Further, each office is responsible for receiving and investigating public communications or complaints related to labor law issues in the territorial domain of another Party. The decision to initiate a formal review of such complaints depends upon the discretion of the Secretary of the National Administrative Office. [Accordingly,] . . . review by a National Administrative Office offers citizens, businesses, and other non-governmental organizations a public forum where they may present a complaint against a *NAFTA* member nation . . . .[10]

Thus, with respect to dispute resolution, the purpose of an NAO review is to collect information, which may ultimately trigger formal proceedings, and consult with NAOs in other *NAFTA* Parties.

There are eight broad steps associated with an enforcement proceeding. That is, the *Labor Side Agreement* establishes an eight-level dispute resolution mechanism for resolving allegations that a *NAFTA* Party is not enforcing its labor laws.

- **Eight Levels of Dispute Resolution**

Level 1: NAO Consultations

Suppose an NAO elects to review complaints submitted by private petitioners. While it can issue a report of its findings, it is not empowered to invoke formal dispute resolution proceedings against a *NAFTA* Party. Rather, under Article 21, an NAO can enter into consultations with the NAO of the other *NAFTA* Party. The

---

9. *See* Articles 8:2 and 9–16. The U.S. NAO is housed in the DOC in Washington, D.C.

10. Michael J. McGuinness, Recent Development, *The Protection of Labor Rights in North America: A Commentary on the North American Agreement on Labor Cooperation*, 30 STANFORD JOURNAL OF INTERNATIONAL LAW 579, 584 (1994). *See also* Lance Compa, *International Labor Rights and the Sovereignty Question: NAFTA and Guatemala, Two Case Studies*, 9 AMERICAN UNIVERSITY JOURNAL OF INTERNATIONAL LAW AND POLICY 117, 134 (1993).

NAOs are obligated to share publicly available information with each other. No time limit is established for NAO consultations.

The first request for a formal review submitted to a NAO was made on 14 February 1994.[11] The U.S. NAO received petitions from the International Brotherhood of Teamsters and the United Electrical, Radio and Machine Workers of America. The UE complaint was brought against a GE motor plant. It accused GE of violating the first, sixth, and ninth principles in Annex 1 of the *Labor Side Agreement* (concerning freedom of association, minimum employment standards, and prevention of workplace injuries, respectively) by firing union activists, and allowing salary, safety, and health standards to fall below minimally acceptable standards. UE's petition also alleged GE's actions violated Mexican labor law. The petition called for the NAO to review Mexico's enforcement of its labor laws. GE stated the workers were fired for violating company work rules. The IBT petition, brought against Honeywell, Inc., focused only on anti-union activities in Honeywell's Chihuahua, Mexico facility. IBT alleged Honeywell fired 20 production workers for trying to form an independent union. Honeywell stated the workers were laid off as a result of downsizing.

On 20 April 1994, the U.S. NAO agreed to review the UE and IBT petitions. It was satisfied the petitions related to labor matters in Mexico and furthered the objectives of the *Labor Side Agreement*. However, after conducting its review, the NAO declined to recommend that the Secretary of Labor pursue ministerial consultations with Mexico under Article 22 of the *Agreement*. In its 12 October 1994 report, the NAO stated the petitioners had not exhausted fully Mexico's own dispute resolution mechanisms, hence the NAO could not conclude Mexico had failed to enforce its labor laws.

Level 2: Ministerial Consultations

The second level of the dispute resolution scheme is specified in Article 22. A complaining Party can request consultations between the labor ministers of the complaining and responding Parties. Any matter within the scope of the *Labor Side Agreement* may be the subject of such consultations. No time limit is set for these consultations.

The first case to reach this level of the dispute resolution scheme was filed with the U.S. NAO in August 1994 by American and Mexican labor unions against Sony's Magneticos subsidiary in Mexico. One charge concerned union registration. After a public hearing, the NAO issued its report on 11 April 1995, recommending that consultations be held between the American Secretary of Labor and Mexican Minister of Labor. These consultations led to an agreement on 12 June 1995 on a series of programs that would educate Sony's workers about their union registration rights. Because the matter concerned freedom of association and protection of the

---

11. *See* United States International Trade Commission, The Year in Trade—Operation of the Trade Agreements Program, U.S. ITC Pub. 2894, 49 (July 1995).

right to organize, it is unlikely it could have been taken to subsequent levels in the dispute settlement scheme.

Level 3: ECE

If the labor ministers are unable to resolve a dispute through consultations, then either consulting Party may ask the Council to appoint an Evaluation Committee of Experts to investigate the dispute. The ECE has three members, with the Chairperson selected by the Council from a roster of experts developed in consultation with the ILO.[12] The members must be labor experts, objective, and independent of the disputing Parties and the Secretariat.[13]

The Council can appoint an ECE only if the matter in dispute is "trade-related" *or* "covered by mutually recognized labor laws."[14] What is the rationale for these criteria? They hedge against one Party using the dispute resolution process to impose its own labor standards on another Party. Thus, suppose a Party is not fulfilling its obligation to enforce labor standards. But, suppose also its failure has nothing to do with companies or sectors in that Party competing against imported goods or services from another Party. In this scenario, only consultations are possible. There can be no further steps in the process, because the matter is not trade related.

Despite this rationale, the limits create uncertainties. No test is set forth to determine whether a dispute is "trade related." Consider workers in a factory where 5% of the factory's output is exported. Is a labor-management dispute in this factory "trade-related"? Article 49 teaches that a "mutually recognized" labor law of a *NAFTA* Party is one that addresses the same general subject matter as the law of the other Party to the dispute. Suppose Canada provides medical care treatment at the government's expense for workers who develop repetitive stress injuries on the job. In the U.S., some state's general worker compensation laws might be interpreted as encompassing such injuries. Is the Canadian law "mutually recognized"? More generally, does this term mean "equivalent," or "reasonably analogous"?

If the disputing Parties disagree as to whether the criteria for appointing an ECE are satisfied, then an expert may be appointed to rule on the dispute within 15 days.[15] Assuming an ECE is appointed, its job is to analyze the "patterns of practice" in a Party's enforcement of its "occupational safety and health or other technical labor standards."[16] Curiously, this language omits reference to child labor or minimum wage standards. Thus, it would appear the ECE cannot consider such matters.

Each Party's NAO must give publicly available information to the ECE to help the ECE in its work.[17] The ECE must present a final report to the Council within

---

12. *See* Articles 24:1(a)-(b), 45.
13. *See* Article 24:1(c).
14. Article 23:3.
15. *See* Annex 23.
16. Article 23:2.
17. *See* Article 16:2(d).

180 days after it is established. (It must present a draft report within 120 days. The remaining 60 days allow the disputing Parties to comment on the draft and the ECE to prepare the final version.[18]) Significantly, this report is not binding on those Parties. The ECE's final report is published 30 days after it is presented to the Council, and the disputing Parties must give comments on it to the Secretariat within 90 days of its publication.[19] The Council may consider the final report and comments at its next meeting.[20]

Level 4: Direct Consultations

Following the presentation to the Council of a final ECE evaluation report, Article 27:1 indicates that the disputing Parties may again engage in consultations "regarding whether there has been a persistent pattern of failure" by one Party in the effective enforcement of "occupational safety and health, child labor or minimum wage technical labor standards" with respect to "the general subject matter addressed in the report." No doubt the wording of Article 27:1 is confusing, and the result is anomalous.

On the one hand, there is an express reference to child labor and minimum wage standards. On the other hand, the language of Article 27:1 expressly refers to the subject matter of the ECE's report. By virtue of Article 23:2, that report can cover only occupational safety and health or technical labor standards. Thus, whereas the ECE could not consider such matters, the Parties are free to consult in these areas. But, without the benefit of an ECE report on child labor and minimum wage standards, what distinguishes direct consultations (Level 3) from consultations between labor ministers (Level 1)?

Level 5: Special Session of Council

If after 60 days direct consultations fail, either consulting Party may call for a special session of the Council under Article 28 in order to take advantage of the Council's informal dispute settlement tools.[21] The Council must convene within 20 days of the request.[22] Further, it must "endeavor to resolve the dispute promptly." Its tools include calling upon technical advisors, creating expert groups, using its own good offices, providing conciliation or mediation services, and making recommendations.[23]

Level 6: Arbitral Panel

Suppose a dispute remains unresolved after a further 60 days. Then, either disputing Party may ask the Council to convene a five-member arbitral Panel under

---

18. *See* Articles 25-26.
19. *See* Article 26:2-3.
20. *See* Article 26:4.
21. *See* Article 28:1.
22. *See* Article 28:3.
23. *See* Article 28:3-4.

Article 29.[24] Because a Panel is appointed upon a two-thirds vote of the Council, it is impossible for any *NAFTA* Party to block commencement of arbitration proceedings. Members of the Panel are drawn from a roster maintained by the Council of 45 experts representing the Parties.[25] The individuals listed on the roster must be experts in labor law, have experience in resolving international disputes, or possess other relevant credentials.[26]

The disputing Parties are charged with the responsibility of agreeing to a chair of the arbitral Panel within 15 days after the Council votes to convene a Panel.[27] If they cannot agree to a chair within 15 days, then by lot a chair is selected within an additional five days. (Article 32:2(b) specifies a different period when there are more than two disputing parties.) Within 15 days after the chair is chosen, each disputing Party must select two Panelists who are citizens of the other disputing Party.[28] (Again, Article 32:2(c) specifies a different period and procedure when there are more than two disputing parties.) The terms of reference of the Panel are standard and set forth in Article 33:3, namely, to investigate whether there has been a "persistent pattern of failure" by the responding Party "to effectively enforce [*sic*] its occupational safety and health, child labor or minimum wage technical labor standards."

At first glance, Article 29:1, which concerns a request for an arbitral Panel, and 23:3, which pertains to the establishment of an ECE, seems redundant. In fact, they are not. Whereas Article 23:3 uses the disjunctive "or," Article 29:1 indicates that a Panel cannot be convened unless the dispute is trade-related "and" covered by mutually recognized labor laws. What is the point of this requirement? It ensures a Panel is not used as a vehicle to coerce one Party to adopt labor standards that are not mutually recognized between or among the Parties. Also, it circumscribes the scope of application of mutually recognized labor standards to cases involving competition in a goods or services sector between or among the Parties.

Use of the conjunctive "and" in Article 29:1 suggests the eight levels in the dispute resolution scheme may be conceptualized as a pyramid. As the disputing Parties ascend through the levels, the requirements to invoke a particular mechanism become more stringent. As another example of this phenomenon, recall that ministerial consultations may concern any matter covered by the *Labor Side Agreement*, but an ECE can consider only occupational safety and health or other technical labor standards.[29]

Within 240 days of its formation, an arbitral Panel must submit to the Council a report that states the judgment of a Panel as to whether the responding Party

---

24. *See* Article 29:1.
25. *See* Articles 30–32.
26. *See* Articles 30:2, 31:1.
27. *See* Article 32:1(b).
28. *See* Article 32:1(c).
29. *See* Articles 22:1, 23:2.

exhibits a persistent pattern of failure to enforce effectively its labor laws. (A draft report, on which the complaining and responding Parties may comment, is due within 180 days of its formation.[30] During the remaining 60 days, the Panel receives comments and drafts the final report.[31]) The final report, which is binding on the disputing Parties, must be transmitted along with comments from the complaining and responding Parties within 15 days of presenting it to the disputants.[32]

If an arbitral Panel renders an affirmative finding, then it also must recommend a remedy. An affirmative report, including the recommended remedy, is implemented by incorporating the report into an "action plan" agreed to by the disputing Parties.[33] The plan should be agreed to within 60 days of the date the Panel issues its final report.[34]

Level 7: Reconvening Arbitral Panel

What if the disputing Parties cannot agree to such a plan? Or, what if the complaining Party believes the responding Party has not implemented the plan? In these instances, either disputing Party may ask the Council to reconvene the arbitral Panel.[35]

Where no action plan was agreed to, the request to reconvene an arbitral Panel must be made no earlier than 60 days, and no later than 120 days, after the date of the Panel's final report.[36] The reconvened Panel determines an action plan and imposes a "monetary enforcement assessment," i.e., a fine.[37] The Panel must make its determination and impose a fine within 90 days of the date it is reconvened.[38] Payment of any fine is due within 180 days of its imposition.[39]

Where it is alleged the responding Party has not implemented an action plan, the request to reconvene the Panel cannot be made any earlier than 180 days after the disputing Parties agreed to the plan.[40] (This time period ensures the responding Party has a chance to implement the plan.) The reconvened Panel has 60 days to determine whether the respondent has failed to implement fully the action plan.[41] If the reconvened Panel finds the respondent has not complied with the action plan, then it must impose a monetary enforcement assessment against the respondent.[42] Presumably to ensure compliance with an action plan is obtained, Article 40

---

30. *See* Article 36:2.
31. *See* Article 37.
32. *See* Article 37:2.
33. *See* Article 38.
34. *See* Article 39:1(b).
35. *See* Article 39:1.
36. *See* Article 39:2.
37. Article 39:4(b).
38. *See* Article 39:4.
39. *See* Article 41:1(a).
40. *See* Article 39:3(a).
41. *See* Article 39:5.
42. *See* Article 39:5(b).

provides the complaining Party with a right to reconvene again the Panel within 180 days of the Panel's finding of non-compliance to determine whether the responding Party is fully implementing the action plan. (In effect, the responding Party gets a "second chance," via a second 180-day period, to implement the plan.) The Panel must make its decision within 60 days.

During the first year in which *NAFTA* was effective, *i.e.*, 1994, the maximum fine that could be imposed was $20 million. Since then, the cap has been set at 0.007% of the total trade in goods among the *NAFTA* Parties.[43] Fines are paid into a fund established by the Council and used to improve labor law enforcement in the responding Party.[44]

Level 8: Retaliation

What if the responding Party fails to pay the fine (either in a case where no action plan was agreed to, or where the plan was not implemented)? It is subject to retaliation, namely, the complaining Party may suspend *NAFTA* benefits (*e.g.,* duty-free treatment) otherwise owed to the respondent in an amount equal to the fine.[45] Special procedures are set forth in Annex 41 and 41A for sanctioning Canada. The Canadian government modified its laws to ensure that any fine imposed by a *NAFTA* arbitral Panel is given the same force and effect as an order of a Canadian court, and hence is immediately enforceable in Canada. So, rather than suspending trade benefits against Canada, a complaining Party would collect a fine and enforce an action plan in Canadian court.

- **Justice Delayed and, Therefore, Denied?**

How long might it take before retaliation occurs? To answer this question, consider a hypothetical dispute between two *NAFTA* Parties about one Party's enforcement of its labor laws. Three assumptions are useful.

First, the maximum time periods specified above are applicable, but there is no time lag associated with moving from one level in the dispute resolution pyramid to the next level. Second, NAO consultations under Article 21 fail to achieve a solution. Third, ministerial consultations under Article 22 end unsuccessfully on Day 1. No assumption is made about how long Level 1 NAO consultations or Level 2 ministerial consultations take. The period for such consultations must be factored into the bottom line calculation.

The answer to the question "how long?" is calculated as follows:

Level 3 — ECE:
On Day 1, an ECE is established. However, one of the disputing Parties contends that the matter is either not trade-related, or not covered by mutually

---

43. *See* Annex 39:1.
44. *See* Article 39:3.
45. *See* Article 41.

recognized labor laws.[46] Thus, an independent expert is appointed to resolve this matter.[47] On Day 15, the expert determines that both criteria are met.[48] On Day 195 (180 days after the expert's determination), the ECE issues a final report and presents it to the Council.[49] This report is published on Day 225 (30 days after it is presented to the Council).[50] The disputing Parties transmit comments on the final report to the Secretariat on Day 315 (90 days after the report is published).[51]

Level 4 — Direct Consultations:
On Day 315, one of the disputing Parties requests consultations with the other disputing Party.[52] The consultations are held until Day 375 (using the full 60-day period), but are unsuccessful.[53]

Level 5 — Special Council Session:
On Day 375, one of the disputing Parties requests a special session of the Council.[54] The Council convenes on Day 395 (within 20 days of the request).[55] The special session is held until Day 455 (again using the full 60-day period), yet the dispute still is not resolved.[56]

Level 6 — Arbitral Panel:
On Day 455 the Council votes to convene an arbitral Panel.[57] However, the disputing Parties are unable to agree upon a Chair for the Panel by Day 470 (15 days after the Council vote). On Day 475, a Chair is selected by lot (five days after the deadlock concerning the chair). On Day 490, each disputing Party selects two Panelists from the other Party (using the maximum 15 days allotted).[58] The Panel issues a report on Day 730 (240 days after it was convened).[59] On Day 790, the disputing Parties agree to an action plan (using the full 60-day period).[60]

Level 7 — Arbitral Panel Reconvened:
But, the disputing Parties cannot agree on whether the responding Party has implemented fully the action plan.[61] On Day 970 (180 days after the

---

46. *See* Article 23:3.
47. *See* Annex 23:1.
48. *See* Annex 23:2.
49. *See* Articles 25:1, 26:1.
50. *See* Article 26:2.
51. *See* Article 26:3.
52. *See* Article 27:1.
53. *See* Article 28:1.
54. *See* Article 28:1.
55. *See* Article 28:3.
56. *See* Article 29:1.
57. *See* Article 29:1.
58. *See* Article 32:1(b).
59. *See* Articles 36:2, 37:1.
60. *See* Articles 38, 39:1(a).
61. *See* Article 39:1(b)(i).

action plan was agreed to) the complaining Party requests the arbitral Panel be reconvened.[62] The reconvened Panel renders a decision on Day 1030 (60 days after it has been reconvened).[63] It orders the respondent to implement the plan and imposes a fine. By day 1210 (180 days after the reconvened Panel acted), it appears the respondent has failed in both respects. So, on Day 1210, the complaining Party requests that the Panel again be reconvened. The reconvened Panel renders its determination on Day 1270 (60 days after it is reconvened for the second time).[64] It holds the responding Party has failed to meet its obligations.

Level 8 — Retaliation:
On Day 1270 — which is about three and one-half years after the ministerial consultations ended unsuccessfully — the complaining Party is entitled to retaliate by suspending *NAFTA* benefits with respect to the responding Party.

Observe this calculation does not include time used for NAO or ministerial consultations.

• **Workers as Victims**

It might be argued three-to-four years is about the same time it would take to obtain a comparable remedy (assuming there is one) under the domestic law of a *NAFTA* Party. This argument amounts to nothing more than an apology for the *Labor Side Agreement*. It merely says the *Agreement* is no worse than existing domestic adjudicatory mechanisms, which most would agree are inefficient, expensive, and uncertain. The ultimate losers could be the workers in the responding Party. For three-to-four years, they may have been exploited because their government failed to enforce its own labor laws.

The *Labor Side Agreement's* dispute resolution scheme is protracted and torturous. What defense did the Clinton Administration offer in the Congressional debate over *NAFTA*? President Clinton's Labor Secretary Robert Reich (1946–) testified as follows.

> I want to stress one other point — we continue to have Section 301 authority. We continue to have the authority to impose unilaterally trade sanctions against any nation that violates internationally accepted rules with regard to labor — labor treatment, labor relations. Nothing in *NAFTA* takes away from that authority we already have under Section 301 of the international trade laws to unilaterally stop trading [*sic*] with a nation that we feel abrogates those basic rights.[65]

---

62. *See* Article 39:3.
63. *See* Article 39:5.
64. *See* Article 40.
65. *NAFTA Labor Issues: Hearings Before the Senate Finance Committee*, 103D CONGRESS, 1ST SESSION 8 (21 September 1993).

Manifestly, this argument elides the *Labor Side Agreement*. It shifts the focus to the most controversial weapon in America's trade arsenal, Section 301 of the *Trade Act of 1974*, as amended. Worse still, the argument is self-defeating. A Section 301 action against another *NAFTA* Party would undermine whatever credibility the *Side Agreement* has.

Unconvinced by the above argument, the AFL-CIO published *NAFTA at 20*. This March 2014 study said "the complaint procedures for violations of labor or environmental standards are exceedingly slow and cumbersome, and provide no reasonable possibility of sanctions being imposed for non-compliance."[66] The study faulted *NAFTA* for failing to "include the same robust trade sanctions for labor violations as for commercial violations and automatic deadlines to advance complaints."

A different argument in defense of the *Labor Side Agreement* is suggested by considering whether labor issues should be addressed at all in the *NAFTA* context. Is the *Agreement* an instance of thinly-veiled protectionism that seeks to repeal the law of comparative advantage? Is it disingenuous for American labor unions to complain about the plight of Mexican workers—the very workers who are the beneficiaries of *NAFTA*? If the answer to these questions is "yes," then ironically all of the aforementioned weaknesses of the *Labor Side Agreement* may be strengths: a protectionist in free trader's garb will have difficulty in attacking Mexico under the *Agreement*.

· **No Cases, and April 2012 Complaint against State Anti-Immigrant Laws**

Small wonder, then, there never has been a fully adjudicated case under the *NAFTA Labor Side Agreement*. Indeed, that is true for all of America's FTAs. Critics charge the labor provisions in the FTAs are of no practical importance. That disappointing record is not for lack of trying. Many claims have been lodged. For example, in April 2012, the Service Employees International Union (SEIU) and the National Association of Democratic Lawyers (ANAD, a labor lawyer organization based in Mexico City) filed a complaint with the Mexican government. They complainants charged that the immigration law of Alabama (House Bill 56), which entered into force in June 2011, violated commitments in the *NAFTA Labor Side Agreement*, namely: (1) the right to organize and bargain collectively; (2) minimum employment standards, including minimum wages and overtime pay; (3) elimination of employment discrimination; (4) prevention of and compensation for occupational illness or injury; and (5) protection of rights of migrant workers. Their complaint extended to the immigration laws of Arizona, Georgia, South Carolina, and Utah.

---

66. AFL-CIO, *NAFTA at 20* (March 2014), www.aflcio.org/content/download/121921/3393031 /March2014_NAFTA20_nb.pdf; Michael Rose, *AFL-CIO Report Denounces NAFTA, Argues for New Approach to Trade Pacts*, 31 International Trade Reporter (BNA) 621 (3 April 2014).

The logic of the complaint was that the tough state immigration laws create a climate of fear and intimidation in the workplace that makes migrant workers afraid to contact authorities about abuses they suffer. Workers are driven deep into the shadows, and confined to a fearful isolation in which they do not exercise their rights. That in itself is a violation of the commitment of the *NAFTA* Parties under the *Labor Side Agreement* to protect the rights of workers to organize and bargain collectively. Such isolation also supports wage theft from migrant immigrants, who are too scared to complain about unpaid earnings, and to their reluctance to seek workers' compensation when injured on the job. Moreover, by creating a subclass of exploitable migrant workers, the complainants charged that the state immigration laws violate the duty of the *NAFTA* Parties to afford the same legal protection on working conditions as to migrant as to workers who are citizens.

The logic of the complaint also was that provisions in those laws are discriminatory and punitive. Examples the complainant cited were: (1) categorizing as a misdemeanor offense an instance in which an unauthorized alien seeks employment; (2) barring an employer from claiming a tax deduction for wages paid to unauthorized aliens; (3) establishing a civil claim against an employer that fails to hire, or that fires, a U.S. citizen or authorized alien while simultaneously hiring or retaining an unauthorized alien; and (4) making it unlawful to conceal, harbor, or transport an unauthorized alien.

II. Procedures under 2012 *Colombia TPA*

- Overview

Although the trade promotion agreement between the U.S. and Colombia was signed by both countries on 22 November 2006, and approved by the Colombian Congress in June 2007, it did not enter into force until 15 May 2012. Labor concerns were the reason for this delay.

Following the expiration of Presidential fast-track trade negotiating authority (*i.e.*, TPA), many experts considered the FTA with Colombia to be facing significant hurdles not for their economic impact but for political reasons.[67] In his 2008 State of the Union Address, President George W. Bush (1946–, President, 2001–2009) made the Colombia agreement a central part of his trade policy for the term. As a friend of America confronting violence, terror, and fighting drug traffickers, President Bush suggested failure to pass the agreement "will embolden the purveyors or false

---

67. Lee Hudson Teslik, *Fast-Track Trade Promotion Authority and Its Impact on U.S. Trade Policy*, COUNCIL ON FOREIGN RELATIONS, 25 June 2007, www.cfr.org/trade/fast-track-trade-promotion-authority-its-impact-us-trade-policy/p13663.

populism in our hemisphere" and urged Congress to pass the agreement and "show our neighbors in the region that democracy leads to a better life."[68]

However, numerous members of Congress opposed passage due to concerns about alleged targeted violence against union members in Colombia, inadequate efforts to bring perpetrators to justice, and weak protection of worker rights.[69] The International Confederation of Free Trade Unions named Colombia "the most perilous place in the world for union activity" due to the violence committed against union leaders and members.[70] Those in favor of passage of the agreement cited progress Colombia made over the past 10 years to curb violence and enhance security in addition to the potential loss of market share for American exporters.[71]

To move the agreement forward, President Barack H. Obama (1961, President, 2009–2017) insisted the government address serious labor concerns before he would send the agreement to Congress including violence against Colombian labor union members, inadequate efforts to bring justice for such action, and insufficient protections of worker rights in Colombia.[72] Negotiators for both countries went back to work and created an Action Plan that was agreed to by President Obama and President Juan Manuel Santos (1951–, 2010–2018) on 7 April 2011.[73] Successful implementation of the Action Plan was a precondition for the trade agreement to enter into force.

- LAP[74]

The *Action Plan Related to Labor Rights*, or *Labor Action Plan (LAP)* for short, under the *Colombia FTA* was a series of major, swift, and concrete steps addressing labor rights for the Colombian government to undertake within specific time frames in order for President Obama to submit the trade promotion agreement to Congress. The Action Plan listed a series of policies Colombia could implement to protect labor rights in the following areas: labor ministry (currently the Ministry of Social Protection (MSP)), criminal code reform, cooperatives, temporary service agencies, collective pacts, essential services, ILO office, protection programs, criminal justice reforms, and follow up mechanisms. Under the *LAP*, legislation

---

68. *President Bush Delivers State of the Union Address*, http://georgewbush-whitehouse.archives .gov/news/releases/2008/01/20080128-13.html.

69. M. Angeles Villarreal, *The U.S.-Colombia Free Trade Agreement: Background and Issues*, CONGRESSIONAL RESEARCH SERVICE (9 November 2012), www.fas.org/sgp/crs/row/RL34470.pdf. [Hereinafter, CONGRESSIONAL RESEARCH SERVICE.]

70. *Deal with Colombia*, WASHINGTON POST EDITORIALS (9 November 2007), www.washingtonpost .com/wp-dyn/content/article/2007/11/08/AR2007110802095.html.

71. CONGRESSIONAL RESEARCH SERVICE.

72. Labor in the U.S.-Colombia Trade Promotion Agreement, OFFICE OF THE UNITED STATES TRADE REPRESENTATIVE, www.ustr.gov/uscolombiatpa/labor.

73. *See* Colombian Action Plan Related to Labor Rights, OFFICE OF THE UNITED STATES TRADE REPRESENTATIVE, https://ustr.gov/sites/default/files/uploads/agreements/morocco/pdfs /Colombian%20Action%20Plan%20Related%20to%20Labor%20Rights.pdf. [Hereinafter, *LAP*.]

74. *See LAP*.

established criminal penalties for employers who undermine the right to organize and bargain collectively or threaten workers exercising their labor rights and established a separate Labor Ministry to implement and protect labor rights. Regulations were issued to include fines against companies who violated legal provisions on cooperatives and employment laws and created tools for the Government to promote the establishment and maintenance of direct employment relationships between user companies and affected workers. New labor inspectors were hired and trained with the commitment to hire 480 new inspectors over a four-year period. A number of inspectors were designated to address workers' rights abuses in the commercial sectors of palm oil, sugar, mines, ports, and flowers. The *Plan* also provided for improved methods for citizens to file labor-related complaints, including anonymously, via phone, or web-based.

In addressing violence against unionists, the criminal justice system was reformed by directing prosecutors to accelerate action on labor violence cases with leads, with a special focus on priority labor cases identified by Colombian labor unions as well as an early identification system in all homicide cases as to whether the victim with a union member or not. Training for police investigators was improved, as was strengthening the capacity of prosecutors and police investigators in regional offices of the Prosecutor General. In a show of transparency, sentences from all labor violence cases since 1 January 2011 were posted on the Prosecutor General's website and a methodology was developed for posting aggregate information about all completed criminal cases involving labor violence. Additionally, the Colombian government formally requested the ILO to increase its presence in Colombia to assist with implementation of the *LAP* and monitoring the use of collective pacts and supporting the tripartite process.

On 15 June 2011, USTR Ron Kirk (1954–) announced Colombia had met the milestones agreed to under the *LAP*. Ambassador Kirk called for swift congressional action on legislation for the trade agreement as President Obama submitted the legislation to Congress on 3 October 2011. Ambassador Kirk stressed the importance of passing the three pending trade agreements by connecting growing American exports with supporting domestic jobs for American workers. Although the White House claimed the *Plan* as a success, many congressman and union groups believed granting the agreement too hasty a move.

The AFL-CIO argued the *Plan* was too limited in its scope as it failed to fully resolve violations of union freedoms and did not include a specific prevision requiring Colombia to establish a record of enforcement of any of the commitments prior to a congressional vote on or official entry-into-force of the trade agreement.[75] The AFL-CIO contended Colombian workers were still unable to exercise the rights

---

75. AFL-CIO, Section on Trade in Colombia, www.aflcio.org/Issues/Trade/Colombia /Colombia. [Hereinafter, Section.]

of free expression, association, and collective bargaining.[76] On 12 October 2011, Congress passed the legislation, which had been updated to include the principles from the May 2007 BTD, and was signed into law by President Obama on 21 October 2011.[77]

The USTR hailed the *Action Plan* as a success following three years of its implementation. In April 2014, the USTR said Colombia had fulfilled its obligations by (1) strengthening workers' rights, (2) hiring hundreds of new inspectors, (3) hiring and training 100 new police investigators and over 20 prosecutors, whose mandate was to focus on violence against trade unionists, and (4) launching enforcement actions against third party contractors committing labor rights abuses.[78] The AFL-CIO, along with labor groups in Colombia, gave this rebuttal: the *Plan* had failed, simply because since its implementation, a further 73 trade unionists had been murdered in Colombia.

· **Harbinger of Future Labor Provisions**

In the decades since the *NAFTA Labor Side Agreement*, labor provisions have evolved. From setting forth of lofty goals via the *NAFTA Labor Side Agreement*, to the modest standard that Parties enforce their own labor laws, the post-May 2007 Bipartisan Trade Deal agreements represent a large leap forward for labor rights considering labor principles and standards are not subject to WTO rules. Critics of prior free trade agreements voiced disappointment with weak enforcement standards and unequal access to dispute settlement procedures.

Those critics may find some comfort in the new agreements based on the principles voiced in the May 2007 BTD. The agreements each reflect four conceptual changes from prior agreements by introducing "adopt and maintain" language, prohibiting Parties from lowering their labor standards, setting limitations on prosecutorial and enforcement discretion, and making available the same dispute settlement mechanisms or penalties that are available for other free trade agreement obligations.[79] The Peru, Colombia, Panama, and South Korea trade agreements incorporate four concepts from the May 2007 deal and are virtually identical in form. However, given the serious labor concerns in Colombia, the *Colombia FTA*, coupled with the *LAP*, indicate the growing importance of labor rights in trade negotiations. Is it reasonable to presume future labor negotiations will or should follow a similar course as the Colombian deal?

---

76. Section.

77. M. Angeles Villarreal, *The U.S.-Colombia Free Trade Agreement: Background and Issues*, Congressional Research Service (9 November 2012), www.fas.org/sgp/crs/row/RL34470.pdf.

78. *See* United States Trade Representative, *Update: The Colombia Labor Action Plan: Three Years Later*, 7 April 2014, www.ustr.gov; AFL-CIO, *Making the Colombia Labor Action Plan Work for Workers*, April 2014, www.aflcio.org/content/download/123141/3414471/version/1/file/April2014 _ColombiaReport.pdf; Rossella Brevetti, *USTR, Colombia Say Action Plan Improved Labor Rights; Trade Unionists Disagree*, 31 International Trade Reporter (BNA) 702 (10 April 2014).

79. Mary Jane Bolle, *Overview of Labor Enforcement Issues in Free Trade Agreements*, Congressional Research Service (31 January 2013), www.fas.org/sgp/crs/misc/RS22823.pdf.

The Labor Chapter has its main obligation via Article 17:2, addressing and making clear the fundamental labor rights of the Chapter. What is noteworthy about this provision is its specificity. The provision requires each Party "adopt and maintain" in its statutes, regulations, and practices the following rights as stated in the *ILO Declaration on Fundamental Principles and Rights at Work and its Follow-Up (1998)*:

(1) freedom of association;

(2) the effective recognition of the right to collective bargaining;

(3) the elimination of all forms of compulsory or forced labor;

(4) the effective abolition of child labor and, for purposes of this Agreement, a prohibition on the worst forms of child labor; and

(5) the elimination of discrimination in respect of employment and occupation.

Previous agreements had referenced the *ILO Declaration* in its statement of shared commitment and referenced "internationally recognized labor rights" as defined in each Agreements' definitions provision under the Chapter.

Additionally, the scope of the obligation is limited via Article 17:2(1) footnote 1, which indicates that the obligation refers only to the *ILO Declaration*. The footnote suggests that Partners would not be held liable to the *Follow Up* procedures or other ILO Conventions. The "adopt and maintain" language incorporated from the May 2007 agreement raises the standard of obligation for Parties much greater than prior requirements on countries to "enforce its labor laws." Language of the Article is further strengthened by providing that "neither Party shall waive or otherwise derogate from" its statutes or regulations implementing the *ILO Declaration* where the waiver would be inconsistent with the fundamental rights listed. In prior agreements, Parties were to "strive to ensure" that they did not waive or derogate from laws in a manner that encouraged trade or the establishment, acquisition, expansion, or retention of an investment in its territory.

A review of enforcement procedures of the Chapter indicates that in order to establish a violation, it is vital to demonstrate a failure to adopt and maintain ILO core labor principles in a manner affecting trade or investment between the Parties pursuant to footnote 2 of Article 17:2(1). Additionally, Article 17:3(1)(b) distinguishes itself from prior trade agreements by denying enforcement resource distribution decisions made by a Party as grounds for non-compliance with the labor chapter. This provision represents a greater sense of sovereignty offered in exchange for the free trade agreement. In the application and enforcement of labor laws in previous agreements, Parties recognized that each Party retained discretion with respect to investigatory, prosecutorial, regulatory, and compliance matters and to allocate resources with respect to other labor matters determined to have a higher priority. In fact, prior agreements explicitly provided an excuse for Parties to not enforce its labor laws by permitting a course of action or inaction as a result of such discretion or result or a *bona fide* decision regarding the allocation of resources. The revised trade agreements close the loophole for Parties to claim a lack of resources as reason for non-enforcement of the ILO fundament principles. However, Parties do retain enforcement discretion as to labor laws other than those relating to the fundamental rights.

Article 17:5, under Institutional Arrangements, establishes a Labor Affairs Council and outlined specific roles for the Council and each Party's contact point. Similar to the roles played by Labor Affairs Councils and Joint Committees under prior agreements, Article 17:5 provided much more detailed actions for the Council to implement within the first year of the date of entry of the agreement. Additionally, the position description for the contact point in each Party emphasizes assistance to the Council and cooperation with opposing contact points to carry out work and coordinate priorities, develop specific cooperation and capacity-building activities, and to exchange information on labor laws and best practices between Parties. By specifically outlining the institutional arrangement, the provision takes a much friendlier and cooperative position encouraging relationship building between Parties.

All this said, it is not clear the *LAP* is an appropriate model for future FTAs. In October 2013, more than two years after the *Colombia FTA* entered into force (on 15 May 2012), Congress issued a report stating labor rights conditions in Colombia had worsened, with continued murders (22 in 2012) and threats of violence (413 in 2012) against union members, and sub-contracting to circumvent unionization. No convictions were obtained in over 90% of cases of violence against union activists. Colombia still failed to adhere to ILO standards.[80] In effect, Colombia was not in full compliance with the *LAP*. Consequently, in November, the two countries agreed to continue meeting on the *LAP*, with a view to ensuring Colombia would: (1) hire more labor inspectors, (2) conduct investigations in five key sectors (flowers, mines, palm oil, ports, and sugar), (3) collect fines it imposed for labor violations, (4) sanction firms that hire contract workers instead of direct hires, and (5) deal with threats and violence against unionists. In a January 2017 report, the DOL OTLA stated Colombia still needed to strengthen its labor inspection and fine collection systems, fight abusive sub-contracting and collective arrangements, and clamp down on anti-union violence.[81]

- **Dispute Resolution Overview**

All Labor Provisions Technically Enforceable:

The dispute resolution system revamped itself under the *Colombia FTA* by making all labor provisions in the agreement subject to enforcement. The potential

---

80. *See* United States House of Representatives, Staff Report on Behalf of U.S. Representatives George Miller and Jim McGovern to the Congressional Monitoring Group on Labor Rights in Colombia, *The U.S.—Colombia Labor Action Plan: Failing on the Ground* (29 October 2013).

81. Office of Trade and Labor Affairs, Bureau of International Labor Affairs, U.S. Department of Labor, *United States—Colombia Trade Promotion Agreement, Public Report of Review of U.S. Submission 2016-02 (Colombia)*, (11 January 2017), www.dol.gov/sites/default/files/documents/ilab/PublicReportofReviewofUSSubmission2016-02_Final.pdf.

for violation increased. That is because Parties must do more than enforce effectively their labor laws, defined in Article 17:8, and the internationally recognized labor rights such as acceptable work conditions and labor protections for children. They also must enforce fundamental labor rights, as defined in the *ILO Declaration*.

Additionally, all labor violations have recourse to dispute settlement procedures of Chapter 21 without distinction. The distinction refers to provisions in prior agreements in which a Party would only have recourse to dispute settlement if the matter concerned a violation of an obligation to enforce its labor laws in a manner affecting trade between the Parties. By eliminating the prerequisite, Parties under the agreement can seek dispute settlement for non-commercial activities.

Institutional Infrastructure:

What are the mechanics of an enforcement proceeding brought under the Colombian accord? The process is similar to prior agreements in that Parties must first pursue the matter through labor consultations within the Chapter in order to have recourse to dispute settlement under the Agreement. Article 17:7 outlines the cooperative labor consultation procedure in order to access dispute settlement. The levels of engagement are as follows.

- **Article 17 Cooperative Labor Consultations**

Step 1: Request for Cooperative Consultation

Under Article 17:7, a Party may request labor consultations with another Party regarding any matter arising under the chapter by submitting a request to the other Party's designated contact point. The consultations are to begin promptly. Parties shall make every attempt to bring the matter to a satisfactory resolution.

Step 2: Request for Convening of Council

Parties may request the Labor Affairs Council be convened if consulting Parties fail to resolve the issue under Step 1. The Council shall consist of cabinet-level representatives of consulting Parties and shall endeavor to resolve the matter.

Step 3: 60 Day Limit

Complainant may resort to Chapter 21 (Dispute Settlement) by requesting consultations (Article 21:4) or a meeting of the Commission (Article 21:5) if consulting Parties fail to resolve the matter within 60 days of a request. This 60 day clock adds pressure to the Labor Affairs Council to settle the matter promptly before the dispute escalates into the dispute settlement chapter.

- **Chapter 21 Dispute Settlement**

Step 1: Fork in Road

Parties may decide whether to pursue additional consultations under Article 21:4 or request a meeting of the Commission under Article 21:5. The consultation period is similar to that which occurred under the cooperative consultations except for a few minor changes. For example, under Article 21:4(3), any Party with a substantial trade interest in the matter may participate in consultations provided written notice was given to both Parties within seven days of the formal request for consultations. Additionally, the provision has accounted for changes in technology by permitting consultations to be held in person or via technological means. All information provided during consultations is treated as confidential. If after 60 days of consultations, the matter remains unresolved, consulting Parties may move forward to Intervention of the Free Trade Commission.

Step 2: Free Trade Commission

Assuming Parties did not immediately request a meeting of the Free Trade Commission pursuant to Article 17:7(6), consulting Parties may request a meeting and shall indicate the measure or matter at issue between the Parties. The Commission must convene within 10 days and seek to resolve the dispute promptly. The Commission has the ability to create working groups to address the situation, make recommendations, or have recourse to conciliation or mediation. If after 30 days the issue remains unsolved, Parties may request an arbitral Panel.

Step 3: Arbitral Panel

An arbitral Panel is established following the delivery of a request by any consulting Party. Interested Parties may request to join Panel proceedings as a complaining Party as long as notice is given within seven days after the request for establishment. If third parties do not join, then they shall refrain from initiating or continuing dispute settlement procedures under the Agreement, the *WTO Agreement*, or other FTAs involving the respondent Party.

Panels must comprise of three members. Each Party appoints a Panelist in consultation with each other within 15 days of the delivery of the request for the establishment of a Panel. Failure to select results in a selection made from the labor roster. The last Panelist, the Chair, must be selected within 15 days of the second Panelist's appointment, failure to do so will result in a default pick from the roster.

The Rules of Procedure in Article 21:10 are default rules, which the Parties may modify. The rules provide for a public hearing and opportunity for submissions by each Party as well as non-governmental entities in the disputing Parties' territories to provide additional views. An interesting point to the procedures is that oral arguments and written submissions may be conducted in English or Spanish. And, Panel hearings are to be conducted in the capital of the Party complained against. Therefore, if the U.S. were to bring a claim against Colombia, then there is a high likelihood the hearing would be in Spanish in Bogota. The role of a translator or bilingual attorney is heightened in such an occasion. The terms of reference of the Panel are standard and set forth in Article 21:10(4), namely, to examine the matter, in light of relevant provisions to the *Agreement*, and make findings, determinations, and recommendations.

Within 120 days of the selection of the last Panelist, an arbitral Panel shall present to disputing Parties and initial report containing findings of fact, determinations as to whether a Party has not conformed with its obligation, and recommendations for resolution of the dispute is requested by disputing Parties. The final report shall be presented to disputing Parties within 30 days of the initial report unless otherwise agreed by Parties. The report shall then be released to the public within 15 days.

Parties shall agree on a resolution of the dispute, conforming with the determination and recommendations of the Panel, after receiving the final report. However, if an arbitral Panel renders an affirmative finding that disputing Party has not conformed with its obligation under the agreement, then the resolution shall be to eliminate the non-conformity or the nullification or impairment. If there is an affirmative finding and parties cannot agree to a resolution within 45 days of receiving the final report, the Parties shall begin negotiations on a mutually acceptable compensation. Failure to agree on compensation after 30 days allows a complaining Party to give notice of its intention to suspend the benefits of equivalent effect of the Party complained against. Suspension of benefits may begin 30 days after providing notice.

Step 4: Reconvening Arbitral Panel

A request to reconvene the Panel may occur within 30 days following notice of suspension of benefits if the Party complained against (a) considered the level of benefits proposed to be suspended is manifestly excess or (b) it has eliminated the non-conformity or impairment found by the Panel. The Panel shall reconvene immediately and present its determination within 90 days or 120 days if the request is under both (a) and (b).

If the benefits are determined to be excessive by the Panel, then the Panel shall determine an equivalent level of benefit by taking into account adverse trade effects if the terms of reference provided such in the Rules for Procedures. Benefits shall be suspended first in the same sector affected by the dispute and if the complaining party finds that suspension not practical, it may suspend benefits in other sectors.

Step 5: Compliance Review and 5 Year Review

If the Party complained against eliminates the impairment, then it may provide notice to the Panel and complaining Parties to which the Panel must issue a report within 90 days. If the matter is rectified in the view of the Panel, then benefits must be reinstated promptly reinstated, and no further monetary assessments are allowed. The Commission shall review the effectiveness of the non-implementation — suspension of benefits procedures within five years after the *Agreement* enters into force or within six months after benefits have been suspended or monetary assessments in five proceedings under the Chapter.

• Justice Delayed and, Therefore, Denied?

How long might it take before retaliation occurs? To answer this question, consider a hypothetical dispute between Colombia and the U.S. about one of the Party's enforcement of its labor laws. Two assumptions are useful.

First, the maximum time periods specified above are applicable. Second, cooperative labor consultations under Article 17:7 do not specify the time consulting

Parties shall attempt to arrive at a mutually satisfactory resolution of the matter prior to requesting that the Council be convened. Consultations between Parties and the Council's attempt to resolve the matter is limited to 60 days from the request for consultations. After the 60-day period, a complaining Party may request consultations or a meeting of the Commission as provided in Dispute Settlement Chapter 21.

The answer to the question "how long?" is calculated as follows:

Step 1: Cooperative Labor Consultations

Assume on Day 1, one Party delivers a request for consultation. Cooperative labor consultations begin promptly after delivery. After making every attempt to come to a resolution, a consulting Party may request that the Council be convened via written request to the contact point for each Party. The Council shall promptly convene and aim to resolve the matter by consulting with outside experts or utilizing good offices, conciliation, or mediation. If there is still no resolution on Day 60, then the complaining Party may request consultations or a meeting of the Commission pursuant to Chapter 21 (Dispute Settlement).

Step 2: Consultations under Dispute Settlement

Presuming Parties aim to make every effort to reconcile the situation, Parties may select the longer course of pursuing further consultations. Suppose on Day 60, one of the disputing Parties requests consultations with the other disputing Party.[82] The consultations are held until Day 120 (using the full 60-day period), but are unsuccessful.[83]

Step 3: Intervention of Commission

On Day 120, one of the disputing Parties requests a meeting of the Commission.[84] The Council convenes on Day 130 (within 10 days of the request).[85] The meeting is held until Day 160 (again using the full 30-day period), yet the dispute still is not resolved.[86]

Step 4: Arbitral Panel

On Day 160 a consulting Party requests the establishment of an arbitral Panel to consider the matter.[87] Parties each appoint one Panelist, in consultation with each out by Day 175 (15 days after the request for establishment of Panel). However, one Panelist is unable to be appointed during the period.

So, on Day 178, a Panelist is selected from the labor roster (three days after the 15-day deadline to appoint Panelists). On Day 193, Parties attempt to agree on a

82. *See* Article 21:4.
83. *See* Article 21:5.
84. *See* Article 21:5.
85. *See* Article 21:5(4).
86. *See* Article 21:6.
87. *See* Article 21:6.

third Panelist to serve as the Chair (within 15 days following the date the second Panelist is appointed). But, they are unable to agree, so the Chair is selected by lot on Day 196 (three days following the maximum 15-day limit).

Assume the Panel issues an initial report on Day 316 (120 days after the last Panelist was selected).[88] On Day 346, the Panel presents its final report to the disputing Parties. On Day 361, the final report is released to the public (within the maximum 15-day time limit). Alas, suppose on Day 406, the disputing Parties fail to agree to a resolution (using the full 45-day period after the final report was received).[89]

Step 5: Level Seven — Arbitral Panel Reconvened

On Day 406, as disputing Parties have failed to reach an agreement, negotiations begin between the Parties to develop mutually acceptable compensation. But, assume the disputing Parties are unable to agree to such compensation.[90] On Day 436 (30 days after negotiations for compensation failed to come to fruition), the complaining Party provides written notice to the Party complained against that it intends to suspend benefits to the Party complained against including the plan of proposed suspended benefits.

On Day 466 (utilizing the maximum 30 days allowed), the Party complained against, believing the level of proposed benefits to be suspended is manifestly excessive and that it has eliminated the non-conformity found by the arbitral Panel, requests the Panel be reconvened.[91] The reconvened Panel renders a decision on the level of benefits that may be suspended on Day 586 (120 days after the request to be reconvened).

Suppose on Day 606, the Party complained against concedes it will pay an annual monetary assessment, instead of being subject to suspension of benefits as provided by the Panel's determination. Parties begin consultations within 10 days, but fail to compromise on the amount the monetary assessment should be set, and exhaust the 30-day maximum consultation period.[92] On Day 646, the Parties still are unable to reach an agreement.

Given that impasse, the amount is set equal to 50% of the level that the complaining Party previously proposed to suspend benefits. On Day 691, the first of the quarterly installments of the monetary assessment begin. If the Party complained against fails to meet its payment obligations, then the complaining Party may suspend benefits. In total, therefore, nearly 700 days — just under two years.

---

88. *See* Article 21:13.
89. *See* Articles 21:15–21:16.
90. *See* Article 21:16(2)(a).
91. *See* Article 21:16(3).
92. *See* Article 21:16(6)

III. Cases under 1994 *NAFTA*
Labor Side Agreement

Although *NAFTA* and all subsequent American FTAs provide for a dispute settlement mechanism for complaints arising under labor provisions, that mechanism typically goes unused. In its November 2013 study, *Social Dimensions of Free Trade Agreements*, the ILO found that complaint settlement provisions "have rarely been activated."[93] Between 1995 and 30 June 2013, in only four instances were they triggered, all being cases arising under U.S. FTAs.

That is, since labor provisions were introduced to U.S. bilateral trade negotiations in 1994, complaints alleging violations of labor provisions of FTAs have included Guatemala, Honduras, the Dominican Republic, Mexico, and Peru. Submissions have proceeded under the *NAFTA Side Agreement* with submissions from each Party and *CAFTA-DR* agreement in reference to a complaint against Guatemala.

Pursuant to the *NAFTA Side Agreement*, 37 submissions have been filed, twenty-three of which were filed with the U.S. NAO, nine filed with the Mexican NAO, and six submissions.[94] Of those 23, four were withdrawn by the submitters, hearings were held on 10, and eight rose to Ministerial-level consultations.[95] The filings were often filed by labor unions of the U.S. involving issues of freedom of association, the right to bargain collectively, use of child labor, minimum employment standards, occupational health and safety, the right to strike, and one case of pregnancy-based gender discrimination.

The results of the complaints under the *NAFTA Side Agreement* are varied. The majority of submissions were concluded at the NAO Stage as information was insufficient to establish the government's failure to enforce its labor laws. Some of the NAO recommendations have included recommendations to development joint cooperative programs to address the freedom of association and right to organize and research projects on evaluating how each Party reconciles the right to strike with national interests of safety, security, and general welfare.

For those that rose to the level of ministerial consultations, the implementation agreements varied and often involved public education on a labor rights issue. For example, one implementation agreement entailed a series of programs to publically address the freedom of association, the right to organize, and minimum employment standards in all three countries. Some agreements involved public seminars and conferences to educate workers on the freedom of association, employment discrimination, workers' legal protections, collective bargaining, and the different types of unions and union rights in each country.

---

93. ILO, *Social Dimensions of Free Trade*, at 3 (November 2013), www.ilo.org.

94. Status of Submissions under the NAALC, DEPARTMENT OF LABOR, www.dol.gov/ilab/trade /agreements/naalc.htm. [Hereinafter, Status.]

95. Status.

On the issue of collective bargaining, the Mexican Department of Labor and Social Welfare promoted the registry of collective bargaining contracts in conformity with established labor legislation and conducted a trilateral seminar to discuss law and practice governing Mexican labor boards. Additionally, the Mexican government provided workers with information pertaining to collective bargaining agreements existing in their place of employment and promoted the use of eligible voter lists and secret ballot elections in disputes over the right to hold the collective bargaining contract. Cooperative activities amongst Parties was a common remedy in the field of occupational safety and health management.

IV. 2001 *Jordan FTA* and Jordanian Labor Conditions

Whatever mechanisms exist in an FTA to adjudicate and enforce labor or environmental disputes, they almost certainly need supplementation and amendment after the FTA operates for a few years. For example, in May 2006 the National Labor Committee, a New York-based workers' advocacy group, said some apparel manufacturers in Jordan, and contractors that supplied them with workers from Bangladesh, engaged in human trafficking. The NLC said Bangladeshi workers suffered 20-hour work days, went unpaid for months, and were imprisoned if they complained. Jordan took the complaints seriously, responding in June 2006 by:

(1) Creating an inter-ministerial committee to respond to the complaints, plus a separate labor subcommittee under the *Jordan FTA* Joint Committee to ensure proper enforcement.

(2) Forming nine inspection teams to check factories in Jordan, thereby boosting the number of labor inspectors from 88.

(3) Establishing telephone hot lines in Bengali and other languages spoken by foreign workers for them to make complaints.

(4) Consulting directly with the government of Bangladesh.

(5) Shutting down three textile factories, and pledging to take further action.

The NLC alleged Bangladeshi workers, as well as workers from China, the Philippines, and Sri Lanka, are abused physically and psychologically, sexually harassed and raped, and put in unsanitary living conditions.

Also, in June, the Jordanian Minister of Trade, Sharif Al Zu'bi, met personally with each of the companies operating in Jordan's QIZs (discussed in a separate Chapter) to explain worker abuse would not be tolerated. "Our inspection regime may have failed us, and may have failed us miserably," he remarked.[96] Also, said

---

96. *Quoted in* Gary G. Yerkey, *Jordan Cracks Down on Firms Exploiting Foreign Workers in Violation of Trade Pact*, 23 International Trade Reporter (BNA) 1075, 1076 (13 July 2006).

the Minister: "We want trade and investment, but not at any price. We want clean investors . . . . They either shape up or ship out. . . . " [Jordan will continue to] "do the right thing" [and] "flush out" [the] "bad apples," which he estimated at about 10% of all companies operating in Jordan making T&A for the American market.[97] Subsequently, Jordan went further:

(1) In August 2006, the Jordanian Minister of Labor oversaw the transfer of 623 Bangladeshi workers from seven textile companies in QIZs implicated in worker rights violations to seven other firms.

(2) In September 2006, Jordan and the U.S. signed an agreement to collaborate on, via independent assessment, compliance with internationally recognized workers' rights in QIZs.

The key point is all of Jordan's measures go beyond the basic requirements in the *Jordan FTA*, namely, to consult with the U.S. and, if consultations fail, to entertain "appropriate and commensurate" measures, meaning trade sanctions.

Nevertheless, the U.S. National Textile Association was not impressed. In September 2006, the NTA filed with the USTR the first *Jordan FTA* Article 17 case. The NTA alleged Jordan's labor inspectors are underpaid and known to take bribes from employers to overlook labor violations, and faulted Jordan's labor code for the following rules:[98]

(1) Only workers of Jordanian nationality can join a trade union.

(2) Government employees, domestic servants, and most agricultural workers cannot join a trade union.

(3) Workers under 25, any person convicted of a criminal offense, or anyone convicted of a misdemeanor involving dishonorable or immoral conduct, cannot join a trade union.

(4) A union cannot be formed by less than 50 workers.

(5) The government may decide which industries may unionize, and no more than one union is permitted per industry.

(6) A worker cannot run for office in a union without having been a member for at least two years.

(7) The Ministry of Interior both endorses candidates and keeps tabs on activities of unions and union office candidates.

(8) Unions must establish a general confederation, which the government subsidizes and audits.

---

97. *Quoted in* Gary G. Yerkey, *U.S., Jordan Sign Agreement to Cooperate In Crackdown on Workers' Rights Violations*, 23 International Trade Reporter (BNA) 1310–11 (7 September 2006).

98. *See* Susan J. McGolrick, *AFL-CIO, Textile Producers Accuse Jordan of Violating Trade Pact with U.S.*, 23 International Trade Reporter (BNA) 1416–18 (28 September 2006).

(9) Unions must give employers 14 days' notice before a strike, and 28 days' notice if the work is related to a public service, but in practice they must obtain government authorization as well, and the government typically declares proposed strikes illegal.

(10) The Ministry of Labor can seek judicial dissolution of a union for a labor code violation, or instigation of an illegal work stoppage.

Further, alleged the NTA, Jordanian law mandates a government license for any organization seeking to hold a public rally or meeting, forbids newspapers from publishing encouragement for an unauthorized work stoppage, and bars individual or collective action intended to change Jordan's economy or society. To be sure, the NTA had an economic motivation for its case. In 2000, the last year before the *FTA* took effect, Jordan exported to the U.S. $43 million worth of T&A exports. In 2005, after four years of operation, exports of this merchandise had increased to $1.083 billion.

The U.S. and Jordan resolved the case via the Joint Committee and Labor Sub-committee the FTA created. In 2008, they set up a process of visits and inspections. They also funded an ILO "Better Work Program," which commenced in 2009, to monitor and publish reports about the conditions of migrant workers in QIZ garment factories.

V. 2006 *Bahrain FTA* and Arab Spring

The existence of even the best enforcement mechanisms does not mean they will be used. Consider the *Bahrain FTA*, which has dispute settlement procedures for each party to enforce effectively its labor laws, and mandates that workers to have access to fair, equitable, and transparent settlement mechanisms. In April 2011, amidst the Arab Spring, the AFL-CIO called for the U.S. to withdraw from the FTA because of the "ongoing brutal repression of peaceful protest carried out by the police and armed forces of Bahrain and the Gulf Cooperation Council."[99]

In August 2012, in the wake of the Arab Spring, the AFL-CIO accused Bahrain of discriminating against trade unions and union activists in contravention of Article 15:1 of the *FTA*, which expresses a shared Bahraini-American commitment to ILO principles. The AFL-CIO said this violation, coupled with what it dubbed "ongoing brutal repression of peaceful protest carried out by the police and armed forces of Bahrain and the Gulf Cooperation Council," were grounds for the U.S. to invoke Article 21:5(2) of the FTA and withdraw from it.[100]

---

99. *Quoted in* Susan R. Hobbs, *DOL Report Faults Bahrain 2011 Actions as Inconsistent with FTA Labor Chapter*, 30 International Trade Reporter (BNA) 37 (3 January 2013).

100. *Quoted in Labor Department Report on Bahrain FTA Compliance Under Interagency Review*, 29 International Trade Reporter (BNA) 1455 (6 September 2012). *See also U.S. Seeks Meeting with*

The Office of Trade and Labor Affairs (OTLA) in the Bureau of International Labor Affairs (BILA, or ILAB), in the DOL conducted fact-finding missions to Bahrain in October 2011 and February 2012, plus examination documentary evidence and consulted with the USTR and State Department. DOL then drafted a report in response to the AFL-CIO complaint. But, following circulation to the AFL-CIO and Bahrain, and publication, of the response, DOL took no further action. Was any necessary, or was the "reputational name-and-shame" sanction enough to bring about change in Bahrain?

Perhaps not, and DOL upped the pressure on the Emirate. In December 2012, the ILAB issued a Report calling compliance by Bahrain with labor commitments under the FTA inconsistent. The Report said Bahrain apparently failed to recognize and protect by law freedom of association and the right to organize and bargain collectively. The Report cited Bahrain for possible violations of Article 15:1 of the FTA, which bars discrimination against trade unions and union activists, and articulates a "shared standard of commitment" to ILO standards. Why?

Because after a February–March 2011 general strike, Bahrain fired and prosecuted criminally trade unionists. The DOL said Bahrain especially targeted *Shī'īte* workers, and made reinstatement of them difficult. Bahrain agreed to study the report, but pointed out that 98% of over 4,600 public and private sector workers dismissed from their jobs for striking had been reinstated or re-employed, or their cases were resolved.

VI. 2006 *CAFTA-DR* Chapter 16 and Enforcing and Guatemalan and Dominican Labor Law

- **2008 Guatemalan Workers' Rights Case**

The labor rights case the U.S. brought against Guatemala under *CAFTA-DR* is a landmark, as it was the first time a country filed a labor claim under an FTA. Along with six Guatemalan unions, the AFL-CIO initially lodged the claim with OTLA on 23 April 2008. The claim alleged failure by Guatemala to meet the *CAFTA-DR* standard, effective enforcement of its laws protecting workers' rights, such as the freedom of association, the right to bargain collectively, and the right to work in acceptable conditions. The complaint charged Guatemala failed to do so in five separate cases.

In June 2008, the DOL accepted the complaint. Following a report released by the DOL in early 2009, the U.S. and Guatemala began negotiations over to issue pursuant to the Article 16 of the agreement. On 30 July 2010, Ambassador Ron Kirk sent written notice to the Minister of Economy, Erick Haroldo Coyoy Echceverría,

---

Bahraini Officials To Discuss Labor Issues, Worker Rights, 30 International Trade Reporter (BNA) 698 (9 May 2013) (discussing the Report).

and the Minister of Labor and Social Protection, Edgar Alfredo Rodriguez, request-ing consultations pursuant to Article 16:6(1) of *CAFTA-DR* to discuss issues related to its obligation to "effectively enforce its labor laws" under Article 16:2(1)(a).[101] The U.S. requested consultations following an investigatory period to which it iden-tified numerous occasions of failures to enforce including the Ministry of Labor's failure to investigate alleged labor law violations, failure by the Ministry of Labor to take enforcement action once a violation was identified, and the court's failure to enforce Labor Court orders involving labor violations.[102] Additionally, the U.S. voiced concerns regarding labor-related violence and the government's response to threats of violence in relation to the right of association, the right to organize, and the right to collective bargaining.

Following little progress made in consultations conducted in Guatemala in Sep-tember and December 2010, in May 2011 Ambassador Ron Kirk requested a meet-ing of the Free Trade Commission under Article 20:5(2) *CAFTA-DR*. The request alleged that while Guatemala had made positive steps, "its proposals were insuf-ficient to address what we view as systemic failures."[103] Ambassador Kirk stressed the importance of holding trading partners accountable "in order to maintain the fairness that creates a level-playing field upon which American workers can com-pete and win."[104] After efforts to reach an adequate enforcement plan with the Free Trade Commission stalled, the U.S. took a step forward in the dispute settlement process on 9 August 2011 as Ambassador Kirk submitted a request to establish an Arbitral Panel under Article 20:6 (Dispute Settlement) of *CAFTA-DR*. Ambassador Kirk characterized this move as "sending a strong message that the Obama Admin-istration will act firmly to ensure effective enforcement of labor laws" and urged concrete actions by Guatemala to protect the rights of workers.[105] Further news of progress regarding the Arbitral Panel was put on hold according to the Ministry of Economy, Sergio de la Torre.[106]

---

101. *Letter from Ambassador Ron Kirk and Secretary of Labor Hilda Solis requesting Consulta-tions*, OFFICE OF THE UNITED STATES TRADE REPRESENTATIVE, 30 July 2010, https://ustr.gov/sites /default/files/073010%20Kirk%20Solis%20Letter%20to%20Guatemala%20about%20Labor%20 Rights%20Violations.pdf. [Hereinafter, *Letter.*]

102. *Letter.*

103. Press Release, *USTR Kirk Seeks Enforcement of Labor Laws in Guatemala*, OFFICE OF THE UNITED STATES TRADE REPRESENTATIVE, 16 May 2011, www.ustr.gov/about-us/press-office/press -releases/2011/may/ustr-kirk-seeks-enforcement-labor-laws-guatemala. [Hereinafter, May 2011 USTR Press Release.]

104. USTR Press Release.

105. Press Release, *U.S. Trade Representative Announces Next Step in Labor Rights Enforcement Case against Guatemala*, OFFICE OF THE UNITED STATES TRADE REPRESENTATIVE, 9 August 2011, www.ustr.gov/about-us/press-office/press-releases/2011/august/us-trade-representative-ron-kirk -announces-next-ste.

106. *See* Michael McDonald, *Guatemala Says Arbitration panel with U.S. on Hold*, REUTERS, 25 June 2012, www.reuters.com/article/2012/06/25/us-guatemala-labor-idUSBRE85O1DX2 0120625.

Voicing potential negative effects on commerce between the two countries, according to De La Torre, the U.S. agreed to suspend the work of the Panel as long as Guatemala proved it was taking steps towards improving working conditions. De la Torre noted one sticking point was the request by the U.S. that Guatemala grant authority for labor inspectors to fine businesses violating labor laws. The authority to sanction however remained within the judiciary, and the Guatemalan constitutional court had previously ruled that all penalties must be court sanctioned. America thus was in a bind: Article 16:3(8) states: "for greater certainty, decisions or pending decisions by each Party's administrative, quasi-judicial, judicial, or labor tribunals are not subject to revision or be reopened under the provisions of this Chapter."

In April 2013, America and Guatemala announced a labor rights enforcement accord under *CAFTA-DR*.[107] Their *Mutually Agreed Enforcement Plan* set out 18 points for Guatemala, for it to implement within six months. The *Plan* obliged Guatemala to:

(1) Enhance labor inspections;

(2) Accelerate processes to sanction employers and grant remedies to workers;

(3) Strengthen labor law compliance by Guatemalan exporting companies;

(4) Upgrade monitoring and enforcement of judicial orders in labor law case;

(5) Publish information about labor law enforcement; and

(6) Ensure workers are paid what is due to them if their factories shutter.

The U.S. agreed to suspend the arbitral Panel, giving Guatemala a chance to implement the *Plan*. Notably, the deal did not call for the Guatemalan Labor Ministry to be granted power to sanction firms that violate labor rights. It left that power with local courts.

One year later, in April 2014, the AFL-CIO said Guatemala had failed to implement several points of the *Plan*, blasted the USTR for giving Guatemala another four months to comply, and called for resumption of arbitral Panel proceedings.[108] Among the failures were Guatemala did not:

(1) Enforce standardized time frames for labor inspections.

(2) Devote sufficient resources to inspectors.

(3) Give priority to inspections called for by workers.

---

107. *See* Susan R. Hobbs, *Labor Enforcement Agreement Reached with Guatemala, DOL, USTR Announce*, 30 International Trade Reporter (BNA) 583 (18 April 2013).

108. *See* Rossella Brevetti, *AFL-CIO Blasts USTR for Delaying Decision on Guatemala Labor Complaint*, 31 International Trade Reporter (BNA) 815 (1 May 2014); Brian Flood, *Labor Groups Say Guatemalan Labor Practices Violate Trade Agreement, Call for Arbitration*, 31 International Trade Reporter (BNA) 777 (24 April 2014). *See also* Maureen Taft-Morales, *Guatemala: Political, Security, and Socio-Economic Conditions and U.S. Relations*, Congressional Research Service Report 7-5700, R42580 (7 August 2014), www.crs.org.

(4) Enact legislation to expedite judicial review and procedures to sanction employers that violate labor laws, or strengthen the authority of the Ministry of Labor to impose sanctions when that Ministry uncovered a violation of Guatemalan labor laws.

(5) Follow up on 38 cases of non-compliance with court orders.

Inaction, plus a lack of economic opportunity, drove young Central Americans to migrate illegally to the U.S.

The news was not all bad. Guatemala hired 100 new labor inspectors, implemented legal reforms to facilitate interaction between police and labor inspectors, verified compliance by employers with court orders, and ensured workers were paid wages owed when their factories closed. In August 2014, to the chagrin of the AFL-CIO, the USTR extended the suspension for another month. But, in September 2014, the USTR said it had enough: it opted to proceeding with the case, the first ever labor enforcement litigation under any U.S. FTA.

The outcome of that case was bad. In June 2014, nine years after the AFL-CIO lodged the initial claim, the *CAFTA* dispute settlement Panel issued its final report. The U.S. lost. It proved Guatemala failed repeatedly to enforce effectively its existing labor laws. But, it failed to prove that violation affected trade. *CAFTA* requires the failures are "in a manner affecting trade." The arbitrators defined this phrase to mean "confers some competitive advantage on an employer or employers engaged in trade." AFL-CIO Trade and Globalization Policy Specialist Celeste Drake remarked:

[T]rade is always affected when labor standards aren't enforced . . . .

Trade impact is only included as a qualifier in *CAFTA* labor disputes "to make it harder to show that there's a labor violation," Drake [observed] . . . . "And why would you do that unless your point is 'We don't really intend this to be enforceable.'"

Drake said "in a manner affecting trade," which is now standard inclusion in free trade agreements, should be eliminated from future agreements, beginning with a renegotiated *North American Free Trade Agreement*.[109]

The loss was historic: it was the first labor case America had ever brought under an FTA.

• **2013 Dominican Sugar Case**

A DOL investigation conducted by OTLA revealed evidence of labor law violations in the sugar industry in the Dominican Republic. The investigation was triggered by a labor advocacy non-governmental organization, Verité. Its report said child labor was used, and other labor rights violations committed. The case was

---

109. *Quoted in* Andrew Wallender, *U.S. Labor Dispute Failure Prompts Calls for NAFTA Changes*, 34 International Trade Reporter (BNA) 974 (6 July 2017).

resolved amicably.[110] The DOL Bureau of Labor Affairs started a $10 million project, and pledged to work with the Dominican government, to address violations.

- **Doubts about Honduras**

Organized labor criticized the effects on Honduras of *CAFTA-DR*. In March 2012, the AFL-CIO and 26 Honduran labor unions and civil society NGOs filed a complaint with OTLA alleging Honduras failed to enforce effectively its labor laws, particularly in the agriculture, manufacturing, and port sectors. Violations affected the rights to associate, form unions, bargain collectively, and have acceptable working conditions such as minimum wages, maximum work hours, and decent safety and health standards.

Senior officials from the AFL-CIO and Communications Workers of America visited the country in October 2014. What they found was disturbing:[111]

(1) Corporate farming of banana and palm had displaced subsistence farming of corn, beans, and rice, forcing small farmers to import those foods they previously had cultivated.

(2) Displaced from the land, small farmers moved to cities in search of factory jobs. But, there was an excess demand for such jobs. Displaced farmers who remained unemployed migrated illegally to the U.S.

(3) 70% of factory employers failed to pay the Honduran minimum wage. Socially responsible companies like Fruit of the Loom, which both respected minimum wage levels and allowed unionization, had to compete against companies that violated the minimum wage rules, giving the violators a 30% wage differential advantage.

These effects, the unions claimed, were caused by *CAFTA-DR* trade liberalization rules.

The result was a December 2015 Monitoring and Action Plan (MAP) between the U.S. Department of Labor and Honduran Ministry of Labor. It obliged Honduras to increase access of labor inspectors to worksites, and impose tougher penalties for violations. Unions and NGOs remained frustrated by the constraint in *CAFTA-DR* that the only way to enforce labor rights was through inter-governmental action.

- **Where Next with *CAFTA-DR*?**

As the Guatemalan dispute passed its fifth year without resolution, critics wondered whether enforcement of labor provisions in FTAs is possible. The formal complaint filed against Guatemala was the first official labor case the U.S. filed under an FTA. Would America go through with the enforcement procedures? Critics charged the U.S. failed miserably, and the weakness of its deals exposed. Under *CAFTA-DR*

---

110. *See* United States Department of Labor, Bureau of Labor Affairs, *Public Report of Review of U.S. Submission 2011-03 (Dominican Republic)*, 27 September 2013.

111. *See* Laura D. Francis, *Labor Leaders Decry CAFTA-DR Impact, Address Implications for Immigration Policy*, 31 International Trade Reporter (BNA) 1902 (23 October 2014).

Articles 16 and 20 procedures, the dispute extended well beyond the permitted time frame.

Through press releases claiming it was getting tough with Guatemala and unafraid to utilize dispute settlement to protect the rights of workers, did the U.S. act hypocritically by allowing numerous delays between its steps? Was the Guatemalan dispute worth pursuing? If the U.S. succeeded in the case, monetary assessments under *CAFTA-DR* would be capped at $15 million. Would the Parties have to return to negotiations to figure out how to improve labor protections? Among post-2007 trade agreements, dispute settlement procedures may be more likely to run efficiently and induce a quicker settlement between Parties, given the lack of a cap on monetary assessments and plain obligation to "adopt and maintain" the ILO core principles. Given the length of time passed, were the workers affected the ultimate losers of the dispute?

VII. 2009 *Oman FTA* and Omani Labor Law Reform

It is important to appreciate the definition of what qualifies as a "labor" or "environmental" law, and thus what must be enforced effectively as the essential obligation, may be open to question. For instance, the President of the Teamsters Union, James P. Hoffa (1941–), criticized the labor provisions in Chapter 17 of the *Peru FTA*, saying they are based on the flawed *CAFTA-DR* model. One flaw is anti-employment discrimination rules are not within the definition of "labor laws" in the *Peru FTA*. Hence:

> [t]he many women who compose much of the workforces in export sectors in Peru and in the Andean region, where sexual harassment has been well documented, would be unprotected from employment and workplace discrimination.[112]

In some countries, the aforementioned commitments mean major changes to local law. The AFL-CIO went beyond the boundaries of labor law, casting doubt on the wisdom of an FTA between the U.S. and Colombia because of criminal violence. In a June 2006, *Justice for All: The Struggle for Worker Rights in Colombia*, the AFL-CIO Solidarity Center said since the mid-1980s roughly 4,000 trade unions have been murdered, with more than 2,000 since 1991, mostly because of their participation in labor disputes.

Consider Oman. It started labor law reform in 2003, ratifying several ILO and U.N. conventions. In a May 2006 letter from the Omani Minister of Commerce and Industry to the USTR, Oman agreed its labor law commitments fell within

---

112. *Quoted in* Rossella Brevetti, *State Department Report Warns On Labor Rights Problems in Peru*, 23 International Trade Reporter (BNA) 413–14 (16 March 2006).

the jurisdiction of Chapter 16 of the *Oman FTA*, "as matters arising" under that Chapter, and thus subject to Article 16:6 consultations. In July 2006, Sultan Qaboos bin Said (1940–) issued a *Royal Decree* (supplemented by Ministerial Decisions) to implement ILO *Conventions* 87 and 98, which concern unionization and child labor. In the Omani legal system, a *Royal Decree* takes precedence over any previously enacted inconsistent measure.

The *Decree* (74/2006):

(1) Removed governmental involvement in activities of workers' representative committees (*i.e.*, labor unions), and allows more than one committee to be formed to represent workers at a specific enterprise.

(2) Forbade employee dismissal for lawful activity in a union, and penalizes anti-union discrimination.

(3) Increased (by five times for a first offense, and two times for a second offense) dissuasive penalties for violating Omani rules against child labor or the improper use of female labor.

(4) Prohibited forced or coerced labor, and penalizes violation of this ban (with fines of up to U.S. $1,300 per violation, imprisonment, or both, and a doubling of the penalty for repeat offenders).

(5) Endorsed collective bargaining.

(6) Permitted the right to strike as a collective bargaining technique, and ensured technical requirements for strikes follow ILO standards.

Not all U.S. politicians agreed the reforms, albeit well intentioned, went far enough. The Decree did not bar employers in Oman from withholding documents that release a foreign worker (*e.g.*, from the Indian Subcontinent) from an employment contract.

In May 2006, during mark-up sessions of the *Oman FTA*, the Senate Finance Committee passed 18–0 an amendment to prevent goods made by slave labor, or with the benefit of human trafficking, from receiving duty free treatment. The USTR opposed the "Conrad-Bingaman-Kerry Amendment" (named after its sponsors, Senators Kent Conrad (Democrat-North Dakota), Jeff Bingaman (Democrat-New Mexico), and John Kerry (Democrat-Massachusetts), saying it was redundant with existing U.S. import restrictions on prison, forced, or indentured labor, and violated *TPA* legislation that allows Congress to suggest only "necessary and appropriate" changes to implement trade deals. President George W. Bush (1946–, President, 2001–2009) refused to include the Amendment in the implementing legislation.

To what extent is this kind of resistance to an FTA justified in the case of Oman? Oman is a moderate nation, the only one dominated by the *Ibāḍī* sect (which is neither *Sunni* nor *Shī'īte*), has been a loyal American ally for 170 years, and overlooks the strategic Straits of Hormuz near the mouth of the Persian Gulf. Are these facts relevant, and if so, how, to a labor amendment in a trade accord?

What about Bahrain? It is not a signatory to ILO conventions on strikes. It is headquarters for the U.S. Navy Fifth Fleet. In November 2006, hardly four months after the *Bahrain FTA* took effect, Bahrain banned strikes and demonstrations at vital establishments, where national security could be disrupted. They were air and sea ports, civil defense installations, hospitals, health centers, and pharmacies, and electricity, oil and gas, telecommunication and water areas—plus bakeries and educational firms.

Chapter 25

Theory of TAA[1]

I. Compensating "Losers" from Free Trade

Even staunch free trade advocates ought to admit trade liberalization results in *net* gains to an economy. There are "winners" and "losers," and the benefits accruing to the winners more than offset the injury experienced by the losers. This net gain is little comfort to a worker who experiences real wage declines, or unemployment, because of fair (much less unfair) foreign competition. Nor is it much comfort to a firm forced to downsize significantly or declare bankruptcy, or the community in which the firm is located, which experiences the economic and social externalities associated with the firm's contraction.

Is it possible to realize the net gain from free trade, while at the same time providing redress for injuries to workers, firms, and communities caused by free trade? Free trade economists answer "yes," offering a solution that is both efficient and fair: transfer some of the net gain accruing to the "winners" from free trade to the "losers" from free trade, namely, those parties dislocated on account of import competition:

> Economic theory has long taught that international trade governed by the principle of comparative advantage, or relative factor endowments, will, over the long run, provide maximum benefit to all trading parties. These benefits will generally consist of higher returns to the factors of production, lower prices, and a wider range of choices to consumers than would exist in the absence of this trade. The theory recognizes, however, that overall economic and social benefits may be accompanied by adverse short-term

---

1. Documents References:
   (1) *Havana Charter* Preamble, Articles 1–10
   (2) GATT Preamble
   (3) *WTO Agreement* Preamble

Portions of this Chapter draw on two excellent CRS studies, both of which are *posted at* www .crs.gov: Benjamin Collins, *Trade Adjustment Assistance for Workers*, Congressional Research Service 7-5700, R42012 (17 December 2012); J.F. Hornbeck & Laine Elise Rover, *Trade Adjustment Assistance and Its Role in U.S. Trade Policy*, Congressional Research Service 7-5700, R41922 (19 July 2011). [Hereinafter, December 2012 CRS Report and July 2011 CRS Report, respectively.] The July 2011 CRS Report, in turn, relies on helpful sources, cited below, and also including: *The Trade Expansion Act: President Receives Unique Tariff-Cutting Rights and Adjustment Program After Carefully Planned Campaign*, Congressional Quarterly, CQ Almanac 1962, at 249–277; John T. Woolley & Gerhard Peters, *The American Presidency Project*, *posted at* www.presidency.ucsb/edu.

economic and social effects on selected parts of a national economy. Inasmuch as the social benefits from the trade are thought to be widespread throughout the economy, it is generally accepted that an adjustment assistance program designed to ease the adverse impact of rising imports on workers, firms, and regions is a vital concomitant to lowered trade restrictions.[2]

Thus, beneficiaries may compensate the injured, *i.e.*, specific industries on which the hardship of import competition is visited, and thus which face adjustment costs, through a redistribution scheme that is a non-protectionist alternative to import barriers.

To be sure, TAA programs are a readily apparent government expense, the benefits of which are not necessarily visible to those other than the targeted beneficiaries—at least not in the short term. In the long term, the benefits may be higher employment and output levels, reduced income inequality, and thus greater social stability. But, in the short term, the costs of protection (*i.e.*, tariffs and NTBs) to limit import competition fall on a diffuse and typically poorly organized group of consumers. Moreover, if the government imposes a tariff, then it earns revenue. So, it is often easier to take a protectionist route than the prudent course.

Nevertheless, non-protectionist choices are preferable, because protectionist measures are an expensive way to save jobs. In *Measuring the Costs of Protection in the United States*, Gary Clyde Hufbauer (1939–) and Kimberly Ann Elliott (1960–) estimate it costs American consumers a staggering $170,000 to protect a single job.[3] Their 1990 data set covers 21 sectors of the American economy ranging from ball bearings to women's hand bags. The $170,000 figure is the average amount of consumer surplus lost as a result of protectionist measures in these 21 sectors. In four of the 21 sectors, the amount is $500,000. (In the steel sector, the estimates are as high as $1 million for each job saved.) When Hufbauer and Elliott take the gain to producers benefiting from protection (*i.e.*, increased producer surplus) into account, the average net national welfare cost per protected job is about $54,000. Accordingly, part of the rationale for trade adjustment assistance is a worker can be retrained for far less than $170,000, or even $54,000.

Nothing in the GATT-WTO regime obliges a Member to implement a redistribution scheme, nor does the regime set out parameters with which such a scheme must comply. To be sure, GATT Articles XXXVI–XXXVIII urge developed countries to adopt measures that help expand trade from less developed countries. But, it is difficult to infer from these provisions an obligation to implement a domestic structural adjustment program. Likewise, FTAs and CUs rarely if ever obligate parties to execute a compensatory mechanism for workers dislocated from

---

2. Samuel M. Rosenblatt, *Trade Adjustment Assistance Programs: Crossroads or Dead End?*, 9 Law & Policy in International Business 1065, 1066 (1977).

3. January 1994, at 11–13.

free trade. *NAFTA* is an exception, in that the *NAFTA Implementation Act of 1993* contained provisions on a temporary assistance program for workers adversely affected by *NAFTA*. But, these provisions were necessary for Congressional passage, not part of the FTA itself.

The first efforts at developing a scheme to compensate parties injured by free trade were in Europe. The establishment of the EEC in 1957 resulted in hardship for many workers and firms because of reduced trade barriers. Adjustment assistance was provided to dislocated workers and firms.

Interestingly, in the *Omnibus Trade and Competitiveness Act of 1988* (*1988 OTCA*) Congress urged the President to undertake negotiations in the Uruguay Round to allow any country to impose a small, uniform fee of not more than 0.15% on all imports to fund a country's adjustment assistance scheme. (Unilateral imposition of the fee might violate GATT MFN treatment, tariff bindings, and non-discrimination obligations.) No such deal was reached. The *1988 Act* authorized the President to impose an import fee either after completing that Round, or 2 years following enactment of the *Act*, unless it was "not in the national economic interest" to do so. President George H. W. Bush (1924–) decided the import fee was not in the national interest.

II. Statutory Evolution

• **1953 Randall Commission**

Even before he joined Prime Minister Winston S. Churchill (1874–1965) in the 1941 *Atlantic Charter*, and thus before the end of the Second World War (1939–1945), President Franklin Delano Roosevelt (1882–1945, President 1933–1945) identified cross-border trade as essential to world order. In his 1940 State of the Union Address, the President declared American trade policy to be an "indispensable part of the foundations for any stable and durable world peace."[4] This policy took on even greater importance in the Cold War, as stitching together a coalition of non-Communist countries that were prosperous and could contain Soviet and Chinese Communism was essential. In 1954, President Dwight D. Eisenhower (1890–1969, President 1953–1961) thus equated trade expansion to expansion of the "free world."[5] Trade and national security were explicitly, inextricably linked: boosting trade among America and its Allies, the "First World," would complement their military preparedness against the "Second World," and perhaps might nudge parts of the "Third World" into their orbit.

---

4. *Quoted in* Robert E. Baldwin, *U.S. Trade Policy Since 1934: An Uneven Path Toward Greater Trade Liberalization*, National Bureau of Economic Research Working Paper 15397, 2 (October 2009).

5. Dwight D. Eisenhower, *Document # 908: To John Foster Dulles*, 30 *Department of State Bulletin* number 763, 187 (8 February 1954).

But, how could Congress agree to a free trade agenda when workers and firms felt cutting tariffs would undermine their economic security? Selling this agenda solely as an as an instrument of foreign economic and national security policy was politically unviable. A practical concept was needed to manage domestic protectionist resistance—hence, TAA. The first mention came from the Public Advisory Board for Mutual Security, or "Bell Commission," which convened under President Harry S. Truman (1884–1972, President 1945–1953). In July 1952, President Truman wrote to the Commission:

> We are working night and day to help build up the military and economic strength of friends and allies throughout the free world. We are spending very substantial sums of money to do this, to the end that our friends can grow strong enough to carry on without special aid from us. This is why we have urged upon them programs of increased production, trade expansion and tariff reduction, so that through world trade they can expand their dollar earnings and progressively reduce their dependence on our aid.
>
> Yet, at the same time, we find growing up in this country an increasing body of restrictive laws attempting to further the interests of particular American producers by cutting down the imports of various foreign goods which can offer competition in American markets. The so-called "cheese" amendment to the *Defense Production Act*—enacted despite a number of existing safeguards—is a striking example of this trend. On the one hand, we are insisting that our friends expand their own world trade; on the other hand, we seem to be raising new barriers against imports from abroad. This poses a very real dilemma for our whole foreign policy.
>
> In my judgment, the first step toward clarifying this situation is for a responsible public group to study this problem and recommend to the President and the Congress the course we should follow in our trade policy. I can think of no group better qualified to do this than the Public Advisory Board for Mutual Security. Representatives of business, *labor*, agriculture, education, and the public at large make up your membership. Both major political parties are represented. . . .
>
> I want you to consider *all* aspects of our foreign trade policy as coming within the scope of your investigation. In particular, I think you should examine our tariff policy, with special reference to the expiration of the *Reciprocal Trade Agreements Act in 1953*; import restrictions, including quotas and customs procedures; agricultural policies affecting foreign trade; maritime laws and regulations concerning carriage of American goods; and *what to do about the problems of domestic producers who may be injured by certain types of foreign commerce*. . . .
>
> *It is extremely important that the whole problem be examined.* The effect of raising a tariff to protect a domestic industry, for example, should be evaluated in terms of the counter-restrictions which are raised against American

exports abroad. Our tobacco producers know what this kind of discrimination can mean, but I am sure that there are many others who are not fully aware of it. Neither, I feel, have we really thought through the full implications of our efforts to prevent the rest of the free world from trading with the Iron Curtain bloc. Having insisted that these countries severely restrict their trade in one direction, what can we suggest to replace it?[6]

The Bell Commission did not develop a long-term strategy on how best to deal with adjustment costs from import competition.

The next body that considered the topic, the Randall Commission—officially known as the 1953 Commission on Foreign Economic Policy—did.[7] Congress set up this Commission when it extended for 1 year the trade negotiating authority for President Eisenhower. This Commission considered a proposal for temporary "government assistance to communities, employers, and workers" in the form of financial and technical help. The assistance would take the form of financial and technical help so that industries adversely affected by imports could diversify their products, and injured communities could generate new employment opportunities.

Despite finding the proposal compelling, the Commission rejected it. The Commission could not justify assistance only for trade-related problems. In other words, the Commission wrestled with the theoretical question that continues to plague TAA: why should assistance be limited to groups suffering economic dislocation from the lowering of trade barriers, but not other causes? It was a question early GATT scholars, such as Swarthmore College Economist Clair Wilcox (1898–1970), who presided at GATT Preparatory Conferences is discussed. In a 1950 article, he studied considered the case for TAA in a government universe in which there were no programs to help casualties of economic change caused by shifting business relocation, consumer preferences, or technological shifts.[8] The latter are increasingly relevant, as the WTO estimates (as of October 2016) technological change accounts for 80% of job losses in developed countries.

- **Modern Debate Framed**

Interestingly, the drafter of the Randall Commission proposal was David J. McDonald, a Commission member and President of the United Steel Workers (USW). He gave an answer to that question that still is offered today: "unemployment

---

6. Public Papers of the Presidents: Harry S. Truman, 1945–1953, "203. Letter to Members of the Public Advisory Board for Mutual Security Requesting a Study of Foreign Trade Policies," (13 July 1952), *posted at* http://trumanlibrary.org/publicpapers/index.php?pid=2365&st=&st1=.

7. *See* U.S. Congress, House of Representatives, Report to the President and Congress, Commission of Foreign Economic Policy, H.R. Document Number 290, 83rd Cong., 2nd Sess. 54–55 (23 January 1954) (prepared by Clarence B. Randall, Chairman) [hereinafter, Randall Commission Report]; Klaus Knorr & Gardner Patterson, A Critique of the Randall Commission Report (1954).

8. *See* Clair Wilcox, *Victims of Tariff Cuts*, 40 The American Economic Review number 5 884–889 (December 1950). [Hereinafter, Wilcox.]

caused by government action, as in the lowering of tariffs, should be of particular concern to the government . . . ."[9] The government should be accountable for the net socioeconomic losses its trade liberalization policies cause. During the 1950s, proponents supplemented his argument with 3 others: efficiency; equity; and politics, and the modern debate over TAA took shape.[10]

Efficiency, proponents urged, counseled for TAA, because support for dislocated workers would accelerate the process of adjustment. Idle workers would return to the labor force, and other factors of production would be redeployed, more quickly. Opponents countered assistance would be a disincentive to speedy adjustment: why relocate, or take a lower paying job, if the government subsidizes trade-related injury. Moreover, might such a subsidy be a moral hazard, encouraging workers and firms to begin or persist in a reckless competition with imports that ultimately is doomed?

Proponents said equity, too, demanded TAA. Was it not fair to spread the cost of free trade across society, by doing what Classical and Neo-Classical economists urged, namely, taking some of the gain from the "winners" and redistributing it to the "losers"? Opponents countered with the point made by Commissioner McDonald and covered in the Wilcox article: why is it to tailor help narrowly for one afflicted economic constituency, but not others? Surely the moral obligation is to weave a safety net to assist all factors of production dislocated by economic changes.

As to politics, the issue was pragmatism. First, the best should not be the enemy of the good. It was politically infeasible to help all in society adversely affected by change. The logical conclusion of the desire to help every person injured or threatened with injury would be the end of American capitalism: a welfare state, or worse — socialism. Even if politically possible, casting a limitless net was impossible for lack of resources. But, the fact that all are adversely affected by economic change should not preclude efforts to help at least some who are.

---

9. Randall Commission Report, 55.

10. Following Wilcox, policy analyses of TAA spanned the decades of the latter half of the 20th and first part of the 21st centuries. For example:

(1) In the 1960s, Richard A. Givens, *The Search for an Alternative to Protection*, 30 FORDHAM LAW REVIEW issue 1, 20 (1961).

(2) In the 1970s, WILLIAM DIEBOLD JR., THE UNITED STATES AND THE INDUSTRIAL WORLD: AMERICAN FOREIGN ECONOMIC POLICY IN THE 1970s 150–153 (1984), and ROBERT A. PASTOR, CONGRESS AND THE POLITICS OF U.S. FOREIGN ECONOMIC POLICY 94–95, 100, 143 (1980).

(3) In the 1980s, ROBERT E. BALDWIN & ANNE O. KRUEGER EDS., THE STRUCTURE AND EVOLUTION OF RECENT U.S. TRADE POLICY (1984), specifically, the chapters therein by C. Michael Aho & Thomas O. Bayard (*Costs and Benefits of Trade Adjustment Assistance*) and J. David Richardson (*Comment*), at 153–185 and 192–193, respectively.; and GARY CLYDE HUFBAUER & HOWARD F. ROSEN, TRADE POLICY FOR TROUBLED INDUSTRIES 35–39 (1986). [Hereinafter, HUFBAUER & ROSEN.]

(4) In the early 2000s, I.M. DESTLER, AMERICAN TRADE POLITICS 7, 12–13, 128, 150, 296–298 (4th ed., 2005). [Hereinafter, DESTLER.]

Moreover, politically, TAA was an escape clause of its own. Proponents saw TAA as a positive way to adjust to import competition. Protection, whether via a safeguard remedy or (long expired) Peril Point Provision, was negative, and inflicted costs of its own. Further, if TAA were available, then threatened laborers—who could be anticipated by applying the Stolper-Samuelson Theorem—might be less staunch in resisting trade liberalization ideas. Their acquiescence, if not tacit support, could help GATT multilateral trade rounds in the 1950s and beyond. Indeed, viewed retrospectively, this *quid pro quo*—freer trade for TAA from its untoward effects—was useful in those rounds, and the key trade bills of 1962, 1974, and 2002.[11]

Opponents replied that politically, TAA would be nightmarishly complex to administer. Bureaucracy would be the end result of empty headed pure-heartedness, as bureaucrats would have to define and measure injury from tariff reductions, determine whether domestic and imported goods were "like," decide if producer-exporters of the latter caused or threatened injury to manufacturers of the former, figure out which retraining programs were appropriate, and so forth. The new administrative apparatus for TAA would be expensive, costing resources that ought to go to the truly needy, and its outcomes would be imprecise.[12] The more sclerotic, arbitrary, or costly the bureaucracy, the more difficult it would be to "sell" TAA politically. Why not let the private sector rely on extant unemployment or other social benefits, and adjust on its own?

· **1950s Bills**

Congress saw the first TAA bills in the 1950s. As Senator from Massachusetts in the 83rd Congress, John F. Kennedy (1917–1963) sponsored the *Trade Adjustment Act of 1954*.[13] The man against whom he would run for the 1960 Democratic nomination for President, Minnesota Senator Hubert Humphrey (1911–1978), introduced an identical bill in the 84th Congress.[14] Congress failed to act on either bill, and likewise other bills introduced into the 86th Congress. In the 1960 Presidential campaign, TAA became a partisan issue. The Democratic Party put TAA in its Platform, along with a call to expand trade, while the Republican Party Platform excluded TAA, in favor of two trade remedies—the Escape Clause and Peril Point Provision.[15]

---

11. *See* DESTLER, 296–298.

12. *See* Wilcox, 884–889.

13. Senate Bill 3650.

14. His bill, which Senator Humphrey initially offered on its own, became a proposed amendment to House Resolution 1, which linked TAA to trade negotiating authority to President Eisenhower. *See* Senator Hubert H. Humphrey, *Extension of the Trade Agreements Act—Amendments*, 101 CONGRESSIONAL RECORD part 3, 3,997–3,998 (30 March 1955).

15. Under the Peril Point Provision, the U.S. Tariff Commission had to study the effects of any proposed reduction in tariffs, and identify the point to which a tariff could be cut without harming domestic producers. The *Trade Expansion Act of 1962* eliminated the Provision.

But, the Kennedy-Humphrey proposals contained the essence of what would be enacted once JFK became President: if a reduction in tariffs on imports competing with domestic merchandise "have been found either to threaten or to have caused serious injury to a domestic industry," then employees, organizations representing employees, firms, industrial development corporations, or communities could apply for temporary assistance. A governmental board would consider their applications.

- *1962 Act* Creation

Following the unsuccessful legislative proposals between 1954–1960, the 87th Congress passed the first TAA program under the *Trade Expansion Act of 1962*. Table 25-1 summarizes basic features of this and all subsequent TAA enactments. TAA under the *1962 Act* helped workers dislocated as a result of a Federal policy to reduce barriers to foreign trade. President John F. Kennedy articulated this link:

> I am also recommending as an essential part of the new trade program that companies, farmers, and workers who suffer damage from increased foreign import competition be assisted in their efforts to adjust to that competition. When considerations of national policy make it desirable to avoid higher tariffs, those injured by that competition should not be required to bear the full brunt of the impact. Rather, the burden of economic adjustment should be borne in part by the Federal Government.[16]

Perhaps it was the experience of candidate John F. Kennedy in the 1960 Presidential Election, particularly the primaries in Wisconsin and West Virginia, where this Harvard-educated scion of a wealthy family encountered real blue collar workers, and real poverty, that led JFK as President, to champion TAA.[17] In any event, the assistance was not a permanent subsidy, but rather—as in the Kennedy-Humphrey bills—temporary help to offset the adjustment costs of trade liberalization. That help would ward off protectionism.

Aside from strong Presidential support, two other factors likely contributed to Congressional passage of TAA. High unemployment existed in the early 1960s, and during the 1960–1961 Dillon Round, America agreed to slash tariffs on 61 product categories below their Peril Point. TAA made GATT-based multilateral trade liberalization less threatening to labor constituencies, which bore the brunt of the weak economy, thus allowing them to join the business community in support of trade expansion legislation (or, at least, oppose it less vigorously).

---

16. *Hearings Before the House Comm. on Ways and Means on H.R. 9900: A Bill To Promote the General Welfare, Foreign Policy and Security of the United States Through International Trade Agreements and Through Adjustment Assistance to Domestic Industry Agriculture and Labor, and for Other Purposes*, 87th Cong., 2d Sess. 8 (1962) (message from President John F. Kennedy relative to the Reciprocal Trade Agreements Program).

17. These campaign experiences are masterfully chronicled by Theodore H. White in *The Making of the President 1960* (1961).

Table 25-1. Summary of TAA Legislation[18]

Year of Enactment	Name of Bill	Public Law Number	Length of TAA Programs	Date Through Which TAA Extended	Lapse in Coverage?; Length of Lapse	Packaged with Presidential Trade Negotiating Authority?	Highlights
1962	*Trade Expansion Act of 1962*	87-794	Permanent	Permanent	No	Yes	1st TAA program
1974	*Trade Act of 1974*	93-618	8 years	30 September 1982	No	Yes	Longest lifespan in TAA history
1981	*Omnibus Budget Reconciliation Act of 1981*	97-35	1 year	30 September 1983	No	No; Part of budget bill	
1983	*A Bill To Amend the International Coffee Agreement Act of 1983*	98-120	2 years	30 September 1985	No	No; Mixed with unrelated legislation	
1984	*Deficit Reduction Act of 1984*	98-369	10 weeks	15 November 1985	No	No; Part of budget bill	Temporary extension amidst budget battles
1985	*Emergency Extension Act of 1985*	99-107	5 weeks	19 December 1985	Yes; Coverage lapsed from 19 December 1985 until March 1986	No; Part of budget bill	
1986	*Deficit Reduction Amendments Act of 1985*	99-272	6 years	30 September 1991	Yes; As above	No; Part of budget bill	Long term extension
1988	*Omnibus Trade and Competitiveness Act*	100-418	2 years	30 September 1993	No	Yes	
1993	*Omnibus Budget Reconciliation Act of 1993*	103-66	5 years	30 September 1998	No	No; Part of budget bill	Long term extension

(continued)

---

18. This Table draws on a variety of sources, including July 2011 CRS Report, Table A-1 at 15.

Table 25-1. Summary of TAA Legislation (*continued*)

Year of Enactment	Name of Bill	Public Law Number	Length of TAA Programs	Date Through Which TAA Extended	Lapse in Coverage?; Length of Lapse	Packaged with Presidential Trade Negotiating Authority?	Highlights
1993	*North American Free Trade Implementation Act*				No		Special TAA for workers dislocated owing to NAFTA
1998	*District of Columbia Appropriations*		9 months	30 June 1999	No	No; Mixed with unrelated legislation	
1999	*Consolidated Appropriations Act of 2000*	106–113	2 ¼ years	30 September 2001	Yes; Coverage lapsed from 30 September 2001 to August 2002	No; Part of budget legislation	
2002	*Trade Act of 2002*	107–210	5 years	30 September 2007	Yes; As above	Yes	Long term extension Consolidated NAFTA TAA into general TAA program; Expanded coverage of general program
2007	*TAA Extension Act*	110-89	3 months	31 December 2007	No	No	
2008	*Consolidated Appropriations Act of 2008*	110-161	1 year	31 December 2008	No	No; Part of budget bill	

2009	Consolidated Security, Disaster Assistance, and Continuing Appropriations Act of 2009	110-329	2 months	February 2009	No	No; Part of budget bill	
2009	American Recovery and Reinvestment Act (specifically, Trade and Globalization Adjustment Assistance Act)	111-5	2 years	31 December 2010	No; But, higher funding levels for TAA programs lapsed on 12 February 2011, and levels reverted to 2002 levels	No; Part of economic stimulus package	Introduced reforms to TAA program
2010	Omnibus Trade Act of 2010	111-344	13 months	12 February 2012	No	No	
2011	Trade Adjustment Assistance Extension Act of 2011		1 year and 10 months	31 December 2014	No; But, renewal terms for certain programs changed in the final year (1 January–31 December 2014)	No	Renewed most TAA reforms introduced in 2009 to the 2002 programs
2015	Trade Adjustment Assistance Enhancement Act of 2015 (proposed May 2015) Trade Preferences Extension Act of 2015 (renewing GSP and AGOA as well as TAA)	Senate Bill 568 House Resolution 1295	6 years	30 June 2021	No, because TAA programs re-established as they were on 31 December 2013	No, proposed as a separate bill but considered at same time as TPA renewal No, proposed and passed as a separate bill, considered after TPA passed as a stand-alone bill	See summary below Renewed GSP, AGOA, and TAA

- **Five Shifts**

For five reasons, inclusion of TAA in the *1962 Act* was a watershed in delegation by Congress of negotiating authority to the President, and indeed, in U.S. trade law history.

First, the *1962 Act* broadened the trade authority of the President. Until this *Act*, most legislation focused on granting the President the ability to cut tariffs. The *1962 Act* went beyond tariff cutting authority.

Second, the *Act* took a new approach to dealing with domestic opposition to trade liberalization generally, and competition from fairly priced imports in particular. Until the *Act*, the classic approach (other than not cutting tariffs or NTBs) was to invoke the Escape Clause. Another approach was the so-called "Peril Point" rule, which the *1962 Act* did not contain. Using this remedy might work for an entire petitioning industry, but unlike TAA, it was not targeted to specific workers or firms dislocated from fair trade. For workers, the *Act* introduced (1) higher, longer unemployment benefits, and (2) retraining and relocation allowances. For firms, it provided (1) loans and loan guarantees, (2) technical assistance, and (3) special tax deductions.

Third, TAA in the *1962 Act* forever changed the debate about trade liberalization. The presence of TAA in the legislation was an explicit acknowledgment free trade does not have unmitigated positive benefits for every sector of society; rather, as Ricardo's Law of Comparative Advantage states, it results in net gains to society, *i.e.*, there are losers from free trade. After 1962, no trade bill could be passed without discussing the domestic adjustment costs of free (or freer) trade on workers and firms. Trade law and policy were no longer were about just tariff cutting; they were about reaching an accommodation on a wide variety of trade issues among many interested parties.

Fourth, and following logically from the third point, the presence of TAA in the *1962 Act* meant labor constituencies — unions and other groups of workers — had a louder voice and a better choice. No longer was the choice of labor all-or-nothing, for-or-against a trade bill. With TAA, workers had a more nuanced option than outright protectionism, assuming Congress provided adjustment assistance suitable to garner their support.

Fifth, and following from the third and fourth points, TAA became a hotly contested issue in the debate about trade liberalization. The *1962 Act* passed with a majority of Democrats, and a minority of Republicans, voting for it. Yet, TAA was the most controversial feature of that legislation. In the House of Representatives, some conservative Democrats, and many Republicans, demanded a separate vote on TAA. They were unsuccessful. The House bill passed the bill under a closed rule barring amendment. The Senate rejected proposals to modify or delete TAA.

Still, House opponents were successful in adding the issue to the American trade legislation debate: should workers and firms get special treatment if import competition, as distinct from some other cause, adversely affects them? Or, is TAA an expensive, ineffective mechanism to deal with domestic dislocations? TAA remains a centerpiece of American trade law, with major renewals in 1974, 1981, 1988, 1999, 2002, 2009, and 2011. In each instance, that debate was re-joined.

- **But, Not Used**

The first generation of TAA programs were not widely used, because of strict eligibility criteria set forth in the *1962 Act* and their application by the U.S. Tariff Commission (the predecessor to the ITC). In fact, no adjustment assistance was granted until 1969: between 1963 and 1969, 6 worker groups and 12 industries filed petitions. None was granted, after a time-consuming, expensive process.[19]

Under the *1962 Act*, workers or firms were eligible for assistance only if four criteria were met:

> First: Imports of a product like or directly competitive with the product they produced were increasing;

> Second: The increased imports were in major part a result of trade agreement concessions;

> Third: The firm was seriously injured, or threatened with serious injury (or the workers were unemployed or threatened with unemployment); and

> Fourth: The increased imports were the major factor in causing the serious injury (or unemployment).

Insistence on the adjective "major" (as distinct from other possibilities in other trade statues, such as "significant" or "substantial"), posed a double barrier: the increase in imports had to have been caused "in major part" by tariff reduction, and that increase had to be the "major cause" of injury to the petitioner. "Major" proved to be an impossibly high threshold: it meant increased imports were more important in causing injury than all other causes combined.

With the promise of TAA unfulfilled, labor looked askance at trade liberalization. Adding to its skepticism, if not cynicism, about free (or freer) trade was an historic reversal in America's BOP: in 1971, for the first time since 1888, the U.S. had a balance of trade deficit. With that "red" position came wage declines and job losses against which TAA had failed to compensate workers and firms.

Safeguard and AD-CVD law were not a solution, as these remedies had their own legal hurdles and administrative costs. Well-connected workers or firms adversely affected by import competition could, and did, seek recourse by lobbying their contacts on Capitol Hill and in the White House.[20] But, their doing so was not a systemic solution. Worse yet, direct intervention for politically powerful constituent was orthogonal to the purpose of trade remedies, which were supposed to be apolitical, or minimally so.

---

19. *See* CHARLES R. FRANK, JR., FOREIGN TRADE AND DOMESTIC AID 4–5, 40–47, 63–67 (1977).
20. *See* HUFBAUER & ROSEN, 35.

That Congress had to act was clear by 1972, when the AFL-CIO publicly rejected both TAA and any further trade agreements during hearings in the Subcommittee on Foreign Economic Policy of the House Foreign Affairs Committee. The uptick in the early 1970s in affirmative decisions on TAA by the U.S. Tariff Commission had not mollified organized labor: the trend could reverse itself at any time, and besides, the Commission still granted only a small percentage of petitions.

Moreover, world economic events imperiled American jobs and incomes: the 1973 Arab Oil Embargo, and continued fears for the position of the U.S. dollar vis-à-vis other currencies in a new world of flexible exchange rates following the 15 August 1971 decoupling of the dollar from the gold standard. Perhaps foreign military defeats played an indirect role in the position of labor against TAA: service personnel were returning from jungle battles in Indochina in an unsuccessful attempt to keep Cambodia, Laos, and Vietnam from falling to Soviet- or Chinese-backed Communist insurgencies.

Congress had to act on TAA, and so it did during the Presidency of Republican Richard M. Nixon (1913–1994, President, 1969–1974). Congress attempted to liberalize the eligibility criteria, and increase the amount of benefits, through changes to TAA programs made by the watershed *Trade Act of 1974*, as amended. Those changes were not the intent of the President: his initial bill focused on conventional trade topics, and cut back on TAA. Congress would (and politically could) have none of it: the House and Senate not only restored, but even bolstered, the TAA benefits the Nixon Administration had stripped away, and eased the criteria for getting them. Hence, the *1974 Act* is rightly described as "one of the most far-reaching trade bills in U.S. history."[21]

- *1974 Act* TAA Criteria Changes

Via the *1974 Act*, Congress abolished the second criterion. No longer was it necessary for a petitioner to show tariff reductions were the "major" reason for increased imports. All that was needed was proof that imports indeed had increased.

The *1974 Act* replaced the serious injury test in the third criterion with requirements that a significant number of workers lose their jobs, or be threatened with redundancy, or that sales or output of their firm decrease.

---

21. July 2011 CRS Report, 8. *See also Congress Clears Trade Bill on Final Day*, Congressional Quarterly, CQ Almanac 93rd Congress, 1974, at 553–562 (reviewing the *Act*).

Congress considered assorted stand-alone trade proposals, but opted to reunite President Nixon's request for renewal of trade negotiation authority with TAA, reflecting the Kennedy-era balancing and synthesis, or linkage, in the *1962 Act*. The difference, of course, was Congress in the *1974 Act* "re-tool[ed]" TAA. *Id*. In retrospect, it was right to do so. Aborting TAA after hardly 12 years of life under severe statutory criteria to test its promise would have been premature and unjust.

In the highly polarized partisan climate of Capitol Hill in the early 2000s, efforts at de-coupling TAA from negotiating authority again are commonplace, *i.e.*, TAA reauthorization is separate from authority renewal. The bipartisan imprimatur of support from Congress for a TAA-authority package, through bills like the *1962* and *1974 Acts*, seems fruit of a remote halcyon period.

Vitally, Congress lowered the causation threshold by striking the adjective "major" from the 4th criterion. No longer was it necessary to show increased imports were a "major factor" in causing serious injury. Rather, it was necessary to show increased imports "contributed importantly" to declining sales or production, or to redundancy of a significant number of workers. Other non-trade factors could play a role, and import competition did not have to amount to more than the totality of the other factors.

Procedurally, Congress acted by changing the decision-maker for TAA petitions, and imposing tight deadlines. It renamed the Tariff Commission the "ITC," but transferred authority for TAA determinations to the DOL (for workers) and DOC (for firms). It left the ITC with Escape Clause cases, and insisted the DOL and DOC act within 60 days, not six months, on TAA petitions.

- *1974 Act* **TAA Benefit Changes**

Aside from boosting benefits for workers and firms, the *1974 Act* added a new class of beneficiaries: communities. The *Act* provided grants and loans for entire communities dislocated by import competition. Congress eliminated the community scheme in 1982, but then re-created it in the 2009 *American Recovery and Reinvestment Act* (*ARRA*).

The *Act* introduced another innovation, one concerning worker beneficiaries. It targeted special help for older workers, because of an important but often-missed distinction between "layoffs" and "plant closings."[22] When a factory is not shuttered, but its owners shed workers, commonly they do so based on "LIFO"—last in, first out. Workers with the least seniority typically are least protected from redundancy. Conversely, when a plant is closed all workers—young and old—lose their job. The shuttering is non-discriminatory. Yet, older workers sometimes comprise the largest percentage of the redundancies. Congress thus addressed the special needs of seniors.

- **Post-*1974 Act* Problems, Reagan-Bush Administration Efforts to Eliminate TAA, and 1980s Reauthorizations**

Statutory authorization for TAA remains in Title II of the *1974 Act*, so all subsequent legislation has taken the form of amendments to that *Act*. (The current eligibility criteria are discussed below.) Despite express language Congress inserted in the *1974 Act* that TAA give meaningful relief from import competition, and despite post-*1974 Act* amendments to TAA, overall the scheme seemed to have little positive impact in helping workers and firms that lost out from free trade. One practitioner observed: "[a]s the *1974 Act* program developed, it proved to be no more effective in

---

22. *See* July 2011 CRS Report, fn. 36 at 9.

facilitating adjustment than the *1962 Act* program had been," and the program for firms "has not functioned" since 1987.[23]

Two reasons why assistance was ineffectual are evident from the discussion of the TAA programs below: obtaining TAA was (and still is) a Byzantine process, and the amount of assistance was (and still is) meager. Aside from complexity and money, a third reason accounts for the disappointing results: ideology about budget priorities.

Funding for the programs comes from general Federal revenues and, therefore, is subject to the politics of budget cutting in an era of deficit reduction. From 1975–1979, many workers and some firms obtained assistance. Payments to workers surged to $1.6 billion in 1980, the highest level ever, and amounted to $1.4 billion in 1981. The reason for the jump was TAA appeared to be functioning as it was supposed to: helping parties dislocated by trade.

Starting with the October 1979 shift in Federal Reserve monetary policy (from Keynesian-style interest rate targeting to Monetarist-style setting money supply growth rate commensurate with output growth rate), the American economy entered into a steep recession from which it would not emerge until the early 1980s. The Big Three auto companies suffered from Japanese import competition. With increased layoffs came increased TAA claims and benefit payouts. These large sums

---

23. Bruce E. Clubb, United States Foreign Trade Law, vol. I, § 24.9.2, at 797.

Note that under Section 224(b) of the *1974 Act* (19 U.S.C. § 2274(b)), the DOL must publish in the Federal Register a summary of a Report the DOL submits to the President under Section 224(a) of that *Act* (19 U.S.C. § 2274(a)). Following a notification from the ITC to DOL, this Report is mandated in each global safeguard case, *i.e.*, Section 201 investigation. The purpose of the Report is to identify which workers (if any) are likely to be certified as eligible for, degree to which they can be helped by, TAA.

For an example of such a Report, see, *U.S. Department of Labor's Report of the Study of Domestic Industry Under Section 224 of the Trade Act of 1974 — Large Residential Washers*, www.doleta .gov/tradeact/docs/LRW_Study.pdf. The DOL summary is Department of Labor, *Large Residential Washers (LRWs)*, 82 Federal Register number 247 61329–61330 (27 December 2017). That Report made 4 findings:

(1) The Department received . . . TAA petitions for four worker groups involved in the production of LRWs since January 2012. All four of those worker groups were certified as eligible to apply for TAA, resulting in an estimated 183 workers eligible to apply for individual benefits under the TAA Program.

(2) The Department estimates that 324 additional workers are likely to be covered by certified TAA petitions before the end of 2019.

(3) Sufficient funding is available to provide TAA benefits and services to these workers. In FY 2017, the Department provided $391 million to states to provide training and other activities 2 for TAA participants as well as $294 million in funding for Trade Readjustment Allowances (TRA) and $31 million in Reemployment Trade Adjustment Assistance (RTAA) funds.

(4) The Department believes that training and benefits under the *Trade Act*, other Department programs, and programs available at other federal agencies are sufficient to assist workers in the LRWs industry to adjust to the trade impact.

Id., 2–3.

led even its champions, such as President Jimmy Carter (1924, President, 1977–1981), to worry about its budgetary impact. That recession also led to an unsuccessful Section 201 Escape Clause petition on behalf of the U.S. auto industry, and a VER effectively capping Japanese car imports at 1.25 million vehicles annually (discussed in a separate Chapter). The surge in TAA payments also caused the Administrations of President Ronald Reagan (1911–, President, 1981–1989) and George H.W. Bush (1924, President, 1989–1993) to propose abolition of the TAA programs.

Congress declined to "kill" TAA, but renewal did not come easy. In the immediate aftermath of the *Trade Agreements Act of 1979*, which implemented the Tokyo Round agreements, Congress did not renew TAA authority: the House, but not the Senate, passed a TAA bill.[24] Subsequently, President Carter agreed to 2-year extension, through 1983—but at a diminished level (cutting $2.6 billion from TAA funding), and with tightened eligibility requirements (especially with respect to unemployment benefits)—via the *Omnibus Budget Reconciliation Act (OBRA)* of 1981. Particularly influential in shaping the 1981 *OBRA* TAA scheme was a GAO Report saying TAA paid out benefits, but failed to result in meaningful adjustment to import competition, *i.e.*, it was welfare.[25]

- **Reauthorizations in 1990s**

In subsequent 1980s and early 1990s Reagan-Bush era budget legislation, the pattern of TAA renewal with lower funding, short periods, and tougher criteria continued. Deficit conscious, and influenced by an ideology of small government, Congress resonated with ambivalence at best, and hostility at worst, to TAA. The legislative vehicles Congress used for TAA renewals symbolized this resonance, and made the case for TAA more difficult than ever before. Those vehicles were budget, not trade, bills. The primary rationales, and policy bargain, for TAA—to help workers dislocated from trade and thereby encourage support from labor constituencies for freer trade, and to reduce the need to resort to protectionist trade remedies—were clear when TAA and trade negotiating authority were bundled. Divorcing was a kind of divide-and-conquer strategy, deliberate or not, that sent TAA into "a long period of decline."[26]

Moreover, during this era, Congress was particularly keen on seeing AD, CVD, and safeguard actions flourish, and on enhancing trade remedies through the Uruguay Round and *NAFTA*. TAA and trade remedies might have been mutually reinforcing, the latter for sparing use against egregious contact, the former being the default preference. Instead, the latter became "core negotiating objectives . . . effectively relegating TAA to the back seat of trade policy."[27]

---

24. *See Trade Adjustment Assistance*, Congressional Quarterly, CQ Almanac 1979, 327–328.
25. *See* Congressional Quarterly, Inc., U.S. Trade Policy Since 1945, 23–69 (1984).
26. July 2011 CRS Report, 9.
27. July 2011 CRS Report, 10.

So, for instance, with the 1983 expiry, Congress eschewed eliminating TAA, but extended it for just two years, through 1985, and trimmed support.[28] Thereupon followed two short extensions, and a lapse of three months. Under deficit-reduction legislation in 1986, Congress agreed to a six-year extension of TAA, through 1991. But, with the longer extension came a trade-off on funding: Congress cut all loan, loan guarantee, and other direct financial assistance support for firms. Thereafter, firms could get only technical assistance. Under the *1988 OTCA*, Congress re-authorized both Presidential trade-negotiating authority and TAA, this time for 5 years through FY 1993.

During the first term of the Presidency of Bill Clinton (1946–, President, 1993–2001) came another long-term extension, five years. In the *OBRA* of August 1993, Congress re-authorized TAA for workers and firms through FY 1998, with assistance terminating on 30 September 1998.[29] Again there was a time-for-money trade-off: Congress also reduced the cap on funding for re-training from $80 million to $70 million for FY 1997. Ambivalence and hostility persisted, and as the CRS rightly observed, "[t]he lengthy extensions appeared to be inversely proportional to the budgetary effort in the bills."[30]

Congress again re-authorized the TAA program, and funded it, via its October 1998 omnibus spending package.[31] That package ensured continuation through 30 June 1999. In June 1999, Congress was poised to grant an extension through 30 September 2001. But, the trade bill with the embedded extension got bogged down in the politics of the GSP, CBI, SSA trade preferences, and fast-track trade negotiating authority. Thus, TAA expired on 30 June 1999. Not until November 1999 did Congress pass a renewal bill, and did so retroactively.

- *1993 NAFTA TAA*

Only once in American history did Congress link TAA directly to a specific FTA; in all other instances, it drew that link to renewal Presidential trade negotiating authority renewal, or severed the link to trade, and either considered TAA on its own, or as part of its budget calculus. The exception came in December 1993, with an exceptional FTA, *NAFTA*. Congress passed a separate *NAFTA Worker Security Act* as part of *North American Free Trade Implementation Act of 1993*, the implementing legislation for NAFTA. Congress thereby established a TAA regime for workers harmed by the anticipated adjustment costs *NAFTA* would impose on them,[32] costs predicted by the Stolper-Samuelson Theorem. No other FTA—not even the commercially enormous *KORUS*—has had *sui generis* TAA, and neither *TPP* nor *T-TIP* has attracted serious discussion of a targeted, *NAFTA*-like TAA-FTA linkage.

---

28. *See Trade Adjustment Aid Cut*, Congressional Quarterly, CQ Almanac 1983, 251.

29. *See* Congressional Quarterly, CQ Almanac 1993, 137–175.

30. July 2011 CRS Report, 10.

31. *See* H.R. 4328, § 1012.

32. *See North American Free Trade Agreement Implementation Act*, Public Law Number 103-182 §§ 501–506 (8 December 1993).

That the link occurred in the *NAFTA* context is largely because of Bill Clinton. As a candidate in the 1992 Presidential election, his support for *NAFTA* was tepid, and contingent on the *Labor* and *Environmental Side Agreements* notwithstanding side letters on these topics negotiated by his opponent, President George H.W. Bush. As President, he conditioned his support for the implementing bill on (*inter alia*) a separate *NAFTA* TAA scheme, notwithstanding the fact Congress had renewed the general TAA for 5 years in the 1993 *OBRA*.

Had TAA returned to the mainstream of the free trade debate in American politics? Was a precedent set for a new synthesis of TAA and FTAs? "No" is the answer to both questions. Towards the end of President Clinton's second term, in 1999, Congress reauthorized TAA for just two years, and when it lapsed in 2001, Congress—perhaps focused on the national security crisis triggered by the 9-11 terrorist attacks—did not renew it for another year, as part of the *Trade Act of 2002* of that year.

But, was TAA once again a hallmark of debate over U.S. trade law and policy? Arguably, "yes." At the least, the 2002 renewal marked a return to the traditional link between TAA and Presidential trade negotiating authority, and a discussion of how best to deal with adjustment costs in a 21st century global economy.[33]

• *2002 Act* Consolidation and Expansion

With narrow, bipartisan support, Congress passed the *2002 TAA Reform Act*, and thereby gave TAA a much-needed "shot in the arm." This *Act* renewed TAA for five years. It provided a larger funding appropriation than before, setting the overall TAA amount as of FY 2005 at $ 1.057 billion, of which $12 million was for firms, and $90 million for farmers and livestock producers. Thus, as with previous TAA legislation, the *Act* continued eligibility for two classes of potential beneficiaries: firms, or groups of former employees. (Technically, the application process and funding sources were distinct.) For former employees lodging a petition, at least three workers at a firm of fewer than 50 employees, or 5% of the workforce for a larger firm, had to be adversely affected by a covered trade agreement to be eligible for TAA.

But, the *Act* introduced two key inter-related innovations: consolidation; and expanded coverage.[34] The *2002 TAA Reform Act* incorporated the *NAFTA* TAA program, which had been separate since its debut, into the mainstream TAA scheme. It broadened coverage under the general scheme to include workers affected by a shift in production associated with under any FTA, or under *AGOA*, *ATPA*, or *CBERA*.

The *2002 TAA Reform Act* also expanded the scope of eligibility to include "secondary workers." That term connotes workers employed by an upstream supplier

---

33. *See* Congressional Quarterly, Inc., CQ Almanac 2002, 184–185.

34. *See* U.S. Congress, House Committee on Ways and Means, Subcommittee on Trade, Trade Act of 2002, Conference Report to Accompany H.R. 3009, 107th Cong., 2nd Sess., House Report 107–624, 26 July 2002, 14–25 (2002).

(*i.e.*, a firm providing inputs into a finished product made by a firm that already has been certified as eligible for TAA), or with a downstream producer (*i.e.*, a firm using in its product components made by a firm already certified as eligible). The *Act* contained a subsidy for health care insurance through a Federal tax credit, a demonstration project for Older Workers (over 50 years old), and aid for farmers and livestock producers (including fisherman) managed by the USDA.

- *2009 TGAAA* Reauthorization and Expansion

TAA was scheduled for renewal in 2007, but amidst the fog of continuing post-9/11 wars in Afghanistan and Iraq, stalled Doha Round negotiations, and limited FTA initiatives, the best Congress could muster was a short-term extension through 31 December 2007. Thereafter, the program expired, but Congress replenished funding for it through 31 December 2008 via the *Consolidated Appropriations Act of 2008*, and into part of 2009 via the *Consolidated Security, Disaster Assistance, and Continuing Appropriations Act of 2009*. It seemed TAA was back to where it had been in the 1980s, namely, part of deficit reduction politics and budget bills.

However, the Great Recession, which commenced in 2008, was a watershed for TAA. Never before had TAA been thought of as an economic stimulus measure. In the response to that Recession by the Administration of Barack H. Obama (1961–, President, 2009–2017), it was. The *American Recovery and Reinvestment Act of 2009* (*2009 ARRA*) extended and expanded TAA under the *1974 Act*. The *2009 Act* was a controversial stimulus package designed to boost the American economy out of the Recession. The relevant portion of this *Act* is the *Trade and Globalization Adjustment Assistance Act* (*TGAAA*). *TGAAA* reauthorized and altered significantly the TAA to deal with adverse effects of globalization, specifically, dislocations caused by international trade competition, via income support, re-training, and re-allocation expenses to adversely affected parties.

Dislocations there were. Between 2000 and 2009, the American manufacturing sector lost nearly one-third of its labor force. Not all of the workers made redundant did, or even could, find new work in that sector. They needed help—all the more so in the Great Recession. Between 2009 and 2013, over 400,000 American workers were approved for TAA benefits. So, the *TGAAA* introduced innovations to TAA, expanding coverage for workers and firms in services sectors, and offering support for communities. The legislation also boosted the health care insurance subsidy. It was "the first time" in American history that "TAA received such a large increase in funding and mission without being part of a major trade bill."[35]

That was because of the new justification for TAA: it was one of several economic stimulus measures, *i.e.*, part of Keynesian fiscal policy to fight a downturn. This justification meant TAA was not tethered to trade-related injury or threats. Indeed, a persuasive case for trade-caused dislocations would have been hard to mount: Wall Street excesses, inadequate financial laws and regulations, poor bank supervision,

---

35. July 2011 CRS Report, 11.

and most of all, a lack of ethical conduct among commercial and investment bankers, were to blame for the Great Recession. There was no set of Doha Round agreements, and precious few new FTAs, at which to point the blame for woes on Main Street.

The essence of *TGAAA* is manifest in its amendments to Chapters 3 and 4 of the *1974 Act*. The *2009 ARRA*, including *TGAAA*, entered into force on 17 February 2009. However, most of those amendments expired on 31 December 2010, and applied only to workers covered by petitions filed between 18 May 2009 and 1 January 2011.

The portion of the *2009 ARRA* stimulus package amending TAA was contained in Subtitle I, Sections 1800–1899K. These provisions broke down logically into 6 Parts:

Part I: TAA for Workers
Part II: TAA for Firms
Part III: TAA for Communities
Part IV: TAA for Farmers
Part V: General Provisions
Part VI: Health Coverage Improvement

The salient features of these Parts are discussed below.[36]

- **2011 Renewal and Expansion of *TGAAA***

Following expiry of the 2009 *ARRA* amendments to TAA, on 1 January 2011, the TAA program fell back on 2002 eligibility criteria and funding levels, corresponding to the previous major TAA legislation. In the *Omnibus Trade Act of 2011*, Congress extended TAA only through 12 February 2011, albeit with the expanded coverage and higher funding levels of the *2009 ARRA*. Thereafter, TAA slumped back to the 2002 amounts. After months of bitter partisan rancor over whether, when, and by how much to renew the 2009 reforms, on 21 October 2011 Congress did so.

The legislation, the *Trade Adjustment Assistance Extension Act of 2011* (*TAAEA*) renewed through 31 December 2014 nearly all of the expansions to TAA, established via the 2009 *ARRA* reforms, to the basic 2002 TAA program.[37] (However, the renewal terms changed for certain programs in the final year, 1 January–31 December 2014.) The vote in the Senate evinced just how partisan the legislative battle was: 70–27, with the 27 "No" votes being cast only by Republicans. (The 70 "Yes" votes came from 51 Democrats, 17 Republicans, and 2 Independents.) Generally, under

---

36. The General Provisions (Part V) of the *2009 Act* indicated changes to TAA wrought by the *Act* were effective "upon the expiration of the 90-day period beginning on the date of the enactment of this *Act*." The *Act* became a Public Law on 17 February 2009. So, the *Act* took full effect by mid-May 2009.

37. *See* H.R. 2832, Public Law Number 112-40, Title II.

TAAEA took effect on 21 October 2011. But, it applied retroactively in the sense that workers certified between 15 February–20 October 2011 could seek benefits under the terms of *TAAEA*.

TGAAA, as renewed in the 2011 legislation, TAA coverage expanded for workers, firms, communities, and farmers vis-à-vis areas where assistance had been offered to a lesser extent, or not at all. In addition, *TGAAA* improved healthcare coverage to TAA beneficiaries.

- **2015 Renewal (Senate Proposal)**

In May 2015, the Senate Finance Committee released the following summary of a proposed 2015 TAA bill that accompanied legislation to renew Presidential fast track trade negotiating authority:

United States Senate, Committee on Finance,

Summary of Trade Adjustment Assistance (TAA) Enhancement Act of 2015
(May 2015)[38]

The *Trade Adjustment Assistance (TAA) Enhancement Act of 2015* re-establishes the TAA programs in effect as of December 31, 2013, and extends the program through June 30, 2021. TAA currently applies only to trade-affected production sector workers, and only if those jobs were moved overseas to a country with which we have a free-trade agreement. **By re-establishing the program as of 2013, this bill will make eligible for TAA service sector workers and workers affected by offshoring or outsourcing to countries like China or India.** Extending TAA ensures that the program's training and reemployment benefits remain accessible and flexible. It also continues accountability measures and the streamlining of TAA programs. Key provisions of this TAA extension bill are set out below:

Maintains and Expands Eligibility Requirements

- *Provides TAA benefits to service sector workers and firms.* The bill ensures that workers and firms in both the service and manufacturing sectors are eligible for TAA. It also offers the same coverage to secondary workers in those sectors.

- *Covers workers whose firms shift production to non-FTA partner countries.* The bill ensures that workers whose firms shift production to any country, including China or India—not just countries with which the United States has free trade agreements—are eligible for TAA.

- *Provides TAA coverage for U.S. suppliers of component parts.* The bill ensures that workers at firms supplying component parts to other firms are eligible for TAA without requiring TAA certification for the firm that buys the component parts. It maintains coverage for firms that petition for TAA benefits if they supply component parts to foreign customers and their customers switch to component parts made outside the United States.

- *Ensures automatic eligibility for workers suffering from unfair trade and import surges.* Unfair foreign subsidies, the dumping of foreign goods, and unexpected

---

38. *Posted at* www.finance.senate.gov/imo/media/doc/TAA Enhancement Act of 2015 Summary.pdf (emphases original).

import surges can harm U.S. industries and affect jobs in those sectors. The bill ensures that workers in such industries will automatically be eligible to receive TAA benefits if their layoffs occurred within one year before or after an affirmative injury determination by the International Trade Commission.

Invests in American Workers

- *Provides a $450 million investment to train workers.* The bill authorizes $450 million annually for fiscal years 2015–2021, ensuring states have ample funding to provide long-term job training.

- *Gives flexible training options and up to 130 weeks of training.* The bill ensures training for up to 117 weeks, giving all workers the opportunity to receive long-term training, and provides an additional 13 weeks of training for workers completing a degree or an industry-recognized credential. TAA allows various training options, including opportunities for part-time and pre-layoff training.

- *Provides accessible wage insurance that works with other benefits.* For workers who seek quick re-employment, TAA provides wage insurance — 50 percent of the wage differential between the old job and the new job, up to $10,000 — to workers 50 years of age or older. The bill ensures workers have the ability to switch from trade readjustment allowances (TRAs) to wage insurance payments at any time during their training. A worker who completes training and is reemployed is eligible to receive reemployment TAA benefits in lieu of TRA benefits for the remainder of the worker's TRA eligibility.

Service and Outreach to Workers in Transition

- *Provides eligibility protections for Americans on active duty military service.* The bill maintains protection for workers called up for active duty military or full-time National Guard service and allows them to restart their TAA enrolment process after completing such service.

- *Re-establishes clarity in enrolment deadlines and ensures fairness.* Workers are currently required to enrol in training within 8 weeks of certification or 16 weeks of layoffs. This bill simplifies the application process by allowing workers to enrol in training within 26 weeks after layoff or certification, whichever is later.

- *Provides funding to help State caseworkers counsel TAA clients.* The bill ensures that not less than five percent of the training funds allocated to States are used for case management services, allowing States to provide proper assessment, career counselling, and other case management services.

Helps Small Businesses and Farmers

- *Provides assistance to small businesses.* The TAA for Firms program helps small businesses adjust to foreign competition and create new jobs by providing assistance to improve their competitiveness. The bill authorizes $16 million annually for the program, which helps small businesses that are able to show a decline in sales or production over one, two, or three years.

- *Provides benefits and technical assistance to farmers and fishermen.* The bill provides targeted training to farmers and fishermen and clarifies that fishermen and aquaculture producers may receive TAA benefits whether they are competing against farmed or wild-caught fish or seafood imports. Producers who complete the training phases become eligible for up to $12,000 in seed money to use their new skills and implement a business plan. The TAA for Farmers and Fishermen Program is authorized at $90 million.

Streamlines Programs and Improves Accountability

- Consolidates and streamlines administrative program costs. The bill continues the consolidation of administration, case management, job search, and relocation funding under the training fund cap. It eliminates separate funding streams, while allowing States more flexibility to use a portion of the training funds for administration and case management costs. States must prioritize these funds for training and case management, but administrative costs are capped at 11.5% of the funds. States can also use these funds to pay for 90% of the cost of job search and relocation, up to $1,250.

- Updates performance measures as requested in the President's budget, in order to conform with the *Workforce Innovation and Opportunity Act of 2014.*

- **Summary Characterization**

No one word—certainly not "generosity"—captures the entire history of TAA. The CRS put it well: "the fortunes of TAA have ebbed and flowed."[39] In 1962 and 1974, with an orthodox, trade-related rationale, Congress authorized TAA for dilated periods and significant funding. In 2002, Congress did the same, synthesizing renewal of TAA and Presidential trade negotiating authority, albeit with a recession-related justification. But, in the 1980s and early 1990s, trade-related orthodoxy fell to budget politics, and despite a modest renaissance connected to *NAFTA*, got only limited renewals and money.

III. Five Non-Fiscal Policy Questions

TAA programs raise serious policy concerns. First, why should the government prefer to assist workers or firms dislocated by free trade as opposed to any other economic phenomenon? Workers lose jobs, and firms go bust, because of changes in IT. Typewriter, musical record, and land-line telephone companies are cases in point. There is no "IT adjustment assistance" for them. Is the distinction that the government promotes trade liberalization (*e.g.*, through FTAs), but not IT progress? Arguably, only where the government catalyzes the dislocation should it be liable to clean up any mess. Or, is that a distinction without a difference. The government encourages IT progress through, for example, defense research (which led to the

---

39. July 2011 CRS Report, 11.

internet—it was initially conceived of as a decentralized communication system for military purposes) and procurement (as in aerospace contracting).

Second, what is to prevent adjustment assistance from becoming a subsidy to inefficient workers and firms? Are some workers simply unwilling or unable to retrain? Should some firms cease to exist through what the noted economist Austrian Joseph A. Schumpeter (1883–1950) calls the creative destruction of capitalism? Conversely, is adjustment assistance "burial insurance" for workers and firms?

Third, is there overlap between TAA and other safety net schemes? To what extent are the same or similar benefits available through multiple Federal or State entitlement programs? Are faith-based initiatives an acceptable alternative?

Fourth, is TAA doomed to political opportunism? Consider the twin facts of economic uncertainty in the U.S. in 2002, when the *TAA Reform Act* was passed, and congressional elections that year. Increased foreign competition hit hard many populous States (*e.g.*, California, Florida, Ohio, and Pennsylvania) wherein key Senatorial of Congressional seats were in play. Was the relief TAA promised an election cycle smoke screen shielding incumbents from constituents disillusioned by trade liberalization?

Fifth, is adjustment assistance "industrial policy"? This term generally refers to official mechanisms "that affect the allocation of a country's resources in terms of industrial sector, region, and time." A key objection to industrial policy is that government plays an inappropriately large, even dominant, role. The forces of the free market lead to more efficient allocations of resources than government decisions. Hence, the argument runs, government bureaucrats should not promote certain domestic industries over others through the provision of adjustment assistance. Of course, a counter-argument is that many governments—including those of some of our important Asian trading partners such as the governments of Japan and Korea—actively engage in planning and support activities with respect to certain sectors of their economies to ensure that these sectors remain internationally competitive.

IV. Generosity, Catholic Social Justice Theory, and Funding

How generous is TAA? One justification for it, complimentary to the Positivistic Utilitarian one of transferring gain from winners to losers, is social justice: helping people and their companies hurt by foreign competition is a hallmark of a compassionate society. The four pillars of Catholic Social Justice Theory are (1) respect for human dignity, (2) advancement of the common good, (3) exercise of a preferential option for the poor, and (4) subsidiarity. Underlying the preferential option is the virtue of magnanimity. How strong is the spirit of giving in the technical rules of a statute like *TGAAA*?

Implementation in practice of any legislation involving expenditures is tied to dollar appropriations. The Federal government funds all TAA program benefits, as well as *NAFTA* Transitional Adjustment Assistance. Funding is an on-budget item from general tax revenues. States then dispense funds. So, there is no "trust fund," akin to the trusts for Social Security or Medicare, for TAA. Thus, at the time TAA legislation enters into force, its implementation future is uncertain if renewal and funding is uncertain. That invariably is the case.

For instance, TRA payments are funded as a general Federal entitlement associated with the Federal Unemployment Benefit Account of the DOL. The amount of such funding is modest: in FY 1995, $274.4 million was appropriated for TRA payments and related administrative expenses. In FY 1997, $276.1 million was appropriated for them. The fact Congress essentially did not increase funding between 1995 and 1997, in spite of the implementation of the Uruguay Round agreements and *NAFTA*, underscores a lack of commitment to, and the uncertain future of, TAA.

As another example, Federal grants to States defray expenses of reemployment services. Similarly, training, job search, and relocation allowances are paid for by an annual appropriated entitlement under the Training and Employment Services account of the DOL. The 2002 *TAA Reform Act* increased funding for program to levels not seen since the early 1980s. Whether higher levels are sustained is uncertain.

Obviously, a key metric of the generosity of an adjustment assistance program is dollars — how many, when, and under what conditions? Generally speaking, the larger the funding, and the easier the access to it, the more generous the program. Applying this general rule is not so easy in practice. Each aspect of TAA must be examined.

For example, job search funding was available under the original TAA statute. The maximum limit per worker initially was $800. The *2009 ARRA* increased the dollar amount available for expenses incurred in these endeavors. The limit was raised to $1,500 from $1,250 per worker. Once a worker found a new job, funding for relocation was increased by the same amount, from $1,250 to $1,500 per worker. Did the boosting of job search and relocation support by $250 per worker America became more generous in its TAA program?

The answer is "not necessarily." Other dimensions of the program must be examined. Perhaps there were offsetting cuts elsewhere. Even if the overall funding declined, the details of funding levels and disbursement criteria must be examined: perhaps "red tape" was cut, so the process for getting money became more efficient. Moreover, the time period for which the answer is formulated can change the answer. Under the *2011 TAAEA*, the limit on job search allowance fell, to 90% of each search, and a maximum of $1,250.[40]

---

40. *See* 20 C.F.R. §§ 617.31(c), 617.41(c).

How, then, does the DOL decide which States get what amounts and when under TAA? The answer to this question changed under the *2009 ARRA*. Overall, the *ARRA* increased the annual funding cap on the TAA training from $220 million to $575 million for each of FY 2009 and 2010. These monies were allocated to the DOL, which in turn distributed them to States under terms prescribed by the TAA program. The *Act* also set a cap of $143,750,000 for the period of 1 October 2010 through 31 December 2010.

The *2009 ARRA* criteria for the DOL to disburse these funds were:

(1) The DOL had to make an initial distribution to the states equal to 65% of the training cap (which was $373.75 of $575 million), and keep the other 35% in reserve to dole out on an as-needed basis, *i.e.*, to give to States that demonstrate a high degree of dislocation. Under prior law, the reserve level was 25%.

(2) In making the initial disbursement, the DOL had to consider 4 variables.

(3) The four variables were the: (a) trend in the number of workers covered by certifications of eligibility, (b) trend in the number of workers engaged in training, (c) estimated number of workers involved in a training program approved under TAA, and (d) estimated funding needed to provide the training.

(4) The DOL (pursuant to its regulations) weighed these four variables equally. As it did prior to the *2009 ARRA*, the DOL calculated the national total for each variable, and the percentage of each State on each variable in relation to the national total. Based on each State's percentage of the national total, the DOL allocated the initial 65% of the cap.

(5) Under a "hold harmless" provision of the *2009 ARRA*, the initial allocation to each State had to be at least 25% of the amount that State obtained in the previous FY. This percentage is a significant drop from prior law, under which each State was guaranteed at least 85% of its initial take from the prior FY.

(6) If the initial unadjusted allocation to a State was less than its hold harmless amount, then the DOL (under its regulations) adjusts the allocation upward to the hold harmless figure. Money to make these upward adjustments was subtracted from the 65% cap available for disbursement. If the unadjusted allocation for any State was less than $100,000, then the DOL continued its practice under prior law of re-apportioning those funds to another State, effectively topping up the 65% cap. A State with a sub-$100,000 allocation could ask the DOL for help from the reserve funds.

(7) By 15 July of each FY, the DOL had to distribute 90% of training funds.

In theory at least, collection of data by the DOL is supposed to help it apply these criteria, so as to distribute funds more quickly to areas in which numbers of displaced workers are the greatest. That is, it is supposed to rectify a long-standing problem with the TAA program, namely, the dilated time between unemployment and receipt of funds where their need is most pressing.[41]

The intricacies of TAA funding and disbursement intimate that TAA is good work for international trade lawyers, in two respects. First, their expertise is needed to comprehend and comply with the rules to get help for the needy. Second, by getting help for the needy, they are doing good.

---

41. *See* 19 U.S.C. § 2296(a)(2).

Chapter 26

Practice of TAA[1]

I. Federal and State Involvement

- **Joint Administration**

Federal and State authorities jointly administer the TAA program. Therefore, workers seeking TAA must deal with two phases and two layers of government. First, they must apply to the Federal government for certification for eligibility. Second, if they receive that certification, then they must apply to their State government for benefits. Each State has a cooperative agreement with the DOL on administration.

At the Federal level, the DOL operates TAA through its ETA. (The USDA administers the program for farmers.) The ETA processes petitions for eligibility submitted by workers, and issues certifications or denials. Petitions are just two pages, but have plenty more pages of supporting documentation. A copy of the petition may be given to the Governor of the State in which the petitioner is located. Obtaining Federal certification for eligibility is a complicated process. A group of three or more workers from a firm with less than 50 employees (or at least 5% of the workforce at a larger firm), a union, or an authorized representative of a group of workers may file a petition with the ETA for certification for eligibility.[2] Only workers adversely affected by increased imports are eligible for benefits.

- **Role of DOL**

The DOL began administering the TAA program in 1975. Its role as the lead governmental agency continued under the *2009 ARRA*. As is clear from the discussion

---

1. Documents References:
   (1) *Havana Charter* Preamble, Articles 1-10
   (2) GATT Preamble
   (3) *WTO Agreement* Preamble

Portions of this Chapter draw on two excellent CRS studies, both of which are *posted at* www .crs.gov: Benjamin Collins, *Trade Adjustment Assistance for Workers*, Congressional Research Service 7-5700, R42012 (17 December 2012); J.F. Hornbeck & Laine Elise Rover, *Trade Adjustment Assistance and Its Role in U.S. Trade Policy*, Congressional Research Service 7-5700, R41922 (19 July 2011). [Hereinafter, December 2012 CRS Report and July 2011 CRS Report, respectively.] The July 2011 CRS Report, in turn, relies on helpful sources, cited below, and also including: *The Trade Expansion Act: President Receives Unique Tariff-Cutting Rights and Adjustment Program After Carefully Planned Campaign*, Congressional Quarterly, CQ Almanac 1962, at 249-277; John T. Woolley & Gerhard Peters, *The American Presidency Project, posted at* www.presidency.ucsb.edu.

2. *See* 19 U.S.C. § 2271(a).

below about disbursing funds, the DOL works with State governments. The DOL set out the details of the administration of the entire TAA program through promulgating new regulations in the CFR.[3] It publishes its petition determinations in the *Federal Register.*

An institutional change wrought by the *ARRA* was establishment of an Office of Trade Adjustment Assistance within the DOL. With principal duties to oversee the implementation of TAA, provide information to workers, and certify applications, this Office is supposed to facilitate the goals of the program. Presumably, this dedicated Office can work exclusively to help needy workers as quickly and effectively.[4]

· **Obtaining Benefits from State**

At the State level, certified workers apply for TAA benefits at the nearest State Employment Security Agency, also called a "Cooperating State Agency." That Agency is supposed to be a "One Stop Career Center." All 50 States, the District of Columbia, and Puerto Rico have such Centers.[5]

In effect, a State acts as a Federal agent to give information, process applications, determine individual eligibility for benefits, issue payments, and provide reemployment services and training opportunities.[6] States apply specified criteria for TRA cash benefits, reemployment services, and training.

In addition to these tasks, States must give written notice to each worker to apply for TAA, in cases where the worker is covered by a Federal certification of eligibility, and publish each certification in a newspaper in the area in which certified workers reside. Finally, States must advise each adversely affected worker at the time the worker applies for unemployment insurance of the TAA program, and counsel each worker to apply for training when the worker seeks a TRA cash benefit.

---

3. *See* 20 C.F.R. Part 618.

An interesting feature of *TGAAA* regulations promulgated by the DOL is that a state must employ only state government merit system personnel to perform functions funded by TAA and implement TAA programs. A state can out-source to the private sector or NGOs training programs or non-inherently governmental functions, like IT and janitorial services. But, it cannot out-source core tasks like the approval of training. Three states — Colorado, Massachusetts, and Michigan — are exempt from this limitation on the use of non-state, non-merit personnel (though they must use state merit personnel to administer trade re-adjustment allowances).

4. *See* 19 U.S.C. § 2311.

5. There are roughly 3,000 such Centers. *See* David H. Bradley, *The Workforce Investment Act and the One-Stop Delivery System,* Congressional Research Service R41135 (14 June 2013), *posted at* www.crs.gov.

6. *See* 19 U.S.C. §§ 2311(a), 2313(a).

II. Primary and Secondary Worker, and Farmer, Eligibility Criteria

- **Statutory Authorization**

Sections 221–250 of the *Trade Act of 1974*, as amended, set forth the TAA scheme for workers.[7] Eligible workers may obtain compensation in the form of TRA, *i.e.*, cash benefits, reemployment services, training, and additional allowances while in training.[8]

Reforms under the 1981 *OBRA* shifted focus from income compensation for temporary layoffs to return to work through retraining and other adjustment measures for the long–term unemployed. The *Deficit Reduction Act of 1984* boosted worker training allowances, and job search and relocation benefits. The *1988 Act* modified significantly the eligibility criteria for cash benefits, and put greater emphasis on worker retraining. For example, the *1988 Act* amendments require a worker to be enrolled in, or complete, training as a condition for receiving a TRA.[9] Since then, both funding levels and emphases have varied.

- **Five Criteria**

To certify petitioning workers as eligible for TAA benefits, the ETA must determine that all of the following criteria are met:[10]

(1) Separation

A significant number or proportion of the workers in a firm have been, or are threatened with, total or partial separation from their firm.

"Significant" means three or more workers in a firm of less than 50 employees, or 5% of the workforce in a firm with 50 or more employees. The distinction between "total" and "partial" separation is numerical. "Total" means the worker is laid off. "Partial" means the wages and hours of work of a worker are cut to less than 80% of her weekly average.[11]

(2) Sales or Production Decline

The firm's sales or production have decreased in absolute terms.

---

7. *See* 19 U.S.C. §§ 2271–2331.

8. *See* 19 U.S.C. §§ 2291–2298.

9. *See* 19 U.S.C. § 2291(a)(5).

10. *See* 19 U.S.C. § 2272(a)(1)–(3); *Former Employees of Home Petroleum Corp. v. United States*, 16 CIT 778, 779 (slip op. 92-156) (CIT 1992); *Former Employees of Bass Enter. v. United States*, 706 F. Supp. 897 (CIT 1989).

A rarely used possibility for eligibility certification involves market disruption. Workers separated from a firm that the ITC identified as part of an industry injured by "market disruption" may seek TAA. In FYs 2010 and 2011, this route accounted for less than 0.5% of all TAA certifications. *See* DECEMBER 2012 CRS REPORT.

11. *See* 20 C.F.R. § 617.3(cc).

(3) Like or Directly Competitive Product

The firm in question makes a product that is "like" or "directly competitive product" with imported merchandise. Alternatively, the firm product made by the firm uses component parts, and the imported merchandise is "like" or "directly competitive" with those components. In other words, the imports compete with the firm directly in either of two ways: as finished goods; or as inputs into a finished good.

(4) Increased Imports or Shift in Production

Imports of the like or directly competitive imported product increased, or the firm from which the petitioning workers were separated moved production from the U.S. to a foreign country.

The "shift in production" possibility, *i.e.*, outsourcing overseas, was created under the 2009 *ARRA*. It means that either the firm of the petitioning workers changed the location of production, moving the facility to a foreign country, or that firm started buying articles from a third-party vendor in a foreign country. The economic result is the same for the workers: separation.

However, under the last year of *2011 TAAEA* renewal, (from 1 January–31 December 2014), only workers adversely affected by a shift in production to a country with which the U.S. has an FTA, or to a BDC under *AGOA, ATPA,* or *CBERA*, were eligible for TAA.

(5) Causation

Increases in like or directly competitive imported products, or the shift in production, "contributed importantly" to both the separation and decline in sales or production.

This determination presumes selection of an appropriate POI. The ETA has 60 days from the filing date of a petition to make the eligibility determination.

It is vital to understand the limited consequence of Federal certification. If the ETA certifies a petition, then the workers technically are eligible for TAA benefits. They do not automatically get benefits. Certification just means they are eligible for them — potentially, they might get those benefits. To obtain them, the eligible workers must proceed to the second step, in which they must prove they meet the federally mandated criteria for eligibility for specific TAA benefits. In other words, in "Step 1" the question is whether workers are eligible for TAA, in "Step 2" the question is whether workers who are eligible for TAA actually qualify for one or more of the specific TAA benefits available. Each TAA benefit schemes has specific eligibility criteria. Also, from Step 1 to 2, the venue shifts from the Federal level (the DOL ETA) to the State level (the "One Stop Career Center"), respectively.

Suppose ETA denies a petition for certification of eligibility. The petitioners can request an administrative reconsideration at the DOL. If the DOL again denies them eligibility certification, then their recourse is judicial review by the CIT of the denial.

- **Causation Problem**

Applying the third and fifth criteria is problematic. There is a threshold question of what constitutes a "like or directly competitive" product.[12] Once that decision is made, the causation issue must be tackled. Imports "contribute importantly" if they are "a cause which is important but not necessarily more important than any other cause."[13] Plainly, this standard is easier for a petitioner to meet than the "substantial cause" standard associated with Section 201 Escape Clause relief.

Still, defining "important" is not easy, as the U.S. Court of Appeals for the D.C. Circuit noted in 1978 in an early TAA case under the *1974 Act*, *United Glass and Ceramic Workers of North America v. Marshall*.[14] In a 1992 case, *Former Employees of Johnson Controls v. United States*, the CIT defined "important" as a "causal nexus" between (1) import penetration and (2) separation of a worker and firm: "[a] causal nexus exists where there is a *direct and substantial* relationship between increased imports and a decline in sales and production."[15]

So, in the July 2013 case of *Former Employees of Weather Shield Manufacturing Inc. v. United States Secretary of Labor*, the CIT ruled against Weather Shield, a producer of doors and windows in Medford, Wisconsin, the administrative support employees of which had lost their jobs.[16] They claimed increased imports were to blame. But, revised data showed their production and sales increased during the POI, 2008 and 2009.

Is the phrase "direct and substantial" misleading? Arguably, it obfuscates an already fuzzy distinction between TAA and Section 201 Escape Clause causation tests. Suppose imports of a product decline nationwide, but imports by competitors of a firm at which workers are laid off increase. Are the increased imports "important"? In 1981, the U.S. Court of Appeals for the 7th Circuit, in *United Rubber Cork, Linoleum and Plastic Workers of America, Local 798 v. Donovan*, gave an affirmative reply.[17]

- **Eligibility for Secondary Workers**

Secondary workers are eligible for TAA. They are defined as employees of either (1) upstream firms, that is, workers in firms that are suppliers to a TAA-certified firm, or (2) downstream firms, meaning workers in firms that make goods using items from a TAA-certified firm.[18]

---

12. *See, e.g.*, *Former Employees of North American Refractories Co. v. United States*, 16 CIT 166, 167–68 (slip op. 92-37) (CIT 1992).

13. 19 U.S.C. § 2272(c)(1).

14. *See* 584 F.2d 398, 407 (D.C. Cir. 1978).

15. 16 CIT 617, 618 (slip. op. 92-114) (CIT 1992) (*citing Former Employees of Health-Tex, Inc. v. United States*, 14 CIT 580 (CIT 1990)) (emphasis added).

16. *See* Number 10-00299 (Slip Opinion 13-85), 1 July 2013.

17. *See* 652 F.2d 702 (7th Cir. 1981).

18. The technical definition of "downstream producer" is "a firm that performs additional, value-added production processes or services directly for another firm." 19 U.S.C. § 2272(c)(3).

For eligibility, secondary workers follow a petition certification process similar to that for primary workers. Secondary workers must satisfy three conditions:

(1) A significant number or proportion of workers in the firm (or subdivision) are totally or partially separated, or are threatened with total or partial separation.

(2) The workers' firm (or subdivision) is a supplier or downstream producer to a firm (or subdivision) that employs a group of workers who received (already) certification of eligibility for a primary firm, and the supply or production is related to the article that is the basis for the (prior) certification.

(3) Either (a) the workers' firm is a supplier and the component part it supplies to the firm (or subdivision) comprises at least 20% of production or sales of the workers' firm, or (b) a loss of business by the workers' firm with the other firm contributed importantly to the workers' actual or threatened separation.

Note the causation standard in the third criterion. What constitutes an "important" contribution? That issue is litigated in the CIT and Federal Circuit. Also note that under the last year of *2011 TAAEA* renewal (from 1 January–31 December 2014), secondary worker eligibility was eliminated.

- **Eligibility for Farmers and Fisherman**

In its full form, TAA has four dimensions: assistance for workers, firms, communities, and farmers. The *TAA Act of 2002* added for the first time help for farmers and agricultural commodity producers, including livestock producers and employees in the fishing industry. The USDA FAS manages their program. Through grants and loans, farmers whose incomes have dropped from levels in the past year are compensated.

The USDA offers farmers for up to half of the difference between (1) 80% of the average national price for a commodity over the preceding five years, and (2) the average national price in the current year. The amount any individual farmer can receive under this program is capped at $ 10,000 per 12-month period. The payment also cannot exceed the limitation on counter cyclical payments in the *Food Security Act of 1985*.[19]

The *2009 ARRA* broadened the definition of members of the farming community eligible for TAA. It widened the term "agricultural commodity producer" to mean:

(A) a person that [*sic*] shares in the risk of producing an agricultural commodity and that is entitled to a share of the commodity for marketing, including an operator, a sharecropper, or a person that owns or rents the land on which the commodity is produced; or (B) a person [*sic*] that reports

---

19. *See* Section 1001(c) of that *Act*.

gain or loss from the trade or business of fishing on the person's annual Federal income tax return for the taxable year that most closely corresponds to the marketing year with respect to which a petition is filed . . . .[20]

More accurately than before, this definition captures workers in the agricultural sector who might be adversely affected by trade, plus includes agricultural firms.

The variables affecting eligibility are prices, production quantities, production values, and cash receipts for an agricultural commodity. In respect of each variable, the issue is whether there has been a decline, and if so, how much. The key criterion for assistance is whether data for the relevant MY are less than 85% of the average for the three MYs preceding that MY. In other words, a farmer (or fisherman) is eligible for help if she experiences a decrease of more than 15% in the national average price, quantity of output, value of output, or cash receipts compared to the average of the preceding three MYs. As always, eligibility requires proof of causation. In turn, causation presumes a showing that "like" or "directly competitive" products entered the market through importation.

What is different as regards TAA for farmers is the need for a credible plan: how would the petitioner use any help they get? Cogent adjustment plans generally are not required of workers (though they are required of firms and communities, as discussed below). Before the *2009 ARRA*, TAA did not tie cash aid to devising such plans. The *Act* made clear a petition from farmers will be unsuccessful if it lacks a long-term business adjustment plan, coupled with an initial adjustment plan. The long-and short-term plans should explain how the recipient of assistance would adjust its farming (or fishing) operations to meet changed economic conditions wrought by import competition. The *Act* offered funding in this respect, namely, up to $4,000 for aid in creating and implementing an initial business model, with a potential for an additional $8,000 to develop and put into practice a long-term business model. Further, FAS can help petitioners develop a plan.

Assuming a successful application, a farmer or agricultural commodity producer is entitled to technical assistance to improve the competitiveness of the commodity it grows or makes. This help may include additional funds to mitigate transportation costs, if the producer must commute to obtain the assistance because it is unavailable locally.

• Odds of Federal Certification

The three-pronged certification test suggests many workers are unlikely to qualify. Some statistics support this expectation. Overall (based on 1990s data), the odds are about two-in-three a petition will be certified and worker will be covered.

---

20. 19 U.S.C. § 2401.

III. Service Sector and Public Agency
Worker Eligibility Criteria

• **Outsourced Software Workers and 2006 *IBM* and *CSC* Cases**

In the technology sector, many software developers have seen their jobs out-sourced to countries like India. Petitions to certify software firms have confounded the DOL. Is software code an "article" the TAA program covers? For example, for-mer employees of Computer Sciences Corporation (CSC), Electronic Data Systems (EDS), and International Business Machines (IBM) filed petitions with the DOL for certification of benefits due to software "source code" development that was off-shored. Initially, the DOL discounted "code" as an "article." Its logic was "code" is not stored on a tangible medium, but rather transmitted electronically.

The CIT disagreed. In the 2006 *IBM* case, the CIT said the HTSUS lists electroni-cally transmitted computer software. Hence, software is an article, even though it is exempt from duty.[21] The 2006 *CSC* case was even more egregious. The plaintiffs endured 5 negative petition reviews by the DOL, and two visits to the CIT with a stern warning the second time from Judge Nicholas Tsoucalas that: "Labor is stub-bornly arguing its position that software code must be embodied on a physical medium . . . . The plain language of the *Trade Act* does not require that an article must be tangible."[22] In April 2006, the DOL acquiesced, expanding the definition of "article" to cover non-physical-medium products.[23]

Why was the DOL challenged by outsourcing of software jobs? Does TAA for outsourced workers presume benefits are for blue collar workers and farmers, but not white-collar workers? Is the presumption that losers from trade are only in dying industries, not infant industries, which may be taking global hold far more rapidly than to what people can react? Evidently, the CIT compelled the DOL to rethink its paradigm.

• **Service Sector Workers**

A seminal contribution of the *2009 ARRA* was expanding the scope of TAA ben-efits to qualifying "service sector" and "public agency" employees, where coverage was lacking previously. This expansion was particularly noteworthy in respect of service sector workers, who had long been, and continue to be, victims of outsourc-ing to the likes of China and India.

The *2009 ARRA* defined "service sector firm" as "a firm engaged in the business of supplying services."[24] The key criteria in a claim by service sector firm workers

---

21. *Former Employees of International Business Machines, Global Services Division v. United States Secretary of Labor,* 462 F. Supp. 2d 1239 (CIT 2006).

22. *Former Employees of Computer Sciences Corporation v. United States Secretary of Labor,* 414 F. Supp. 2d 1334, 1343 (CIT 2006).

23. *See* 71 Fed. Reg. 18,355 (11 April 2006).

24. 19 U.S.C. § 2319.

for TAA are the "directly competitive" and "like product" tests.[25] If importation of directly competitive or foreign like articles or services that a domestic firm otherwise would have supplied causes a shift in jobs overseas for the production and implementation of such articles and services, then workers of that firm may file a TAA claim.

Deciding whether a foreign-provided service is "directly competitive" with, or "like," an American-provided one is dicey. To what extent can the jurisprudence from the world of goods be applied to the world of services?

Moreover, concomitant with satisfying these tests is proof that the U.S. service sector firm otherwise would have provided the article or service. Suppose that firm was abandoning the product or service line in question. Then satisfying those tests would not matter. Why? Because of the link to causation: trade, or offshoring, did not cause the job loss. The firm opted to alter its product or service line, wholly apart from its decision to shift jobs overseas.

TAA coverage for the service sector included primary and secondary workers. However, under the last year of *2011 TAAEA* renewal (from 1 January–31 December 2014), service sector workers no longer were eligible for TAA.

- **Public Agency Workers**

The *2009 ARRA* defined "public agency" as "a department or agency of State or local government or of the Federal Government, or a subdivision thereof."[26] Public agency workers must meet three requirements to become eligible:

(1) A significant number or proportion of the workers in the public agency became totally or partially separated, or are threatened to be totally or partially separated.

(2) The public agency acquired from a foreign country services like or directly competitive with services that this agency supplies.

(3) Third, this acquisition of services described "contributed importantly" to the separation of the workers, or threat of separation.

Once again, the determination is based on the "like" or "directly competitive" nature of the services.[27]

- **Getting More Data**

The *2009 ARRA* authorized the DOL to get additional data it needs to rule on a petition from dislocated workers for certification for TAA eligibility. The DOL may seek any information it deems necessary to certify a group of workers, for example, via questionnaires. The DOL may call on a variety of sources, including the firm, its employees or customers, and unions.

---

25. 19 U.S.C. § 2272.
26. 19 U.S.C. § 2319.
27. 19 U.S.C. § 2272.

Relatedly, Section 1802 of the *ARRA* allowed for a separate basis for certification for firms specifically "identified by the International Trade Commission [ITC]." Suppose the ITC opens an investigation into a firm, designated by name, which ends with an "affirmative determination of injury or threat thereof," or "market disruption" that causes workers to become separated from their job. Then, the DOL will certify the workers' petition. In addition, the DOL must implement monitoring and data collection programs to track numbers, reasons, and industries being adversely affected.[28]

- **Penalties**

The *2009 ARRA* revamped the penalties provision in a predictable fashion.[29] The new provision takes aim at making knowingly false claims, statements, and failure to disclose material facts in an effort to obtain or increase benefits under the TAA program.

IV. Four Types of Worker Benefits

There are four principal types of TAA benefits for workers who have received certification from the DOL ETA as eligible for these benefits:

(1) Trade Readjustment Allowance (TRA)

(2) Reemployment Services

(3) Reemployment Trade Adjustment Assistance (RTAA)

(4) Health Care Tax Credit (HCTC)

The diversity, criteria, and funding for these benefits have evolved over time.

That is, the first two benefits have been associated with TAA since its inception under the *1962 Act*. The latter two schemes were introduced decades thereafter. The intricate requirements to obtain the benefits have changed. And, Federal budget outlays for the benefits have ebbed and flowed.

TAA legislation sets the requirements for specific TAA benefits. The States administer those Federal mandates in deciding whether certified workers qualify for the benefits. Thus, certified workers must apply to their State-level "One Stop Career Center" to receive the benefits. That Center will decide whether they meet the criteria for the specific type of benefit they seek. In theory, at least, a worker could be certified as eligible for TAA in "Step 1" of the process, but not satisfy all the requirements in "Step 2" for a specific type of benefit. Individual workers denied a benefit have a right of appeal.

---

28. 19 U.S.C. § 2272.
29. *See* 19 U.S.C. § 2316

- **Type 1: Cash Benefit and Five Qualifying Requirements**

The TAA cash benefit, or TRA, is the quintessential form of help. It is income support, but only for a worker who (1) has been certified as "eligible," (2) is enrolled in a training program, and (3) exhausted her UI. The most difficult eligibility criterion to prove is causation, *i.e.*, either increased like or directly competitive imports contributed importantly to separation of the worker from employment, or a shift of jobs from America overseas contributed importantly to the job loss. Training programs (discussed below) must be certified by the DOL as "eligible." As for UI, the maximum duration a worker can claim it has varied over time, but a worker cannot claim TRA until she has used up all her UI. Under the *2011 TAAEA*, the maximum duration for UI plus TRA cash help is 117 weeks, or in certain circumstances, 130 weeks.

Qualifying for a TRA cash benefit is hard, because five criteria must be met. The first criterion concerns the timing of the "qualifying separation" between a worker and firm, *i.e.*, the layoff that generates eligibility for a TRA. A worker must be laid off on or after the "Impact Date" set out in a certification for that worker. The DOL identifies that Date as when total or partial layoffs begin, or threaten to begin. It is never more than 1 year before the day a petition is filed.

The petition covers workers laid off between the Impact Date and two years after the date on which the DOL certified the petition are covered. So, a worker must be laid off within two years after the date the DOL issues its certification. Hence, a certified worker has two years to apply for TRA. Suppose the DOL finds the Impact Date is 1 May 2018, and certifies the corresponding petition on 1 July 2018. Anyone among the certified workers laid off between 1 May 2018 and 1 July 2020 is eligible for TAA benefits.

Second, there is a minimum period during which a worker must have served with the adversely affected firm, otherwise an employee who had been at that firm for a short period—say a week—would be eligible for a TRA benefit. (Of course, from a social justice perspective, query why that should matter. The shorter the minimum period, the more generous the TAA program.) That minimum period has changed with different TAA legislation. With the *1988 Act* amendments, a worker must have been employed for one year before the first qualifying separation, and earned at least $30 per week for at least six months. With the *2011 TAAEA*, the rule changed: a worker needed to be employed by the firm for at least 26 of the 52 weeks (*i.e.*, just over six months) preceding the layoff.

Third, the worker must be entitled to UI, but have exhausted all rights to this entitlement, including extended benefits. Consequently, a worker cannot obtain both UI and a TRA benefit. TRA essentially serves as a continuation of UI.

Fourth, the worker must not be disqualified from receiving extended UI benefits because she has accepted a new job. UI disqualification means TAA disqualification.

Fifth, with the *1988 Act* amendments, a worker seeking TAA benefits must be enrolled in, or have completed, a full-time training program. That is, if a worker sought a TRA cash benefit, then she had to seek training so she ultimately could re-enter the workforce. If because of health reasons a worker cannot participate in training, no suitable training is at hand, or enrollment in a training program within 60 days is unavailable, then the worker may obtain a waiver from this requirement.[30]

• **Fifth Qualifying Requirement for TRA Cash Benefit: Training Program**

Section 1821 of the *2009 ARRA* modestly loosened the training requirement. Under the original statute, a worker had to enroll in a training program within 16 weeks. Section 1821 gave workers more time, extending this deadline to 26 weeks.

The *ARRA* added another potential waiver of training requirements if a worker has "marketable skills" such as a post-graduate degree, or specialized certification in a specialized field. This change eased the process for some dislocated workers to receive benefits, and simultaneously freed up funds for ones who truly need extra training.

In other respects, the *ARRA* modestly eased the training requirement. For a dislocated worker who enters a training program, the *ARRA* increased the time allotted for completion of the training program from 52 additional weeks to 78 additional weeks, and allowed for payment during those additional weeks. The eligibility period remained largely the same, but now includes a special rule for reserve military forces.[31] If a member of the reserves "serves a period of duty" during a time while eligible for TAA benefits, the time away is effectively tolled until return so that she may continue to receive benefits and continue training programs after the call to serve.[32]

• **Limits on TRA Cash Benefits**

If the criteria are met (particularly the tie to enrollment in a TAA-approved training program), then a worker may receive a TRA. But, the level and duration of this cash benefit are limited. As to the level, the worker can get cash for each week of unemployment equal to the most recent weekly benefit amount of UI the worker received after her first qualifying separation and before exhausting this insurance. The amount of a TRA is limited to the amount of UI for which a worker qualifies.[33] The *OBRA* of 1981 introduced this limitation to reduce the cost of TAA to the Federal government. So:

Maximum TRA Cash Benefit Level = Final UI Benefit

In turn, the final UI benefit depends on the earnings of a worker during a base period of employment. That base typically is the first four of the last five calendar

---

30. *See* 19 U.S.C. § 2291(c).
31. *See* 19 U.S.C. § 2291(a)(5)(A)(ii).
32. 19 U.S.C. § 2291(c).
33. *See* 19 U.S.C. §§ 2291–2293.

quarters in which the worker completed work. The TRA is reduced by the amount of any training allowance provided.

In real dollars, what do these TRA Cash Benefit limits mean? In FY 2010, the average weekly TRA payment nationwide was $320. The UI benefit to which the TRA Cash Benefit equates usually covers 50% of the wages of a worker, up to a State-imposed maximum limit. There is considerable regional variation on that limit. In January 2011, Massachusetts offered the highest maximum weekly UI benefit, and thus TRA Cash Benefit, for a worker without any dependents — $625. Louisiana provided the lowest, at $235. Plainly, the answer to the question mathematically is "halving of income." The answer in human terms is "significant hardship."

In respect of the duration of TRA, the 1981 *OBRA* called for a one-year limit linked to the period during which UI was received.[34] A worker could get UI, followed by TRA, for a maximum of 52 weeks. Thus, a worker who got UI for 30 weeks thereafter could obtain a TRA for at most 22 weeks. Under that law, she could extend TRA for an additional 26 weeks, if she was participating in training. Hypothetically, a worker entitled to UI for 52 or more weeks would not receive TRA. So, UI both caps at a maximum level, and partly or wholly offsets TRA.

A TRA for 52 weeks or less is the "Basic TRA," while an extension of the cash benefit associated with training is the "Additional TRA." "Basic TRA" thus starts as the week after eligibility for UI benefits expire. Mathematically:

$$\text{Total Maximum Basic TRA} = (52 \text{ weeks}) \cdot \left[\left(\frac{\text{maximum Weekly TRA}}{\text{Cash Benefit Level}}\right) - (\text{UI Benefit})\right]$$

"Additional" TRA commences as soon as a worker exhausts Basic TRA, but only for a worker in a training program.

The *2011 TAAEA* altered the duration limit. Under it, cash payments are available for a maximum of 117 weeks (with a possible extension to 130 weeks) if a worker concurrently is in a full-time training program. In other words, following the 52-week limit on Basic TRA (including UI), a maximum further 65 weeks of Additional TRA is possible, hence, the 117-week figure. A worker can extend this figure for a further 13 weeks, to 130 weeks total, if she is enrolled in, but not yet finished, a training program, and would get an industry-recognized credential by completing it.

Moreover, in relation to the duration limit, the *2011 TAAEA* mandated that a worker must have joined a training program within 26 weeks of redundancy or certification (whichever is later). (For 1 January through 31 December 2014, this latter requirement tightened: the worker had to be enrolled in training by the later of 16 weeks after redundancy or eight weeks after certification.)

---

34. *See* 19 U.S.C. § 2293(a)(1).

In addition to limits on level and duration, the attractiveness of a TRA is reduced because of the lag time between the first qualifying separation and receipt of a TRA. Evidence from 1974–1979 indicates on average workers receive their first TRA payment 14–16 months after becoming unemployed. Notwithstanding regular unemployment compensation from the State within the first two weeks of separation, their income support may be insufficient when they most need it, namely, while out of work, looking for a job, and needing to upgrade their human capital. Yet, equity demands not only prompt administrative action on a TRA application, but also a full, fair, analysis of each case.

- **Type 2: Reemployment Services (including Training)**

Regardless of whether a certified worker exhausts unemployment benefits and is eligible for TRA payments, she may receive reemployment services through an appropriate State agency, including training through a certified provider.[35] The services aim to help the dislocated worker plan for and obtain a new job. The services may be in lieu of, or alongside, training.

Among the specific services are counseling, vocational testing, and job search and placement. A job search allowance is available if a certified worker cannot obtain suitable employment within her local commuting area. The allowance is limited to 90% of necessary job search expenses, up to a defined maximum, such as $800, $1,250, or $1,500 per worker. This allowance covers transportation and subsistence costs relating to job search activities. Payment for transportation is capped at the Federal mileage rate level, and for subsistence at the Federal *per diem* rate.

A relocation allowance is available to a worker obtaining suitable employment outside her commuting area. Its cap is 90% of reasonable and necessary moving expenses for the worker, her family, and their household items, plus a lump sum payment of up to three times her average weekly wage up to a maximum level. That maximum was $800 before the *2009 TGAAA*, and the *2011 TAAEA* bumped it up to $1,250.

The income support associated with reemployment services can help a worker while in between jobs and engaged in full-time training with a view to expected future job. So, even before its amendment by the *TGAAA*, TAA included re-adjustment assistance. For the long term, however, training (or re-training) is essential.

As for training, it is the largest expense among the Reemployment Services. Traditionally, "training" referred to the development of new skills. Thanks to the *1988 Act* amendments, it now includes remedial education. The Federal government covers the costs of training directly, either through the relevant State agency or a voucher system. The *1988 Act* also converted training from an entitlement contingent on the availability of appropriated funds to an entitlement without regard to the availability of funds to pay the costs of training.

---

35. *See* 19 U.S.C. § 2295.

For coverage as a TAA Reemployment Service, a certified entity must provide training. That entity may be a public or private institution. The training program may not exceed 104 weeks (*i.e.*, two years).[36] In reality, most workers get about a year's worth of training: in FY 2011, of the 70% of them who completed a training program, the average duration was 427 days.

There is no TAA rule stating that training must lead to a credential, such as a degree or certification. In FY 2011, 45% of workers who finished a training program obtained some type of credential. However, there must be a reasonable expectation that training will result in employment. The training must be at a "reasonable cost," defined by considering the employment outcome and checking the cost of similar training from a different provider.[37] The Federal government does not impose a limit on the amount of training funds a dislocated worker can receive. But, some States do.

The *2011 TAAEA* capped annual aggregate expenditures on Reemployment Services at $575 million. (From 1 January though 31 December 2014, this cap reverted down to the 2002 ARRA level of $220 million, with an additional allowance for States of 15% of the amount they allocate for those programs.) The Federal government requires States spend at least 5% of their Reemployment Services funds on case management services, and bars them from spending more than 10% on administrative expenses.[38]

With these temporal and fiscal constraints, could a worker apply funds to a life-changing graduate or professional degree? Most do not. In FY 2011, about 90% of workers in a program received occupational skills training, *i.e.*, training for a specific job, provided in a classroom. The remainder got on-the-job, pre-requisite, or remedial training.

- **Limits on Reemployment Services**

Just as there are limits on TRA cash benefits, limits exist on available funding for training. For example, the *1988 Act* established an annual aggregate ceiling on

---

36. *See* 20 C.F.R. § 617.22(f)(2).

37. *See* 19 U.S.C. § 2296(a)(1); 20 C.F.R. § 617.22.

38. *See* 19 U.S.C. § 2295a.

How does the DOL decide the distribution of funds to states for Reemployment Services? The answer is a four-factor formula:

  (1) Weighted average of certified workers in the state during the past four quarters (with the greatest weight given to the most recent quarter);

  (2) Weighted average of workers engaged in training during the last four quarters (again with the greatest weight to latest quarter);

  (3) Estimated number of workers who will be engaged in training in the coming year; and

  (4) Estimated amount of funding needed to give appropriate training (as estimated based on per-trainee expenditures in the last 4 quarters).

See 19 U.S.C. § 2296(A)(C)(ii). Using this formula, the DOL distributes 65% of the funding to the states at the start of the FY, holding 35% in a reserve fund. States with unforeseen training expenditures, or emergencies, apply for those funds. The DOL cannot allocate to any state less than 25% of what it distributed to that state the previous FY. The DOL allocates leftover reserve funds during the FY to the states, using the same formula. *See* 19 C.F.R. §§ 618.910–930.

training costs of $80 million.[39] Moreover, training is given only if 6 conditions are satisfied.[40]

First, there must be no suitable employment available. Second, it is clear the worker would benefit from appropriate training. Third, the worker must be qualified to undertake and complete the training. Fourth, the training is reasonably available from government or private sources. Fifth, the training is offered at reasonable cost. Sixth, there is a reasonable expectation of employment after finishing the training.

Ironically, TRA payments may operate at cross-purposes with reemployment services and training. This irony arises from the fact many workers find their previous job offered better pay and benefits than any new job available through training. Consequently, workers may elect to postpone retraining or a job search in the hope that they will be recalled to their old job. Moreover, they are likely to have many incentives to avoid moving to a new community for a job, *e.g.*, a spouse with a local job, children in nearby schools, family in close proximity, ownership of real property, and long-standing ties to the community. Put simply, TRA payments may exacerbate the adjustment problem. Indeed, data from 1974–1979 indicate this phenomenon occurred.

- **Employment and Case Management Services**

Section 1826 of the *2009 ARRA* provided for "Employment and Case Management Services" to appraise variables that affect success in re-entering the workplace. Those variables include employment goals, job market barriers, and competency levels. A worker may obtain a comprehensive assessment of her skills and needs, and help to target employment objectives.[41] The assessment yields information about suitable local training programs, placement counseling, and applications for services, plus help with applying for financial aid other than benefits through TAA.

- **Pre-Vocational, Pre-Layoff, and On the Job Training**

Beyond the usual training programs, the *2009 ARRA* called for "Pre-Vocational Training" to aid in "development of learning skills, communication skills, and interviewing skills." These skills are critical in getting a worker back into the labor force once she has completed the necessary job training. To pay for Employment and Case Management Services, and Pre-Vocational Training, States received additional funding from the Federal government in an amount equal to 15% of the amount of training funds already made available. The *Act* specified the States have to use the additional appropriation of funds specifically for administrative purposes such as processing waivers, collecting and reporting data, and providing reemployment

---

39. *See* 19 U.S.C. § 2296(a)(2)(A).
40. *See* 19 U.S.C. § 2296(a)(1).
41. *See* 19 U.S.C. § 2295.

assistance. Further, each State received $350,000 during a FY solely for Case Management Services.[42]

In many instances, the *ARRA* allowed for lodging of applications when there is a threat of separation, but that separation has not yet occurred. In such cases, the *Act* provided for "pre-layoff part time training." This amendment was clever, because it allowed workers to prepare for reemployment before actually becoming unemployed. As a result, the change helped (or should have helped) minimize the amount of funding needed to retrain and reemploy affected workers, and save funding for those who were made redundant with no chance to get ready for a new job.

Section 1831 of the *ARRA* also provided for "On the Job Training." That training still was paid for through the TAA program for part time training. But, it carried the benefit of keeping the worker employed throughout, without consuming additional funds for unemployment.[43]

- **Type 3: RTAA**

That the American workforce is aging is no secret. Older workers rendered redundant often have no choice but to take a new job at considerably less pay than their former one. They experience downward mobility, in multiple dimensions—economic, social, and psychological—and as they are nearing the end of their productive lifespan, their time to participate in the labor market is limited, and comprehensive retraining is infeasible, or at least not cost effective. Nevertheless, from both Utilitarian and Social Justice perspectives, the participation of elderly workers matters: they can add to GDP, and facilitating their ability to do so supports their human dignity.

To help offset loss of wages between a job from which a worker is separated and the job in which the worker is reemployed, assistance is necessary. To qualify for RTAA, a worker must be age 50 or over.[44] The essence of the benefit is to pay the worker a wage supplement if that worker obtains new job at a wage level lower than the prior employment. The worker must obtain a new full-time job within 26 weeks of separation from her firm, and not be in a training program. This requirement resulted from a tightening under the *2011 TAAEA*. (Until 1 January 2014, she had the option of getting a part-time job and concurrently being in a training program, and she did not have to find reemployment within 26 weeks of separation.)

The *2009 ARRA* specified the amount of readjustment assistance as an amount equal to 50% of the difference between income level of the higher-paying prior and lower-paying new job. Effectively, the *Act* required an averaging of the two wages, and payment of the average to supplement the lower wage associated with reemployment. However, the *Act* restricted this amount to $12,000. To be sure, any amount

---

42. *See* 19 U.S.C. § 2295.

43. *See* 19 U.S.C. § 2296(c).

44. RTAA previously was called "Alternative Trade Adjustment Assistance," or "ATAA." Both RTAA and ATAA sometimes are referred to as "wage insurance."

helps in the immediate time frame so workers may adjust to a lower standard of living associated with the new pay grade.[45]

Under the *2011 TAAEA*, the 50% rule remained in place, but the eligibility for and limits on RTAA changed. First, a worker is ineligible for RTAA if the annual wage in her new job exceeds $50,000.[46] Second, the maximum benefit dropped to $10,000 over two years. The combined wage and RTAA, however, can exceed $50,000. For instance, a worker whose prior and new jobs paid $57,000 and $49,000, respectively, could obtain RTAA of $4,000 for each of 2 years (50% of the wage differential), with the result being $53,000 annually. Third, an RTAA recipient is ineligible for TRA, job search, or relocation benefits.

- **Type 4: HCTC**

The *2002 TAA Reform Act* ushered in a Federal tax credit to subsidize private health care coverage for displaced workers who are certified to receive TAA benefits. Through the IRC, the IRS administers the HCTC. Hence, the HCTC is unique among TAA benefits in two respects: general revenues (not a specific appropriation based on the budget request to Congress by the President) fund it; and it is not run jointly via the DOL and States. The HCTC is for any worker getting TRA, UI in lieu or TRA, or RTAA.

Under the *2002 Act*, the HCTC covered 65% of premiums a worker pays for qualified health insurance. The *2011 TAAEA* boosted the subsidy to 72.5% of health care premiums. This figure was less generous than the 80% in the 2009 *ARRA*, but more generous than the 65% subsidy in the 2002 legislation.[47] Still, a worker must cover the 27.5% balance. The 2011 legislation also amended the definition of "qualifying insurance and credit." Under the *2011 TAAEA*, for all qualifying individuals, the HCTC sunset on 31 December 2013 (1 year before expiry of the rest of that *Act*).

---

45. *See* 19 U.S.C. § 2297.

46. *See* 19 U.S.C. § 2318.

47. In Part VI, Section 1899B of the *2009 ARRA*, an additional provision was inserted to the extant coverage for "Payment of Premiums Due Prior to Commencement of Advance Payments of Credit." Unlike the rest of the *Act* (with a few other exceptions), this Section went into effect 1 January 2009. The retroactive nature of this Section was unsurprising, because of President Barack H. Obama advocacy for improved health care coverage. Effectively, this Section required the Secretary of Labor to make at least one retroactive payment "equal to 80 percent of the premiums for coverage . . . for eligible coverage months . . . occurring prior to the first month for which advance payment is made."

The *ARRA* made certain changes in the *IRC* regarding a lapse in creditable coverage. *See* p. 42 of the *Act*. In addition, the *Act* references the *Employee Retirement Income Security Act* (*ERISA*), and creates special rules for TAA eligible workers. These special rules also affected *IRC* sections and the *Public Health Services Act*, and are repeated almost *verbatim* for each of these purposes. *See id.*, p. 43. The remainder of Part VI of the *ARRA* was administrative in nature, calling for reporting and data collection on recipients and their demographics. It also extended National Emergency Grants originally created under the *Workforce Investment Act* allowing for payment of administrative costs to start up group health plans. Again, this type of addition was in line with President Obama's policy goal of enhanced health care coverage. *See id.*, pp. 44–47.

The HCTC can be refunded if a worker has no tax liability. It can be advanced to apply to insurance purchases, obviating the need to wait to receive it until filing a tax return. The HCTC can be applied toward purchase of 3 kinds of policies:

(1) *Consolidated Omnibus Budget Reconciliation Act of 1985 (COBRA)* continued employer-sponsored health insurance.

(2) An individual health insurance policy (if already covered by an individual policy 30 days before becoming unemployed).

(3) A group policy offered through a spouse's employer.

The Federal tax credit can apply to certain types of State-provided coverage.

V. Firm Eligibility

Sections 251–264 of the *1974 Act* added a TAA program for firms adversely affected by import competition.[48] The DOC EDA oversees, implements, and disburses matching funds under this program. The EDA operates 11 TAA Centers, each of which is responsible for a different geographical region. The Centers help eligible firms to formulate business recovery plans, obtain certification, and disburse funds.

Compensation to certified firms consists exclusively of technical assistance to develop and implement an economic recovery strategy. Amendments to the program made in 1986 under the *COBRA* eliminated financial assistance benefits, which had included direct loans and loan guarantees.[49]

The *2009 Act* extended the portion of the original statute regarding firms to include service sector firms, plus agricultural firms.[50] The *Act* also loosened requirements for certification for eligibility. The nature of the assistance remained unchanged: a 50-50 cost sharing of projects between the Federal government and an American company, designed to enhance the competitive position of that company. That is, assistance comes as an even split between the government and firm of the costs of projects to enhance the competitive position of the firm vis-à-vis foreign manufacturers. The projects may address manufacturing efficiency, technology, or marketing, and the costs may be for consultants, designers, or engineers.

On what basis is assistance to firms offered? The answer is a decline in "sales or production, or both" of the firm. When looking at this decrease, the POI is a comparison of the most recent 12-month average versus the average of the preceding 24 or 36 months. As with TAA for any other category of petitioner, TAA for firms depends on proof of causation, which in turn depends on proof of importation of a "like" or "directly competitive" product.[51] Additionally, as with TAA for farmers,

---

48. *See* 19 U.S.C. §§ 2341–2355.
49. *See* 19 U.S.C. § 2344(d).
50. 19 U.S.C. § 2341.
51. 19 U.S.C. § 2341(c)(1)(B).

a plan for how the firm would recover business in the wake of changed economic conditions owing to import competition, is essential for a successful petition.

The *2009 ARRA* increased total funding for TAA to firms to $50 million for FYs 2009 and 2010, with an additional $12,501,000 for 1 October 2010 through 31 December 2010. Out of these amounts, $350,000 were designated for full-time positions within the EDA.[52] However, the *Act* capped at a small amount the extent to which the government can finance any single project of an eligible firm: $75,000. The *Act* also increased criminal penalties for fraud, to imprisonment of up to two years, fines, or both, under title 18 of the U.S. Code.

VI. Rebuilding Communities

The provisions of the *2009 ARRA* on assistance for communities ushered in a new dimension to the TAA program.[53] Section 1871 said the purpose:

> is to assist communities impacted by trade with economic adjustment through the coordination of Federal, State, and local resources, the creation of community-based development strategies, and the development and provision of programs that meet the training needs of workers covered by certifications . . . .

To get relief through award grants to communities as fast as possible, the program for them took effect in August 2009. The provisions applied retroactively to 1 January 2007.

There are two essential requirements for qualifying as a community impacted by trade. First, a community must be able to show one or more certifications for assistance under "Paragraph (3)" are made with respect to the community. The elements of "Paragraph (3)" are certification by the:

(1) Secretary of Labor that a group of workers in the community is eligible to apply for assistance;

(2) Secretary of Commerce that a firm located in the community is eligible to apply for adjustment assistance; or

(3) Secretary of Agriculture that a group of agricultural commodity producers in the community is eligible to apply for adjustment assistance.

Satisfying these elements entails navigating a complex admixture of politics and bureaucracy. Second, in connection with a certification, the DOL must determine a threat to, or loss of, jobs significantly affects the community.

---

52. *See* 19 U.S.C. § 2341.

53. Chapter 4 of 19 U.S.C. 2371 *et seq.* adds the new provisions covering TAA for communities, from which the above quotes are drawn.

If the petitioning community is successful, then the relevant Secretary must inform promptly the Governor of the State in which that community is located of the affirmative determination. The Governor must then notify the community of its certification for assistance, and explain how to get succor.

The help should be consistent with a development strategy for the community. The DOL must provide technical assistance to diversify and strengthen the economy of the community. It also must help the community identify "impediments to economic development that result from the impact of trade." Doing so facilitates creation of a strategic plan to address economic adjustment and workforce dislocation, including unemployment among agricultural commodity producers.

The amount any community may receive from a grant cannot exceed $5 million, of which not more that 95% of the grant can come from Federal funding. Though this ceiling is not low, it is a limitation nonetheless. It means no less than 5% of grant funds must come from the community itself (*i.e.*, local government).

As intimated, to receive funding, a community must submit a grant application that includes a proposed strategic plan. That plan must contain (at a minimum) certain elements the 2009 *ARRA* mandated:

(1) Analysis of the capacity of the community to adjust economically to the impact of trade.

(2) Review of the economic development challenges and opportunities the community faces, and the strengths and weaknesses of its economy.

(3) Assessments of the long-term commitment of the community to the plan, and engagement by community members affected by economic dislocation.

(4) Description of the role and participation of entities that developed the plan.

(5) Discussion of the projects the community will undertake pursuant to the plan.

(6) Explanation of how the plan and projects thereunder will facilitate economic adjustment of the community.

(7) Identification of educational and training programs available to workers in the community, and future employment needs of the community.

(8) Study of the cost to implement the plan, and the timing of funding required by the community to implement the plan.

(9) Scheme to continue economic adjustment in the community after completion of the planned projects.

Concocting a successful plan is not easy, and the collaboration of the DOL is essential.

The total amount of funds the *ARRA* authorized for TAA for communities was $150 million for each of FY 2009 and 2010 (with an additional $37,500,000 for 1 October 2010 through 31 December 2010). Of the total, $25 million and $6.25

million, respectively, were for the community grants mentioned above. The law left unclear how the balance of funds was to be used.

The provisions on community TAA also provided for Community College and Career Training grants. The dollar limitation to any single institution was at $1 million. To receive a grant, a Community College had to submit a proposal outlining how it would deploy the funds. That deployment had to be tied to training: a Community College was obliged to use a grant to develop, offer, or improve a training program used by workers adversely affected by trade. Also relevant to the success of a Community College grant application was the extent to which its application was consistent with the petition of an affected community.

Thus, in addition to the $5,000,000 potentially granted to a community, each Community College in that community could receive additional grant funding. It behooved a community to include such Colleges from the beginning in outlining any proposal, so the community and College apportion funding for maximum impact.

Criteria for a Community College grant were mostly the same as for a community. For College grants, Congress appropriated $40 million for each of FYs 2009 and 2010 (with an additional $10 million for 1 October 2010 through 31 December 2010).

Finally, under community TAA, Congress authorized funding for grants to Industry or Sector Partnerships. These grants aimed to revitalize industries, and generate jobs for workers in communities hit by import competition. Congress allotted an identical dollar amount to that of College grants for this purpose.

VII. Proving Causation and 2013 *Western Digital* and 2014 *Boeing* Cases

The significance of proving imports or a shift of production or services abroad "contributed importantly" to the separation of workers from a firm cannot be over stated. It can make or break a case. Consider the January 2013 CIT case of *Former Employees of Western Digital Technologies Inc. v. Secretary of Labor.*[54]

The petitioners were Lake Forest, California engineers who developed prototypes for computer hard drives. They lost their jobs in late 2008 and early 2009, allegedly to engineers in Malaysia. They petitioned for TAA, but DOL turned them down, and the CIT affirmed the negative DOL determination. The petitioners failed to show their job loss was caused by increased imports or a shift abroad of production and services, *i.e.*, they simply did not prove they lost their jobs to import competition or engineers employed overseas. To the contrary, as their former employer, Western Digital argued, they were made redundant in a cost-cutting effort. Moreover, during

---

54. *See* Number 11-000-85, 30 January 2013.

the relevant POI, imports of like or directly competitive hard disk drives into the U.S. declined. And, the work of engineers employed abroad was not like or directly competitive with the work of the California engineers. Their function was not interchangeable with that of foreign workers: they were engaged in design of prototypes, whereas the foreign engineers were involved in hard disk manufacturing.

True, said the CIT, both cohorts of engineers engaged in failure analysis, but the Californians did that in the context of design, while the Malaysians did so in the context of production. Design up to the stage of a prototype, and production of large volumes based on that prototype, are substantially different functions. True also, the Californians helped train the Malaysians. But that was because they designed the product as to which the Malaysians would oversee mass production. Indeed, the training they provided cut against their case, as from it the CIT agreed with the inference drawn by the DOL: the two types of engineers were not substitutes.

Another important example of the causation criterion is the 2014 CIT case of *Former Employees of Boeing Co. v. U.S. Secretary of Labor.*[55] Boeing shut down its facility in Wichita, Kansas and shifted work to other domestic factories. The DOL rejected the application of the Kansas workers Boeing had laid off, because they had serviced military aircraft. In particular, commercial aircraft were not made in the Wichita facility (nor had military aircraft been made there for several years). The redundant workers had maintained and modified military aircraft. Additionally, cuts to the DOD budget partly were to blame for the closure of their facility.

The DOL decision was correct, said the CIT. Any worker of a firm the goods or services of which are covered by ITAR (promulgated by the U.S. Department of State) are ineligible for TAA certification.[56] By law, defense items covered by ITAR, like the aircraft in question the displaced workers maintained and modified, must be made and serviced in America. Because such work can occur only domestically, neither international competition nor outsourcing can be a cause of job loss.

Consider whether all such cases suffer from a measurement problem: how can trade be pinpointed as a cause of injury or threat in a world of multi-jurisdictional manufacturing characterized by global value-added chains? If an American worker or firm claims a need for TAA, then is the competitive import truly of foreign origin? What is the TAA ROO, when the import embodies inputs, technology, and services from one or more foreign countries, and the U.S.? Is TAA justified in that common case? In other words, is TAA designed for a Smith-Ricardo world of simple, single-country products? (The same question plagues AD, CVD, and safeguard law and policy.)

---

55. *See* Number 13-00281, Slip Opinion 14-94, 11 August 2014; Brian Flood, *Trade Court Denies Ex-Boeing Workers' Claim for Trade Adjustment Assistance*, 31 International Trade Reporter (BNA) 1466 (14 August 2014).

56. ITAR are published at 22 CFR Parts 120-130 and implement the *Arms Export Control Act*, 22 U.S.C. §§ 2751 *et seq.* (discussed in a separate Chapter).

VIII. Efficacy

How effective is TAA at changing the economic lives of its recipients for the benefit of the economy as a whole? Is it dis-incentivizing welfare? Or, is it essential support for retooling? Aside from its social just-ness, does TAA work?

TAA is only as good as its funding allows. In the 1980s, the program fared poorly. As part of its efforts to reduce the Federal budget deficits, Congress cut TAA funding, and subjected it only to short-term extensions. The rationales for TAA—equity and fairness toward dislocated workers, and mollifying calls for dramatic import restrictions—were lost. Efficiency was what mattered, and TAA suffered in a utilitarian calculus. That was ironic, because the idea of compensating losers from free trade was consistent with Classical and Neo-Classical theory on comparative advantage.

In the years following enactment of the *Trade Adjustment Assistance Reform Act of 2002*, the GAO analyzed the success of TAA, especially with its new features.[57] The GAO research indicated while some benefits were realized, overall, workers certified as eligible to apply for TAA benefits did not fully utilize them.

(1) A September 2004 Report found workers apply more quickly for benefits, but only because of an increase in the productivity of the DOL in processing petitions—from 238 days to 38 days.[58]

That dramatic time decrease was mandated by a new 40-day maximum rule in the *2002 Act*. States reported more workers in training programs. That was because of a *2002 Act* requirement that a worker be enrolled either (1) eight weeks after petition certification, or (2) 16 weeks after the worker is laid off, whichever is later. The Report also said States struggle to meet administrative demands, and to find training funds to fulfil the needs of workers.

(2) A January 2006 Report examined five plant closings involving many TAA-eligible separated workers.[59] These cases were geographically diverse, and covering urban and rural companies.

In them, 75% or more of workers received some reemployment assistance, and a majority either was working elsewhere or had retired. In three of the five closures, a majority or plurality of workers obtained training at public entities, typically community colleges or vocational schools. In the other two closures, a majority enrolled in training programs offered by for-profit institutions. In none of the five closures did more than 8% of the dislocated

---

57. All GAO Reports are submitted to Congress and *posted at* www.gao.gov (under "trade adjustment assistance").

58. *See* GAO-04-1012.

59. *See Trade Adjustment Assistance: Most Workers in Five Layoffs Received Services, But Better Outreach Needed on Benefits*, GAO-06-43 (January 2006).

workers engage in on-the-job training. For all five closures, the cost of the training program was less than $10,000 for a clear majority (between 64–100%) of workers.

Also, in all five cases, the HCTC was the most underutilized benefit, with only 12% of workers claiming it. They were unaware of it, had other coverage, or found coverage too expensive even with the tax break. Only half of older workers knew a wage subsidy benefit existed, and no more than 20% of them obtained it.

(3) An April 2006 Report found States tend to under-report participation in the TAA program.[60] It also highlighted the desire among States to share lessons about TAA, and improve statistical collection and quality.

(4) A December 2006 Report reviewed the USDA TAA program.[61] It concluded fisherman receive far more of the benefits than farmers.

Salmon and shrimp fisherman received approximately 92% of all funds paid. The USDA FAS reviews petitions under the same 40-day limit as the DOL. Yet, participation is low, with just 101 petitions submitted in FYs 2004–2006. Among other crops the FAS certified for TAA benefits were lychees, olives, catfish, Concord grapes, potatoes, and blueberries.

In sum, TAA benefit petitions increased after the *2002 Act*. But, there was imperfect or no information about new benefits, and coordination between DOL and States needed improvement. Access to TAA improved, but the help was not fully utilized.

Similarly, results for TAA for firms are underwhelming. In a September 2012 Report, the GAO said the *2009 ARRA* was limited in its effect on firms.[62] On the one hand, participation in the TAA program for firms increased. From FYs 2008 through 2010, the EDA certified 26 services firms that had been ineligible under prior law, and 32 other firms because of the relatively more flexible certification requirements under the *Act* than under prior law. On the other hand, subsequently, participation later dropped because of funding uncertainty and the failure of Congress to renew TAA in a timely fashion. TAA lapsed from February to October 2011, hence certifications for firms and approved business recovery plans fell in FY 2011.

---

60. *See* GAO-06-496.
61. *See* GAO-07-201.
62. *See* GAO-12-930.

Part Seven

Trade and the Environment

Chapter 27

GATT Article XX(b) and XX(g) Jurisprudence[1]

I. Extraterritorial Measures, Primary Boycotts, and 1992 *Tuna-Dolphin I* Case

GATT Panel Report,

United States—Restrictions on Imports of Tuna,
B.I.S.D. (39th Supp.) at 155, 156-159, 191, 196-201, 205 (1992)
(Not Adopted) (United States-Mexico Dispute)

2. Factual Aspects

Purse-Seine Fishing of Tuna

2.1 The last three decades have seen the deployment of tuna fishing technology based on the "purse-seine" net in many areas of the world. A fishing vessel using this technique locates a school of fish and sends out a motorboat (a "seine skiff") to hold one end of the purse-seine net. The vessel motors around the perimeter of the school of fish, unfurling the net and encircling the fish, and the seine skiff then attaches its end of the net to the fishing vessel. The fishing vessel then purses the net by winching in a cable at the bottom edge of the net, and draws in the top cables of the net to gather its entire contents.

2.2 Studies monitoring direct and indirect catch levels have shown that fish and dolphins are found together in a number of areas around the world and that this may lead to incidental taking of dolphins during fishing operations. In the Eastern Tropical Pacific Ocean (ETP), a particular association between dolphins and tuna has long been observed, such that fishermen locate schools of underwater tuna by finding and chasing dolphins on the ocean surface and intentionally encircling them with nets to catch the tuna underneath. This type of association has not been observed in other areas of the world; consequently, intentional encirclement of dolphins with purse-seine nets is used as a tuna fishing technique only in the Eastern Tropical Pacific Ocean. When dolphins and tuna together have been surrounded by

---

1. Documents References:
   (1) *Havana (ITO) Charter* Articles 1, 45:1(a)(iii), (viii)
   (2) GATT Preamble and Article XX(b) and XX(g)
   (3) *WTO Agreement* Preamble

purse-seine nets, it is possible to reduce or eliminate the catch of dolphins through using certain procedures.

Marine Mammals Protection Act of the United States
(Measures on Imports from Mexico)

2.3 The *Marine Mammal Protection Act of 1972*, as revised (*MMPA*) [16 U.S.C. §§ 1361 *et seq.*], requires a general prohibition of "taking" (harassment, hunting, capture, killing or attempt thereof) and importation into the United States of marine mammals, except where an exception is explicitly authorized. Its stated goal is that the incidental kill or serious injury of marine mammals in the course of commercial fishing be reduced to insignificant levels approaching zero. The *MMPA* contains special provisions applicable to tuna caught in the ETP, defined as the area of the Pacific Ocean bounded by 40 degrees north latitude, 40 degrees south latitude, 160 degrees west longitude, and the coasts of North, Central and South America. These provisions govern the taking of marine mammals incidental to harvesting of yellowfin tuna in the ETP, as well as importation of yellowfin tuna and tuna products harvested in the ETP. The *MMPA* is enforced by the National Marine Fisheries Service (NMFS) of the National Oceanic and Atmospheric Administration (NOAA) of the Department of Commerce, except for its provisions regarding importation which are enforced by the United States Customs Service under the Department of the Treasury [now CBP under the Department of Homeland Security].

2.4 Section 101(a)(2) of the *MMPA* authorizes limited incidental taking of marine mammals by United States fishermen in the course of commercial fishing pursuant to a permit issued by NMFS, in conformity with and governed by certain statutory criteria in sections 103 and 104 and implementing regulations. Only one such permit has been issued, to the American Tuna-boat Association, covering all domestic tuna fishing operations in the ETP. Under the general permit issued to this Association, no more than 20,500 dolphins may be incidentally killed or injured each year by the United States fleet fishing in the ETP. Among this number, no more than 250 may be coastal spotted dolphin . . . and no more than 2,750 may be Eastern spinner dolphin . . . . The *MMPA* and its implementing regulations include extensive provisions regarding commercial tuna fishing in the ETP, particularly the use of purse-seine nets to encircle dolphin in order to catch tuna beneath (referred to as "setting on" dolphin). These provisions apply to all persons subject to United States jurisdiction and vessels subject to United States jurisdiction, on the high seas and in United States territory, including the territorial sea of the United States and the United States Exclusive Economic Zone. Although *MMPA* enforcement provisions provide for forfeiture of cargo as a penalty for violation of its regulations on harvesting of tuna, neither the *MMPA* provisions nor their implementing regulations otherwise prohibit or regulate the sale, offer for sale, purchase, transportation, distribution or use of yellowfin tuna caught by the United States fleet.

2.5 Section 101(a)(2) of the *MMPA* also states that "[t]he Secretary of Treasury shall ban the importation of commercial fish or products from fish which have been caught with commercial fishing technology which results in the incidental kill or incidental serious injury of ocean mammals in excess of United States standards." This prohibition is mandatory. Special ETP provisions in section 101(a)(2)(B) provide that importation of yellowfin tuna harvested with purse-seine nets in the ETP and products therefrom is prohibited unless the Secretary of Commerce finds that (i) the government of the harvesting country has a program regulating taking of marine mammals that is comparable to that of the United States, and (ii) the average rate of incidental taking of marine mammals by vessels of the harvesting nation is comparable to the average rate of such taking by United States vessels. The Secretary need not act unless a harvesting country requests a finding. If it does, the burden is on that country to prove through documentary evidence that its regulatory regime and taking rates are comparable. If the data show that they are, the Secretary must make a positive finding.

2.6 The provisions for ETP yellowfin tuna in section 101(a)(2)(B) of the *MMPA* provide special prerequisites for a positive finding on comparability of a harvesting country's regulatory regime and incidental taking rates. The regulatory regime must include the same prohibitions as are applicable under United States rules to United States vessels. The average incidental taking rate (in terms of dolphins killed each time the purse-seine nets are set) for that country's tuna fleet must not exceed 1.25 times the average taking rate of United States vessels in the same period. Also, the share of Eastern spinner dolphin and coastal spotted dolphin relative to total incidental takings of dolphin during each entire (one-year) fishing season must not exceed 15 per cent and 2 per cent respectively. NMFS regulations have specified a method of comparing incidental taking rates by calculating the kill per set of the United States tuna fleet as an unweighted average, then weighting this figure for each harvesting country based on differences in mortality by type of dolphin and location of sets; these regulations have also otherwise implemented the *MMPA* provisions on importation.

2.7 On 28 August 1990, the United States Government imposed an embargo, pursuant to a court order, on imports of commercial yellowfin tuna and yellowfin tuna products harvested with purse-seine nets in the ETP until the Secretary of Commerce made positive findings based on documentary evidence of compliance with the *MMPA* standards. This action affected Mexico, Venezuela, Vanuatu, Panama and Ecuador. On 7 September, this measure was removed for Mexico, Venezuela and Vanuatu, pursuant to positive Commerce Department findings; also, Panama and Ecuador later prohibited their fleets from setting on dolphin and were exempted from the embargo. On 10 October 1990, the United States Government, pursuant to court order, imposed an embargo on imports of such tuna from Mexico until the Secretary made a positive finding based on documentary evidence that the percentage of Eastern spinner dolphins killed by the Mexican fleet over the course of an entire fishing season did not exceed 15 per cent of dolphins killed by it in that period. An appeals court ordered on 14 November 1990 that the embargo be stayed, but when it lifted the stay on 22 February 1991, the embargo on imports of such tuna from Mexico went into effect.

2.8 On 3 April 1991, the United States Customs Service issued guidance implementing a further embargo, pursuant to another court order of 26 March, on imports of yellowfin tuna and tuna products harvested in the ETP with purse-seine nets by vessels of Mexico, Venezuela and Vanuatu. Under this embargo, effective 26 March 1991, the importation of yellowfin tuna, and "light meat" tuna products which can contain yellowfin tuna, under specified Harmonized System tariff headings is prohibited unless the importer provides a declaration that, based on appropriate inquiry and the written evidence in his possession, no yellowfin tuna or tuna products in the shipment were harvested with purse-seines in the ETP by vessels from Mexico, Venezuela or Vanuatu.

. . .

[Omitted are the factual aspects, main arguments, findings, and conclusions regarding the *Fishermen's Protective Act of 1967* (the *Pelly Amendment*), *MMPA* measures on intermediary country imports, and *Dolphin Protection Consumer Information Act*. Also omitted are the main arguments and submissions by third parties concerning the *MMPA*. Finally, omitted are the Panel's discussion of categorizing the disputed measures as internal regulations under GATT Article III or as quantitative restrictions under Article XI, and its holding—essentially uncontested by the U.S.—that the *MMPA* violated Article XI.]

. . .

5. Findings

. . .

Article XX

General

5.22 . . . [T]he United States had argued that its direct embargo under the *MMPA* could be justified under Article XX(b) or Article XX(g), and that Mexico had argued that a contracting party could not simultaneously argue that a measure is compatible with the general rules of the General Agreement and invoke Article XX for that measure. . . . [P]revious panels had established that Article XX is a limited and conditional exception from obligations under other provisions of the General Agreement, and not a positive rule establishing obligations in itself. [The Panel cited *United States—Section 337 of the Tariff Act of 1930*, GATT B.I.S.D. (36th Supp.) at 345, 385 ¶ 5.9 (1990) (adopted 7 November 1989), which a later Chapter discusses.] Therefore, the practice of panels has been to interpret Article XX narrowly, to place the burden on the party invoking Article XX to justify its invocation, and not to examine Article XX exceptions unless invoked. Nevertheless, . . . a party to a dispute could argue in the alternative that Article XX might apply, without this argument constituting *ipso facto* an admission that the measures in question would otherwise be inconsistent with the General Agreement. Indeed, the efficient operation of the dispute settlement process required that such arguments in the alternative be possible.

5.23 The Panel proceeded to examine whether Article XX(b) or Article XX(g) could justify the *MMPA* provisions . . . . Article XX provides that:

> Subject to the requirement that such measures are not applied in a manner which would constitute a means of arbitrary or unjustifiable discrimination between countries where the same conditions prevail, or a disguised restriction on international trade, nothing in this Agreement shall be construed to prevent the adoption or enforcement by any contracting party of measures . . .
>
> (b) necessary to protect human, animal or plant life or health;
>
> . . .
>
> (g) relating to the conservation of exhaustible natural resources if such measures are made effective in conjunction with restrictions on domestic production or consumption . . . .

Article XX(b)

5.24 . . . [T]he United States considered the prohibition of imports of certain yellowfin tuna and certain yellowfin tuna products from Mexico, and the provisions of the *MMPA* on which this prohibition is based, to be justified by Article XX(b) because they served solely the purpose of protecting dolphin life and health and were "necessary" within the meaning of that provision because, in respect of the protection of dolphin life and health outside its jurisdiction, there was no alternative measure reasonably available to the United States to achieve this objective. Mexico considered that Article XX(b) was not applicable to a measure imposed to protect the life or health of animals outside the jurisdiction of the contracting party taking it and that the import prohibition imposed by the United States was not necessary because alternative means consistent with the General Agreement were available to it to protect dolphin lives or health, namely international co-operation between the countries concerned.

5.25 . . . [T]he basic question raised by these arguments . . . [is] whether Article XX(b) covers measures necessary to protect human, animal or plant life or health outside the jurisdiction of the contracting party taking the measure, is not clearly answered by the text of that provision. It refers to life and health protection generally without expressly limiting that protection to the jurisdiction of the contracting party concerned. The Panel therefore decided to analyze this issue in the light of the drafting history of Article XX(b), the purpose of this provision, and the consequences that the interpretations proposed by the parties would have for the operation of the General Agreement as a whole.

5.26 . . . [T]he proposal for Article XX(b) dated from the *Draft Charter of the International Trade Organization* (ITO) proposed by the United States, which stated in Article 32, "Nothing in Chapter IV [on commercial policy] of this *Charter* shall be construed to prevent the adoption or enforcement by any Member of measures: . . .(b) necessary to protect human, animal or plant life or health." In the *New York Draft of the ITO Charter*, the preamble had been revised to read as it does at present, and exception (b) read: "For the purpose of protecting human, animal or plant life or health, if corresponding domestic safeguards under similar conditions exist in the importing country." This added proviso reflected concerns regarding the abuse of sanitary regulations by importing countries. Later, Commission A of the Second Session of the Preparatory Committee in Geneva agreed to drop this proviso as unnecessary. Thus, the record indicates that the concerns of the drafters of Article XX(b) focused on the use of sanitary measures to safeguard life or health of humans, animals or plants within the jurisdiction of the importing country.

5.27 . . . Article XX(b) allows each contracting party to set its human, animal or plant life or health standards. The conditions set out in Article XX(b) which limit resort to this exception, namely that the measure taken must be "necessary" and not "constitute a means of arbitrary or unjustifiable discrimination or a disguised restriction on international trade," refer to the trade measure requiring justification under Article XX(b), not however to the life or health standard chosen by the contracting party. [T]his paragraph of Article XX was intended to allow contracting parties to impose trade restrictive measures inconsistent with the General Agreement to pursue overriding public policy goals to the extent that such inconsistencies were unavoidable. The Panel considered that if the broad interpretation of Article XX(b) suggested by the United States were accepted, each contracting party could unilaterally determine the life or health protection policies from which other contracting parties could not deviate without jeopardizing their rights under the General Agreement. The General Agreement would then no longer constitute a multilateral framework for trade among all contracting parties but would provide legal security only in respect of trade between a limited number of contracting parties with identical internal regulations.

5.28 . . . [T]he United States' measures, even if Article XX(b) were interpreted to permit extra-jurisdictional protection of life and health, would not meet the requirement of necessity set out in that provision. The United States had not demonstrated to the Panel — as required of the party invoking an Article XX exception — that it had exhausted all options reasonably available to it to pursue its dolphin protection objectives through measures consistent with the General Agreement, in particular through the negotiation of international cooperative arrangements, which would seem to be desirable in view of the fact that dolphins roam the waters of many states and the high seas. Moreover, even assuming that an import prohibition were the only resort reasonably available to the United States, the particular measure chosen by the United States could in the Panel's view not be considered to be necessary within the meaning of Article XX(b). The United States linked the maximum incidental dolphin taking rate which Mexico had to meet during a particular period in order to be able to export tuna to the United States to the taking rate actually recorded for United States fishermen during the same period. Consequently, the

Mexican authorities could not know whether, at a given point of time, their policies conformed to the United States' dolphin protection standards. The Panel considered that a limitation on trade based on such unpredictable conditions could not be regarded as necessary to protect the health or life of dolphins.

5.29 On the basis of the above considerations, the Panel found that the United States' direct import prohibition imposed on certain yellowfin tuna and certain yellowfin tuna products of Mexico and the provisions of the *MMPA* under which it is imposed could not be justified under the exception in Article XX(b).

Article XX(g)

5.30 The Panel proceeded to examine whether the prohibition on imports of certain yellowfin tuna and certain yellowfin tuna products from Mexico and the *MMPA* provisions under which it was imposed could be justified under the exception in Article XX(g). The Panel noted that the United States, in invoking Article XX(g) with respect to its direct import prohibition under the *MMPA*, had argued that the measures taken under the *MMPA* are measures primarily aimed at the conservation of dolphin, and that the import restrictions on certain tuna and tuna products under the *MMPA* are "primarily aimed at rendering effective restrictions on domestic production or consumption" of dolphin. The Panel also noted that Mexico had argued that the United States measures were not justified under the exception in Article XX(g) because, *inter alia*, this provision could not be applied extra-jurisdictionally.

5.31 The Panel noted that Article XX(g) required that the measures relating to the conservation of exhaustible natural resources be taken "in conjunction with restrictions on domestic production or consumption." A previous panel had found that a measure could only be considered to have been taken "in conjunction with" production restrictions "if it was primarily aimed at rendering effective these restrictions." [*Canada—Measures Affecting Exports of Unprocessed Herring and Salmon*, GATT B.I.S.D. (35th Supp.) at 98, 114 ¶ 4.6 (1989) (adopted 22 March 1988).] A country can effectively control the production or consumption of an exhaustible natural resource only to the extent that the production or consumption is under its jurisdiction. This suggests that Article XX(g) was intended to permit contracting parties to take trade measures primarily aimed at rendering effective restrictions on production or consumption within their jurisdiction.

5.32 The Panel further noted that Article XX(g) allows each contracting party to adopt its own conservation policies. The conditions set out in Article XX(g) which limit resort to this exception, namely that the measures taken must be related to the conservation of exhaustible natural resources, and that they not "constitute a means of arbitrary or unjustifiable discrimination . . . or a disguised restriction on international trade" refer to the trade measure requiring justification under Article XX(g), not however to the conservation policies adopted by the contracting party. The Panel considered that if the extra-jurisdictional interpretation of Article XX(g) suggested by the United States were accepted, each contracting party could unilaterally determine the conservation policies from which other contracting parties could not deviate without jeopardizing their rights under the General Agreement. The considerations that led the Panel to reject an extra-jurisdictional application of Article XX(b) therefore apply also to Article XX(g).

5.33 The Panel did not consider that the United States measures, even if Article XX(g) could be applied extra-jurisdictionally, would meet the conditions set out in that provision. A previous panel [in the 1988 *Canada — Herring and Salmon* case] found that a measure could be considered as "relating to the conservation of exhaustible natural resources" within the meaning of Article XX(g) only if it was primarily aimed at such conservation. The Panel recalled that the United States linked the maximum incidental dolphin-taking rate which Mexico had to meet during a particular period in order to be able to export tuna to the United States to the taking rate actually recorded for United States fishermen during the same period. Consequently, the Mexican authorities could not know whether, at a given point of time, their conservation policies conformed to the United States conservation standards. The Panel considered that a limitation on trade based on such unpredictable conditions could not be regarded as being primarily aimed at the conservation of dolphins.

5.34 On the basis of the above considerations, the Panel found that the United States direct import prohibition on certain yellowfin tuna and certain yellowfin tuna products of Mexico directly imported from Mexico, and the provisions of the *MMPA* under which it is imposed, could not be justified under Article XX(g).

II. Extraterritorial Measures, Secondary Boycotts, and 1994 *Tuna-Dolphin II* Case

GATT Panel Report,

United States — Restrictions on Imports of Tuna,
Reprinted in 33 International Legal Materials 839, 887-899 (1994)
(Not Adopted) (United States-EEC dispute)

V. Findings

A. Introduction

. . .

3. United States Restrictions Affecting Indirect Imports of Tuna ("Intermediary Nation Embargo")

5.5 The *Act* [*i.e., Marine Mammal Protection Act*, or *MMPA*] provides that any nation ("intermediary nation") that exports yellowfin tuna or yellowfin tuna products to the United States, and that imports yellowfin tuna or yellowfin tuna products that are subject to a direct prohibition on import into the United States, must certify and provide reasonable proof that it has not imported products subject to the direct prohibition within the preceding six months. This provision, effective

26 October 1992, is an amendment of an earlier provision, interpreted by a United States court to require that proof be made that each country identified as an intermediary nation had itself prohibited the import of any tuna that was barred from direct importation into the United States. . . .

. . .

F. Concluding Observations

5.42 . . . [T]he objective of sustainable development, which includes the protection and preservation of the environment, has been widely recognized by the contracting parties to the General Agreement. . . . [T]he issue in this dispute was not the validity of the environmental objectives of the United States to protect and conserve dolphins. The issue was whether, in the pursuit of its environmental objectives, the United States could impose trade embargoes to secure changes in the policies which other contracting parties pursued within their own jurisdiction. The Panel therefore had to resolve whether the contracting parties, by agreeing to give each other in Article XX the right to take trade measures necessary to protect the health and life of plants, animals and persons or aimed at the conservation of exhaustible natural resources, had agreed to accord each other the right to impose trade embargoes for such purposes. The Panel had examined this issue in the light of the recognized methods of interpretation and had found that none of them lent any support to the view that such an agreement was reflected in Article XX.

. . .

VI. Conclusions

. . .

[Using analysis redolent of its *Tuna–Dolphin I* Report, the GATT Panel held the primary and intermediary nation embargoes violated GATT Article XI:1 and could not be excused by Article XX(b), (g), or (d). As in *Tuna-Dolphin I*, the Panel recommended the United States bring its law into conformity with its GATT obligations.]

III. Eco-Labeling and 2012 *Tuna Dolphin* Case

Is eco-labeling the answer to some trade issues? Does its efficacy depend on the nature and content of, and criteria for, a label, and vigorous enforcement mechanisms? Consider *Earth Island institute v. Hogarth*, a case in which the U.S. government sought unsuccessfully to weaken labeling rules so as to permit a dolphin-safe label on tuna imports from Mexico and other countries if no dolphins were observed to be killed or maimed.[2]

In 2012, the WTO Appellate Body ruled that American dolphin-safe tuna labeling requirements under the 1990 *Dolphin Protection Consumer Information Act*

---

2. Number 04-17018, CV-03-00007 (9th Cir., 27 April 2007).

(*DPCIA*) violated GATT-WTO non-discriminatory rules.[3] The *DPCIA* contains three key rules for obtaining a label on a tuna product that represents that product as dolphin safe, *i.e.*, it has been harvested in a way that does not kill the air-breathing mammals. Specifically, the *DPCIA* says no producer, exporter, importer, distributor, or seller may label any tuna as "dolphin-safe" if it was harvested:

(1) In international waters by a vessel using driftnet fishing.

(2) In the ETP Ocean by a vessel using a purse seine net with a carrying capacity of 400 short tons or more, unless accompanied by a certification from the Captain of the vessel, and a certification from an observer, that no dolphins (a) were intentionally encircled during the fishing trip, and (b) were killed or seriously injured during the setting of the net. In other words, a dual certification is needed.

(3) Outside the ETP Ocean by a vessel using a purse seine net, unless the Captain certifies that no dolphins were intentionally encircled during the fishing trip. However, to obtain the "dolphin safe" label, there is no need for the Captain to certify that no dolphins were killed or seriously injured during the tuna catch.

Simply put, the *DPCIA* banned the use of the "dolphin friendly" label if tuna in the ETP Ocean:

> is caught by intentionally encircling and deploying nets on dolphins that follow tuna schools, and if any dolphins are killed or seriously injured in the harvesting of tuna. In contrast, tuna caught outside the ETP was not subject to these standards, but still qualified for the label on the grounds that dolphins to not tend to follow tuna schools outside the ETP, and that fishing boats therefore do not set on dolphins to catch tuna.[4]

The statute applies to all tuna products exported from or offered for sale in the U.S.

However, the Appellate Body ruled *DPCIA* implementing regulations—the measures determining eligibility for a dolphin-safe label—treated Mexican tuna less favorably than American tuna. The discrimination arose because the requirements did not establish conditions for using a label in a manner that reflected risks faced by dolphins in different oceans. The Mexican tuna finishing fleet generally operates in the ETP Ocean, so it was subject to the dual certification requirement. Consequently, the labeling measures precluded most Mexican tuna from getting a dolphin-safe label. In contrast, tuna fishing vessels that are American-owned and flagged typically operate in the Western Pacific. So, the American tuna fishing fleet (and other non-Mexican fleets) generally was not subject to the dual certification

---

3. *See* WTO Appellate Body Report, *United States—Measures Concerning the Importation, Marketing and Sale of Tuna and Tuna Products*, WT/DS381/AB/R (adopted 13 June 2012) (also called *U.S.—Tuna Dolphin II (Mexico)*). The U.S. statute is codified at 16 U.S.C. § 1385.

4. Daniel Pruzin, *Mexico Contests U.S. Compliance Claims With WTO Tuna-Dolphin Ruling*, 30 International Trade Reporter (BNA) 1381 (5 September 2013).

requirement. Tuna from the American (and other non-Mexican) fisherman tended to get qualify for the dolphin-safe label.

So, Mexico pointed out that tuna products sold in the U.S. tend to come from the Western Pacific, and the three leading brand name processors of tuna sold in America—Bumblebee, Chicken of the Sea, and StarKist—refuse to buy Mexican tuna, because the Mexican fishermen cannot meet the tougher rules imposed on them. Mexico won. As the WTO summarized:

> This dispute arises out of a challenge brought by Mexico against certain legal instruments of the United States (the "measure at issue") establishing the conditions for the use of a "dolphin-safe" label on tuna products. The legal instruments identified by Mexico in its panel request comprised the . . . DPCIA, implementing regulations, and a ruling by a U.S. federal appeals court in *Earth Island Institute v. Hogarth* relating to the application of the DPCIA. The measure at issue does not make the use of a "dolphin-safe" label obligatory for the importation or sale of tuna products in the United States. The conditions established in the measure at issue vary depending on the area where the tuna contained in the tuna product is caught and the type of vessel and fishing method by which it is harvested. . . . [T]una products made from tuna caught by "setting on" dolphins (that is, chasing and encircling dolphins with a net in order to catch the tuna associating with them) are not eligible for a "dolphin-safe" label in the United States. . . .
>
> Regarding the question of whether the measure . . . constitutes a "technical regulation," the Appellate Body **found** that the Panel did not err in characterizing the measure . . . as a "technical regulation" within the meaning of Annex 1:1 to the *TBT Agreement*. The Appellate Body noted that the challenged measure is composed of legislative and regulatory acts of the U.S. federal authorities and includes administrative provisions. The Appellate Body added that the measure sets out a single and legally mandated definition of a "dolphin-safe" tuna product and disallows the use of other labels on tuna products that use the terms "dolphin-safe," dolphins, porpoises and marine mammals and do not satisfy this definition. In doing so, the U.S. measure prescribes in a broad and exhaustive manner the conditions that apply for making any assertion on a tuna product as to its "dolphin-safety", regardless of the manner in which that statement is made.
>
> With respect to Mexico's claim under Article 2:1 of the *TBT Agreement*, the Appellate Body **reversed** the Panel's finding that the U.S. "dolphin-safe" labelling provisions are not inconsistent with [*i.e.*, is legal under] Article 2:1 . . . , and **found**, instead, that the U.S. measure is inconsistent with [*i.e.*, is illegal under] Article 2:1. The Appellate Body reasoned, first, that, by excluding most Mexican tuna products from access to the "dolphin-safe" label while granting access to most U.S. tuna products and tuna products from other countries, the measure *modifies the conditions*

of competition in the U.S. market to the detriment of Mexican tuna products. Next, the Appellate Body scrutinized whether, ... the detrimental impact from the measure stems exclusively from a legitimate regulatory distinction. ... [T]he Appellate Body examined whether the different conditions for access to a "dolphin-safe" label are "calibrated" to the risks to dolphins arising from different fishing methods in different areas of the ocean, as the United States had claimed. The Appellate Body noted the Panel's finding that the fishing technique of setting on dolphins is particularly harmful to dolphins and that this fishing method has the capacity of resulting in observed and unobserved adverse effects on dolphins. At the same time, the Panel was not persuaded that the risks to dolphins from other fishing techniques are insignificant and do not under some circumstances rise to the same level as the risks from setting on dolphins. The Appellate Body further noted the Panel's finding that, while the U.S. measure fully addresses the adverse effects on dolphins resulting (including observed and unobserved effects) from setting on dolphins in the ETP, it does not address mortality arising from fishing methods other than setting on dolphins in other areas of the ocean. In these circumstances, the Appellate Body **found** that the measure at issue is not even-handed in the manner in which it addresses the risks to dolphins arising from different fishing techniques in different areas of the ocean.[5]

Manifestly, the U.S. defended the distinction between rules (1) and (2) above by pointing out dolphins do not follow tuna schools outside the ETP Ocean. So, a fishing vessel does not need to set nets on dolphins there to catch tuna, and the additional certification (item (b) in rule (1)) is unnecessary. The Appellate Body rejected the American argument.

To comply with the ruling, in July 2013 the U.S. National Marine Fisheries Service adopted new labeling rules.[6] The rules concern documentation needed to support a dolphin-safe label on a tuna product. Their thrust was to rectify the lack of even-handedness in the treatment of tuna harvested in different oceans by imposing the same rules on tuna harvested anywhere: vessel captains, and in certain cases observers, would have to provide a statement that "no dolphins were killed or seriously injured" for any tuna product labeled dolphin-safe, whether or not the tuna was harvested using a purse seine net in the ETP Ocean. Simply put, the U.S. extended rule (1) globally to all vessels and fishing methods.

Specifically, first, the requirement for certification by vessel captains, and sometimes observers, that "no dolphins were killed or seriously injured" expanded beyond large purse-seine net vessels operating in the ETP Ocean to all vessels in all

---

5. World Trade Organization, Dispute Settlement: DS 381, United States—Measures Concerning the Importation, Marketing and Sale of Tuna and Tuna Products, www.wto.org/english/tratop_e/dispu_e/cases_e/ds381_e.htm (bold emphases original, italicized emphases added).

6. *See* Federal Register, 9 July 2013, at 16508.

locations. That is, a Captain must certify no dolphin was killed or seriously injured during the sets of the deployment of other fishing equipment, regardless of the type of fishing gear used or the place of fishing.

Second, the new regulations strengthened the system for tracking domestic tuna canning and processing operations. They also set new metrics for processors other than tuna canners to qualify for a tuna product label of dolphin-safe.

Third, to avoid commingling and thereby undermine the integrity of the dolphin-safe label, the new regulations altered requirements for both dolphin-safe and non-dolphin-safe tuna that is harvested on the same fishing trip or stored on board the same fishing vessel.[7] The two types of tuna must be kept in separately, by using netting or other differentiating material, containers, or spaces. Fourth, the new regulations expanded the requirement of an observer to fisheries outside the ETP Ocean, subject to the NOAA agreeing the observers are qualified and authorized by the relevant authority to make dolphin-safe certifications.

Mexico argued the new regulations failed to comply with the Appellate Body ruling, as they continued to discriminate in fact against Mexican tuna, and a compliance dispute ensured. In 2016, the U.S. again revised the *DPCIA* by increasing the labeling rules applicable to tuna fishing vessels outside the ETP Ocean. But, it did not change its labeling rules for tuna harvested using the purse seine method by vessels in that Ocean. "Not good enough," Mexico urged, and in May 2017 won the right to impose $163 million annually in retaliatory tariffs against the U.S.

Consider the same questions raised in this case in a different context: "fair trade" labels to certify production in keeping with labor rights. Note the use of the *TBT Agreement* in environmental and labor rights contexts. What happens if the context is a "women's rights" label, or a "human rights" label?

IV. Two-Step Test, Differential Regulations, and 1996 *Reformulated Gas* Case

• *Gasoline Rule*

The "*Gasoline Rule*" is short hand of the Appellate Body for a controversial EPA regulation. The *Rule* was formally entitled "Regulation of Fuels and Fuel Additives—Standards for Reformulated and Conventional Gasoline."[8] The EPA promulgated it pursuant to the 1963 *Clean Air Act*, as amended, for reformulated and conventional gasoline. The *Rule*, which took effect on 1 January 1995, mandated reductions in certain gasoline constituents to reduce vehicle emissions. By reducing harmful constituents in gasoline, exhaust pollution would decrease. Using 1990

---

7. *See* 50 C.F.R. § 216.93.
8. *See* 40 C.F.R. Part 80, 59 Federal Register 7,716 (16 February 1994).

figures, the *Gasoline Rule* set baseline "ozone-forming constituent" levels that gasoline could contain.

The *Gasoline Rule* identified nine highly-populated areas—areas most in need of a quick decrease in exhaust pollution. (These were large metropolitan areas that had experienced the worst summertime ozone pollution. In addition to these nine cities, various additional areas were included at the request of certain state governors.) In these so-called "non-attainment areas," only "reformulated" gasoline could be used. Reduction of particularly troublesome constituents (*e.g.*, benzene, oxygen, and Reid Vapor Pressure) was called for between 1995–1998. In all other areas of the U.S., "conventional" gasoline—gasoline as clean as gasoline in 1990—could be used. For conventional gasoline, no specific period for reductions in harmful constituents was set, but all constituents in this type of gasoline ultimately would be subject to regulation.

What were the compositional and performance specifications for "reformulated" gasoline set forth in the *Clean Air Act*? There were three compositional standards: (1) the oxygen content could not be less than 2.0% by weight; (2) the benzene content could not exceed 1.0% by volume; and (3) the gasoline must be free of heavy metals, including lead and manganese. There were also 3 performance standards: (1) a 15% reduction in the emission of volatile organic compounds (VOCs); (2) a 15% reduction in the emission of toxic air pollutants (toxics); and (3) no increase in the emission of nitrogen oxides (NO_x). The statute explained the methodologies for satisfying these compositional and performance specifications. It established a "Simple Model" methodology to be used between 1 January 1995 and 1 January 1998, and a "Complex Model" methodology for use thereafter. The Complex Model more accurately predicted emissions performance than the former Model, but it the Simple Model was at issue in the dispute.

What about "conventional" gasoline? Congress and the EPA worried that refiners, blenders, and importers might dump pollutants they extracted from reformulated gasoline into conventional gasoline. Therefore, the *Clean Air Act* mandated all conventional gasoline remain at least as clean as 1990 baseline levels. The mandate was strict. The Simple Model for reformulated gasoline covered only certain qualities of that type of gasoline, namely, sulphur, olefins, and T-90. The Simple Model said these constituents had to remain at or below 1990 levels—a "non-degradation" requirement. However, the non-degradation requirement for conventional gasoline was much broader: it covered not only sulphur, olefins, and T-90, but also all other qualities of that kind of gasoline. There was to be no degradation from the 1990 level for all of the qualities.

How would the EPA judge compliance with the non-degradation mandates for conventional and reformulated gasoline? Each year, it would compare emissions of gasoline sold by domestic refiners, blenders, and importers against emissions from a 1990 baseline. But, that begged the question of how the baselines would be established—and that question was the "rub" of the WTO dispute excepted below. After all, baselines were at the heart of the enforcement process.

• Two-Step Test

WTO Appellate Body Report,

United States—Standards for Reformulated and Conventional Gasoline,
WT/DS2/AB/R (Adopted 20 May 1996)

III. The Issue of Justification Under Article XX(g) of the General Agreement

. . .

B. "Relating to the Conservation of Exhaustible Natural Resources"

The Panel Report took the view that clean air was a "natural resource" that could be "depleted." Accordingly, . . . the Panel concluded that a policy to reduce the depletion of clean air was a policy to conserve an exhaustible natural resource within the meaning of Article XX(g). Shortly thereafter, however, the Panel Report also concluded that "the less favorable baseline establishments methods" were *not* primarily aimed at the conservation of exhaustible natural resources and thus fell outside the justifying scope of Article XX(g).

The Panel, addressing the task of interpreting the words "relating to," quoted with approval the following passage from the panel report in the 1987 *Herring and Salmon* case [*i.e., Canada—Measures Affecting Exports of Unprocessed Herring and Salmon,* GATT B.I.S.D. (35th Supp.) 98 at 114 ¶ 4.6 (1989) (adopted 22 March 1988)]:

> as the preamble of Article XX indicates, the purpose of including Article XX:(g) in the General Agreement was not to widen the scope for measures serving trade policy purposes but merely to ensure that the commitments under the General Agreement do not hinder the pursuit of policies aimed at the conservation of exhaustive natural resources. The Panel concluded for these reasons that, while a trade measure did not have to be necessary or essential to the conservation of an exhaustible natural resource, it had to be *primarily aimed* at the conservation of an exhaustible natural resource to be considered as "relating to" conservation within the meaning of Article XX:(g). (emphasis added by the Panel)

The Panel Report then went on to apply the . . . *Herring and Salmon* reasoning and conclusion to the baseline establishment rules of the *Gasoline Rule* in the following manner:

> The Panel then considered whether the precise aspects of the *Gasoline Rule* that it had found to violate Article III—the less favorable baseline establishments methods that adversely affected the conditions of competition for imported gasoline—were primarily aimed at the conservation of natural resources. The Panel saw no direct connection between less favorable treatment of imported gasoline that was chemically identical to domestic gasoline, and the U.S. objective of improving air quality in the United States. Indeed, in the view of the Panel, being consistent with the obligation to provide no less favorable treatment would not prevent the attainment of the

desired level of conservation of natural resources under the *Gasoline Rule*. Accordingly, it could not be said that the baseline establishment methods that afforded less favorable treatment to imported gasoline were primarily aimed at the conservation of natural resources. In the Panel's view, the above-noted lack of connection was underscored by the fact that affording treatment of imported gasoline consistent with its Article III:4 obligations would not in any way hinder the United States in its pursuit of its conservation policies under the *Gasoline Rule*. Indeed, the United States remained free to regulate in order to obtain whatever air quality it wished. The Panel therefore concluded that the less favorable baseline establishments methods at issue in this case were not primarily aimed at the conservation of natural resources.

. . .

A principal difficulty . . . with the Panel Report's application of Article XX(g) to the baseline establishment rules is that the Panel there overlooked a fundamental rule of treaty interpretation. This rule has received its most authoritative and succinct expression in the *Vienna Convention on the Law of Treaties* (the "*Vienna Convention*"), which provides in relevant part:

Article 31
General Rule of Interpretation

1. A treaty shall be interpreted in good faith in accordance with the ordinary meaning to be given to the terms of the treaty in their context and in the light of its object and purpose.

The "general rule of interpretation" set out above has been relied upon by all of the participants and third participants, although not always in relation to the same issue. That general rule of interpretation has attained the status of a rule of customary or general international law. As such, it forms part of the "customary rules of interpretation of public international law" which the Appellate Body has been directed, by Article 3(2) of the *DSU*, to apply in seeking to clarify the provisions of the *General Agreement* and the other "covered agreements" of the . . . [*WTO Agreement*]. That direction reflects a measure of recognition that the *General Agreement* is not to be read in clinical isolation from public international law.

Applying the basic principle of interpretation that the words of a treaty, like the *General Agreement*, are to be given their ordinary meaning, in their context and in the light of the treaty's object and purpose, the Appellate Body observes that the Panel Report failed to take adequate account of the words actually used by Article XX in its several paragraphs. In enumerating the various categories of governmental acts, laws or regulations which WTO Members may carry out or promulgate in pursuit of differing legitimate state policies or interests outside the realm of trade liberalization, Article XX uses different terms in respect of different categories:

| "necessary" | — in paragraphs (a), (b) and (d); |
| "essential" | — in paragraph (j); |

"relating to"   —   in paragraphs (c), (e) and (g);
"for the protection of"   —   in paragraph (f);
"in pursuance of"   —   in paragraph (h); and
"involving"   —   in paragraph (i).

It does not seem reasonable to suppose that the WTO Members intended to require, in respect of each and every category, the same kind or degree of connection or relationship between the measure under appraisal and the state interest or policy sought to be promoted or realized.

At the same time, Article XX(g) and its phrase, "relating to the conservation of exhaustible natural resources," need to be read in context and in such a manner as to give effect to the purposes and objects of the *General Agreement*. The context of Article XX(g) includes the provisions of the rest of the *General Agreement*, including in particular Articles I, III and XI; conversely, the context of Articles I and III and XI includes Article XX. Accordingly, the phrase "relating to the conservation of exhaustible natural resources" may not be read so expansively as seriously to subvert the purpose and object of Article III:4. Nor may Article III:4 be given so broad a reach as effectively to emasculate Article XX(g) and the policies and interests it embodies. The relationship between the affirmative commitments set out in, *e.g.*, Articles I, III and XI, and the policies and interests embodied in the "General Exceptions" listed in Article XX, can be given meaning within the framework of the *General Agreement* and its object and purpose by a treaty interpreter only on a case-to-case basis, by careful scrutiny of the factual and legal context in a given dispute, without disregarding the words actually used by the WTO Members themselves to express their intent and purpose.

. . .

All the participants . . . in this appeal accept the propriety and applicability of the view of the *Herring and Salmon* report and the Panel Report that a measure must be "primarily aimed at" the conservation of exhaustible natural resources in order to fall within the scope of Article XX(g). Accordingly, we see no need to examine this point further, save, perhaps, to note that the phrase "primarily aimed at" is not itself treaty language and was not designed as a simple litmus test for inclusion or exclusion from Article XX(g).

. . . [W]e turn to the specific question of whether the baseline establishment rules are appropriately regarded as "primarily aimed at" the conservation of natural resources for the purposes of Article XX(g). . . . [T]his question must be answered in the affirmative.

The baseline establishment rules, taken as a whole (that is, the provisions relating to establishment of baselines for domestic refiners, along with the provisions relating to baselines for blenders and importers of gasoline), need to be related to the "non-degradation" requirements set out elsewhere in the *Gasoline Rule*. Those provisions can scarcely be understood if scrutinized strictly by themselves, totally divorced from other sections of the *Gasoline Rule* which certainly constitute part of the context of these provisions. The baseline establishment rules whether individual or statutory, were designed to permit scrutiny and monitoring of the level of compliance of refiners, importers and blenders with the "non-degradation" requirements. Without baselines of some kind, such scrutiny would not be possible and the *Gasoline Rule's* objective of stabilizing and preventing further deterioration of the level of air pollution prevailing in 1990, would be substantially frustrated. The relationship between the baseline establishment rules and the "non-degradation" requirements of the *Gasoline Rule* is not negated by the inconsistency, found by the Panel, of the baseline establishment rules with the terms of [GATT] Article III:4. We consider that, given that substantial relationship, the baseline establishment rules cannot be regarded as merely incidentally or inadvertently aimed at the conservation of clean air in the United States for the purposes of Article XX(g).

C. "If Such Measures are Made Effective in Conjunction with Restrictions on Domestic Production or Consumption"

The Panel did not find it necessary to deal with the issue of whether the baseline establishment rules "are made effective in conjunction with restrictions on domestic production or consumption," since it had earlier concluded that those rules had not even satisfied the preceding requirement of "relating to" in the sense of being "primarily aimed at" the conservation of clean air. Having been unable to concur with that earlier conclusion of the Panel, we must now address this second requirement of Article XX(g) . . . .

The claim of the United States is that the second clause of Article XX(g) requires that the burdens entailed by regulating the level of pollutants in the air emitted in the course of combustion of gasoline, must not be imposed solely on, or in respect of, imported gasoline.

. . .

There is, of course, no textual basis for requiring identical treatment of domestic and imported products. Indeed, where there is identity of treatment — constituting real, not merely formal, equality of treatment — it is difficult to see how inconsistency with Article III:4 would have arisen in the first place. On the other hand, if *no* restrictions on domestically-produced like products are imposed at all, and all limitations are placed upon imported products *alone*, the measure cannot be accepted as primarily or even substantially designed for implementing conservationist goals. The measure would simply be naked discrimination for protecting locally-produced goods.

. . . [T]he baseline establishment rules affect both domestic gasoline and imported gasoline, providing for — generally speaking — individual baselines for domestic refiners and blenders and statutory baselines for importers. Thus, restrictions on the consumption or depletion of clean air by regulating the domestic production of "dirty" gasoline are established jointly with corresponding restrictions with respect to imported gasoline. That imported gasoline has been determined to have been accorded "less favorable treatment" than the domestic gasoline in terms of Article

III:4, is not material for purposes of analysis under Article XX(g). It might also be noted that the second clause of Article XX(g) speaks disjunctively of "domestic production *or* consumption."

We do not believe, finally, that the clause "if made effective in conjunction with restrictions on domestic production or consumption" was intended to establish an empirical "effects test" for the availability of the Article XX(g) exception. In the first place, the problem of determining causation, well-known in both domestic and international law, is always a difficult one. In the second place, in the field of conservation of exhaustible natural resources, a substantial period of time, perhaps years, may have to elapse before the effects attributable to implementation of a given measure may be observable. The legal characterization of such a measure is not reasonably made contingent upon occurrence of subsequent events. We are not, however, suggesting that consideration of the predictable effects of a measure is never relevant. In a particular case, should it become clear that realistically, a specific measure cannot in any possible situation have any positive effect on conservation goals, it would very probably be because that measure was not designed as a conservation regulation to begin with. In other words, it would not have been "primarily aimed at" conservation of natural resources at all.

V. The Introductory Provisions of Article XX of the General Agreement: Applying the *Chapeau* of the General Exceptions

. . .

The *chapeau* . . . prohibits such application of a measure at issue (otherwise falling within the scope of Article XX(g)) as would constitute

(a) "arbitrary discrimination" (between countries where the same conditions prevail);

(b) "unjustifiable discrimination" (with the same qualifier); or

(c) "disguised restriction" on international trade.

. . .

"Arbitrary discrimination," "unjustifiable discrimination" and "disguised restriction" on international trade may, accordingly, be read side-by-side; they impart meaning to one another. It is clear to us that "disguised restriction" includes disguised *discrimination* in international trade. It is equally clear that *concealed* or *unannounced* restriction or discrimination in international trade does *not* exhaust the meaning of "disguised restriction." We consider that "disguised restriction," whatever else it covers, may properly be read as embracing restrictions amounting to arbitrary or unjustifiable discrimination in international trade taken under the guise of a measure formally within the terms of an exception listed in Article

XX. Put in a somewhat different manner, the kinds of considerations pertinent in deciding whether the application of a particular measure amounts to "arbitrary or unjustifiable discrimination," may also be taken into account in determining the presence of a "disguised restriction" on international trade. The fundamental theme is to be found in the purpose and object of avoiding abuse or illegitimate use of the exceptions to substantive rules available in Article XX.

There was more than one alternative course of action available to the United States in promulgating regulations implementing the *CAA* [the 1970 *Clean Air Act*, as amended]. These included the imposition of statutory baselines without differentiation as between domestic and imported gasoline. This approach, if properly implemented, could have avoided any discrimination at all. Among the other options open to the United States was to make available individual baselines to foreign refiners as well as domestic refiners. The United States has put forward a series of reasons why either of these courses was not, in its view, realistically open to it and why, instead, it had to devise and apply the baseline establishment rules contained in the *Gasoline Rule*.

In explaining why individual baselines for foreign refiners had not been put in place, the United States laid heavy stress upon the difficulties which the EPA would have had to face. These difficulties related to anticipated administrative problems that individual baselines for foreign refiners would have generated. This argument was made succinctly by the United States in the following terms:

> Verification on foreign soil of foreign baselines, and subsequent enforcement actions, present substantial difficulties relating to problems arising whenever a country exercises enforcement jurisdiction over foreign persons. In addition, even if individual baselines were established for several foreign refiners, the importer would be tempted to claim the refinery of origin that presented the most benefits in terms of baseline restrictions, and tracking the refinery or origin would be very difficult because gasoline is a fungible commodity. The United States should not have to prove that it cannot verify information and enforce its regulations in every instance in order to show that the same enforcement conditions do not prevail in the United States and other countries. . . . The impracticability of verification and enforcement of foreign refiner baselines in this instance shows that the "discrimination" is based on serious, not arbitrary or unjustifiable, concerns stemming from different conditions between enforcement of its laws in the United States and abroad.

Thus, according to the United States, imported gasoline was relegated to the more exacting statutory baseline requirement because of these difficulties of verification and enforcement. The United States stated that verification and enforcement of the *Gasoline Rule's* requirements for imported gasoline are "much easier when the statutory baseline is used" and that there would be a "dramatic difference" in the burden of administering requirements for imported gasoline if individual baselines were allowed.

. . .

Clearly, the United States did not feel it feasible to require its domestic refiners to incur the physical and financial costs and burdens entailed by immediate compliance with a statutory baseline. The United States wished to give domestic refiners time to restructure their operations and adjust to the requirements in the *Gasoline Rule*. This may very well have constituted sound domestic policy from the viewpoint of the EPA and U.S. refiners. At the same time, we are bound to note that, while the United States counted the costs for its domestic refiners of statutory baselines, there is nothing in the record to indicate that it did other than disregard that kind of consideration when it came to foreign refiners.

We have above located two omissions on the part of the United States: to explore adequately means, including in particular cooperation with the governments of Venezuela and Brazil, of mitigating the administrative problems relied on as justification by the United States for rejecting individual baselines for foreign refiners; and to count the costs for foreign refiners that would result from the imposition of statutory baselines. In our view, these two omissions go well beyond what was necessary for the Panel to determine that a violation of Article III:4 had occurred in the first place. The resulting discrimination must have been foreseen, and was not merely inadvertent or unavoidable. In the light of the foregoing, our conclusion is that the baseline establishment rules in the *Gasoline Rule*, in their application, constitute "unjustifiable discrimination" and a "disguised restriction on international trade." We hold, in sum, that the baseline establishment rules, although within the terms of Article XX(g), are not entitled to the justifying protection afforded by Article XX as a whole.

VI. Two-Step Test, Species Protection, and 1998 *Turtle-Shrimp* Case

WTO Appellate Body Report,

United States — Import Prohibition of Certain Shrimp and Shrimp Products, WT/DS58/AB/R (Adopted 6 November 1998)

I. Introduction: Statement of the Appeal

1. This is an appeal by the United States from certain issues of law and legal interpretations in the Panel Report, *United States — Import Prohibition of Certain Shrimp and Shrimp Products.* . . . India, Malaysia, Pakistan and Thailand . . . requested . . . that the Dispute Settlement Body (the "DSB") establish a panel to examine their complaint regarding a prohibition imposed by the United States on the importation of certain shrimp and shrimp products by Section 609 of Public Law 101-162 ("Section 609") [16 U.S.C. § 1537] and associated regulations and judicial rulings. . . .

2. . . . The United States issued regulations in 1987 pursuant to the *Endangered Species Act of 1973* [16 U.S.C. §§ 1531 *et seq.*] requiring all United States shrimp trawl

vessels to use approved Turtle Excluder Devices ("TEDs") or tow-time restrictions in specified areas where there was a significant mortality of sea turtles in shrimp harvesting. [*See* 52 Fed. Reg. 24,244 (29 June 1987) — the *"1987 Regulations".*] These regulations, which became fully effective in 1990, were modified so as to require the use of approved TEDs at all times and in all areas where there is a likelihood that shrimp trawling will interact with sea turtles, with certain limited exceptions.

7. . . . [T]he Panel reached the following conclusions:

> In the light of the findings above, we conclude that the import ban on shrimp and shrimp products as applied by the United States on the basis of Section 609 of Public Law 101-162 is not consistent with Article XI:1 of GATT 1994, and cannot be justified under Article XX of GATT 1994.

. . .

VI. Appraising Section 609 Under Article XX of the GATT 1994

. . .

A. The Panel's Findings and Interpretative Analysis

. . .

117. . . . The Panel defined its approach as first "determin[ing] whether the measure at issue satisfies the conditions contained in the *chapeau.*" If the Panel found that to be the case, it said that it "shall then examine whether the U.S. measure is covered by the terms of Article XX(b) or (g)." The Panel attempted to justify its interpretative approach in the following manner:

> As mentioned by the Appellate Body in its report in the *Gasoline* case, in order for the justification of Article XX to be extended to a given measure, it must not only come under one or another of the particular exceptions — paragraphs (a) to (j) — listed under Article XX; it must also satisfy the requirements imposed by the opening clause of Article XX. We note that panels have in the past considered the specific paragraphs of Article XX before reviewing the applicability of the conditions contained in the *chapeau.* However, *as the conditions contained in the introductory provision apply to any of the paragraphs of Article XX, it seems equally appropriate to analyze first the introductory provision of Article XX.* (emphasis added)

118. In *United States-Gasoline*, we enunciated the appropriate method for applying Article XX of the GATT 1994:

> In order that the justifying protection of Article XX may be extended to it, the measure at issue must not only come under one or another of the particular exceptions — paragraphs (a) to (j) — listed under Article XX; it must also satisfy the requirements imposed by the opening clauses of Article XX. *The analysis is,* in other words, *two-tiered: first, provisional justification by reason of characterization of the measure under XX(g); second, further*

appraisal of the same measure under the introductory clauses of Article XX. (emphasis added)

119. The sequence of steps indicated above in the analysis of a claim of justification under Article XX reflects, not inadvertence or random choice, but rather the fundamental structure and logic of Article XX. The Panel appears to suggest, albeit indirectly, that following the indicated sequence of steps, or the inverse thereof, does not make any difference. To the Panel, reversing the sequence set out in *United States-Gasoline* "seems equally appropriate." We do not agree.

120. The task of interpreting the *chapeau* so as to prevent the abuse or misuse of the specific exemptions provided for in Article XX is rendered very difficult, if indeed it remains possible at all, where the interpreter (like the Panel in this case) has not first identified and examined the specific exception threatened with abuse. The standards established in the *chapeau* are, moreover, necessarily broad in scope and reach: the prohibition of the *application* of a measure "in a manner which would constitute a means of *arbitrary* or *unjustifiable discrimination* between countries where the same conditions prevail" or "a *disguised restriction* on international trade" (emphasis added). When applied in a particular case, the actual contours and contents of these standards will vary as the kind of measure under examination varies. What is appropriately characterizable as "arbitrary discrimination" or "unjustifiable discrimination," or as a "disguised restriction on international trade" in respect of one category of measures, need not be so with respect to another group or type of measures. The standard of "arbitrary discrimination," for example, under the *chapeau* may be different for a measure that purports to be necessary to protect public morals than for one relating to the products of prison labor.

121. The consequences of the interpretative approach adopted by the Panel are apparent in its findings. The Panel formulated a broad standard and a test for appraising measures sought to be justified under the *chapeau*; it is a standard or a test that finds no basis either in the text of the *chapeau* or in that of either of the two specific exceptions claimed by the United States. The Panel, in effect, constructed an *a priori* test that purports to define a category of measures which, *ratione materiae* [by reason of the matter involved, *i.e.*, from the nature of the subject matter], fall outside the justifying protection of Article XX's *chapeau*. In the present case, the Panel found that the United States measure at stake fell within that class of excluded measures because Section 609 conditions access to the domestic shrimp market of the United States on the adoption by exporting countries of certain conservation policies prescribed by the United States. It appears to us, however, that conditioning access to a Member's domestic market on whether exporting Members comply with, or adopt, a policy or policies unilaterally prescribed by the importing Member may, to some degree, be a common aspect of measures falling within the scope of one or another of the exceptions (a) to (j) of Article XX. Paragraphs (a) to (j) comprise measures that are recognized as *exceptions to substantive obligations*

established in the GATT 1994, because the domestic policies embodied in such measures have been recognized as important and legitimate in character. It is not necessary to assume that requiring from exporting countries compliance with, or adoption of, certain policies (although covered in principle by one or another of the exceptions) prescribed by the importing country, renders a measure *a priori* incapable of justification under Article XX. Such an interpretation renders most, if not all, of the specific exceptions of Article XX inutile, a result abhorrent to the principles of interpretation we are bound to apply.

122. We hold that the findings of the Panel . . ., and . . . [its] interpretative analysis, constitute error in legal interpretation and accordingly reverse them.

123. Having reversed the Panel's legal conclusion that the United States measure at issue "is not within the scope of measures permitted under the *chapeau* of Article XX," . . . it is our duty and our responsibility to complete the legal analysis in this case in order to determine whether Section 609 qualifies for justification under Article XX. . . .

. . .

B. Article XX(g): Provisional Justification of Section 609

125. In claiming justification for its measure, the United States primarily invokes Article XX(g). Justification under Article XX(b) is claimed only in the alternative . . . .

. . .

1. "Exhaustible Natural Resources"

. . .

129. The words of Article XX(g), "exhaustible natural resources," were actually crafted more than 50 years ago. They must be read by a treaty interpreter in the light of contemporary concerns of the community of nations about the protection and conservation of the environment. While Article XX was not modified in the Uruguay Round, the preamble attached to the *WTO Agreement* shows that the signatories to that *Agreement* were, in 1994, fully aware of the importance and legitimacy of environmental protection as a goal of national and international policy. The Preamble of the *WTO Agreement*—which informs not only the GATT 1994, but also the other covered agreements—explicitly acknowledges "the objective of *sustainable development*" . . . .

130. From the perspective embodied in the preamble of the *WTO Agreement*, we note that the generic term "natural resources" in Article XX(g) is not "static" in its content or reference but is rather "by definition, evolutionary." It is, therefore, pertinent to note that modern international conventions and declarations make frequent references to natural resources as embracing both living and non-living resources. For instance, the 1982 *United Nations Convention on the Law of the Sea* ("*UNCLOS*") [done at Montego Bay, 10 December 1982, U.N. Doc. A/CONF.62/122, *reprinted in* 21 INTERNATIONAL LEGAL MATERIALS 1261], in defining the jurisdictional rights of coastal states in their exclusive economic zones, provides:

Article 56
Rights, jurisdiction and duties of the coastal State
in the exclusive economic zone

1. In the exclusive economic zone, the coastal State has:

> (a) sovereign rights for the purpose of exploring and exploiting, conserving and managing the *natural resources, whether living or non-living,* of the waters superjacent to the sea-bed and of the sea-bed and its subsoil, . . . (emphasis added)

The *UNCLOS* also repeatedly refers in Articles 61 and 62 to "living resources" in specifying rights and duties of states in their exclusive economic zones. . . . [The U.S. has not joined *UNCLOS*. The Appellate Body proceeded by (1) observing the *Convention on Biological Diversity*, done at Rio de Janeiro, 5 June 1992, UNEP/Bio. Div./N7-INC5/4, *reprinted in* 31 INTERNATIONAL LEGAL MATERIALS 818, which Thailand and the U.S. have signed, but not ratified, and which India, Malaysia, and Pakistan have ratified, uses the concept of "biological resources," (2) explaining *Agenda 21*, adopted by the United Nations Conference on Environment and Development, 14 June 1992, U.N. Doc. A/CONF.151/26/Rev.1, speaks broadly of "natural resources" and in detail about "marine living resources," and (3) quoting from the *Final Act of the Conference to Conclude a Convention on the Conservation of Migratory Species of Wild Animals*, done at Bonn, 23 June 1979, *reprinted in* 19 INTERNATIONAL LEGAL MATERIALS 11, 15, which states migratory species are "living natural resources."]

131. Given the recent acknowledgement by the international community of the importance of concerted bilateral or multilateral action to protect living natural resources, and recalling the explicit recognition by WTO Members of the objective of sustainable development in the preamble of the *WTO Agreement*, we believe it is too late in the day to suppose that Article XX(g) . . . may be read as referring only to the conservation of exhaustible mineral or other non-living natural resources. [Plus, as the Appellate Body stated in Footnote 114, there is no evidence from the drafting history that the GATT framers intended to exclude "living" natural resources from the scope of application of Article XX:(g).] Moreover, two adopted GATT 1947 panel reports previously found fish to be an "exhaustible natural resource" within the meaning of Article XX(g). [*See United States-Prohibition of Imports of Tuna and Tuna Products from Canada*, GATT B.I.S.D. (29th Supp.) at 91 ¶ 4.9 (1983) (adopted 22 February 1982); *Canada — Measures Affecting Exports of Unprocessed Herring and Salmon*, GATT B.I.S.D. (35th Supp.) at 98 ¶ 4.4 (1989) (adopted 22 March 1988).] We hold that, in line with the principle of effectiveness in treaty interpretation, measures to conserve exhaustible natural resources, whether *living* or *non-living*, may fall within Article XX(g).

132. We turn next to the issue of whether the living natural resources sought to be conserved by the measure are "exhaustible" under Article XX(g). That this element is present in respect of the five species of sea turtles here involved appears to be

conceded by all the participants and third participants in this case. The exhaustibility of sea turtles would in fact have been very difficult to controvert since all of the seven recognized species of sea turtles are today listed in Appendix 1 of the *Convention on International Trade in Endangered Species of Wild Fauna and Flora* (*"CITES"*). The list in Appendix 1 includes "all species *threatened with extinction* which are or may be affected by trade" (emphasis added).

133. Finally, we observe that sea turtles are highly migratory animals, passing in and out of waters subject to the rights of jurisdiction of various coastal states and the high seas. . . . The sea turtle species here at stake, *i.e.*, covered by Section 609, are all known to occur in waters over which the United States exercises jurisdiction. Of course, it is not claimed that *all* populations of these species migrate to, or traverse, at one time or another, waters subject to United States jurisdiction. Neither the appellant nor any of the appellees claims any rights of exclusive ownership over the sea turtles, at least not while they are swimming freely in their natural habitat — the oceans. We do not pass upon the question of whether there is an implied jurisdictional limitation in Article XX(g), and if so, the nature or extent of that limitation. We note only that in the specific circumstances of the case before us, there is a sufficient nexus between the migratory and endangered marine populations involved and the United States for purposes of Article XX(g).

134. . . . [W]e find that the sea turtles here involved constitute "exhaustible natural resources" for purposes of Article XX(g) of the GATT 1994.

2. "Relating to the Conservation of"

135. Article XX(g) requires that the measure sought to be justified be one which "relat[es] to" the conservation of exhaustible natural resources. In making this determination, the treaty interpreter essentially looks into the relationship between the measure at stake and the legitimate policy of conserving exhaustible natural resources. . . . [T]he policy of protecting and conserving the endangered sea turtles here involved is shared by all participants and third participants in this appeal, indeed, by the vast majority of the nations of the world. None of the parties to this dispute question the genuineness of the commitment of the others to that policy.

136. In *United States-Gasoline*, we inquired into the relationship between the baseline establishment rules of the United States Environmental Protection Agency (the "EPA") and the conservation of natural resources for the purposes of Article XX(g). There, we answered in the affirmative the question posed before the panel of whether the baseline establishment rules were "primarily aimed at" the conservation of clean air. . . . [The Appellate Body quoted from its holding in that case.] The substantial relationship we found there between the EPA baseline establishment rules and the conservation of clean air in the United States was a close and genuine relationship of ends and means.

137. In the present case, we must examine the relationship between the general structure and design of the measure here at stake, Section 609, and the policy goal it purports to serve, that is, the conservation of sea turtles.

138. Section 609(b)(1) imposes an import ban on shrimp that have been harvested with commercial fishing technology which may adversely affect sea turtles. This provision is designed to influence countries to adopt national regulatory programs requiring the use of TEDs by their shrimp fishermen.... There are two basic exemptions from the import ban, both of which relate clearly and directly to the policy goal of conserving sea turtles. First, Section 609, as elaborated in the *1996 Guidelines*, excludes from the import ban shrimp harvested "under conditions that do not adversely affect sea turtles." Thus, the measure, by its terms, excludes from the import ban: aquaculture shrimp; shrimp species (such as *pandalid* shrimp) harvested in water areas where sea turtles do not normally occur; and shrimp harvested exclusively by artisanal methods, even from non-certified countries. The harvesting of such shrimp clearly does not affect sea turtles. Second, under Section 609(b)(2), the measure exempts from the import ban shrimp caught in waters subject to the jurisdiction of certified countries.

139. There are two types of certification for countries under Section 609(b)(2). First, under Section 609(b)(2)(C), a country may be certified as having a fishing environment that does not pose a threat of incidental taking of sea turtles in the course of commercial shrimp trawl harvesting. There is no risk, or only a negligible risk, that sea turtles will be harmed by shrimp trawling in such an environment.

140. The second type of certification is provided by Section 609(b)(2)(A) and (B). Under these provisions, as further elaborated in the *1996 Guidelines*, a country wishing to export shrimp to the United States is required to adopt a regulatory program that is comparable to that of the United States program and to have a rate of incidental take of sea turtles that is comparable to the average rate of United States' vessels. This is, essentially, a requirement that a country adopt a regulatory program requiring the use of TEDs by commercial shrimp trawling vessels in areas where there is a likelihood of intercepting sea turtles. This requirement is, in our view, directly connected with the policy of conservation of sea turtles. It is undisputed among the participants, and recognized by the experts consulted by the Panel, that the harvesting of shrimp by commercial shrimp trawling vessels with mechanical retrieval devices in waters where shrimp and sea turtles coincide is a significant cause of sea turtle mortality.... [T]he Panel did "not question ... the fact generally acknowledged by the experts that TEDs, when properly installed and adapted to the local area, would be an effective tool for the preservation of sea turtles."

141. In its general design and structure, therefore, Section 609 is not a simple, blanket prohibition of the importation of shrimp imposed without regard to the consequences (or lack thereof) of the mode of harvesting employed upon the incidental capture and mortality of sea turtles. Focusing on the design of the measure here at stake, it appears to us that Section 609, *cum* implementing guidelines, is not disproportionately wide in its scope and reach in relation to the policy objective of protection and conservation of sea turtle species. The means are, in principle, reasonably related to the ends. The means and ends relationship between Section 609 and the

legitimate policy of conserving an exhaustible, and, in fact, endangered species, is observably a close and real one, a relationship that is every bit as substantial as that which we found in *United States-Gasoline* between the EPA baseline establishment rules and the conservation of clean air in the United States.

142. In our view, therefore, Section 609 is a measure "relating to" the conservation of an exhaustible natural resource within the meaning of Article XX(g) of the GATT 1994.

3. "If Such Measures are Made Effective in Conjunction with Restrictions on Domestic Production or Consumption"

143. In *United States-Gasoline*, we held that . . . Article XX(g),

> . . . is appropriately read as a requirement that the measures concerned impose restrictions, not just in respect of imported gasoline but also with respect to domestic gasoline. The clause is a requirement of *even-handedness* in the imposition of restrictions, in the name of conservation, upon the production or consumption of exhaustible natural resources.

In this case, we need to examine whether the restrictions imposed by Section 609 with respect to imported shrimp are also imposed in respect of shrimp caught by United States shrimp trawl vessels.

144. . . . Section 609, enacted in 1989, addresses the mode of harvesting of imported shrimp only. However, two years earlier, in 1987, the United States issued regulations pursuant to the *Endangered Species Act* requiring all United States shrimp trawl vessels to use approved TEDs, or to restrict the duration of tow-times, in specified areas where there was significant incidental mortality of sea turtles in shrimp trawls. These regulations became fully effective in 1990 and were later modified. They now require United States shrimp trawlers to use approved TEDs "in areas and at times when there is a likelihood of intercepting sea turtles," with certain limited exceptions. Penalties for violation of the *Endangered Species Act*, or the regulations issued thereunder, include civil and criminal sanctions. The United States government currently relies on monetary sanctions and civil penalties for enforcement. The government has the ability to seize shrimp catch from trawl vessels fishing in United States waters and has done so in cases of egregious violations. We believe that, in principle, Section 609 is an even-handed measure.

145. Accordingly, we hold that Section 609 is a measure made effective in conjunction with the restrictions on domestic harvesting of shrimp, as required by Article XX(g).

C. The Introductory Clauses of Article XX: Characterizing Section 609 under the *Chapeau's* Standards

146. . . . Having found that Section 609 does come within the terms of Article XX(g), it is not, therefore, necessary to analyze the measure in terms of Article XX(b).

147. Although provisionally justified under Article XX(g), Section 609, if it is ultimately to be justified as an exception under Article XX, must also satisfy the

requirements of the introductory clauses — the *"chapeau"* — of Article XX . . . . We turn . . . to the second part of the two-tier analysis required under Article XX.

1. General Considerations

. . .

156. Turning then to the *chapeau* of Article XX, . . . it embodies the recognition on the part of WTO Members of the need to maintain a balance of rights and obligations between the right of a Member to invoke one or another of the exceptions of Article XX, specified in paragraphs (a) to (j), on the one hand, and the substantive rights of the other Members under the GATT 1994, on the other hand. Exercise by one Member of its right to invoke an exception, such as Article XX(g), if abused or misused, will, to that extent, erode or render naught the substantive treaty rights in, for example, Article XI:1, of other Members. Similarly, because the GATT 1994 itself makes available the exceptions of Article XX, in recognition of the legitimate nature of the policies and interests there embodied, the right to invoke one of those exceptions is not to be rendered illusory. The same concept may be expressed from a slightly different angle of vision, thus, a balance must be struck between the *right* of a Member to invoke an exception under Article XX and the *duty* of that same Member to respect the treaty rights of the other Members. To permit one Member to abuse or misuse its right to invoke an exception would be effectively to allow that Member to degrade its own treaty obligations as well as to devalue the treaty rights of other Members. If the abuse or misuse is sufficiently grave or extensive, the Member, in effect, reduces its treaty obligation to a merely facultative one and dissolves its juridical character, and, in so doing, negates altogether the treaty rights of other Members. The *chapeau* was installed at the head of the list of "General Exceptions" in Article XX to prevent such far-reaching consequences.

157. . . . [T]he language of the *chapeau* makes clear that each of the exceptions in paragraphs (a) to (j) of Article XX is a *limited and conditional* exception from the substantive obligations contained in the other provisions of the GATT 1994, that is to say, the ultimate availability of the exception is subject to the compliance by the invoking Member with the requirements of the *chapeau*. This interpretation of the *chapeau* is confirmed by its negotiating history. [The Appellate Body observed in footnote 152 of its Report that Article 32 of the *Vienna Convention* permits recourse to "supplementary means of interpretation, including the preparatory work of the treaty and the circumstances of its conclusion," in order to confirm a meaning resulting from the application of Article 31, or to determine a meaning when the application of Article 31 leaves the meaning ambiguous or obscure, or leads to a manifestly absurd or unreasonable result. The Appellate Body said it was resorting to legislative history to confirm a meaning.] The language initially proposed by the United States in 1946 for the *chapeau* of what would later become Article XX was unqualified and unconditional. Several proposals were made during the First Session of the Preparatory Committee of the United Nations Conference on Trade and Employment in 1946 suggesting modifications. In November 1946, the United Kingdom proposed that "in order to prevent abuse of the exceptions of Article 32 [which

would subsequently become Article XX]," the *chapeau* of this provision should be qualified. This proposal was generally accepted, subject to later review of its precise wording. Thus, the negotiating history of Article XX confirms that the paragraphs of Article XX set forth *limited and conditional* exceptions from the obligations of the substantive provisions of the GATT. Any measure, to qualify finally for exception, must also satisfy the requirements of the *chapeau*. This is a fundamental part of the balance of rights and obligations struck by the original framers of the GATT 1947.

. . .

159. The task of interpreting and applying the *chapeau* is, hence, essentially the delicate one of locating and marking out a line of equilibrium between the right of a Member to invoke an exception under Article XX and the rights of the other Members under varying substantive provisions (*e.g.*, Article XI) of the GATT 1994, so that neither of the competing rights will cancel out the other and thereby distort and nullify or impair the balance of rights and obligations constructed by the Members themselves in that Agreement. The location of the line of equilibrium, as expressed in the *chapeau*, is not fixed and unchanging; the line moves as the kind and the shape of the measures at stake vary and as the facts making up specific cases differ.

160. . . . [W]e address now the issue of whether the *application* of the United States measure, although the measure itself falls within the terms of Article XX(g), nevertheless constitutes "a means of arbitrary or unjustifiable discrimination between countries where the same conditions prevail" or "a disguised restriction on international trade." We address, in other words, whether the application of this measure constitutes an abuse or misuse of the provisional justification made available by Article XX(g). . . . [T]he application of a measure may be characterized as amounting to an abuse or misuse of an exception of Article XX not only when the detailed operating provisions of the measure prescribe the arbitrary or unjustifiable activity, but also where a measure, otherwise fair and just on its face, is actually applied in an arbitrary or unjustifiable manner. The standards of the *chapeau* . . . project both substantive and procedural requirements.

2. "Unjustifiable Discrimination"

161. We scrutinize first whether Section 609 has been applied in a manner constituting "unjustifiable discrimination between countries where the same conditions prevail." Perhaps the most conspicuous flaw in this measure's application relates to its intended and actual coercive effect on the specific policy decisions made by foreign governments, Members of the WTO. Section 609, in its application, is, in effect, an economic embargo which requires *all other exporting Members*, if they wish to exercise their GATT rights, to adopt *essentially the same* policy (together with an approved enforcement program) as that applied to, and enforced on, United States domestic shrimp trawlers. As enacted by the Congress of the United States, the *statutory* provisions of Section 609(b)(2)(A) and (B) do not, in themselves, *require* that other WTO Members adopt *essentially the same* policies and enforcement practices

as the United States. Viewed alone, the statute appears to permit a degree of discretion or flexibility in how the standards for determining comparability might be applied, in practice, to other countries. However, any flexibility that may have been intended by Congress when it enacted the statutory provision has been effectively eliminated in the implementation of that policy through the *1996 Guidelines* promulgated by the Department of State and through the practice of the administrators in making certification determinations.

. . .

164. . . . [T]he United States also applies a uniform standard throughout its territory, regardless of the particular conditions existing in certain parts of the country. The United States requires the use of approved TEDs at all times by domestic, commercial shrimp trawl vessels operating in waters where there is any likelihood that they may interact with sea turtles, regardless of the actual incidence of sea turtles in those waters, the species of those sea turtles, or other differences or disparities that may exist in different parts of the United States. It may be quite acceptable for a government, in adopting and implementing a domestic policy, to adopt a single standard applicable to all its citizens throughout that country. However, it is not acceptable, in international trade relations, for one WTO Member to use an economic embargo to *require* other Members to adopt essentially the same comprehensive regulatory program, to achieve a certain policy goal, as that in force within that Member's territory, *without* taking into consideration different conditions which may occur in the territories of those other Members.

. . .

166. Another aspect of the application of Section 609 that bears heavily in any appraisal of justifiable or unjustifiable discrimination is the failure of the United States to engage the appellees, as well as other Members exporting shrimp to the United States, in serious, across-the-board negotiations with the objective of concluding bilateral or multilateral agreements for the protection and conservation of sea turtles, before enforcing the import prohibition against the shrimp exports of those other Members. . . .

167. . . . First, the Congress of the United States expressly recognized the importance of securing international agreements for the protection and conservation of the sea turtle species in enacting this law. . . . [The Appellate Body quoted to this effect from Section 609(a), which directs the Secretary of State to enter into bilateral accords or MEAs to protect and conserve sea turtles.] Apart from the negotiation of the *Inter-American Convention for the Protection and Conservation of Sea Turtles* (the "*Inter-American Convention*") which concluded in 1996, the record before the Panel does not indicate any serious, substantial efforts to carry out these express directions of Congress.

168. Second, the protection and conservation of highly migratory species of sea turtles, that is, the very policy objective of the measure, demands concerted and cooperative efforts on the part of the many countries whose waters are traversed in the

course of recurrent sea turtle migrations. The need for, and the appropriateness of, such efforts have been recognized in the WTO itself as well as in a significant number of other international instruments and declarations. . . . [T]he [WTO] *Decision on Trade and Environment*, which provided for the establishment of the CTE [Committee on Trade and the Environment] and set out its terms of reference, refers to both the *Rio Declaration on Environment and Development* and *Agenda 21*. Of particular relevance is Principle 12 of the *Rio Declaration* . . ., which states, in part:

> Unilateral actions to deal with environmental challenges outside the jurisdiction of the importing country should be avoided. *Environmental measures addressing transboundary or global environmental problems should, as far as possible, be based on international consensus.* (emphasis added)

. . . [The Appellate Body quoted generously from comparable provisions in *Agenda 21* (para. 2.22(i), the *Convention on Biological Diversity* (Article 5), and the *Convention on the Conservation of Migratory Species of Wild Animals* (Annex I).] . . . Furthermore, . . . WTO Members in the Report of the CTE, forming part of the Report of the General Council to Ministers on the occasion of the [December 1996] Singapore Ministerial Conference, endorsed and supported [as "best and most effective" multilateral solutions to trans-boundary or global environmental problems] . . . .

169. Third, the United States did negotiate and conclude one regional international agreement for the protection and conservation of sea turtles: The *Inter-American Convention*. This *Convention* was opened for signature on 1 December 1996 and has been signed by five countries, in addition to the United States, and four of these countries are currently certified under Section 609. This *Convention* has not yet been ratified by any of its signatories. [The Appellate Body quoted generously from this *Convention*, too.]

   . . .

171. The *Inter-American Convention* thus provides convincing demonstration that an alternative course of action was reasonably open to the United States for securing the legitimate policy goal of its measure, a course of action other than the unilateral and non-consensual procedures of the import prohibition under Section 609. It is relevant to observe that an import prohibition is, ordinarily, the heaviest "weapon" in a Member's armory of trade measures. The record does not, however, show that serious efforts were made by the United States to negotiate similar agreements with any other country or group of countries before (and, as far as the record shows, after) Section 609 was enforced on a world-wide basis on 1 May 1996. . . .

172. Clearly, the United States negotiated seriously with some, but not with other Members (including the appellees), that export shrimp to the United States. The effect is plainly discriminatory and, in our view, unjustifiable. The unjustifiable nature of this discrimination emerges clearly when we consider the cumulative effects of the failure of the United States to pursue negotiations for establishing consensual means of protection and conservation of the living marine resources here involved, notwithstanding the explicit statutory direction in Section 609 itself to

initiate negotiations as soon as possible for the development of bilateral and multilateral agreements. The principal consequence of this failure may be seen in the
resulting unilateralism evident in the application of Section 609. . . . [T]he policies
relating to the necessity for use of particular kinds of TEDs in various maritime
areas, and the operating details of these policies, are all shaped by the Department
of State, without the participation of the exporting Members. The system and processes of certification are established and administered by the United States agencies
alone. The decision-making involved in the grant, denial or withdrawal of certification to the exporting Members, is, accordingly, also unilateral. The unilateral character of the application of Section 609 heightens the disruptive and discriminatory
influence of the import prohibition and underscores its unjustifiability.

. . .

[The Appellate Body pointed out that transition periods and TED technology sharing by the U.S., under the *1991* and *1993 Guidelines*, discriminated against certain
countries.]

176. . . . [W]e find, and so hold, that . . . [the cumulative effect of differences in the
means of application of Section 609 to various shrimp exporting countries] . . .
constitute "unjustifiable discrimination" between exporting countries desiring
certification in order to gain access to the United States shrimp market within the
meaning of the *chapeau* of Article XX.

3. "Arbitrary Discrimination"

177. We next consider whether Section 609 has been applied in a manner constituting "arbitrary discrimination between countries where the same conditions
prevail." . . . Section 609, in its application, imposes a single, rigid and unbending
requirement that countries applying for certification under Section 609(b)(2)(A)
and (B) adopt a comprehensive regulatory program that is essentially the same as
the United States' program, without inquiring into the appropriateness of that program for the conditions prevailing in the exporting countries. Furthermore, there is
little or no flexibility in how officials make the determination for certification pursuant to these provisions. . . . [T]his rigidity and inflexibility also constitute "arbitrary discrimination" within the meaning of the *chapeau*.

. . .

180. . . . [W]ith respect to neither type of certification under Section 609(b)(2)
[*i.e.*, under Section 609(b)(2)(A) and (B), or under Section 609(b)(2)(C)] is there
a transparent, predictable certification process that is followed by the competent
United States government officials. The certification processes under Section 609
consist principally of administrative *ex parte* inquiry or verification by staff of the
Office of Marine Conservation in the Department of State with staff of the United
States National Marine Fisheries Service. With respect to both types of certification,
there is no formal opportunity for an applicant country to be heard, or to respond
to any arguments that may be made against it, in the course of the certification process before a decision to grant or to deny certification is made. Moreover, no formal

written, reasoned decision, whether of acceptance or rejection, is rendered on applications for either type of certification . . . . Countries which are granted certification are included in a list of approved applications published in the *Federal Register*; however, they are not notified specifically. Countries whose applications are denied also do not receive notice of such denial (other than by omission from the list of approved applications) or of the reasons for the denial. No procedure for review of, or appeal from, a denial of an application is provided.

181. The certification processes followed by the United States thus appear to be singularly informal and casual, and to be conducted in a manner such that these processes could result in the negation of rights of Members. There appears to be no way that exporting Members can be certain whether the terms of Section 609, in particular, the *1996 Guidelines*, are being applied in a fair and just manner by the appropriate governmental agencies of the United States. It appears to us that, effectively, exporting Members applying for certification whose applications are rejected are denied basic fairness and due process, and are discriminated against, *vis-à-vis* those Members which are granted certification.

. . .

184. We find . . . the United States measure is applied in a manner which amounts to a means not just of "unjustifiable discrimination," but also of "arbitrary discrimination" between countries where the same conditions prevail, contrary to the requirements of the *chapeau* of Article XX. The measure, therefore, is not entitled to the justifying protection of Article XX of the GATT 1994. Having made this finding, it is not necessary for us to examine also whether the United States measure is applied in a manner that constitutes a "disguised restriction on international trade" under the *chapeau* of Article XX.

185. In reaching these conclusions, we wish to underscore what we have *not* decided in this appeal. We have *not* decided that the protection and preservation of the environment is of no significance to the Members of the WTO. Clearly, it is. We have *not* decided that the sovereign nations that are Members of the WTO cannot adopt effective measures to protect endangered species, such as sea turtles. Clearly, they can and should. And we have *not* decided that sovereign states should not act together bilaterally, plurilaterally or multilaterally, either within the WTO or in other international fora, to protect endangered species or to otherwise protect the environment. Clearly, they should and do.

186. What we *have* decided in this appeal is simply this: although the measure of the United States in dispute in this appeal serves an environmental objective that is recognized as legitimate under paragraph (g) of Article XX of the GATT 1994, this measure has been applied by the United States in a manner which constitutes arbitrary and unjustifiable discrimination between Members of the WTO, contrary to the requirements of the *chapeau* of Article XX. . . . [T]his measure does not qualify for the exemption that Article XX . . . affords to measures which serve certain recognized, legitimate environmental purposes but which, at the same time, are not

applied in a manner that constitutes a means of arbitrary or unjustifiable discrimination between countries where the same conditions prevail or a disguised restriction on international trade. As we emphasized in *United States-Gasoline*, WTO Members are free to adopt their own policies aimed at protecting the environment as long as, in so doing, they fulfill their obligations and respect the rights of other Members under the *WTO Agreement*.

[For a critique of the *Turtle-Shrimp* decision, see Mervyn Martin, *The Power-Based Influence within a Rule-Based System through "Extended" Interpretation in U.S.—Shrimp: Is All Lost for the WTO DSU?*, 24 INTERNATIONAL TRADE LAW & REGULATION issue 1, 7-20 (2018). Dr. Martin argues (*inter alia*) the Appellate Body undermined the rules-based *DSU* regime by accommodating developing country interests to expand the regulatory coverage of GATT by "'smuggling in' new, especially non-trade, issues into the *DSU*, thereby adjusting the parameters or extent of consent to be bound, and displacing the intended rule-based system." In effect, its extended approach exemplifies its judicial activism.]

VII. Passing Two-Step Test and 2001 *Asbestos* Case

- **Overview**

The Appellate Body Report in the 2001 *Asbestos* case is a cause for both cheer and disappointment.[9] "Cheer," at least among environmentalists. It is the first instance in which the Appellate Body holds a disputed measure passes muster under both steps in the Two-Step Article XX test. "Necessity" is not to be interpreted in a highly restrictive manner, but as "reasonable availability," thereby according deference and flexibility to national authorities. "Disappointment," because aside from elaborating on the meaning of "necessity" under Article XX(b), the Appellate Body provides no insights to Article XX—in particular, on how to interpret key terms in the *chapeau*. On appeal, Canada did not raise a challenge under the *chapeau*. Hence, the case is not the quintessential example of successful invocation, following full adjudication, of Article XX(b) and the *chapeau*.

The disputed measure was a French import ban on asbestos and asbestos-containing products. On Step 1, Paragraph (b) of Article XX, the Appellate Body asked whether the ban "protected" human life or health, and whether it was "necessary" to do so with a ban. The Panel looked at a large amount of scientific evidence. All four scientific experts it consulted agreed chrysotile asbestos fibers, and cement-based products containing these fibers, constitute a risk to human health. The Panel observed that since 1977, international bodies like the WHO and International Agency for Research on Cancer have acknowledged this risk. Chrysotile, in specific, posed a risk of lung cancer and mesothelioma (another form of cancer) to humans

---

9. *See European Communities—Measures Affecting Asbestos and Asbestos-Containing Products*, WT/DS135/AB/R (adopted 12 March 2001). [Hereinafter, *Asbestos* Appellate Body Report.]

in occupational sectors downstream of production and processing. Cement-based products containing chrysotile posed the same risks for the public in general. As the Panel did not exceed the bounds of its discretion in making these deductions, the Appellate Body found no reason to interfere with them. After all, panels, not the Appellate Body, are the triers of fact.

- **Definition of "Necessity"**

In the *Asbestos* case, both the Panel and Appellate Body agreed the disputed measure was "necessary," within the meaning of GATT Article XX(b), for protecting human life. There was no reasonably available alternative to banning chrysotile and products containing chrysotile. On appeal, Canada urged the Panel committed legal errors by not quantifying the risk of chrysotile and chrysotile-containing products, and by failing to consider the risk of substitute goods permitted by the French government. Canada also argued the Panel was legally incorrect to hold that controlled use of chrysotile and chrysotile-containing products is not a reasonably available alternative to banning asbestos and products with asbestos. On both arguments, Canada lost.

First, held the Appellate Body, neither Article XX(b), nor any provision of the WTO *SPS Agreement*, requires a quantitative measurement of risks to human life or health. Rather, they permit either a quantitative or qualitative evaluation. The Panel looked at the scientific evidence, which indicated no minimum threshold level of exposure or duration has been identified for any risk (except for asbestosis) posed by chrysotile, and which also proved a clear link to cancer. Second, as Canada ought to have known, "it is undisputed that WTO Members have the right to determine the level of protection of health that they consider appropriate in a given situation."[10] France chose to "halt" the spread of asbestos-related health risks, and the word "necessary" in Article XX(b) must not be misconstrued to undermine this sovereign right. True, the substitute good (PCG fibers and cement-based products containing PCG fibers), might pose health risks too. But, these risks are less than those posed by chrysotile asbestos fibers and products containing them. In other words, said the Appellate Body, "it seems to us perfectly legitimate for a Member to seek to halt the spread of a highly risky product while allowing the use of a less risky product in its place."[11]

Canada's argument—that the Panel should have found controlled use of asbestos and products containing asbestos is not a reasonably available alternative to banning these products—raises the interpretive question of what, at bottom, "necessity" in Article XX(b) means. What factors must be checked to see whether an alternative measure, short of a ban, is "necessary" for the importing country to protect human life or health?

---

10. *Asbestos* Appellate Body Report, ¶ 168. *See also id.* ¶¶ 157-63.
11. *Asbestos* Appellate Body Report, ¶ 168.

In *Reformulated Gasoline* case, the Panel held that an alternative measure is reasonably available even if there are administrative difficulties associated with implementing that measure. As this holding was not appealed, in *Asbestos* the Appellate Body had its first opportunity to opine on the point.

Predictably, the Appellate Body looked to three precedents:

(1) The 1989 GATT Panel Report, *United States—Section 337 of the Tariff Act of 1930.*[12]

(2) The 1990 GATT Panel Report, *Thailand—Restrictions on Importation of and Internal Taxes on Cigarettes.*[13]

(3) The 2001 Appellate Body Report, *Korea—Measures Affecting Imports of Fresh, Chilled and Frozen Beef.*[14]

In the *Thai Cigarettes* case, the GATT Panel faced the same issue—how to evaluate whether a measure is "necessary" under Article XX(b). The import restrictions on cigarettes imposed by Thailand, said the Panel, could be considered "'necessary'... only if there were *no alternative measure consistent with the General Agreement, or less inconsistent with it*, which Thailand could *reasonably be expected to employ to achieve* its health *policy objectives.*"[15]

Parsed carefully, the italicized words set a four-pronged test for "necessity" under Paragraph (b). The prongs apply *in seriatim, i.e.*, each one builds on its predecessor.

First: There must be no measure that is an alternative to the measure in dispute.

Second: Assuming there is an alternative measure, it must be either consistent with GATT, or less inconsistent with GATT than the disputed measure.

Third: Assuming there is a GATT-consistent, or less-GATT-inconsistent, alternative measure, it must be reasonable to expect the importing country to employ the alternative.

Fourth: Assuming the first three prongs are met, the alternative measure furthers the health policy goal of the importing country.

The GATT Panel faced nearly the same issue in the *Section 337* case, as did the Appellate Body in *Korea Beef*. What does "necessary" under Article XX(d) mean? The adjudicators established essentially the same test as the *Thai Cigarettes* Panel.

---

12. *See* B.I.S.D. (36th Supp.) 345 at ¶ 5.26 (adopted 7 November 1989).

13. *See* B.I.S.D. (37th Supp.) 200 (adopted 20 February 1990).

14. *See* WT/DS161/AB/R, WT/DS169/AB/R (adopted 10 January 2001).

15. B.I.S.D. (37th Supp.) 200 at ¶ 75 (adopted 20 February 1990) (emphasis added).

Thus, in *Section 337*, the Panel ruled the proper standard for testing "necessity" under Paragraph (d) is whether:

(1) An alternative measure exists that is available to the importing country,

(2) It is reasonable to expect the importing country to use the alternative measure, and

(3) The alternative measure is not inconsistent with other GATT provisions.

In one important respect, the *Section 337* Panel supplemented this test. It considered the possibility no GATT-consistent measure is reasonably available to an importing country. What should the country do? The Panel said the country would be bound to choose from among the alternative measures reasonably available to it the one least inconsistent with other GATT provisions. Put differently, the country would have to choose the least trade restrictive measure, because this least-worst choice would be most consistent with the trade-liberalizing aim of GATT. In *Korea Beef*, the Appellate Body affirmed the *Section 337* test, and did so again in *EC Asbestos*.

Following and building on precedent, the Appellate Body in *Asbestos* applied the same test for Article XX(b) from *Thai Cigarettes*, and Article XX(d) from *Section 337* and *Korea Beef*. The Appellate Body agreed (1) no alternative measure existed that (2) France could reasonably be expected to employ that (3) was consistent with GATT, or less inconsistent with GATT, than a complete ban on asbestos and asbestos-containing products, which (4) also would achieve France's health policy aim.

Observe, too, the Appellate Body's reiteration of a point it had made in *Korea Beef* about judicial decision-making under Article XX(b) and (d). The "necessity" test requires weighing and balancing to see whether a GATT-consistent, WTO-consistent alternative not only is reasonably available, but also whether it advances a policy goal of the importing country. That country must show how vital the stakes are. The more important the common interests or values at stake, the easier it is to accept a measure is "necessary" to achieve its stated goal. In this regard, the French ban was the perfect case.

The ban was designed to further a value "both vital and important in the highest degree," namely, the preservation of human life and health by eliminating "well-known, and life-threatening health risks posed by asbestos fibers."[16] No alternative measure simultaneously could achieve the same goal and be less restrictive of trade than a prohibition. Canada's proposed alternative—controlled use of asbestos and asbestos-containing products—could not achieve the French aim of halting these risks, but it would undermine France's sovereign right to choose its level of health protection.

---

16. *Asbestos* Appellate Body Report, ¶ 172.

VIII. Failing Two-Step Test and 2014 *China Rare Earths* Case

- **GATT Article XX(g) "Relating to" Conservation**[17]

In the 2014 *China Rare Earths* case, aside from the appellate issue of the relationship between the Chinese *Accession Protocol* and GATT-WTO rules, the second Chinese appeal concerned the Panel finding that Chinese export quotas on rare earths, tungsten, and molybdenum did not meet the "relating to" conservation requirement of GATT Article XX(g), and thus could not be justified. The Panel found that although the Chinese export quotas may "signal to the world its limited resources and conservation policy," they could also send a perverse signal to increase domestic consumption that could not be offset through its measures on domestic production caps or conservation policy.[18] In other words, China flunked Step One in the Two-Step Test for successful invocation of an Article XX defense.

On appeal, China claimed the Panel (1) mistakenly interpreted the "relating to" conservation requirement to mean a Panel can assess only whether the design and structure of the challenged measure is closely and genuinely related to its purported objective, and (2) erroneously focused on the design and structure of the measure to the detriment of other factors, such as market effects. Based on this faulty interpretation, the Panel failed to determine whether the "perverse signals" or risk of "perverse signals" was real. China also asserted the "contribution test" of GATT Article XX(a), (b), and (d) may be used to determine "whether there is a close and genuine relationship of ends and means between the measure at issue and the conservation objective."[19]

The Appellate Body rejected the Chinese points and upheld the Panel findings. The Appellate Body stated the Panel was not required to assess the effects of a disputed measure, although it was also not precluded from doing so. According to the Appellate Body, the Panel reasonably found, "as a matter of design and structure," the domestic production caps on rare earths and tungsten were not "capable of mitigating" the perverse signals generally sent out by export quotas to domestic consumers.[20]

Additionally, the Appellate Body pointed to previous findings that the distinctions between the connecting words "necessary" and "relating to" require different tests. "[M]ixing of the different tests under Article XX(b) and Article XX(g), absent of context, would result in an approach that ignores the important distinctions between the various subparagraphs of Article XX."[21] In other words, "neces-

---

17. This case is cited, and its facts summarized, in an earlier Chapter. *See China Rare Earths* Appellate Body Report, ¶¶ 5.75-5.118; 5.142-5.162.

18. *China Rare Earths* Appellate Body Report, ¶¶ 5.143, 5.149.

19. *China Rare Earths* Appellate Body Report, ¶ 5.105.

20. *China Rare Earths* Appellate Body Report, ¶¶ 5.157-5.159.

21. *China Rare Earths* Appellate Body Report, ¶ 5.115.

sary" under Paragraph (b) does not mean the same as "relating to" under Paragraph (g). That finding was obvious enough: to view the two as equivalent would violate a fundamental norm of treaty and statutory interpretation that words in a text must be given their meaning, and the drafters must have intended different meanings for different terms, unless they said so otherwise.

Inching toward one Chinese point, the Appellate Body agreed it is conceivable in some cases that addition of the Article XX(b) "contribution" test could help to decide whether a "close and genuine relationship" exists between the challenged measure and its purported conservation objective for the purposes of the Article XX(g) "relating to" test.

- **GATT Article XX(g) "Made Effective in Conjunction with" Domestic Restrictions**[22]

The third Chinese appeal concerned the finding Chinese export quotas on rare earths, tungsten, and molybdenum are not "made effective in conjunction with" domestic restrictions. Here again, China could not pass the first of the Steps in the Two-Step Test. Specifically, China asserted the Panel incorrectly interpreted GATT Article XX(g) and applied an extra "even-handedness" obligation that would require the burden of the domestic restriction and restriction on international trade to be balanced evenly between domestic and foreign producers and consumers. China also claimed the Panel incorrectly limited its analysis to the design and structure of the challenged export quotas.

In accordance with its 1996 *Reformulated Gasoline* opinion, the Appellate Body found "evenhandedness," in the context of Article XX(g), is not an additional obligation. It simply requires a challenged measure apply to both international trade and domestic production and consumption. The phrase "made effective in conjunction with" domestic restrictions requires the challenged measure be imposed on domestic producers and consumers in a "real" way, as opposed to "existing merely 'on the books,'" and the domestic restrictions must "reinforce and complement the restriction on international trade."[23] So, it would be hard to satisfy all Article XX(g) requirements if a measure is considerably more burdensome on foreign consumers or producers.

The Appellate Body also found the Panel did not error in focusing on the design and structure of the challenged measure, and noted again that an "effects test" is not required. The Appellate Body agreed with China the Panel erred to the extent it found (1) a separate "even-handedness" requirement and (2) the burden of conservation must be evenly distributed between domestic and foreign producers and consumers. But, these errors were inconsequential, as they did not affect the other elements under Article XX(g) and were not ultimately applied in the analysis by the Panel.

---

22. *See China Rare Earths* Appellate Body Report, ¶¶ 5.75-5.101; 5.119-5.141; 5.163-5.175.
23. *China Rare Earths* Appellate Body Report, ¶ 5.136.

IX. Products versus Processes

Is the way in which a product is made—the process and production method (PPM) a justifiable basis for an import restriction? Major jurisprudence under GATT Articles XX(b) and XX(g)—namely, the *Tuna Dolphin I* and *II*, *Reformulated Gasoline*, and *Turtle Shrimp* cases—suggest a negative response. None of these cases yields a prophylactic ruling against a particular PPM. The decision in the 1998 *Beef Hormones* case, however, and possibly the 2006 *GMO* decision too, suggest use of certain PPMs directly related to the product, and reflected in it, could support an import ban.

Is the difference between a product *per se*, and the way it is grown, raised, harvested, raised, or manufactured, a distinction about the appropriate level at which to regulate? A product embodying a scientifically demonstrable risk of harm is a legitimate target for an import restriction. To ensure protectionism with respect to that product is not afoot, GATT-WTO disciplines apply. But, neither GATT nor the WTO *SPS Agreement* is a document designed to deal with harmful production methods that apply to whole categories of merchandise, or that might cause systemic problems like global warming. Those methods are to be regulated through MEAs. What role does, and should, preservation of sovereignty play in the product—process distinction?

Chapter 28

Environmental Provisions in FTAs[1]

I. Six Metrics to Compare FTA Environmental Provisions

With nearly 20 FTAs in effect between America and foreign countries, and hundreds of other FTAs around the world to which America is not a party, including *CPTPP*, it is impracticable to pour through each one of them in detail in respect of their environmental provisions (or lack thereof). However, it is feasible to see, by way of overview, what the most salient environmental rules in U.S. FTAs look like. Toward that end, it is vital to appreciate there have been important shifts in American FTA policy on the environment, as there have been with respect to labor.

For example, environmental provisions moved in terms of placement, from a *Side Agreement* (*e.g., NAFTA*), to the core text of FTAs (starting with the 2001 *U.S-Jordan* FTA). That change is partly symbolic: a provision in the main body of a treaty may capture more attention (pleasing supporters), at least among politicians and the general public, than a provision buried in a side deal. The change also raises the legal question of the status of a provision in (1) a core text, (2) *Side Agreement*, or (3) *Side Letter*. Is the provision equally enforceable regardless of placement? Or, does its enforceability depend on whether Congress voted on the provision when approving the FTA—did it, for instance, approve all the *Side Letters* to an FTA when it passed the FTA?

Similarly, in respect of evolution, the focus of environmental provisions in America's FTAs has expanded from preventing a "race to the bottom" among the FTA Parties (*e.g.*, to attract FDI from MNCs) by mandating effective enforcement of existing rules (as under the *NAFTA Environmental Side Agreement*) to requiring, or at least encouraging, membership in one or more *Multilateral Environmental Agreements*. That is, starting in 2007, environmental provisions in America's FTAs become more rigorous than before, supplementing the typical minimum obligation with a duty to adhere to standards in *MEAs*. That change recognized the reality that in some countries, effective enforcement of existing domestic environmental protection measures is too low a benchmark, because those measures are paltry and parlous.

---

1. Documents References:
   (1) *NAFTA Environmental Side Agreement*
   (2) Environmental Chapters in other FTAs

So, environmental rules in America's FTAs have evolved over time, not unlike those concerning labor. In this respect, consider six questions:

(1) Does the FTA contain environmental provisions?

(2) In what place are the environmental provisions, namely, in a *Side Letter* or *Side Agreement* to the FTA, or the core text of the FTA?

(3) What are the key substantive obligations, and what are the pertinent additional duties, demanded?

(4) Is there a dispute resolution mechanism to handle alleged failures to meet these obligations?

(5) To what extent, if any, has the dispute resolution mechanism been used, and with what results?[2]

(6) To what extent, if any, are the provisions of one FTA the same as, similar to, or different from those of other FTAs, *i.e.*, to what extent does one FTA establish a template for others?

Consider these questions in relation to prominent FTAs to which America is not a Party, most notably, Chapter 20 of *CPTPP* and its *Side Letters*.

II. Case Study: 1994 *NAFTA Environmental Side Agreement*

• **Trade Promotion, Environmental Protection, and FTA Context**

It is a bland truism to say there is an increased understanding of a nexus between environmental law and international trade law. Certain environmental problems cannot be resolved by one country alone. Global warming, ozone depletion, pollution on contiguous borders, and protecting endangered species are obvious examples. Trade laws can affect the pattern of environmental protection. For example, the environment is less protected in a "pollution haven" country that aggressively encourages the growth of export industries. That kind of environmentally unfriendly trade regime does not lead to sustainable development, because it risks destroying the resource base on which trade occurs.

Likewise, FTAs arguably can facilitate environmental degradation. Consider mining for natural resources in Mexico. That activity causes environmental

---

2. As the discussion below makes clear, a persistent problem associated with America's FTAs is a lack of systematic monitoring and vigorous enforcement by both the U.S. and foreign countries that are Parties to an FTA with the U.S. That problem was caused by a decline in resources for collaborative activities. *See* U.S. Government Accountability Office, *Free Trade Agreements: Office of the U.S. Trade Representative Should Continue to Improve Its Monitoring of Environmental Commitments*, GAO-15-161 (6 November 2014), www.gao.gov.

contamination. As a developing country, how is Mexico to pay for the clean up? Does *NAFTA* help?

As another illustration, consider the development of tar sands in Alberta. Extraction of oil from them is carbon intensive, demands considerable water, and disrupts the ecology. Yet, a provision in *NAFTA* known as the "Proportionality Clause" requires Canada to reduce any petrochemical or gas product exports only if it also cuts its own energy consumption. Thus, the FTA rule may inhibit Canada from slowing tar sand development, assuming export demand continues or increases.

Thus, from a global systemic perspective, there is a legitimate concern environmental regulations may have a negative impact on trade. Such a regulation may be a disguised barrier to trade, and simply burden trade too much—"too much" as against the degree of environmental protection it affords. At the same time, it is not in the interests of the international trade community to see certain countries become pollution havens. Aside from long-term negative environmental damages wrought by such havens, in the short term they would enjoy huge comparative cost advantages. As yet, there is no WTO agreement on the environment. Thus, the tension between trade promotion and environmental protection plays out in FTA negotiations.

- **Background to *NAFTA Environmental Side Agreement***

As with labor, *NAFTA* deals with environmental issues—save for SPS through a side agreement. While post-*NAFTA* accords treat these matters in the core text of the agreement, the *NAFTA Side Agreements* are significant for three reasons. First, of U.S. FTAs, *NAFTA* itself is the commercial colossus. For the U.S., and most American states, the bulk of trade is conducted with Canada and Mexico. Second, as a consequence of the first reason, a labor or environmental dispute is especially likely to arise under *NAFTA*. While labor and environmental concerns exist in other FTA partners, the sheer transactional value and volume ensures disputes arise in these areas among the *NAFTA* Parties. Third, the *Side Agreements* established standards for the future. From these precedents, as it were, the U.S. developed and refined its negotiating stance on both the text and placement of labor and environmental provisions.

The *NAFTA Environmental Side Agreement* is formally titled the *North American Agreement on Environmental Cooperation (NAAEC)*. What concerns—or, better put, fears—motivated the *Side Agreement*? The U.S. believed:

(1) Mexican economic growth, stimulated by *NAFTA*, might give rise to ever-larger volumes of air pollution blowing north, and ever-larger volumes of raw sewage floating north.

(2) Lower trade restrictions achieved by *NAFTA* could lead to pesticide-laden Mexican vegetables being sold in the U.S.

(3) Some American companies might be attracted to Mexico because of its low environmental standards, and lax enforcement of these low standards,

translating into not only lower operating costs for the companies, but also a massive shift of jobs from the U.S. southward.

(4) Other companies in the U.S. would not be able to compete with Mexican companies that benefit from escaping from tough, expensive pollution standards, *i.e.*, they cannot match Mexican companies, which engage in "environmental dumping" — polluting Mexican plants that sell goods more cheaply than clean American plants, thereby driving high-cost "environmentally good" American production of business by low-cost "environmentally bad" Mexican production.

Mexico, too, had worries:

(1) The U.S. and Canada could, or would, not empathize with Mexico's plight as a developing country.

(2) The U.S. and Canada did not appreciate the huge disparities of income between Mexico, on the one hand, and themselves, on the other hand, and thus would not be tolerant toward Mexico's policy priorities, only one of which was addressing local pollution problems to prevent cross-border environmental degradation.

(3) The U.S. would cater to domestic environmental lobbies and use *NAFTA* to impose American environmental solutions on local Mexican problems, rather than allowing local pollution problems to be addressed locally.

America and Mexico addressed these matters not only through a Clinton Administration *Report on NAFTA Environmental Issues*, and *NAFTA* Chapter 7B, but also through the *Environmental Side Agreement*.

• **Seven Parts of *NAFTA Environmental Side Agreement***

What does the *NAFTA Environmental Side Agreement* say? It consists of seven parts with certain key provisions — and ambiguities:

Part One: Objectives
        (Article 1)

This Part sets out 10 broadly-worded aims, including "support [for] the environmental goals and objectives of the *NAFTA*." It is unclear what, precisely, the "goals and objectives" are.

Part Two: Obligations
        (Articles 2–7)

This Part contains general commitments, which include most notably (in Article 5:1), "each Party shall effectively enforce its environmental laws and regulations through appropriate governmental action . . .," with enforcement procedures to include remedies for violations, such as the cost of containing or cleaning up pollution, and private access to remedies (such as the right to seek an injunction to obey an environmental law, if the local law provides this right). What constitutes "effective enforcement" is not clear.

The general commitments also include assessing environmental impacts of *NAFTA*, promoting "education in environmental matters," using "economic instruments for the efficient achievement of environmental goals," considering the prohibition on exports of pesticides or toxic substances when one Party bans such substances, ensuring that laws provide for "high levels of environmental protection," and striving "to continue to improve those laws." Again, several key terms are left undefined.

Part Three: Commission for Environmental Cooperation (CEC) (Articles 8–19)

This Part establishes the CEC to "strengthen cooperation on the development and continuing improvement of environmental laws and regulations . . . ." A Council governs the CEC. The Council operates by consensus, which effectively means unanimity. The exception is a decision (for which it is responsible) to establish an arbitral panel. That decision may be made by a two-thirds vote. The Council consists of cabinet-level environmental ministers from the *NAFTA* Parties, which cooperates with the *NAFTA* FTC and is assisted by a Joint Public Advisory Committee of five members from each of the Parties, and which has a Secretariat led by an Executive Director. Day to day work of the CEC is conducted by a Secretariat, which is headed by an Executive Director.

Part Four: Cooperation and Provision of Information (Articles 20–21)

This Part commits the *NAFTA* Parties to cooperate on environmental matters, including the sharing of information (when not prohibited by local law).

Part Five: Consultation and Resolution of Disputes (Articles 22–36)

This Part, the longest of the *Side Agreement*, concerns dispute resolution. It authorizes the CEC Council to convene an arbitral panel to consider an allegation from a *NAFTA* Party that another Party is not effectively enforcing its environmental laws. The Council may convene a panel, but only after the issue in question is not resolved pursuant to an investigation by the Council. The Council chooses the panel from a roster of persons expertise and experience.

A "persistent pattern" exists if there is "sustained or recurring course of action or inaction." Part Five does not explain how an arbitral panel should ascertain whether a "persistent pattern" exists. For instance, submissions to arbitral panels under the *Environmental*, as well as *Labor, Side Agreement* are strictly government-to-government. Private parties are not directly involved. It is unclear whether a panel may entertain *amicus curiae* briefs, though a panel may—if the disputing Parties agree—seek advice from outside experts. The Panel cannot decide there has been ineffective enforcement (*i.e.*, the Party complained against has as a defense) if the respondent Party (1) engaged in a "reasonable exercise" of its investigatory, prosecutorial, or regulatory discretion, suggesting that nothing in the *Side Agreement* strips a Party of its discretion, or (2) made a *bona fide* decision to allocate resources to enforce higher priority environmental matters, indicating nothing in the *Side Agreement* commits a *NAFTA* party to increase agency enforcement budgets.

Four limits exist on the subject matter jurisdiction of an arbitral panel. First, if the issue is the subject of domestic adjudication, then it cannot come before the CEC—and thus an arbitral panel. Preclusion provides some protection against parallel proceedings. Second, the alleged failure to enforce environmental laws must relate to goods traded in North America. Third, "environmental law" is defined narrowly to mean only rules whose "primary purpose" concerns the conditions for harvesting natural resources. Query whether laws affecting coastal fishing, energy extraction, strip mining, and timber harvesting fit within this definition. Fourth, laws concerning wildlife outside the territory of a party are not subject to review. There is no extraterritoriality beyond *NAFTA* Parties. So, the controversial American bans on tuna caught using the purse-seine method, or on shrimp obtained without turtle excluder devices would not be subject to review under the *Side Agreement* if the underlying facts transpired outside of American, Canadian, and Mexican waters.

An arbitral Panel must issue a written report. The disputing Parties—but not the public—get the opportunity to comment on the draft report. If the panel finds in the affirmative, then it may propose an "action plan" to rectify the persistent pattern. Specifically, if the Panel finds the respondent Party is engaged in a persistent pattern of ineffectively enforcing its environmental laws (and has not reasonably exercised discretion or allocated a funds to a higher budget priority), then the disputing Parties try to agree upon a plan. This plan has the advantages of (1) providing an objective way to measure enforcement, (2) serving as an excuse for an environmental agency in a Party to argue that it needs a larger enforcement budget, and (3) embarrassing a *NAFTA* Party into mending its ways. Interestingly, the action plan was the idea of environmental groups, not the USTR. These groups supported it because they felt Mexico lacked the infrastructure needed to enforce its laws. In that context, Mexico needed plans, not financial penalties.

Suppose the prevailing *NAFTA* Party feels the losing Party is not implementing the action plan? Then, it may reconvene the panel, and if the panel agrees, then the panel must impose a "monetary enforcement assessment." In effect, the assessment is a fine, the amount of which the panel has broad discretion to set, and which is paid to the CEC for use in improving the environment or enforcement of environmental law. What if, despite the fine, the losing Party still does not implement the action plan? Continued failure to implement the action plan empowers the prevailing Party, with panel approval, to increase tariffs up to the amount of the fine on goods from the violating Party. The tariff increase is a trade sanction designed to collect an unpaid fine. Notably, this scenario applies only if the violator is the U.S. or Mexico. Canada negotiated an exemption from being targeted for trade sanctions, because it committed to treating a panel decision an "order of the court."

Throughout the process, strict deadlines apply. For example, an arbitral panel must render a written opinion as to whether a "persistent pattern" of failure to enforce effectively "environmental law" exists. The panel has 180 days after formation to prepare a draft report. The Panel's final report must be issued within 60 days of the initial report. If the disputing Parties cannot agree on an action plan within 60 days, then the Panel is reconvened, and within 90 days the panel proposes a plan. If the Panel decides that the defendant Party is not implementing the Action Plan, then the Panel must impose a fine within 60 days.

Still, the total time for completion (from complaint to trade sanction) is a minimum of 755 days. Observe this figure—about two years—is only marginally swifter than under the *Labor Side Agreement*. In sharp contrast to both *Side Agreement* dispute resolution timeframes, the regular *NAFTA* Chapter 19 dispute settlement process is 240 days.

Part Six: General Provisions
(Articles 37–45)

This Part contains general provisions and definitions.

Part Seven: Final Provisions
(Articles 46–51)

This Part contains final provisions typical of an international agreement, dealing with entry into force, amendments, accession, withdrawal, and authentic texts.

Following these Parts are several annexes. Two of them pertain specifically to Canada. Annex 36A, on Canadian Domestic Enforcement and Collection, contains the trade sanction exemption (noted above), and explains that a panel decision "shall become an order of the [*i.e.*, treated as if it were issued by a Canadian] court." Annex 41 states that *Environmental Side Agreement* obligations apply only to matters under Canadian federal jurisdiction, and not to matters within the jurisdiction of a Canadian province.

• **Success?**

Is the *NAFTA Environmental Side Agreement* a "success"? To be sure, it is positive for the *Environmental Side Agreement* to establish a lofty commitment, namely, each *NAFTA* party shall ensure that its laws provide for "high levels" of environmental protection and strive to continue to improve those levels. The central enforcement obligation—enforcing existing environmental laws—also is noteworthy. It is significant the *Agreement* requires each *NAFTA* Party provide procedural guarantees in its administrative, quasi-judicial, and judicial systems, and that eschew proceedings that are unnecessarily complicated or unreasonably delayed (problems plaguing some American proceedings). No less important is the effort of the Parties to give arbitral decisions "teeth" by subjecting recalcitrant respondents to fines and trade retaliation.

Notwithstanding these advantages, there are weighty reasons to believe the *NAFTA Environmental Side Agreement* is not a "success." Professor Steve Charnovitz writes:

> First, the NAAEC enforcement procedures only apply to domestic laws and therefore do not apply to international obligations that are not self-executing as domestic law. Thus, the one substantive obligation in the NAAEC, to provide for "high levels" of environmental protection is not subject to dispute settlement under the NAAEC or the *NAFTA*.

> Second, neither the NAAEC Secretariat nor the dispute panels have subpoena power. . . .

> Whether the absence of subpoena power impedes the panels will depend on whether they search for patterns of inadequate enforcement in the practices of regulatory agencies or in actual pollution levels. Whether the panel will be able to compel governments to provide information from regulatory agencies is unclear. The lack of subpoena power may prove to be a significant constraint on actual pollution level information if governments are not forthcoming with information.

> Third, the NAAEC relies exclusively on *ad hoc* panels. In contrast, the European Community has an on-going Court that develops case law for Community-wide rules. Over time, this Court has developed useful environmental norms, but whether useful norms will emerge from the NAAEC's narrow procedures remains to be seen.[3]

This critique is worth pondering. On the first point, of what value is a commitment regarding "high levels" of environmental protection that is vague? To supplement the first and second points, might it be argued that the focus on environmental enforcement, however sloppy that enforcement may be in practice, has diminished efforts toward making specific policy commitments? If a *NAFTA* Party need only enforce the laws existing on its books, then the recipe is for a "stand still," not progress. That is, the *Side Agreement* has a retrogressive focus, namely, the domestic standards of each *NAFTA* Party. Turning to the third point, is the emphasis in the *Side Agreement* on domestic standards in an international agreement is inappropriate. Perhaps the parochial laws of a country may be inadequate for the country's own environmental needs, as well as for the rest of North America. If those laws are inadequate, then enforcement of them does not matter.

---

3. Steve Charnovitz, *The NAFTA Environmental Side Agreement: Implications for Environmental Cooperation, Trade Policy, and American Treaty Making*, 8 TEMPLE INTERNATIONAL AND COMPARATIVE LAW JOURNAL 257, 260–283 (1994).

A number of additional critical points indicate the *NAFTA Environmental Side Agreement* is flawed. For instance:

(1) Independence of the CEC?

To what extent is the CEC truly independent of the governments of the *NAFTA* Parties? Arguably, it is semi-independent at best. The Council governing the CEC consists of senior cabinet officials, thus ensuring top-level representation of the Parties. But, if its members served fixed terms, and were not answerable to their home country governments, then its independence would be enhanced. Moreover, the CEC is not financially self-sustaining. It has no fiscal powers to raise revenue. Instead, it must submit its annual program and budget to the Council for approval.

(2) Private Enforcement?

Does the *Environmental Side Agreement* create a meaningful private right of action? Arguably, the answer is "no." Private parties must work through the relevant governmental trade bureaucracies. Thus, private parties must go through the USTR. Further, the CEC Secretariat has broad discretion to disregard any submission it considers aimed at "harassing industry" rather than promoting enforcement. Finally, even where a case is brought, complaints are against a *NAFTA* Party for failing to enforce effectively its environmental laws. That is, claims are not made against individual companies for despoiling the environment. Yet, as a practical matter, private companies often are culprits.

(3) Too Slow?

Before a complaint is heard by an arbitral panel, indeed, before a panel even is formed, the CEC Secretariat must review that complaint for appropriateness. The Secretariat issues a recommendation as to whether it believes a factual record should be developed in the case. If so, then the Secretariat prepares it. But, the record does not set forth conclusions or recommendations. This process considerably delays actual consideration of complaints.

Moreover, the CEC Secretariat finding is not binding on the *NAFTA* Party at issue. For instance, in November 2013, the Secretariat recommended investigation of the refusal by Canada to protect polar bears under the Canadian *Species At Risk Act*. Canada itself, along with Mexico, opposed the investigation (which the U.S. favored). So, the expert Secretariat staff calling for Canada to be investigated for failure to comply with its own laws was ignored, and in June 2014, the process was terminated.

(4) Flaws in the System Design?

Questions about sovereignty, defenses, and remedies cast doubt on the design of the dispute resolution system. On sovereignty, is it more difficult for an international arbitral panel to determine whether a government is complying with its own law than for a court in the defendant country to determine whether a government is complying with its own law (assuming the judiciary is independent)? If the answer is "yes," then why not focus efforts on upgrading the domestic enforcement procedures in each *NAFTA* Party? Would it be less intrusive on the sovereignty of each Party to agree on a set of regional environmental standards for panels to enforce, rather than charge panels with the responsibility of deciding cases about local law?

As to defenses, are justifications of "reasonable discretion" and "higher budget priority environmental enforcement matter" so broad it is hard to hold a respondent Party guilty of a persistent pattern of ineffective enforcement? Concerning remedies, are trade sanctions, if imposed, a useful tool, given they harm consumers in the prevailing Party by raising prices (by the amount of the punitive tariff) on imports from the losing Party? While spending proceeds of a fine on environmental improvement rehabilitates the environment, is there a deterrent value to paying a fine to the CEC? Is the process too protracted?

(5) Harmonization and Trade Barriers?

Consider whether environmental standards are disguised barriers to trade. Should environmental laws be harmonized so the U.S., Canada, and Mexico deal with the same standards? The trans-boundary reality of pollution counsels an affirmative answer. Yet, many American environmentalists oppose harmonization. They view American laws to be so far ahead of all other countries that harmonization would mean diminution for the U.S. Moreover, harmonization is not thorough even within each *NAFTA* Party. For example, American environmental laws are not harmonized themselves. As California vehicle emission standards illustrate, assuming there is no pre-emptive federal regulation, some state laws may be stricter than others.

Of course, *NAFTA* does not require harmonization of either environmental or labor laws. If it did, would the resulting regime provide better insurance against the abuse of such laws for protectionist purposes? Observe *NAFTA* Chapter 9 concerns TBTs. This Chapter provides that if a law has a "legitimate environmental purpose"—*i.e.*, protection of the environment—then an arbitral panel cannot overturn it. Only a showing that the law is a disguised barrier to trade will result in an adverse decision. Under what conditions may a panel overturn an SPS measure? The criterion is not proof the measure has "no legitimate purpose." That test is too high in this context, and *NAFTA* leaves each Party free to decide and choose, based on a scientific method, its own risk levels. Observe, in the SPS context, penalties for an offending measure are fines of U.S. $20 million, or trade sanctions, but not striking down the measure.

The Center for International Environmental Law showed in a 2015 study that 87 petitions had been filed with the CEC, but in only 22 of them did the cases advance to the stage of the development of a factual record—and that took an average of 5 years.[4] No case led to an arbitration, much less sanctions. This underwhelming

---

4. Center for International Environmental Law, The Trans-Pacific Partnership and the Environment: An Assessment of Commitments and Trade Agreement Enforcement 6–7 (November 2015),

outcome reflects the problems of only allowing governments to arbitrate, instead of private parties and an overall lack of enthusiasm by all three government Parties. Thus, "[t]he majority of cases brought and resolved before the CEC were closed without the development of a factual record, usually on the grounds that the issues are already being dealt with by the national authorities or that the procedural requirements of the NAAEC have not been met."[5]

III. Case Study: Contrasting Environmental Dispute Settlement under 2005 *Singapore FTA*, 2005 *CAFTA-DR*, and 2009 *Peru TPA*

The environmental dispute settlement mechanisms in *NAFTA*, the *Singapore FTA*, *CAFTA-DR*, and *Peru TPA* differ from each another, and each is intricate. The steps under the *NAFTA Environmental Side Agreement* are laid out above. Conceptually, what distinguishes the mechanisms of the other accords? Practically, what do the distinctions mean?

The following points help differentiate the *Singapore FTA* and *CAFTA-DR* mechanisms:

(1) With respect to the *Singapore FTA*, there are six basic steps, as follows:

Step 1: *Consultation under the Environmental Chapter (Article 18:7)*

A Party may request direct consultations with another Party regarding any matter arising under the Environmental Chapter.

Step 2: *Recourse to Sub-Committee under the Environmental Chapter (Article 18:7(3))*

If direct bilateral consultations fail to resolve the issue between the Parties, then either Party may refer the case to a Sub-Committee. The Sub-Committee must work to resolve the issue promptly.

Step 3: *Consultation under the General Dispute Settlement Chapter (Article 20:3(1))*

If the complaint involves failure by a Party to enforce effectively its environmental laws, then a Party may request consultations under the general dispute settlement Chapter of the FTA. This request may be for direct talks with the other Party directly.

---

www.ciel.org/wp-content/uploads/2015/11/TPP-Enforcement-Analysis-Nov2015.pdf.

5. David A. Gantz, *Labor Rights and Environmental Protection under NAFTA and Other U.S. Free Trade Agreements*, 42 University Miami Inter-American Law Review 297, 312 (2011). [Hereinafter, Gantz, *Labor Rights*.]

Step 4: *Referral to the Joint Committee*
(Article 20:3(2))

> If direct consultations between disputing Parties under the general dispute settlement Chapter fail, then the matter may be referred to a Joint Committee. The Joint Committee has 60 days to resolve the dispute, after which the complaining Party may refer the matter to a dispute settlement Panel.

Step 5: *Referral to Dispute Settlement Panel*
(Article 20:3(4))

> A dispute settlement Panel is comprised of three panelists, one chosen by each of the disputing parties and the third panelist chosen by mutual agreement. The Panel has 150 days to issue an initial Report of its findings to both Parties. After the initial Report, the Panel has 45 days to give the Parties its final Report.

Step 6: *Implementation*
(Article 20:5)

> Once the Parties receive the final Report of the Panel, they are to agree on a resolution of the dispute. If the Panel determined that the Party complained against failed to enforce effectively its environmental laws and obligations, then the resolution must be to eliminate any non-conformity or impairment of enforcement.

(2) With respect to *CAFTA-DR*, there are seven basic steps, as follows:

Step 1: *Submissions on Matters Concerning Effective Enforcement of Environmental Laws*
(Article 17:7-8)

> Any person (*i.e.*, individual or enterprise), except a person of the U.S. complaining against the U.S., may file a "submission" with the Secretariat, claiming another Party is failing to enforce effectively its environmental laws. (A person of the U.S. must use the *NAFTA Environmental Side Agreement* to lodge a complaint against the U.S.)

> The Secretariat has discretion to determine whether to ask the Party complained against for a response to the submission. The Secretariat also may develop a factual record, if it feels it necessary to do so from the submission and any response provided by the Party complained against.

> The Environmental Affairs Council (EAC) also can demand the Secretariat prepare a factual record for a submission. The EAC may vote to make any factual records public after the Parties receive those records. The EAC must provide recommendations to the Environmental Cooperation Commission (ECC) (a body consisting of representatives from the *CAFTA-DR* Parties) about the factual record and mechanisms for the Party complained against to

enforce its environmental rules. Note that environmental provisions in other free trade pacts modeled on *CAFTA-DR*, such as the *Panama FTA*, establish ECCs.

Should the Party still fail in its obligations, the person providing the initial submission has no further direct recourse against that Party. Any further action must be brought by a sovereign Party, such as the government of that person. In other words, Step 1 is not a waiver of sovereign immunity by the *CAFTA-DR* government to be sued by private parties on environmental matters.

Step 2: *Consultations under the Environmental Chapter (Article 17:10)*

Any Party may request direct consultations with another Party as to any matter arising under this Chapter.

Step 3: *Recourse to EAC under the Environmental Chapter (Article 17:10)*

If the direct consultations fail to resolve the issue, a Party may request the matter be referred to the EAC.

Step 4: *Consultation under the General Dispute Settlement Chapter (Article 20:4 & 20:5)*

If the issue in dispute involves a failure by a Party to enforce effectively its environmental laws and obligations, a Party may refer the dispute to direct consultations under the general dispute settlement Chapter of the FTA. A Party can skip this Step of the process, and move directly to requesting referral of the matter to the Commission (which supervises all of *CAFTA-DR*), if consultations already occurred under the Environmental Chapter and were unsuccessful.

Step 5: *Referral to the Commission (Article 20:5)*

If direct consultations fail to resolve the issue, then a Party may request that the issue be referred to the Commission, which will consist of Cabinet-level representatives of the consulting Parties. The Commission shall convene with ten days of receiving the request from a Party and work to promptly resolve the issue.

Step 6: *Referral to Arbitration (Article 20:6)*

If the Parties fail to resolve the issue within 30 days of convening the Commission, or 75 days if the Commission has not convened, a Party may request the matter be referred to a dispute settlement Panel. The Panel must consist of three Panelists, one chosen by each Party, and the third mutually agreed upon by both Parties. The Panel must issue its initial report within 120 days, but no later than 180 days, after the last Panelist is selected, and must present its final Report to the Parties within 45 days of the initial Report.

Step 7: *Implementation*
(Article 20:15)

Once the Parties receive the final Report of the Panel, they are to agree on a resolution of the dispute. If the Panel determined that the Party complained against failed to enforce effectively its environmental laws and obligations, then the resolution must be to eliminate any non-conformity or impairment of enforcement.

(3) Comparing the procedures in the respective accords, Step 1 in *CAFTA-DR* (Submissions on Matters about Effective Enforcement) is a feature not in the *Singapore FTA*. This Step gives private parties the right to bring an environmental matter to the attention of a government. Thus, a Submission is an outlet for an individual or organization to complain a government is not enforcing effectively its existing environmental rules. That may resolve the matter, or at least draw public attention to environmental issues and lack of enforcement by one Party.

But, as intimated, the willingness of the *CAFTA-DR* Parties to accept private party submissions does not constitute consent to be sued by an individual or organization on environmental enforcement. This lack of a waiver of sovereign immunity, which contrast with that waiver in investor-state dispute settlement in the context of FDI, indicates *CAFTA-DR* Parties may not be as serious about the environment as about FDI.[6]

What do these procedural distinctions mean in practice? The answer is "not much," if the goal is to facilitate complaints and adjudications on environmental matters. Both procedural mechanisms are rather tortuous. Neither makes it easy to prosecute environmental cases. Offering direct consultations under the Environmental and General Dispute Settlement Chapters is helpful on paper, yet in practice may be redundant.

Suppose a Party follows the steps in the *Singapore FTA*, and initial direct consultations under the Environmental Chapter are unsuccessful. Why would that Party believe further direct consultations under the General Dispute Settlement Chapter will be successful? For example, if Singapore believes the U.S. fails to enforce effectively its environmental laws and obligations, then would Singapore find using the Environmental Chapter consultations a waste of time and money? Would it instead skip to Step 3 of the process, namely, consultations under the General Dispute Settlement Chapter? Might an answer be that the possibility of two levels of consultations avoids automatically forcing a matter to the most serious, and possibly

---

6. Bradley N. Lewis, *Biting Without Teeth: The Citizen Submission Process and Environmental Protection*, 155 UNIVERSITY OF PENNSYLVANIA LAW REVIEW 1229, 1242 (2007). [Hereinafter, *Biting*.]

most politicized, level? That is, the first level can be one for amicable, technical discussions?

Finally, as to the *Peru TPA*, it has four distinguishing features:

(1) It is the first American trade agreement to subject environmental requirements to the same dispute settlement procedures and sanctions as commercial obligations.

(2) It contains specific provisions on forest sector governance, set out in the Annex on Forest Sector Governance (specifically, 18:3:4, also called the "Timber Annex"), which is part of the Environment Chapter. In February 2017, Peru published Legislative Decree 1319, which centralized the collection of data on forest matters, particularly deforestation, under a National System of Control and Surveillance on Forest and Wildlife, and distribution of those data on a real-time basis to sub-central governments. The new System linked directly to the battle against climate change. Between 2001–2015, Peru lost 4.4 million acres of forest, and though the country was responsible for just 0.3% to total global greenhouse gas emissions, 40% of that contribution was due to deforestation. Monitoring deforestation was the key step in slowing it and, in turn, those emissions.

(3) It emphasizes—indeed, Article 18:2 expressly mentions—*MEAs*. No other American FTA before the *Peru TPA* mentions *MEAs* as exhaustively, or with such emphasis, nor does *KORUS*, which follows after the *TPA*. Only Colombia and Panama give *MEAs* the same prominence as the *Peru TPA*. The *Peru TPA* obliges the United States and Peru to cooperate on the sustainable management of species protected by the *Convention on International Trade in Endangered Species of Wild Fauna and Flora* (*CITES*), such as bigleaf mahogany and Spanish cedar trees.

(4) It contains provisions to combat illegal logging. One such provision mandates that the Peruvian government body responsible for regulating logging be an independent agency. In January 2019, the USTR triggered the dispute settlement provisions of the *TPA*, arguing against a December 2018 decision by Peru to fold this agency (*Organismo de Supervisión de los Recursos Forestales y de Fauna Silvestre*, or *OSINFOR*) into its Ministry of the Environment. Bilateral consultations followed, and Peru's Environmental Affairs Council considered the USTR's argument that putting the agency under the Ministry would compromise its ability to enforce effectively Peru's laws against illegal harvesting of forests and exportation of logs. In April 2019, Peru revoked the decision, thus scoring a victory under the *TPA* dispute settlement rules in favor of for environmentally-friendly forest management.

Thus, the *Peru TPA* is a watershed. It occurred in part because of the May 2007 BTD (discussed below and in a separate Chapter). Congress pressured the USTR to spotlight *MEAs* in new trade deals, starting with the *Peru* accord.

The BTD covers five areas: environment; labor; IP; FDI; government procurement; and port security.[7] However, the most significant changes relate to labor and environmental provisions. Specifically, thanks to the BTD, environmental violations under the *Peru TPA* are subject to trade sanctions, whereas in previous FTAs they are subject only to monetary assessments. That appears to be an improvement in enforcement of environmental protection and obligations, *i.e.*, the Parties seem to have focused more on serious enforcement in the *Peru TPA* than preceding FTAs. Whether this improvement remains part of the structure of future FTAs is unclear. After all, focusing on trade sanctions and dispute settlement, rather than on cutting tariff and non-tariff barriers, could be counterproductive to promoting free trade and cooperation among Parties.

The *Peru TPA* not only lists *MEAs*, but also allows a Party to seek dispute settlement procedures under the *TPA* for failure to enforce a listed *MEA*. It gives the U.S. and Peru the discretion to emphasize compliance with an *MEA* over a *TPA* obligation in order to avoid a dispute. To be sure, the *TPA* does not specify an *MEA* trumps a *TPA* obligation. Still, might that be a harbinger of a "race to the top"?

All this is not to say the *Peru TPA* is an environmentalist's dream. The *TPA* does not recognize any outlet for citizen complaints, unlike the preceding *CAFTA-DR*. Professor David Gantz identifies the primary focus of the *TPA* as "assuring the existence of binding dispute settlement and trade sanctions for enforcing environmental violations," and argues that focus is misplaced.[8] Binding dispute settlement language is not necessarily the key to enforcing environmental provisions. That is because the history of those dispute settlement procedures in American FTAs shows they are rarely used. So, a more efficacious mechanism may be a dedicated outlet for citizen complaints, insofar as it would mobilize public attention and create political pressure to address alleged environmental violations.[9]

IV. Case Study: 2012 *KORUS* *Environmental Chapter*

· **Background to *KORUS Environmental Chapter***

As with labor, *KORUS* deals with environmental issues in its core text. These environmental provisions are important for at least three reasons.

First, they reflect the maturity of Korea. After the suffering the devastation of the 1950–1953 Korean War, and experiencing hard-earned growth as an Asian

---

7. David Gants, *Regional Trade Agreements: Law, Policy and Practice* 97–98 (Durham, North Carolina: Carolina Academic Press, 2009).

8. David Gantz, Regional Trade Agreements: Law, Policy and Practice 99–100 (Durham, North Carolina: Carolina Academic Press, 2009). [Hereinafter, Gantz, Regional Trade Agreements.]

9. *Biting*, 1264–1265.

Tiger in the 1960s through 1990s, Korea firmly established itself as a modern, developed country. With that status, if not before it, came recognition within Korea of the need to pay attention to the environmental effects of economic progress. The stimuli also were exogenous: air pollution drifting from Chinese factories into the Korean atmosphere; and the threat of another war, this time one with WMDs with the North. Ironically, remaining largely undeveloped since 1953, the perilous DMZ is a remarkably pristine environmental sanctuary for flora and fauna, as few humans tread there.

Second, Korea is the seventh largest goods trading partner of the U.S.[10] This general prominence of Korea casts a halo over the environmental provisions: they get attention because Korea is so significant economically. To be sure, just because a trading partner is large does not mean it will generate a concomitantly large number of environmental cases. Many of the most serious environmental problems are in small, poor countries. The point, rather, is public awareness associated with size.

Third, the environmental provisions of *KORUS* are a model (or ante-model) for the rest of the Asia-Pacific region. The FTA itself was the first one between the U.S. and a North Asian country, and had obvious national security benefits to both parties. But, those benefits did not distract them from environmental protection.

- **Seven Parts of *KORUS Environmental Chapter***

What, then, does the *KORUS FTA Environmental Chapter* say? As follows, it consists of seven parts with certain key environmental provisions—and ambiguities. A review of these provisions, especially those emphasizing *MEAs*, suggests *KORUS* continues in the line from *NAFTA* through the Peru *TPA*.

Part One: Objectives
        (Article 20:1)

This Part acknowledges the ability of each Party to regulate its own environmental policy. This Part also sets out broadly-worded goals, including "encourag[ing] high levels of environmental protection," and "striv[ing] to continue to improve . . . respective levels of environmental protection."[11] It is unclear what, precisely, a "high level" of protection is, or how a Party may improve its current protection of the environment to meet the "high level" standard.

Part Two: Obligations
        (Articles 20:2–20:5)

This Part contains general commitments. Most notably, Article 20:3(1)(a) is the familiar "effective enforcement of existing laws" rule: "neither Party shall fail to effectively enforce its environmental laws, and its laws, regulations, and other

---

10. "Fact Sheet of Economic Value," www.whitehouse.gov/sites/default/files/fact_sheet
_economic_value_us_korea_free_trade_agreement.pdf (using 2010 statistics).

11. *KORUS* Chapter 20:1: Levels of Protection.

measures to fulfill its obligations under the covered agreements."[12] Article 20:3(2) adds the "no race to the bottom" undertaking, *i.e.*, it is "inappropriate to encourage trade or investment by weakening or reducing the protections afforded in its environmental laws," and assures appropriate and effective remedies for violations.

What does the Article 20:3(1)(a) language, "through a sustained or recurring course of action or inaction, in a manner effecting trade or investment," mean? An isolated incident of noncompliance is not subject to dispute resolution; rather, there must be a recurring issue, and only recurring issues of noncompliance that effect trade or investment may be disciplined. While Article 20:11 defines "covered agreements" what constitutes "effective enforcement" is not clear.

The general commitments also include encouraging voluntary and incentive-based programs to increase levels of environmental protection, sharing information among authorities, and using (under Article 20:5(1)) "market-based incentives where appropriate, to encourage conservation, restoration, and protection of natural resources and the environment." There also is a procedural fairness guarantee within these general commitments. Again, several key terms are left undefined.

Part Three: Environmental Affairs Council and Opportunities for Public Participation (Article 20:6–7)

This Part establishes the Environmental Affairs Council (EAC) to oversee the implementation of the Environmental Chapter, and to "promote public participation in its work, . . . by seeking advice from the public in developing agendas for Council meetings and by engaging in a dialogue with the public on environmental issues of interest to the public."[13] The Council is comprised of senior officials from each Party, including those with environmental responsibilities.

Each Party also must promote public awareness of its environmental laws. To do so, under Article 20:7(3), each "Party shall convene a new, or consult an existing, national advisory committee," and the EAC must consider the views each Party receives from its national advisory committee about implementation of Chapter 20.

Such provisions are designed to ensure all stakeholders have the opportunity to make written submissions to the American and Korean governments. They can request information, and express their views, on whether the governments are implementing fully the Chapter 20 provisions. The governments are obliged to provide responses.

Part Four: Cooperation (Article 20:8)

This Part commits the *KORUS* Parties to cooperate on environmental matters arising under Chapter 20, and in respect of provisions in the *Agreement between the*

---

12. *KORUS* Chapter 20:3(1)(a): Application and Enforcement of Environmental Laws.
13. *KORUS* Chapter 20:6(3): Environmental Affairs Council.

Government of the United States of America and the Government of the Republic of Korea on Environmental Cooperation (ECA). Cooperation under Chapter 20 requires the Parties to share with each other and the public, as appropriate, information on the positive and negative effects of trade and trade agreements on the environment.

Part Five: Environmental Consultations and Panel Procedure
(Article 20:9)

This Part concerns dispute resolution. It authorizes each Party to seek direct consultations if one Party feels the other fails to enforce effectively its environmental laws. It also authorizes the Council to convene to hear a complaint from one Party that the other Party is not enforcing effectively its environmental laws.

The Parties must make every attempt to find a mutually satisfactory solution by working through direct consultations with one another under Chapter 20. The Council may be convened, but only after resolution between the Parties directly fails. If, after 60 days after the initial request for direct consultations under this Chapter, the issue still is unresolved, then the complaining Party may resort to other methods of dispute settlement located within the FTA, such as Article 22:7 (Consultations), Article 22:8 (Referral to the Joint Committee) or other Chapter 22 mechanisms (Dispute Settlement). But, neither Party may avail itself of the Chapter 22 Dispute Settlement provisions without first exhausting all consultative and EAC procedures under Article 20:9 for resolution of the issue.

If a dispute between the Parties arises under Article 20:2, specifically enforcement by a Party of its environmental laws, or is an issue under both that and another Article in Chapter 20, then a Dispute Settlement Panel may be convened. In rendering the final determination on the issue, the Panel must consult any entity authorized to address the issue under the relevant agreement. If guidance on the issue exists, then the Panel must defer to it, and if there is more than one interpretation of the issue, then the Panel must accept the interpretation relied on by a complaining party.

A Panel must follow the rules of procedure contained in Chapter 22 for Dispute Settlement, and resolution of an environmental dispute is subject to all other rules found in that Chapter as well.

Part Six: Relation to MEAs
(Article 20:10)

In this Part, the Parties recognize the listed *MEAs*. The Parties must seek to continue to support one another in *MEAs* of which they are both members. They also must consult one another with respect to negotiations on environmental issues of mutual interest.

Part Seven: General Provisions
(Article 20:11)

This Part contains general provisions and definitions.

Following these Parts is an Annex, which describes all of the covered agreements mentioned throughout the Chapter.

- **Synopsis**

The resolution process for disputes arising under environmental provisions of FTAs to which the U.S. is a Party has evolved, as have many features of American FTAs. Unlike *NAFTA*, *KORUS* does away with the Secretariat and requirement that environmental issues be submitted to the Secretariat under the NAAEC before a Panel may be convened. *KORUS* requires only that the Parties directly consult each other. If the Parties cannot resolve the matter between themselves, then they may request the EAC be convened, and it must work to resolve the matter quickly.

Environmental matters also can be subject to dispute resolution procedures governing the FTA. Making environmental disputes subject to these general mechanisms was an important development in American FTAs, beginning with the *Jordan FTA*, and continuing through *KORUS*.[8] That is, for all post-*Jordan* FTAs, the ability to access the general dispute settlement procedure in environmental cases effectively "mainstreams" such cases with traditional trade disputes, and distinguishes them from *NAFTA*.

But, is the result faster dispute resolution? Apparently, no. That is because typically it is not possible to access the general mechanism without exhausting the procedures specific to the environmental chapter (such as *KORUS* Chapter 20). A cynic might say sequencing of mechanisms actually slows the cause of environmental justice.

- **Success?**

KORUS was implemented in March 2012. Already from the relatively short life of *KORUS*, it is evident that the success of the environmental provisions depends largely on the actions of the American and Korean governments. As Professor David Gantz writes:

> if—and this is an enormous "if"—the United States complies with the . . . environmental FTA provisions, and provides adequate funding and technical support to its developing country partners, the other Parties may ultimately regard compliance with environmental . . . obligations as important as compliance with trade obligations under the agreements.[14]

If the Parties do not dedicate and properly allocate sufficient resources to support their environment obligations, then *KORUS* will be of paper significance, and the DMZ may end up as one of the areas in the two countries more environmentally friendly to non-human species.

---

14. Gantz, *Labor Rights*, 297–366.

V. May 2007 Bipartisan Trade Deal and Expansion of *NAFTA*

The BTD set new criteria for future *FTA* environmental rules the U.S. negotiates with other countries. The BTD requires the environmental chapter of any new FTA to include a specific list of *MEAs*, and subjects all FTA environmental obligations to the same enforcement rules as all commercial provisions of the agreements:[15]

> The May 2007 BTD was negotiated by U.S. Trade Representative Susan Schwab and the Congressional and Senate leadership for the principal purpose of obtaining the support of the Democratically controlled Congress and Senate for the four then-pending FTAs, particularly for the three with the Latin American nations of Peru, Colombia and Panama, although the results applied to the *KORUS* FTA as well.[16]

So, *KORUS* includes a comprehensive list of *MEAs*, which *NAFTA* lacks.

If a dispute arises between environmental obligations a Party owes, on the one hand, under *KORUS* and, on the other hand, a covered *MEA*, then that Party must try to balance obligations under both agreements. But, *MEA* obligations take precedence over *KORUS*. Failure of a Party to comply with an *MEA* is a violation of *KORUS* that also is subject to *KORUS* dispute settlement.[17]

With such features, not surprisingly, champions of *KORUS* tout it as having the most effective environmental chapter of any FTA up to its time. Critics charge the formal government-to-government dispute settlement procedures are rarely used.[18] And, funding is the key to enforcement. Professor Gantz thus takes a cautiously optimistic approach: "One may hope that governments that are prepared to comply in good faith with the obligations they have entered into with regard to the trade and commercial aspects of an FTA would be prepared to do the same with the labor and environmental provisions."[19]

VI. Case Study on Wildlife and Timber Trafficking, and IUU Fishing: *NAFTA* 2.0

NAFTA 2.0 repositions the *NAFTA* 1.0 *Environmental Side Agreement*, putting it into the core text of the FTA and making them enforceable therein. Is it, then, "the most advanced, most comprehensive, highest-standard Chapter on the

---

15. Trade Facts, *Office of the United States Trade Representative,* www.ustr.gov/sites/default /files/uploads/factsheets/2007/asset_upload_file127_11319.pdf.

16. Gantz, *Labor Rights*, 340.

17. *See* Gantz, *Labor Rights*, 345.

18. *See* Gantz, *Labor Rights*, 349.

19. Gantz, *Labor Rights*, 305, 313–315, 324.

Environment of any trade agreement"?[20] How does it compare with *CPTPP*? On the one hand, there is no discussion in *NAFTA* 2.0 of climate change, the most important of all environmental issues. There is no provision about encouraging investment in renewable energy, nor about shifting to a carbon-neutral economy. In these respects, the *USMCA* is not *CPTPP* Plus.

On the other hand, *NAFTA* 2.0 does contain *CPTPP*-like provisions on trade in illegally harvested wood products, so as to promote sustainable forestry, and on IUU fishing, so as to promote sustainable fishing.

- **27 August 2018 U.S.-Mexico Bilateral Agreement**

Office of the United States Trade Representative,
United States–Mexico Trade Fact Sheet, *Modernizing NAFTA to Be a 21st Century Trade Agreement*
(28 August 2018)[21]

Key Achievement: Most Comprehensive Set of Enforceable Environmental Obligations

The Environment Chapter includes the most comprehensive set of enforceable environmental obligations of any previous United States agreement, including obligations to combat trafficking in wildlife, timber, and fish; to strengthen law enforcement networks to stem such trafficking; and to address pressing environmental issues such as air quality and marine litter.

Environment obligations include:

(1) Prohibitions on some of the most harmful fisheries subsidies, such as those that benefit vessels or operators involved in illegal, unreported, and unregulated (IUU) fishing.

(2) New protections for marine species like whales and sea turtles, including a prohibition on shark-finning and commitment to work together to protect marine habitat.

(3) Obligations to enhance the effectiveness of customs inspections of shipments containing wild fauna and flora at ports of entry, and ensure strong enforcement to combat IUU fishing.

(4) First-ever articles to improve air quality, prevent and reduce marine litter, support sustainable forest management, and ensure appropriate procedures for environmental impact assessments.

(5) Robust and modernized mechanisms for public participation and environmental cooperation.

---

20. Office of the United States Trade Representative, United States-Mexico Trade Fact Sheet, *Modernizing NAFTA to be a 21st Century Trade Agreement* (28 August 2018), https://ustr.gov/about-us/policy-offices/press-office/press-releases/2018/august/modernizing-nafta-be-21st-century.

21. https://ustr.gov/about-us/policy-offices/press-office/press-releases/2018/august/modernizing-nafta-be-21st-century (emphasis original).

- **30 September 2018 Trilateral *NAFTA* 2.0 (*USMCA*)**

Office of the United States Trade Representative,

United States–Mexico–Canada Fact Sheet: *Modernizing
NAFTA into a 21st Century Agreement*
(1 October 2018)[22]

. . .

The United States, Mexico, and Canada have agreed to the most advanced, most comprehensive, highest-standard Chapter on the Environment of any trade agreement.

Like the Labor Chapter, the Environment Chapter brings all environmental provisions into the core of the agreement [as distinct from a *Side Agreement*, where labor provisions were located in *NAFTA* 1.0] and makes them enforceable.

Key Achievement: Most Comprehensive Set of Enforceable Environmental Obligations

The Environment Chapter includes the most comprehensive set of enforceable environmental obligations of any previous United States agreement, including obligations to combat trafficking in wildlife, timber, and fish; to strengthen law enforcement networks to stem such trafficking; and to address pressing environmental issues such as air quality and marine litter.

Environment obligations include:

(1) Prohibitions on some of the most harmful fisheries subsidies, such as those that benefit vessels or operators involved in illegal, unreported, and unregulated (IUU) fishing.

(2) New protections for marine species like whales and sea turtles, including a prohibition on shark-finning and commitment to work together to protect marine habitat.

(3) Obligations to enhance the effectiveness of customs inspections of shipments containing wild fauna and flora at ports of entry, and ensure strong enforcement to combat IUU fishing.

(4) First-ever articles to improve air quality, prevent and reduce marine litter, support sustainable forest management, and ensure appropriate procedures for environmental impact assessments.

(5) Robust and modernized mechanisms for public participation and environmental cooperation.

---

22. https://ustr.gov/about-us/policy-offices/press-office/fact-sheets/2018/october/united
-states-mexico-canada-trade-fa-1.

Chapter 29

Trade and Climate Change[1]

I. Synopsis of Scientific Evidence Concerning Climate Change

- Global Warming[2]

In 2009, the Intergovernmental Panel on Climate Change (IPCC) reviewed a voluminous amount of scientific data on climate change on Earth, and concluded:

(1) Warming of the climate system is "unequivocal."

(2) Human activities are "very likely" the cause of this warming, primarily via greenhouse gas emissions to the atmosphere.

(3) Suppose greenhouse gas emissions were significantly reduced today. Because many such gasses linger in the atmosphere for long periods, global warming will continue for several hundred years. Unfortunately, emission levels continue to grow. That trend is projected to continue indefinitely, unless current laws and policies change swiftly and markedly.

(4) Over the last 50 years, greenhouse gas emissions per person in industrialized countries have been roughly four times higher than those in developing countries, and the difference is even more striking for LDCs.

(5) Emissions from developing countries are becoming more significant. Developing countries account for two-thirds of new greenhouse gas emissions.

The ineluctable consequence of unabated, or even slowed, emissions are further global temperature increases. Indeed, 2014 had been the hottest year on record, besting 2010, 2005, and 1998, and "the 10 warmest years since records began in the 19th century . . . occurred since 1997."[3] Subsequently, new annual "hottest ever" records were set.

---

1. Documents References:
    (1) *Havana Charter* Article _____
    (2) GATT Article XX(b), (g).

2. This discussion draws on Ludivine Tamiotti, Robert Teh, Vesile Kulaço lu, Anne Olhoff, Benjamin Simmons & Hussein Abaza, World Trade Organization-United Nations Environment Program, Trade and Climate Change vii–viii (2009). [Hereinafter, Tamiotti et al.]

3. *2014: Hottest Year on Record and Humans to Blame, Says NASA*, Al Jazeera, 16 January 2015, http://america.aljazeera.com/articles/2015/1/16/2014-hottest-yearonrecord.html.

In its 2014 *Synthesis Report*, the IPCC:[4]

(1) Again intoned global warming is "unequivocal," and the "[h]uman influence on the climate system is clear."

(2) Recounted that 1983 to 2012 probably was the warmest 30-year period in the previous 1,400 years.

(3) Listed impacts of global warming, such as acidification of oceans, melting of arctic ice, and diminished crop yields.

In the *Synthesis Report*, the IPCC called for:

(1) By 2010, an end to unrestricted use of fossil fuels, specifically, a phasing out almost entirely of all fossil fuel power generation without carbon capture and storage (CCS) technology.

(2) By 2050, production of most of the world's electricity from low-carbon sources, in particular, a growth in the share of renewable energy in the power sector from 30% in 2014 to 80% in 2050.

Without these actions, which require multilateral action on carbon emissions, global temperatures would rise steadily and by 2100 would be 5 °C (41 °F) above pre-industrial levels. The result would be "severe, pervasive and irreversible damage."[5]

- **Heat Stress and Heat Death**

The most obvious and immediate "damage" to human civilization from global warming is "heat stress," and ultimately, "heat death":

> Humans, like all mammals, are heat engines; surviving means having to continually cool off, like panting dogs. For that, the temperature needs to be low enough for the air to act as a kind of refrigerant, drawing heat off the skin so the engine can keep pumping. At seven degrees of warming, that would become impossible for large portions of the planet's equatorial band, and especially the tropics, where humidity adds to the problem; in the jungles of Costa Rica, for instance, where humidity routinely tops 90 percent, simply moving around outside when it's over 105 degrees Fahrenheit would be lethal. And the effect would be fast: Within a few hours, a human body would be cooked to death from both inside and out.
>
> . . .
>
> Since 1980, the planet has experienced a 50-fold increase in the number of places experiencing dangerous or extreme heat; a bigger increase is to come. The five warmest summers in Europe since 1500 have all occurred since 2002, and soon, the IPCC warns, simply being outdoors that time of year will be unhealthy for much of the globe. Even if we meet the Paris

---

4. *See* Climate Change 2014, IPCC Synthesis Report 2014, www.ipcc.ch/report/ar5/syr/.

5. *See* Matt McGrath, *Fossil Fuels Should be Phased Out by 2100 Says IPCC*, BBC News, 2 November 2014, www.bbc.com/news/science-environment-29855884.

goals of two degrees warming, cities like Karachi and Kolkata will become close to uninhabitable, annually encountering deadly heat waves like those that crippled them in 2015. At four degrees, the deadly European heat wave of 2003, which killed as many as 2,000 people a day, will be a normal summer. At six, according to an assessment focused only on effects within the U.S. from the National Oceanic and Atmospheric Administration, summer labor of any kind would become impossible in the lower Mississippi Valley, and everybody in the country east of the Rockies would be under more heat stress than anyone, anywhere, in the world today. As Joseph Romm has put it in his authoritative primer *Climate Change: What Everyone Needs to Know* [2015], heat stress in New York City would exceed that of present-day Bahrain, one of the planet's hottest spots, and the temperature in Bahrain "would induce hyperthermia in even sleeping humans." . . . Air-conditioning can help but will ultimately only add to the carbon problem; plus, the climate-controlled malls of the Arab Emirates aside, it is not remotely plausible to wholesale air-condition all the hottest parts of the world, many of them also the poorest. And indeed, the crisis will be most dramatic across the Middle East and Persian Gulf, where in 2015 the heat index registered temperatures as high as 163 degrees Fahrenheit. As soon as several decades from now, the Ḥajj will become physically impossible for the 2 million Muslims who make the pilgrimage each year.[6]

Succinctly put, human civilization already is under heat stress.[7] At issue is whether heat death can be averted.

---

6. David Wallace-Wells, *The Uninhabitable Earth*, New York Magazine, 19 July 2017, http://nymag.com/daily/intelligencer/2017/07/climate-change-earth-too-hot-for-humans.html. [Hereinafter, *Uninhabitable*.]

7. This stress is worsened by smog:

Our lungs need oxygen, but that is only a fraction of what we breathe. The fraction of carbon dioxide is growing: It just crossed 400 parts per million, and high-end estimates extrapolating from current trends suggest it will hit 1,000 ppm by 2100. At that concentration, compared to the air we breathe now, human cognitive ability declines by 21 percent. Other stuff in the hotter air is even scarier, with small increases in pollution capable of shortening life spans by ten years. The warmer the planet gets, the more ozone forms, and by mid-century, Americans will likely suffer a 70 percent increase in unhealthy ozone smog, the National Center for Atmospheric Research has projected.

. . .

. . . In 2013, melting Arctic ice remodeled Asian weather patterns, depriving industrial China of the natural ventilation systems it had come to depend on, which blanketed much of the country's north in an unbreathable smog. Literally unbreathable. A metric called the Air Quality Index categorizes the risks and tops out at the 301-to-500 range, warning of "serious aggravation of heart or lung disease and premature mortality in persons with cardiopulmonary disease and the elderly" and, for all others, "serious risk of respiratory effects"; at that level, "everyone should avoid all outdoor exertion." The Chinese "airpocalypse" of 2013 peaked at what would have been an Air Quality Index of over 800. That year, smog was responsible for a third of all deaths in the country.

Uninhabitable.

• "Hothouse" Effect

Damage from global warming could be caused by, and accelerated because of, a "hothouse" effect. Research by British Professor James Lovelock (1919–), CH, CBE, FRS, who pioneered the theory of "Gaia," which posits that the earth is alive, a living super-organism, shows that once average global temperatures rise by more than 2 °C (3.6 °F), the effects of climate change become irreversible.[8] The economic, political, and demographic implications are horrific:

> In Lovelock's view, the scale of the catastrophe that awaits us will soon become obvious. By 2020, droughts and other extreme weather will be commonplace. By 2040, the Sahara will be moving into Europe, and Berlin will be as hot as Baghdad. Atlanta will end up a kudzu jungle. Phoenix will become uninhabitable, as will parts of Beijing (desert), Miami (rising seas) and London (floods). Food shortages will drive millions of people north, raising political tensions. "The Chinese have nowhere to go but up into Siberia," Lovelock says. "How will the Russians feel about that? I fear that war between Russia and China is probably inevitable." With hardship and mass migrations will come epidemics, which are likely to kill millions. By 2100, Lovelock believes, the Earth's population will be culled from today's 6.6 billion to as few as 500 million, with most of the survivors living in the far latitudes — Canada, Iceland, Scandinavia, the Arctic Basin.[9]

To be sure, the exact timing of the Lovelockian effects is debatable, as is the likelihood of a Sino-Russian conflagration.

But, the underlying scientific point is accepted: even if the December 2015 *Paris Climate Change Agreement* (discussed below) carbon emissions targets are met, "a

---

8. In October 2018, an IPCC *Report* commissioned by the U.N. stated that keeping average global temperature increases to 1.5 °C still would result in grave problems, yet the world was entirely off track, heading toward a rise of 3 °C in the 21st century. *See* Intergovernmental Panel on Climate Change, *Global Warming of 1.5 °C* (October 2018), https://report.ipcc.ch/sr15/pdf/sr15 _spm_final.pdf; Matt McGrath, *Katowice: COP24 Climate Change Deal to Bring Pact to Life*, BBC News, 16 December 2018, www.bbc.com/news/science-environment-46582025. America, Kuwait, Russia, and Saudi Arabia objected to delegates at the December 2018 Katowice, Poland U.N. Climate Change Conference "welcoming" this *Report*. Nevertheless, at that two-week long Conference knowns as "COP 24," 196 nations agreed on technical regulations (memorialized in 156-page rule book, organized by topics such as reporting on country-specific obligations to cut greenhouse gas emissions, updates on emissions plans, and accounting rules for monitoring carbon credits) to help implement the December 2015 *Paris Agreement* goals of keeping average global temperature increases to "well below" 2.0 °C above pre-industrial levels. *See* Nancy Chestney, Bate Felix & Agnieszka Barteczko, *Nations Agree on Global Climate Pact Rules, but They Are Seen as Weak*, REUTERS, 15 December 2018, www.reuters.com/article/us-climate-change-accord/nations-agree -on-global-climate-pact-rules-but-they-are-seen-as-weak-idUSKBN1OE0N9.

9. Jeff Goodell, *Hothouse Earth is Merely the Beginning of the End*, ROLLING STONE, 9 August 2018, www.rollingstone.com/politics/politics-features/hothouse-earth-climate-change-709470/ (emphasis original). [Hereinafter, *Hothouse Earth*.]

series of accelerating climate-system feedback loops that would push the climate into a permanent hothouse state, with a warming of four, five or even six degrees Celsius" still might be triggered:[10]

> Hothouse Earth is likely to be uncontrollable and dangerous to many, particularly if we transition into it in only a century or two, and it poses severe risks for health, economies, political stability (especially for the most climate vulnerable), and ultimately, the habitability of the planet for humans.[11]

Indeed, many other scientists have reached the same conclusion about an irreversible degradation of the biosphere, "an essentially irreversible pathway driven by intrinsic biogeophysical feedbacks."[12]

There are various possible specific causal chains in this pathway toward degradation. For example, with average temperatures rising above the 2 °C above pre-Industrial Revolution level, bacteria increase in forest soil, and they emit greenhouse gasses—"warming the soil increases microbial respiration, releasing CO_2 back into the atmosphere." Rather than absorbing those gasses, forests thus become net emitters of the gasses. Other possible "feedback processes include permafrost thawing, decomposition of ocean methane hydrates, increased marine bacterial respiration, and loss of polar ice sheets accompanied by a rise in sea levels and potential amplification of temperature rise through changes in ocean circulation."[13] Regardless of the exact mechanism, the "tipping element," the vital challenge is to avoid a rise in global temperatures that create a "tipping cascade," which put the planet beyond the "tipping point":

> A critical issue is that, if a planetary threshold is crossed toward the Hothouse Earth pathway, accessing the Stabilized Earth pathway would become very difficult no matter what actions human societies might take. Beyond the threshold, positive (reinforcing) feedbacks within the Earth System—outside of human influence or control—could become the dominant driver of the system's pathway, as individual tipping elements create linked cascades through time and with rising temperature.[14]

Scientists appreciate that "[t]here is much uncertainty and debate about how this [the 'deliberate, integral, and adaptive steps to reduce dangerous impacts on the

---

10. *Hothouse Earth.*

11. Will Steffen, Johan Rockström, Katherine Richardson, Timothy M. Lenton, Carl Folke, Diana Liverman, Colin P. Summerhayes, Anthony D. Barnosky, Sarah E. Cornell, Michel Crucifix, Jonathan F. Donges, Ingo Fetzer, Steven J. Lade, Marten Scheffer, Ricarda Winkelmann, & Hans Joachim Schellnhuber, *Trajectories of the Earth System in the Anthropocene*, Proceedings of the National Academy of Sciences 1–8, at 5 (6 August 2018), www.pnas.org/content/early /2018/07/31/1810141115. [Hereinafter, *Trajectories.*]

12. *Trajectories,* 3.

13. *Trajectories.* 4.

14. *Trajectories,* 5.

Earth System, effectively monitoring and changing behavior to form feedback loops that stabilize this [current] intermediate state'] can be done—technically, ethically, equitably, and economically—and there is no doubt that the normative, policy, and institutional aspects are highly challenging."[15] There is an opportunity for International Trade Law, because an underlying causal factor is that "[t]he present dominant socioeconomic system . . . is based on high-carbon economic growth and exploitative resource use," hence reforms in this Law to de-incentivize this use are needed.[16]

- **Impacts of Global Warming**[17]

To appreciate the link between climate change and International Trade Law, it is first necessary to understand the effects of climate change. Then, it is possible to propose and evaluate trade measures to address those effects. Climate change has a diverse array of consequences. They can be grouped into five categories: effects on (1) weather patterns; (2) poor countries; (3) specific economic sectors; (4) trade routes; and (5) national security.

First: Weather Patterns

Even with small increases in average global temperature, the type, frequency, and intensity of extreme weather are increasing. The distribution of extreme weather events is expected to vary considerably among countries and regions, and the knock-on effects will depend primarily on the vulnerability of populations or ecosystems. "Extreme weather" refers to hurricanes, typhoons, cyclones, floods, droughts, thunder, snow, and hail storms, and tornadoes), and nearly every person on the planet already has observed or experienced such events and recent oddities in their timing and location.

Second: Poor Countries

Generally, developing countries are the most adversely affected by climate change. That is partly because of their vulnerability: with fewer resources and a less sophisticated infrastructure, they are less able to adapt than developed countries. The poorest and most marginalized populations within these countries suffer the most.

Third: Specific Economic Sectors and Immiserizing Growth

While climate change is visited on all economic sectors, its repercussions are particularly acute for two of them: agriculture and tourism. Both sectors are prominent in the global economy, and the subject of WTO agreements (the *Agreement on Agriculture* and *GATS*, respectively) and Chapters in certain FTAs.

---

15. *Trajectories*, 5.
16. *Trajectories*, 5.
17. This discussion draws on TAMIOTTI ET AL., vii–xi.

Agriculture probably is the single most vulnerable sector to climate change. Depending on location, agriculture is prone to water shortages, because of loss of glacial meltwater and reduced rainfall or droughts:

> Climates differ and plants vary, but the basic rule for staple cereal crops grown at optimal temperature is that for every degree of warming, yields decline by 10 percent. Some estimates run as high as 15 or even 17 percent. Which means that if the planet is five degrees warmer at the end of the century, we may have as many as 50 percent more people to feed and 50 percent less grain to give them. And proteins are worse: It takes 16 calories of grain to produce just a single calorie of hamburger meat, butchered from a cow that spent its life polluting the climate with methane farts.
>
> . . .
>
> Drought might be an even bigger problem than heat, with some of the world's most arable land turning quickly to desert. Precipitation is notoriously hard to model, yet predictions for later this century are basically unanimous: unprecedented droughts nearly everywhere food is today produced. By 2080, without dramatic reductions in emissions, southern Europe will be in permanent extreme drought, much worse than the American dust bowl ever was. The same will be true in Iraq and Syria and much of the rest of the Middle East; some of the most densely populated parts of Australia, Africa, and South America; and the breadbasket regions of China. None of these places, which today supply much of the world's food, will be reliable sources of any.[18]

Agricultural output declines cannot always, or not easily, be overcome by GM of organisms to produce drought-resistance, and such GM itself is controversial.

Tourism is affected by global warming and the extreme weather it brings, because of loss of coastal areas and changes in snow cover. Australia is a case in point. For instance, the adverse effects on coastal ecosystems, such as loss of coral reefs and disappearance of marine biodiversity mean the loss of billions of dollars in hotel, restaurant, and sports and recreational services associated with snorkeling, scuba diving, and other activities around the Great Barrier Reef. Conversely, some regions may experience benefits. For example, Colorado ski lodges may enjoy revenue increases, with extended ski seasons afforded by heavier snowfall.

Perhaps the most ominous concern about the economic effects of climate change transcend any particular sector, and relate to the Capitalism model of growth and development:

> . . . in the aftermath of the 2008 crash, a growing number of historians studying what they call "fossil capitalism" have begun to suggest that the entire history of swift economic growth, which began somewhat suddenly

---

18. *Uninhabitable.*

in the 18th century, is not the result of innovation or trade or the dynamics of global capitalism but simply our discovery of fossil fuels and all their raw power—a onetime injection of new "value" into a system that had previously been characterized by global subsistence living. Before fossil fuels, nobody lived better than their parents or grandparents or ancestors from 500 years before, except in the immediate aftermath of a great plague like the Black Death, which allowed the lucky survivors to gobble up the resources liberated by mass graves. After we've burned all the fossil fuels, these scholars suggest, perhaps we will return to a "steady state" global economy. Of course, that onetime injection has a devastating long-term cost: climate change.

. . . [Research by Solomon Hsiang, Chancellor's Associate Professor of Public Policy at the University of California, Berkeley, projects that] [e]very degree Celsius of warming costs, on average, 1.2 percent of GDP (an enormous number, considering we count growth in the low single digits as "strong"). . . . [T]heir median projection is for a 23 percent loss in *per capita* earning globally by the end of this century (resulting from changes in agriculture, crime, storms, energy, mortality, and labor). Tracing the shape of the probability curve is even scarier: There is a 12 percent chance that climate change will reduce global output by more than 50 percent by 2100, . . . and a 51 percent chance that it lowers per capita GDP by 20 percent or more by then, unless emissions decline. By comparison, the Great Recession lowered global GDP by about 6 percent, in a onetime shock. . . . [19]

Accordingly, the prevailing model favoring trade liberalization, that more output and trade enhances human welfare, measured using conventional economic growth metric of GDP, could be flat wrong. Increases in output and trade that contribute to global warming, such as those that rely on hydrocarbons, could be detract from GDP growth. In effect, hydrocarbon-based trade liberalization could lead to immiserizing growth—not of the kind caused by being a large player in a commodity market, discussed in a separate Chapter, but rather of the kind that destroys growth because of its unsustainable sources.

Fourth: Trade Routes

One of the clearest impacts of global climate change is on trade routes and infrastructure. The IPCC identifies several types of infrastructure, such as railways, ports, airports, as at serious risk of damage from rising sea levels and increased frequency of extreme weather. Changes in sea ice, especially in the Arctic, already have led to new shipping routes, which in turn engender the need for new infrastructure on these routes.

New routes also catalyze territorial disputes among Canada, Denmark (including Greenland), Norway, Russia, and the U.S. over the famed Northwest Passage

---

19. *Uninhabitable.*

and the rights to explore and exploit natural resources that previously were inaccessible (or accessible at a prohibitive cost) under snow and ice. These countries jockey for passageways and territorial rights over the rich oil, gas, and natural resources in the Arctic region, while China—lacking an Arctic boundary—calls for the territory to be international and open to all.

Fifth: National Security

In June 2014, the U.S. DOD issued a report on the national security implications of climate change.[20] Politicians inside-the-Beltway argued about the causes (man-made or otherwise) of environmental shifts, but the Pentagon bluntly explained it did not care why climate change was happening: the fact was, it was happening. Sea levels were rising. Cyclones and hurricanes were wreaking monstrous devastation. A new sea lane through the Arctic Ocean appeared. So, the military had to deal with:

(1) Droughts and water shortages

(2) Crop failures and food shortages

(3) Rapid disease transmission[21]

(4) Interruptions of commercial transactions

(5) Displacement of persons

(6) Mass migration

Overall, these effects exacerbated global instability.

Syria is just one of many potential theatres for violence:

> Climatologists are very careful when talking about Syria. . . . [W]hile climate change did produce a drought that contributed to [the Syrian] civil war, it is not exactly fair to say that the conflict is the result of warming; next door, for instance, Lebanon suffered the same crop failures. But researchers like Marshall Burke [Professor of Earth Science at Stanford] and Solomon Hsiang [noted above] have managed to quantify some of the non-obvious relationships between temperature and violence: For every half-degree of warming, they say, societies will see between a 10 and 20 percent increase in the likelihood of armed conflict. . . . A planet five degrees warmer would have at least half again as many wars as we do today. . . .

> This is one reason that . . . the U.S. military is obsessed with climate change: The drowning of all American Navy bases by sea-level rise is trouble enough,

---

20. *See* U.S. Department of Defense, *2014 Climate Change Adaptation Roadmap* (June 2014), *posted at* www.acq.osd.mil/ie/download/CCARprint.pdf; Renee Lewis, *Climate Change Poses Urgent National Security Threats, Says Pentagon*, AL JAZEERA, 13 October 2014, america.aljazeera .com/articles/2014/10/13/climate-change-arctic.html.

21. Associated with the rapidity of disease transmission caused by climate change is "climate plague," which refers both to the mutation of existing diseases, and the release from melting ice of disease-carrying organisms, some of which are ancient, and against which humans may lack resistance. *See Uninhabitable.*

but being the world's policeman is quite a bit harder when the crime rate doubles. Of course, it's not just Syria where climate has contributed to conflict. Some speculate that the elevated level of strife across the Middle East over the past generation reflects the pressures of global warming—a hypothesis all the more cruel considering that warming began accelerating when the industrialized world extracted and then burned the region's oil.[22]

Rightly so, therefore, the Pentagon is resolved to integrate the conflict-inducing effect of climate change into every dimension of its strategic and operational planning about peace and security.

II. Environmental Kuznets Curve[23]

Is there an inverse relationship between *per capita* GDP and emissions of greenhouse gases? That is, as a nation grows as measured by income per head, does its carbon footprint fall?

An affirmative answer is known as the "Environmental Kuznets Curve," depicted in Graph 29-1. It is named after the Nobel Prize winning development economist Simon Kuznets (1901–1985), who proposed an Inverted U Curve to describe the relationship between growth in *per capita* income and inequality. (This Curve is treated in another Chapter.)

The "Environmental Kuznets Curve" for greenhouse gases describes the relationship between higher *per capita* incomes and lower greenhouse gas emissions. In theory, as income per capita rises as a country develops through agricultural and industrial stages, greenhouse gas emissions rise, particularly with industrialization. However, as that country advances to post-industrial status, relying on services, greenhouse gas emissions ought to fall. That decrease should be reinforced by demands from the people in that country, as they get wealthier, for cleaner technologies and a better environment. So, the Curve ought to look like an inverted U.

Empirical studies as to whether this Curve exists in reality produce inconsistent results. Recent studies tend to show there is no relationship between higher incomes and lower greenhouse gas emissions. In other words, there is no global Curve covering all countries. But, studies that differentiate between industrialized and developing countries tend to find evidence of an Environmental Kuznets Curve for the industrialized countries, but not developing countries.

---

22. *Uninhabitable*. The empirical study on climate change and war is Marshall Burke, Solomon M. Hsiang & Edward Miguel, *Climate and Conflict*, National Bureau of Economic Research (NBER) Working Paper Number 20598 (October 2014), www.nber.org/papers/w20598.pdf (also published in 7 ANNUAL REVIEW OF ECONOMICS 577–617 (August 2015)); Solomon M. Hsiang, Marshall Burke & Edward Miguel *et al.*, *Quantifying the Influence of Climate on Human Conflict*, 341 SCIENCE issue 6151 (13 September 2013).

23. This discussion draws on TAMIOTTI ET AL., xii–xiii.

Graph 29-1. Environmental Kuznets Curve

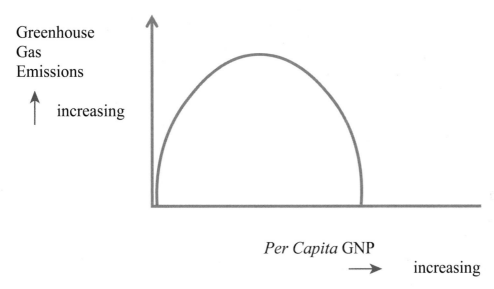

These empirical results suggest two countries. First, why is there no global Curve? The answer may be many industrialized countries require environmental assessments of trade agreements to which they enter. These assessments focus on national issues and goals, not global pollutants and international problems with climate change. In other words, even countries with high *per capita* GDPs do not necessarily focus on greenhouse gas reductions, from a global perspective, as they develop.

Second, what accounts for the existence of a Curve in some developed, but not less developed, countries? Here the explanation may be, in line with the theory, on the "dirtiness" of the different stages of development, the environmental law framework in the countries, and the environmental consciousness of the people in those countries and their legal ability to express their concerns.

China exemplifies a country in transition from developing to developed status. Countless news stories chronicle environmental protests by its citizens to pollution-generating industrial projects. Such stories were fewer in the 1980s and 1990s, as most citizens accepted the relentless drive for higher levels of manufacturing output, regardless of environmental externalities, orchestrated by the Communist Party. But, after horrific smog, toxic water, and other environmental problems, average citizens are expressing openly their opposition to a blindly ambitious go-for-growth strategy.

III. Three Relationships between Trade and Climate Change

It may seem obvious climate change worsens with increased economic activity, and such activity includes the cross-border flow of goods, services, and IP. To be precise, how exactly does international trade affect climate change? There are three relationships:

- **Scale Effect**[24]

The Scale Effect refers to the expansion of economic activity arising from lowering trade barriers, and the effect of that greater activity on greenhouse gas emissions. *Á propos* the theories of absolute and comparative advantage of Adam Smith (1723–1790) and David Ricardo (1772–1823), trade liberalization should result in greater overall output via production specialization and finer division of labor, and concomitant increases in consumption opportunity. The increases in output (measured by higher levels of GDP) require greater energy and fuel use. Burning more energy and fuel generates more greenhouse gas emissions, *i.e.*, as the scale of production grows, so do the emissions of greenhouse gases.

Additionally, the increased consumption opportunities, when realized, reinforce the problem. For example, the availability of more sport utility vehicles (SUVs) to buy, when purchased and driven, leads to greater demand for and use of gasoline.

- **Composition Effect**[25]

The Composition Effect is the way increased international trade alters the structure of production in a country in response to changes in relative prices, and the consequences of these alterations on the levels of greenhouse gas emissions. Exactly how the structure of production changes in a country liberalizing trade by lowering tariff and non-tariff barriers, and cutting subsidies, depends on the comparative advantages it holds.

Recall the Heckscher-Ohlin Theorem (discussed in a separate Chapter), which holds that a country will specialize in the production of, and export, a good that uses intensively in its production the factor with which that country is relatively well endowed. So, a country relatively well-endowed with labor and physical capital can be expected to emphasize labor-intensive and capital-intensive manufacturing. Conversely, a country relatively well endowed with human capital and technology likely will emphasize high-tech and services sectors. These sectors may well be less environmentally degrading than the traditional manufacturing in which the first country specializes. Note these specializations are not static for eternity. As relative factor endowments change, the composition of output of the countries alters.

Moreover, the effect of free (or freer) trade on greenhouse gas emissions depends on the relative growth rates of sectors in which a liberalizing country holds a competitive advantage. If those sectors are emission-intensive, and are expanding, the level of greenhouse gas emissions from the liberalizing country will increase due to the Composition Effect. A competitively advantaged sector may be a contracting emission-intensive one. While this sector emits greenhouse gases, the Composition

---

24. This discussion draws on TAMIOTTI ET AL., xi.
25. This discussion draws on TAMIOTTI ET AL., xi–xii.

Effect on the environment will not be as substantial as that of the growing sector. China and the U.S. furnish examples of expanding and contracting emission-intensive industries, respectively: smokestack industries, like autos, chemicals, steel, and paper, all of which in the last few decades of the 20th century and early part of the 21st century experienced outsourcing from America to the Mainland.

- **Technique Effect**[26]

The Technique Effect refers to improvements in methods of production of goods and services. Through environmentally friendly processes for producing (and, presumably, delivering) goods, services, and IP—the emission intensity of output is reduced. Whereas the Scale and Composition Effects of trade liberalization tend to boost greenhouse gas emissions, the Technique Effect is the way to help lower them and thereby mitigate climate change.

Decreasing emission intensity via this Effect can occur in two ways. First, international trade can increase the supply, and cut price, of, climate-friendly goods and services. By lowering tariffs and NTBs on items used to clean up and protect the environment, these items are more widely available to more countries at cheaper prices. Such countries, particularly ones lacking domestic manufacturing capacity in these items, can import them affordably, and deploy them in making other goods and supplying other services. Ideally, and obviously, there would be multilateral agreement under WTO auspices creating free trade in environmental goods and services. It could be modeled after the 1996 *ITA*. WTO Members pursued this ideal in the Doha Round. They failed.

Second, as income levels rise because of increased trade, people may demand lower greenhouse gas emissions. Redolent of the Environmental Kuznets Curve, greater income tends to lead to environmental improvements. So, governments should provide appropriate tax and regulatory measures to meet public demand. Only when such laws and policies are in place will firms adopt cleaner production technologies to improve the production methods for goods and services and reduce emission intensity of output.

The Technique Effect implicates the method by which a good is produced or service provided. In GATT-WTO jurisprudence, particularly on GATT Article XX(b) and (g) in cases such as the 1992 and 1994 *Tuna-Dolphin I and II* disputes, a distinction between "product" and "process" sometimes has been made. To what extent does this jurisprudence accommodate the distinction, and thereby allow for regulation of goods and services to mitigate climate change based on their "technique"?

Note, too, the way in which farm subsidies in developed countries can have a negative Technique Effect in developing and least developed countries. When American and European agricultural subsidies make crops cheaper, farmers in poor countries face increased difficulties in selling their produce. To face the larger-volume,

---

26. This discussion draws on Tamiotti et al., xii.

lower-price competition, they may start producing on marginal lands, use inefficient nutrients and pesticides, *i.e.*, they may eschew environmentally friendly farming techniques, possibly even contributing to deforestation.[27]

IV. International Efforts to Mitigate Climate Change

International efforts to reduce the extent and speed of climate change may be
divided into three categories: (1) non-legal (technological) initiatives; (2) non-trade
multilateral initiatives; and (3) trade-related initiatives. They are discussed below,
but emphasis is on the third, as it obviously raises issues under GATT-WTO law. (To
be sure, an additional category covers local and national levels within a particular
country.)

- **Non-Legal (Technological) Initiatives**[28]

These efforts do not involve negotiation or implementation of a new international agreement, nor modification of an existing accord. Likewise, they do not pertain to changing domestic laws. Rather, they are technological in nature.

Technological innovation, plus the transfer and widespread implementation of
technologies, is central to global efforts to mitigate the adverse effects of climate
change. The cost of these new technologies has not been estimated precisely, but
surely is substantial. The theory is the benefit from the innovation and implementation of new technologies will markedly outweigh the costs.

International transfer of technology occurs in two dimensions: the transfer of
technologies that are physically embodied in tangible assets or capital goods, such
as industrial plant and equipment, machinery; and the transfer of intangible knowledge and information associated with the technology or technological system.
Because it is largely private companies that own a wide variety of technologies, it is
necessary to identify ways within the private sector to facilitate technology transfers, such as FDI, license agreements, or royalty agreements.

Does IPR protection impede or assist the transfer of climate change technologies to developing countries? Proponents in this long-standing and vigorous debate,
which extends far beyond the context of climate change, insist the protections are
necessary to encourage innovation. Without protection, private companies would
be unwilling to invest substantially in R&D for new technology, because it would be
unlikely they would be able to recover the costs and reap any of the benefits of their
advancements.

---

27. *See* LaTrina Antoine, *Analysts: Higher U.S. Farm Subsidies May Lead to Environmental Damage Abroad*, 30 International Trade Reporter (BNA) 1275 (15 August 2013).

28. This discussion draws on Tᴀᴍɪᴏᴛᴛɪ ᴇᴛ ᴀʟ. ix–xi.

Of course, this debate assumes IP protection is feasible and pertinent. Patents or other IPRs may not protect many technologies, such as insulation in buildings (*e.g.*, choosing higher or lower quality wall interiors, or windows and door treatments) or better energy management (*e.g.*, to setting thermostats higher in the summer and lower in the winter), needed to address climate change. In other words, some technological initiatives to combat climate change are not susceptible to IP protection, so the question of ramifications of such protection for poor countries is immaterial. Those technologies are widely accessible, but the challenge is to ensure their widespread use.

- **Non-Trade Multilateral Legal Initiatives**[29]

The UNEP and WMO launched the IPCC in 1988 to undertake the first authoritative assessment of scientific literature on climate change. In its first report, released in 1990, the IPCC confirmed climate change represents a severe threat, and called for a global treaty to address the challenge.

The IPCC report was a catalyst for government support and helped initiate international negotiations on climate change. They began in 1991, and ended with the adoption of the *UNFCCC*, to which is linked to the *Kyoto Protocol*. (That Protocol was adopted in 1997 and entered into force in 2005.) The objective of the *Convention* is stabilization of greenhouse gases in the atmosphere at a level that would prevent dangerous human interference with the climate system. The *Convention* represents the first global effort to tackle climate change.

The *Convention* is a general framework for international climate change action. It elaborates principles to help the parties in reaching the objective, such as the principle of "common but different responsibility," which was first developed in the 1992 Earth Summit *Rio Declaration*. This principle recognizes the fact that even though all countries have a responsibility to address climate change, not all countries have contributed equally to the cause of the problem, and not all are equally equipped to deal with it.

The *Convention* lacks mandatory emission limits and reduction commitments from the parties. As the scientific consensus surrounding climate change has built, however, the international community has called for inclusion of a supplementary agreement with legally binding commitments for reducing greenhouse gas emissions. Their energy led to the signing of the *Kyoto Protocol*, which established specific, binding emission reduction commitments for industrialized countries. However, several major countries, including the U.S., China, and India, declined to join.

Building on *Convention* principles, the *Kyoto Protocol* created different obligations for developing and industrialized countries based on past responsibility. Developing countries had no binding emission reduction duties. In contrast, industrialized countries and economies in transition had to meet agreed levels of emission

---

29. This discussion draws on TAMIOTTI ET AL., xiv–xvi.

reductions over an initial commitment period that ran from 2008 to 2012. The *Protocol* also required economies in transition to monitor and report their greenhouse gas emissions.

Within the *Protocol* are three "flexibility mechanisms": (1) emissions trading; (2) Joint Implementation; and (3) the Clean Development Mechanism (CDM). These mechanisms were designed to help parties meet their obligations and achieve their emission reduction commitments in cost-efficient ways. Emission trading allows one party to buy "emission credits" from other parties. These credits can be the unused emission allowances from other parties, or may derived from either of the other two mechanisms.

Joint Implementation allows a country with an economy in transition toward market principles to invest in emission-reducing projects in the territory of another country with a transitional economy in transition, so as to earn emission reduction credits the first country can apply to its own emission target. That is, if one transition country helps mitigate climate change in another transition country, then this help counts at home. Similarly, CDM allows a transition economy country to meet its emission obligations by earning emission reduction credits from projects it initiates in developing countries. (These developing countries, while poor, do not have transitional economies.) The CDM requires evidence that the reductions in emissions achieved by the project in the developing country are additional, meaning the cuts would not have occurred without the CDM project implementation and financing.

One of the most significant non-trade multilateral accords was the December 2015 *Paris Agreement*, to which 196 countries—including the U.S.—were signatories. The *Agreement*, under the *UNFCCC* auspices, committed the signatories, as per Article 2, to "enhancing the implementation" of the *UNFCCC*, via three key obligations:

(a) Holding the increase in the global average temperature to "well below" 2 °C (*i.e.*, to "well below" 3.6 °F) above pre-industrial levels and to pursue efforts to limit the temperature increase to 1.5 °C above pre-industrial levels, recognizing that this would significantly reduce the risks and impacts of climate change;

(b) Increasing the ability to adapt to the adverse impacts of climate change and foster climate resilience and low greenhouse gas emissions development, in a manner that does not threaten food production;

(c) Making finance flows consistent with a pathway towards low greenhouse gas emissions and climate-resilient development.

In June 2017, President Donald J. Trump (1946–, President, 2017–) withdrew America from the *Paris Agreement*, and his USTR, Robert Lighthizer, called it "another unfair trade barrier that America cannot afford."[30]

---

30. *Quoted in* Len Bracken, *Lighthizer to Hold Bilateral Meetings on Margins of OECD Meeting*, International Trade Daily (BNA) (2 June 2017).

- **Trade Law Initiatives: Pollution Pricing Mechanisms — Carbon Taxes**[31]

An emerging strategy in environmental policy to meet the objective of mitigating climate change is to put a price tag on pollution, typically referred to as carbon taxes. There are, generally speaking, two types of pollution pricing mechanisms used to reduce greenhouse gas emissions: taxes and cap-and-trade systems.

These tools set a price on either the:

(1) Carbon content of energy consumed (*e.g.*, differential taxation based on burning one type of fossil fuel, which has a larger carbon footprint, than another type of fossil fuel, which has a smaller footprint), or

(2) CO_2 emissions generated in production or consumption (*e.g.*, taxation based on the total amount of carbon dioxide emitted).

These pricing mechanisms create an incentive for both producers and consumers to limit their uses of carbon-intensive fuels and products, because paying for carbon creates an additional cost to both sides. Adding taxes creates higher prices for inputs and end products, therefore driving both producers and consumers to use less carbon-intensive means of production and consumption. Tax and emission trading schemes also hold the potential to be a significant source of revenue for the general public purse. As tax revenue grows, more money can be invested in environmentally friendly means of production, a kind of financial recycling.

As to pricing under item (1) above, a number of countries have put a price on CO_2 released into the atmosphere. They have done so by imposing taxes on the consumption of fossil fuels based on the unique level of carbon content of that fuel. For example, crude oil has a different carbon content than coal, so the taxes imposed on those two types of fuels would be different.

- **Trade Law Initiatives: Pollution Pricing Mechanisms — Emission Trading Schemes**[32]

Other countries have introduced general taxes on the consumption of energy, eschewing an explicit "carbon tax" on specific fossil fuel types. Still other countries have fixed a cap on the total emissions of greenhouse gases, used this cap to create allowances to cover such emissions, and then created a market to trade these allowances at a price determined by the market, usually termed "emission trading schemes" (ETSs). One example is the EU Emission Trading Scheme, introduced in 2005. It was the first trading scheme for greenhouse gas emissions, and the most wide-ranging. Today, Australia, China, Japan, and the Northeastern U.S. all have emission trading schemes.[33]

---

31. This discussion draws on TAMIOTTI ET AL., xvi–xxii, 87–128.

32. This discussion draws on TAMIOTTI ET AL., xvi–xxii and 87–128.

33. *FactBox: Carbon Trading Schemes Around the World*, REUTERS, 26 September 2012, www
.reuters.com/article/2012/09/26/us-carbon-trading-idUSBRE88P0ZN20120926.

There are economic pitfalls with an ETS. For an ETS to operate properly, emission permits are issued and then traded privately among participant in the created market.[34] Ideally, the permits will be bought and used by the parties who value them the most. This means that pollution occurs from sources where there is the greatest productivity.[35] Traditionally, however, permits tend to be "grandfathered," or distributed to existing polluters at no cost in proportion to their current level of emissions.[36] Of course, grandfathering spawns two economic problems: (1) barriers to entry in industries with heavy pollution, and (2) perverse incentives.[37]

First, the permits create high barriers to entry because it is difficult for a new entrant to gain a "costless" permit, thereby driving up the startup cost. This roots current producers in the industry and protects them. If new producers were to enter, then the incumbents still hold a competitive advantage in the form of lower operating costs due to their cost free permits.[38] Second, this type of market creates an incentive for producers that receive a costless permit to drive up their emissions to maximize their allocation of permits prior to the issue of permits.[39]

Overall, carbon taxes and an ETS are the primary methods debated and used, because they each incorporate a market mechanism and thereby internalize the cost of pollution on the polluter.[40] This point is crucial because imposing the cost on the polluter through a market mechanism is what creates change through the market actors:

> In particular, imposing the cost of pollution on the polluter has two distinct benefits: (1) natural forces of demand and supply will act to push the level of activity closer to that which is socially optimal; and (2) producers have an incentive to lower emissions through some voluntary means, such as improvements in technology that will lower emissions without changing production processes (such as carbon capture and storage technology) or adopting lower carbon-emitting processes (since lower emissions lead to lower costs).[41]

A carbon tax may be more easily analyzed under WTO law than an ETS, because the "WTO has indicated that measures affecting price are economically preferable to quantitative restrictions, noting that the former [carbon taxes] are more

---

34. Keith Kendall, *Carbon Taxes and the WTO: A Carbon Charge Without Trade Concerns?*, 29 Arizona Journal of International and Comparative Law 49, 57 (2012) [hereinafter, *Carbon Taxes*].

35. *Carbon Taxes*, 57.

36. *See Carbon Taxes*, 58.

37. *Carbon Taxes*, 58.

38. *Carbon Taxes*, 58.

39. *Carbon Taxes*, 58.

40. *Carbon Taxes*, 57.

41. *Carbon Taxes*, 57.

transparent in their operation."[42] A carbon tax removes the perverse incentives from producers because if a producer increases their emission output, they must pay for it.

These mechanisms, especially a unilateral carbon tax imposed on a domestic industry, will have an adverse impact on that domestic industry's international competitiveness. One possible way to address this issue is through the use of a BTA.

• **Trade Law Initiatives: Remedies**

Experts also discuss imposing an AD duty or CVD against *de facto*, or "hidden," subsidies or "environmental dumping," respectively, on imported goods from countries that do not have regulations to help mitigate climate change. The trade remedy would offset the emission-reduction costs producer-exporters have avoided paying owing to lax regulations in their countries. The justification would be that a producer-exporter from a country that does not impose methods to mitigate climate change receives a hidden subsidy, because it has not paid the costs of emission-reduction that its competitors in the importing country, which has stricter environmental rules, have paid. The exporting country avoids the cost of fighting climate change, and confers a benefit on its exporters through its inaction, while competitors in the importing country are relatively disadvantaged by the costs of the tougher climate change regulations in that country.

Using orthodox trade remedies to fight climate change is fraught with legal difficulties. For example, it could be difficult to measure one country's failure to adopt climate change legislation in terms of a "subsidy" or environmental "dumping." What exactly would the net subsidization rate, or dumping margin, be? What adjustments might be appropriate?

V. BTAs and GATT-WTO Rules[43]

• **Defining BTAs**

Two kinds of trade law initiatives draw the most attention in respect of the application of GATT-WTO rules. They are the extent to which:

(1) Domestic carbon and energy taxes, which are imposed on inputs like energy, are eligible for BTAs; and

(2) BTAs may be limited to inputs that are physically incorporated into a final product.

A "BTA" is an adjustment by an importing country of taxes imposed domestically on a product when that product is imported.

---

42. *Carbon Taxes*, 61.
43. This discussion draws on Tamiotti et al., xvi–xxii and 87–128.

If a country imposes carbon or energy taxes on domestically-produced merchandise, then can it impose those taxes on foreign goods, when it imports those goods, via a BTA? Intuitively, an affirmative answer seems reasonable: a BTA levels the competitive playing field between domestic and foreign merchandise, when the latter goods are made with more carbon or energy-intensive processes or inputs. Moreover, without a BTA, manufacturers might migrate to jurisdictions with lax climate change rules, thus creating a "race to the bottom" on those rules (as countries compete to attract FDI), and exacerbating global warming. It might even be said that allowing a firm to produce blithely without regard to the carbon footprint of its operations or products is an implicit subsidy against other firms held to higher standards.

However, the intuitive answer is misleading. All of the same points can be made in respect of labor or environmental rights. Yet, BTAs are not imposed on merchandise made by cheap labor or in poor environmental conditions. Furthermore, the idea of a carbon or energy BTA is based on a distinction between "product" and "process," which is controversial in the annals of GATT-WTO jurisprudence.

- **Origin and Destination Principles**

  BTAs may be imposed (if at all) under one of two tax paradigms:

  > These are referred to as the *origin* and the *destination principles*. Under the destination principle, imports are subjected to the relevant tax upon importation. Exports have the relevant tax that had been imposed up to the point of export rebated at the border. The origin principle acts in the opposite fashion, exempting imports from the tax and not rebating the tax on exports as they leave the country.[44]

In other words, under the destination principle, merchandise is taxed when it enters an importing country, but not when it is exported from its country of origin.

Under the origin principle, merchandise is taxed as an export in the country of its origin (the exporting country). Once imported in a foreign country, the exporter does not get a rebate from its home (the exporting) country for the tax it paid. Consequently, there are two basic options as to where to impose a BTA: under the destination principle, by the importing country, upon importation; under the origin principle, by the exporting country, upon exportation. The options are (or should be) mutually exclusive: merchandise should not be double-taxed, with a BTA at both origin and destination.

Tax experts and environmentalists argue about which form of tax, origin-based or destination-based, would have the greatest effect on carbon emission reduction. Origin-based BTAs impose a burden on production, while destination-based BTAs impose the burden on consumption.[45] However, a destination based tax might be

---

44. *Carbon Taxes*, 64–65 (emphasis added).
45. *Carbon Taxes*, 66.

relatively easier to implement: "jurisdictions may act unilaterally to introduce the tax, yet not suffer any loss of international competitive advantage, because exports enter the world market free of the tax, and imports have the tax imposed at the border."[46] Stated differently, with a destination-based BTA, domestic producers and exporters are protected, because the tax is imposed on their foreign competition upon entry.

In respect of trade law initiatives, several GATT-WTO rules are implicated by an explicit carbon tax or general energy tax, or an emission-trading scheme. That also is true for adjustments under such a scheme (*i.e.*, raising or lowering a cap) affect international trade. The pertinent GATT rules are pillar obligations covering tariff bindings and non-discriminatory treatment, and the relevant WTO rules include provisions on subsidies.

- **GATT Article II:2 Tariff Bindings**[47]

GATT Articles II:2(a) and III:2, first sentence, are at the heart of the extensive debate over BTAs on carbon and energy taxes. Article II:2(a) and its phrase "articles from which the imported product has been manufactured or produced in whole or in part," and Article III:2, first sentence and the terms "applied, directly or indirectly, to like domestic products," divide environmentalists and policy makers. Article II:2(a) allows two types of BTAs: those imposed on (1) imported products that are like domestic products, and (2) articles from which the imported product has been manufactured. For example, a finished solar panel would be in the first category, while a solar battery cell used in a watch would be in the second category. It is this second type of BTA charge on which most of the debate is focused. To what extent can energy and fossil fuels used in the production of a particular product be considered "articles from which the imported product has been manufactured or produced in whole or in part"?[48]

One argument is the wording of Article II:2(a) was intended to mean only inputs physically incorporated into a finished product, *e.g.*, a solar battery in a watch. Therefore, GATT Article II:2(a) would not allow adjustment of taxes for energy or fossil fuels used in production of goods. What if a good is derived wholly from fossil fuels or energy? Is it a fair reading of GATT, and the intentions of its drafters to liberalize trade, to categorize "articles" in Article II:2(a) as meaning only those inputs which are physical? Simply put, can a country impose a BTA tax purely on energy that is expended (*e.g.*, fossil fuels burned) in the manufacturing process of an article?

Many European countries read that wording expansively. They are eager to impose a BTA on items manufactured in countries that burn a significant amount of fossil fuels in the production of goods. Those countries are not just the traditional

---

46. *Carbon Taxes*, 69.
47. This discussion draws on Tamiotti et al., xvi–xxii, 87–128.
48. GATT Article II:2(a).

industrialized ones, like the U.S., but also many oil-exporting countries, like Saudi Arabia, which have significant petrochemical product operations.

Note there are additional GATT constraints on taxation. Article II:2(a) also states that internal taxes and equivalent charges on imported products must be imposed consistently with GATT Article III:2 and the preamble to *Ad Note Article III*. Under Article III:2, BTAs on imported goods are only allowed in respect of indirect taxes. Taxes that are imposed on products are indirect taxes, while taxes not directly levied on products, *i.e.*, direct taxes, are those on income and property, for example.

- **GATT Article III National Treatment Rule**[49]

Article II:2(a) makes clear an internal tax on a like domestic product may be imposed on an import, so long as it is done consistently with Article III:2.[50] Article III tries to ensure imports are treated equally with competing domestic products.

The GATT Article III national treatment principle is pertinent in cases where climate change related regulation is applied differently to domestic and foreign products. Under this principle, a WTO Member shall not discriminate between its own products and like foreign products. Article III:2 explains that a tax on imports must apply "directly or indirectly, to all like products" to fall under the national treatment principle. Problems arise because it is uncertain whether a potential tax on carbon emissions released during the production of a good will be considered a tax applied indirectly to products, thus allowing BTAs to be charged on imported goods.

- **BTAs and GATT Article I MFN Rule**[51]

A WTO member must not discriminate between "like" products from different trading partners under the most-favored nation clause. The reference of "like" products is critical and was the focus of the 1992 *Tuna-Dolphin I* GATT Panel decision (discussed in a separate Chapter). To determine the meaning of the phrase "like product," the Panel held that the reference was to the physical characteristics of a product, not the process by which the product was produced. This Panel decision often is said to stand for the proposition that taxes cannot be imposed based on processes and production methods. This conclusion stems from the interpretation that imposition of a tax based on a process and production method constitutes a point of differentiation between two products that qualify as "like" under GATT-WTO rules.[52]

In the carbon tax context, imposing a BTA on imports based on carbon emitted during the production process could result in differing treatment between physically indistinguishable imports. For example, suppose China and Germany both produce steel. In this example, China emits a high amount of carbon in its production

---

49. This discussion draws on TAMIOTTI ET AL., xvi–xxii, 87–128.
50. *Carbon Taxes*, 73.
51. This discussion draws on TAMIOTTI ET AL., xvi–xxii, 87–128.
52. *Carbon Taxes*, 71–72.

process by burning fossil fuels, but Germany emits little carbon by primarily harnessing solar power. When the steel is imported into the U.S., the Chinese steel will receive a much higher tax rate than the German steel, under the destination-based BTA principle. The different taxes imposed at the border, based on the different amounts of carbon emitted during production of the steel, constitute the differing, and thereby illegal, treatment.[53]

- **BTAs and Subsidies**[54]

GATT and WTO rules permit, under specific circumstances, the use of BTAs on exported products. The circumstances must be specific and unique indeed, because export BTAs arguably cannot be subject to AD duties imposed on goods that are "dumped," nor can they be subject to CVDs. With an export BTA, presumably a producer-exporter will seek to pass that tax onto consumers, if it can. So, it will try to raise both the price of the merchandise it sells in its home country (Normal Value), and the price of goods it ships to an importing country (Export or Constructed Export Price). If so, then there is no net effect on any dumping margin (the difference between Normal Value and Export or Constructed Export Price).

As for CVDs, export BTAs are not subsidies. To the contrary, a tax is imposed at origin (*i.e.*, by the country of export) and, therefore, there is no prohibited or actionable subsidy under the WTO *SCM Agreement*.

VI. Failed Doha Round Environmental Negotiations

- **NAMA Context and Goals**

Within the context of Doha Round NAMA negotiations, WTO Members discussed free (or freer) trade in environmental goods. The December 2008 Draft NAMA Modalities Text indicates all Members agreed the WTO Committee on Trade and Environment in Special Session (CTESS) should work toward an understanding on the reduction, if not outright elimination, of tariffs and NTBs on non-agricultural environmental goods.[55]

---

53. *Carbon Taxes*, 71–72.

54. This discussion draws on TAMIOTTI ET AL., xvi–xxii, 87–128 (2009). *See also* Daniel Peat, *The Perfect FIT: Lessons for Renewable Energy Subsidies in the World Trade Organization*, 1 LSU JOURNAL OF ENERGY LAW & RESOURCES 43–66 (2012) (concerning WTO compatibility of renewable energy subsidies).

55. *See* World Trade Organization, Negotiating Group on Market Access, Fourth Revision of Draft Modalities for Non-Agricultural Market Access, TN/MA/W/103/Rev.3 (6 December 2008), www.wto.org. [Hereinafter, December 2008 Draft NAMA Modalities Text.] *Compare* December 2008 Draft NAMA Modalities Text, ¶ 31 *with* its predecessor, July 2008 Draft NAMA Modalities Text, ¶ 31.

Their goals were laudable enough, as they set out in an April 2011 Trade and Environment Document explained:

13. . . . Members agree that a successful outcome of the negotiations under Paragraph 31(iii) [*i.e.*, Paragraph 31(3) of the DDA] should deliver a triple-win in terms of trade, environment and development for WTO Members. First, the negotiations can benefit the environment by improving countries' ability to obtain high quality environmental goods at low cost or by enhancing the ability to increase production, exports and trade in environmentally beneficial products. This can directly improve the quality of life for citizens in all countries by providing a cleaner environment and better access to safe water, sanitation or clean energy.

14. The liberalization of trade in environmental goods and services can be beneficial for development by assisting developing countries in obtaining the tools needed to address key environmental priorities as part of their ongoing development strategies. Finally, trade wins because these products become less costly and efficient producers of such technologies can find new markets. In addition, liberalizing trade in environmental goods will encourage the use of environmental technologies, which can in turn stimulate innovation and technology transfer.[56]

Note there is a reasonably clear link between these goals and the broader Doha Round aim of combatting poverty and terrorism: enhancements in the environmental quality in which poor people find themselves represent tangible gains, which in turn may impress upon them a sense that they can benefit from trade liberalization. Seeing such progress, they develop hope in the world trading system, and their hope in the world trading system can supplant vulnerability to extremist ideologies. Unfortunately, these goals, and the December 2008 agreement language, are little else than a repetition of Article 31:3 of the DDA, which called for negotiations on environmental goods and services.

Likewise, agreement in the December 2008 Text that Members seek greater coherence between GATT-WTO rules and *MEAs* simply repeats the obligation they set for themselves when they launched the Doha Round. After all, Article 31:1 of the DDA called for an examination of the relationship between those trade rules and *MEAs*, and Article 31:2 urged greater collaboration between the WTO and *MEA* Secretariats.

Indubitably, a more open market for environmental goods and services would bolster the ability of an importing country to obtain high-quality items to help it deal with air pollution, renewable energy, waste management, water, and wastewater

---

56. *See* World Trade Organization, Negotiating Group on Market Access, *Textual Report by the Chairman, Ambassador Luzius Wasescha, on the State of Play of the NAMA Negotiations*, TN/MA/W/103/Rev.3/Add.1 (21 April 2011). [Hereinafter, April 2011 NAMA Document.] *See id.*, Part II ¶¶ 13–14.

treatment.[57] Developing countries were keenly interested in technology transfer and S&D treatment in respect of these goods and services. The topic took on particular poignancy as discussions about climate change continued amidst a new, more flexible approach signaled by President Barack H. Obama (1961–, President, 2009–2017) than had been taken by his predecessor.

- **Three Issues**

Frustrated by the lack of progress under WTO auspices on liberalizing trade in environmental goods and services, some American politicians and business groups advocated removal of the topic from the Doha Round agenda. They wanted fast action, namely, an FTA on "green" goods and services akin to the 1997 *ITA*. They pointed out developing countries like China and India have the highest tariffs and NTBs to such goods and services. If they removed these obstacles, considerable progress could be made on reducing greenhouse gas emissions that cause global warming. There would be a larger volume of trade, at cheaper prices, in environmental goods and services, thus more firms and individuals would have access to them.

But, advocates for breaking off this topic from the DDA met with two arguments. First, doing so would imperil further the Round. Having removed the promising topics, what would be left in the Round would be the hardest issues. Second, doing so would help American businesses, which have an international competitive advantage in goods like wind turbines, smart meters used to make electricity grids more efficient, and replacement parts for extant power plants. In other words, dominant MNCs like General Electric were motivated by market access that would benefit them, particularly because they feared a loss of their competitive advantage.[58]

Not surprisingly, therefore, the WTO Secretariat announcement in January 2011 that Members were ready "to move forward on environmental negotiations" was more bluster than substance.[59] The Members were set to discuss the same issues:

(1) relationship between GATT-WTO rules and *MEAs*;

(2) cooperation among Secretariats of relevant international organizations, including the WTO and *MEA* entities; and

(3) trade liberalization, *i.e.*, the elimination of tariffs and NTBs, in environmental goods and services.

But, all they did was identify options. They laid out no clear road map for a consensus.

---

57. World Trade Organization, *Briefing Notes — Trade and Environment*, www.wto.org. These Notes were posted in connection with the Seventh Ministerial Conference held in Geneva from 30 November–2 December 2009.

58. Indeed, among the 30 leading companies (as of October 2009) in international trade in environmental goods and services, only six were American firms. *See* Amy Tsui, *Environmental Goods, Services Agreement Critical to Green Exports, DOC Official Says*, 26 International Trade Reporter (BNA) 1382 (15 October 2009).

59. World Trade Organization, *Members Ready to Move Forward on Environment Negotiations*, 10 and 14 January 2011, www.wto.org.

The first topic involved issues such as national coordination, technical assistance, capacity building, and special trade obligations (STOs) set out in *MEAs*. On the second topic, the EU asserted *MEAs* already at work in the WTO should be given official status in the WTO as Observers. As to the third topic, Members could not agree on how to define an "environmental good." They talked about tariff cuts on roughly 400 products, in categories such as air pollution control, environmental technologies (including carbon capture and control), renewable energy, waste management, and water treatment.

But, should "environmental goods" be defined by using the approach of a list, a project, or the classic GATT request-offer? What about technical assistance and capacity building to facilitate the acquisition of environmental technologies by poor countries, and S&D treatment for them? Liberalizing trade in environmental services hardly was simpler than goods. It, too, involved the same kinds of issues.

Despite its rhetoric to the contrary, the April 2011 Trade and Environment Document showed WTO Members had made little substantive progress on these three issues since the issuance of the December 2008 NAMA Text. Indeed, as to the first two issues, they made no progress at all. The Document contained an Annex (namely, Annex I), with an introductory comment and draft ministerial decision on trade and the environment. The proposed comment and decision were largely a summary of bland discussions among Members: the importance of national-level coordination of STOs in *MEAs* should be highlighted;[60] information exchange is important;[61] a textual formulation to facilitate appropriate observer status had yet to be agreed;[62] an outcome on technical assistance and capacity-building is needed;[63] and perhaps a non-mandatory approach to the relationship between WTO rules and STOs in *MEAs*, in the context of dispute settlement, might be appropriate.[64] On these and related topics, the Members had not taken the key step of making choices.

On the third issue, as to the definition of an "environmental good," the April 2011 contained an Annex (specifically, Annex II.A and II.B) that did nothing more than compile all merchandise, at the HS 6-digit level, which various Members proposed should qualify as such a good. By its own admission, the compilation is a "work in

60. *See* April 2011 Trade and Environment Document, Annex I, Introductory Comment, first 3 bullet points; Draft Ministerial Decision on Trade and Environment, Preambular Language and ¶ 1. [Hereinafter, April 2011 Document.]

61. *See* April 2011 Document, Annex I, Introductory Comment, 4th bullet points; Introductory Comment, first 3 bullet points; Draft Ministerial Decision on Trade and Environment, Preambular Language and ¶¶ 1–2, 5(a)-(b).

62. *See* April 2011 Document, Annex I, Introductory Comment, 5th bullet point; Draft Ministerial Decision on Trade and Environment, Preambular Language and ¶¶ 2–4.

63. *See* April 2011 Document, Annex I, Introductory Comment, 6th bullet point; Draft Ministerial Decision on Trade and Environment, ¶ 5(c)-(d), Annex I:A ("Proposed Elements Relating to a Group of Experts").

64. *See* April 2011 Document, Annex I, Introductory Comment, 7th bullet point; Draft Ministerial Decision on Trade and Environment, ¶ 5(e), Annex I:B ("Proposed Elements on Dispute Settlement").

progress" and a mere "*starting point* for discussion . . . towards a credible core list of environmental goods . . . ."[65] Annex II covered 6 broad product categories:

(1) Air pollution control.

(2) Carbon capture and storage.

(3) Environmental technologies.

(4) Renewable energy.

(5) Waste Management and Water Treatment.

(6) Other.

Thus, by no means did the Members reach consensus on the proposals. In WTO-speak, the compilation was a "reference universe."[66] That "universe" did not expand to environmental services, which the Members—despite the DDA negotiating mandate—seemed to have all but forgotten.

• **Disputes Over Lists and Methodologies**

Indeed, the Introductory Comment to Annex II shows how far apart the Members were after a decade of negotiations:

4. According to a submission presented [by Mexico and Chile on 11 March 2011] during the recent intensification of negotiations, there would be two lists, one for developed and one for developing country Members with both being self-selected from the reference universe and subject to an agreed *alpha* minimum number of tariff lines for developed country Members and a *beta* minimum number of tariff lines for developing country Members, with *alpha* being greater in number than *beta*.

5. The idea of developing two lists had been put forward by two proposals in the past. In one of these proposals [from the U.S., in July 2003], there would be a *core list* of environment products that could deliver an ambitious and significant outcome. In addition, there will be a *complementary list* on which consensus could not be reached from which Members would have to self-select a certain *x* per cent of tariff lines.

6. According to another proposal [from China, in July 2004], there would be a *common list* for all Members, which comprises specific product lines that constitute environmental goods. The second list would be a *development list* which could comprise products selected from the common list by developing countries for exemption or a lower level of tariff treatment.

---

65. *See* April 2011 Document, Annex II.A—Reference Universe of Environmental Goods: Official HS Descriptions ¶ 1; Annex II.B—Sample Core List of Environmental Goods by Official HS 2002 Description ¶ 1 (emphasis original).

66. April 2011 Document, Part II ¶¶ 7–8; Annex II—Structure of the Outcome, Environmental Goods Coverage Under Paragraph 31(III), Introductory Comment, ¶ 2.

7. In an effort to combine the various elements of all proposals on the table, the *hybrid* approach includes the following components: (i) an agreed core list which would comprise a targeted set of environmental goods on which all Members would take commitments; (ii) a complementary self-selected list: developed countries would individually select a number of environmental products for tariff elimination and developing countries are encouraged to participate; (iii) as a complement to the common core list and complementary lists, products would be identified through a request/offer process, the outcome of which would be multilateralized in accordance with the MFN principle; and (iv) environmental projects could be used to identify lines for inclusion in the common core list, the complementary self-selected list or the request-offer list or by unilateral liberalization if used in environmental projects.[67]

Worse yet, the Members failed to agree on a methodology to discipline, and on the disciplines for, tariffs on the goods in this universe.

Some WTO Members (such as Argentina and Brazil) called for application of the old-fashioned request-offer approach, whereby an interested country would seek a tariff concession on a good it deemed "environmental" with an importing country.[68] Trade liberalization, as well as the identification of what articles qualified as "environmental," then would occur only on a product-by-product basis. Other Members sought a more ambitious approach, calling for a reduction of tariffs to zero. Still other Members advocated a zero-for-X strategy, *i.e.*, duty-free treatment on some environmental goods in exchange for a certain minimum cut of X on other goods. And, there were Members who proposed a formula that would cut tariffs by 50% quickly, followed by an eventual elimination of all tariffs.[69]

- **No Standstill Agreement**

Regrettably, the Members could not reach even a "standstill agreement." In July 2011, the U.S. proposed all Members pledge to freeze their applied duty rates on 155 "green" tariff lines. Brazil and India balked at the proposal, arguing they and other developing countries would be most affected. Why?

Because developed countries already apply tariff rates up at their bound levels. Hence, while rich countries cannot raise their green tariffs anymore, poor countries would be unable to do so. In effect, their applied rates would become their *de facto* bound rates. Developing countries countered with a proposal for a standstill

---

67. April 2011 Document, Annex II — Structure of the Outcome, Environmental Goods Coverage Under Paragraph 31(III), Introductory Comment, ¶¶ 4–6 (emphasis original, footnotes omitted). For the identification of countries associated with various proposals, see fn. 5 to ¶ 4, fn. 6 to ¶ 5, and fn. 9 to ¶ 6.

68. April 2011 Document, Annex II — Structure of the Outcome, Environmental Goods Coverage Under Paragraph 31(III), Introductory Comment, ¶ 2.

69. *See* April 2011 Document, Part II ¶ 17.

agreement on 25 green tariff lines. Here, the U.S. balked, arguing the number of lines was too low to give the proposal credibility.

- **No Agreement on NTBs or S&D Treatment**

Likewise, there was no consensus among Members on reducing NTBs on environmental goods, nor on S&D treatment (*e.g.*, in the form of flexibilities from tariff cuts) for poor countries.[70] The juxtaposition of the lofty goals of trade liberalization in environmental goods, along with their link to poverty and extremism, on the one hand, and lack of progress in this area of the Doha Round, on the other hand, illustrates well how the Round betrayed its original purposes as time passed. However "environmental goods" may be defined, it is axiomatic that this universe is smaller than that of all industrial products (and for that matter, agricultural goods). To have achieved next-to-nothing in a decade in a smaller-scale universe — a decade in which the science of climate change advanced considerably to emphasize a commonality of interests among all countries — is nothing short of scandalous.

Frustrated at the stagnation, the U.S. and other like-minded countries turned to a different forum: the APEC group. In September 2012, APEC foreign and trade ministers agreed to a list of environmental goods on which they pledged to apply tariff rates of 5% or less by 2015.[71] This commitment fulfilled a 2011 APEC Directive to establish a "List of Environmental Goods." The List agreed upon included air pollution control technologies, environmental monitoring and assessment equipment, renewable and clean energy technologies, and wastewater treatment equipment. Applying duties of 5% or less entailed a substantial reduction from existing rates, which were as high as 35%. However, reducing duties was voluntary, *i.e.*, the commitment was non-binding.

- **Solar Panels and Trade Remedies**

The Technique Effect (discussed earlier) presumes that a country follows Smith-Ricardo production specialization and division of labor patterns. That may be true for a country that neither has nor seeks to build an industry in, say, solar panels. But, some countries want to get into that market, and others already in it may fear unfair foreign competition from potential or actual new entrants.

So, for example, in the aftermath of the Doha Round failure came several high-profile AD and CVD actions by the U.S. and EU against solar panel imports from China. China (as of July 2013) is the largest producer of solar panels in the world, but its rapid expansion of production between 2008 and 2012 caused an excess supply of them on world markets. Predictably, solar panel prices tumbled. China also is a large importer of ingredients for solar panels, such as polysilicon and specializes manufacturing equipment. The U.S. and EU are its preeminent suppliers.

---

70. *See* April 2011 Document, Part II ¶ 18.

71. *See* Len Bracken, *APEC Agrees on List of Environmental Goods Set to Receive 5 Percent Tariff Limit by 2015*, 29 International Trade Reporter (BNA) 1485 (13 September 2013).

In 2012, the U.S. imposed AD duties and CVDs against Chinese solar panel imports. Within a year, in July 2013, July, China retaliated by imposing AD duties on American (and Korean) solar-grade polysilicon ranging from 53.5% to 57% (and 2.4% to 48.7% on Korean merchandise). Among the American producer-exporters were subsidiaries of Dow Corning and SunEdison. China claimed the dumped imports caused substantial damage to its polysilicon producers.

Next up was the EU, which sought to protect its solar panel industry from unfairly traded Chinese merchandise. European polysilicon producers, like Wacker Chemie of Germany, feared China and the fate of the likes of Dow Corning and SunEditon, so they lobbied against any European action. Nevertheless, the EU imposed on 6 June 2013 the largest AD duties in its history on Chinese solar panels. The AD duty rates initially were set at 11.8%, and rose to 47.6% in August. The purpose of the phased increase was to give China time to settle the case. With Chinese insistence that the EU phase out AD duties by the end of 2014, and exclude solar panel components (*e.g.,* wafers), no settlement occurred. The final rate itself equated to U.S. $1.10 per watt, which the EU said offset Chinese dumping. That dumping had cost over 15,000 European jobs and 60 European insolvencies and plant closures. Immaturely, China retaliated literally the next day, 7 June, in a tit-for-tat fashion, launching an AD investigation of EU wine imports: China sought to penalize France, Italy, and Spain, which backed the EU AD case, and which are the major wine exporters to China. Ironically, the main Chinese losers from any AD duties on European wine would be some Communist Party cadres and their cronies, those who fancy themselves as oenological connoisseurs.[72]

Such cases suggest WTO Members may agree in theory that free trade in environmental goods should exist to help mitigate climate change. But, in practice they approach the matter from a mercantilist perspective: some want that trade to consist of their exports, while others do not want to be dependent on imports, and still others feel a need to protect a domestic industry. Hence, environmental goods, for all their special importance, become the subject of bargaining as if they were widgets.

---

72. Ultimately, the sides did settle the case, with a managed trade solution through 2015 that favored China. In August 2013, the EU agreed to give China 70% of its solar panel market, but at a set price. The minimum price was 73 U.S. cents per watt for a total of 7 gigawatts worth of solar panel exports, or 70% of the European market. (European, Japanese, and Korean producers were left battling for the remaining 30%.) Chinese producer-exporters thus escaped the 47.6% AD duty. China did not have to agree to drop its AD investigation of wine, or of silicon materials used to make solar panels. *See* Joe Kirwin, *EU Approves Deal with China on Dumping Of Solar Panels, Though Some States Object*, 30 International Trade Reporter (BNA) 1239 (8 August 2013).

VII. Toward a Plurilateral
Environmental Goods Agreement

Following the Ninth WTO Ministerial Conference in Bali, Indonesia in December 2013, the U.S., EU, and China, plus 11 other WTO Members commenced negotiations toward a plurilateral free trade arrangement covering environmental goods.[73] The idea originated in a 25 June 2013 "Climate Action Plan" of President Barack H. Obama. In that Plan, the President said America would seek an accord on duty-free treatment covering 90% of global trade in environmental goods. But, that Plan surely was borne of frustration with Doha Round discussions on green goods, which bogged down over disagreements about the (1) definition of "environmental good" and (2) coverage list of over 400 products.

The 14 Members launching the talks accounted for 86%, or almost $1 trillion annually, so that goal seemed realizable. The 11 other Members were Australia, Canada, Costa Rica, Hong Kong, Japan, Korea, New Zealand, Norway, Singapore, Switzerland, and Taiwan. They expected Israel would join, too.

In their 24 January 2014 announcement, made amidst the World Economic Forum in Davos, Switzerland, they articulated a goal of building on a September 2012 agreement reached by the countries in the Asia Pacific Economic Cooperation forum, namely, to cut tariffs to 5% or less on 54 environmental goods by the end of 2015.[74] The APEC arrangement covered air pollution control technologies (*e.g.*, catalytic converters and soot removers), environmental monitoring and assessment equipment (*e.g.*, air and water quality monitors), gas and wind turbines, solar panels, solid and hazardous waste treatment technologies (*e.g.*, crushing and sorting machinery, and waste incinerators), and wastewater treatment technologies (*e.g.*, filters and ultraviolet disinfection equipment).[75] It also covered bamboo flooring, photovoltaic cells, or steam boilers.[76] Implementation commenced on schedule, resulting in some dramatic duty declines, such as China's cut from 25% to 5% on water-purifying machinery, and from 10% to 5% on renewable fuel generators.[77]

---

73. *See* Daniel Pruzin, *U.S., Others Launch Global Talks On Free Trade in Environmental Goods*, 31 International Trade Reporter (BNA) 195 (30 January 2014). [Hereinafter, *U.S., Others Launch.*]

74. *See* Carlos Kuriyama, *The APEC List of Environmental Goods*, APEC Policy Support Unit, Policy Brief Number 5 (28 November 2012), http://www.apec.org.

75. *See U.S., Others Launch.*

76. *See U.S. Cuts Tariffs on Environmental Goods*, 33 International Trade Reporter (BNA) (7 January 2016). The United States implemented this agreement, cutting tariffs to 5 percent or less, as of 31 December 2015. *See id.*

77. *See* Asia Pacific Economic Cooperation, *APEC Economies' Implementation Plans for Tariff Reductions on Environmental Goods* (28 January 2016), www.apec.org/Groups/Committee-on-Trade-and-Investment/APEC-Economies-Implementation-Plans.aspx; Murray Griffin, *Asia-Pacific Countries Cut Tariffs on Environmental Goods*, 33 International Trade Reporter (BNA) (4 February 2016).

WTO Members said the APEC deal was a good start, but their ambitions were higher. The Members aimed to eliminate all duties on environmental goods so as to bolster protections for the environment (*e.g.*, cut air, soil, and water pollution), address climate change, contribute to green growth, encourage the use of clean and renewable energy (as well as improve energy and resource efficiency), abate noise, and most broadly, help set the world on a path of sustainable development. Moreover, Members criticized the APEC list as reflecting interests of manufacturers clamoring to ensure their products were included.[78] Since it was created, consumer groups lobbied for inclusion of environmentally friendly products. For example, the "People For Bikes Coalition" (along with the Bicycle Products Suppliers Coalition), said bikes and bike parts should be on the list: they faced tariffs of up to 11%, but are a cheap, zero-emission mode of transport.[79] And, all Members understood NTBs impeded market access for environmental goods.

So, WTO Members agreed the key parameters for a potential WTO green goods agreement, or *EGA — Environmental Goods Agreement —* were:

(1) Participation in negotiations would be open to any WTO Member willing to eliminate tariffs on environmental goods, staring with the 54-item APEC list.

(2) The agreement would be a "living" one, with green goods added over time, and eventually services included.

(3) Duty-free treatment would be extended on an unconditional MFN basis to all WTO Members, whether or not they participated in the negotiations.

(4) The agreement would enter into force upon acceptance by a critical mass of Members.

To be sure, U.S. was not motivated entirely by green-friendly ideals. Tariffs on such goods were high, some being 35%, whereas the average American tariff on such goods was 3.5%.

So, an *EGA* would enhance market access — and profits — for American producer-exporters of environmental goods vis-à-vis foreign competitors, and generate jobs in America. The USTR, Ambassador Michael Froman (1962–), admitted as much: "One of the benefits of a negotiation like this is that it helps open markets that have higher barriers to our exports and therefore help increase our exports as well."[80] Moreover, he noted that duty-free treatment for environmental goods would not weaken American trade defense instruments, like AD duties and CVDs against such goods.[81]

---

78. *See* Mark Lihn, *Organizations Want More Products In Environmental Goods Agreement*, 31 International Trade Reporter (BNA) 1058 (12 June 2014). [Hereinafter, *Organizations Want.*]

79. *See Organizations Want.*

80. *See U.S., Others Launch.*

81. On 21 March 2014, the USTR notified Congress of its intent to launch negotiations on the environmental deal. *See* Len Bracken, *USTR Notifies Congress of Intent To Launch Environmental*

In May 2015, the sixth round of *EGA* talks was held. By then, tariffs on environmental goods remained in the range of 0 to 35%. And, by this round, 17 WTO Members participated covering 44 countries (given the presence of the European Union) and representing 90% of global trade. Their ambition remained to "eliminate tariffs on goods that make a credible contribution to the environment."[82] The participants nominated over 650 such goods, from bicycles to electric motors, gas, hydraulic, and wind turbines to solar panels, and from catalytic converters to wastewater filters.[83] They were evaluating each one on a product-by-product basis. Examples included items pertaining to clean air, energy, and water technologies, such as ceramic substrates (used in mobile emissions), to diesel filters, made by the American company Corning, Inc., and to mechanical seals, which the John Crane Group, an American subsidiary of British-based Smiths Group, manufactured.[84] The examples showed the keen interest of United States firms in duty free, quota free treatment for environmental goods. Corning, for one, faced a 17.5% tariff in China on its ceramic substrates.

By June 2015, there appeared to be some convergence on a product list. Australia, Canada, China, EU, Japan, Korea, New Zealand, Switzerland, and U.S. all called for inclusion in an *EGA* of the following 10 environmental goods and services categories: (1) air pollution control; (2) energy efficiency; (3) environmental monitoring and analysis; (4) environmentally preferable products; (5) environmental remediation and clean up; (6) noise and vibration abatement; (7) renewable energy generation; (8) resource efficiency; (9) solid and hazardous waste management; and (10) water waste management and water treatment.[85] A leaked version of the product list in September 2015 suggested over 50 product categories containing more than 2,400 goods, but there was no consensus on this list.[86] The U.S. also suggested a phase-out mechanism:

> The proposal suggests that EGA parties may apply their tariff reductions in four phases: immediately, three years, five years and seven years after the agreement enters into force . . . .

> The U.S. proposal suggests that EGA participants should completely eliminate tariffs on at least 75 percent of the products on the entry date of the

---

Goods Talks, 31 International Trade Reporter (BNA) 570 (27 March 2014).

82. Len Bracken, *Sixth Round of Environmental Goods Talks Set for Early May, Moving into Second Phase*, International Trade Daily (BNA) (8 April 2015). [Hereinafter, *Sixth Round*.]

83. *See* Bryce Baschuk, *EGA Negotiators Hope U.N. Climate Change Talks May Spur Agreement on Trade Benefits*, 32 International Trade Reporter (BNA) 1148 (25 June 2015). [Hereinafter, *EGA Negotiators*.]

84. *See Sixth Round.*

85. *See EGA Negotiators.*

86. *See* Bryce Baschuk, *Environmental Group Leaks Preliminary EGA Product List*, International Trade Daily (BNA) (16 September 2015).

agreement and no more than 5 percent of the products should be subject to seven-year tariff elimination schedules.[87]

A strong precedent existed for the American proposal. The *ITA* used the same phase out mechanism.

In March 2016, China tried to persuade WTO Members engaged in *EGA* talks to accept a "Snapback Provision" whereby any Member that joined the *EGA* later could withdraw from it.[88] Specifically:

> If the percentage of world trade covered under the agreement falls below 70 percent or if trade in such products by a non-participant of the agreement — such as India — exceeds 3 percent of world trade, a withdrawal mechanism would be triggered automatically.

> After the snapback mechanism is triggered, any party to the *EGA* would have the right to withdraw their tariff concessions without being challenged by other parties to the agreement . . . .[89]

In effect, the Snapback would allow "participants to withdraw their *EGA* tariff concessions if at any point in the future the deal no longer covers a 'critical mass' of environmental products."[90] The result would be re-instatement of pre-*EGA* tariffs on the covered products, which would be tantamount to withdrawal from the deal. As intimated, China was concerned about free riders, like India, which was benefitting from the *ITA* and its 2015 expansion in coverage, but not a formal party to that deal. Thresholds like 70% overall or 3% for a country would put an end to the free-riding. Though Members rejected the idea as undermining the fundamental goal of the *EGA*, namely, eradicating all tariffs on roughly 350 environmental goods covered by the accord, China stuck to the idea.

Instead, the following month, Members sought to classify goods into one of three groups:[91]

(1) Category 1:

Goods in this grouping would see tariffs eliminated as soon as the EGA took effect.

(2) Category 2:

Tariffs on these goods would fall across three, five, or seven years.

---

87. *See* Bryce Baschuk, *Trade Negotiators Pan Chinese EGA Snapback Proposal*, 33 International Trade Reporter (BNA) (10 March 2016). [Hereinafter, *Trade Negotiators Pan.*]

88. *See Trade Negotiators Pan.*

89. *See Trade Negotiators Pan.*

90. Bryce Baschuk, *Environmental Goods Talks Lag as Agreement Window Narrows*, 33 International Trade Reporter (BNA) 1529 (27 October 2016).

91. *See* Bryce Baschuk, *China Says No to Environmental Goods Pact at G-20 Meeting*, 33 International Trade Reporter (BNA) 686 (12 May 2016).

(3) Category 3:

> These goods were too sensitive for inclusion in the *EGA*, hence their tariffs would not be eliminated or phased out.

These groups were staging categories, and they adduced that Members could not agree on immediate duty-free treatment for all goods.

What was China's reply to the response of the Member's? China "refused to budge":

> Chinese trade negotiators refused to back down from their various demands related to an . . . *EGA* during a recent trade meeting in Paris, saying they don't want any "free riders" to benefit from the pact.
>
> For months the Chinese delegation refused to present its market access offer, has sought more flexible tariff reduction terms and demanded specific provisions to prevent non-*EGA* participants from benefitting from the deal.
>
> Chinese Assistant Commerce Minister Wang Shouwen stuck to those demands in Paris. He said any World Trade Organization member that accounts for more than 1 percent of global trade in *EGA* products must either join the accord or lose its WTO most-favored nation status, according to officials familiar with the meeting.
>
> . . .
>
> China has said it wants to ensure that the deal includes as many WTO members as possible and is working to ensure the agreement covers a critical mass of global trade in environmental products.
>
> . . .
>
> The *Environmental Goods Agreement* is being negotiated among a subset of 17 WTO members that account for roughly 80 percent of global trade in such products, such as China, the European Union, Japan, South Korea and the U.S.
>
> The 145 WTO members that don't participate in the *Environmental Goods Agreement* would still benefit as "free riders" to the deal because *EGA* signatories would apply their tariff cuts on a most-favored nation basis to all members once a critical mass threshold is met.
>
> China is seeking an automatic withdrawal mechanism, also known as a snapback, that would allow Environmental Goods Agreement parties to raise tariffs if at any point the percentage of world trade in products covered by the agreement falls below 70 percent.
>
> China also is seeking special and differential treatment that, in principle, would provide developing countries with more flexible tariff reduction terms than developed nations.[92]

---

92. Bryce Baschuk, *Chinese Negotiators Don't Budge in Environmental Goods Talks*, 33 International Trade Reporter (BNA) 811 (9 June 2016).

It seemed clear the two sides were far off from completing an *EGA*.

That they were was manifest in September 2016:

> Influential participants in the 44-country *EGA* have expressed their reluctance to fully eliminate tariffs in several core areas—like air pollution abatement technology, clean water technology, and clean energy technology, among others.

> A particularly contentious disagreement centers on the European Union, which has repeatedly rebuffed China's calls to cut tariffs on more than a dozen bicycle parts . . . .

> The EU, which is home to cycling companies like Peugeot, and Bianchi, argues that bicycles are not necessarily environmental products despite the fact that they help reduce the amount of cars on the road and thus the proliferation of greenhouse gasses.[93]

The differences continued to year-end 2016. At the November 2016 APEC meeting in Lima, Peru:[94]

> China demanded that *EGA* participants cut their tariffs on 36 key products—such as bicycles and bicycle parts—which could flood the U.S. and the European Union with cheap Chinese bicycles.

> In addition, China refused to cut its own tariffs on environmental products such as small gas turbines, programmable controllers, batteries, polysilicon, carbon fiber and valves, among others.

> China also demanded inclusion of an automatic withdrawal mechanism, also known as a snapback provision, that would allow *EGA* parties to raise tariffs if at any point the percentage of world trade in products covered by the agreement fell below 70 percent.[95]

---

93. Bryce Baschuk, *Environmental Goods Negotiators Make Incremental Progress*, 33 International Trade Reporter (BNA) 1338 (29 September 2016).

A similar issue existed with respect to wood, specifically, coniferous wood products used in construction:

> Japan argued that cutting tariffs on trade in wood products would lead to unsustainable forestry practices and undermine international efforts to crack down on illegal logging.
> Canada, New Zealand, and Norway countered that sustainable harvesting of coniferous wood products involves a negligible percentage of illegal logging when compared to trade in deciduous trees from certain tropical regions.
> Japan is among the world's top importers of wood products and in 2015. Canada, New Zealand, and Norway collectively exported about $1.4 billion of wood products to Japan, according to World Bank statistics.

Bryce Baschuk, *Wood-Tariffs Fight Splinters Environmental Goods Talks*, 33 International Trade Reporter (BNA) 1529 (27 October 2016).

94. Bryce Baschuk, *Chinese Demands Threaten Environmental Goods Accord*, 33 International Trade Reporter (BNA) 1659 (24 November 2016).

95. Bryce Baschuk, *Chinese Demands Threaten Environmental Goods Accord*, 33 International Trade Reporter (BNA) 1659 (24 November 2016).

The Sino-European-American debate suggested a philosophical schism: if bicycles are defined within the ambit of green goods, then countries might be propelling down a slippery slope in which a broad array of items should be in the *EGA* scope, which nearly ensures more corporate interests in exporting and importing countries crashing against each other.

By December 2016, there were 19 *EGA* participants, encompassing 46 countries (thanks to the EU members): Australia; Canada; China; Costa Rica; the European Union (representing Austria, Belgium, Bulgaria, Croatia, Republic of Cyprus, Czech Republic, Denmark, Estonia, Finland, France, Germany, Greece, Hungary, Ireland, Italy, Latvia, Lithuania, Luxembourg, Malta, Netherlands, Poland, Portugal, Romania, Slovakia, Slovenia, Spain, Sweden and the United Kingdom); Hong Kong, China; Iceland; Israel; Japan; Korea; New Zealand; Norway; Singapore; Switzerland; Liechtenstein; Chinese Taipei; Turkey; and the U.S. These participants accounted for almost all the global trade in environmental goods. At the end of their early December negotiating session, the WTO Director General, Roberto Azevêdo (1957–) said:

> Participants negotiated in good faith and made good progress towards an agreement. I believe that the knowledge and understanding gained in these discussions will help us to move forward in the near future. I urge participants to show whatever flexibility they can to help conclude the deal.[96]

His first sentence was "spin" for the media, and his last sentence went unheard. China, the EU alleged, had scuppered the talks, partly over bicycles:

> . . . [European Trade Commissioner Cecilia] Malmstrom said bicycles had become totemic for China and nobody else, and the agreement went far wider, adding that the EU had "quite cheap bicycles already."[97]

The EU resisted those demands, as well as bicycles because of its insistence on "impossible late demands" made by China, covering a range of new elements and perspectives that could not be accommodated.[98]

Those demands amounted to a rejection by China of an ambitious *EGA* list of 250 products, and a counter-proposal for a slimmed down list excluding items such as solar panels and wind turbines. Reportedly, "Chinese negotiators were unwilling to find a compromise, sought unbalanced demands and offered an eleventh-hour counterproposal that wasn't constructive . . . . China's counterproposal sought to include 35 of its 36 priority items and excluded more than half of the U.S. and EU's

---

96. World Trade Organization, *Progress Made on Environmental Goods Agreement, Setting Stage for Further Talks*, 4 December 2016, www.wto.org/english/news_e/news16_e/ega_04dec16_e.htm.

97. *Quoted in* Tom Miles, *EU Blames China for WTO Environmental Trade Talks Collapse*, REUTERS, 4 December 2016, www.reuters.com/article/us-trade-environment-idUSKBN13T0MX. [Hereinafter, *EU Blames.*]

98. *EU Blames.*

most important items."[99] China also demanded special and differential treatment for developing countries, whereby their responsibilities under the *EGA* would be reduced vis-à-vis developed countries.

The counterproposal also was met with a distinct lack of interest in the *EGA* by the Administration of President Donald J. Trump.[100] By June 2017, there were 18 WTO Members participating in *EGA* negotiations, and 12 of them were enthusiastic about concluding a deal before the December 2017 WTO Ministerial Conference in Buenos Aires. Canada and the EU were among them, America was not. That was unsurprising, as earlier in June, Mr. Trump pulled the U.S. out of the 2015 *Paris Agreement* on climate change.

---

99. Bryce Baschuk, *Environmental Trade Talks Collapse Over Product List Discord*, 33 International Trade Reporter (BNA) 1723 (8 December 2016).

100. Bryce Baschuk, *U.S. "Reviewing" Environmental Trade Pact*, 34 International Trade Reporter (BNA) 949 (29 June 2017).

Part Eight

Trade and Intellectual Property

Chapter 30

Overview of IP[1]

I. IP Types

IP is a unique form of intangible property that protects a creator's right to their inventions or works. IPRs are like other property rights in that they allow the creator (or owner) to own an idea and benefit from it. IP encourages the creation and invention of new ideas and technology, by protecting those that invest time and resources into inventing something new. Over the last 150 years, IP has expanded to include Patents, Copyrights, Trademarks, and Integrated Circuits

- **Patents**

A patent is an IPR granted to the inventor that makes a new product or process. The inventor (or patent holder) is granted an exclusive right to make, use, distribute, import, and sell her invention for a limited period of time. In exchange for the patent right, the patent holder is required to publicly disclose information about their inventions. This publicly disclosed information serves the public and promotes further creativity and innovation.

The IPR is transferable like property in that the patent holder may give permission, license, or sell the patented invention to a third party. Regardless of who owns the patent, patents only offer protection for a limited period of time. Generally, Patent protection expires after 20 years. After expiration, the protection ends and the invention becomes available for commercial exploitation by others.

To qualify for a patent, generally an invention must meet four requirements. First, the invention must be of practical use and show an element of novelty. In other words, show some "new characteristic which is not known in the body of existing knowledge in its technical field."[2] Second, the invention must be "non-obvious." Non-obvious requires that a "person having ordinary skill in the art" would not know how to solve the problem the invention was created to solve by using exactly the same mechanism. Third, the invention must be capable of industrial application. The invention cannot be merely theoretical; it must have an industrial or business purpose. Fourth, the subject matter must be accepted as "patentable." In many

---

1. Documents References:
    (1) *Havana (ITO) Charter* Articles 19, 37:7, 45:1(a)(vii)
    (2) GATT Articles IV, IX:6, XX(f)
    (3) WTO *Agreement on Trade Related Aspects of Intellectual Property Rights (TRIPs)*
2. *See* www.wipo.int/patents/en/faq_patents.html.

countries, scientific theories, aesthetic creations, mathematical methods, plant or animal varieties, discoveries of natural substances, commercial methods, methods for medical treatment, and computer programs are generally not patentable.[3]

- **Copyrights**

A copyright is an IPR that protects literary and artistic works. Copyrights are granted to authors, artists, or other creators of literary and artistic works including, but not limited to performances, films, computer programs, and electronic databases. Specifically, a copyright holder (or person that has obtained a license from the holder, *i.e.*, a publisher) is given the exclusive right to copy, import, or distribute the work. Like patents, copyrights are only granted for a limited period of time, typically defined in terms of the life of the author ("life in being") plus a defined number of years (with the *Berne Convention* setting a minimum of life in being plus 50 years, but U.S. and U.K. law with "life in being plus 70 years" rules).

It is important to note a copyright only protects the expression of an idea. A common misunderstanding is that copyrights protect the idea itself. For example, a copyright protects the particular arrangement of words in Romeo and Juliet, however it does not protect the idea of two star-crossed lovers.

Copyright is unique in that it does not have to be registered to have an IPR. A work receives copyright protection the moment it is created and fixed in a tangible form. Generally, registration of a copyright is voluntary, however in order to bring a lawsuit for infringement, the work must be registered.

- **Trademarks**

A distinctive word, phrase, symbol, or design that represents a company or product is a Trademark. Trademarks are extended the same IPRs as Copyrights and Patents, ensuring the owner's exclusive right to use the IP. Trademarks are used to prevent competitors from using similar designs to market lower quality or different products and services. If a competitor uses the same design or a similar one, courts have able to stop trademark infringement.

Even a company that chooses to not register its mark receives some protection. Under the common law, trademark rights are automatically acquired when a business uses a distinctive mark in commerce. These trademarks are enforceable at the state court level and are easily identified by a ™ next to the name or logo. However, trademarks that are officially registered with the U.S. Patent and Trademark Office receive more protection in federal court than unregistered trademarks. Trademarks that have gone through the registration process and have been officially registered are accompanied by a ® symbol next to the mark.

The amount of protection also depends on the level of distinctiveness. There are four categories: Generic (no protection); Description (weak protection); Suggestive (medium protection); and Arbitrary and Fanciful (strongest protection). Fanciful

---

3. *See* www.wipo.int/patents/en/faq_patents.html.

marks are devices invented for the sole purpose to function as a trademark, and have no other meaning (*i.e.*, Zappos—online shoe store). Arbitrary marks are pre-existing words used in an arbitrary way (*i.e.*, Amazon—online store). Suggestive Marks insinuate a quality or characteristic of a good or services (*i.e.*, "Microsoft," which suggests software for microcomputers).[4] Generic marks name a product and are not able to be trademarks. Valid trademarks run the risk of becoming generic marks if the trademark becomes a commonly used name for the product. Companies such as Kleenex were once almost considered Generic Marks and had to spend money advertising to prevent misuse of their trademark.

- **Integrated Circuits**

In the last several decades, IP law was extended to protect integrated circuits, or a chip or microchip. An integrated circuit is a product in its final form or an intermediate form, which some or all of the interconnections are integrally formed in or on a piece of material, an which is intended to perform an electronic function. Integrated circuits are given similar protection as a copyright, protecting against reproduction, importation, and distribution, however derivative works are similarly not protected. Additionally, if a integrated circuit is reverse engineered by a third party, it is permitted by law and the lawful owner of the integrated circuit does not have any recourse.[5]

Generally, in order to receive protection an integrated circuit must be registered with a national office such as the U.S. Copyright Office. In order to qualify for protection, an integrated circuit must either be registered or is first commercially exploited anywhere in the world. Additionally, the owner must be one of the following: a national or domiciliary of the U.S.; a national, domiciliary, or sovereign authority of a foreign nation that is a party to a treaty which the U.S. is a party; or a stateless person. The integrated circuit must be first to commercially exploit in America. However, protection is not extended to unoriginal integrated circuits or designs that are commonplace to the industry.

- **Trade Secrets**

A trade secret is a broad term encompassing any confidential business information that provides a company with an economic advantage over competitors. Examples of trade secrets include, but are not limited to: formulas, sales methods, distribution methods, consumer profiles, advertising strategies, lists of suppliers and clients, and manufacturing processes. The requirements of a trade secret vary from jurisdiction to jurisdiction, but there are general standards which are referred in the Article 39 of the *TRIPS Agreement*. The information (1) must be secret (*i.e.*, not generally known by industry); (2) confer commercial value because it is a secret;

---

4. *See* www.bitlaw.com/trademark/degrees.html.
5. 17 U.S.C. §906.

and (3) must have been subject to reasonable efforts by the holder to maintain its secrecy.[6]

These requirements are more difficult to meet than they may appear, however if they are met a trade secret is automatically protected without any procedural formalities. Additionally, trade secrets are protected for an unlimited period of time, as long as the holder continues to meet the jurisdiction's requirements. Some companies choose to protect information through a trade secret over a patent due to the indefinite protection period of a trade secret. Coca-Cola is a prime example of a company that has used trade secret to protect its product. It has been an effective method for protecting the secret Coca-Cola formula for longer than the 20 years of patent protection. However, the downfall of trade secrets is that once information is made public, through disclosure or reverse engineering, the trade secret is no longer protected.

II. Leading International IP Treaties

• 1883 *Paris Convention*

The *Paris Convention for the Protection of Industrial Property* was one of the first intellectual property treaties, originally signed in 1883.[7] It was created in response to the "increasingly international flow of technology and increase in international trade" and established a Union for the protection of utility models, industrial designs, trademarks, service marks, trade names, indication of origin and most important to this treaty, patents.[8]

The treaty provides greater harmonization of protection by establishing international protocols to provide for multinational patent filings. It protects the rights of those who file applications internationally, and requires contracting states treat foreigners' filings the same as their own nationals. Most importantly, the *Paris Convention* creates an International Priority Right.[9] Once an application is filed in one contracting state, the claimant retains the right to apply and obtain IPRs in other contracting states.[10] However, this right to apply is only available for a limited period of time; patents holders must file within 12 months while holders of trademarks must file within six months. Therefore, a subsequent application in a contracting state has priority over any similar prior applications, if the subsequent application was the first to file in a different contracting state and retained the priority right.

---

6. *See* www.wipo.int/sme/en/ip_business/trade_secrets/protection.htm.

7. *Paris Convention for the Protection of Industrial Property*, 20 March 1883, as revised at the Stockholm Revision Conference, July 14, 1967, 21 U.S.T. 1538, 828 U.N.T.S. 305.

8. Susan K. Sell, *Intellectual Property as a Trade Issue: From the Pairs Convention to GATT*, 13 LEGAL STUDIES FORUM 408 (1989).

9. *Paris Convention 1983*, Article 4.

10. *Paris Convention 1983*, Article 4.

Although innovative in 1883, the *Paris Convention* does not provide for much substantive IP law. This treaty leaves a contracting party to determine the level or protection it wishes to implement in its domestic laws. Many developing countries and LDCs do not provide the same level of patent protection and patent holders are not afforded all economic benefits from the patent. The U.S. and EU, both with sophisticated IP regimes, continue to dedicate resources and training to help developing countries and LDCs increase the level of IP protection. However, for many of these countries, they have yet to fulfill their *TRIPs* obligations, let alone implement a higher standard, providing substantial protection to patents.

- **1886 *Berne Convention***

The *Berne Convention for the Protection of Literary and Artistic Works*[11] (most commonly referred to as the *Berne Convention*) was the first multilateral copyright treaty, signed in 1886.[12] The *Berne Convention* was enacted to protect authors and booksellers from international pirating. Since the creation of the printing press in 1436, pirating books has become a serious concern for booksellers and authors. Providing international protection to authors has allowed authors the right to copy, distribute, and import the work and a means of redress.

An author is provided automatic protection under the *Berne Convention*. Contracting states are prohibited from instituting any formalities that could prevent an author's IPR.[13] Once a work is first published, or the author's country of origin (which is where the author is a national), is in a contracting state, all other member states must extend the same protection they grant their nationals to the author.[14] The basic protection required of all contracting states is that they protect "every production in the literary, scientific, and artistic domain, whatever may be the mode or form of its expression."[15] Furthermore, the *Convention* requires a minimum period of protection for a copyright to extend to the life of the author plus 50 years. A contracting state may provide for much longer, as does the *Copyright Term Extension Act of 1998*, for example, which protects copyrights for the author's life plus 75 years.[16]

Originally, the *Berne Convention* drafters considered removing the national treatment rule in favor of a uniform law for copyright. Ultimately, the attractiveness waned, and they wrote national treatment into the final draft. However, national treatment continues to be criticized. The downfall of national treatment is it provides only the same treatment to other countries' nationals as their own

---

11. *Berne Convention for the Protection of Literary and Artistic Works*, 9 September 1886, as revised at Stockholm on 14 July 1967, 828 U.N.T.S. 222.

12. *See* AMANDA REID & CAMILLE S. BROADWAY, ON THE CULTURE BORDER: ENFORCEMENT ISSUES FOR INTELLECTUAL PROPERTY RIGHTS IN DEVELOPING COUNTRIES 8 (2009).

13. *Berne Convention* 1971, Article 5(2).

14. *Berne Convention* 1971, Article 3.

15. *Berne Convention* 1971, Article 2(1).

16. 17 U.S.C. § 302(a) (2000).

nationals. For example, if Bangladesh provides limited protection of copyrights to their nationals, copyright owners in the EU will only receive that same limited protection, that may not properly guard their IPRs.

- **1964 *Rome Convention***

Copyright protection was extended under the *Rome Convention for the Protection of Performer, Producers of Phonograms and Broadcasting Organizations* of 1964.[17] The *Rome Convention* was a response to new technology, such as audiocassettes, that allowed sounds and images to be reproduced in an easier and cheaper manner. As the treaty name suggests, the protection extended to performers, producers of phonograms (*i.e.*, records, CDs, and DVDs), and broadcasting organizations.

The term "performers" is construed as a large group consisting of actors, singers, musicians, dancers, and other persons who act, sing, deliver, declaim, play in, or otherwise perform literary or artistic works.[18] Performers are granted national treatment if the performance:

(1) takes place in a contracting state;

(2) is incorporated in a phonograph in a contracting state; or

(3) is transmitted in a broadcast in a contracting state.

A phonogram is the exclusive aural fixation of sounds of a performance or of other sounds. The producers of phonograms are granted national treatment when:

(1) the producer of the phonogram is a national of a contracting state;

(2) the first fixation of the sound was made in a contracting state; and

(3) when the phonogram is first published in a contracting state.[19]

Lastly, a broadcasting organization is one that transmits by wireless means for public reception of sounds, or of images and sounds. Broadcasting organizations enjoy the right to authorize or prohibit certain acts such as the rebroadcasting of their broadcasts, fixation of their broadcasts, reproduction of fixations, and communications of their television broadcasts if made in the public against payment of an entrance fee. They are granted national treatment protection if the broadcasting organization's headquarters is located in a contracting state, or the transmission of a broadcast is in a contracting state.

The *Rome Convention* provides a minimum of 20 years of protection.[20] However, Article 12 of the *TRIPs Agreement* extends protection for performers and producers of phonograms to a minimum of 50 years.

---

17. *Rome Convention for the Protection of Performers, Producers of Phonograms and Broadcasting Organizations*, 26 October 1964, 469 U.N.T.S. 43.

18. *Rome Convention*, Article 3(a).

19. *Rome Convention*, Article 5.

20. *Rome Convention*, Article. 14.

Critics argue broadcasters do not need as strong of protection, and that such protection could hinder access to copyrighted material by requiring permission from the copyright owner and the broadcaster. Furthermore, there is concern that broadcasters would have exclusive rights over materials that would otherwise not qualify for copyrights (*i.e.*, films out of the period of protection, sport or news events) and thereby, privatizing materials that are public. But, others argue that the materials themselves would remain public for others to play, record, or broadcast, and therefore would not affect access to the material.

- **1989 *Washington Treaty***

The *Treaty on Intellectual Property in Respect of Integrated Circuits (IPIC Treaty)* is known as the *Washington Treaty*, because it was adopted in Washington, D.C., in 1989.[21] Bosnia and Herzegovina (acceded 8 March 2007), Egypt (ratified July 26, 1990), and Saint Lucia (acceded 18 December 2000) have ratified or acceded to the treaty. However, the *Treaty* is not yet in force and is the only "piggy back" agreement mentioned in *TRIPS* that has not entered into force.

That is because the *Washington Treaty* requires 5 States or Intergovernmental Organizations to ratify or accede to it for it to enter into force.[22] Developing countries originally objected to the drafts proposed, and the *Treaty* was amended to include compulsory licenses and provide the WIPO Assembly as the dispute resolution panel. The U.S. and Japan found these amendments to the original draft unacceptable, so the *Treaty* never received enough support to enter into force. Instead, developed countries engineered a partial incorporation of the *Washington Treaty* into the *TRIPs Agreement*, intentionally excluding those provisions developing countries later added to the *Treaty*.

A creator of an integrated circuit is provided exclusive rights to sell, copy, distribute, or import the protected integrated circuit for commercial purposes.[23] It is illegal not only to reproduce the integrated circuit, but it also to incorporate a protected layout design in its entirety or any part thereof in an integrated circuit. However, protection is limited only to those integrated circuits that meet the originality requirement. The originality requirement has two elements: (1) the integrated circuit is made by the creator's own intellectual effort; and (2) the integrated circuit is not commonplace among creators and manufacturers in the industry.[24] A combination of elements or interconnections that are commonplace still may be protected, as long as the combination itself is not common.[25] Furthermore, integrated circuit holders are granted protection internationally through the

---

21. *Treaty on Intellectual Property in Respect of Integrated Circuits*, 26 May 1989, 28 I.L.M. 1477 (1989).
22. *IPIC Treaty*, Article 16.
23. *IPIC Treaty*, Article 6(1).
24. *IPIC Treaty*, Article 3(2).
25. *IPIC Treaty*, Article 3(2).

national treatment rule, requiring contracting states to provide the same treatment it accords its own national to all individuals that are nationals or domiciled in a contracting party.[26]

The partial integration of the *Washington Treaty* into the *TRIPs Agreement* is criticized by many developing countries and LDCs. Compulsory licenses were necessary for developing countries and LDCs to be able to commit to the burdensome obligations of the *Washington Treaty*. These countries also sought protection by having disputes heard by the WIPO Assembly. The U.S. and Japan found the amendments unacceptable, and not in furtherance of their interests to protect their large amount of integrated circuits. They simply disregarded what developing countries and LDCs can realistically commit to, and forced the obligations on them through the Grand Bargain of the Uruguay Round.

III. Importance of IP in Manufactured Products

Over 30% of the value of all manufactured products in the world consists of IP or other intangible capital. Put differently, the intensiveness of labor and other traditional factors of production is relatively less important than IP, even in tangible "stuff" like coffee, smartphones, and solar panels. Consequently, companies that produce and export "stuff" have a keen interest in the cross-border protection of the patents, trademarks, and copyrights embodied in that "stuff." Companies rely on IP to differentiate their product, which they then can brand, and monetize the value of their brand. That is, IP allows them to avoid commodification of their product, and thus avoid price declines.

World Intellectual Property Organization,

World Intellectual Property Report 2017, Intangible Capital in
Global Value Chains, Executive Summary, 9–12, November 2017[27]

A consumer buys a new smartphone. What exactly is she paying for?

The phone consists of many parts and components manufactured all over the world, and the price needs to cover the cost of those. She is also paying for the labor of the people who made the components and assembled the final product, and for services such as transportation and the retailing of the product in a physical store or online. And, very importantly, she is paying for intangible capital—the technology that runs the smartphone, its design and its brand name.

. . .

Is it possible to quantify the importance of intangible capital? What types of intangibles are most valuable at different production stages and for different consumer

---

26. *IPIC Treaty*, Article 5.
27. *See* www.wipo.int/edocs/pubdocs/en/wipo_pub_944_2017.pdf.

products? How do companies manage their intangible assets in global value chains, and what role does intellectual property (IP) play in generating a return on these assets?

. . .

Global value chain production in the 21st century is popularly characterized by the so-called smile curve first proposed in the early 1990s by the chief executive of Acer of the company Acer, Inc. . . .[T]he Smile Curve [redrawn from Figure 2 in the *Report*] recognizes the increased importance of pre- and post-manufacturing stages and posits that those stages account for ever-higher shares of overall production value. The growing Smile . . . reflects that intangible capital—in the form of technology, design and brand value as well as workers' skills and managerial know-how—has become critically important in dynamically competitive markets. Firms continuously invest in intangible capital to stay ahead of their rivals.

As economies have grown richer, consumers' preferences have shifted toward goods that respond to differentiated tastes and offer a broader "brand experience."

. . .

While appealing and intuitive, the concept of the smile curve has its limitations. It may reasonably portray the distribution of value added for firms performing all production stages. But it is more difficult to apply at the economy-wide level, where firms' value chains intersect and overlap. In addition, it does not provide any insight into what precisely generates value added at different production stages. For example, "higher value added" does not necessarily coincide with underlying

Figure 2. Production in the 21st century—A Growing Smile [Redrawn]

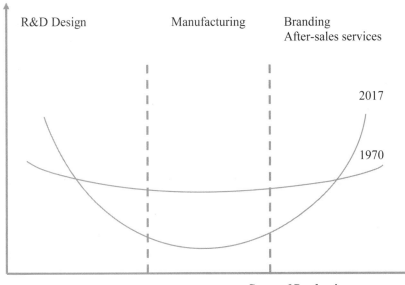

Stage of Production

activities being more pro table, associated with better paying jobs, or generally "more desirable."

...

Intangible capital accounts for around one-third of production value . . .

. . .[Consider the data on] the resulting income shares accruing to the three production factors [labor, tangible (*i.e.*, physical) capital, and IP and intangible capital] for all products manufactured and sold worldwide from 2000 to 2014. The intangibles share averaged 30.4 percent throughout this period, almost double the share for tangibles. Interestingly, it rose from 27.8 percent in 2000 to 31.9 percent in 2007, but has stagnated since then. Overall income from intangibles in the 19 manufacturing industries increased by 75 percent from 2000 to 2014 in real terms. It amounted to 5.9 trillion United States dollars (USD) in 2014.

. . . with food products, motor vehicles and textiles accounting for around one-half of income to intangibles

Which product global value chains use intangibles most intensively? . . .[Consider data on] factor income shares in 2014 for the 19 manufacturing product groups in descending order of their global output size. [Those product groups are: (1) food, beverages, and tobacco; (2) motor vehicles and trailers; (3) T&A and leather; (4) other machinery and equipment; (5) computer, electronic, and optical; (6) furniture and other manufacturing; (7) petroleum; (8) other transport equipment; (9) electrical equipment; (10) chemicals; (11) pharmaceuticals; (12) fabricated metals; (13) rubber and plastics; (14) basic metals; (15) repair and installation of machinery; (16) paper; (17) other non-metallic minerals; (18) wood; and (19) printing products.] For all product groups, intangible capital accounts for a higher share of value added than tangible capital.

The intangibles share is especially high—and more than double the tangibles share—for pharmaceutical, chemical and petroleum products. It is also relatively high for food products as well as computer, electronic and optical products. In terms of absolute returns, the three largest product groups—food products, motor vehicles and textiles—account for close to 50 percent of the total income generated by intangible capital in the 19 manufacturing global value chains.

...

The case of coffee

Coffee is one of the most important traded agricultural commodities. It is the source of income for nearly 26 million farmers in over 50 developing economies, but 70 percent of coffee demand comes from high-income countries. Most of the value added of coffee sold also accrues to high-income countries. This partly reflects the short shelf life of roasted coffee, which implies that most of the roasting is done close to where the coffee is consumed. More importantly, it reflects the economic importance of downstream activities in the global value chain.

Intangible capital in the coffee supply chain mainly consists of downstream techno-logical innovations and branding

The case study on coffee highlights two key forms of intangible capital in the global value chain: . . .

- Technology associated with coffee farming and with turning coffee into a high-quality and appealing consumer product. Patent data suggest that the most innovative value chain stages are those closer to the consumer, including the processing of beans and especially the final distribution of coffee products . . . . The latter stage includes the modern espresso machines and coffee capsules found in many homes and of offices.

- Brand reputation and image, which allow consumer product firms to differentiate their offering from those of their rivals. Branding plays an important role in all coffee market segments, including soluble and roasted coffee sold in grocery stores, espresso-based coffee products and retail coffeehouses.

Thus, when WIPO "analyzed the development of brand identities for coffee, compared with the more common treatment of the product as an unbranded commodity on the part of coffee growers,"[28] it found:

Coffee growers are seeking to secure brand identities from the point of production, allowing coffee farmers to capture more of the final product's value . . . .

When coffee roasters sell roasted beans for $4.11 a pound for coffee whose original producer has no consumer recognition, the export price from the country of origin is only $1.45 a pound, WIPO said in its report. However, when a farmer builds brand recognition for a single-source roast, the roaster's price goes up to $17.45 a pound and the export price goes up to $5.14 a pound.[29]

IV. Interests of Rich and Poor Countries

American dollars are a critical driving force behind the WTO *TRIPs Agreement*, which is contained in Annex 1C to the *WTO Agreement*. That is, the critical catalyst was, and continues to be, profits lost by American companies because of infringements of their IPRs by foreign producers of "pirated" products.[30] It is tempting for

---

28. Anandashankar Mazumdar, *IP, Other Intangibles Are Big Parts of Manufactured Goods' Value*, 34 International Trade Reporter (BNA) 1547 (23 November 2017). [Hereinafter, *IP, Other Intangibles.*]

29. *IP, Other Intangibles, supra.*

30. *See* Fred Warshofsky, The Patent Wars 90 (1994); World Intellectual Property Organization, Guide to the Berne Convention for the Protection of Literary and Artistic Works 6 *bis.*, 3–6 *bis.* 4 (Paris Act 1971); Karen Kontje Waller, Comment, *NAFTA: The Latest Gun in the Fight to Protect International Intellectual Property Rights*, 13 Dickinson Journal of International Law 347, 348–50 (1995).; Richard M. Brenan, *Intellectual Property Aspects of*

such companies, their industry associations, and the American Chambers of Commerce, to point the finger at a few major NICs and developing countries, notably, China, India, and Russia, along with an assorted bunch of relatively smaller ones, such as Egypt, Thailand, and Vietnam. Hardly a month goes by without publication of a story on rampant piracy of a valid patent, trademark, copyright, or semiconductor mask work, or on the lack of enforcement of IPRs, in these countries.

China, in particular, is singled out for good reason: between 2008 and 2010, 67% of all counterfeited products seized by authorities globally originated in China.[31] That figure includes almost 60% of all counterfeit medicines, and 87% of all goods U.S. CBP seized. Across the world, in the 20 years up to 2013, the problem of counterfeiting and piracy grew by 10,000%. In 2008, over $250 billion in both counterfeit goods (*i.e.*, merchandise with stolen trademarks) and pirated goods (*i.e.*, items with unauthorized copyrighted material) crossed international boundaries. By 2015, international trade in counterfeit goods alone was $1.7 trillion. There also is a link to national security: trade in counterfeit and pirated items is a source of cash for terrorist organizations.

Never mind the forgetfulness, if not hypocrisy in these stories and statistics. As one senior Eritrean government official once reported (to your Textbook author), the advice she received from a prominent, developed South East Asian nation was to steal as many IPRs as possible before signing the *TRIPs Agreement*. IP theft was part of the development history of many of today's rich countries. Never mind, too, the fact that countries like China, India, and Egypt are increasingly interested in strong, enforceable IP protection — because they are producers and exporters, not just consumers and importers, of merchandise or services embodying IP.

The fact is that economic importance to the U.S. of strong international IP protection cannot be overstated. Roughly $600 billion (in 2005) of the world market for goods consists of pirated or counterfeit goods (up from $150–200 billion in 2001). More than 50% of American exports are goods protected by a patent, trademark, copyright, or semiconductor mask work. Of all software used in the world, 35% is pirated. In China, 90% of software is pirated. Piracy has real-world implications for the labor market. The U.S. auto industry could create an estimated 200,000 jobs if fake auto parts were eliminated.

Consider another victim: the American the copyright industry. This industry may be divided into four distinct sectors: (1) the "core" copyright sector, which produces copyrighted works like newspapers, magazines, books, radio and television broadcasts, records and tapes, movies, plays, advertising, computer software, and data processing; (2) the "partial" copyright sector, which produces goods that are partly copyrighted such as business forms and architectural plans; (3) the

---

Canada-U.S. Competitiveness in the World Context, 14 CANADA-UNITED STATES LAW JOURNAL 263, 266 (1989).

31. *See* Rebecca Lowe, *War on Fakes*, 67 IBA GLOBAL INSIGHT number 4, 49–57 (August-September 2013).

"distribution" sector, which distributes copyrighted material to businesses and consumers, such as libraries and wholesale and retail traders; and (4) the "copyright-related" sector, which makes products for use with copyrighted materials such as computers, radios, and televisions. In 1977, the combined share of the U.S. GDP accounted for by these 4 categories was 3.7%. By 1993, this share had risen to 5.7%. During the same period, the share of GDP accounted for by core copyright industries rose from 2.2 to 3.7%. These increases implied that from 1977–1993, the total copyright industries grew twice as fast as the American economy. The core copyright industries grew at 5.6%, while the remainder of the economy grew at 2.6%.

It is stunning to learn that "[t]he core copyright industries contribute more to the U.S. economy and employ more workers than any single manufacturing sector including aircraft manufacturing, primary metals, fabricated metals, textiles, apparel, or chemicals and allied products"[32] The dramatic performance of the copyright industries is due in part to their increasing dominance of markets in other countries. For example, in 1993 foreign sales of the core copyright industries were $45.8 billion, and that figure undoubtedly has risen dramatically. Not surprisingly, the American copyright industries feel seriously threatened by copyright infringements in foreign countries. For instance, it is easy to walk out of one's hotel in Bangkok to a main street and purchase pirated cassette tapes of Michael Jackson, George Michael, Pat Benatar, or any other musician—for roughly $1 a tape! Ironically, it was rumored some American Embassy personnel who were aware of the infringing tapes actually purchased their favorite tapes for their personal collections, or at least to see whether they enjoyed the music enough to buy an authentic CD.

V. 1994 Smith Argument on *TRIPs Agreement* Implementation

Trade Agreements Resulting from the Uruguay Round Of Multilateral Trade Negotiations,

Hearings before the House Committee on Ways and Means,
103d Cong., 2d Sess. 127–132 (1 February 1994)
(Testimony of Eric H. Smith, Executive Director and General Counsel,
International Intellectual Property Alliance (IIPA) on Behalf of the IIPA)

Mr. Chairman and Members of the Committee:

. . .

The IIPA is comprised of . . . trade associations that collectively represent the U.S. copyright-based industries—the motion picture, recording, computer software and music and book publishing industries. . . .

---

32. Stephen E. Siwek & Harold Furchtgott-Roth, Copyright Industries in the U.S. Economy: 1977–1993 iv–v (January 1995). *See also id.*, 5–6.

. . .

These industries represent the leading edge of the world's high technology, entertainment and publishing industries and are among the fastest growing and largest segments of our economy. . . .

. . . IIPA has estimated that the U.S. economy was already losing $15–17 billion in 1992 [the eve of completion of Uruguay Round negotiations, which produced the *TRIPs Agreement*] due to piracy outside this country.

. . .

While none of our members will seek to oppose the *WTO Agreement* [including the *TRIPs Agreement*,] many of them will not be able to warmly endorse it. However, on careful balance, our members believe that, with the help of a resolute U.S. bilateral trade policy on intellectual property, the impact of the deficiencies in the *TRIPs . . . Agreement*[] can be mitigated.

. . .[T]he final agreement contains many positive elements.

. . .

[However,] [t]he two major flaws in the final *TRIPs Agreement* . . . detract from these overall well-recognized gains.

1. National Treatment

U.S. negotiators sought in vain to obtain agreement of the European Union to fill the gaps and clarify the ambiguities in the national treatment provisions in the Dunkel text [a prior draft of proposed Uruguay Round trade agreements]. In his testimony last week before the Subcommittee, Ambassador [Mickey] Kantor [President Clinton's first USTR] emphasized that he was "bitterly disappointed by the European Union's intransigence with respect to national treatment and market access for our entertainment industries." Had the EU been willing to cease its discrimination against U.S. rightholders, the chances of worldwide acceptance of the U.S.' improved proposal (known as Article 14 *bis*) would have been vastly increased. However, notwithstanding the failure to eliminate these gaps and ambiguities, IIPA firmly believes that the existing national treatment obligation in Article 3 of the *TRIPs Agreement* does provide national treatment for many classes of U.S. rightholders.

In some cases, however, WTO members will argue that they are free, without violating their international WTO obligations, for example, to discriminate against U.S. record companies by denying them the critical right to control the public performance and broadcasting of their works by digital means while extending that right to their domestic recording companies. As another example, under this national treatment provision, they could also seek to deny to U.S. record companies the proceeds resulting from blank tape levies to provide some, however inadequate, payment to rights owners for the home taping of their recording. This could happen at the same time as the United States extends full national treatment under its recently adopted blank tape levy on digital recordings to that country's recording companies and performers whose recordings are copied here. The U.S. motion picture industry and U.S. artists and performers could continue to be denied appropriate shares of blank tape video levies on the grounds that the *TRIPs* national treatment provision authorizes this continuing discrimination and subsidy to their own industry. In the end, if these efforts by our trading partners are successful, the U.S. stands to lose millions of dollars in royalties justly due its industries and the American jobs that could be created with those funds will never materialize.

2. Overly Long Transition Periods

The *TRIPs Agreement* [under Article 66:1] continues to permit those countries that qualify as . . . ["developing" or "least developed"] an additional . . . [5 and 10 years, respectively] . . . before they must bring their domestic legislation and enforcement regimes into full compliance with the obligations in the *Agreement*. The countries in transition to market economies also may benefit from this additional transition period. . . .

[The extension for developing and transition economy countries ended on 31 December 1999. For least developed countries (the status of 34 of the 159 WTO Members as of March 2013), 1 January 2006 was the original deadline for compliance with the *Agreement*. The subsequent history of S&D treatment for LDCs — that is, for *TRIPs Agreement* compliance — is discussed below.]

At present, there are a large number of developing countries that, as a result of inadequate legislation or lax enforcement, cause, collectively, billions of dollars in lost jobs and income to the United States. As the result of an aggressive bilateral program using Special 301, Section 301, the Generalized System of Preferences [GSP] Program and similar programs, the U.S. Government has succeeded in bringing many of these countries to within months of compliance with the basic obligations in the *TRIPs Agreement*. Countries like Thailand, Turkey, Egypt, South Korea, Indonesia, Brazil, Venezuela, Philippines, India and Poland (all GATT members), to name but a few, together account for close to *$1.8 billion* in losses due to piracy of U.S. copyrights [emphasis original]. Were all these countries to take full advantage of their transition period rights under the *Agreement* (and assuming losses remain at the same level as in 1992; though they are likely to increase), the U.S. economy would lose an additional *$7 billion* over that four-year period [emphasis original]. This is a staggering blow to these industries and to the U.S. economy as they seek to add the new high-tech and high-wage jobs necessary for this country to be competitive into the next century.

What is plainly apparent is that none of these ten named countries needs or deserves to take an additional four-year period to deal with the problem of copyright piracy. USTR has been negotiating with each of these countries for well over five years already; many have indicated their commitment to significantly reduce piracy in 1994 or are already in breach of existing bilateral commitments to the United States. For any of these countries to take advantage of their rights under the

TRIPs Agreement would be an outrage that the United States simply must not tolerate. Unfortunately, the *TRIPs Agreement* could condone such action.

In addition to these two major flaws in the text, the final *TRIPs* text also contains a new concession—this time to the *developed* countries—permitting them to have the benefit of a five-year moratorium on the application of the "nullification and impairment" provisions of the *Agreement*. IIPA has always viewed this remedy, which gets at the "spirit" rather than the letter of the obligations in the *Agreement*, as providing key leverage to ensure that our major trading partners cannot undermine the *Agreement* for protectionist reasons. We regret that this concession was made but believe its absence can be compensated for by a clear and unequivocal U.S. trade policy that would result in punishing any country, at the end of the five-year moratorium, for any actions during the moratorium which had the effect of "nullifying or impairing" any benefit in the *Agreement* which the U.S. had bargained for.

. . .

IIPA members are still in the process of evaluating and considering trade and non-trade policy options in the intellectual property area to ensure that our trading partners promptly open their markets to U.S. copyrighted works and avoid taking advantage of actual and potential national treatment loopholes in the *TRIPs Agreement*. Similar consideration is being given to dealing with the issue of broadcast and new technology quotas and similar restrictions faced by our audiovisual industry, particularly in the European Union. Finally, consideration must also be given to ensuring that multilateral obligations in the intellectual property area continue to keep pace with technological developments. Clearly, it will not be possible to secure quickly major changes to the *TRIPs Agreement* which may become necessary due to unforeseen technological developments. A continuing and aggressive bilateral program must also be able to safeguard U.S. interests in this event as well.

. . .

While the procedures under Special 301, including the identification of countries that pose IPR problems to the U.S. under Section 182 [19 U.S.C. § 2242] and the commencement of investigations against countries named as Priority Foreign Countries, should continue in effect and should be aggressively used by the Administration, remedies available to the U.S. under its bilateral programs—because of the wider coverage of, and bindings in, the WTO—become more limited. [Mr. Smith noted the IIPA's strong agreement "with statements recently made by Administration officials that where the U.S. national interest is demonstrably at stake, the U.S. should not hesitate to take sanctions even in WTO-bound areas if it would be fruitful in ending the conduct which is damaging to those interests."] However, withdrawal of preferential benefits extended to any country under programs like the GSP, CBI and ATPA [,which lapsed but renewed in a different form] may still occur for failure to meet IPR criteria established for these programs. Countries that unfairly take advantage of the WTO authorized transition period to continue to steal U.S. intellectual property should also be made vulnerable to removal of other trade and non-trade benefits that they receive from the U.S.

Concerted efforts should be made to encourage our trading partners, in appropriate cases, to join the *NAFTA* and adhere to the strong IPR text of this *Agreement*. We note in particular that the *NAFTA* contains a straight-forward national treatment provision of the type the U.S. was unable to achieve in the GATT.

VI. 1990 Raghavan Recolonization Argument

As the testimony (above) of Eric H. Smith, IIPA Executive Director and General Counsel, indicates, delayed implementation period of the *TRIPs Agreement* for NICs and poor countries undermined the force of the *Agreement*. The NICs had until 1 July 2000, and least developed countries had until 1 July 2006, to implement the *Agreement*. From a cynical perspective, the delays were a license to continue to violate IPRs at the expense of the profits of the rights holders. The Smith testimony suggests ways to combat future IP piracy—direct, even unilateral, action by the U.S. against.

Is S&D treatment in the *TRIPs Agreement* too generous, as Smith argues? One response of NICs and poor countries to Smith's criticisms bespeaks a radically different perspective on international intellectual property protection. IP is seen as the common heritage of humankind. It is a government-granted privilege, not a natural property right.

Chakravarthi Raghavan, the Geneva Representative of Malaysia-based Third World Network, and Chief Editor of the *South-North Development Monitors* newsletter, argues:

> Patents and other intellectual or industrial property are thus statutory rights—benefits created by law by the State. Even to call them "rights" is a misnomer. They are really "privileges" granted by the State by statute—a form of government intervention in the market place, a government subsidy not unlike tax credits, export incentives etc.

> Gradually there has been the development of the concept of Science and Technology as a common heritage of mankind but this is now being challenged. In the postwar decades, patents etc. have been garnered by the TNCs [transnational corporations] who have created a monopoly right for themselves. Patent laws were originally established to reward invention and promote industrialization as well as prevent import monopolies within the country concerned. However, through efforts to universalize patent laws that give owners the right to exploit the patent at [the] international level (and not only at [the] national level), the industrialized countries are in fact trying to reward export monopolies in the industrial centers which would slow down industrialization and [the] spread of technology in the Third World.

. . .

In bringing the issue on the Uruguay Round agenda and by using the term "intellectual property right," the U.S. and other ICs [industrialized countries] have managed to inject some value-loaded words, like "piracy" and "counterfeiting," to describe those who are not prepared to accept their demands. With the help of the media, they have made these terms current coin, confusing the public and legitimizing their own demands, and painting those opposing them as indulging in some immoral acts or near criminal conduct . . . .

. . .

In international trade, "patents" and "trade marks" far from expanding trade are really trade barriers in as much as the owners are given some monopoly import privileges.[33]

This argument seems to underlie the *ordre public* exception to the scope of patentability contained in Article 27:2 of the *TRIPs Agreement*.

The argument also suggests public interests, broadly defined, ought to be given priority over the interest of a private party to obtain and exploit a technological monopoly.

Being a statutorily granted right, the most important consideration in granting IPR protection is public interest — counter-balancing the rights of IPR owners by their obligations to the country granting them such rights, such as through local working, and compulsory licensing in the absence of local working. It may be in the interests of the dominant industrialized nations now to shift the balance more to private rights of their corporations than public interest; but this cannot negate the right of the Third World to maintain this balance and ensure public good and public welfare.[34]

Put bluntly, IP should be used to help improve the lot of poor people, not enrich the coffers of American or European corporations. From this perspective, the *TRIPs Agreement* is biased in favor of private interests from developed countries. Notice the implicit assumption here: NICs, most developing countries, and probably all least developed countries are doomed for the foreseeable future to be net consumers, not net producers, of IP products.

This perspective may be analyzed in economic terms. A key benefit of IPR protection is that it ensures that inventors, artists, writers, and other producers of intellectual property will earn monopoly profits on their work. This assurance is credible because the work is destined to command a price higher than it would in the absence of protection, and it provides a motivation to create the work. However,

---

33. Chakravarthi Raghavan Recolonization: GATT, the Uruguay Round & the Third World 116–17, 121–22 (1990). [Hereinafter, Raghavan.] *See also id.*, 124–125, 129.
34. Raghavan, 134.

monopoly profits represent a transfer of wealth from consumers to producers of IP. Moreover, as in any monopoly situation, the quantity of output and consumption is sub-optimal. The result of this monopoly situation is a deadweight loss, which gives rise to an argument that requiring every country in the world to provide IPR protection might be inefficient. For example, with respect to patents:

> as protection is extended to a larger and larger portion of the world, the marginal benefits of extending it further decline and the marginal costs increase. Therefore if the two are equal for some particular extent of patent protection, then this will be an optimal situation.
>
> To see that the marginal benefits and costs behave in this way, consider the effect of extending protection to an additional market of some given size. The benefits from doing so arise entirely from the new inventions that this additional market will make profitable but that would not have been profitable to invent with the previous protected market size. The larger the previously protected market, however, the greater will be the number of inventions already invented, and the less desirable will be the ones that remain. Hence, the marginal benefit declines.
>
> Similarly, the cost of extending patent protection to this additional market is some fraction of the consumer surplus generated in this market by the inventions that would be undertaken anyway. This fraction is the amount by which consumer surplus declines on these goods when consumers are charged a monopoly price, minus the monopoly profits that are earned on the goods. This is therefore a deadweight loss to the world as a whole. The size of this fraction depends on the elasticity of demand for invented goods, and hence on the size of the monopoly markup, but there is no reason to expect this fraction to decline systematically as protection is extended. Therefore, as protection is extended further, and as more and more inventions are therefore stimulated and become subject to this markup, the deadweight loss due to extending to the additional market will grow.
>
> All of this suggests, therefore, that there will be an optimal geographical extent of patent protection that need not be the whole world.[35]

If, indeed, extension of IPR protection to all countries is not supported by a marginal cost-benefit analysis, then what countries should be exempt from the requirement of providing such protection?

Perhaps poor countries should be exempt from patent protection because (1) transfers from poor to rich countries exacerbate income inequality and, therefore, are unfair, (2) patent protection leads to more inventions in developed than less developed countries, because there are more resources in the former than the

---

35. Alan V. Deardorff, *Should Patent Protection Be Extended to All Developing Countries?*, in THE MULTILATERAL TRADING SYSTEM 443–444 (Robert M. Stern ed., 1993). *See also id.*, 431–432, 435, 438, 443–446.

latter, thus the technology gap between rich and poor countries is worsened, and (3) political constituencies in developed countries favor IPR protection, while interest groups in poor countries tend to oppose such protection.

VII. 1994 Ringo African Dilemma Argument

Frederick S. Ringo, an advocate of the High Court of Tanzania, writes about the dilemma facing middle- and low-income countries of SSA. He argues the MFN obligation in Article 3 of the *TRIPs Agreement*—whereby each WTO Member must have an MFN clause in its IP law to ensure favored treatment is extended immediately and unconditionally to all other Members—will expand "the legal hegemony . . . of former imperial States over their colonial territories" so that rights holders from other countries can "claim territorial rights" in SSA countries and other poor nations. The transition periods of which Smith (and others) complain actually provides "breathing space" for SSA to develop their technological bases. Ringo's thesis is

> [t]he present era has been hailed as the information age where knowledge constitutes power and a competitive edge over competitors. It is, therefore, in the interest of technology owners that knowledge is not easily dissipated and they have, therefore, pressed for the introduction of *TRIPs* as another barrier to access, and as one of the means of controlling, knowledge.
>
>   . . .
>
> . . . It is perceived by least-developed countries (LDCs) as ironic that the relatively loose international IPR system, which has been in existence for more than one hundred and fifty years and which has served as the basis for the technology transfer, copying, learning and adaptation that permitted the current industrialized countries (not least Japan, but also, at an earlier stage, the United States, France, Germany etc.) to catch up with the technological leaders and to achieve technological parity, is now being made more restrictive in order to make it more costly and difficult for newcomers to enter the field. This does raise questions as to the real intentions of industrial countries in GATT. Further, these moves are in opposition to the internationally accepted transfer-of-technology principles as formulated in the [United Nations] Program of Action for the Establishment of a New International Economic Order [U.N. General Assembly Resolution 3202, (S-VI), May 1974)]. The one-sided formulations of the *TRIPs Agreement*, which insist on the rights of sellers without juxtaposing the same with the right to economic development of African countries, provide grounds for skepticism as to the acceptability of the *TRIPs Agreement* by these countries despite the legal measures which could be taken.[36]

---

36. Frederick S. Ringo, *The Trade-Related Aspects of Intellectual Property Rights Agreement in the GATT and Legal Implications for Sub-Saharan Africa*, 28 JOURNAL OF WORLD TRADE number 6, 121–39, at 122–123 (December 1994). [Hereinafter, *Sub-Saharan Africa*.]

Does the strength of Ringo's argument vary with the protected product in question?

For example, perhaps trademark protection held by Nike and the National Football League is acceptable to SSA, because athletic shoes and logo apparel are not products central to economic development. In contrast, patents for pharmaceuticals, and trademarks associated with the marketing of pharmaceuticals, may be difficult to justify. Ringo contends:

> Technologies such as those used in the pharmaceutical and chemical industries depend heavily on patents in both products and processes, as well as trade marks in marketing. This sector's moral and commercial practices in LDCs [less developed countries], such as in the SSA countries, have been under close research and criticism. Drugs being a basic need in many LDCs and the costs being exorbitant ensure that many African countries, and some industrial countries, do not offer patent protection to these processes and prefer the use of generic rather than brand-name products. Indeed, some industrial countries have only recently introduced patent protection in pharmaceuticals and chemicals after ensuring the development of their own domestic industries. They have been taken as examples by the LDCs against stricter *TRIPS* enforcement. These measures, which are partly political and partly economic, ensured that needed drugs were acquired at reasonable prices.[37]

There would seem to be at least two difficulties associated with any attempt to justify IP protection on a product-specific basis.

First, delineating products that are crucial to economic development is sure to generate argument. At one extreme, any product that contributes to development as measured by value-added or increases in gross domestic product could be regarded as critical. Thus, athletic shoes and logo apparel would be included. At the other extreme, only those items that impart sustenance to the human body could be regarded as keys to economic development. Examples would include food (particularly species of crops) and medicines, but not clothes or school books (much less law books!). With respect to patent protection for food, Ringo argues:

> Patented plant life in the food industry has resulted in serious food insecurity in some areas and the disappearance of drought- and sickness-resistant strains. The TNC [transnational corporation] agribusiness industries are stated to hold a substantial share of responsibility in this unfortunate event. . . .

> For the agricultural-based economies of the SSA, bio-technologies present a double-edged sword, and several issues will face the WTO and African governments in relation to the *TRIPS Agreement*. First, with the increasing pressures by industrialized countries on African and other LDCs, how

---

37. *Sub-Saharan Africa*, 123–124.

can the increased intellectual property rights protection ensure the linking of research to the requirements of the local economies, and the com-
mercialization of agricultural research results? Second, most SSA countries
are being forced to implement World Bank/International Monetary Fund
(IMF) structural adjustment programs (SAPS) with the aim of introducing market economies. These programs have severely reduced the purchasing capacities of the peoples of these countries. How can bio-technologies
be effectively introduced (especially in seed, animal and health sectors)
when stronger IPR protection will increase prices, therefore hindering
their acceptability? Third, it is well known that the theoretical premises of
IPR protection lead to anti-competitive practices which are in conformity
neither with internationally agreed principles nor with the aims of SAPS;
how can the WTO technically assist SSA countries to counterbalance the
adverse effects of such measures in their economies? Fourth, the most challenging aspect facing the WTO in this area is how to shake off the image
of GATT as the "rich countries' forum" by ensuring that the *TRIPS Agreement* is not abused by its sponsors, *i.e.*, TNCs and their home governments,
to the detriment of the economies of SSA countries. These abuses include
using IPRs to create monopoly conditions, destroying bio-diversity, and the
destruction of LDC agricultural sectors and environments.[38]

Interestingly, Article 27:3(b) of the *TRIPs Agreement* allows WTO Members to
exclude from patentability plants and animals other than micro-organisms. It also
authorizes them to exclude from patentability a process that is essentially biological whose purpose is the production of plants or animals. However, Members must
allow for protection of plant varieties either by patents or an effective *sui generis*
system, or by a combination thereof.

A similar argument could be made with respect to the pharmaceutical and chemical industries. Indeed, before the *TRIPs Agreement* entered into force, Argentina,
Brazil, Egypt, Ghana, India, Mexico, Korea, Taiwan, and Thailand did not provide
patent protection for pharmaceutical processes. (Interestingly, they were not alone.
This protection also was unavailable in Australia, Finland, New Zealand, and Norway.) Chemicals were not patentable in Brazil, Colombia, India, Mexico, and Venezuela. (Here again, NICs and poor countries were not alone. This protection also
was lacking in Japan and Switzerland.) These facts helped generate the 1998 *India
Patent* case.

Significantly, Article 27:2 of the *TRIPs Agreement* provides a potentially broad
exception to the scope of patentable subject matter:

> Members may exclude from patentability inventions, the prevention
> within their territory of the commercial exploitation of which is necessary
> to protect *ordre public* or morality, including to protect human, animal or

---

38. *Sub-Saharan Africa*, 131–132.

plant life or health or to avoid serious prejudice to the environment, provided that such exclusion is not made merely because their exploitation is prohibited by their law.

In the interest of public health, could a Member decline to provide patent protection for a pharmaceutical company's process for making a particular drug? Could a Member refuse to offer patent protection for an insecticide because it is valuable in protecting the Member's food supply from pests? Because *ordre public* is a vague concept, a Member may interpret it broadly, hence suggesting an affirmative answer to both questions.

However, even some scholars sympathetic to the plight of NICs, developing, and least developed countries question the utility of IP protection for "essential" sectors.

> Ensuring worldwide rights for processes and products for drugs, it is argued, is essential to encourage new research and discovery of new drugs. But, patents no longer seem to serve their original purpose of innovation of things useful to society and spread of knowledge. In the area of pharmaceuticals, patents and excessive secrecy associated with them appear to be reducing innovation and scientific research, and have not helped produce new drugs needed for the ailments afflicting humanity, particularly the poor.

> According to an article in *The Economist* magazine: "Two-thirds of the 50 top selling drugs are retreads of old therapies. Drug research used to be simple . . . Now, biotechnology has made cleverness essential again . . . Unfortunately academic culture and drug-industry culture seem to react as tastelessly as port poured into gin . . . Those scientists who come to the drug industry to get rich and recognized are soon disappointed. Researchers in the industry rarely get a share of the profits from the products they discover."[39]

Moreover, a number of products fall on a continuum between the above two extremes. For example, Ringo asserts computers and allied products are essential to the development of SSA countries. But, owners of computer technology "are only willing to transfer technology where IPR protection is such that it allows the maximum exploitation of their technological rights," and it is not in the self-interest of SSA countries to develop such legal regimes.[40] Thus, he finds the extension of copyright protection for "literary and artistic works" under the *Berne Convention* to include computer programs irksome.

A second difficulty associated with any attempt to link IP protection to product type concerns the dynamic nature of Third World economic development. The product mix manufactured domestically changes as a country develops. In 1945, who would have thought Japan would mass produce consumer electronics

---

39. RAGHAVAN, 118.
40. *Sub-Saharan Africa*, 125.

domestically, and subsequently transfer production to Malaysia, Indonesia, Thailand, and Vietnam? More generally, the hidden assumption of Ringo's argument is Third World countries are forever dependent on, and consumers of, foreign technology. Yet, India has its own versions of Silicon Valley in Bangalore and Hyderabad, and Malaysia has impressive hardware and software research facilities in Penang. The inventors of tomorrow who need IP rights and enforcement for creative expression are as likely to come from poor as rich countries.

One interesting omission from the *TRIPs Agreement* concerns the process of checking for counterfeit goods before they are exported. This issue is also not addressed in the WTO *PSI Agreement*. One reason may be inspection of goods for pirated materials before export is a costly process. Third World countries are unwilling to incur such costs without financial or logistical assistance from First World counterparts.

VIII. Extended Transition Periods and December 2005 Hong Kong Ministerial Conference

As explained earlier, the extension to comply with *TRIPs Agreement* obligations for developing and transition economy countries ended on 31 December 1999. For least developed countries (the status of 34 of the 159 WTO Members as of March 2013), 1 January 2006 was the original deadline for compliance with the *Agreement*. The transition period then became indefinite, by virtue of an extension WTO Members granted on the eve of the 2005 Hong Kong Ministerial Conference to 1 July 2013 (which was 8 years later than the original 10-year transition period set in the *Agreement*), and then an indefinite extension they granted at the 2011 Geneva Ministerial Conference.

Notably, among the precious few lasting achievements of the entire Doha Round (November 2001–March 2018), two lay at the intersection of IP and trade, namely, (1) transition periods and (2) compulsory licensing, and they occurred in connection with the December 2005 Hong Kong Ministerial Conference.[41] (The latter topic is discussed in a separate Chapter. A third achievement, concerning trade facilitation, also is discussed in a separate Chapter.) as to the transition periods, on 30 November 2005, WTO Members agreed to extend preferential treatment to least developed countries under the *TRIPs Agreement* from 10 to 16 years (counting from the entry into force date, which for developed countries typically was 1 January 1996). That is, recognizing the "special needs" and "economic, financial, and administrative constraints" in the poorest of poor countries, *TRIPs* Article 66:1 affords them a decade-long transition period. Thus, LDCs were supposed to have implemented all *TRIPs Agreement* obligations by 31 December 2005. But, as this

---

41. Technically, these achievements occurred at a WTO General Council session on 6 December 2005, before the Conference opened.

date approached, many of them asked for more time, such as an additional 15-year general exemption from *TRIPs* obligations, lasting until 2020.

The compromise reached on the eve of the Hong Kong Ministerial Conference was to give LDCs until 1 July 2013.[42] The extended S&D treatment to 2013 did not affect new WTO Members, which joined the club after its establishment on 1 January 2005. These countries, such as China, KSA, Russia, and Vietnam, were supposed to apply *TRIPs* obligations as specified in their accession terms. Generally, those specifications call for immediate compliance. Finally, the 2013 extension did not affect developing or economies in transition from central planning. They already benefited from the Article 65:2-3 grace period of five years, which lapsed on 1 January 2000.

The extensions granted at the Hong Kong and Geneva Ministerial Conferences meant LDCs did not have to protect copyrights, patents, trademarks, or GIs. But, if they chose to do so, then they had to adhere to the national treatment and MFN rules in Articles 3 and 4, respectively, of the *TRIPs Agreement*. Moreover, under the binding "non-rollback" provision of the original 2005 extension, any LDC that was complying with *TRIPs* obligations could not reduce the level of IP protection it afforded during the transition period.

As of March 2013, WTO Members failed to agree on how much additional time, if any, LDCs should get to implement the *Agreement*. Nepal argued for the transition period to last as long as a Member is "least developed," meaning a Member would not incur *TRIPs* obligations until it graduates to the status of a developing country. While the U.N. AIDS agency, Oxfam, and some Members agreed, the U.S. and EU objected to any open-ended extension. In June 2013, the WTO agreed to a compromise proposal: LDCs would have eight additional years, until 1 July 2021, to bring their IP laws into compliance with the *TRIPs Agreement*, but the binding non-roll back provision from the original extension was dropped. Consequently, LDCs would "express their determination" to preserve and continue to progress toward putting *TRIPs* commitments into practice, but could during the eight-year transition period cut back on them.

---

42. The extension granted in Hong Kong did not alter an earlier deal set out in the 2002 Doha *Declaration on TRIPs and Public Health*. In that *Declaration*, LDCs were exempt until 1 January 2016 from protecting pharmaceutical patents. That is, for these countries, in respect of pharmaceutical patent protection, the extension was to 1 January 2016 by virtue of the special Doha *Declaration*. Thereafter, they had to must protect patented pharmaceuticals.

Chapter 31

Substantive *TRIPs Agreement* Obligations[1]

I. Purposes and Cornerstones

The *TRIPs Agreement* is an effort to respond to the concerns of not only the American IP industry, but any industry, wherever located, whose product relies on a copyright, semiconductor mask work, patent, or trademark. In fact, it is important to realize that IP can be produced anywhere—wherever there is creative human capital. That means poor countries ought to see themselves not only as consumers of IP products from overseas, but also—sooner or later—as actual or potential producers of IP exports for the rest of the world. Of course, this Janus-faced perspective is not the one that predominates in most parts of the developing and least developed world.

The overall objective of *TRIPs*, stated in Article 7, is to "contribute to the promotion of technological innovation and to the transfer and dissemination of technology, to the mutual advantage of producers and users of technological knowledge and in a manner conducive to social and economic welfare, and to a balance of rights and obligations." Clearly, the *Agreement* is not simply about IP protection. Rather, it is about the tension between such protection, on the one hand, and the need to disseminate knowledge, especially to developing countries that require technology for economic growth, on the other hand.

Articles 3 and 4 are the cornerstones of the *TRIPs Agreement*. Article 3 of the *Agreement* mandates national treatment for IP protection. Article 4 creates an MFN obligation for such protection. But, these cornerstones do not establish a specific level of protection. National or MFN treatment has little value if such treatment provides poor protection. In this regard, it must be remembered the *Agreement* is not the first attempt at cross-border IPR. There are many pre-Uruguay Round multilateral accords dealing with the protection of specific types of IP that continue in force. The *Agreement* supplements and strengthens the earlier accords and,

---

1. Documents References:
   (1) *Havana (ITO) Charter* Articles 19, 37:7, 45:1(a)(vii)
   (2) GATT Articles IV, IX:6, XX(f)
   (3) WTO *TRIPs Agreement*

therefore, presumably harmonizes international IP protection, at a higher level than under previous accords.

II. Summary Table to Navigate *TRIPs Agreement*

At least for the non-IP specialist, an overview of the *TRIPs Agreement*, which has 73 Articles, is helpful. Table 31-1 provides that overview, evincing that the *Agreement* is logically structured. The *Agreement* contains a *Preamble* that amalgamates the importance of IPR protection and enforcement, private nature of those rights, special needs of LDCs, and need for a multilateral framework in cooperation with WIPO. Thereafter, the *Agreement* has the following key provisions.

Table 31-1. Navigating *TRIPs Agreement*

Part I: "General Provisions and Basic Principles"	
Articles 1–8	Articles 1–2 incorporate the "piggy back" strategy (*i.e.*, expressly mandating compliance with existing named IPR treaties), and allow WTO Members to provide *TRIPs* Plus IPR protection (*i.e.*, implement in their domestic law more extensive protection than the *TRIPs Agreement* mandates)
	Article 3 mandates national treatment
	Article 4 is the MFN rule
Part II: "Standards Concerning the Availability, Scope, and Use of Intellectual Property Rights"	
Section 1: Copyright	
Articles 9–14	Article 10 defines computer programs and data compilations within the ambit of copyright protection
	Article 11 does so for commercial rental of computer programs and cinematographic works
	Article 12 sets the minimum term of copyright protection as the life in being of the author plus 50 years
Section 2: Trademarks	
Articles 15–21	Article 15 defines broadly the goods or services subject to protection of a mark
	Article 17 contains a fair use exception
	Article 18 sets the minimum term of trademark protection at 7 years, subject to renewal
	Article 19 requires that if use is a requirement to maintain registration of a trademark, then cancellation of registration may occur only after at least 3 years of non-use
	Article 21 preserves sovereignty of WTO Members to set conditions on trademark licensing and assignment, and bars compulsory licensing of trademarks

(continued)

Table 55-1. Navigating *TRIPs Agreement* (*continued*)

Part II: **"Standards Concerning the Availability, Scope, and Use of Intellectual Property Rights"**	
Section 3: Geographical Indications	
Articles 22–24	Article 22 establishes defines "GI" and requires WTO Members to provide a legal means to prevent abusive use or unfair competition with GIs
	Article 23 mandates Members to provide special GI protection for wines and spirits
	Article 24 pledges Members to continued negotiations over GIs
Section 4: Industrial Designs	
Articles 25–26	Article 25 requires WTO Members to provide industrial design protection, including for textile designs, without imposing unreasonable burdens to secure this protection
	Article 26 sets out the parameters for industrial design protection
Section 5: Patents	
Articles 27–34	Article 27 defines broadly patentable subject matter, with limited exceptions (1) "necessary to protect *ordre public* or morality, including to protect human, animal, or plant life or health, or to avoid serious prejudice to the environment," (2) for "diagnostic, therapeutic, and surgical methods," and (3) for plants, animals, and "essentially biological processes"
	Articles 28 and 30 explain what exclusive rights a patent confers
	Article 29 establishes minimum conditions for patent applications
	Article 31 covers compulsory licensing, and is the only Uruguay Round text to have been amended (as discussed in a separate Chapter)
	Article 32 mandates an opportunity for judicial review of any decision to revoke or forfeit a patent
	Article 33 set the minimum period of patent protection at 20 years from the filing date
	Article 34 concerns burdens of proof for process patents
Section 6: Layout Designs for Integrated Circuits (Chips)	
Articles 35–38	Article 38 sets the minimum protection for protection of a layout design at 10 years from the date of filing
Section 7: Undisclosed Information (Trade Secrets)	
Article 39	Article 39 requires WTO Members to provide for protection of trade secrets
Section 8: Anti-Competitive Practices	
Article 40	Article 40 acknowledges IPR licensing may restrain competition, thereby impeding the transfer and dissemination of technology, and thus permits WTO Members to legislate against abuse of IPRs that have these adverse effects

(*continued*)

Table 55-1. Navigating *TRIPs Agreement* (*continued*)

Part III: **"Enforcement of Intellectual Property Rights" (Divided into 5 Sections)**	
Articles 41–61	Article 41 mandates WTO Members implement enforcement procedures, as called for in subsequent provisions, against IPR infringement
	Articles 44, 45, and 46 require Members to have as civil penalties injunctions, damages, and other remedies
	Article 51 requires Members to allow Customs authorities to seize and hold merchandise suspected to infringe on an IPR
	Articles 52–58 explain procedures for Customs seizure
	Article 59 mandates as a remedy destruction of seized goods that infringe on an IPR, subject to judicial review
	Article 61 mandates criminal penalties for "willful trademark counterfeiting or copyright piracy on a commercial scale"
Part IV: **"Acquisition and Maintenance of Intellectual Property Rights and Related *Inter Partes* Procedures"**	
Article 62	Article 62 allows WTO Members to impose "reasonable procedures and formalities" to obtain and maintain an IPR
Part V: **"Dispute Prevention and Settlement"**	
Articles 63–64	Article 63 contains transparency requirements
	Article 64 explains the relationship among the *TRIPs Agreement*, *DSU*, and GATT, and bars non-violation nullification or impairment claims
Part VI: **"Transitional Arrangements"**	
Articles 65–67	Article 65 granted developing countries an additional 5 years to phase in the *TRIPs Agreement*
	Article 66 granted LDCs an additional 10 years phase-in period
	Article 67 obligates developed countries to help developing countries and LDCs in meeting their *TRIPs* commitments
Part VII: **"Institutional Arrangements; Final Provisions"**	
Articles 68–73	Article 70 contains the "Mailbox Rule" at issue in the 1998 *India Patent Protection* case
	Article 68 and 71, respectively, establish the WTO Council for TRIPs and set out procedures for review of the implementation of the *TRIPs Agreement* and amendment of its text
	Article 69 mandates international cooperation against IPR infringement, including the establishment by each WTO Member of an administrative contact point, and exchange of information among those points and with Customs authorities
	Article 72 prohibits reservations to the *TRIPs Agreement*
	Article 73 contains a National Security exception to all TRIPs commitments

III. Special Points about Copyright Protection

As regards adding to and fortifying international lPR protection, for copyrights, Article 9:1 of the *TRIPs Agreement* requires all WTO Members to comply with the 1971 version of the *Berne Convention for the Protection of Literary and Artistic Works* (*Berne Convention*). (Recall the *Berne Convention* protects copyrights. The U.S. acceded to the *Berne Convention* in 1989.) Interestingly, however, this Article does not require Members to respect the concept of "moral rights" of an author of copyrighted material set forth in the *Berne Convention*.

"Moral rights," which are recognized by Article 6 *bis* of the *Berne Convention*, "are author's rights that are separate and distinct from the pecuniary or economic benefits deriving from copyright, which reflect that the author's work is a reflection of the personality of its creator."[2] There are two key moral rights:

(1) "the right of paternity," which is the author's right to claim the work as her own and put her name on the work, and

(2) "the right of integrity" (sometimes known as the "right of respect"), which is the author's right to object to any distortion, mutilation, or derogatory action with respect to the work that would harm the author's honor or reputation.

American copyright law does not recognize moral rights. Why not? Observe they are found in the copyright laws of almost all civil law countries, and typically they are inalienable by the author.

Significantly, the *TRIPs Agreement* does clarify several ambiguities in the *Berne Convention*. First—and perhaps most importantly—disputes arising under the *Agreement* are subject to the WTO *DSU*. As one practitioner points out, this contrasts with the inefficacious method of dispute resolution under the *Berne Convention*:

> No longer does membership in the *Berne Convention* suffice to protect member nations from the perils of copyright non-compliance. An inherent deficiency plagues enforcement of *Berne Convention* strictures, inasmuch as the mechanism of enforcement under the treaty is limited to actions brought by one country against another country in the International Court of Justice, a cumbersome procedure which has never been invoked. In a world service economy, for which the copyright industries produce works that account for billions of dollars of international trade, the lack of effective enforcement mechanisms in the *Berne Convention* renders it insufficiently potent to safeguard authors' rights.[3]

---

2. RICHARD E. NEFF & FRAN SMALLSON, NAFTA: PROTECTING AND ENFORCING INTELLECTUAL PROPERTY RIGHTS IN NORTH AMERICA 17 n. 6 (1994).

3. David Nimmer, *GATT's Entertainment: Before and NAFTA*, 15 LOYOLA OF LOS ANGELES ENTERTAINMENT LAW JOURNAL 133, 135. *See also id.*, 143–146.

Second, Article 10:1 states that computer programs and databases must be given protection as literary works under the *Berne Convention*.

Third, Articles 12 and 14:5 essentially require that performers, producers of phonograms, and authors must receive protection for their works for 50 years.

Fourth, both the *Berne Convention* and *TRIPs Agreement* confer the exclusive right to authorize a public performance or broadcast on a performer. (The IPRs of performers, producers of phonograms, and broadcasting organizations are known as "neighboring rights.") But, the *Convention* does not provide the performer with a right to prohibit commercial rentals to the public of originals or copies of the copyrighted work, unauthorized taping of live performances, or broadcasting of live performances.

Under Articles 11 and 14:1-2 of the *TRIPs Agreement*, performers, producers of phonograms, and authors of computer programs and films must be permitted to authorize or prohibit commercial rental to the public of their works. Fortunately for video rental stores and their customers, Article 11 contains an exception for "cinematographic works unless such [commercial] rental has led to widespread copying of such works which is materially impairing the exclusive right of reproduction conferred in . . .[a] Member on authors and their successors in title." Finally, Article 61 of the *Agreement* requires WTO Members to impose criminal penalties for willful copyright piracy on a commercial scale.

IV. Mail Boxes and 1998 *India Patent Protection* Case

At the end of the Uruguay Round, many developing countries and LDCs did not have laws in place to protect patents for pharmaceuticals and agricultural chemicals. India—which, in the past, was one of the world's worst offenders of patent rights—was an example. India granted only process patents. Hence, domestic companies were free to re-produce any new product entering the international marketplace. American pharmaceutical companies complained this piracy cost them $500 million annually.

To be sure, under Article 66:1 of the *TRIPs Agreement*, LDC Members were supposed to establish patent laws by 1 January 2006.[4] But, what happened until then, *i.e.*, during the 1st decade of life of the WTO and *Agreement*? Many pharmaceutical

---

4. In 2002, the WTO TRIPs Council extended for another 10 years (to 1 January 2016) the period in which pharmaceuticals were exempt from *TRIPs Agreement* patent rules, specifically, Articles 66:1 and 70:8-9. As the expiry date approached, LDCs called for a permanent extension under Article 66:1 for any WTO Member as long as it has the status of an LDC. Developed countries such as Australia, Canada, Switzerland, and the U.S. refused an indefinite extension, arguing it was not helpful to LDCs to exempt them indefinitely from obligations of a system of which they were Members, and into which they were seeking to integrate.

and agricultural chemical companies sought to apply for patent protection in such countries in anticipation of forthcoming patent laws. How could these applicants be confident such countries would recognize their inventions as novel given that legal void? These companies also sought to sell their products in such countries and retain the exclusive right to do so. How could they obtain this right?

The *TRIPs Agreement* answers these questions. Article 70 contains two key transitional rules. First, Article 70:8 requires any WTO Member that did not protect patents for pharmaceuticals and agricultural chemicals to have established by 1 January 1995 a "mail box" system for filing patent applications. Under this "Mail Box Rule," the original date on which an applicant files for patent protection pursuant to a yet-to-be-established legal regime is preserved. A mail box applicant stands a better chance in the future, when the legal regime is in place, of arguing successfully its invention is novel, because its application must be reviewed on the basis of the date it was filed (*i.e.*, placed in the mail box).

Second, Article 70:9 requires a WTO Member to provide exclusive marketing rights for a product that is the subject of a mail box patent application. The rights period must be the earlier of (1) five years from the date of obtaining marketing approval or (2) the granting or rejection of the patent. Exclusive marketing rights are conditional on the applicant having filed a patent application, and been granted both a patent and marketing approval, in a different Member.

In December 1994, India implemented temporary rules for a mail box system through the *Patents (Amendment) Ordinance*. The *Ordinance* expired in March 1995. The Indian government, then led by the Congress Party, also proposed the *Patents (Amendment) Bill of 1995* to amend the *Patents Act of 1970* to make the rules permanent. This proposal also granted exclusive marketing rights for five years to newly patented drugs, pharmaceuticals, and agricultural chemicals.

But, writing IP rules in a way that might benefit foreign companies evokes strong emotions in India, a country unusually sensitive about foreign political or economic influence. The government of former Prime Minister Indira Gandhi (1917–1984, PM, 1966–1977, 1980–1984) forced Coca-Cola to withdraw from India in the 1970s when Coke refused to yield its secret "7X" formula. Both the right-wing BJP and the

---

In October 2015, the U.S. offered an additional 10 year extension (to 1 January 2026). LDCs rejected that offer. But, in November 2015, LDCs accepted an American counterproposal: LDCs would be exempt from pharmaceutical patent rules until 1 January 2033, *i.e.*, a 17 year waiver under Article 66:1 based on the "special needs and requirements of least developed country Members, their economic, financial, and administrative constraints, and their need for flexibility to create a viable technological base." The waiver covered most *TRIPs Agreement* obligations (other than the National Treatment and MFN rules in Articles 3 and 4, respectively, and the related Article 5 provision about WIPO agreements). The waiver also applied to the "Mailbox Rule" and five-year exclusive marketing rights provision in Articles 70:8 and 70:9, respectively.

Accordingly, the type of problem India faced in the *Mailbox* case could arise again in any LDC: like India, the LDC would have the benefit of the Article 66:1 waiver, but could be accused of not fulfilling its Article 70:8 or 70:9 obligations.

Communist Party (otherwise strange bedfellows) fought the proposed amendment. While the *Lok Sabha*, India's Lower House of Parliament, approved the proposal, the Upper House (the *Rajya Sabha*) rejected it. So, in March 1995 when the temporary Mail Box system expired and no exclusive marketing rights system was in place, India was vulnerable to the charge it was in breach of its *TRIPs* obligations.

The U.S. formally made the charge in July 1996. It commenced a Special 301 investigation and a WTO action against India. In September 1997, a WTO Panel ruled in favor of the U.S. In its report, the Panel found India had failed to establish a mail box system. India argued it received Mail Box applications under an unpublished administrative system. But, the U.S. successfully countered administrative instructions are not legally secure, *i.e.*, not a legally valid Mail Box, in contravention of Article 70:8. The U.S. doubted the instructions would be upheld under India's *Patents Act*, because drugs, pharmaceuticals, and agricultural chemicals are not patentable under that *Act*.

The Panel also found India ran afoul of two other *TRIPs Agreement* provisions. It violated Article 63:2, because it did not notify the WTO of the legal basis for its administrative Mail Box scheme, and it violated Article 70:9 by failing to provide exclusive marketing rights. The USTR hailed the decision as an important precedent for the enforcement of American rights. It was the first WTO adjudication under the *TRIPs Agreement*, and it served notice on developing countries to abide by that accord.

India appealed the adverse decision. But, in December 1997 the Appellate Body (whose decision is excerpted below) largely affirmed the Panel report. The Appellate Body upheld the Article 70:8 and 70:9 findings. It overturned the Article 63:2 ruling, on the grounds the Panel had strayed outside of its jurisdiction as the U.S. had not raised this provision when it called for formation of a Panel. As it had done with the Panel Report, the USTR praised the Appellate Body Report for its precedential value. One of many interesting features of the Report is the extensive discussion of the concept of "legitimate expectations," the difference between violation and non-violation nullification or impairment, and the relevance of this concept and the distinction to the case at bar.

India and the U.S. argued about the time period for implementing the Appellate Body decision. India contended it needed until 16 June 1999 to comply, partly in view of general elections that brought to power a new government led by the BJP. The U.S. hoped for near-immediate implementation, especially in view of the fact India should have amended its law in 1994 in the wake of the Uruguay Round. In April 1998, the sides agreed to the usual 15 month implementation period, backdated to the date the Dispute Settlement Body adopted the Appellate Body Report (16 January 1998). Thus, India was given until 16 July 1999 to bring its legal regime into compliance.

Not only does the case present an admixture of the *TRIPs Agreement*, IP protection issues in the Third World context, and domestic Indian politics, but it also underscores the variables affecting FDI flows in the global economy. Ultimately, the BJP recognized the stakes: India's poor record of IPR enforcement was one reason why it is an unattractive destination for FDI, even (or perhaps especially) in comparison with China. The Indian government also seemed to realize just how important a center of IP activity India had become. It was producing IP products. For the government to view the country as a net consumer of IP products was to see the India of the past, and not imagine the India of the future whose IP entrepreneurs would need *TRIPs* protections abroad.

V. Substantive Holdings of 1998 *India Patent Protection* Case

WTO Appellate Body Report,

India — Patent Protection for Pharmaceutical and Agricultural Chemical Products, WT/DS50/AB/R (Adopted 16 January 1998)

I. Introduction

1. India appeals from certain issues of law and legal interpretations in the Panel Report ....

. . .

(9) Under Indian patent law, patent applications for pharmaceutical or agricultural chemical products made by any person entitled to apply under Section 6 of the *Patents Act 1970* are subject to the same fee as any other patent application being received and allotted a filing date and advertised in the *Official Gazette* with serial number, filing date, name of applicant and title of invention. But, under the administrative arrangements of the Indian patent offices pursuant to the decision taken in April 1995, these applications are unlike other patent applications. They are stored separately and not referred by the Controller to an examiner as specified in Section 12 of the *Act.*

(10) The legal authority for these administrative arrangements that India cited is Article 73(1)(a) of the Indian Constitution, along with the *Indian Patents Act 1970.* Article 73(1) reads as follows:

> "*Extent of executive power of the Union.* (1) Subject to the provisions of this Constitution, the executive power of the Union shall extend
>
> (a) to the matters with respect to which Parliament has power to make laws; and
>
> (b) to the exercise of such rights, authority and jurisdiction as are exercisable by the Government of India by virtue of any treaty or agreement:
>
> Provided that the executive power referred to in sub-clause (a) shall not, save as expressly provided in this Constitution or in any law made by

Parliament, extend in any State to matters with respect to which the Legislature of the State has also power to make laws."

(11) As for the *Patents Act*, the relevant provisions are:

— Chapter III (Sections 6 through 11) deals with applications for patents. These provisions do not require that applications for patents must be limited to patentable subject matter. They only require that such applications should be for inventions.

— Inventions are defined in Section 2(1)(j) as, *inter alia*, any new and useful substance produced by manufacture, including any new and useful improvement of such a substance.

— Section 5 makes it clear that inventions claiming substances intended for use, or capable of being used, as a food, medicine or drug or relating to substances prepared or produced by chemical processes are not in themselves patentable. But, methods or processes for the manufacture of these products are patentable. Under Section 2(1)(l)(iv) the term "medicine or drug" includes insecticides, germicides, fungicides, weedicides and all other substances intended to be used for the protection or preservation of plants.

— Chapter IV of the *Patents Act* concerns the examination of applications. Section 12 requires that, when the complete specification has been filed with respect to an application for a patent, the application shall be referred by the Controller General of Patents, Designs and Trademarks to an examiner. The examiner shall ordinarily report to the Controller within a period of 18 months on, *inter alia*, whether the application and the specification are in accordance with the requirements of the *Act* and whether there is any lawful ground for objecting to the grant of the patent under the *Act*.

— Paragraph 2 of Section 15 states that, if it appears to the Controller that the invention claimed in the specification is not patentable under the *Act*, he shall refuse the application.

(12) Between 1 January 1995 and 15 February 1997, a total of 1,339 applications for pharmaceutical and agricultural chemical products had been received and registered. Of these applications, American companies had filed 318 applications for pharmaceutical product patents and 45 applications for agricultural chemical product patents. On the day the *Patents (Amendment) Ordinance 1994* had lapsed, 125 applications had been received and filed (41 by American companies). Before 15 February 1997, out of the other 1,214 applications (322 by American companies), 605 had been received and filed prior to the day the *Patents (Amendment) Bill 1995* had lapsed.

(13) The Indian executive authorities do not have the legal powers under present Indian law to accord exclusive marketing rights in accordance with *TRIPs* Article 70:9. [No request for grant of exclusive marketing rights was submitted to Indian authorities.]

III. Issues Raised In This Appeal

28. The appellant, India, raises the following issues in this appeal:

    (a) What is the proper interpretation to be given to the requirement in Article 70:8(a) of the *TRIPS Agreement* that a Member shall provide "a means" by which applications for patents for inventions relating to pharmaceutical or agricultural chemical products can be filed?

    (b) Did the Panel err in its treatment of Indian municipal law, or in its application of the burden of proof, in examining whether India had complied with its obligations under Article 70:8(a) of the *TRIPS Agreement*?

    (c) Does Article 70:9 of the *TRIPS Agreement* require that there must be a "mechanism" in place to provide for the grant of exclusive marketing rights effective as from the date of entry into force of the *WTO Agreement*?

[The portion of the Appellate Body report dealing with the alternative U.S. claim under Article 63 is omitted. The Appellate Body reversed the Panel's finding India had violated Article 63:1-2, because the matter was outside of the Panel's terms of reference.]

IV. The *TRIPS Agreement*

29. . . . The dispute that gives rise to this case represents the first time the *TRIPS Agreement* has been submitted to the scrutiny of the WTO dispute settlement system.

30. Among the many provisions of the *TRIPS Agreement* are certain specific obligations relating to patent protection for pharmaceutical and agricultural chemical products [such as in Article 27:1] . . . .

31. However, Article 65 of the *TRIPS Agreement* provides, in pertinent part:

> 1. Subject to the provisions of paragraphs 2, 3 and 4, no Member shall be obliged to apply the provisions of this *Agreement* before the expiry of a general period of one year following the date of entry into force of the *WTO Agreement*.

> 2. A developing country Member is entitled to delay for a further period of four years the date of application, as defined in paragraph 1, of the provisions of this *Agreement* other than Articles 3, 4 and 5.

>   . . .

> 4. To the extent that a developing country Member is obliged by this Agreement to extend product patent protection to areas of technology not so protectable in its territory on the general date of application of this Agreement for that Member, as defined in paragraph 2, it may delay the application of the provisions on product patents of Section 5 of Part II to such areas of technology for an additional period of five years.

> 5. A Member availing itself of a transitional period under paragraphs 1, 2, 3 or 4 shall ensure that any changes in its laws, regulations and practice made

during that period do not result in a lesser degree of consistency with the provisions of this *Agreement.*

32. With respect to patent protection for pharmaceutical and agricultural chemical products, certain specific obligations are found in Articles 70:8 and 70:9 of the *TRIPS Agreement.* The interpretation of these specific obligations is the subject of this dispute.

. . .

[Omitted is the Appellate Body's extended discussion, and rejection, in Section V (Paragraphs 33–48) of the Panel's interpretative theory that legitimate expectations always must be considered when appraising the words of the *TRIPs Agreement*—or, by extension, any WTO text. The Panel said protection of legitimate expectations is a well-established principle of GATT, deriving from GATT Article XXIII. The Appellate Body explained the Panel had confused 2 different strains in prior GATT practice—violation nullification or impairment cases under Article XXIII:1(a), and non-violation nullification or impairment cases arising under Article XXIII:1(b).

Almost all GATT panel cases arose under the first of these provisions. In such cases involving substantive claims under Articles III and XI, panels often would mention the importance of the Articles in protecting legitimate expectations of contracting parties. But, typically, panels made statements only after finding a violation of one of the articles. Only a handful of pre-*DSU* claims were brought under the second provision, and in only 4 of the 14 of them did a GATT panel find non-violation nullification or impairment. The doctrine of protecting reasonable expectations arose under, and is connected with, with non-violation claims. Article 26:1 of the *DSU* imports some GATT Article XXIII:1(b) non-violation concepts. But, Article 64:2 of the *TRIPs Agreement* makes clear that non-violation claims may not be brought under that *Agreement* for the first 5 years of its life, *i.e.,* between 1 January 1996 and 31 December 2000. The *India Patent Protection* case arose during this period. WTO Members have renewed periodically this moratorium against non-violation nullification or impairment IP claims.

In sum, whether legitimate expectations may be used as an interpretative basis is a violation nullification or impairment case is highly dubious, and as a practical matter, impossible in the present dispute.]

VI. Article 70:8

. . .

54. Article 70:8(a) imposes an obligation on Members to provide "a means" by which mailbox applications can be filed "from the date of entry into force of the WTO Agreement." Thus, this obligation has been in force since 1 January 1995. The issue before us in this appeal is not whether this obligation exists or whether this obligation is now in force. Clearly, it exists, and, equally clearly, it is in force now. The issue before us in this appeal is: what precisely is the "means" for filing mailbox

applications that is contemplated and required by Article 70:8(a)? To answer this question, we must interpret the terms of Article 70:8(a).

55. We agree with the Panel that "[t]he analysis of the ordinary meaning of these terms alone does not lead to a definitive interpretation as to what sort of 'means' is required by this subparagraph." Therefore, in accordance with the general rules of treaty interpretation set out in Article 31 of the *Vienna Convention,* to discern the meaning of the terms in Article 70:8(a), we must also read this provision in its context, and in light of the object and purpose of the *TRIPS Agreement.*

56. Paragraphs (b) and (c) of Article 70:8 constitute part of the context for interpreting Article 70:8(a). Paragraphs (b) and (c) of Article 70:8 require that the "means" provided by a Member under Article 70:8(a) must allow the filing of applications for patents for pharmaceutical and agricultural chemical products from 1 January 1995 and preserve the dates of filing and priority of those applications, so that the criteria for patentability may be applied as of those dates, and so that the patent protection eventually granted is dated back to the filing date. In this respect, we agree with the Panel that,

> . . . in order to prevent the loss of the novelty of an invention . . . filing and priority dates need to have a sound legal basis if the provisions of Article 70:8 are to fulfill their purpose. Moreover, if available, a filing must entitle the applicant to claim priority on the basis of an earlier filing in respect of the claimed invention over applications with subsequent filing or priority dates. Without legally sound filing and priority dates, the mechanism to be established on the basis of Article 70:8 will be rendered inoperational.

57. On this, the Panel is clearly correct. The Panel's interpretation here is consistent also with the object and purpose of the *TRIPS Agreement.* The *Agreement* [in the Preamble] takes into account, *inter alia,* "the need to promote effective and adequate protection of intellectual property rights." We believe the Panel was correct in finding that the "means" that the Member concerned is obliged to provide under Article 70:8(a) must allow for "the entitlement to file mailbox applications and the allocation of filing and priority dates to them." Furthermore, the Panel was correct in finding that the "means" established under Article 70:8(a) must also provide "a sound legal basis to preserve novelty and priority as of those dates." These findings flow inescapably from the necessary operation of paragraphs (b) and (c) of Article 70:8.

58. However, we do *not* agree with the Panel that Article 70:8(a) requires a Member to establish a means "so as to eliminate any reasonable doubts regarding whether mailbox applications and eventual patents based on them could be rejected or invalidated because, at the filing or priority date, the matter for which protection was sought was unpatentable in the country in question." India is *entitled,* by the "transitional arrangements" in paragraphs 1, 2 and 4 of Article 65, to delay application of Article 27 for patents for pharmaceutical and agricultural chemical products until 1 January 2005. In our view, India is obliged, by Article 70:8(a), to provide a

legal mechanism for the filing of mailbox applications that provides a sound legal basis to preserve both the novelty of the inventions and the priority of the applications as of the relevant filing and priority dates. No more.

59. But what constitutes such a sound legal basis in Indian law? To answer this question, we must recall first an important general rule in the *TRIPS Agreement*. Article 1.1 of the *TRIPS Agreement* states, in pertinent part:

> ... Members shall be free to determine the appropriate method of implementing the provisions of this Agreement within their own legal system and practice.

Members, therefore, are free to determine how best to meet their obligations under the *TRIPS Agreement* within the context of their own legal systems. And, as a Member, India is "free to determine the appropriate method of implementing" its obligations under the *TRIPS Agreement* within the context of its own legal system.

60. India insists that it has done that. India contends that it has established, through "administrative instructions," a "means" consistent with Article 70:8(a) of the *TRIPS Agreement*. According to India, these "administrative instructions" establish a mechanism that provides a sound legal basis to preserve the novelty of the inventions and the priority of the applications as of the relevant filing and priority dates consistent with Article 70:8(a) of the *TRIPS Agreement*. According to India, pursuant to these "administrative instructions," the Patent Office has been directed to store applications for patents for pharmaceutical and agricultural chemical products separately for future action pursuant to Article 70:8, and the Controller General of Patents Designs and Trademarks ("the Controller") has been instructed not to refer them to an examiner until 1 January 2005. According to India, these "administrative instructions" are legally valid in Indian law, as they are reflected in the Minister's Statement to Parliament of 2 August 1996. And, according to India:

> There is ... *absolute certainty* that India can, when patents are due in accordance with subparagraphs (b) and (c) of Article 70:8, decide to grant such patents on the basis of the applications currently submitted and determine the novelty and priority of the inventions in accordance with the date of these applications. (emphasis added)

61. India has not provided any text of these "administrative instructions" either to the Panel or to us.

62. Whatever their substance or their import, these "administrative instructions" were not the initial "means" chosen by the Government of India to meet India's obligations under Article 70:8(a) of the *TRIPS Agreement*. The Government of India's initial preference for establishing a "means" for filing mailbox applications under Article 70:8(a) was the *Patents (Amendment) Ordinance* (the "*Ordinance*"), promulgated by the President of India on 31 December 1994 pursuant to Article 123 of India's Constitution. Article 123 enables the President to promulgate an ordinance when Parliament is not in session, and when the President is satisfied "that circumstances exist which render it necessary for him to take immediate

action." India notified the *Ordinance* to the Council for *TRIPS*, pursuant to Article 63:2 of the *TRIPS Agreement*, on 6 March 1995. In accordance with the terms of Article 123 of India's Constitution, the *Ordinance* expired on 26 March 1995, six weeks after the reassembly of Parliament. This was followed by an unsuccessful effort to enact the *Patents (Amendment) Bill 1995* to implement the contents of the *Ordinance* on a permanent basis. This *Bill* was introduced in the *Lok Sabha* (Lower House) in March 1995. After being passed by the *Lok Sabha*, it was referred to a Select Committee of the *Rajya Sabha* (Upper House) for examination and report. However, the *Bill* was subsequently not enacted due to the dissolution of Parliament on 10 May 1996. From these actions, it is apparent that the Government of India initially considered the enactment of amending legislation to be necessary in order to implement its obligations under Article 70:8(a). However, India maintains that the "administrative instructions" issued in April 1995 effectively continued the mailbox system established by the *Ordinance*, thus obviating the need for a formal amendment to the *Patents Act* or for a new notification to the Council for *TRIPS*.

63. With respect to India's "administrative instructions," the Panel found that "the current administrative practice creates a certain degree of legal insecurity in that it requires Indian officials to ignore certain mandatory provisions of the *Patents Act*;" and that "even if Patent Office officials do not examine and reject mailbox applications, a competitor might seek a judicial order to do so in order to obtain rejection of a patent claim."

64. India asserts that the Panel erred in its treatment of India's municipal law because municipal law is a fact that must be established before an international tribunal by the party relying on it. In India's view, the Panel did not assess the Indian law as a fact to be established by the United States, but rather as a law to be interpreted by the Panel. India argues that the Panel should have given India the benefit of the doubt as to the status of its mailbox system under Indian domestic law. India claims, furthermore, that the Panel should have sought guidance from India on matters relating to the interpretation of Indian law.

65. In public international law, an international tribunal may treat municipal law in several ways. Municipal law may serve as evidence of facts and may provide evidence of state practice. However, municipal law may also constitute evidence of compliance or non-compliance with international obligations. For example, in *Certain German Interests in Polish Upper Silesia*, the Permanent Court of International Justice observed:

> It might be asked whether a difficulty does not arise from the fact that the Court would have to deal with the Polish law of July 14th, 1920. This, however, does not appear to be the case. From the standpoint of International Law and of the Court which is its organ, municipal laws are merely facts which express the will and constitute the activities of States, in the same manner as do legal decisions and administrative measures. *The Court is certainly not called upon to interpret the Polish law as such; but there is nothing to*

prevent the Court's giving judgment on the question whether or not, in apply-
ing that law, Poland is acting in conformity with its obligations towards Ger-
many under the Geneva Convention. (emphasis added) [1926 P.C.I.J. Rep.,
Series A, No. 7, p. 19]

66. In this case, the Panel was simply performing its task in determining whether
India's "administrative instructions" for receiving mailbox applications were in
conformity with India's obligations under Article 70:8(a) of the *TRIPS Agreement.*
It is clear that an examination of the relevant aspects of Indian municipal law and,
in particular, the relevant provisions of the *Patents Act* as they relate to the "administrative instructions," is essential to determining whether India has complied with
its obligations under Article 70:8(a). There was simply no way for the Panel to
make this determination without engaging in an examination of Indian law. But,
as in the case cited above before the Permanent Court of International Justice, in
this case, the Panel was not interpreting Indian law "as such;" rather, the Panel was
examining Indian law solely for the purpose of determining whether India had
met its obligations under the *TRIPS Agreement.* To say that the Panel should have
done otherwise would be to say that only India can assess whether Indian law is
consistent with India's obligations under the *WTO Agreement.* This, clearly, cannot
be so.

67. Previous GATT/WTO panels also have conducted a detailed examination of the
domestic law of a Member in assessing the conformity of that domestic law with
the relevant GATT/WTO obligations. For example, in *United States—Section 337
of the Tariff Act of 1930,* the panel conducted a detailed examination of the relevant
United States' legislation and practice, including the remedies available under Section 337 as well as the differences between patent-based Section 337 proceedings and
federal district court proceedings, in order to determine whether Section 337 was
inconsistent with Article III:4 of the GATT 1947. [*See* GATT B.I.S.D. (36th Supp.) at
345 (adopted 7 November 1989).] This seems to us to be a comparable case.

. . .

69. To do so, we must look at the specific provisions of the *Patents Act.* Section 5(a)
of the *Patents Act* provides that substances "intended for use, or capable of being
used, as food or as medicine or drug" are not patentable. "When the complete specification has been led in respect of an application for a patent," section 12(1) *requires*
the Controller to refer that application and that specification to an examiner. Moreover, section 15(2) of the *Patents Act* states that the Controller "shall refuse" an
application in respect of a substance that is not patentable. We agree with the Panel
that these provisions of the *Patents Act* are mandatory. And, like the Panel, we are
not persuaded that India's "administrative instructions" would prevail over the
contradictory mandatory provisions of the *Patents Act.* We note also that, in issuing
these "administrative instructions," the Government of India did not avail itself of
the provisions of section 159 of the *Patents Act,* which allows the Central Government "to make rules for carrying out the provisions of [the] *Act*" or section 160
of the *Patents Act,* which requires that such rules be laid before each House of the

Indian Parliament. We are told by India that such rulemaking was not required for the "administrative instructions" at issue here. But this, too, seems to be inconsistent with the mandatory provisions of the *Patents Act*.

70. We are not persuaded by India's explanation of these seeming contradictions. Accordingly, we are not persuaded that India's "administrative instructions" would survive a legal challenge under the *Patents Act*. And, consequently, we are not persuaded that India's "administrative instructions" provide a sound legal basis to preserve novelty of inventions and priority of applications as of the relevant filing and priority dates.

71. For these reasons, we agree with the Panel's conclusion that India's "administrative instructions" for receiving mailbox applications are inconsistent with Article 70:8(a) of the *TRIPS Agreement*.

  . . .

VII. Article 70:9

  . . .

78. India argues that Article 70:9 establishes an obligation to grant exclusive marketing rights for a product that is the subject of a patent application under Article 70:8(a) after all the other conditions specified in Article 70:9 have been fulfilled. India asserts that there are many provisions in the *TRIPS Agreement* that, unlike Article 70:9, explicitly oblige Members to change their domestic laws to authorize their domestic authorities to take certain action before the need to take such action actually arises. India maintains that the Panel's interpretation of Article 70:9 has the consequence that the transitional arrangements in Article 65 allow developing country Members to postpone legislative changes in all fields of technology except the most "sensitive" ones, pharmaceutical and agricultural chemical products. India claims that the Panel turned an obligation to take action in the future into an obligation to take action immediately.

79. India's arguments must be examined in the light of Article XVI:4 of the *WTO Agreement*, which requires that:

> Each Member shall ensure the conformity of its laws, regulations and administrative procedures with its obligations as provided in the annexed Agreements.

80. Moreover, India acknowledged before the Panel and in this appeal that, under Indian law, it is necessary to enact legislation in order to grant exclusive marketing rights in compliance with the provisions of Article 70:9. This was already implied in the *Ordinance*, which contained detailed provisions for the grant of exclusive marketing rights in India effective 1 January 1995. However, with the expiry of the *Ordinance* on 26 March 1995, no legal basis remained, and with the failure to enact the *Patents (Amendment) Bill 1995* due to the dissolution of Parliament on 10 May 1996, no legal basis currently exists, for the grant of exclusive marketing rights in India. India notified the Council for *TRIPS* of the promulgation of the *Ordinance* pursuant

to Article 63:2 of the *TRIPS Agreement*, but has failed as yet to notify the Council for *TRIPS* that the *Ordinance* has expired.

81. Given India's admissions that legislation is necessary in order to grant exclusive marketing rights in compliance with Article 70:9 and that it does not currently have such legislation, the issue for us to consider in this appeal is whether a failure to have in place a mechanism ready for the grant of exclusive marketing rights, effective *as from the date of entry into force* of the *WTO Agreement*, constitutes a violation of India's obligations under Article 70:9 of the *TRIPS Agreement*.

82. By its terms, Article 70:9 applies only in situations where a product patent application is filed under Article 70.8(a). Like Article 70:8(a), Article 70:9 applies "notwithstanding the provisions of Part VI." Article 70:9 specifically refers to Article 70:8(a), and they operate in tandem to provide a package of rights and obligations that apply *during* the transitional periods contemplated in Article 65. It is obvious, therefore, that both Article 70:8(a) *and* Article 70:9 are intended to apply as from the date of entry into force of the *WTO Agreement*.

83. India has an obligation to implement the provisions of Article 70:9 of the *TRIPS Agreement* effective as from the date of entry into force of the *WTO Agreement*, that is, 1 January 1995. India concedes that legislation is needed to implement this obligation. India has not enacted such legislation. To give meaning and effect to the rights and obligations under Article 70:9 of the *TRIPS Agreement*, such legislation should have been in effect since 1 January 1995.

84. For these reasons, we agree with the Panel that India should have had a mechanism in place to provide for the grant of exclusive marketing rights effective as from the date of entry into force of the *WTO Agreement*, and, therefore, we agree with the Panel that India is in violation of Article 70:9 of the *TRIPS Agreement*.

VI. Jurisprudential Hypocrisy as to What "Law" Is?

A fascinating dimension of the *India Patent* case is jurisprudential. Indeed, it is one of the most fundamental questions in legal philosophy: what is "law"? India argues its unpublished administrative system is, indeed, "law." The U.S. demands greater formality, looking for a statute with the imprimatur of the Indian Parliament. But, is there not something to the Indian point?

The answer to the question "what is law" may depend on the context of application. Any visitor to India knows there is often quite a difference between the written rule and actual practice. Custom and other informal sources of rules typically are what really matter. Why adhere to formalistic notions about the sources of law grounded in Judeo-Christian tradition when India, and many Non-Western countries, present a different context?

Moreover, is the American pressure on India hypocritical? In the 2000 *Section 301* case (treated in a separate Chapter), the U.S. "got off the hook" because of the custom and practice surrounding Section 301. The Appellate Body was content with the fact the U.S. did not use the discretionary authority granted by statute in a unilateral matter. In other words, even in the developed country context, informalities like actual practice matter. If the behavior and representations of the American government as regards an offending statute count, then why not count the assurances of the Indian government to fill a void of formal law? Is it a question of the credibility of the governments involved? If so, then is there a presumption favoring First World governments? Is such a presumption fair?

Chapter 32

Compulsory Licensing, Evergreening, and Patented Pharmaceuticals[1]

I. Dreaded Diseases and Generic Medicines

A rare achievement of the November 2001-March 2018 Doha Round, finalized at the December 2005 Hong Kong Ministerial Conference, concerned compulsory licensing. WTO Members agreed to ease restrictions on imports of generic copies of life-saving medicines by poor countries that do not have the capacity to manufacture generics. They did so against a backdrop of three stark facts: in developing countries, about 90% of the population pays for medicines out-of-pocket; after food, medicines are the largest household expenditure in these countries; and many such countries cannot take advantage of the compulsory licensing under Article 31(f) of the *TRIPs Agreement*.

Article 31(f) allows the government of a Member to issue a compulsory license only if it would be used "predominantly" to supply the domestic market in that country. If a country lacks manufacturing capacity (*e.g.*, Mali), then its only viable alternative is to import generics. But, such importation could imply the exporting Member (*e.g.*, the EU) might not be supplying predominantly its own market. The Doha *Ministerial Declaration* on compulsory licensing did not fix the anomaly. The special *Declaration on TRIPs and Public Health*, while referring to the problem in Paragraph 6 — hence, the rubric "Paragraph 6 issue" — did not fix it either.

So, in August 2003, the Members agreed to grant three temporary waivers, two from Article 31(f) and 1 from Article 31(h) of the *TRIPs Agreement*, to deal with the problem of manufacturing capacity. The waivers sometimes are called the "August 2003 Medicines Agreement," or the "Paragraph 6 Decision." The waivers allow a country to issue a compulsory license and thereby override patent rights, and import generic drugs to treat public health matters, including HIV/AIDS, malaria, and tuberculosis. That is, the waivers remove the constraint that generics

---

1. Documents References:
   (1) *Havana (ITO) Charter* Articles 19, 37:7, 45:1(a)(vii)
   (2) GATT Articles IV, IX:6, XX(f)
   (3) WTO *TRIPs Agreement*

made under a compulsory license should be primarily for the domestic market of the country granting the license, and thus permit exportation of generics to countries lacking manufacturing capacity. At the December 2005 Hong Kong Ministerial Conference, the Members made the waivers permanent, subject to approval by two-thirds of the Membership. That occurred on 23 January 2017.

II. Doha Round December 2005 Hong Kong Ministerial Conference and First Waiver from Article 31(f)

Any WTO Member can export generic pharmaceutical products made under a compulsory license to meet the needs of an importing country. Thus, a country lacking production capacity may import medicine that is under a compulsory license, and producers in an exporting country in which the pharmaceutical is subject to a patent may manufacture and export them under the license. However, checks must be established checks to ensure beneficiary countries import generics without undermining the patent systems of developed countries. To ensure a beneficiary is not constrained by burdensome or impractical checks inuring to the benefit of rich countries, the waiver affords that country flexibility. The measures must be "reasonable," within its "means," and "proportionate" to its "administrative capacities." There are three kinds of checks.

First, generic medicines must not be diverted to the wrong markets. Second, while no WTO approval is required, a developing or least developed country invoking the waiver must notify the WTO before importing a generic version of a patented medicine. It must explain what it is importing, in what expected quantities, affirm that it has insufficient or no manufacturing capacity for the product in question, and (if the product is patented in its territory) confirm it has granted a compulsory license in accordance with the *TRIPs Agreement*. Similarly, a developed or developing country that exports pharmaceuticals under a compulsory license must notify the WTO it is doing so. The exporting Member must explain the conditions on (including length of) the license, identify the licensee and product, and state the expected export quantities destinations.

Technically, any Member—rich or poor—can invoke the Article 31(f) waiver. However, in 2003, 23 developed countries declared voluntarily they would not import generic pharmaceutical products. In 2004, the 10 newly acceding countries to the EU added themselves to this list. Thus, the 33 Members abstaining from waiver rights are:

Australia	Czech Republic
Austria	Cyprus
Belgium	Denmark
Canada	Estonia

Finland	Netherlands
France	New Zealand
Germany	Norway
Greece	Poland
Hungary	Portugal
Iceland	Slovak Republic
Ireland	Slovenia
Italy	Spain
Japan	Sweden
Latvia	Switzerland
Lithuania	United Kingdom
Luxembourg	U.S.
Malta	

Significantly, 11 additional Members voluntarily declared (in connection with the December 2005 *Statement* of the General Council Chairperson, discussed below) they would use the waiver system to import generics only in a national emergency or other circumstance of extreme urgency:

Hong Kong

Israel

Korea

Kuwait

Macao

Mexico

Qatar

Singapore

Taiwan (Chinese Taipei)

Turkey

United Arab Emirates

Which Members are the most likely exporters of generics? The answer includes the ones that changed their laws to implement the waiver and permit manufacturing of generics under a compulsory license exclusively for export. These countries include Canada, the EU, India, and Norway. For instance, in 2005, the Indian Parliament amended the country's patent law to make illegal copying patented drugs. Hence, an Indian drug companies cannot lawfully supply African countries with an unauthorized version of a patented medicine.

III. 2007 *Rwanda* Case Invoking Article 31(f) Waiver

Rwanda was the first WTO Member to invoke the generics import waiver under the amendment to Article 31(f) of the *TRIPs Agreement*. In July 2007, it notified the Membership it would import (in 2008 and 2009) 260,000 packs of a generic version of a patented medicine. The generic product, TriAvir, was made in Canada by Apotex, Inc. This medicine is a fixed dose tablet that is an admixture of Zidovudine (300 mg, used to treat HIV), Lamivudine (150 mg, for HIV and hepatitis B), and Nevirapine (200 mg, for HIV/AIDS). Rwanda explained it could not make the generic medicine domestically. Canada followed suit in October 2007, becoming the first Member to notify the WTO it would export drugs—15.6 million TriAvir tablets to Rwanda—under the new compulsory licensing regime.

Notably, though, Apotex, along with *Medecins Sans Frontieres* (Doctors Without Borders), and Members such as Brazil, Canada, China, Ecuador, and Pakistan, have said the Waiver from Article 31(f) is deeply flawed, in a part because it is too cumbersome to comply with. In the Apotex experience, the company received fast-track approval from Canada for its generic in June 2006 (having asked in December 2005), found an interested importing country in July 2007, contacted the patent holders and sought (unsuccessfully) a voluntary license (a step normally required before moving to a compulsory license, even under the Paragraph 6 system), requested and got a compulsory license in Canada in two weeks, in September 2007, participated in the public tender in Rwanda in May 2008, when Apotex also started production of the generic, and finally made first delivery in September 2008. The fact that the process took over two years is one reason why critics charge the Waiver is so rarely used.

Is the correct measure of the success of the Waiver the extent to which it is used, or the effect the mere existence of the Waiver has cajoling pharmaceutical companies to lower their prices in poor countries? Are foundation funds for buying medicines a reliable alternative to the Waiver? Further, are pharmaceutical companies at least partly correct in arguing the reason medicines are highly-priced and difficult to access in those countries are infrastructural and financial: barriers to distribution and storage of medicines, and inadequate health care budgets? Survey evidence (as of 2008) from 30 low-income countries shows the price of medicines sold in the private sector exceeds the international reference prices by more than six-fold. There are considerable add-ons in the supply chain for medicines, for which these countries are to blame. Tajikistan imposes a 20% VAT. Sudan levies a 10% tariff, 1% Ministry of Defense charge, and 1% pharmacy fee.

Finally, note how EU customs authorities treat some shipments of generic medicines—detaining them, if not seizing them—that are in transit through EU ports destined for developing countries and LDCs. Brazil and India complained in 2009 that Dutch authorities wrongly seized genuine (not counterfeit) generics, violating GATT provisions on goods in transit, plus the *TRIPs Agreement* and the Doha

Declaration on TRIPs and Public Health. They said the EU imposing "*TRIPs* Plus" enforcement standards on other WTO Members. The EU countered it was not trying to hinder exportation of generic medicines, but rather interdicting dangerous fake medicines.

IV. Doha Round December 2005 Hong Kong Ministerial Conference and Two Additional Waivers

At the December 2005 Hong Kong Ministerial Conference, WTO Members agreed to two further changes to the *TRIPs Agreement.*

- **Second Waiver from Article 31(f)**

Developing and least developed WTO Members are not bound by the constraints on exports with respect to exporting in a RTA, as long as at least half of the members of that RTA are least developed (as of August 2003, when the *Medicines Agreement* was forged). This waiver allows such countries to take advantage of economies of scale associated with an FTA or CU in which they participate.

This waiver is inapplicable to *NAFTA*, because no *NAFTA* Party is least developed. It would apply to the *SACU*. Would this waiver apply to the *CAFTA-DR*, the members of which are Costa Rica, El Salvador, Guatemala, Honduras, Nicaragua, the U.S., plus the Dominican Republic?

- **Waiver from Article 31(h)**

A WTO Member importing generic pharmaceuticals made under a compulsory license is not liable for payment of compensation to the patent holder of the medicine subject to the license. Rather, liability is owed by the exporting country. This waiver avoids the possibility of double payment to the right holder, and relieves importing countries, which are likely to be acutely poor, from a possible burden.

- **Permanence of Waivers**

Not surprisingly, developing countries sought to make the *Medicines Agreement* permanent. On 6 December 2005, the WTO Members made the waivers permanent. (Technically, they remained temporary until 31 December 2007, the original target date by which ⅔ of WTO Members were to ratify the changes. Via a Decision of the *TRIPS* Council of 23 October 2007, the WTO extended the ratification deadline from 1 December 2007 to 31 December 2009. It had little choice. Ironically, by May 2008, only 15 of the then 151 Members had ratified the changes—and no African Member had done so, despite SSACs being at the forefront of compulsory licensing reform. Yet by October 2009, only 26 of the 153 WTO Members had ratified the changes. Thus, following a *TRIPS* Council Decision of 27 October 2009, the WTO extended the ratification again from 31 December 2009 until 31 December 2011. Following further extensions, on 23 January 2017, Members achieved the ⅔ approval threshold, and the new flexibilities on compulsory licensing took effect.) The results—new Article 31 *bis*, which is a direct translation of the waivers, plus Annex to the *TRIPs Agreement*—made legal history. It is the first amendment to a Uruguay Round accord. However, the result came about only after considerable controversy.

Led by the U.S., developed countries queried whether the *Medicines Agreement* was a solution searching for a problem. No poor country had invoked Article 31 of the *TRIPs Agreement*. Decrepit distribution systems, dreadful health care, and monstrous corruption are the real impediments to distributing medicines in many parts of the world. Developed countries and their pharmaceutical industries feared export-oriented compulsory licensing would be used to achieve commercial or industrial goals, not for public health reasons. Unscrupulous behavior could occur whereby generics were diverted away from poor people in an intended recipient country to paying customers in rich countries, thereby undermining the market for patented medicines. In response, on 6 December 2005, when the Members adopted the waivers as a "*Decision*," the Chairman of the WTO General Council issued a "*Statement*" about these concerns.

To make it part of a binding deal with the *Medicines Agreement*, the U.S. and other developed countries sought express reference in the text of the *TRIPs Agreement* to the Chairperson's *Statement*, thus giving it legal status. Led by India (a major source of generics) and Kenya (a large consumer of them), plus Argentina, Brazil, and the Philippines, poor countries objected. They saw the *Statement* as creating "best endeavor" duties, but not hard obligations on monitoring and enforcement. They noted since August 2003 deal, drug prices had fallen by 70%-80%. In the end, the U.S. dropped its demand for a reference, agreeing to have the *Statement* re-read at the 6 December General Council meeting. Poor countries agreed not to change the *Medicines Agreement*.

V. 2007 Thai and Brazilian, and 2012 Indian, Compulsory License Cases

In the spring 2007, Thailand became the first country to invoke the compulsory license provisions of the *TRIPs Agreement*, the *Doha Declaration on TRIPs*, and *Medicines Agreement*.[2] Thailand has an ambitious healthcare program to make life-saving treatments for certain diseases available free or at reduced prices. Accordingly, Thailand issued a compulsory license for two HIV/AIDS drugs, efavirenz (also called STOCRIN), on which Merck held the patent, and kaletra (also called lopinavir/ritonavir), on which Abbott Laboratories held the patent, plus a third compulsory license for a TB medicine on which Sanofi-Aventis (a Franco-German drug maker) held the patent. (The Thai government also pressed, with success, Sanofi-Aventis to cut the price it charges to patients in the Thai public health system

---

2. *See* Amy Kazmin & Andrew Jack, *Abbott Pulls HIV Drug in Thai Patents Protest*, Financial Times, 14 March 2007, at 7.

for its malaria treatment.) Thailand went even further, issuing a compulsory license for Plavix, which is a blood-thinning drug used to treat heart disease and strokes, on which Abbott held the patent. Considerable controversy ensued.

In respect of efavirenz, Thailand authorized domestic production of generic versions until 2011, and importation from India of generic copies until it gains manufacturing capacity. The Pharmaceutical Research and Manufacturers of America (PhRMA) castigated Thailand for not consulting or negotiating first with Merck. But, was Thailand obligated to do so for a compulsory license in a public health emergency to be used for a non-commercial treatment program?

For kaletra, Thailand argued Abbott had been selling the non-heat stable version to it at U.S. $2,200 per patient, whereas Abbott sold the drug at $500 per patient in Africa. Abbott said Thailand was using compulsory licensing as a tool for price negotiations. It retaliated by withholding seven drugs from the Thai market, including the heat-stable version of kaletra, which is widely sought after in hot, humid countries for patients for whom the first-line drug therapies has failed. Unabashedly, Thailand announced in March 2008 that it would go ahead with compulsory licenses on four anti-cancer drugs—Sanofi-Aventis's docetaxel (branded as Taxotere), Roche/Genetech's erlotinib (branded as Tarceva), Novartis's imatinib (branded as Gleevec), and Novartis's letrozole (branded as Femara)—and import generic copies of these medicines from overseas countries like India until it had built its own plant, which met WHO standards, to make them.

Notably, for efavirenz, Brazil asked Merck to cut the price from $1.57 per patient per day to 65 cents—the amount at which Merck sold it in Thailand. Merck refused. Merck distinguished these countries: AIDS is more prevalent in Thailand than Brazil, and Brazil is larger and wealthier than Thailand. Therefore, Thailand—but not Brazil—is in Merck's category for pricing at cost. Brazil simply can afford to pay more for drugs than a poorer, harder hit country like Thailand. Not persuaded by a utilitarian calculus, in May 2007, Brazil became the second country to invoke compulsory licenses, overriding Merck's efavirenz patent. The drug would be available, sourced from India, at 45 cents. Observe that of 180,000 Brazilians who get free anti-retroviral AIDS medicines from the government, 75,000 Brazilians use efavirenz.

In March 2012, India granted its first compulsory license since implementing the *TRIPs Agreement* in 2005.[3] The facts for its move were compelling. In March 2008, India granted a patent to Swiss pharmaceutical giant Bayer to sell Nexavar, to treat kidney and lung cancer, in India. Nexavar is the name for the drug patented by Bayer known as "sorafenib tosylate." Bayer sold the drug at $5,600 per month, a prohibitive cost for most Indians, who must pay for their medications out of pocket. Natco Pharma, an Indian generic pharmaceutical company, sought from Bayer a license for

---

3. *See* Madhur Singh, *Compulsory License Awarded to Natco to Sell Generic of Bayer's Nexavar in India*, 29 International Trade Reporter (BNA) 414 (15 March 2012).

the patent so that Natco could produce a generic version, called "Sorafenib," of Nexavar. Bayer refused, even though the availability of Sorafenib in India was limited to less than 1% of the patients requiring it. This supply constraint existed because Bayer controlled and imported into India all supplies of the generic version of Nexavar, and Bayer sold them only in a few of India's major cities and certain states.

Natco then applied for a compulsory license to the Indian Controller General of Patents, Designs, and Trademarks. The Controller was impressed Natco could manufacture and sell Sorafenib at 74 *rupees* ($1.48) per tablet, or 8,800 rupees ($176) per patient per month, and could provide the generic free to patients who could not afford it. Bayer fought the application, saying it could not lower its price because of the research and development it had invested in the medication. Ironically, Bayer also argued pirated (or "at risk") copies were plentiful in the Indian market, so there was no need for an authorized generic version of Nexavar.

The Controller sided with Natco, on the grounds that Bayer not only sold Nexavar at too high a price for Indian patients, but also that it had not worked the patent, *i.e.*, it had not manufactured Nexavar to a reasonable extent. The compulsory license for Natco on the generic version, Sorafenib, mandated that Natco (1) charge no more than 8,880 rupees for a pack for 120 tablets (the amount for one month of therapy), (2) pay to Bayer a quarterly royalty of 6% of net sales of Sorafenib, and (3) supply Sorafenib free to at least 600 indigent patients annually. The compulsory license was for the remaining life of the patent Bayer had received on Nexavar, namely until 2020. It so happened the price actually fell from $5,300 to $160 per month, as the multinational producers like Bayer had to drop their prices to at or below the compulsory license price set for Natco.[4]

In March 2013, the Intellectual Property Appellate Board upheld the decision of the Controller, thus allowing the first compulsory license in India to be issued. Soon thereafter, health officials in India declared they would seek a compulsory license for Herceptin (used to treat breast cancer) from Roche, and for Sprycel (used to treat leukemia) and Ixempra (also for breast cancer) from Bristol-Myers Squibb.

VI. Evergreening and 2013 Indian Supreme Court *Novartis* Case

While not technically a compulsory license case, India again found itself at the center of controversy in the international IP world with an April 2013 decision by its Supreme Court.[5] Swiss pharmaceutical giant Novartis AG applied to the Controller

---

4. *See* Daniel Pruzin, *Indian Minister Defends Court's Denial of Patent Protection for Cancer Drug Glivec*, 30 International Trade Reporter (BNA) 531 (11 April 2013). [Hereinafter, *Indian Minister.*]

5. *See* Madhur Singh, *Top India Court Denies Novartis Appeal On Patent for Cancer Medication Glivec*, 30 International Trade Reporter (BNA) 489 (4 April 2013); Soutik Biswas, *Is Novartis Ruling*

of Patents under Section 3(d) of the *Indian Patents Act* for a patent on Glivec, a new form of a drug for which Novartis held a patent on the earlier version. Both versions are for fighting chronic myeloid leukemia and other cancers.

Section 3(d), which India amended to conform to the *TRIPs Agreement*, aims to prevent pharmaceutical companies from "evergreening." This practice refers to the use (or abuse) of IP laws in a tactical way to extend patent protection and keep competitors, particularly of generic products, out of the market. Typically, a drug company makes a small change in a patented pharmaceutical, and then seeks a new patent on the modified drug. The goal of the practice is to extend the life of the original patent through a trivial change to the existing drug. The Controller rejected the application, and in 2009 the Intellectual Property Appellate Board upheld its decision.

Glivec was the *beta* crystal form of the molecule generically known as "imatinib mesylate." The existing drug, on which Novartis held a patent, was the *alpha* crystal version of that molecule. The difference between them concerned absorption in the human body: Novartis claimed it had poured in years of research to improve the extent to which the human body absorbs the molecule, hence the *beta* version deserved protection as a new, more effective, medicine.

The Supreme Court of India held otherwise, saying the *beta* form did not improve the "therapeutic efficacy" of the *alpha* form, though it left open for future cases the question of what change is needed to yield "therapeutic efficacy." More significantly, without condemning all incremental inventions in pharmaceuticals, the Court said simply the change Novartis made in absorption capacity lacked novelty and inventiveness, which are criteria for granting a new patent. In brief, the Court ruled against what it described as "repetitive patenting." After all, once the period of patent protection (*e.g.*, 20 years) ends, then the patent holder no longer has the right to exclude others from making or selling the "off-patent" drug. A generic producer can attempt to make a cheaper copy of that drug. And, under Indian law, the first producer to do so gets an exclusive right to sell its generic for 180 days. That surely leads to a price drop, and once the 180-day period is over, other generic producers can enter the market, resulting in further price drops.

So, Indian generic producers and many non-governmental organizations (NGOs) supported the decision. They pointed out Novartis sold Glivec at U.S. $2,600 per month, whereas the generic version sold at $175 per month. Moreover, holding 147 patents under Indian law, Novartis was the third largest beneficiary of patent registrations in India.[6] Novartis and the PhRMA trade group decried the decision as creating a disincentive to innovation in India.

---

a Watershed?, BBC News, 1 April 2013, *posted at* www.bbc.co.uk; *Novartis: India Rejects Patent Plea for Cancer Drug Glivec*, BBC News, 1 April 2013, *posted at* www.bbc.co.uk.

6. *See Indian Minister.*

Chapter 33

IP Enforcement[1]

I. Infringement, Exclusion and Seizure, and Section 337 Elements

Section 337 of the *Tariff Act of 1930*, as amended, makes it unlawful to import into the U.S. any article that infringes on a patent, trademark, or copyright that is valid and enforceable in the U.S., or a semiconductor chip that infringes on a registered mask work that is valid and enforceable in the U.S.[2] As the statute heading intimates, importing infringing articles is considered "unfair." The list of unfair trade practices (and it is a list, not a general theory of fairness) embraces dumping, certain subsidies, and infringement of an IPR. Note, however, an "article" must be tangible; Section 337 does not confer authority on the government, specifically, the ITC, to bar importation of patent-infringing data transmissions.[3]

The *Omnibus Trade and Competitiveness Act of 1988* changes an important threshold requirement for Section 337 relief.[4] Before the *Act*, a complainant had to show it constituted or was part of an "efficiently and economically operated" domestic industry. The *1988 Act* eliminated that rule. Importing infringing articles is unlawful if "an industry in the United States" exists "relating to" articles

---

1. Documents References:
   (1) *Havana (ITO) Charter* Articles 19, 37:7, 45:1(a)(vii)
   (2) GATT Articles IV, IX:6, XX(f)
   (3) WTO *Agreement on Trade Related Aspects of Intellectual Property Rights (TRIPs)*

2. *See* 19 U.S.C. § 1337(a)(1)(B)-(D).

3. *See ClearCorrect Operating, LLC v. International Trade Commission*, Federal Circuit Number No. 2014-1527 (31 March 2016). In this case, patent holder Align Technology Inc. unsuccessfully confronted the business model of ClearCorrect, whereby ClearCorrect made data models of orthodontic aligners in Pakistan, transmitted the data about a dental patient's needs to its facility in the U.S., and through 3D printing made the aligners in America. Align Technology invoked Section 337, which grants the ITC had authority over "articles protected by the patent, copyright, trademark, mask work, or design concerned." The Dissent pointed out Congress wrote in the 1920s, before cross-border electronic data transmissions, so "article" now should cover intangible as well as tangible items. But, the Majority said it was for Congress to change the statute to include digital transmissions and e commerce.

4. *See* Public Law Number 100-418, 102 Stat. 1107.

protected by the patent, trademark, copyright, or mask work at issue.[5] An industry is defined to "exist" if there is:

(1) significant investment in plant and equipment,

(2) significant employment of labor or capital, or

(3) substantial investment in the exploitation of the patent, trademark, copyright, or mask work as evidenced by expenditures on research, development, or licensing.[6]

The 3rd prong of this definition means it no longer is necessary to have extensive production facilities located in the U.S. Yet, the meaning of "significant" and "substantial" is apparent neither from the statute nor legislative history.

Alternatively, because of the *1988 Act* amendments, importing infringing articles is unlawful if an industry in the U.S. relating to a patent, trademark, copyright, or mask work is "in the process of being established."[7] Unfortunately, neither the *1988 Act* nor Section 337 has criteria to determine when an industry is "being established." There are few if any analogies from which to reason. Jurisprudence from AD, specifically, determinations concerning whether dumping materially retards the establishment of an industry in the U.S., is scant.

Significantly, the *1988 Act* (at § 1341(b)) also eliminates the need to show injury to an industry in the U.S. Congress wanted to make Section 337 "a more effective remedy for the protection of United States intellectual property rights." Thus, the House Ways and Means Committee stated:

> [u]nlike dumping or countervailing duties, or even other unfair trade practices such as false advertising or other business torts, the owner of intellectual property has been granted a temporary statutory right to exclude others from making, using, or selling the protected property. The purpose of such temporary protection, which is provided for in Article I, Section 8, Clause 8 of the United States Constitution, is "to promote the Progress of Science and Useful Arts, by securing for limited Times to Authors and Inventors the exclusive Rights to their respective Writings and Discoveries." In return for temporary protection, the owner agrees to make public the intellectual property in question. It is this trade-off which creates a public interest in the enforcement of protected intellectual property rights. *Any sale in the United States of an infringing product is a sale that rightfully belongs only to the holder or licensee of that property. The importation of any infringing merchandise derogates from the statutory right, diminishes the value of the intellectual property, and thus indirectly harms the public interest.* Under such circumstances, the Committee believes that requiring proof of

---

5. 19 U.S.C. § 1337(a)(2).

6. *See* 19 U.S.C § 1337(a)(3).

7. 19 U.S.C. § 1337(a)(2).

injury, beyond that shown by proof of the infringement of a valid intellectual property right, should not be necessary.[8]

As an attorney explains, this amendment has an important practical effect.

> Although complainants were denied relief in only a few cases because of a failure to meet these [injury] requirements, it is estimated that over half of the total expenses in litigating section 337 cases were incurred in establishing the injury and other economic requirements. These expenses tended to make section 337 proceedings inaccessible to prospective complainants with small pocketbooks.[9]

In sum, to establish a violation of Section 337, 4 elements are necessary:

(1) a valid and enforceable IPR;

(2) infringement of that IPR by imports;

(3) an "industry in the United States" that either "exists" or is "in the process of being established"; and

(4) a relationship between that industry and the articles protected by the IPR.

In establishing the claim, do the *Federal Rules of Civil Procedure* and *Federal Rules of Evidence* apply? Why or why not?

Notably, Section 337 declares unlawful any unfair method of competition and unfair acts in importation, other than those relating to IP, if the threat of effect of such methods or acts is to (1) destroy or substantially injure an industry in the U.S., (2) prevent establishment of an industry in the U.S., or (3) restrain or monopolize trade and commerce in the U.S.[10] The unfair method or act provision of Section 337 reflects the statute's history: Section 337 was originally enacted in the *Tariff Act of 1922*. Its aim was a panoply of unfair acts not then covered by other unfair import laws. Indeed, the provision was used in antitrust and false advertising cases.

Amendments in the *1988 Act* narrowed the scope of actions that may be brought before the ITC, yet it is still remarkable. The unfair method or act provision in Section 337 remains applicable to allegations such as common law trademark infringement, unfair competition, trade secret misappropriation, trademark dilution, false designation of origin, and grey market importations. Certainly, Section 337 is best known for its use in cases of alleged IPR—especially patent—infringements. However, Subsection (a)(1)(A) of the statute (19 U.S.C. Section 1337) is of increasing interest. It allows the ITC to issue an exclusion order based on the importer's "[u]nfair methods of competition and unfair acts in the importation of articles." That means stopping products at the American border, even if they do not infringe on a U.S. IPR. This authority has raised two major issues.

---

8. H.R. Rep. No. 40, 100th Cong., 1st Sess., pt. 1, at 156 (1987) (emphasis added).

9. Andrew S. Newman, *The Amendments to Section 337: Increased Protection for Intellectual Property Rights*, 20 Law & Policy in International Business 571, 576 (1989).

10. *See* 19 U.S.C. § 1337(a)(1)(A).

First, must the unfair competition occur, at least in part, in the U.S.? The answer is "no." In the 2011 case of *TianRui Group Company v. International Trade Commission*, the Federal Circuit held the ITC can issue a Section 337 exclusion order even if all conduct occurs outside the U.S.[11] Second, does misappropriation of trade secrets constitute an "unfair method of competition"? The answer is "yes." In the 2017 case of *Sino Legend (Zhangjiagang) Chemical Company v. International Trade Commission*, the U.S. Supreme Court declined to review a Federal Circuit decision upholding a CIT ruling in favor of a 10-year ITC ban against imports of synthetic rubber components that were made in China thanks to stealing American trade secrets.[12] Two employees left their jobs in China with SI Group Inc. to join Sino Legend. The Group accused them of stealing trade secrets on synthetic rubbers that have so-called "tackifiers," which increase the strength of adhesive bonds between layers. Chinese courts, through the Supreme Court, exonerated the producer-exporter, Sino Legend. So, Sino Legend argued the ITC should drop its ban on the basis of comity (the Public International Law principle of mutual respect among countries for legal decisions rendered in other countries). Otherwise, American companies might face retaliation from the Chinese government. The Group prevailed in U.S. litigation: the *TianRui* precedent was controlling, meaning that even though all trade secret misappropriation occurred outside the U.S., the ITC still had the authority to issue a Section 337 order against the unfairly competitive products.

II. Section 337 Operation

The ITC has sole authority to investigate alleged Section 337 violations. A case may be commenced by filing a petition with the ITC.[13] Typically, the complainant is a right holder seeking to enforce its IPR against allegedly infringing goods and seeks an order excluding those goods from entry into America. The complainant need not be an American business or citizen. Foreign companies can and do bring Section 337 actions.

> Not only are the Japanese improving their U.S. court techniques, but they are learning to play the patent game quite well. In 1992, Japanese companies again led the world in gaining U.S. patents. Canon, Hitachi, and Toshiba ranked one, two, and three, respectively, in the number of American patents received. Number four was IBM. The increase in the Japanese patent portfolio means an inevitable move on the part of the Japanese to litigate in U.S. courts to protect *their* intellectual property.[14]

---

11. *See* 661 F.3d. 1322 (Fed. Cir. 2011).

12. *See* U.S. Number 16-428 (*writ of certiorari* denied, 9 January 2017); Tony Dutra, *Chinese Company Fails to Win High Court Review of ITC Ban*, 34 International Trade Reporter (BNA) 87 (12 January 2017).

13. *See* 19 U.S.C. § 1337(b)(1).

14. Fred Warshofsky, The Patent Wars 100 (1994) (emphasis original). *See also id.*, 90, 94–97.

Alternatively, the ITC may self-initiate a Section 337 action. Under pre-Uruguay Round law, regardless of who initiated a Section 337 investigation, it had to be completed within one year (or 18 months in complicated cases).[15]

Section 337 is unique among trade remedy laws in that it is the only such law subject to the *Administrative Procedure Act (APA)*.[16] Therefore, all ITC investigations and determinations under Section 337 must be conducted on the record before an ALJ, after publication of notice and opportunity for hearing in conformity with *APA* requirements. An ALJ decision may be appealed to the ITC and, thereafter, the Federal Circuit. Interestingly, the 1-year (or 18-month) period starts on the day after the ITC publishes a Section 337 investigation notice in the *Federal Register*. It was, and still is, required to publish it upon commencing an investigation.[17] Presumably, the ITC could delay publication of the notice to "buy" itself additional time, though it could not conduct a formal investigation in the pre-notice period.

Section 321(a) of the *Uruguay Round Agreements Act of 1994*, the legislation implementing the Uruguay Round accords, eliminated the one year (and 18 month) time limits on Section 337 actions.[18] Presently, the ITC must conclude its investigation and make a determination "at the earliest practicable time after the date of publication of notice of such investigation."[19] To promote expeditious adjudication, the statute requires the ITC to set a target date for its final determination. It must set this date within 45 days after initiating an investigation.

III. Exclusion Orders

• **Temporary Exclusion Orders**

Arguably, the defining feature of Section 337 is the ITC's authority to prescribe provisional relief. Infringing imports may pose an imminent threat to a complainant's business. Hence, the complainant may not be able to wait 1 year for a final ITC determination. Instead, the complainant may seek a Temporary Exclusion Order.

> In 1982, that was the situation faced by the dozen U.S. companies that had created the once-thriving double-sided floppy disk drive industry. "We had a very viable U.S. industry with 12 floppy disk drive companies," recalls Ray Lupo [a private attorney in Washington, D.C.]. "In November 1982, 14 Japanese companies showed up at an American trade show with double-sided floppy disk drives. At the time the drives were selling in the U.S. for $150 to $200. The Japanese were offering theirs for $30 less. Within a year

---

15. *See* 19 U.S.C. § 1337(b)(1).

16. 5 U.S.C. §§ 551 *et seq.* 19 U.S.C. § 1337(c).

17. *See* 19 U.S.C. § 1337(b)(1).

18. *See Uruguay Round Trade Agreement*, H.R. Doc. No. 316, 103d Cong., 2d Sess., vol. 1, 360 (27 September 1994).

19. 19 U.S.C. § 1337(b)(1).

to a year and a half there were only two American companies left—Tandon and Shugart. By the time we brought the suit [against the Mitsubishi Electric Corporation, TEAC Corporation, Sony Corporation, and other Japanese companies] and obtained a preliminary injunction three months later, there was just Tandon. The whole U.S. industry had been wiped out in the space of just 18 months by the importation of infringing products."[20]

To avoid this result, the ITC is empowered to seal off America's borders to goods that it preliminarily suspects violate an IPR.

In specific, suppose the ITC "determines that there is reason to believe that there is a violation" of Section 337.[21] Then it "may direct that the articles concerned . . . be excluded from entry into the United States . . . ."[22] As a result of the *1988 Act* amendments to Section 337, the ITC has 90 days (or up to 150 days in complicated cases) to render a decision about preliminary relief. (The 90- or 150-day period begins the day after the date on which the ITC publishes its investigation notice in the *Federal Register.*) When the ITC issues a TEO, it notifies the Secretary of the Treasury of its decision. In turn, the Secretary orders CBP to exclude infringing goods from entry into the U.S.

For three reasons, obtaining a TEO order may be difficult. First, even if the ITC suspects an IPR violation, it may decline to impose an order because of an offsetting, and relatively greater, public interest. The ITC makes exceptions if admitting allegedly infringing articles is justified because of the adverse effect exclusion would have on public health and welfare, competitive conditions in the U.S. economy, production of like or directly competitive products, or U.S. consumers. In effect, before imposing a TEO, the ITC does a balancing test, weighing the common good against private gain to the complainant. Even if the exceptions are inapplicable, allegedly infringing goods may be admitted to the U.S. under bond.[23]

Second, thanks to the *1988 Act*, the ITC must apply the same standards to a request for a TEO that a federal district court would apply in a motion for a preliminary injunction.[24] These standards are in the *Federal Rules of Civil Procedure*. They weigh:

(1) the complainant's likelihood of success on the merits,

(2) whether the complainant would suffer irreparable injury during the pendency of the litigation if the temporary relief were not granted,

(3) whether that injury would outweigh harm to other parties if the temporary relief were granted, and

(4) whether temporary relief is in the public interest.

---

20. WARSHOFSKY, *supra*, (emphasis original).

21. 19 U.S.C. § 1337(e)(1).

22. 19 U.S.C. § 1337(e)(1).

23. *See* 19 U.S.C. § 1337(e)(1); *Biocraft Laboratories, Inc. v. U.S. International Trade Commission*, 947 F.2d 483 (Fed. Cir. 1991).

24. *See* 19 U.S.C. § 1337(e)(3).

Why is it logical that TEO requisites would follow preliminary injunction criteria?

Third, the ITC may require a complainant to post a bond as a prerequisite to issuance of a TEO.[25] The bond must be forfeited to the government if the complainant is unsuccessful in obtaining the order. This requirement, also added by the *1988 Act*, raises several practical concerns for complainants.

> The purpose of the provision is to deter complainants from filing frivolous motions for temporary relief. However, it is difficult to envisage the permanent criteria the [International Trade] [C]ommission will use to determine the size of the bond. Will complainants ever be excused from posting a bond? At what time will the bond need to be posted? At what amount should the bond be set? Presumably, the bond should reflect at a minimum the potential gain to the complainant of excluding its competitor's goods during the period of a temporary exclusion order. Moreover, under what circumstances should the bond be forfeited to the U.S. Treasury?[26]

In brief, the bond requirement forces a complainant to engage in a careful risk-return calculation before applying for provisional relief.

- **Permanent Exclusion Orders**

If the ITC renders a final determination that Section 337 is violated, then it may order the "permanent" exclusion of the offending articles from entry into the U.S.[27] The aforementioned exceptions for public health and welfare, competitive conditions, production, and consumer interests exist. Thus, the ITC must balance the interest of the complainant in getting complete relief against the interest of the public in avoiding disruption to legitimate trade caused by relief. However, the ITC

> rarely declines to grant relief on public interest grounds, and only when the dual requirements are met that (1) a strong public interest exists in maintaining an adequate supply of the goods under investigation; and (2) either that the domestic industry cannot maintain an adequate supply of the goods or the domestic users of the goods cannot obtain sufficient substitutes. The effect of rising consumer prices due to imposition of a Commission remedy is not sufficient grounds by itself for denying relief.[28]

A "Permanent" Exclusion Order remains in effect until the violation ends.[29] That can be a long time. For example, in December 2015 the U.S. Court of Appeals for the Federal Circuit upheld the extension of a 10-year exclusion of certain rubber

---

25. *See* 19 U.S.C. § 1337(e)(2).

26. Newman, 571, 583.

27. *See* 19 U.S.C. § 1337(d).

28. William L. Lafuze & Patricia F. Stanford, *An Overview of Section 337 of the Tariff Act of 1930: A Primer for Practice Before the International Trade Commission*, 25 John Marshall Law Review 459, 466–67 (1992). *See also id.*, 463, 465–68, 474–90 (1992).

29. *See* 19 U.S.C. § 1337(k)(1).

resins from China.[30] The ITC had found Chinese producer-exporters of the resins misappropriated trade secrets belonging to the SI Group Inc. of Schenectady, New York. Any article subject to a PEO that is imported in violation of the order are subject to seizure and forfeiture.[31]

PEOs, which are the primary weapon against infringing imports, take 1 of 2 forms. A "limited" exclusion order directs the CBP to bar infringing articles originating from a source the order identifies, such as a specific country or a group of companies within a country. A "general" exclusion order tells the CBP to stop infringing articles regardless of source. The focus is on the nature of an article, not its country of origin or whether the respondent produced it. Thus, a general PEO is the strongest remedy.

Not surprisingly, a limited exclusion order is more commonly granted than a general one. Obtaining a general PEO is difficult. In its 1981 determination in *Certain Airless Paint Spray Pumps and Components Thereof* (*Spray Pumps*), the ITC formulated a high burden of proof. A complaint must prove "both a *widespread pattern of unauthorized use* of its patented invention and *certain business conditions* from which one might reasonably infer that foreign manufacturers other than the respondents to the investigation may attempt to enter the U.S. market with infringing articles."[32] A variety of facts are potentially relevant:

> Factors relevant to proof of whether a "widespread pattern of unauthorized use" exists include: (1) a Commission determination of unauthorized importation by numerous foreign manufacturers; (2) the pendency of foreign infringement suits based upon the intellectual property right at issue; and (3) other evidence which demonstrates a history of unauthorized foreign use of the patented invention. In order to prove that "certain business conditions" exist which make new foreign entrants into the United States markets likely, the Commission would consider the following: (1) the existence of an established market for the patented product in the United States; (2) the availability of marketing and distributing networks in the United States for potential foreign manufacturers; (3) the cost to foreign entrepreneurs of building a facility capable of producing the article; (4) the number of foreign manufacturers whose facilities could be retooled to produce the patented article; and (5) the cost to foreign manufacturers of retooling their facilities. The "certain business conditions" analysis is essentially an inquiry into barriers to market entry facing the infringing article.[33]

---

30. *See Sino Legend (Zhangjiagang) v. United States,* Number 2015-1209 (11 December 2015).
31. *See* 19 U.S.C. § 1337(i).
32. 216 U.S.P.Q. (BNA) 465, 473 (U.S. ITC 1981) (emphasis added).
33. Lafuze & Stanford, *supra,* 459, 468.

Section 321(a) of the *1994 Act* codified part of the *Spray Pumps* test.[34] The ITC cannot issue a general PEO unless that order "is necessary to prevent circumvention of an exclusion order limited to products of named persons" and "there is a pattern of violation of . . . Section [337] and it is difficult to identify the source of infringing products."

It is the CBP that must enforce a TEO or PEO. So, as a practical matter an individual CBP officer at a port of entry must determine whether an import is infringing on an IPR and, therefore, within the scope of the ITC's order. In many cases this task may be difficult. The officer's decision may be contested in the CIT.

• **Other Remedies**

One other remedy is available to a complainant in the event of a final affirmative Section 337 determination by the ITC. In addition to, or in lieu of, excluding goods from entry, the ITC may issue a temporary or permanent cease and desist order.[35] If IPR violators disobey the order, then the ITC may levy a civil money penalty (*i.e.,* a fine) against them.[36] The reason for the availability of different remedies is to ensure a complainant can obtain complete relief, and the ITC has broad discretion in selecting an appropriate remedy.[37]

Remedies available under Section 337 are not based on the ITC having *in personam* jurisdiction over a respondent. Instead, Section 337 confers nation-wide *in rem* jurisdiction. As the Court stated in in 1981 in *Sealed Air Corporation v. U.S. International Trade Commission*, the statute was "intended to provide an adequate remedy . . . against unfair methods of competition and unfair acts instigated by foreign concerns operating beyond the *in personam* jurisdiction of domestic courts."[38]

IV. Presidential Discretion, Patent Hold Up Behavior, and 2011–2013 Apple-Samsung Cell Phone Patent War

A TEO, PEO, seizure and forfeiture order, temporary or permanent cease and desist order, or fine is subject to Presidential disapproval. Section 337 requires the ITC to forward a copy of a final determination, and a preliminary determination calling for a TEO, to the President.[39] The President has 60 days to overturn, "for

---

34. *See Uruguay Round Trade Agreement*, H.R. Doc. No. 316, 103d Cong., 2d Sess., vol. 1, 364 (27 September).

35. *See* 19 U.S.C. § 1337(f)(1).

36. *See* 19 U.S.C. § 1337(f)(2).

37. *See, e.g., Viscofan, S.A. v. U.S. International Trade Commission*, 787 F.2d 544, 548 (Fed. Cir. 1986).

38. 645 F.2d 976, 985 (C.C.P.A. 1981).

39. *See* 19 U.S.C. § 1337(j)(1)(B).

policy reasons," the ITC's determination.[40] The statute does not delineate the policy reasons that would serve as a basis for overturning an ITC order, hence considerable discretion rests with the President. If the President does not disapprove of the ITC order, then it becomes effective upon publication in the *Federal Register*. The actions taken against the offending articles and culpable parties are effective as provided in the statute.[41]

In August 2013, President Barack H. Obama (1961, President, 2009–2017) used his discretion to overturn an affirmative ITC decision. That decision came in response to a 2011 complaint filed by Samsung Electronics Co. against Apple Inc. Samsung sought an exclusion order against imports by Apple of older iPhone and iPad models. Samsung said those Apple smartphones and tablets infringed on five Samsung patents. Those patents, said Samsung, were the basis for part of the Universal Mobile Telecommunications System (UMTS), which is a standard in the wireless communications industry. Apple devices adhere to that standard. So, Samsung claimed it held a valid "Standard-Essential Patent" (SEP), which concerns inclusion in merchandise of technology to satisfy a standard. That is, an SEP is a patent covering inventions that must be used for those inventions to comply with a technical standard. Samsung said it was the SEP owner.

The ITC agreed with Samsung. The ITC granted it what is the equivalent of an injunction, an exclusion order, against Apple from importing those older models sold through ATT&T Wireless, but not covering newer models (*i.e.*, iPhone 4S or 5, or iPad 4).[42] Apple disagreed with Samsung and the ITC, saying the Samsung patents were invalid, or did not merit SEP status, and its devices did not infringe on them anyway.

Siding with Apple, President Obama was the first President to overturn an ITC Section 337 decision since Ronald Reagan. That decision, in favour of Samsung Electronics Co., barred rival Apple Inc. from importation of older iPhone and iPad models. The Presidential reversal meant Apple could proceed with their importation.

The USTR, Ambassador Michael Froman, defended the decision of the President saying Samsung was using the ITC to "hold out," meaning Samsung was trying to get a higher price for the use of its SEP. That is, Samsung was engaging in "patent hold up" behavior: Samsung participated in the creation of the pertinent industry technical standard, and became an SEP owner. In so doing, it voluntarily agreed to license its technology on fair, reasonable, and non-discriminatory (FRAND) terms.

---

40. 19 U.S.C. § 1337(j)(1)-(2). The 60-day period begins on the day after the day on which the President receives a copy of the ITC determination.

41. *See* 19 U.S.C. § 1337(j)(3).

42. *See* International Trade Commission, *Certain Electronic Devices, Including Wireless Communication Devices, Portable Music and Data Processing Devices, and Tablet Computers*, Number 337-TA-794 (4 June 2013); Tony Dutra, *President Reverses ITC Decision to Ban Imports of Apple iPhone, iPad Models*, 30 International Trade Reporter 1227 (BNA) (8 August 2013).

Yet, thereafter it sought a higher price for its SEP than possible before the industry set the standard, when multiple alternative technologies were available.

So, the USTR said the ITC should use a "Relevant Factors Analysis," with one such factor being hold out behaviour, in deciding whether to grant a TEO or PEO on merchandise with an SEP. Here, said the USTR, Samsung (the SEP holder) sought to compel Apple (the licensee of the SEP technology) to pay Samsung a higher royalty than Apple thought reasonable. If the ITC would grant Samsung an exclusion order, then Apple would not be able to import its devices and sell them in the U.S. In a thus weakened position, Apple would be forced to pay Samsung a higher royalty fee.

Certainly, if an SEP holder chooses to participate in creating an industry standard, and thereby agrees to license its technologies to third parties on FRAND terms, then it should not be allowed to use Section 337 as leverage to extract unreasonable royalties. Otherwise, Section 337 would become an instrument for undermining FRAND licensing commitments. But, whether Samsung was an uncompromising hold out, using Section 337 to extract more money from Apple, or whether Apple was correct that the technology at issue was not worthy of an SEP, invalid, or was not being offered on FRAND terms, was debateable. Consider the perspective of Samsung (and other companies that participate in standard-setting): if it has no effective way to increase pressure on a recalcitrant licensee, then it may eschew making commitments to help set standards. In turn, the public interest in encouraging efficient standard setting may be compromised.

It may well be that for SEP holders, monetary damages, not Section 337, are the most realistic source of relief. This point leads to comparison between filing Section 337 relief before the ITC and lodging a complaint in a Federal district court.[43] Administrative Law Judges at the ITC are bound neither by the *Federal Rules of Evidence* nor the *Federal Rules of Civil Procedure*. The ITC cannot entertain counterclaims, nor can it award monetary damages. Rather, its remedies are TEOs, PEOs (limited or general), and cease and desist orders. ALJ decisions take about 14 months.

For Samsung, the veto of the ITC decision by President Obama was the second of two blows. Hardly a week later, also in August 2013, the ITC ruled Samsung smartphones and tablet computers infringed on valid Apple patents.[44] Apple had filed the complaint against Samsung in 2011, and the ITC agreed with it that Samsung infringed on its graphical interface and hardware patents. So, the ITC issued an exclusion order precluding entry of the Samsung devices.

---

43. *See* Rossella Brevetti, *Drop in 2012 of Section 337 Cases Could Be Related to Economic Factors, Attorney Says*, 30 International Trade Reporter (BNA) 1277 (15 August 2013).

44. *See* International Trade Commission, *Certain Electronic Digital Media Devices and Components Thereof,* Investigation Number 337-TA-796 (9 August 2013); Tony Dutra, *Samsung Phones, Tablets, Infringe Apple Patents, Trade Commission Rules*, 30 International Trade Reporter (BNA) 1277 (15 August 2013).

Though empowered to overturn the decision on policy grounds, the President in October 2013 decided not to do so. The USTR defended the President as "*continuing the practice of successive Administrations of exercising Section 337 policy review authority with restraint.*"[45] In view of the August veto, was this statement ironic, even disingenuous? Putting the merits of the two cases aside, was the double-victory of Apple against arch rival Samsung evidence of American mercantilism?

V. GATT Consistency of Section 337 and 1989 *Section 337* Case

The GATT consistency of Section 337 is a source of controversy in Euro-American trade relations. The controversy escalated to a pre-WTO dispute settlement case, *United States—Section 337 of the Tariff Act of 1930.*[46] The EU claimed Section 337 violated GATT Article III:4 and could not be justified as necessary under Article XX(d).

The EU argued, in brief, Section 337 treated foreign merchandise less favorably than American merchandise, because it established different procedures in a patent infringement case if allegedly infringing merchandise is foreign, rather than domestic. Domestic-origin goods could be subject to a Section 337 case or a federal district court action. Foreign-origin goods had to endure a Section 337 action. The EU highlighted critical differences between Section 337 and federal district court actions. The differences included forum, decision-makers, procedural rules, jurisdiction, time limits, counter-claims, public interest considerations, presidential review, remedies, and enforcement.

The Panel, in one of the longest reports in pre-WTO history, accepted the European argument. In doing so, it made clear Article III:4 applies to procedural as well as substantive law. The Panel also rejected the American defense of administrative necessity under GATT Article XX(d). How did the U.S. respond to the loss? Did compliance become a bargaining chip in the Uruguay Round, *i.e.*, did America condition amending Section 337 to conform to GATT if *TRIPs Agreement* negotiations proved satisfactory to it? What amendments did it make under the *1994 Uruguay Round Agreements Act*? Do they satisfy the EU? Do they weaken American defenses against infringing goods?[47]

---

45. *Quoted in* Brian Flood, *Administration Refuses to Veto Decision Favoring Apple in Dispute with Samsung*, 30 International Trade Reporter (BNA) 1588 (17 October 2013) (emphasis added).

46. *See* B.I.S.D. (36th Supp.) 345 (1990) (adopted 7 November 1989).

47. In *DBN Holding, Inc. v. International Trade Commission*, the U.S. Supreme Court denied a *writ of certiorari* to consider whether the jurisdiction of the ITC under 19 U.S.C. § 1337(a)(1)(B)(i) concerning imports of "articles that . . . infringe a valid and enforceable" patent extends to articles that do not infringe any patent. *Petition for a Writ of Certiorari*, Brief of DBN Holding, 13 July 2016. "In a series of recent cases that have repeatedly and deeply divided the Federal Circuit, the Commission has been permitted to expand its jurisdiction to regulate the importation of articles that do

VI. Gray Market, Section 337, 1999 *Gamut* Case, and 2005 *SKF* Case

- What Is the "Gray Market"?

In its 1999 decision in *Gamut Trading Company v. United States International Trade Commission*, the U.S. Court of Appeals for the Federal Circuit defined the "gray market" as:

> The principle of gray market law is that the importation of a product that was produced by the owner of the United States trademark or with its consent, but not authorized for sale in the United States, may, in appropriate cases, infringe the United States trademark.
>
> . . .
>
> The term "gray market goods" refers to genuine goods that in this case are of foreign manufacture, bearing a legally affixed foreign trademark that is the same mark as is registered in the United States; gray goods are legally acquired abroad and then imported without the consent of the United States trademark holder. See *K Mart Corp. v. Cartier, Inc.*, 486 U.S. 281, 286–87 (1987) . . . . The conditions under which gray-market goods have been excluded implement the territorial nature of trademark registration, and reflect a legal recognition of the role of domestic business in establishing and maintaining the reputation and goodwill of a domestic trademark.[48]

The *TRIPs Agreement* does not directly address gray market issues. They are dealt with in U.S. law by Section 337, and the *Gamut* Court nicely summarized decades of jurisprudence as follows:

> Until the Supreme Court's decision in *A. Bourjois & Co. v. Katzel*, 260 U.S. 689 (1923), . . . the prevailing rule in the United States was that the authorized sale of a validly trademarked product, anywhere in the world, exhausted the trademark's exclusionary right; thus the holder of the corresponding registered United States trademark was believed to have no right

---

not infringe any patent but are merely associated with the alleged infringing conduct of U.S. companies on U.S. soil." DBN Brief, i (emphasis original). In the *DBN* case, the Federal Circuit agreed with "the Commission exercise[] [of] its expanded jurisdiction to enforce a patent that has been finally adjudicated to be invalid by the federal courts." *Id.* DBN, which imported two-way satellite communication devices, was supported by Dell, Google, and other IT companies, in the argument that the expanded ITC jurisdiction gave patent owners greater rights than they could obtain in Federal Court. "Nonpracticing entities, which acquire patents and make money solely from their licensing or litigation, can't threaten alleged infringers with an injunction in court, . . . [DBN argued]. But the import ban that the ITC can impose is equivalent to an injunction and gives an NPE 'leverage in extracting outsized license payments,' . . . Further, . . . 'practitioners understand that the ITC systematically favors patent holders.'" Tony Dutra, *Supreme Court Won't Review ITC Jurisdiction in Patent Suits*, 33 International Trade Reporter (BNA) 1688 (1 December 2016) (*quoting* the DBN Brief).

48. 200 F.3d 775 (1999).

to bar the importation and sale of authentically marked foreign goods. However, in the *Bourjois* case the Court recognized the territorial boundaries of trademarks, stressing that the reputation and goodwill of the holder of the corresponding United States mark warrants protection against unauthorized importation of goods bearing the same mark, although the mark was validly affixed in the foreign country. In *Bourjois* the foreign-origin goods were produced by an unrelated commercial entity and imported by a third person, although the goods themselves were related in that the United States trademark owner bought its materials from the foreign producer. . . .

Since the *Bourjois* decision, the regional circuits and the Federal Circuit have drawn a variety of distinctions in applying gray market jurisprudence, primarily in consideration of whether the foreign source of the trademarked goods and the United States trademark holder are related commercial entities and whether the imported goods bearing the foreign mark are the same as (or not materially different from) the goods that are sold under the United States trademark, applying a standard of materiality suitable to considerations of consumer protection and support for the integrity of the trademarks of domestic purveyors, all with due consideration to the territorial nature of registered trademarks in the context of international trade.[49]

So, the key issue in gray market cases is whether parallel importation of goods carrying a valid U.S. trademark, but authorized for sale by the trademark owner in the U.S., may be blocked from entry into the customs territory of the U.S.

• **Physical Differences and 1999 *Gamut* Case**[50]

Gamut Trading Company v. United States International Trade Commission,

United States Court of Appeals for the Federal Circuit,
200 F.3d 775 (1999)

NEWMAN, CIRCUIT JUDGE:

This action for violation of Section 337 of the *Tariff Act of 1930*, 19 U.S.C. § 1337, was initiated at the United States International Trade Commission ("ITC") on the

---

49. 200 F.3D 775 (1999).

50. For another case involving material physical differences, see *Milecrest Corporation v. U.S.*, CIT Number 17-00125 (17 September 2017), involving gray market Duracell batteries, specifically, OEM bulk packaged batteries and foreign retail packaged batteries with a valid Duracell trademark. The gray market batteries differed from batteries that Duracell authorized for sale in the U.S. with respect to consumer assistance information, guarantees and warranties, and label warnings, label warnings. New Jersey-based Milecrest was the gray market importer, which Duracell did not authorize to import the batteries that Milecrest bought overseas and sold at a discount in the U.S. Duracell obtained a ban on the gray market goods under the so-called "Lever Rule," whereby a trademark holder (*e.g.*, Duracell) can ask CBP to importation of merchandise that bears a valid trademark, if that merchandise would sow confusion among consumers, as where the "goods sold overseas differ from those sold under the same trademark in the U.S.," and possibly

complaint of the Kubota Corporation, a Japanese company ("Kubota-Japan"), owner of the registered United States trademark "Kubota," and its United States affiliated companies Kubota Tractor Corporation ("Kubota-US") and Kubota Manufacturing of America ("KMA"). Kubota-US is the exclusive licensee of the "Kubota" trademark in the United States, by agreement with Kubota-Japan which provides that the United States trademark and associated goodwill remain the exclusive property of Kubota-Japan.

The respondents are Gamut Trading Company and other entities (collectively "Gamut") that import from Japan and resell in the United States various models of used tractors of under 50 horsepower, all manufactured in Japan by the Kubota Corporation, used in Japan, and bearing the mark "Kubota" that had been properly affixed in Japan. Gamut was charged with violation of Section 337 of the *Tariff Act of 1930*, 19 U.S.C. § 1337, which provides for exclusion of product bearing infringing marks and other remedies, based on asserted infringement of the United States trademark "Kubota":

19 U.S.C. § 1337   Unfair practices in import trade

(a)(1)(C)   The importation into the United States, the sale for importation, or the sale within the United States after importation by the owner, importer, or consignee, of articles that infringe a valid and enforceable United States trademark registered under the Trademark Act of 1946.

Describing this case as one of "gray-market goods," the ITC issued a General Exclusion Order against importation of used Japanese tractors bearing the "Kubota" trademark, and Cease and Desist Orders against sale of such tractors that had already been imported into the United States. . . .

On Gamut's appeal, we now affirm the decision of the ITC.

. . .

Kubota-Japan manufactures in Japan a large number of models of agricultural tractors, for use in Japan and other countries. Various tractor models are custom-designed for a particular use in a particular country. For example, tractor models that are designed for rice paddy farming are constructed for traction and manoeuvrability under wet, muddy conditions; these tractors have smaller tire separation in order to make tight turns in rice paddies, and are designed to function with rice paddy tillers, which contain narrow, light-weight blades. No corresponding model is designed for export to the United States.

---

also lead to consumer disappointment, thereby harming the trademark brand. Milecrest, which had been importing Duracell batteries for 27 years, challenged Duracell's efforts. *See* XYZ Corporation v. United States, CIT Number 17-0025 (12 September 2017); Brian Flood, *Duracell Loses Bid to Stop "Gray-Market" Batteries Challenge*, 34 International Trade Reporter (BNA) 1250 (21 September 2017); Brian Flood, *Duracell Battery Importer Forced to Unmask to Pursue Challenge*, 34 International Trade Reporter (BNA) 1250 (21 September 2017).

In contrast, some tractor models that are intended to be used in the United States are specially constructed for lifting and transporting earth and rocks, and to function with rear cutters that contain heavy blades capable of cutting rough undergrowth; these models do not have a direct Japanese counterpart. The tractor models intended for sale and use in the United States bear English-language controls and warnings, and have English-language dealers and users manuals. They are imported by Kubota-US and sold through a nationwide dealership network which provides full maintenance and repair service and maintains an inventory of parts for these specific tractor models. Kubota-US conducts training classes for its dealership employees, instructing them on service and maintenance procedures.

Gamut purchases used Kubota tractors in Japan and imports them into the United States. The majority of the imported tractors are described as between 13 and 25 years old. All bear the mark "Kubota." The Kubota companies state that the importation and its extent came to their attention when United States purchasers sought service and repair or maintenance from Kubota-US dealerships.

The Gray Market

. . .

Gamut directs our attention to cases in which the courts have refused to exclude gray market goods. For example, in *NEC Electronics v. CAL Circuit Abco*, 810 F.2d 1506 (9th Cir. 1987), . . . the court held that the importation of genuine NEC computer chips by the defendant, an entity unrelated to any NEC company, did not constitute infringement of the United States "NEC" trademark when there was no material difference between the NEC product imported by the defendant and the NEC product imported by the NEC United States subsidiary; the court distinguished *Bourjois* on the ground that in *Bourjois* the United States trademark owner could not control the quality of the unaffiliated foreign producer's goods, whereas when the companies are commonly controlled there is a reasonable assurance of similar quality.

A similar refusal to exclude was reached in *Weil Ceramics & Glass, Inc. v. Dash*, 878 F.2d 659 (3rd Cir. 1989), . . . wherein the court held that the United States trademark "Lladro" was not infringed by importation and sale of authentic "Lladro" figurines by one other than the trademark holder. The court reasoned that there is no need to protect the consumer against confusion when the goods imported by the defendant are identical to the goods imported by the United States trademark holder. . . . The court also reasoned that when the foreign manufacturer and the United States trademark holder are related companies, there is no need to protect the domestic company's investment in goodwill based on the quality of the trademarked goods, for the foreign manufacturer has control over their quality and the goods (porcelain figurines) are unchanged from their original quality.

However, when there are material differences between the domestic product and the foreign product bearing the same mark, most of the courts that have considered the issue have excluded the gray goods, even when the holders of the domestic and foreign trademarks are related companies, on grounds of both safeguarding the goodwill of the domestic enterprise, and protecting consumers from confusion or deception as to the quality and nature of the product bearing the mark. Thus, in *Societe des Produits Nestle v. Casa Helvetia, Inc.*, 982 F.2d 633 (1st Cir. 1992), . . . the court held that the foreign owner of the United States trademark "Perugina" and its Puerto Rican subsidiary that imported Italian-made "Perugina" chocolate could prevent the importation of "Perugina" chocolate made under license in Venezuela, because the product is materially different in taste; the court referred to the likelihood of consumer confusion and loss of goodwill and integrity of the mark.

Similarly in *Original Appalachian Artworks v. Granada Electronics*, 816 F.2d 68, 73 (2nd Cir. 1987), . . . the court held that the United States owner of the "Cabbage Patch" mark can prevent importation of "Cabbage Patch" dolls that were made and sold abroad under license from the United States owner, on the ground that the foreign dolls were materially different from the dolls authorized for sale in the United States because their instructions and adoption papers were in the Spanish language. . . .

These decisions implement the reasoning that the consuming public, associating a trademark with goods having certain characteristics, would be likely to be confused or deceived by goods bearing the same mark but having materially different characteristics; this confusion or deception would also erode the goodwill achieved by the United States trademark holder's business. Thus the basic question in gray market cases concerning goods of foreign origin is not whether the mark was validly affixed, but whether there are differences between the foreign and domestic product and if so whether the differences are material.

The Courts have applied a low threshold of materiality, requiring no more than showing that consumers would be likely to consider the differences between the foreign and domestic products to be significant when purchasing the product, for such differences would suffice to erode the goodwill of the domestic source. As explained in *Nestle*, "any higher threshold would endanger a manufacturer's investment in product goodwill and unduly subject consumers to potential confusion by severing the tie between a manufacturer's protected mark and its associated bundle of traits." . . . This criterion readily reconciles cases that have permitted parallel importation of identical goods, such as the Lladro figurines in *Weil Ceramics* (consumers not deceived, and no erosion of goodwill) and those that have barred importation based on material differences, such as the "Perugina" chocolate in *Nestle*. This criterion was applied by the Commission in reviewing the used "Kubota" tractor importations.

. . .

The Question of Material Differences

Gamut argues that the ITC erred in finding that there are material differences between their imported tractors and those imported by Kubota-U.S. Gamut points out that materiality of product differences is determined by the likelihood of confusion of those whose purchasing choice would be affected by knowledge of the differences, . . . and that its purchasers know that they are purchasing a used Japanese tractor. Gamut states that a purchaser of a used tractor bearing Japanese labels would not be deceived into thinking that he/she is buying a new tractor designed for the United States market. Gamut states that any differences between the imported models and the United States models are readily apparent, and thus can not be a material difference.

The ITC rejected this argument, finding that it is not reasonable to expect that purchasers of used Kubota tractors will be aware of structural differences from the United States models and of the consequences of these differences for purposes of maintenance, service, and parts. This finding was supported by substantial evidence. Indeed, the marking of these tractors with the "Kubota" mark weighs against an inference that purchasers would be expected to be aware of or expect structural differences.

As precedent illustrates, differences that may be readily apparent to consumers may nevertheless be material. In *Nestle*, the court found differences in quality, composition, and packaging to be material. In *Martin's Herend* the court found differences in the color, pattern or shape of porcelain figures to be material, although they would be apparent to an observer of the products side-by-side. [*See Martin's Herend Imports, Inc. v. Diamond & Gem Trading USA*, Co., 112 F.3d 1296 (5th Cir. 1997).] Differences in labelling and other written materials have been deemed material, on the criteria of likelihood of consumer confusion and concerns for the effect of failed consumer expectations on the trademark holder's reputation and goodwill. . . .

The Commission found that the imported used "Kubota" tractors lacked English instructional and warning labels, operator manuals, and service manuals. Labels are attached at various places on the tractor to instruct the user on the proper operation of the tractor and to warn of potential hazards, and include instructions on the direction of the engine speed hand throttle, the function of the transmission, the four-wheel drive, the power take-off speed, hydraulic power lift, and other controls on the tractor. The Commission found that such labels are necessary to safe and effective operation. The authorized "Kubota" tractors bear these labels in English; the permanent labels on the used imported tractors are in Japanese.

While it would be obvious to the purchaser that the warning and instructional labels are in Japanese, there was evidence before the ITC of consumer belief that the used tractors were sponsored by or otherwise associated with the Kubota-U.S. distributorship/service system. The ALJ heard evidence that a purchaser of such a used tractor knew the tractor bore Japanese labels, but did not realize that he was not buying an authorized tractor or that service and parts were not available from the Kubota-U.S. dealerships. Gamut contends that Kubota-Japan and Kubota-U.S. form a single enterprise and thus that Kubota-U.S. can and should provide any parts, service, maintenance, and repairs required by these used tractors. The ALJ found that in order to service the Gamut-imported tractors in the same manner as

Kubota-U.S. provides for its authorized tractors, the dealerships and service agencies would require an additional inventory of parts for the various Japan-only models, English-language operator manuals and service manuals that do not now exist, and additional service training as to the different models. There was testimony from a Kubota-U.S. dealer that he had tried to service several of the imported used tractors in order to preserve the reputation and goodwill of the mark, but that he was unable to do so satisfactorily since he had neither technical information nor replacement parts. He testified to customer dissatisfaction and anger with his dealership. The ALJ heard testimony that it would cost millions of dollars to provide equivalent support in the United States for the tractors that are made for use only in Japan. Gamut disputes these assertions and argues that most of the used tractors could be readily serviced without extraordinary effort. However, the record contains substantial evidence in support of the ALJ's findings. Further, materiality does not turn on whether extraordinary effort would be required for Kubota to service the Gamut-imported tractors; the threshold is not so high or the burden of establishing materiality so heavy.

The Kubota companies are not required to arrange to provide service to Gamut's imports in order to ratify these importations by mitigating their injury to the goodwill associated with the "Kubota" trademark. Whether or not the Kubota companies could arrange to service these tractors does not convert an otherwise infringing activity into an authorized importation. . . .

In addition to the differences in labelling, service, and parts, the ALJ found that many of the tractors designed by Kubota for use in the United States are stronger structurally than the corresponding tractors made for use in Japan. For example, the ALJ found that some of the intended United States tractors were made with stronger front and rear axles, front axle brackets, chassis, power trail, and parts contained in the transmission, such as gears. . . . The ALJ heard evidence that these structural differences significantly increase the likelihood of breakdowns of the less strong Japanese models. Although Gamut points to the absence of evidence of actual breakdown, the conceded or established differences in structural strength are relevant to the finding of material differences, and were properly considered by the Commission, along with the evidence concerning labelling, warnings, service, and parts.

Gamut raises the additional argument that in all events the Commission erred in law by applying the material differences test with the low threshold of precedent, because the imported tractors are not new but used. Gamut states that the Commission should have applied a more stringent test, namely, that differences which are easily ascertained by the consumer cannot be material. Gamut also argues that the Commission erred in ruling that differences that are easily apparent to the consumer, such as differences in structural strength and availability of parts and service, are material. We conclude that the Commission applied the correct standard, for this standard implements the two fundamental policies of trademark law: to protect the consumer and to safeguard the goodwill of the producer. . . .

Substantial evidence supports the Commission's finding that consumers would consider the differences between the used imported tractors and the authorized Kubota-U.S. tractors to be important to their purchasing decision, and thus material.

Effect of the Fact that the Goods are Used

Gamut argues that this is not a "gray market" case because the imported tractors are simply durable used goods, rendering it irrelevant whether the trademark owner authorized their sale in the United States. Gamut also argues that imported goods must be sold in competition with the goods of the owner of the United States trademark in order for authentic foreign-marked goods to infringe any trademark rights, citing *K Mart v. Cartier* . . . . Gamut asserts that because Kubota-U.S. sells new tractors in the United States and the respondents sell only used tractors, the goods are not in direct competition and the imported used tractors can not be held to be infringing gray market goods.

Direct competition between substantially identical goods is a factor to be considered, but it is not a prerequisite to trademark infringement. In *Safety-Kleen Corp. v. Dresser Indus.*, 518 F.2d 1399, 1404 (CCPA 1975), . . . the court explained that "While the similarity or dissimilarity of the goods or service should, in appropriate cases, be considered in determining likelihood of confusion . . . the law has long protected the legitimate interests of trademark owners from confusion among noncompetitive, but related, products bearing confusingly similar marks." Similar reasoning applies to products of the gray market.

. . .[T]rademark law as applied to gray market goods embodies a composite of likelihood of consumer confusion as to the source of the goods, likelihood of consumer confusion arising from differences between the foreign and the domestic goods, impositions on the goodwill and burdens on the integrity of the United States trademark owner due to consumer response to any differences, and recognition of the territorial scope of national trademarks. Various of these factors acquire more or less weight depending on the particular situation. Although it is relevant to consider whether the imported product is new or used, other factors that may affect the reputation and the goodwill enuring to the holder of a trademark are not overridden by the fact that the product is known to be second-hand.

Courts that have considered the question and concluded that used goods can be gray market goods include *Red Baron-Franklin Park, Inc. v. Taito Corp.*, 883 F.2d 275 (4th Cir. 1989) (used circuit boards purchased abroad and imported into the United States without the copyright holder's consent were gray market goods); . . . *Sims v. Florida Dep't of Highway Safety and Motor Vehicles*, 862 F.2d 1449, 1451 (11th Cir. 1989) (used Mercedes Benz automobiles were gray market goods under definition of Clean Air and Safety Act); . . . *Sturges v. Clark D. Pease, Inc.*, 48 F.2d 1035, 1038 (2nd Cir. 1931) (barring importation of used HISPANO SUIZA automobile because it bore United States registered trademark).

The ALJ found that Kubota-U.S. has established a reputation for safety, reliability, and service that consumers associate with the "Kubota" mark, and that the used tractors bearing the "Kubota" mark undermine the investment that Kubota-U.S. made in consumer goodwill for "Kubota" products. These findings are supported by substantial evidence. The fact that the imported tractors are used does not prevent a finding of infringement of the United States "Kubota" trademark.

Goodwill of the United States Trademark

Gamut points out that according to the trademark license agreement, Kubota-Japan owns the "Kubota" trademark in the United States and associated goodwill. Gamut argues that there can be no infringement of the United States trademark unless Kubota-Japan, as the trademark owner, demonstrates that it "has developed domestic goodwill, that is, independent of the goodwill associated with the mark world wide." The goodwill of a trademark is developed by use of the mark. The ALJ found that Kubota-U.S., through its large network of authorized dealers in "Kubota"-brand products, had established a reputation for product quality and service throughout the United States, establishing use of the mark accompanied by goodwill. This goodwill enures to the benefit of the trademark owner. Gamut's challenge to the standing of the complainants is not well founded.

Remedy

The ALJ recommended imposition of a general exclusion order as to the infringing tractor models, barring their importation and sale unless the tractors bore a permanent, non-removable label alerting the consumer to the origin of the used tractors and containing other information deemed necessary to mitigate consumer confusion. The ALJ also recommended that cease and desist orders be issued to bar the respondents from selling infringing used tractors already imported unless the tractors were appropriately labelled. The Commission, . . . affirmed the ALJ's ruling that the vinyl decal label that was proposed by Gamut would not eliminate the likelihood of consumer confusion because of the high likelihood that the labels would be removed after importation and prior to sale.

. . .

An exclusion order is the Commission's statutory remedy for trademark infringement. 19 U.S.C. § 1337(d). In addition, the Commission may issue cease and desist orders when it has personal jurisdiction over the party against whom the order is directed. 19 U.S.C. § 1337(f). . . .

• **Non-Physical Differences and 2005 *SKF* Case**

In *Gamut*, the Court did not face the issue of whether the distinction between domestic and gray market goods must be physical in nature to satisfy the "material difference test." The respondent, Gamut, infringed on Kubota's trademark because the 24 models of the "Kubota" tractors it imported from Japan did not have English language warning labels, and Kubota-U.S. dealers did not have English language operator or service manuals for them. The labelling, service, and parts differences were material as between authorized and gray market merchandise, thus supporting the invocation of Section 337. The issue of non-physical differences was presented on first impression in *SKF USA Inc. v. ITC*.[51]

In *SKF*, the Federal Circuit (per Circuit Judge Lourie) upheld the finding of the ITC that differences between authorized and gray market goods need not be physical, *i.e.*, need not be manifest in the product or its packaging, to be material. Differences in sellers of the product, or the services offered by sellers, may be material and thus establish a trademark infringement. That is because trademarked goods may have non-physical characteristics originating with the trademark owner. But, consumers may believe similar goods lacking those characteristics also originate with the owner. That erroneous impression could mislead consumers and damage the goodwill of the trademark owner.

The *SKF* Court stressed its reasoning, while "a step further" than in *Gamut*, simply made "explicit what may have only been implicit in *Gamut*." Notably, the *Gamut* court used the term "material differences," not "physical differences," and relied on prior case law in which non-physical material differences were held sufficient to avoid trademark infringement. In sum, to establish a Section 337 case based on trademark infringement in the context of the gray market, it does not matter whether differences — so long as they are material — between authorized, domestic goods and imported merchandise are physical or non-physical.

VII. Refusing Protection and 2002 *Havana Club* Case

- **Family, Business, and Political Intrigue**

The facts of the *Havana Club* case are an amalgam of family, business, and political intrigue fit for a novel or movie. In 1862, a 15-year-old named José Arechabala y Aldama migrated from Spain to Cuba. The same year, Facundo Bacardi Massó, who also had migrated from Spain to Cuba, established a rum distillery in Santiago de Cuba. Mr. Bacardi's distillery was called Bacardi, Bouteller & Co. In 1878, in Cárdenas, Mr. Arechabala set up a rum distillery, which became a quick success and one of the wealthiest businesses in Cuba. In 1934, Mr. Arechabala launched a new rum product, and called it "Havana Club." He marketed this product in the U.S., and registered the "Havana Club" mark with the PTO.

Until 1960, the Arechabala family owned the name "Havana Club" and applied it to its product, white rum. In 1960, with the Communist Revolution in Cuba, Fidel Castro seized the assets of José Arechabla S.A., and turned them over to a government entity, *Empresa Cubana Exportadora de Alimentos y Varios*, *i.e.*, the Cuban Food and Varied Products Export Enterprise, or Cubaexport. Castro expropriated

---

51. 27 ITRD 1705 (Fed. Cir., 14 September 2005) (No. 04-1460).

the name "Havana Club." Originally, Mr. Bacardi supported the Revolution. Subsequently, the Castro regime caused Bacardi's operations to shift to the Bahamas and Puerto Rico.

In 1963, pursuant to the *Trading with the Enemy Act of 1917*, President John F. Kennedy initiated the U.S. trade embargo on Cuba, forbidding importation and exportation of goods to that country. Cubaexport is a state-owned rum enterprise, controlled by the Cuban government. Because of the U.S. trade embargo against Cuba, importation into the U.S. is prohibited. The Cuban Asset Control Regulations cut off trade with Cuba, but allowed the administering authority—the Department of the Treasury—to make certain exceptions.[52] One such exception is for the registration of trademarks by Cuban entities.

In 1994, a JV between the Cuban distiller, Cubaexport, and a French company, Pernod-Ricard S.A., was established. (Pernod-Ricard produces some of the most famous alcoholic brands in the world, including Absolut, Beefeater, Chivas Regal, Glenlivet, Kahlúa, Seagram's, and Stolichnaya. It has an American subsidiary in Purchase, New York.) The JV is called "Havana Club Holdings SA." The JV produces white rum in Cuba, and sells it globally under the "Havana Club" brand name. Exports of the rum are managed by Cubaexport.

Pernod-Ricard says it was in 1994 the Cuban government gave it the right to the Havana Club brand. Notably, even before the Revolution, the Arechabala family let lapse its rights in the "Havana Club" name in some countries. In 1973, the family failed to renew its trademark registration in the U.S., a process that would have cost just $25. In contrast, Pernod-Ricard and Cubaexport registered the "Havana Club" brand in many countries, including the U.S. in 1976 through the PTO and Cuba in 1984, without protest from the family. There were 8 such registrations between 1995–2000 under Section 44 of the U.S. *Lanham Act*.[53] Pernod-Ricard says two factors account for the success of the brand, and make it necessary for its products to have a stamp of authenticity and thereby avoid misleading customers: it uses Cuban sugar cane and a special distillation process established in Cuba.[54]

Also in 1994, the Arechabala family signed a sales agreement with another company, Bacardi Ltd., a private company owned by over 200 descendants of the Bacardi founder. The Bacardi enterprise is based in the Bahamas and has a subsidiary in the U.S. The American subsidiary sells a brand of rum in the U.S. called "Havana Club." Under the deal with the Arechabala family, Bacardi can make Havana Club rum in Puerto Rico using the original recipe of the Arechabala family. Ultimately,

---

52. *See* 31 C.F.R. § 515.201.

53. *See* 15 U.S.C. § 1126.

54. *See* Anandashankar Mazumdar, *Bacardi Has "Cuban Heritage" and Thus Does Not Mislead With Its Use of "Havana Club,"* 27 International Trade Reporter (BNA) 594 (22 April 2010); *PTO Cancels Cuban "Havana Club" Mark; Bacardi Set to Sell Rum Under Same Mark*, 23 International Trade Reporter (BNA) 1216–1217 (17 August 2006).

in 1994, Bacardi bought the entire interest (the trademark and associated goodwill) of the Arechabala family in the "Havana Club" mark.

According to Bacardi, Pernod-Ricard tried unsuccessfully to buy the rights to "Havana Club" from the Arechabala family shortly after it formed the JV—a clear indication, says Bacardi, Pernod-Ricard recognized the family as the rightful owner of the mark. Bacardi tried to register the mark in America, and began selling the product in 1996. (It distilled rum in the Bahamas and Puerto Rico to avoid any difficulties with the American embargo on imports of Cuban products.)

In 1995, under 31 C.F.R. Section 515.318, OFAC (which administers the Cuban trade embargo, and which the Department of the Treasury houses) granted a license to Cubaexport to assign its American trademark rights to the JV, Havana Club Holdings SA. But, in July 1996, OFAC revoked this license and refused to allow Cubaexport to file an application with the PTO to renew its trademark. Consequently, in 2006, the registration by the JV expired. Bacardi then stepped in and tried to register the "Havana Club" mark with the PTO. In 1997, *In re Bacardi*, the U.S. Trademark Trial and Appeal Board upheld the denial by the PTO of the application by Bacardi to register the "Havana Club" name.[55] The Board reasoned that this term was geographically inaccurate and deceptive.

In 1998, Congress enacted a budget bill, the *Omnibus Consolidated and Emergency Supplemental Appropriations Act of 1999*,[56] which (*inter alia*) contained Section 211. The bill was signed into law on 21 October 1998. Section 211 states no trademark or trade name of Cuban origin can be protected by law in America if that mark or name had been used in connection with a business confiscated by the Castro regime. That is, registration or renewal in America of a trademark is forbidden, if the mark previously was abandoned by its owner whose business and assets were confiscated under Cuban law. Moreover, Section 211 prohibits an American court from recognizing or enforcing any assertion of such trademark rights. Section 211(a) states:

> [forbids authorization of any transaction or payment for a trademark] used in connection with a business or assets that were confiscated unless the original owner of the mark . . . or the *bona fide* successor in interest has expressly consented.

In other words, Section 211(a), and its implementing regulation, 31 C.F.R. Section 515.527, prohibited any further renewal of the registration of the "Havana Club" mark by entities affiliated with the Cuban government or a Cuban national. Thus, in 2006, OFAC rejected the application of Cubaexport to renew its registration of the mark.

---

55. *See In re Bacardi & Co.*, 48 U.S.P.Q 2d 1031 (T.T.A.B. 1997).
56. *See* Public Law Number 105-277, 112 Stat. 2681 (21 October 1988).

Section 211(b) of the *1999 Omnibus Act* says:

> No U.S. court shall recognize, enforce or otherwise validate an asser-
> tion of treaty rights by a designated national or its successor-in-interest
> under sections 44(b) or (e) of the *Trademark Act of 1946* . . . for a mark,
> trade name, or commercial name that is the same or substantially similar
> to a mark, trade name, or commercial name that was used in connection
> with a business or assets that were confiscated unless the original owner of
> such mark, trade name, or commercial name, or the *bona fide* successor-in-
> interest has expressly consented.

Consequently, no Court in the U.S. can recognize or enforce an assertion of rights
by a Cuban national related to a mark that is the same or similar to a mark used by
a business confiscated by Cuba. The only exception is where the original trademark
owner expressly agrees to the use of the trademark or trade name. The principal,
and indeed only, beneficiary of Section 211 is Bacardi.

In 1996, Havana Club Holdings S.A., the JV involving Pernod-Ricard, commenced litigation in federal court in New York against Bacardi to stop Bacardi from
using the "Havana Club" name to sell rum in the U.S. (Bacardi suspended sales,
pending outcome of the case.) The plaintiff argued it had been assigned the world
wide rights to the "Havana Club" trademark by the Cuban government, and Bacardi
was using its mark illegally. Based on Section 211 of the *Omnibus Act*, in April 1999,
the U.S. District Court in threw out the case. The plaintiff accused Bacardi of
deploying lobbying power to effect a change in U.S. law for its sole benefit. It said
the case was about Bacardi's desperate attempt to hold onto 50% of the American
rum market, and Congress' desire to "get tough" on Castro.

In February 2000, a Federal Appeals Court upheld the right of Bacardi to use the
"Havana Club" rum label in the U.S., affirming the District Court ruling that the
Cuban–French JV had no rights to the trademark in the U.S.[57] The Second Circuit
Court of Appeals rested its holding on two bases. First, in 1960, the Cuban government illegally confiscated the Havana Club rum distillery from its rightful owner,
the Arechabala family. Second, the efforts of Pernod-Ricard to protect the mark
violated Section 211. Essentially, the Court held that the American trade embargo
against Cuba barred the JV from pursuing any claims in American courts.

In the meantime, Bacardi test marketed its "Havana Club" rum, made some
adjustments to the production process (namely, changing the type of wood it used
for its aging barrels), and in 2006 began selling the product in Florida. That same
year, 2006, Pernod-Ricard filed a case in U.S. District Court arguing use of the
"Havana Club" name by Bacardi was a false and misleading representation of the
true origin of the rum in contravention of Section 43(a) of the *Lanham Act*.[58] This

---

57. *See Havana Club Holding, S.A. v. Galleon S.A.*, 203 F.3d 116 (2d Cir. 2000); *Havana Club
Holding, S.A. v. Galleon S.A.*, 62 F.Supp.2d 1085 (S.D.N.Y. 1999).

58. *See* 15 U.S.C. Section 1125(a).

Section bars misrepresentation of the "geographic origin" of a product, including geographical indications that convey the place of manufacture, or the "heritage," of the product.

In 2010, the District Court ruled that use by Bacardi of the term "Havana Club" is not misleading or deceptive, and thus does not violate the *Lanham Act*.[59] The Court rested its judgment on the fact Bacardi clearly labeled its rum to state that it made the rum in Puerto Rico. The label said "Puerto Rican Rum" below the "Havana Club" logo, and further stated "Crafted in Puerto Rico." The Court also reasoned that the product was not deceptive as to its geographic origin, because Havana Club rum has a Cuban history, and Bacardi uses the recipe of the Arechabala family. The modifications of this recipe do not annul the heritage of the product. Disappointed by the ruling, Pernod-Ricard appealed to the Court of Appeals for the Third Circuit.[60]

On appeal, Pernod-Ricard argued the District Court failed to consider carefully certain evidence, namely, a consumer survey. The Third Circuit held that the

---

59. *See Pernod Ricard USA LLC v. Bacardi U.S.A. Inc.*, D. Del. (No. 06-505-SLR, 6 April 2010).

60. Still another set of lawsuits over the "Havana Club" occurred in the District Court for the District of Columbia and the Court of Appeals for the D.C. Circuit. In 1998, Cubaexport argued in the D.C. District Court that (1) Section 211 was an unconstitutional violation of substantive due process (because of the Constitutional presumption against the retroactive application of a statute), (2) amendments to the C.F.R. to implement the *1999 Omnibus Act* violated both due process and the *Administrative Procedure Act*, and (3) the denial of the 2006 trademark renewal application of Cubaexport by OFAC was arbitrary and capricious. The District Court granted summary judgment for the U.S. government, and Cubaexport appealed to the D.C. Circuit. In March 2011, the Appeals Court rejected the appeal. *See Empresa Cubana Exportadora De Alimentos Y Productos Varios v. United States Department of the Treasury*, D.C. Cir. (No. 09-5196, 29 March 2011).

The Appeals Court held Section 211(a)(1) applies to both new registrations and renewals of existing registrations, and the presumption against retroactive application of a statute exists only if (1) the statute does not clearly specify its temporal scope, and (2) applying the statute retroactively would affect the "vested rights" of a party. The Appeals Court said Cubaexport lacked a "vested right" to renewal of its trademark registration, because the 1963 Cuban Asset Control Regulations clearly indicate that exceptions to the trade embargo with Cuba, such as for trademark registrations, could be amended, modified, or revoked at any time. Consequently, from 1963 on, Cuban entities had notice their trademark rights in the U.S. might not be renewed—hence their lack of a "vested interest." (In a dissent, one judge opined that "vested rights" refer to substantive, not procedural, rights, and Cubaexport did have a substantive right in trademark registration.) As for denial of substantive due process, the Appeals Court applied the highly deferential standard of review, namely the rational basis test: whether the governmental restriction at issue is rationally related to a legitimate governmental interest. Under this scrutiny, it was easy to show the *1999 Omnibus Act* is rationally related to the legitimate goal of isolating the Communist government in Cuba and hastening democratic reform in that country. Denying Cuban-affiliated entities the use of U.S. trademarks related to American businesses or assets confiscated by the Cuban government helps pursue this goal. Similarly, the Court rejected Cubaexport's arguments made under the *Administrative Procedure Act*, as OFAC provided Cubaexport with sufficient notice via a letter sent to it in 2006 about the change in regulations and offered it the opportunity to apply for an individualized license, called a "specific license." Finally, in implementing the will of Congress, the Appeals Court held OFAC did not behave arbitrarily or capriciously.

lower court did not err.[61] The survey evidence was irrelevant. The label Bacardi uses on its "Havana Club" brand clearly indicates the rum is "Puerto Rican Rum." Consequently, no reasonable consumer could be misled as to the true geographic origin of the product—Puerto Rico. Pernod-Ricard was wrong in its contention that only the "Havana Club" mark should be analyzed, *i.e.*, it should not be read in conjunction with the label "Puerto Rican Rum." Moreover, Pernod-Ricard was trying to disguise a claim it is barred from making in U.S. courts (concerning trademark infringement) as a claim of false advertising. After all, the real, underlying fight in the Havana Club case is which party has the exclusive right to the famed geographically-indicated trademark.

Did Bacardi abandon the "Havana Club" name? Is Bacardi trying to seize control of the name to fend off competition from Pernod? Section 211 was applied against Havana Club International retroactively—is that unfair? The New York litigation was brought in 1996, the law was enacted in 1998, and the courts applied it in 1999. To be sure, the arguments are not all one way. One argument for Bacardi is Section 211 is no different from legal rights the EU established to protect property expropriated by the Nazis during the Second World War, or by communist regimes during the Cold War.

In July 1999, the EU and Cuba took up the cause of Havana Club Holdings SA, lodging against the U.S. a WTO complaint. Canada, Japan, and Nicaragua reserved third party rights, and only with the intercession of the WTO Director General was a Panel composed. The complainants, led by the EC, argued Section 211 of the *Omnibus Appropriations Act* violated *TRIPs Agreement* provisions:

(1) Article 2, which incorporates by reference relevant provisions of the 1967 *Paris Convention for the Protection of Industrial Property*, as amended by the *Stockholm Act of 1967*.

(2) Article 3, which guarantees national treatment with respect to IP protection.

(3) Article 4, which guarantees MFN treatment with respect to IP protection.

(4) Articles 15–21, which set out obligations for the protection of trademarks.

(5) Article 41, covering general obligations about the enforcement of IP rights.

(6) Article 42, dealing with fair and equitable procedures in IP enforcement.

(7) Article 62, on acquiring and maintaining IPR and related *inter partes* (between two or more parties) procedures.

The Panel rejected most EC claims. But, it agreed Section 211(a)(2) inconsistent with *TRIPs Agreement* Article 42. That is because it restricts, in certain circumstances, effective access to, and availability of civil judicial procedures, for IPR holders.

---

61. *See Pernod-Ricard U.S.A. LL.C. v. Bacardi U.S.A. Inc.*, 3d Cir. (No. 10-2354, 4 August 2011).

The EC appealed in October 2001, and the Appellate Body rendered a decision in January 2002. That decision presents far more mixed results for the U.S. than the Panel findings. In brief, the Appellate Body reached the following conclusions:

(1) It affirmed the Panel conclusion Section 211 does not violate the American obligations under Article 2:1 of the *TRIPs Agreement* in conjunction with Article 6 *quinquies* A(1) of the 1967 *Paris Convention*. ("*Quinquies*," from Latin, means "five" or "fifth.")

(2) It agreed with the Panel that Section 211 does not violate *TRIPs Agreement* Articles 15 and 16.

(3) As to Section 211(b), it upheld the Panel finding under Article 42 of the *TRIPs Agreement* of consistency between the two provisions. However, the Appellate Body reversed the Panel holding that Section 211(a)(2) violates Article 42 of the *TRIPs Agreement*. The Appellate Body said Article 42 contains procedural obligations, while Section 211 affects substantive trademark rights.

(4) In respect of trademark protection, it said Sections 211(a)(2) and (b) violate the national treatment and MFN obligations in the *TRIPs Agreement*, as well as the analogous provisions in the *Paris Convention* (1967). Thus, it reversed the Panel's contrary findings on *TRIPs Agreement* Articles 2, 3, and 4.

(5) It reversed the Panel finding that trade names are not a category of IP the *TRIPs Agreement* protects The Appellate Body completed the analysis, reaching the same conclusion for trade names and trademarks. The Appellate Body also ruled Sections 211(a)(2) and (b) are not inconsistent with Article 2:1 of the *TRIPs Agreement* in conjunction with Article 8 of the *Paris Convention*.

After the January 2002 Appellate Body Report, the U.S. and EC, with Cuba, reached an agreement on an RPT for compliance—a maximum of 1 year (until 3 January 2003).

In 2002, to the consternation of the EC and Cuba, the administration of President George W. Bush announced it was unnecessary to clarify Section 211 does not apply to cases in which a trademark has been abandoned by its original owner. The EC said American officials had assured the Panel, and the Panel accepted the assurances, that Section 211 would not apply to a new trademark after a former trademark, to which the Section might have applied, had been abandoned. The problem was American federal courts disagreed. Adhering to the opposite view, they applied Section 211 to trademarks succeeding abandoned trademarks. The EC and Cuba said there was legal uncertainty. Any solution to the dispute had to address the issue of abandoned trademarks.

After the verbal scuffle, the parties agreed to repeated RPT extensions—to 30 June 2003, 31 December 2003, 31 December 2004, and 30 June 2005. In July 2005, the EU agreed to refrain from seeking WTO authorization to retaliate. Yet, Section 211 remains un-repealed and un-amended. Might a technical clarification to Section 211, stating that it applies to any party, regardless of nationality, claiming a right in a Cuban-confiscated trademark, bring the statute into compliance with *TRIPs Agreement*? Or, would it be better to do away with not only the statute, but the trade embargo itself?

As indicated above, in July 2006, OFAC denied an application by Cubaexport a license to renew U.S. registration of the "Havana Club" trademark. In turn, in August 2006, the PTO declared the "Havana Club" trademark of Pernod-Ricard "cancelled/expired." The PTO rejected the argument of Pernod-Ricard: regardless of OFAC's decision, Pernod-Ricard lodged a timely application with the PTO to renew the trademark; and, the PTO should focus solely on the status of the trademark in evaluating the right to renewal (not bring in other political issues). The PTO also rejected the argument it should not void the trademark until a U.S. court has the opportunity to review the legitimacy of OFAC's denial in respect of the Cubaexport application. Of course, Pernod-Ricard also intoned the PTO's took its decision to cancellation its trademark under Section 211—which the WTO Appellate Body ruled illegal under Article 42 of the *TRIPs Agreement*.

Was Pernod-Ricard caught between two parts of the U.S. government in a pincer-like move? Alternatively, was there official confusion as to what mattered more—enforcing the Cuban trade embargo, or maintaining the integrity of IPR protection? Did international law matter in the case, and if so, how? What solution was reached?

- **Scope of Article 6** *quinquies* **A(1) of the** *Paris Convention* **(1967)**

Does the *Paris Convention* bar a host country regulator from dictating the form and registration process of a trademark or patent? The Appellate body in *Havana Club* defined the scope of Article 6 *quinquies* A(1).

The Appellate Body in U*nited States—Section 211 Omnibus Appropriations Act of 1998*, interpreted a non-WTO treaty. It did so because the *TRIPS Agreement* incorporates the *Paris Convention* of 1967 by reference. To be a WTO Member, a country must adhere to the *TRIPs Agreement*, and to follow that *Agreement*, the country must agree to the provisions of the *Paris Convention* of 1967. Article 2:1 of the *TRIPS Agreement* states: "[i]n respect of Parts II, III and IV of this *Agreement*, Members shall comply with Articles 1 through 12, and Article 19, of the *Paris Convention* (1967)."[62]

Article 6(1) of the 1967 revision of the *Paris Convention* provides a means for a foreign national "of a country of the Paris Union" to *register* a patent or trademark.[63] The general rule is "each country of the Paris Union has the right to determine the

---

62. Appellate Body Report, *United States—Section 211 Omnibus Appropriations Act of 1998*, WT/DS176/AB/R, ¶ 124 (adopted 2, January 2002 [hereafter *Havana Club* Appellate Body Report].

63. *Havana Club* Appellate Body Report, ¶ 132 (*emphasis added*).

conditions for filing and registration of trademarks in its domestic legislation."[64] That is, in respect to registration of patents and trademarks, a foreign national must follow the domestic laws within the territory of each member country.

Although a foreign national of a member must still register in a host country, Article 6 *quinquies* A(1) of the *Paris Convention* grants a national additional rights, *i.e.*, rights available to a national in her own country. The Appellate Body in *Havana Club* asked whether these additional rights relate only to the "*form* of the trademark as registered in the applicant's country of origin" or whether the rights "encompass other features and aspects of that trademark as registered in the country of origin."[65]

Article 6 *quinquies* A(1) requires a member country to register a trademark of a national of another member country, "as is." The EU in *Havana Club* argued Article 6 *quinquies* A(1) creates a "global system" of "trademark ownership" where members must adhere to the registration processes of other members.[66] The EU believed the U.S. *must* allow a national to register a patent or trademark if the patent or trademark was registered in the EU. The Panel and Appellate Body disagreed with this argument. After a textual analysis of the term "as is," the Appellate Body held Article 6 *quinquies* A(1) "does *not* encompass all the features and aspects of that trademark."[67]

All members have the "right to right to determine the conditions for filing and registration of trademarks . . . ."[68] In other words, member countries may still limit trademark ownership by independently regulating filings and registrations. However, if registered in home and host countries, a host-member must accept the trademark *form* as it is in the national's country of origin. The appellate body agreed with the Panel, holding the Section 211 registration ban on IP appropriated by the Cuban Government dealt with the "ownership of a defined category of trademarks" and was thus permissible under Article 6 *quinquies* A(1).[69]

- **National Treatment, MFN, Article 2(1) of *Paris Convention* (1967) and Article 3:1 of *TRIPS Agreement***

Can a Member discriminate against applicants from other member countries in favor of its domestic applicants? May a Member treat applicants from some member countries better than applicants from other Members? The Appellate Body in *Havana Club* addressed these questions.

The *Paris Convention* and the *TRIPS Agreement* address national treatment. Much like national treatment under GATT Article III:4, "[t]he national treatment

---

64. *Havana Club* Appellate Body Report, ¶ 132 (*emphasis added*).
65. *Havana Club* Appellate Body Report, ¶ 137.
66. *Havana Club* Appellate Body Report, ¶ 141.
67. *Havana Club* Appellate Body Report, ¶ 139.
68. *Havana Club* Appellate Body Report, ¶ 139.
69. *Havana Club* Appellate Body Report, ¶ 147.

obligation is a fundamental principle underlying the *TRIPs Areement*."[70] For "matters affecting availability, scope, maintenance and enforcement of intellectual property rights as well as those matters affecting the use of intellectual property rights," Article 3:1 of the *TRIPs Agreement* requires members "accord no less favorable treatment to non-nationals than to nationals."[71]

The EU argued sections 211(a)(2) and (b) treated non-US nationals "less favorably" than U.S. nationals in two different situations: first, in situations involving "*bona fide* successors-in-interest," and second, in situations involving original owners.[72]

In situations involving "successors-in-interest," the U.S. Under the *CACR*, OFAC may issue licenses to U.S. nationals to own intellectual property "that was confiscated by the Cuban government."[73] The U.S. and Panel believed, that article 211(a)(2) could not discriminate in favor of US nationals because it did not apply to U.S. nationals. U.S. nationals could not practically obtain property confiscated by the Cuban Government.

That is, OFAC'S discretion to issue licenses had "little practical effect," because it "never issued such a license to a U.S. National."[74] The Panel cited the holding in *United States Measures Affecting the Importation, Internal Sale and Use of Tobacco*: "where discretionary authority is vested in the executive branch of a WTO Member, it cannot be assumed that the Member will exercise the authority in the violations of its obligations . . . ."[75] The mere fact an executive agency has the *discretion* to discriminate is not dispositive. The Panel must review how the agency *uses* its discretion. Because OFAC never granted such a license to U.S. nationals, the Panel held the practical effect of its discretion was not inconsistent with its national treatment obligations.

The EU argued, despite OFAC'S discretion to grant licenses, the ban on foreign successors in interest still discriminated against non-U.S. nationals because it created a procedural "extra hurdle that non-United States nationals face." A U.S. Court will never recognize a foreign successor-interest, while a U.S. Court must assume "no action by OFAC" in order to reject an *American* successor in interest.[76]

The Appellate Body agreed with EU, holding this "procedural hurdle" existed on the statute's face because Section 211(a)(2) applied *only* to non-U.S. successors-in

---

70. *Havana Club* Appellate Body Report, ¶ 242.
71. *Havana Club* Appellate Body Report, ¶ 243.
72. *Havana Club* Appellate Body Report, ¶ 244.
73. *Havana Club* Appellate Body Report, ¶ 249.
74. *Havana Club* Appellate Body Report, ¶ 251.
75. *Havana Club* Appellate Body Report, ¶ 251 (Adopted 2, January 2002) (*citing United States Measures Affecting the Importation, Internal Sale and Use of Tobacco* ("*US—Tobacco*") [B.I.S.D. (41st Supp. I) at 131, ¶ 118 (adopted 4 October 1994).
76. *Havana Club* Appellate Body Report, ¶ 264.

interest. It cited the GATT Panel ruling in the 1989 *Section 337* case, and held the "mere *possibility* of this extra hurdle is inherently less favorable."[77]

> The United States may be right that the likelihood of having to over-come the hurdles of both Section 515.201 of Title 31 CFR and Section 211(a)(2) may, echoing the panel in *U.S. — Section 337,* be *small.* But, ... even the *possibility* that non-United States successors-in-interest face two hur-dles is *inherently less favorable* than the undisputed fact that United States successors-in-interest face only one.[78]

Because of this extra hurdle, the Appellate body held Section 211(a)(2) violated the "national treatment obligations of Article 2(1) of the *Paris Convention* and Article 3:1 of the *TRIPS Agreement.*"[79]

The Appellate Body then addressed the EU claim that Section 211(a)(2) and (b) discriminated against non-U.S. original owners. The Panel held the two provisions do not treat foreign original owners less favorably than U.S. nationals. The EU and Appellate Body disagreed. The Appellate Body agreed with the EU contention that "a particular set of circumstances that exist under the statute" demonstrate the "discriminatory treatment implicit in Sections 211(a)(2) and (b)."[80] The EU illus-trated a particular situation where discrimination may exist.

> There are two separate owners who acquired rights, either at common law or based on registration, in two separate United States trademarks, before the Cuban confiscation occurred. Each of these two United States trade-marks is the same, or substantially similar to, the signs or combination of signs of which a trademark registered in Cuba is composed. That same or similar Cuban trademark was used in connection with a business or assets that were confiscated in Cuba. Neither of the two original owners of the two United States trademarks was the owner of that same or similar trademark that was registered in Cuba. Those two original owners each seek to assert rights in the United States in their two respective United States trademarks. The situation of these two original owners of these two United States trade-marks is identical in every relevant respect, but one. That one difference is this: one original owner is a national of Cuba, and the other original owner is a national of the United States.[81]

In this situation, the Cuban national is "subject to Sections 211(a)(2) and (b)" and therefore is not barred from enforcing the trademark. Yet, the American original owner is not subject to these Sections. The Appellate body held Sections 211(a)(2) and (b) were "discriminatory on their face," "because they applied to original

---

77. *Havana Club* Appellate Body Report, ¶ 265 (*citing* GATT, B.I.S.D. (36th Supp.) 345 (adopted 7 November 1989)).

78. *Havana Club* Appellate Body Report, ¶ 265.

79. *Havana Club* Appellate Body Report, ¶ 268.

80. *Havana Club* Appellate Body Report, ¶ 275.

81. *Havana Club* Appellate Body Report, ¶ 276.

owners that are Cuban nationals" while "original owners that are United States nationals are not covered."[82]

- **National Treatment, MFN, Article 2(1) of *Paris Convention* (1967) and Article 3:1 of *TRIPs Agreement***

Regarding how MFN obligations apply to IP, the *TRIPs Agreement* steps in to fill a void in the *Paris Convention*. "Unlike the national treatment principle, there is no provision in the *Paris Convention* (1967) that establishes an MFN obligation with respect to rights in trademarks or other industrial property."[83] In *Havana Club*, the Appellate Body addressed the scope of the IP MFN obligations of a WTO Member under Article 4 of the *TRIPS Agreement*.

The Panel rejected the EU claims, holding Sections 211(a)(2) and (b) do not deny Cuban nationals any advantage, favor, privilege or immunity that it accords to other nations. The EU allegations for MFN treatment "of original owners are similar to those described in the previous section on national treatment."[84]

The EU cited a similar situation as the circumstance described in the context of the national treatment exception for original owners. The EU and Appellate Body substituted "for the sake of convenience," the original American owner with "a non-Cuban foreign national." The EU argued "a Cuban national is subject to Sections 211(a)(2) and (b), and the original owner who is a non-Cuban foreign national is not."[85] The Appellate Body agreed with this exception and held the Sections facially discriminate against Cuban nationals in favor of other foreign nationals. Therefore, they violate Article 4 of the *TRIPS Agreement*.

VIII. Special 301 Black Listing

"Special 301" is Section 182 of the *Trade Act of 1974*, as amended.[86] It was added to the *1974 Act* by Section 1303 of the *Omnibus Trade and Competitiveness Act of 1988*. Special 301 requires the USTR annually to give Congress (specifically, the House Ways and Means and Senate Finance Committees) information on countries that lack or fail to enforce IPRs, The USTR must do so within 30 days after issuing its yearly study of foreign trade barriers under Section 301 of the *1974 Act*. The Section 301 analysis is called the *National Trade Estimate Report* (NTE).[87] The 30 day rule means the USTR must put out the Special 301 Report on or before 30 April

---

82. *Havana Club* Appellate Body Report, ¶ 279.

83. *Havana Club* Appellate Body Report, ¶ 297.

84. *Havana Club* Appellate Body Report, ¶ 305.

85. *Havana Club* Appellate Body Report, ¶ 307.

86. *See* 19 U.S.C. Section 2242; URUGUAY ROUND TRADE AGREEMENT, STATEMENT OF ADMINISTRATIVE ACTION, UNDERSTANDING ON RULES AND PROCEDURES GOVERNING THE SETTLEMENT OF DISPUTES, H.R.DOC. No. 316, 103D CONG., 2D SESS., VOL. 1, 1031–32 (27 September 1994).

87. *See* 19 U.S.C. § 2241(b).

each year. The Special 301 Report must address not only conventional IPRs, *i.e.*, patents, trademarks, and copyrights, but also semiconductor mask works, textile designs, trade secrets, and plant breeder's rights. Critically, it must cover market access issues relevant to IPR holders.

What are the fundamental purposes of blacklisting under Special 301? One answer is to increase the leverage of the USTR in trade negotiations. Another answer is that public proclamation of countries with lax IPR regimes is a sanction in itself—shame. Presumably, most countries seek to avoid the reputation of being an IP brigand. A third answer is that advocates in a foreign country of strong IP protection and vigorous enforcement can use the actuality, or spectre, of being put on the Special 301 list as leverage in their domestic political environments. They can point to Special 301 to persuade recalcitrant constituencies in their country that IP reform is required. Otherwise, they can say, American businesses will eschew trade and investment with their country.

In respect of all three responses, consider whether overt American pressure might be counterproductive. Is every country crestfallen when the American government publicly proclaims displeasure with it? Might there be rally-around-the-flag effect in blacklisted countries against heavy-handedness by a hegemonic power? To be even-handed, query whether any other country has the willingness or ability to take a resolute stand on IP protection and enforcement? Is Special 301 a particular instance of the broad international role in which the U.S. finds, or casts itself, in—the reluctant sheriff?

Under Special 301, the USTR must identify any country, whether a WTO Member or not, and whether a party to an FTA or not, which

(1) denies "adequate and effective" IPR protection, specifically, patent, trademark, copyright, or semiconductor mask work protection, or

(2) "fair and equitable market access" to U.S. persons relying on such protection.[88]

The USTR's annual Special 301 review process can lead to a trading partner being placed on one of three lists. In order of ascending severity, they are:

(1) "Watch List"

A "Watch List" country requires American attention about specific IPR problems.

(2) "Priority Watch List"

A "Priority Watch List" country is one about which the U.S. has significant concerns its protection and enforcement of IPRs are insufficient, or that access to its market for businesses relying on IPR is limited.

---

88. *See* 19 U.S.C. § 2242(a).

(3) "Priority List"

> A "Priority" Foreign Country, or "PFC," is one in which the most egregious IP offenses occur, *i.e.*, whose IP regimes are deemed to constitute trade barriers, and thus are targeted for retaliatory measures.

The Special 301 statute does not mandate the first two lists. Rather, the USTR created them by administrative fiat, as alternatives to the severest black listing category. Countries on these Lists warrant attention on account of their dubious IPR regimes or enforcement regimens.

As the USTR's Watch List is the least severe form of black listing, it simply names countries warranting special attention. They are of particular concern, because they engage in IP practices that pose market access barriers. The Priority Watch List is a moderately severe form of black listing. Countries on this list meet some, but not all, of the criteria for PFC designation. The USTR carefully monitors these countries to determine whether further Special 301 action is needed, and takes active, bilateral steps to resolve deficiencies in their legal apparatus for IPR protection.

From the Priority Watch List, a country can move "up." China, India, and Thailand are among countries the USTR placed (on 26 May 1989, following the USTR's first annual review) on the Priority Watch List. Failing (in the USTR's view) to make significant improvements to IP protection while on that list, they graduated (on 26 April 1991) to the Priority List. Attention on these countries is not without justification. In 2012, as in several previous years, China accounted for more counterfeit and pirated goods seized by CBP than any other country—72%. China had the top spot in 2014, too. India, along with Hong Kong and Singapore, also ranked high on the list of sources of CBP IPR seizures. The most commonly seized items were handbags and wallets.

"Downward" mobility also is possible. Indonesia was on the Priority Watch List from 2001 until 6 November 2006. On that date, the USTR pronounced itself pleased with Indonesian reforms, and downgraded the country to the Watch List. What had Indonesia done to justify the lesser black listing? It took action against illegal manufacturing of pirated optical discs, namely, stronger licensing requirements on factories and additional raids on both production facilities and retail outlets. It also enacted a new customs law clarifying the authority of the government to seize infringing goods. And, it commenced public awareness campaigns.

The change in Indonesia's status occurred through an OCR. Accordingly, the USTR need not wed itself to annual reviews. What factors might influence the decision to conduct an OCR? To be sure, all Special 301 reviews, in contrast to Section 337 actions, can be initiated only by the USTR. But, this arrangement does not mean private parties are without a voice. To the contrary, an IPR holder can petition the USTR to initiate a Special 301 action if it feels a foreign country merits investigation.[89] Of course, whether it is successful may depend in part on its economic significance and its lobbying clout.

Israel is another example of downward mobility from the Priority Watch List to the Watch List. That happened to Israel in September 2012. In a 2010 *MOU*, the U.S. agreed to remove Israel from the Priority Watch List once it submitted three new laws to its parliament to improve terms (1) on patents on pharmaceuticals, (2) provisions on publications for patent applications, and (3) data protection. The first law granted patent term extensions as compensation for delays in obtaining regulatory approval for a pharmaceutical. The second and third laws contained protections against unfair commercial use of undisclosed test and other data generated to obtain approval to market a pharmaceutical product. The USTR changed the Israeli status once Israel introduced the three laws to the Knesset. The 2010 *MOU* obligated the USTR to remove Israel from the Watch List entirely, as soon as the Knesset enacted these laws. Query whether the USTR would be satisfied with mere submission of laws to a legislature, as distinct from both enactment and enforcement, for other countries. After all, to be downgraded from the Priority Watch List to the Watch List means a country has made progress in resolving issues that led to the blacklisting in the first place. What constitutes "progress," and are the benchmarks the same for every foreign country?

Three statutory criteria must be satisfied before the USTR affixes to a country the label "PFC" and places it on the Priority List.

(1) The country must have the "most onerous or egregious" acts, policies, or practices that deny either "adequate and effective" IPRs or "fair and equitable" market access to U.S. persons that rely on IP protection.

(2) The country's IP acts, practices, or policies must have the "greatest adverse impact," whether actual or potential, on American products.

(3) The country must not have entered into good faith negotiations, either multilateral or bilateral, to provide adequate and effective IP protection.[90]

Simply put, PFC countries are the worst offenders of IPRs in the world.

At any point, the USTR can make or revoke a PFC designation—but, it must explain such a move to Congress.[91] In addition to these criteria, the USTR must consider the history of IP law and practice in an investigated country, whether it has been listed as a "PFC" previously, and its behavior on enhanced IP protection and enforcement. The USTR may put a country on the Priority List even if it is in compliance with the *TRIPs Agreement*. That is because the *Agreement* does not cover all aspects of IP that might affect U.S. persons seeking to protect or enforce rights overseas. Is it, therefore, fair to characterize Special 301 as a unilateral tool to push for *TRIPs* Plus obligations?

---

89. *See* 19 U.S.C. § 2412(a).
90. *See* 19 U.S.C. § 2242(b)(1)(A)-(C).
91. *See* 19 U.S.C. § 2242(c).

Undoubtedly, Priority List designation is the most severe form of black listing. That is because of the link between Special 301 and Section 301. Within 30 days after identifying a PFC, the USTR must initiate a Section 301 investigation of that country.[92] That is, within one month of being put on the Special 301 list, a country can expect to be the target of a Section 301 inquiry. Only in two circumstances is the link not automatic. First, if the USTR decides a Section 301 investigation would be detrimental to American economic interests, and explains to Congress why, then it does not commence an inquiry.[93] Second, the USTR need not initiate a case if it believes retaliatory action against an allegedly violating country would be ineffective.[94]

Obviously, a Section 301 investigation of a Priority List country focuses on alleged IPR violations in that country. The USTR must consult with the Commissioner of Patents and Trademarks and the Register of Copyrights.[95] The investigation must be finished within six (or, if there are complex issues or substantial progress is being made, nine) months.[96] These times are tighter than a Section 301 case not triggered by Special 301.

Section 301 investigations, including those triggered by Special 301, entail the threat of retaliatory action by the U.S. against another country's behavior. If the acts, practices, or policies in question of the other country continue, then the USTR must take "appropriate and feasible" action to enforce America's trade rights and eliminate the violating behavior.[97] Retaliation is subject to the direction of the President.[98]

One of two prerequisites must be fulfilled before retaliation can occur. The first condition is the USTR affirmatively determines that "the rights to which the United States is entitled under any trade agreement are being denied . . . ."[99] Thus, for example, violation of a bilateral IP agreement, *NAFTA* Chapter 17, or the *TRIPs Agreement* would satisfy this prerequisite.

The other prerequisite is somewhat confusing. It has two alternative prongs: the USTR must find that an act, policy, or practice of a country under investigation either:

(1) "violates, . . . or otherwise denies benefits to the United States under, any trade agreement" or "is unjustifiable and burdens or restricts United States commerce,"[100] or

---

92. *See* 19 U.S.C. § 2412(b)(2)(A).
93. *See* 19 U.S.C. § 2412(b)(2)(B)-(C).
94. *See* 19 U.S.C. § 2412(c).
95. *See* 19 U.S.C. § 2412(b)(2)(D).
96. *See* 19 U.S.C. § 2414(a)(3)(A)-(B).
97. 19 U.S.C. § 2411(a)(1), (b).
98. *See* §§ 2411(a)-(b), 2415(a)(1).
99. 19 U.S.C. § 2414(a)(1)(A)(i).
100. 19 U.S.C. §§ 2411(a)(1)(B), (i)-(ii), 2414 (a)(1)(A)(ii).

(2) is "unreasonable or discriminatory and burdens or restricts United States commerce."[101]

The rubric for the 1st prong is "mandatory action," and for the 2nd is "discretionary action." Before making a final determination (unless expeditious action is required), the USTR must give opportunity for public comment and consult with advisory committees. It may request the views of the ITC on the probable impact of retaliatory action on the American economy.[102]

Retaliation may take the form of suspension of benefits of concessions otherwise due to the violating country under a trade agreement, or an increase in tariffs on, or erection of non-tariff barriers against, its imports.[103] With certain exceptions, retaliatory action must take effect within 30 days after the USTR's affirmative determination.[104]

IX. 2014 Case of India on Special 301 Priority List

In spring 2014, the USTR came under pressure from American trade lobbies to designate India as a PFC under Special 301. The USTR acknowledged problems in India with respect to securing and enforcing patents, protecting trade secrets, counterfeiting trademarked goods, IP piracy (e.g., illegally downloading and distributing books, movies, and music), and localization rules.[105] The reaction in India was anger: to Indians, the action was an American bullying tactic, and unjustified legally. Indian Ambassador to the U.S., S. Jaishankar, intoned in a March 2014 Chicago speech that "it would be a mistake [for America] to pile up public pressure, especially through a misrepresentation of the facts."[106] Did India have a point?

First, India had amended its IP rules to conform to the *TRIPs Agreement*. The changes bolstered protection for patents and copyrights. It also created the Intellectual Property Appellate Board, with jurisdiction over patents, trademarks, and GIs. Overall, the Indian IPR regime reflected the same balance as the *Agreement*: protection of commercial interests vis-à-vis access to products.

---

101. 19 U.S.C. §§ 2411(b)(1), 2414(a)(1)(A)(ii).

102. *See* 19 U.S.C. § 2414(b).

103. *See* 19 U.S.C. §§ 2411(c)(1)(A)-(B), 2416(b).

104. *See* 19 U.S.C. § 2415(a)(1)). The USTR may delay implementing retaliation for up to 180 days in conditions set forth in § 2415(a)(2).

105. Localization measures favor a domestic industry or service provider, or domestic IP, vis-à-vis foreign competitors. Some of them have a legitimate purpose, such as protecting data privacy or national security. Others are protectionist. Indigenous innovation policies are related, as they prefer IP innovation from domestic over foreign firms, typically in the pursuit of enhancing domestic R&D capacity and boosting the share of value added by domestic firms to GDP.

106. *Quoted in* Indrani Bagchi, *India's Fresh Attack in U.S. Trade War*, THE TIMES OF INDIA, 4 March 2014, at 19. [Hereinafter, *India's Fresh Attack*.]

Second, India pointed out America was displeased by its stands on an array of non-IP matters. For example, India stood up to the U.S. for its allegedly abusive treatment in January 2014 of one of its diplomats in New York, Devyani Khobragade, whom law enforcement authorities strip-searched and tossed in jail with common criminal defendants for alleged false statements on immigration and visa forms. (She was the target of a grand jury indictment, and expelled.) Further, several American MNCs were embroiled in income tax disputes with Indian revenue authorities.

Still another instance was India's import prohibition on American solar panels using thin-film technology. India claimed they contained environmentally unfriendly components (particularly cadmium telluride, which Japan and other WTO Members banned), in contrast to the like domestic product, which used crystalline technology. The Indian product was more efficient in power generation (using less land to generate power, about 4.5 acres per megawatt (MW), versus 6–7 acres per MW by the U.S. product), faster to reach stabilized output levels, slower to degrade, less prone to breakage, and cheaper, than the U.S. competitor. India also mandated U.S. products meet central-government level domestic content rules. (That dispute triggered an American WTO complaint against India in February 2014, with India rebutting that its local sourcing rules were GATT-WTO compliant, partly because India had not joined the WTO *GPA*.)

These non-IP issues should be irrelevant to a decision about Section 301 blacklisting. To India, they were not, and they reinforced the USTR determination to punish India. Yet, the IP issues gave the USTR no sound basis to put India on the Priority List. Indeed, America was legally incorrect with respect to each of the 3 issues:

- **Issue 1: Compulsory Licensing**

In March 2012, India granted its first compulsory license to a domestic generic pharmaceutical company, Natco, for medication, Nexavar, used to treat kidney and lung cancer, over the objections of the Swiss patent holder, Bayer. (This case is discussed in a separate Chapter.) The U.S. worried about a slippery slope on which Indian authorities would grant compulsory licenses on a range of medications unconnected with a public health emergency like HIV-AIDS, malaria, or tuberculosis. The Americans had reason to worry. India's November 2011 National Manufacturing Policy promoted compulsory licensing of patented products to encourage transfer of clean energy technologies.[107]

India viewed the USTR Special 301 action as unveiled pressure to restrict its grants of compulsory licenses. India noted Nexavar had been the only instance of it granting such a license, and pointed out its procedures for doing so were more

---

107. *See* Michael F. Martin, Shayerah Ilias Akhtar, K. Alan Kronstadt, Samir Kumar & Alison Siskin, *India — U.S. Economic Relations: In Brief*, Congressional Research Service 7-5700, R43741 at 5 (26 September 2014), *posted at* www.crs.org. [Hereinafter, September 2014 CRS Report.]

"nuanced and balanced" than those of America, which permits compulsory licensing by "executive fiat."[108] Besides, India had to attend to the public health concerns of a population 4 times the size of that of America living on one-third the land mass. Indeed, as *Médecins Sans Frontières* (MSF) pointed out, Indian generic producers helped provide affordable access across the globe to medicines to treat AIDS, malaria, and TB.[109]

- **Issue 2: Patent Evergreening**

In 2005, India amended its patent laws to comply with the *TRIPs Agreement*, specifically allowing for product patents on chemicals, food, and pharmaceuticals.[110] But, starting in 2012, India denied or revoked patents on certain foreign medicines, saying they failed to satisfy its patent laws. Most notably, in April 2013, the Supreme Court of India rejected an evergreening patent application of Novartis AG. (This case is discussed in an earlier Chapter.) Under Section 3(d) of *The Patents Act 1970 (India)*, novelty is construed to exclude patent evergreening. Section 3, appears within Chapter II, which covers "Inventions Not Patentable," and states:

3. What are not inventions.—The following are not inventions within the meaning of this *Act*,—

(a) an invention which is frivolous or which claims anything obviously contrary to well established natural laws;

(b) an invention the primary or intended use or commercial exploitation of which could be contrary public order or morality or which causes serious prejudice to human, animal or plant life or health or to the environment;

(c) the mere discovery of a scientific principle or the formulation of an abstract theory or discovery of any living thing or non-living substance occurring in nature;

(d) the mere discovery of a new form of a known substance which does not result in the enhancement of the known efficacy of that substance or the mere discovery of any new property or new use for a known substance or of the mere use of a known process, machine or apparatus unless such known process results in a new product or employs at least one new reactant.

Explanation.—For the purposes of this clause, salts, esters, ethers, polymorphs, metabolites, pure form, particle size, isomers, mixtures of isomers, complexes, combinations and other derivatives of known

---

108. Madhur Singh, *U.S. Concerned Over Indian Drug Licenses, State Department Official Says*, 31 International Trade Reporter (BNA) 508 (13 March 2014).

109. *See* Len Bracken, *Industry Alliance, NGOs Take Sides On India's Intellectual Property Regime*, 31 International Trade Reporter (BNA) 1972 (6 November 2014).

110. *See* September 2014 CRS Report at 4.

substance shall be considered to be the same substance, unless they differ significantly in properties with regard to efficacy;

(e) a substance obtained by a mere admixture resulting only in the aggregation of the properties of the components thereof or a process for producing such substance;

(f) the mere arrangement or re-arrangement or duplication of known devices each functioning independently of one another in a known way;

(g) Omitted by the *Patents (Amendment) Act, 2002*;

(h) a method of agriculture or horticulture;

(i) any process for the medicinal, surgical, curative, prophylactic diagnostic, therapeutic or other treatment of human beings or any process for a similar treatment of animals to render them free of disease or to increase their economic value or that of their products;

(j) plants and animals in whole or any part thereof other than micro organisms but including seeds, varieties and species and essentially biological processes for production or propagation of plants and animals;

(k) a mathematical or business method or a computer program *per se* or algorithms;

(l) a literary, dramatic, musical or artistic work or any other aesthetic creation whatsoever including cinematographic works and television productions;

(m) a mere scheme or rule or method of performing mental act or method of playing game;

(n) a presentation of information;

(o) topography of integrated circuits;

(p) an invention which in effect, is traditional knowledge or which is an aggregation or duplication of known properties of traditionally known component or components.[111]

The essence of the *Novartis* decision was India takes seriously its requirement of "enhanced efficiency." That is, even if a pharmaceutical satisfies international standards for patentability, it also must meet India's requirement of "enhanced efficiency," which meant a company could not make minor modifications of its patented product to extend the life of that patent — *i.e.*, it could not engage in evergreening.[112]

---

111. Indian federal statutes are readily available online on a variety of websites, in this case, Intellectual Property India, http://ipindia.nic.in/ipr/patent/eVersion_ActRules/sections/ps3.html.

112. *See* September 2014 CRS Report at 4.

From the American perspective, India was restricting the patentability of potentially innovative and useful drugs. From the Indian standpoint, America was pushing it via Special 301 to change Section 3(d) to create a *TRIPs* Plus obligation (allowing evergreening) for which India was not liable. The dispute involved tricky issues as to whether better delivery systems, decreased toxicity, fewer side effects, or greater storage and temperature stability were significant enough modifications to a patented drug to justify a new (or extended) patent.

- **Issue 3: Generic Pharmaceutical Importation**

For years, leading Indian generic pharmaceutical producers like Ranbaxy Laboratories Ltd. and Wockhardt Ltd. shipped medicines from their factories in India to the U.S. Overall (as of May 2014), the Indian generic drug industry accounts for $34 billion in output. India is the second largest exporter of OTC generic drugs to America, second only to Canada. In February 2014, the FDA barred entry into the U.S. of medications produced in the fourth of 4 Ranbaxy factories, having banned shipments earlier from the other facilities. The FDA alleged Ranbaxy employees wrongly re-tested ingredients that had failed to pass initial testing, and then certified those ingredients and generics that incorporated them as safe. The FDA also banned imports from Wockhardt.

Ranbaxy replied it was doing nothing different in its facilities than it had over the previous decade, and that a reputable Japanese company had acquired it, which surely enhanced its reputation for scrupulous adherence to quality conformity assessment procedures. Besides, India and the U.S. had a shared interest in safe generics, and India had no desire to have the adverse reputation among American consumers that Chinese companies have for poor quality, unsafe products. To that end, in May 2014, G.N. Singh, the Drug Controller General of India, pledged to boost the number of inspectors for India's 10,000 generic factories from 1,500 to 5,000 by 2017–2018.[113] Also that month, the Indian Commerce Ministry announced a "zero tolerance" policy and the expenditure of 30 billion *rupees* across three years to (1) double (to 1,000) its drug inspectors at the central government level, (2) hire 3,000 inspectors at state agencies, and (3) set up new testing labs at ports, all to ensure the quality of pharmaceuticals exported from India. For its part, the FDA said it would expand its offices in India, help train Indian inspectors, and increase its inspections in India and other countries.

Three years later, in March 2017, the FDA sent warning letters to two Indian pharmaceutical companies (USV Private Limited, and Badrivishal Chemicals & Pharmaceuticals). The FDA alleged problems such as (1) a lack of appropriate lab controls to ensure products are free from microbiological contamination, and computer systems are safe from unauthorized personnel altering production and

---

113. *See* Ketaki Gokhale, *India To Double Drug Regulators Staffing, Test Drugs at Ports*, 31 International Trade Reporter (BNA) 993 (29 May 2014); Amrit Dhillon, *India Steps Up to Improve Image of Generic Drug Industry*, 31 International Trade Reporter (BNA) 867 (8 May 2014).

control records, and (2) incomplete data in lab records to ensure compliance with applicable specifications. The dispute continued.

- **Still Another Issue: Data Exclusivity and Patent Linkage**

Similarly, on a fourth issue—data exclusivity via a patent linkage system—what the U.S. sought from India was an American policy preference, not a multilateral IP obligation. The U.S. wanted India to ensure holders of branded patented biologic medicines would not have to compete with generic pharmaceuticals during patent life. That protection could occur through a non-patent form of IP, data exclusivity, whereby generic manufacturers cannot, for purposes of getting regulatory authorizations, use clinical trial data generated by the original patent holders to obtain their patents.[114] How long that prohibition (if it exists) lasts is a matter for negotiation. From the perspective of original patent holders, the longer the better. As its name suggests, a "patent linkage" system connects the introduction of a generic drug to the expiry of a patent (plus any data exclusivity period). U.S. FTA partners (*e.g.*, Australia, Canada, Korea, and Singapore) have them, so why not India, if India wants to upgrade its bilateral trade relationship?

On all such disputes, India viewed the underlying problem to be with the increasingly uneconomic nature of American pharmaceutical manufacturers, coupled with a corporatization of U.S. trade policy that lacked empathy for poor countries. American pharmaceutical giants, said India, are uncompetitive globally without ever-longer and more draconian patent monopolies. They are saddled with large overhead expenses thanks to bloated bureaucracies, on top of the roughly $1 billion in costs they incur to secure FDA approval for a medication. Wall Street investment banks are unwilling to finance promising, but unproven, technologies: even though transformative drugs are needed for dreaded diseases, funding cosmetics research for products like Botox or wrinkle creams is less risky.[115] No longer are "PhRMA" firms innovative. Promising new medications come out of university laboratories or Steve Jobs-like garages. That explains why "dinosaur" companies seek to acquire entrepreneurial ventures and their patents. It also highlights why they try to survive by extending patents through evergreening as they approach a patent cliff (the end of the 20 year protection period), collaborating with universities, and demanding *TRIPs* Plus rules in bilateral trade talks with India or FTA negotiations (*e.g.*, via 12 year data exclusivity periods in *TPP*).

Not to be bullied, Indian Commerce Minister Anand Sharma resisted pressure to make *TRIPs* Plus commitments. The FICCI intoned:

> India has a well-established legislative, administrative, and judicial framework to safeguard IPRs which meets its obligations under *TRIPs* . . . . The

---

114. *See* Yu-Tzu Chu, *Taiwan to Create Patent Linkage System For Drugs in Quest for TPP Membership*, 31 International Trade Reporter (BNA) 1530 (21 August 2014).

115. *See* David Shaywitz, *Addiction to Deals Reveals the Depth of Pharma's Ills*, Financial Times, 2 May 2014, at 7.

two Trade Policy Reviews conducted by [the] WTO in respect of India in 2007 and 2011 have found the Indian IPR regime to be adequate. India has an independent authority and appellate board and courts to decide on due processes . . . . There has been no concerted effort by the Indian system discriminating [against] foreign companies, and there have been a number of Indian patents also being invalidated.[116]

Further, India listed its demands with which America had failed to comply. Said Ambassador Jaishankar: "Our concerns include immigration reform provisions that attack our service industry's viability in the U.S., [tax] revenues [from American multinational corporations doing business in India] forfeited by the absence of progress on a totalization agreement, and restricted market access. Localization [*i.e.*, local content rules], too, is apparently an issue where preaching against it abroad does not include practicing it at home [as 16 American states, but no Indian state, has sourcing requirements]."[117] Notwithstanding its presentation of its list, Indian trade officials said "discussions with U.S. trade officials are like a 'dialogue of the deaf.'"[118]

Much was at stake for both sides. The U.S. threatened India with loss of GSP benefits. India, in turn, could make life for American exporters and investors yet more difficult in a country to which they sought market access in a variety of agricultural, industrial, and services sectors. In April 2014, the USTR backed off: it opted not to designate India a PFC, though it kept India on the Priority Watch List, and said it would subject India to an OCR of its IP rules.[119] (India remained on the list as of 2017.) The USTR did not single out India. Others on the List that year were Algeria, Argentina, Chile, China, Indonesia, Kuwait (which also underwent an OCR), Pakistan, Russia, Thailand, and Venezuela.

Five months later, following the thumping victory of Narendra Modi (1950–, PM, 2014–) and his BJP in India's 16th general election held in April–May, the new Prime Minister met President Obama. They produced a September 2014 deal to create an IP Working Group, within the framework of the existing Indo-American Trade Policy Forum. The Group was to meet annually, with frequent technical

---

116. *Quoted in* Madhur Singh, *U.S. Concerned Over Indian Drug Licenses, State Department Official Says*, 31 International Trade Reporter (BNA) 508 (13 March 2014).

117. *Quoted in India's Fresh Attack.*

The November 2011 National Manufacturing Policy sought to boost employment in India's industrial sector. It calls for government procurement in certain sectors, such as clean energy and ICT, to follow greater local content rules — in effect, to use more Indian inputs, intermediate goods, and finished products. For example, effective July 2014, all telecommunication equipment vendors had to test their products in a laboratory in India. Pursuant to this Policy, India issued a Preferential Market Access Mandate, which sets local content rules for government procurement of electronic goods. These examples, as well as Indian local content rules and government subsidies for solar panel products, were a source of Indo-American trade friction and WTO litigation. *See* September 2014 CRS Report at 5.

118. *Quoted in India's Fresh Attack.*

119. *See* September 2014 CRS Report at 3–4.

discussions, and given "appropriate decision-making" authority.[120] The ambiguity in what that meant was worrying, given the range of IP issues the two sides had to resolve. The leaders also expressed their desire, manifest in an "Indo-U.S. Investment Initiative," to boost capital markets and flows to finance Indian infrastructure projects under an "Infrastructure Collaboration Platform" that would ensure participation of American companies in those projects. But, might legal uncertainty over IPRs dampen enthusiasm to participate?

---

120. Stephanie Cohen, *Obama, Modi Agree to High-Level IP Working Group, Financing, Infrastructure Initiative*, 31 International Trade Reporter (BNA) 1748 (2 October 2014).

Index

References are to Chapter and Sections.

A

Africa
African Growth and Opportunity
Act (AGOA), 21[I]
Economic dependency, 21[IV]
Protectionist details, 21[II]
Ringo African dilemma argument
(1994), 21[V]
Social justice, 21[V]
Trade distortion, 21[III]

C

Catholic Social Justice Theory
Trade adjustment assistance (TAA),
25[IV]
Climate Change, Trade and
Bilateral trade agreements (BTAs)
and GATT-WTO rules, 29[V]
Environmental Goods Agreement,
toward a plurilateral, 29[VII]
Environmental Kuznets Curve, 29[II]
Failed DOHA Round environmental
negotiations, 29[VI]
GATT-WTO rules and bilateral trade
agreements (BTAs), 29[V]
International efforts to mitigate
climate change, 29[IV]
Mitigate climate change, interna-
tional efforts to, 29[IV]
Plurilateral *Environmental Goods
Agreement*, toward, 29[VII]
Scientific evidence concerning cli-
mate change, synopsis of, 29[I]

Trade and climate change, relation-
ship between, 29[III]
Compulsory Licensing, Evergreening,
and Patented Pharmaceuticals
Brazilian and *Thai* (2007), and
Indian (2012) compulsory license
cases, 32[V]
Compulsory license cases: *Brazil-
ian* and *Thai* (2007), and *Indian*
(2012), 32[V]
Doha Round December 2005 Hong
Kong Ministerial Conference
First waiver from Article 31(f),
32[II]
Second additional waivers, 32[IV]
Dreaded diseases and generic medi-
cines, 32[I]
Evergreening and 2013 Indian
Supreme Court *Novartis* case,
32[VI]
Generic medicines, 32[I]
Indian (2012) and *Thai* and *Brazilian*
(2007) compulsory license cases,
32[V]
Rwanda case invoking Article 31(f)
waiver (2007), 32[III]
Thai and *Brazilian* (2007), and
Indian (2012) compulsory license
cases, 32[V]
2013 Indian Supreme Court *Novartis*
case, evergreening and, 32[VI]

D

Doha Round
  Doha Round December 2005 Hong
    Kong Ministerial Conference
  First waiver from Article 31(f),
    32[II]
  Second additional waivers, 32[IV]
  Failed DOHA Round environmental
    negotiations, 29[VI]

E

Economic Growth Models
  Industrialization and labor surplus
    Agriculture to industry, transfor-
      mation, 15[1]
    Chenery-Syrquin study, 1975,
      15[VII]
    Labor surplus concept and shift,
      15[II]
    Labor surplus models
      Background, 15[III]
      Critique, 15[IV]
      Fei-Ranis model, 1964, 15[IV]
      Neo-classical two-sector
        model, 15[VI]
    Patterns of development, 15[VII]
  Labor surplus (See subhead: Indus-
    trialization and labor surplus)
  Poor countries, preferences for (See
    Preferential Programs, subhead:
    Development and poverty)
  Stages and sources of growth
    Essential growth model concepts,
      14[II]
    Growth accounting, sources of,
      14[IV]
    Harrod-Domar 1-sector growth
      model, 14[III]
    Rostow stages of growth theory,
      14[I]
Environmental Issues
  Climate change (See Climate
    Change, Trade and)
  Free trade agreements and (See Free
    Trade Agreements (FTAs), sub-
    head: Environment provisions)

F

FDI
  (See Foreign Direct Investment
    (FDI))
Fei-Ranis Labor Surplus Models
  Generally, 15[IV]
Foreign Direct Investment (FDI)
  Competition policy and state owned
    enterprise (SOE), 11[VIII]
  Dispute resolution mechanisms,
    11[V]; 11[VI]; 11[VII]
  Expropriation, rules on compensa-
    tion for, 11[IV]
  Free trade agreements (FTA), liber-
    alization and protection through
    (See subhead: Liberalization and
    protection through free trade
    agreements)
  Institutions and dispute resolution
    mechanisms, 11[V]
  Investor-state dispute settlement
    (ISDS)
    Mechanisms, critique of, 11[VI]
    NAFTA 2.0 cut back, 11[VII]
  Liberalization and protection
    through free trade agreements
    Expropriation, rules on compen-
      sation for, 11[IV]
    FDI and competition policy and
      state owned enterprise (SOE),
      11[VIII]
    Free trade agreements (FTAs)
      investment chapters, 11[I]
    Institutions and dispute resolu-
      tion mechanisms, 11[V]
    Investor-state dispute settlement
      (ISDS) mechanisms, critique
      of, 11[VI]
    Market access rules, 11[II]

Non-discrimination rules, 11[III]

Rules on compensation for expropriation, 11[IV]

Market access rules, 11[II]

NAFTA 2.0 ISDS cut back, 11[VII]

Non-discrimination rules, 11[III]

Rules on compensation for expropriation, 11[IV]

State owned enterprise (SOE), competition policy and, 11[VIII]

Free Trade Agreements (FTAs)

Commitments in

Cultural industries exceptions and 1997 *Canada Magazines* case, 12[IX]

"Deep," "second generation," or "21st century" FTAs, 12[I]

Exporting American IP standards and pushing *TRIPs* plus commitments, 12[VI]

Government procurement

Economic significance of, 12[III]

Malaysian social engineering through, 12[V]

Managed trade in, 12[IV]

International digital trade

Generally, 12[XI]

NAFTA 2.0 case study, 12[XII]

North American Free Trade Agreement (NAFTA) Chapter 20 case study, 12[II]

"Second generation," "deep," or "21st century" FTAs, 12[I]

Securitization and relationship between Trade Related Aspects of Intellectual Property Rights (TRIPS) plus and other FTA obligations, 12[IX]

Trade Related Aspects of Intellectual Property Rights (TRIPS) plus commitments (See subhead: Trade Related Aspects of Intellectual Property Rights (TRIPS))

"21st century," "second generation," or "deep" FTAs, 12[I]

Diversity in ambition of, 1[VII]

Economic aspects of

CAFTA-DR case study, 1[VIII]

Diversity in ambition of FTAs, 1[VII]

Job creation or destruction, 1[IV]

Statistics, 1[II]

Stepping stones or fortresses, 1[VI]

Terminological distinctions and examples, 1[I]

Trade creation or diversion, 1[V]

Trends, 1[II]

U.S. FTAs, 1[III]

Environment provisions

Bipartisan trade deal and expansion of *NAFTA*, 28[V]

Contrasting environmental dispute settlement under 2005 *Singapore FTA, CAFTA-DR,* and 2009 *Peru TPA*, 28[III]

Environmental dispute settlement under 2005 *Singapore FTA, CAFTA-DR,* and 2009 *Peru TPA*, 28[III]

Fishing, illegal, unreported and unregulated: *NAFTA* 2.0 case study, 28[VI]

KORUS Environmental Chapter, 28[IV]

Metrics to compare, 28[I]

NAFTA Environmental Side Agreement, 28[II]

Timber tracking: *NAFTA* 2.0 case study, 28[VI]

Wildlife and timber tracking: *NAFTA* 2.0 case study, 28[VI]

Foreign direct investment (FDI) liberalization and protection through FTAs (See Foreign Direct Investment (FDI), subhead: Liberalization and protection through free trade agreements)

GATT-WTO disciplines on
  Article XXIV:11: August 1947
    British Partition of India, 5[I]
  Article XXIV:11 to Indo-Pakistani
    trade, 5[II]
  Compensatory adjustments, Arti-
    cle XXIV:6, and EU enlarge-
    ment, 4[V]
  EU and Gabon case studies, 4[V]
  Gabon and EU case studies, 4[V]
  "Higher or more restrictive" test
    in Article XXIV:5, 4[IV]
  Indian subcontinent and Article
    XXIV:11, questions about, 5[III]
  Notification under Article
    XXIV:7, 4[VI]
  Poor countries, ITO Charter
    Article 15 and GATT Article
    XXIV origins, 4[I]
  Purpose of RTAs, Article XXIV:4,
    and Article XXIV:10 waiver,
    4[II]
  Regional trade agreement (RTA)
    disciplines parlous, 4[VII]
  "Substantially all" test in Article
    XXIV:8, 4[III]
India special disciplines (See sub-
  head: GATT-WTO disciplines on)
Labor disputes under, resolving (See
  International Labor Law and
  Trade Restrictions, subhead: Free
  trade agreements (FTAs), disputes
  under)
Liberalizing trade in services
  through
  Data localization and non-dis-
    crimination: NAFTA 2.0 case
    study, 10[III]
  Financial services and capital
    controls, 10[I]
  Freer trade vs. road safety, 10[II]
  Managed trade in services, 10[IV]
  NAFTA Cross Border Trucking
    case, 10[II]

NAFTA 2.0, 10[III]
Non-discrimination and data
  localization: NAFTA 2.0 case
  study, 10[III]
Road safety vs. freer trade, 10[II]
Market access obligations
  Agricultural products and textiles
    and apparel (T&A)
    Enhanced market access case
      study, 9[VII]
    NAFTA 2.0, 9[VII]
    Sensitive products case studies,
      9[VI]
  Ambition
    Elimination of trade barriers,
      9[II]
    Singapore and Chile FTAs,
      9[III]
  Australia FTA, 9[IV]
  Check list, 9[I]
  Elimination of trade barriers,
    9[II]
  Industrial goods: case study on
    enhanced market access under
    NAFTA 2.0, 9[X]
  Managed trade in goods, 9[XI]
  NAFTA Corn Brooms case, 9[IX]
  Safeguards
    Bilateral and special, 9[VIII]
    NAFTA Corn Brooms case,
      9[IX]
    Sensitivities and bilateral and
      special, 9[VIII]
  Sensitive products
    Agricultural products and
      T&A, 9[VI]
    Sectors, and, 9[V]
  Singapore and Chile FTAs, 9[III]
  Trade barriers, elimination of,
    9[II]
Pakistan special disciplines (See sub-
  head: GATT-WTO disciplines on)
Partners, choosing, 2[II]
Political and security aspects of

Competitive imperialism, 3[VII]

Competitive liberalization and its defects, 2[I]

Criteria, political, 2[III]

Economy, political

Generally, 2[VI]

Egypt, QIZs and Israeli content: case study, 3[II]

Israeli content, Egypt, and QIZs: case study, 3[II]

Korea and *KORUS*, 3[III]

Qualified industrial zone, Egypt and Israel, 3[II]

Security case study, and, 3[II]; 3[III]

Panama and 3 FTA issues, 2[V]

Partners, choosing, 2[II]; 3[I]

Security case study

Kaesong and *KORUS*, 3[IV]

Pakistan, ROZs, and Islamist extremism, 3[V]

Turkey, 3[VI]

Taiwan, *TIFA*, but no FTA, 2[IV]

Preferential Rules of Origin (ROOs) (See Preferential Rules of Origin (ROOs))

Rules of Origin (ROOs), preferential (See Preferential Rules of Origin (ROOs))

Security aspects of (See subhead: Political and security aspects of)

Substantive labor rules in (See International Labor Law and Trade Restrictions, subhead: Free trade agreements (FTAs), substantive labor rules in)

Trade Related Aspects of Intellectual Property Rights (TRIPS) (See Trade Related Aspects of Intellectual Property Rights (TRIPS) Agreement)

FTAS (See Free Trade Agreements (FTAs))

H

Hong Kong Ministerial Conference Doha Round

First waiver from Article 31(f), 32[II]

Second additional waivers, 32[IV]

Extended transition periods and, 30[VIII]

I

ILO (See International Labor Organization (ILO))

India

Anti-colonialism, 18[II]

Compulsory license case: *Indian* (2012), 32[V]

Evergreening and 2013 Indian Supreme Court *Novartis* case, 32[VI]

GATT-WTO disciplines on

Article XXIV:11: August 1947 British Partition of India, 5[I]

Article XXIV:11 to Indo-Pakistani trade, 5[II]

Indian subcontinent and Article XXIV:11, questions about, 5[III]

Inefficiencies of 1970s, 18[IV]

Intellectual property

India Patent Protection case (1998)

Jurisprudential considerations, 31[VI]

Mailboxes and, 31[IV]

Substantive holdings of, 31[V]

2014 Case of India on special 301 priority list, 33[IX]

Modi era, 18[VIII]

Nationalism, 18[II]

1970s inefficiencies, 18[IV]

Reforms

First generation, 1991, 18[V]

Sputter of reforms, 1990s and 2000s, 18[VI]

Path ahead, 18[VII]

Partition of 15 August 1947, 18[I]

Socialism, 18[II]

Socialist planning, post-partition, 18[III]

Intellectual Property

Compulsory licensing, evergreening, and patented pharmaceuticals (See Compulsory Licensing, Evergreening, and Patented Pharmaceuticals)

Enforcement

Apple (2011-2013), 33[IV]

Black listing, 33[VIII]

Exclusion orders, 33[III]

GATT consistency of Section 337, 33[V]

Gray market and Section 337, 33[VI]

Infringement, exclusion and seizure, and Section 337, 33[I]

Patent hold up behavior, 33[IV]

Presidential discretion, 33[IV]

Refusing protection and 2002 *Havana Club* case, 33[VII]

Samsung cell phone patent war, 33[IV]

Section 337

Gray market and, 33[VI]

Infringement, exclusion and seizure, and, 3[I]

1999 *Gamut* case, 33[VI]

Operation, 33[II]

2005 *SKF* case, 33[VI]

2014 Case of India on special 301 priority list, 33[IX]

Exporting American IP standards and pushing TRIPs plus commitments, 12[VI]

Extended transition periods and 2005 Hong Kong Ministerial Conference, 30[VIII]

Free trade agreements (FTAs)

Case study: *NAFTA* 2.0, 12[VIII]

Exporting American IP standards and TRIPs plus commitments, 12[VI]

El Said argument on, 12[VII]

Exporting American IP standards and pushing, 12[VI]

NAFTA 2.0, 12[VIII]

Securitization and relationship between *TRIPs* plus and other FTA obligations, 12[VIII]

Manufactured products, importance of IP to, 30[III]

Raghavan recolonization argument (1990), 30[VI]

Rich and poor countries, interests of, 30[IV]

Ringo African dilemma argument (1994), 30[VII]

Securitization and FTA obligations, 12[IX]

Trade Related Aspects of Intellectual Property Rights (TRIPS) Agreement (See Trade Related Aspects of Intellectual Property Rights (TRIPS) Agreement)

Treaties, 30[II]

Types, 30[I]

International Labor Law and Trade Restrictions

Consumptive demand exception, end of, 22[VIII]

Debate on labor rights in poor countries, 22[IV]

EU Social Charter, 22[III]

Free trade agreements (FTAs), disputes under

Bahrain FTA and Arab spring, 24[V]

CAFTA-DR Chapter 16 and enforcing and Guatemalan and dominican labor law, 24[VI]

Cases under 1994 *NAFTA Labor Side Agreement*, 24[III]

Jordan FTA and Jordanian labor conditions, 24[IV]

NAFTA Labor Side Agreement
Cases under, 24[III]
Procedures under, 24[I]

Oman FTA and Omani Labor Law reform, 24[VII]

Procedures
Colombia TPA, under, 24[II]
NAFTA Labor Side Agreement, under, 24[I]

Free trade agreements (FTAs), substantive labor rules in
Generally, 23[I]
Collective bargaining: NAFTA 2.0 case study, 23[V]
ILO implementation: NAFTA 2.0 case study, 9[V]
LGBTQ+, provisions for, 23[VI]
Models, 23[II]
Model 4, special importance of, 23[IV]
November 2013 ILO study on significance, 23[II]
Women, provisions for, 23[VI]

GATT Article XX(e) prison labor exception, 22[V]

International Labor Organization (ILO)
Generally, 22[I]
Internationally recognized worker rights based on ILO *Conventions*, 22[II]

Labor surplus concept and shift, 15[II]

Labor surplus models
Background, 15[III]
Critique, 15[IV]
Fei-Ranis model, 1964, 15[IV]
Neo-classical two-sector model, 15[VI]

Section 307 cases, 22[VII]

Substantive labor rules in FTAs
Generally, 23[I]
Collective bargaining: NAFTA 2.0 case study, 23[V]
ILO implementation: NAFTA 2.0 case study, 9[V]
LGBTQ+, provisions for, 23[VI]
Models, 23[II]
Model 4, special importance of, 23[IV]
November 2013 ILO study on significance, 23[II]
Women, provisions for, 23[VI]

U.S. Section 307 ban on merchandise from convict, forced, or indentured labor, 22[VI]

International Labor Organization (ILO)
Generally, 22[I]
Collective bargaining and ILO implementation case study: *NAFTA* 2.0, 23[V]
Internationally recognized worker rights based on ILO *Conventions*, 22[II]
NAFTA 2.0 and collective bargaining, 23[V]
November 2013 ILO study, 23[II]

J

Jurisprudence of GATT ARTICLE XX(B) and (G)
Chapeau of the general exceptions, 27[V]
ECO-labeling and 2012 *Tuna-Dolphin* case, 27[III]
Extraterritorial measures
Primary boycotts and 1992 *Tuna-Dolphin I* case, 27[I]
Secondary boycotts and 1994 *Tuna-Dolphin II* CASE, 27[II]
Introductory provisions, 27[V]
General exceptions and *Chapeau*, 27[V]

Products versus processes, 27[IX]

Two step test

Differential regulations, and 1996 *Reformulated Gas* case, 27[IV]

Failing 2 step test and 2014 *China Rare Earths* case, 27[VIII]

Passing 2 step test and 2001 *Asbestos* case, 27[VII]

Species protection, and 1998 *Turtle-Shrimp* case, 27[VI]

L

Labor, Trade and

Free trade agreements (FTAs), resolving labor disputes under (See Free Trade Agreements (FTAs), subhead: Labor disputes under, resolving)

International labor law and trade restrictions (See International Labor Law and Trade Restrictions)

Substantive labor rules in free trade agreements (FTAs) (See Free Trade Agreements (FTAs), subhead: Substantive labor rules in)

N

NAFTA 2.0

Agricultural products and textiles and apparel (T&A), 9[VII]

Collective bargaining, 23[V]

Data localization and non-discrimination, 10[III]

Fishing, illegal, unreported and unregulated, 28[VI]

Industrial goods and enhanced market access, 9[X]

International digital trade and, 12[XII]

International Labor Organization (ILO) implementation, 9[V]

Investor-state dispute settlement (ISDS) cut back, 11[VII]

Non-discrimination and data localization, 10[III]

Preferential Rules of Origin (ROOs), 7[VIII]

Textiles and apparel (T&A), 9[VII]

Trade Related Aspects of Intellectual Property Rights (TRIPS) and, 12[VIII]

National Security

(See Free Trade Agreements (FTAs), subhead: Political and security aspects of)

Neo-Classical 2-Sector Model

Generally, 15[VI]

P

Preferential Programs

Africa, special help for (See Africa)

Development and poverty, measuring

Absolute poverty, 13[III]

Development, 13[II]

Gini coefficient, 13[V]

Growth defined, 13[I]

ITO Charter Article 15 and GATT Article XXIV origins, 4[I]

Top-bottom ration, 13[IV]

Generalized system of preferences (GSP)

Generally, 20[I]

Bangladeshi worker rights, case study of, 20[III]

Beneficiary developing country (BDC), designation as, 20[II]

Discretionary graduation and competitive need limitation (CNL), 20[VII]

Eligible articles and extensive ineligibility list, 20[IV]

European GSP case, 20[VIII]

Non-tariff measures (NTMs)

Tokyo Round defenses, 20[IX]

2019 *Brazil Tax* case, 20[IX]

Preferential ROOs, 20[VI]

Regional trade agreements (RTAs)
   Tokyo Round defenses, 20[IX]
   2019 Brazil Tax case, 20[IX]
   Sleeping bags, import sensitivity,
      and politics, 20[V]

Growth models
   Accounting, sources of, 14[IV]
   Agriculture to industry, transfor-
      mation, 15[1]
   Chenery-Syrquin study, 1975,
      15[VII]
   Essential growth model concepts,
      14[II]
   Growth accounting, sources of,
      14[IV]
   Harrod-Domar 1-sector growth
      model, 14[III]
   Labor surplus concept and shift,
      15[II]
   Labor surplus models
      Background, 15[III]
      Critique, 15[IV]
      Fei-Ranis model, 1964, 15[IV]
      Neo-classical two-sector
         model, 15[VI]
   Patterns of development, 15[VII]
   Poverty, absolute, 13[III]
   Rostow stages of growth theory,
      14[I]

Labor surplus models
   Background, 15[III]
   Critique, 15[IV]
   Fei-Ranis model, 1964, 15[IV]
   Neo-classical two-sector model,
      15[VI]

Poor countries, preferences for (See
   subhead: Development and poverty, measuring)

Special and differential (S&D) treatment (See Special and Differential
   (S&D) Treatment)

Special help for Africa (See Africa)

Trade policies, growth, and poverty
   (See Trade, Growth, and Poverty)

Preferential Rules of Origin (ROOs)
   Cummins case, 8[I]
   Generic categories, 6[II]
   Indispensability, 6[I]
   Israeli origin, occupied territories,
      and February 2010 ECJ *Brita* case,
      6[IV]
   Middle East politics and qualified
      industrial zone (QIZs), 6[V]
   NAFTA Certificate of Origin and
      2006 *Corrpro* case, 8[II]
   Problem, 6[III]
   Tariff shift and *Cummins* case, 8[I]
   Trans-shipment and *Singapore FTA*,
      8[III]
   Types of preferential ROOs in
      NAFTA and other FTAs
      Generally, 7[I]
      NAFTA renegotiations, 7[VI]
      Type 1: Goods wholly obtained
         rule, 7[II]
      Type 2: Originating materials
         rule, 7[III]
      Type 3: Substantial transforma-
         tion rule, 7[IV]
      Type 5: Hybrid rule
         Generally, 7[VI]
         Automobiles, 6.25% ROO,
            7[VII]
         Hybrid automobiles under
            NAFTA ROO, 7[VIII]
         Minimum wage and hybrid
            automobiles, 7[VIII]
         NAFTA renegotiation on 62.5%
            auto ROO, 7[VII]
         NAFTA 2.0 hybrid auto ROO,
            7[VIII]
         Regional value content 75% for
            hybrid autos, 7[VIII]
         Trilateral deal, 7[IX]
      Type 6: Assembled goods rule,
         7[X]

Type 7: Specified process rule,
  7[XI]
Type 8: *De minimus* test, 7[XII]

R

Rostow Stages of Growth Theory
  Generally, 14[I]
Rules of Origin (ROOs)
  (See Preferential Rules of Origin
    (ROOs))

S

S&D Treatment
  (See Special and Differential (S&D)
    Treatment)
Special and Differential (S&D)
  Treatment
  Bali *Monitoring Mechanism Decision*,
    December 2013, 19[VII]
  Collaboration, GATT Article
    XXXIII, and 1980 *Sugar Refunds*
    case, 19[IV]
  European preferences for former
    colonies, 19[VI]
  GATT-WTO texts, in, 19[V]
  Haberler Report, 19[II]
  Non-reciprocal trade preferences and
    GATT Part IV, Prebisch, Baran,
    and intellectual background for,
    19[I]
  Substantive content of Article
    XXXVI:8, 19[III]

T

TAA
  (See Trade Adjustment Assistance
    (TAA))
Trade, Growth, and Poverty
  Export orientation
    Evidence for, 16[VIII]
    Evidence questioning, 16[IX]
    Immiserizing growth, rish of,
      16[VII]

Import substitution, versus, 16[V]
Industrialization and unbalanced
  growth, 16[I]
Kuznets Inverted U Theory,
  growth, poverty, and, 16[II]
Market-based theory for, 16[VI]
Piketty critique of Kuznets curve,
  16[III]
Terms of trade (TOT), 16[IV]
Import substitution
  Dependency theory, 17[II]
  Evidence for, 17[V]
  Export orientation versus, 97[IV]
  Frank theory, 17[II]
  Lord Bauer rebuttal, 17[VI]
  Marxist intellectual heritage, 17[I]
  Prebisch-Singer Thesis
    Generally, 17[III]
    Policy implications, 17[IV]
Trade Adjustment Assistance (TAA)
  Practice
    Causation, importance of proving,
      26[VII]
    Communities, rebuilding, 26[VI]
    Efficacy, 26[VIII]
    Eligibility criteria
      Farmer, 26[II]
      Primary and secondary worker,
        26[III]
      Public agency worker, 26[III]
      Service sector and public
        agency worker, 26[III]
    Farmer eligibility criteria, 26[II]
    Federal and state involvement,
      26[I]
    Firm eligibility, 26[V]
    Primary and secondary worker,
      26[II]
    Rebuilding communities, 26[VI]
    Secondary worker, 26[II]
    Worker
      Benefits, types of, 26[IV]
      Primary and secondary, 26[II]
  Theory

Causation, proof of, 26[VII]

Catholic Social Justice Theory, 25[IV]

Compensating "losers" from free trade, 25[I]

Free trade, compensating "losers" from, 25[I]

Funding, 25[IV]

Generosity, 25[IV]

Non-fiscal policy questions, 25[III]

Statutory evolution, 25[II]

2013 *Western Digital* case, 26[VII]

2014 *Boeing* case, 26[VII]

Trade Related Aspects of Intellectual Property Rights (TRIPS) Agreement

Generally, 31[I]; 31[II]

Copyright protection, 31[III]

El Said argument on, 12[VII]

Exporting American IP standards and pushing TRIPs plus commitments, 12[VI]

Foreign trade agreements exporting American IP standards and TRIPs plus commitments, 12[VI]

Free trade agreements (FTAs), relationship between TRIPS and, 12(IX)

India Patent Protection case (1998)

Jurisprudential considerations, 31[VI]

Mailboxes and, 31[IV]

Substantive holdings of, 31[V]

Mailboxes and 1998 *India Patent Protection* case, 31[IV]

NAFTA 2.0, 12[VIII]

Pushing TRIPs plus commitments through FTAs, 12[VI]

Securitization and other FTA obligations, 12[IX]

Smith argument on TRIPS agreement implementation (1994), 30[V]